BROKEN FORTUNES

South Carolina Soldiers, Sailors and Citizens
Who Died in the Service of Their Country and State
in the War for Southern Independence, 1861–1865

Randolph W. Kirkland, Jr.
For the South Carolina Historical Society

The University of South Carolina Press

© 1995 South Carolina Historical Society

Cloth edition published by the South Carolina Historical Society, 1995
Paperback edition published in Columbia, South Carolina,
by the University of South Carolina Press, 2012

www.sc.edu/uscpress

Manufactured in the United States of America

21 20 19 18 17 16 15 14 13 12
10 9 8 7 6 5 4 3 2 1

ISBN 978-1-61117-143-3 (pbk)

DEDICATION

This register of South Carolinians who died in Confederate service
1861-1865
is dedicated to the memory of
Private Charles H. Wate
Company G, 1st South Carolina Volunteer Infantry (Gregg's),
Perrin's Brigade, Pender's Division,
A. P. Hill's Corps,
Army of Northern Virginia,
who at age sixteen volunteered to serve his state and nation.
He fought with steady courage in all eleven major battles
of his regiment,
fell in victorious charge,
July 1, 1863,
at Gettysburg, Pennsylvania,
and now lies with his comrades in an unmarked grave on that battlefield,
never having known defeat.

INSCRIPTION ON THE CONFEDERATE MONUMENT AT COLUMBIA, SOUTH CAROLINA

To South Carolina's Dead
1861   of the   1865
Confederate Army
Erected by the Women of South Carolina

This Monument
Perpetuates the Memory
Of those who
True to the instincts of their birth,
Faithful to the teaching of their fathers,
Constant in their love for the State,
Died in the performance of their duty,
Who
Have glorified a fallen cause
By the simple manhood of their lives,
The patient endurance of suffering
And the heroism of death;
And who
In the dark hours of imprisonment,
And the hopelessness of the hospital,
In the short sharp agony of the field,
Found support and consolation
In the belief
That at home they would not be forgotten.

Let the stranger
Who may in future times
Read this inscription
Recognize that these were men
Whom Power could not corrupt,
Whom Death could not terrify,
Whom Defeat could not dishonor,
And let their virtue plead for just judgment
Of the cause in which they perished;
Let the South Carolinian
Of another generation
Remember
That the state taught them
How to live and how to die,
And that from her broken fortunes
She has preserved for her children
The priceless treasure of their memories;
Teaching all who may claim
The same birthright
That Truth, Courage, and Patriotism,
Endureth Forever.

[William Henry Trescot]

TABLE OF CONTENTS

PREFACE
  By Alexander Moore   Page vii
ACKNOWLEDGEMENTS   ix
INTRODUCTION   xi
LIST A   1
LIST B   13
LIST C   53
LIST D   85
LIST E   101
LIST F   109
LIST G   123
LIST H   143
LIST I   177
LIST J   179
LIST K   191
LIST L   201
LIST M   217
LIST Mc   241
LIST N   257
LIST O   263
LIST P   269
LIST Q   287
LIST R   289
LIST S   307
LIST T   341
LIST U   355
LIST V   357
LIST W   361
LIST XYZ   389
APPENDICES
  Source Codes & Abbreviations   393
  Secession Convention Resolution   403
  Report of William B. Johnston
    to the General Assembly   404
  William J. Rivers's Advertisement   406
  William J. Rivers on the "Roll of Honor" 407
  Statistical Summaries   411
  Photo Credits   413

PREFACE

We need to know their names. Much of recorded history and the enduring works of world literature catalog the names of those who died in combat. The *Iliad* and *Old Testament* are all the more true histories because they have immortalized men fallen in battle. We Americans share this need to know their names and to record them for posterity. Town squares from Hope, Maine, to Allendale, South Carolina, and beyond contain monuments to warriors fallen in our nation's conflicts. Those monuments invariably record the names of the dead.

Randolph W. Kirkland's *Broken Fortunes* is a monument in paper, a roster of 18,666 South Carolina casualties of the American Civil War. In 1862 the state's Secession Convention mandated that a roster be compiled of South Carolina's war dead and wounded. Work on the roster began at that time and continued, under several guises, to the present. Mr. Kirkland has substantially finished the work of his predecessors, William B. Johnston, William James Rivers, John Peyre Thomas, and Alexander S. Salley, Jr., who compiled South Carolina rosters. *Broken Fortunes* includes names found in Johnston's and Rivers's "Roll of the Dead" and "Roll of Honor" and complements their lists with new research in newspapers, cemetery registers, unit histories, and other primary sources.

Broken Fortunes is a milestone in the study of South Carolina's Civil War history. Its value is obvious as a research tool for genealogists and students of the war. But all people who care about South Carolina history must welcome this book. It works strongly upon our historical imaginations. We learn these men's names and their personal fates. We realize that so many men — a book full of them — fought and died for South Carolina and the Confederate States of America. *Broken Fortunes* accomplishes two remarkable tasks. It tells more than 18,000 individual stories and, also, repeats a single story 18,000 times. The death of Private James L. Campbell, Company K, 22nd Regiment, South Carolina Infantry, killed at the Battle of the Crater, makes us pause and think of his family and his neighbors. But we cannot pause and think too long. For there are so many others. Private Campbell's life history — and those of more than 18,000 others — is the Civil War history of our state and nation.

Mr. Kirkland includes appendices that recount the history of his predecessors' compilations. He also applied statistical analysis to his roster and his arithmetic revelations enrich our understanding. Nearly 13 percent of South Carolina's white male population died as a result of the war. York, Williamsburg, and Kershaw counties suffered the highest casualty rates. In York County more than 18 percent of the white male population died. The talents, skills, and love of two of every eleven men in York were lost to their families, their neighbors, and their state in the war. The state capital and its largest city was in ruins. The slave economy had disappeared. And the cemeteries were full.

The South Carolina Historical Society is proud to cooperate with Mr. Kirkland in publishing *Broken Fortunes*. The Society was active in the work of his predecessors and has been a partner in his labors. We at the South Carolina Historical Society honor Lieutenant Benjamin Taylor Gibbes, Company D, 16th Regiment, S.C. Infantry and Private R.A. Mullins, Company B, 12th S.C. Infantry, as representatives of all those whose names Mr. Kirkland has recorded. And we honor Randolph W. Kirkland for his achievement. Mr. Kirkland estimates with authority that the names of about 2,500 South Carolina casualties still await discovery. He and the South Carolina Historical Society actively seek to know their names.

    Alexander Moore
    Executive Director
    South Carolina Historical Society
    Charleston, South Carolina

ACKNOWLEDGEMENTS

This compilation is founded upon the contributions of many, many people. The basic work done by Mr. William B. Johnston and Professor William J. Rivers was built upon the contributions of officials and veterans unknown and forgotten. Many of the later compilations of county rolls, unit histories, and graveyard records that have been referred to were also prepared by forgotten people in the United Daughters of the Confederacy, the United Confederate Veterans, the Sons of Confederate Veterans, and various county historical societies. This publication in a small measure ensures that their work is at last available to the general public.

The following contributors to this edition have earned the gratitude of all those who use it in their own research:

Gregory S. (Mrs. Lewis A.) Arthur
    Lynchburg, Virginia
Charles Kelly Barrow
    Georgia Division Historian, Sons of Confederate Veterans, Thomasville, Georgia
Trudy McC. Bazemore
    Georgetown County Library, Georgetown, South Carolina
John R. Davis, Jr.
    Chief of Interpretation, National Park Service, Petersburg National Battlefield
Susan E. Dick
    Publications and Library Assistant, South Carolina Historical Society, Charleston
C. Patton Hash
    Research Consultant, South Carolina Historical Society, Charleston
Stephen Hoffius
    Director of Publications, South Carolina Historical Society, Charleston
Eugene W. Jones, Jr.
    Goose Creek, South Carolina
Ruth M. Leland
    Newberry, South Carolina
Patrick McCawley
    Archivist, Reference Services, South Carolina Department of Archives and History, Columbia
Keith C. Morgan
    Chief of Interpretation, National Park Service, Richmond National Battlefield Park
Margaret M. O'Bryant
    Librarian, Albemarle County Historical Society, Charlottesville, Virginia
Dennis E. Todd
    Historian, South Carolina Division, Sons of Confederate Veterans
Steven D. Tuttle, Jr.
    Supervisor, Reference Services, South Carolina Department of Archives and History, Columbia
Raymond F. Watkins
    Springfield, Virginia
Robert Welsh
    Arlington, Virginia
Peter L. Wilkerson
    Archivist, South Carolina Historical Society, Charleston
Mac Wyckoff
    Historian, National Park Service, Fredericksburg and Spotsylvania County Battlefields Memorial National Military Park

INTRODUCTION

HISTORY

The American Civil War has no formal beginning or ending dates. The war in South Carolina probably began with the call-up of the Charleston militia on December 27, 1860. Uniformed units of the Fourth Brigade, South Carolina militia, occupied Fort Moultrie and Castle Pinckney in Charleston harbor. This action was caused by U.S. Major Robert Anderson's surprise move of his garrison from Fort Moultrie to Fort Sumter on December 26. From this day until the end of the war, South Carolina men were in uniformed service under military discipline. They also began to die from the contagious diseases common to military camps and primitive medical facilities.

The first man to die in the Civil War was a South Carolinian: Private Robert Little Holmes of Company L, First South Carolina Volunteer Infantry (SCVI) (Gregg's). He died of accidentally inflicted bayonet wounds at Castle Pinckney on January 7, 1861. The wound was delivered by a friend during silly horseplay with bayoneted rifles. This senseless death was but the first in a relentless flood. The shocking casualty lists from the Virginia campaigns of 1862 were such that the Secession Convention recognized an obligation to remember and honor those who had fallen, and would fall, in state and Confederate service. On September 17, 1862, the convention passed a resolution (see appendix) requesting the executive authority of the state to collect and record the names of all those who died in service, this record to be preserved in the state archives.

Governor Francis W. Pickens responded to this resolution by appointing William B. Johnston, an editor of a Columbia newspaper, *The Daily South Carolinian*, as agent to record the names of soldiers and sailors who died in service. Mr. Johnston seems to have depended initially upon reports from the commanders of South Carolina military units. His December 1, 1863 report to the General Assembly (see appendix) summarizes the returns from ten regiments. This report explains that private sources had been asked to help through advertisements in public journals. In this report Mr. Johnston states that the deaths of 4089 men had been recorded. On December 3, 1863, the legislative Committee on the Military decreed that the work had been faithfully performed and that it should be continued. Mr. Johnston dutifully placed in newspapers additional appeals to the general public and unit commanders. (See appendix for Mr. Johnston's report, the legislative response, and a sample of Mr. Johnston's notice from the December 24, 1863 issue of the *Charleston Daily Courier*.)

In the next year, however, the Committee on the Military was not pleased with Mr. Johnston's continued work. On December 22, 1864, the committee reviewed Mr. Johnston's record and found it so full of obvious errors as to render it untrustworthy. Mr. Johnston was dropped and, upon recommendation of the committee, Professor William J. Rivers of the South Carolina College was appointed to complete what has become known as "the Roll of the Dead." Mr. Johnston's ledgers were stored with other state papers and they managed to survive the war.

Professor Rivers manfully attempted to honor his assignment, but the end was near. In a letter written on November 15, 1897, to Colonel J.P. Thomas, state historian of Confederate records, Professor Rivers described his efforts to complete the Death Rolls up to 1867. (See appendix.) He noted that he was never given a chance to use the material collected by his predecessor, William B. Johnston. The two compilations thus were prepared without reference to one another. The advent of Reconstruction ended official support and interest in the Rolls.

On November 18, 1869, the first annual meeting of the Survivors' Association of the State of South Carolina met at the South Carolina Society Hall in Charleston. One of the principal purposes of this Survivors' Association was the collection and protection of Confederate records. Professor Rivers turned over his collected material to the group. He had been forced by circumstances to move to Baltimore, Maryland, and therefore could not participate directly in the organization or completion of his work.

The second annual meeting of the Survivors' Association was held in Columbia on November 10, 1870. The executive board's report on that occasion summarized the actions taken to finish and publish what had become known as "Rivers' Roll of Honor." An extract from that report follows:

"But the most valuable material offered to the Association by Prof. Rivers, in the opinion of the Board, are the names of the dead collected by him. This roll he had made up from all sources within his reach, newspaper reports, reports of friends, and some official reports. Thus collected they had been put down only in alphabetical order, that is, the names were only collected together by the initial letters and so in looking for any given name, in many cases hundreds had to be read. Gathered, moreover, from various sources and put down from time to time, it was impossible but that it should happen that some names be twice or even thrice entered, and this was more likely to happen in the hurry of the official reports, the difficulty of deciphering illegible writing, and through the mistakes of the press, combined with the arbitrary method of spelling names. The same name reported from different sources was often so varied as to make a doubt as to its identity.

"The board, therefore, undertook to have this collection of names re-arranged lexicographically and fairly written out, and engaged a lady, the widow of a Confederate officer, to perform the task. This work has been done and supervised with the assistance of Professor Rivers, and we herewith present to the Association a roll of ten thousand South Carolinians who gave their lives to the Southern cause, with an appendix of two thousand more collected from sources not as authentic. The Lady who undertook the work agreed to do it for the sum of one hundred dollars and that amount has been advanced to her by members of this Board. But it is not considered a sufficient remuneration for the labor it has cost. She has been obliged to procure assistance, and the task has occupied the whole summer. The Board thinks that an inspection of the work will show that the Association is still indebted to the ladies who have performed it, and recommend that the Treasurer be authorized and instructed to pay to them the further sum of twenty-five dollars as soon as in funds.

"The Board are well aware that some names are still wanting; they themselves could supply a few omissions, but they have determined to recommend that it be published as it is, in two editions. The first with a preface, inviting corrections and additions, to be submitted to the Board, by the friends of those who fell; the second, with the additions and corrections thus made in a better and more permanent form.

"The Board have obtained estimates of the cost of publishing this Roll, together with Professor Rivers' history of the raising of troops in this State, in the two editions, and report that Messrs. Walker, Evans & Cogswell, of Charleston, offer to publish 1,000 copies of each edition for $2.50 a copy, to be paid on delivery. If then we can obtain 1,000 subscribers at $5 for the two editions, this great memorial of our dead and valuable historical work for our State will be secured.

"The Board did not feel themselves authorized to employ a Librarian until some definite arrangement had been made in regard to the finances of the Association. But they are anxious to have this office filled at once. The correspondence in regard to the rolls (unit rolls) now being prepared is large, the custody of the papers a matter of responsibility, and their arrangement a work requiring more time and attention than can be given, but by a person regularly employed to attend to it. They think that for the small salary of $100, they could obtain the services of a competent person to perform these duties. It is of great consequence, too, that the records should be kept in a secure place accessible to all. They think that they can effect an arrangement by which such a place of deposit will be found, and this only at the cost of fixing a few shelves and boxes for these books and records.

"The Board cannot close this report without calling attention of the Association still more particularly to the patriotic and laborious efforts of Professor Rivers to collect and preserve the material collected by him, as well as to the generous manner in which he has placed the results of his labor at the disposal of this Association.

"Professor Rivers, it is true, was engaged by the Legislature of the State in 1864 to undertake this work, but it should be known that he never received one cent for his services during the time he was acting under its authority. His work had indeed but been commenced when the war ended, and his official connection with the matter ceased. The great mass of the material has been collected since the end of the war by his disinterested efforts. The people of the State generally, but particularly those of whose services he has endeavored to preserve the record, owe to him a debt of gratitude. The friends of those whose names, through his exertion, are found upon the glorious roll of South Carolina's martyred dead, should appreciate and gratefully remember the services he has rendered them."

There is no evidence that the Survivors' Association ever published "Rivers' Roll of Honor." No copy is known. Mr. Patrick McCawley, state archivist at the South Carolina Department of Archives and History, has determined that "Rivers' Roll of Honor" had been deposited in the vaults of the South Carolina National Bank in Charleston. A vice president of that bank turned the volume over to the U.S. War Department sometime in 1947. The volume was then turned over to the custody of the National Archives. The National Archives microfilmed the volume under the title "Roll of the Dead South Carolina Troops, Confederate States Service," Record Group 109. This microfilm copy was used as the foundation for this compilation. In 1994 the South Carolina Department of Archives and History successfully petitioned the National Archives for the return to South Carolina of the original copy of "Rivers' Roll of Honor."

The history of "Johnston's Rolls" is more curious and humbling. The rolls were preserved

INTRODUCTION

in ledger form in the state archives and in some unknown manner became known and indexed as "Rivers' Roll of Honor." This might have been brought about by the mounting in the ledger front of a copy of Professor Rivers's November 15, 1897 letter. (See appendix.) In any case this roll was consulted and cited by many researchers, including A. S. Salley in his three-volume *South Carolina Troops in Confederate Service*. In the preparation of my own augmented compilation a review of the "Roll of Honor" in the state archives turned up the fact that there were glaring errors that would not have been condoned by a scholar of Professor Rivers's stature, mistakes such as the listing of nonexistent regiments. Also, the total list was much smaller than the 12,000 names reputed to be in "Rivers' Roll." Mr. McCawley's research into the provenance of these records has resulted in a belated but welcome reidentification of these valuable sources.

This publication thus is the end of a project that was defined and begun by the Secession Convention 134 years ago.

The last South Carolinian to die in the war within the final year of 1865 appears from this listing to be Sergeant R.H. Ward of Darlington District, Company E, 8th SCVI, who died a prisoner of war at Camp Chase, Ohio, on December 19, 1865. He had been captured at Winchester, Virginia, on September 13, 1864.

ORGANIZATION OF THIS RECORD

The organization of the individual records in this register of South Carolina dead generally follows that used in Professor Rivers's "Roll of Honor" with the addition of burial location data and the inclusion of codes identifying the information sources. Each individual record is limited to one line. This layout severely limits the information that can be included but facilitates the location of a specific record. It is intended that this compilation be a register of the South Carolina dead rather than a complete record of each individual's service. The space limitations imposed by the single-line layout has required the frequent use of unconventional punctuation and abbreviations. The appendix carries expansions of these abbreviations.

It has been assumed that this compilation will be of most value to genealogists and descendants seeking to identify a lost forebear. For this reason the location of the place of death is listed wherever it is known rather than the location of the battle that may have been the cause of death. If the place of death is not known, the battle site is listed under the assumption that death occurred in the field. It is recognized that this is a questionable arrangement but it provides help in tracing further the history of each individual. This procedure is illustrated particularly in the records of those men who died of wounds suffered at the battle of Second Manassas. It is known that most, if not all, of the South Carolina wounded were sent to hospitals in Warrenton, Virginia. There are few records, however, of those who died of wounds in Warrenton following the battle, so that it is not certain that any given casualty reached there alive.

The age data provided in the records is intended to be the individuals' ages at death. The ages cited can be of considerable value in separating the records of members of the same family bearing identical names. However the ages included in this list should be regarded with some caution, for it is suspected that the ages given in some sources were derived from records that used the individuals' ages at times of enlistment.

Every record in this compilation is based on at least one known and durable source. Many records are supported by multiple sources. These multiple sources may not agree with each other in all details. The sources cited do agree as to the individuals' identities and existence, though spellings may vary. This is of some importance, for many phantom records have been created over the years through the misspelling of names and the confusion of unit assignments. Care has been taken to eliminate these phantom records, but it must be recognized that records with multiple source citations are most likely to be dependable in spelling and record accuracy.

In many records it will be noted that certain cryptic notes have been placed in otherwise empty data columns. These notes are carried in parentheses. They are temporary comments provided as research aids. They will be removed in later editions following the completion of the record data.

INCLUDED DUPLICATIONS

Some known duplicate records have been left in this compilation as an aid to further research. This is particularly true of some cemetery records that have fragmentary names or questionable unit data. Many of the records in Hollywood Cemetery in Richmond, Virginia, are not matched with other supporting records and are thus very likely to be seriously misspelled. A number of spelling errors found in the Hollywood Cemetery roster have been identified and corrected in this compilation though the original incorrect spelling remains in the cemetery records. It is planned that later editions of this compilation will remove all known duplications.

ELIGIBILITY FOR ENTRY

Professor Rivers included in his "Roll of Honor" only those South Carolinians who died in military and naval organizations. He included South Carolinians who served in organizations from other states. A review of the many unit rosters now available, the federal prison records, and contemporary newspaper accounts shows that it may not be correct to limit the death rolls from the war to well-defined military organizations. Some civilians died as a result of enemy action. Some died in militia turnouts during Sherman's and Potter's invasions. The inclusion of South Carolinians in this compilation raises questions as to duplication in rolls prepared by other states. It also raises a question as to the identification and treatment of individuals from other states serving in South Carolina units. The following general rules have been adopted in the preparation of this listing:

■ Soldiers and sailors on active duty in South Carolina units are to be included, regardless of out-of-state origin.

■ Any and all South Carolinians not enrolled in other state organizations who died as a result of enemy action are eligible.

■ South Carolinians enrolled in other states' service are excluded under the assumption that they will be included in the rolls compiled by other states.

■ Deaths that occurred between January 1, 1861 and December 31, 1865 are eligible. Deaths that occurred after 1865 are considered only upon evidence of severe and continuous effects of service-connected disabilities.

SUMMARY

There are 18,666 records in this compilation. There are some unidentified duplications. Not all records are complete. The burial sites of the majority are unknown. The list is the most complete and accurate summary of South Carolina dead in the Confederate War that has been made.

Mr. John P. Thomas, South Carolina historian of Confederate records, reported to the state General Assembly in 1899 that a review of unit rolls in the state archives put the total deaths in service at 20,101. He further stated that the number of missing rolls raised the probable total to about 21,146. A review of the tabulations of deaths by units and by districts included in the appendix supports this estimate. This suggests that approximately 2500 names still are missing.

There are 16,235 records with known causes of death. These can be tabulated as follows:

Killed in Action	5,226
Died of Wounds	2,647
Died of Disease	6,755
Died in Prison	1,408
Accidental Deaths	155
Murdered	28
Executed	9
Suicides	3
Killed in Duels	2
Died of Exposure	2

This shows that 48.5 percent died in action, 50 percent died of disease in service or in prison, and 1.5 percent died from miscellaneous causes.

The death rates in the various regiments and other units varied widely. Some of the regiments are underrepresented in the regimental death summary in the appendix. A tabulation of the five regiments with the highest number of dead is as follows:

Orr's Rifles	745
13th SCVI	652
14th SCVI	624
Palmetto Sharp Shooters	603
6th SCVI	583

These totals are much greater than those cited by J.F.J. Caldwell in his *History of a Brigade of South Carolinians*. Caldwell lists the total dead from all causes in Orr's Rifles, the 13th SCVI, and the 14th SCVI as 535, 482, and 550 respectively. There is no ready explanation for this discrepancy, though Caldwell does indicate in his book that he had trouble accounting for men who were prisoners.

The deaths suffered by the various districts show that some, such as Barnwell, are underrepresented in the following pages. It is perhaps significant that the underrepresented districts are those without detailed published histories of the Confederate War period. The five districts with the highest deaths per thousand white, male population are:

York	183.8
Williamsburg	150.1
Kershaw	143.4
Spartanburg	137.7
Newberry	133.3

THE PERFECTION OF THE ROLL

The attainment of the 2500 or so additional names needed to complete the list of names of South Carolina's dead in Confederate service is not an impossible task since there are many records that have yet to be researched. However

INTRODUCTION

perfecting the totals and assuring the accuracy of each record will require a large amount of research. Many people are diligently involved in tracing the records of Confederate ancestors. The publication and maintenance of this register provides a means for capturing and preserving the names and service records that are known, or will be found, by these many dedicated researchers. All those who are interested in preserving this record of South Carolina's heritage are urged to share the results of their efforts by sending the material that they may find to:

<u>Research Consultant</u>
The South Carolina Historical Society
100 Meeting Street
Charleston, SC 29401-2299

Copies of all documents supporting the data reported should be included.

BROKEN FORTUNES

SOUTH CAROLINA DEAD IN CSA SERVICE 1861-1865

NAME	RANK	C	REGIMENT	AGE	DS	DIED	WHERE	WHY	BURIED	SOURCES
Abbott, Ancrum P.	Pvt.	C	1st SCVIG		RD	05/03/63	Chancellorsville	KIA	(JR=5/9/63 @ Pbg.)	ROH,SA1,JR
Abbott, Cary	Pvt.	G	24th SCVI			09/20/63	Chickamauga, GA	KIA		ROH,CDC,JR
Abbott, Daniel	Pvt.	B	7th SCVIBn	31	RD	08/21/64	Petersburg, VA	KIA		ROH
Abbott, Hamilton H.	Pvt.	K	P.S.S.		SG	06/30/62	Frayser's Farm	KIA		ROH,HOS,CDC,JR
Abbott, J.T.	Pvt.	B	P.S.S.		PS	07/01/62	Richmond, VA	DOW	(Wdd @ Gaines's Mill)	ROH,CDC,JR
Abbott, Nathaniel	Pvt.	D	2nd SCVA		DN	06/26/64	Adams Run, SC	DOD	(Inglis Lt. Arty.)	ROH,PP
Abbott, Robert R.	Pvt.	K	P.S.S.		SG	07/15/62	Manchester, VA	DOW	(Wdd @ Frayser's Farm)	HOS,JR
Abell, W.H.	Pvt.	F	6th SCVI		CR	12/20/61	Dranesville, VA	KIA		ROH,CDC,JR
Abercrombie, A.	Pvt.	B	1st SCVC		LS	01/29/64	Pt. Lookout, MD	DIP	C.C. Pt. Lookout, MD	ROH,FPH,P113
Abercrombie, A.	Pvt.		2nd SCVIRi			01/22/64	Camp Morton, IN	DIP	Green Lawn C. Indianapolis	FPH,CV,P12
Abercrombie, Houston	Pvt.	E	2nd SCVIRi		PS	08/16/64	Fussel's Mill VA	KIA		ROH,CDC,JR
Abercrombie, J.	Pvt.	G	14th SCVI		LS	06/10/62	Richmond, VA	DOD	Hollywood Cem.Rchmd. L185	ROH,HC
Abercrombie, J.K.	Pvt.	A	6th SCVC			06/15/64		DOW	(Wdd 6/11/64)	ROH
Abercrombie, James	Pvt.	C	14th SCVI		LS	06/10/62	Richmond, VA	DOD	Hollywood Cem.Rchmd. P156	ROH,HC,JR
Abercrombie, L.	Pvt.	C	14th SCVI			08/04/62	Richmond, VA	DOD	(Fever)	JR
Abernathy, A.L.	Pvt.	D	Ham.Leg.		AN	06/15/65	Richmond, VA	DOD		GRS
Abernathy, C.P.	2nd Lt.	D	3rd SCVI		SG	09/17/62	Sharpsburg, MD	KIA	Rose Hill C. Hagerstown	ROH,SA2,JR,BOD
Abernathy, E.H.	Pvt.	H	18th SCVI	28	YK	/ /		DOD		YEB
Abernathy, J.D.C.	1st Cpl.	D	3rd SCVI		SG	06/29/62	Savage Stn., VA	KIA		ROH,SA2,JR
Abernathy, J.W.	Sgt.	B	15th SCVI		UN	12/15/62	Fredericksburg	DOW	(Wdd 12/13/62)	CDC,KEB,JR
Abernathy, L.H.	Pvt.	H	18th SCVI		YK	03/19/64	Madison, FL	DOD		PP,YEB
Able, A.R.	Pvt.	F	P.S.S.			07/29/64		DOD		ROH,JR
Able, Milton	Pvt.	K	9th SCVIB			12/15/61	Manassas, VA	DOD		JR
Abney, George P.	Pvt.	C	Hol.Leg.		ED	02/15/62	Adams Run, SC	DOD		HOE,JR,PP,UD2
Abney, J.J.	Pvt.		Ham.Leg.			09/15/62	Virginia	DOD	(Measles)	JR
Abney, J.R.	Pvt.	B	7th SCVI		ED	08/04/64	Richmond, VA		Hollywood Cem.Rchmd. V653	ROH,HC
Abney, John P.	Pvt.	D	19th SCVI	25	ED	02/16/65	Columbia, SC	KIA		ROH,HOE,PP,UD3
Abney, Michael George W.	Pvt.	M	7th SCVI	29	CD	07/21/62	Manchester, VA	DOW	(Wdd @ Savage Stn.6/29/62)	EDN,CNM
Abraham, John H.	Pvt.	H	15th SCVI			/ /		DOD		JR
Abrahams, H.J. (H.F.?)	Pvt.	A	13th SCVI			03/18/62	Richmond, VA	DOD	(JR= 3/17/63)	ROH,JR
Abrams, J.A.	Pvt.	E	3rd SCVI			08/15/62	Richmond, VA	DOD		JR
Abrams, Jasper N.	Pvt.	E	3rd SCVI		NY	03/15/62	Charlottesville	DOD	(8/15/61 Culpepper/SA2)	ROH,SA2,ANY
Abrams, John B.	Pvt.	G	15th SCVI	24	WG	01/25/63	Hardeeville, SC	DOD	(HOW =1861)	ROH,CTA,HOW
Abrams, R.A.	Pvt.	I	3rd SCVI		LS	07/12/62	Richmond, VA	DOD	(To Hosp 5/25/62)	SA2,ANY,JR
Abrams, Robert	Pvt.		8th SCVI		WG	/ /	Richmond, VA			ROH
Abshear, Joseph	Pvt.	K	17th SCVI	33	YK	07/17/64	Petersburg, VA	DOW	Blandford Church Pbg., VA	ROH,BLC,YEB,PP
Acker, James	Pvt.	D	Ham.Leg.		GE	06/15/62	7 Pines, VA	DOW		GRS
Ackerman, D.S.	Pvt.	C	5th SCVC			06/23/64	Richmond, VA		Hollywood Cem.Rchmd. U415	ROH,HC
Ackerman, David	Pvt.		5th SCVC		CO	01/01/64	Virginia	DOD		ROH
Ackerman, George G.	Pvt.		5th SCVC		CO	11/23/63	Charleston, SC	DOD		ROH
Ackerman, H.F.	Pvt.	H	11th SCVI		CO	01/01/62		DOD		ROH
Ackerman, J.K.	Pvt.	H	11th SCVI	24	CO	06/25/64	Petersburg, VA	DOW	Blandford Church Pbg., VA	ROH,BLC,PP
Ackerman, J.O.	Pvt.	I	1st SCVC	19	CO	08/31/64	Mt. Pleasant, SC	DOD		ROH
Ackerman, Joseph	Pvt.		1st SCVC		CO	01/01/64		DOD		ROH
Ackerman, N.S.D.	Pvt.	H	11th SCVI		CO	01/01/64	At home			ROH
Ackis, Richard William	Cpl.		Brooks Gd.	25	CN	07/03/63	Gettysburg, PA	KIA	(KEB=Ackison)	ROH,JR,GDR,SA2
Adair, T.E.	Pvt.	F	14th SCVI		LS	02/04/62	McPhersonville	DOD	(Rheumatism)	JR
Adam, J.G.	Pvt.	B	24th SCVI		MO	04/04/64	M.C. Hos Atlanta	DOD	Oakland C. Atlanta R17#16	BIG
Adam, Wyatt	Pvt.		17th SCVI	34		08/30/62	2nd Manassas, VA	KIA		ROH
Adams,	Pvt.	C	2nd SCVA	28	OG	01/01/65	Charleston, SC	DOD		ROH
Adams, A.	Pvt.	H	25th SCVI		CN	02/17/65	Elmira, NY	DIP	Woodlawn N.C.#2219 Elmira	FPH,HAG,P65

SOUTH CAROLINA DEAD IN CSA SERVICE 1861-1865

NAME	RANK	C REGIMENT	AGE	DS	DIED	WHERE	WHY	BURIED	SOURCES
Adams, A.	Pvt.	2nd SCV			07/21/62	Richmond, VA		Hollywood Cem.Rchmd. M262	HC
Adams, A.B.	Pvt.	K 14th SCVI		ED	08/05/63	Davids Island NY	DOW	Cyprus Hills N.C.#748, NY	ROH,JR,FPH,GDR
Adams, B.	Pvt.	Post Guard			05/19/64	Columbia, SC	DOD		ROH,PP
Adams, B.F.	Pvt.	B 8th SCVI			05/24/62	Richmond, VA	DOD	(Fever)	JR
Adams, Belton O'Neall	Pvt.	K 7th SCVI	22	ED	09/13/62	Maryland Hts, MD	KIA		ROH,JR
Adams, C. Matthew	Pvt.	B 6th SCVC		ED	03/10/65	Monroe's X Rd NC	KIA	(Kilpatrick's Camp)	HOE,BHC,UD3
Adams, Calvin	Sgt.	A 1st SCVIR			09/22/61	Ft. Moultrie, SC	DOD		SA1
Adams, D.	Pvt.	F 20th SCVI		NY	08/12/64	Richmond, VA	DOW	Hollywood Cem.Rchmd. V221	ROH,HC,ANY,P12
Adams, David Sumter	Pvt.	D 19th SCVI	30	ED	07/13/62	Enterprise, MS	DOD	(UD3=Charleston, SC)	HOE,EDN,PP,UD3
Adams, Edwin	Pvt.	H 18th SCVI			08/04/64	Petersburg, VA	DOW		ROH,PP
Adams, Elijah	Color Sgt.	G 8th SCVI	24	MO	07/15/63	Gettysburg, PA	DOW	Magnolia Cem. Charleston	JR,GDR,P1,UD1
Adams, Elvin	Pvt.	H 18th SCVI		YK	/ /	At home	DOW	(Dup of Edward?)	YEB
Adams, H.	Pvt.	A 27th SCVI			11/01/62	Richmond, VA		Hollywood Cem.Rchmd. C45	HC
Adams, H.C.	Pvt.	E 24th SCVI	40	CO	06/01/64	New Hope Ch., GA	KIA	(JR= Near Marietta, GA)	ROH,CDC,JR
Adams, Harris R.	2nd Lt.	G 8th SCVI		MO	07/02/63	Gettysburg, PA	KIA	UD2	JR,GDR,UD1,KEB
Adams, Hiram L.	2nd Sgt.	C 19th SCVI		ED	05/15/65	Nashville, TN	DOW	(Wdd 12/16/64)	HOE,UD3
Adams, Ira P.	Pvt.	C 15th SCVI		LN	09/18/64	Sandy Hook, MD	DOW		TOD,KEB,P12
Adams, J. Henry	Pvt.	D 1st SCVC	25	CR	02/15/63	Lynchburg, VA	DOD	(HMC=Richmond, VA)	ROH,HMC
Adams, J. Matthew	Pvt.	B 6th SCVC		ED	03/12/65	Fayetteville, NC	KIA		ROH
Adams, J. Washington	Pvt.	C 2nd SCVI	32	UN	11/15/62	Mt. Jackson, VA	DOW	Mt. Joy B.C. UN Cty., SC	ROH,SA2,UNC,PP
Adams, J.R.	Pvt.	F 21st SCVI		MO	06/04/64	Cold Harbor, VA	KIA		ROH,HOM
Adams, J.R.	Pvt.	D 2nd SCVI			02/11/64	Richmond, VA		(Prob. John R. CMO)	ROH
Adams, J.T.	Pvt.	E 4th SCVC			07/11/64	Trevillian Stn.	KIA		JR
Adams, J.W.	Pvt.	G 1st SCVIR			09/02/62	Ft. Moultrie, SC	ACD	(Gun exploded)	SA1
Adams, James	Pvt.	C 2nd SCVA	17	OG	03/19/65	Bentonville, NC	KIA		ROH
Adams, James M. (A.?)	Pvt.	K Orr's Ri.	22	AN	08/29/62	2nd Manassas, VA	KIA		ROH,JR
Adams, Joel C.	Cpl.	H 6th SCVI		FD	06/30/62	Frayser's Farm	KIA	Oakwood C. #20,Row A,Div C	ROH,OWC,WDB
Adams, John	Pvt.	D 1st SCVIH	25	LR	09/06/62	Petersburg, VA	DOD	Blandford Church Pbg., VA	ROH,LAN,BLC,PP
Adams, John Dixon	Cpl.	G 6th SCVI	20	CR	10/24/61	Charlottesville	DOD		ROH,CMR,HHC
Adams, M.C.	Pvt.	C 4th SCVIBn			05/31/62	Philadelphia, PA	DIP		ROH
Adams, Peter L.	Pvt.	E 4th SCVC		MO	/ /	Georgetown, SC	DOD	(1862)	HOM
Adams, R.J.	Pvt.	F 15th SCVI			12/08/62	Richmond, VA	DOD		ROH
Adams, Robert W.	Pvt.	B 4th SCVC		CR	01/03/65	Elmira, NY	DIP	Woodlawn N.C.#1267 Elmira	FPH,P65,HHC,CB
Adams, Ransom	Pvt.	E Orr's Ri.	21	PS	08/01/62	Dill's Spgs., VA	DOD	(JR= Adams, Rains)	ROH,JR
Adams, Richard W.	Pvt.	C 19th SCVI		ED	08/15/64	Atlanta, GA	DOW		HOE,UD3
Adams, Robert	Pvt.	D 5th SCV			01/21/63	Summerville, SC	DOD	(Inflamation of the brain)	JR
Adams, Samuel W.	Pvt.	A 12th SCVI	19	YK	08/14/62	Richmond, VA	DOD	(Typhoid Fever)	JR,YEB
Adams, Serginsk (SP?)	Pvt.	B 1st SCV			/ /	Fts. Monroe, VA			P6
Adams, Sim	Pvt.	G 7th SCV			/ /		KIA		UD2
Adams, Simeon J.	4th Sgt.	G 7th SCVI		ED	09/17/62	Sharpsburg, MD	KIA		JR,HOE
Adams, T.L.	Pvt.	I 12th SCVI			05/16/64	Drury's Bluff VA	KIA	(Dup of T.M.?)	JR
Adams, T.M.	Pvt.	I 12th SCVI		LR	05/12/64	Wilderness, VA	KIA		LAN,JR
Adams, Thomas C.	Pvt.	A 4th SCVC		CD	08/17/63		DOD		ROH
Adams, W.	Pvt.	A 17th SCVI			11/01/62	Richmond, VA	DOD		ROH
Adams, W.	Pvt.	K 7th SCVI			09/14/62	Pleasant Val. MD	DOW	(Wdd. Maryland Hts)	JR
Adams, W.D,	Pvt.	H 25th SCVI			07/17/63	Charleston, SC	DOW	Magnolia C. Charleston	ROH,JR,MAG
Adams, W.L.	Pvt.	F 21st SCVI		MO	01/01/64	At home,sick Lv.	DOD		ROH,HOM
Adams, W.S.	Pvt.	I 4th SCVC			08/18/63		DOD	(Congestive Fever)	JR
Adams, Watson	Pvt.	A 6th SCVI		CR	05/30/62	7 Pines	KIA		CB
Adams, Wiley T.	4th Cpl.	C 19th SCVI		ED	02/07/62	Charleston, SC	DOD		HOE,UD3
Adams, William	Pvt.	A 17th SCVI	23	CR	08/25/62	Richmond, VA	DOD	(Acute Rheumatism)	ROH,JR,HHC,CB

SOUTH CAROLINA DEAD IN CSA SERVICE 1861-1865

NAME	RANK	C REGIMENT	AGE	DS	DIED	WHERE	WHY	BURIED	SOURCES
Adams, William	Pvt.	B 2nd SCRi.		PS	/ /				ROH
Adams, William	Pvt.	B 6th SCVI		YK	01/01/64	At home	DOD	(YEB= Wm. E Co.A, 12th SC)	ROH
Adamson, John L.	Pvt.	C 7th SCVI	22	AE	05/08/63	Hanover Jctn. VA	DOD	(JR= 5/22/63)	ROH,JR
Adcock, W.T.	Pvt.	G 2nd SCVIRi			10/07/64	Darbytown Rd. VA	KIA		JR
Addis, James	Pvt.	h 15th SCVI			05/06/64	Wilderness, VA	dow	Fredericksburg C.C. R6S13	JR,FBG,KEB
Addis, Robert	Pvt.	H 15th SCVI	08	UN	08/06/64	Richmond, VA	DOD	Hollywood Cem.Rchmd. V716	ROH,HC,JR,KEB
Addis, W.M.	Pvt.	K 22nd SCVI		PS	03/01/62	Columbia, SC	DOD		ROH,PP
Addison, Capers P.	Pvt.	A 27th SCVI		CN	05/07/64	Pt.Walthal Jctn.	KIA	(JR= S.P.)	ROH,JR,CDC,HAG
Addison, H.B.	Pvt.	F 5th SCVI	24	LN	01/26/62	Charleston, SC	DOD		ROH
Addison, Joseph J.	Pvt.	H 7th SCVIBn	36	RD	05/16/64	Drury's Bluff VA	KIA		ROH,JR
Addison, R.H.	Pvt.	A 5th SCVI		LR	05/31/62	7 Pines, VA	KIA		SA3,LAN,JR
Addison, W.S.	Pvt.	B 14th SCVI		ED	10/30/64	Pt. Lookout, MD	DIP	C.C. Pt. Lookout, MD	FPH,P114
Addy, John Calvin	Pvt.	15th SCVI	26	ED	08/16/64	Atlanta, GA	KIA		ROH
Addy, Simeon Lloyd	Pvt.	C 15th SCVI	19	LN	06/06/64	Lynchburg, VA	DOW	Lynchburg CSA Cem. #9 R1	ROH,JR,H15,KEB
Adger,Jr., James	Pvt.	K 4th SCVC		CN	/ /				CLD
Adicks, Henry	Pvt.	I 27th SCVI	22	CN	08/26/64	Petersburg, VA	DOW	(Wdd Ream's Stn. 8/21/64)	ROH,CDC
Adkins, Benjamin F.	Pvt.	A 16th SCVI		GE	/ /	Charleston, SC	DOD		16R
Adkins, Gilbert	Pvt.	H 5th SCVI	22	YK	/ /		DOD		YEB
Adkins, Jasper	Pvt.	H 18th SCVI	18	YK	07/30/64	Crater, Pbg., VA	KIA	(YEB=B,6th SC KIA in MS)	ROH,JR,BLM
Adkins, R.J.	Pvt.	D 22nd SCVI		PS	10/31/62	Winchester, VA		Stonewall C. Winchester VA	WIN,P12
Adkins, Thomas (SP?)	Pvt.	E 13th SCVI			11/02/61	Columbia, SC	DOD	(Typhoid Fever)	JR
Adkins, Thomas D.	Pvt.	I 12th SCVI		LR	04/17/63	Moss Neck, VA	DOD	(Pneumonia @ Camp Gregg)	LAN,JR
Adkins, William J.	Pvt.	H 5th SCVI	21	YK	11/13/61	Charlottesville	DOD	(JR= Co. B)	JR,SA3,YEB
Adkinson, Benjamin	Pvt.	B 8th SCVI		CD	07/01/63	Gettysburg, PA	KIA		GDR,JR
Adkinson, S.S.	Pvt.	H 5th SCVI			03/20/65	Ft. Delaware, DE	DIP	Finn's Pt., NJ Nat. Cem.	ROH,FPH,P41,SA
Agerton, J.A.	Pvt.	B 26th SCVI			07/16/64	Richmond, VA	DOD	(Jackson Hospital)	ROH,JR
Agnes, William	Pvt.	D 21st SCVI		CD	07/15/64	Petersburg, VA		Blandford Church Pbg., VA	BLC
Agnew, Elijah	Pvt.	A 16th SCVI		GE	05/19/65	Camp Chase, OH	DIP	Con.Cem.#1987 Columbus, OH	FPH,16R,P22,P2
Agnew, George W.	Pvt.	H 24th SCVI	20	CR	05/14/64	Atlanta M.C. Hos	DOD	Oakland C. Atlanta R4#5	CMO,BIG,HHC,CB
Agnew, J. Calvin	Pvt.	B 6th SCVI		CR	10/15/62	Union Ford, VA	DOW	Elmwood C. Shepherdstown	CRM,BOD,HHC,CB
Agnew, James	Pvt.	A 1st SCVIH		BL	08/29/62	2nd Manassas, VA	KIA		JR,SA1,UD3
Aiken, George W.	Pvt.	K 17th SCVI	20	YK	08/30/62	2nd Manassas, VA	DOW	(YEB=DOD)	JR,YEB
Aiken, Hugh Kerr	Colonel	6th SCVC	42	FD	02/24/65	Darlington, SC	KIA	(On active duty?)	BHC,LC,PP
Aiken, R.A.	Pvt.	Macbeth LA		UN	06/16/62	Columbia, SC	DOD		PP
Aiken, W.B.	Pvt.	E 15th SCVI		FD	05/12/64	Spotsylvania, VA	KIA	Spotsylvania, C.H., VA	JR,SCH,KEB
Aiton, Robert	Pvt.	C 19th SCVI		ED	/ /		DOD	(1862)	HOE,UD3
Aiton, Thomas L.	Cpl.	G 7th SCVI		ED	07/02/63	Gettysburg, PA	KIA		ROH,JR,HOE,GDR
Alaway, Simon	Pvt.	C 1st SCV			08/13/63	Gettysburg, PA	DOW	#23 5th Sec. Gbg. Gen Hos	P5,P12
Albergotti, W.M.	Pvt.	A 5th SCVC	36	CN	02/26/65	Columbia, SC	DOD	Trinity Ch. Charleston, SC	MAG,RCD
Albers, H.K.	Pvt.	A 24th SCVI		CN	06/19/64	Marietta, GA	KIA		ROH,JR
Albertson, J.D. (J.O.?)	Pvt.	A Orr's Ri.			05/03/63	Chancellorsville	KIA		JR
Albright, W.C.	Pvt.	D 1st SCVC		CR	10/11/64	James Island, SC	DOD		CDC
Albritton, Joseph	Pvt.	C 3rd SCVI		NY	05/06/64	Wilderness, VA	KIA		JR,ANY,SA2,KEB
Aldrich, C.F.	Pvt.	D 27th SCVI		CN	06/16/64	Hare's Hill, VA	KIA	(JR= Aldridge)	JR,CDC,HAG
Alewine, Chesly M.	Pvt.	C 15th SCVI	25	LN	12/26/61	Jonesville, SC	DOD	(Camp Gist)	JR,H15,TOD
Alewine, J. Lemuel	Pvt.	C 15th SCVI	40	LN	/ /	Richmond, VA	DOD	(Detailed shoemaker)	TOD,KEB
Alewine, J.E.	Pvt.	C 15th SCVI		LN	/ /			Charlottesville, VA	ROH
Alewine, J.P.	Pvt.	C 20th SCVI		LN	10/01/63	Columbia, SC	DOD		PP
Alewine, Phillip	Pvt.	C 15th SCVI	60	LN	/ /	At home	DOD		TOD,KEB
Alexander, C.	Pvt.				/ /	Columbia, SC		Elmwood Cem. Columbia, SC	MP
Alexander, D.F.	Pvt.	G 12th SCVI		PS	06/27/62	Gaines' Mill, VA	KIA		ROH,JR,CNM

3

SOUTH CAROLINA DEAD IN CSA SERVICE 1861-1865

NAME	RANK	C	REGIMENT	AGE	DS	DIED	WHERE	WHY	BURIED	SOURCES
Alexander, D.F.	Pvt.	G	12th SCVI		PS	06/27/62	Gaines' Mill, VA	KIA		ROH,JR,CNM
Alexander, Henson	Pvt.					04/02/65	Sutherland Stn.	KIA		LSS
Alexander, J.	Pvt.		Orr's Ri.			08/03/64	Richmond, VA		Hollywood Cem.Rchmd. V56	HC
Alexander, J.P.	Pvt.	K	Orr's Ri.			07/17/62	Cold Harbor, VA	KIA		JR
Alexander, J.W.	Pvt.	D	27th SCVI		CN	02/17/65	Richmond, VA		Hollywood Cem.Rchmd. W3	HC
Alexander, J.W.	Pvt.					08/10/64	Richmond, VA		Hollywood Cem.Rchmd. V224	HC
Alexander, Jasper	Pvt.	F	22nd SCVI		PS	03/20/62	Columbia, SC	DOD		PP
Alexander, John	Pvt.	B	12th SCVI			09/06/61		DOD		JR
Alexander, John Jennings	Pvt.	B	12th SCVI			09/21/61	Lightwood Knot S	DOD	(Measles)	JR
Alexander, Prier	Pvt.	A	Orr's Ri.		AN	05/27/63	Chancellorsville	DOW		JR
Alexander, R.C.M.	Pvt.	E	3rd SCVBn		CR	/ /		KIA		HHC
Alexander, R.J.	Pvt.	C	2nd SCVIRi			11/21/62	Staunton, VA			ROH
Alexander, William J.	2nd Lt.	K	16th SCVI		GE	07/29/64	Lovejoy's St. GA	KIA		16R,R47
Alford, Artemus	Pvt.	L	8th SCVI		MN	07/13/62	Richmond, VA	DOD	(Typhoid Fever)	JR,HMC,KEB
Alford, Douglas	Pvt.	H	Orr's Ri		MN	/ /	At home	DOD	(1865)	HMC
Alford, J.T.	Pvt.	G	10th SCVI		HY	/ /		DOD		RAS
Alford, J.T.	Pvt.	E	26th SCVI			01/01/63		DOD		JR
Alford, Jesse T.	Cpl.	D	9th SCVIBn		HY	06/16/62	Secessionville	KIA		ROH,PP
Alford, M.N.	Pvt.	K	8th SCVI		MO	/ /	Richmond, VA		Oakwood C.#113,Row L,Div G	ROH,OWC
Alford, Malcom A.	Pvt.	H	Orr's Ri.	17	MN	06/24/64	Richmond, VA	DOW	(Wdd @ Jericho Ford)	ROH,HMC,CDC
Alford, Michael N.	1st Sgt.	K	8th SCVI		MO	/ /		DIP	(P22 says released at end)	HOM,P22,KEB
Aliancie, U.R.	Pvt.	K	26th SCVI			08/17/64	Petersburg, VA	KIA		ROH
Alison, W. Vincent	Pvt.	I	2nd SCVI		CN	/ /	Warwick Crk., VA	KIA	(On picket)	SA2
Alison, William Terry	Pvt.	A	3rd SCVI		LS	12/22/61	Centreville, VA	DOD		JR,SA2
All, A.E.	Pvt.	G	17th SCVI			/ /		DOD		JR
Allemong, Alexander A.	1st Lt.	H	27th SCVI		CN	06/22/64	Petersburg, VA	DOW	St.Mary's R.C. Charleston	ROH,MAG,HHS,HAG
Allen, B.J. (Init?)	Pvt.	A	P.S.S.			/ /		DOD		JR
Allen, B.G.	Pvt.	D	18th SCVI		AN	02/15/62	At home	DOD		ROH
Allen, C.	Pvt.	A	23rd SCVI			10/08/64	Richmond, VA			ROH
Allen, Clardy (SP?)	Pvt.	F	Orr's Ri.			04/12/62	Danville, VA	DOD		JR
Allen, Daniel T.	Pvt.	M	10th SCVI			02/04/63			Mt. Olive B.C., Georgetown	GMG
Allen, Drury A.	Pvt.	C	25th SCVI		WG	02/20/65	Elmira, NY	DIP	Woodlawn N.C.#2308 Elmira	FPH,P65,HAG,P12
Allen, Edens	1st Lt.	E	4th SCVC		MO	/ /	At home	DOD		HOM
Allen, Ezra	Pvt.	A	23rd SCVI		SR	10/07/64	Richmond, VA	DOD	Hollywood Cem.Rchmd. V400	ROH,HC
Allen, Ezra Ellerby	Pvt.	G	Ham.Leg.			07/27/62	Gaines' Mill, VA	DOW		JR
Allen, Garland	5th Cpl.	D	3rd SCVI	27	SG	07/21/62	Savage Stn., VA	DOW	(JR= Sgt.)	ROH,JR,SA2,HOS
Allen, George	Pvt.	C	1st SCVIR		CN	07/30/62	Adams Run, SC	DOD		SA1
Allen, H. Wiley	Pvt.			24		06/24/65			Magnolia Cem. Charleston	MAG
Allen, H.C.A. (?)	Pvt.	A	12th SCVI			05/06/64	Wilderness, VA	KIA		JR
Allen, H.J. (SP?)	Pvt.	B	Wash. Arty			09/17/62	Sharpsburg, MD	KIA		JR
Allen, Henry	Pvt.	G	Orr's Ri.		AE	09/30/64	Petersburg, VA	KIA	(JR= Weldon RR)	ROH,JR,CDC
Allen, J.H.	Pvt.	H	12th SCVI	24	YK	05/12/64	Spotsylvania, VA	KIA		JR,CWC,YEB
Allen, J.H.	Pvt.	F	P.S.S.			/ /		DOW	(Dup of James H.?)	JR
Allen, J.L.	Pvt.	A	5th SCVI		RD	05/31/62	7 Pines, VA	KIA		JR,SA3,LAN
Allen, J.W.	Pvt.	F	1st SCVI			07/19/62	Richmond, VA		Hollywood Cem.Rchmd. Q147	ROH,HC
Allen, J.W.	Pvt.	D	2nd SCVI			08/13/63	Richmond, VA		Hollywood Cem.Rchmd. D105	ROH,HC
Allen, J.W.	Cpl.	G	2_th SCVI			08/30/62	2nd Manassas, VA	KIA	(JR=28th SCVI, no such	JR
Allen, Jacob W.	Pvt.	D	7th SCVIBn	24	KW	07/12/63	Bty. Wagner, SC	DOW	Magnolia Cem. Charleston	ROH,JR,MAG,HAG
Allen, James C.	Pvt.					02/19/61	Sullivan's I. SC	ACD	(Bayonet in eye, horseplay	CDC
Allen, James H.	Pvt.	K	P.S.S.		SG	/ /	At home	DOD		JR,HOS
Allen, John	Pvt.	B	22nd SCVI		SG	07/30/64	Crater, Pbg., VA	KIA		ROH,JR,HOS,BLM

SOUTH CAROLINA DEAD IN CSA SERVICE 1861-1865

NAME	RANK	C REGIMENT	AGE	DS	DIED	WHERE	WHY	BURIED	SOURCES
Allen, L.W.	Pvt.	F Orr's Ri.		PS	07/30/64			Hollywood Cem.Rchmd. V522	ROH,HC,CDC
Allen, Paul C.	2nd Lt.	A 1st SCVIH		BL	05/16/64	Lynchburg, VA	DOW	(Wdd @ Wilderness) UD3	ROH,JR,SA1,JRH
Allen, Samuel H.	Pvt.	E 1st SCVIR		RD	06/05/64	Mt. Pleasant, SC	DOD		SA1
Allen, T.W.	Pvt.	Orr's Ri.			07/29/64	Richmond, VA		Hollywood Cem.Rchmd. V529	HC
Allen, Thomas	Cpl.	C 16th SCVI		GE	/ /	Newman, GA	DOW		16R
Allen, Thomas	Pvt.	C 6th SCVI		KW	/ /		KIA		HIC
Allen, Thomas J.	Pvt.	E 6th SCVI	30	CR	04/29/62	Charlottesville	DOD	Univ. C. Charlottesville	ROH,ACH,HHC
Allen, W. Riley	Pvt.	E 2nd SCVI		KW	07/01/63	Gettysburg, PA	KIA	Magnolia Cem. Charleston	JR,GDR,SA2,HIC
Allen, W.H.	Musician	C 6th SCVC		RD	06/21/63	Columbia, SC	DOD		ROH,PP
Allen, W.S.	Pvt.	K 6th SCVI		WG	/ /		DOD	(1864, also Wdd @ 7 Pines)	CTA,HOW
Allen, W.T.	2nd Cpl.	G 23rd SCVI		MO	/ /	Rappahannock, VA	KIA	(7 Pines probably)	HOM,CDC
Allen, W.T.	Pvt.	B 10th SCVI			/ /	Cat Island, SC	DOD		RAS
Allen, Wade	3rd Lt.	D 3rd SCVI		SG	05/07/64	Ft. Delaware, DE	DIP	Finn's Pt., NJ Nat. Cem.	ROH,SA2,FPH,P3
Allen, Wiley A.	Pvt.	E 5th SCVI		YK	07/10/62	Richmond, VA	DOW	Oakwood C.#24,Row D,Div C	ROH,JR,SA3,OWC
Allen, Wiley Warren	Pvt.	A 7th SCVIBn	38	CD	08/15/64	At home	DOD	(Perhaps from KW)	ROH,HIC,HAG
Allen, William	Pvt.	H 23rd SCVI		MN	/ /	Morris Island SC	DOD		HMC
Allen, William Bell	1st Lt.	B 23rd SCVI	29	CN	08/30/62	2nd Manassas	KIA	(Eulogy in CDC)	ROH,JR,CDC
Allewalt, F.	Pvt.	Hart's HA			09/17/62	Sharpsburg, MD	KIA	(JR=Washington Arty)	JR,CDC
Alley, Thomas J.	Pvt.	C 13th SCVI		SG	07/16/62	Laurel Hill, VA	DOW	(ROH=Wdd @ Gaines' Mill)	ROH,JR,HOS,CDC
Allgood, J.E.	Pvt.	P.S.S.	23	PS	05/08/64	Spotsylvania, VA	KIA	(JR= Fickling's Bty.)	JR,PCS
Allison, Casey	Pvt.	F Orr's Ri.			05/03/63	Chancelorsville	KIA		JR
Allison, Daniel M.	Pvt.	G 5th SCVI		YK	10/10/61	Richmond, VA	DOD	Hollywood Cem.Rchmd. F34	ROH,SA3
Allison, Dock	Pvt.	M P.S.S.			/ /		DOD	(May be Doe M. in P.S.S.)	JR
Allison, Doe M.	Pvt.	G 5th SCVI	20	SG	10/09/61	Richmond, VA	DOD		ROH,SA3
Allison, J.B.	Pvt.	B 7th SCVI			09/07/62	Pleasant Val. MD	DOW	(Date seems wrong)	JR
Allison, James R.	Pvt.	M P.S.S.			/ /	Charlottesville	DOD		ROH,JR
Allison, Newton Jasper	Cpl.	D 3rd SCVIBn		LS	06/29/62	Adams Run, SC	DOD	(Typhoid Fever PP=Co.G)	ROH,JR,PP
Allison, W.D.	Pvt.	K 18th SCVI	19		02/15/62	Charleston, SC	DOD		ROH,JR
Allison, William Alford	Pvt.	F Ham.Leg.			/ /		DOD	(Consumption)	JR
Alston, J. Julius P.	1st Lt.	E 1st SCVA	26	CN	09/20/63	Charleston, SC	DOD	Christ Ch. Greenville, SC	ROH,SCA,WLI,PP
Alston, John William	Pvt.	B 6th SCVI		FD	07/20/62	Richmond, VA	DOW	(Wdd 6/30 @ Frayser's Fm.)	ROH,JR,WDB
Alston, Marion K.	Pvt.	F 15th SCVI	26	GE	09/14/62	South Mtn., MD	KIA	Christ Ch. Greenville, SC	JR,GEE,KEB,PP
Alston, Peter	Pvt.	H 6th SCVI	17	YK	06/29/62	Savage Stn., VA	KIA		YEB
Alston, Thomas Pinckney	Lt. Col.	1st SCVIG	32	CN	06/19/64	Richmond, VA	DOW	Magnolia Cem., Charleston	ROH,JR,SA1,CV
Alston, Washington	2nd Sgt.	L 1st SCVIG	18	CN	12/13/62	Fredericksburg	KIA	All Saints, Pawleys I. SC	ROH,JR,GNG,SA1
Altman, Adam Miles	Pvt.	B 3rd SCVC			12/18/62		DOD	(Pneumonia)	JR
Altman, Calvin T.	Pvt.	I 10th SCVI	24	WG	09/20/63	Chickamauga, GA	KIA	(Perhaps MN district)	RAS,CTA,HOW,HM
Altman, Dempsey	Pvt.	F P.S.S.		LN	06/06/62	Fts. Monroe, VA	DOW	(Wdd @ 7 Pines)	ROH,JR,CDC,CNM
Altman, J.	Pvt.	H 8th SCVI		MN	12/30/61	Charlottesville	DOW	Univ. C. Charlottesville	JR,HMC,ACH,KEB
Altman, J. Benjamin	Pvt.	I 21st SCVI		MN	03/28/62	Georgetown, SC	DOD	(JR=4/13/62)	JR,HMC,HAG,PP
Altman, J. Wesley	Pvt.	I 21st SCVI		MN	05/09/64	Swift Creek, VA	DOW	(JR & PP= DOD 3/28/62)	JR,HMC,CDC,PP
Altman, James P.	Pvt.	A 21st SCVI		GN	03/29/65	Elmira, NY	DIP	Woodlawn N.C, Elmira 2536W	ROH,FPH,P65,HA
Altman, John A.	4th Cpl.	E 1st SCVIG		MN	06/15/63	Gordonsville, VA	DOD	(Promoted for bravery)	SA1,PDL,HMC
Altman, John Alfred	Pvt.	G 15th SCVI	19	WG	05/06/64	Wilderness, VA	DOW	Lynchburg CSA Cem. #9 R1	ROH,BBW,UD1,HO
Altman, Samuel S.	Pvt.	I 21st SCVI		MN	04/06/62	Georgetown, SC	DOD		JR,HMC,HAG
Altman, Solomon	Pvt.	F P.S.S.			/ /		DOD		JR
Altman, W.J.	Cpl.	K 25th SCVI			01/01/63	Wilmington, NC	DOD	(HAG=Pvt. W.T.)	JR
Alton, J.P.	1st Sgt.	A 22nd SCVI			07/30/64	Crater, Pbg., VA	KIA		BLM
Alton, Thomas	Pvt.	G 7th SCV			/ /		KIA		UD2
Alverson, James B.	Pvt.	B 16th SCVI		GE	/ /	At home	DOD	(1861)	16R
Alverson, John L.	Pvt.	F 13th SCVI		SG	07/28/64	New Market Hts.	KIA	(HOS=Riddle's Shop)	ROH,JR,HOS

SOUTH CAROLINA DEAD IN CSA SERVICE 1861-1865

NAME	RANK	C	REGIMENT	AGE	DS	DIED	WHERE	WHY	BURIED	SOURCES
Amaker, Abram	Pvt.	I	2nd SCVA	18	OG	03/19/65	Bentonville, NC	DOW		ROH
Amaker, William H.	Pvt.	I	2nd SCVA	21	OG	06/16/62	Secessionville	KIA		ROH,CDC,PP
Amerson, J.W.	Pvt.	A	14th SCVI	30	DN	08/03/62	Richmond, VA	DOD (JR= J.D.)		ROH,JR
Amerson, James	Pvt.	A	14th SCVI	20	DN	06/30/62	Malvern Hill, VA	KIA (JR=Frayer's Farm)		ROH,JR
Amerson, John	Pvt.	A	14th SCVI		DN	02/22/65	Petersburg, VA	KIA		ROH
Ames,	Pvt.		2nd SCVC			07/07/64	James Island, SC	KIA		CDC
Ames, E.S.	Pvt.	E	P.S.S.			05/23/62	Washington, DC	DOW (Cliffborne Hos.)		JR,P12
Amick, David W.	Pvt.	C	20th SCVI	20	LN	07/15/63	Mt.Pleasant, SC	DOD		ROH,KEB
Amick, Drayton J.	Pvt.	I	15th SCVI	18	LN	07/02/63	Hagerstown, MD	DOW (Arm amputated)		P12,GDR,KEB,H15,TOD
Amick, Elijah R.	Pvt.	C	15th SCVI	20	LN	09/06/63	Gettysburg, PA	DOW	Magnolia Cem. Charleston	GDR,H15,KEB,P1
Amick, Henry Luther	3rd Sgt.	I	15th SCVI	28	LN	07/02/63	Gettysburg, PA	KIA	TOD	ROH,JR,KEB,H15
Amick, James Joshua	Pvt.	I	15th SCVI	34	LN	06/20/65	Pt. Lookout, MD	DIP	C.C. Pt. Lookout, MD	FPH,KEB,P22,TOD
Amick, Joseph Wesley	Pvt.	I	15th SCVI	19	LN	09/14/62	South Mtn., MD	KIA		ROH,KEB,TOD
Amick, S.R.	Pvt.	C	15th SCVI		LN	07/14/63	Gettysburg, PA	DOW (Letterman G.H.)		CDC,P1
Amick, Solomon D.W.	Pvt.	I	15th SCVI	34	LN	09/15/63	Frederick, MD	DOW (POW @ Boonesboro, MD)		JR,H15,KEB,TOD
Amker, W.H.	Pvt.	I	1st SCVA			06/15/62	Secessionsville	KIA		JR
Ammons, W.W.	Pvt.	D	15th SCVI			/ /		DOD		JR
Ammons, Asa	Pvt.	I	1st SCVIH		MN	05/28/63	Columbia, SC	DOD (JR= Co.L, 8th SCVI)		JR,SA1,HMC
Ammons, H. (K.?)	Pvt.	D	15th SCVI			/ /		DOD		JR
Ammons, J.	Pvt.	C	10th SCVI		MN	12/15/64	Nashville, TN	DOW		ROH,RAS
Ammons, Thomas	Pvt.	C	6th SCVI		KW	06/15/62	Richmond, VA	DOD (JR= Co.E, 9th SCVIB)		JR,HIC
Amos, James	Pvt.	K	18th SCVI			06/12/65	Pt. Lookout, MD	DIP	C.C. Pt. Lookout, MD	FPH,P114,P12
Amyet, E.J.N.	Pvt.	L	10th SCVI		MN	12/31/62	Murfreesboro, TN	KIA		ROH,JR,CDC
Ancrum, Douglas J.	Pvt.	A	2nd SCVC		KW	06/20/64	Charleston, SC	DOD	Magnolia C, Charleston	ROH,MAG,HIC
Ancrum, William Heyward	Pvt.	A	1st SCVA			12/25/63	Johns Island, SC	DOW		ROH,LCA,STR
Anderson,	Pvt.	C	7th SCV			01/20/62	Columbia, SC	DOD		JR
Anderson, A. George	Pvt.	A	2nd SCVI	25	RD	11/08/61	Richmond, VA	DOD	Oakwood C.#160 Row A,Div A	ROH,SA2,OWC
Anderson, Abijah	Pvt.	F	19th SCVI		ED	02/11/65	Camp Chase, OH	DIP	Con.Cem.#1188 Columbus, OH	FPH,P22,P27,HOE
Anderson, Alexander	Pvt.	B	16th SCVI		GE	/ /		DIP		16R
Anderson, Alexander	Pvt.	B	10th SCVI		HY	06/26/62	Brandon, MS	DOD (RAS=Tupelo, MS)		RAS,PP
Anderson, Amos G.	Pvt.	K	12th SCVI			09/27/63	Richmond, VA	DOD (Typhoid @ Chimarazo Hos.)		JR
Anderson, B.	Pvt.					02/14/63	Johns Island, SC			CV
Anderson, Bachellor	Pvt.	D	4th SCVC	39	CN	07/31/63	McPhersonville	DOD	Magnolia C.(PL)Charleston	ROH,MAG,JR
Anderson, Brylie H.	Pvt.	K	21st SCVI			07/05/63		DOD		JR
Anderson, C.W.	Pvt.	A	Orr's Ri.			03/13/63	Fredericksburg	DOW		JR
Anderson, D.J.	Pvt.	K	7th SCVC			/ /	VA	DOD		HIC
Anderson, Daniel H.	5th Sgt.	I	1st SCVIG		CN	06/27/62	Richmond, VA	DOW (JR=D.W. & 7/31/62)		ROH,JR,SA1
Anderson, Edward McK.	Major		Bgd. Staff		SR	05/05/62	Williamsburg, VA	KIA		ROH
Anderson, Elvin	Pvt.	C	15th SCVI	18	LN	07/07/62		DOD		JR,H15,TOD
Anderson, Enoch W.	Pvt.	C	15th SCVI	20	LN	04/26/62	Richmond, VA	DOD		JR,H15,KEB,TOD
Anderson, Frank	Asst. Surg		1st LA Hos		CR	10/15/64	Charleston, SC	DOD	Magnolia C.(PL) Charleston	MAG
Anderson, G.W.	Pvt.	F	7th SCVI			02/14/65	Richmond, VA		(Not in KEB or HAG)	ROH
Anderson, George Olin	Pvt.	D	Orr's Ri.		AN	07/10/62	Gaines' Mill, VA	DOW		JR,CDC
Anderson, H. Franklin	Pvt.	F	9th SCVIB	25	SR	09/06/61	Germantown, VA	DOD		ROH,JR
Anderson, H. James	2nd Lt.	E	5th SCVC	36	CN	08/18/64	at home	DOW	Christ Church Parish	ROH,CDC,R43
Anderson, H.T.	Pvt.	E	8th SCVI		DN	06/04/64	Richmond, VA			ROH
Anderson, Hiram	Pvt.	D	1st SCVC	18	CR	10/12/62	Richmond, VA	DOD		ROH,HHC
Anderson, J.	Pvt.	B	1st SCVIBn			06/19/62	Secessionville	KIA (JR=27th SCVI,not yet Fmd)		JR
Anderson, J. Gamble	Pvt.	K	23rd SCVI	38	SR	10/15/64	Charleston, SC	DOD		ROH,K23
Anderson, J.B.	Pvt.		13th SCVI			04/07/64	Richmond, VA		Hollywood Cem.Rchmd. I174	HC
Anderson, J.C.	Pvt.	B	7th SCVI		AE	08/05/63	Chickamauga, GA	DOW (JR=9/22/63)		ROH,JR,CDC,KEB

SOUTH CAROLINA DEAD IN CSA SERVICE 1861-1865

NAME	RANK	C	REGIMENT	AGE	DS	DIED	WHERE	WHY	BURIED	SOURCES
Anderson, J.C.	Pvt.	B	7th SCVI		AE	08/05/63	Chickamauga, GA	DOW	(JR=9/22/63)	ROH,JR,CDC,KEB
Anderson, J.G.	Pvt.	D	21st SCVI		MO	06/24/64	Petersburg, VA	KIA		ROH,HOM
Anderson, J.H.	Pvt.	G	6th SCVI		CR	10/31/61	Richmond, VA	DOD	Hollywood Cem.Rchmd. B127	ROH,HC,CDC,HHC
Anderson, J.J.	2nd Sgt.	F	1st SCVIG		HY	06/27/62	Gaines' Mill, VA	KIA	(JR= Cold Harbor)	JR,SA1,PDL
Anderson, James	Pvt.		Ferguson's			12/09/63	Empire S.Atlanta	DOD	Oakland C. Atlanta R40#8	BIG
Anderson, James	Pvt.	D	3rd SCVI			11/20/62	Winchester, VA	DOD	(NI SA2 3rd Bn?)	JR
Anderson, James	Pvt.	I	1st SCV			/ /	Raleigh, NC		Oakwood C. Raleigh, NC	TOD
Anderson, James E.	Pvt.		Ham.Leg.		LS	10/14/64	Richmond, VA	DOD	Hollywood Cem.Rchmd. V189	ROH,HC,RHL,UD3
Anderson, James H.	Pvt.	E	13th SCVI			05/25/62	Ashland Hospital	DOD	(Typhoid Fever)	JR
Anderson, James Robert	Pvt.	L	21st SCVI		MN	08/12/63	Summerville, SC	DOD		ROH,JR,HMC,HAG
Anderson, James S.	1st Cpl.	F	1st SCVIG		HY	11/11/61	Norfolk, VA	DOD	(JR=Portsmouth, VA)	JR,SA1,PDL
Anderson, Jesse R.	Pvt.	K	21st SCVI		DN	12/04/62	Florence, SC	DOD		JR,PP
Anderson, Joel	Cpl.	K	21st SCVI		DN	07/10/63	Morris Island SC	KIA	(Battery Wagner)	JR,CDC,HAG
Anderson, John	Pvt.	F	Hol.Leg.	38	AE	11/05/62	Gordonsville, VA	DOD	Gordonsville, VA	ROH,GOR
Anderson, John	Pvt.			39	GE	02/15/65	Smithfield, NC	DOD	Fairview P.C. GE Cty.	GEE
Anderson, John Henry	4th Cpl.	H	4th SCVI		GE	07/06/61	Leesburg, VA	DOD		SA2,HOF
Anderson, John J.	1st Lt.	F	6th SCVI	20	CR	09/30/64	Ft. Harrison, VA	KIA		ROH,R46
Anderson, John J.	Sgt.	E	6th SCVI		CR	/ /	Petersburg, VA	KIA		HHC
Anderson, John Kincaid	Cpl.	B	24th SCVI	18	FD	08/30/64	Forsyth, GA	DOW	(Wdd @ Atlanta)	ROH,JR
Anderson, John M.	2nd Lt.	E	18th SCVI	31	SG	07/30/64	Crater, Pbg. VA	KIA		ROH,JR,BLM,R47
Anderson, John W.	1st Lt.	A	3rd SCVIBn		LS	09/26/62		DOD	Stonewall C. Winchester	ROH,WIN,KEB
Anderson, John White	Pvt.	F	2nd SCVI	25	LS	09/04/64	Winchester, VA	DOW	Stonewall C. Winchester	ROH,WIN,SA2,KE
Anderson, L.	Pvt.	B	1st SCV			/ /	Fts. Monroe, VA			P6
Anderson, L.G.	Pvt.	I	23rd SCVI		CL	09/16/62	Staunton, VA	DOD	Thornrose C. Staunton, VA	ROH,TOD
Anderson, Lewis	Pvt.	C	7th SCVIBn	18	RD	01/05/63	At home	DOD		ROH
Anderson, Love	Pvt.	B	1st SCVIG		NY	04/25/65	Petersburg, VA	DOW	Nat. Cem. Hampton, VA	SA1,ANY,PP
Anderson, M.R.	Pvt.	K	21st SCVI		DN	05/16/64	Drury's Bluff VA	KIA		ROH,JR,CDC,HAG
Anderson, M.Y.	Pvt.	I	3rd SCVI		LS	10/20/64	Strasburg, VA	DOW	(Wdd 10/13/64)	SA2,KEB
Anderson, M.Y.	Pvt.	C	2nd SCV			10/17/64	Mt. Jackson, VA			PP
Anderson, R.T.	Pvt.	L	7th SCVI		HY	06/29/62	Savage Stn., VA	KIA	(Not in KEB)	ROH,CDC,CNM
Anderson, Richard	Pvt.	E	12th SCVI	30	LR	10/21/61	Columbia, SC	DOD		ROH,JR,LAN,PP
Anderson, Richard	Lt. Col.		15th SCVI		RD	10/18/61	Columbia, SC	DOD	(Lightwood Knot Springs)	ROH,JR,LC
Anderson, Robert	Pvt.	C	19th SCVI		LS	07/22/64	Atlanta, GA	KIA		HOE,UD3
Anderson, Robert	Pvt.				WG	/ /		KIA		HOW
Anderson, Robert C.	Pvt.	F	1st SCVIG		HY	07/06/62	Danville, VA	DOD	(JR=Richmond, 1861)	JR,SA1,PDL
Anderson, S.	Pvt.	B	1st SCV			04/24/65	Fts. Monroe, VA		Nat. Cem. Hampton, VA	TOD
Anderson, Samuel W.	Pvt.	A	25th SCVI		CN	10/31/63	Ft. Sumter, SC	KIA	Magnolia C.(PL)Charleston	ROH,JR,WLI,PP
Anderson, Stephen	Pvt.	F	19th SCVI	30	ED	05/28/62	Okolona, MS	DOD	(ROH=Tupelo, MS)	ROH,PP
Anderson, Tapley Andrew	5th Sgt.	K	2nd SCVRi.	35	AE	09/30/64	Ft. Harrison, VA	KIA		ROH,JR
Anderson, Thomas	Pvt.	B	15th SCVI			/ /		DOW		JR,KEB
Anderson, W.	Sgt.	F	14th SCVI		LS	04/01/65	Richmond, VA		Hollywood Cem.Rchmd. W574	HC
Anderson, W.B.	Pvt.	F	P.S.S.		LN	05/23/64	Hanover Jctn. VA	KIA		ROH,JR
Anderson, W.D. (T.?)	Pvt.	E	8th SCVI			09/17/62	MD		DOW (Wdd @ Maryland Hts.)	JR
Anderson, W.F.	3rd Cpl.	F	21st SCVI		MO	06/15/64	NC		DOW (Dup of William T.?)	ROH
Anderson, W.H.	Pvt.	K	23rd SCVI	28	SR	09/15/63	Charleston, SC	DOD		ROH
Anderson, W.H.	Pvt.	I	3rd SCVI		LS	05/16/63	Fredericksburg	DOD	Spotsylvania C.H., VA	JR,SCH,SA2
Anderson, W.J.	Pvt.	K	19th SCVI		ED	07/22/64	Atlanta, GA	KIA	(NI HOE)	ROH,JR
Anderson, William	Major		P.S.S.	29	AN	07/04/62	Frayser's Farm	DOW	1st Baptist C. Anderson SC	ROH,JR,CDC,LC
Anderson, William D.	Pvt.	G	Orr's Ri.		AE	10/22/62	At home	DOW	(Wdd@2M JR=DOD@Hodges SC)	ROH,JR,CDC
Anderson, William D.	2nd Lt.	K	P.S.S.	23	SG	11/16/63	Campbell Stn. TN	KIA	Fairview P.C. Greenville	ROH,HOS,GDC,R4
Anderson, William Frank	3rd Cpl.	B	3rd SCVI		NY	03/25/62	Richmond, VA	DOD	(W.A. in KEB)	ROH,SA2,ANY,KE

SOUTH CAROLINA DEAD IN CSA SERVICE 1861-1865

NAME	RANK	C REGIMENT	AGE	DS	DIED	WHERE	WHY	BURIED	SOURCES
Anderson, William L.	Pvt.	C 5th SCRes			02/01/62	Columbia, SC	DOD	Elmwood Cem. Columbia, SC	PP
Anderson, William T.	Pvt.	F 21st SCVI		MO	06/21/64	Richmond, VA	DOD	Hollywood Cem.Rchmd. U663	ROH,HC,HOM,HAG
Anderson, Wm. Franklin	Pvt.	Orr's Ri.			08/10/62	Virginia	DOD	(Sunstroke on the march)	JR
Anderson, Thomas	Pvt.	1st SCV			/ /	Raleigh, NC	DOD		WAT
Andrews,	Pvt.	F 2nd SCVC		GE	08/01/63	Brandy Stn., VA	KIA		ROH
Andrews, B.	Pvt.	G 2nd SCVIRi			/ /			Oakwood C.# 44 Row L,Div C	ROH,OWC
Andrews, C.J.	Cpl.	A 14th SCVI		DN	07/03/62	Richmond, VA	DOD	(Typhoid RR=7/15/62)	ROH,JR
Andrews, D.J.	Pvt.	I 10th SCVI		MN	05/14/64	Resaca, GA	DOW		RAS,HMC
Andrews, George	Pvt.	G 1st SCVA			07/24/63	Bty. Wagner, SC	KIA	Magnolia C. Charleston	ROH,MAG
Andrews, H.M.	Sgt.	I 17th SCVI		LR	04/16/62	Johns Island, SC	DOW	(JR=W.W.)	ROH,JR,LAN
Andrews, Henry A.	Pvt.	F 3rd SCVI	22	LS	04/22/63	Lynchburg, VA	DOD	(Consumption)	ROH,JR,SA2
Andrews, J.H.	Pvt.	F 13th SCVI		SG	05/25/62	Virginia	DOD		JR,HOS
Andrews, James	Pvt.	Beaufort A		BT	03/04/64	Camp Morton, IN	DIP	Green Lawn C. Indianapolis	FPH,CV
Andrews, James	Pvt.	D 3rd SCVI		SG	09/14/62	Maryland Hts. MD	KIA	(SA2 says sick in Hos.)	HOS,SA2
Andrews, John B.	Pvt.	B 1st SCVIBn	21	CN	06/14/62	James Island, SC	KIA	(Gunboat shell)	ROH,CDC
Andrews, Joseph	Pvt.	F 13th SCVI		SG	06/21/64	Richmond, VA	DOD	Hollywood Cem.Rchmd. U57	ROH,HC,HOS
Andrews, Newton C.	Cpl.	A 8th SCVI		DN	11/22/63	Dalton, GA			ROH,PP
Andrews, Peter	Pvt.	F 13th SCVI		SG	08/15/62	Virginia		(Day date is approximate)	HOS
Andrews, R.E.	Pvt.	A 14th SCVI	32	DN	12/08/63	Columbia, SC	DOD	Elmwood Cem. Columbia, SC	ROH,JR,MP,PP
Andrews, W.J.	Sgt.	A 14th SCVI	22	DN	10/18/61	At home	DOD	(See P89,DEB Carterville)	ROH,JR,DEB
Andry, John (Addy, J.M.?	Pvt.	H 3rd SCVI		LN	09/20/64	Chickamauga, GA	KIA	Mayer Family Gvyd. NY, SC	NCC
Angel, Alfred Henry	Pvt.	A 18th SCVAB	29	CN	04/24/65	Averysboro, NC	DOW	Chicora C. Harnett Cty. NC	ROH,WAT,PP
Anglesea,	Pvt.	A 1st SCVA			07/18/63	Bty. Wagner, SC	KIA		ROH
Angleser, R.	Pvt.	Ferguson's			01/23/64	M.C.Hos Atlanta	DOD	Oakland C. Atlanta R13#13	BIG
Angley, A.M.	Pvt.	D 17th SCVI		BL	12/18/62	Columbia, SC	DOD	(JR= Co.G @ Goldsboro)	ROH,JR
Angus, W.G.	2nd Lt.	H 22nd SCVI			06/05/64				R48
Antonio, L.W.	Pvt.	C 7th SCVIBn		RD	12/22/62	Columbia, SC	DOD		ROH,HAG,PP
Appleby, Albert R.	Sgt.	C 24th SCVI	21	CO	12/16/64	Nashville, TN	KIA	(PP=Franklin, TN)	ROH,TEB,PP
Appleby, D.C.	Sgt.	C 24th SCVI		CN	/ /	Atlanta, GA	DOW		DRE
Appleby, Franklin B.	Sgt.	F 6th SCVC	26	CO	10/20/64	Richmond, VA	DOD	(Exchanged POW)	CAG,P41,P42,P47
Arant, A.	Pvt.	E 9th SCVI			02/19/62	Camden, SC	DOD		JR
Arant, B.J.	Pvt.	C 25th SCVI		WG	08/15/64	Richmond, VA		(Not in HAG or HOW)	ROH
Arant, Daniel	Pvt.	B 20th SCVI		OG	/ /	At home	DOD	(mem to CNM 2/15/62)	CNM
Arant, F.	Pvt.	C 1st SCVIR			06/18/63	Charleston, SC	DOD	Magnolia C. Charleston	ROH,MAG
Arant, George	Pvt.	H Ham.Leg.		OG	09/06/62	Virginia	DOD		ROH
Arant, J.G.	Color Sgt.	Hood's Rgt			09/14/62		DOD		JR
Arant, J.W.	Pvt.	A 5th SCVC		OG	02/21/65	Pt. Lookout, MD	DIP	C.C. Pt. Lookout, MD	ROH,FPH
Arant, L.A.	Pvt.	I 20th SCVI		LN	07/25/64	Richmond, VA		(NI KEB)	ROH
Arant, M.R.	Pvt.	F 2nd SCVA	3	OG	08/24/64		DOD		ROH
Archer, H.S.	Pvt.	G 18th SCVI			07/30/64	Crater Pbg., VA	KIA		ROH,JR
Archer, Smith	Pvt.	G 18th SCVI	21	YK	07/30/64	Crater, Pbg., VA	KIA		JR,YEB
Ard, Andrew J.	Cpl.	F 10th SCVI		MN	/ /	Saltillo, MS	DOD		RAS,HMC,PP
Ard, Benjamin R.	Cpl.	K 25th SCVI		WG	06/01/65	Elmira, NY	DIP	Woodlawn N.C.#2904 Elmira	FPH,HAG,P6,P65
Ard, E. Frank	Pvt.	G 15th SCVI		WG	02/25/63	Frederick, MD	DOW	Mt. Olivet Cem. C.S.#190	ROH,JR,FPH,BOD
Ard, Emanuel H.	Pvt.	K 21st SCVI		WG	09/20/64	Elmira, NY	DIP	Woodlawn N.C.#340 Elmira	FPH,HOW,P120,HAG
Ard, J.	Pvt.	K 25th SCVI	28	WG	05/09/64	Swift Creek, VA	KIA	(May be James Co. C)	CTA,HOW,HAG
Ard, John J.	Pvt.	G 15th SCVI	23	WG	11/28/63	Ft. Delaware, DE	DIP	Finn's Pt., NJ Nat. Cem.	FPH,CDC,P5,P40
Ard, Joseph O.	Pvt.	C 25th SCVI	28	WG	10/20/64	Raleigh, NC	DOD	Oakwood Cem. Raleigh, NC	CTA,HOW,HAG,TOD
Ard, R.	Pvt.	G 15th SCVI		WG	05/02/63	Chancellorsville	KIA		JR,CDC,KEB
Ard, Samuel R.	Pvt.	G 15th SCVI	37	WG	05/24/63	Chancellorsville	DOW	Fredericksburg C.C.R6S13	FBG,CTA,HOW,KEB
Areheart, Henry	Pvt.	I 3rd SCVC		LN	04/10/64	Charleston, SC	DOD		ROH

SOUTH CAROLINA DEAD IN CSA SERVICE 1861-1865

NAME	RANK	C	REGIMENT	AGE	DS	DIED	WHERE	WHY	BURIED	SOURCES
Areheart, Henry M.	Pvt.	C	20th SCVI		LN	04/15/64	Sullivan's I. SC	DOD	(Archart in KEB)	ROH,KEB
Argoe, Leven	Pvt.	I	22nd SCVI		OG	02/27/63	Richmond, VA			ROH
Argoe, R.M.	Pvt.	K	1st SCVIH		OG	11/01/62	Richmond, VA	DOD	(Died of Peritonitis)	ROH,SA1,JRH
Arial, John Harvey	Cpl.	F	1st SCVC	30	PS	04/05/62	Adams Run, SC	DOD	Arial Family C. Easley, SC	PP,UD1
Arledge, J.L.	Pvt.	B	3rd SCV			04/03/65	Raleigh, NC		Oakwood Cem. Raleigh, NC	TOD
Arledge, Joseph	Pvt.	C	7th SCVIBn	18	FD	01/11/65	Wilmington, NC	DOD		ROH
Arms, E.C.	1st Sgt.	D	P.S.S.		SR	05/15/62	Williamsburg, VA	DOW		ROH
Arms, Edward S.	Pvt.	E	P.S.S.		WG	05/22/62	Cliffburn GH, DC	DOW	Arlington N.C. Sec 15	ROH,CDC,P6,PP
Armstrong, A.	Pvt.	B	1st SCVC		LS	01/01/63		DIP		ROH
Armstrong, A.C.	Pvt.	F	1st SCVC			09/19/62	Richmond, VA	DOD	Hollywood Cem.Rchmd. A92	ROH,JR,HC
Armstrong, Alexander	1st Sgt.	F	Orr's Ri.		PS	07/17/62	Richmond, VA		Hollywood Cem.Rchmd. H165	HC,CDC
Armstrong, Archibald D.	Pvt.	D	27th SCVI		CN	08/15/65	Chester, SC		(D.A. in HAG)	ROH,HAG
Armstrong, Edward C.	Pvt.	H	5th SCVI	22	UN	09/15/62	Warrenton, VA	DOD	(JR=Staunton, VA)	ROH,JR,SA3
Armstrong, George W.	Pvt.	F	18th SCVI	29	UN	02/10/62	Charleston, SC	DOD	Skull Shoals Ch. UN Cty.	ROH,JR,UNC
Armstrong, J. Bryant	Pvt.	K	P.S.S.		UN	07/21/62	Charlottesville	DOD	Univ. C. Charlottesville	ROH,JR,SA3,ACH
Armstrong, James A.	Pvt.	I	14th SCVI		AE	05/12/64	Spotsylvania, VA	KIA	(RR=Fraser's Fm. 7/28/64)	HOL,JR
Armstrong, Joel	Pvt.	E	17th SCVI	23	YK	07/30/64	Crater Pbg., VA	KIA	(JR=7/17/64)	ROH,JR,YEB
Armstrong, John A.	Pvt.	I	14th SCVI	21	AE	06/30/64	Fussell's Mill	KIA		ROH
Armstrong, Robert J.	Pvt.	F	5th SCVI	24	YK	05/06/64	Wilderness, VA	KIA	(JR= Lt.) CB	ROH,JR,SA3,YEB
Armstrong, Thomas H.	Pvt.	d	7th SCVI		UN	10/09/64	Richmond, VA		Hollywood Cem.Rchmd. V323	ROH,HC
Arnett, Benjamin O.	Pvt.	B	24th SCVI		MN	06/15/64	Atlanta, GA	DOD	Oakland C. Atlanta, R4#6	ROH,BIG
Arnett, J.A.	Pvt.	I	4th SCVC		WG	/ /		DOD	(1863)	CTA,HOW
Arnett, K.	Pvt.	H	23rd SCVI		MN	08/15/64				HMC
Arnold, Aaron	Pvt.	B	1st SCVIBn		CN	08/10/63		DOD	(Typhoid Fever)	ROH,JR
Arnold, Elias	Pvt.	C	22nd SCVI		SG	08/26/62	At home	DOD	(Intermitent Fever)	ROH,JR
Arnold, H. Berry	1st Sgt.	L	Orr's Ri.		AN	12/16/62	Fredericksburg	DOW		ROH,CDC,JR
Arnold, J.H.	Pvt.	G	14th SCVI			07/10/62	Richmond, VA	DOD	(Typhoid Fever)	JR
Arnold, James	Pvt.	C	22nd SCVI			09/15/62		DOD	(Typhoid, Nimrod?)	JR
Arnold, John	Pvt.	I	P.S.S.		PS	07/20/62	Petersburg	DOD	Blandford Church Pbg., VA	ROH,BLC,PP
Arnold, John	Pvt.	H	14th SCVI			06/27/62	Gaines' Mill VA	KIA		JR,CNM
Arnold, John	Pvt.	H	14th SCV			/ /	(June 1862)	KIA		UD2
Arnold, John C.	2nd Lt.	E	16th SCVI		GE	11/30/64	Franklin, TN	DOW	Macgavock C. Frkln Gv #38	ROH,16R,WCT,PP
Arnold, John W.	Pvt.	E	7th SCVC	32	LS	/ /	Williamsburg, VA	KIA	(1863, scouting)	ANY,RHL,UD3
Arnold, Malun David	Cpl.	G	19th SCVI		AE	03/15/63	Dalton, GA	DOD		HOL
Arnold, Nimrod	Pvt.	C	22nd SCVI		SG	11/11/62	At home	DOD	(Consumption)	ROH,JR
Arnold, Silas	Pvt.	I	P.S.S.		PS	07/17/62	Staunton, VA	DOD	(ROH=Petersburg, VA)	ROH,JR
Arnold, William A.	Pvt.	C	14th SCVI		LS	07/01/63	Staunton, VA	DOD	Thornrose C. Staunton, VA	JR,TOD
Arrant, David	Pvt.	I	3rd SCVI		LS	11/08/62	Staunton, VA	DOD		ROH,JR,SA2
Arrant, J.W.	Pvt.	I	3rd SCVI		LS	11/17/62	Richmond, VA	DOD	Hollywood Cem.Rchmd. S246	HC,SA2,JR
Arrant, James H.	Pvt.	D	1st SCVIH		LR	06/12/62	Charleston, SC	DOD	(Died, Remittant Fever)	ROH,LAN,SA1,JR
Arrants, Harmon	Pvt.	K	7th SCVC		KW	/ /		DOD		HIC
Arrants, Joseph H.	Pvt.	E	2nd SCVI	25	KW	09/17/62	Sharpsburg, MD	KIA		ROH,SA2,HIC,ED
Arrants, Robert Benj.	Pvt.	E	2nd SCVI		KW	09/20/63	Chickamauga, GA	KIA		ROH,JR,SA2,HIC
Arthur, Marshall	Pvt.	B	19th SCVI		ED	11/25/63	Missionary Ridge	KIA		HOE
Arthurs, Stephen E.	Pvt.	H	9th SCVIB		ED	09/07/61	Germantown, VA	DOD	(JR= 9/20/61)	ROH,JR
Asbill, Arion B.	Pvt.	F	19th SCVI	30	ED	10/25/62	Knoxville, TN	DOD	Bethel C. Knoxville, TN	ROH
Asbill, Jefferson J.	Pvt.	A	19th SCVI	30	ED	10/03/62	Danville, KY	DOD		ROH,HOE,UD3
Asbill, Loy P.	Pvt.	A	19th SCVI	32	ED	10/16/62	Wildcat Mtn., KY	DOD		ROH,HOE,UD3
Asbury, Oscar	Pvt.	I	6th SCVI		CR	08/30/62	2nd Manassas, VA	KIA	CB	ROH,JR,WDB,HHC
Asbury, W.E.	Sgt.	A	15th SCVI		RD	05/08/64	Spotsylvania, VA	KIA	(Pvt. in KEB)	ROH,JR,KEB
Ashby, John H.	Pvt.		Tucker's C	32	GN	04/02/62	Pawleys Isl., SC	DOD	Elmwood Cem. Georgetown SC	PP,GNT

SOUTH CAROLINA DEAD IN CSA SERVICE 1861-1865

NAME	RANK	C	REGIMENT	AGE	DS	DIED	WHERE	WHY	BURIED	SOURCES
Ashley, A.J.	1st Lt.	A	1st SCVIG		BL	06/27/62	Gaines' Mill, VA	KIA		ROH,JR,SA1
Ashley, Aaron	Pvt.	I	19th SCVI	42	AE	08/28/64	Griffin, GA	DOW (Wdd 7/28/64)		ROH
Ashley, G.	Pvt.	F	Hol.Leg.		AE	12/11/62	Warrenton, VA	DOW (Wdd @ 2nd Manassas)		ROH
Ashley, J.R.	Pvt.	D	19th SCVI		ED	10/03/62	Danville, KY	DOD	Danville Cem. C.L.#11 KY	FPH,CV
Ashley, James D.	Pvt.	I	19th SCVI	22	AE	02/10/62	Charleston, SC	DOD		ROH
Ashley, Joshua Jackson	Pvt.	I	19th SCVI	22	AE	06/01/62	Guntown, MS	DOD		ROH,PP
Ashley, Newton	Pvt.	B	7th SCVI		AE	04/24/65	Richmond, VA	DOD	Hollywood Cem.Rchmd. W570	ROH,HC
Ashley, Perry	Pvt.	B	13th SCVI		SG	07/24/62	Richmond, VA	DOD (Winder Hospital)		HOS,JR
Ashley, Reuben T.	Pvt.	I	19th SCVI	18	AE	05/16/65	Chester, SC	DOD		ROH
Ashley, Richard S.	Pvt.	G	Orr's Ri.		AE	08/24/64	Pt. Lookout, MD	DIP	C.C. Pt. Lookout, MD	ROH,FPH,P113,P5
Ashley, W.N.	Pvt.	B	7th SCVI		AE	07/16/63	Gettysburg, PA	DOW (JR=Typhoid Fever)		JR,GDR
Ashmore, G.E.	Pvt.	I	3rd SCVABn		GE	11/30/63	At home	DOD		PP
Ashmore, J.H.	Pvt.	E	16th SCVI		GE	/ /	At home	DOD (1863)		16R
Ashmore, John W.	Pvt.	B	16th SCVI	27	GE	10/17/63	At home	DOD		ROH,16R,PP
Ashworth, William (SP?)	Pvt.	H	2nd SCVIRi			09/20/62		DOD (Consumption)		JR
Askew, M.	Pvt.	G	7th SCVC		CN	04/30/65	Richmond, VA	DOD (Scurvy)		ROH,P12
Askin, William K.	Pvt.	A	7th SCVC			04/03/65	Richmond, VA	DOW	Hollywood Cem.Rchmd.	JR,P6
Askins, J.A.	Pvt.	I	10th SCVI		MN	/ /	MS	DOD		RAS,HMC
Askins, John A.J.	Pvt.	E	8th SCVI		DN	05/25/65	Camp Chase, OH	DIP	C.C.#2001 Columbus OH	FPH,P22,P27,KEB
Askins, W. Thomas	Pvt.	G	9th SCVIB		DN	02/15/62	Centreville, VA	DOD (JR=9/13/62)		ROH,JR,JLC
Atchison, J.R.	Pvt.	F	2nd SCVI			05/06/64	Wilderness, VA	KIA (NI SA2 or KEB, 2nd Ri.?)		CDC
Atkins, D.	Pvt.				AE	/ /			Fredericksburg C.C,R1S11	FBG
Atkins, Green	Pvt.	F	13th SCVI		SG	07/22/62	Charlottesville	DOD	Univ. C., Charlottesville	JR,HOS,ACH
Atkins, J.H.	Pvt.	I	15th SCVI			07/28/64	Fraser's Farm VA	KIA		JR
Atkins, John Perry	Pvt.	B	22nd SCVI		SG	03/27/65	Richmond, VA			ROH
Atkins, M. Jackson	Pvt.	B	22nd SCVI		SG	07/30/64	Crater, Pbg., VA	KIA		ROH,BLM
Atkins, R.D.	Pvt.	B	22nd SCVI		SG	10/31/62	Winchester, VA			ROH,CGH
Atkins, R.W.	Pvt.	E	3rd SCVI	17	NY	08/31/61	Culpepper, VA	DOD	Fairview C. Culpepper, VA	ROH,JR,CUL,SA2
Atkins, Ravenna	Pvt.					/ /				UD1
Atkinson, A.	Pvt.	G	Ham.Leg.			/ /	Charlottesville		Univ. C. Charlottesville	ACH
Atkinson, Abraham	Pvt.	D	23rd SCVI		CN	09/14/62	South Mtn., MD	KIA		ROH,JR,CDC
Atkinson, Alexander	Pvt.	D	21st SCVI		CD	07/14/64	Petersburg, VA	DOD		ROH,HAG,PP
Atkinson, B.	Pvt.	B	8th SCVI		CD	07/02/63	Gettysburg, PA	KIA (JR= Co.B)		ROH,JR
Atkinson, Charles Moody	Sgt.	E	7th SCVIBn	25	SR	08/21/64	City Point, VA	DOW	City Pt. N.C. Hopewell, VA	ROH,HAG,TOD,P12
Atkinson, Charles S.	Pvt.	A	Ham.Leg.	21	GN	09/01/62	Gainesville, VA	DOW (Wdd @ 2nd Man. p15 LED)		ROH,LED,CDC,WLI
Atkinson, F.	Pvt.	A	16th SCVI		GE	06/22/64	Kennesaw Mtn.,GA	KIA (NI 16R)		ROH
Atkinson, J.A.	Pvt.	A	Ham.Leg.		GN	08/30/62	2nd Manassas VA	KIA		FLR
Atkinson, J.H.	Pvt.	D	27th SCVI			05/15/64		DOW (Day date is approximate)		JR
Atkinson, J.H.	Pvt.	A	16th SCVI		GE	06/20/64	Marietta, GA	KIA		JR,16R
Atkinson, J.J.	Cpl.	A	7th SCVIBn		KW	03/14/64	Raleigh, NC		Oakwood C. Raleigh, NC	HIC,HAG,TOD
Atkinson, James S.F.	Pvt.	D	21st SCVI		CD	05/07/64	Walthall Jctn.	KIA (JR=Wilderness)		ROH,JR,CDC,HAG
Atkinson, John	Pvt.	E	2nd SCVA			07/05/64	Charleston, SC	DOD	Magnolia Cem. Charleston	MAG,ROH
Atkinson, John	Pvt.	D	23rd SCVI		CN	06/15/62				ROH,CDC
Atkinson, John L.	Pvt.	F	7th SCVI	26	ED	/ /	At home	DOD		HOE,KEB
Atkinson, John W.	Pvt.	A	16th SCVI		GE	06/23/64	Kennesaw Mtn. GA	KIA		ROH,16
Atkinson, Richard	Pvt.	D	21st SCVI		CD	05/06/62	At home	DOD (Cheraw, SC)		ROH,JR,HAG
Atkinson, S.S.	Pvt.	H	5th SCVC			03/20/65	Ft. Delaware, DE	DIP	Finn's Pt., NJ Nat. Cem.	FPH,P47
Atkinson, Samuel	Pvt.	G	Ham.Leg.			/ /			Oakwood C. #28 Row H,Div A	ROH,OWC
Atkinson, Thomas	Pvt.	G	21st SCVI		CD	04/06/65	Elmira, NY	DIP	Woodlawn N.C.#2631 Elmira	FPH,P65
Atkinson, Thomas A.	Pvt.	A	16th SCVI	27	GE	06/15/64	Marietta, GA	KIA (Kenesaw Mtn/16R)		ROH,16R
Atkinson, Thomas W.	Pvt.	D	27th SCVI	26	CO	06/01/64	Cold Harbor, VA	KIA		ROH,JR,CDC,HAG

SOUTH CAROLINA DEAD IN CSA SERVICE 1861-1865

NAME	RANK	C	REGIMENT	AGE	DS	DIED	WHERE	WHY	BURIED	SOURCES
Atkinson, Thomas W.	Pvt.	D	27th SCVI	26	CO	06/01/64	Cold Harbor, VA	KIA		ROH,JR,CDC,HAG
Atkinson, W.H.	Pvt.	B	P.S.S.		AN	01/07/64		DOD		ROH
Atkinson, W.M.	Sgt.	G	Ham.Leg.			07/13/64	Riddle's Shop VA	KIA (JR=6/13/64)		ROH,JR
Atkinson, Wiley K.	Pvt.	E	6th SCVI		DN	05/06/64	Wilderness, VA	KIA		ROH,JR,JLC
Atkinson, William	Pvt.	D	21st SCVI		CD	08/08/63		DIP	NC Beaufort, SC #53-6358	ROH,HAG,PP,P12
Atkinson, William	Pvt.		Ham.Leg.			/ /	Farmville, VA			ROH
Atkinson, William H.	Cpl.	A	7th SCVIBn	30	KW	05/16/64	Drury's Bluff,VA	KIA		ROH,JR,HIC,HAG
Atkinson, William R.	Pvt.	F	26th SCVI	25	CD	01/01/63	Church Flats, SC	DOD		ROH,JR
Atkinson, Willis	Pvt.	B	11th SCVI		CO	12/31/64	Goldsboro, NC	DOD	Willow Dale C. Goldsboro	ROH,HAG,PP
Attaway, J. Simon	Pvt.	G	1st SCVIG		ED	08/08/63	Gettysburg, PA	DOW (Wdd 7/1)	HOE	ROH,SA1,GDR,P1
Attaway, J.A.	Pvt.	F	27th SCVI	19	ED	12/21/62	At home	DOW (Wdd @ Pocotaligo)		HOE,HAG,UD3
Attaway, T.G.	3rd Cpl.	F	27th SCVI	27	ED	06/18/65	Pt. Lookout, MD	DIP	C.C. Pt. Lookout, MD	FPH,HAG,P114,P
Attaway, Towles	Pvt.	G	7th SCVI		ED	/ /		DOD		HOE,KEB,UD2
Atterbury, A.	Pvt.	H	17th SCVI		BL	07/15/64	Petersburg, VA	DOW	Oakwood C.#19,Row C,Div A	ROH,OWC
Atwell, A. (Arnold?)	Pvt.	C	7th SCVC			09/30/64	Richmond, VA	KIA		JR
Augley, A.M.	Pvt.	G	17th SCVI		BL	12/18/62	Goldsboro, NC	DOD	Willowdale C. Goldsboro NC	PP
Augustine, Samuel W.	Pvt.	G	7th SCVIBn	18	RD	05/17/64	Drury's Bluff VA	DOW		ROH,JR,HAG,HIC
Aul, Greene	Pvt.	E	11th SCVI			01/01/62		DOD		JR,HAG
Aull, W.C.	Pvt.	G	13th SCVI		NY	05/19/63	Richmond, VA	DOW	Hollywood Cem.Rchmnd. T98	ROH,ANY,HC
Aultry, Robert	Pvt.	E	Ham.Leg.		GE	07/21/61	1st Manassas, VA	KIA		ROH,JR,CDC,ETT
Austell, Samuel S.	Pvt.	I	5th SCVI		SG	06/30/62	Frayser's Farm	KIA (? NI SA3)		HOS
Austin, A.	Pvt.	F	17th SCVI		YK	10/02/62	Richmond, VA			ROH
Austin, A.M.	Pvt.		Ham.Leg.			04/25/62	Richmond, VA		Hollywood Cem.Rchmd. B21	HC
Austin, Aaron	2nd Lt.	D	6th SCVC	33	CN	09/28/63	Adams Run, SC	DOD		R43,PP
Austin, Andrew	Cpl.	K	10th SCVI		CN	02/05/62		DOD (Measles)		JR,RAS
Austin, B.F.	Pvt.		1st SCMil.			02/09/65	Charleston, SC	DOD	Magnolia C. Charleston	ROH,MAG
Austin, F.C.	Pvt.	H	Ham.Leg.			06/15/62	Richmond, VA			ROH
Austin, F.D.	Pvt.	F	3rd SCVI		LS	06/29/62	Savage Stn., VA	KIA		ROH,JR,SA2
Austin, Green B.	Pvt.	A	16th SCVI		GE	06/24/64	Kennesaw Mtn. GA	KIA	Oakland C. Atlanta, GA	ROH,16R,CVGA
Austin, J.G.	Pvt.	B	3rd SCVIBn		LS	05/08/64	Spotsylvania, VA	KIA	Spotsylvania C.H., VA	ROH,JR,SCH,R45
Austin, J.W.	Pvt.	G	6th SCVI			10/24/64	Richmond, VA		Hollywood Cem.Rchmd. E41	ROH,HC
Austin, John Thomas	Pvt.	I	16th SCVI		GE	06/22/64	Kennesaw Mtn. GA	KIA		16R
Austin, John W.	Cpl.	F	1st SCVIR		CN	02/10/62		DOD		SA1
Austin, Joseph Manning	Cpt.	I	16th SCVI	22	GE	07/28/62	West Point, GA	DOD	Christ Ch. Greenville, SC	16R,GEE,R47,PP
Austin, Lawrence M.	Surgeon		Barksdale		GE	07/19/63	At home	DOD		ROH,JR
Austin, Morgan L.	Cpl.	G	25th SCVI		BL	05/16/64	Drury's Bluff VA	KIA		ROH,JR,CV,HAG
Austin, Nathaniel	2nd Lt.	E	14th SCVI		LS	08/22/63	Gettysburg, PA	DOW	Magnolia C. Charleston	ROH,JR,MAG,GDR
Austin, T. Manning	Pvt.	A	16th SCVI		GE	/ /	At home	DOD		16R
Austin, Thomas J.	Pvt,	I	SDVI			09/15/64	LaGrange, GA		Con. Cem. LaGrange, GA	TOD
Austin, W.D.	Pvt.	F	3rd SCVI		LS	06/29/62	Savage Stn., VA	KIA		ROH
Austin, W.R.	Pvt.	C	14th SCVI			08/10/63	Gettysburg, PA	DOW		P5
Austin, Wesley	Pvt.	B	20th SCVI		OG	/ /	Sullivan's I. SC	DOD		ROH
Austin, William	Cpt.	F	Ham.Leg.	58	GE	07/21/61	1st Manassas, VA	KIA	Bethel M.C. GE Cty.	R48,GEE
Ava, E.T.	Pvt.	G	15th SCVI		WG	02/25/63	Frederick, MD	DOW		ROH
Avant, Allen	Pvt.	D	10th SCVI		MN	/ /	Okolona, MS	DOD (Prob in Con. Cem. there)		RAS,HMC,PP
Avant, B.J.	Pvt.				WG	/ /		DOD (1864)		HOW
Avant, J.W.	Pvt.	A	5th SCVC			02/22/65	Pt. Lookout, MD	DIP	C.C. Pt. Lookout, MD	FPH,P114,P6,P1
Avant, Jerry R.	3rd Sgt.	A	21st SCVI		CN	01/15/65	Pt. Lookout, MD	DIP	C.C. Pt. Lookout, MD	FPH,HAG,P6
Avant, Jordan	Pvt.	L	21st SCVI		MN	05/07/64	Petersburg, VA			PP
Avant, L.A.	Pvt.	I	21st SCVI		MN	07/25/64	Richmond, VA	DOD	Hollywood Cem.Rchmd. V159	FPH,HC,P12
Avant, M.E.G.	Pvt.	D	2nd SCVI		MN	11/15/62	Virginia	DOD		SA2

SOUTH CAROLINA DEAD IN CSA SERVICE 1861-1865

NAME	RANK	C REGIMENT	AGE	DS	DIED	WHERE	WHY	BURIED	SOURCES
Avant, Orlando R.	Pvt.	I 21st SCVI		MN	/ /	Columbia, SC	DOD		HMC,HAG
Avant, Samuel	5th Sgt.	A 21st SCVI		CN	09/26/64	Elmira, NY	DIP	Woodlawn N.C.#447 Elmira	FPH,HAG,P65,P6
Avery, Thomas M.	Pvt.	G 3rd SCVI	24	LS	09/16/61	Flint Hill, VA	DOD		ROH,JR,SA2,KEB
Avery, William L.	Pvt.	C 14th SCVI		LS	06/30/62	Frayser's Farm	KIA	(JR= Co. G)	ROH,JR
Avinger, C.J.	Sgt.	D 8th SCRes.	48	OG	01/05/65	Columbia, SC	DOW	(P.P.=J.C.)	ROH,PP
Axson, Charles Henry	Cpt.	M 1st SCVIG		CN	07/30/61	On cars to VA	MUR	St. Michael's Charleston	ROH,MAG,RCD,ALH
Axson, J. Waring	Cpt.	A 27th SCVI	35	CN	06/24/64	Petersburg, VA	KIA	1st Baptist C.Charleston	ROH,MAG,RR,DOC
Axson, Lewis S.	Pvt.			CN	01/23/62	Charleston, SC		Magnolia Cem. Charleston	MAG
Axson, R. Edwards	Pvt.	K 1st SCVIH	33	OG	12/16/62	Manchester, VA	DOD		ROH,SA1,CDC,JRH
Ayers, A.C.	Pvt.	F 11th SCVI		BT	/ /	Richmond, VA		Oakwood C.#57 Row F,Div B	ROH,OWC
Ayers, D.	Pvt.	G 22nd SCVI		CN	07/30/64	Crater, Pbg., VA	KIA		BLM,RCD
Ayers, D. Dwight	Pvt.	L 8th SCVI		MN	05/22/63	Richmond, VA	DOD	Oakwood C.#57 Row F,Div B	ROH,JR,KEB,OWC
Ayers, E.D.	Pvt.	H 22nd SCVI			07/30/64	Crater, Pbg., VA	KIA	(Dup of D. in Co.G?)	JR
Ayers, Jefferson	Pvt.	K 17th SCVI		YK	07/02/65	Pt. Lookout, MD	DIP	C.C. Pt. Lookout, MD	FPH
Ayers, John	Pvt.	C 12th SCVI		FD	/ /		DOD		HFC
Ayers, Joseph E.	Pvt.	L 21st SCVI	19	MN	05/08/64	Petersburg, VA	DOW	(Wdd @ Port Walthal Jctn.)	ROH,HMC,HAG

SOUTH CAROLINA DEAD IN CSA SERVICE 1861-1865

NAME	RANK	C	REGIMENT	AGE	DS	DIED	WHERE	WHY	BURIED	SOURCES
B___, J.B.	Cpl.	A	20th SCVI		PS	11/08/64	Winchester, VA	DOW	(Leg Amptd. by enemy)	P12
Babb, J.E.	Pvt.	E	14th SCVI		LS	06/16/62	Richmond, VA	DOD	Hollywood Cem.Rchmd. O164	HC,CGS
Babb, James M.	Pvt.	A	6th SCVC			06/24/64	Ladd's Store, VA	KIA		ROH,R47
Babb, John T.						/ /	Richmond, VA			CDC
Babb, Newton	Cpt.	I	16th SCVI	33	GE	11/06/63	AL	DOD	Fairview Cem. Greenville	16R,GEE
Babb, Samson	Pvt.	B	1st SCVC	18	LS	06/15/62	Johns Island, SC	DOD		ROH
Babcock, Frederick	Pvt.	F	6th SCVI	24	CR	05/31/62	Seven Pines, VA	KIA		ROH,WDB,HHC,JR
Bachman, C.	Pvt.	H	20th SCVI		LN	10/19/63	Bristoe Stn., VA	KIA		ROH,KEB
Bachman, T.F.	Pvt.	G	Orr's Ri.			08/01/62	Richmond, VA	DOW		JR
Backstrom, B.F.	Pvt.	A	6th SCVI	28	CR	05/31/62	Seven Pines, VA	KIA	CB	ROH,JR,WDB,HHC
Backstrom, Isaac M.	Pvt.	A	6th SCVI			06/13/61	Charleston, SC	DOD		JR
Backus, John A.	Pvt.	B	21st SCVI	18	DN	01/15/65	Ft. Fisher, NC	KIA		ROH,HAG
Bacon, Randolph	Color Sgt.	B	2nd SCVI		GE	09/25/64	Charlestown, VA	DOW	(Wdd '62, POW Gtsbg,Xcgd ?)	ROH,JR,SA2,P1
Baers, L.N.	Pvt.	K	18th SCVI			07/15/62	Charleston, SC	DOD	Magnolia Cem. Charleston	ROH,MAG
Baggett, Isom	Pvt.	G	4th SCVC		CO	03/27/64	Green Pond, SC			PP
Baggott, James M.	Sgt.	B	1st SCVA	25	LN	06/16/62	Secessionville	KIA	Old Mt. Herman B.C. Lxngtn	ROH,JR,TOD,PP
Bagley, W.L.	Pvt.	G	7th SCVIBn	26	FD	05/16/64	Drury's Bluff VA	KIA		ROH,JR,HIC,HAG
Bagnall, T.	Pvt.	G	13th SCVI			07/23/61	Richmond, VA		Hollywood Cem.Rchmd. H200	HC
Bagnall, W.A.	Sgt.	E	Ham.Leg.		CL	05/31/62	7 Pines, VA	KIA		ROH,JR,CDC
Bagwell, Berryman W.	Pvt.	I	Hol.Leg.		SG	06/15/62	Adams Run, SC	DOD	(HOS=Benjamin)	ROH,HOS
Bagwell, Enoch	Pvt.	C	14th SCVI			03/13/63	Guinea Stn., VA	DOD		JR
Bagwell, G.M.	Pvt.	F	11th SCVI			/ /			Richmond, VA	ROH
Bagwell, George W.	Pvt.	K	Orr's Ri.	23	AN	01/13/62	Richmond, VA	DOW		ROH,JR,CDC
Bagwell, H.J.	Pvt.		15th SCVI			/ /	Farmville, VA			ROH
Bagwell, Hiram S.	Pvt.	I	13th SCVI	40	SG	07/17/62		DOD		ROH
Bagwell, J.L.	Pvt.	C	14th SCVI		LS	07/28/64	Fraysers Farm VA	KIA		ROH,JR
Bagwell, James	Pvt.	I	13th SCVI	23	SG	12/08/63	Lynchburg, VA	DOD	Lynchburg CSA Cem. #3 R5	ROH,JR,BBW
Bagwell, James	Pvt.	E	16th SCVI	22	AN	01/17/62	Charleston, SC	DOD		ROH,16R
Bagwell, James W.	Pvt.	I	13th SCVI	32	SG	07/03/63	Gettysburg, PA	KIA		ROH,JR,HOS
Bagwell, Jasper	Pvt.	E	16th SCVI	39	LS	06/15/63	At home	DOD		ROH,16R
Bagwell, John J.	Pvt.	K	Orr's Ri.	21	AN	06/18/62	Dill Farm, VA	DOD		ROH,JR,CDC
Bagwell, Kelsey	Pvt.	A	5th SC Res	36		01/04/63	Adams Run, SC	DOD		PP
Bagwell, Lewis	Pvt.	G	2nd SCVIRi			06/15/64	White Sulpher Ss			PP
Bagwell, P.	Pvt.	H	7th SCVI			/ /	Charlottesville		University Cem. Ch'ville	ACH
Bagwell, Samuel	Pvt.	B	6th SCVC		ED	06/15/64				ROH
Bagwell, Samuel	Pvt.	I	13th SCVI	19	SG	09/29/62	Richmond, VA	DOD	(Also Wdd @ 2M)	ROH,JR,HOS
Bagwell, Sandford V.	Pvt.	E	16th SCVI	30	GE	01/25/63	Adams Run, SC	DOD		ROH,16R,PP
Bagwell, Simpson	Pvt.	I	13th SCVI	35	SG	09/09/62	2nd Manassas	DOW	(Prob in Warrenton)	ROH,JR,HOS
Bagwell, Thomas	Pvt.	I	13th SCVI		SG	06/15/62	Ashland Sta., VA	DOD		ROH
Bagwell, Thomas T.	Pvt.	C	4th SCVI	18	AN	08/25/61	Culpepper, VA	DOD	Fairview C. Culpepper, VA	JR,CGH,SA2,CDC
Bagwell, W.H.	Pvt.	C	Hol.Leg.			04/25/62	Richmond, VA	DOD	Hollywood CEm.Rchmd. W634	HC
Bagwell, Wiley H.	2nd Lt.	C	Hol.Leg.	25	SG	11/05/64	Petersburg, VA	KIA		ROH,HOS
Bagwell, William	Pvt.	C	4th SCVI		AN	08/24/61	Germantown, VA	DOD		SA2,HOF
Bagwell, William A.	Pvt.	K	Orr's Ri.	25	AN	08/08/62	Richmond, VA	DOW	Oakwood C.#16,Row S,Div C	ROH,JR,OWC,CDC
Bagwell, William T.	Pvt.	I	13th SCVI			08/08/62	Richmond, VA	DOD		ROH,JR
Bagwell, William W.	Pvt.	G	7th SCVI		ED	02/19/65	Camp Chase, OH	DIP	Con.Cem.#1346 Columbus, OH	FPH,P6,UD2,KEB
Bail, James E.	Pvt.	H	1st SCVIG		CN	08/29/62	2nd Manassas	KIA		ROH,JR,SA1,BBC
Bailee, W.	Pvt.	E	3rd SCVI			12/31/62	Fredericksburg	DOW	(3rd Bn?)	JR
Bailes, Charles N.	Pvt.	B	6th SCVI	25	YK	05/21/62	Richmond, VA	DOD	Hollywood Cem.Rchmd. F14	HC,ROH,YEB
Bailes, Joseph	Pvt.	H	6th SCVI		YK	03/29/62	Orange C.H., VA	DOD		ROH
Bailey, Charles	Pvt.	G	25th SCVI		OG	04/17/65	Elmira, NY	DIP	Woodlawn N.C.#1377W Elmira	ROH,FPH,P6,P65

B

SOUTH CAROLINA DEAD IN CSA SERVICE 1861-1865

NAME	RANK	C REGIMENT	AGE	DS	DIED	WHERE	WHY	BURIED	SOURCES
Bailey, Daniel	Pvt.	D 7th SCVIBn		KW	/ /		DIP	(Wdd & POW maybe DOW)	HIC,P114,HAG
Bailey, David Harrison	Pvt.	C 18th SCVI		UN	10/28/62	Staunton, VA	DOD		ROH,JR,UNC
Bailey, E.J.	Pvt.	D 1st SCVIH		OG	07/12/64		DOD	(To Hos 4/24/64)	ROH,SA1,LAN
Bailey, Ebenezer C.	Pvt.	C 13th SCVI		SG	05/12/64	Spotsylvania, VA	KIA		ROH,HOS
Bailey, Eli B.	Pvt.	K 18th SCVI	21	SG	07/14/64	Petersburg, VA	DOW	Blandford Church Pbg., VA	ROH,BLC,PP
Bailey, Elmore C.	Sgt.	C 18th SCVI	45	UN	07/30/64	Crater, Pbg., VA	KIA		ROH,JR,BLM
Bailey, Henry	Pvt.	I 3rd SCVC	27	CN	10/18/64	Charleston, SC	DOD		ROH
Bailey, Henry L.	Pvt.	G 25th SCVI	36	OG	03/12/65	Elmira, NY	DIP	Woodlawn N.C.#2426W Elmira	ROH,FPH,P6,P65
Bailey, J.	Pvt.	E 23rd SCVI		MN	09/17/62	Sharpsburg, MD	KIA	(JR=South Mtn. 9/14/62)	ROH,JR,CDC
Bailey, J. Pressley	Pvt.	A 3rd SCVIBn		LS	02/12/62	Adams Run, SC	DOD	(NI HAG)	PP
Bailey, J.C.	Pvt.	D 2nd SCV			10/26/62			Winchester, VA	ROH
Bailey, John M.	Pvt.	C P.S.S.			01/31/63	Manchester, VA	DOD		ROH,JR,GMJ
Bailey, J.M.	Pvt.	I 12th SCVI			05/15/62	SC Coast	DOD	(Measles)	JR
Bailey, J.N.	Pvt.	H 3rd SCVBn			11/30/62	Richmond, VA		Hollywood Cem.Rchmd. S241	ROH,HC
Bailey, J.N.D.	Pvt.	2nd SCVIRi			01/23/65	Columbia, SC		Elmwood Cem. Columbia, SC	ROH,MP,PP
Bailey, James	Pvt.	D 16th SCVI		GE	07/21/63	Lauderdale Spgs.	DOD	Prob in UK part C.C. there	PP,16R
Bailey, James A.	Pvt.	B 7th SCVIBn	23	KW	05/25/63	Church Flats, SC	DOD		ROH,HAG
Bailey, James D.	Pvt.	H 2nd SCVI		LR	08/25/62	Richmond, VA	DOD	(SA2=in HOS @ Culpepper)	LAN,SA2,KEB,H2
Bailey, Jehu W.	Pvt.	H 2nd SCVI		LR	04/15/62	Richmond, VA	DOD	(SA2=on rolls 6/30/64)	LAN,SA2
Bailey, John	Pvt.	F 16th SCVI		GE	11/30/64	Franklin, TN	KIA		ROH,16R,CDC,PP
Bailey, John	Pvt.	K 2nd SCVI		CN	09/28/64	Burkeville, VA	ACD	(Fell from train)	H2,SA2,KEB
Bailey, John (James D.?)	Pvt.	2nd SCVI			08/26/61	Richmond, VA		Hollywood Cem.Rchmd. K64	ROH,HC
Bailey, John B.	Pvt.	I 11th SCVI		CO	03/19/65	Elmira, NY	DIP	Woodlawn N.C.#1726 Elmira	FPH,HAG,P65,P120
Bailey, John C.		Sgt.		D	SCVA			06/24/65 Augusta, GA	
Bailey, John D.	Pvt.	H 7th SCVIBn			05/16/64	Drury's Bluff,VA	KIA	(ROH= Co.G)	ROH,JR,HAG
Bailey, John M.	Pvt.	1 12th SCVI		LR	/ /	McPhersonville	DOD		LAN
Bailey, John T.	Pvt.	C 18th SCVI	20	UN	09/17/62	Sharpsburg, MD	KIA	(JR=South Mtn. 9/14/62)	ROH,JR
Bailey, John W.	Pvt.	C 18th SCVI		UN	07/30/64	Crater, Pbg., VA	KIA		ROH,JR,BLM
Bailey, Morgan	Pvt.	E 2nd SCVIRi			09/22/63	Petersburg, VA	DOW		ROH
Bailey, Newton F.	Pvt.	C 18th SCVI		UN	03/29/65	Petersburg, VA	DOW		ROH
Bailey, R.	Pvt.	K P.S.S.			06/24/64	Petersburg, VA	KIA	(Might be 5/24/64)	ROH
Bailey, Rix	Pvt.	F 4th SCVC		GN	05/15/64	Old Church, VA	DOW	(Wdd @ Hawes Shop, VA)	ROH,JR,LOR,CDC
Bailey, Robert	Pvt.	F 16th SCVI		GE	/ /	Charleston, SC	KIA		16R
Bailey, Robert W.	Pvt.	G 1st SCVC		GE	10/15/64	James Island, SC	DOD		ROH
Bailey, Solomon	Pvt.	G 10th SCVI		HY	05/23/63	Empire H.Atlanta		Oakland C. Atlanta R9#4	BGA
Bailey, T.	Pvt.	G 24th SCVI		CR	07/20/64	Atlanta, GA	KIA	(Peachtree Creek)	HHC
Bailey, W.C.	Pvt.	G 1st SCVC	35	GE	10/15/64	James Island, SC	DOD		ROH,CDC
Bailey, W.H.	Pvt.	C 18th SCVI	20	UN	08/10/62	Columbia, SC	DOD		ROH,JR,PP
Bailey, W.J.	Pvt.	I 12th SCVI		LR	05/15/62	McPhersonville	DOD	(Measles)	JR,LAN
Bailey, William	Pvt.	G 7th SCVIBn	20		11/16/63	At home	DOD		ROH
Bailey, William	Pvt.	H 7th SCVIBn			05/16/64	Drury's Bluff VA	KIA		JR,HAG
Bailey, William A.	Pvt.	D 27th SCVI	21	CN	08/06/63	Bty. Wagner, SC	DOW	Magnolia C.(PL) Charleston	ROH,JR.MAG,HAG
Bailey, William M.	Pvt.	C 18th SCVI	30	UN	03/14/62	At home	DOD		ROH,JR
Bails, Charles				OG	/ /	Virginia	DOD		ROH
Bair, Jacob	Pvt.	B 20th SCVI	20	OG	06/15/64	At home	DOD		ROH,KEB
Bair, John	Cpl.	I 2nd SCVA	32	OG	06/15/65		DOD		ROH
Bair, P.W.	Pvt.	I 2nd SCVA	34	OG	09/12/62	James Island, SC	DOD		ROH
Bair, W.B.	Pvt.	I 3rd SCVI		OG	11/15/62	At home	DOD		JR,SA2
Baird, John W.	2nd Lt.	F 23rd SCVI		CR	09/11/62	2nd Manassas, VA	DOW		ROH,HHC,R48,CMO
Baker, A.J.	Sgt.	D 8th SCVI			01/16/62	Charlottesville	DOD	(Typhoid Fever)	JR,KEB
Baker, Andrew Jackson	Pvt.	K 23rd SCVI	35	SR	11/15/62	Winchester, VA	DOD	Stonewall C. Winchester	ROH,WIN,K23,UD3

SOUTH CAROLINA DEAD IN CSA SERVICE 1861-1865

NAME	RANK	C	REGIMENT	AGE	DS	DIED	WHERE	WHY	BURIED	SOURCES
Baker, B.	Sgt.	K	7th SCVC		KW	06/15/64	Richmond, VA	DOD		ROH
Baker, B.C.	Pvt.					/ /				ROH
Baker, B.E.	Pvt.		21st SCVI			10/24/64	Richmond, VA		(Benjamin B.?)	ROH
Baker, B.J.	Pvt.	K	7th SCVC		KW	06/28/64	Richmond, VA		Hollywood Cem.Rchmd. U79	ROH,HC,HIC
Baker, C.C.	Pvt.	A	14th SCVI	20	DN	11/07/62	Winchester, VA		Stonewall C. Winchester	ROH,JR,WIN
Baker, Charles S.	Pvt.	C	13th SCVI		SG	08/16/64	Fussells Mill VA	KIA	(JR=Barker)	ROH,JR,HOS
Baker, Cornelius M.	Pvt.	K	23rd SCVI	20	SR	09/17/63	Sharpsburg, MD	KIA	(JR=South Mtn. 9/14/62)	ROH,JR,K23,UD3
Baker, E.F.	Pvt.	D	14th SCVI	23	DN	07/03/63	Gettysburg, PA	KIA	(JR=Co. A)	ROH,JR
Baker, Eugene B.	Cpl.	E	1st SCVIBn		CN	08/18/63	Bty. Wagner, SC	KIA	(JR=A, 27th SCVI)	ROH,JR,CDC
Baker, F.M.	Pvt.				CD	06/06/63	Virginia	DOD		ROH
Baker, Francis	Sgt.	C	15th SCVAB			08/20/63	Bty. Wagner, SC	KIA	Magnolia C. Charleston	ROH,JR,MAG,CDC
Baker, Henry	Pvt.	D	15th SCMil		LN	04/15/65	New Bern, NC	DIP		ROH
Baker, Henry Griggs	Pvt.	A	25th SCVI	25	CN	01/15/65	Ft. Fisher, NC	KIA		ROH,WL1,HAG,PP
Baker, Henry J.	Pvt.	K	23rd SCVI		SR	01/31/63	Goldsboro, NC	DOD		ROH
Baker, J.	Pvt.					02/11/65	Columbia, SC		Elmwood Cem. Columbia, SC	MP
Baker, J.P.	Pvt.		18th SCVAB			10/03/63	Charleston, SC		Magnolia C. Charleston	ROH,MAG
Baker, J.T.	Pvt.	A	Alston's B			07/30/62	Charleston, SC		Magnolia C. Charleston	ROH,MAG
Baker, Jacob L.	Pvt.	A	2nd SCVI		RD	03/15/64	Winchester, VA	DOD		SA2,KEB,H2
Baker, James A.	Pvt.	D	5th SCVC		CN	08/07/63	Charleston, SC	DOD	St. Lawrence C. Charleston	ROH,MAG
Baker, James S.	Pvt.	K	23rd SCVI	25	SR	01/15/63	Goldsboro, NC	DOD		ROH,K23,UD3
Baker, John	Pvt.	I	8th SCVI		MN	10/05/61	Charleston, SC	DOD	(Typhoid)	JR,HMC,KEB
Baker, John L.	Pvt.	K	10th SCVI		CN	06/12/62	Canton, MS	DOD	Con. Cem. Canton, MS Gv#66	RAS,PP,TOD
Baker, M.R.D.	Cpl.	C	25th SCVI	28	WG	03/31/65	Elmira, NY	DIP	Woodlawn N.C.#2601 Elmira	FPH,HAG,P6,P65
Baker, Neill	Pvt.	H	Orr's Ri.		MN	/ /	At home	DOW	(05/? /64)	HMC
Baker, O.R.	Pvt.	I	12th SCVI		LR	05/11/62	McPhersonville	DOD		LAN,JR
Baker, Thomas	Pvt.	E	1st SCVIG		MN	09/15/62	Warrenton, VA	DOW	(Wdd 2nd Man)	ROH,SA1,HMC
Baker, Thomas McDonald	Lt. Col.		1st SCVIR	47	SR	01/20/64	At home	DOD		ROH,SA1
Baker, Turner M.	Pvt.		Ch'fld LA	24	CD	04/28/63	Petersburg, VA	DOD	Blandford Church Pbg., VA	BLC,PP
Baker, V.	Pvt.	A	27th SCVI			10/26/64	Richmond, VA		Hollywood Cem.Rchmd. E13	HC
Baker, William	Pvt.	C	7th SCVI	24	AE	10/01/62	At home	DOD	(New Market, SC)	ROH,JR,KEB
Baker, William	Pvt.	H	2nd SCVI		LR	02/01/62	Centreville, VA	DOD	(Pneumonia)	H2,SA2,LAN
Baker, William Henry	Sgt.	B	15th SCMil		LN	04/01/65	New Bern, NC	DOW	Cedar Grove C. NewBern, NC	ROH,P1,P6,PP
Baker, William L.	Pvt.	K	16th SCVI	41	GE	08/06/62	Adams Run, SC	DOD		ROH,JR,16R,PP
Balcom, Aaron	Pvt.	E	20th SCVI			05/17/65	Pt. Lookout, MD	DIP	C.C. Pt. Lookout, MD	FPH,P6,P114,KE
Baldwin, Benjamin F.	Pvt.	B	18th SCVI			02/15/62	Charleston, SC	DOD		JR
Baldwin, Josiah C.	Pvt.	I	16th SCVI		GE	10/21/63	At home	DOD	(NI 16R)	PP
Baldwin, William W.	Pvt.	B	2nd SCVI	31	GE	04/15/65	Goldsboro, NC	DOD	(PP=Greensboro, NC)	ROH,SA2,KEB,PP
Bale, A.	Pvt.	H	8th SCVI			03/06/65	Pt. Lookout, MD	DIP	(POW N. Anna R. 5/24/64)	P7,P113
Balentine, B.		D	4th SCVC			07/23/64	Pt. Lookout, MD	DIP	C.C. Pt. Lookout, MD	ROH
Balentine, H.	Pvt.	I	11th SCVI		CO	08/23/64	Virginia	DOD	(NI HAG)	ROH
Balentine, J.B.	Pvt.	H	13th SCVI		LN	06/18/62	Richmond, VA		Hollywood Cem.Rchmd. O180	ROH,HC
Balentine, J.E.	Pvt.	K	1st SCVIG		LS	08/16/64	Fussells Mill VA	KIA	(CDC & JR = T.C.)	JR,SA1,CDC
Bales, Thomas	Cpl.	A	7th SCVC		GN	/ /		DOD		FLR
Balew, Franklin	Pvt.	H	3rd SCVABn		GE	01/06/63	Columbia, SC	DOD	(PP=Co. G)	ROH,PP
Balew, Franklin	Pvt.	G	3rd SCVABn		GE	01/06/63	Columbia, SC	DOD		PP
Balick, William A.	Pvt.	K	1st SCVC			/ /	Virginia			ROH
Ball, Albert	Pvt.	F	3rd SCVI		LS	01/12/62	Charlottesville	DOD	(KEB= Bale, A.)	ROH,SA2,KEB
Ball, H.P.	Pvt.	G	3rd SCVI	18	LS	08/24/61	At home	DOD		ROH,SA2,KEB
Ball, J.F.	Pvt.	E	14th SCVI			06/16/62	Richmond, VA	DOD	(Typhoid Fever)	JR
Ball, J.J.	Pvt.	D	27th SCVI	19	LS	12/18/64	Pt. Lookout, MD	DIP	C.C. Pt. Lookout, MD	ROH,FPH,P113,H
Ball, James K.	Pvt.	A	6th SCVC			06/22/64		KIA		JR

B

SOUTH CAROLINA DEAD IN CSA SERVICE 1861-1865

NAME	RANK	C	REGIMENT	AGE	DS	DIED	WHERE	WHY	BURIED	SOURCES
Ball, T.J.	Pvt.	D	27th SCVI	36	LS	09/01/63		DOD	(NI HAG, J.J.?)	ROH
Ballard, E.P.	Cpl.	F	Hol.Leg.	29	AE	12/26/62	At home	DOD	(Due West, SC)	ROH
Ballard, F.M.	Cpl.	K	15th SCVI			/ /		DOD	(KEB=F.S.)	JR,KEB
Ballard, Martin Luther	Pvt.	A	3rd SCVABn		GE	/ /	At home	DOD		PP
Ballard, William	Pvt.	H	Orr's Ri.			11/21/61	Sullivans I., SC	DOD		JR
Ballard, William R.	Pvt.	D	2nd SCVI		SR	07/02/63	Gettysburg, PA	KIA	Magnolia Cem. Charleston	MAG,GDR,SA2,H2
Ballenger, Dillingham	2nd Lt.	B	22nd SCVI	37	SG	11/27/63	Charleston, SC	DOD		ROH,HOS,R48
Ballenger, Henry M.	Pvt.	I	Hol.Leg.		SG	09/01/62	At home	DOD		ROH,HOS
Ballenger, John M.	Pvt.	C	13th SCVI		SG	08/16/64	City Point, VA		City Pt. N.C. Hopewell, VA	PP
Ballenger, Joseph	Pvt.	C	13th SCVI		SG	06/30/62	Frayser's Farm	KIA		HOS
Ballenger, Richard D.	2nd Lt.	D	P.S.S.		SG	05/06/64	Wilderness, VA	KIA	(Bio.in HOS,JR=DOW 5/31)	ROH,JR,HOS
Ballentine, Belton	Pvt.	H	13th SCVI		LN	/ /		DOD		ROH,JR
Ballentine, D.O.S.	Pvt.	D	4th SCVC		CN	07/23/64	Pt. Lookout, MD	DIP	C.C. Pt. Lookout, MD	ROH,FPH,P6,P113
Ballentine, Frederick D.	Pvt.	H	13th SCVI		LN	06/23/62	Ashland Stn., VA	DOD	(Typhoid)	ROH,JR,ANY
Ballentine, George	Pvt.	E	1st SCVIR		CN	05/23/63	Ft. Moultrie, SC	DOD		SA1
Ballentine, George P.	Pvt.	D	27th SCVI	18	LS	08/10/63	Bty. Wagner, SC	DOW		ROH,JR,HAG
Ballentine, H. Belton	Pvt.	H	13th SCVI			06/23/62	Winder Hos Rchmd	DOD	(Typhoid Fever)	JR
Ballentine, J.L.	Pvt.	C	1st SCVC			02/28/65	Raleigh, NC		Oakwood C. Raleigh, NC	TOD
Ballentine, John Calvin	Cpl.	I	15th SCVI	21	LN	/ /	Hardeeville, SC	DOD	(Prob Nov., 1861)	JR,TOD
Ballentine, Thomas	Pvt.	H	1st SCVIG		CN	10/15/62		DOD		ROH,SA1
Ballentine, William F.	Pvt.	H	1st SCVIG		CN	08/29/62	2nd Manassas, VA	DOW		ROH,JR,SA1,CDC
Ballentine, William P.	Pvt.	H	13th SCVI	22	LN	06/15/62	Cold Harbor, VA	DOW	Spotsylvania C.H. C.C., VA	ROH,JR,SCH
Ballew, James S.	Pvt.	C	1st SCVIG	31	LS	12/29/64	Raleigh, NC	DOD	Oakwood C. Raleigh, NC	ROH,SA1,TOD
Ballew, Jefferson F.	Pvt.	F	22nd SCVI		PS	/ /	Mt. Jackson, VA		Mt. Jackson, VA	PP
Ballin, James	Pvt.	A	Ballins Bn			01/16/65	Charleston, SC	DOD	Magnolia Cem. Charleston	MAG
Ballinger, J.	Pvt.	C	13th SCVI		SG	08/15/64	City Point, VA	DOW	City Pt. N.C. Hopewell, VA	TOD
Ballinger, J.R.	Pvt.	F	Orr's Ri.		PS	04/15/62	Sullivans I., SC	DOD		JR,CDC
Ballot, F.G.	Pvt.	A	25th SCVI		CN	08/06/62	Charleston, SC	DOD	Magnolia Cem. Charleston	ROH,JR,MAG,HAG
Balls, James	Pvt.	G	24th SCVI			01/31/65	Camp Chase, OH	DIP	Con.Cem.#974 Columbus, OH	FPH,P6,P23,P27
Balt, John	Pvt.	C	14th SCVI			06/30/62	Frayser's Farm	KIA		ROH
Baltzeggar, John	Pvt.	C	2nd SCVA	40	OG	01/01/65	NC	DOD		ROH
Bamboo, J.	Pvt.	A	7th SCVI			09/22/63	Chickamauga, GA	DOW		ROH,JR
Bancroft, Matthew V.	Major		23rd SCVI	25	CN	06/22/64	Petersburg, VA	DOW	St. Philips C. Charleston	ROH,JR,MAG,K23
Banion, B.O.	Pvt.	E	SCVA			04/03/65	High Point, NC		Oakwood C. High Point, NC	CV
Banister, Thompson	Pvt.	K	Orr's Ri.	22	AN	09/22/63		DOD	(ROH= Thomas)	ROH,CDC
Banks, C. Columbus	Pvt.	A	2nd SCVI	28	RD	07/24/61	Culpepper, VA	DOD	Fairview Cem., Culpepper	ROH,JR,CGH,SA2
Banks, Ephraim F.	Pvt.	F	12th SCVI	18	FD	09/05/62	2nd Manassas, VA	DOW		ROH,JR,HFC
Banks, J.M.	Pvt.	D	7th SCVIBn	37	KW	07/06/64	Petersburg, VA	KIA		ROH,JR,HIC,HAG
Banks, John W.	Pvt.	H	6th SCVI	20	FD	09/17/62	Sharpsburg, MD	DOW	Rose Hill C. Hagerstown MD	ROH,JR,WDB,BOD
Banks, M.	Pvt.	C	Ham.Leg.			/ /	Shepherdstown VA	DOW	Elmwood Cem. Shepherdstown	ROH,CV,BOD
Banks, R.A.	Pvt.	H	4th SCVI		PS	01/01/62	Charlottesville	DOD		SA2
Banks, T.C.	Pvt.	D	14th SCVI	36	ED	/ /		DOD	(1864)	HOE
Banks, Warren T.	Pvt.	H	2nd SCVIRi		AE	12/02/62	White Sulpher Ss	DOD		PP
Banks, William Henry	Pvt.	D	19th SCVI	17	ED	06/18/62	Enterprise, MS	DOD	(Prob Bd in UK C.C. there)	PP,HOE
Bannister, W.L.	Pvt.		Hol.Leg.			08/25/62	Staunton, VA			ROH
Barber, C.A.	Pvt.	F	5th SCVI			05/25/62	Washington, DC	DOW	(Wdd & POW @ Williamsburg)	ROH,CDC
Barber, Edward	Pvt.	C	11th SCVI		CO	01/01/62	Hardeeville, SC	DOD	(JR=12/31/62)	ROH,JR,HAG
Barber, G.D.	Pvt.	F	25th SCVI	22	OG	06/25/65	Elmira, NY	DIP	Woodlawn N.C.#2823 Elmira	ROH,FPH,P6,P65
Barber, Hilliard A.	Pvt.	F	6th SCVI	25	CR	05/15/62	Washington, DC	DOW	Arlington N.C. Sec. 16	ROH,CV,P6,HHC,PP
Barber, J.C.	Pvt.	B	12th SCVI	20	YK	09/15/61		DOD		JR,YEB
Barber, John T.	Pvt.	A	12th SCVI	21	YK	06/28/62	Richmond, VA	DOD		JR,YEB

SOUTH CAROLINA DEAD IN CSA SERVICE 1861-1865

NAME	RANK	C	REGIMENT	AGE	DS	DIED	WHERE	WHY	BURIED	SOURCES
Barber, Joseph	Pvt.	C	11th SCVI		CO	06/19/64	Richmond, VA		Hollywood Cem.Rchmd. U323	ROH,HC,HAG
Barbour, John G.	Pvt.	B	6th SCVI		CR	12/20/61	Dranesville, VA	KIA		ROH,JR,CB,GLS
Barbry, James	Pvt.	F	16th SCVI		GE	/ /	At home	DOD		16R
Barbry, Washington	Pvt.	F	16th SCVI		GE	/ /	Charleston, SC	DOD		16R
Barclay, R.H.	Pvt.	E	P.S.S.		SR	06/30/62	Fraysers Farm VA	KIA		ROH,JR
Barden, J.						/ /			(Rchmd effects list 12/62)	CDC
Barden, Pickens B.	Pvt.		7th SCVI		ED	09/07/61	Charlottesville	DOD	University Cem. Ch'ville	ROH,ACH
Barden, Shelley	Pvt.	H	19th SCVI		AE	01/01/62		DOD		ROH
Barefield, Alfred	Pvt.	C	1st SCVIG		RD	05/31/64		DOD		SA1
Barefoot, David M.	Pvt.	E	8th SCVI		DN	01/15/62	Richmond, VA	dod	Oakwood C.#43,Row D,Div A	JR,OWC
Barefoot, William	Pvt.				RD	04/13/65	Columbia, SC	DOD	Elmwood Cem. Columbia, SC	MP,PP
Barfield, David M.	Pvt.	E	8th SCVI		LR	09/30/62	Richmond, VA		Hollywood Cem.Rchmd. C78	ROH,HC
Barfield, H.M.	Pvt.	E	P.S.S.		CL	06/30/62	Fraysers Farm VA	KIA		ROH,JR,CDC
Barfield, Harvey	Pvt.				WG	11/25/63	Missionary Ridge	KIA		CTA,HOW
Barfield, Henry	Pvt.	E	1st SCVIG		MN	08/07/62	Richmond, VA	DOD	Hollywood Cem.Rchmd. H121	HC,HMC,SA1
Barfield, John	Pvt.					02/16/65	Charleston, SC	DOD	Magnolia CEm. Charleston	MAG
Barham, John		A	1st SCVA			04/07/65	Raleigh, NC		Oakwood C. Raleigh, NC	TOD
Barker, A.J.	Pvt.	C	Orr's Ri.		PS	06/27/62	Lynchburg, VA	DOW	Lynchburg CSA Cem. #2 R2	ROH,JR,BBW
Barker, G.B.	Pvt.	M	10th SCVI		HY	/ /	Okolona, MS	DOD	(Prob in Con. Cem. there)	RAS,PP,TOD
Barker, Isham	Pvt.	B	22nd SCVI		SG	05/03/62	Charleston, SC	DOD	(J.A. in HOS?)	ROH
Barker, J.C.	Pvt.	G	17th SCVI		BL	08/30/62	2nd Manassas, VA	KIA		ROH,JR
Barker, J.M.	Pvt.	D	22nd SCVI		PS	09/22/62	Frederick, MD	DOW	Mt. Olivet Cem. Frederick	FPH,BOD,P6,P12
Barker, J.W.	Pvt.	A	17th SCVI			09/17/62	Sharpsburg, MD	KIA		JR
Barker, J.W.	Pvt.	D	18th SCVI			09/17/62	Sharpsberg, MD	KIA	(DUP/?)	JR
Barker, John H.	Pvt.	E	17th SCVI	21	BL	08/20/64	Petersburg, VA			ROH,PP
Barker, Joshua	Pvt.	A	Orr's Ri.		AN	02/09/65	Elmira, NY	DIP	Woodlawn N.C.#1949 Elmira	FPH,P1,P6,P65
Barker, Josiah A.	Pvt.	B	22nd SCVI		SG	07/30/64	Crater, Pbg., VA	KIA	(Also Wdd in '62)	ROH,HOS,BLM
Barker, L.M.	Pvt.	A	Orr's Ri.			05/28/63	Richmond, VA	DOW	(Co. C?)	ROH,JR
Barker, M.J.	Pvt.	M	10th SCVI		HY	/ /	Tazewell, KY	DOD		RAS
Barker, W. Thomas	Pvt.	B	22nd SCVI		SG	07/30/64	Crater, Pbg., VA	KIA		ROH,HOS,BLM
Barker, W.R.	Pvt.	D	22nd SCVI		PS	07/30/64	Crater, Pbg., VA	KIA		JR,BLM
Barker, Wheeler W.	Pvt.	B	13th SCVI		SG	08/19/64	Fussels Mill, VA	DOW		HOS
Barker, William J.	Pvt.	E	15th SCVI		FD	12/31/64	Rock Island, IL	DIP	Con.Cem.#1237 Rock Isl. IL	FPH,KEB,P5
Barker, Wilson D.	Pvt.	I	2nd SCVI		CN	05/07/63	Fredericksburg	DOD	(In camp)	SA2,H2
Barkley, B.H.	Pvt.	B	1st SCVI			/ /	Richmond, VA		Oakwood C.#108 Row L,Div C	ROH,OWC
Barkley, G.R.	Pvt.	D	18th SCVI		AN	03/10/64	Lake City, FL	DOD		ROH,PP
Barkley, T.M.J.	Pvt.		7th SCVC			09/17/64	Richmond, VA	MUR	(Killed By Wm. Brandon)	CDC
Barksdale, Collyar D.	Cpt.	L	1st SCVIG	34	LS	09/01/62	2nd Manassas, VA	DOW	Laurens Cem., SC UD3	ROH,JR,SA1,LSC
Barksdale, James C.	Pvt.	D	27th SCVI	20	LS	06/24/64		KIA		ROH,HAG
Barksdale, John A.	Cpl.	D	27th SCVI	30	LS	06/24/64	Petersburg	KIA		ROH,JR,CDC,HAG
Barksdale, Thomas B.	1st Cpl.	G	3rd SCVI	21	LS	09/20/63	Chickamauga, GA	KIA	Highland Home B.C. AE	ROH,JR,SA2,LSC
Barksdale, W.S.	Pvt.	C	7th SCVI		AE	05/06/64	Wilderness, VA	KIA		ROH,JR,KEB
Barley, D.H.	Pvt.	C	18th SCVI		UN	10/23/62	Staunton, VA		Thornrose C. Staunton, VA	TOD
Barlow, J.W.F.	Pvt.	F	6th SCVI		CR	/ /	Richmond, VA		Oakwood C. #29,Row O,Div B	ROH,OWC
Barmore, William C.	Pvt.	B	7th SCVI		AE	07/02/63	Gettysburg, PA	KIA		ROH,JR,GDR,KEB
Barnadore, Thomas	Pvt.	H	6th SCVI		FD	09/08/61	Monkely, VA	DOD		ROH
Barnes, B.J.	Pvt.	I	10th SCVI		MN	07/22/64	Atlanta, GA	DOW	(MIA with severe leg Wd.)	RAS,HMC,CDC
Barnes, C.R.	Pvt.	L	Orr's Ri.		AN	06/27/62	Gaines' Mill, VA	KIA		ROH,JR,CDC
Barnes, D.	Pvt.		SCV			08/23/64	Salisbury, NC		Prob Lutheran C. Salisbury	PP
Barnes, Dixon	Col.		12th SCVI	46	KW	09/27/62	Sharpsburg, MD	DOW	(Biography in BOS)	ROH,JR,LC,BOS
Barnes, F.	Pvt.	B	7th SCVIBn			06/15/64		KIA		JR

B

SOUTH CAROLINA DEAD IN CSA SERVICE 1861-1865

NAME	RANK	C REGIMENT	AGE	DS	DIED	WHERE	WHY	BURIED	SOURCES
Barnes, F.H.	Pvt.	I 25th SCVI		CL	04/01/65	Elmira, NY	DIP	Woodlawn N.C.#2587 Elmira	FPH,HAG,P6,P65
Barnes, H.A.	Pvt.	C 6th SCVI		KW	/ /		KIA		HIC
Barnes, J.C.	Pvt.	I 5th SCVC		BL	08/03/64	Kittrell Spgs NC	DOD	Con. Cem. Kittrell Spgs NC	CV,WAT,PP
Barnes, John	Pvt.	D 11th SCVI	26	BT	01/07/62	Hardeesville, SC	DOD	(NI HAG)	ROH
Barnes, John N.	Pvt.	F Orr's Ri.		PS	08/08/62	Howard Grove Hos	DOD	Oakwood C.#16,Row B,Div C	ROH,JR,OWC,CDC
Barnes, John O.	Pvt.	A 12th SCVI	43	YK	05/12/64	Spotsylvania, VA	KIA		YEB
Barnes, Morgan	Pvt.	H 24th SCVI	34	CR	09/21/63	Chickamauga, GA	DOW		ROH,CDC,HHC,CB
Barnes, N.K.	Pvt.	H 24th SCVI		CR	/ /	Chickamauga, GA	KIA	(Prob Nickerson, POW)	HHC
Barnes, Nickerson	Pvt.	H 24th SCVI		CR	11/16/64	Camp Douglas, IL	DIP	Oak Woods Cem. Chicago, IL	FPH,P6,P53,P12
Barnes, Reddin E.	Pvt.	F 7th SCVIBn		KW	06/21/64	Petersburg, VA	KIA		ROH,JR,HIC,HAG
Barnes, Robert	Pvt.	A 8th SCVI		DN	11/08/61	Charlottesville	DOD	University Cem. Ch'ville	ROH,JR,ACH,KEB
Barnes, William	Pvt.	B 21st SCVI		DN	02/06/65	Pt. Lookout, MD	DOW	C.C. Pt. Lookout, MD	P12,HAG
Barnett, C.M.	Pvt.	D 16th SCVI		GE	/ /	Montgomery, AL	DOD		16R
Barnett, Cary	Pvt.	B 18th SCVI		UN	01/27/63	Wilson, NC	DOD		JR,PP
Barnett, F.B.	Pvt.	D 16th SCVI		GE	06/22/64	Kennesaw Mtn. GA	KIA		16R
Barnett, H.O.M. (N.?)	Pvt.	D Ham.Leg.		AN	/ /	(?dup in D,PSS)	DOD	Oakwood C.#10,Row 17,Div D	ROH,GRS,OWC
Barnett, Hezekiah	Pvt.	D 5th SCVI		OG	05/31/62	7 Pines, VA	KIA		ROH,JR,SA3
Barnett, Isaac	Pvt.	G 22nd SCVI	40	AN	08/15/64	Farmville, VA	DOD	(Dup of J. in OWC?)	ROH
Barnett, J.	Pvt.	D P.S.S.			/ /	Richmond, VA		Oakwood C.#23,Row 17,Div D	ROH,OWC
Barnett, J. (Isaac?)	Pvt.	G 22nd SCVI			07/31/64	Richmond, VA		Hollywood Cem.Rchmd. V681	HC
Barnett, J. Sutcliff	Pvt.				08/07/64	Petersburg, VA	DOD	(C, 27th SCVI? see P65)	ROH
Barnett, J.M.C.	Pvt.	B 5th SCVI	21	YK	08/23/64	Virginia	DOD		SA3,YEB
Barnett, J.P.	2nd Lt.	B 15th SCVI			05/03/63	Chancellorsville	KIA	(NI KEB or R47)	ROH
Barnett, J.S.	Pvt.	B 27th SCVI		CN	07/05/64	Petersburg, VA	KIA	(John in HAG?)	ROH
Barnett, Jareal R.	Pvt.	H 16th SCVI		GE	04/13/62	Adams Run, SC	DOD		PP
Barnett, John N.	Pvt.	H 18th SCVI	24	YK	/ /	At home	DOW	(1865)	YEB
Barnett, Josiah	Pvt.	B 22nd SCVI		SG	04/20/62	Charleston, SC	DOD	(HOS=Joseph)	ROH,HOS
Barnett, Josiah J.	Pvt.	B 5th SCVI	28	YK	04/06/63	Jerusalem, VA	DOD		JR,SA3,YEB
Barnett, M.C.	Cpl.	7th SCVI			/ /			Manchester, VA	ROH
Barnett, Robert A.	Pvt.	H 18th SCVI	25	YK	07/15/64	Petersburg, VA	KIA		ROH,YEB
Barnett, S.	Pvt.	G 22nd SCVI		AN	08/01/64			Hollywood Cem.Rchmd. V681	ROH,HC
Barnett, Thomas	Pvt.	H 2nd SCV			/ /	Lynchburg, VA		Lynchburg CSA Cem. #4 R2	BBW
Barnett, W.A.	Pvt.	C 12th SCVI			/ /	Richmond, VA		Oakwood C.#6,Row 6,Div D	OWC
Barnett, William H.	Pvt.	C 13th SCVI	24	SG	04/07/63	Richmond, VA	DOD	(Earlier in K, 3rd SCVI)	ROH,SA2,HOS
Barnett, William S.	Pvt.	D 6th SCVI	33	YK	11/17/62	White Sulpher S.	DOD		PP,YEB
Barnhill, Benjamin	Pvt.	F 1st SCVIG		HY	05/03/63	Chancellorsville	KIA		ROH,SA1,PDL
Barnhill, J.G.	Pvt.	C 10th SCVI		HY	/ /	Georgetown, SC	DOD		RAS
Barnhill, Joseph	Pvt.	G 10th SCVI		HY	06/15/62	Meridian, MS	DOD	(Prob Rose Hill C. there)	RAS,PP
Barnhill, Josiah	Pvt.	G 10th SCVI		HY	/ /		DOD		RAS
Barnhill, R.	Pvt.	C 10th SCVI		HY	/ /	Chickamauga, GA	DOD		RAS
Barnhill, R.J.	Pvt.	M 10th SCVI		HY	/ /	Barbourville, KY	DOD	(1863)	RAS
Barnhill, Stafford	Pvt.	C 10th SCVI		HY	07/22/64	Forsyth, GA	DOW	Forsyth, GA	RAS,CDC,CRB
Barns, J.M.					/ /			(Rchmd effects list 12/62)	CDC
Barnum, Elisha	Pvt.	H.L. Arty			10/18/64			Richmond, VA	ROH
Barnwell, James Stuart	Pvt.	B 7th SCVC	19	BT	07/08/64	Richmond, VA	DOW		ROH,CDC
Barnwell, Robert W.	Chaplain				/ /	Virginia	DOD	Trinity Ch. Columbia, SC	MP,PP
Barnwell, Thomas Gibbes	Pvt.	I 2nd SCVIRi	31	BT	10/26/62	Greenville, SC	DOD		ROH,PP
Barnwell, William F.	1st Lt.	S.D. Lee A		CN	06/15/61	Charleston, SC	ACD	(Pistol Dschg,JR=12/20/62)	ROH,JR
Barr, Ernest	Pvt.	A Tucker's R			03/03/65	Salisbury, NC		Prob Old Lutheran Cem. UK	PP
Barr, James Michael	Pvt.	I 5th SCVC	37	LN	08/29/64	Charlottesville	DOW	Barr F.C. Leesville, SC	LGS
Barr, John J.	Cpl.	K 13th SCVI		LN	05/05/64	VA	KIA		ROH,JR,JMB

SOUTH CAROLINA DEAD IN CSA SERVICE 1861-1865

NAME	RANK	C REGIMENT	AGE	DS	DIED	WHERE	WHY	BURIED	SOURCES
Barr, Leroy	Pvt.	D 18th SCVI		AN	07/16/62	Charleston, SC	DOD	Magnolia Cem. Charleston	ROH,MAG
Barr, T.H. (H.H.?)	Pvt.	D 18th SCVI		AN	07/12/62	Charleston, SC	DOD		ROH,JR
Barr, Walter N.	2nd Lt.	K 9th SCVIB	21	LN	12/30/61	Germantown, VA	DOD	Barr Cem. Lexington Cty.SC	JR,LGS,CNM
Barratt, John S.G.	Pvt.	F 2nd SCVI	31	AE	09/17/62	Sharpsburg, MD	KIA	(JR=MD Hts. 9/13/62)	ROH,JR,SA2,KEB
Barrentine, Nelson	Pvt.	D 25th SCVI		MN	06/20/63	James Island, Sc	KIA	Magnolia Cem. Charleston	ROH,JR,MAG,HAG
Barrentine, T.L.	Pvt.	F 21st SCVI			06/23/62	Charleston, SC	DOD		JR
Barrentine, Wilson	Pvt.	B 25th SCVI		MN	06/27/63	Charleston, SC	DOD	Magnolia Cem. Charleston	ROH,JR,MAG
Barret, John W.	Pvt.	F 23rd SCVI		CR	10/05/62	Warrenton, VA	DOW	(Wdd @ 2nd Manassas)	CRM
Barrett, Benjamin C.	Pvt.	C 2nd SCVIRi		PS	08/02/62	Richmond, VA	DOW	(Rchmd effects list)	ROH,CDC,CUS
Barrett, C.	Pvt.	C 7th SCVI		PS	/ /	Winchester, VA		Stonewall C. Winchester	ROH,WIN
Barrett, Edward R.	Pvt.	E 2nd SCVI		KW	07/21/61	1st Manassas, VA	KIA		ROH,HIC,SA2,KE
Barrett, Joseph	Pvt.	G 22nd SCVI	33	AN	03/07/62	Columbia, SC	DOD		ROH,CEN,PP
Barrett, Lawrence	Pvt.	Ham.Leg.		PS	/ /	VA	MIA	(1864)	CUS
Barrett, Richard	Pvt.	Brook's LA		CN	10/13/62		DOW	(Wdd @ Sharpsburg)	JR,SA2,H2
Barrett, William M.	Pvt.	F 1st SCVC	31	PS	08/30/62	Summerville, SC	DOD	Ponder Cem. Lathem, SC	PCS
Barrineau, J. Thomas	Pvt.	C 25th SCVI		WG	05/16/64	Drury's Bluff VA	KIA		CTA,HOW,HAG
Barrineau, J.J.	Pvt.	E 15th SCVI	19	WG	01/29/63	Richmond, VA	DOD	(Dup James J.?)	ROH,JR,CDC,KEB
Barrineau, James E.	Pvt.	I 4th SCVC		WG	/ /	('63)	DOD		CTA,HOW
Barrineau, James J.	Pvt.	E 15th SCVI	28	WG	03/10/63	Richmond, VA	DOD	(Dup. of J.J.?)	ROH,JR
Barrineau, S.I.	Pvt.			WG	06/02/64	Cold Harbor, VA	KIA		CTA,HOW
Barrineau, W.J.	Pvt.	I 4th SCVC			08/15/63	McPhersonville	DOD		JR
Barringer, H.A.	Pvt.				/ /			Stonewall C. Winchester VA	WIN
Barrington, Peter L.	Pvt.	F 21st SCVI		MO	06/20/62	Charleston, SC	DOD	(ROH & HOM= P.L.)	ROH,HAG,HOM
Barrington, Phillip	Pvt.	F 21st SCVI		MO	07/12/64	Kitrell Sps., NC	DOW		ROH,HAG,HOM,PP
Barrington, William	Pvt.	F 21st SCVI		MO	06/18/64	Petersburg, VA	DOD	(HAG= Barrentine)	ROH,JR,HAG,HOM
Barron, Alexander A.	4th Cpl.	B 6th SCVI	28	YK	07/20/64	Petersburg, VA	KIA	(YEB=Co. H)	ROH,YMD,YEB
Barron, J.	Pvt.	H 25th SCVI			10/19/62		DOD		JR
Barron, J.T.	Pvt.	PSS			05/15/62	7 Pines	KIA		UD2
Barron, James Philo	Pvt.	G P.S.S.	19	YK	06/04/62	7 Pines, VA	DOW	(JR=5/31/62) SA3	JR,DEM,BIG,YEB
Barron, John B.	Pvt.	H 5th SCVI	32	YK	/ /	Petersburg, VA	KIA		YEB
Barron, Samuel H.P.	Pvt.	I 5th SCVI	19	YK	02/11/62	Raleigh, NC	DOD	(JR=Co. F, P.S.S.)	JR,YMD,DEM,SA3
Barron, Samuel Watson	1st Cpl.	E 17th SCVI	23	YK	12/23/62	At home	DOD	(JR & YEB=Goldsboro, NC)	ROH,JR,DEM,YEB
Barrow, John L.	Pvt.	B 24th SCVI	25	MO	05/14/64	Rock Island, IL	DIP	C.C. Rock Island, IL #237	ROH,FPH,P1,P6
Barrow, Robert W.J.	Pvt.	K 6th SCVI		CL	09/22/62	Sharpsburg, MD	DOD	(Wdd 9/15/62)	ROH,3RC
Barrs, William W.	Pvt.	C 24th SCVI			/ /	Charleston, SC			ROH
Barry, Walter N.	2nd Lt.	K 9th SCVIBn			12/30/61		DOD	(? No Co. K in this Bn.)	R46
Bars, Benjamin J.	Pvt.	H Ham.Leg.	36		10/28/63	Lookout Valley	KIA	(JR= Racoon Mtn.)	ROH,JR,CDC
Bars, Daniel	Pvt.	H Ham.Leg.	40		07/09/64	NC			ROH
Barta, B.	Pvt.	G 5th SCV			09/14/64			Hollywood Cem.Rchmd. V346	HC
Bartell, William	Sgt.	I 10th SCVI		MN	/ /	TN	DOD		RAS,HMC
Barter, G.V.	Pvt.	D 14th SCVI	26	ED	11/01/64	Fts. Monroe, VA	DOW	(Bartee, W.V./D14? HOE)	ROH
Barth, Frederick S.	Pvt.	A 10th SCVI	25	GN	06/11/62	Okalona, MS	DOD		ROH,JR,PP,RAS
Bartless, L.W.				CN	/ /			(Bartlett ?)	ROH
Bartless, William H.	Cpt.	A 8th SCResB		CN	03/27/65	Columbia, SC	DOD		ROH,CEN,R46,PP
Bartlett, Leonard White	Cpt.	D 2nd SCVI		SR	07/01/62	Richmond, VA	DOW	(Wdd @ Savage Stn.)	ROH,KEB,H2,SA2
Bartlett, Millage	Pvt.				/ /	Petersburg, VA	KIA		LSS
Bartley, Andrew	Pvt.	B 14th SCVI	23	ED	01/02/62	Port Royal, SC	DOW	UD3	ROH,JR,HOE,PP
Bartley, Charles	Pvt.	H 8th SCVI		MN	07/02/63	Getttysburg, PA	KIA		ROH,JR,GDR,CDC
Bartley, Elias	Pvt.	E 9th SCVIBn		HY	03/20/62		DOD	(JR= Co.E, 26th SCVI)	ROH,JR
Bartley, J.L.	Pvt.			WG	05/09/64	Swift Creek, VA	KIA		CTA,HOW
Bartley, Nathan L.	Pvt.	D 14th SCVI	32	ED	07/01/63	Gettysburg, PA	KIA		ROH,JR,GDR,HOE

B

SOUTH CAROLINA DEAD IN CSA SERVICE 1861-1865

NAME	RANK	C REGIMENT	AGE	DS	DIED	WHERE	WHY	BURIED	SOURCES
Barton, A.W.	Pvt.	B 1st SC Res			/ /			Charlotte, NC	ROH
Barton, Benjamin F.	Pvt.	F 4th SCVI		GE	11/12/61	Culpepper, VA	DOD	Fairview C, Culpepper, VA	CGH,SA2
Barton, E.B.	Pvt.	1st SCVA			08/18/62	Charleston, SC	DOD	Magnolia Cem. Charleston	ROH,MAG
Barton, Francis J.	Pvt.	D 16th SCVI			02/07/64	Nashville, TN	DOW		P2,P5,16R
Barton, G.B.	Pvt.				05/29/65	Pickens, SC	DOD	Liberty Cem. Pickens, SC	PCS
Barton, Isaac A.	Pvt.	A Orr's Ri.		AN	05/03/63	Chancellorsville	KIA		ROH,JR,CDC
Barton, J.J.	Pvt.	I P.S.S.			/ /		KIA		JR
Barton, James G.	Pvt.	A 16th SCVI		GE	/ /	At home	DOD	(In service ?)	16R
Barton, Joseph	Pvt.	K Ham.Leg.			03/13/65	Pt. Lookout, MD	DIP	C.C. Pt. Lookout, MD	FPH,P6,P10,P114
Barton, O.	Pvt.	F 13th SCVI		SG	/ /	(1864)			HOS
Barton, O.H.P.	Sgt.	A 22nd SCVI			03/02/64	Petersburg, VA	DOW		ROH
Barton, S.	Pvt.	I 1st SCV			07/05/64	Richmond, VA		Hollywood Cem.Rchmd. U434	HC
Barton,Jr., William M.	Pvt.	I 12th SCVI		LR	05/05/64	Wilderness, VA	KIA		JR,LAN
Barton,Sr., William M.	Cpl.	I 12th SCVI		LR	07/01/63	Gettysburg, PA	KIA		JR,LAN,GDR
Barwick, Edward N.	Pvt.	G 14th SCVI	35	AE	04/23/65	Hart's Island NY	DIP		ROH,P6,P79
Barwick, George W.	Pvt.	I 25th SCVI		CL	/ /	Richmond, VA		(ROH= Bostwick)	ROH,HAG
Barwick, H.	Pvt.	G 14th SCVI	30	AE	01/17/63	Fredericksburg	DOW	(Berwick?)	ROH
Barwick, J.H.	Pvt.	2nd SCV			10/15/62	Mt. Jackson H.VA	DOW		JR
Barwick, J.N.	Pvt.	I 25th SCVI		CL	08/05/64	Petersburg, VA	DOW	(George W. in HAG?)	ROH
Barwick, Robert T.	Pvt.	C 6th SCVI		KW	09/14/62	South Mtn., MD	KIA	(ROH & JR= Sharpsburg, MD)	ROH,JR,CDC,WDB
Barwick,, R.S.	Pvt.	G 14th SCVI	25	AE	07/01/63	Gettysburg, PA	KIA	(JR= Co.F 7/2/63)	ROH,JR
Basin, David	Pvt.	E 1st SCVIG		MN	12/01/61	Suffolk, VA	DOD	(Bazen in SA1)	SA1,PDL,HMC
Baskin, Edward C.	Pvt.	G 2nd SCVI		KW	05/31/62	Manchester, VA	DOD		HIC,SA2,H2
Baskin, John G.	2nd Lt.	I 14th SCVI	40	AE	05/01/63	Richmond, VA	DOD	(Also Wdd. @ Frayser's Fm)	ROH,HOL,R47
Baskin,Jr., John C.	Pvt.	G 2nd SCVI		KW	06/29/62	Savage Stn., VA	KIA		SA2,HIC
Baskins, John E.	Pvt.	I 12th SCVI		LR	08/11/62	Richmond, VA	DOD	Oakwood C.#65,Row G,Div C	ROH,JR,LAN,OWC
Baskins, Joseph W.	Pvt.	A 17th SCVI		CR	09/17/62	Sharpsburg, MD	KIA		ROH,JR,HHC
Bason, M.	Pvt.	F 22nd SCVI		PS	07/03/64	Pt. Lookout, MD	DIP		ROH,P113
Bass, A.M.	Pvt.	I 1st SCVIR			07/18/63	Bty. Wagner, SC	KIA	(JR=7/16/63)	ROH,JR,CDC,SA1
Bass, D.J.	Sgt.	K ?28th SCVI			09/05/64	Richmond, VA		Hollywood Cem.Rchmd. V409	HC
Bass, E.C.	Pvt.	C 6th SCVI		KW	05/22/62	Richmond, VA	DOD	Hollywood Cem.Rchmd. J27	ROH,HC,HIC
Bass, Edmon	Pvt.	G 17th SCVI			09/17/62	Sharpsburg, MD	KIA		JR
Bass, Eli	Pvt.	1st SCVI			05/25/61	Richmond, VA	DOD		ROH
Bass, H.E.	Pvt.	G 17th SCVI			09/17/62	Sharpsburg, MD	KIA		JR
Bass, John N.	Pvt.	A 3rd SCVI		LS	08/16/64	(in enemy hands)	DOW	(Wdd 7/28/64 limb Amptd)	P12,KEB,SA2
Bass, Joseph	Pvt.	PeeDee LA		DN	/ /				ROH
Bassett, J.J.	Pvt.	G 1st SCVIH		BL	11/16/63	Campbell Stn. TN	KIA		ROH,SA1
Bassett, Simpson	Pvt.	G 17th SCVI			/ /	Johns Island, SC	DOD		JR
Basterskin, W.W.	Pvt.	A 1st SCV			09/04/62	Richmond, VA		Hollywood Cem.Rchmd. A37	HC
Bateman, J.D.	Pvt.	I Ham.Leg.			02/04/65	Elmira, NY	DIP		P65
Bateman, Thomas L.	Pvt.	G 21st SCVI	18	DN	07/25/64	Petersburg, VA	DOD	(Wdd @ 7 Pines E,6th)	ROH,JLC
Bates, Andrew	Pvt.	I 2nd SCVC		ED	07/07/64	Johns Island, SC	KIA		ROH,HOE,CDC,JMB
Bates, C.W.	Pvt.	C 23rd SCVI		CN	09/15/63			Magnolia Cem. Charleston	MAG
Bates, Chesley	Pvt.	B 1st SCVA		BL	06/18/62	Secessionville	DOW	(JR=6/30/62)	ROH,JR,CDC,PP
Bates, Daniel	Pvt.	B P.S.S.			10/12/64		DOD		JR
Bates, Elbert	Pvt.	B 2nd SCVA		BL	06/16/62	Secessionville	KIA		PP
Bates, Henry D.	Pvt.	B 27th SCVI		CN	06/24/64	Petersburg, VA	KIA		ROH,CDC,HAG
Bates, James	Pvt.	E 1st SCVIH		BL	07/03/62		DOD		ROH,SA1
Bates, James	Pvt.	D Hol.Leg.		BL	05/20/62	Charleston, SC	DOD		ROH
Bates, John A.	Pvt.	D Orr's Ri.			02/02/63	Guinea Stn., VA	DOD		JR,CDC
Bates, John Pearson	Ord. Sgt.	I 2nd SCVC		ED	11/05/64	Green Pond, SC	DOD	Willowbrook B.C. Edgefield	ROH,HOE,PP

B

SOUTH CAROLINA DEAD IN CSA SERVICE 1861-1865

NAME	RANK	C REGIMENT	AGE	DS	DIED	WHERE	WHY	BURIED	SOURCES
Bates, Joseph H.	Pvt.	D Hol.Leg.			05/18/62	Adams Run, SC	DOD	(Cattarhal Fever)	JR
Bates, Joseph S.	1st Lt.	D Hol.Leg.		BL	08/30/62	2nd Manassas, VA	KIA	(JR= Sharpsburg)	ROH,JR,R48
Bates, R.R.	Pvt.	B 1st SCVA		BL	06/16/62	Secessionville	KIA		ROH,JR,CDC,PP
Bates, Thomas	Pvt.	SCVC		GN	03/27/62	Georgetown, SC	DOD		PP
Batson, A.J.	Pvt.	H 3rd SCVABn	28	GE	12/02/63	Green Pond, SC	DOD	(Furman Artillery)	ROH,PP
Batson, Elliot	Pvt.	K 16th SCVI		GE	03/13/65	Camp Chase, OH	DIP	Con.Cem.#1647 Columbus, OH	FPH,P23
Batson, Fountain P.	Pvt.	G 16th SCVI		GE	06/17/62	Adams Run, SC	DOD		16R,PP
Batson, Hezekiah Y.	Pvt.	G 16th SCVI	35	GE	11/30/64	Franklin, TN	KIA	Macgavock C. Frkln Gv #19	ROH,16R,WCT,PP
Batson, Thornton	Pvt.	I Ham.Leg.			08/11/63	Petersburg, VA			ROH
Batson, W.P.	Pvt.	H 16th SCVI		GE	01/01/64	At home		(Might be in Co.G)	PP
Bauer, John	Sgt.	C 23rd SCVI		CN	10/24/62	Charlottesville	ACD	University Cem. Ch'ville	ROH,CDC,AHC
Baugh, M.	Pvt.	H 25th SCVI		CN	06/24/64	Petersburg, VA	DOW		ROH,CDC,HAG
Baughknight, S.N.	Pvt.	H 13th SCVI		LN	08/30/62	2nd Manassas, VA	KIA		ROH,CDC
Baughman, H. Lafayette	Pvt.	C 1st SCVIG	24	LN	05/21/65	Hart's Island NY	DIP	Cypress Hill N.C. #2844	ROH,FPH,SA1,P1
Baughman, J.M. (J.P.)	Pvt.	D Hol.Leg.		BL	08/23/62	Rappahanock Stn.	KIA	(JR= Sharpsburg)	ROH,JR
Baughman, W.W.	Pvt.	K 15th SCVI		AE	12/13/62	Fredericksburg	KIA	(JR=12/15/62)	ROH,JR,KEB
Baum, M.H.	Pvt.	A 15th SCVI		RD	05/08/64	Wilderness, VA	KIA		ROH,JR,KEB
Baum, Marcus	Pvt.	E 2nd SCVI	32	KW	05/06/64	Wilderness, VA	KIA	(Shot with Longstreet)	ROH,SA2,HIC,KE
Bawlin, B.F.	Pvt.				/ /	Camp Gurin,Chstn	DOD	Measles (Jan or Feb 62)	UD2
Baxley, Barney	Pvt.	D 10th SCVI		MN	06/15/62	Holly Springs MS	DOD		RAS,HMC,PP
Baxley, C.W.	Pvt.		18	WG	05/02/63	Chancellorsville	KIA		CTA
Baxley, David W.	Pvt.	E 10th SCVI	32	WG	09/10/62	Shelbyville, TN	DOD	Willowmount C. Shelbyville	ROH,RAS,PP,TOD
Baxley, Henry C.	Pvt.	E 10th SCVI	20	WG	09/15/62	Corinth, MS	DOD		ROH,RAS,CTA,HO
Baxley, J.P.	Pvt.	A 1st SCVIG		BL	06/29/62	Richmond, VA	DOD	Richmond, VA	ROH,JR,SA1
Baxley, James W.	Pvt.	E 10th SCVI	40	WG	07/20/62	Saltillo, MS	DOD	(PP=John W.)	ROH,RAS,PP,HOW
Baxley, Oliver W.	Pvt.	G 15th SCVI	29	WG	05/04/63	Chancellorsville	KIA		ROH,JR,HOW
Baxley, William James	Pvt.	F 4th SCVC	36	WG	06/27/64	Richmond, VA	DOD	Hollywood Cem. Rchmd U33	ROH,HMC,HC,P12
Baxter, David	Pvt.	E 1st SCVIG		MN	/ /		KIA	(SA1=Baxley & OR 12/31/64)	HMC,SA1
Baxter, Francis D.	Pvt.	C 11th SCVI		CN	05/09/64	Swift Creek, VA	DOW	Blandford Church Pbg., VA	ROH,BLC,P1
Baxter, Lewis	Pvt.	20th SCVI		OG	03/15/62	James Island, SC	DOD		ROH
Bay, A.	Pvt.	C 22nd SCVI			11/29/64	Petersburg, VA	DOW		ROH
Baylis, Earle Boozer	Pvt.		22	LN	12/16/61			Baylis Fam.C. Lexington SC	TOD
Bayly, Joseph	Pvt.	McQueen LA			/ /		DOD		CDC
Baynard, William E.	Pvt.	JD Legion		CN	/ /			(Tfd frm I, 2nd SCVI)	H2,SA2
Bayne, T.C.					/ /	Richmond, VA		(Rchmd effects list)	CDC
Bazille, J.O.	Pvt.	K 2nd SCVI		BL	10/14/62	Winchester, VA	DOD		H2,SA2
Beacham, William S.	Pvt.	F 5th SCVI		SG	12/19/61	Centreville, VA	DOD	(HOS & JR=D,PSS)	ROH,JR,SA3,HOS
Beacham, William V.	Pvt.	B P.S.S.			06/10/62	Petersburg, VA	DOD	(Might be W.S. in 5th SC)	PP
Beadle, R.T.	Cpl.	D 27th SCVI	40	LS	06/18/64	Petersburg, VA	KIA	(JR=6/19/64)	ROH,JR,CDC,HAG
Beakham, B.	Pvt.	F 1st SCVA		LR	05/06/65	Newport News, VA	DIP		P6
Beam, Judge	Pvt.	E 6th SCVI		CR	/ /	Centreville, VA	DOD	(Camp Pettus)	HHC
Beam, R. Hampton	Pvt.	B 16th SCVI		GE	/ /	Atlanta, GA	DOD	(1864)	16R
Beamguard, Samuel W.	Pvt.	F 17th SCVI	26	YK	05/12/62	Johns Island, SC	DOD	(Carolina Rifles)	JR,YMD
Bean, A.Y.	Pvt.	F 23rd SCVI		CR	07/30/64	Crater, Pbg., VA	KIA		JR,BLM
Bean, H.	Pvt.	B 10th SCVI		HY	05/17/64	Med.C.H. Atlanta		Oakland C. Atlanta R5#13	BGA
Bean, James	Pvt.	B 2nd SCRes		ED	12/22/62		DOD		ROH,CEN
Bear, John	Pvt.	A 14th SCMil	17	OG	04/01/65	Goldsboro, NC	DIP		ROH
Beard L.W.	Pvt.	I 3rd SCVI			/ /	(OWC says B,3rd)		Oakwood C.#52,Row J,Div A	ROH,OWC
Beard, Daniel	Pvt.	D 2nd SCVI			09/20/63	Chickamauga, GA	KIA		ROH,JR,SA2,KEB
Beard, Henry		CSN Hunley			10/16/63	Charleston, SC	DOD	Magnolia Cem. Charleston	RCD
Beard, Jackson	Pvt.	A 12th SCVI		YK	/ /		KIA		YEB

B

SOUTH CAROLINA DEAD IN CSA SERVICE 1861-1865

NAME	RANK	C REGIMENT	AGE	DS	DIED	WHERE	WHY	BURIED	SOURCES
Beard, James Clough	Pvt.	K 3rd SCVI	19	SG	01/02/64	At home	DOD	(To hosp 9/2/62)	ROH,SA2,HOS
Beard, James O.	Pvt.	A Orr's Ri.			05/23/65	Hart's Island NY	DIP	Cyprus Hills N.C.#2861 NYC	FPH,P6,P12,P79
Beard, R.	Pvt.	B 9th SCVIB			02/09/62	Richmond, VA	DOD		JR
Beard, William	Pvt.	G 18th SCVI	36	YK	/ /	Charleston, SC	DOD		YEB
Beard, William F.	Pvt.			GE	/ /			Christ E.C. Greenville, SC	PP
Bearde, W.S.	Pvt.	C 27th SCVI			08/15/63		DOD	(NI HAG)	JR
Bearden, Berry	Pvt.	SCVA			/ /			Gilead C. Jonesville UN Cy	UD3
Bearden, C.	Pvt.	D 22nd SCVI		PS	08/02/64	Richmond, VA		Richmond, VA	ROH
Bearden, David T.	Pvt.	K P.S.S.	31	SG	08/30/62	2nd Manassas, VA	KIA	Manassas Con. Cemetary VA	ROH,JR,CDC
Bearden, E.M.	Pvt.nd	K 3rd SCVI		SG	03/21/63	Lynchburg, VA	DOD	(JR=Richmond)	ROH,JR,SA2
Bearden, Isaac M.	1st Cpl.	H 1st SCVIH		SG	09/05/62	2nd Manassas, VA	DOW		ROH,JR,SA1,HOS
Bearden, O.P.	Pvt.	H 1st SCVIH		SG	04/15/65	Richmond, VA	DOD		ROH,SA1,P12
Bearden, Robert	Pvt.	G 14th SCVI	18	AE	02/12/63	Fredericksburg	DOD	(Measles)	ROH,JR
Bearden, Thomas M.	Pvt.	I 3rd SCVI		LS	05/02/62	Richmond, VA	DOD		ROH,JR,SA2,KEB
Bearden, W.T.	Pvt.	F Orr's Ri.			07/12/62	Cold Harbor, VA	DOW	Oakwood C.#59,Row J,Div C	ROH,JR,OWC,CDC
Bearden, William	2nd Lt.	K 3rd SCVI	34	SG	07/05/63	Gettysburg, PA	DOW	HOS	ROH,JR,SA2,GDR
Bearden, William S.	Pvt.	K 3rd SCVI		SG	/ /	Richmond, VA	KIA	(HOS=1862)	HOS,SA2,KEB
Beasley, Edward Bland	Pvt.	A 25th SCVI	21	CN	07/31/62	Charleston, SC	DOD	St.Michael's Ch. Charltn.	ROH,JR,MAG,WLI
Beasly, George L.	Pvt.	I 3rd SCVI	20	LS	07/10/63	Sharpsburg, MD	KIA	Memorial @ Duncan's Creek	JR,SA2,LSC,KEB
Beasly, J.F.	Pvt.	A 14th SCVI	22	DN	05/03/63	Chancellorsville	KIA	Oakwood C.#52,Row L,Div B	ROH,OWC
Beasly, James R.	Pvt.	I 5th SCRes	44	AE	01/21/63	Jacksonboro, SC	DOD		ROH
Beasly, M.A.	Pvt.				05/15/65	Columbia, SC	DOD		ROH,PP
Beasly, William	Pvt.	PeeDee LA			/ /				ROH
Beason, Thomas H.	Pvt.	K 16th SCVI		GE	03/10/64	(Batson?)		Mt. Olivet C. Nashville TN	PP
Beason,Jr., John	Pvt.	E 18th SCVI	19	SG	04/01/65	Five Forks, VA	KIA		ROH,HOS
Beattie, Robert	3rd Sgt.	G 5th SCVI	33	YK	09/13/64	Richmond, VA	DOD	(YEB=Beatty)	ROH,SA3,YEB
Beatty, Alexander	Pvt.	D 17th SCVI		CR	01/14/65	At home/POW Xchg	DOD		ROH,P65,HHC,CB
Beatty, C.B.	Pvt.	A 18th SCVI		UN	02/24/65	Elmira, NY	DIP	Woodlawn N.C.#2255 Elmira	FPH
Beatty, Christopher L.	Cpt.	A P.S.S.	25	UN	08/15/64	Deep Bottom, VA	DOW	Mt. Vernon Cem. Union, SC	ROH,JR,UNC,P10
Beatty, James G.	Lt.	A 9th SCVIBn			06/12/62	Secessionville	KIA	Magnolia Cem. Charleston	ROH,MAG,R46
Beatty, Joseph R.	Pvt.	B 4th SCVI		AN	09/07/61	Culpepper, VA	DOD	Fairview C. Culpepper, VA	CGH,SA2,GMJ
Beatty, P.F.	Pvt.	D Orr's Ri			/ /	Richmond, VA		Oakwood C.#110,Row M,Div B	JR,OWC
Beatty, R.R.	Pvt.	D Orr's Ri.			06/16/62	Richmond, VA	DOD		JR,CDC
Beatty, Robert L.	Cpl.	G 6th SCVI	26	CR	12/25/61	Centreville, VA	DOD		ROH,HHC
Beatty, Thomas E.	Pvt.	G 6th SCVI	24	CR	08/30/61	Germantown, VA	DOD		ROH,HHC
Beatty, Thomas M.	Surgeon		31		07/29/63	Vicksburg, TN	DOD		ROH
Beaty, J.	Pvt.	K 7th SCVC			/ /	Atlanta, GA	KIA		HIC
Beaty, James G.	1st Lt.	E 9th SCVIBn	40	HY	06/16/62	Secessionville	KIA	(R48=J.E.)	ROH,R48
Beaty, John M.	2nd Sgt.	B 10th SCVI		HY	07/22/64	Atlanta, GA	DOW	Stonewall Cem. Griffin, GA	RAS,FLR,CDC,BGA
Beaufort, Monroe	Pvt.	H 19th SCVI	19	AE	08/15/63		DOD		ROH
Beaur, John	Sgt.	C 23rd SCVI		CN	10/24/62	Charlottesville	ACD	(Central RR wreck)	CDC
Beaver, Levy	Pvt.	I 17th SCVI		LR	/ /	Johns Island SC	DOD		LAN
Beck, Caleb M.	Cpl.	B 21st SCVI	29	DN	05/16/64	Drury's Bluff VA	KIA		ROH,JR,CDC,HAG
Beck, James D.	Pvt.	A 8th SCVI		DN	11/05/61	Culpepper C.H.	DOD	(KEB=W.D.,JR=Lynchburg)	ROH,JR
Beck, Robert C.	Pvt.	A 15th SCVI	37	RD	07/22/64	Richmond, VA	DOW	1st P.C. Columbia, SC	ROH,JR,KEB,PP
Beckham, Bolivar S.	Pvt.	F 1st SCVA		LR	05/06/65	Newport News, VA	DIP	Greenlawn C. Newport News	PP,P6
Beckham, James R.	Pvt.	H 4th SCVC		LR	07/20/64	Richmond, VA	DOW	Hollywood Cem.Rchmd. U202	HC,LAN
Beckham, William W.	Pvt.	A 6th SCVI	28	CR	07/15/64		DOD	(ROH= KIA @ 7 Pines)	ROH,GLS,HHC,CB
Beckham,Sr., William	Pvt.	I 12th SCVI		LR	06/15/61	Columbia, SC	DOD		LAN
Beckhouse, Ernest	Cpl.	B 1st SCVIR		CN	07/01/63	Summerville, SC	DOD		ROH,SA1
Beckman, William W.	1st Sgt.	D 27th SCVI	34	CN	06/25/64	Petersburg, VA	DOW	Magnolia C.(PL) Charleston	ROH,MAG,CDC,HAG

SOUTH CAROLINA DEAD IN CSA SERVICE 1861-1865

NAME	RANK	C REGIMENT	AGE	DS	DIED	WHERE	WHY	BURIED	SOURCES
Becknell,	Pvt.	I P.S.S.		PS	01/09/64		DOD		ROH
Beckwith, William H.	Pvt.	A 15th SCVI		RD	01/04/62	Red Bluff, SC	DOD	Trinity C. Columbia, SC	ROH,JR,MP,KEB,
Bedenbaugh, W.A.	Pvt.	G 13th SCVI		NY	07/08/63	Richmond, VA	DOD		ROH,ANY
Bedford, John	Pvt.	E 1st SCVIG		MN	05/03/63	Chancellorsville	KIA		ROH,SA1,PDL,HM
Bedon, Josiah	Pvt.	K 4th SCVC		CO	05/28/64	Hawe's Shop, VA	KIA		ROH,CV,CLD
Bee, Bernard E.	Brig. Gen.		37	CN	07/22/61	1st Manassas, VA	DOW	Pendleton, SC	ROH,JR,CMH5,GI
Bee, James Ladson	Pvt.	K 4th SCVC	22	CN	07/07/64	Washington, DC	DOW	Magnolia Cem. Charleston	ROH,MAG,P5,CLD
Bee, John Stock	2nd Lt.	I 1st SCVA	23	CN	07/28/63	Hilton Head, SC	DOW	Magnolia C.(PL) Charleston	ROH,PP,P2,WLI
Bee, Sandiford	Pvt.	D 27th SCVI	21	CN	10/04/64	at home	DOD	(Frm Pbg. to Summerville)	ROH,CDC,HAG
Bee, William Edwards	Pvt.	D 27th SCVI	21	CN	05/09/64	Swift Creek, VA	KIA	Unitarian C. Charleston	ROH,MAG,PP,HAG
Bee, William Foster	Pvt.	H 1st SCVIG		CN	08/29/62	2nd Manassas, VA	DOW	Old Scotch P.C. Charleston	ROH,JR,SA1,CDC
Beecham, Jeff T.	Pvt.	G Orr's Ri.		AE	07/15/62	Dill Farm, VA	DOD		ROH
Beecham, Thomas P.	Pvt.	B 13th SCVI		SG	07/01/63	Gettysburg, PA	KIA		HOS
Beechum, W.D.	Pvt.	B P.S.S.		PS	06/30/62	Frayser's Farm	KIA		ROH
Beek, William C.	Pvt.	19th SCVI			07/31/62	Alton, IL	DIP	Con. Cem. Alton, IL	FPH
Beerly, J.W.	Pvt.	1st SCV			/ /			Charlestown, VA	ROH
Beggs, Thomas	2nd Lt.	D Hol.Leg.	47	BL	08/30/62	2nd Manassas, VA	KIA	(JR=Sharpsburg)	ROH,JR,SAS,EDN
Beheler, J.	Pvt.	F 17th SCVI		YK	09/01/64	Elmira, NY	DIP	Woodlawn N.C.#77 Elmira	FPH
Beiglin, John	Pvt.	C 24th SCVI	29	CO	07/25/63	Jackson, MS	DOW	(Beagling?)	ROH,DRE,PP
Belcher, Alexander	Pvt.	A 13th SCVI		LS	07/10/62	Richmond, VA		Hollywood Cem.Rchmd. H260	HC
Belcher, Barney	Pvt.	E 13th SCVI			/ /		DOD	(1863)	JR
Belcher, Robert	Pvt.	D 5th SCVI			12/15/61	Manassas, VA	DOD		JR,SA3
Belcher, Thomas	Pvt.	E 13th SCVI			07/01/63	Gettysburg, PA	KIA		JR
Belew, J.F.	Pvt.	22nd SCVI			/ /	Mt. Jackson, VA		Mt. Jackson, VA	ROH,CDC
Belk, D.B.	Pvt.			UN	/ /	Petersburg, VA	DOD	Blandford Church Pbg., VA	ROH,BLC
Belk, Henry J.	Pvt.	E 12th SCVI	28	LR	10/20/64	Bellefield, VA	DOD		ROH,LAN
Belk, J.R.	Pvt.	I 12th SCVI		LR	05/12/64	Spotsylvania, VA	KIA		JR,LAN
Belk, John M.	Pvt.	G 2nd SCVI		LS	12/31/62	Manchester, VA	DOD	(Typhoid)	ROH,SA2,H2,KEB
Belk, S. Lawson	Pvt.	E 7th SCVIBn	18	SR	04/14/62	Adams Run, SC	DOD	(ROH= Bilk)	ROH,JR,HAG,PP
Bell, A.F.	Pvt.	E P.S.S.			/ /		DOD		JR
Bell, Andrew J.	Pvt.	H 12th SCVI	43	YK	03/05/65	Pt. Lookout, MD	DIP	C.C. Pt. Lookout, MD	ROH,FPH,P6,YEB
Bell, Charles W.	Pvt.	K 2nd SCVI		CO	08/14/63	Gettysburg, PA	DOW	(P12=died 7/15/63)	ROH,JR,GDR,SA2
Bell, E.	Pvt.	A 14th SCVI	27	DN	10/20/63	Culpepper C.H.			ROH,JR
Bell, Edward H.	1st Lt.	C 7th SCVIBn		RD	03/19/65	Bentonville, NC	KIA		ROH,HAG,PP
Bell, Eugene B.	Pvt.	D 5th SCVC	35	CN	04/13/64	Savannah, GA	ACD	(Eng. DTL Torpedo expl'n)	ROH,CDC
Bell, J.L.	Pvt.	A 5th SCVI			03/21/63	South Keys, VA	DOD		JR
Bell, Jacob H. (M.?)	3rd Sgt.	C 2nd SCVI		RD	04/13/62	Williamsburg, VA	DOD	(Typhoid)	ROH,SA2,KEB,H2
Bell, John F.	Pvt.	D 9th SCVIB		CL	11/27/62	Manchester, VA	DOD	Hollywood Cem.Rchmd. B160	ROH,HC
Bell, John J.	Pvt.	H 7th SCVIBn	33	ED	11/10/62	Adams Run, SC	DOD		ROH,JR,HAG,PP
Bell, Joseph B.	Sgt.	H 24th SCVI	23	CR	10/15/63	Chickamauga, GA	DOW	(Not on Chester Memorial)	ROH,HHC,CB
Bell, Lewis A.	Pvt.	B Orr's Ri.	19	AE	05/20/63	At home	DOD		ROH,JR
Bell, M.J.	Pvt.	E 9th SCVIB		KW	09/27/61	Germantown, VA	DOD		ROH,JR,HIC
Bell, Nathaniel E.	1st Sgt.	B Orr's Ri.	21	AE	10/05/64	Richmond, VA	DOD	Oakwood C.#21,Row H,Div G	ROH,OWC,CDC,P4
Bell, Samuel N.	Pvt.	I 12th SCVI		LR	05/29/63	Richmond, VA	DOD	Hollywood Cem.Rchmd. T215	ROH,JR,HC,LAN
Bell, Sanders W.	Pvt.	A 1st SCVIG		BL	06/18/64	Pt. Lookout, MD	DIP	C.C. Pt. Lookout, MD	ROH,FPH,P6,P11
Bell, W.H. (Henry/HAG?)	Pvt.	H 7th SCVIBn		ED	07/24/64	Pt. Lookout, MD	DIP	C.C. Pt. Lookout, MD	ROH,FPH,P6,P12
Bell, W.N.	Pvt.	A 14th SCVI	27	DN	12/01/63	Staunton, VA	DOD		ROH
Bell, William E.	4th Cpl.	H 4th SCVC		LR	05/30/64	Cold Harbor, VA	KIA	(JR=Old Church, VA)	ROH,JR,LAN
Bell, William F.	Pvt.	F 2nd SCVI	21	AE	04/15/62	Williamsburg, VA	DOD	Oakwood C.#47,Row J,Div A	ROH,SA2,OWC,KE
Bellamy, C.A.	Cpl.	F 1st SCVIG		HY	06/12/61	Richmond, VA	DOD		JR
Bellamy,Jr., William A.	3rd Cpl.	F 1st SCVIG		HY	06/19/62	Manchester, VA	DOD		SA1,PDL

B

SOUTH CAROLINA DEAD IN CSA SERVICE 1861-1865

NAME	RANK	C REGIMENT	AGE	DS	DIED	WHERE	WHY	BURIED	SOURCES
Bellflowers, H.	Pvt.	McQueen LA		MN	/ /		DOD	(1862)	HMC,CDC
Bellflowers, J.J.	Pvt.	F 10th SCVI		MN	03/01/62	Corinth, MS	DOD	(PP=Macon, MS)	RAS,HMC,PP
Bellflowers, Jesse	Pvt.	I 21st SCVI		MN	07/12/63	Bty. Wagner, SC	KIA	(JR=7/27/63)	HMC,JR,R48,HAG
Bellinger, Edmond W.	2nd Sgt.	K 1st SCVIH	21	BL	09/30/64	Ft. Harrison, VA	KIA	(1st in I, 2nd SCVI)	ROH,SA1,SA2,H2
Bellinger, John A.	1st Lt.	B 2nd SCVA	30	BL	04/20/63	James Island, SC	DID	(Duel)	HAG,R44
Bellinger, John Skottowe	Pvt.	A 1st SCVIH	17	BL	08/30/62	2nd Manassas, VA	KIA	(JR=14th SCVI) UD3	ROH,JR,SA1,JRH
Bellot, John E.	Pvt.	C 7th SCVI	32	AE	02/17/63	Gordonsville, VA	DOD	(Pneumonia)	ROH,JR,KEB
Bellotte, John D.	Pvt.	C 4th SCVC	17	AN	03/16/65	Elmira, NY	DIP	Woodlawn N.C.#1700 Elmira	ROH,JR,FPH,P6
Bellotte, Michael A.	3rd Lt.	K 4th SCVI	35	AN	07/23/61	Culpepper C.H.	ACD	Fairview Cem. Culpepper VA	ROH,JR,CGH,SA2
Bellotte, Thomas D.	1st Lt.	C 4th SCVC		AN	05/28/64	Hawes Shop, VA	KIA		JR,BHC,R43
Bellune, W.S.	Pvt.	A 7th SCVC			06/15/65	Georgetown, SC	DOD	Elmwood C. Georgetown, SC	GNG
Belot, E.	Pvt.	F 14th SCVI		LS	11/11/62	Mt. Jackson, VA	DOD	Mt. Jackson, VA	PP
Belvin, John W.	Pvt.	E 9th SCVIB		SR	10/27/61	Manchester, VA	DOD	Hollywood Cem.Rchmd. B244	JR,HC,HIC
Belvin, William T.	2nd Lt.	G 20th SCVI		SR	08/28/63				R48,KEB
Bendott, R.H.	Pvt.	E 4th Bn.Res			12/01/64	Charleston, SC	DOD	(1st Louisiana Hos.)	CDC
Benenhaile, F.	Pvt.	C 7th SCVIBn		SR	04/24/62	Adams Run, SC	DOD	(NI HAG)	PP
Benjamin, J.H.	Pvt.	F 22nd SCVI		PS	/ /	Petersburg, VA	DOW	(1864)	ROH
Bennet, Joseph	Pvt.	F 23rd SCVI		CR	05/03/62	Charleston, SC	DOD	(HHC=James)	CRM,HHC
Bennett, A.J.	Pvt.	C 1st SCVIR		LR	09/08/63	Ft. Moultrie, SC	DOW		ROH,SA1,CDC,LAN
Bennett, Berryman	Pvt.	B 22nd SCVI		SG	05/27/62	Charleston, SC	DOD		ROH,HOS
Bennett, C.L.	Pvt.	D 24th SCVI		BT	08/05/62	Columbia, SC	DOD		ROH,PP
Bennett, Charles F.	Pvt.	I 24th SCVI	20	ED	05/15/64	Potato Hill, ?	KIA	(PP=Dalton, GA 5/10)	ROH,PP
Bennett, G.W.	Pvt.	H 2nd SCVI		LR	/ /	Chickamauga, GA	DOW	(SA2=Wdd,on rolls 6/30/64)	LAN,SA2,KEB
Bennett, J.M.	Pvt.	G 1st SCVIH		BL	05/01/63	Charleston, SC	DOD	(Variola)	ROH,SA1,JRH
Bennett, James K.	2nd Sgt.	D 1st SCVIH		LR	06/09/64		DOD	(NI JRH)	SA1,LAN
Bennett, James W.	2nd Lt.	B 13th SCVI		SG	09/30/64	Jones Farm, VA	KIA		ROH,JR,BOS,HOS
Bennett, T.B.	Pvt.	D Ham.Leg.		AN	06/01/62	7 Pines, VA	DOW		ROH,JR,CDC
Bennett, T.S.	Pvt.	E 11th SCVI			06/21/64	Petersburg, VA	KIA	(J.L. in HAG?)	JR
Bennett, Thomas	Pvt.	Bachman's		CN	01/01/65			NC Beaufort, SC #53-6325	PP,BNC
Bennett, W.D.	Cpl.	D Ham.Leg.		AN	10/28/63	Lookout Valley	DOW	(JR=Racoon Mtn., TN)	ROH,JR,GRS,CDC
Bennett, West	Pvt.	B 22nd SCVI		SG	05/26/62	Charleston, SC	DOD		ROH,HOS
Bennett, William	Pvt.	F 23rd SCVI		CR	08/30/62	2nd Manassas, VA	KIA	(JR=28th SCVI)	ROH,JR,CDC
Bennifield, George	Pvt.	Ferguson's			12/28/63	Dalton, GA			PP
Bennifield, H.	Pvt.	Ferguson's			01/09/64	Med.C.H. Atlanta		Oakland C. Atlanta R$#12	BGA
Bennifield, John	Pvt.	Ferguson's			01/07/65	Camp Chase, OH	DIP	Con. Cem.#719 Columbus, OH	FPH,P6,P10,P23
Bennifield, Joseph J.	Pvt.	Ferguson's			01/05/64	Med.C.H. Atlanta	DOW	Oakland C. Atlanta R12#9	BGA,PP
Benson, E.	Pvt.	H 22nd SCVI			08/05/64	Richmond, VA			ROH
Benson, G.A.	Pvt.	F 6th SCVI			08/30/62	2nd Manassas, VA	KIA		JR
Benson, J.F.	Pvt.	A 2nd SCV			11/03/62	2nd Manassas, VA	DOW		JR
Benson, Jacob	Pvt.	F 4th SCVC		WG	01/05/63	Georgeton, SC	DOD		HMC,PP
Benson, Thomas	Pvt.	F 2nd SCVI	21	AE	06/22/64	Petersburg, VA	KIA		ROH,SA2,KEB
Benson, Thomas B.	Sgt	Orr's Ri.	30	AN	09/15/62	Charlottesville	DOD	(Probably on Rgtl. Staff)	ROH,CDC
Benson, Thomas H.	Pvt.	K 16th SCVI		GE	03/10/64	Nashville, TN	DOW	Nashville Con.Cem. TN	P2,CV,P5
Benson, Virgil S.	Pvt.	F 2nd SCVI	21	AE	07/04/62	Savage Stn., VA	DOW	(JR=6/30/62)	ROH,JR,SA2,H2
Benson, W. Alexander	Cpt.	B 22nd SCVI	32	SG	06/18/64	Petersburg, VA	KIA	(JR=6/17/64)	ROH,JR,HOS,R48
Benson, Zachariah	Pvt.	H 1st SCVIG		GE	08/10/64	Wilderness, VA	DOW		ROH,SA1,BBC
Bentley, E.B.	Pvt.			WG	05/09/64	Swift Creek, VA	KIA		CTA,HOW
Bentley, James	Pvt.	H 15th SCVI			10/19/64	Strasburg, VA	KIA		JR,KEB
Bentley, W.H.	Pvt.	B Orr's Ri.			11/19/62	Richmond, VA	DOD		ROH,JR
Benton, E.H.	2nd Lt.	E 24th SCVI	30	CO	07/22/64	Atlanta, GA	KIA		ROH,JR,CDC,R48
Benton, George W.	Pvt.	I 8th SCVI		MN	/ /		KIA	(1st or 2nd Man.)	HMC,KEB

SOUTH CAROLINA DEAD IN CSA SERVICE 1861-1865

NAME	RANK	C	REGIMENT	AGE	DS	DIED	WHERE	WHY	BURIED	SOURCES
Benton, Henry E.	Pvt.	E	24th SCVI	20	CO	02/24/65	Camp Chase, OH	DIP	Nat.Cem.#1415 Columbus, OH	ROH,FPH,P6,P23
Benton, Hugh	Pvt.	G	1st SCVA			07/15/62	Ft. Moultrie, SC	DOW	(Bursting gun)	ROH
Benton, J.D.	Pvt.	E	24th SCVI	20	CO	05/21/64	Calhoun, GA	DOW	Con. Cem. Cobb Cty., GA	ROH,BGA
Benton, J.R.	Pvt.	E	24th SCVI	22	CO	08/21/64	U.S. Prison Hosp	DOW	(Wdd 6/20/64, arm Amputa.)	ROH,CDC
Benton, John M.	Pvt.	C	1st SCVA			04/17/65	Pt. Lookout, MD	DIP	C.C. Pt. Lookout, MD	FPH,P114
Benton, Joseph W.	Pvt.	E	7th SCVIBn	37	SR	05/16/64	Drury's Bluff VA	KIA	(HAG= Cpl.)(JR=Co.D)	ROH,JR,HAG
Benton, Joshua	Pvt.	I	11th SCVI		CO	10/01/64	Elmira, NY	DIP	Woodlawn N.C.#419 Elmira	ROH,FPH,P6,HAG
Benton, S.S.	Pvt.	E	24th SCVI	35	CO	09/30/63	Marietta, GA	DOD	Con. Cem. Marietta, GA	ROH,CCM
Benton, Thomas	Pvt.	B	3rd SCVC	24	CO	09/28/63	Hardeeville, SC	DOD		ROH
Berly, William Thomas	1st Sgt.	I	3rd SCVI	25	LS	09/20/63	Chickamauga, GA	KIA	Shady Grove Ch. Joanna, SC	SA2,KEB,CDC,LS
Berney, W.	Pvt.					/ /	Richmond, VA		Oakwood C.#33,Row K,Div E	ROH,OWC
Bernhard, Henry C.	Pvt.	E	3rd SCVI		LN	05/02/62	Richmond, VA	DOD		ROH,JR,SA2,ANY
Berry, Elison A.	Pvt.	E	19th SCVI	23	KW	06/26/62	Boonsville, MS	DOD		CDN
Berry, F.M.	Pvt.	I	18th SCVI	25	DN	07/30/64	Crater, Pbg. VA	KIA		ROH
Berry, J.P.	Pvt.	K	14th SCVI			07/30/62	Piedmont Inst VA	DOW	Oakwood C.#89,Row K,Div B	ROH,JR,HOE,OWC
Berry, James J.	Cpl.	E	7th SCVIBn		KW	/ /		KIA		HIC,HAG
Berry, James Welborn	Pvt.	A	7th SCVIBn	23	KW	05/16/64	Drury's Bluff VA	DOW		ROH,HIC,KEB
Berry, Jesse J.	Pvt.	K	14th SCVI		ED	06/05/62	Richmond, VA	DOD		ROH,JR,HOE
Berry, John	Pvt.	M	7th SCVI		ED	09/20/63	Chickamauga, GA	KIA	(Co. M not listed in KEB)	CDC,JR
Berry, N.C.	Pvt.		Ham.Leg.			10/07/64	Richmond, VA		Hollywood Cem.Rchmd. V449	ROH,HC
Berry, R.S.	Pvt.	K	17th SCVI		YK	/ /	At home	DOD		JR
Berry, Samuel Obediah	Pvt.	D	19th SCVI			02/09/64	Louisville, KY	DIP	Cave Hill C. Louisville KY	FPH,ROH,CV,P5
Berry, T.W.	Pvt.	I	18th SCVI	23	DN	08/01/64	Petersburg, VA			PP
Berry, Thomas	Pvt.	H	Hol.Leg.	24	ED	08/30/62	2nd Manassas, VA	KIA	(JR=Sharpsburg)	ROH,JR
Berry, Tredaway	Pvt.	H	20th SCVI		LN	07/17/62		DOD		ROH,ANY,KEB
Berry, W.G.	Pvt.	I	7th SCVI		ED	07/23/63	Chester, PA	DOW		GDR,P1
Berry, W.S.	Pvt.	G	7th SCVI		ED	07/25/63	Chester, PA	DIP	Phila.N.C. Confed. Section	ROH,FPH,P6,CV
Berry, William	Pvt.	K	2nd SCVA		ED	/ /		DOD		HOE
Bertin, J.M.	Pvt.	C	1st SCV			04/16/65	Pt. Lookout, MD	DIP		ROH
Beshears, L.S.	Pvt.	B	22nd SCVI		SG	03/21/62	Charleston, SC	DOD		ROH,HOS
Besinger, G.	Pvt.	A	1st SCVIH		BL	09/30/64	Ft. Harrison, VA	KIA		SA1,UD3
Besinger, J.	Pvt.	G	7th SCVI			08/29/62	2nd Manassas, VA	KIA		JR
Besinger, Jonce J.	Pvt.	G	1st SCVIH		BL	08/29/62	Groveton, VA	KIA		ROH,SA1,JRH,CD
Bessent, Thomas W.	Pvt.		Ward's LA	20	HY	07/09/63	Georgetown, SC	DOD		PP,CEN
Best, George	Pvt.	B	21st SCVI			09/07/63	At home	DOD		JR
Betenbaugh, John J.	Pvt.	F	15th SCVI		UN	03/24/65	Pt. Lookout, MD	DIP	C.C. Pt. Lookout, MD	ROH,FPH,P6,P11
Bethany, Jesse	Pvt.	B	15th SCVI			/ /		DOD		JR,KEB
Bethea, Henry P.	Pvt.	L	8th SCVI		MN	02/15/65	Camp Chase, OH	DIP	Con.Cem.#1274 Columbus, OH	FPH,HMC,P6,P23
Bethea, J.E.	Pvt.	B	24th SCVI	20	MO	06/24/63	Yazoo, MS	DOD		ROH,R48,PP
Bethea, Pickett P.	2nd Lt.	D	25th SCVI	26	MN	08/21/64	Reams Sta., VA	KIA	(Welden RR)	ROH,HAG,DOC,HM
Bethea, Redden	Pvt.	H	Orr's Ri.		MN	04/02/65	McIlwain's Hill	KIA		LSS,HMC
Bethea, Tristram T.	Pvt.	B	24th SCVI		MO	11/30/64	Franklin, TN	KIA		ROH,HOM
Beverly, Daniel B.	Pvt.	D	10th SCVI		MN	05/30/62	Brandon, MS	DOD		RAS,HMC,PP
Beverly, F.	Pvt.	D	10th SCVI		MN	06/15/62	Brandon, MS	DOD		RAS,HMC,PP
Beverly, John	Pvt.	D	25th SCVI		MN	02/27/65	Elmira, NY	DIP	Woodlawn N.C.#2123 Elmira	FPH,P6,P65,P66
Beverly, John B.	Pvt.	K	11th SCVI	45	MN	04/21/65	Pt. Lookout, MD	DIP	C.C. Pt. Lookout, MD	ROH,FPH,P6,P11
Beverly, Robert A.	Cpl.	B	24th SCVI	26	MO	05/16/64	Calhoun, GA	KIA		ROH,JR,HOM,CDC
Beverly, Wm. Douglass	Pvt.	D	25th SCVI		MN	06/07/64	Swift Creek, VA	DOW	Blandford Church Pbg., VA	HMC,HAG,BLC,PP
Bevill, James	Pvt.	H	1st SCVIR		CD	03/19/65	Bentonville, NC	KIA		ROH,SA1,WAT,PP
Bevill, W.A.	2nd Lt.	G	21st SCVI		CD	05/09/64	Swift Creek, VA	KIA	(JR=Drury's Bluff 5/16/64	ROH,JR,CDC,HAG
Bibb, S.P. (S.R.?)	Pvt.	B	P.S.S.		PS	10/18/62	Richmond, VA	DOW	Hollywood Cem.Rchmd. V317	ROH,JR,HC,P12

B

SOUTH CAROLINA DEAD IN CSA SERVICE 1861-1865

NAME	RANK	C REGIMENT	AGE	DS	DIED	WHERE	WHY	BURIED	SOURCES
Bice, Pinckney	Pvt.	I 13th SCVI			07/16/62		DOD		JR
Bickett, John	Pvt.	G 14th SCVI	30	AE	01/17/63	Fredericksburg	DOW	(JR=Fraysers Fm 7/28/64)	ROH,JR
Bickley, Deidrich W.	Pvt.	I 15th SCVI	29	LN	12/28/61	Hardeeville, SC	DOD		ROH,KEB,H15,TOD
Bickley, Jacob H.	Pvt.	I 15th SCVI	33	LN	05/03/65	At home	MUR	St. Peters L.C. Lexington	TOD,KEB
Bickley, Jefferson J.	Pvt.	I 15th SCVI		LN	07/17/65	Pt. Lookout, MD	DIP	(? Rlsd 6/23/65 per P114)	ROH,P12,P114,TOD
Bicknell, John	Pvt.	I P.S.S.			02/15/64	Virginia	DOD		ROH
Bidault, H. Robert	Pvt.	A 25th SCVI		CN	06/21/64	Petersburg, VA	DOW	(NI HAG)	ROH,WLI
Bideault, Alexander	Pvt.	Ham.Leg.		CN	/ /	VA	KIA		DRE
Bigger, Alexander B.	Pvt.	H 1st SCVC	42	YK	07/15/63	Mt. Jackson, VA	DOD	Mt. Jackson, VA	ROH,CV,SHS,YEB
Biggers, Andrew Jackson	Pvt.	C 27th SCVI	27	YK	07/19/64	Petersburg, VA	DOW		ROH,HAG,YEB
Bigham, Elijah	Pvt.	A 17th SCVI	19	CR	05/26/65	Pt. Lookout, MD	DIP	C.C. Pt. Lookout, MD	ROH,FPH,P6,HHC
Bigham, Hugh C.	Cpl.	A 17th SCVI	24	CR	09/15/63	Mt. Pleasant, SC	DOD		ROH,JR,HHC,CB
Bigham, J.H.	Pvt.	A 5th SCVI		DN	09/21/64	Richmond, VA	DOD	Hollywood Cem.Rchmd. V277	ROH,HC,SA3
Bigham, J.H.	2nd Lt.	B 12th SCVI		YK	09/14/62	Warrenton, VA	DOW	(Wdd @ 2nd Manassas)	JR,YMD,CDC,R47
Bigham, J.R.	Pvt.	E 17th SCVI	15	YK	05/23/62	At home	DOD		ROH,JR
Bigham, James H.	Pvt.	A 17th SCVI	21	CR	08/30/62	2nd Manassas, VA	KIA		ROH,JR,HHC,CB
Bigham, John	Pvt.	A 6th SCVI	30	CR	05/28/62	Richmond, VA	DOD	Hollywood Cem.Rchmd. L87	ROH,HC,GLS,HHC
Bigham, Joseph H.	Pvt.	A 17th SCVI	20	CR	06/27/65	Fts. Monroe, VA	DIP	Nat. Cem. Hampton, VA	ROH,HHC,PP,CB
Bigham, Lawson	Pvt.	A 17th SCVI	19	CR	12/15/63	At home	DOD		ROH,HHC,CB
Bigler, J.	Pvt.	H 1st SCVC		YK	09/28/64	Ft. Delaware, DE	DIP	Finn's Pt., NJ Nat. Cem.	ROH,FPH,P5,P47
Billings, C.T.	Pvt.	D 7th SCVIBn	25	KW	07/25/65	Charleston, SC	DOW	(Wdd 7/10 action?)	ROH,JR,HIC,HAG
Bilton, William H.	Pvt.	E 25th SCVI	21	CN	03/20/65	Richmond, VA	DOD	Oakwood C.#117,Row K,Div G	ROH,OWC,HAG,P65
Bingham, J.F.	Pvt.	K 6th SCVI			09/27/62	Bunker Hill, VA	DOD		3RC
Binniker, Nathan	Pvt.	H Ham.Leg.	25	OG	08/14/63	VA	DOD		ROH
Birch, Thomas B.	Pvt.	A Hol.Leg.	19	SG	09/04/62	Culpepper, VA	DOW	Fairview C. Culpepper, VA	CGH,HOS
Bird, Daniel	Pvt.	K 15th SCVI		AE	02/07/65	Camp Chase, OH	DIP	Con.Cem.#1094 Columbus, OH	FPH,P5,P23,KEB
Bird, Edward	Pvt.	B 5th SCVI		YK	08/21/61	Charlottesville	DOD	University Cem. Ch'ville	SA3,ACH,CB
Bird, H.G.	Pvt.	D 10th SCVI		MN	/ /	Franklin, KY	DOD		HMC,RAS
Bird, Hugh G.	Pvt.	L 21st SCVI	21	MN	06/04/64	Richmond, VA	DOD		ROH,HMC,HAG
Bird, Isaac Bailey	Pvt.	I 2nd SCVI	26	CN	08/19/64	Wilmington, NC	DOW	2nd Presb. C. Charleston	ROH,MAG,CDC
Bird, J.	Pvt.	D 10th SCVI		MN	/ /	Kentucky	DOD		RAS,HMC
Bird, Joseph	Pvt.	K 1st SCVC	25	PS	/ /	At home	DOD		ROH
Bird, Malachi	Pvt.	K 7th SCVI		ED	06/29/62	Savage Stn., VA	KIA	(JR=Cpl.)	ROH,JR,CDC,CNM
Bird, Peter C.	Pvt.	A 9th SCVIB		DN	10/07/61	Richmond, VA	DOD	Hollywood Cem.Rchmd. F166	ROH,JR,HC,JLC
Bird, W.L.	Pvt.	G 2nd SCVI		KW	08/29/63	Davids Island NY	DOW	Cypress Hills N.C.#830 NYC	FPH,GDR,P1,P5
Bird, W.W.	Pvt.			CR	07/23/64	Petersburg, VA		Blandford Church Pbg., VA	BLC
Birt, C.	Pvt.	H 17th SCVI			09/14/62	South Mtn., MD	KIA		JR
Birt, M.W.	Pvt.	H 17th SCVI		BL	07/01/64	Petersburg, VA	KIA		ROH,JR
Bishop, A.J.	Pvt.	D 16th SCVI		GE	/ /	MS	DOD	(1863)	16R
Bishop, C.C.	Pvt.	D P.S.S.		SG	06/18/63	Weldon, NC	DOW	(JR=DOD)	ROH,JR,HOS,PP
Bishop, Elmore G.	Pvt.	C 18th SCVI	45	UN	07/30/64	Crater, Pbg., VA	KIA		ROH,JR,BLM
Bishop, George W.	Pvt.	I Hol.Leg.		SG	/ /	At home	DOD	(POW Stoney Ck. xchd & Dd)	HOS,P120
Bishop, Hampton	Pvt.	H 2nd SCVIRi			07/08/62	Richmond, VA	DOW	(JR=6/29/62)	ROH,JR,CDC
Bishop, Henry M.	Sgt.	D 16th SCVI		GE	/ /	GA	DOD		16R
Bishop, J.	Pvt.	K 5th SCVI			/ /		DOD		JR
Bishop, J.C.	Pvt.	A 4th Bn Res		NY	10/02/64	Charleston, SC	DOD		ROH,ANY,CDC
Bishop, J.M.	Pvt.	G 1st SCVIH		BL	04/24/63	Charleston, SC	DOD		ROH,SA1
Bishop, J.W.	Pvt.	K 3rd SCVI	20	SG	06/01/64	Richmond, VA	KIA	(HOS=Md. Hts.)	ROH,JR,SA2,HOS
Bishop, James	Pvt.	D 17th SCVI		CR	11/09/64	Elmira, NY	DIP	Woodlawn N.C.#784 Elmira	ROH,FPH,P6,P65
Bishop, John	Pvt.	F 1st SCVIH		GE	07/05/62	Charleston, SC	DOD	Magnolia Cem. Charleston	ROH,SA1,MAG,RCD
Bishop, John F.	Pvt.	D 5th SCVI		UN	05/31/62	7 Pines, VA	KIA		ROH,JR,SA3

SOUTH CAROLINA DEAD IN CSA SERVICE 1861-1865

NAME	RANK	C	REGIMENT	AGE	DS	DIED	WHERE	WHY	BURIED	SOURCES
Bishop, Miles B.	Pvt.	H	2nd SCVIRi			06/30/62	Richmond, VA	KIA		JR
Bishop, Silas	Pvt.	D	3rd SCVIBn		NY	06/15/63	Bunker's Hill VA	DOD	(Date aprox)	ANY
Bishop, William C.	Pvt.	I	27th SCVI		CN	07/25/64	Fts. Monroe, VA	DOW		ROH,P12
Bishop, William F.	Pvt.	B	3rd SCVI		NY	08/30/64	At home	DOD		SA2,ANY,KEB
Bishop, Wilson	Pvt.	G	16th SCVI		GE	/ /	Lauderdale, MS	DOD	(Prob Con. Cem. there)	16R,PP
Bishop, Zachariah	Pvt.	D	17th SCVI	24	CR	08/30/62	2nd Manassas, VA	KIA	(JR=Groveton)	ROH,JR,CDC,HHC
Biter, John	Pvt.	C	22nd SCVI		SG	10/09/64	Elmira, NY	DIP	Woodlawn N.C.#664 Elmira	ROH,FPH,P6,P65
Biter, Peter	Pvt.	C	22nd SCVI	19	SG	08/19/63	Virginia	DOD		ROH,HOS
Biter, Willis	Pvt.	C	22nd SCVI		SG	07/01/64	Elmira, NY	DIP		ROH,CDC
Bittle, James H.	Pvt.	D	26th SCVI		MO	07/15/64	Petersburg, VA	DOW	(Date approx 6/17-7/27/64)	ROH,HOM,CDC
Black, A.H.	Pvt.	D	1st SCV			02/25/65	Raleigh, NC		Oakwood C. Raleigh, NC	TOD
Black, Alpheus	Pvt.	D	6th SCVI		CR	08/17/64	Petersburg, VA	KIA	(HHC=17th SCVI)	ROH,HHC
Black, Daniel L.	Pvt.	G	7th SCVC		CN	09/26/64	Elmira, NY	DIP	Woodlawn N.C.#377 Elmira	FPH,P5,P65,P11
Black, David M.	Pvt.	K	P.S.S.	41	UN	12/09/64	Richmond, VA	DOD	Fair Forest P.C. Union, SC	UNC
Black, Edward	Pvt.	I	6th SCVI		CR	06/30/62	Frayser's Fm. VA	KIA	Oakwood C.#4,Row L,Div C	OWC,WDB,HHC,CB
Black, Gaines W.	Pvt.	I	6th SCVI		CR	02/24/64	At home	DOD		CRM,HFC,HHC,CB
Black, J.	Pvt.	B	18th SCVI		UN	07/17/64	Richmond, VA		Hollywood Cem.Rchmd. U651	HC
Black, J. Benjamin	Pvt.	K	2nd SCVI		CN	01/17/62		DOD		SA2,KEB
Black, J.H.	Pvt.	C	21st SCVI			04/15/62	At home	DOD	(No Co.C in HAG)	JR
Black, J.J.	Pvt.	H	7th SCVIBn			11/10/62	Adams Run, SC	DOD		JR
Black, Jacob Wilson	Pvt.	E	7th SCVI		ED	09/13/62	Maryland Hts. MD	KIA		ROH,JR,HOE,UD3
Black, James J.	2nd Lt.	G	P.S.S.	25	YK	08/05/62	7 Pines, VA	DOW	(Wdd earlier 6/1/62)	ROH,JR,YEB,SA3
Black, Jasper	Pvt.	D	17th SCVI	33	CR	07/29/62	At home	DOD	(HHC & CB=Joseph)	ROH,JR,HHC,CB
Black, John	Pvt.	F	18th SCVI		UN	08/15/62	Charleston, SC	DOD		ROH,JR
Black, John	2nd Lt.	B	11th SCVI	32	CO	07/17/64	Drury's Bluff VA	DOW	(Wdd 5/16/64)	ROH,HAG,R47
Black, John H.	Pvt.	L	P.S.S.		PS	/ /	Richmond, VA	KIA		ROH,JR
Black, R.R.	Cpt.	B	11th SCVI	38	CO	12/22/62	Pocotaligo, SC	DOD	(NI HAG, Prob 9th SCVIH)	ROH
Black, Robert	Pvt.	C	4th SCResB	16	YK	/ /	At home	DOD	(Gill's Bn. Florence Gd.)	YEB
Black, Thomas	Pvt.	D	17th SCVI	24	CR	08/30/62	2nd Manassas, VA	KIA	(JR=8/29/62)	ROH,JR,HHC,CB
Black, Thomas	Pvt.	G	18th SCVI	23	YK	/ /		DOD	(Measles 1862)	YEB
Black, Thomas P.	Pvt.	E	P.S.S.	20	SR	10/10/64	At home	DOD	(JR=T.B.)	ROH,JR
Black, Wesley A.	Pvt.	D	19th SCVI	19	ED	12/15/64	Nashville, TN	KIA		HOE,UD3
Black, William	Pvt.	F	1st SCVA			12/15/62	Charleston, SC	DOD	Magnolia Cem. Charleston	ROH,MAG
Black, William	Pvt.	M	P.S.S.		SG	09/17/62	Sharpsburg, MD	KIA		JR,HOS,CDC
Black, William Pickens	Pvt.	D	7th SCVI	17	AE	09/22/61	At home	DOD	Shiloh M.C. Antreville	ROH,CAE
Blackburn, D.	Pvt.	C	10th SCVIRi		HY	/ /	Georgetown, SC	DOD		RAS
Blackburn, Daniel M.	Pvt.	L	7th SCVI	20	MN	06/26/61	Culpepper, VA	DOD	Fairview C. Culpepper, VA	CGH
Blackburn, J.H.	Pvt.	G	7th SCVC		CN	03/08/65	Pt. Lookout, MD	DIP	C.C. Pt. Lookout, MD	P12,FPH
Blackburn, John	Pvt.	B	Orr's Ri.		AE	06/27/62	Gaines' Mill, VA	KIA		ROH,JR,CDC
Blackenstine, Jacob	Pvt.	A	15th SCVI		RD	05/02/63	Chancellorsville	KIA		ROH,CDC,KEB,R4
Blackman, H.J.	2nd Lt.	D	10th SCVI		MN	11/01/62		DOD		RAS,HMC
Blackman, Hugh G.	Pvt.	F	4th SCVC		MN	08/18/64	Pt. Lookout, MD	DIP	C.C. Pt. Lookout, MD	ROH,FPH,P5,P11
Blackman, J.W. (22ndSC?)	Pvt.	E	12th SCVI		LR	10/04/64	Richmond, VA		Hollywood Cem.Rchmd. V138	ROH,HC
Blackman, James	Pvt.	B	21st SCVI		DN	03/06/65	Elmira, NY	DIP	Woodlawn N.C.#2416 Elmira	ROH,FPH,P6,P65
Blackman, John J.	Pvt.	A	8th SCVI		DN	05/28/62	Petersburg, VA	DOD	Blandford Ch. Pbg., VA PP	ROH,JR,BLC,KEB
Blackman, O.H.	Pvt.	F	12th SCVI			08/28/64	Ream's St., VA	KIA		JR
Blackmon, Andrew J.	Pvt.	E	12th SCVI	17	LR	09/17/62	Sharpsburg, MD	KIA		ROH,LAN
Blackmon, J. Burdock	1st Lt.	E	12th SCVI	27	LR	05/12/64	Spotsylvania, VA	KIA	(Also Wdd.@ 2nd M.)	ROH,JR,HCD,LAN
Blackmon, Jerry	Pvt.	G	1st SCVC		AE	03/15/63	Staunton, VA	DOD		ROH
Blackmon, John A.	Pvt.	E	22nd SCVI		LR	03/11/62	Columbia, SC	DOD		PP,LAN
Blackmon, John C.	Pvt.	G	2nd SCVI			09/20/63	Chickamauga, GA	KIA		ROH,SA2,HIC,H2

B

SOUTH CAROLINA DEAD IN CSA SERVICE 1861-1865

NAME	RANK	C	REGIMENT	AGE	DS	DIED	WHERE	WHY	BURIED	SOURCES
Blackmon, John E.	3rd Sgt.	E	12th SCVI	45	LR	08/03/64	Ft. Delaware, DE	DIP	Finn's Pt., NJ Nat. Cem.	ROH,FPH,P5,P43
Blackmon, K.C.	Pvt.	D	10th SCVI		MN	/ /		DOD		RAS,HMC
Blackmon, Samuel W.	Pvt.	H	2nd SCVI		LR	08/15/61	Richmond, VA	DOD	Hollywood Cem.Rchmd. K63	HC,LAN
Blackmon, Simpson	Pvt.	D	1st SCVIH		LR	03/04/63	Liberty, VA	DOD	Piedmont Jctn, VA	ROH,SA1,LAN,JRH
Blackmon, W.H.	Pvt.	F	Hol.Leg.		AE	12/03/64	Richmond, VA	DOW	(Wdd @ Ptsbg.)	ROH
Blackmon, William J.	Pvt.	E	12th SCVI	21	LR	09/30/64	Petersburg, VA	KIA	(LAN=Bloody Angle)	ROH,LAN
Blackmon,Jr., James B.	2nd Lt.	E	12th SCVI		LR	09/17/62	Sharpsburg, MD	KIA	(Also Wdd 7 Days battles)	ROH,BOS,LAN,R47
Blacknell,	Pvt.	K	1st SCV			06/29/62	Richmond, VA		Hollywood Cem.Rchmd. P28	HC
Blackwell, Berry H.	Pvt.	F	18th SCVI			03/15/62	Charleston, SC	DOD	(Measles)	JR
Blackwell, C.	Pvt.	I	Hol.Leg.	18	SG	07/30/62	Adams Run, VA	DOD		ROH
Blackwell, F.M.	Pvt.	B	Ham.Leg.			12/17/62	Kinston, NC	KIA		JR
Blackwell, H.	Pvt.	B	21st SCVI			07/28/63	Charleston, SC			ROH,RCD
Blackwell, H.H.	Pvt.	A	21st SCVI			07/31/62		DOD		JR
Blackwell, James	Pvt.	H	21st SCVI		DN	08/05/63	Charleston, SC	DOD	Magnolia Cem. Charleston	JR,MAG,RCD,HAG
Blackwell, James L.	Pvt.	A	2nd SCVI		RD	12/13/62	Fredericksburg	KIA		ROH,JR,SA2,KEB
Blackwell, John	Pvt.	D	9th SCVIBn			07/12/62	Charleston, SC	DOD	Magnolia Cem. Charleston	JR,MAG
Blackwell, John A.	Pvt.	G	2nd SCVI		KW	08/18/61	Orange C.H., VA	DOD	(Typhoid)	SA2,HIC,KEB,H2
Blackwell, Joseph P.	Pvt.	I	14th SCVI	28	AE	06/13/62	Richmond, VA	DOD	(HOL= John P.)	ROH,JR,HOL
Blackwell, Micajo Thomas	Pvt.	A	7th SCVIBn	20	CD	05/24/64	Drury's Bluff VA	DOW	Oakwood C.#8,Row J,Div F	ROH,HIC,HAG,OWC
Blackwell, Samuel	Pvt.	B	6th SCVC		ED	02/03/65	Elmira, NY	DIP	Woodlawn N.C.#1752 Elmira	ROH,FPH,P6,UD3
Blackwell, Thomas J.	Pvt.	K	6th SCVI	35	CL	06/27/62	Gaines' Mill, VA	KIA		ROH,CTA,HOW,3RC
Blackwell, W.D.	Pvt.	H	2nd SCV			03/15/63	Richmond, VA			ROH
Blackwood, Alexander	Pvt.	F	13th SCVI		SG	08/29/62	2nd Manassas, VA	KIA		ROH,JR,HOS,CDC
Blackwood, John C.	Pvt.	A	25th SCVI	34	CN	03/29/64	James Island, SC	DOD	(PP=Greenville, SC)	ROH,HAG,PP,WLI
Blackwood, John K.	Pvt.	E	Hol.leg.			12/15/64	Elmira, NY	DIP	Woodlawn N.C.#1118 Elmira	FPH,P6
Blackwood, Thomas W.	Pvt.	C	1st SCVIH		BL	09/30/62	Warrenton, VA	DOW	(Wdd @ 2nd Manassas)	ROH,SJR,A1,JRH
Bladson, N.M.	Pvt.	K	12th SCVI		PS	/ /	Richmond, VA		Oakwood C.#85,Row B,Div B	ROH,OWC
Blain, Andrew Melville	Pvt.	H	6th SCVI	19	FD	11/16/63	Campbell Stn. TN	DOW		ROH,JR,HFC
Blair, David	Pvt.	G	Hol.Leg.	22	FD	12/17/62	Goldsboro, NC	DOW		ROH,ANY
Blair, William T.	Pvt.	E	4th SCVI		PS	07/31/61	Orange C.H., VA	DOW	(Wdd @ 1st Manassas)	ROH,JR,SA2
Blake, Alexander	Pvt.	K	18th SCVI			09/07/63	At home	DOD		JR
Blake, Caswell	Pvt.	M	10th SCVI		HY	/ /		DOD	(1862)	RAS
Blake, J.J.	Pvt.	M	10th SCVI		HY	/ /		DOD	(1862)	RAS
Blake, John	Pvt.	D	Hol.Leg.	27	BL	05/04/62	Adams Run, SC	DOD		PP
Blake, Thomas	Pvt.	I	1st SCVIR		GA	10/21/64	Charleston, SC	DOD	Magnolia Cem. Charleston	ROH,MAG,SA1,CDC
Blake, William	Cpl.	K	18th SCVI			06/15/63	Meridian, MS	DOD	(19th SCVI?)	JR
Blakeley, L.L.	Pvt.	F	14th SCVI		LS	10/02/64	Richmond, VA		Hollywood Cem.Rchmd. V386	ROH,HC
Blakeley, R.R.	Pvt.	B	25th SCVI		WG	05/16/64	Drury's Bluff VA	KIA		ROH,JR,HAG,WLI
Blakeley, William	Pvt.	A	20th SCVI		PS	07/04/64	Richmond, VA			ROH
Blakely, B.	Sgt.	F	14th SCVI			09/17/62	Sharpsburg, MD	KIA		JR
Blakely, D.	Sgt.	F	14th SCVI			09/20/62	Shepherdstown VA	KIA		JR
Blakely, E.T.	Pvt.	F	14th SCVI			07/16/62	Fraysers Farm VA	DOW		JR
Blakely, M.L.	Pvt.	F	14th SCVI		LS	08/30/62	2nd Manassas, VA	KIA	(JR=8/29/62)	ROH,JR,CDC
Blakely, M.M.	Sgt.	F	14th SCVI			06/30/62	McPhersonville	DOD		JR
Blakely, Thomas W.	Pvt.	K	25th SCVI		WG	07/17/63	James Island, SC	DOD	(Brain Fever)	JR,CTA,HOW,HAG
Blakely, W.R.	Pvt.	F	14th SCVI		LS	07/02/63	Gettysburg, PA	DOW		ROH,JR
Blakely, William J.	Pvt.	K	25th SCVI		WG	07/17/63		DOD	(1863)	JR,CTA,HOW
Blakeney, Hugh	1st Lt.	D	8th SCVI	20	CD	05/09/64	Spotsylvania, VA	KIA	C.C. Spotsylvania C.H., VA	ROH,JR,SCH,CDC
Blakeney, Louis N.	1st Lt.		Ch'fld. LA	20	CD	06/15/63	Jerusalem, VA	DOD		ROH,R44
Blakewood, John S.	Cpt.	B	1st Mtd Ma		BT	01/05/62		DOD		R43
Blalock, J.B.	Pvt.	E	17th SCVI	23	YK	08/01/64	Petersburg, VA	DOW	(Wdd 6/30/64)	ROH,PP

SOUTH CAROLINA DEAD IN CSA SERVICE 1861-1865

NAME	RANK	C REGIMENT	AGE	DS	DIED	WHERE	WHY	BURIED	SOURCES
Blalock, J.D.	Pvt.	Barnwell A		BL	01/04/65	Charleston, SC	DOD	Magnolia Cem. Charleston	ROH,MAG
Blalock, J.D.	Pvt.	I 17th SCVI		LR	07/30/64	Crater, Pbg., VA	KIA		ROH,JR,BLM,LAN
Blalock, James N.	Pvt.	I 12th SCVI		LR	08/15/62	Laurel Hill, VA	DOD		JR,LAN
Blanckenstein, Jacob	Pvt.	A 15th SCVI			05/28/62	Richmond, VA	KIA		JR,KEB
Bland, Elbert	Lt. Col.	7th SCVI	38	ED	09/20/63	Chickamauga, TN	KIA	(See KEB p78)	ROH,JR,LC,KEB,
Bland, J.M.	Pvt.	2nd SCV			10/16/62	Winchester, VA	DOD	Stonewall Cem. Winchester	ROH,WIN
Blankensea, Claborne	Pvt.	M P.S.S.	26	UN	/ /		DOD	(JR=Blanton)	ROH,JR
Blankensea, Robert	Pvt.	A Ham.Leg.	25	BL	07/21/61	1st Manassas, VA	KIA	(Henry per WLI)	ROH,CDC,WLI
Blankensea, Samuel	Pvt.	M P.S.S.	22	UN	/ /		DOD	(JR=Blanton)	ROH,JR
Blankensea, Thomas	Pvt.	M P.S.S.	24	UN	/ /		DOD	(JR=Blanton)	ROH,JR
Blankheart, M.P.	Pvt.	H 26th SCVI		SR	12/24/62	Richmond, VA		Hollywood Cem.Rchmd. Q51	HC
Blanton, Ambrose	Pvt.	F 15th SCVI		UN	10/01/62	Frederick, MD	DOD	Mt. Olivet C. C.S.#72	JR,FPH,P1,P6,B
Blanton, B.F.					/ /			(Rchmd effects list 12/62)	CDC
Blanton, C.D.	Pvt.	H P.S.S.			/ /		DOD	(Dup of Clayton?)	JR
Blanton, Clayton	Pvt.	M P.S.S.			/ /		DOD		JR
Blanton, D.D.	Pvt.	F 15th SCVI		UN	/ /		DOD		JR,KEB
Blanton, D.J.	Pvt.	K 26th SCVI	30	HY	02/20/65	Richmond, VA	DOD	Hollywood Cem.Rchmd. W52	ROH,HC
Blanton, Franklin	Pvt.	I 5th SCVI		SG	/ /		DOD		HOS
Blanton, James C.	Pvt.	G 5th SCVI	22	UN	12/27/61	Richmond, VA	DOD	Oakwood C.#62,Row D,Div A	ROH,SA3,OWC
Blanton, Joseph	Pvt.			M				04/05/65 Washington, DC	
Blanton, Michael	Pvt.	M P.S.S.	20	UN	10/24/64	Richmond, VA	DOD		ROH,RR
Blanton, Samuel D.	Pvt.	G 5th SCVI		SG	12/26/61	Manchester, VA	DOD	(JR=M, P.S.S.)	JR,SA3
Blanton, Tom	Pvt.	M P.S.S.			/ /		DOD		JR
Blanton, W.H.	Pvt.	M P.S.S.		UN	10/25/64	Richmond, VA			ROH
Blanton, W.H.	Pvt.	A 1st SCVIG		BL	06/27/62	Gaines' Mill, VA	KIA		JR,SA1
Blanton, W.M.	Pvt.	K Hol.Leg.			/ /	At sea	DIP		CDC,P114
Blanton, William L.	Pvt.	K 3rd SCVI			11/06/64	Fts. Monroe, VA	DOW	(NI SA@ or KEB 3rd SCVC?)	ROH
Blanton,Sr., James	Pvt.	M P.S.S.		UN	06/30/62	Frayser's Farm	KIA		ROH,JR,CDC
Blassingame, W.H.	Pvt.	A 4th SCVIBn		AN	05/05/62	Williamsburg, VA	KIA		ROH,CNM
Blaylock, William	Pvt.	F 7th SCVI			09/19/62	Pleasant Val. MD	DOW		JR
Bledsoe, Lewis	Pvt.	K 14th SCVI	59	ED	11/25/61	At home	DOD		HOE,EDN
Bledsoe, Vinson B.	Pvt.	K 14th SCVI		ED	09/04/62	Richmond, VA	DOD	(JR=7/30/62)	JR,HOE,CDC,EDN
Blichington, A.	Pvt.	A 1st SCVIH			10/24/63	Med.C.H. Atlanta		Oakland C. Atlanta R14#9	BGA
Bligh, John	Pvt.	D 2nd SCVI		SR	07/02/63	Gettysburg, PA	KIA	Magnolia Cem. Charleston	ROH,JR,GDR,SA2
Blitchington, O.B.	Pvt.	A 1st SCVIH		BL	10/28/63	Chattanooga, TN	DOW	(Wdd 9/27/63)	ROH,SA1,JRH,UD
Blizzard, E. Jacob	Pvt.	B 7th SCVIBn		RD	05/16/64	Drury's Bluff VA	KIA		ROH,JR,HAG
Blizzard, James T.	Pvt.	B 7th SCVIBn		RD	12/28/64	Washington, DC	DOW		ROH,P1,P5,HAG
Blocker, A.B.	Pvt.	I 11th SCVI		CO	06/01/65	SC Coast	DOD		ROH
Blocker, Arthur P.	Cpl.	F 11th SCVI	19	CO	05/09/64	Swift Creek, VA	KIA	(HAG=A.W.)	ROH,JR,HAG
Blocker, Benjamin B.	Pvt.			CO	08/29/61	South Carolina	DOD		ROH
Blocker, Edwin	Pvt.	K 1st SCVIR		CO	08/02/62	Camp Evans, SC	DOD		SA1
Blocker, John R.	Major	Butler's D		ED	06/06/64	Richmond, VA	DOW	Blocker Fam. Cem. ED Cty.	ROH,JR,EDN,BHC
Blocker, T.J.	Pvt.	K 1st SCVIR		CO	05/26/65	Pt. Lookout, MD	DIP	C.C. Pt. Lookout, MD	FPH,SA1,P6,P11
Blood, Marshall D.	Pvt.	H 2nd SCVC	28	RD	07/04/64	Georgetown, SC	DOD		ROH,PP
Blott, E.	Pvt.	14th SCVI			/ /	Mt. Jackson, VA	DOD	Mt. Jackson, VA	ROH,CDC
Blue, Henry. A.	Sgt.	C 8th SCVI		CD	07/13/61	Richmond, VA	DOD	Hollywood Cem.Rchmd. K110	ROH,JR,HC
Blue, William	2nd Sgt.	I 1st SCVIH		MN	05/06/64	Wilderness, VA	KIA		SA1,HMC
Blue, William A.	Sgt.	B 26th SCVI	21	CD	05/04/64	New Bern, NC		(PP=3/4/64)	ROH,PP
Bluff, George	Pvt.	H 7th SCVI		CR	/ /		KIA		HHC
Bluffkin, Burrell	Pvt.	K 26th SCVI	36	HY	07/09/62	Columbia, SC	DOD		ROH,JR
Bluffkin, Kinchen	Pvt.	F 1st SCVIG		HY	05/05/64	Wilderness, VA	KIA		JR,SA1,PDL,CDC

B

SOUTH CAROLINA DEAD IN CSA SERVICE 1861-1865

NAME	RANK	C	REGIMENT	AGE	DS	DIED	WHERE	WHY	BURIED	SOURCES
Bluffkin, Sylvester	Pvt.	F	1st SCVIG		HY	05/23/64	Noel Station, VA	KIA		SA1,PDL,CDC
Bluffkin, William H.	Pvt.	F	1st SCVIG		HY	07/01/63	Gettysburg, PA	KIA		JR,GDR,SA1,PDL
Blum, Robert A.	1st Lt.	B	25th SCVI	31	CN	09/05/63	Bty. Wagner, SC	KIA	St.John's L.C. Charleston	ROH,JR,DOC,HAG
Blum, Jr., John A.	Pvt.	A	Ham.Leg.	22	CN	10/21/62	Richmond, VA	DOD	English L.C. Charleston SC	ROH,JR,CDC,WLI
Blume, John H.	Pvt.	A	14th SCVI	53	DN	04/19/65	New Bern, NC	DOW	Cedar Grove C. Newbern, NC	P1,P6,P12,PP
Boag, Charles Lawton.	Cpt.	I	1st SCVIG		CN	06/27/62	Gaines's Mill VA	KIA	Magnolia C.(PL)Charleston	ROH,JR,MAG,SA1
Boan, C.J.	Pvt.	B	8th SCVI			11/15/61	Richmond, VA	DOD	(Typhoid)	JR
Boan, V.R.	Pvt.	B	8th SCVI			11/15/61	Richmond, VA	DOD	(Typhoid)	JR
Boan, William	Cpt.		Chstrfld A	28	CD	07/04/62	Petersburg, VA			PP
Board, W.H.	Pvt.	A	14th SCVI	40	DN	03/10/63	Fredericksburg	DOD	(Pneumonia @ Camp Gregg)	ROH,JR,DEB
Boatwright, Thomas	Pvt.	F	4th SCVC		GN	06/11/64	Trevillian Stn.	KIA	(JR=7/10)	ROH,JR,LOR,HMC
Boatwright, W.N.	Pvt.				WG	/ /		DOD	(1864)	CTA,HOW
Boatwright, W.W.	Pvt.	A	10th SCVI			02/08/64	Cassville, GA	KIA	(NI RAS, 19th SCVI?)	ROH
Boazman, David H.	Pvt.	B	Orr's Ri.			06/01/62	Richmond, VA	DOD	Hollywood Cem.Rchmd. L162	ROH,JR,HC
Boazman, L.J.	3rd Lt.	F	3rd SCVI		LS	10/17/62	Sharpsburg, MD	DOW	Rose Hill C. Hagerstown	ROH,JR,SA2,BOD
Bobb, F.W.B.	Pvt.	G	13th SCVI		NY	08/29/62	2nd Manassas, VA	KIA		ROH,JR,ANY,CDC
Bobb, G.L. (G.S.?)	Pvt.	G	13th SCVI		NY	08/29/62	2nd Manassas, VA	DOW		ROH,JR,ANY,CDC
Bobb, Jacob F.	Pvt.	G	13th SCVI		NY	05/14/62	Ashland C.H., VA	DOD		ROH,JR,ANY
Bobbett, W.J.	Pvt.	H	18th SCVI		YK	06/30/62	Charleston, SC	DOD	Magnolia Cem. Charleston	ROH,JR,MAG
Bobo, Charles Burwell	2nd Lt.	E	18th SCVI	30	UN	05/20/64	Clay's Farm, VA	DOW	Blandford Church Pbg., VA	ROH,JR,BLC,UNC
Bobo, D.	Pvt.	K	1st SCVIR			07/15/63	Columbia, SC	DOD		ROH,SA1,PP
Bobo, Howard T.	Pvt.	C	13th SCVI		SG	08/16/64	Fussell's Mill	KIA	(JR=8/10/64)	ROH,JR,HOS
Bobo, John	Pvt.	I	1st SCVIR		GA	11/17/64	At home	DOD		SA1
Bobo, Robert	Pvt.	C	18th SCVI	27	UN	08/30/62	2nd Manassas, VA	KIA	(JR=DOW 9/1)	ROH,JR
Bobo, S. Williams	Pvt.	E	2nd SCVC		SG	11/03/64	Adams Run, SC	DOD		HOS,PP
Bobo, S.N.	Pvt.	C	18th SCVI	23	UN	08/08/62	Petersburg, VA	DOD	New Prospect Ch. Union, SC	ROH,JR,UNC
Bodie, David S.	Pvt.	B	14th SCVI	23	ED	04/02/65	Petersburg, VA	KIA		HOE,UD3
Bodie, Felix	Pvt.	B	14th SCVI	45	ED	/ /	Richmond, VA	DOD	(1864)	HOE,UD3
Bodie, Mitchell	Pvt.	F	27th SCVI		ED	08/07/64	Petersburg, VA	KIA	(HAG= Brodie)	ROH,HAG
Bodie, Morgan D.	Sgt.	A	19th SCVI	19	ED	10/30/62	Knoxville, TN	DOD	Bethel C. Knoxville, TN	JR,HOE,UD3,TOD
Bodie, Obediah	Pvt.	B	14th SCVI	30	ED	06/21/62	Richmond, VA '62	DOD	Oakwood C.#26,Row K,Div B	ROH,JR,UD3,OWC
Bodie, Wiley	Pvt.	A	19th SCVI	40	ED	/ /	Augusta, GA	DOD		HOE,UD3
Bodom, H.	Pvt.	A	27th SCVI		CN	/ /	Virginia	DOW	(Leg amputated)	DRE
Body, Joseph	Pvt.	I	22nd SCVI		OG	07/14/64	Petersburg, VA	DOD	Blandford Church Pbg., VA	ROH,BLC,PP
Bogan, Benjamin G.	Pvt.	H	1st SCVIG		CN	12/09/64	Elmira, NY	DIP	Woodlawn N.C.#1160 Elmira	FPH,SA1,P6,P65
Boggs, George W.B.	Pvt.	B	Ham.Leg.		PS	05/04/62	Williamsburg, VA	KIA	Liberty Cem. Pickens, SC	PCS,BC,CDC,R48
Boggs, Thomas A.	Pvt.	G	6th SCVI	20	FD	06/30/62	Frayser's Farm	KIA	Presbyterian Ch. Winnsboro	ROH,CV,PP
Boggs, Thomas Hamilton	Lt. Col.		2nd SCVIRi	35	PS	07/06/62	Richmond, VA	DOD	Carmel P.C. Liberty SC	ROH,JR,PCS
Boland, J.B.	Pvt.	G	13th SCVI		NY	08/01/62	Laurel Hill, VA	DOD		ROH,ANY
Boland, S.D.	Cpl.	I	15th SCVI	21	LN	04/30/62		DOD		H15,KEB,TOD
Bold, William	Pvt.	A	24th SCVI	54		/ /	Charleston, SC	DOD		CDC
Bolen,	Pvt.	A				/ /			Stonewall C. Winchester VA	ROH,WIN
Boles, Samuel F.	Pvt.	K	20th SCVI		LN	06/15/65		DOD		ROH,KEB
Bolick, E.D.	Cpl.	F	6th SCVI	25	CR	07/19/64	Weldon RR, VA	KIA		ROH,JR,HHC
Bolin, Benjamin	Pvt.	K	17th SCVI	41	YK	/ /	Adams Run, SC	DOD		JR,YEB
Bolin, John	Pvt.	C	17th SCVI	38	YK	/ /	Staunton, VA	DOD	(YEB=KIA @ Crater Pbg.)	JR,YEB
Bolin, John	Pvt.	C	17th SCVI		YK	11/10/62	Warrenton, VA	DOW		PP
Bolin, Lewis	Cpl.	C	17th SCVI	29	YK	07/30/64	Crater, Pbg., VA	KIA	(YEB=DOD)	BLM,YEB
Bolin, R.V.	Pvt.	G	5th SCVI		YK	06/15/63	Lynchburg, VA	DOD		ROH,SA3
Bolin, Thomas	Cpl.	K	Ham.Leg.			07/28/64	Ft. Delaware, DE	DIP	Finn's Pt. NJ, Nat. Cem.	FPH,P5,P47
Bolin, William	Pvt.	C	17th SCVI	26	YK	/ /	Johns Island, SC	DOD	(1862)	JR,YEB

SOUTH CAROLINA DEAD IN CSA SERVICE 1861-1865

NAME	RANK	C	REGIMENT	AGE	DS	DIED	WHERE	WHY	BURIED	SOURCES
Boling, E.P.	Sgt.	K	1st SCResB			01/26/65	Raleigh, NC		Oakwood C. Raleigh, NC	TOD
Boling, J.M.	Pvt.	I	P.S.S.			06/19/64	Petersburg, VA	KIA		ROH,JR
Boling, James E.	Pvt.	G	16th SCVI		GE	/ /	Atlanta, GA	DOD		16R
Bolins, E.	Pvt.	C	7th SCVI			11/07/62	Staunton, VA		Thornrose C. Staunton, VA	TOD
Bollen, S.E.	Pvt.		22nd SCVI	50	OG	06/15/64	Columbia, SC	DOD	(Date approximate)	ROH,PP
Boller, John	Cpl.	C	9th SCVIBn		LN	07/13/62	Charleston, SC		Magnolia Cem. Charleston	ROH,RCD
Bolt, C.C.	Pvt.	L	Orr's Ri.		AN	/ /	Charlottesville		University Cem. Ch'ville	ACH
Bolt, Edward	Pvt.	L	Orr's Ri.			07/16/62	Dill Springs, VA	DOD		JR,CDC
Bolt, John L.	Pvt.	A	3rd SCVI		LS	07/19/62	At home	DOD	(NI SA2, JR=J.S.)	ROH,JR,KEB
Bolt, Lewis Martin	Pvt.	L	Orr's Ri.			01/26/62	Guinea Stn., VA	DOD		JR
Bolt, Robert	Pvt.	G	22nd SCVI	53	AN	08/27/64	Charlotte, NC	DOD		ROH
Bolt, Thomas	Pvt.	G	22nd SCVI	25	AN	07/30/64	Crater, Pbg., VA	KIA		ROH
Bolt, Thomas W.	Pvt.	G	22nd SCVI	27	AN	07/16/64	Petersburg, VA	DOD		ROH
Bolt, William T.	Pvt.	A	3rd SCVI		LS	07/26/62	At home	DOD		ROH,JR,SA2,KEB
Bolton, Britton	Pvt.	I	1st SCVIH		MN	01/03/64	Petersburg, VA		(SA1=AWOL since 3/64	ROH,HMC,SA1
Bolton, Britton	Pvt.	D	26th SCVI		MO	/ /	At home	DOD	(? also in I, 1st SCVIH)	HOM
Bolton, Edmund	Pvt.	A	22nd SCVI		ED	06/18/64	Petersburg, VA	KIA		ROH,JR
Bolton, John	Pvt.	G	7th SCVI		ED	/ /		KIA		HOE,UD2
Bolton, W.L.	Pvt.	I	2nd SCVC			07/07/64	Johns Island, SC	KIA		ROH,CDC
Bolton, William H.	Pvt.	I	2nd SCVC		ED	06/15/64	Johns Island, SC	KIA		ROH,HOE
Bomar, E. Thomas	Pvt.	B	22nd SCVI		SG	07/30/64	Crater, Pbg., VA	KIA		HOS
Bomar, George Washington	Pvt.	B	22nd SCVI		SG	07/30/64	Crater, Pbg., VA	KIA		HOS,BLM
Bomar, J.	Pvt.	H	25th SCVI			10/09/63	Charleston, SC	DOD		JR
Bomar, J. Edward	2nd Lt.	B	25th SCVI	26	CN	05/16/64	Drury's Bluff VA	KIA	(JR=Bowen)	ROH,JR,HAG,WLI
Bomar, John W.	Pvt.	B	22nd SCVI		SG	06/17/64	Petersburg, VA	KIA		ROH,JR,HOS
Bomar, Robert	Pvt.	A	Ham.Leg.		CN	07/21/61	1st Manassas, VA	KIA		ROH,CDC
Bomar, T.M.	Pvt.	K	2nd SCVIRi			09/30/64	Ft. Harrison, VA	KIA		JR
Bomar, Thomas N.	Pvt.	C	5th SCVI			07/25/62	Richmond, VA	DOD	(JR=January, 1862)	ROH,JR
Bonds, L.J.	Pvt.	H	15th SCVI			/ /		DOD		JR
Bonds, Robert	Pvt.	H	15th SCVI		UN	07/01/63	Gettysburg, PA	KIA	(NI KEB, Bends?)	ROH,JR,CDC,GDR
Bonds, William	Pvt.	H	2nd SCVA		BL	08/01/63	Bty Wagner, SC	KIA		ROH
Bone, Jacob W.	Pvt.	A	7th SCVIBn	36	CD	10/28/64	Darbytown, VA	DOD		ROH,HIC,HAG
Bone, John D.	Pvt.	I	21st		MN	02/14/62	At home	DOD	(2nd entry in JR=7/11/62)	JR,HMC,HAG
Bone, N.	Pvt.		Arty			/ /	Richmond, VA		Oakwood C.#162,Row N,Div A	OWC
Bone, Thomas	Pvt.	E	10th SCVI		GN	/ /	MS	DOD		RAS
Bone, W.R.	Pvt.	B	8th SCVI			/ /	Richmond, VA	DOD	(Typhoid)	JR
Boney, John T.	Pvt.	B	7th SCVIBn	23	FD	10/06/62	Church Flats, SC	DOD	(ROH= John F.)	ROH,JR,HAG
Bong, James	Pvt.	E	3rd SCVBn		CR	/ /		KIA		HHC
Bonham, G.L.	Pvt.	H	6th SCVC			01/14/65	Weldon, NC		(Yeadon Rangers)	PP
Bonham, J.H.	Pvt.	H	6th SCVC	38		05/29/63	Adams Run, SC	DOD		PP
Bonham, W.C.	Pvt.	E	13th SCVI		SG	09/18/63	Ft. Delaware, DE	DIP	Finn's Pt., NJ Nat. Cem.	FPH,HOS,P5,P47
Bonner, Luther	3rd Lt.	M	P.S.S.	23	SG	06/30/62	Frayser's Farm	KIA		ROH,JR,HOS,R48
Bonner, Pinckney	Pvt.	M	P.S.S.	25	SG	05/31/62	7 Pines, VA	KIA		ROH,JR,HOS,CDC
Bonner, Wiley	Pvt.	A	24th SCVI	23	CO	02/13/65	Camp Morton, IN	DIP	(POW, New Hope Ch.6/24/64)	ROH,CDC,P3,P6
Bonnett,	Pvt.		SCVA	17	OG	04/15/65	Summerville, SC	DOD		ROH
Bonnett, Daniel	Pvt.	I	25th SCVI	50	OG	04/15/65		DOD		ROH
Bonnett, George	Pvt.	I	2nd SCVA	35	OG	06/15/63	James Island, SC	ACD		ROH
Bonney, Usher P.	1st Lt.	H	7th SCVC		KW	/ /	Johnsons Isl.,OH	DIP	(P43=Rlsd Ft. Del.6/16/65)	HIC,P43,PP
Booker, John L.	Pvt.	C	13th SCVI		SG	11/26/61	Coosawatchie, SC	DOD	(Pneumonia, RR=Co.G)	ROH,JR,HOS
Booker, Thomas P.	Pvt.	D	P.S.S.		SG	06/15/65	At home	DOD		ROH,HOS
Booker, Thomas W.	Pvt.	D	P.S.S.		SG	05/29/64	Wilderness, VA	DOW	(JR&HOS=Campbells Stn TN)	ROH,JR,HOS

B

SOUTH CAROLINA DEAD IN CSA SERVICE 1861-1865

NAME	RANK	C REGIMENT	AGE	DS	DIED	WHERE	WHY	BURIED	SOURCES
Bookhart, Joel T.	Pvt.	E Ham.Leg.	17	RD	08/29/61	Culpepper, VA	DOW	Fairview C. Culpepper, VA	JR,CGH,CDC
Bookheart, S.					09/04/61	Richmond, VA		Hollywood Cem.Rchmd. G44	HC
Bookman, Oscar H.	Pvt.	F 12th SCVI		FD	08/25/64	Ream's Stn., VA	KIA	(See p194,LSS)	HFC,LSS
Bookter, Edwin Faust	Col.	12th SCVI	27	RD	09/30/64	Jones Farm, VA	KIA	Mt. Pleasant P.C. RD Cty.	ROH,JR,BOS,HCD
Bookter, Nathan R.	2nd Lt.	D 12th SCVI	23	RD	06/22/64	Jerusalem Pl. Rd	KIA	Mt. Pleasant P.C. RD Cty.	ROH,JR,HCD,RCD
Boone, Godfrey	Pvt.	H 13th SCVI		LN	10/24/62	Lynchburg, VA	DOD	Lynchburg CSA Cem.#7 R3	ROH,JR,CDC,BBW
Boone, J.H.W.	Pvt.	K 4th SCVC		CN	06/11/64	Trevillian Stn.	KIA	(See p67,BHC)	ROH,JR,BHC,CDC
Boone, Joseph W.	Pvt.	A 8th SCVI		DN	08/07/61	Culpepper, VA	DOD	Fairview Cem. Culpepper VA	ROH,JR,CGH,CDC
Boone, Silas	Pvt.	D 7th SCVIBn	50	KW	03/31/62	Adams Run, SC	DOD	(HAG= Boon) PP	ROH,JR,HIC,HAG
Booshe, A.J.	Pvt.	A 1st SCVI			01/13/64	Pt. Lookout, MD	DIP	(NI SA1, FPH or POW Rcds)	ROH
Booth, John A.	Pvt.	B 10th SCVI		HY	06/05/63	Shelbyville, TN	DOD	(JR=Chattanooga)	JR,RAS
Boothe, J.W.	Pvt.	G 26th SCVI		DN	12/12/64	Richmond, VA			ROH
Boozer, Burr A.	2nd Cpl.	G 13th SCVI		NY	07/03/63	Gettysburg, PA	DOW	(CDC=D.A.)	ROH,ANY,CDC,GDR
Boozer, David C.	Pvt.	E 3rd SCVI		NY	05/09/64	Lynchburg, VA	DOW	(Wdd @ Wilderness)	ROH,JR,SA2,ANY
Boozer, David W.	2nd Cpl.	C 3rd SCVI		NY	07/27/61	Fairfax, VA	DOD	(JR=E.W.& 7/7/61)	ROH,JR,SA2,ANY
Boozer, Erskine P.	Pvt.	E 3rd SCVI		NY	10/13/64	Strasburg, VA	KIA		ROH,SA2,ANY,KEB
Boozer, F.S.	Pvt.	K 5th SCVC		NY	07/21/64	Lincoln Hos., Dc	DOW	(Wdd leg Price's Fm 6/28)	ANY,CDC,P6
Boozer, Henry	Pvt.	F 20th SCVI		NY	06/15/62	At home	DOD		ANY,KEB
Boozer, Jacob	4th Sgt.	F 27th SCVI	21	ED	09/05/64	Danville, VA	DOD		HOE,HAG,UD3
Boozer, Jacob W.	Pvt.	H Hol.Leg.	34	NY	05/23/63	At home	DOD	St.Lukes L.C. Prosperity	ROH,JR,NCC
Boozer, James M.	Pvt.	D 13th SCVI	19	NY	01/12/62	Roper Hos. Chn.	DOD	Head Springs Cem. Newberry	JR,NCC,ANY
Boozer, John	Pvt.	G 2nd SC Res		NY	06/15/64	At home	DOD	(Date approx)	ANY
Boozer, Stanmore S.	Pvt.	H Hol.Leg.	20	NY	07/14/64	At home	DOD		ROH,ANY
Boren, M.	Pvt.	F 22nd SCVI		PS	07/15/64		DIP	(Date & place obscure ?)	P12
Borroughs, John Thomas	Pvt.	C 4th SCVI		AN	09/18/61	Germantown, VA	DOD		HOF,SA2
Borum, W.H.	Pvt.	B 15th SCVI		GN	07/28/64	Petersburg, VA	KIA	(JR=Brown & Frayser's Fm)	ROH,JR,KEB
Bost, Joseph M.	Cpt.	C Hol.Leg.	40	SG	07/01/64	Sappony Ch., VA	DOW	(HOS=Stoney Creek)	ROH,HOS,R48
Bostick, Benjamin R.	Pvt.	K 4th SCVC	17	BT	10/05/64	Wilson, NC	DOW	(Wdd 10/1/64,Peebles Fm.)	ROH,CDC,PP
Bostick, Edward	Cpt.	E 26th SCVI		BT	02/15/64	Petersburg, VA	KIA		ROH
Bostick, J.H.	Pvt.	I 10th SCVI		MN	/ /	Kentucky	DOD		RAS,HMC
Bostick, James	Pvt.	A 10th SCVI		GN	07/21/64	Atlanta, GA	KIA		FLR,RAS
Bostick, L.F.	Pvt.	Ham.Leg.			07/08/62	Richmond, VA		Hollywood Cem.Rchmd. M291	ROH,HC
Bostick, T.J.	2nd Lt.	I 10th SCVI		MN	11/30/64	Franklin, TN	KIA	Williamson Cty TN Con. C.	ROH,RAS,WCT,PP
Boswell, J.L.	Pvt.	G 7th SCV		MN	08/20/61	Flint Hill, VA	DOD	Hollywood Cem. Rchmd. K14	HC,CDC
Boswick, James	Pvt.	H			/ /	Enterprise, MS	ACD		PP
Bosworth, John W.	Pvt.	C 7th SCVI	19	AE	08/23/61	Culpepper, VA	DOD	(JR=5/23 Brain Fever)	ROH,JR,KEB
Botenstine, H.W.	Pvt.	A 1st SCVIG		BL	09/04/62	Richmond, VA	DOD	Hollywood Cem.Rchmd. A37	ROH,JR,SA1,HC
Bott, John	Pvt.	C 14th SCVI			06/30/62	Fraysers Farm VA	KIA		JR
Botts, F.A.	Pvt.	F Hol.Leg.		AE	05/04/65	Elmira, NY	DIP	Woodlawn N.C.#2801 Elmira	FPH,P6,P65,P120
Bouknight, Daniel Reuben	Sgt.	H 13th SCVI	23	LN	07/03/63	Gettysburg, PA	DOW		ROH,JR
Bouknight, F.	Pvt.	F 4th SCVC			05/28/64	VA	KIA		JR
Bouknight, Jacob R.	1st Lt.	M 7th SCVI		ED	07/29/62	Malvern Hill, VA	DOW	(RR=7/24/62)	JR,HOE,CV,R46
Bouknight, Jeremiah S.	Pvt.	H 13th SCVI	25	LN	08/28/62	2nd Manassas, VA	KIA		ROH
Bouknight, John M.	Pvt.	C 20th SCVI		LN	02/16/62	Charleston, SC	DOD	(J.W. in KEB)	ROH,KEB
Bouknight, Sanders J.	Pvt.	H 13th SCVI		NY	08/29/62	2nd Manassas, VA	KIA	(NI ANY)	JR,CDC
Bouknight, T.W.	Pvt.	H 13th SCVI			/ /		DOD		JR
Boulware, D.P.	Pvt.	B 17th SCVI	19	UN	07/31/61	(JR=KIA 6/18/64)	DOD	Gilead B.C. Jonesville, SC	JR,UNC,UD3
Boulware, George F.	Pvt.	H 24th SCVI	34	CR	09/20/63	Chickamauga, Tn	KIA	(HHC=Green F.)	ROH,JR,HHC,CB
Boulware, O.	Pvt.	B 17th SCVI			09/21/62	Lynchburg, VA	DOD		JR
Boulware, Pinkney	Pvt.	B 17th SCVI			07/30/64	Crater, Pbg., VA	KIA		JR,BLM
Boulware, R.J.	2nd Sgt.	B 17th SCVI			/ /	Warrenton, VA	DOW	(Wdd @ 2M)	JR

SOUTH CAROLINA DEAD IN CSA SERVICE 1861-1865

NAME	RANK	C REGIMENT	AGE	DS	DIED	WHERE	WHY	BURIED	SOURCES
Boulware, Thomas E.	Sgt. Maj.	17th SCVI	23	FD	06/13/62		DOD	Stevens/Crosby Fam.C. FD	JR,UNC,HFC
Bounds, J.M.	Pvt.	G 20th SCVI		SR	01/29/62	Charleston, SC		Magnolia Cem. Charleston	ROH,MAG,KEB
Bourne, T.J.	Pvt.	A 10th SCVI		GN	06/13/62	Macon, MS	DOD		JR,GRG,RAS,PP
Bowen, A. Cornelius	Pvt.	G Orr's Ri.		AE	07/08/63	Chester, PA	DIP	Magnolia C. Charleston	ROH,FPH,GDR,P1
Bowen, E.B.	2nd Lt.	D Ham.Leg.		AN	/ /	At home	DOD		GRS
Bowen, Farley	Pvt.	F 21st SCVI		MO	05/16/64	Drury's Bluff VA	KIA	(PP=9/10/64)	ROH,HOM,HAG,PP
Bowen, James	Pvt.	C Ham.Leg.			02/15/65	Camp Chase, OH	DIP		P22
Bowen, James Oliver	Pvt.	B 7th SCVI	23	AE	12/22/61	Richmond, VA	DOD	Shiloh M.C. Abbeville, SC	JR,,KEB
Bowen, John M.	Cpl.	K 6th SCVI		GE	09/10/61	Fairfax C.H., VA	DOD		ROH
Bowen, John W.	Pvt.	I 14th SCVI		AE	08/15/64	At home	DOD	(Also wdd. @ 2nd M.)	ROH,HOL
Bowen, L.M.	Cpl.	D 7th SCVI			09/15/62	Maryland Hts. MD	KIA	(JR=Co.B & 9/13/62)	ROH,JR,KEB
Bowen, R.L.	Pvt.	C 17th SCVI			/ /		DOW	(2nd Manassas)	JR
Bowen, R.T.	Pvt.	A 11th SCVI			10/13/62	(?no Co.A then)		Stonewall C. Winchester VA	ROH,WIN
Bowen, Samuel Newton	Pvt.	G Orr's Ri.	21	AE	07/08/62	Dill's Farm, VA	DOD	Shiloh M.C. AE Cty.	ROH,CAE,CDC
Bowen, Thomas M.	Pvt.	L 2nd SCVIRi	33	AN	10/30/64	Ft. Harrison, VA	DOW		ROH
Bowen, William	Pvt.	E 2nd SCVI		KW	05/15/62	Richmond, VA	DOD	Oakwood C.#27,Row A,Div A	ROH,SA2,HIC,OW
Bowen, William Benton	Pvt.	G Ham.Leg.			11/12/61	Bethel Ch., VA	DOD	(JR=Typhoid 11/16)	ROH,JR
Bowers, A.	Sgt.	H 22nd SCVI		GE	03/07/65	Elmira, NY	DIP	Woodlawn N.C.#2395 Elmira	FPH,P6,P65,P12
Bowers, A.E.	Cpt.	D 24th SCVI	34	BT	12/25/63	Nashville, TN	DOW	(Date obscure in P12)	R48,P12
Bowers, Charles E.	Sgt.	D 24th SCVI		BT	01/15/65	Camp Chase, OH	DIP	Con.Cem.#759 Columbus, OH	FPH,P6,P23,P27
Bowers, George McQueen	Pvt.	G 2nd SCVI		KW	08/14/61	Richmond, VA	DOD	(Typhoid)	HIC,KEB,H2
Bowers, J.	Pvt.	A Hol.Leg.			04/10/65	Petersburg, VA	DOW	Near Fair Gds. Hospital	ROH,P6
Bowers, J.F.	Pvt.	C Ham.Leg.		CL	02/15/65	Camp Chase, OH	DIP	Con.Cem.#1261 Columbus, OH	FPH,P6,P27
Bowers, J.J.	Pvt.	H 7th SCVIBn			11/10/62	Adams Run, SC	DOD		JR
Bowers, J.S.	1st Lt.	G 13th SCVI		NY	05/03/65	Farmville, VA	DOW	Farmville Hos. Cem.	ROH,P6
Bowers, Jacob A.	Cpl.	H Hol.Leg.		NY	11/06/64	Petersburg, VA	DOW	Zion U.M.C. Prosperity SC	ROH,NCC
Bowers, Jacob Andrews	Pvt.	I 15th SCVI	19	LN	10/10/62	Frederick, MD	DOW	Rose Hill C. Hagerstown VA	ROH,FPH,BOD,P6
Bowers, James Smiley	Cpl.	H Hol.Leg.		NY	06/03/65	Pt. Lookout, MD	DIP	C.C. Pt. Lookout, MD	FPH,ANY,P6,P11
Bowers, Jarrott F.	Pvt.	I 12th SCVI		LR	11/28/62	Danville, VA	DOW	(Wdd @ Gaines Mill)	JR,LAN
Bowers, Joseph T.	Pvt.	A 23rd SCVI		KW	03/09/65		DOD		ROH
Bowers, L.S.	Pvt.	B 27th SCVI		SG	05/07/64	Walthall Jctn.	KIA		ROH,JR,HOS,HAG
Bowers, M.H.	1st Lt.	D 24th SCVI	19	BT	09/20/63	Chickamauga, GA	KIA	(CDC=H.M.)	ROH,JR,CDC,R48
Bowers, Malcom	Pvt.	C 1st SCVIH		BL	10/10/63	Dalton, GA	DOD		ROH,SA1
Bowers, Mc.R.	3rd Cpl.	C 1st SCVIH		BL	09/11/62	Warrenton, VA	DOW	(Wdd @ 2nd Manassas)	ROH,SA1,JRH
Bowers, W.	Pvt.	E 21st SCVI			05/12/64	Spotsylvania, VA	KIA	(?21st not there)	JR
Bowers, William J.	Pvt.	E 12th SCVI	19	LR	05/12/64	Spotsylvania, VA	KIA	(Bloody Angle)	ROH,JR,LAN
Bowick, James F.	Pvt.	H 19th SCVI	41	AE	04/24/62	Enterprise, MS	ACD	(RR accident)	ROH,CDC
Bowick, John	Pvt.	H 19th SCVI	18	AE	04/15/64		DOD		ROH
Bowie, Andrew	Pvt.	K P.S.S.		SG	07/22/63	(In camp)	DOD	(Brain Fever, JR=Lt.)	HOS,JR
Bowie, E.P.	Pvt.	A 2nd SCVIRi			06/29/62	Savage Stn., VA	KIA		ROH,JR,CDC
Bowlin, Benjamin	Pvt.	K 17th SCVI	41	YK	06/15/62	Charleston, SC	DOD	(Date approximate)	YEB
Bowlin, D.P.	Pvt.	A Orr's Ri.			11/23/61	Sullivans I., SC	DOD		JR,CDC
Bowlin, G.B.	Pvt.	I 12th SCVI			01/08/62	Pocotaligo, SC	DOD		JR
Bowlin, John	Pvt.	C 17th SCVI	38	YK	07/30/64	Crater Pbg., VA	KIA		YEB
Bowlin, Lewis	Pvt.	C 17th SCVI	29	YK	06/15/64		DOD	(Date approximate)	YEB
Bowlin, W. Riley	Pvt.	C 17th SCVI	36	YK	09/15/64	Petersburg, VA	DOW	Blandford Church Pbg., VA	ROH,BLC,YEB,PP
Bowlin, William	Pvt.	C 17th SCVI	34	YK	06/15/62	Charleston, SC	DOD	(Date approximate)	YEB
Bowling, Ellet	Pvt.	C 16th SCVI		GE	/ /	Charleston, SC	DOD		16R
Bowling, G.E.	Pvt.	A 20th SCVI		PS	10/13/64	Strasburg, VA	KIA		ROH,JR,CDC
Bowling, W.M.	Pvt.	F 13th SCVI		SG	12/13/62	Fredericksburg	KIA		ROH,JR,HOS
Bowman,	Pvt.	23rd SCVI			/ /		KIA		CDC

B

SOUTH CAROLINA DEAD IN CSA SERVICE 1861-1865

NAME	RANK	C	REGIMENT	AGE	DS	DIED	WHERE	WHY	BURIED	SOURCES
Bowman, D.P.	Col.Sgt.		11th SCVI			09/22/64		DOW	(In enemy hands)	P12
Bowman, Daniel P.	Pvt.	A	5th SCVC	31	OG	09/10/64	Raleigh, NC	DOD		ROH,CDC
Box, Edward W.	Pvt.	H	1st SCVIG	20	BT	06/27/62	Gaines' Mill, VA	KIA		ROH,JR,SA1,BBC
Boyce, Albert K.	Pvt.	E	14th SCVI	21	NY	06/27/62	Gaines' Mill, VA	DOW		ROH,JR,ANY,CGS
Boyce, Hampton W.	Pvt.	E	P.S.S.		SR	12/21/64	Columbia, SC	DOD	Elmwood C. Columbia, SC	ROH,JR,MP
Boyce, James E.	Pvt.	K	23rd SCVI		SR	09/30/62	Staunton, VA		Thornrose C. Staunton, VA	ROH,K23,UD3,TOD
Boyce, John S.	Pvt.	A	13th SCVI	22	LS	05/03/63	Richmond, VA	DOD		ROH
Boyce, L.R.	Pvt.	D	14th SCVI	17	ED	05/25/63		DOD		D14,HOE
Boyce, Robert	Cpt.		McBeth LA		UN	04/26/63	Wilmington, NC	DOD		ROH,R44,HOS
Boyce, William W.	Pvt.	K	23rd SCVI	21	SR	09/08/62	2nd Manassas, VA	DOW		ROH
Boyd, A.F.	Pvt.	C	14th SCVI		LS	05/18/63	Richmond, VA			ROH
Boyd, A.F.	Pvt.	E	1st SCV			09/17/62	Sharpsburg, MD	KIA		ROH
Boyd, Andrew	Pvt.	D	7th SCVI			/ /	Lynchburg, VA		Lynchburg CSA Cem. #3 R1	BBW
Boyd, Charles A.	Pvt.	A	17th SCVI	45	CR	05/10/64	At home	DOD	(HHC=DOW)	ROH,HHC
Boyd, Charles J.	Cpl.	B	27th SCVI		SG	05/07/64	Walthall Jctn.	KIA	(CDC=C.W.)	ROH,CDC,HAG
Boyd, Charles Wesley	Cpt.	F	15th SCVI	28	UN	05/03/63	Chancellorsville	KIA	(5/2/63 per NHU & JR)	ROH,JR,NHU,UD3
Boyd, David Caswell	Pvt.	B	1st SCVIG	21	LS	07/03/63	Gettysburg, PA	KIA		ROH,JR,SA1,GDR
Boyd, Francis J.	Pvt.	H	18th SCVI	20	YK	/ /	Kinston, NC	DOD		YEB
Boyd, J. Thomas	Pvt.	G	19th SCVI		AE	12/31/62	Murfreesboro, TN	KIA		ROH,JR,HOL
Boyd, J. Wesley	Cpl.	F	3rd SCVI	23	LS	07/02/62	Manchester, VA	DOW	(Wdd Malvern Hill)	ROH,JR,SA2,YMD
Boyd, James	Pvt.	D	14th SCVI	44	ED	05/23/64	Noel Station, VA	KIA		D14,HOE
Boyd, James A.	Pvt.	D	13th SCVI	27	NY	07/20/63	Baltimore, MD	DOW	Loudon Park Cem. Balto, MD	ROH,JR,ANY,GDR
Boyd, James Brown	2nd Sgt.	I	2nd SCVI		CN	09/17/62	Sharpsburg, MD	DOW	Old Scotch P.C. Charleston	ROH,JR,SA2,KEB
Boyd, Jesse	Cpl.	G	10th SCVI		HY	01/26/63	Murfreesboro, TN	DOW	(RAS=Mission Ridge)	RAS,P12,P38
Boyd, John H.	Pvt.	A	13th SCVI	52	LS	05/03/63	Chancellorsville	KIA	Chestnut Ridge B.C. LS Cty	ROH,JR,LSC
Boyd, John H.	Pvt.		Kanapaughs	39	YK	06/09/64	Coosewatchie, SC	DOD	(YEB=Gillisonville)	YMD,YEB
Boyd, John L.	Pvt.	H	24th SCVI		CR	11/30/64	Franklin, TN	KIA	Williamson C.C.,TN S84 #29	ROH,WCT,HHC,CB
Boyd, N.F. (M.T.?)	Cpl.	C	14th SCVI	23	LS	05/17/63	Richmond(WDD@CV)	DOW	Hollywood Cem. Rchmd. T559	ROH,JR,HC
Boyd, P.G.	Pvt.	H	18th SCVI		YK	07/30/64	Sharpsburg, PA			ROH
Boyd, R.G.G.	2nd Cpl.	E	17th SCVI	27	YK	09/29/62	Winchester, VA	DOW	Stonewall C. Winchester VA	ROH,JR,WIN
Boyd, R.P.	Pvt.	D	7th SCVI			09/15/62	Maryland Hts. MD	KIA	(JR=9/16/62)	ROH,JR,KEB
Boyd, Robert Amzi	Pvt.	A	17th SCVI		CR	05/10/64	At home	DOD		CB
Boyd, Robert Watson	Pvt.	F	6th SCVC	24	CR	07/31/64	Lee's Mill, VA	KIA		ROH,CAG,HHC
Boyd, S.N.	Pvt.	F	24th SCVI	19	AN	10/10/63	Atlanta, GA Hos.	DOW	(Wdd @ Chickamauga)	HOL
Boyd, Samuel L.	Cpl.	E	14th SCVI	25	LS	01/01/62	Port Royal Ferry	KIA		ROH,JR,CGS,PP
Boyd, Thomas	Pvt.	H	18th SCVI		YK	/ /	Raleigh, NC	DOD	(YEB=25 @ enlstmt)	YEB
Boyd, Thomas J.	Pvt.	H	18th SCVI	21	YK	08/11/62	Petersburg, VA	DOD	Blandford Ch. Pbg., VA PP	ROH,JR,YMD,BLC
Boyd, Thomas M.	Pvt.	H	18th SCVI	33	YK	07/30/64	Crater, Pbg. VA	KIA		ROH,JR,BLM,YEB
Boyd, W.M.J.	Pvt.	F	3rd SCVI		LS	12/13/62	Fredericksburg	KIA		ROH,JR,SA2,KEB
Boyd, W.T.	Pvt.	C	14th SCVI			12/09/61	Gardens Crnr.,SC	DOD		JR
Boyd, Warren	Pvt.	F	12th SCVI		FD	08/25/64	Ream's Stn., VA	KIA		HFC
Boyd, William	Pvt.	G	Orr's Ri.		AE	07/21/62	Farmville, VA	DOW	(Wdd @ Gaines' Mill, VA)	ROH,JR
Boyd, William	Cpl.	D	17th SCVI	29	CR	08/21/62	At home	DOD		ROH,JR,CB
Boyer, Thomas			C.S. Navy		RD	/ /				ROH
Boyer, Wesley			C.S. Navy		RD	/ /				ROH
Boykin, Harrison	Pvt.	H	21st SCVI	42	DN	04/15/62	Georgetown, SC	DOD	(PP=H.H.)	JR,HAG,PP
Boykin, Henry	Pvt.	H	21st SCVI		DN	02/15/62		DOD		JR,HAG
Boykin, James F.	Pvt.	E	2nd SCVI		KW	03/23/64	Ft. Delaware, DE	DIP	Finn's Pt., NJ Nat. Cem.	P40,H2,SA2
Boykin, John	Pvt.	A	2nd SCVC		KW	03/23/64	Ft. Delaware, DE	DIP	Finn's Pt., NJ Nat. Cem.	ROH,FPH,P5,P47
Boykin, Thomas Lang	Sgt.	K	7th SCVC	21	KW	05/30/64	Old Church, VA	KIA	Quaker Cem. Camden, SC	ROH,HIC,CDN,PP
Boyle,	Pvt.	K	7th SCVC		KW	/ /		KIA		HIC

SOUTH CAROLINA DEAD IN CSA SERVICE 1861-1865

NAME	RANK	C	REGIMENT	AGE	DS	DIED	WHERE	WHY	BURIED	SOURCES
Boyle, Edward	Pvt.	D	3rd SC			11/25/62	At home	DOD		JR
Boyle, John	Pvt.	H	1st SCVIR			07/18/63	Bty. Wagner, SC	KIA		ROH,SA1
Boyle, N.C.	Pvt.	M	P.S.S.	40	RD	10/28/63	Lookout Valley	KIA	(JR=Racoon Mtn., TN)	ROH,JR,CDC
Boyle, Patrick	Pvt.	F	1st SCVIR		CN	02/14/64	Ft. Moultrie, SC	KIA		SA1
Boyles, William	Pvt.	C	17th SCVI	26	YK	/ /	Charleston, SC	DOD	(1862, JR=Richmond)	JR,YEB
Boyleston, L.A.	Pvt.	I	5th SCVC		BL	09/29/64	Wyatt's Farm, VA	KIA		ROH,JR,CDC
Boyleston, T.R.	Pvt.		5th SCVC		BL	07/19/64	Richmond, VA			ROH
Boynton, Ephraim S.	1st Sgt.	F	17th SCVI	18	BL	03/02/62	Johns Island, SC	DOD	(JR=Co.H, 3/27 & Typhoid)	ROH,JR
Boynton, Stephen D.	Pvt.	C	Ham.Leg. C	24	CO	05/04/62	Williamsburg, VA	KIA	Williamsburg, VA	ROH,CDC,AOA
Bozeman, Brunson C.	Pvt.	F	8th SCVI	18	DN	05/20/62	Richmond, VA	DOD	Hollywood Cem.Rchmd. J140	ROH,JR,HC,KEB
Bozeman, D. Tilman	Sgt.	F	24th SCVI	47	AN	09/25/63	At home	DOD		ROH,HOL
Bozeman, G. (J.?)	Pvt.	F	8th SCVI			07/02/63	Gettysburg, PA	DOW	(KEB= J.)	CDC,KEB
Bozeman, Henry	Pvt.	F	8th SCVI	25	DN	06/15/64	At home	DOW	(Wdd at Gettysburg)	ROH,KEB
Bozeman, James S.	Pvt.	F	8th SCVI	27	DN	04/04/62	Lynchburg, VA	DOD	Lynchburg CSA Cem.#5 R5	ROH,JR,BBW,KEB
Bozeman, Peter W.	Pvt.	F	8th SCVI	35	DN	10/02/62	Sharpsburg, MD	DOW	(JR=Co.M)	ROH,JR,KEB,P12
Bozeman, William	Cpl.	F	8th SCVI	28	DN	07/10/62	At home	DOW	(Wdd @ Malvern Hill)	ROH,JR,KEB
Brace, Thomas Jefferson	Pvt.			28	KW	03/25/65	Bentonville, NC	KIA		CDN
Bracher, S.T.						/ /	Richmond, VA		(Rchmd effects list)	CDC
Bradberry, J.P.	Pvt.	F	Orr's Ri.			12/21/61	Sullivans I., SC	DOD		JR,CDC
Braddock, Franklyn	Pvt.	D	21st SCVI		CD	06/15/63	Pt. Lookout, MD	DIP	Laurel Grove C. Savannah	ROH,HAG,P114,B
Braddock, George W.	Pvt.	D	21st SCVI		CD	06/15/63	Morris Island SC	DOD		ROH,HAG
Braddock, James F.	Pvt.	A	13th SCVI	18	LS	10/05/62	Culpepper, VA	DOD	Duncan Creek P.C. LS Cty.	ROH,JR,LSC
Braddock, Joseph	Pvt.	D	21st SCVI		CD	05/16/64	Drury's Bluff VA	KIA		ROH,JR,CDC,HAG
Braddock, Wm. Ellerbe	Pvt.	D	21st SCVI		CD	07/18/63	Bty. Wagner, SC	KIA	(JR=8/18/63)	ROH,JR,KEB
Braddox, Dr.						/ /	Sharpsburg, MD		Rose Hill C. Hagerstown MD	BOD
Braddy, James G.	Cpl.	H	7th SCVIBn	30	RD	07/01/64	Drury's Bluff VA	DOW	(ROH & JR=J.E.)	ROH,JR,HAG
Braddy, Russell	Pvt.	E	1st SCVC	24	OG	07/15/62	Charleston, SC	DOD		ROH
Bradford, James	Pvt.	G	14th SCVI	20	AE	02/03/62	McPhersonville	DOD	(JR=02/06/62)	ROH,JR
Bradford, Robert M.	Pvt.		SC Militia	17	SR	02/01/65	Adam's Run, SC	DOD		ROH
Bradford, Walter A.	Pvt.	A	3rd SCVI		LS	02/15/64	Pt. Lookout, MD	DIP	C.C. Pt. Lookout, MD P5	ROH,P113,UD3,S
Bradford, William	Pvt.	G	1st SCVC	51	AE	03/15/62	Adam's Run, SC	DOD		ROH,PP
Bradham, Robert J.	Pvt.	D	9th SCVIB	18	WG	12/26/61	Culpepper, VA	DOD	Fairview C. Culpepper, VA	ROH,JR,CGH
Bradkins, John D.	Pvt.		1st Bn Res			03/12/65	Camden, SC	DOD		CDN
Bradley, George W.	1st Sgt.	E	2nd SCVIRi	24	PS	10/28/63	Lookout Valley	KIA	(JR=Racoon Mtn., TN)	ROH,JR,CDC,CUS
Bradley, J.	Pvt.	F	3rd SCVC			12/06/64	25 Mile Stn., GA	KIA		R43
Bradley, J.F.	Pvt.	F	7th SCVC		ED	07/27/64	Pt. Lookout, MD	DIP	C.C. Pt.Lookout, MD	ROH,FPH,P6
Bradley, John	Pvt.	G	14th SCVI	30	AE	09/01/62	Ox Hill, VA	KIA		ROH,JR
Bradley, John R.	Pvt.	B	5th SCVI	23		11/18/64	Petersburg, VA	DOD		SA3,PP
Bradley, Nelson	Pvt.	D	1st SCVIH		LR	09/17/62	Sharpsburg, MD	DOW		LAN,HAG,JRH
Bradley, R.L.	Pvt.		2nd SCRes		NY	/ /		DOD	(1863-2nd SCRes, 6 mths)	ANY
Bradley, Robert Newton	Pvt.	D	Ham.Leg.		PS	06/27/62	7 Pines, VA	DOW		ROH,GRS
Bradley, Samuel	Pvt.	D	5th SCVI		UN	10/06/61	Richmond, VA	DOD	(JR=10/01/61)	JR,SA3
Bradley, Thomas C.	Cpl.	C	6th SCVC	23	AE	06/11/64	Trevillian Stn.	KIA		ROH,JR
Bradley, W.H.	Pvt.	B	1st SCV			11/08/62	Richmond, VA		Hollywood Cem.Rchmd. S195	HC
Bradley, W.R.	Pvt.	C	7th SCVI			05/20/62	Chickahominy, VA	DOW		JR,KEB
Bradley, Warren Davis	Pvt.	K	22nd SCVI		PS	10/09/64		DOD		ROH
Bradley, William	Cpl.	G	14th SCVI	30	AE	05/20/63	Chancellorsville	DOW	Hollywood Cem.Rchmd. T97	ROH,JR,HC
Bradshaw, J.J.	Pvt.	A	8th SCVI		DN	06/15/61	Richmond, VA	DOD	Oakwood C.#16,Row D,Div B	ROH,JR,OWC,KEB
Bradshaw, John	Pvt.	H	Orr's Ri.		MN	10/18/62	Bunker Hill, VA	DOD		JR,HMC
Bradshaw, Eli M.	Pvt.	A	8th SCVI		DN	02/07/65	Camp Chase, OH	DIP	C.C.#1086 Columbus, OH	ROH,FPH,P6,P23
Brady, G.M.	Pvt.	K	22nd SCVI		PS	10/19/62			Stonewall C. Winchester VA	ROH,WIN

B

SOUTH CAROLINA DEAD IN CSA SERVICE 1861-1865

NAME	RANK	C REGIMENT	AGE	DS	DIED	WHERE	WHY	BURIED	SOURCES
Brady, Peter	Cpl.	H 24th SCVI	30	CR	06/22/62	Columbia, SC	DOD		ROH,HHC,PP,CB
Brady, R.M.	Pvt.	B 2nd SCVIRi			05/16/65	City Point, VA	DOW	City Pt. N.C. Hopewell, VA	PP,TOD
Brady, T.D. (F.D.?0	Pvt.	D Orr's Ri.		AN	06/30/62	Savage Stn., VA	KIA		JR,CDC,CNM
Brady, Thomas C.	Cpt.	A Hol.Leg.		SG	/ /		DOD		HOS
Brady, William	Sgt.	B 1st SCVIR		CN	03/19/65	Bentonville, NC	KIA		ROH,SA1,WAT,PP
Braezel, M.A.	Pvt.	F 2nd BnSCRi			01/09/65	Columbia, SC	DOD		ROH
Bragg, D.W.	Pvt.	K 27th SCVI			10/01/63		DOD		JR,HAG
Brakefield, James M.	Pvt.	A 12th SCVI	30	YK	05/27/62	Ashland, VA	DOD		JR,YEB
Bramblitt, James M.	Pvt.,	G 3rd SCVABn			09/01/63	Columbia, SC	DOD	(PP=Co. E)	ROH,PP
Bramblitt, R.R.	Pvt.	Hol.Leg.			12/04/62	Richmond, VA			ROH
Bramlet, J.A.H.	Pvt.	E 6th SCVC			10/27/64	Burgess Mills VA	DOW		CDC
Bramlett, Charles	Pvt.	G 3rd SCVI		RD	11/26/62	Mt. Jackson, VA	DOD	Mt. Jackson, VA PP	ROH,JR,SA2,KEB
Bramlett, Henry	Pvt.	E 3rd SCVIBn		LS	08/02/64	Richmond, VA			ROH,KEB
Bramlett, John L.	Pvt.	E 3rd SCVIBn		LS	04/22/64	Rock Island, IL	DIP	C.C.#1079 Rock Island, IL	FPH,P6,KEB
Bramlett, Robert	Pvt.	E 3rd SCVIBn		LS	05/07/64	Wilderness, VA	KIA		ROH,KEB
Bramlett, W.H.	Pvt.	E 6th SCVI		LS	04/20/64	Charleston, SC	DOD	Magnolia Cem. Charleston	ROH,MAG,CDC
Bramlette, James	Pvt.	I 16th SCVI		GE	11/30/64	Franklin, TN	KIA		16R
Bramlette, Josiah W.	Pvt.	A 16th SCVI		GE	11/30/64	Franklin, TN	KIA		ROH,16R,PP
Branard, C.	Pvt.	C 14th SCVI		LS	/ /	Richmond, VA		Oakwood C.#35,Row L,Div B	ROH,OWC
Branch, George	Pvt.	C 15th SCVAB			12/25/61	Charleston, SC	DOD	Magnolia Cem. Charleston	ROH,MAG
Brandenburg, John	Pvt.	E 1st SCVC	20	OG	07/06/63	Boonsboro, MD	DOW	(Died in enemy hands)	ROH
Brandley, C.W.	Pvt.	G 15th SCVI		WG	/ /	Richmond, VA		Oakwood C.#18,Row 24,Div D	ROH,OWC
Brandon, James R.	Pvt.	E 5th SCVI	22	YK	01/01/63	Staunton, VA	DOD	Thornrose C. Staunton, VA	ROH,JR,SA3,YEB
Brandon, John C.	Pvt.	B 5th SCVI		YK	11/18/64	Ft. Harrison, VA	DOW	Hollywood Cem.Rchmd. W643	ROH,SA3,YEB,HC
Brandon, William A.	Pvt.	Kanapaux's	33	YK	/ /	Mississippi	DOD	(1864)	YEB
Brandt, J.	Pvt.	A German Art		CN	/ /		DOD	Bethany Cem. Charleston	MAG,RCD
Brandt, John F.	Pvt.	C 19th SCVCB			05/31/65	Pt. Lookout, MD	DIP	C.C. Pt. Lookout, MD	FPH,P6,P12
Brannigan, Richard A.	Pvt.	K Orr's Ri.			06/27/62	Richmond, VA	KIA		JR
Brannon, Hugh	Pvt.	H 18th SCVI	45	YK	09/07/64	Elmira, NY	DIP	Woodlawn N.C.#219 Elmira	FPH,P5,P65,YEB
Brannon, J.	Pvt.	A 25th SCVI		CN	09/08/64	Richmond, VA		(NI HAG)	ROH
Brannon, James Ellis	Pvt.	A 7th SCVIBn	27	KW	09/09/62	At home	DOD	(JR=Lynchburg 8/14/62)	ROH,JR,HIC,HAG
Brannon, John	Pvt.	D 15th SCVI		KW	/ /	Virginia	KIA		HIC,KEB
Brannon, Richard A.	Pvt.	K Orr's Ri.		AN	06/27/62	Gaines' Mill, VA	KIA		ROH,JR,CDC
Brannon, Robert	Pvt.	D 15th SCVI		KW	/ /	VA	DOD		JR,HIC
Brannon, W.C.	Pvt.	F 13th SCVI		SG	08/19/62	Lynchburg, VA	DOD	Lynchburg CSA Cem.#6 R1	ROH,JR,CDC,BBW
Brannon, W.C.	Pvt.	E 13th SCVI			08/26/62	Winder Hos Rchmd	DOD	(Typhoid, DUP ?)	JR
Brant, A.	Lt.	I 21st SCVI		MN	/ /	Richmond, VA		Oakwood C.#27,Row R,Div F	ROH,OWC
Brant, John	Pvt.	G 17th SCVI	22	BL	08/30/62	2nd Manassas, VA	KIA		ROH,JR
Brant, W.J.	Pvt.	G 17th SCVI			07/30/64	Crater, Pbg., VA	KIA		JR
Brantley, Beverly Blake	Pvt.	A Ham.Leg.	20	CN	08/30/62	2nd Manassas, VA	KIA		ROH,JR,CDC,WLI
Brantley, F. Marion	Pvt.	A 4th SCVC		CD	06/26/65	Greensboro, NC	DOW		ROH,PP,P12
Branton, S.P.	Pvt.	G 10th SCVI	17	HY	07/22/64	Atlanta, GA	KIA		ROH,RAS,CDC
Branyan, E.P. (R.P.?)	Cpl.	F 24th SCVI		AN	08/17/65	Camp Chase, OH	DIP	Con.Cem.#2061 Columbus, OH	FPH,HOL,P6,P23
Branyan, John Robert	Pvt.	I 19th SCVI	20	AE	07/30/62	Saltillo, MS	DOD		ROH,PP
Branyan, Samuel T.	Pvt.	A 19th SCVI		AE	10/12/62	Danville, KY	DOD		ROH
Branyan, T.M.	Pvt.	G 6th SCVC			12/08/62	Adams Run, SC	DOD		PP
Branyan, W.S.	Pvt.	G 2ns SCResB			02/05/65	Columbia, SC		Elmwood Cem. Columbia, SC	MP,PP
Branyon, J.S.	Pvt.	B 7th SCVI			10/15/62		DOD		JR
Branyon, John W.	Pvt.	K Orr's Ri.	18	AN	07/13/62	Richmond, VA	DOD		ROH
Branyon, William C.	Pvt.	L 2nd SCVIRi	18	AN	09/15/63	Petersburg, VA	KIA		ROH
Brasher, Silas R.	Pvt.	K 16th SCVI		GE	09/02/63	Yazoo City, MS	DOD		PP,16R

SOUTH CAROLINA DEAD IN CSA SERVICE 1861-1865

NAME	RANK	C REGIMENT	AGE	DS	DIED	WHERE	WHY	BURIED	SOURCES
Brasington, George C.	2nd Lt.	H 2nd SCVI		LR	07/06/63	Gettysburg, PA	DOW	Magnolia Cem. Charleston	JR,MAG,GDR,SA2
Brasington, William M.	Pvt.	H 2nd SCVI		LR	10/28/63	At home	DOW	Magnolia Cem. Augusta, GA	JR,SA2,KEB,BGA
Brassell, John	Pvt.	K 10th SCVI		CN	06/11/62	Brandon, MS	DOD		RAS,PP
Braswell, A. Clark	Pvt.	C 12th SCVI		FD	06/27/62	Gaines' Mill, VA	KIA	(JR=Cold Harbor 6/17)	ROH,JR,HFC,CNM
Braswell, J.O.	Pvt.	Brook's LA			/ /		KIA		JR
Braswell, John	Pvt.	H 23rd SCVI		MN	/ /	NC	DOD	('62)	HMC
Braswell, Owen L.	Pvt.	B 7th SCVIBn	18	FD	01/30/64	Sullivans I., SC	DOD	(NI HAG,HFC Brazil,D.L.?)	ROH
Braswell, Thomas P.	Pvt.	K 2nd SCVI	23	PS	06/15/65	At home	DOD	Crossroads B.B. Easley, SC	H2,SA2,PCS
Braswell, William	Pvt.	A 19th SCVI	23	ED	01/20/62	Charleston, SC	DOD		ROH,HOE,UD3
Bratcher, S.	Pvt.	B 7th SCVI			/ /	Richmond, VA		(NI KEB)	ROH
Brazeale, F.M.	Pvt.	K Orr's Ri.	29	AN	08/15/62	Lynchburg, VA	DOD		ROH,JR
Brazeale, John T.	Pvt.	K Orr's Ri.	20	AN	09/01/63	At home	DOD	(JR=7/24/63)	ROH,JR
Brazel, M.A.	Pvt.	F 2nd SCResB			01/09/65	Columbia, SC			PP
Brazell, A.T.	Pvt.	7th SCVIBn			07/24/61	Richmond, VA	DOD	Hollywood Cem.Rchmd. V161	ROH,HC
Brazell, B. (R.?)	Pvt.	D 12th SCVI		RD	05/05/64	At home	DOD		ROH,JR
Brazell, H.	Pvt.	D 12th SCVI		RD	07/01/64	Ft. Delaware, DE	DIP	Finn's Pt., NJ Nat. Cem.	ROH,FPH,P5,P47
Brazell, Henry	Pvt.	D 12th SCVI		RD	05/05/64	Columbia, SC	DOD		PP
Brazell, J.	Pvt.	D 12th SCVI		RD	08/30/64	Ft. Delaware, DE	DIP	Finn's Pt., NJ Nat. Cem.	ROH,FPH,P43,P4
Brazil J.	Pvt.	K 13th SCVI		LN	/ /	Ft. Delaware, DE	DIP	Finn's Pt., NJ Nat. Cem.	ROH,CDC
Brazil, James P.	Pvt.	C 7th SCVIBn	20	RD	07/28/64	Petersburg, VA	DOD		ROH
Brazil, R.	Pvt.	K 12th SCVI		PS	/ /	Ft. Delaware, DE	DIP	Finn's Pt., NJ Nat. Cem.	ROH
Brazill, D.L.	Pvt.	B 7th SCVIBn			10/05/63	Bty.Marshall, SC	KIA		JR,HAG
Brazzell, B.	Pvt.	K 2nd SCVIRi			/ /			Stonewall C. Winchester VA	ROH,WIN
Breaker, H.M.	Pvt.	I 1st SCVC	18	CO	06/09/63	Brandy Stn., VA	KIA		ROH
Breakfield, George W.	Pvt.	E 6th SCVI		CR	12/20/61	Dranesville, VA	KIA		JR,CDC,HHC
Breakfield, William	Pvt.	E 5th SCVI		CR	09/15/63	Griffin, GA	DOD	(Wdd @ Lookout Valley)	SA3
Brearley, James W.	Sgt.	F 8th SCVI	22	DN	07/28/64	Malvern Hill, VA	KIA	(Bearly, J.M. in KEB)	ROH,JLC,KEB
Breckenridge, J.L.	Sgt.	A Orr's Ri.	21	PS	05/12/64	Spotsylvania, VA	KIA	(John in CDC,James in ROH)	ROH,JR,CDC
Breeden, A.T.	Pvt.	K 23rd SCVI		SR	07/09/64	Richmond, VA			ROH
Breeden, John L.	Pvt.	E 4th SCVC		MO	/ /		KIA	(1864)	HOM
Breese, Stewart V.V.	Pvt.	A 25th SCVI	18	CN	01/05/63	Charleston, SC	DOD	Magnolia C.(PL) Charleston	ROH,MAG,RRC,HA
Breland, A.B.	Pvt.	E 24th SCVI	35	CO	12/31/63	Kingston, GA	DOD		ROH
Breland, Isaiah B.	Pvt.	D 24th SCVI	47	BT	02/21/65	Camp Douglas, IL	DIP	Oak Woods C. Chicago, IL	ROH,FPH,CDC,P6
Breland, J.R.	Pvt.	E 24th SCVI	36	CO	05/24/63	Selma, AL			ROH
Bresman, Thomas	Cpl.	C 1st SCVIBn		CN	06/02/62	Secessionville	KIA	St. Lawrence Cem. Ch'ston	ROH,JR,CDC,HAG
Brewer, A.J.	Pvt.	SCVA	21	CD	12/17/63	Raleigh, NC	DOD		ROH
Brewer, J.T.	Pvt.				10/15/62	WinchesterVA	ACD	(Fell off RR handcar)	UD2
Brewer, Thomas	Sgt.	B 26th SCVI	37	CD	07/30/64	Petersburg, VA	KIA		ROH
Brewer, W.A.	Pvt.	K 12th SCVI		PS	07/04/62	Richmond, VA		Hollywood Cem.Rchmd. M446	ROH,HC
Brewer, W.C.	Pvt.	5th SCV			/ /			Gordonsville, VA	ROH
Brewer, W.P.G.	Pvt.	B 21st SCVI			05/16/64	Drury's Bluff VA	KIA		JR
Brewer, W.S.G.	Pvt.	K 12th SCVI		PS	07/15/62	Richmond, VA			ROH
Brewer, William	Pvt.	B 26th SCVI	20	CD	07/12/62	Augusta, GA	DOD		ROH
Brewerton, Henry W.	Pvt.	A 7th SCVC			05/17/65	Newport News, VA	DIP	Greenlawn N.C.Newport News	P6,PP,P12
Brewton, Wyllis L.	Sgt.	A Hol.Leg.	28	SG	08/30/62	2nd Manassas	KIA	(JR=Sharpsburg)	ROH,JR,HOS
Breycock, T.	Pvt.	15th SCVI			08/11/64	Petersburg, VA	KIA	(Prob Goudlock, T. Co. F)	ROH
Briant, Alfred B.	Cpt.	B Hol.Leg.		SG	03/25/65	Ft. Steadman, VA	DOW		ROH,HOS
Briant, Alfred T.	Pvt.	G 18th SCVI		SG	12/16/64	Elmira, NY	DIP	(P65= Co.F,FPH=N.C.)	FPH,P6,P65,P12
Briant, Columbus N.P.	Pvt.	B Hol.Leg.	18	SG	07/11/63	Meridian, MS	DOD		ROH,HOS,PP
Briant, David	Pvt.	B Hol.Leg.		SG	/ /	Mississippi	DOD		HOS
Briant, Harcamus	Pvt.	B Hol.Leg.	39	SG	03/31/63	Columbia, SC	DOW	(Wdd @ 2nd Manassas)	ROH,HOS,PP

B

SOUTH CAROLINA DEAD IN CSA SERVICE 1861-1865

NAME	RANK	C REGIMENT	AGE	DS	DIED	WHERE	WHY	BURIED	SOURCES
Briant, J.Boylin	Cpl.	B Hol.Leg.	34	SG	09/28/62	At home	DOD		ROH,HOS
Briant, Warren J.	Pvt.	B 2nd SCVIRi	26	PS	05/25/62	Adams Run, SC	DOD		ROH,PP
Brice, C.S.	Pvt.	F 6th SCVI		CR	/ /		DOW		HHC
Brice, J.A.	Pvt.	C 27th SCVI		CN	02/03/64	Charleston, SC	DOD		ROH,HAG
Brice, James	Pvt.	F Ham.Leg.		GE	06/15/61	Brentsville, VA	DOD		ROH
Brice, James Michael	Cpt.	G 6th SCVI	32	FD	09/30/64	Ft. Harrison, VA	KIA	(Once POW @ Frederick, MD)	ROH,JR,R46,HFC
Brice, James Price.	Pvt.	F Ham.Leg.	20	FD	11/06/61	Manassas, VA	DOD		ROH
Brice, John Moore	Pvt.	H 6th SCVI	25	FD	06/03/64	Cold Harbor, VA	KIA	(On picket duty)	ROH,JR,HFC
Brice, Pinckney	Pvt.	I 13th SCVI		SG	07/29/62		DOD	(Typhoid)	JR,HOS
Brice, Thomas K.	Pvt.	F 1st SCVIH		GE	02/23/65	Pt. Lookout, MD	DIP	(POW 8/14/64)	ROH,HAG,SA1,P113
Brice, W.M.	Pvt.	G 6th SCVI		FD	07/19/64	Petersburg, VA	DOW	(Wdd 7/18/64)	ROH,HFC
Brice, Walter Scott	Pvt.	F 12th SCVI	28	FD	07/13/62	Richmond, VA	DOD	(Typhoid)	ROH,JR,HFC
Bridges, A.	Pvt.	F 1st SCVIH		GE	10/18/63	TN	DOD	(Chronic Diarrhea)	ROH,SA1,JRH
Bridges, Arthur D.	Pvt.	G 16th SCVI		GE	/ /	Covington, GA	DOD		16R
Bridges, Franklin C.	Pvt.	E 15th SCVI	21	FD	04/13/63	Monticello, SC	DOD		ROH,JR,KEB
Bridges, G.H.	Pvt.	K 27th SCVI	45	SG	07/25/64	Pt. Lookout, MD	DIP	C.C. Pt. Lookout, MD	ROH,FPH,P6,P113
Bridges, H.P.	Sgt.	A 18th SCVI		UN	08/27/62	Rappahannock Stn	KIA		ROH,JR,CDC
Bridges, Jonathan	Pvt.	C 17th SCVI		CR	07/24/62	Adams Run, SC	DOD	(JR=James I. 9/15/62)	JR,PP,CB
Bridges, P.H.	Pvt.	H 2nd SCVI		LR	10/02/62	Winchester, VA	DOD	Stonewall C. Winchester VA	ROH,WIN,LAN,SA2
Bridges, W. Lewis	Pvt.	B 16th SCVI		GE	11/30/64	Franklin, TN	KIA		16R
Bridges, W.M.	Pvt.	F 1st SCVIH		GE	10/10/62	VA	DOD	(Chronic Diarrhea)	ROH,SA1,HAG,JRH
Bridges, William P.	Cpt.	K 18th SCVI	29	SG	07/30/64	Crater, Pbg., VA	KIA		ROH,JR,BLM,TCC
Bridwell, James	Pvt.	F 16th SCVI		GE	/ /	Macon, GA	DOD		16R
Bridwell, John	Pvt.	D 14th SCVI	21	ED	07/01/63	Gettysburg, PA	KIA		JR,D14,HOE,GDR
Bridwell, W.C.	Sgt.	C 18th SCVI		UN	07/30/64	Petersburg, VA	KIA		ROH,JR
Bridwell, W.J.	Pvt.	C 18th SCVI	19	UN	07/30/64	Crater, Pbg., VA	KIA		ROH,BLM
Briggs, A.J.	Pvt.	I 7th SCVI		ED	/ /				HOE,KEB
Briggs, Henry	Pvt.	I 7th SCVI	25	AE	/ /	Richmond, VA	DOD	Oakwood C.#172,Row A,Div A	ROH,OWC,KEB,ACC
Briggs, James M.	Pvt.	B 6th SCVC		ED	08/29/64	Richmond, VA	DOD	Hollywood Cem. Rchmd. V538	ROH,HC,HOE
Briggs, Pickens	Pvt.	Ham.Leg.		ED	/ /		DOW	(Wdd @ Gettysburg)	ROH
Briggs, Richard P.	Cpl.	Ham.Leg.	22	AE	09/17/62	Sharpsburg, MD	KIA	Plum Branch Ch. AE Cty.	ROH,MCC
Briggs, T.J.	Pvt.				09/26/62	Richmond, VA	DOD		ROH
Briggs, Thomas	Pvt.	Ham.Leg.		ED	/ /	Richmond, VA		(Prob. Dup Briggs, T.J.)	ROH
Brigham, Eli	Pvt.	D 26th SCVI		MO	08/25/64	Ream's Stn. VA	KIA		ROH,HOM
Bright, Adam G.	Pvt.	B 13th SCVI		SG	10/09/62	Richmond, VA	DOD	(Typhoid)	HOS,JR
Bright, Robert	Pvt.	B 13th SCVI		SG	/ /	Columbia, SC	DOD		HOS
Bright, Robert B.	Pvt.	H 22nd SCVI			09/13/64	Elmira, NY	DIP	Woodlawn N.C.#262 Elmira	FPH,P5
Bright, Thomas B.	Pvt.	K P.S.S.		SG	/ /		DIP		HOS
Bright, William J.	Pvt.	C 22nd SCVI	28	SG	09/23/64	Elmira, NY	DIP	Woodlawn N.C.#469W Elmira	ROH,FPH,HOS,P5
Brigman,	Pvt.	E 23rd SCVI		MN	/ /			(1864)	HMC
Brigman, Archibald	Pvt.	I 8th SCVI		MN	07/08/62	Charlottesville	DOD	University Cem. Ch'ville	JR,HMC,ACH,KEB
Brigman, E.J.	Pvt.	D 26th SCVI		MO	08/23/64	Petersburg, VA	DOW	(ROH=Bigman)	ROH
Brigman, J.F.	Pvt.	K 6th SCVI		MO	09/22/62	Bunker Hill, VA	DOD		ROH,WDB
Brigman, J.W.	Pvt.	C 10th SCVI		AN	01/15/64	Dalton, GA	DOD		RAS,PP
Brigman, James B.	Pvt.	B 12th SCVI	27	YK	07/01/63	Gettysburg, PA	KIA		JR,YEB
Brigman, William	Pvt.	D 26th SCVI		MO	04/18/65	Newbern, NC	DIP	Cedar Grove C. Newbern, NC	HOM,WAT,P6,PP
Brigman, William	Pvt.	E 4th SCVC		MO	/ /	At home	MUR		HOM
Brigman, William S.	Pvt.	H 1st SCVIR		DN	07/18/63	Bty. Wagner, SC	KIA		ROH,SA1,CDC
Bringenath, William	Pvt.	B German Art		CN	11/07/61	Pt. Royal, SC	KIA		ROH,JR,CDC
Bringleton, James	Pvt.	Artillery			01/03/65	Charleston, SC	DOD	Magnolia Cem. Charleston	MAG
Brinks, J.	Pvt.	H 6th SCVI			09/17/62	Sharpsburg, MD	KIA		ROH,CDC

B

SOUTH CAROLINA DEAD IN CSA SERVICE 1861-1865

NAME	RANK	C REGIMENT	AGE	DS	DIED	WHERE	WHY	BURIED	SOURCES
Brinson, Benjamin	Pvt.	K 10th SCVI		CN	06/12/62	Canton, MS	DOD	Con. Cem. Canton, MS Gv#68	RAS,PP,TOD
Brinson, H.	Pvt.	E 5th SCVC			05/16/64	Drury's Bluff VA	KIA		JR,CDC
Brisden, T.W.	Pvt.	D 23rd SCVI		CN	03/22/65	Petersburg, VA	ACD		ROH
Brison, M.H.	Pvt.	C 5th SCVI			10/28/63	Lookout Valley	KIA	(Bryson, H.C. in SA3?)	ROH,CDC
Bristow, Daniel M.	Pvt.	F 21st SCVI		MO	03/03/65	Elmira, NY	DIP	Woodlawn N.C.#1998W Elmira	ROH,FPH,P6,P65
Bristow, J.Y.	Sgt.	E 8th SCVI			09/13/62	Maryland Hts. MD	KIA	(J.N. in KEB?)	JR
Bristow, Robert N.	Pvt.	F 21st SCVI		MO	03/18/65	Elmira, NY	DIP	Woodlawn N.C.#1719W Elmira	ROH,FPH,P6,P65
Bristow, Wiley J.	Pvt.	F 21st SCVI		MO	09/02/62	Morris Island SC	ACD	(Gunshot)	ROH,JR,HOM,HAG
Britt, John	Pvt.	F 19th SCVI		ED	02/05/65	Camp Chase, OH	DIP	Con.Cem.#1059 Columbus, OH	FPH,HOE,P6,P27
Britt, John L.	Pvt.	H 23rd SCVI	23	MN	07/30/64	Crater, Pbg., VA	KIA	(PP=8/1/64)	ROH,BLM,HMC,PP
Britt, T.J.	Pvt.	G 14th SCVI	27	AE	07/23/62	Gaines' Mill, VA	DOW		ROH,JR
Britton, Benjamin F.	Pvt.	E 10th SCVI		WG	11/10/62	Tullahoma, TN	DOD		RAS,HOW,PP
Britton, Henry	Pvt.	E 6th SCVI		SR	09/06/62	Warrenton, VA	DOW	(Wdd @ 2nd Manassas)	ROH,JR,JLC
Britton, J.W.	Pvt.	A 7th SCVC		WG	04/05/65	Farmville, VA	KIA		CTA,HOW
Britton, S.F.	Pvt.	K 23rd SCVI		SR	09/17/62	Sharpsburg, MD	KIA		JR
Britton, T.G.	Lt.	I 4th SCVC		WG	05/28/64	Hawe's Shop, VA	KIA	(ROH= Button)	ROH,HOM
Britton, Thomas M.	Pvt.	K 23rd SCVI	33	SR	08/30/62	2nd Manassas, VA	KIA		ROH,JR,K23,UD3
Broach, G.W.	Pvt.	H 8th SCVI		MN	/ /		DOD	(1861)	HMC,KEB
Broach, J.K.	Cpl.	C 23rd SCVI		CN	07/15/64		KIA	(? Bunch)	JR
Broach, J.R.	Pvt.	A 8th SCVI		DN	07/02/63	Gettysburg, PA	KIA		ROH,JR,GDR,CDC
Broach, R.	Pvt.	F 10th SCVI		MN	/ /		DOD		RAS,HMC
Broadwater, Y.J.	Pvt.	I 7th SCVI		ED	05/15/64	Piedmont Inst.VA		(NI KEB or HOE)	ROH
Brochet, T.	Pvt.	B 7th SCVI			/ /	(OWC=Brockett)		Oakwood C.62,Row D,Div B	ROH,OWC
Brock, A.M.	Pvt.	E 18th BnArt			09/30/64	Charleston, SC	DOD	Magnolia Cem. Charleston	ROH,MAG
Brock, Calvin	Pvt.	B 8th SCVI	33	CD	02/09/65	Camp Chase, OH	DIP	Con.Cem.#1141 Columbus, OH	ROH,FPH,P6,KEB
Brock, F.J.	Pvt.	I P.S.S.		PS	07/01/62	Frayser's Farm	DOW		ROH
Brock, H.	Civilian			CD	06/12/65	Pt. Lookout, MD	DIP	C.C. Pt. Lookout, MD	FPH,P6,P114
Brock, Joel W.	Pvt.	21st SCVI		CD	03/01/65	Charleston, SC			ROH
Brock, John W.	Pvt.	G Orr's Ri.		AE	06/22/64	Richmond, VA	DOD	(Also Wdd 6/27/62)	ROH
Brock, Samuel W.	Pvt.	21st SCVI	35	CD	06/15/65	Charleston, SC		(Prob Co. D)	ROH
Brock, Thomas	Pvt.	D 21st SCVI	24	CD	10/17/63	Columbia, SC	DOD		ROH,JR,HAG,PP
Brock, William	Pvt.	B 13th SCVI		SG	/ /	Columbia, SC	DOD	(1861)	HOS
Brockinton, John S.	Pvt.	E 10th SCVI	17	WG	06/03/62	Chickasaw, MS	DOD	(JR= Palo Alto, MS)	JR,RAS,HOW,CDC
Brockman, Benjamin T.	Col.	13th SCVI	33	SG	06/08/64	Richmond, VA	DOW	(Wdd @ Spots'a 5/12) UD1	ROH,JR,LC,BOS
Brockman, Jesse Kilgore	Cpt.	B 13th SCVI	25	SG	05/28/64	Spotsylvania, VA	DOW	Spotsylvania C.H., VA	ROH,JR,SCH,UD1
Brog, M.A.	Pvt.				/ /	Columbia, SC		Elmwood Cem. Columbia, SC	MP,PP
Brogden, Joel Davis	Pvt.	D 2nd SCVI	21	SR	06/29/62	Malvern Hill, VA	KIA	(H2=Savage Stn.)	ROH,SA2,KEB,H2
Brogden, John	Pvt.	K 19th SCVI	28	ED	04/24/62	Enterprise, MS	ACD	Phillipi B.C. Johnson, SC	ROH,JR,PP,EDN
Brogden, Robert	Pvt.	F P.S.S.			/ /		KIA		JR
Brois, H.	Pvt.				/ /	Richmond, VA		Oakwood C.#48,Row R,Div C	OWC
Brook, J.(Brooks, H.J.?)	Pvt.	F 20th SCVI		NY	/ /	Richmond, VA		Oakwood C.#55,Row B,Div G	ROH,OWC
Brookbanks, R.		CSN Hunley			12/16/63	Charleston, SC	ACD	Magnolia Cem. Charleston	RCD
Brooker, A. Fuller	3rd Sgt.	K 1st SCVIH		LN	08/30/64	2nd Manassas, VA	KIA	(JR= Sharpsburg)	ROH,JR,SA1,JRH
Brooker, B.D.	Pvt.	E 27th SCVI			06/18/64	Petersburg, VA	KIA	(JR=Booker)	ROH,JR,HAG
Brooker, J. Edward	Pvt.	E 11th SCVI	31	BT	09/20/64	Greensboro, NC	DOD	(PP=9/29/64)	ROH,HAG,PP
Brooker, James	4th Sgt.	K 1st SCVIH			06/22/64	Welden RR, Pbg.	KIA	(Pvt. in Co. A per HAG)	ROH,SA1,HAG
Brooker, John R.	Pvt.	E 11th SCVI	37	BT	09/10/64	Petersburg, VA	DOW	(Wdd 6/24/64,d:enemy hands)	ROH,HAG,P12
Brooks, Andrew P.	Pvt.	G Orr's Ri.		AE	06/15/65	Elmira, NY	DIP	Woodlawn N.C.#2879W Elmira	ROH,FPH,P6,P65
Brooks, Caleb W.	Pvt.	I 6th SCVI	24	CR	08/09/62	Richmond, VA	DOD		ROH,HHC,CB
Brooks, Charles Elisha	3rd Sgt.	F 2nd SCVI		AE	01/23/65	Camp Chase, OH	DIP	Con. Cem. Columbus, OH	ROH,JR,FPH,P23
Brooks, Henry J.	Pvt.	F 20th SCVI		NY	/ /	Petersburg, VA	KIA		ANY,KEB

B

SOUTH CAROLINA DEAD IN CSA SERVICE 1861-1865

NAME	RANK	C	REGIMENT	AGE	DS	DIED	WHERE	WHY	BURIED	SOURCES
Brooks, Isaac	Pvt.	F	7th SCVI	18	ED	05/06/64	Wilderness, VA	KIA	(Brooks, G. in KEB?)	JR,HOE
Brooks, J. DeLoach	Pvt.	E	25th SCVI		CN	09/19/62	Charleston, SC	DOD	Magnolia Cem. Charleston	ROH,JR,MAG,HAG
Brooks, James	Pvt.	F	Hol.Leg.	41	AE	05/20/64	Raleigh, NC	DOD	Oakwood C. Raleigh, NC	ROH,TOD
Brooks, Jason T.	Pvt.	G	19th SCVI		AE	12/15/64	Nashville, TN	KIA		ROH,HOL
Brooks, John	Pvt.	I	6th SCVI	21	CR	09/30/64	Ft. Harrison, VA	KIA		ROH,HHC,CB
Brooks, Josiah W.	Pvt.	G	1st SCVIG		ED	09/20/62		DOW	(Wdd @ 2nd Man)	JR,SA1,HOE,EDN
Brooks, R.H.	Pvt.	I	7th SCVI		ED	06/29/62	Savage Stn., VA	DOW		HOE,CDC,CNM
Brooks, Robert	Pvt.	A	1st SCV			10/24/63	Med.C.H. Atlanta		Oakland C. Atlanta R14#9	BGA
Brooks, W.J.	Pvt.	G	3rd SCVI		LS	12/13/62	Fredericksburg	KIA		ROH,JR,SA2,KEB
Brooks, Warren D.	Cpt.	F	7th SCVI	19	ED	05/06/64	Wilderness, VA	KIA		JR,HOE,KEB,UD3
Brooks, Whitfield Butler	Pvt.	B	6th SCVC	18	ED	06/12/64	Trevillian Stn.	KIA	Willowbrook C. Edgefield	ROH,BHC,UD3,PP
Brooks, Willie	Pvt.		1st SCV			03/06/65	Cheraw, SC	DIP	(In enemy hands)	P1,P6
Broom, Abel	Pvt.	E	12th SCVI	40	LR	08/29/62	Warrenton, VA	DOW	(Wdd @ 2nd Manassas)	ROH,LAN
Broom, James F.	Pvt.	E	Orr's Ri.	19	PS	12/13/62	Fredericksburg	KIA		ROH
Broom, John W.	Sgt.	C	12th SCVI		FD	07/02/63	Gettysburg, PA	KIA		JR,HFC,GDR
Broom, Michael	Pvt.	I	2nd SCVI			12/01/62	Richmond, VA	DOD		SA2,H2
Broom, Reuben	Pvt.	D	Hol.Leg.		BL	/ /	Staunton, VA		Thornrose Cem. Staunton VA	PP
Broom, William M.	Pvt.	B	2nd SCVIRi		PS	/ /			Hall G.Y. Westminster, SC	ROH,OCS
Broome, Green E.	Pvt.	G	5th SCVI		YK	05/06/64	Wilderness, VA	KIA	(ROH & JR= Brown)	ROH,JR,SA3
Broughton, Wilson W.	2nd Lt.	B	2nd SCVC		BT	09/13/63	Martinsburg, VA	DOW	(Wdd @ Frederick, MD)	CDC,R43
Brourton, J.A.	Pvt.	A	7th SCVC		GN	/ /	Richmond, VA	DOD		FLR
Browder, Edwin	Pvt.	K	25th SCVI	27	WG	05/06/64	Walthall Jctn.	KIA		CTA,HOW,HAG
Browder, J.W.	Pvt.	K	25th SCVI			06/02/62	Wilmington, NC	DOD	(Pneumonia)	JR
Browder, S. Warren	Pvt.	C	25th SCVI		WG	05/17/65	Elmira, NY	DIP	Woodlawn C.C.#2954 Elmira	FPH,P6,HAG
Browdley, J.W.	Pvt.	G	18th SCVI		UN	07/30/64	Crater, Pbg., VA	KIA	(Bradley ?)	ROH
Brown,	Pvt.		1st SCVI			07/05/62	Richmond, VA		Hollywood Cem.Rchmd. Q261	HC
Brown,	Pvt.		PSS			01/07/64	Near Richmond	KIA		UD2
Brown, A.B.	Pvt.	A	20th SCVI		PS	06/22/63	Charleston, SC	DOD	Magnolia Cem. Charleston	ROH,MAG
Brown, A.E.	Pvt.	D	9th SCVIB		SR	11/27/61	Richmond, VA	DOD	(Typhoid)	ROH,JR
Brown, A.E.	Pvt.	F	21st SCVI			/ /	Virginia	KIA	(1864)	ROH
Brown, A.H.	Pvt.	L	1st SCVIG		CN	06/05/65	Pt. Lookout, MD	DIP	C.C. Pt. Lookout, MD	FPH,SA1,P6,P113
Brown, A.J.	Pvt.	B	1st SCVIH		OG	09/17/62	Sharpsburg, MD	KIA		ROH,JR,SA1,JRH
Brown, A.R.	Pvt.		22nd SCVI			10/15/62			Stonewall C. Winchester VA	ROH,WIN
Brown, Addison D.	Pvt.		Hart's Bty	19	BL	10/27/64	Boydton Plank Rd	DOW		ROH
Brown, Albert	Pvt.	K	P.S.S.		SG	06/30/62	Frayser's Farm	KIA		ROH,JR,HOS,CDC
Brown, Albert	Pvt.	B	22nd SCVI		SG	07/30/64	Crater, Pbg., VA	KIA		ROH,BLM
Brown, Alexander	Pvt.	D	10th SCVI		MN	06/30/62	Holly Springs MS	DOD		RAS,PP
Brown, Alfred	Pvt.	A	26th SCVI	18	HY	08/15/64	Petersburg, VA	KIA	(PP=9/18/64)	ROH,PP
Brown, Asa	Pvt.	F	4th SCVC		GN	10/10/64	Elmira, NY	DIP	Woodlawn N.C.#672 Elmira	FPH,HMC,P65
Brown, B.F.	Pvt.	B	13th SCVI		SG	07/01/62	Richmond, VA	DOD	(Typhoid)	JR
Brown, Burrell	Pvt.	B	22nd SCVI		SG	/ /				ROH
Brown, C.R.	Pvt.	A	2nd SCVI		RD	09/24/63	Chickamauga, GA	DOW	(Wdd 9/20/63)	JR,SA2,KEB
Brown, Carter	Pvt.	B	15th SCVAB			08/17/63	Bty. Wagner, SC	KIA		ROH,CDC
Brown, Charles J.	Pvt.	I	2nd SCVI	32	BL	07/18/61	Fairfax C.H., VA	DOD	(Sunstroke)	ROH,JR,SA2,HO2
Brown, Charles Pinckney	Pvt.	A	27th SCVI	39	CN	05/14/64	Drury's Bluff VA	KIA	(Magnolia Cem., Charleston	ROH,JR,HAG,CDC
Brown, Columbus	Pvt.	F	19th SCVI		ED	07/22/64	Atlanta, GA	KIA		ROH,JR
Brown, D.	Pvt.	F	4th SCVC		GN	06/11/64	Trevillian Stn.	KIA		HMC
Brown, D.R.	Pvt.	B	22nd SCVI		SG	06/16/62	At home	DOD		ROH,HOS
Brown, D.R.	Pvt.	C	Orr's Ri.		PS	05/03/63	Chancellorsville	KIA		ROH,JR
Brown, Daniel Edward	Adjt.		14th SCVI	22	AE	05/25/64	Judiciary Hos DC	DOW	(Wdd @ Spotsylvania 5/12)	ROH,CGS,P6
Brown, Daniel M.	Pvt.	F	12th SCVI		FD	04/26/62	At home	DOD	(HFC=Feb., 1862)	JR,HFC

SOUTH CAROLINA DEAD IN CSA SERVICE 1861-1865

NAME	RANK	C REGIMENT	AGE	DS	DIED	WHERE	WHY	BURIED	SOURCES
Brown, David	Pvt.	G 25th SCVI		OG	05/07/65	Pt. Lookout, MD	DIP	C.C. Pt. Lookout, MD	ROH,FPH,EDR,P6
Brown, David	Pvt.	B 8th SCVI		CD	/ /	Richmond, VA		Oakwood C.#102,Row L,Div A	ROH,OWC,KEB
Brown, E.	Pvt.	D 15th SCVI			06/28/64	Fraysers Farm VA	KIA	(NI KEB)	JR
Brown, E.A.	Pvt.	D 6th SCVI			03/04/61	Richmond, VA	DOD		JR
Brown, E.P.	Pvt.	D 1st SCV			04/15/64	Gordonsville, VA		Gordonsville, VA	GOR
Brown, E.R.	Pvt.	I 5th SCVI		SG	05/31/62	7 Pines, VA	KIA		JR,SA3
Brown, E.T.	Pvt.	G 7th SCVIBn		KW	05/16/64	Drury's Bluff VA	KIA		HIC,HAG
Brown, E.T.	Pvt.	F Orr's Ri.			09/15/62		DOW		JR
Brown, Edward	Pvt.	E 11th SCVI		BT	01/23/65	Elmira, NY	DIP	Woodlawn N.C.#1607 Elmira	FPH,P65,HAG,P6
Brown, Evander	Pvt.	I 21st SCVI		MN	/ /	Elmira, NY	DIP	(POW @ Pbg. 5/9/64)	HMC,HAG
Brown, F.	Pvt.	G 1st SCVI			05/13/63	(OWC=10th SCVI)		Oakwood C.#32,Row 35,Div D	ROH
Brown, F.	Pvt.	G 14th SCVI		AE	05/15/63	Lynchburg, VA	DOW	(Wdd @ Chancellorsville)	ROH
Brown, F.W.	Pvt.	D 20th SCVI		OG	05/11/65	Pt. Lookout, MD	DIP	C.C. Pt. Lookout, MD	FPH,P6,P114,KE
Brown, Francis H.	Pvt.	D 2nd SCVI		SR	07/21/61	1st Manassas, VA	KIA		ROH,KEB,SA2
Brown, Fred T.A.	Pvt.	B 27th SCVI		CN	11/14/62	Charleston, SC	DOD		ROH,JR,CDC
Brown, G.	Pvt.	12th SCVI			/ /	Richmond, VA			ROH
Brown, G.F.M.	Pvt.	F Orr's Ri.		PS	06/27/62	Gaines' Mill, VA	KIA		ROH,JR,CDC
Brown, G.W.	Pvt.	G 3rd SCVI			11/01/62	Staunton, VA		Thornrose C. Staunton, VA	ROH,TOD
Brown, G.W.	Pvt.	D Ham.Leg.		AN	07/21/61	1st Manassas, VA	DOW		GRS
Brown, George W.	Cpt.	C 27th SCVI		CN	06/21/64	Petersburg, VA	DOW	1st P.C.(Scotch)Charleston	ROH,JR,MAG,HAG
Brown, H.	Pvt.	H 22nd SCVI		GE	03/11/65	Elmira, NY	DIP	Woodlawn N.C.#1842 Elmira	FPH,P6,P65
Brown, H.H.	Pvt.	F 24th SCVI	31	AN	05/13/64	LaGrange, GA	DOD	Con. Cem. LaGrange, GA	HOL,TOD
Brown, H.N.	Adjt.	23rd SCVI			06/17/64	Petersburg, VA	KIA	(JR=6/18)	ROH,JR,R48,UD3
Brown, H.R.	Pvt.	B 3rd SCVIBn		LS	05/08/64	Spotsylvania, VA	KIA	Spotsylvania C.H., VA	ROH,JR,SCH,KEB
Brown, Harrison	Pvt.	F Orr's Ri.			01/16/62		DOD		JR
Brown, Herrington E.	Pvt.	B 13th SCVI		SG	10/12/63	Davids Island NY	DOW	Cypress Hills N.C.#898 NYC	FPH,HOS,P6,GDR
Brown, Horatio	2nd Lt.	K 25th SCVI	28	SR	06/17/64	Petersburg, VA	KIA	(NI HAG)	ROH
Brown, Hugh W.	Pvt.	B 26th SCVI	24	HY	01/23/65	Kittrell Spgs.NC	DOD	Con. Cem. Kittrell Spgs NC	ROH,CV,WAT,PP
Brown, I.F.	Pvt.	G 14th SCVI		AE	12/20/61	Coosawatchie, SC	DOD		ROH
Brown, Irvins	Pvt.	SC Militia	16	BL	06/15/65		DIP		ROH
Brown, Isaac	Pvt.	E 9th SCVIBn		HY	04/15/62	Camp Lookout, MD	DIP	(JR=26th SCVI DOD 3/15)	ROH,JR
Brown, J.	Pvt.	A 25th SCVI		CN	09/07/64	Richmond, VA		Hollywood Cem.Rchmd. V213	HC
Brown, J. Franklin	Pvt.	E 13th SCVI		SG	05/23/64	Jericho Ford, VA	KIA		HOS
Brown, J. Graham	2nd Lt.	H Orr's Ri.		MN	06/27/62	Gaines' Mill, VA	KIA		ROH,JR,HMC,R45
Brown, J. Nardin	Cpl.	C P.S.S.	21	AN	08/30/62	2nd Manassas, VA	KIA	Con. Cem. Manassas, VA	ROH,JR,CDC,GMJ
Brown, J.C. (T.C./HC)	Pvt.	A 7th SCVI			07/31/64	Richmond, VA		Hollywood Cem.Rchmd. V571	HC,KEB
Brown, J.E.	Pvt.	A 7th SCVI			/ /	Lynchburg, VA	DOD	Lynchburg CSA Cem. #5 R5	SA1,BBW
Brown, J.F.	Pvt.	F 15th SCVI		UN	07/05/64	Richmond, VA		Oakwood C.#4,Row P,Div F	ROH,OWC
Brown, J.J.	Pvt.	I 6th SCVC		CR	05/06/65	Davids Island NY	DIP	Cypress Hills N.C.#2686 NY	FPH,P1,P6,P12
Brown, J.K.	Pvt.	D 24th SCVI		BT	05/16/64	Calhoun Stn., GA	KIA		ROH,JR,CDC
Brown, J.L.	Pvt.	B 7th SCVIBN	18	FD	02/09/62	Charleston, SC	DOD	(ROH= J.T.)	ROH,JR,HAG
Brown, J.L.	Pvt.	I 14th SCVI			08/14/61	Camp Butler, SC	DOD	(Measles)	JR
Brown, J.M.	Pvt.	E 13th SCVI		SG	10/12/63	Davids Island NY	DOW	(Joseph M. in P1 Co. B?)	ROH,CDC
Brown, J.M.	Pvt.	B 13th SCVI		SG	07/05/64	Richmond, VA		Hollywood Cem.Rchmd.U466	HC
Brown, J.N.	Pvt.	I 14th SCVI		AE	/ /	Richmond, VA	DOD	Oakwood C.#46,Row R,Div C	ROH,OWC,HOL
Brown, J.P.	Pvt.	K 1st SCVIH		OG	07/01/64	Petersburg, VA	KIA		SA1,HAG
Brown, J.R.Y.	Pvt.	G 13th SCVI		NY	09/03/62	2nd Manassas, VA	DOW		ROH,JR,ANY,CDC
Brown, J.S.	Pvt.	F 6th SCVI			05/06/64	Wilderness, VA	KIA		JR
Brown, J.T.	Pvt.	C 7th SCVIBn	39	RD	08/07/64	Poplar Hosp., VA	DOD		ROH
Brown, J.T.	Pvt.	B 12th SCVI		YK	08/15/63	Chester, PA	DOW	Charleston, SC	JR,FPH,P1,P6,P
Brown, J.W.	Pvt.	D Hol.Leg.	52	BL	12/06/64	Petersburg, VA	KIA		ROH

B

SOUTH CAROLINA DEAD IN CSA SERVICE 1861-1865

NAME	RANK	C REGIMENT	AGE	DS	DIED	WHERE	WHY	BURIED	SOURCES
Brown, J.W.	Pvt.	C 12th SCVI		FD	07/01/63	Gettysburg, PA	KIA		ROH
Brown, James	Pvt.	B 22nd SCVI		SG	09/14/62	South Mtn., MD	KIA		ROH,HOS
Brown, James	Pvt.	H 19th SCVI	30	AE	02/10/64	Rock Island, IL	DIP	C.C. Rock Island, IL	ROH,FPH,P5,P39
Brown, James	Pvt.	G 6th SCVI		CR	08/30/61	Germantown, VA	DOD		ROH,HHC
Brown, James	Pvt.	B 22nd SCVI		SG	07/30/64	Crater, Pbg., VA	KIA		BLM
Brown, James C.	Pvt.	I 14th SCVI	18	AE	07/14/62	Richmond, VA	DOD	(JR=June, 1862)	ROH,JR,HOL
Brown, James F.	Pvt.	E Orr's Ri.			12/13/62	Fredericksburg	KIA		JR,CDC
Brown, James M.	Pvt.	C 25th SCVI	28	WG	08/21/64	Weldon RR, VA	KIA		HOW,HAG,CTA
Brown, James Robert	Sgt.	G 18th SCVI	22	YK	07/30/64	Crater, Pbg., VA	KIA	Beersheba P.C. YK, SC	ROH,YMD,YEB
Brown, James T.	Pvt.	E 19th SCVI			06/05/63	Dalton, GA			PP
Brown, Jesse	Cpl.	E 2nd SCVC		SG	11/13/63	Pt. Lookout, MD	DIP	(HOS=KIA @ Brandy Stn.)	HOS,FPH,P5
Brown, Jesse C.	Pvt.	I 21st SCVI		MN	08/23/63	At home	DOD		JR,HMC,HAG
Brown, Jesse J.	Pvt.	L 1st SCVIG		CN	04/29/65	Elmira, NY	DIP	Woodlawn N.C.#2731 Elmira	FPH,P6,P65,SA1
Brown, Jesse T.	Pvt.	A 2nd SCVI		RD	/ /	At home	DOD	(POW Xchd 3/17/64)	ROH,KEB,SA2,P113
Brown, Joel L.	Pvt.	L 10th SCVI		MN	06/30/62	Goodman, MS	DOD		RAS,HMC,PP
Brown, John	Pvt.	D Hol.Leg.	29	BL	12/06/64	Petersburg, VA	KIA		ROH
Brown, John	Pvt.	Hol.Leg.			02/11/62			Magnolia Cem. Charleston	MAG
Brown, John	Bosun	CS Chicora			02/07/65	Charleston	DOD	St.Lawrence C. Charleston	MAG,RCD
Brown, John	Pvt.	B 14th SCVI		ED	07/02/63	Gettysburg, PA	KIA		JR,HOE,UD3
Brown, John	Pvt.	B 13th SCVI		SG	08/31/62	Ox Hill, VA	DOW		HOS
Brown, John B.	Pvt.	5th SCVI	23	YK	08/15/64	Petersburg, VA	DOW	(Wdd7/29/64)(Co.H<reorg)	ROH,SA3,YMD
Brown, John J.	Pvt.	L 2nd SCVIRi	42	AN	10/15/62	Anderson, SC	DOW	(Wdd prob @ Gaines' Mill)	ROH
Brown, John J.	1st Cpl.	G 15th SCVI	22	WG	05/02/63	Chancellorsville	KIA	(CTA= 5/24)	CTA,HOW,KEB
Brown, John L.	Pvt.	A 18th SCVI		UN	07/30/64	Crater, Pbg., VA	KIA		ROH,JR,BLM
Brown, John L.	Pvt.	I 14th SCVI	17	AE	10/12/61	Camp Butler, SC	DOD		ROH,HOL
Brown, John M.	Pvt.	K 15th SCVI		AE	12/08/64	Camp Chase, OH	DIP	C.C.#574 Columbus, OH	FPH,P6,P23,P26
Brown, John S.	Pvt.	E 2nd SCVI		KW	06/21/61	Manassas, VA	DOD		SA2,KEB,H2
Brown, John W.	Pvt.	C 7th SCVIBn	18	RD	08/30/64	Danville, VA	DOD		ROH
Brown, John W.	Pvt.	G 3rd SCVIBn		FD	04/15/62	Adams Run, VA	DOD		PP
Brown, Joseph	Pvt.	D 16th SCVI		GE	/ /	MS	DOD	(1863)	16R
Brown, Joseph F.	5th Sgt.	B 1st SCVIH		OG	07/03/62	Richmond, VA	ACD	(On picket)	ROH,SA1
Brown, Joseph White	Pvt.	H 10th SCVI	28	WG	11/15/64	Nashville, TN	KIA	(HOW says 18 in 64)	CTA,HOW,RAS
Brown, L.	Pvt.	C 22nd SCVI		SG	/ /			Stonewall C.Winchester VA	ROH,WIN
Brown, L.	Pvt.	A 17th SCVI		CR	11/18/62	Richmond, VA		Hollywood Cem.Rchmd. S304	HC,HHC
Brown, L.	Pvt.	L 10th SCVI		MN	/ /		DOD		RAS,HMC
Brown, Lee	Pvt.	D 24th SCVI	17	BT	08/19/64	Atlanta, GA	KIA		EJM
Brown, M.	Sgt.	F 10th SCVI		MN	07/22/64	Atlanta, GA	DOW	Stonewall C. Griffin, GA	ROH,RAS,HMC,BGA
Brown, M.	Pvt.	B 10th SCV			/ /	Griffin Hosp	SOW	Spaulding Cnty GA	UD2
Brown, M.P.	Pvt.	Matthews A			10/06/64	Charleston, SC	DOD	Magnolia Cem. Charleston	ROH,MAG
Brown, M.S.	Pvt.	I 1st SCVIR		AN	11/18/64	Charleston, SC	DOD	Magnolia Cem.(Brow, M.L.)	ROH,SA1,MAG
Brown, Madison H.	Pvt.	C 25th SCVI		WG	05/16/64	Drury's Bluff VA	KIA		CTA,HOW,HAG,CDC
Brown, N.	Pvt.	A 24th SCVI		CN	02/13/65	Camp Morton, IN	DIP	Green Lawn C. Indianpls.IN	FPH,CV
Brown, N. Cope	Pvt.	H Ham.Leg.	38	OG	09/12/62	2nd Manassas, VA	DOW		ROH,CDC
Brown, N.A.	Pvt.	G 28th SCVI			/ /	Richmond, VA		Oakwood C.#11,Row K,Div F	ROH,OWC
Brown, Newton	Pvt.	F Orr's Ri.			08/15/62		DOD		JR
Brown, Noble Jackson	Pvt.	E 4th SCResB	49	CR	03/30/64	At home	DOD	(Gill's Bn. Florence Pris)	ROH
Brown, P.F.	Pvt.	2nd SCVA			07/16/64	Charleston, SC	DOD	Magnolia Cem. Charleston	ROH,MAG
Brown, Philip	Sgt.	A 16th SCVI		GE	07/17/63	Yazoo City, MS	DOD		ROH,16R,PP
Brown, Ralph L.	2nd Lt.	A 2nd SCVI		RD	09/19/63	Chickamauga, GA	KIA		ROH,JR,SA2,KEB
Brown, Ransom	Pvt.	F 4th SCVC		GN	07/14/64	Hawes Shop, VA	DOW	Hollywood Cem.Rchmd. U118	ROH,HC,HMC,FLR
Brown, Reuben	Pvt.	D Hol.Leg.	23	BL	11/07/62	Staunton, VA	DOD		ROH

SOUTH CAROLINA DEAD IN CSA SERVICE 1861-1865

NAME	RANK	C	REGIMENT	AGE	DS	DIED	WHERE	WHY	BURIED	SOURCES
Brown, Richard	Pvt.	F	7th SCVC			07/15/65	Fts. Monroe, VA	DIP	Greenlawn C. Newport News	P6,JES
Brown, Richard Evander	Pvt.	I	21st SCVI		MN	10/01/64	Elmira, NY	DIP	Woodlawn N.C.#404 Elmira	FPH,P6,P113,HM
Brown, Richard M.	Pvt.	B	2nd SCVI			11/07/62	Frederick, MD	DOW	Mt. Olivet C. Frederick MD	ROH,FPH,P6,BOD
Brown, Robert M.	Pvt.	L	10th SCVI		MN	02/14/63	Shelbyville, TN	DOD	Willowmount C. Shelbyville	RAS,HMC,PP,TOD
Brown, Roland T.	Pvt.	I	5th SCVI		SG	05/31/62	7 Pines, VA	KIA		JR,SA3,HOS
Brown, S.B.	Pvt.				WG	/ /		DOD	(1862)	CTA,HOW
Brown, S.J. (Samuel?)	Pvt.	K	21st SCVI		DN	/ /	Richmond, VA		Oakwood C.#5,Row B,Div G	ROH,OWC
Brown, S.K.	Pvt.	G	18th SCVI		UN	07/30/64	Crater, Pbg., VA	KIA		BLM
Brown, Samuel	Pvt.	D	17th SCVI		CR	11/17/62	Richmond, VA	DOD		ROH,HHC,CB
Brown, Samuel	Pvt.	F	6th SCVI	18	CR	05/06/64	Wilderness, VA	KIA		ROH,HHC
Brown, Samuel	Pvt.	C	2nd SCVI		RD	10/22/64	Winchester, VA	DOD	Stonewall Cem. Winchester	ROH,WIN,P12,SA
Brown, Samuel	Pvt.	F	24th SCVI	64		/ /		DOD		HOL
Brown, T.	Pvt.	B	13th SCVI		SG	/ /			Richmond, VA	ROH
Brown, T.	Pvt.	B	12th SCVI		YK	07/01/63	Chester, PA	DOW	Magnolia Cem. Charleston	MAG
Brown, T.F.	Pvt.	E	2nd SCVA			07/16/64			Magnolia Cem. Charleston	RCD
Brown, Thomas	Pvt.	H	14th SCVI		BL	04/09/62	Richmond, VA	DOD		ROH,JR
Brown, Thomas	Pvt.	A	1st SCVIR			04/30/62	Ft. Moultrie, SC	DOD		SA1
Brown, Thomas	Pvt.	B	16th SCVI		GE	/ /	At home	DOD	(? in service)	16R
Brown, Thomas	Pvt.	H	14th SCV			/ /	Hospital 7/62			UD2
Brown, Thomas D.	Pvt.	K	1st SCVIH		OG	08/30/62	2nd Manassas, VA	KIA	Con. Cem. Manassas, VA	ROH,JR.SA1,CDC
Brown, Thomas E.	Pvt.	I	2nd SCVA	26	OG	09/09/63	James Island, SC	ACD		ROH
Brown, Thomas J.	Pvt.	B	26th SCVI			08/21/64	Petersburg, VA			PP
Brown, Vincent	Pvt.	C	8th Res Bn Bn		BL	10/12/64	Charleston, SC	DOD	Magnolia Cem. Charleston	ROH,MAG,CDC
Brown, W.						/ /			(Rchmd effects list 12/62)	CDC
Brown, W.C.	Pvt.	B	7th SCVIBn	37	FD	07/01/64	Drury's Bluff, V	DOW	Oakwood C.#15,Row J,Div F	ROH,OWC,HAG
Brown, W.C.	Pvt.	H	Ham.Leg.		RD	08/30/62	2nd Manassas, VA	KIA		ROH,JR
Brown, W.E.	Pvt.	H	14th SCVI			08/02/62	Danville, VA	DOD		JR
Brown, W.H.	Pvt.	B	8th SCVI		CD	06/15/62	Richmond, VA			ROH
Brown, W.J.	Pvt.	B	13th SCVI		SG	05/15/64	Virginia	KIA	(Prob. Dup of William B.)	ROH
Brown, W.J.	Pvt.	K	10th SCVI		CN	/ /		DOD		RAS
Brown, W.P. (W.L.?)	Pvt.	D	17th SCVI	21	CR	08/09/64	Crater, Pbg., VA	DOW	Blandford Church Pbg., VA	ROH,BLM,BLC,PP
Brown, William	Pvt.		PeeDee LA		DN	12/13/62	Fredericksburg	KIA		ROH,PDL
Brown, William	Pvt.	F	15th SCVI		UN	07/01/63	Gettysburg, PA	KIA		ROH,JR,GDR,KEB
Brown, William	Pvt.	A	13th SCVI		LS	07/01/63	Gettysburg, PA	KIA		ROH,JR,CDC,GDR
Brown, William	Pvt.	D	15th SCVI		KW	05/12/64	Spotsylvania, VA	KIA		JR,HIC,KEB
Brown, William	Pvt.				WG	05/08/63	Rappahanock, VA	KIA		CTA,HOW
Brown, William	Pvt.	K	13th SCVI			05/12/64	Wilderness, VA	KIA		JR
Brown, William B.	Pvt.	B	13th SCVI		SG	05/12/64	Spotsylvania, VA	KIA		HOS
Brown, William D	Pvt.	C	1st SCVIR		SG	12/10/61	Charleston, SC	DOD		SA1
Brown, William J.	Pvt.	I	18th SCVI	21	DN	05/20/64	Clay's Farm, VA	KIA		ROH,JR
Brown, William Leslie	Pvt.	E	16th SCVI	19	LS	06/25/64	Kennesaw Mt. GA	KIA	Con. Cem. Marietta, GA	ROH,16R,CCM
Brown, William M.	Sgt.	B	12th SCVI	30	YK	07/08/62	Richmond, VA	DOD		YMD,YEB
Brown, Wilson S.	Pvt.	A	16th SCVI		GE	11/30/64	Franklin, TN	KIA	Macgavock C., Frkln Gv# 17	ROH,16R,WCT,PP
Browne, A. Daniel	Pvt.	A	4th SCVI		AN	07/21/61	1st Manassas, VA	KIA		ROH,SA2,GMJ
Browne, H.N.	Lt.	K	23rd SCVI		SR	06/18/64	Petersburg, VA	KIA	(As Rgtl. Adjutant)	K23,R48
Brownfield, Thomas S.	1st Lt.	I	2nd SCVI		SR	07/02/62	Malvern Hill, VA	DOW		ROH,SA2,KEB,R4
Browning, R.A.	Pvt.	B	23rd SCVI		CN	09/10/62	Lynchburg, VA	DOD	Lynchburg CSA Cem. #6 R2	ROH,JR,CDC,BBW
Browning, R.W.	Pvt.	B	23rd SCVI	51	CN	08/15/63	MS			ROH
Browning, William B.	2nd Lt.	E	16th SCVI	35	LS	04/08/64	Greensboro, NC	DOD	(?RES 2/5/62?)	ROH,16R,R47
Brownlee, C.D.	Pvt.	D	2nd SCVIRi		LS	06/29/62	Savage Stn., VA	KIA		ROH,CDC
Brownlee, David D.	2nd Cpl.	G	3rd SCVI	29	LS	06/29/62	Savage Stn., VA	KIA	(D.J.G. in KEB)	ROH,JR,SA2,KEB

B

SOUTH CAROLINA DEAD IN CSA SERVICE 1861-1865

NAME	RANK	C	REGIMENT	AGE	DS	DIED	WHERE	WHY	BURIED	SOURCES
Brownlee, F.L.	Pvt.	G	11th SCVI		CO	05/16/65	Elmira, NY	DIP	Woodlawn N.C.#2961 Elmira	JR,FPH,P6,P65
Brownlee, G.R.	Pvt.	G	11th SCVI		CO	10/19/64	Richmond, VA	DOD		ROH
Brownlee, George W.	5th Sgt.	I	19th SCVI	29	AE	05/31/64	Richmond, VA	DOD	Hollywood Cem.Rchmd. W414	ROH,HC,P39
Brownlee, James R.	Pvt.	B	7th SCVI			08/15/62		DOD		JR
Brownlee, James W.	Pvt.	G	11th SCVI		CO	06/16/64	Richmond, VA	DOD	Hollywood Cem.Rchmd. U20	ROH,JR,HC,HAG
Brownlee, John H.	2nd Lt.	G	11th SCVI		CO	11/10/64	Raleigh, NC	DOD	Oakwood C. Raleigh, NC	ROH,HAG,TOD
Brownlee, Samuel R.	5th Sgt.	I	19th SCVI	39	AE	05/11/62	Saltillo, MS	DOD	(JR=5/18)	ROH,JR,PP
Brownter, G.A.	Cpl.					/ /	Richmond, VA		Oakwood C.#13,Row T,Div F	ROH,OWC
Broxton, John K.	Sgt.	K	9th SCVIB	23	CO	11/11/61	Lady's Isl., SC	DOD	(CNM=Sand's Pt.)	ROH,JR,HAG,CNM
Brubaker, Nathan	Pvt.	B	9th SCVIB		RD	09/11/61	Germantown, VA	DOD		ROH
Bruce, B.S.	Pvt.	F	Orr's Ri.			06/15/62	Howard Grove Hos	DOD		JR
Bruce, C.	Pvt.	D	16th SCVI		GE	09/23/63	Rome, GA	DOD	Myrtle Hill Cem. Rome, GA	ROH,16R,BGA
Bruce, E.C.	Pvt.	G	1st SCVIR		AN	07/16/64	Charleston, SC	DOD	Magnolia Cem, Charleston	ROH,MAG,SA1
Bruce, George W.			Pvt.		I	14th SCVI			04/25/65 Pt. Lookout, MD	
Bruce, J. Marion	Pvt.	I	12th SCVI		LR	06/27/62	Gaines' Mill, VA	KIA		ROH,JR,LAN,CNM
Bruce, J.W.	Pvt.	L	1st SCVIG		CN	01/22/63	Lynchburg, VA	DOD	Lynchburg CSA Cem. #9 R1	JR,SA1,BBW
Bruce, James	Pvt.	F	7th SCVIBn	42	LR	12/05/62	McPhersonville	DOW	(Wdd 10/62 @ Pocotaligo)	ROH,JR,PP,HAG
Bruce, James A.	Pvt.			20	AN	04/25/62	Richmond, VA		Townville B.C. Anderson SC	ACC
Bruce, James H.	Pvt.	G	2nd SCVI		KW	09/03/61	Lynchburg, VA	DOD	Lynchburg CSA Cem. lot 159	ROH,SA2,HIC,BBW
Bruce, John	Pvt.	D	16th SCVI		GE	06/30/62	Kingston, GA	DOD	(PP=At home)	16R,PP
Bruce, John C.	1st Sgt.	D	Ham.Leg.	28	AN	04/09/65	Appomatox, VA	KIA		ROH,GRS
Bruce, John Daniel	Pvt.	D	19th SCVI	19	ED	06/27/62	Enterprise, MS	DOD		HOE,PP,UD3
Bruce, John R.	Pvt.	C	1st SC Res			04/30/64	Charleston, SC	DOD	Magnolia Cem. Charleston	ROH,MAG,CDC
Bruce, M.C.	Pvt.	A	2nd SCVA			10/20/64	James Island, SC	DOD		ROH,CDC
Bruce, Moses	Pvt.	I	2nd SCVC		ED	07/05/64	Johns Island, SC	KIA		ROH,HOE
Bruce, Robert	Pvt.	F	21st SCVI			10/21/63	Cassville, GA		(?21st NI GA?, 24th ?)	ROH
Bruce, Samuel	Pvt.	D	16th SCVI		GE	08/01/63	Marion, MS	DOD	(2nd PP entry=Lauderdale)	16R,PP
Bruce, T.R.	Pvt.	K	8th SCVI			06/10/63	Gordonsville, VA	DOD		JR,KEB
Bruce, W.B.	Pvt.	D	16th SCVI		GE	/ /	Kingston, GA	DOD	(1864)	16R
Bruce, W.M.	Pvt.	D	16th SCVI		GE	/ /	Rome, GA	DOD	(1863)	16R
Brun, E.P.	Pvt.	D	1st SCV			/ /	Gordonsville, VA		(NI SA1, Orr's Ri., Cav?)	ROH
Brunson, John A.	Pvt.	E	6th SCVI	37	DN	08/30/62	2nd Manassas, VA	KIA		ROH,JLC,WDB,UD3
Brunson, W.D.	Pvt.	F	1st SCVIG			02/28/64	Orange C.H., VA	DOD		SA1,PDL
Brunson, W.L.	Pvt.	I	23rd SCVI		CL	09/15/62	Warrenton, VA	DOW	(Wdd @ 2nd Manassas)	ROH,CDC
Brunson, William E.	Pvt.	E	P.S.S.		SR	10/12/64	Ft. Harrison, VA	DOW	(1st in Co. D, 2nd SCVI)	JR,H2,SA2,P12
Brunswick, J.M.	Pvt.	K	13th SCVI		LN	09/09/62		DOD	Richmond, VA	ROH
Brunton, J.A.	Cpt.		SCVC		GN	06/15/64	Richmond, VA		(Prob. Cpl. no such Cpt.)	ROH
Bryan, Artemas M.	2nd Sgt.	G	7th SCVI		ED	06/15/63		KIA		ROH,HOE,KEB
Bryan, Goodwyn B.	Pvt.	K	14th SCVI		ED	06/27/62	Gaines' Mill VA	KIA	(JR=J.G.)	ROH,JR,HOE,CNM
Bryan, J.T.	Pvt.	E	24th SCVI	22	CO	01/13/64	Columbia, SC	DOD		ROH,PP
Bryan, M.T.	Pvt.	K	P.S.S.			05/31/62	Chickahominy R.	KIA		JR
Bryan, Robert	Pvt.	A	22nd SCVI			/ /		KIA	(1864)	ROH
Bryan, Robert	Pvt.	G	7th SCV			/ /		DOW		UD2
Bryan, Robert C.	Pvt.	G	7th SCVI		ED	/ /		DOD		HOE,KEB
Bryan, Robert S.	Pvt.	A	27th SCVI		CN	11/28/64	Elmira, NY	DIP	Woodlawn N.C.#991 Elmira	FPH,P12
Bryan, S.T.	Pvt.		19th SCVI			03/05/63	Jefferson Bks MO	DIP	St. Louis N.C.#4783 MO	FPH,PP,P12
Bryan, W. Hudson	Cpt.		Hol.Leg.			03/07/63		DOD	(Typhoid)	JR
Bryan, W.C.	Pvt.	D	3rd SC			09/11/63		DOD		JR
Bryan, William	Pvt.	B	27th SCVI			05/09/64	Swift Creek, VA	KIA		JR
Bryan, William	Pvt.	B	9th SCVIBn			/ /		DOD	(JR=26th SCVI)	JR
Bryan,, L.T.	Pvt.	I	19th SCVI			11/02/62	Danville, KY		Con. Lot #56 Danville C.	FPH,P12

SOUTH CAROLINA DEAD IN CSA SERVICE 1861-1865

NAME	RANK	C	REGIMENT	AGE	DS	DIED	WHERE	WHY	BURIED	SOURCES
Bryant, Art.	Pvt.	G	7th SCV			/ /		KIA		UD2
Bryant, Evan T.	Pvt.	H	Orr's Ri.		MN	07/02/62	Richmond, VA	DOD		JR,HMC
Bryant, Isaac	Pvt.	H	14th SCVI			01/01/63	Richmond, VA	DOD	(Typhoid,may be 12th SCVI)	ROH,JR
Bryant, J.W.	Pvt.	A	8th SCVI		DN	11/28/62	Charlottesville	DOD	University Cem. Ch'ville	ROH,JR,ACH
Bryant, James R.	Pvt.	E	5th SCVI	37	YK	02/01/63	Richmond, VA	DOD	Oakwood C.#7,Row P,Div C	ROH,JR,SA3,OWC
Bryant, John G.	2nd Lt.	D	18th SCVI		AN	07/30/64	Crater, Pbg., VA	KIA		ROH,JR,BLM,R47
Bryant, K.S.	Pvt.	H	Orr's Ri.			05/27/63		DOW	(Wdd @ Chancellorsville)	JR
Bryant, L.	Pvt.	G	3rd SCVI			05/20/64	Spotsylvania, VA	KIA		ROH,JR
Bryant, McRady	Pvt.	H	11th SCVI			/ /	Marietta, GA	KIA	(? 11th SCVI NI GA)	DRE
Bryant, Rowland	Pvt.	E	13th SCVI		SG	07/01/63	Gettysburg, PA	KIA	(JR=DOD 7/13/63)	HOS,JR,ROH
Bryant, Solomon	Sgt.	H	Orr's Ri.	40	MN	12/13/62	Fredericksburg	KIA	(Bryon in ROH)	HMC,ROH
Bryant, W.M.	Pvt.	C	18th SCVI			07/30/64	Crater, Pbg., VA	KIA		JR
Bryant, William	Pvt.	B	21st SCVI		DN	05/10/64	Petersburg, VA			ROH,HAG,PP
Bryant, William A.	Pvt.	I	5th SCVI		SG	09/19/63	Chickamauga, GA	KIA	(SA3=On Roster 2/28/65)	HOS,SA3
Bryant, William F.	Pvt.	D	7th SCVIBn	48	HY	06/15/64	At home	DOD		ROH,HAG
Bryant, William H.	Pvt.	M	10th SCVI		HY	03/03/64	Rock Island, IL	DIP	C.C.#722 Rock Island, IL	FPH,RAS,P5,P39
Bryant, William N.	Sgt.	D	18th SCVI		AN	01/29/65	Elmira, NY	DIP	Woodlawn N.C.#1652W Elmira	ROH,FPH,P6,P65
Bryce, Robert Power	5th Sgt.	C	2nd SCVI	21	RD	09/20/63	Chickamauga, GA	KIA	(Pvt. in KEB)	ROH,JR,SA2,KEB
Bryson, H.J.	Pvt.	F	3rd SCVI		LS	07/02/63	Gettysburg, PA	KIA		ROH,JR,GDR,SA2
Bryson, J.G.	Pvt.	F	3rd SCVI		LS	06/04/62	Danville, VA	DOD	(J.A. in KEB)	ROH,JR,SA2,KEB
Bryson, John E.	Pvt.	F	3rd SCVI		LS	10/29/62	Winchester, VA	DOD		ROH,JR,SA2
Bryson, John H.	Pvt.	D	27th SCVI	38	LS	07/25/64	Petersburg, VA	DOD		ROH,HAG
Bryson, M.H.	Pvt.	C	5th SCVI			10/28/63	Chattanooga, TN	KIA	(H.C.?)	JR
Bryson, Marsh S.	Pvt.	K	P.S.S.		SG	05/31/62	7 Pines, VA	KIA	(Bryan ?)	HOS,CDC
Bryson, T.J.	Pvt.	D	27th SCVI	18	LS	06/16/64	Petersburg, VA	KIA	(JR=6/18)	ROH,JR,CDC,HAG
Buchanan, J.A.	Sgt.	F	Hol.Leg.	21	AE	08/30/62	2nd Manassas, VA	KIA	(JRR=J.T. & Sharpsburg)	ROH,JR
Buchanan, J.W.	Pvt.	F	Hol.Leg.	27	AE	08/30/62	2nd Manassas, VA	KIA	(JR=Sharpsburg)	ROH,JR
Buchanan, James B.	Pvt.	I	11th SCVI		CO	07/15/64	Virginia	DOD		ROH,HAG
Buchanan, James R.	Pvt.	A	6th SCVI		CR	03/01/62	Richmond, VA	DOD	(Pneumonia)	JR,HHC,CB
Buchanan, W.C.	Pvt.	C	12th SCVI		FD	09/01/62	Ox Hill, VA	KIA	(JR=Adjutant)	ROH,JR,HFC,BOS
Buchannon, F. Maxim	Pvt.	K	5th SCVC		UN	06/17/64	Richmond, VA	DOW	Hollywood Cem.Rchmd. U226	ROH,HC
Buck, George O.	Cadet		Citadel	19	HY	01/23/65	Charleston, SC	DOD		ROH
Buck, J.F.	Pvt.	I	P.S.S.			/ /		DOD		JR
Buckhalter, Raymond	Pvt.	B	19th SCVI		ED	01/25/64	Cassville, GA		(HOE= Burkhalter)	ROH,HOE
Buckles, Henry	Pvt.	G	15th SCVI	28	WG	06/15/64	Lynchburg, VA	DOW	Lynchburg CSA Cem. #9 R3	JR,HOW,BBW,KEB
Bucknell, J.W.	Pvt.	I	P.S.S.			01/19/64		DOD		JR
Buckner, J.A.	Pvt.	D	23rd SCVI		CN	11/12/62	Charleston, SC	DOD	Magnolia Cem. Charleston	ROH,RCD
Buckner, J.W.	Pvt.	A	9th SCVIB			10/13/62	(Rgt.Disbdd?)		Stonewall C. Winchester VA	WIN
Buckner, T.G.	1st Lt.	C	Ham.leg. C		BT	05/29/62	Pocotaligo, SC	DOW		ROH
Buckon, Edward J.	Cpl.	E	12th SCVI	34	LR	04/20/63	Guinea Stn., VA	DOD		ROH,JR,LAN
Budd, Joseph	Pvt.	K	Ham.Leg.		WG	09/28/62	Frederick, MD	DOW	Mt. Olivet C. CS #57	ROH,FPH,BOD
Budd, Nathan	Pvt.	D	5th SC			07/21/63		DOD	(Prob Byars, Nathan)	JR
Buddin, Archibald F.	Pvt.	K	23rd SCVI		SR	07/08/64	Richmond, VA	DOW	Hollywood Cem.Rchmd. U397	ROH,HC,K23,UD3
Buddin, William Pierson	Cpl.	H	10th SCVI	24	WG	09/14/62	Glasgow, KY	DOD	(JR=2nd Lt.)	JR,RAS,CTA,HOW
Buff, H.E.	Pvt.	F	5th SCVC	26	LN	02/15/62	Grahamville, SC	DOD		ROH
Buie, William F.	Pvt.	I	1st SCVIH		MN	11/25/63	Newman, GA	DOD	Oak Hill Cem. Newman, GA	ROH,SA1,HMC,BG
Buist, Edward Somers	Asst. Surg		1st SCVA	25	CN	11/07/61	Port Royal, SC	KIA	2nd P.C. Charleston, SC	ROH,JR,MAG,CGS
Bull, A.W.	Pvt.	I	2nd SCVA	25	OG	06/15/65	NC	DOD	(EDR= W.A.)	ROH,EDR
Bull, Charles J.	Pvt.	K	2nd SCVI		OG	05/14/64	Spotsylvania, VA	KIA		ROH,SA2,KEB,H2
Bull, E.	Pvt.		15th SCVI			/ /		DOD		JR
Bull, E.P.	Pvt.	I	2nd SCVA	10	OG	06/15/62	At home	DOD		ROH

B

SOUTH CAROLINA DEAD IN CSA SERVICE 1861-1865

NAME	RANK	C REGIMENT	AGE	DS	DIED	WHERE	WHY	BURIED	SOURCES
Bull, John C.	Pvt.	K 7th SCVI			11/18/61	Charlottesville	DOD		JR
Bull, L.	Pvt.	K 2nd SC			05/08/64	Spotsylvania, VA	KIA		JR
Bull, William W.	Pvt.	K 15th SCVI		AE	10/07/62		DOW	(Wdd @ Sharpsburg)	ROH,JR,KEB
Bullard, Wesley	Pvt.	H Orr's Ri.		MN	02/15/62	Sullivans I., SC	DOD		ROH,CDC,CNM
Bullard, William	Pvt.	E 23rd SCVI		MN	01/17/64		KIA		HMC
Bulley, W.B.	Pvt.	E 7th RegCav	22		05/31/64	Cold Harbor	KIA		UD2
Bulling, Benjamin	Pvt.	C 11th SCVI		CO	01/30/65	Ft. Anderson, VA	DOD	(Barber, Benjamin? HAG)	ROH
Bulling, Mattison	Pvt.	I P.S.S.		PS	06/21/64	Petersburg, VA	KIA		ROH
Bullington, Alexander	Pvt.	P.S.S.		SG	/ /		DOD	(? Bullman, orig Co. C)	HOS
Bullington, Robert J.	Pvt.	A Hol.Leg.	19	SG	06/03/62	Adams Run, SC	DOD		ROH,HOS,PP
Bullman, H. Spencer	Pvt.	C 13th SCVI		SG	07/02/63	Gettysburg, PA	DOW		ROH,JR,GDR,HOS
Bullman, J.L.	Pvt.	I Hol.Leg.		SG	02/04/65	Elmira, NY	DIP	Woodlawn N.C.#1748 Elmira	FPH,P6,P113,HOS
Bullock, Charles B.	Pvt.	F 1st SCVIG		HY	11/12/62	Sharpsburg, MD	DOD		JR,SA1,PDL
Bullock, G.N.	Pvt.	D 7th SCVIBn	22	KW	02/08/64	Charleston, SC	DOD	Magnolia Cem. Charleston	ROH,MAG,HIC,HAG
Bulman, Alexander	Pvt.	K 5th SCVI		SG	09/21/61		DOD	(JR=P.S.S.)	JR,SA3
Bulware, O.	Pvt.	B 17th SCVI		FD	09/21/62	Lynchburg, VA	DOD	Lynchburg CSA Cem. #10 R4	ROH,CDC,BBW
Bunch, Daniel	Pvt.	K 10th SCVI			/ /	Okolona, MS	DOD		JR,RAS,PP,TOD
Bunch, Henry	Pvt.	K 10th SCVI		CN	05/17/62	Charleston, SC	DOD		JR,RAS
Bunch, J.	Pvt.	G 1st SCVA		CN	12/07/61	Charleston, SC	DOD	Magnolia Cem. Charleston	ROH,MAG
Bunch, J.H.	Pvt.	K 10th SCVI		CN	/ /		DOD		RAS
Bunch, J.W.H.	Pvt.	K 10th SCVI		CN	12/30/62	Murfreesboro, TN	KIA		ROH,JR,RAS,CDC
Bunch, Jacob N.	Cpl.	A 23rd SCVI	19	CN	02/07/63	Goldsboro, NC	DOW	(ROH=3/8/65)	ROH,CDC,PP
Bunch, W.C.	Pvt.	K 10th SCVI		CN	08/15/64	Near Atlanta, G	KIA		RAS
Bunch, Washington J.	Pvt.	H 11th SCVI	21	CN	08/25/64	Petersburg, VA	DOD		ROH,HAG,PP
Bunch, William	Pvt.	C 15th SCMil			04/17/65	Newbern, NC	DIP	Cedar Grove. C. Newbern NC	P6,PP
Bunch, William M.	Pvt.	C 11th SCVI		CN	04/17/65	New Bern, NC	DOW	Cedar Grove C. Newbern, NC	P1,P6,HAG,WAT
Bundrick, C.W.	Pvt.	H 13th SCVI			/ /		DOD		JR
Bundrick, James N.	Pvt.	H 13th SCVI			09/08/62	Winder Hos Rchmd	DOD	(Typhoid)	JR
Bundrick, John A.	Pvt.	C 20th SCVI	28	LN	07/24/63	Bty. Wagner, SC	KIA	(JR=7/20/63)	ROH,JR,CDC,KEB
Bundy, George Washington	Pvt.	F 21st SCVI		MO	03/05/65	Elmira, NY	DIP	Woodlawn N.C.#2377W Elmira	ROH,FPH,P6,P65
Bunford, L.F.	Pvt.	G 25th SCVI			02/01/65	Richmond, VA			ROH
Bunker,	Cpl.			CN	05/23/65	Richmond, VA			ROH
Bunn, D.L.	Pvt.	F 7th SCVI		FD	07/11/64	Pt. Lookout, MD	DIP		ROH
Bunson, H.	Pvt.	E 5th SCVC			05/15/64	Drury's Bluff VA	KIA		ROH
Bunton, James L.	Pvt.	I 14th SCVI	18	AE	05/12/64	Spotsylvania, VA	KIA		ROH,JR
Burbage, Alexander	Pvt.	F 3rd SCVABn	35	CN	10/15/62	James Island, SC	DOD	Magnolia Cem. Charleston	ROH,MAG
Burch, Christopher F.	Pvt.	K 3rd SCVI		SG	/ /	Richmond, VA	DOD	(Between 6/61 & 11/62)	ROH,HOS,SA2,KEB
Burckhalter, Claude.	Pvt.	A 1st SCVIG		BL	12/30/63	Ft. Delaware, DE	DIP	Finn's Pt., NJ Nat. Cem.	FPH,P47,P6,SA1
Burckhalter, J.A.	1st Cpl.	A 1st SCVIG		BL	01/31/64	Charlottesville	DOD		SA1
Burdell, Hiram W.	Pvt.	I 14th SCVI	17	AE	05/03/64	Lynchburg, VA	DOD	Lynchburg CSA Cem. #6 R3	ROH,BBW
Burdell, John W.	Pvt.	I 14th SCVI		AE	/ /				ROH
Burdell, R.	Pvt.	B 27th SCVI			05/25/63		DOD		JR
Burdett, J.R.	Pvt.	D 3rd SCVIBn		LS	/ /	Virginia		(KEB=G.W.)(1863)	ROH
Burdett, J.W.					/ /			(Rchmd effects list 12/62)	CDC
Burdett, R.C.	Pvt.	F Ham.Leg.		GE	06/01/62	7 Pines, VA	KIA	(5/31?)	ROH,JR,CDC
Burdett, W.H.	Pvt.	F Orr's Ri.			06/10/62	Howard Grove, VA		Hollywood Cem.Rchmd. L184	ROH,JR,HC
Burdett, _.J.	Pvt.	F Orr's Ri.			/ /	Howard Grove Hos	DOD		JR
Burdett,Sr. Samuel G.	Sgt.	F 24th SCVI	40	AN	05/14/63	Jackson, MS	DOW	(PP=6/30/64)	HOL,PP
Burdette, George F.	Pvt.	I 14th SCVI	18	AE	05/12/64	Spotsylvania, VA	KIA		ROH,HOL
Burdette, J. Thompson	Pvt.	I 14th SCVI		AE	05/12/64	Spotsylvania, VA	KIA		ROH,JR
Burdette, John W.	Pvt.	I 14th SCVI	24	AE	07/07/62	Richmond, VA	DOD	(JR=Typhoid 8/11/62)	ROH,JR,HOL

SOUTH CAROLINA DEAD IN CSA SERVICE 1861-1865

NAME	RANK	C REGIMENT	AGE	DS	DIED	WHERE	WHY	BURIED	SOURCES
Burdick, E.W.C.	Pvt.	G 14th SCVI		AE	04/23/65	Hart's Island NY	DIP	Cypress Hills N.C.#2591 NY	FPH,P12
Burdine, F.M.	Pvt.	A 2nd SCV		PS	07/15/64	Petersburg, VA	DOW	(Wdd 7/1/64)	ROH
Burdine, James F.	Pvt.	E 2nd SCVIRi			11/16/63	Knoxville, TN	KIA		JR
Burdine, James H.	Pvt.	D Ham.Leg.			10/28/63	Lookout Valley	KIA	(JR=Racoon Mtn., TN)	ROH,JR,CDC
Burdine, John W.	Pvt.	C 16th SCVI		GE	03/16/64	Dalton, GA	DOD		16R,PP
Burdine, Richard H.	Pvt.	I 4th SCVI			06/01/62	Washington, DC	DOW	(Wdd & POW Williamsburg)	JR,SA2
Burdine, W.C.	2nd Lt.	C 16th SCVI		AN	11/30/64	Franklin, TN	KIA	Macgavock C., Frkln Gv# 43	ROH,16R,WCT,PP
Burditt, R.A.	Pvt.	E 1st SC Res		PS	10/01/64	Charleston, SC	DOD	Magnolia Cem. Charleston	ROH,MAG,RCD
Burell, William J. Lewis	Pvt.	F 2nd SCVI	28	AE	11/03/62	Sharpsburg, MD	DOW	(JR=Co.A & 2nd Man.)	ROH,JR,SA2,H2
Burfield, William	Pvt.				10/07/62			Richmond, VA	ROH
Burger, George W.	Cpl.	F 1st SCVA		NY	09/04/62	Sullivans I., SC	EXC	Sullivans I. Soldiers Gvyd	CDC
Burgess, William	Pvt.	A 18th SCVI		UN	06/28/65	Newport News, VA		Greenlawn C. Newport News	PP,P12
Burgess, A.	Pvt.	G Orr's Ri.		AE	08/09/62	Richmond, VA		Oakwood C.#81, Row D, Div G	ROH,OWC
Burgess, Arthur F.	Pvt.	C 9th SCVIB	22	CL	12/06/61	Centreville, MD	SUI	(JR=DOD)	ROH,JR
Burgess, E.M.	Pvt.	A 15th SCVI			07/01/63	Gettysburg, PA	KIA	Magnolia Cem. Charleston	MAG,RCD
Burgess, Franklin M.	Pvt.	H 15th SCVI		UN	07/16/63	Gettysburg, PA	DOW		ROH,JR,P1,GDR
Burgess, Hiram	Pvt.	K 9th SCVIB		CL	09/04/61	Germantown, VA	DOD		ROH,JR
Burgess, J.	Pvt.	G 27th SCVI		SG	/ /		DOD		HOS,HAG
Burgess, J. Calvin	Pvt.	I 25th SCVI		CL	07/10/65	Elmira, NY	DIP	Woodlawn N.C.#2844 Elmira	FPH,P6,P65,HAG
Burgess, John	Pvt.	E 9th SCVIBn	23	HY	03/09/62	Camp Lookout, SC	DOD	(JR=26th SC 3/19)	ROH,JR,PP
Burgess, John A.J.	Pvt.	C 9th SCVIB		CL	03/16/62	Manchester, VA	DOD		ROH,JR
Burgess, Joseph	Pvt.	B 18th SCVI		UN	02/20/65	Elmira, NY	DIP	Woodlawn N.C.#2307 Elmira	FPH,P65
Burgess, McKinsey	Pvt.	E 9th SCVIBn	18	HY	03/14/62	Camp Lookout, SC	DOD		ROH,JR,PP
Burgess, R.	Pvt.	15th SCVI			/ /	(NI KEB)		Gordonsville, VA	ROH
Burgess, Robert Warren	Pvt.	I 25th SCVI	24	CL	05/30/64	Drury's Bluff VA	DOW	Hollywood Cem.Rchmd. I132	ROH,HC,HAG
Burgess, Thomas	Sgt.	F SCVA		UN	/ /			Gilead C. Jonesville UN Cy	UD3
Burgess, W.	Pvt.	F 1st SCV			06/29/62	Richmond, VA		Hollywood Cem.Rchmd. P149	HC
Burham, W.A.	Pvt.	1st SCVI			07/15/61	Richmond, VA			ROH
Burk, I.J.	Cpl.	G 27th SCVI		SG	04/11/65	Elmira, NY	DIP	Woodlawn N.C.#2675 Elmira	FPH,P6,P120,HA
Burk, Redman	Cpt.	Ham.Leg.			/ /	Shepherdstown VA	DOW	Shepherdstown C.C., VA	CV
Burke, M.P.	1st Sgt.	D 1st SCVIR			12/15/63	Charleston, SC	DOD	(POW 3/21/63 but Rtd 9/20)	SA1,P40,P42
Burke, Morgan	Pvt.	A 6th Bn Res	48	OG	06/15/64	At home	DOD		ROH
Burkett, John L.	Pvt.	D 2nd SCVI	23	SR	04/15/64	Bristol, TN	DOD		ROH,SA2,KEB
Burkett, S.B.	2nd Lt.	H 10th SCVI		WG	12/31/62	Murfreesboro, TN	KIA		RAS,HOW
Burkhalter, James	Pvt.	3rd SCVABn			04/17/65	Pt. Lookout, MD	DIP	C.C. Point Lookout, MD	FPH,P6
Burkhalter, John E.	Asst Surg	B Ham.Leg.		ED	06/29/62	Savage Stn., VA	KIA		JR,CNM
Burkhalter, W.P.	Cpl.	E 7th SCVC	21	ED	/ /	At home	DOD	(1864)	ANY,HOE,UD2
Burkhalter, John E.	Pvt.	B Ham.Leg.		ED	06/29/62	Savage's Stn. VA	KIA		ROH,CDC
Burmick, J.H.	Pvt.	2nd SCVIRi			10/19/62	Sharpsburg, MD	DOW		ROH,CDC
Burn, Charles Lide	Pvt.	G 1st SCVIG		ED	05/06/64	Spotsylvania, VA	KIA	(SA1 says POW)	ROH,SA1,HOE
Burn, Orville J.	Pvt.	A 25th SCVI	31	CN	10/31/63	Ft. Sumter, SC	KIA	Magnolia Cem. Charleston	ROH,JR,MAG,PP
Burnet, Burgh Smith	Cpt.	F 1st SCVIR	27	CN	03/28/65	High Point, NC	DOW	St. Phillips Cem., Ch'ston	ROH,SA1,PP,WAT
Burnett,	Pvt.	F 9th SCVIH			11/07/61	Port Royal, SC	KIA		ROH
Burnett, C.F.	Pvt.	I 24th SCVI			06/19/64	Petersburg, VA	KIA		JR
Burnett, Carter	Pvt.	G 7th SCVI		ED	/ /		DOD		HOE,UD2
Burnett, D.D.	Pvt.	D 20th SCVI			03/15/65	(OWC=26th SCVI)		Oakwood C.#65, Row K, Div G	ROH,OWC
Burnett, Daniel A.	Pvt.	E 27th SCVI			/ /	Mt. Jackson, VA		Mt.Jackson, VA	ROH,CDC,CV
Burnett, James	Pvt.	P.S.S.			03/15/63				ROH
Burnett, James B.	Pvt.	D P.S.S.		SG	09/20/62	Sharpsburg, MD	DOW		ROH,JR,HOS,CDC
Burnett, James S.	Pvt.	G 7th SCVI		ED	09/13/62	Maryland Hts. MD	KIA	(JR=R.S.)	ROH,JR,HOE
Burnett, Jim	Pvt.	K 7th SCV			/ /		KIA		UD2

B

SOUTH CAROLINA DEAD IN CSA SERVICE 1861-1865

NAME	RANK	C REGIMENT	AGE	DS	DIED	WHERE	WHY	BURIED	SOURCES
Burnett, John E.	Pvt.	C 22nd SCVI		SG	12/07/64	Elmira, NY	DIP	Woodlawn N.C.#1182 Elmira	ROH,FPH,P6,P65
Burnett, John M.	Pvt.	C 13th SCVI		SG	07/01/63	Gettysburg, PA	DOW		HOS,GDR
Burnett, Jordan A.	Pvt.	A 22nd SCVI		ED	11/24/62	Mt. Jackson, VA		Mt. Jackson, VA	ROH,CV,PP
Burnett, Joseph	Pvt.	D P.S.S.		SG	/ /		DOD		ROH,JR
Burnett, M.C.	Pvt.	C Orr's Ri.			07/05/62	Manchester, VA	DOD		JR
Burnett, Mortimer P.	Pvt.	G 1st SCVIG		ED	05/18/63	Richmond, VA	DOD	Oakwood C.#31,Row 33,Div D	ROH,SA1,HOE,OWC
Burnett, Perry	Pvt.	C Hol.Leg.		SG	12/14/62	Kinston, NC	KIA		HOS
Burnett, Richard	Pvt.	D P.S.S.		SG	08/30/62	2nd Manassas, VA	KIA	(JR=DOD)	ROH,JR,HOS
Burnett, W.M.	Pvt.	C 18th SCVI		UN	07/30/64	Crater, Pbg., VA	KIA		ROH,BLM
Burnett, William	Pvt.	C 18th SCVI	27	UN	08/30/62	2nd Manassas, VA	KIA		ROH
Burnett, William	Pvt.	B 15th SCVI		UN	/ /	Richmond, VA		Oakwood C.#19,Row 34,Div D	ROH,JR,OWC,KEB
Burnett, William T.	Pvt.	E 13th SCVI		SG	05/11/65	Hart's Island NY	DIP	Cypress Hills N.C.#2750 NY	FPH,P6,P12,P79
Burnham, H.J.L.	Pvt.	C 14th SCVI		LS	04/05/65	Petersburg, VA	DOW	Fair Gds. Hos. Cem. Pbg.	ROH,P6,P12
Burnham, Richard	Surgeon	16th SCVI	31	GE	04/28/63	Charleston, SC	DOD		ROH,CDC,16R
Burnham, William A.	Pvt.	B 1st SCVIG	18	NY	07/15/61		DOD		ANY
Burns, B.C.	Pvt.	B 22nd SCVI		SG	/ /				HOS
Burns, B.F.	Pvt.	E 14th SCVI		LS	11/28/62	Mt. Jackson Hos.	DOD	Oakwood C.#53,Row L,Div C	ROH,OWC,CGS,CDC
Burns, C.R.	Pvt.	L Orr's Ri.			06/27/62	Cold Harbor, VA	KIA	(Burns, D.S.?)	JR
Burns, D.S.	Pvt.	Orr's Ri.			06/29/62	Richmond, VA		Hollywood Cem.Rchmd. P148	HC
Burns, David S.	Pvt.	D P.S.S.		SG	01/19/64	Petersburg, PA	KIA	(JR=S.D.)	HOS,JR
Burns, Edward	Pvt.	B 1st SCVIR		CN	08/16/63	Bty. Wagner, SC	DOW		ROH,R45
Burns, Equilla	Pvt.	F 13th SCVI		SG	09/17/62	Sharpsburg, MD	KIA	(JR=Co.E & DOW 10/5/62)	HOS,JR
Burns, Henry	Pvt.	H 11th SCVI		CO	06/15/64	Lynchburg, VA		Lynchburg CSA Cem. #9 R2	ROH,BBW
Burns, Isaac Wilson	1st Sgt.	A 7th SCVIBn	23	KW	09/03/64	Weldon RR, VA	DOW	(Wdd 8/31/64)	ROH,HIC,HAG
Burns, James	Pvt.	K 1st SCVIG		CN	09/10/62	Frederick, MD	ACD	(JR=9/15/62)	SA1,JR
Burns, James Edward	1st Sgt.	A 12th SCVI	20	YK	11/16/62	At home	DOD	Beersheba P.C. YK, SC	JR,YMD,YEB
Burns, James P.	Pvt.	F 17th SCVI		YK	/ /	Richmond, VA	DOD	(YEB=26 @ Enlistmt)	JR,YEB
Burns, John	Pvt.	E 2nd SCVC		SG	01/15/63			Gordonsville, VA	ROH,GOR,HOS
Burns, John	Pvt.	F 1st SCV			04/02/65	Raleigh, NC		Oakwood C. Raleigh, NC	TOD
Burns, Lawrence T.	Pvt.	B 25th SCVI		CN	/ /	Charleston, SC	DOD	St.Lawrence C. Charleston	MAG,WLI
Burns, P.	Pvt.	B 27th SCVI			08/19/63	Bty. Wagner, SC	DOW		JR
Burns, Perry	Pvt.	G 16th SCVI		GE	/ /	Charleston, SC	DOD		16R
Burns, Robert	Pvt.	C 14th SCVI			11/02/61	Aiken, SC	DOD	(Typhoid)	JR
Burns, Thomas	Pvt.			GE	/ /		DOD	(1864)	ROH
Burns, Thomas C.	Pvt.	D Orr's Ri.		AN	06/29/62	Savage Stn., VA	KIA	(JR=6/27/62)	ROH,JR,CDC,CNM
Burns, W.R.	Sgt.	D Orr's Ri.		AN	06/27/62	Gaines' Mill, VA	KIA		ROH,CDC
Burns, William	Pvt.	D 7th SCVC		RD	05/04/62	Richmond, VA			ROH
Burr, Alston	Pvt.	E 21st SCVI	20	CD	05/16/64	Drury's Bluff VA	KIA		ROH,JR,HAG,UD3
Burr, Burwell	Pvt.	6th SCVC	24	CD	01/23/64	Adams Run, SC	DOD	(PP=Green Pond, SC)	ROH,PP
Burr, George	Pvt.	A 4th SCVC		CD	05/30/64	Cold Harbor, VA	KIA	(JR=Old Church, VA)	ROH,JR
Burr, William	Pvt.	A 4th SCVC		CD	05/28/64	Hawes Shop, VA	KIA		ROH
Burr, William C.	Pvt.	D 6th SCVC		CN	/ /	Lynchburg, VA		Lynchburg CSA Cem. #7 R3	BBW
Burrell, B.	Pvt.	F 1st SCVC		PS	07/01/63	Gettysburg, PA	KIA		ROH,JR
Burress, C.M.	Color Sgt.	K 7th SCVI			10/10/62		DOW	(Wdd @ Maryland Hts)	JR
Burress, Riley	Pvt.				07/01/62	Malvern Hill, VA	KIA		HOF
Burress, Thomas	Pvt.	L P.S.S.			/ /		DOD		JR
Burris, E.D.	1st Lt.	K 17th SCVI		YK	06/15/62	At home	DOD		JR,YEB
Burris, George Ross	1st Sgt.	E 5th SCVI	29	YK	05/29/64	Gordonsville, VA	DOW	Bethesda Cem. York, SC	SA3,YMD,YEB,UD3
Burris, John T.	Pvt.	E 5th SCVI	31	YK	07/10/62	7 Pines, VA	DOW	Bethesda Cem. York, SC	ROH,JR,SA3,YEB
Burris, John W.	Pvt.	I 18th SCVI	19	DN	05/20/64	Petersburg, VA	KIA		ROH,JR
Burris, Thomas E.	Pvt.	E 5th SCVI	23	YK	05/16/64	Orange C.H., VA	DOW	(Wdd @ Wilderness)	ROH,SA3,YEB,UD3

SOUTH CAROLINA DEAD IN CSA SERVICE 1861-1865

NAME	RANK	C REGIMENT	AGE	DS	DIED	WHERE	WHY	BURIED	SOURCES
Burris, W.D.	Pvt.	H 10th SCVI		CN	12/31/62	Murfreesboro, TN	KIA	(Buddin, W.P.? see RAS)	ROH,JR,CDC
Burris, William W.	Pvt.	I 18th SCVI	24	DN	05/20/64	Petersburg, VA	KIA		ROH,JR
Burriss, G.W.	Sgt. Maj.	17th SCVI			07/30/64	Crater, Pbg., VA	KIA		BLM
Burriss, R.J.	Pvt.	K 10th SCVI		CN	/ /		DOD		RAS
Burroughs, Bryant	Pvt.	I P.S.S.		PS	08/30/62	2nd Manassas, VA	KIA	(JR=J.B.)	ROH,JR
Burroughs, DeSaussure	Pvt.	A 15th SCVI		RD	10/19/64	Cedar Creek, VA	KIA	(JR=W.D.)	ROH,JR,KEB
Burroughs, Henry C.	Pvt.	C 7th SCVC		UN	05/17/65	Ft. McHenry, MD	DOW	Loudon Park Cem. Balto, MD	FPH,P4,P6,PP
Burrow, R.W.G.	Pvt.	2nd SCVIRi			09/30/62	Jackson Hos Rchd	DOW	(Wdd @ Sharpsburg)	ROH,JR,CDC
Burrows, Francis Marion	Pvt.	A 25th SCVI		CN	10/31/63	Ft. Sumter, SC	KIA	Magnolia C.(PL) Chstn., SC	ROH,JR,PP,WLI
Burrows, George W.	Pvt.	H 10th SCVI	34	WG	12/15/64	Nashville, TN	KIA		RAS,HOW,ROH
Burrows, John Thomas	Pvt.	G 15th SCVI		WG	12/22/63	Bean's Stn., TN	DOW		ROH,HOW,KEB,R4
Burrows, P.M.	Pvt.	H 26th SCVI			09/14/63		DOD		JR
Burrows, Samuel	Cpt.	(Ship?)		CN	05/04/63	City Point, VA	DIP	(Exchd POW)	ROH,CDC
Burrows, Samuel Lambeth	Pvt.	A 25th SCVI		CN	10/31/63	Ft. Sumter, SC	KIA	Magnolia C.(PL) Chstn., SC	ROH,JR,PP,DOC
Burrows, W. Riley	Sgt.	D Orr's Ri.		AN	06/29/62	Savage Stn., VA	KIA	(JR=Co.B)	ROH,JR,CDC,CNM
Burruss, Charles	Pvt.	K 7th SCVI			10/10/62	Pleasant Val. MD	DOW		JR
Burruss, W.	Pvt.				05/03/62	Richmond, VA		Hollywood Cem.Rchmd. F114	HC
Burt, J.W.	Pvt.	A 1st SCVIG			05/05/64	Wilderness, VA	DOW	Fredericksburg C.C. R8S12	ROH,JR,SA1,FBG
Burt, Thomas	Pvt.	G 7th SCVI		ED	/ /		KIA		HOE,UD2
Burt, William B.	Pvt.	H 17th SCVI		BL	08/30/64	Elmira, NY	DIP	Woodlawn N.C.#56 Elmira	FPH,P5,P65,P12
Burton, A.M.	Pvt.	C 1st SCVA						04/17/65 Pt. Lookout, MD	
Burton, Albert M.	Pvt.	G 19th SCVI		AE	03/04/63	Rome, GA	DOD		HOL
Burton, James	Pvt.	I 14th SCVI		AE	/ /	Spotsylvania, VA	KIA	(Perhaps in Wilderness)	HOL
Burton, John A.	Cpl.	G Orr's Ri.		AE	07/15/62	Gaines' Mill, VA	DOW	(JR=DOD at home 7/26)	ROH,JR
Burton, John J.	Pvt.	I 4th SCVI		AN	07/21/61	1st Manassas, VA	KIA		ROH,SA2
Burton, Oliver Hazard P.	Sgt.	A 22nd SCVI		ED	03/25/65	Petersburg, VA			PP
Burton, R.H.	Pvt.	D 7th SCVI			06/29/62	Savage's Stn. VA	KIA		ROH,JR,CDC,KEB
Burton, Thomas	Pvt.	I 1st SCVIG		LS	07/05/64	Richmond, VA	DOD		ROH,SA1
Burton, Thomas	Pvt.	I Orr's Ri.			/ /	Charlottesville	DOD		JR
Burton, Timothy	Pvt.	G 16th SCVI		GE	11/30/64	Franklin, TN	KIA		ROH,16R,PP
Burton, William	Pvt.	G 7th SCVI		ED	/ /		DOD		HOE,UD2
Burton, William	Pvt.	G 7th SCV			/ /		SOW		UD2
Burton, William M.	Pvt.	E 17th SCVI	25	YK	07/08/64	At home	DOD		ROH,DEM
Busbee, Allan	Pvt.	G 19th SCVI		AE	12/19/64	Nashville, TN	DOW	(Cumberland Gen.Hos.)	P4,P6,P12
Busbee, E.	Pvt.	C SCVIBn			/ /	High Point, NC		Oakwood Cem. High Point NC	CV,WAT,TOD
Busbee, J.M.	Pvt.	H 3rd SCVI		LN	05/06/64	Wilderness, VA	KIA	(Busby in KEB)	SA2,KEB
Busbee, William	Pvt.	H 3rd SCVI		LN	12/17/62	Fredericksburg	DOW	(Busby in KEB)	ROH,SA2,KEB
Busby, J. Swancy	Pvt.	A 3rd SCVIBn		AE	08/28/62	Staunton, VA	DOD	Thornrose C. Staunton, VA	ROH,KEB,TOD
Busby, Jacob J.	Pvt.	H 13th SCVI	16	NY	07/28/64	New Market Hts.	KIA	(ANY=Deep Bottom)	ROH,ANY
Busby, James Wesley	Pvt.	L Orr's Ri.		AN	08/09/62	Richmond, VA	DOD		ROH,JR,NCC
Busby, John Jacob	Pvt.	G 6th SCVC	52	RD	06/11/64	Trevillian Stn.	KIA	(Tfd frm F, 19th SCVI)	ROH,JR,NCC,UD3
Busby, R.T.	Pvt.	L Orr's Ri.			07/27/62	Dill Farm, VA	DOD		JR,CDC
Bush, C.A.	Pvt.	E German Art		GN	05/15/65		DIP		FLR
Bush, Govan	Pvt.	K P.S.S.		SG	06/19/64	Petersburg, VA	KIA		ROH,JR,HOS
Bush, Jesse D.	Pvt.	A 7th SCVIBn			05/16/64	Drury's Bluff VA	KIA		JR
Bush, John G.	Pvt.	K 1st SCVC	18	ED	10/07/64	Charleston, SC	DOD	Magnolia Cem. Charleston	ROH,MAG,CDC
Bush, T.	Pvt.	K P.S.S.			06/15/64	Petersburg, VA	KIA		ROH
Bush, Thomas	Pvt.	A 26th SCVI		HY	09/14/63			Magnolia Cem. Charleston	MAG,RCD
Bush, Thomas J.	Refugee				03/05/64	Hilton Head, SC	DOD	Hilton Head N.C.#288	P6
Bush, W.H.	1st Sgt.	K 5th SCVI			05/31/62	7 Pines, VA	KIA		SA3,JR
Bush, Washington W.	Pvt.	A 19th SCVI	28	ED	/ /	Atlanta, GA	DOW	(Wdd @ Missionary Ridge)	HOE,UD3

B

SOUTH CAROLINA DEAD IN CSA SERVICE 1861-1865

NAME	RANK	C REGIMENT	AGE	DS	DIED	WHERE	WHY	BURIED	SOURCES
Bush, William Burges	Pvt.	A 19th SCVI	24	ED	/ /	Chattanooga, TN	DOD		HOE,UD3
Busshart, Richard N.	Pvt.	B Orr's Ri.	35	AE	12/13/62	Fredericksburg	KIA	(JR=DOW 1/18/63)	ROH,JR
Bussy, J.A. (Co. I?)	Pvt.	G 7th SCVI		ED	04/15/62	Charlottesville	DOD	University Cem. Ch'ville	ROH,CDC,ACH,EDN
Bussy, J.E.	Pvt.	K 24th SCVI		ED	06/16/62	Secessionville	KIA		ROH,JR,HOE,PP
Bussy, J.T.	Pvt.	I 7th SCVI		ED	/ /			(KEB=Bussey, J.A.)	HOE,KEB
Bussy, John L.	Pvt.	G 14th SCVI	19	ED	06/27/62	Gaines' Mill, VA	KIA		ROH,JR,HOE,EDN
Butler, Andrew Pickens	1st Lt.	B 1st SCVIR	24	LS	12/21/63	Wilmington, NC			ROH,SA1
Butler, Arthur Pierce	3rd Cpl.	I 3rd SCVI	19	LS	09/13/62	Maryland Hts. MD	KIA	(KEB=Butler, P.M.)	ROH,JR,SA1,KEB
Butler, E.	Pvt.	G 8th SCVI		MO	02/22/65	Columbia, SC	DOD	Elmwood Cem. Columbia, SC	ROH,MP,KEB,PP
Butler, Edward J.	Cpl.	A 7th SCVI		ED	07/01/62	Malvern Hill, VA	KIA		ROH,JR,EDN,KEB
Butler, Ephriam A.	Pvt.	B 3rd SCVI	21	NY	12/13/62	Fredericksburg	KIA	Bush River B.C. Newberry	ROH,JR,NCC,ANY
Butler, G.J.	Pvt.	K 14th SCVI		ED	04/27/65	Pt. Lookout, MD	DIP	(NI FPH or HOE)	ROH
Butler, H.	Pvt.	F 1st SCVC		PS	06/09/63	Brandy Stn., VA	KIA	(JR=Co.C)	ROH,JR
Butler, Jere F.	Pvt.	H 1st SCVIG		CN	08/15/64	Richmond, VA	DOW	Richmond area	ROH,SA1
Butler, John A.	Pvt.	I 8th SCVI		MN	06/15/62	Richmond, VA	DOD	(KEB= Cpl.)	JR,HMC,KEB
Butler, M.L.C.	Pvt.	L 2nd SCVC			07/31/63	Culpepper, VA	DOD	(Scarlet Fever)	JR
Butler, O.	Pvt.	B P.S.S.		PS	06/30/62	Frayser's Farm	KIA		ROH,JR
Butler, Sampson	Pvt.	I 2nd SCVC		ED	/ /	Martinsburg, VA	DOD		HOE
Butler, Silas W.	Pvt.	I 8th SCVI		MN	11/28/61	At home	DOD	(KEB= Cpl., JR=Pneumonia)	JR,HMC,KEB
Butler, Thomas Loundes	3rd Sgt.	I 2nd SCVC	22	ED	07/03/63	Gettysburg, PA	KIA	Christ Ch. Greenville, SC	ROH,JR,BHC,GEE
Butler, Thomas Pickens	Pvt.	I 7th SCVI	50	ED	02/21/62	Richmond, VA	SUI	Butler Fam. Cem. ED Cty.	ROH,EDN,CNM
Butler, William	Pvt.	G 8th SCVI	18	MO	/ /		DOD	(1863)	HOM,UD2
Butler, William	Pvt.	F 21st SCVI		MO	/ /		DOD	(Jr. or Sr. in HAG)	HOM,HAG
Butler, William Calvin	Pvt.	E 3rd SCVI		NY	07/02/63	Gettysburg, PA	KIA	Head Springs Cem. NY	ROH,JR,GDR,SA2
Butler,Jr., Allen	2nd Lt.	B P.S.S.		PS	11/16/63	Campbell Stn. TN	KIA		ROH,JR,R48
Butner, John J.	Pvt.	E 15th SCVI	23	FD	10/13/64	Strasburg, VA	KIA		ROH,JR,KEB
Butt, John F.	Pvt.	c 27th SCVI		CN	05/09/64	Charleston, SC	DOD	(Soldiers Relief Hos.)	CDC,HAG
Butts, Charles H.	Pvt.	A 24th SCVI		CN	/ /	Marietta, GA	DOD		EJM
Buzhardt, Abner M.	Pvt.	K 14th SCVI		ED	12/09/63	Alexandria, VA	DOW	Christ Ch. Alexandria, VA	HOE,CV,P6,P12
Buzhardt, Beauford S.	Pvt.	E 3rd SCVI		NY	06/29/62	Savage Stn. VA	KIA	Buzhardt Gvyd #2 NY	ROH,JR,NCC,SA2
Buzhardt, J.S. (T.S.?)	Pvt.	K 5th SCVC		UN			DOW	(In enemy hands)	P12
Buzhardt, Milton P.	3rd Lt.	B 3rd SCVI	21	NY	07/02/63	Gettysburg, PA	KIA	Magnolia Cem. Charleston	ROH,SA1,CSL,GDR
Buzhardt, W. Jefferson	Pvt.	F 20th SCVI		NY	/ /	Sullivans I., SC	DOD	(1862)	ANY,KEB
Buzhardt, Walter F.	Pvt.	F 20th SCVI		NY	/ /		DIP		ANY,KEB
Buzhardt, Williamson L.	Pvt.	F 20th SCVI		NY	10/12/64	Charleston, SC	DOD	Mt.Bethel P.C. Newberry	ROH,NCC,ANY
Buzzard, Pressley	Pvt.	B 14th SCVI	20	ED	06/06/62	Lynchburg, VA	DOD	Lynchburg CSA Cem. #4 R5	ROH,JR,UD3,BBW
Buzzardt, Joseph T.	1st Lt.	C 19th SCVI		ED	09/20/63	Chickamauga, GA	KIA	Con. Cem. Marietta, GA	ROH,JR,HOE,UD3
Byars, Bedford	Pvt.	K 18th SCVI	20	SG	10/15/64	Petersburg, VA	KIA		ROH
Byars, Henry Jonas	Pvt.	K 18th SCVI	17	SG	02/26/62	Charleston, SC	ACD	(Lightning bolt)	ROH,JR,TCC
Byars, Robert S.	Pvt.	I 5th SCVI		SG	05/06/64	Wilderness, VA	KIA		HOS
Byers, A.L.	Pvt.	F 17th SCVI			/ /	Charleston, SC	DOD		JR
Byers, Edward	Pvt.	K 17th SCVI	35	YK	/ /		DOD		YEB
Byers, Jackson	Pvt.	F 18th SCVI			03/04/62	Charleston, SC	DOD		JR
Byers, L.N.	Sgt.	K 18th SCVI			06/04/62	Charleston, SC	DOD		JR
Byers, W.C.	Cpl.	H 6th SCVI	30	FD	01/15/62	Dranesville, VA	DOW	(? duplicate/William C.)	ROH
Byers, William C.	Cpl.	C 6th SCVI	26	UN	12/24/61	Dranesville, VA	DOW		ROH,CDC
Byles, W.M.	Pvt.	G 27th SCVI		SR	07/27/64	Pt. Lookout, MD	DIP	(NI FPH or HAG, Bryant?)	ROH
Byrd,	Pvt.	A 13th SCVI		LS	05/03/63	Chancellorsville	KIA		ROH,CDC
Byrd, A.K.	Pvt.	F 14th SCVI	23	LS	04/17/62	At home	DOD	Bethany P.C. Laurens, SC	JR,LSG
Byrd, Alexander F.	Pvt.	E 6th SCVI	27	DN	09/14/62	South Mtn., MD	DOW	Rose Hill C. Hagerstown RR	ROH,JLC,BOD,WDB
Byrd, F.P.	Pvt.	H 18th SCVI			03/01/63	Wilmington, NC	DOD		JR

SOUTH CAROLINA DEAD IN CSA SERVICE 1861-1865

NAME	RANK	C	REGIMENT	AGE	DS	DIED	WHERE	WHY	BURIED	SOURCES
Byrd, G.F.	Pvt.	M	8th SCVI			05/06/63	Richmond, VA	DOD	(Pneumonia)	JR
Byrd, G.P.	Pvt.	I	3rd SCVI			04/05/62	Fredericksburg	DOD		JR
Byrd, G.W.	Sgt.	A	2nd SC			12/15/61		DOD	(Typhoid pneumonia)	JR
Byrd, G.W.	Pvt	A	PeeDee Leg			12/25/62	Georgetown, SC	DOD	(Measles)	JR
Byrd, George F.	Pvt.	M	8th SCVI	25	DN	05/06/63	Richmond, VA	DOD	(ROH= Bird)	ROH,JR,KEB
Byrd, J.	Pvt.	D	4th SCVC		WG	07/15/63		DOD		ROH
Byrd, J.D.	Pvt.	D	19th SCVCB	44	WG	12/13/64	Georgetown, SC	DOD		PP,HOW
Byrd, J.M.	Sgt.		7th Militi			02/11/65	Charleston, SC	DOD	Magnolia Cem. Charleston	ROH,MAG
Byrd, John	Pvt.	C	2nd SCVA			05/11/64	Charleston, SC	DOD		ROH,CDC
Byrd, John F.	2nd Lt.	F	14th SCVI		LS	07/12/62		DOD	Bethany P.C. Laurens, SC	LSC,R47
Byrd, Joseph	Pvt.	C	26th SCVI		MN	06/24/63	McLellanville SC	DOD	(JR=Bird)	JR,HMC
Byrd, Matthew	Pvt.	G	21st SCVI		CD	03/28/65	Elmira, NY	DIP	Woodlawn N.C.#2508 Elmira	FPH,P2,P65,HAG
Byrd, N.A.	Pvt.	G	4th SCVC		CO	09/26/63	Green Pond, SC	DOD		PP
Byrd, Peter	Pvt.	H	11th SCVI		CN	/ /	Marietta, GA	DOW	(? 11th SCVI NI GA)	DRE
Byrd, W.B.	1st Lt.	I	3rd SCVI		LS	05/20/64	Wilderness, VA	DOW	University Cem. Ch'ville	SA2,KEB,ACH
Byrd, W.F.	Pvt.	M	8th SCVI		DN	02/12/64	Rock Island, IL	DIP	C.C.#446 Rock Island, IL	FPH,P5
Byrd, Wesley Winnfield	Pvt.	D	4th SCVI	21	AN	10/17/61	Culpepper, VA	DOD	Fairview C. Culpepper, VA	CGH,SA2
Byrdick, William R.	Pvt.	K	25th SCVI		WG	05/09/64	Swift Creek, VA	KIA	(Burdick in HOW)	CTA,HOW,HAG
Byrne, James	Pvt.	B	1st SCVA		OG	06/03/64	Charleston, SC	DOD		ROH
Bysander, H. Baxter	Pvt.	C	7th SCVIBn	35	RD	03/25/64	Charleston, SC	DOD		ROH,CDC,HAG

SOUTH CAROLINA DEAD IN CSA SERVICE 1861-1865

NAME	RANK	C	REGIMENT	AGE	DS	DIED	WHERE	WHY	BURIED	SOURCES
C____, J.		A	15th SCVI		RD	/ /			Con. Cem. Marietta, GA	CCM
Cabeen, Richard	Cpl.	F	Ham. Leg.	26	FD	11/16/63	Campbell Stn. TN	KIA		ROH,CDC
Cadden, Richard	Cpl.	C	24th SCVI		CO	/ /	At home			ROH
Cade, J.J.	Pvt.	C	9th SCVIB		CL	01/15/62	Richmond, VA	DOD		JR
Cadle,	Pvt.	E	13th SCVI		SG	/ /		DOD	(Wdd @ Chancellorsville)	HOS
Cadle, James	Pvt.	F	7th SCVI			07/02/63	Gettysburg, PA	KIA		CV
Cahil,	Pvt.	F	1st SCVA			07/07/62	Ft. Sumter, SC	ACD	(Fell from ramparts)	ROH
Cahon, James S.	Pvt.	K	21st SCVI			/ /			Oakwood C.#14 Row L Div C	ROH,OWC
Cahoon, George	Pvt.	C	6th SCVI		KW	/ /	Virginia	DOD		HIC
Cain, Aaron	Pvt.	K	22nd SCVI			07/30/64	Crater, Pbg., VA	KIA		BLM
Cain, E.E.	Pvt.	I	10th SCVI		MN	/ /	Georgia	DOD	(Perhaps WG district)	RAS,HOW,HMC
Cain, J.G.	Pvt.	I	14th SCVI		AE	/ /		DIP		HOL
Cain, J.J.	Pvt.	H	8th SCVI		MN	11/28/62	Richmond, VA	DOD	Oakwood C.#77 Row M Div C	ROH,JR,HMC,OWC
Cain, Joel	Pvt.	K	22nd SCVI			07/30/64	Crater, Pbg., VA	KIA		BLM
Cain, John	Pvt.	G	14th SCVI	22	AE	05/03/63	Chancellorsville	KIA		ROH,JR
Cain, John E.	Pvt.	K	5th SCVC	26	UN	06/11/64	Trevillian Stn.	KIA	(JR=7/12/64)	ROH,JR,CDC
Cain, K.S.	Pvt.	H	8th SCVI			06/29/61	Culpepper, VA	DOD	Fairview C. Culpepper, VA	JR,CGH,CDC,KEB
Cain, S.G.	Pvt.	C	26th SCVI		MN	03/15/65	Pt. Lookout, MD	DIP	C.C. Pt. Lookout, MD	ROH,FPH,P6,HMC
Cain, T.C.	Pvt.	C	26th SCVI		MN	/ /	Petersburg, VA			HMC
Cain, W.E.	Pvt.	C	26th SCVI		MN	07/27/64	Richmond, VA	DOD	Hollywood Cm. Rchmd. V3	HMC,HC,P12
Calby, E.W.	Pvt.	L	20th SCVI			08/29/62	Charleston, SC	DOD	Magnolia CEm. Charleston	ROH,MAG
Calder, Alexander	Sgt.	B	23rd SCVI	23	CN	07/01/64	Petersburg, VA	DOW	(Wdd 6/17/64	ROH
Calder, Daniel	Pvt.	D	26th SCVI		MO	/ /	At home	DOD		HOM,JR
Calder, Henry	Pvt.	B	24th SCVI		MO	08/17/64	Atlanta, GA	KIA		HOM
Calder, James	Pvt.	A	25th SCVI	38	CN	10/31/63	Ft. Sumter, SC	KIA	Magnolia Cem. Charleston	ROH,RR,DOC,WLI
Calder, John D.	Pvt.	F	21st SCVI		MO	09/03/63		DIP	NC Beaufort, SC #53-6382	ROH,PP,BNC
Calder, John W.	Pvt.			33	WG	/ /		DOD	(1863)	CTA,HOW
Calder, Samuel C.	Pvt.	I	2nd SCVI		CN	/ /	At home	DOD	(SA2-DIS unfit 9/3/62)	SA2,H2,KEB
Calder, William C.	Pvt.	H	23rd SCVI		MN	/ /	Virginia	DOW		HMC
Calder,Sr., William	Pvt.	D	25th SCVI		MN	/ /	James Island, SC	DOD	(HAG=Candler)	HMC,HAG
Caldwell, A.P.	Pvt.	C	27th SCVI		CN	07/04/64	Richmond, VA			ROH
Caldwell, Edward T.	Pvt.	G	P.S.S.	21	YK	/ /	Petersburg, VA	KIA		YEB
Caldwell, Hugh G. (T.?)	Sgt.	K	17th SCVI	23	YK	05/01/65	Pt. Lookout, MD	DIP	C.C. Pt. Lookout, MD	ROH,FPH,P114,P
Caldwell, J.M.	Pvt.	G	1st SCVIR		AE	05/15/61	Charleston, SC	DOD		SA1
Caldwell, J.S.	Pvt.	B	25th SCVI			/ /		DOW		ROH,WLI
Caldwell, J.W	Pvt.	A	1st SCV			09/15/64	Richmond, VA	DOW		JR
Caldwell, J.W.	Pvt.	K	15th SCVI			/ /		DOW	(JR=G.W.)	JR
Caldwell, James E.	Pvt.	D	7th SCVIBn	21	KW	05/05/62	Petersburg, VA	DOD	Blandford Church Pbg., VA	ROH,BLC,PP
Caldwell, James T.	Pvt.	G	6th SCVI	21	CR	12/20/61	Dranesville, VA	KIA		ROH,JR,HHC,R46
Caldwell, James W.	Pvt.	K	2nd SCVIRi	18		09/30/64	Ft. Harrison, VA	KIA		ROH
Caldwell, John McM.	Pvt.	B	1st SCVIG	18	NY	01/19/63	Manchester, VA	DOD	Head Springs Cem. Nwby, SC	ROH,JR,NCC,SA1
Caldwell, John W.	4th Sgt.	D	13th SCVI	21	NY	08/30/62	2nd Manassas, VA	KIA		ROH,JR,ANY,CDC
Caldwell, Joseph	Pvt.?		6th SCVI		CR	12/20/61	Dranesville, VA	KIA		UD2
Caldwell, P.M.	Pvt.	K	17th SCVI			07/30/64	Crater, Pbg., VA	KIA		BLM
Caldwell, Robert	Pvt.	F	17th SCVI	43	YK	/ /	Petersburg, VA	KIA		YEB
Caldwell, Spencer J.	Pvt.	D	13th SCVI	21	NY	09/30/64	Jones' Farm, VA	KIA		ROH,JR,ANY,CSL
Caldwell, T.E.			PSS			09/12/64	Near Petersburg	KIA		UD2
Caldwell, W.N.	Pvt.	F	17th SCVI	28	YK	03/27/65	Petersburg, VA	KIA		ROH,PP
Caldwell, William	Pvt.	F	17th SCVI		YK	08/30/62	2nd Manassas, VA	KIA		YEB
Caldwell, William Henry	3rd Lt.	F	13th SCVI	22	SG	03/15/62	Whitehall, SC	DOD	Nazareth M.C. SG Cty.	JR,GEC,GEE,R47
Calear, John	Pvt.	I	1st SCV	20	CO	12/15/62	Lynchburg, VA	DOD		ROH

C

SOUTH CAROLINA DEAD IN CSA SERVICE 1861-1865

NAME	RANK	C REGIMENT	AGE	DS	DIED	WHERE	WHY	BURIED	SOURCES
Calear, Richard	Pvt.	I 1st SCV	37	CO	10/25/63	Culpepper, VA	DOD		ROH
Calee, James F.	Pvt.	E 9th SCVIB		CN	/ /	Richmond, VA		Oakwood C.#76 Row D,Div A	ROH,OWC
Cales, C.A.	Pvt.	K 10th SCVI		CN	/ /		DOD		RAS
Calhoun, James	Pvt.	C 1st SCVIBn		CN	07/24/63	Bty. Wagner, SC	DOW	(JR=H,27th)	JR
Calhoun, John C.	Pvt.	G 23rd SCVI		MO	07/30/64	Crater, Pbg., VA	KIA		ROH,HOM,BLM
Calhoun, John William	Pvt.	A 3rd SCV			09/17/62	Sharpsburg, MD	KIA		JR
Calhoun, N.	Pvt.	F Hol.Leg.	35	AE	09/14/64	Elmira, NY	DIP	Woodlawn N.C.#264 Elmira	FPH,P5,P65,P120
Calhoun, P.L.	Lt.	H 13th SCVI		LN	07/28/64	Deep bottom, VA	KIA		ROH,JR,BOS,R47
Calhoun, T.H.	Pvt.	B 3rd SCVIBn		LS	06/10/64	Cold Harbor, VA	KIA		R45,KEB
Calhoun, Warren R.D.	Pvt.	E Orr's Ri.	20	PS	10/01/62	Winchester, VA	DOW		ROH,JR
Calhoun, William Ransom	Col.	1st SCVA		AE	09/15/62	Charleston, SC	DID	(Duel/Lt.Col. A. Rhett)	ROH,CDC
Callaghan, Daniel	Pvt.	K 1st SCVIG		CN	08/29/62	2nd Manassas VA	DOW		JR,SA1,CDC
Callahan, Andrew H.	Pvt.	I 19th SCVI	33	AE	07/14/62	Columbus, MS	DOD		ROH
Callahan, J.	Pvt.	E 25th SCVI			05/16/64	Drury's Bluff VA	KIA	(JR=5/15/64)	ROH,JR
Callahan, J. Flemming	2nd Lt.	H 16th SCVI		GE	11/30/64	Franklin, TN	KIA		ROH,16R,R47,PP
Callahan, John William	2nd Sgt.	G 22nd SCVI	28	PS	07/30/64	Crater, Pbg., VA	KIA		ROH,BLM
Callahan, Logan A.	Pvt.	G Orr's Ri.		AE	06/27/62	Gaines' Mill, VA	KIA		ROH,JR,CDC
Callahan, Sherod W.	2nd Lt.	B 7th SCVI	32	AE	07/18/63	Gettysburg, PA	DOW	(Wdd @ Gbg. 7/2/63)	ROH,JR,GDR,R46
Callahan, T.H.					/ /			(F,1st SCVIBn? Wd Bty W)	ROH
Callis, James H.	Pvt.	E Orr's Ri.	20	PS	08/31/62	2nd Manassas, VA	DOW		ROH,CDC
Calloway, J.	Pvt.	I 7th SCMil		GE	02/19/65	Charleston, SC	DOD	Magnolia Cem. Charleston	ROH,MAG
Calloway, James F.	Pvt.	H 22nd SCVI		GE	07/10/62	At home	DOD		PP
Callsken, Levi	Pvt.	D 2nd SCVIRi			09/19/62	Mt. Jackson, VA	DOW	(Wdd @ Sharpsburg, MD)	ROH,JR,CDC
Calvert, Decatur	Pvt.	K 5th SC			/ /		DOD		JR
Calvert, Eben J.	2nd Lt.	C 22nd SCVI		SG	09/14/62	South Mtn., MD	KIA		ROH,HOS,R48
Calvert, John	Citizen	Charleston		CN	05/31/65	Hart's Island NY	DIP	Cypress Hills N.C. NY	P6,P79
Calvert, John H.	Pvt.	F 2nd SCVI	24	AE	10/19/64	Cedar Creek, VA	KIA		ROH,JR,SA2
Calvert, William H.	Pvt.	B 23rd SCVI		CN	09/10/62		DOD		ROH,RCD
Calvert, William James	Pvt.	G Orr's Ri.	19	AE	09/23/62	Warrenton, VA	DOW	(Wdd @ 2nd Manassas)	ROH,JR,CDC
Calvin, A.D.	Pvt.	H 17th SCVI		BL	10/02/63	Frederick, MD	DOW	(Wdd @ Sharpsburg)	ROH,CDC,P1,P6,P12
Camack, Andrew F.	Cpl.	E 15th SCVI		FD	05/27/65	Pt. Lookout, MD	DIP	C.C. Pt. Lookout, MD	FPH,P6,P114,KEB
Camack, James B.	Pvt.	F 6th SCVI		FD	05/11/62	Petersburg, VA	DOD		PP
Camack, Samuel	Pvt.	E 15th SCVI	30	FD	07/02/63	Gettysburg, PA	KIA		ROH,JR,KEB,GDR
Camack, Samuel Y.	Cpl.	G 6th SCVI		FD	05/31/62	7 Pines, VA	KIA	Oakwood C.#1 Row B Div A	ROH,JR,OWC,WDB
Cambra, E.	Pvt.	E Ham.Leg.			/ /	Manassas, VA		Manassas Con. Cem.	CV
Cameron, Alexander W.	2nd Lt.	I 8th SCVI		MN	08/20/62	At home	DOW	(?R46=RES 8/16/62?)	JR,HMC,R46
Cameron, D.P.	Pvt.	K 1st SCVIG		BL	05/12/64	Spotsylvania, VA	KIA	(TFD from 1st SCVIH?)	ROH,JR,SA1,CDC
Cameron, George V.	Pvt.	I 26th SCVI	21	WG	10/06/64	Richmond, VA			ROH,HOW
Cameron, J.C.	Pvt.				07/24/64	Richmond, VA			ROH
Cameron, John W.	Pvt.	I 26th SCVI		WG	07/16/64	Richmond, VA	DOW	(Wdd @ Pbg, L.leg amptd)	ROH,JR,CDC,HOW
Cameron, Joseph D.	Pvt.	E 1st SCVIH		BL	02/19/63		DOD		SA1,HAG
Cameron, Robert F.	Pvt.	B 4th SCVC		CR	12/28/64	Elmira, NY	DIP	Woodlawn N.C.#1092W Elmira	FPH,P5,P65,HHC
Caminade, John C.	Pvt.	B P.S.S.		AN	/ /	Fts. Monroe, VA	DOW	(In enemy hands)	ROH
Caminade, M.	Pvt.	1st SCV			07/03/62	Fts. Monroe, VA	DOW	(Wdd @ 7 Pines)	ROH,CDC,CNM
Camminade, J.B.	Pvt.	B P.S.S.			/ /		DOD	(Dup of John C.?)	JR
Camminade, J.J.	Color Sgt.	A 24th SCVI		CN	09/20/63	Chickamauga, GA	KIA	(JR=9/30/63)	ROH,JR,CDC
Camp, J.L.	Pvt.	B P.S.S.			/ /		DOD		JR
Camp, J.P.	Cpl.	I 5th SCVI	19	SG	10/28/63	Will's Valley TN	KIA	(HOS=Chickamauga)	ROH,JR,SA3,HOS
Camp, James M.	Pvt.	I Hol.Leg.	23	SG	12/15/64	Spartanburg, SC	DOD	(HOS=DIP @ Elmira)	ROH,HOS
Camp, N. Stafford	Pvt.	A 12th SCVI	24	YK	06/27/62	Gaines' Mill, VA	KIA	(YEB=Stafford, J.)	ROH,JR,YEB,CNM
Camp, William E.	Pvt.	M P.S.S.	20	SG	04/05/65	Amelia C.H., VA	KIA	(HOS=KIA @ Appomatox)	ROH,HOS

54

SOUTH CAROLINA DEAD IN CSA SERVICE 1861-1865

NAME	RANK	C	REGIMENT	AGE	DS	DIED	WHERE	WHY	BURIED	SOURCES
Campbell, A.D.	Pvt.	D	Orr's Ri.		AN	07/07/62	Gaines' Mill, VA	DOW	(JR=H.D.)	JR,CDC
Campbell, A.F.C.	Pvt.	G	22nd SCVI		AN	07/30/64	Crater, Pbg., VA	KIA		ROH
Campbell, A.M.	Pvt.	L	Orr's Ri.		AN	08/18/62	Richmond, VA	DOD		JR
Campbell, Alexander	Pvt.	A	4th SCVC		CD	06/11/64	Trevillian Stn.	KIA	(JR=7/12/64)	ROH,JR,CDC
Campbell, Alexander	Pvt.	E	2nd SCVI		KW	07/15/61	Richmond, VA	DOD	Oakwood C.#61 Row R Div C	SA2,HIC,OWC
Campbell, Alexander	Pvt.	B	18th SCVI		UN	06/03/65	Newport News, VA		Greenlawn C. Newport News	PP
Campbell, Ancel Hudgins	Pvt.	E	4th SCVI		AN	01/13/62	Warren Sprgs, VA	DOD	(JR=P.S.S.)	SA2,JR
Campbell, Archibald E.	Pvt.	F	14th SCVI		LS	04/06/65	City Point, VA	DOW	City Point, VA #8 R6 Sec 1	P6,P12
Campbell, Austin	2nd Lt.	L	Orr's Ri.	25	AN	05/08/63	Chancellorsville	DOW	(ROH=KIA @ Sharpsburg)	ROH,JR,R45
Campbell, Charles	Cpl.	A	7th SCVIBn	23	KW	09/17/63	Columbia, SC	DOD	(JR=Charleston)	ROH,JR,CDN,HAG
Campbell, D.M.	Pvt.	B	37th VAVCB			09/15/64		DOD		37V
Campbell, D.W.	Cpl.	G	6th SCVI	22	FD	10/04/64	Richmond, VA	DOW	Presbyterian Ch. Winnsboro	PP
Campbell, Daniel	Pvt.	C	7th SCVIBn	45	RD	11/13/63	Charleston, SC	DOD	Magnolia Cem. Charleston	ROH,JR,MAG,HAG
Campbell, Daniel	Pvt.	C	26th SCVI		MN	09/25/63	Mt. Pleasant, SC	DOD		JR,HMC
Campbell, Daniel A.(L.?)	Sgt.	D	21st SCVI		CD	05/07/64	Pt. Walthal Jctn	DOW	Blandford Church Pbg., VA	ROH,BLC,PP
Campbell, Daniel P.	Pvt.	I	11th SCVI	22	CN	10/22/62	Pocotaligo, SC	KIA	Pon Pon Chapel CO Cty. SC	ROH,JR,PP,RCD
Campbell, E.	Pvt.	A	14th SCMil			05/06/65	Hart's Island NY	DIP	Cypress Hills N.C.#2729 NY	FPH,P79
Campbell, E.M.	Pvt.	G	2nd SCVIRi			09/30/64	Ft. Harrison, VA	KIA		ROH,JR
Campbell, G.F.	Pvt.	L	10th SCVI		MN	/ /		DOD		RAS,HMC
Campbell, H.	Pvt.	D	12th SCVI		RD	02/25/63	Lynchburg, VA		Lynchburg CSA Cem.#5 R1	BBW,JR
Campbell, H.W.	Pvt.	I	17th SCVI		LR	07/30/64	Crater, Pbg., VA	KIA		ROH,JR,BLM,LAN
Campbell, Hugh W.	1st Lt.	I	12th SCVI		YK	06/15/64	Petersburg, VA	KIA	(?R47=RET 5/17/62)	ROH,DEM,LAN,R4
Campbell, Isaac A.	Pvt.	H	18th SCVI	20	YK	/ /	Mt. Pleasant, SC	DOD		YEB
Campbell, J.	Pvt.					04/13/62	Charleston, SC		Magnolia Cem. Charleston	ROH,MAG
Campbell, J.A.	Pvt.	B	2nd SCVA		AN	/ /	North Carolina	DOD		ROH
Campbell, J.C.	Pvt.	K	1st SCEng			07/10/64	Richmond, VA	DOD	Hollywood Cem.Rchmd. U557	HC,P12
Campbell, J.M.	Pvt.	G	27th SCVI		PS	07/01/64	Petersburg, VA	DOW	(Wdd 6/27/64)	ROH,HAG
Campbell, J.M.	Pvt.	D	6th SCVC			04/02/65	Pt. Lookout, MD	DIP	C.C. Pt. Lookout, MD	ROH,FPH,P6,P11
Campbell, J.M.	Pvt.	A	1st SCVC			/ /	Lynchburg, VA		Lynchburg CSA Cem. #9 R5	BBW
Campbell, J.P.	Pvt.	I	22nd SCVI		OG	08/12/64	Richmond, VA			ROH
Campbell, J.W.	Pvt.	F	2nd SCVI		SR	/ /	Lynchburg, VA		Lynchburg CSA Cem. #2 R3	BBW
Campbell, James	Pvt.	F	3rd SCVIBn	25	RD	06/15/63	Lynchburg, VA	DOD	Lynchburg CSA Cem. #3 R5	ROH,BBW,KEB
Campbell, James H.	Pvt.	H	21st SCVI		DN	01/05/65	Ft. Fisher, NC	KIA		PP
Campbell, James J.	Pvt.	H	Orr's Ri.		MN	07/01/64	Petersburg, VA	DOW	(Wdd 6/27/64)	ROH,HMC,CDC
Campbell, James L.	Pvt.	K	22nd SCVI		PS	07/30/64	Crater, Pbg., VA	KIA		BLM
Campbell, James M.	Pvt.	F	24th SCVI		AN	10/19/63	Chattanooga, TN	DOD		HOL
Campbell, James P.	Pvt.	I	14th SCVI	41	AE	07/12/64	Richmond, VA	DOD	Hollywood Cem.Rchmd. V347	ROH,HC,HOL
Campbell, James R.	1st Sgt.	D	13th SCVI	18	NY	06/12/64	Richmond, VA	DOW	Hollywood Cem.Rchmd. U41	ROH,HC,ANY,P12
Campbell, Jesse T.	Pvt.	I	14th SCVI	20	SG	05/04/65	At home	DOD	(Wdd & DIS @ Chance'ville)	ROH,HOL
Campbell, John	Cpl.	A	7th SCVIBn	25	KW	07/21/62	Adams Run, SC	DOD		ROH,JR,CDN,PP
Campbell, John	Pvt.	A	6th SCVI		CR	09/15/61	Richmond, VA	DOD		CB,HHC
Campbell, John A.	Pvt.	B	8th SCVI		CD	02/10/62	Culpepper, VA	DOD	Fairview C. Culpepper, VA	CGH
Campbell, John C.	Pvt.	I	1st SCVIH	17	MN	12/07/64	Florence, SC	MUR	(EXC at home mistaken DES)	ROH,HMC,SA1
Campbell, Leonard	Pvt.	B	18th SCVI		UN	03/28/65	Elmira, NY	DIP	Woodlawn N.C.#2485 Elmira	FPH,P6,P65,P12
Campbell, Malcom H.	Pvt.	A	4th SCVC		CD	02/04/62		DOD		ROH
Campbell, Martin	Pvt.	B	3rd SCVC	26	CO	06/27/62	At home	DOD		ROH
Campbell, Michael C.	Pvt.	L	21st SCVI	29	MN	09/06/63	Morris Island SC	KIA		ROH,JR,HMC,HAG
Campbell, O.B.	Pvt.	F	24th SCVI	19	AN	05/21/64		DOD		HOL
Campbell, Patillo	Pvt.	I	3rd SCVI		LS	09/20/63	Chickamauga, GA	DOW		SA2,CDC,KEB
Campbell, R.J.	Pvt.	C	4th SCVABn			04/19/65	Hart's Island NY	DIP	Cypress Hills N.C.#2571 NY	FPH,P6,P79
Campbell, Robert	Pvt.	H	1st SCVIR			05/18/65	Hart's Island NY	DIP	Cypress Hills N.C.#2814 NY	FPH,SA1,P6,P79

C

SOUTH CAROLINA DEAD IN CSA SERVICE 1861-1865

NAME	RANK	C REGIMENT	AGE	DS	DIED	WHERE	WHY	BURIED	SOURCES
Campbell, S.M.	Pvt.	L 2nd SCVIRi			/ /	Richmond, VA		Oakwood C.#81 Row G Div B	ROH,OWC
Campbell, Steven A.	Pvt.	K 2nd SCVA		ED	/ /		DOD		HOE
Campbell, W.	Pvt.	E 4th SCVI		PS	/ /	Charlottesville	DOD	Univ. Cem. Charlottesville	ACH,SA2
Campbell, W. Scott	Pvt.	A 16th SCVI		GE	01/05/64	Rock Island, IL	DIP	C.C.#124 Rock Island, IL	FPH,P5,16R
Campbell, W.J.	Pvt.	K 1st SCV			07/08/62	Richmond, VA		Hollywood Cem.Rchmd. M70	ROH,HC
Campbell, W.J.	Pvt.	I 14th SCVI	25	AE	06/30/62	Frayser's Farm	KIA		ROH,JR,HOL
Campbell, W.O.	Pvt.	F 3rd SCVI			09/17/62	Sharpsburg, MD	KIA	(NI SA2,KEB. 3rd Bn?)	ROH,CDC
Campbell, W.T.	Pvt.	B 22nd SCVI		SG	09/04/62	Richmond, VA	DOD	Hollywood Cem.Rchmd. A28	ROH,HC,CDC
Campbell, William J.	3rd Lt.	B 6th SCVI	36	YK	05/05/62	Williamsburg, VA	KIA		ROH,WDB,R46,YEB
Campbell,Jr., Thomas	Pvt.	C 7th SCVIBn	35	RD	10/24/63	Charleston, SC	DOD		ROH,HAG
Campton, T.H.	Pvt.	F 14th SCVI		LS	07/17/62	Richmond, VA		Hollywood Cem.Rchmd. Q154	HC
Camy, H.L.		D 3rd SCVI			/ /			Con. Cem. Marietta, GA	CCM
Canaday, J.S.	Pvt.	C 24th SCVI		CO	02/22/62				ROH
Canady, J.W.	Pvt.	I 3rd SCVI		LS	07/02/63	Gettysburg, PA	KIA		SA2,ANY,GDR
Canady, John	Pvt.	E 6th SCVI		DN	08/30/62	2nd Manassas, VA	KIA		ROH,JR,JLC,WDB
Canady, S.S.	Pvt.	G 4th SCVC		CD	05/29/64	Hawes Shop, VA	KIA		ROH,SSO
Canady, Wesley	Pvt.	C 7th SCVC		LS	/ /	Gettysburg, PA	KIA	(NI NY Monument list)	ANY
Canady, William	Pvt.	B 15th SCVI		UN	10/27/64	Burgess Mills VA	KIA		ROH,JR
Candle, Watty	Pvt.	1st SCVA		GE	06/01/63	Charleston, SC	DOD	Magnolia Cem. Charleston	ROH,MAG
Candy, Samuel	Pvt.	L 8th SCVI		MN	05/15/63	At home	DOD	(JR=Co.I, Pneumonia)	HMC,JR,KEB
Cannaday William B.	Pvt.	G 4th SCVC	35	CO	11/22/64	Petersburg, VA	DOW	Blandford Church Pbg., VA	ROH,BLC,PP
Cannaday, J.M.	Pvt.	I 2nd SCVI			07/23/63	Gettysburg, VA	DOW	(Amputation Dup of J.W.?)	ROH,JR
Cannaday, John	Pvt.	D 6th SCVI		CR	05/23/62	Lynchburg, VA	DOD	Lynchburg CSA Cem. #6 R5	ROH,CDC,BBW
Cannady, Austin	Pvt.	I 1st SCVIG		LS	06/25/64	Petersburg, VA	KIA		SA1
Cannady, Charles T.	Pvt.	H 11th SCVI		CO	07/05/64	Petersburg, VA	KIA	(JR=6/18/64)	ROH,JR,HAG
Cannady, Henry C.	Pvt.	H 11th SCVI		CO	02/28/62	Hardeeville, SC	DOD		ROH,JR,HAG
Cannady, James	4th Sgt.	F 1st SCVIG		HY	07/02/63	Gettysburg, PA	DOW	(Wdd 7/1/63)	GDR,SA1,PDL,CDC
Cannady, James Preston	Pvt.	H 11th SCVI	24	CO	05/24/64	Drury's Bluff VA	DOW	Blandford Church Pbg., VA	ROH,HAG,PP,BLC
Cannady, Joseph	Pvt.	F 1st SCVIG		HY	07/28/64	Riddle's Shop VA	KIA	(AKA New Market Heights)	JR,SA1,PDL,CDC
Canniel, E.	Pvt.	A 14th SCMil			05/06/65	Hart's Island NY	DIP	Cypress Hills N.C. NY	P6
Cannon, A.C.	Pvt.	A 2nd SCVI			09/13/62	Maryland Hts. MD	KIA		ROH,JR
Cannon, C.B.	Pvt.	A 3rd SCVIBn			05/08/64	Spotsylvania, VA	KIA	Spotsylvania C.H., VA	ROH,JR,SCH,KEB
Cannon, D.F.	Pvt.	A 10th SCVI		GN	/ /		DOD		GRG,RAS
Cannon, E.	Pvt.	A 2nd SCVC		DN	/ /		KIA	(Boykin Rangers)	JLC
Cannon, George D.	Pvt.	F 20th SCVI		NY	/ /	Strasburg, VA	KIA	(KEB=George W.)	ANY,KEB
Cannon, H.H.	Pvt.	I 3rd SCVI		LS	09/25/62	Pleasant Valley	DOW	(Wdd Md. Hts. 9/13/62)	JR,SA2,KEB
Cannon, Henry Ulmer	1st Sgt.	A 8th SCVCBn	22	CO	06/15/62	At home	DOD	(Marion Men of Combahee)	ROH,CNM
Cannon, Isaac P.	Pvt.	B 3rd SCVI		NY	09/04/61	Richmond, VA	DOD	Bush River B.C. Newberry	ROH,JR,NCC,SA2
Cannon, J.C.	Pvt.				07/24/64	Richmond, VA		Hollywood Cem.Rchmd. V660	HC
Cannon, J.M.	Pvt.	C 10th SCVI		HY	/ /	At home	DOD		RAS
Cannon, J.R.	Pvt.	F 3rd SCVI		LS	12/13/62	Fredericksburg	KIA	(KEB=J.L.)	ROH,JR,KEB,SA2
Cannon, John Hunter	2nd Lt.	G 22nd SCVI	28	AN	05/24/62	Charleston, SC	DOD		ROH,R48
Cannon, L.A.	Pvt.	F 3rd SCVI		LS	10/22/62	Winchester, VA	DOD	Stonewall C. Winchester VA	ROH,JR,WIN,SA2
Cannon, M.	Pvt.	A 2nd SCVI		CD	09/17/62	Sharpsburg, MD	KIA		ROH,SA2,KEB
Cannon, R.J.	Pvt.	K 25th SCVI		WG	03/09/65	Elmira, NY	DIP	Woodlawn N.C.#1872 Elmira	FPH,P6,P65,HAG
Cannon, W.F.	Pvt.	I 9th SCVI			10/12/61	Meadville, VA	DOD		JR
Cannon, W.H.	Pvt.	D 16th SCVI		GE	03/23/62	Adams Run, SCC	DOD		16R,PP
Cannon, Warren R.	Pvt.	E Orr's Ri.	25	PS	06/27/62	Gaines' Mill, VA	KIA	(JR=12/15/62)	ROH,JR,CDC
Canter, R.	Pvt.	L Orr's Ri.			06/27/62	Gaines' Mill, VA	KIA		ROH,CDC
Cantey, W.J.R.	Cpt.	I 23rd SCVI		CL	04/01/65	Five Forks, VA	KIA		ACL
Cantrell, C.M.	Pvt.	E 13th SCVI		SG	06/28/64	Richmond, VA		Hollywood Cem.Rchmd. U14	ROH,HC,P12

SOUTH CAROLINA DEAD IN CSA SERVICE 1861-1865

NAME	RANK	C REGIMENT	AGE	DS	DIED	WHERE	WHY	BURIED	SOURCES
Cantrell, E.	Pvt.	K 27th SCVI		SG	05/16/64	Drury's Bluff VA	DOW		ROH,HAG
Cantrell, J.D.	Pvt.	K 5th SCVI		SG	03/24/65	Salisbury, NC	DOD	Prob Old Lutheran C. there	PP,SA3
Cantrell, Ladson	Pvt.	H 16th SCVI		GE	/ /		DOD		16R
Cantrell, W.	Pvt.	H 5th SCV			/ /		DOD		JR
Cantrell, William	Pvt.	K Hol.Leg.	26	SG	07/26/62	Adams Run, SC	DOD	(JR=Lt., Typhoid)	ROH,JR,PP
Cantrell, William	Pvt.	G 12th SCVI		PS	/ /		DOD	(1862 Hol.Leg.?)	JR
Cantwell, S.	Pvt.	G 1st SCVC			11/04/62			Stonewall C. Winchester VA	ROH,WIN
Canty, Samuel	Pvt.	D 16th SCVI			/ /	(?16th NI VA)		Elmwood C. Shepherdstown,	ROH,CV,BOD
Canty, William	Pvt.	H 12th SCVI	23	YK	01/15/65		DOW	(Indian Wdd 5/5/64)	YEB
Cape, W.	Pvt.	C 2nd SCV			/ /	Lynchburg, VA		Lynchburg CSA Cem. #1 R4	BBW
Capehart, H.R.	Pvt.	B 2nd SCVIRi		PS	09/30/62	Richmond, VA	DOD	Hollywood Cem.Rchmd. S191	ROH,HC
Capehart, W.F.	Pvt.	A Orr's Ri.		PS	05/23/62	Virginia	DOD		JR
Capehart, J.H.	Pvt.	B 2nd SCVIRi		PS	/ /				ROH
Capell, Joseph B.	Pvt.	D 15th SCVI			/ /		KIA	(KEB=Copell)	JR,KEB
Capell, Sydney B.	Pvt.	D 15th SCVI		KW	10/13/61	Columbia, SC	DOD	(KEB=Copell)	ROH,JR,HIC,CDN
Capell, Hartwell	Pvt.	D 7th SCVIBn	38	KW	07/11/63	Bty Wagner, SC	KIA		ROH,JR,HIC,HAG
Capers, John S.	Lt.	H 7th SCVC	23	KW	04/05/65	Amelia C.H., VA	KIA	(acting Adjutant)	ROH,HIC,CDN
Capers, Theodotus LeG.	Pvt.	K P.S.S.	22	SG	08/30/62	2nd Manassas, VA	KIA	Manassas Cem., VA	ROH,JR,HOS,CV
Capps, J.M.	Pvt.	G 12th SCVI		PS	06/07/62	Richmond, SC	DOD	Hollywood Cem.Rchmd. P158	ROH,JR,HC
Caps, J.L.	Pvt.	B 1st SCRes		GE	02/11/65	Columbia, SC	DOD		ROH,PP
Caraway, W.	Pvt.	H 10th SCVI		WG	/ /	Gainesville, AL	DOD	Gainesville, AL	RAS,TOD
Carbright, Alva	Pvt.	K 26th SCVI	17	HY	05/10/64	Clay's Farm, VA	KIA		ROH
Carden, C.J.	Sgt.	B P.S.S.		PS	10/05/64	Richmond, VA	DOW	(Wdd at Ft. Harrison)	ROH
Cardwell, A.P.	Pvt.	C 26th SCVI			07/03/64	Richmond, VA		Hollywood Cem.Rchmd. U286	HC
Carley, R.W.	Pvt.	2nd SCMil		CN	02/10/65	Charleston, SC	DOD	Magnolia Cem. Charleston	ROH,MAG
Carlisle, John H.	Pvt.	E 15th SCVI	22	FD	08/11/62	Columbia, SC	DOD		ROH,KEB,PP
Carlisle, L.A.	Pvt.	D Orr's Ri.		AN	12/13/62	Fredericksburg	KIA		JR
Carlisle, R.E.	Pvt.	A 2nd SCVIRi			08/29/62	Richmond, VA	DOD	Hollywood Cem.Rchmd. S86	ROH,HC
Carlisle, Robert Harris	2nd Lt.	D 7th SCVI		AE	09/22/62	Mt. Jackson, VA	DOW	(Wdd @ Sharpsburg)	ROH,JR,KEB,R46
Carlson, F.	Pvt.	A German Art			02/17/64	Crew on "Hunley"	KIA	Bethany C., Charleston, SC	MAG,RCD
Carlton, Elias	Pvt.	E Hol.Leg.		SG	02/21/65	Richmond, VA	DOD	Hollywood Cem.Rchmd. W78	HC,HOS
Carlton, Elijah	Pvt.	E Hol.Leg.	22	SG	12/10/63	At home	DOD		ROH,HOS
Carlton, J.M.	Pvt.	D 16th SCVI		GE	/ /	Lovejoy, GA	KIA		16R
Carlton, John	Pvt.	F Hol.Leg.	20	SG	08/30/64	2nd Manassas, VA	KIA		ROH,JR,HOS
Carlton, Thomas	Pvt.	H 1st SCVA			03/03/65	Columbia, SC	DOD		ROH,PP
Carmichael, Alexander	1st Cpl.	L 8th SCVI		MN	09/13/62	Maryland Hts. MD	KIA		JR,HMC,KEB
Carmichael, Alexander J.	Pvt.	I 1st SCVIH		MN	02/19/63	White Sulpher Ss	DOW	(Wdd 8/30 @ 2nd Manassas)	ROH,SA1,HMC,PP
Carmichael, D.	2nd Lt.	E 23rd SCVI		MN	/ /	(Prob at home)		(? RES 11/25/64 per R48)	HMC,R48
Carmichael, D.M.	Pvt.	D 10th SCVI		MN	12/31/62	Murfreesboro, TN	KIA		ROH,RAS,HMC,CD
Carmichael, Daniel A.	Cpl.	I 1st SCVIH		MN	08/28/62	Charleston, SC	DOD		HMC,HAG,JRH
Carmichael, Evander	Pvt.	L 21st SCVI	21	MN	06/16/64	Petersburg, VA	KIA	(HMC=Darbytown Rd.)	ROH,JR,HMC,HAG
Carmichael, Franklin	Pvt.	L 21st SCVI	30	MN	06/16/64	Petersburg, VA	KIA	(HMC=Darbytown Rd.)	ROH,JR,HMC,HAG
Carmichael, J.L.	Pvt.	L 10th SCVI		MN	11/30/64	Franklin, TN	DOW		RAS,HMC
Carmichael, John	Pvt.	C 26th SCVI		MN	/ /	Petersburg, VA			HMC
Carmichael, Joseph B.	Pvt.	L 21st SCVI	30	MN	06/05/64	Cold Harbor, VA	DOW	Hollywood Cem.Rchmd. U400	ROH,HC,HAG
Carmichael, Judson D.	Pvt.	L 21st SCVI	25	MN	03/30/65	Elmira, NY	DIP	Woodlawn N.C.#2592 Elmira	ROH,FPH,P6,P65
Carnes, Jacob G.	Pvt.	E 1st SCVIR	23	CD	07/29/62	Adams Run, SC	DOD		ROH,SA1
Carnes, Jonas A.	Pvt.	E 22nd SCVI		LR	04/17/65	Elmira, NY	DIP	Woodlawn N.C.#2592 Elmira	FPH,LAN,P65,P1
Carnes, Nathan	Pvt.	E 1st SCVIR	21	CD	10/11/63	Charleston, SC	DOW	Magnolia Cem. Charleston	ROH,MAG,SA1
Carnes, W. Harper	Pvt.	A 12th SCVI	22	YK	01/05/64	Orange C.H., VA	DOD	(YEB=Cairmes)	JR,YEB
Carnes, W.T.	Pvt.	E 14th SCVI			09/15/62	Richmond, VA	DOD		JR

C

SOUTH CAROLINA DEAD IN CSA SERVICE 1861-1865

NAME	RANK	C REGIMENT	AGE	DS	DIED	WHERE	WHY	BURIED	SOURCES
Carnes, William	Pvt.	B 26th SCVI	37	CD	10/27/63	Mt. Pleasant, SC	DOD		ROH,JR
Carnes, William	Musician	25th SCVI		OG	08/20/64	Petersburg, VA			ROH
Carney, C.	Pvt	SCV			08/21/64	City Point, VA		City Pt. N.C. Hopewell, VA	PP
Carney, E.	Pvt.	B 22nd SCVI		SG	09/21/64	Richmond, VA			ROH
Carney, John	Pvt.	C 16th SCVI		GE	08/19/64	Atlanta, GA	KIA		ROH,16R
Carnighan, John				CN	/ /			Magnolia C.(PL) Charleston	MAG
Carol, James	Pvt.	K 22nd SCVI		PS	07/09/64	Summerville, SC	DOD		ROH
Carol, R.D.	Pvt.	G 18th SCVI			08/07/63	(RR in Alabama)	ACD		ROH
Caroll, John	Pvt.	D 7th SCVIBn	30	RD	/ /	Richmond, VA	DOD	(HIC says Pbg)	ROH,HIC,HAG
Caroll, Vincent	Pvt.	C 7th SCVI	21	AE	10/01/62	Gordonsville, VA	DOD	(JR=Orange C.H. 3/62)	ROH,JR,KEB
Caroll, W.J.	Pvt.	K 22nd SCVI		PS	07/08/64	Pickens, SC	DOD		ROH
Caron, E.P.	Pvt.	Hol.Leg.			02/23/65	Richmond, VA			ROH
Carothers, James R.	Pvt.	H 12th SCVI	31	2K	10/29/62	Winchester, VA	DOD	(YEB=H, 18th SCVI)	ROH,YEB
Carothers, W.H.	Pvt.	E 17th SCVI	26	YK	10/20/63	At home	DOD		ROH,CWC,YEB
Carpenter, J.J.	Pvt.	I 21st SCVI	39	CL	11/04/64	Petersburg, VA	DOW	Blandford Church Pbg., VA	ROH,BLC,PP
Carpenter, J.Q.	Cpt.	M P.S.S.	35	SG	05/31/62	7 Pines, VA	KIA		ROH,JR,HOS,CMH5
Carpenter, J.S.	Pvt.	I 23rd SCVI		CL	03/03/64	Petersburg, VA			ROH,HCL
Carpenter, John B.	Color Sgt.	I 23rd SCVI		CL	08/29/62	2nd Manassas, VA	KIA	(JR=28th SCVI & 8/30/62)	JR,CDC,HCL
Carpenter, John T.	Pvt.	F Orr's Ri.		PS	/ /		DOD	(Brain Fever 1863)	JR,CDC
Carpenter, Thomas J.	Pvt.		23	PS	09/30/63		DOD		ROH
Carpenter, W.	Pvt.				02/16/65			Magnolia Cem. Charleston	MAG
Carpenter, Wickliffe	Pvt.	F 4th SCV			/ /				ROH,CDC
Carr, G.H.	Pvt.	H 6th SCVI		FD	10/31/62	Winchester, VA	DOD	Stonewall C. Winchester VA	ROH,WIN,P12
Carr, J.L.	Pvt.	I 2nd SCVC			12/29/64	Wilmington, NC	KIA		ROH
Carr, J.M.	Pvt.	I 2nd SCVA	23	OG	08/13/62		DOD		ROH
Carr, John		CSN			04/29/65	Richmond, VA			ROH
Carr, John J.	Pvt.	D Ham.Leg.			05/31/62	7 Pines, VA	KIA		ROH,JR,GRS,CDC
Carr, John W.	1st Sgt.				05/15/63	Charleston, SC	DOD		ROH
Carr, R.D.	Sgt.	K 10th SCVI		CN	10/20/62	Cumberland Gap	DOD		RAS,PP
Carr, W.E.	Pvt.	C 26th SCVI			07/29/64	Richmond, VA			ROH
Carraway, James Henry	Pvt.	K 23rd SCVI		SR	11/24/64	Elmira, NY	DIP	Woodlawn N.C.#914 Elmira	ROH,FPH,P6,UD3
Carraway, Joshua	Pvt.	C 6th SCVIBn			08/15/62		DOD	(Typhoid)	JR
Carraway, Washington G.	Pvt.	D 9th SCVIB		WG	08/29/61	Germantown, VA	DOD		ROH,JR,HOW
Carraway, William J.	Pvt.	D 1st SCV			08/29/62		DOD		JR
Carrer, William A.	Musician	F 25th SCVI	49	OG	08/20/64	Petersburg, VA			PP
Carribo, Henry	Pvt.	G 23rd SCVI		MO	/ /	Petersburg, VA	KIA		HOM
Carroll, A.	Pvt.	P.S.S.			07/05/62	Richmond, VA		Hollywood Cem.Rchmd. M284	ROH,HC
Carroll, Anderson	Pvt.	L 2nd SCVIRi	16	AN	06/30/62	Frayser's Farm	KIA		ROH
Carroll, Henry		2nd SCVA			/ /	Averysboro, NC	KIA		UD1
Carroll, Isaac	Pvt.	A 19th SCVI	24	ED	/ /	Charleston, SC	DOD		HOE,UD3
Carroll, J.C.	Lt.	B 5th SCVI			09/15/62	Sharpsburg, MD	KIA	(Very Suspect record)	JR
Carroll, J.J.	Pvt.	K 3rd SCVABn			02/01/64	Charleston, SC	DOD	(K,1st SCVIG ?)	ROH
Carroll, Jacob	Pvt.	2nd SCVA			/ /	Aversboro, NC	KIA		UD1
Carroll, James	Pvt.	H 27th SCVI		CN	06/24/64	Petersburg, VA	KIA		ROH,CDC,HAG
Carroll, James	Pvt.	G 1st SCV			/ /	Lynchburg, VA		CSA Cem. Lynchburg #10 R4	BBW
Carroll, James	Pvt.	A P.S.S.			08/21/64		DOW		JR
Carroll, Matthew	Pvt.	F 1st SCVIG		HY	06/12/62	Richmond, VA	DOD		JR,SA1,PDL
Carroll, R.	Pvt.	D 2nd SCVIRi			/ /			Oakwood C.#29 Row O Div F	ROH,OWC
Carroll, R.J.	Pvt.	B Ham.Leg.			/ /			Oakwood C.#9 Row 39 Div D	ROH,OWC
Carroll, Robert D.	Pvt.	G 18th SCVI	24	YK	08/07/62	Montgomery, AL	ACD	(Railroad ACD)	JR,YEB
Carroll, William B.	Cpl.	A 24th SCVI	18		10/16/64	Shipp's Gap, GA	KIA		EJM

SOUTH CAROLINA DEAD IN CSA SERVICE 1861-1865

NAME	RANK	C REGIMENT	AGE	DS	DIED	WHERE	WHY	BURIED	SOURCES
Carson, Edward	Pvt.	B 12th SCVI	25	YK	/ /		KIA	(Dup of Edward B. 17th?)	YEB
Carson, Edward B.	Pvt.	F 17th SCVI		YK	02/15/62	Winchester, VA	DOD	Stonewall C. Winchester VA	ROH,JR,WIN
Carson, F.S.	4th Sgt.	G 5th SCVI		YK	12/21/62	Lynchburg, VA	DOD	Lynchburg CSA Cem. #5 R2	JR,SA3,BBW
Carson, H.	Pvt.	D 16th SCVI		GE	11/30/64	Franklin, TN	KIA	Macgavock C. Fr'kln GV#22	16R,WCT
Carson, John M.	Pvt.	B 7th SCVC		CN	06/23/64	Richmond, VA	DOW	(Wdd @ Riddell's Shop, VA)	ROH,JES
Carson, James P.	Pvt.	B 20th SCVI	30	OG	08/13/64	Strasburg, VA	KIA	(JR=Co.D)	ROH,JR,CDC
Carson, Jehu	Pvt.	I 7th SCVI		FD	10/08/61	Charlottesville	DOD		EDN
Carson, John L.	Pvt.	I 1st SCVA			02/21/65	Elmira, NY	DIP	Woodlawn N.C. Elmira #2238	FPH,P1,P6,P65
Carson, John W.	Pvt.	D 3rd SCVI		SG	10/11/64	At home	DOD	(Home wdd around 2/29/64)	SA2,KEB
Carson, Joseph M.	Pvt.	B 2nd SCVI		GE	07/29/61	Charlottesville	DOW	(Wd.1st Man., ROH=John M.)	ROH,KEB,SA2
Carson, N.C.	Pvt.	D Ham. Leg.	23	PS	09/15/64	Richmond, VA	DOW	(GRS=7/29 Fussel's Mills)	ROH,GRS
Carson, Robert J.	1st Sgt.	F 25th SCVI	32	OG	09/06/63	Bty. Wagner, SC	KIA	(JR=9/4/63)	ROH,JR,HAG,R48
Carson, Roland	Pvt.	B 14th SCMil			05/09/65	Newbern, NC	DIP	Cedar Grove C. Newbern NC	WAT,P6,PP
Carson, W.	Pvt.	D 16th SCVI		GE	11/30/64	Franklin, TN	KIA	Macgavock C. Fr'kln GV#23	16R
Carson, W.C.	Pvt.	G 12th SCVI		PS	08/20/64	Ft. Delaware, DE	DIP	Finn's Point, NJ N.C.	ROH,FPH,P6,P41
Carson, W.D.	Pvt.	F 14th SCVI		SG	09/30/64	Richmond, VA	KIA		JR
Carson, William	Pvt.	H Ham.Leg.	36	OG	03/26/63	Petersburg, VA	DOW	Blandford Church Pbg., VA	ROH,BLC,PP
Carter, A.J.	Pvt.	C 12th SCVI		FD	08/09/64	Richmond, VA	DOD	Hollywood Cem.Rchmd. V236	ROH,JR,HC,HFC
Carter, Adam	Pvt.	E 24th SCVI	38	BL	06/02/65	Camp Chase, OH	DIP	Con.Cem.#2013 Columbus, OH	ROH,FPH,CDC,P6
Carter, Asbury B.	Pvt.	G 15th SCVI	23	WG	06/15/62	Lynchburg, VA	DOD	Lynchburg CSA Cem. #7 R4	JR,HOW,BBW,KEB
Carter, B.	Pvt.	A 7th SCVC		WG	08/12/63	Georgetown, SC	DOD		R43,PP
Carter, B.A.	Pvt.	I 6th SCVI		CR	/ /		KIA		CB,HHC
Carter, D.W.	Cpt.	G 26th SCVI		DN	08/19/64	Petersburg, VA	KIA		R48
Carter, G.W.	Pvt.	H 17th SCVI			08/30/62	2nd Manassas, VA	KIA		JR
Carter, Garrett D.	Pvt.	K 25th SCVI	41	WG	09/30/64	Petersburg, VA			PP
Carter, George W.	Pvt.	G 15th SCVI	52	WG	08/18/62	Richmond, VA	DOD	Hollywood Cem.Rchmd. M249	ROH,JR,HC,HOW
Carter, Henry	Pvt.	D 25th SCVI		MN	08/15/64	Swift Creek, VA	DOW	(Wdd 8/3/64)	ROH,HMC,HAG
Carter, Isaac	Pvt.	E 24th SCVI	37	CO	02/13/64	Atlanta, GA	DOD		ROH
Carter, J.S.	5th Sgt.	E 5th SCVI			06/29/62	Savage Stn., VA	KIA	(JR=Gaines' Mill 6/27/62)	JR,SA3
Carter, J.W.	Pvt.	D 18th SCVI		AN	08/30/64	2nd Manassas, VA	KIA	Manassas Cem., VA	ROH,JR,CDC
Carter, J.W.	Pvt.	H 10th SCVI	25	WG	12/15/64	Nashville, TN	KIA	(PP=Okolona, MS 6/3/62)	RAS,CTA,HOW
Carter, J.Z.	Pvt.	I 1st SCVI	35	CO	10/15/62	Stevensburg, VA	DOD	(Prob 1st SCVC)	ROH
Carter, Jackson	Pvt.	K 5th SCVI		SG	/ /	Virginia	DOD	(SA3=DES in 1863)	HOS,SA3
Carter, James	Pvt.	F 4th SCVC		MN	06/01/64	Cold Harbor, VA	KIA	(Same as J.R.P. POW?)	HMC
Carter, James	Pvt.	C 12th SCVI		FD	/ /		DOD	(1862)	JR
Carter, James R.	Pvt.	K 11th SCVI	25	CO	11/06/64	At home	DOD		ROH,HAG
Carter, James T.	Pvt.	E 1st SCVIR		AN	03/16/65	Averysboro, NC	DOW		ROH,SA1,WAT,PP
Carter, Jesse	Pvt.	G 26th SCVI		DN	07/10/63		KIA		JR
Carter, Jesse S.	Pvt.	E 6th SCVI		CR	/ /	Richmond, VA	KIA		HHC
Carter, John	Pvt.	A 21st SCVI			07/10/63	Bty. Wagner, SC	KIA	(? Co. L)	ROH,JR,CDC
Carter, John	Pvt.	E 6th SCVI		CR	/ /	Richmond, VA	KIA		HHC
Carter, John A.	Pvt.	G 9th SCVIB			01/14/62	Cheraw, SC	DOD		JR
Carter, John H.	Pvt.			WG	/ /		DOD	(1862)	CTA,HOW
Carter, John M.	Pvt.	G 1st SCVIG		ED	/ /	Virginia, 1864	DOD		HOE,SA1
Carter, John M.T.	Pvt.	H 10th SCVI	25	WG	07/07/62	Columbus, MS	DOD	Friendship C. Columbus, MS	RAS,CTA,HOW,PP
Carter, John Morgan	Sgt.	A 14th SCVI	30	DN	05/03/63	Chancellorsville	KIA		ROH,JR,DEB
Carter, Johnson	Pvt.	I 6th SCVI		CR	02/04/63			Piedmont Institute, VA	ROH,HHC,CB
Carter, Joseph	Pvt.	I 6th SCVI		CR	/ /			(May be Johnson Carter)	CB
Carter, Joseph R.P.	Pvt.	F 4th SCVC			10/17/64	Elmira, NY	DIP	Woodlawn N.C.#543 Elmira	FPH,P6,P65,P12
Carter, Joseph S.	Pvt.	I 11th SCVI		CO	05/09/64	Swift Creek, VA	KIA		ROH,HAG
Carter, Larkin	Pvt.	A 22nd SCVI		ED	08/14/62	Columbia, SC	DOD	(Typhoid)	ROH,JR,PP

C

SOUTH CAROLINA DEAD IN CSA SERVICE 1861-1865

NAME	RANK	C REGIMENT	AGE	DS	DIED	WHERE	WHY	BURIED	SOURCES
Carter, Osborne	Pvt.	B 3rd SCVC	22	CO	09/14/63	Hardeeville SC	DOD		ROH
Carter, Philip	Pvt.	B 3rd SCVC	22	CO	09/15/62	At home	DOD		ROH
Carter, R.	Pvt.	K Orr's Ri.			06/27/62	Gaines' Mill, VA	KIA		JR
Carter, R.E.	Pvt.	F Orr's Ri.		AN	06/27/62	Gaines' Mill, VA	KIA	(CDC=CO.L)	JR,CDC
Carter, Ransom	Pvt.	E 13th SCVI			12/11/62		DOD	(Typhoid)	JR
Carter, Richard Daniel	Cpl.	A 14th SCVI	27	DN	04/18/62	McPhersonville	DOD	(JR=D.R. & 4/6/62)	ROH,JR,DEB
Carter, S.G.	Pvt.	E 27th SCVI			08/10/64	Richmond, VA		Hollywood Cem.Rchmd. V52	ROH,HC
Carter, S.G.A.	Pvt.	I 12th SCVI		LR	/ /	Virginia	DOD	(1862)	LAN
Carter, S.J.N.	Cpl.	E 8th SCVI		DN	07/02/63	Gettysburg, PA	KIA	(KEB=N.S.J.)	ROH,JR,KEB,GDR
Carter, Sidney	2nd Lt.	A 14th SCVI	33	DN	07/08/63	Gettysburg, PA	DOW	(See p100,DEB)	ROH,JR,DEB,GDR
Carter, Thomas	Pvt.	D 3rd SCVI		SG	09/13/62	Maryland Hts. MD	KIA		ROH,JR,SA2,CDC
Carter, Thomas	Pvt.	E 6th SCVI		CR	/ /	Germantown, VA	DOD		HHC
Carter, Timothy	Pvt.	H 1st SCVIR			05/19/65	Hart's Island NY	DIP	Cypress Hills N.C.#2819 NY	FPH,SA1,P6
Carter, V.S.	Pvt.	H 1st SCVIH	33	UN	11/16/63	Campbells St. TN	DOW		ROH,SA1
Carter, Vinton C.	Pvt.	F 2nd SCVI	20	AE	07/11/61	Culpepper, VA	DOD	Fairview C. Culpepper, VA	ROH,JR,CGH,SA2
Carter, W.F.R.	Pvt.	K 8th SCVI		BL	10/26/62			Stonewall C. Winchester VA	ROH,WIN
Carter, W.J.H.	Pvt.	K 11th SCVI	28	CO	/ /	At home	DOD		ROH,HAG
Carter, W.M.R.	Cpl.	A 8th SCVI		DN	06/02/64	Cold Harber, VA	KIA	Oakwood C.#60 Row A Div G	ROH,OWC,KEB
Carter, W.T.	Pvt.	B 26th SCVI			04/11/63		DOD		JR
Carter, Wesley	Pvt.	Ferguson's			01/30/64	Med.Col. Atlanta		Oakland C. Atlanta R28#12	BGA
Carter, William E.	Pvt.	I 10th SCVI		MN	/ /	Chattanooga, TN	DOD	City C. Chattanooga, TN	RAS,HMC,TOD
Carter, William Henry	1st Lt.	E 16th SCVI	30	LS	03/03/63	Adams Run, SC	DOD	Carter/Ellison F.C. LS Cty	ROH,JR,16R,LSC
Cartin, James A.	Pvt.	F 7th SCVI		ED	/ /	At home	DOD	(KEB=Corten)	HOE,KEB
Cartledge, Robert Wade	Pvt.	K 17th SCVI	27	ED	08/26/61	Charlottesville	DOD	(Typhoid)	ROH,JR
Cartledge, William	Pvt.	D 5th SCVC	27	ED	02/01/65	Reams Stn. VA	KIA		ROH
Cartrett, Hezekiah	Pvt.	G 10th SCVI		HY	03/29/64	Rock Island, IL	DIP	(Cautrell, Cotrell ?)	RAS,P6,P12
Cartright, H.B.	Pvt.	F 1st SCVIG		HY	05/28/64	Wilderness, VA	DOW	(Wdd 5/5/64)	SA1,PDL
Caruthers, J.R.	Pvt.	H 18th SCVI		YK	/ /	Lynchburg, VA		Lynchburg CSA Cem. #6 R3	BBW
Caruthers, John	Sgt.	F 6th SCVI		CR	12/20/61	Dranesville, VA	KIA		ROH,JR,CDC,HHC
Carver, A.	Pvt.	G SCVA		PS	12/12/61	Charleston, SC	DOD	Magnolia Cem. Charleston	ROH,MAG
Carver, Alfred	Pvt.	K 22nd SCVI		PS	06/16/62	Secessionville	KIA		ROH,CDC,PP
Carver, Allison	Pvt.	F Orr's Ri.		PS	05/03/63	Chancellorsville	KIA		ROH,JR,CDC
Carvin, J.H.	Pvt.	G 12th SCVI		PS	08/07/62	Richmond, VA			ROH
Casaway, Charles	Pvt.	A P.S.S.		UN	06/30/62	Frayser's Farm	KIA		ROH,JR,CDC
Casey, A.M.	Pvt.	Marion Art			05/08/65	Ft. Columbus, NY	DIP	Cypress Hills N.C.#2605 NY	FPH,P6,P79
Casey, Christopher C.	Pvt.	K 5th SCVC		SG	05/21/65	Bentonville, NC	KIA		ROH,CV
Casey, David	Pvt.	E 18th SCVAB		SG	/ /	Sullivans Island	ACD	(Drowned)	HOS
Casey, Ivy R.	Pvt.	D 3rd SCVI		SG	11/15/61	Charlottesville	DOD		JR,SA2
Casey, John	Pvt.	K 1st SCVIG		CN	05/03/63	Chancellorsville	KIA	(Also wdd. @ 2nd M.)	ROH,SA1,CDC
Casey, Martin	Pvt.	E 1st SCVIR			10/12/63	Ft. Moultrie, SC	ACD	(Explosion 9/8/63)	ROH,SA1,CDC
Casey, William Parker	Pvt.	Brook's GA	20	CN	07/02/63	Gettysburg, PA	DOW	Crawford Farm, Gbg.	ROH,JR,GDR,WV,H2
Cash, Benjamin F.	Pvt.	A 13th SCVI	33		06/17/62	Richmond, VA		(Measles)(ROH=Co.I)	ROH,JR
Cash, Dillard	Pvt.	H P.S.S.			/ /		DOW		JR
Cash, John B.	Pvt.	I 5th SCVI		SG	05/04/63	Columbia, SC	DOD	(Pneumonia, Wdd 2nd Man.)	JR,SA3,HOS
Cash, Joseph	Pvt.	I 5th SCVI		SG	/ /	Sweetwater, TN	DOD		HOS
Cash, Lawson	Pvt.	E 13th SCVI		SG	06/23/62	Winder Hos Rchmd	DOD	(Typhoid)	JR,HOS
Cash, Lee	Pvt.	E 13th SCVI		SG	06/24/62	Charleston, SC	DOD	(Dysentery)	ROH,JR,HOS
Cash, Moses	Pvt.	E 13th SCVI		SG	08/15/62	At home	DOD		JR
Cash, Robert	Pvt.	E 7th SCVI		ED	/ /		KIA		HOE,UD3
Caskey, Frank M.	Pvt.	H 24th SCVI		CR	04/18/64	Dalton, GA	DOD		ROH,HHC,CB,PP
Caskey, Grandison M.	3rd Lt.	D 5th SCVI		LR	06/30/62	Frayser's Farm	KIA	Hollywood Cem.Rchmd. M283	JR,HC,SA3,LAN

SOUTH CAROLINA DEAD IN CSA SERVICE 1861-1865

NAME	RANK	C REGIMENT	AGE	DS	DIED	WHERE	WHY	BURIED	SOURCES
Caskey, J.P.C.	Pvt.	I 12th SCVI		LR	07/01/63	Gettysburg, PA	KIA		JR,LAN
Caskey, John D.	Pvt.	D 1st SCVIH		LR	07/05/64	Lynchburg, VA	DOW	Lynchburg CSA Cem. #3 R2	ROH,SA1,LAN,BB
Caskey, Jonas B.	4th Cpl.	A 5th SCVI		LR	07/15/62	Frayser's Farm	DOW	(Wdd 6/30/62)	JR,LAN,SA3
Caskey, William Reed	Pvt.	D 1st SCVIH	15	LR	08/23/62	Petersburg, VA	DOD	Blandford Church Pbg., VA	LAN,HAG,BLC,PP
Cason, Nicholas O.	Pvt.	F 2nd SCVI		AE	06/20/64	Petersburg, VA	KIA		ROH,SA2
Cason, William H.	Pvt.	E 14th SCVI		LS	08/29/62	2nd Manassas, VA	KIA	(RHL=A,3rd,W.B. in 3rd/KEB)	ROH,JR,CGS,RHL
Casson, J.	Pvt.	I 7th SCVI		ED	/ /	Charlottesville		Univ. Cem. Charlottesville	ACH
Casson, James H.	Pvt.	A 2nd SCVI		RD	07/07/63	Gettysburg, PA	DOW	Magnolia Cem. Charleston	ROH,JR,P1,GDR
Castin, W.J.	2nd Cpl.	E 27th SCVI		CN	05/16/64	Drury's Bluff VA	KIA		ROH,JR,CDC,HAG
Castleman, Jacob D.	Pvt.	I 26th SCVI		WG	06/17/64	Pt. Lookout, MD	DOW	C.C. Pt. Lookout, MD	ROH,FPH,P12,HO
Castlereigh, H.C.	Pvt.	1st SCVA			10/29/63	Ft. Sunter, SC	KIA	Magnolia Cem. Charleston	MAG,CDC
Castles, Barnett	Pvt.	G P.S.S.		CR	06/30/62	Frayser's Farm	KIA	(JR=Bennett)	ROH,JR,CDC,HHC
Castles, John F.	Pvt.	F 6th SCVI		CR	/ /	Richmond, VA	DOW	(1861)	ROH,HHC
Castles, John S.	Pvt.	B 7th SCVIBn	58	FD	09/10/64	Petersburg, VA	DOD		ROH,HAG,PP,UD4
Castles, T.L.	Pvt.	B 12th SCVI		YK	01/15/63		DOD		JR
Caston, A.D.	Pvt.	F 1st SCVI	40	CO	10/15/63	Raccoon Ford VA	DOW	(? 1st SCVC)	ROH
Caston, A.H.	Pvt.	I 1st SCV			/ /	Lynchburg, VA		Lynchburg CSA Cem. #9 R1	BBW
Caston, John Wilson	Pvt.	F 7th SCVIBn	19	LR	08/10/62	Adams Run, SC	DOD	(JR=At home)	ROH,JR,HIC,HAG
Caston, P.	Pvt.	H 2nd SCV			10/22/63	Chickamauga, GA	DOW		JR
Caston, S.G.A.	Pvt.	I 12th SCVI		LR	05/03/62	McPhersonville	DOD		JR
Caston, W.J.	Pvt.	H 2nd SCVI		LR	10/20/63	Chickamauga, GA	DOW	(P. in ROH)	ROH,HIC,
Caston, William G.	Pvt.	I 12th SCVI		LR	04/30/62	McPhersonville	DOD	Magnolia Cem. Charleston	ROH,JR,MAG,LAN
Cater, Franklin M.	Pvt.	D 5th SCVI		UN	05/31/62	7 Pines, VA	KIA		ROH,JR,SA3
Caterton, F.	Pvt,		35	CO	/ /		DOD		ROH
Cathcart, H.P.	Pvt.	D 3rd SCVI			08/24/64	Petersburg, VA	DOD	Blandford Church Pbg., VA	SA2,BLC
Cathcart, Henry H.	Pvt.	D 3rd SCVIBn		SG	07/01/64	Petersburg, VA	KIA	Blandford Church Pbg., VA	ROH,BLC,PP
Cathcart, J.	Pvt.	F 1st SCVA			02/17/65	Charleston, SC	DOD	Magnolia Cem. Charleston	ROH,MAG
Cathcart, James H.	Pvt.	B 1st SCVC	21	SG	06/15/65	At home	DOD		ROH,HOS
Cathcart, James H.	Pvt.	H 5th SCVI	25	YK	08/20/61	Charlottesville	DOD	(JR= Co.B & 8/14/61)	JR,SA3,YEB
Cathcart, Robert	Pvt.	B 1st SCVC	28	SG	06/15/62	Johns Island, SC	KIA		ROH
Cato, A.D.	Pvt.	G 2nd SCVI		KW	/ /		DOD	(SA2=Cato dtld Treasury)	HIC,KEB,SA2
Cato, Hiram	Sgt.	A 19th SCVI	23	ED	06/15/64	New Hope Ch., GA	KIA		ROH,HOE,UD3
Cato, R.E.	Pvt.	H 2nd SCVI		LR	08/31/61	Richmond, VA	DOD	Hollywood Cem.Rchmd. K66	ROH,HC,SA2,KEB
Cato, William Thomas	Pvt.	F 7th SCVIBn	17	LR	05/02/64	Wilmington, NC	DOD		ROH,JR,HIC,HAG
Catoe, Lewis	Pvt.	E 12th SCVI	22	LR	08/01/62	Lexington, VA	DOD		ROH,JR,LAN
Catoe, William T.	Pvt.	B 26th SCVI	18	CD	04/15/63	Church Flats, SC	DOD		ROH
Caton, Sylvester	Pvt.				/ /	Petersburg, VA			ROH
Catrist, H.B.	Pvt.	1st SCVI			/ /			Gordonsville, VA	ROH
Caughman, Christopher	Cpt.	K 13th SCVI	27	LN	09/30/64	Jones' Farm, VA	KIA		ROH,JR,BOS,R47
Caughman, G.E.	Pvt.	F 13th SCVI		LN	07/03/62	Richmond, VA			ROH
Caughman, G.E.	Pvt.	F 1st SCVI			11/30/61	Richmond, VA		Hollywood Cem.Rchmd. M133	HC
Caughman, James A.	Sgt.		37	LN	08/04/64	Atlanta, GA	KIA		ROH
Caughman, Joshua	Pvt.	I 26th SCVI		WG	07/08/63		DOD		JR
Caughman, M.L.	Pvt.	H 3rd SCVI	25	LN	10/17/61	Culpepper, VA	DOD	Fairview C. Culpepper, VA	ROH,JR,SA2,CGH
Caughman, N. Fred	Pvt.	K 20th SCVI		LN	10/19/64	Cedar Creek, VA	KIA		ROH,KEB
Caulder, J.W.	Pvt.	H 10th SCVI		WG	/ /	Chattanooga, TN	DOD	City C. Chattanooga, TN	RAS,TOD
Caulk, Daniel	Pvt.	G 2nd SCVC	21	MO	09/15/64	SC coast	DOD		ROH
Caulk, James	Pvt.	B 24th SCVI		MO	/ /		DOD	(1862)	HOM
Causey, H.L.	Pvt.	D 4th SCVC		HY	02/25/65	Richmond, VA		Hollywood Cem.Rchmd. W31	ROH,HC
Causey, Philip	Pvt.	E 9th SCVIBn	22	HY	03/07/62	Camp Lookout, SC	DOD		ROH,PP
Cauthen, Andrew J.	2nd Sgt.	G 2nd SCVI		KW	05/15/62	At home	DOD		HIC,SA2,KEB

C

SOUTH CAROLINA DEAD IN CSA SERVICE 1861-1865

NAME	RANK	C REGIMENT	AGE	DS	DIED	WHERE	WHY	BURIED	SOURCES
Cauthen, G.C.	Pvt.	H 2nd SCVI		LR	11/20/62		DOD	(G.L. ?)	LAN
Cauthen, J.M.	Pvt.	D 7th SCVIBn		KW	02/25/65	Pt. Lookout, MD	DIP	(POW 8/21/64)	FPH,HIC,HAG,P6
Cauthen, R.D.	Pvt.	H 2nd SCVI		LR	11/01/62		DOD		SA2,LAN,KEB
Cauthen, Samuel	Pvt.	H 7th SCVI		LR	10/03/64	Charleston, SC	DOD	Magnolia Cem. Charleston	ROH,MAG
Cauthen, W.B.	Pvt.	D 7th SCVIBn	25	KW	08/21/64	Weldon RR, VA	KIA	(JR=July)	ROH,JR,HAG
Cauthen, William	Pvt.	D 1st SCVIH		LR	08/30/62	2nd Manassas, VA	KIA		ROH,LAN,CDC,JRH
Cauthorn, H.	Pvt.	B 5th SCVI			08/29/62	Richmond, VA		Hollywood Cem.Rchmd. S37	HC
Cauthorn, W.J.	Pvt.	I 15th SCVI			02/26/65	Elmira, NY	DIP	Woodlawn N.C.#2279 Elmira	FPH,P12
Cavanaugh, J.P.	Pvt.	F 17th SCVI		YK	10/14/62	Frederick, MD	DOW	Mt.Olivet C. Con.Sec.#119	JR,FPH,P1,P6,BOD
Caveny, John	Pvt.	F 17th SCVI		YK	09/14/62	South Mtn., MD	KIA		CB
Caver, James	Pvt.	B 1st SCVIH		OG	10/15/62		DOD		ROH,SA1
Cay, Thaddeus L.	Pvt.	A Ham.Leg.		CN	09/09/62	Warrenton, VA	DOD		ROH,CDC,WLI
Cely, William	Pvt.	C 16th SCVI		GE	07/23/63	Lauderdale Ss MS	DOD		PP,16R
Center, Bright	Pvt.	H 22nd SCVI	30	GE	11/13/64	Petersburg, VA	KIA		ROH,PP
Cerpt, Charles C.	Pvt.	1st SCVI			11/21/63	Charleston, SC	DOD	Magnolia Cem. Charleston	ROH,MAG
Chadwick, J.G.	Pvt.	A 10th SCVI		GN	07/15/62		DOD	(JR=J.B.)	JR,GRG,RAS
Chalmers, John C.	Pvt.	C Hol.Leg.		NY	/ /	Virginia	DOD		ANY
Chalmers, Joseph H.	Pvt.	B 1st SCVIG	24	NY	06/27/62	Gaines' Mill, VA	KIA	Head Springs C. NY	ROH,JR,NCC,ANY
Chalmers, R.	Sgt.	A 1st SCVC	30	AE	/ /	Virginia			ROH
Chambers, A.J.	Pvt.	E 17th SCVI	29	YK	01/13/63	Kinston, NC	DOD		ROH,JR,PP
Chambers, Alexander M.	Pvt.	B 1st SCVIG	24	NY	07/15/63		DIP		SA1,ANY
Chambers, B.W.	Pvt.	D 2nd SCVA		DN	10/12/63	Columbia, SC	DOD		ROH,PP
Chambers, Daniel Gibbes	Pvt.	B 1st SCVIG	17	NY	07/01/63	Gettysburg, PA	KIA	ANY	ROH,JR,SA1,GDR
Chambers, E.T.	Pvt.	L Orr's Ri.		AN	06/27/62	Gaines' Mill, VA	KIA	(Prob Chamblee, R.T./CDC)	JR
Chambers, John W.	Cpt.	L 1st SCVIG		CN	07/13/63	Hagerstown, MD	KIA		ROH,BOS,SA1,R45
Chambers, Joseph	Pvt.	B 1st SCV			06/27/61		DOW		JR
Chambers, R.P.	Pvt.	E 17th SCVI	33	YK	11/01/62	Richmond, VA	DOW	(Wdd @ Sharpsburg)	ROH,JR
Chambers, Robert	Pvt.	E 6th SCVI		CR	/ /	Virginia			HHC
Chambers, Robert S.	Cpl.	A 12th SCVI	30	YK	05/12/64	Spotsylvania, VA	KIA		JR,YEB
Chambers, W.E.	Pvt.	L 1st SCVIG		YK	10/23/63	Petersburg, VA	DOD		SA1
Chambers, Williams H.	Cpl.	C 17th SCVI	22	YK	07/30/64	Crater, Pbg., VA	KIA		ROH,JR,YMD,BLM
Chamblee, Anderson F.	Pvt.	G 22nd SCVI	22	AN	07/30/64	Crater, Pbg. VA	KIA	(Chambler per BLM)	ROH,BLM
Chamblin, Dallas	Pvt.	A 2nd SCVC		SG	/ /		DOD	(1865)	HOS
Chamblin, Samuel J.	Pvt.	B 13th SCVI		SG	08/14/62	Richmond, VA	DOD	(Consumption, JR=At home)	JR,HOS
Chamblin, W.W.	Pvt.	D P.S.S.		SG	03/30/64	Bristoe Stn. VA	DOD	(HOS=Bristol, TN)	ROH,JR,HOS,
Champart, G.A.	Pvt.	E 19th SCVI			09/20/63	Chickamauga, GA	KIA	(10th/19th Consolidated)	CDC
Champion, J.W.	Pvt.	K 14th SCVI			/ /			Oakwood C.#11 Row R Div C	ROH,OWC
Champion, Richard	Pvt.	H P.S.S.		GE	06/30/62	Frayser's Farm	KIA		JR
Champlin, A.J.	Pvt.	A 27th SCVI	51		08/25/64	Petersburg, VA	DOW	(Wdd 8/19/64)	ROH,PP
Champlin, William Ewing	1st Sgt.	I 1st SCVIG	24	CN	01/01/63	Richmond, VA	DOW	Hollywood Cem.Rchmd. D24	ROH,JR,HC,SA1
Chandler, Crayton	2nd Sgt.	F 16th SCVI		GE	/ /		DOD		16R
Chandler, Josiah	Pvt.	E 16th SCVI	19	GE	02/23/62	Charleston, SC	DOD		ROH,16R
Chandler, Robert W.	5th Sgt.	K 6th SCVI	24	WG	07/15/64	Petersburg, VA	DOW		ROH,CTA,HOW,3RC
Chandler, S.M.	Cpl.	H 26th SCVI		CN	07/30/64	Crater, Pbg., VA	KIA		BLM,PP
Chandler, S.W.	Pvt.	D 7th SCVI			08/03/64	(NI KEB,HAG)		Hollywood Cem.Rchmd. V531	ROH,HC
Chandler, Samuel Thomas	Pvt.	D Ham.Leg.	38	CL	06/26/62	Fts.Monroe, VA	DOW	(Wdd & POW @ 7 Pines)	ROH,CDC,CNM,P12
Chandler, T.A.	Pvt.	E 8th SCVI			04/15/62	Charlottesville	DOD	Univ, C., Ch'ville, VA	ROH,JR,CDC,ACH
Chandler, Thomas Sidney	Pvt.	K 6th SCVI	30	WG	09/27/62	South Mtn., MD	DOW	(Wdd 9/14/62)	ROH,JR,HOW,LOR
Chandler, W.H.	Pvt.	I 3rd SCVI		GE	10/31/62	Winchester, VA	DOD	Stonewall C. Winchester VA	ROH,WIN,SA2
Chaney, Jacob H.	Sgt.	K 13th SCVI		LN	08/09/63	Gettysburg, PA	DOW	Magnolia Cem. Charleston	ROH,MAG,GDR,P1
Chaney, S.	Pvt.	I 27th SCVI			09/27/64	Elmira, NY	DIP	Woodlawn N.C.#395 Elmira	FPH,HAG,CDC,P6

SOUTH CAROLINA DEAD IN CSA SERVICE 1861-1865

NAME	RANK	C	REGIMENT	AGE	DS	DIED	WHERE	WHY	BURIED	SOURCES
Chaney, William H.	Pvt.	A	4th SCVC		CD	06/11/64	Trevillian STn.	KIA		ROH,JR
Chaney, Willis	Pvt.	F	2nd SCVI	26	AE	10/15/62	Sharpsburg, MD	DOW		ROH,SA2
Chapell, L.H.	1st Sgt.	F	12th SCVI		FD	06/27/62	Gaines' Mill, VA	KIA		ROH,JR
Chapin, J.R.	Pvt.	A	Ham.Leg.	22	GN	01/01/62	Richmond, VA	DOW (Wdd @ 1st Manassas)		ROH,LOR,WLI
Chaplin, Eugene T.	Pvt.	D	5th SCVI	19	BT	03/15/65	Goldsboro, NC	DIP		ROH
Chaplin, Jacob C.	Pvt.	D	5th SCVI		UN	08/27/61	Culpepper, VA	DOD	Fairview C. Culpepper, VA	JR,CGH,SA3,CDC
Chapline, John S.	2nd Lt.	G	Hol.Leg.		NY	11/26/62	At home	DOD	Boshart Cem. Newberry, SC	NCC,ANY
Chapman, A. Quinton	Pvt.	E	16th SCVI	23	GE	11/30/64	Franklin, TN	KIA		ROH,16R,PP
Chapman, A.A.	Pvt.	I	18th SCVI	33	DN	04/18/65	Elmira, NY	DIP	Woodlawn N.C.#2655 Elmira	ROH,FPH,P6,P65
Chapman, B.F.	Pvt.	H	3rd SCVI		LN	07/25/64	Lynchburg, VA	DOW	Lynchburg CSA Cem. #9 R2	SA2,ANY,KEB,BB
Chapman, B.M.	Pvt.	H	6th SCVI			08/09/64	Richmond, VA		Hollywood Cem.Rchmd. V337	ROH,HC
Chapman, Berry	Pvt.	I	P.S.S.		PS	01/17/64	Danbridge, VA	KIA		ROH
Chapman, Charles E.	Pvt.	A	4th SCVC	21	CD	10/06/64	At home	DOD		ROH,UD4
Chapman, David	Pvt.	E	16th SCVI	19	GE	02/01/65	Rock Island, IL	DIP	C.C.#1847 Rock Island, IL	ROH,FPH,16R,P6
Chapman, G.E.	Cpl.	E	2nd SCVIRi			09/30/64	Ft. Harrison, VA	KIA		ROH,JR
Chapman, G.E.	Pvt.	F	P.S.S.			/ /		DOD		JR
Chapman, G.F.	1st Lt.	C	5th SCVI		SG	12/04/61	Charlottesville	DOD		JR,SA3,R46
Chapman, Hembry	Pvt.	E	16th SCVI	18	GE	11/30/64	Franklin, TN	KIA	McGavock C. Franklin Gv#2	ROH,16R,PP
Chapman, Henry Z.	Pvt.	F	20th SCVI		NY	11/10/64	Baltimore, MD	DIP	Loudon Pk. C. B-42 Balto.	FPH,ANY,PP,P3
Chapman, J.	Pvt.	G	12th SCVI		PS	05/05/64	Wilderness, VA	KIA		JR
Chapman, J.C.	Pvt.	E	Ham.Leg.			10/28/63	Lookout Valley	KIA (JR=Racoon Mtn.)		ROH,JR,CDC
Chapman, J.F.	Pvt.	G	12th SCVI		PS	05/12/64	Spotsylvania, VA	KIA		JR
Chapman, John W.N.	1st Sgt..	H	13th SCVI	24	NY	11/12/62	At home	DOD	Chapman Cem. Pomaria, SC	JR,NCC,ANY
Chapman, M.	Pvt.	H	7th SCVI			10/25/62	Winchester, VA		Stonewall C. Winchester VA	ROH,WIN,P12
Chapman, R.	Pvt.	H	1st SCVI			/ /	(OWC=Co.K,NI SA1		Oakwood C.#68 Row R Div C	ROH,OWC
Chapman, T.J.	Pvt.	C	22nd SCVI	48	SG	07/30/64	Crater, Pbg VA	KIA		ROH,JR,BLM
Chapman, T.P.	Pvt.	H	22nd SCVI		GE	/ /	At home	DOD		PP
Chapman, Thomas	Pvt.	E	16th SCVI	24	GE	02/03/62	Charleston, SC	DOD		ROH,16R
Chapman, Thomas E.	Sgt.	D	19th SCVI	32	ED	08/15/64	At home	DOW (Wdd @ Atlanta or N.Hope)		ANY,HOE,UD3
Chapman, Thomas N.	Pvt.	A	25th SCVI		CN	06/16/62	Seccessionville	KIA (HAG=Thomas B.)		LED,HAG
Chapman, W.A.	Pvt.	I	P.S.S.			06/17/64	Danbridge, TN	KIA (JR=1/17/64)		ROH,JR
Chapman, W.H.	2nd Lt.	F	13th SCVI		SG	04/02/65	Sutherland Stn.	KIA		HOS,BOS
Chapman, W.W.	Hos. Stwd.	H	13th SCVI		LN	/ /		DOD		JR
Chapman, Warren D.	Cpl.	K	27th SCVI	37	SG	06/02/64	Drury's Bluff VA	DOW	Blandford Church Pbg., VA	HOS,BLC,PP.HAG
Chapman, Washington C.	Pvt.	E	16th SCVI	27	GE	05/14/62	At home	DOD (PP=Charles W.)		ROH,16R,PP
Chapman, William	Pvt.	G	13th SCVI		NY	01/19/63	Lynchburg, VA	DOD	Lynchburg CSA Cem. #6 R4	ROH,ANY,BBW
Chapman, William J.	Pvt.	E	16th SCVI	27	GE	06/27/62	Adams Run, SC	DOD (ROH=6/22/62)		ROH,16R,PP
Chapman, William R.	Pvt.	G	Hol.Leg.	43	NY	11/17/64	Petersburg, VA	DOW	Blandford Church Pbg., VA	ROH,ANY,BLC
Chappell, Henry H.	2nd Lt.	F	12th SCVI		FD	01/12/62	At home	DOD		ROH,JR,HFC,R47
Chappell, Henry J. (C.?)	1st Lt.	I	21st SCVI	26	MN	07/02/64	Petersburg, VA	DOW	Blandford Church Pbg., VA	ROH,PP,BLC,HMC
Chappell, Hix	Pvt.	F	12th SCVI		FD	04/01/65	Five Forks, VA	KIA		HFC
Chappell, Joel	Pvt.	F	12th SCVI		FD	07/17/63	Gettysburg, PA	DOW		JR,HFC,GDR
Chappell, L.H.	1st Sgt.	F	12th SCVI		FD	06/27/62	Gaines' Mill, VA	KIA		HFC,CNM
Charles, C.	Pvt.		1st SCV			/ /			Magnolia Cem. Charleston	RCD
Charles, James F.	Pvt.	F	Ham.Leg.		GE	/ /	Brentsville, VA	DOD (1861)		ROH
Charles, James O.	Sgt.	B	16th SCVI	34	DN	08/24/64	Forsyth, GA	DOD	Forsyth, GA	ROH,JR,16R,CKB
Charles, John B.	2nd Cpl.	B	16th SCVI		GE	08/09/62	Adams Run, SC	DOD		16R,PP
Charles, Peter G.	Sgt.	B	16th SCVI		GE	09/02/64	At home	DOW (Wdd @ Kennesaw Mtn.)		ROH,16R
Charpie, Henry L.	Pvt.	I	1st SCVIG	31	CN	07/29/62	Gaines' Mill, VA	DOW		JR,SA1,CDC
Charvis, E.W.	Pvt.	I	22nd SCVI		SR	07/01/64	Petersburg, VA	DOW (Wdd 6/22/64)		ROH
Chasereau, G.C.	Pvt.	G	17th SCVI		BL	07/30/64	Crater, Pbg., VA	KIA		ROH,JR,BLM

C

SOUTH CAROLINA DEAD IN CSA SERVICE 1861-1865

NAME	RANK	C	REGIMENT	AGE	DS	DIED	WHERE	WHY	BURIED	SOURCES
Chasereau, J.W.	Pvt.	G	17th SCVI			08/30/62	2nd Manassas, VA	DOW		JR
Chastain, Alfred	Pvt.	D	2nd SCVIRi		AN	06/29/62	Savage Stn., VA	KIA		ROH,CDC
Chastain, James E.	Pvt.	L	2nd SCVIRi	40	AN	12/16/62	Lynchburg, VA	DOD	Lynchburg CSA Cem. #2 R5	ROH,BBW
Chastain, King Edward	Pvt.	F	22nd SCVI			08/22/62	Rappahanock R.	KIA		JR
Chastain, Thomas	Pvt.	E	Orr's Ri.		PS	06/27/62	Gaines' Mill, VA	KIA		ROH,JR,CDC
Chasteen, R.L.	Pvt.	G	22nd SCVI	28	AN	07/30/64	Crater, Pbg., VA	KIA	(Chastine per BLM)	ROH,BLM
Chasteen, W.B.	Pvt.	H	25th SCVI		AN	09/05/63	Bty. Wagner, SC	DOW	(ROH=DOD 10/13/64)	ROH,JR,HAG
Chastene, John W.	Pvt.	D	2nd SCVIRi			02/12/65	Rock Island, IL	DIP	C.C.#1875 Rock Island, IL	FPH,P6
Chatman, W.A.	4th Cpl.	A	1st SCVIG			09/30/64	Chaffin's Farm	KIA		JR,SA1
Chavis, Alfred	Pvt.	D	26th SCVI		MO	08/16/64	Petersburg, VA	KIA		HOM
Chavis, Bithel	Pvt.	D	26th SCVI		MO	/ /	At home	DOD		HOM
Chavis, Bytha J.	Pvt.	D	26th SCVI		MO	05/05/62	At home	DOD		JR,HOM
Chavis, George	Pvt.	B	24th SCVI		MO	01/28/62	Charleston, SC	DOD		ROH,HOM
Chavis, Harris	Pvt.	D	26th SCVI		MO	11/02/63		DOD		JR
Chavis, John	Pvt.	D	26th SCVI		MO	07/25/62	Charleston, SC	DOD		JR,HOM
Chavis, Levi	Pvt.	D	26th SCVI	34	MO	05/20/64	Clay's Farm, VA	KIA		HOM,PP
Chavis, M.	Pvt.	I	2nd SCVA	19	OG	06/11/63	Columbia, SC	DOD		ROH
Chavis, William	Pvt.	D	26th SCVI		MO	05/16/64	Drury's Bluff VA	KIA		ROH,HOM
Cheatham, Alfred	Pvt.	H	7th SCVIBn	40	AE	05/16/64	Drury's Bluff VA	KIA	(JR=Alford)	ROH,JR,HAG
Cheatham, C.A.	Pvt.	I	2nd SCVC		ED	/ /		DOW		HOE
Cheatham, J.W.	Cpt.	K	7th SCVI			01/08/65			(Chetham in KEB)	R46,KEB
Cheatham, Robert M.	Cpt.	G	19th SCVI		AE	05/25/64	New Hope Ch., GA	ACD		JR,HOL,R47,UD1
Cheatham, W.T.	Pvt.	G	1st SCVC	26	AE	08/09/63	Richmond, VA	DOW	Hollywood Cem.Rchmd. T388	ROH,JR,HC
Cheatham, W.W.	Pvt.	L	P.S.S.			08/30/62	2nd Manassas, VA	KIA		ROH,JR,CDC
Check, E.V.	Pvt.	F	14th SCVI			06/30/62	Richmond, VA	DOD	(Cheek?)	JR
Check, J.M.	Pvt.	E	14th SCVI			08/11/62	Richmond, VA	DOD	(Typhoid, Dup of J.W.?)	JR
Check, James	Pvt.	B	1st SCVC	32	LS	06/15/64	James Island, SC	DOD		ROH
Check, John P.	Pvt.	E	3rd SCVIBn			07/02/63	Gettysburg, PA	KIA	(KEB=Cheek)	ROH,JR,GDR,KEB
Check, William	Pvt.	G	3rd SCVI		LS	10/15/62	Winchester, VA	DOD	Stonewall C. Winchester VA	ROH,WIN,KEB
Cheek, Ellis	Pvt.	E	6th SCVC	26	LS	04/27/63	Adams Run, SC	DOD		PP
Cheek, J.W.	Pvt.	E	14th SCVI		LS	07/05/62	Richmond, VA	KIA		ROH,JR,CGS
Chency, W.C.	Pvt.		2nd SCVIRi			10/18/62	Sharpsburg, MD	DOW		ROH,JR,CDC
Cheney, D. Stockton K.	Pvt.	I	27th SCVI	27	CN	09/28/64	Elmira, NY	DIP	Woodlawn Cem. Elmira NY	ROH,HAG,CDC,P65
Cherry, Columbus D.	Pvt.	A	6th SCVI	18	CR	03/30/62	7 Pines, VA	KIA	(HHC=Gaines' Mill)	ROH,HHC,CB
Cherry, Elijah	Pvt.	H	24th SCVI		CR	03/14/64	At home	ACD		ROH,HHC,CB
Cherry, Isaac	Pvt.	F	23rd SCVI			08/30/62	2nd Manassas, VA	KIA	(JR=28th SCVI)	JR
Cherry, Isaiah	Pvt.		6th SCVI		CR	08/30/62	2nd Manassas, VA	KIA		HHC
Cherry, John H.	Pvt.	H	24th SCVI		CR	11/20/64	Lookout Mtn., TN	DOD		ROH,HHC,CB
Cherry, R.S.	Pvt.	H	18th SCVI		YK	01/22/62	Charleston, SC	DOD		JR
Chesenthal, S.	Pvt.	G	11th SCVI		CN	05/07/64	Pt. Lookout, MD	DIP		ROH
Chesney, George	Pvt.	G	3rd SCVI		SG	12/05/62	Staunton, VA	DOD	Thornrose C. Staunton, VA	ROH,JR,SA2,TOD
Chesney, George W.	Pvt.	C	27th SCVI	23	SG	06/06/64	Petersburg, VA	DOW	Blandford Church Pbg., VA	ROH,HAG,BLC,PP
Chesney, J.N.	Pvt.	G	3rd SCVI		SG	11/18/62	Staunton, VA	DOD	Thornrose C. Staunton, VA	ROH,SA2,HOS,TOD
Chesney, N.	Pvt.	G	3rd SCVI		SG	12/06/62	Staunton, VA	DOD		ROH,SA2,KEB
Chesney, R.J.	Pvt.	G	3rd SCVI		SG	11/21/62	White Sulpher Ss	DOD	(JR=11/24/62) PP	ROH,JR,SA2,KEB
Chesney, Thomas	Pvt.	E	18th SCVI		SG	01/23/62	Charleston, SC	DOD		HOS,JR
Chesnut, Rufus M.	Pvt.	F	1st SCVIG		HY	07/07/62	Richmond, VA	DOD	(JR=1861)	JR,SA1,PDL
Chesnut, Wilson C.	Pvt.		Allston's			07/10/62	Columbia, SC	DOD		JR
Chevers, Levi	Pvt.	D	26th SCVI		MN	05/21/64	Petersburg, VA		Blandford Church Pbg., VA	BLC
Cheves, Edward	Cpt. ADC		Gn. Lawton		BT	06/27/62	Gaines' Mill, VA	KIA	(May have moved to GA)	CNM
Cheves, Langdon	Cpt.		Eng'r Corp	50	CN	07/10/63	Morris Island SC	KIA	Magnolia Cem. Chlstn.	ROH,DOC,RCD

SOUTH CAROLINA DEAD IN CSA SERVICE 1861-1865

NAME	RANK	C REGIMENT	AGE	DS	DIED	WHERE	WHY	BURIED	SOURCES
Cheves, William	Pvt.	24th SCVI		DN	02/03/62			Magnolia Cem. Charleston	MAG,RCD
Chevis, J.T.	Pvt.	I 22nd SCVI			08/04/64	Richmond, VA		Hollywood Cem.Rchmd. V302	ROH,HC
Chew, Thomas R.	Pvt.	Hart's LA			03/19/65	Bentonville, NC	KIA		WAT,PP
Chewning, J.W.	Pvt.	I 23rd SCVI			06/13/65	Pt. Lookout, MD	DIP	C.C. Pt. Lookout, MD	FPH,P6,P114
Childers, J.	Pvt.	C 27th SCVI			06/29/64	Richmond, VA		Hollywood Cem.Rchmd. U193	ROH,HC,HAG
Childers, J.W.	Pvt.	B 16th SCVI		GE	/ /	At home	DOD		16R
Childers, John	Pvt.	C 17th SCVI	33	YK	05/20/64	Clay's Farm, VA	KIA		YEB
Childers, John C.	Pvt.	C 17th SCVI	22	YK	/ /	Charleston, SC	DOD	(1865)	YEB
Childers, W.W.	Pvt.	B 12th SCVI	19	YK	06/15/62	Richmond, VA	DOD	Hollywood Cem.Rchmd. O77	ROH,JR,HC,YEB
Childers, Ware E.	Pvt.	B 16th SCVI		GE	/ /	At home	DOD	(1862)	16R
Childers, Washington	Pvt.	G 5th SCVI	35	YK	12/15/62	Manchester, VA	DOD		JR,SA3,YEB
Childers, William	Pvt.	E 14th SCVI		LS	/ /		DOD		CGS
Childress, D.M.	Pvt.	G 3rd SCVI	23	LS	08/25/61	Culpepper, VA	DOD	New Harmony B.C.	ROH,JR,CGH,SA2
Childress, Elias	Pvt.	K 2nd SCVIRi	18	PS	11/29/63	Knoxville, TN	KIA		ROH
Childress, Josiah.	Pvt.	E 17th SCVI	24	YK	08/07/62	Richmond, VA	DOW	Hollywood Cem.Rchmd. H138	JR,HC,YEB
Childress, L. Thomas	Pvt.	C 22nd SCVI	33	SG	10/22/64	Winchester, VA	DOD		ROH
Childress, R.	Pvt.	K 18th SCVI			11/25/62	Staunton, VA		Thornrose C. Staunton, VA	ROH,TOD
Childress, R.F.	Pvt.	E 14th SCVI	25	GE	07/05/62	Richmond, VA	DOD	New Harmony P.C.	JR,GEC,LSC,CGS
Childress, T.T.	Pvt.	Ham.Leg.		AN	08/07/62	Richmond, VA		Hollywood Cem.Rchmd. S54	ROH,HC
Childress, W.A.	Pvt.	G 3rd SCVI	21	LS	02/09/62	Manassas, VA	DOD	New Harmony B.C.	ROH,JR,SA2,LSC
Childs, Thomas M.	1st Lt.	C 7th SCVI	25	AE	09/13/62	Maryland Hts. MD	KIA	(Acting Adjutant)	ROH,JR,KEB,CDC
Childs, W.R.	Pvt.	SC Arty			01/03/62	Charleston, SC	DOD		ROH
Chiles, Franklin Perry	Pvt.	G 4th SCVI		GE	07/21/61	1st Manassas, VA	KIA		ROH,JR,SA2
Chiles, William	Pvt.	G 4th SCVI	26	GE	09/11/61	Culpepper, VA	DOD		JR,CGH,SA2
China, J. Randolph	2nd Lt.	E 1st SCVIH	24	WG	/ /		DOD	('64 prob NI Rgt at death)	CTA,HOW
China, Thomas J.	Cpt.	C 25th SCVI	37	WG	05/18/64	Drury's Bluff, V	DOW	(Wdd 5/16/64)	ROH,JR,HAG,HOW
Chisolm, William T.	Pvt.	I 1st SCVIG			09/05/62	(Prob Warrenton)	DOW	(Wdd 2nd Man 8/29/62)	JR,SA1
Choate, Henry E.	Pvt.	A 27th SCVI		CN	06/15/65	At home		Magnolia Cem. Charleston	MAG,HAG
Choate, John Arthur	Pvt.	E 17th SCVI	18	YK	10/03/64	Petersburg, VA	DOW	Blandford Church Pbg., VA	ROH,DEM,BLC
Choate, Robert Walker	Cpl.	B 13th SCVI	29	YK	05/21/64	Spotsylvania, VA	KIA	(YEB=DOW at home)	ROH,YEB
Choate,Jr., Augustine D.	Pvt.	B 13th SCVI	29	YK	06/27/62	Gaines' Mill. VA	KIA		ROH,YEB
Christian, A.H.	Pvt.	D 2nd SCVIRi			05/16/64	Drury's Bluff VA	KIA		JR
Christian, Alfred	Pvt.	D 2nd SCVIRi			06/28/62	Richmond, VA	KIA		JR
Christian, Thomas R.	Pvt.	E Orr's Ri.		PS	06/27/62	Gaines' Mill, VA	KIA		ROH,JR,CDC
Christman, Jarrott	Pvt.	H 8th SCVI		MN	/ /	Charlottesville	DOD	(1862, ? Christmas, C.L.)	HMC
Christmas, Andrew J.	Pvt.	B 27th SCVI		CN	04/07/64	Petersburg, VA		Blandford Church Pbg., VA	BLC,HAG,PP
Christmas, C.	Cpl.	A 14th SCVI	35	DN	07/01/62	Malvern Hill, VA	KIA	Oakwood C.#107 Row M Div C	ROH,JR,OWC
Christmas, Charles W.	Pvt.	C 17th SCVI	25	YK	/ /		DOD	(1862)	JR,YEB
Christmas, J.	Pvt.	E 23rd SCVI1		MN	11/07/62	(Chrisman/ OWC)		Oakwood C.#19 Row L Div B	ROH,OWC
Christmas, Smith	Pvt.	C			08/11/64			Magnolia Cem. Charleston	MAG
Christmas, T.C.H.	Pvt.	C 17th SCVI		YK	/ /	John's Island SC	DOD		JR
Christmas, Thomas H.	Pvt.	B 7th SCVIBn	27	SR	01/01/64	Drury's Bluff VA	DOW	Oakwood C. #6 Row J Div F	ROH,OWC,HAG
Christmas, William G.	Pvt.	G 15th SCVI	27	WG	01/26/63	Richmond, VA	DOD	Oakwood C.#1 Row C Div E	ROH,JR,KEB,OWC
Christopher, Benjamin	Pvt.	G 16th SCVI		GE	/ /	Adams Run, SC	DOD		16R
Christopher, D. Lewis	Pvt.	I 14th SCVI	21	AE	01/31/63	Fredericksburg	DOD	Fredericksburg C.C. R1S11	ROH,JR,FBG,HOL
Christopher, Ellison G.	Pvt.	B 13th SCVI		SG	03/12/63	Richmond, VA	DOD	(Dysentery)	ROH,JR,HOS
Christopher, James	Pvt.	G 16th SCVI		GE	/ /	At home	DOD		16R
Christopher, John H.	Pvt.	A 16th SCVI		GE	02/10/62	At home	DOD		PP
Christopher, T.C.	Pvt.	D 14th SCVI		ED	05/24/62	Washington, DC	DOW	Arlington N.C. Sec. 16.	CV,P6,PP
Christopher, W. Griffin	Pvt.	I 14th SCVI	18	AE	07/12/63	Richmond, VA	DOW	(Wdd @ Chancellorsville)	ROH,JR,HOL
Chumbler, Earl	Pvt.	H 2nd SCVIRi			05/16/64	Drury's Bluff VA	KIA		ROH,JR

C

SOUTH CAROLINA DEAD IN CSA SERVICE 1861-1865

NAME	RANK	C REGIMENT	AGE	DS	DIED	WHERE	WHY	BURIED	SOURCES
Chumley, George W.	Pvt.	K 3rd SCVI	21	SG	07/27/64	Camp Douglas, IL	DIP	Oak Woods C. Chicago, IL	ROH,FPH,SA2,P5
Chumley, Joseph	Pvt.	K 3rd SCVI	27	SG	10/13/64	Cedar Creek, VA	KIA		ROH,HOS,SA2,KEB
Chupp, Joseph G.	Pvt.	B 3rd SCVI		NY	05/15/64		DOD		ROH,SA2,ANY,KEB
Claggett, W.T.	Pvt.	B 17th SCVCB		ED	06/27/62	Green Pond, SC	ACD	(Disch. of gun at parade)	ROH,CDC,MDM,PP
Clamp, C. Calvin	Pvt.	D 13th SCVI	23	NY	08/29/62	2nd Manassas, VA	KIA	(JR=Co.B,12th SCVI)	ROH,JR,ANY,CDC
Clamp, George	Pvt.	E 3rd SCVI		NY	06/01/64	Cold Harbor, VA	KIA		ROH,ANY,SA2
Clamp, H.	Pvt.	B 1st SCVIG	17	NY	12/15/61		DOD	(NI SA1 or NY Monument)	ANY
Clamp, Henry E.	Pvt.	B 14th SCMil	59	LN	04/05/65	Newbern, NC	DIP	Cedar Grove C. Newbern NC	ROH,P6,WAT,PP
Clamp, James Belton	Pvt.	K 13th SCVI		LN	09/01/62	(Prob Warrenton)	DOW	(Wdd 2nd Manassas)	ROH,JR,CDC
Clamp, James R.	Pvt.	B 1st SCVIG		NY	12/15/61	Suffolk, VA	DOD	(JR=6/27/62)	ROH,JR,SA1
Clamp, William	Pvt.	I 19th SCVI	33	AE	07/14/62	Columbus, MS	DOD	Con. Cem. Marietta, GA	ROH,BGA,CCM,UD2
Clamp, William H.	Pvt.	B 1st SCVIG		NY	10/15/61	Suffolk, VA	DOD		ROH,SA1
Clapton, W.B.	Pvt.	A 13th SCVI		LS	06/04/63	Fredericksburg	DOD		JR
Clardy, L.G.	Pvt.	D 18th SCVI		AN	07/01/64	Richmond, VA		Hollywood Cem.Rchmd. U346	ROH,HC
Clardy, R.M.	Pvt.	A 2nd SCVI		AN	10/16/62	Winchester, VA	DOD	Stonewall C. Winchester VA	ROH,WIN,SA2
Clardy, Reuben	Pvt.	A 6th SCVC			08/27/64	Wilson, NC	DOD		JR,PP
Clardy, Thomas	Pvt.	K 6th SCVC	16	CD	11/24/63	Adams Run, SC	DOD		PP
Clark,		2nd SCV			09/11/63	Petersburg	EXC	(Capt.Phillip's Co.)	UD2
Clark, A.	Pvt.	D 6th SCVI			06/15/64	Petersburg, VA	DOW	(Wdd 6/17/64)	ROH
Clark, A.D.	Sgt.	D 7th SCVI			09/20/63	Chickamauga, GA	KIA		ROH,JR,CDC,KEB
Clark, Alexander	Pvt.	D 1st SCVC		CR	03/19/65	Bentonville, NC	KIA		ROH,WAT,PP
Clark, Amzi	Pvt.	H 6th SCVI	20	YK	/ /		DOD		YEB
Clark, Archibald C.	Pvt.	F 21st SCVI		MO	07/10/63	Morris Island SC	KIA	(PP=Hilton Head)	ROH,JR,HAG,PP
Clark, Caleb	Cpt.(ADC)	15th SCVI			09/14/62	South Mtn., MD	KIA		ROH,JR
Clark, Charles	Pvt.	1st SCVA	34	GB	08/26/63	FT. Sumter, SC	DOW	(1st in 1st SCVIR)	ROH
Clark, Daniel	Pvt.	F 5th SCVI		YK	07/19/62	Richmond, VA	DOD		JR,SA3,CB
Clark, E. Gilbert	Pvt.	B 3rd SCVI		NY	04/23/62	Richmond, VA	DOD	Oakwood C.#74 Row I Div A	ROH,JR,ANY,OWC
Clark, Elsey	Pvt.	G 23rd SCVI		MO	08/30/62	2nd Manassas, VA	KIA	(JR=28th SCVI)	JR,HOM,CDC
Clark, F.E.	1st Sgt.	A 3rd SCVC	26	CO	06/15/64	Hardeeville, SC	DOD		ROH
Clark, G.B.	Pvt.	G 14th SCVI	20	AE	06/27/62	Gaines' Mill, VA	KIA		ROH,JR,CNM
Clark, George	Pvt.	G 7th SCVI		ED	09/28/61	Orange C.H., VA	DOD		HOE,KEB,UD2
Clark, Henry	Pvt.	G 22nd SCVI	30	AN	07/30/64	Crater, Pbg., VA	KIA		ROH,BLM
Clark, J. Frank	1st Cpl.	B 3rd SCVI		LR	11/14/62	At home on leave	DOD		ROH,JR,SA2,ANY
Clark, J. Newton	Pvt.	A 12th SCVI	28	YK	05/23/64	Jericho Ford, VA	KIA		JR,YEB
Clark, J.H.	Pvt.	B 19th SCVI		ED	/ /	Murfreesboro, TN		Evergreen C. Murfreesboro	TOD
Clark, J.J.	Pvt.	F 17th SCVI		YK	07/02/64	Petersburg, VA	KIA	(B, 12th SCVI?)	ROH,JR
Clark, James	Pvt.	C 24th SCVI	20	CO	08/24/62	James Island, SC	DOD		ROH
Clark, James	Pvt.	G Tucker's R			01/19/65	Salisbury, NC		Prob Old Lutheran C. there	PP
Clark, James S.	Pvt.	E 15th SCVI	34	FD	05/08/64	Spotsylvania, VA	KIA	Spotsylvania C.H., VA	ROH,JR,SCH,KEB
Clark, Jason Adolphus	4th Sgt.	A 5th SCVI	29	LR	10/27/64	Williamsburg Rd.	KIA		SA3,LAN,UD1
Clark, Jesse	Pvt.	D 3rd SCRes		MO	/ /	Charleston, SC	DOD		HOM
Clark, John Calvin	2nd Lt.	L 8th SCVI		MN	07/28/64	Deep Bottom, VA	KIA		HMC,R46
Clark, John L.	Pvt.	G 5th SCVC			06/18/64	Washington, DC	DOW	(P12= Sgt. 4th SCVC)	P5,P12
Clark, John W.	Pvt.	A 19th SCVI	21	ED	09/20/63	Chickamauga, GA	DOW		HOE,UD3
Clark, Joseph	Pvt.	B 5th SCVI		YK	11/14/61	Manassas, VA	DOD	(CB=Co. F)	SA3,CB
Clark, Kenneth	Pvt.	I 1st SCVIH		MN	11/07/62	Winchester, VA	DOD	Stonewall C. Winchester VA	ROH,WIN,SA1,HMC
Clark, Lawson	Pvt.	I 6th SCVI	35	YK	04/19/63	Franklin Stn. VA	DOD		YMD,YEB.CB
Clark, Luther	Pvt.	D 14th SCVI		ED	06/28/62	Gaines' Mill, VA	KIA	(Dup of W.L.?)	JR
Clark, M.	Pvt.	K 10th SCVI		CN	06/16/62	Meridian, MS	DOD	(Prob Rose Hill C. there)	RAS,PP
Clark, M.W.	Pvt.	B 6th SCVC			/ /				EDN
Clark, R.M.	Pvt.	H 6th SCVI	27	FD	09/17/62	Sharpsburg, MD	DOW	(In enemy hands)	ROH,JR,CDC

SOUTH CAROLINA DEAD IN CSA SERVICE 1861-1865

NAME	RANK	C	REGIMENT	AGE	DS	DIED	WHERE	WHY	BURIED	SOURCES
Clark, W.C.	Cpl.	A	3rd SCVC	35	CO	06/15/63		DOD		ROH
Clark, W.H.	Pvt.	E	7th SCVI		ED	10/05/64	Richmond, VA		Hollywood Cem.Rchmd. V252	ROH,HC
Clark, W.H.	Pvt.	E	7th SCVC	18	LS	/ /	At home	DOD	(Dup of same in HC?)	ANY
Clark, William	Pvt.	H	18th SCVI	27	YK	09/02/64	Elmira, NY	DIP	Woodlawn N.C.#78 Elmira	FPH,P5,P65,YEB
Clark, William	Pvt.	C	17th SCVI		YK	09/17/62	Sharpsburg, MD	KIA	(Lowry Diary)	CV
Clark, William	Pvt.	D	14th SCVI			07/07/62	Richmond, VA	DOW	(Wdd @ Gaines' Mill)	JR
Clark, William	Pvt.	D	26th SCVI			12/15/62		DOD		JR,HOE
Clark, William Coffee	Pvt.	A	3rd SCVC	36	CO	01/09/63		DOD		ROH,CDC
Clark, William E.	Cpt.	G	7th SCVI		ED	09/20/62	Maryland Hts. MD	DOW		KEB,HOE,R46,UD
Clark, William H.	Pvt.	F	17th SCVI		YK	09/14/62	South Mtn., MD	DOW		JR,CB
Clark, William H.	Pvt.	H	2nd SCVIRi	28	PS	09/11/63	Petersburg, VA			PP
Clark, William L.	Pvt.	D	14th SCVI	22	ED	05/23/64	Jericho Ford, VA	KIA		ROH,D14,HOE
Clarke, August J.	Pvt.	F	4th SCVC		MN	03/25/65	Hawes Shop, VA	DOW	Hollywood Cem.Rchmd. W737	ROH,HC,HMC
Clarke, G.W.	Pvt.	H	6th SCVI		FD	08/22/62	At home	DOD	(Typhoid)	JR
Clarke, James	Pvt.	H	7th SCVIBn		CR	05/12/64	Drury's Bluff VA	KIA	(NI HAG)	HHC
Clarke, James Caleb	Lt.	C	15th SCVI	23	FD	09/14/62	South Mtn., MD	KIA		ROH,HIC
Clarke, Robert Council	Cpl.	L	21st SCVI	26	MN	01/17/65	Ft. Fisher, NC	DOW		ROH,HMC,HAG,PP
Clarke, T.A.G.	1st Lt.	H	Ham.Leg.		CN	01/12/64	Dandridge, TN	DOW		ROH,R48,CDC
Clary, Obie	Pvt.	M	P.S.S.		SG	06/15/63	Franklin, VA	DOD		JR,HOS
Clary, William	Pvt.	F	15th SCVI		UN	10/06/62	Columbia, SC	DOD		ROH,JR,KEB,PP
Claxton, William L.	Pvt.	B	6th SCVC		ED	07/10/64	Charlottesville	DOW	Univ. Cem. Charlottesville	ROH,HOE,ACH,UD
Clayton,	Pvt.		2nd SCVC			07/07/64	James Island, SC	KIA		CDC
Clayton, Frank R.	Pvt.	F	25th SCVI	20	OG	03/23/65	Elmira, NY	DIP	Woodlawn N.C.#2439 Elmira	ROH,FPH,P6,HAG
Clayton, Jasper	Pvt.	B	22nd SCVI		SG	07/30/64	Crater, Pbg., VA	KIA		HOS
Clayton, Jesse M.	Pvt.	A	Orr's Ri.		AN	06/27/62	Gaines' Mill, VA	KIA		ROH,JR,CDC
Clayton, John	Pvt.	D	26th SCVI		MO	/ /	At home	DOD		HOM
Clayton, John	Pvt.	F	1st SCVA			05/13/65	Newport News, VA	DIP	Greenlawn C. Newport News	P6,PP
Clayton, John W.	Cpl.	A	24th SCVI	21	AE	/ /	Atlanta, GA	KIA		HOL
Clayton, Joseph	Pvt.	B	22nd SCVI		SG	07/30/64	Crater, Pbg., VA	KIA	(Jasper per BLM)	ROH,BLM
Clayton, W.C.	1st Sgt.	I	P.S.S.			07/15/62	Frayser's Farm	DOW		ROH,JR
Clayton, W.W.	Pvt.	F	25th SCVI	22	OG	11/10/64	Baltimore, MD	DIP	Loudon Pk. Cem. Balto. MD	ROH,FPH,HAG,PP
Cleary, O.V.	Pvt.	M	P.S.S.	25	SG	06/02/63	Franklin, TN	DOD	(HOS=I,5th SCVI, in VA)	ROH,HOS
Cleary, Stephen	Pvt.	F	18th SCVI	19	UN	07/07/62	Charleston, SC	DOD	(JR=Clary, Steven)	ROH,JR,PP
Clegg, Irvin	Pvt.	G	1st SCVIG		ED	05/31/64	Wilderness, VA	DOW	Univ. Cem. Charlottesville	ROH,SA1,HOE,AC
Cleland, David	Pvt.	G	Orr's Ri.		AE	05/21/64	Noel's Stn. VA	DOW	Hollywood Cem.Rchmd. I36	ROH,HC,P12
Cleland, Jesse P.	Pvt.	B	3rd SCVI		NY	12/01/62	At home	DOD		ROH,JR,SA2,ANY
Clemens, G.	Pvt.	K	23rd SCVI		SR	/ /		DOD		ROH
Clement, Edwin William	1st Cpl.	I	3rd SCVC	20	CN	04/12/63	Johns Island, SC	DOW	(Wdd 4/11/63)	ROH,JR,CDC
Clement, Ira Augustus	Pvt.	L	Orr's Ri.	21	AN	06/28/62	Richmond, VA	DOD	(JR=Joshua)	ROH,JR,CDC
Clendening, E.C.	Pvt.	H	12th SCVI	21	YK	08/07/63	North Carolina	DOD		JR,CWC,YEB
Cleveland, J.C.	Pvt.	B	7th SCVI			06/15/64	Richmond, VA		(NI KEB, 7th SCVC?)	ROH
Clifton, Benjamin F.	5th Sgt.	C	5th SCVI			10/04/64	Chaffin's Farm	DOW	(Wdd 9/30/64)	ROH,SA3
Clifton, James E.	Pvt.	B	2nd SCVC	24	BT	07/07/64	Johns Island, SC	KIA	(Beaufort District Troop)	ROH,CDC,AOA
Clifton, Robert	Pvt.	C	18th SCVI	28	UN	09/14/62	South Mtn., MD	KIA		ROH,JR
Cline, M.P.	Pvt.	G	2nd SCVC		NY	/ /		DIP	(Not on NY Monument list)	ANY
Clinkscales, Frank	Hos. Stwd.	G	Orr's Ri.		AE	06/27/62	Gaines' Mill, VA	KIA		ROH,JR,CV,CDC
Clinkscales, J.K.	Pvt.	D	Orr's Ri.		AN	12/13/62	Fredericksburg	KIA	(JR=J.R.)	JR,CDC
Clinkscales, James L.	Cpl.	F	24th SCVI	18	AN	07/20/64	Peachtree Ck. GA	KIA		HOL
Clinton, Andrew Jackson	Pvt.	K	17th SCVI	23	YK	11/12/63	Ft. Sumter, SC	KIA	Magnolia Cem. Charleston	ROH,JR,YEB,YMD
Clinton, Edward B.	1st Lt.	I	5th SCVI	24	YK	12/24/61	Warrenton, VA	DOD	(JR=Co.G, P.S.S.)	ROH,JR,SA3,YEB
Clinton, Jackson A.	Pvt.	F	5th SCVI	22	YK	05/31/62	7 Pines, VA	KIA	(YEB=James A.)	JR,SA3,YEB,CD

C

SOUTH CAROLINA DEAD IN CSA SERVICE 1861-1865

NAME	RANK	C REGIMENT	AGE	DS	DIED	WHERE	WHY	BURIED	SOURCES
Clinton, Thomas W.	Pvt.	I 6th SCVI		CR	11/03/62	At home	DOD		JR,HHC
Clinton, Williamson	Pvt.	K 17th SCVI	41	YK	/ /	At home	DOD	(1862)	YEB
Clopton, B.	Pvt.				/ /			Fredericksburg C.C. R4S11	FBG
Clowney, John	Sgt.	C 6th SCVC			06/11/64	Trevillian Stn.	KIA		ROH,JR
Clybern, Jesse N.	Pvt.	G 7th SCVIBn	35	KW	05/16/64	Drury's Bluff VA	KIA		ROH,JR,HIC,HAG
Clybern, John C.	Pvt.	D 7th SCVIBn	23	KW	06/13/63	Adams Run, SC	DOD	(PP=1/15/63)	JR,HIC,HAG,PP
Clybern, Thomas J.	1st Lt.	G 2nd SCVI		KW	08/20/61	Fairfax, VA	DOD	(Cpt. in KEB)	SA2,HIC,KEB,R45
Clyburn, George W.	Pvt.	E 22nd SCVI	29	LR	09/14/62	South Mtn., MD	KIA		ROH,JR,LAN
Clyburn, John	Pvt.	E 12th SCVI	34	LR	04/28/64	At home	DOD	(LAN=age 40, JR=4/9/64)	ROH,JR,LAN
Coachman, Edgar F.	2nd Sgt.	A Ham.Leg.	22	GN	08/06/62	Fts. Monroe, VA	DOW	Nat. Cem. Hampton, VA	ROH,JR,PP,TOD
Coachman, Walter R.	Pvt.	A 18th SCVAB			07/18/62	James Island, SC	DOD	Magnolia Cem. Charleston	JR,RCD
Coal, W.J.	Pvt.	I 9th SCVIB		CO	09/12/61	Germantown, VA	DOD		ROH
Coan, William H.	1st Lt.	E 2nd SCVC		SG	/ /	At home	DOD	(Coner, W.H. in 4th Bn?)	HOS
Coate, Henry	Pvt.	D 13th SCVI	21	NY	07/11/62	Richmond, VA	DOD		ROH,JR,ANY
Coats, D.G.	Pvt.	G 2nd SCV			/ /			Oakwood C.#42 Row G Div A	OWC
Coats, Daniel W.	1st Cpl.	G 2nd SCVI		KW	04/06/62	Richmond, VA	DOD	(Pneu., HIC=Samuel W.)	HIC,SA2,KEB,H2
Coats, H.	Pvt.	B 13th SCVI			/ /	Richmond		Oakwood C.#106 Row H Div C	ROH,OWC
Coats, Henry J.	Pvt.	G 2nd SCVI		KW	03/10/61	Vienna, VA	DOD		ROH,SA2,HIC,KEB
Coats, James P.	Pvt.	B 21st SCVI			05/16/64	Drury's Bluff VA	KIA		ROH,JR,CDC,HAG
Cobb, George W.	Pvt.	B 12th SCVI	42	YK	11/25/63	Pt. Lookout, MD	DIP	C.C. Pt. Lookout, MD YEB	ROH,JR,FPH,P5
Cobb, H.A.	Pvt.	K Orr's Ri.	42	AN	06/26/64	Richmond, VA	DOD	Hollywood Cem.Rchmd. U348	ROH,HC
Cobb, J.D.	Pvt.	K 12th SCVI		PS	08/09/62	Richmond, VA			ROH
Cobb, Richmond S.	2nd Lt.	C 6th SCVC	30	AE	10/01/64	Armstrong Mills	KIA	Methodist C. Greenwood, SC	BHC,R43,UD3
Cobb, Robert A.	Cpl.	K 12th SCVI	21	PS	04/22/64	Pt. Lookout, MD	DIP	C.C. Pt. Lookout, MD	ROH,JRR,FPH,P5
Cobb, Robert J.	1st Sgt.	F 7th SCVI	23	ED	09/26/63	Chickamauga, GA	DOW		ROH,JR,HOE,KEB
Cobb, W.P.	Pvt.	I 2nd SCVI		RD	12/26/62	Lynchburg, VA	DOD	Lynchburg CSA Cem. #10 R3	SA2,BBW
Cobb, William G.	Pvt.	F 5th SCVI	31	YK	06/19/64	Petersburg, VA	KIA	(YEB=Co. G)	JR,SA3,YEB,CB
Cobb,Jr., J.C.	Pvt.	K 12th SCVI		PS	05/06/62	Richmond, VA	DOD		ROH,JR
Cochran, A.W.	Pvt.	I 25th SCVI			03/18/65	Elmira, NY	DIP	Woodlawn N.C.#2373 Elmira	FPH,P6,P65,HAG
Cochran, H.	Pvt.	F P.S.S.			/ /		DOW		JR
Cochran, Samuel	Pvt.	B 6th SCVC		ED	/ /	Rockfish Crk. NC	KIA		HOE,UD3
Cochran, William H.	Cpl.	G 19th SCVI		AE	05/20/62	Columbia, SC	DOD	(On way home)	HOL
Cocke, S.	Pvt.	D 2nd SCV			01/05/63	Richmond, VA			ROH
Cocker, C.A.	Pvt.	H 14th SCVI		BL	05/16/64		KIA		JR
Cocker, O.W.	Sgt.	8th SCVI			06/15/62	Richmond	KIA		ROH
Cockfield, Cleland W.	Sgt.	E 10th SCVI	42	WG	12/31/62	Murfreesboro, TN	KIA		ROH,JR,RAS,HOW
Cockfield, John H.	Pvt.	E 10th SCVI	24	WG	12/31/62	Murfreesboro, TN	KIA		ROH,JR,RAS,HOW
Cockfield, Joseph C.	Pvt.	G 15th SCVI	19	WG	07/02/63	Gettysburg, PA	KIA		ROH,JR,CDC,HOW
Cockfield, Samuel W.	4th Sgt.	K 6th SCVI	27	WG	02/22/65	Richmond, VA	DOD		ROH,CTA,HOW,3RC
Cockran, George	Pvt.	H 1st SCVA			09/25/64	Charleston, SC	DOD	Magnolia Cem. Charleston	ROH,MAG
Cocksey, J.L.	Pvt.	K 27th SCVI			05/16/64	Drury's Bluff VA	KIA		ROH
Coder, Henry M.	Pvt.	C 7th SCVI			/ /			Magnolia Cem. Charleston	MAG
Cofer, J.B.	Pvt.	G 14th SCVI	19	AE	02/09/62	McPhersonville	DOD	(RR=6/1/62 in VA)	ROH
Coffee, Daniel	Pvt.	K 1st SCVIG		CN	08/29/62	2nd Manassas, VA	KIA		ROH,JR,SA1,CDC
Coffee, Joseph A.	Pvt.	E Orr's Ri.	18	PS	01/15/63	Manchester, VA	DOS	Oakwood C.#146 Row M Div A	ROH,JR,OWC
Coffee, William N.	Pvt.	E Orr's Ri.	20	PS	07/04/62	Dill Spring, VA	DOW	Hollywood Cem.Rchmd. M469	ROH,JR,HC
Coffer, J.W.	Cpt.	Ham.Leg.			10/22/62	Richmond		Hollywood Cem.Rchmd. B230	HC
Coffer, Joseph	Pvt.	G 14th SCVI		AE	06/15/62	Virginia			ROH
Coffield, S.H.	Pvt.	B 4th SCMil			02/19/65	Charleston, SC	DOD	Magnolia Cem. Charleston	ROH,MAG
Coffin, James	Pvt.	G 12th SCVI		PS	06/02/62	Richmond, VA		Hollywood Cem.Rchmd. L117	HC
Coffin, W.	Pvt.	D 1st SCVIH			08/30/62	2nd Manassas, VA	KIA		ROH,JR,CDC

SOUTH CAROLINA DEAD IN CSA SERVICE 1861-1865

NAME	RANK	C REGIMENT	AGE	DS	DIED	WHERE	WHY	BURIED	SOURCES
Coffin, W.F.	Pvt.	I 13th SCVI		SG	06/26/62	Richmond, VA		Hollywood Cem.Rchmd. L129	HC
Cofield, Robert R.	Pvt.		19		01/29/65	Columbia, SC		Elmwood Cem., Columbia, SC	WAT,PP
Cogburn, B.J.	Pvt.	A 7th SCVI			/ /			Spotsylvania C.H., VA	SCH
Cogburn, J.H.	Pvt.	K 14th SCVI		ED	06/21/62	Richmond, VA	DOD	Hollywood Cem.Rchmd. O204	ROH,HC,HOE,CDC
Cogburn, Lafayette	Pvt.	B 6th SCVC		ED	03/12/65	Fayetteville, NC	KIA		PP ROH,HOE,BAC,UD
Cogburn, Randolph M.	Pvt.	H 7th SCVIBn	22	ED	07/18/64	At home	DOW	(Wdd @ Drury's Bluff)	ROH,JR,HAG
Coggin, H.	Pvt.	I 13th SCVI		SG	08/13/62	Richmond, VA		Hollywood Cem.Rchmd. Q233	HC
Coggins, David W.	Pvt.	I 13th SCVI	20	SG	05/05/64	Wilderness, VA	DOW	Univ. Cem. Charlottesville	ROH,HOS,ACH
Coggins, E.	Pvt.	I 13th SCVI	25	SG	/ /	Richmond, VA	DOD		ROH
Coggins, John Lewis	Pvt.	I 13th SCVI		SG	08/11/62	Richmond, VA	DOD	Hollywood Cem.Rchmd. Q210	ROH,HC,HOS
Coggins, T.T.	Pvt.	I 13th SCVI		SG	08/14/62		DOD		JR
Coggins, W. Franklin	Pvt.	I 13th SCVI			06/30/62	Winder H. Rchmd.	DOD	(Typhoid)	JR
Cohen, A.P.	Cook	D 24th SCVI	32		11/15/62	Savannah, GA	DOD	(Free black)	EJM
Cohen, Henry F.	Pvt.	Hart's LA		CN	/ /	Richmond, VA	KIA	(Seven Days battles)	CNM,STC
Cohen, Isaac B.	Sgt.	A 21st SCVI		CN	01/15/65	Ft. Fisher, NC	KIA	(Cohen, Jacob B.in HAG)	ROH,PP,HAG
Cohen, James					/ /	Richmond, VA		(Richmond effects list)	CDC
Cohen, Max Edward	Pvt.	Hart's Bty	35	CN	03/19/65	Bentonville, NC	KIA	Beth Elohim, Chlstn.	ROH,PP,CAG,RCD
Cohen, Robert	Pvt.	A 22nd SCVI			06/16/62	Secessionville	KIA		ROH,CDC
Coit, George E.	1st Lt.	Palmetto A		SR	05/03/63	Suffolk, VA	KIA		ROH,JR,CV,SOB
Coit, Henry W.	Pvt.	F 9th SCVIB		SR	02/22/63	Cheraw, SC	DOD		JR
Coke, J. (Coker?)	Pvt.				/ /			Oakwood C.#64 Row N Div A	ROH,OWC
Coker, Asa	Pvt.	I 1st SCVA			09/25/64	Elmira, NY	DIP	Woodlawn N.C.#375 Elmira	FPH,P5,P65,P11
Coker, Berry	Pvt.	K Orr's Ri.		AN	05/05/64	Wilderness, VA	KIA	(JR=Benjamin)	ROH,JR
Coker, Charles W.	Ord.Sgt.	M 8th SCVI		DN	07/01/62	Malvern Hill, VA	KIA		ROH,JR
Coker, Daniel C.	1st Sgt.	E 6th SCVI	25	DN	12/18/64	At home	DOW	(Wdd @ Ft. Harrison)	ROH,JLC
Coker, Hugh	Pvt.	E 6th SCVI		DN	11/15/62	Winchester, VA	DOD		ROH,JLC
Coker, Isaac	Pvt.	I 26th SCVI			07/17/64	Richmond, VA		Hollywood Cem.Rchmd. U423	ROH,HC
Coker, J. Thomas	Pvt.	G 9th SCVI		DN	10/13/61	Richmond, VA	DOD	Hollywood Cem.Rchmd. F181	ROH,HC,JLC
Coker, J.W.	Pvt.	B 9th SCVIB		WG	/ /		DOD	(1861)	JR,CTA,HOW
Coker, John H.	Pvt.	G 9th SCVIB		DN	01/15/62	Charlottesville	DOD	Univ. Cem. Charlottesville	ROH,JLC,ACH
Coker, John S.	Pvt.	I 4th SCVC			12/10/64	Elmira, NY	DIP	Woodlawn N.C.#1046 Elmira	FPH,P65,P120,P
Coker, Josiah F.	Pvt.	E 6th SCVI		DN	02/15/63	At home	DOD		ROH,JLC
Coker, Robert H.	Pvt.	E 6th SCVI		DN	03/15/63	At home	DOD		ROH
Coker, William	Pvt.	A 4th SCVC		CD	05/28/64	Hawes Shop, VA	KIA		ROH
Coker, William C.	Pvt.	A 5th SCVC			06/19/64	Lincoln Hos., DC	DIP	Soldier's Burial Gds., DC	P6,P12
Colben, A.	Pvt.	E 2nd SCVIRi			01/18/64	Knoxville, TN	DIP		P5,P12
Colbert, H. Decatur	Pvt.	C 5th SCVI		OG	10/29/61	Richmond, VA	DOD		ROH,SA3
Colbert, V.W.	Pvt.	G 15th SCVI			02/24/64	Richmond, VA		Hollywood Cem.Rchmd. D162	HC
Colclasure, A.D.	Pvt.	H Ham.Leg.		RD	01/17/64	Danbridge, TN	KIA		ROH,CDC
Colclasure, J.T.	Pvt.	H Ham.Leg.		RD	01/17/64	Danbridge, TN	KIA		ROH
Colclough, Alexander	Cpt.	E P.S.S.		SR	/ /	Richmond, VA	KIA	(1862)	ROH
Cole, Andrew B.	Pvt.	I Hol.Leg.	39	SG	11/08/62	Richmond, VA	DOD	(HOS=DIP @ Elmira)	ROH,HOS
Cole, D. Jackson	Pvt.	B 13th SCVI		SG	11/09/62	Richmond	DOD	Hollywood Cem.Rchmd. C7	HC,HOS
Cole, Elijah W.	Pvt.	I Hol.Leg.		SG	09/19/64	Elmira, NY	DIP	Woodlawn N.C.#323 Elmira	FPH,HOS,P5,P65
Cole, H.P.	Pvt.	C 17th SCVI			07/30/64	Crater, Pbg., VA	KIA		ROH,JR,BLM
Cole, Howard	Pvt.	K 17th SCVI	41	YK	/ /	Petersburg, VA	KIA	(Dup of Cole, H.P.?)	YEB
Cole, J.J.	Pvt.	B 13th SCVI		SG	08/14/62	At home	DOD	(Consumption)	JR
Cole, James J.	Pvt.	K 23rd SCVI		SR	06/18/64	Petersburg, VA	KIA		JR,UD3
Cole, John	Pvt.	I 6th SCVI		SG	03/15/62	Richmond, VA	DOD	Oakwood C.#81 Row F Div A	HOS,JR,OWC
Cole, John A.	Pvt.	B 3rd SCVI		NY	10/05/62	Richmond, VA	DOD	Hollywood Cem. Rchmd S299	ROH,JR,ANY,SA2
Cole, Joseph	Pvt.	F 3rd SCVI		LS	05/06/64	Wilderness, VA	KIA		ROH,JR,SA2,KEB

C

SOUTH CAROLINA DEAD IN CSA SERVICE 1861-1865

NAME	RANK	C REGIMENT	AGE	DS	DIED	WHERE	WHY	BURIED	SOURCES
Cole, Matthew	Pvt.	I Hol.Leg.	18	SG	12/14/62	Kinston, NC	KIA	(JR=DOW @ Fredericksburg)	ROH,JR,HOS,PP
Cole, Pinckney	Pvt.	C 17th SCVI	43	YK	05/20/64	Clay's Farm, VA	KIA		YEB
Cole, Samuel	4th Sgt.	I 5th SCVI	27	SG	06/30/62	Frayser's Farm	KIA		JR,SA3,HOS
Cole, W.D.	Pvt.	A 13th SCVI	18	LS	04/25/63	Petersburg, VA		Blandford Church Pbg., VA	BLC,PP
Cole, W.J.	Pvt.	I 9th SCVIB			09/12/61	Germantown, VA	DOD		JR
Cole, William M.	Pvt.	B 13th SCVI		SG	03/27/63	Laurel hill, VA	DOD	Oakwood C.#20 Row 17 Div D	ROH,OWC,HOS
Coleman,	Sgt.	D 17th SCVI		CR	08/30/62	2nd Manassas, VA	KIA	(Prob Martin see HHC)	JR
Coleman, Allan G.	Pvt.	B 17th SCVI	28	FD	07/04/64	Petersburg, VA	DOW	(PP=7/7/64)	ROH,BLC,PP,UD3
Coleman, B. Franklin	1st Lt.	B 17th SCVI		FD	10/28/62	Winchester, VA	DOD	Crane Brick Chapel SC	JR,R47,UD3
Coleman, C.C.	Pvt.	A 22nd SCVI	21	ED	07/30/64	Crater, Pbg., VA	KIA		ROH,JR,BLM
Coleman, C.J.	Pvt.	B 18th SCVI	20	UN	06/18/64	Petersburg, VA	KIA	Gilead B.C. Union Cty, SC	ROH,UNC,UD3
Coleman, Charles	Pvt.	B 18th SCVI		UN	02/15/62	Charleston, SC	DOD		JR
Coleman, Edward A.	Pvt.	B 17th SCVI	27	FD	08/18/62	Petersburg, VA	DOD	(Born in Heckley, NC)	JR,BLC,HFC,PP
Coleman, H.R.	Pvt.	B 17th SCVI			/ /		DOW	(Wdd @ 2nd Manassas)	JR
Coleman, Henry A.	Pvt.	A 18th SCVI		UN	07/30/64	Crater, Pbg., VA	KIA		BLM
Coleman, Isaac M.	Pvt.	C 22nd SCVI	26	SG	11/12/64	Elmira, NY	DIP	Woodlawn N.C.#827 Elmira	ROH,FPH,P5,P65
Coleman, J.M.	Pvt.	K 14th SCVI		ED	06/27/62	Gaines' Mill, VA	KIA		HOE,CNM
Coleman, J.W.	Pvt.	D 10th SCVI		MN	/ /	Chattanooga, TN	DOD	City C. Chattanooga, TN	RAS,HMC,TOD
Coleman, Jacob	Pvt.	B 17th SCVI		FD	05/20/64	Wilmington, NC	DOD	Feaster Cem. Lyles Ford SC	UD3
Coleman, James D.	Pvt.	I 1st SCVIG		LS	06/19/62	Richmond, VA	DOD	Oakwood C.#11 Row N Div B	ROH,JR,SA1,OWC
Coleman, James E.	1st Lt.	I 20th SCVI		LN	08/05/62		DOD		ROH,JR,R48
Coleman, John	Pvt.	A 6th SCVC	42	GE	06/11/64	Trevillian Stn.	KIA	M.@ Rabon Creek B.C. GE	ROH,JR,GEC
Coleman, Lewis	5th Sgt.	D 14th SCVI	29	ED	08/30/62	2nd Manassas, VA	KIA		ROH,JR,D14,HOE
Coleman, M.A.	Pvt.	3rd SCVC		ED	06/15/64	Virginia	KIA		ROH
Coleman, R.C.	3rd Sgt.	B 17th SCVI		FD	/ /	Church Flats, SC	DOD		JR,HFC
Coleman, Robert	Pvt.	E 20th SCVI			06/01/64	Beulah Church VA	KIA		ROH
Coleman, Robert C.	Pvt.	B 17th SCVI			07/30/64	Crater, Pbg., VA	KIA		BLM
Coleman, Robert H.	Pvt.	E 15th SCVI	37	FD	06/30/62	Augusta, GA	DOD		ROH,JR,KEB
Coleman, T.J.	Pvt.	B 7th SCVI	20	AE	08/28/61	Culpepper, VA	DOD	Fairview C. Culpepper, VA	JR,CGH
Coleman, Thomas J.	Pvt.	G 14th SCVI	19	ED	02/09/62	McPhersonville	DOD		ROH,JR,HOE
Coleman, Thomas W.	Pvt.	C 16th SCVI		GE	01/13/64	At home	DOD	(PP=Co.K)	PP,16R
Coleman, W. Preston	Cpt.	B 17th SCVI		FD	01/31/63	(Prob Warrenton)	DOW	(Wdd @ 2nd Man.)	JR,R47,HFC,UD3
Coleman, W.B.	Pvt.	G 7th SCVI		ED	10/19/64	Cedar Creek, VA	KIA	(Dup of W.M.?)	JR
Coleman, W.L.	Pvt.	K 7th SCVI		ED	09/13/62	Maryland Hts. MD	KIA		JR,KEB
Coleman, William	Pvt.	G 7th SCV			/ /		KIA		UD2
Coleman, William M.	Pvt.	G 7th SCVI		ED	/ /		KIA		HOE
Colgan, James A.	Pvt.	D 14th SCVI	20	ED	06/30/62	Frayser's Farm	KIA	(HOE=Wdd @ Man & Gbg?)	ROH,D14,HOE
Collar, W.S.	Cpl.	A Orr's Ri.			07/09/63	Gettysburg, PA	DOW		ROH,P1
Collett, William A.	Pvt.	K 16th SCVI		GE	06/25/64	Kennesaw Mtn. GA	DOW	(Prob in CN in 1860 CEN)	ROH,16R,CUS
Collier, E.	Pvt.	A 7th SCVI		ED	06/29/62	Savage Stn., VA	DOW		CNM
Collier, E.J.	Pvt.	I 8th SCVI		MN	12/14/61	Richmond, VA	DOD	(Collins, E.H.?)	JR
Collier, James Daniel W.	Cpt.	D 1st SCVIH		OG	12/15/61	at home	DOD	(Date approx)	ROH,JR,SA1,R45
Collier, Joseph	Pvt.	A 27th SCVI		CN	06/15/65	At home	DOD	Magnolia Cem. Charleston	MAG
Collier, Thomas	Pvt.		22		12/21/61	Warren Spgs., VA	DOD		EDN
Collins, A. Bryan	Pvt.	F 20th SCVI		NY	06/19/64	Petersburg, VA	KIA		ROH,JR,ANY,CDC
Collins, A.D.	Cpl.	H 17th SCVI		BL	10/02/62	Frederick, MD	DOW	Mt. Olivet Cem. C.S.#78	ROH,JR,FPH,BOD
Collins, Albert T.	Pvt.	H 13th SCVI		SG	07/01/63	Gettysburg, PA	KIA		HOS
Collins, Andrew J.	Pvt.	L 10th SCVI		MN	06/15/62	Tazewell, TN	DOD		RAS,HMC,PP
Collins, B.	Pvt.	K 7th SCVC			05/02/65	Farmville, VA	DOW	Farmville Hos. Cem., VA	P6
Collins, C.D.	Pvt.				10/23/64	Petersburg, VA		Blandford Church Pbg., VA	BLC
Collins, D.B.	Pvt.	M P.S.S.		SG	06/15/63	Richmond, VA	DOD		ROH,HOS

SOUTH CAROLINA DEAD IN CSA SERVICE 1861-1865

NAME	RANK	C REGIMENT	AGE	DS	DIED	WHERE	WHY	BURIED	SOURCES
Collins, D.F.	Cpl.	L 10th SCVI		MN	/ /	Georgetown, SC	DOD	(Winter of '61-'62)	RAS,HMC
Collins, David	Pvt.	D 10th SCVI		MN	07/23/62	Columbus, MS	DOD	Friendship C. Columbus, MS	RAS,HMC,PP
Collins, David C.	Pvt.	L 21st SCVI	27	MN	05/16/64	Petersburg, VA	DOW	(Wdd @ Port Walthal Jctn.)	ROH,HMC,BLC,PP
Collins, E.O.	Pvt.	F 1st SCVIH	27	BL	01/07/65	Pt. Lookout, MD	DIP	C.C. Pt. Lookout, MD	ROH,FPH,P6,SA1
Collins, Edward H.	Pvt.	I 8th SCVI		MN	/ /	Virginia	DOD		JR,HMC
Collins, Frank	Pvt.	C 26th SCVI		MN	/ /	Mt. Pleasant, SC	DOD		HMC
Collins, J.D.	Pvt.	L 10th SCVI		MN	/ /		DOD		RAS,HMC
Collins, J.G.	Pvt.	L 10th SCVI		MN	/ /		DOD		RAS,HMC
Collins, J.H.	Pvt.	B 2nd SCVIRi		PS	/ /	Richmond, VA			ROH
Collins, J.H.	Pvt.	SCVA	30	CD	01/23/63	Virginia	DOD		ROH
Collins, J.R.	Pvt.	H 17th SCVI			08/30/62	2nd Manassas, VA	KIA		ROH,JR
Collins, J.S.	Pvt.	K 22nd SCVI			07/30/64	Crater, Pbg., VA	KIA		BLM
Collins, J.T.	5th Sgt.	E 5th SCVI			10/28/63	Lookout Valley	KIA	(JR=Racoon Mtn., TN)	ROH,JR,SA3,UD3
Collins, Joel Burt	Pvt.	L 21st SCVI		MN	06/16/64	Hares Hill, VA	KIA	(JR=6/18/64)	JR,HMC,CDC,HAG
Collins, John	Pvt.			OG	09/14/62	MD	KIA		ROH
Collins, John B.	Pvt.	G 1st SCVIG		ED	07/27/62		DOD	(Chronic Diarrhea)	JR,SA1,HOE
Collins, John E. (A.?)	Sgt.	H Orr's Ri.		MN	05/29/64	Richmond, VA	DOW	Hollywood Cem.Rchmd. S139	ROH,HC,CDC,HMC
Collins, John W.	Pvt.	L 21st SCVI	26	MN	10/15/64	Petersburg, VA	DOW		ROH,HMC,HAG
Collins, John W.	Pvt.	I 26th SCVI	22	WG	05/20/64	Drury's Bluff VA	DOW	Blandford Church Pbg., VA	CTA,HOW,BLC,PP
Collins, Jonathan	Pvt.	H 24th SCVI	34	CR	04/19/64	Atlanta, GA	DOD		ROH,HHC,CB
Collins, Joseph	Pvt.	L 21st SCVI	21	MN	11/10/64	Petersburg, VA			PP
Collins, Joseph B.	Cpl.	F 10th SCVI	24	MN	10/27/62	Cleveland, TN	DOW	(Wdd @ Chattanooga, TN)	ROH,JR,HMC,RAS
Collins, Lazareth S.	Pvt.	B 22nd SCVI		SG	/ /				ROH,HOS
Collins, Lorenzo D.	Pvt.	B 22nd SCVI	35	SG	10/23/64	Crater, Pbg., VA	DOW	(PP=10/23/64)	ROH,HOS,BLM,PP
Collins, M.	Pvt.	H 6th SCVC		SG	/ /	Virginia			HOS
Collins, Mark C.	Pvt.	M P.S.S.	35	SG	05/03/62	7 Pines, VA	KIA		ROH,JR,HOS
Collins, P.	Pvt.	H 6th SCVC		SG	/ /	Adams Run, SC	DOD		HOS
Collins, P.	Pvt.	H 13th SCVI		LN	05/15/64		KIA		JR
Collins, P.A.	Pvt.	C 4th SCVC			04/11/65	Elmira, NY	DIP	Woodlawn N.C.#2698 Elmira	FPH,P6,P65,P12
Collins, R.	Pvt.	F 4th SCVC		MN	06/11/64	Trevillian Stn.	KIA		HMC
Collins, R.F.	Pvt.	A 10th SCVI		GN	12/15/61	South Island, SC	DOD		JR,GRG,RAS
Collins, Richard H.	Pvt.	L 21st SCVI	22	MN	02/09/65	Elmira, NY	DIP	Woodlawn N.C.#1848 Elmira	ROH,FPH,HAG,P6
Collins, Samuel	Pvt.	I 27th SCVI		CN	12/24/62	King St. Chlstn.	MUR	Magnolia Cem. Charleston	JR,MAG,HAG
Collins, Thomas	Pvt.	K 24th SCVI		ED	/ /	(1863)	DOD		HOE
Collins, W.H.	Pvt.	C 5th SCVC			05/28/64	Price's Farm, VA	DOW	(In enemy hands)	JR,CDC
Collins, W.M.	Pvt.	H 12th SCVI	25	YK	06/18/63	Ashland, VA	DOD		JR,CWC,YEB
Collins, Washington	Pvt.	H 10th SCVI	28	WG	09/20/63	Chickamauga, Tn	KIA		ROH,JR,RAS,HOW
Collins, William	Pvt.	H 17th SCVI			09/17/62	Sharpsburg, MD	KIA		JR
Collins, William H.	Pvt.	B 6th SCVI			01/18/63	White Sulpher Ss	DOD		PP
Collins, William S.	Pvt.	H 6th SCVC	35		08/08/63	Adams Run, SC	DOD	(Yeadon Rangers)	PP
Collins, William T.	3rd Sgt.	L 21st SCVI	32	MN	06/15/64	Petersburg, VA	KIA		ROH,HMC,HAG
Collins,Jr., John	Pvt.			OG	/ /	North Carolina			ROH
Collison, C.J.	Pvt.	A 3rd SCVI		CD	/ /			Oakwood C.#109 Row J Div A	ROH,OWC
Colman, Charles	Pvt.				/ /	Camp Gurin,Chstn	DOD	Measles (Jan or Feb 62)	UD2
Coltharp, Brantly	Pvt.	B 6th SCVI		YK	/ /		DOD		ROH
Colvin, Dennis	Cpt.	I 6th SCVI		CR	04/22/62		DOD	(R46=2nd Lt.)	JR,R46,HHC,CB
Colvin, John	Pvt.	F 6th SCVI		CR	08/31/61		DOD	(Typhoid)	JR,HHC
Colvin, Martin	Pvt.	D 17th SCVI	21	CR	02/17/62	At home	DOD	(JR=DOW @ Sharpsburg)	ROH,JR,HHC
Colvin, Martin Franklin	Pvt.	I 6th SCVI	19	CR	09/01/64	At home	DOD		ROH,HHC
Comeck, James B.	Pvt.	F 6th SCVI		CR	03/11/64	Petersburg, VA			ROH
Comel, J.J.	Pvt.	K 3rd SCVABn			02/01/64			Magnolia Cem. Charleston	MAG

C

SOUTH CAROLINA DEAD IN CSA SERVICE 1861-1865

NAME	RANK	C REGIMENT	AGE	DS	DIED	WHERE	WHY	BURIED	SOURCES
Comer, Franklin	Pvt.	D 5th SCVI		UN	06/09/62	7 Pines, VA	DOW	Oakwood C.#35 Row K Div. B	ROH,JR,SA3,OWC
Commander, James E.	Pvt.	A 14th SCVI	30	DN	06/28/62	Petersburg, VA	DOD	Blandford Church Pbg, VA	ROH,JR,BLC,PP
Commander, Joseph G.	Pvt.	A 14th SCVI	22	DN	07/01/63	Gettysburg, PA	KIA		ROH,JR,CDC,GDR
Compton, J.A.	Pvt.	K 3rd SCVI	30	LS	05/05/64	Charlottesville	DOW	Univ. Cem. Charlottesville	ROH,SA2,ACH
Compton, J.R.	Pvt.	F 3rd SCVC			04/29/65	Ft. Delaware, DE	DIP	Finn's Point, NJ Nat Cem.	ROH,FPH,P6,P12
Compton, James F.	Pvt.	G 16th SCVI		GE	/ /	LaGrange, GA	DOD	Con. Cem. LaGrange, GA	16R,TOD
Compton, T.H.	Pvt.	F 14th SCVI		LS	07/17/62	Richmond, VA			ROH
Comstock, Charles Henry	Pvt.	H 1st SCVIG		BT	08/29/62	2nd Manassas, VA	KIA		ROH,JR,SA1,CDC
Comstock, James B.	Pvt.	F 6th SCVI		FD	05/11/62	Petersburg, VA	DOD	Blandford Church Pbg., VA	BLC
Conaugh, J.P.	Pvt.	I 17th SCVI		LR	10/15/62	Frederick, MD	DOW	Rose Hill C. Hagerstown MD	ROH,BOD
Condon, Jerome F.	Pvt.	F 11th SCVI			06/30/64	Pt. Lookout, MD	DOW	C.C. Pt. Lookout, MD	FPH,P5,HAG,P12
Condon, Nicholas J.	4th Cpl.	I 1st SCVIG			06/27/62	Gaines' Mill, VA	KIA		JR,SA1
Cone, George	Color Cpl.	A 8th SCVCBn		CO	/ /	At home	DOD	(Mem. to CNM 2/1562)	CNM
Cone, George P.	Pvt.	C 1st SCVIH		BL	06/15/62	Augusta, GA	DOD		ROH,SA1
Cone, L.G.	Sgt.	D 25th SCVI		MN	10/25/64	Richmond, VA			ROH
Cone, R.	Pvt.	E 8th SCVI		DN	08/24/61	Petersburg, VA	DOD	(Typhoid)	JR,KEB
Conlin, J.B.	Pvt.	K 27th SCVI		CN	09/22/64	Elmira, NY	DIP	Woodlawn N.C.#483 Elmira	FPH,P5,P65,HAG
Connel, S.D.	Pvt.	D 16th SCVI		GE	09/04/64	Lovejoy's Stn GA	KIA	(16R=DOD @ Adams Run)	ROH,16R
Connell, J.F.	Pvt.	E 22nd SCVI		LR	10/22/64	Charleston, SC	DOD	(Not a casualty in LAN)	ROH,LAN
Connell, William R.	Pvt.	E 22nd SCVI		LR	06/26/62	Charleston, SC	DOW	Magnolia Cem. Charleston	ROH,JR,PP,LAN
Connelly, Thomas	Pvt.	H 6th SCVC			05/22/64	Charleston, SC	DOD	(Soldiers Relief Hos.)	ROH,CDC
Conner, Franklin H.	Pvt.	G Hol.Leg.	20		07/18/62	Adams Run, SC	DOD		ROH
Conner, George McD.	Pvt.	B Orr's Ri.	27	AE	11/30/61	At home	DOD	(JR=Richmond 8/11/62)	ROH,JR,CDC
Conner, J.B.	Pvt.	F 3rd SCVI		LS	12/29/62	Richmond, VA	DOW	(Wdd @ Fredericksburg)	ROH,JR,SA2,KEB
Conner, James W.	Adjt.	17th SCVI		CR	06/20/64	Petersburg, VA	DOW	(Wdd 6/17/64)	ROH,HHC,CB
Conner, Martin B.	Pvt.	G 19th SCVI		AE	07/22/64	Atlanta, GA	KIA		CDC
Conner, Robert F.	Pvt.	4th Cavlry	20		/ /	Hosp. 1862			UD2
Conner, Robert T.D.	Pvt.	4th SCVC		MO	/ /	Charlottesville	DOD	Univ. Cem. Charlottesville	HOM,ACH
Conner, Spartan	Pvt.	D 16th SCVI		GE	09/03/64	Lovejoy Stn., GA	KIA	(NI 16R)	ROH
Connerly, Dempsey C.	Pvt.	K 11th SCVI	45	CO	10/01/63	At home	DOD		ROH,JR,HAG
Conners, Andrew J.	Pvt.	I 12th SCVI		LR	08/29/62	2nd Manassas VA	KIA		JR,LAN
Connor, Patrick	Pvt.	C 1st SCVA			04/27/65	Hart's Island NY	DIP	(Probably Cypress Hills)	P6,P79
Connor, W. Dukes	Cpl.	2nd SCVIRi			07/27/62		DOW		JR
Conolly, John M.	Pvt.	G 1st SCVIG		ED	12/01/62	Winchester, VA	DOD		SA1,HOE
Conrad, J.C.	Pvt.	E 10th SCVI		WG	10/15/62	Chattanooga, TN	DOD		ROH,RAS
Conroy, S.P.	Pvt.	15th SCVI		CN	06/05/62	Richmond, VVA		Hollywood Cem.Rchmd. M73	ROH,HC
Conroy, Timothy	Pvt.	B 1st SCVIBn		CN	08/19/63	Bty. Wagner, SC	DOW	(JR=Co.B, 27th SCVI)	ROH,JR
Contreras, Peter	Pvt.	Ham.Leg.			/ /			(Saved Metz @ Weldon, NC)	UD1
Conway, B.	Pvt.		26	LS	06/29/62	Savage Stn., VA	KIA	Laurens Cem. SC	PP
Conway, Stephen	Pvt.	I 2_th SCVI	25		06/07/64	Petersburg, VA			PP
Conwell, Amos S.	Pvt.	D 13th SCVI	21	NY	08/10/62	Gaines' Mill, VA	DOW	(Connel, A.J. in ROH)	ROH,ANY,PP
Conyers, John	Pvt.	D 9th SCVIB		CL	11/16/61	Culpepper, VA	DOD	Fairview Cem. Culpepper VA	ROH,JR,CGH
Coogler, Robert Edmond	Pvt.	C 20th SCVI	35	LN	04/15/62	Sullivans I., SC	DOD		ROH
Cook, A.	Pvt.	F 11th SCVI			08/04/64	Richmond		Hollywood Cem.Rchmd, V521	HC
Cook, A.J.	Pvt.			WG	/ /		DOD	(1863)	CTA,HOW
Cook, A.W.	Pvt.	D 27th SCVI		CN	06/26/64		KIA		JR
Cook, Alexander	Pvt.			WG	03/21/64	Weldon RR, VA	KIA	(May be Cook,A. F,11th)	CTA,HOW
Cook, Allen	Pvt.	H 10th SCVI		WG	/ /	Okolona, MS	DOD		RAS,PP,TOD
Cook, Allen	Pvt.	D 25th SCVI		MN	07/16/63	James Island, SC	DOD		JR
Cook, Allen A.	Pvt.	F 20th SCVI		OG	08/05/64	Richmond, VA	DOD	St. Mark's L.C. Saluda, SC	ROH,TOD
Cook, C.A.	Pvt.	H 14th SCVI		BL	05/12/64	Spotsylvania, VA	KIA		ROH,UD2

SOUTH CAROLINA DEAD IN CSA SERVICE 1861-1865

NAME	RANK	C REGIMENT	AGE	DS	DIED	WHERE	WHY	BURIED	SOURCES
Cook, Culberson	Pvt.	K 6th SCVC		LR	/ /				ROH
Cook, D.J.	Pvt.	K 7th SCVC		KW	/ /		DIP		HIC
Cook, E.F.	Sgt.			CN	06/15/61	Rantowles, SC	DOD	(Goose Creek Company)	ROH,CNM
Cook, E.R.	Pvt.	C Orr's Ri.		PS	01/06/62	Richmond, VA	DOD	(Enoch B./CDC?)	JR
Cook, E.W.	Pvt.	H 10th SCVI	21	WG	/ /		DOD	(1863)	RAS,CTA,HOW
Cook, Emory	Cpl.	H 9th SCVIB			01/25/62	Charlottesville	DOD		JR
Cook, G.S.	Pvt.			WG	07/22/64	Atlanta, GA	KIA		HOW
Cook, George	Pvt.	G 3rd SCVI	20	LS	01/22/62	Manassas, VA	DOD	(JR=Richmond 1/5/62)	ROH,JR,SA2,KEB
Cook, George	Pvt.	C 12th SCVI			09/06/62	Richmond, VA	DOD	Oakwood C.#87 Row B Div B	JR,OWC
Cook, George F.	Pvt.	A 10th SCVI		HY	07/22/64	Atlanta, GA	KIA		ROH,JR,RAS,GRG
Cook, Henry H.	Pvt.	A 3rd SCVIBn		LS	07/26/64	Petersburg, VA		Blandford Church Pbg., VA	ROH,BLC,PP
Cook, I.M.	Pvt.	A 10th SCVI		GN	02/11/63	St. Louis, MO	DIP	Jefferson Bks. N.C.#4906	FPH,RAS,PP,P12
Cook, Isaac B.	Pvt.	H 10th SCVI		WG	09/20/63	St. Louis, MO	DOW	(P5=POW @ Arkansas Post)	CTA,HOW,P5
Cook, J.B.	Pvt.	H Ham.Leg.		CN	08/30/62	2nd Manassas, VA	KIA		ROH,JR,CDC
Cook, J.E.	Pvt.	G 2nd SCVI		SR	07/15/64	Richmond, VA	DOD	Hollywood Cem.Rchmd. P198	HC,SA2,KEB
Cook, J.W.	Pvt.	H 10th SCVI	25	WG	/ /		DOD	(1862)	CTA,HOW
Cook, James	Pvt.	E 2nd SCVI		KW	/ /	Richmond, VA	DOD	(1863)	HIC,KEB,SA2
Cook, James A.	Color Sgt.	F 12th SCVI	26	FD	10/15/62	2nd Manassas, VA	DOW		ROH,JR,HFC
Cook, James C.	Pvt.	D Orr's Ri.	23	LR	01/05/63	Richmond, VA	DOD	(Pneumonia @ Chimborazo)	ROH,JR
Cook, James C.	Pvt.	D 27th SCVI	19	LS	06/24/64	Petersburg, VA	KIA		ROH,CDC,HAG
Cook, James Crawford	Pvt.	D 1st SCVIH		LR	01/08/63	Richmond, VA	DOD		ROH,SA1,LAN
Cook, James Ervin	Pvt.	I 21st SCVI		MN	02/19/62	Georgetown, SC	DOD		JR,HMC,HAG
Cook, Jesse	Pvt.	C 12th SCVI		FD	05/12/64	Spotsylvania, VA	KIA	(JR=Wilderness 5/6/64)	ROH,JR,HFC
Cook, Jethro G.	Pvt.	E 17th SCVI	20	YK	06/25/64	Petersburg, VA			ROH,PP,YEB
Cook, John	Pvt.	F 11th SCVI		BT	04/12/64	Camp Milton, FL	DOD		ROH,HAG
Cook, John	Pvt.	L 8th SCVI		MN	/ /	Lynchburg, VA		Lynchburg CSA Cem. #6 R4	BBW,KEB,HMC
Cook, John	Pvt.	H 17th SCVI			06/28/62	Gaines' Mill, VA	DOW		JR
Cook, John	Pvt.	H 14th SCV			/ /	June 1862	KIA		UD2
Cook, John A.	Pvt.	D 5th SCVC			09/29/64	Wyatt's Farm, VA	KIA	(JR=Trevillian Stn.)	JR,CDC
Cook, John C.	Pvt.	K 6th SCVC	26	LR	08/23/64	Ream's Stn., VA	KIA	(? Dup. Cook, Culberson)	ROH,JR
Cook, John M.	Pvt.	E 2nd SCVI		KW	06/12/62	Richmond, VA	DOD	(Measles)	H2,SA2,KEB
Cook, Joseph M.	Pvt.	E 2nd SCVI		KW	06/13/62	Richmond, VA	DOD	(Typhoid)	ROH,SA2,H2,KEB
Cook, Kinsey	Pvt.	D 11th SCVI	23	BT	07/27/63	McPhersonville	DOD	(JR=8/3/63)	ROH,JR,HAG
Cook, Matthew	Pvt.	E 2nd SCVI		KW	05/31/63	Richmond, VA	DOD	(H2=Madison)	SA2,KEB,H2
Cook, Middleton	Pvt.	F 11th SCVI	20	BT	03/05/62	Hardeeville, SC	DOD	(JR=1/14/62)	ROH,JR,HAG
Cook, Nimrod J.	Pvt.	K 3rd SCVI		SG	/ /	Florence, SC		(HOS=1865)	HOS,SA2,KEB
Cook, P.B.	Pvt.	G 13th SCVI		NY	08/29/62	2nd Manassas, VA	KIA	(JR=Gettysburg 7/2/63)	ROH,JR,ANY,CDC
Cook, Philip C.	Pvt.	G 13th SCVI		NY	11/06/62	At home	DOD	(ANY says KIA @ 2nd Man)	ROH,JR,ANY,
Cook, Samuel	Pvt.	H 7th SCVI			10/07/62	Staunton, VA		Thornrose C. Staunton, VA	ROH,TOD
Cook, Samuel	Pvt.	K 15th SCVI			/ /		KIA		JR,KEB
Cook, Samuel J.	Pvt.	H 3rd SCVI		LN	09/20/63	Chickamauga, GA	KIA		ROH,JR,SA2,ANY
Cook, Smith	Pvt.	F 18th SCVI		YK	10/15/62	Virginia	DOD		JR
Cook, T.J.	Pvt.	G 10th SCVI		HY	/ /		DOD		RAS
Cook, W.	Pvt.	E			06/01/63	Richmond, VA		(Perhaps 3rd SCVIBn)	ROH
Cook, W. Dorsey	Pvt.	C 25th SCVI	32	WG	03/29/65	Elmira, NY	DIP	Woodlawn N.C.#2521 Elmira	FPH,P6,P65,HAG
Cook, W. Ira	Pvt.	K 20th SCVI		LN	10/20/64	Charlottesville	DOD	Univ. Cem. Charlottesville	ROH,ACH,KEB
Cook, W.B.	Pvt.	C 24th SCVI			09/20/63	Chickamauga, GA	KIA		JR
Cook, W.H.	Pvt.	F 18th SCVI			11/04/62	Staunton, VA		Thornrose C. Staunton, VA	ROH,TOD
Cook, W.J.	Pvt.	C 15th SCVAB			05/16/65	Pt. Lookout, MD	DIP	C.C. Pt. Lookout MD	ROH,FPH,P6,P11
Cook, W.P.	Pvt.	I 26th SCVI		WG	11/07/63		DOD		JR
Cook, Washington	4th Sgt.	D 11th SCVI	28	BT	05/09/64	Swift Creek, VA	KIA		ROH,JR,HAG

C

SOUTH CAROLINA DEAD IN CSA SERVICE 1861-1865

NAME	RANK	C REGIMENT	AGE	DS	DIED	WHERE	WHY	BURIED	SOURCES
Cook, William	Pvt.	C 7th SCVI	25	AE	08/14/61	Richmond, VA	DOD	(Diarrhea)	ROH,JR
Cook, William D.	2nd Lt.	F 21st SCVI		MO	04/29/65	Pt. Lookout, MD	DOW	C.C. Pt. Lookout, MD	ROH,FPH,P6,P12
Cook, Willis M.	Pvt.	H 20th SCVI		LN	03/16/64		DOD		ROH
Cook,Jr., John A.	Pvt.	D 5th SCVC	23	CN	09/29/64	Ream's Stn., VA	KIA		ROH
Cooke, J.	Pvt.	I 22nd SCVI		OG	08/20/64	Petersburg, VA			ROH
Cooksey, T.L.	Pvt.	K 27th SCVI		CN	05/16/64	Drury's Bluff VA	KIA	(JR=G.L.)	JR,CDC,HAG
Cooley, A.C.	Pvt.	H P.S.S.		SG	06/27/62	Gaines' Mill, VA	KIA		ROH,JR,HOS,CDC
Cooley, Jacob M.	Pvt.	E 6th SCVC		SG	10/11/63	Adams Run, SC	DOD		ROH,PP
Cooley, Joel	Pvt.	B 22nd SCVI		SG	08/23/62	Rappahanock, VA	KIA	(Artillery Shell)	HOS,ROH
Coon, Davies	Pvt.	B 9th SCVIB			/ /	Charlottesville	DOD	Univ. Cem. Charlottesville	JR,ACH
Coon, Gideon J.	Pvt.	B 9th SCVIB			10/11/61	Virginia	DOD		JR
Coon, S.C.	Pvt.	G 2nd SCVI		LR	07/23/63	Gettysburg, PA	DOW	(KEB=Coon, S.S.)	SA2,HIC,LAN,P1
Cooner, E.J.	Pvt.	E 1st SCVCBn		OG	10/29/61	Branchville, SC	MUR	(Shot by William Blair)	ROH,CDC
Cooner, William M.	Pvt.	E 7th SCVI		ED	/ /		KIA	(KEB=Cooner, W.E.)	HOE,KEB,UD3
Cooney, Michael	Pvt.	I 1st SCVIR		CN	11/29/63	Charleston, SC	DOD	Magnolia Cem. Charleston	ROH,MAG,SA1
Coons, S.	Pvt.	D 22nd SCVI		PS	07/23/62	Charleston, SC	DOD	Magnolia Cem. Charleston	ROH,MAG
Cooper, B.	Pvt.	C 23rd SCVI		CN	07/16/64	Petersburg, VA			ROH
Cooper, B.A.	Pvt.	H 2nd SCVIRi			05/06/64	Wilderness, VA	KIA		ROH,JR
Cooper, Davis	Pvt.	F 22nd SCVI		PS	08/20/62	Columbia, SC	DOD		PP
Cooper, Elijah M.	Pvt.	F 13th SCVI		SG	05/22/62	Ashland, VA	DOD	(Thomas in HOS,JR=Co.E)	ROH,JR,HOS
Cooper, Fry	Pvt.	C 26th SCVI		MN	/ /	Petersville, VA	DOD		HMC
Cooper, George	Pvt.	I 22nd SCVI	25	OG	/ /	Catawba River NC	ACD	(Drowned)	ROH
Cooper, George	Pvt.	A 26th SCVI	21	HY	08/18/63	Jackson, MS	DOW	(Leg amputated)	ROH,JR,CDC,PP
Cooper, Henry	Pvt.	A 9th SCVIBn			07/10/62	Charleston, SC	DOW	Magnolia Cem. Charleston	ROH,JR,MAG
Cooper, Isaac N.	1st Lt.	C 3rd SCVIBn		LS	05/12/64	Spotsylvania, VA	KIA	(JR=Chickamauga)	JR,R45,KEB
Cooper, J.J.	Sgt.	K 25th SCVI		WG	12/29/62	Wilmington, NC	DOD	(Pneumonia)	JR,HAG
Cooper, Jacob	Pvt.	I 22nd SCVI	25	OG	07/16/63	Jackson, MS	KIA	(PP=7/4/63)	ROH,PP
Cooper, James	Pvt.	2nd SCVC		GE	07/15/64	Johns Island, SC	KIA		ROH
Cooper, Jesse	Pvt.	D 3rd SCVI		SG	07/01/62	Malvern Hill, VA	KIA	(SA2 says sick 9/16/62)	HOS,SA2,KEB
Cooper, Joel J.	Pvt.	K 21st SCVI		DN	01/15/65	Ft. Fisher, NC	KIA		PP,HAG
Cooper, John C.	Pvt.	E 2nd SCVI		KW	09/17/62	Sharpsburg, MD	KIA		HIC,SA2,KEB
Cooper, John D.	Pvt.	E 2nd SCVI		KW	09/17/62	Sharpsburg, MD	KIA	(JR=Co.A & Md. Hts.)	ROH,JR,SA2,HIC
Cooper, John E.	Pvt.	I 5th SCVI		SG	/ /	Virginia	KIA		HOS
Cooper, John Franklin	Pvt.	E Hol. Leg.	21	SG	12/20/62	Richmond, VA	DOD		ROH,HOS
Cooper, Julius J.	Cpl	E 3rd SCVABn	25	KW	04/13/63	Columbia, SC	DOD	(ROH=15th SCVI)	ROH,CDN,PP
Cooper, Levi	Pvt.	G 16th SCVI		GE	/ /	Dallas, TX	DOW	(Prob Dalton, GA)	16R
Cooper, Noah C.	Cpl.	K 16th SCVI		GE	07/22/62		DOD		16R,PP
Cooper, P.F.	Pvt.	B 22nd SCVI		SG	/ /				HOS
Cooper, Presley	Color Sgt.	G 7th SCVIBn		FD	07/15/64	Petersburg, VA	KIA		JR,HIC,HAG
Cooper, S.D.	Pvt.	A 3rd SCVABn			01/25/65	Charleston, SC	DOD	Magnolia Cem. Charleston	ROH,MAG
Cooper, Samuel	Pvt.	SCV			05/26/65	Raleigh, NC		Oakwood C. Raleigh, NC	TOD
Cooper, Thomas	Pvt.	K 16th SCVI		GE	/ /		DOD		16R
Cooper, Vernon H.	Pvt.	G 8th SCVI	22	MO	01/02/63	Richmond, VA	DOW	(Wdd @ Fbg) UD2	ROH,JR,HOM,KEB
Cooper, W.H.	Pvt.	A 1st SCVIG		BL	07/15/63	Guinea Stn., VA			SA1
Cooper, W.J.	Pvt.	B 7th SCVIBn		FD	11/05/64	Elmira, NY	DIP	Woodlawn N.C.#838 Elmira	FPH,P5,P65,HAG
Cooper, W.N.	Pvt	SCVC			04/29/62	Georgetown, SC	DOD		PP
Cooper, W.P.	Pvt.	D 1st SCMil			12/24/61	Charleston, SC	DOD	Magnolia Cem. Charleston	ROH,MAG
Cooper, William	Pvt.	C 27th SCVI		CN	10/03/64	Petersburg, VA			ROH,HAG
Cooper, William A.	Pvt.	Calhoun's			10/22/63	Columbia, SC	DOD		ROH
Cope, Daniel	Pvt.	E 4th SCVC		MO	10/31/64	Savannah, GA	DIP	(Date approx Xchd 10/29)	HOM,P114
Cope, James	Pvt.				11/16/64	Savannah, GA	DOD	Laurel Grove C. Savannah	ROH,BGA

SOUTH CAROLINA DEAD IN CSA SERVICE 1861-1865

NAME	RANK	C REGIMENT	AGE	DS	DIED	WHERE	WHY	BURIED	SOURCES
Cope, John J.	Pvt.	B 24th SCVI		MO	11/15/63	Atlanta, GA	DOD	Oak Hill C. Newman, GA	ROH,HOM,BGA
Copeland, Isaac L.E.	Pvt.	E 24th SCVI	33	CO	09/20/63	Chickamauga, GA	KIA		ROH,JR,CDC
Copeland, J. Anderson	2nd Sgt.	B 3rd SCVI	24	NY	09/24/63	Chickamauga, GA	DOW	Marietta C.C. GA	ROH,JR,NCC,SA2
Copeland, J.H.	Pvt.	G 17th SCVI			08/30/62	2nd Manassas, VA	KIA		JR
Copeland, J.J.T.	Pvt.	E 24th SCVI	23	CO	08/01/64	Atlanta, GA	KIA		ROH
Copeland, James L.	Pvt.	C 2nd SCVI		RD	07/17/63	Gettysburg, PA	DOW	P1	ROH,JR,GDR,SA2
Copeland, John W.	Pvt.	G 3rd SCVABn		SR	09/28/62		DOD		ROH
Copeland, Nicholas W.	Pvt.	K 23rd SCVI	25	SR	09/24/62	Gordonsville, GA	DOD		ROH,K23
Copeland, W. Jefferson	Pvt.	K 2nd SCVI		BL	10/22/62	Winchester, VA	DOD	(JR=9/27/62)	JR,SA2,KEB
Copeland, William	Pvt.	K 1st SCVIR		LR	02/19/64	Charleston, SC	DOD		ROH,SA1
Copps, John					/ /	Virginia	DOD		ROH
Corbett, H.F.	Pvt.	D 15th SCVI		KW	10/16/61	Columbia, SC	DOD		ROH,JR,HIC,CDN
Corbett, Julius Clement	Pvt.	D 15th SCVI		KW	07/02/63	Gettysburg, PA	KIA		ROH,JR,KEB,GDR
Corbett, L.	Pvt.	A 1st SCVA			06/22/63			Magnolia Cem. Charleston	RCD
Corbett, William M.	Pvt.	K 1st SCVIH		OG	11/12/62	Culpepper, VA	DOD		ROH,SA1,JRH
Corbin, Edward	Pvt.	D 11th SCVI		CO	05/23/65	Elmira, NY	DIP	Woodlawn N.C.#2926 Elmira	FPH,P6,P65,HAG
Corbin, John S.	Pvt.	A Orr's Ri.		PS	01/01/62	Richmond, VA	DOD	Hollywood Cem.Rchmd. D21	ROH,HC,CDC
Corbin, William	Pvt.	H 4th SCVI		PS	02/04/62	Manassas, VA	DOD	C.C. Manassas, VA	SA2,CV
Corbin, William F.	Pvt.	A Orr's Ri.		PS	05/20/62	Richmond, VA		Hollywood Cem.Rchmd. L15	HC,CDC
Corby, James	Pvt.	B 23rd SCVI	47	CN	06/17/64	Petersburg, VA	KIA		ROH,RCD
Corcoran, B.		CSN			02/20/65			Richmond, VA	ROH
Corcoran, H.	Pvt.	F P.S.S.		DN	06/30/62	Frayser's Farm	KIA	(JR=Co.E)	ROH,JR,CDC
Corcoran, J.	Pvt.	H 1st SCVA			06/22/63	Charleston, SC	DOD	Magnolia Cem. Charleston	ROH,MAG
Corder, D.A.	Pvt.	D 17th SCVI		CR	07/04/65	Elmira, NY	DIP	Woodlawn N.C.#2834W Elmira	FPH,P65,P120,H
Corder, Henry M.	Pvt.	C 7th SCVIBn	35	RD	10/24/63	Charleston, SC	DOD		ROH,HAG
Corder, Morgan C.	Pvt.	F 19th SCVI			07/22/64	Atlanta, GA	KIA	(JR=7/26/64)	ROH,JR
Corder, S.		F 19th SCV			/ /	Griffin Hosp.	SOW	Spaulding Cnty GA	UD2
Cordero, John W.	2nd Sgt.	C 1st SCVIG		RD	01/21/63	Richmond, VA	DOW	Elmwood C. Columbia, SC	ROH,MP,SA1,PP
Cordes, David A.	Pvt.	D 17th SCVI		CR	07/04/65	Elmira, NY	DIP	Woodlawn N.C.#2834 Elmira	ROH,FPH,P6,CB
Cork, John	Pvt.	B 7th SCVIBn	35	FD	08/10/64	At home	DOD		ROH,HAG
Corley, C.S.	Pvt.	D 14th SCVI	22	ED	12/05/62	Charlottesville	DOD	Univ. Cem. Charlottesville	JR,D14,HOE,ACH
Corley, Edward W.	Pvt.	G 1st SCVIG		ED	08/16/62	Richmond, VA	DOD	Oakwood C.#29 Row H Div C	ROH,JR,SA1,OWC
Corley, Edwin T.	Pvt.	I 5th SCVI	27	LN	03/01/65	Winnsboro, SC	DOD		ROH
Corley, Frank	Pvt.	E 7th SCVI		ED	/ /		KIA		HOE,KEB,UD3
Corley, Freeman H.	Pvt.	D 14th SCVI	20	ED	07/06/63	Gettysburg, PA	DOW		JR,D14,HOE,GDR
Corley, H.N.	Pvt.	K 13th SCVI		LN	07/02/63	Gettysburg, PA	KIA		ROH
Corley, J.A.	Pvt.	K 15th SCVI		ED	02/07/65	Camp Chase, OH	DIP	C.C.#1093 Columbus, OH	FPH,P6,P23,KEB
Corley, J.P.	Pvt.	F	20	LN	08/11/62	Pocotaligo, SC	ACD		ROH
Corley, Jacob C.	Pvt.	G 1st SCVIG		ED	05/29/62	Richmond, VA	DOD		JR,SA1,HOE
Corley, Joseph E.	1st Sgt.	K 13th SCVI		LN	10/15/62	Charlottesville	ACD	(Railroad wreck,ROH=Co.I)	ROH,JR
Corley, R.C.	Pvt.	F 3rd SCVC		BT	02/02/65	Ft. Delaware, DE	DIP	Finn's Point, NJ Nat. Cem.	ROH,FPH,P6,P41
Corley, Wesley	Pvt.	SC Militia	38	LN	03/15/65	Fayetteville, NC	DIP		ROH
Cornelius, Alexander	Pvt.	G 24th SCVI		CO	12/29/63	Atlanta, GA	DOD	Oakland C. Atlanta R7#7	BGA
Cornell, J.F.	Pvt.	E 22nd SCVI			10/22/63			Magnolia Cem. Charleston	MAG
Cornwall, Thomas	Pvt.				/ /	1861			ROH
Cornwell, Eli C.	Pvt.	E 6th SCVI	18	CR	09/06/61	Germantown, VA	DOD		ROH,HHC
Cornwell, J.P.	Pvt.	D 1st SCVC	28	CR	10/12/62	Richmond, VA	DOD	(Sgt. John B. in HHC?)	ROH
Cornwell, John	Pvt.	B 16th SCVI		GE	09/05/62	Charleston, SC	DOD	Magnolia Cem. Charleston	ROH,JR,PP,16R
Cornwell, W.D.J.	Pvt.	I 6th SCVI		CR	01/04/62		DOD		JR,HHC,CB
Corthan, W.					/ /			(Rchmd effects list 12/62)	CDC
Cosby, J.W.	Pvt.	I 19th SCVI			12/23/64	Nashville, TN	DOW	(Wdd:12/15)	P4,P6

C

SOUTH CAROLINA DEAD IN CSA SERVICE 1861-1865

NAME	RANK	C REGIMENT	AGE	DS	DIED	WHERE	WHY	BURIED	SOURCES
Cosby, John W.	Cpt.	G 19th SCVI		AE	12/31/62	Murfreesboro, TN	DOW	(In enemy hands)	HOL,P6
Coster, William	Pvt.	C 27th SCVI		CN	08/26/64	Petersburg, VA		(Cooper, W.in HAG?)	ROH,PP
Cotes, L.	Pvt.	G Ham.Leg.			09/17/62	Sharpsburg, MD	KIA		ROH,JR
Cothern, Henry	Pvt.	K 5th SCVI		SG	08/29/62	Richmond, VA	DOD	Hollywood Cem.Rchmd. C169	ROH,HC,HOS,SA2
Cothran, J.C.	Pvt.	E 16th SCVI		GE	06/14/64	Marietta, GA	KIA		JR,16R
Cothran, J.R.	Pvt.	H 18th SCVI		YK	10/15/62		DOD		JR
Cothran, Samuel G.	Sgt.	B 6th SCVC		ED	03/10/65	Fayetteville, NC	KIA		PP ROH,HOE,BHC,UD3
Cothran, Samuel N.B.	Pvt.	H 7th SCVIBn	26	AE	09/30/63	Sullivans Isl.SC	DOD	(JR=KIA 5/16/64)	ROH,JR,HAG
Cothran, William	Pvt.	E Orr's Ri.	20	PS	07/20/62	Gaines' Mill, VA	DOW	Oakwood C.#56 Row L Div C	ROH,JR,OWC,CDC
Cottingham, Charles	Pvt.	K 8th SCVI		MO	06/05/61	At home	DOD	(Typhoid)	JR,HOM,KEB
Cottingham, Conner	Pvt.	L 8th SCVI		MN	07/19/62	Williamsburg, VA	DOD	(Typhoid)	JR,HMC,KEB
Cottingham, Quitman	Pvt.	F 21st SCVI	46	MO	08/02/64	Petersburg, VA	DOW		ROH,HAG,HOM,PP
Cottingham, Stewart	Pvt.	I 1st SCVIH		MN	03/21/64	(Wdd 2nd M.)	DOW	(In hospital 12/31/63)	HMC,SA1,JRH
Cottingham, Ucal	Pvt.	E 4th SCVC		MO	/ /	Trevillian Stn.	DOW		HOM
Cotton, John L.	Pvt.	H 7th SCVIBn	21	RD	05/22/64	Drury's Bluff VA	DOW	Oakwood C.#4 Row J Div F	ROH,JR,OWC,HAG
Cotton, Joseph	Pvt.	B 7th SCVIBn	31	FD	03/17/64	Ridgeway, SC	DOD	Magnolia Cem. Charleston	ROH,MAG,CDC
Cotton, William J.	Pvt.	E 15th SCVI	35	FD	09/14/62	South Mtn., MD	KIA	(JR=2nd Lt.)	ROH,JR,KEB
Couch, Enoch	Pvt.	D P.S.S.		SG	/ /	Richmond, VA		(1862)	HOS
Couch, Ezekiel	Pvt.	C 5th SCVI		SG	10/04/61	Richmond, VA	DOD	Hollywood Cem.Rchmd. G126	ROH,JR,HC,SA3
Couch, J.	Pvt.	G 7th SCVIBn			11/06/62	Winchester, VA	DOD	(Croach, J.S. 7th?)	ROH
Couch, J.L.	Pvt.	E 18th SCVI		SG	08/15/62	Charleston, SC	DOD		JR
Couch, Jesse A.	Pvt.	E 18th SCVI	27	SG	02/12/65	Elmira, NY	DIP	Woodlawn N.C.#2056 Elmira	ROH,FPH,P6,P65
Couch, S.H.	Pvt.	L P.S.S.			07/26/64		DOD		ROH,JR
Couch, Siebern	Pvt.	D 2nd SCVI			01/04/63	Richmond, VA	DOD	(Typhoid, SA2=Couch, C.)	H2,SA2
Couch, Simeon	Pvt.	I 9th SCVIB		SG	/ /	Richmond, VA		Oakwood C.#83 Row B Div A	ROH,OWC,HOS
Council, Andrew J.	Pvt.	E 10th SCVI	41	WG	08/10/64	Macon, GA	DOW	Rose Hill C. Macon, GA	RAS,BGA,HOW,PP
Counts, Henry A.	Pvt.	C 20th SCVI		LN	06/01/64	Cold Harbor, VA	KIA		JR,KEB
Counts, James A.	Pvt.	G 13th SCVI		NY	07/07/62	Richmond, VA	DOD	(Typhoid, Winder Hospital)	ROH,JR,ANY
Counts, James W.	Pvt.	H 6th SCVI	18	FD	12/26/63	Ft. Harrison, VA	DOW		ROH
Counts, John Henry	Pvt.	C 20th SCVI	20	LN	06/01/64	Cold Harbor, VA	KIA		ROH,JR
Counts, John William	Pvt.	H 13th SCVI		LN	10/12/62	At home	DOD	(Measles)	JR
Counts, Jonah	Pvt.			LN	/ /				ROH
Counts, Joseph	1st Lt.	H 13th SCVI		LN	02/26/62	Whitehall, SC	DOD	(Erysipelas)	JR,R47
Counts, Paul Washington	Pvt.	H 13th SCVI		LN	07/16/62	Richmond, VA	DOD	Hollywood Cem.Rchmd. H31	JR,HC
Counts, Peter W.	Pvt.	G 13th SCVI		NY	02/24/64	At home	DOD	Zion U.M.C. Prosperity SC	ROH,NCC,ANY
Counts, Waller H.	2nd Sgt.	H 13th SCVI	28	LN	10/25/62	Lynchburg, VA	DOW	(Wdd @ 2nd M., JR=Co.K)	ROH
Counts, Waller Ruggles	Pvt.	H 6th SCVI	19	FD	05/31/62	7 Pines, VA	DOW	Oakwood C. #7 Row C Div. A	ROH,JR,OWC,WDB
Counts, William Junius	Cpl.	H 3rd SCVI		LN	03/14/62	Richmond, VA	DOD	Counts/Summer Gvyd Newby	ROH,JR,NCC,SA2
Counts, William Pierce	Pvt.	G 13th SCVI		NY	07/05/62	Gaines' Mill, VA	DOW	Zion U.M.C. Prosperity SC	ROH,JR,NCC,ANY
Courtenay, J.R.	2nd Lt.	H 14th SCVI		BL	04/15/65	Hatcher's Run VA	DOW	Oakwood C.#92 Row C Div A	BOS,OWC
Courteney, J.S.	Pvt.	H 14th SCVI		BL	11/29/63		KIA		JR
Courteney, W.B.	Sgt.	H 14th SCVI		BL	05/25/63	Virginia	DOD	(Pneumonia)	JR
Courtney, Aaron	Pvt.	K 6th SCVC	20	CD	08/23/64	Ream's Stn., VA	KIA		ROH,JR
Courtney, Brooks	2nd Sgt.	H 14th SCV			/ /	Camp Gregg	?	(5/ /63)	UD2
Courtney, Isaac	Pvt.	B 8th SCVI	30	CD	12/15/61	Richmond, VA	DOD	(Typhoid)	ROH,JR,KEB
Courtney, John	Pvt.	H 14th SCV			/ /	Mine Run 11/63	KIA		UD2
Covar, Charles Lewis	Pvt.	D 14th SCVI	23	ED	11/18/62	Manchester, VA	DOD	Hollywood Cem.Rchmd. S133	ROH,JR,HC,D14
Covert, W.H.					/ /	Columbia, SC		Elmwood Cem. Columbia, SC	MP,PP
Covin, Oscar W.	Pvt.	K 15th SCVI	20	ED	08/11/63	Chester, PA	DOW	Magnolia Cem. Charleston	ROH,JR,P1,P6,MAG
Covington, Elijah	Pvt.	D 1st SCV			05/24/65	Hart's Island NY	DIP	Cypress Hills N.C.#2874 NY	FPH,P6,P79
Covington, Henry	Pvt.	D 26th SCVI		MO	07/15/64	Petersburg, VA	KIA	(Date approx 6/17 to 7/27)	HOM,CDC

76

C

SOUTH CAROLINA DEAD IN CSA SERVICE 1861-1865

NAME	RANK	C REGIMENT	AGE	DS	DIED	WHERE	WHY	BURIED	SOURCES
Covington, J.A.	Pvt.	G 23rd SCVI		MO	07/15/65	Petersburg, VA	DOW	Near the hospital	ROH,HOM,P6
Covington, W.W.	1st Lt.	G 23rd SCVI		MO	06/15/64	Petersburg, VA	KIA	(HOM=died after war)	JR,HOM
Cowan, J.E.	Cpl.	A 20th SCVI		PS	10/15/64	Richmond, VA			ROH
Cowan, James	Pvt.	B 19th SCVI		ED	/ /		DOD		HOE
Cowan, Robert Andrew	Pvt.	A 22nd SCVI	34	AN	06/16/62	Secessionville	KIA		ROH,EDN,PP
Cowan, William	Pvt.	D 6th SCVI			/ /			Oakwood C.#16 Row G Div B	ROH,OWC
Coward, Harvey	Pvt.	L 8th SCVI		MN	08/22/62	Richmond, VA	DOD	(Typhoid)	JR,HMC,KEB
Coward, Henry	Pvt.	22nd SCVI			10/08/62	Richmond, VA			ROH
Coward, J.F.	Pvt.	I 26th SCVI		WG	10/06/63		DOD		JR
Coward, J.W.	Pvt.	D 26th SCVI		MO	08/28/63		DOD		JR
Coward, James J.	Sgt. Major	5th SCVI	21	YK	10/20/64	Darbytown Rd.	DOW	(Wdd 10/07/64)	SA3,YMD,TSC,YE
Coward, Lewis M.	Pvt.	4th SCVC		MO	/ /	(1862)	DOD	(Trfd frm G, 8th SCVI)	HOM
Coward, N.M.	Pvt.	B 14th SCMil			05/10/65	Hart's Island NY	DIP	Note says grave not found	FPH,P6,P79
Coward, Samuel	Pvt.	D 26th SCVI		MO	06/05/63		DOD		JR
Coward, W.	Pvt.	E 8th SCVI		DN	10/08/62	Richmond, VA		Hollywood Cem.Rchmd. C58	HC,KEB
Cowford, T.J.	Pvt.	B 11th SCVI			/ /	(OWC= J.J.)		Oakwood C.#15 Row F Div C	ROH,OWC
Cox,	Pvt.	D 24th SCVI			07/15/63	Jackson, MS	KIA	(ROH=22nd,unit not in MS)	ROH
Cox, A.M.	Sgt.	B 2nd SCVIRi		PS	/ /				ROH
Cox, A.T. (B.T.?)	Pvt.	F Orr's Ri.			/ /	Richmond, VA	DOD	Oakwood C.#100 Row L Div A	ROH,JR,OWC,CDC
Cox, Abraham S.	Pvt.	A 16th SCVI		GE	02/10/65	Camp Douglas, IL	DIP	Oak Woods C. Chicago, IL	FPH,P6,,CDC,P1
Cox, Andrew P.	Pvt.	C Orr's Ri.		PS	01/28/65	Ft. Delaware, DE	DIP	Finn's Pt., NJ Nat. Cem.	ROH,FPH,P5,CDC
Cox, B.	Pvt.	C 22nd SCVI			12/21/64	Richmond, VA			ROH
Cox, C.B.	Pvt.	G 2nd SCVIRi			06/29/62	Savage's Stn. VA	KIA		ROH,JR,CDC
Cox, Charles Edward	Pvt.	G 13th SCVI		RD	07/28/62	Frayser's Farm	KIA	(ANY= DOD in 1864)	ROH,JR,ANY
Cox, Charles G.	Pvt.	B 16th SCVI		GE	07/22/62	Adams Run, SC	DOD		16R,PP
Cox, D.	Pvt.	D 22nd SCVI		PS	12/20/64	Richmond, VA		Hollywood Cem.Rchmd. W676	HC
Cox, D.V.	Pvt.	L 7th SCVI		HY	/ /	Charlottesville	DOD	Univ. Cem. Charlottesville	ACH,KEB
Cox, Dempsey	Pvt.	L 2nd SCVIRi	44	AN	06/29/62	Savage Stn., VA	KIA	(JR=6/27/62)	ROH,JR,CDC,CNM
Cox, E.A.	Pvt.	D 18th SCVI		AN	09/13/62	Culpepper, VA	DOW		ROH,JR
Cox, E.P.	Pvt.	A 25th SCVI		CN	/ /	Charleston, SC	DOD		ROH,HAG
Cox, Edward M.	Pvt.	H Ham.Leg.		RD	06/23/65	Newport News, VA		Greenlawn C. Newport News	PP
Cox, Elisha	Pvt.	F 4th SCVI		GE	11/29/61		DOD		SA2
Cox, Ely	Pvt.	G 23rd SCVI		MO	/ /				HOM
Cox, Frank	Pvt.			WG	07/02/63	Gettysburg, PA	KIA		HOW
Cox, J.B.	Pvt.	C 1st SCVI			06/14/62			Hollywood Cem.Rchmd. P215	ROH,HC
Cox, J.F.	Pvt.	E 14th SCVI		LS	06/27/62	Gaines' Mill VA	KIA	Oakwood C.#121 Row N Div C	ROH,JR,OWC,CGS
Cox, J.S.	Pvt.	E 3rd SCVIBn		LS	09/06/62	Richmond, VA		Hollywood Cem.Rchmd. A60	ROH,HC,KEB
Cox, James	Pvt.	E 16th SCVI	32	AN	02/17/64	Rock Island, IL	DIP	C.C.#527 Rock Island, IL	ROH,FPH,P5,16R
Cox, Joel H.	Pvt.	K Orr's Ri.		AN	07/14/64	Dill Farms, VA	DOD		ROH,JR,CDC
Cox, John B.	3rd Sgt.	D 22nd SCVI	21	PS	08/08/64	Crater, Pbg., VA	DOW	Blandford Church Pbg., VA	ROH,BLM,BLC,PP
Cox, John M.	Cpl.	K Orr's Ri.	27	AN	05/05/64	Wilderness, VA	KIA		ROH
Cox, John Milton	1st Lt.	G 2nd SCVIRi		PS	06/29/62	Savage's Stn. VA	KIA		ROH,JR,CDC,R45
Cox, John T.	Pvt.	G 15th SCVI	24	WG	06/18/62	James Island, SC	DOD		ROH,JR,HOW,KEB
Cox, Kenneth	Cpl.	2nd SCVA			/ /	NC	KIA		UD1
Cox, L.D.	Pvt	C 10th SCVI		HY	01/07/64	Rock Island, IL	DIP	C.C.#142 Rock Island, IL	FPH,P5,RAS
Cox, L.D.	Pvt.	G 25th SCVI			10/23/64	Richmond, VA		Hollywood Cem.Rchmd. E25	HC
Cox, Lee	Pvt.	G 15th SCVI		WG	05/12/64	Spotsylvania, VA	KIA		UD1
Cox, Lewis J.	Cpl.	D 25th SCVI		MN	/ /	Petersburg, VA	KIA		HMC,HAG
Cox, M.L.	Pvt.	A 1st SCVC			06/30/64	Ft. Delaware, DE	DIP	Finn's Pt., NJ Nat. Cem.	ROH,FPH,P5,CDC
Cox, N.	Pvt.	B 2nd SCVIRi			06/27/62	Gaines' Mill, VA	KIA		JR
Cox, N.D.	Pvt.	F 4th SCVC		MN	06/20/64	Hawes Shop VA	DOW	Hollywood Cem.Rchmd. U59	ROH,JR,HC,HMC

C

SOUTH CAROLINA DEAD IN CSA SERVICE 1861-1865

NAME	RANK	C REGIMENT	AGE	DS	DIED	WHERE	WHY	BURIED	SOURCES
Cox, R. Franklin	Pvt.	G 15th SCVI	20	WG	01/04/63	(Wwdd @ 2nd Man)	DOW	Oakwood C.#10 Row N Div A	ROH,CTA,HOW,OWC
Cox, R.J.	Pvt.	L P.S.S.			/ /	Richmond, VA	DOW		ROH,JR
Cox, R.L.	Pvt.	G 15th SCVI		WG	/ /		DOD		JR
Cox, Samuel	Pvt.	D 15th SCMil			04/30/65	Pt. Lookout, MD	DIP	C.C. Pt. Lookout, MD	FPH,P6,P12
Cox, W. Jasper	Pvt.	A 16th SCVI		GE	12/30/63	Atlanta, GA	DOD	Oakland C. Atlanta R1#11	ROH,JR,16R,BGA
Cox, W.F.	Pvt.	C 10th SCVI		HY	/ /	Corinth, MS	DOD		RAS
Cox, W.H.	Pvt.	I 3rd SCVABn			05/26/64	Charleston, SC	DOD	Magnolia Cem. Charleston	ROH,MAG,CDC
Cox, W.J.	Pvt.			WG	06/30/64	Cold Harbor, VA	KIA		HOW
Cox, W.R.	Pvt.	G 2nd SCRes?		AN	02/06/65	Columbia, SC	DOD		ROH,PP
Cox, William	Pvt.	7th SCVI			09/17/62	Sharpsburg, MD	KIA	Rose Hill C. Hagerstown MD	ROH,BOD,P12
Cox, William F.	Pvt.	K Orr's Ri.	27	AN	07/12/62	Richmond, VA	DOW	Oakwood C.#43 Row R Div C	ROH,JR,OWC,CDC
Cox, William G.	Sgt.	G 15th SCVI	34	WG	10/19/64	Cedar Creek, VA	KIA		ROH,JR,KEB
Cox, William M.	Pvt.	H 22nd SCVI		GE	08/01/62	Columbia, SC	DOD		PP
Cox, William W.	Pvt.	E 16th SCVI	30	AN	03/06/64	Rock Island, IL	DIP	Con. Cem.#754 Rock Isl. IL	ROH,FPH,P5,16R
Coxe, C. Edwin	Pvt.	A Ham. Leg.		MO	/ /		DIP		HOM,WLI
Coy, J.M.	Pvt.				/ /			Fredericksburg C.C. R4S12	FBG
Coyer, H.S.		CSN			11/07/64	Richmond, VA			ROH
Crabtree, George	Pvt.	K 1st SCVIG			04/17/65	Pt. Lookout, MD	DIP	C.C. Pt. Lookout, MD	
Craddock, H.A.	Lt.	B 3rd SCVI			05/29/62	Richmond, VA		Hollywood Cem.Rchmd. L40	HC
Craddock, Henry Milton	Pvt.	H 13th SCVI		LN	07/07/62	Richmond, VA	DOD	Hollywood Cem.Rchmd. C186	ROH,JR,HC,CDC
Craddock, J.	Pvt.	23rd SCVI			07/15/64	Petersburg, VA			ROH
Craddock, Theodore	Pvt.	B 3rd SCVI		NY	05/15/62	Richmond, VA	DOD		ROH,JR,SA2,ANY
Craddock, W.A.	Pvt.	B 1st SCVC	35	LS	06/25/62	Columbia, SC	DOD	Beaverdam B.C. LS Cty.	ROH,LSC
Craddock, William P.	Pvt.	C 1st SCVIH		BL	07/27/63	At home	DOD		ROH,SA1
Craddock, Y.					/ /	Richmond, VA		(Richmond effects list)	CDC
Craft, J.S.	Pvt.	K 1st SCVIH		OG	09/30/64	Jones' Farm, VA	KIA		SA1
Craft, Jacob	Pvt.	E 2nd SCVI		KW	06/18/64	Petersburg, VA	KIA	(KEB=Croft)	SA2,KEB,HIC,H2
Craft, James	Pvt.	D 12th SCVI		RD	07/31/64	City Point, VA	DOW	City Pt. N.C. Hopewell, VA	ROH,PP,TOD,P12
Craft, L.S.	Pvt.	K 6th SCVI			/ /			Oakwood C.#46 Row R Div C	ROH,OWC
Crafton, Thomas M.	Pvt.	I 2nd SCVC		ED	07/05/64	Johns Island, SC	KIA		ROH,HOE,CDC
Cragham, J.	Pvt.	2nd SCV			08/21/61	Culpepper, VA	DOD	(JR=DOW in 7th SCV)	JR,CDC
Craig, Alexander J.	Pvt.	I 17th SCVI		LR	/ /	Charleston, SC	DOD		JR,LAN
Craig, Daniel	Pvt.	I 17th SCVI		LR	/ /	Wilmington, NC	DOD	(JR=B.M.)	JR,LAN
Craig, G.W.	Pvt.	F 17th SCVI		YK	08/21/64	Petersburg, VA	KIA		ROH,JR
Craig, George W.D.	Pvt.	I 3rd SCVI		LS	07/30/63	Mt. Jackson, VA	DOD		JR,SA2,KEB,PP
Craig, J.R.	Pvt.	I 12th SCVI		LR	/ /	Virginia	DOD		LAN
Craig, James	Pvt.	G 3rd SCVI		LS	12/28/62	Lynchburg, VA	DOD	(JR=Liberty, VA)	ROH,JR,SA2,HOS
Craig, James Pringle	Pvt.	I 12th SCVI		LR	04/10/62	White Hall, SC	DOD		JR,LAN
Craig, John A.	2nd Lt.	E 21st SCVI	21	CD	05/16/64	Drury's Bluff VA	KIA		ROH,R48,HAG,UD3
Craig, Lawrence C.	4th Cpl.	A P.S.S.		PS	10/03/64			Craig F. Gvyd Pickens, SC	PCS,CDC
Craig, R.M.	Pvt.	I 12th SCVI		LR	09/15/61	Lightwood Knot	DOD		JR,LAN
Crain, E.	Pvt.	G 13th SCVI			08/29/62	2nd Manassas, VA	KIA		JR
Crain, E.M.	Pvt.	D 16th SCVI		GE	09/13/63	Lauderdale, MS	DOD	(16R=KIA @ Franklin, TN)	16R,PP
Crain, S.J.	Pvt.	F 3rd SCVI		LS	09/17/62	Sharpsburg, MD	KIA	Rose Hill C. Hagerstown MD	ROH,JR,SA2,BOD
Crane, E.	Pvt.	E 20th SCVI		OG	06/13/63	Charleston, SC	DOD	Magnolia Cem. Charleston	ROH,MAG
Crane, Henderson	Pvt.	A Orr's Ri.		AN	/ /			Oakwood C.#12 Row G Div B	ROH,OWC,CDC
Crane, Jasper	Pvt.	A Orr's Ri.			06/27/62	Gaines' Mill, VA	KIA		ROH,JR,CDC
Crane, W.O.	Pvt.	D 5th SCVC	28	CN	05/28/64	Price's Farm, VA	DOW	(In enemy hands)	ROH,CDC
Crane, William J.	Pvt.	A 20th SCVI		PS	08/23/63	Bty. Wagner, SC	KIA	(KEB=Craine)	ROH,CDC,KEB
Cranner, G.W.	Pvt.	C 16th SCV			/ /		DOW	Marietta GA	UD2
Crapps, Edwin Boyd	Pvt.	C 15th SCVI	19	LN	07/24/63	Richmond, VA	DOW	Oakwood C.#4 Row 39 Div D	ROH,JR,OWC,H15

SOUTH CAROLINA DEAD IN CSA SERVICE 1861-1865

NAME	RANK	C REGIMENT	AGE	DS	DIED	WHERE	WHY	BURIED	SOURCES
Crapps, Patrick E.	Pvt.	K 15th SCVI		LN	07/08/62	Richmond, VA	DOD	Hollywood CEm.Rchmd. M187	ROH,JR,HC
Crapps, S.W.	Cpl.	I 4th SCVC	42	WG	05/29/64	Old Church, VA	DOW	Mrs. Wm. Wenton's, Hanover	ROH,CTA,HOW,CD
Craps, Harrison F.	Pvt.	K 13th SCVI	21	LN	10/04/61	At home	DOD	Craps Fam. C. Lexington SC	ROH,JR,TOD
Craps, William J.	Pvt.	D 24th SCVI	37	BT	03/11/65	Nashville, TN	DIP	(Wdd. @ Franklin, TN)	P4,P12
Crapse, James I.	Pvt.	E 11th SCVI	22	BT	12/26/62	Hardeeville, SC	DOD		ROH
Crapse, Jonas I.	Pvt.	E 11th SCVI		BT	03/20/65	Bentonville, NC	KIA	(HAG=Crapes, Jonas)	ROH,WAT,HAG,PP
Craven, Thomas	Pvt.	I 11th SCVI		CO	12/02/64	Elmira, NY	DIP	Woodlawn N.C.#1010 Elmira	FPH,P5,P65,HAG
Crawford,	Pvt.	PSS			10/02/64	Chaffins FarmVA	KIA	(date uncertain)	UD2
Crawford, B.	Pvt.	Home Gd.		UN	/ /		ACD	(Rail Rd trestle collapse)	NHU
Crawford, Benjamin F.	Cpl.	I 1st SCVIR			10/19/64	Charleston, SC	DOD	Magnolia Cem. Charleston	ROH,MAG,SA1,CD
Crawford, Charles		CSN			11/07/64	Richmond, VA			ROH
Crawford, Daniel A.	Pvt.	C 23rd SCVI		CN	06/18/65	Pt. Lookout, MD	DIP	C.C. Pt. Lookout, MD	FPH,P6,P114
Crawford, Dixon L.	Pvt.	H 1st SCVIG		BT	06/27/62	Gaines' Mill, VA	KIA	(JR=L.L.)	ROH,JR,SA1
Crawford, George J.	Pvt.	D 2nd SCVC	24	CN	11/12/62	Winchester, VA	DOD	Wassamaw B.C. Berkeley Cty	ROH,CDC,BCI
Crawford, H.	Pvt.				04/25/62	Richmond, VA		Hollywood Cem.Rchmd. B20	HC
Crawford, H.C.	Pvt.	E 12th SCVI			08/29/62	2nd Manassas, VA	KIA		JR
Crawford, Henry L.	Pvt.	E 1st SCVIG		MN	08/29/62	2nd Manassas, VA	KIA		ROH,JR,HMC,CDC
Crawford, J. Pinckney	Pvt.	A 6th SCVI		CR	09/15/61	Virginia	DOD	CB	ROH,JR,GLS,HHC
Crawford, J.P.	2nd Lt.	B 10th SCVI		HY	12/09/62	Atlanta, GA	DOD	Oakland C. Atlanta R10#22	ROH,RAS,R47,BG
Crawford, James Franklin	Pvt.	I 19th SCVI	41	AE	05/08/64	Rock Island, IL	DIP	C.C.#1102 Rock Island, IL	ROH,FPH,P5,P12
Crawford, James P.	Pvt.	B Orr's Ri.		AE	08/01/62	Richmond, VA	DOD		ROH,JR
Crawford, Jesse R.	Pvt.	K 15th SCVI		AE	10/21/62	Winchester, VA	DOW	Stonewall C. Winchester VA	ROH,JR,WIN,KEB
Crawford, John H.	2nd Lt.	G Orr's Ri.		AE	/ /	Pontotoc, MS		(Prob from Johnson's Isl.)	PP,P7
Crawford, John J.	Pvt.	D 2nd SCVC	23	CN	09/22/63	Jack's Shop, VA	KIA		ROH,BCI
Crawford, John W.	Pvt.	B 3rd SCVIBn		NY	09/14/62	Maryland Hts. MD	KIA	Little River P.C. Newby SC	NCC,KEB
Crawford, Martin P.	3rd Cpl.	A 9th SCVIB	37	LR	04/04/62	Richmond, VA	DOD	Old Presb. Ch. Cem. LR	ROH,LAN
Crawford, Pinckney T.	Pvt.	D 21st SCVI	35	CD	01/28/62	Georgetown, SC	DOD	(John T.?)	ROH,JR,PP
Crawford, R. Douglas	Pvt.	D 6th SCVI	29	YK	10/19/62	Sharpsburg, MD	DOW	Rose Hill C. Hagerstown MD	ROH,JR,YMD,BOD
Crawford, Robert	Pvt.	G 5th SCVI		YK	04/22/63		DOD		JR,SA3
Crawford, Robert L.	Cpt.	D 1st SCVIH	37	LR	04/20/63	Suffolk, VA	KIA	(Hill's Point,Nasemond R.)	ROH,JR,SA1,JLC
Crawford, Robert W.	1st Lt.	D 1st SCVC	27	CR	11/07/62	Staunton, VA	ACD	(Thrown by horse, dragged)	ROH,CDC,R43,HH
Crawford, S.J.	Cpl.	M 10th SCVI		HY	/ /		DOD	(1862)	RAS
Crawford, V.	Pvt.	D 3rd SCResB			03/24/64	Raleigh, NC		Oakwood C. Raleigh, NC	TOD
Crawford, W.D.	Pvt.	L P.S.S.			12/15/63		DOD		ROH,JR
Crawford, Wiley	Pvt.	H 7th SCVI			09/13/62	Maryland Hts. MD	KIA		JR
Crawford, William	Pvt.	F 6th SCVI	25	CR	05/31/62	7 Pines, VA	KIA		ROH,JR,WDB,HHC
Crawford, William B.	Pvt.	A 12th SCVI	39	YK	06/16/65	Chester, SC	DIP	(YEB=W.T.)(POW Rlsd 6/6)	YEB,P114
Crawford, William Elias	Pvt.	G 25th SCVI	33	BL	03/07/65	Elmira, NY	DIP	Woodlawn N.C.#2406 Elmira	ROH,FPH,P6,P65
Crawford, William G.	Pvt.	A 17th SCVI	33	CR	02/16/62	At home	DOD	(JR=7/30/63)	ROH,JR,HHC,CB
Crawford,Jr., Edward	Pvt.	F 6th SCVI	31	YK	09/29/64	Ft. Harrison, VA	KIA		YEB
Crawley, James	Pvt.	B P.S.S.		SG	/ /	Richmond, VA		Oakwood C.#62 Row P Div B	ROH,OWC
Creamer, George W.	Pvt.	E 16th SCVI	33	GE	03/11/64	Marietta, GA	DOD	Con. Cem. Marietta, GA	ROH,16R,BGA
Creamer, William H.	Pvt.	E 16th SCVI	23	GE	11/30/64	Franklin, TN	KIA	Macgavock C. Frkln Gv# 3	ROH,16R,PP
Creech, David L.	Pvt.	F 21st SCVI		MO	06/03/65	Elmira, NY	DIP	Woodlawn N.C.#2900 Elmira	ROH,FPH,P6,P65
Creed, J. Ellis	Cpl.	A 19th SCVI	30	ED	/ /		DOD	(1862)	HOE
Creek, T.		5th SCVI			/ /	(Not in SA3)		Oakwood C.#6 Row C Div C	ROH,OWC
Creekmore, Arthur	Pvt.	K 2nd SCVI		CN	02/04/62		DOD	(KEB=Creekins)	SA2,KEB
Creel, N.B.	Pvt.	I 10th SCVI		MN	06/17/62	MS	DOD	(JR=W.B.)	JR,RAS,HMC
Cregg, George	Pvt.	F 17th SCVI	20	YK	/ /	Richmond, VA	DOD		YEB
Creighton, James	Pvt.	K 4th SCVC		CN	09/15/62	McPhersonville	DOD		ROH,CLD
Crenshaw, Hezekiah N.	Pvt.	C Orr's Ri.		PS	01/06/63	Richmond, VA		Hollywood cem.Rchmd. D35	ROH,JR,HC,CDC

C

SOUTH CAROLINA DEAD IN CSA SERVICE 1861-1865

NAME	RANK	C REGIMENT	AGE	DS	DIED	WHERE	WHY	BURIED	SOURCES
Crenshaw, J. William	Pvt.	I 12th SCVI		LR	07/15/63	Gettysburg, PA	DOW		JR,LAN
Crenshaw, John S.	Pvt.	D 1st SCVIH		LR	09/30/64	Ft. Harrison, VA	KIA		SA1,LAN
Crenshaw, Joseph	Pvt.	I 12th SCVI		LR	05/15/61	McPhersonville	DOD		JR,LAN
Crenshaw, Troy L.	Pvt.	I 12th SCVI		LR	09/15/62	2nd Manassas, VA	DOW	(LAN=DOD)	JR,LAN
Crepps, Nestley	Pvt.	A 12th SCVI	24	YK	07/01/62	Malvern Hill, VA	KIA	(Dup of Wesley?)	YEB
Creps, Wesley C.	Cpl.	A 12th SCVI	36	YK	11/23/62	Richmond, VA	DOW	(Richmond effects list)	JR,CDC,YEB
Crespo, W.E.	Pvt.	A 12th SCVI		YK	11/25/62	Richmond, VA			ROH
Cresswell, D.E.	Pvt.	3rd SCVABn			/ /	Raleigh, NC	DOD	Oakwood C. Raleigh, NC	WAT,TOD
Cresswell, John	Pvt.	H 19th SCVI	35	AE	05/15/65	At home	DOD		ROH
Cresswell, Perryman	Pvt.	F 2nd SCVI		AE	/ /	At home	DOD		ROH,SA2,KEB
Cresswell, Thomas	Pvt.	H 19th SCVI	40	AE	06/15/64	Augusta, GA	DOD	Magnolia Cem. Augusta, GA	ROH,BGA
Crews, C.F.	Pvt.	D 17th SCVI			08/20/64	Petersburg, VA			ROH
Crews, Charles E.	Pvt.	D 11th SCVI	27	BT	06/19/64	Petersburg, VA	KIA		ROH,JR,HAG
Crews, Edward	Pvt.	F 11th SCVI	20	BT	03/06/62	Hardeeville, SC	DOD		ROH,HAG
Crews, J.W.	Sgt.	B 17th SCVI			07/30/64	Petersburg, VA			ROH
Crews, Marcus Aurelius	Pvt.	F 2nd SCVI	36	AE	10/25/64	Armory Sq. H. DC	DOW	(Wdd & POW @ Cold Harbor)	ROH,P6,KEB,P12
Crews, Moses	Pvt.	D 24th SCVI	28	BT	12/04/64	Camp Morton, IN	DIP	Green Lawn C. Indianapolis	FPH,P5,CDC,CV
Crews, Samuel	Pvt.	D 11th SCVI	17	BT	08/20/61	Bay Point, SC	DOD	(Isham?)	ROH
Crews, William L.	Pvt.	D 11th SCVI		BT	04/16/65	Hardeeville, SC	DOD		ROH,JR,HAG
Cribb, A.	Pvt.	I 7th SCV			08/09/63	McPhersonville	DOD	(Prob Cav Co. ante 7SCVC)	JR
Cribb, Benjamin	Pvt.	A 21st SCVI		GN	06/16/64	Petersburg, VA	DOW	(In enemy hands)	ROH,CDC,HAG
Cribb, Dempsey	Pvt.	E 1st SCVIG		MN	08/31/62	2nd Manassas, VA	DOW		ROH,JR,HMC,CDC
Cribb, Haly	Pvt.	A 21st SCVI		GN	12/21/62	Morris Island SC	DOD	(HAG & JR= Italy)	ROH,JR,HAG
Cribb, Levi	Pvt.	I 8th SCVI		MN	11/25/61	Warrenton Spgs.	DOD	(Pneumonia)	JR,KEB
Cribb, Noah	Pvt.	A 10th SCVI		GN	12/15/61	South Island, SC	DOD		JR,GRG,RAS
Cribb, R.	Pvt.	A 21st SCVI		GN	/ /	Weldon RR, VA	DOE	(Froze to death 1864)	ROH
Cribb, Samuel	Pvt.	A 21st SCVI		GN	06/16/64	Petersburg, VA	KIA	(Emanuel?)	ROH
Crider, A.L.	Pvt.	D 20th SCVI		OG	10/26/64	Mt. Jackson, VA			PP,KEB
Crider, C.W.	Pvt.	C 5th SCVI		OG	09/30/62	Lynchburg, VA	DOD	Lynchburg CSA Cem. #2 R4	BBW,SA3
Crider, David H.	Pvt.	K 1st SCVIH		OG	02/14/64	Rock Island, IL	DIP	C.C. #488 Rock Island, IL	SA1,P5,P39,P12
Crider, George B.	Pvt.	G 25th SCVI		OG	09/01/64	Philadelphia, PA	DOW	N.C.#271 Philadelphia, PA	ROH,FPH,P6,HAG
Crig, William (Craig?)	Pvt.	4th SCVI ?			/ /	(?H,2nd SCVI)		Oakwood C.#146 Row A Div A	ROH,OWC
Crim, D.L.	Pvt.	K 1st SCVIH		OG	12/13/62	Charlottesville	DOD	Univ. Cem. Charlottesville	ROH,SA1,ACH
Crim, Harvey	Pvt.			LN	/ /			Oakwood C.#41 Row F Div A	OWC
Crim, Henry E.	Pvt.	C 14th SCVCB	21	LN	11/03/62	McPhersonville	DOW	(Wdd 10/22/62 Leg Amptd)	ROH,PP,UD1
Crim, P.L.	Pvt.	B 1st SCVIH		OG	06/20/62	Charleston, SC	DOD	Magnolia Cem. Charleston	ROH,MAG,SA1
Crim, S.	Citizen	Columbia		RD	04/28/65	Hart's Island NY	DIP	(Probably Cypress Hills)	P6,P12,P79
Crim, T.J.	Pvt.	B 1st SCVIH		OG	10/12/62	Shepherdstown VA	DOD	Shepherdstown WVA Con. Cem	ROH,SA1,CV
Crimes, George	Pvt.	K Orr's Ri.			06/27/62	Gaines' Mill, VA	KIA	(Grimes?)	JR
Criminger, Rufus	Pvt.	A 1st SCVC		LR	08/15/63	Gordonsville, VA		Gordonsville, VA	ROH,GOR
Crisp, A.R.	Pvt.	D 3rd SCVIBn		LS	05/06/64	Wilderness, VA	KIA		ROH,JR,KEB
Crisp, Lewis R.	Pvt.	L 1st SCVIG		CN	08/29/62	2nd Manassas, VA	KIA		ROH,JR,SA1,CDC
Crisp, S.D.	Cpl.	G 5th SCVI			05/05/64	Wilderness, VA	KIA		JR
Crittenden, Kichard T.	Pvt.	K P.S.S.		SG	12/15/63	Louisiana	DOD	(Wdd also @ Gaines Mill)	ROH,JR,HOS
Crocker, Anthony C.	Pvt.	I 13th SCVI	20	SG	09/16/62	2nd Manassas, VA	DOW		ROH,JR
Crocker, Edward	Pvt.	H 5th SCVI			06/30/62	Frayser's Farm	KIA		JR,SA3
Crocker, H.	Pvt.	L 10th SCVI		MN	/ /		DOD		RAS,HMC
Crocker, Harvey D.	2nd Lt.	D 14th SCVI	29	ED	07/02/63	Gettysburg, PA	KIA	(JR=7/3/63)	ROH,JR,GDR,HOE
Crocker, James	Pvt.	B 18th SCVI		UN	06/17/62	Charleston, SC	DOD	Magnolia Cem. Charleston	ROH,JR,MAG
Crocker, James L.	Pvt.	B Hol.Leg.	31	SG	12/14/62	Kinston, NC	KIA	Bethesda B.C. SG Cty., SC	ROH,JR,PP,SSC
Crocker, James M.	Pvt.	I 13th SCVI	25	SG	12/13/62	Fredericksburg	KIA		ROH,JR

SOUTH CAROLINA DEAD IN CSA SERVICE 1861-1865

NAME	RANK	C REGIMENT	AGE	DS	DIED	WHERE	WHY	BURIED	SOURCES
Crocker, John A.	Pvt.	H P.S.S.		SG	06/27/62	Gaines' Mill, VA	KIA	(JR=J.E.)	ROH,JR,HOS,CDC
Crocker, M.	Pvt.	H P.S.S.			09/17/62	Sharpsburg, MD	KIA		ROH,JR,CDC
Crocker, Robert	Pvt.	G 10th SCVI			11/12/63	Med.Col. Atlanta		Oakland C. Atlanta R24#7	BGA
Crocker, T.C.	Pvt.	E 5th SCVI		YK	05/31/62	7 Pines, VA	KIA	(JR=2/21/62)	JR,SA3
Crocker, W.C.	Pvt.	E 6th SCVI		CR	/ /	Richmond, VA	KIA		HHC
Crocker, W.M.	Pvt.	C 18th SCVI	30	UN	07/18/62	Ft. Johnson, SC	DOD		ROH,JR
Crocker, W.W.	Pvt.	I 13th SCVI		SG	08/05/62	Winder Hos Rchmd	DOD	(Typhoid)	JR,HOS
Crocker, William C.	Pvt.	I 13th SCVI	20	SG	08/31/62	Warrenton, VA	DOW	(Wdd @ 2nd Manassas)	ROH,JR
Crockett, James E.	Pvt.	D 1st SCVIH		LR	11/01/62	Lynchburg, VA	DOD	(5th Sgt. per LAN)	ROH,SA1,LAN
Croft, Benjamin S.	Pvt.	K 6th SCVI	25	WG	07/16/62	Richmond, VA	DOW	(Wdd @ Fraysers Farm)	ROH,JR,CTA,3RC
Croft, F.	Pvt.	D 18th SCVI		AN	07/02/64	Petersburg, VA	KIA		ROH
Croft, L.S.	Pvt.	K 6th SCVI			/ /	Richmond, VA			ROH
Croft, Randall	1st Lt.	I 1st SCVA	23	BT	07/25/62	At home	DOD	(JR=7/26/62)	ROH,JR,EDN,R44
Crofton, Snowdon H.	Pvt.	I 24th SCVI	26	ED	07/22/64	Atlanta, GA	KIA	(Decatur)	CDC
Cromer, Daniel	Pvt.	D 15th SCMil	58	LN	04/15/65	Newbern, NC	DIP	Cedar Grove C. Newbern, NC	ROH,P6,WAT,PP
Cromer, Franklin H.	Pvt.	G Hol.Leg.			06/30/62	Adams Run, SC	DOD		ANY
Cromer, G.M.	Pvt.	5th SCVI			08/05/61	Charleston, SC	DOD		ROH
Cromer, George Henry	Pvt.	D 13th SCVI	24	NY	05/15/64	Spotsylvania, VA	KIA		ROH,JR,ANY
Cromer, J. Preston	Pvt.	D 13th SCVI	19	NY	05/12/64	Spotsylvania, VA	KIA		ROH,ANY
Cromer, James	Ord. Sgt.	D 15th SCMil		LN	04/15/65	(On road as POW)	DOW		ROH
Cromer, John D.	Pvt.	B 1st SCVIG	18	NY	06/24/62	Danville, VA	DOD		ROH,JR,SA1,ANY
Cromer, John L.	Pvt.	F 20th SCVI		NY	12/21/64	Pt. Lookout, MD	DIP	C.C. Pt. Lookout, MD	FPH,KEB,P5,P11
Cromer, John P.	Pvt.	K 2nd SCVIRi		AE	11/22/62	Manchester, VA	DOD	(ROH=KIA, Fraysers Fm.)	ROH,JR
Cromer, John S. (R.?)	Pvt.	F 20th SCVI			12/28/64	Richmond, VA		Hollywood Cem.Rchmd. W152	ROH,HC
Cromer, John William	Pvt.	H 13th SCVI	18	NY	10/12/61	Camp Johnson	DOD	(JR=At home)	JR,ANY
Cromer, Stephen	Pvt.	G Hol.Leg.			08/29/62	2nd Manassas, VA	KIA		ANY,ROH
Cromer, W.	Pvt.	D 2nd SCVIRi			/ /			Stonewall C. Winchester VA	ROH,WIN
Cromer, W.W.	Pvt.	H 15th SCVI		UN	05/15/64		KIA	(Prob Conner per KEB)	JR
Cromer, Whitfield	Pvt.	G Hol.Leg.		NY	11/06/64	Petersburg, VA	KIA		ROH,ANY
Cromer, William P.	Cpt.	D 13th SCVI	26	NY	07/02/63	Gettysburg, PA	KIA		ROH,JR,ANY,GDR
Crompton, S.N.	Pvt.	C 6th SCVI			07/18/64	Richmond, VA			ROH
Crook, W. Benjamin	Pvt.	C 24th SCVI	42	CO	09/20/63	Chickamauga, GA	DOW	Con. Cem. Marietta, GA	ROH,CDC,CCM
Crook, W. Hemphill	Pvt.	H 24th SCVI		CR	08/31/64	Georgia	DOD		ROH,HHC,CB
Crooker, J.D.	Pvt.	Orr's Ri.			05/25/64	Richmond, VA		Hollywood Cem.Rchmd. I90	ROH,HC
Crooks, Lewis T.	Pvt.	B 3rd SCVI		NY	09/24/63	Chickamauga, GA	DOW		ROH,SA2,ANY,KE
Crooks, W.	Pvt.	C 2nd SCVIRi			09/17/62	Sharpsburg, MD	DOW		JR,CDC
Crooks, William T.	Pvt.	D 5th SCVI		UN	10/05/64		DOD		SA3
Crosby,	Pvt.	23rd SCVI			/ /				ROH,CDC
Crosby,	Pvt.	G 27th SCVI		SG	05/16/64	Drury's Bluff VA	KIA	(Crossley, E.? in HAG)	ROH
Crosby, B.D.	Pvt.	D 8th SCVI		CD	01/14/62	Charlottesville	DOD	(KEB=Crowley)	JR
Crosby, Cornelius N.	Pvt.	B 7th SCVIBn	18	FD	07/15/64	Petersburg, VA		Stevens/Crosby F.C. FD Cty	ROH,UNC,HAG,PP
Crosby, Daniel	Pvt.	F 11th SCVI	28	BT	05/25/64	Fts. Monroe, VA	DOW	Nat. Cem. Hampton, VA	ROH,PP,TOD,P12
Crosby, Daniel W.	Pvt.	E 5th SCVI	19	YK	10/28/63	Lookout Val., TN	KIA	(CDC= D.H.)	SA3,CDC,YEB,UD
Crosby, David	Pvt.	F 11th SCVI	29	BT	05/09/64	Swift Creek, VA	KIA		ROH,JR,HAG
Crosby, Dennis	Pvt.	I 6th SCVI		CR	09/30/64	Chaffin's Farm	KIA		ROH,HHC
Crosby, Dennis H.	3rd Lt.	H 6th SCVI	31	YK	03/06/62	Centreville, VA	DOD	(Pneumonia)	ROH,JR,YEB
Crosby, J.J.	Pvt.	K 27th SCVI		CN	05/17/64	Drury's Bluff VA	KIA	(5/21/64?)	ROH,JR,CDC,HAG
Crosby, J.W.	Pvt.	F 10th SCVI		MN	/ /	Mississippi	DOD		RAS,HMC
Crosby, James	Pvt.	E 25th SCVI		CN	10/08/62	Green Pond, SC	DOD		JR,HAG,PP
Crosby, James M.	Cpt.	I 6th SCVI		CR	06/30/62	Frayser's Farm	KIA		WDB,R46,HHC
Crosby, John L.	Pvt.	F 10th SCVI		MN	/ /	At home	DOD	(JR=Co.A)	JR,RAS,HMC

C

SOUTH CAROLINA DEAD IN CSA SERVICE 1861-1865

NAME	RANK	C REGIMENT	AGE	DS	DIED	WHERE	WHY	BURIED	SOURCES
Crosby, John L.	Pvt.	A 1st SCV			11/20/62	At home	DOD (Diarrhea)		JR
Crosby, M.F.	Pvt.	I 6th SCVI		CR	/ /		DOD		CB,HHC
Crosby, Rufus Felder	Pvt.	B 7th SCVIBn	18	CR	07/01/64	Petersburg, VA	DOD	CB	ROH,JR,HAG,HHC
Crosby, T. Nevitt	Pvt.	B 7th SCVIBn	19	FD	06/25/64	Bermuda Hundred	DOW (HAG= C.N.)		ROH,HAG,HOF
Crosby, Walter Scott	Pvt.	D 12th SCVI		CR	07/15/63	Gettysburg, PA	DOW		JR,HHC
Crosby, William	2nd Lt.	E 5th SCVI	27	YK	12/13/63	Nashville, TN	DOW	Mt. Olivet C. Nashville	SA3,YEB,PP,P6
Crosland, Samuel	Pvt.	G 8th SCV	20		/ /	LynchburgVA 61			UD2
Cross, H.	Pvt.	E 21st SCVI		CD	07/10/63	Bty. Wagner, SC	KIA		ROH,JR,HAG
Cross, Isaac C.	Pvt.	C 19th SCVI		ED	03/23/62	Charleston, SC	DOD	Magnolia C. Charleston	ROH,MAG,HOE,UD3
Cross, J.	Pvt.	F 1st SCVA		CN	03/31/62	Ft. Sumter, SC	DOD	Magnolia C. Charleston	ROH,MAG
Cross, P.	Pvt.	B 8th SCVI		CD	02/15/62	Charlottesville	DOD	Univ. Cem. Charlottesville	JR,ACH
Cross, W.C.	Pvt.	12th SCVI			/ /			Oakwood C.#44 Row L Div C	OWC
Crossland, Abraham T.	Pvt.	E 15th SCVI	18	FD	05/24/64	Richmond, VA	DOD		ROH,KEB
Crossland, J.W.	Pvt.	F 1st SCVIR		FD	10/16/61		DOD		SA1
Crossland, John C.	Pvt.	A 23rd SCVI		CN	07/02/64	Petersburg, VA	DOW		ROH
Crossland, Samuel	Pvt.	G 8th SCVI		MO	09/15/61	Lynchburg, VA	DOD (JR=Charlottesville)		JR,HOM,KEB,UD1
Croston, J.	Pvt.	F 2nd SC			07/21/63		DOD (Erysipelas)		JR
Crouch, Hillery D.	Pvt.	E 7th SCVI	29	ED	02/07/62	Centreville, VA	DOD	Butler Ch. Edgefield, SC	EDN,HOE,UD3
Crouch, Jacob	Pvt.	D 19th SCVI	30	ED	07/22/64	Atlanta, GA	KIA (UD2=8/63)		ANY,HOE,UD3,UD2
Crouch, John S.	Pvt.	G 7th SCVI		ED	11/06/62	Winchester, VA	DOD	Stonewall C. Winchester VA	HOE,KEB,WIN
Crouch, Levi M.	Cpl.	D 19th SCVI	25	ED	/ /	Kentucky	DOD (1862)		HOE,UD3
Crouch, Levi McD.	2nd Lt.	D 19th SCVI		ED	09/30/62		KIA		MOE,R47
Crouch, T.	Pvt.	E 18th SCVI			07/30/62	Charleston, SC	DOD	Magnolia Cem. Charleston	ROH,MAG
Crouch, Vastine	Pvt.	2nd SCVA			/ /		DOW	In the field	UD3
Crouder, William	Pvt.	A 15th SCVAB			05/11/65	Hart's Island NY	DIP	Cypress Hills N.C. #2764	FPH,P6,P79
Crout, Elias	Pvt.	E 7th SCVI	30	LN	10/06/63	Chickamauga, GA	DOW	Crout C. Atlas Dr., Saluda	ROH,JR,TOD
Crout, Jacob T.	Pvt.	K 20th SCVI		LN	10/19/64	Mt. Jackson, VA	DOW	Mt. Jackson, VA Con. Cem.	ROH,SHS,PP,KEB
Crout, Jeremiah	Pvt.	I 15th SCVI	28	LN	12/15/62	Hardeeville, SC	DOD	Crout C. Atlas Dr. Saluda	JR,KEB,TOD,UD2
Crout, John	Pvt.	C 15th SCVI	22	LN	12/27/62	Fredericksburg	DOW		ROH,JR,KEB,TOD
Crout, Levi	Pvt.	K 9th SCVIB			10/17/61	Charlottesville	DOD	Univ. Cem. Charlottesville	JR,ACH
Crout, Samuel	Pvt.	H 7th SCVI	21	ED	/ /	(1865)		Crout C. Atlas Dr. Saluda	TOD
Crow, D.	Pvt.	E 1st SCVI			07/04/62	Richmond, VA		Hollywood Cem.Rchmd. M472	HC
Crow, H.B.	Pvt.	F 1st SCVC			08/13/63	Staunton, VA	DOW	Thornhill C. Staunton, VA	ROH,TOD
Crow, John T.	Pvt.	Macbeth LA			12/01/62	Goldsboro, NC	DOD (Quinsy, Willowdale C.?)		JR,PP
Crow, Pinckney	Pvt.	B 1st SCVC	26	SG	06/15/62	Church Flats, SC	DOD		ROH,HOS
Crow, Silas	Pvt.	G 2nd SCVIRi			07/01/62	Malvern Hill, VA	KIA (JR=6/28/62)		ROH,JR,HOF,CDC
Crow, Silas N.	Pvt.	Macbeth LA		UN	11/21/62	Kinston, NC	DOD		PP
Crowder, B.	Pvt.	B 17th SCVI			08/30/62	2nd Manassas, VA	KIA		ROH
Crowder, J.D.	2nd Cpl.	G 5th SCVI			05/06/64	Wilderness, VA	KIA (JR=5/5/64)		ROH,JR,SA3
Crowder, J.W.	Sgt.	B 17th SCVI			07/30/64	Crater, Pbg., VA	KIA		ROH,JR,BLM
Crowder, John A.	Major	19th SCVI	29	GE	02/14/63	At home	DOW (Wdd @ Murfreesboro)		CGW,HOE,R47
Crowder, Robert	Pvt.	B 17th SCVI		FD	08/30/62	2nd Manassas, VA	KIA		JR,HFC,UD3
Crowley, Alexander L.	Pvt.	E 6th SCVI		DN	06/15/63	Blackwater R. VA	DOD (POW @ 7 Pines & Xchd)		ROH,JLC,CDC
Crowley, W. Harrison	Pvt.	D 21st SCVI		CD	09/25/63	Charleston, SC	DOD	Magnolia CEm. Charleston	ROH,JR,MAG,HAG
Crowley, William F.	Pvt.	H 6th SCVC	39	CD	12/24/63	Adams Run, SC	DOD (ROH=4th SCVC)		ROH,PP
Crowly, W.	Pvt.	G 23rd SCVI		MO	/ /	2nd Manassas, VA	KIA		HOM
Crowther, J.	Pvt.	B Orr's Ri.		AE	06/15/64	Richmond, VA	DOW		ROH,P12
Croxton, John Quincy.	Pvt.	G 2nd SCVI		LR	07/21/63	Gettysburg, PA	DOW	P1,LAN	ROH,JR,GDR,SA2
Cruber, W.R.	Cpl.	P.S.S.			03/26/65	Richmond, VA		Hollywood Cem.Rchmd. W139	HC
Crumpton, Benjamin G.	Pvt.	C 1st SCVIR			11/13/63	Morris Island SC	KIA		ROH,SA1
Crumpton, Samuel H.	Pvt.	C 6th SCVC			07/24/64	Richmond, VA	DOW (Wdd @ Trevillian Stn.)		ROH,JR

NAME	RANK	C	REGIMENT	AGE	DS	DIED	WHERE	WHY	BURIED	SOURCES
Crumpton, Thomas H.	Pvt.	E	15th SCVI	18	FD	12/30/63	Abington, VA	DOD		ROH
Crumpton, W.C.	Cpl.	E	15th SCVI	22	FD	06/19/64	Gordonsville, VA	DOW (Wdd 5/6/64)		ROH,KEB,HOF
Crymes, William	Cpl.	D	Ham.Leg.		AN	/ /	Bacon Race, VA	DOD		GRS
Cubstead, J.E.	Pvt.	K	25th SCVI		WG	05/09/64	Swift Creek, VA	KIA		CTA,HOW,HAG
Cubsted, Jacob	Pvt.	F	20th SCVI	40	LN	02/12/62	At home	DOD		CNM
Cudd, John Henry	Pvt.	I	Hol.Leg.	20	SG	05/09/62	Adams Run, SC	DOD (ROH=At home)		ROH,HOS,PP
Cudd, Joseph	Pvt.	K	Hol.Leg.	21	SG	09/26/62		DOW (Wdd @ South Mtn.)		ROH
Culberson, A.J.	Pvt.	B	1st SCVIR		AN	03/16/65	Averysboro, NC	KIA		ROH,SA1,WAT,PP
Culberson, G.W.	Pvt.	G	1st SCVIR			03/16/65	Averysboro, NC	KIA		ROH,SA1,WAT,PP
Culberson, J.M. (W./OWC)	Pvt.	F	16th SCVI			07/10/63	(?16th NI VA)		Oakwood C.#51 Row M Div G	ROH,OWC
Culbertson, J.B.	Pvt.	C	3rd SCVIBn		LS	10/19/63	Strasburg, VA	KIA		ROH,JRR,KEB
Culbertson, J.W.	Pvt.		13th SCVI			01/10/63	Richmond, VA		Hollywood Cem.Rchmd. D195	ROH,HC
Culbertson, T.H.	Pvt.	C	3rd SCVIBn		LS	12/07/62	Richmond, VA			ROH,KEB
Culbertson, Y.J.	Sgt.	C	3rd SCVIBn		LS	07/02/63	Gettysburg, PA	KIA	Magnolia Cem. Charleston	ROH,JR,GDR,KEB
Culbreath, John	Cpl.	A	SC RES Bn	20	ED	04/15/65	Greenville, SC	DOD (State Cadet Battalion)		ROH,PP
Culbreath, John	3rd Sgt.	K	7th SCVI	25	ED	06/02/64	Cold Harbor, VA	KIA		ROH,KEB
Culburth, H.L.	Pvt.		5th SCV		ED	11/30/62	Richmond, VA		Hollywood Cem.Rchmd. B225	HC
Culclasure, A.D.	Pvt.	B	1st SCVIH		OG	09/15/62		DOD (Date approx)		SA1
Culclasure, Davis	Pvt.	H	Ham.Leg.		OG	01/12/64	Tennessee	DOW		ROH
Culclasure, John	Pvt.	H	Ham.Leg.		OG	01/12/64	Tennessee	DOW		ROH
Culler, Henry L.	Cpl.	E	1st SCVC	23	SG	07/06/63	Gettysburg, PA	DOW (Wdd 7/2/63)		ROH,HOS,P12
Culler, Jacob	Pvt.	G	25th SCVI		OG	08/21/64	Petersburg, PA	KIA		ROH,HAG
Culler, James	4th Cpl.	H	14th SCV			09/17/63		KIA		UD2
Culler, James Whitford	Pvt.	H	14th SCVI	23	BL	09/20/62	Shepherdstown MD	KIA		ROH,JR
Cullum, J.T.	Pvt.	K	9th SCVIB			11/10/61	Manassas, VA	DOD		JR
Cullum, Peter	Pvt.	H	14th SCV			05/05/64		KIA		UD2
Cullum, William	Pvt.	A	19th SCVI	45	ED	02/15/65	Camp Chase, OH	DIP	C.C.#1258 Columbus, OH	FPH,HOE,P6,UD3
Culough, W.C.	Pvt.	K	6th SCVI			11/14/64	Richmond			ROH
Culp, Benjamin Franklin	Pvt.	A	6th SCVI		CR	10/06/62	Virginia	DOD (Typhoid)	CB	ROH,JR,HHC,GLS
Culp, Drewry	Pvt.	B	6th SCVI		YK	06/30/62	Frayser's Farm	KIA		ROH
Culp, John M.	Pvt.	A	6th SCVI		CR	09/01/62	2nd Manassas, VA	DOW		JR
Culp, John Rivers	Cpl.	A	6th SCVI	25	CR	05/12/64	Hanover Jctn. VA	KIA (CB=5/15/64)		ROH,GLS,HHC,CB
Culp, John Wesley	Pvt.	A	6th SCVI		CR	08/29/62	2nd Manassas, VA	DOW (Groveton)	CB	JR,WDB,GLS,HHC
Culp, W.B.	Lt.		Signal C.			03/15/63		DOD		ROH
Cumming, A.	Pvt.	C	14th SCVI		LS	08/03/62	Richmond, VA			ROH
Cummings, Frank W.	4th Cpl.	K	11th SCVI	25	CO	08/30/64	Weldon RR, VA	KIA	Hollywood Cem.Rchmd. V57	ROH,HC,HAG
Cummins, John	Pvt.	K	Orr's Ri.	24	AN	06/27/62	At home	DOD (JR=8/1/62)		ROH,JR
Cummins, Patrick	Pvt.	K	1st SCVIG		CN	09/01/62	Ox Hill, VA	KIA		JR,SA1
Cummins, Reuben M.	Pvt.	K	Orr's Ri.	28	AN	08/27/62	Richmond, VA	DOD (JR=July)		ROH,JR,CDC
Cumpton, L.H.	Pvt.	C	6th SCVI			07/17/64	Richmond, VA		Hollywood Cem.Rchmd. U561	HC
Cunningham, A.F.	2nd Lt.	F	24th SCVI	22	AN	05/14/63	Jackson, MS	KIA		ROH,JR,CDC,R48
Cunningham, Absalom J.	Cpl.	H	4th SCVC		LR	07/03/64	Hawes Shop, VA	DOW	Hollywood Cem.Rchmd. X145	HC,LAN,ROH
Cunningham, C.	Pvt.	I	8th SCVI			04/20/62	Richmond, VA	DOD		ROH
Cunningham, H.	Pvt.	C	4th SCVC			07/31/64	Richmond			ROH
Cunningham, Henry M.	Pvt.	K	3rd SCVI	27	SG	01/08/65	Pt. Lookout, MD	DIP	C.C. Pt. Lookout, MD	ROH,FPH,P6,HOS
Cunningham, J.R.McC.	Pvt.	F	24th SCVI		AN	09/21/63	Chickamauga, GA	DOW	Con. Cem. Marietta, GA	ROH,HOL,CDC,CC
Cunningham, J.W.	Pvt.	E	12th SCVI	24	LR	06/27/62	Gaines' Mill, VA	KIA		ROH,JR,LAN
Cunningham, James	Cpl.	B	2nd SCVIRi		PS	/ /				ROH
Cunningham, James	Pvt.	K	P.S.S.		SG	/ /	Farmville, VA	DOD		JR,HOS
Cunningham, John H.	Pvt.	C	6th SCVC		SG	08/25/64	Ream's Stn., VA	KIA (HOS=Gravely Run,RR=8/23)		ROH,JR,HOS
Cunningham, John H.	Pvt.	A	13th SCVI		LS	07/02/63	Gettysburg, PA	KIA (JR=Co.E & 7/1/63)		ROH,JR,CDC,GDR

C

SOUTH CAROLINA DEAD IN CSA SERVICE 1861-1865

NAME	RANK	C REGIMENT	AGE	DS	DIED	WHERE	WHY	BURIED	SOURCES
Cunningham, John Wesley	Pvt.	F Hol.Leg.	20	AE	02/03/62	Adams Run, SC	DOD		ROH,PP
Cunningham, Joseph	Cpt.	G 19th SCVI		AE	06/09/62	Meridian, MS	DOD	(? R47=Dropped 5/8/62)	HOL,R47,PP
Cunningham, Joseph Henry	Cpt.	K 3rd SCVI	29	SG	10/31/63	Chickamauga, GA	DOW	Fair Forest Cem. UN Cty.	ROH,SA2,HOS,CDC
Cunningham, Joseph L.	Sgt.	A 13th SCVI	23	LS	06/27/62	Richmond, VA	DOD	(JR=Consumption at home)	ROH,JR
Cunningham, Joseph P.	Cpt.	G 2nd SCVI	29	LW	07/02/63	Gettysburg, PA	KIA	Magnolia Cem. Charleston	ROH,JR,GDR,SA2
Cunningham, M.M.	Cpt.	D 4th SCVIBn	24	GE	07/04/62	Malvern Hill, VA	DOW	Bailey Family C. GE	JR,GEC,R47,GEE
Cunningham, R.C.	Pvt.	B 22nd SCVI		SG	11/03/63	Charleston, SC	DOD	Magnolia C. Charleston	ROH,MAG
Cunningham, Reuben J.	Pvt.	G 16th SCVI	19	GE	09/03/64	Covington, GA	DOW	(Wdd @ Atlanta)	ROH,16R
Cunningham, Robert F.	Pvt.	G Orr's Ri.		AE	06/27/62	Gaines' Mill, VA	KIA		ROH,JR,CV,CDC
Cunningham, William W.	2nd Cpl.	K 6th SCVI	20	WG	09/17/62	Sharpsburg, MD	KIA		WDB ROH,JR,HOW,UD1
Cureton, Drayton T.	Pvt.	G 2nd SC Res		NY	02/15/64	At home	DOD	(Date approx)	ANY
Cureton,Jr., James B.M.	Cpl.	H 7th SCVC		KW	05/30/64	Old Church, VA	KIA		ROH,JR,HIC,CDN
Curlee, John	Pvt.	F 3rd SCVIBn	34	RD	06/15/63	Richmond, VA			ROH,KEB
Currence, Bishop B.	Pvt.	H 18th SCVI		YK	08/30/62	2nd Manassas, VA	KIA		ROH,JR,CDC,YEB
Currence, D.A.	Pvt.	F 17th SCVI		YK	05/08/65	Pt. Lookout, MD	DIP	C.C. Pt. Lookout, MD	FPH,P6,P114
Currie, Archibald	Pvt.	A 23rd SCVI		CD	07/30/64	Crater, Pbg., VA	KIA		ROH,JR,BLM
Currie, Neal R.	Pvt.	F 21st SCVI		MO	05/14/65	Elmira, NY	DIP	Woodlawn N.C.#2802 Elmira	ROH,FPH,P6,HOM
Currie, W. Thomas I.	Pvt.	A 21st SCVI		GN	07/15/64	Richmond, VA	DOW	(Curry in ROH)	ROH,HAG
Curry, Barnett B.	Pvt.	A 6th SCVI	26	GE	07/22/64	Charlottesville	DOW	Dials Methodist C. GE Cty.	GEC,ACH,LSC
Curry, D.	Pvt.	F 10th SCVI		MN	/ /	At home	DOD		RAS,HMC
Curry, H.S.	Pvt.	D 3rd SCVIBn		LS	09/20/63	Chickamauga, GA	KIA	(Curry, L. in KEB?)	ROH,CDC
Curry, J.	Pvt.	F 10th SCVI		MN	/ /	At home	DOD		RAS,HMC
Curry, John A.	Pvt.	G 3rd SCVI		LS	01/05/62	Richmond, VA	DOD		ROH,JR,SA2,KEB
Curry, John C.	Pvt.	D 21st SCVI		CD	07/15/64	Boydton Plank Rd	KIA		ROH,HAG
Curry, N.W.	Pvt.	A 6th SCVI		LS	08/08/64	Richmond, VA		Hollywood Cem.Rchmd. V468	ROH,HC
Curry, W.T.	Pvt.	E 14th SCVI		LS	09/20/62	Shepherdstown VA	KIA		CGS
Curry, William H.T.	Pvt.				07/16/64	Petersburg, VA		Blandford Church Pbg., VA	BLC
Curry, Wilmot W.	Sgt.	Wash. Arty		BT	11/16/61	Camp Butler, VA	DOD		ROH
Curtis, James S.	Pvt.	I 1st SCVIG			08/11/64	Gordonsville, VA	DOD	Gordonsville, VA	ROH,SA1,GOR
Cusack, H.D.	Pvt.	A 7th SCVC	29	WG	/ /	Richmond, VA	KIA		CTA,LOR,HOW
Cushman, Robert	Pvt.	F 7th SCVI	22	BL	/ /	At home	DOD	(KEB= Cashman)	HOE,KEB
Cuthbert, George B.	Cpt.	I 2nd SCVI	33	BT	05/10/63	Manchester, VA	DOW	(Wdd 5/3/63 @ Chanc'ville)	ROH,SA2,R45,CDC
Cutley, A.P.	Pvt.	F 20th SCVI		NY	08/18/64	(Collins, A.B.?)		Hollywood Cem.Rchmd. V305	ROH,HC
Cymes, George	Pvt.	K Orr's Ri.		AN	06/27/62	Gaines' Mill, VA	KIA		ROH,JR,CDC
Cynes, William A.	Pvt.	D Ham.Leg.			06/27/62	Gaines' Mill, VA	KIA		JR

D

SOUTH CAROLINA DEAD IN CSA SERVICE 1861-1865

NAME	RANK	C REGIMENT	AGE	DS	DIED	WHERE	WHY	BURIED	SOURCES
Daber, F.	Pvt.	Wash. Arty			09/17/62	Sharpsburg, MD	KIA	(Hart's Battery?)	JR,CDC
Dacus, D.N.M.	Pvt.	F Ham.Leg.		GE	05/15/64	Richmond, VA		Hollywood Cem.Rchmd. U85	ROH,HC
Dadgin, Wiley	Pvt.	G 7th SCV			/ /		KIA		UD2
Daggett, John W.	Pvt.	E 25th SCVI		CN	03/23/64	Charleston, SC	DOD	Magnolia Cem.(PL) Ch'ston	ROH,MAG,HAG
Daggett, Theodore L.D.	Pvt.	E 25th SCVI	19	CN	09/23/63	Bty. Gregg, SC	DOW	Magnolia Cem.Charleston	ROH,JR,MAG
Dagnell, Marion	Pvt.	E 18th SCABn		LS	07/27/64	Charleston, SC	KIA	Magnolia Cem. Charleston	ROH,MAG,CGS
Daily, J. Isaiah	Pvt.	H 13th SCVI	21	LN	03/24/65	Jones Farm, VA	DOW	(Wdd 3/21)	ROH
Daily, Timothy	Pvt.	H 1st SCVIR		LN	05/29/63	Battery Bee, SC	DOD		SA1
Dale,	Pvt.				/ /	Petersburg, VA	KIA		LSS
Daley, Robert H.	Pvt.		26	ED	02/26/62	At home	DOD		EDN
Dalrymple, John	Pvt.	D 2nd SCVA		DN	08/06/62	Ft. Johnson, SC	DOD		ROH
Dalrymple, Peter L.	Sgt.	H 21st SCVI		DN	05/16/64	Drury's Bluff VA	KIA		ROH,JR,JLC,HAG
Dalrymple, Robert B.	Pvt.	G 9th SCVIB		DN	12/24/61	At home	DOD		ROH,JR,JLC
Dalrymple, Thomas H.	1st Lt.	H 21st SCVI		DN	07/10/63	Bty. Wagner, SC	KIA	1st B.Ch. Hartsville, SC	ROH,JR,HAG,PP
Dalton, Amos H.	Pvt.	F Ham.Leg.			03/23/64	Camp Morton, IN	DIP	Green Lawn C. Indianapolis	FPH,CV,P12
Dalton, C.T.	Pvt.	F			/ /	Danville, VA	DOD		JR
Dalton, Jesse	Pvt.	F Orr's Ri.		PS	08/29/62	2nd Manassas, VA	KIA		JR,CDC
Dalton, M.V.	Pvt.	G 13th SCVI		NY	07/01/62	Richmond, VA	DOD	Hollywood Cem.Rchmd. M308	ROH,JR,ANY,HC
Dalton, W.J. (A.J.?)	Pvt.	F Orr's Ri.		PS	08/17/63	At home	DOD		JR
Dalton, W.M.	Pvt.	I 3rd SCVI		LS	01/01/63	Richmond, VA	DOD		JR,SA2
Dameron, William W.	Pvt.	F 17th SCVI		YK	/ /	Virginia	DOD		JR,CB
Dampier, Amos M.	Pvt.	G 9th SCVIB		DN	09/10/61	Germantown, VA	DOD		ROH,JR,JLC
Dandridge, Richard J.	2nd Lt.	I 11th SCVI		CO	08/10/62	Pocotaligo, SC	DOD		ROH,JR,R47
Dangerfield, S.J.	Pvt.	C 11th SCVI		CN	07/10/64	Petersburg, VA	KIA		ROH
Daniel, A.M.	Pvt.	I 1st SCV			/ /	(Orr's Ri.?)		Spotsylvania C.H. Cem.	SCH
Daniel, Isham H.	Pvt.	C Hol.Leg.		SG	06/09/65	Pt. Lookout, MD	DIP	C.C. Pt. Lookout, MD	FPH,HOS,P6,P11
Daniel, J.H.	Pvt.	F 13th SCVI		SG	/ /	Virginia		(1863)	HOS
Daniel, James Madison	2nd Lt.	E 7th SCVI		ED	07/03/63	Gettysburg, PA	DOW		JR,WV,GDR,UD1
Daniel, R.A.	Pvt.	A 3rd SCVI		SG	02/08/63	Richmond, VA	DOD	Hollywood Cem.Rchmd. D61	ROH,JR,HC,SA2
Daniel, W.C.	Pvt.	D			03/29/65			Con. Cem. Thomasville, NC	PP
Daniel, William Lowndes	1st Lt.	I 2nd SCVI		CN	07/02/63	Gettysburg, PA	KIA	UD1	JR,WV,GDR,SA2
Daniels, Columbus A.	Sgt.	L P.S.S.			09/30/64	Ft. Harrison VA	KIA		ROH,JR
Daniels, Dandy	Pvt.	C Hol.Leg.			/ /	Baltimore, MD	DIP	Loudon Pk. Cem. Balto., MD	CV
Daniels, Edmond Erastus	Pvt	E 3rd SCVABn	22		01/09/63	Columbia, SC	DOD		ROH,PP
Daniels, Edmund G.	Cpl.	G 7th SCVIBn		KW	04/19/65	Pt. Lookout, MD	DIP	C.C. Pt. Lookout, MD	ROH,FPH,P6,HIC
Daniels, J.G.	Pvt.	F 10th SCVI	30	MN	/ /	South Island, SC	DOD		ROH,RAS,HMC
Daniels, John L.	Pvt.	McQueen LA	18	WG	03/15/63		DOD		CTA,CDC
Daniels, L.	Pvt.	B 15th SCVI		UN	04/14/65	Elmira, NY	DIP	Woodlawn N.C.#2704 Elmira	FPH,P12
Daniels, Nathan S.	Pvt.	C 7th SCVIBn		RD	07/10/63	Morris Island SC	KIA		ROH,JR,HAG
Daniels, William	Pvt.	H 1st SCVIR		CN	07/21/63	Bty. Wagner, SC	DOW	Magnolia Cem. Charleston	ROH,MAG
Danion, G.B.	Pvt.	E 2nd SCVA			/ /	High Point, NC		Oakwood C. High Point, NC	WAT
Dannely, J.W.	Pvt.	E 1st SCVI			/ /	(?Lt.G.W. B,VIH)		Oakwood C.#35 Row M Div C	ROH,OWC
Dannely, James	Pvt.	H Ham.Leg.	18	OG	06/15/64	Tennessee	KIA		ROH
Dannely, Mathias P.	Sgt.	H Ham.Leg.	26	OG	08/14/64	Deep Bottom, VA	DOW		ROH,CDC
Dansby, Isaac	Pvt.	C 24th SCVI		CO	/ /	At home	DOD		EJM
Dansler, J.R.F.	Pvt.	C 2nd SCVA		CN	05/17/64	Charleston, SC	DOD	(may be "Jr." and not "F."	ROH,CDC
Dant, F.D.	Pvt.	A 5th SCV			06/01/64			Oakwood C.#28 Row R Div F	ROH,OWC
Dantler, Q.	Pvt.	2nd SCV			05/29/64	Richmond, VA		Hollywood Cem.Rchmd. U82	HC
Dantzler, Benjamin M.	Sgt.	F 25th SCVI	30	OG	02/23/65	Elmira, NY	DIP	Woodlawn N.C.#2321 Elmira	ROH,FPH,HAG,P6
Dantzler, Daniel	Pvt.	G 25th SCVI	25	OG	06/15/65	Elmira, NY	DIP		ROH
Dantzler, David W.	Cpl.	G 25th SCVI	23	OG	04/01/65	Elmira, NY	DIP	Woodlawn N.C.#2588 Elmira	ROH,FPH,EDR,P6

D

SOUTH CAROLINA DEAD IN CSA SERVICE 1861-1865

NAME	RANK	C REGIMENT	AGE	DS	DIED	WHERE	WHY	BURIED	SOURCES
Dantzler, Edward D.	Pvt.	A 5th SCVC	30	OG	06/02/64	Hawes Shop, VA	DOW	(Wdd 6/1)	ROH
Dantzler, J. Marshall	Pvt.	F 25th SCVI	20	OG	06/20/64	Petersburg, VA	KIA	(killed by sniper)	ROH,CDC,HAG
Dantzler, John	Pvt.	G 25th SCVI		OG	07/15/65	Virginia			ROH
Dantzler, John R.	Pvt.	A 5th SCVC		OG	12/15/63	At home	DOD		ROH,JR
Dantzler, Lewis E.	4th Cpl.	D 1st SCVIH	30	OG	11/15/61	SC	DOD		ROH,SA1
Dantzler, Olin M.	Col.	22nd SCVI	38	OG	06/02/64	Bermuda Hundred	KIA	Tabernacle M.C. St.Math SC	ROH,JR,LC,R48
Darby, David	Pvt.	B 22nd SCVI		SG	09/14/62	South Mtn., MD	KIA		ROH,HOS
Darby, Edward H.	4th Sgt.	L 1st SCVIG	21	CN	08/29/62	2nd Manassas, VA	KIA		ROH,JR,SA1,CDC
Darby, George M.	Pvt.	K Orr's Ri.	25	AE	05/12/64	Spotsylvania, VA	KIA		ROH,CDC
Darby, James	Pvt.	I 19th SCVI	38	AE	12/29/64	Nashville, TN	DOW	Mt. Olivet C. Nashville TN	ROH,P3,P6,PP
Darby, James W.	Pvt.	B 22nd SCVI		SG	08/23/62	Rappahannock Stn	KIA	(Artillery shell)	ROH,HOS
Darby, John C.	Pvt.	B 22nd SCVI		SG	07/30/64	Crater, Pbg., VA	KIA		ROH,BLM
Darby, John Calvin	Pvt.	E 4th SCVI	23	PS	09/12/61	Culpepper, VA	DOD	Fairview Cem. Culpepper VA	ROH,JR,CGH,SA2
Darby, John W.	Pvt.	2nd SCV		AE	07/19/61	Charleston, SC	DOD		ROH
Darby, W.J.	Pvt.	F 23rd SCVI			08/26/62	Richmond, VA		Hollywood Cem.Rchmd. Q223	ROH,HC
Darby, W.J.	Pvt.	B 4th SCVC		CR	/ /	At home	DOD	(1864)	CB
Darby, William	Pvt.	G 22nd SCVI	28	AN	02/24/65	Petersburg, VA	DOD		ROH
Darby, William Thompson	3rd Lt.	I 2nd SCVI		OG	09/17/62	Sharpsburg, MD	DOW	Charlestown, VA	ROH,JR,SA2,H2
Dargan, Alonzo T.	Lt.Col.	21st SCVI	26	DN	05/07/64	Walthall Jctn VA	KIA	Blandford Church Pbg., VA	ROH,JR,TRR,BLC
Dargan, C. Dubose	Pvt.	D 2nd SCVABn		DN	01/09/64	At home	DOD		ROH
Daring, J. Thomas	Pvt.	E 11th SCVI		BT	05/20/65	Elmira, NY	DIP	Woodlawn N.C.#2940 Elmira	FPH,HAG,P6,P65
Darity, J.	Pvt.	A 14th SCVI	35	DN	06/15/62	Lynchburg, VA			ROH
Darlington, H. Manly	Pvt.	B 4th SCVI		AN	10/15/61	Centreville, VA	DOD	(Typhoid, Palmetto Rifles)	JR,SA2,CNM,GMJ
Darlington, Hamish	Pvt.	1st SCV	19	BL	07/15/61	Orangeburg, SC	DOD		ROH
Darlton, J.	Pvt.	A 24th SCVI		CN	10/23/62	Richmond, VA		Hollywood Cem.Rchmd. B241	HC
Darnall, J.L.	Pvt.	B 7th SCVI		AE	12/15/62		DOD	(KEB=Donald)	JR,KEB
Darnall, T.P.	Pvt.	F 3rd SCVI		LS	12/18/62	Richmond, VA	DOW	(Wdd @ Fredericksburg)	ROH,JR,SA2
Darnell, W.	Pvt.	B 1st SCResB	18	KW	01/26/65	Columbia, SC	DOD		ROH
Darnett, F.P.	Pvt.	F 1st SCV			01/01/63	Richmond, VA		Hollywood Cem.Rchmd. D12	HC
Darnold, Samuel C.	Pvt.	G 25th SCVI		OG	/ /	Charleston, SC	DOD		ROH,HAG
Darracott, James T.	Pvt.	K 4th SCVI	29	AN	08/15/61	Culpepper, VA	DOD	Fairview Cem. Culpepper VA	ROH,JR,CGH,SA2
Darrell, J.	Pvt.	B		CN	01/26/65	Columbia, SC	DOD	Elmwood Cem. Columbia, SC	MP,PP
Darwin, Presley P.	Pvt.	I 5th SCVI	20	YK	09/02/61	Richmond, VA	DOD		JR,SA3,YMD,YEB
Dasson, S.	Pvt.	A 23rd SCVI		CN	09/02/64	Richmond, VA		(Dawson?)	ROH
Davenport, Charles S.	2nd Lt.	B 3rd SCVI		NY	09/17/62	Sharpsburg, MD	DOW	Shepherdstown, WVA C.C.	ROH,JR,SA2,ANY
Davenport, D.N.	Pvt.	E 16th SCVI	27	GE	06/15/64	Pine Mountain GA	KIA		ROH,16R
Davenport, Ephriam W.	Pvt.	B 3rd SCVI		NY	11/28/63	Dalton, GA	DOW		ROH,SA2,ANY,PP
Davenport, H.W.	Pvt.	E 27th SCVI			09/10/64	Pt. Lookout, MD	DIP	C.C. Pt. Lookout, MD	ROH,FPH,P6,HAG
Davenport, Isaac	Pvt.	B 16th SCVI		GE	/ /	Dalton, GA	DOD	(1864)	16R
Davenport, J.	Pvt.	K Orr's Ri.		AN	06/27/62	Gaines' Mill, VA	KIA		ROH,JR,CDC
Davenport, J.M.	Pvt.	C 23rd SCVI		CN	02/15/65	Richmond, VA		Hollywood Cem.Rchmd. W55	ROH,HC
Davenport, James M.	Pvt.	C 3rd SCVI		NY	06/15/63	Richmond, VA	DOD		ROH,SA2,ANY
Davenport, Jesse	Pvt.	K Orr's Ri.	25	AN	/ /				ROH
Davenport, John M.	Pvt.	E 7th SCVC	27	NY	03/01/65	Columbia, SC	DOD	Elmwood Cem. Columbia, SC	ROH,MP,PP,NCC
Davenport, R.W.	Pvt.	F 3rd SCVI		NY	07/02/63	Gettysburg, PA	KIA		ROH,JR,GDR,SA2
Davenport, Thomas T.	Pvt.	B 1st SCVIG		NY	06/25/65	Cape Hatteras NC	ACD	(Storm at sea frm prison)	LSS,ANY
Davenport, William C.	Pvt.	C 3rd SCVI		NY	09/30/63	Chickamauga, GA	KIA	C.C. Marietta, GA	ROH,JR,SA2,CCM
Davey, J.R.	Pvt.			CN	/ /		DOD		ROH
David, Henry L.	Pvt.	C 6th SCVI		KW	10/03/62	Richmond, VA	DOD	Hollywood Cem.Rchmd. A55	ROH,HC,HIC,H2
David, J.A.	Pvt.	B 16th SCVI		GE	/ /	Atlanta, GA	KIA		16R
David, James Joshua	2nd Lt.	D 16th SCVI	21	GE	07/22/64	Atlanta, GA	KIA	Christ Ch. Greenville, SC	ROH,16R,GEE,R47

D

SOUTH CAROLINA DEAD IN CSA SERVICE 1861-1865

NAME	RANK	C	REGIMENT	AGE	DS	DIED	WHERE	WHY	BURIED	SOURCES
David, Robert J.	Pvt.	G	8th SCVI	24	MO	01/15/63	Richmond, VA	DOW	(Wdd @ Fredericksburg)	ROH,JR,HOM,UD2
Davidson, G.W.	Pvt.	H	6th SCVI		YK	06/15/61	Charlottesville	DOD		ROH
Davidson, James	Pvt.	E	13th SCVI		SG	11/20/62	Winchester, VA	DOD	Stonewall Cem. Winchester	ROH,WIN,HOS
Davidson, James T.	Pvt.	A	12th SCVI	27	YK	07/04/63	Gettysburg, VA	DOW		JR,YEB
Davidson, John H.	Pvt.	F	6th SCVI	23	YK	07/20/64	Petersburg, VA	KIA	(YEB=Co. H)	ROH,YEB,HHC
Davidson, Robert L.	Pvt.	A	12th SCVI	31	YK	08/20/62	Richmond, VA	DOW	Bethesda Ch. York, SC	JR,RCD,YEB
Davidson, Samuel N.	Cpt.	B	3rd SCVI		NY	06/19/62	Petersburg VA	DOD	(Typhoid)	ROH,JR,SA2,ANY
Davidson, Thadeus M.	Pvt.	K	17th SCVI	20	YK	06/18/63	Petersburg, VA	DOD	(YEB=Wilmington, NC)	ROH,YEB
Davidson, W.W.	Pvt.	F	17th SCVI		YK	08/30/62		DOD		JR
Davidson, William G.	Pvt.	H	6th SCVI	21	YK	/ /	Charlottesville	DOD		YEB
Davis,	Pvt.			25	CD	08/05/63	Petersburg, VA			ROH
Davis,	Pvt.	F	5th SCVI		YK	/ /			Oakwood C.#94 Row M Div A	ROH,OWC
Davis,	Pvt.	B	Orr's Ri.	30	AE	08/27/64	Petersburg, VA	KIA		ROH
Davis,	Pvt.		Arty			07/18/63	Bty. Wagner, SC	KIA		ROH
Davis, A. Asbury	Pvt.	E	16th SCVI	26	GE	03/13/64	Rock Island, IL	DIP	C.C. #806 Rock Island, IL	ROH,FPH,P6,16R
Davis, A.E.	Pvt.	D	7th SCVIBn	19	KW	05/27/64	Petersburg, VA	DOW	(Wdd 6/19/64)	ROH,HIC
Davis, A.M.	Pvt.	E	20th SCVI		AN	08/22/64	Richmond, VA		Oakwood C.#15 Row 23 Div D	ROH,OWC,KEB
Davis, Adolphus T.	Cpl.	K	3rd SCVI	25	SG	02/14/62	Centreville, VA	DOD	(JR=Manassas, VA)	ROH,JR,SA2,HOS
Davis, Alfred	Cpl.	I	1st SCVC	30	CO	11/16/62	Staunton, VA	DOD		ROH
Davis, Arthur	Pvt.	H	Orr's Ri		MN	09/01/62	Ox Hill, VA	KIA	On the field	JR,HMC,CDC
Davis, Arthur	Pvt.	H	Orr's Ri.			03/14/63	Camp Gregg, VA	DOD	(? Two confl. records)	JR
Davis, Arthur W.	Pvt.	D	19th SCVI	24	ED	03/19/65	High Point, NC	DOW	Oakwood Cem. High Point NC	HOE,CV,UD3,TOD
Davis, B. Thomas	Cpt.	E	21st SCVI	34	CD	05/28/64	Ft. Stevens, VA	KIA	(AKA Bermuda Hundred)	ROH,HAG,R48,UD
Davis, B.W.			CS Navy			07/29/64	Pt. Lookout, MD	DIP	C.C. Pt. Lookout, MD	ROH
Davis, C.C.	Pvt.	A	5th SCVI		GN	11/01/63	Lookout Valley	DOW		SA3,LAN,CDC
Davis, Columbus	Pvt.	K	8th SCVI		MO	03/17/65	Camp Chase, OH	DIP	C.C.#1689 Columbus, OH	FPH,P6,KEB,HOM
Davis, D.D.	Pvt.	A	13th SCVI		LS	/ /	Ft. Delaware, DE	DIP		ROH,CDC
Davis, Daniel	Pvt.	K	13th SCVI		LN	11/26/63	Ft. Delaware, DE	DIP	Finn's Pt. NJ Nat. Cem.	ROH,FPH,P5,P40
Davis, Daniel P.	Pvt.	B	3rd SCVI	19	NY	12/13/62	Fredericksburg	KIA	KEB	ROH,JR,SA2,ANY
Davis, David R.	Pvt.	C	7th SCVIBn	25	RD	08/01/64	Richmond, VA	DOW		ROH,HAG
Davis, E. Lewis	Pvt.	K	2nd SCV	36	AE	03/05/63	Lynchburg, VA	DOD	Lynchburg CSA Cem. #5 R2	ROH,BBW
Davis, E.A. (E.J.?)	Pvt.	E	3rd SCVABn		LS	04/20/63	Columbia, SC	DOD		ROH,PP
Davis, Edward W.	Pvt.	I	23rd SCVI		CL	05/27/65	Pt. Lookout, MD	DIP	C.C. Pt. Lookout, MD	FPH,P6,P114
Davis, Elihu L.	1st Sgt.	C	7th SCVIBn	30	RD	08/05/63	Columbia, SC	DOW		ROH,HAG,PP
Davis, Epaminondas W.	1st Lt.	I	14th SCVI	21	AE	06/30/62	Frayser's Farm	KIA		ROH,JR,HOL,R47
Davis, Francis M.	Pvt.	L	2nd SCVIRi	18	AN	01/06/64	Knoxville, TN	DOW		ROH,P1,P5
Davis, Franklin	Pvt.	K	5th SCVI		SG	08/02/62	Richmond, VA	DOD	Hollywood Cem.Rchmd. H93	ROH,JR,HC,SA3
Davis, G.A.	Pvt.	G	14th SCVI	36	AE	06/22/63	Lynchburg, VA	DOD	Lynchburg CSA Cem. #9 R3	ROH,JR,BBW
Davis, G.E.	Pvt.	H	7th SCVIBn			05/16/65	Drury's Bluff VA	KIA		JR
Davis, George	Pvt.	L	2nd SCVIRi	18	AN	01/15/64	Morristown, TN	DOD		ROH
Davis, George W.	Pvt.	I	19th SCVI	17	AE	07/25/64	Atlanta area	DOW		ROH
Davis, George W. (H.?)	Pvt.	K	Orr's Ri.	40	AN	09/30/64	Jones Farm, VA	KIA	(George M.?)	ROH,JR
Davis, H.E.	Pvt.	C	2nd SCVIRi			05/12/64	Spotsylvania, VA	KIA		ROH
Davis, Henry	Pvt.		1st SCVIR			08/23/63	Bty. Wagner, SC	KIA		ROH,CDC
Davis, Henry	Pvt.	A	24th SCVI			01/15/65				EJM
Davis, Hiram M.	Cpl.	C	2nd SCVI		RD	06/06/65	Pt. Lookout, MD	DIP	C.C. Pt. Lookout, MD	FPH,P6,P114,SA
Davis, J.	Pvt.	I	1st SCV			12/26/63	Atlanta, GA		Oakland C. Atlanta R6 #7	BGA
Davis, J. Allen	Pvt.	G	Orr's Ri.		AE	06/27/62	Gaines' Mill VA	KIA	(JR=2nd SCVIRi.)	ROH,JR,CDC
Davis, J. Robertson	Pvt.	E	6th SCVI		DN	09/29/64	Pt. Lookout, MD	DOW	C.C. Pt. Lookout, MD	RUH,FPH,JLC
Davis, J.A.	Pvt.	D	3rd SCV			11/13/63	At home	DOD		JR
Davis, J.F.H.	Pvt.	B	Orr's Ri.			09/30/64	Jones' Farm, VA	KIA		JR

D

SOUTH CAROLINA DEAD IN CSA SERVICE 1861-1865

NAME	RANK	C REGIMENT	AGE	DS	DIED	WHERE	WHY	BURIED	SOURCES
Davis, J.H.	Pvt.	E 1st SCVI			08/19/64	Richmond, VA		(NI SA1, Orr's Ri.?)	ROH
Davis, J.L.	Pvt.	H 8th SCVI		MN	/ /	Charlottesville	DOD	Univ. Cem. Charlottesville	ROH,CDC,ACH
Davis, J.L.	Pvt.	C 1st SCV			/ /		DOD		ROH
Davis, J.L.	Pvt.	H 8th SCVI		MN	03/14/63	Richmond, VA	DOD	(Pneumonia)	JR
Davis, J.N.	Pvt.	K 1st SCV			/ /			Oakwood C.#186 Row M Div A	OWC
Davis, J.P.	Pvt.	K 25th SCVI			03/03/63		DOD		JR
Davis, J. Robertson	Pvt.	E 6th SCVI		DN	09/16/64	Pt. Lookout, MD	DIP	C.C. Pt. Lookout, MD	ROH,JLC,P6,P113
Davis, J.R.	Pvt.	K 7th SCVC		KW	05/11/65	Hart's Island NY	DIP	Cypress Hills N.C.#2759 NY	FPH,P6,HIC,P79
Davis, J.S.	Cpl.	B 2nd SCVIRi		PS	/ /				ROH
Davis, J.W.	Pvt.	B 7th SCVI		AE	06/29/62	Gaines' Mill, VA	DOW	Oakwood C.#15 Row M Div C	ROH,JR,OWC,KEB
Davis, J.W.	1st Sgt.	B 3rd SCVIBn		LS	/ /		DOW	(Wdd at Maryland Hts.)	JR,KEB
Davis, James	Pvt.	H 25th SCVI		CN	06/16/62	Secessionville	KIA	Magnolia Cem. Charleston	ROH,MAG
Davis, James	Pvt.	H 7th SCV			06/07/65	Pt. Lookout, MD	DIP	C.C. Pt. Lookout, MD	FPH,P6
Davis, James	Pvt.	F 1st SCVIBn	35	CN	06/16/62	Secessionville	KIA	(JR=C,27th SCVI)	JR,PP
Davis, James C.	Pvt.	E 16th SCVI	27	GE	10/19/63	Kingston, GA	DOD		ROH,16R
Davis, James D.	Lt.	F		UN	11/07/61	Ft. Walker, SC	DOW	Fernandez Gvyd Pacolet R.	UD3
Davis, James Edward	Pvt.	C 13th SCVI		UN	03/03/65	Jones' Farm, VA	DOW	Hollywood Cem.Rchmd. W598	ROH,HC,HOS
Davis, James G.	Pvt.	F Orr's Ri.		PS	08/24/62	Richmond, VA		Hollywood Cem.Rchmd. Q188	ROH,HC,CDC
Davis, James H.	Pvt.	I 21st SCVI		MN	08/12/64	Richmond, VA	DOW	Hollywood Cem.Rchmd. V677	ROH,HC,HMC,HAG
Davis, James Leonidas	Pvt.	E 3rd SCVI	19	NY	07/04/63	At home	DOD	Kings Creek ARP Newberry	ROH,JR,NCC,SA2
Davis, James M.	Pvt.	B 13th SCVI		SG	07/12/62	Gaines' Mill, VA	DOW		JR,HOS,CDC,CNM
Davis, James M. (W.?)	2nd Lt.	D 26th SCVI		MO	09/23/62	At home	DOD		HOM,R48
Davis, James P.	Pvt.	I 4th SCVC	23	WG	/ /		DOD	(1863)	CTA,HOW
Davis, Jefferson	1st Sgt.	F 7th SCVI	25	ED	/ /	Richmond, VA	DOD		HOE,KEB
Davis, Joel L.	Pvt.	D 2nd SCVI	21	SR	10/18/62	Mt. Jackson, VA	DOW	(Wdd @ Sharpsburg 9/17)	ROH,JR,SA2,H2
Davis, John	Pvt.	SCVA			05/04/62	Richmond, VA	DOD	Hollywood Cem.Rchmd. F72	HC
Davis, John	Pvt.	K 25th SCVI		WG	05/09/64	Swift Creek, VA	KIA		CTA,HOW,HAG
Davis, John A.	Pvt.	H 7th SCVC		KW	/ /		KIA		HIC
Davis, John Alexander	Pvt.	L 10th SCVI			08/26/62	Lauderdale Spgs.	DOD	(PP=4/26/62)	ROH,JR,PP
Davis, John C.	Pvt.	E 3rd SCVI	22	NY	05/02/63	Chancellorsville	KIA	Kings Creek ARP Cem. Newby	ROH,JR,NCC,ANY
Davis, John F.H.	Pvt.	Orr's Ri.		AN	09/30/64	Ft. Harrison, VA	KIA	(1st in 2nd SCVI)	H2,KEB
Davis, John M.	Pvt.	F 8th SCVI	21	DN	08/12/61	Richmond, VA	DOD		ROH,JR,KEB
Davis, John P.	Pvt.	K Hol.Leg.	29	SG	06/06/64	Pt. Lookout, MD	DIP	C.C. Pt. Lookout, MD	ROH,FPH,P6,P113
Davis, John W. (R.?)	Pvt.	B 13th SCVI		SG	04/28/62	At home	DOD		JR,HOS
Davis, Joseph Berry	Pvt.	K 4th SCVI		AN	10/16/61	Charlottesville	DOD	Univ. Cem. Charlottesville	JR,ACH,SA2
Davis, Joseph M.	Pvt.	H 1st SCVIG		AE	05/08/64	Charlottesville	DOW	Univ. Cem. Charlottesville	ROH,SA1,ACH,CDC
Davis, L.C.	Pvt.	B 13th SCVI		SG	05/20/62	Hanover C.H., VA	DOD	Ashland, VA	ROH,JR,HOS
Davis, L.H.	Pvt.	1st SCVA			10/21/64	Charleston, SC	DOD	Magnolia Cem. Charleston	ROH,MAG
Davis, Lewis	Pvt.	K 2nd SCVA		ED	/ /		DOD		HOE,UD3
Davis, Lewis B.	Pvt.	I 2nd SCVI		RD	04/19/63	Richmond, VA	DOD	Oakwood C.#28 Row 52 Div D	ROH,SA2,OWC
Davis, M.	Pvt.	C 14th SCVI		LS	12/07/62			Stonewall Cem. Winchester	ROH,WIN
Davis, Madison L.	Cpl.	G 5th SCVC		AE	03/26/63	Wilson, NC			PP
Davis, Milford	Pvt.	L 2nd SCVIRi	30	AN	09/15/62	Charlotte, NC	DOD		ROH
Davis, Monroe M.	3rd Sgt.	D 3rd SCVI	22	SG	09/21/63	Chickamauga, GA	DOW	Belmont Cem. UN Cty., SC	ROH,SA2
Davis, Moses	Pvt.			CN	06/26/64	Ft. Sumter, VA	KIA	Magnolia Cem. Charleston	ROH,RCD
Davis, N.H.	Pvt.	D 2nd SCV			/ /	Charlottesville		Univ. Cem. Charlottesville	ACH
Davis, O.C.	Pvt.	Ham.Leg.		CL	05/02/62	Ashland, VA	DOD		ROH
Davis, Oliver S.	Pvt.	F 25th SCVI	21	CN	05/16/64	Drury's Bluff VA	KIA		ROH,HAG
Davis, P.	Pvt.	C 27th SCVI		CN	06/29/64	Petersburg, VA	DOW		ROH,JR,HAG
Davis, Pringle	Pvt.	A 24th SCVI		CN	01/15/65	Camp Chase, OH	DIP	C.C. #777 Columbus, OH	ROH,FPH,P6,P23
Davis, R. David	Pvt.	C 2nd SCVI		RD	10/17/63	Lynchburg, VA	DOD	Lynchburg CSA Cem. #2 R3	ROH,JR,SA2,BBW

D

SOUTH CAROLINA DEAD IN CSA SERVICE 1861-1865

NAME	RANK	C	REGIMENT	AGE	DS	DIED	WHERE	WHY	BURIED	SOURCES
Davis, R.J.	Pvt.	A	Ham.Leg.			08/06/63	Petersburg, VA			ROH
Davis, R.J.	Pvt.		8th SCVI			/ /			Oakwood C.#44 Row B Div E	OWC
Davis, R.W.	Pvt.		19th SCVI			/ /	High Point, NC		Oakwood C. High Point, NC	WAT
Davis, Richard P.	Pvt.	G	22nd SCVI	20	AN	02/24/62	Columbia, SC	DOD		ROH,PP
Davis, Riley	Pvt.	C	12th SCVI		FD	05/17/64	Richmond, VA	DOW (Wdd @ Wilderness)		JR,HFC
Davis, Robert	Pvt.	D	P.S.S.		SG	12/10/63	Rutledge, TN	DOD (HOS=Fraysers Farm)		ROH,JR,HOS
Davis, Ross	2nd Lt.	I	15th SCVI	20	FD	07/13/64	Petersburg, VA	DOW	PP	ROH,JR,KEB,CAG
Davis, S.J.	Pvt.	C	Ham.Leg.			08/29/62	2nd Manassas, VA	KIA (JR=8/30/62)		ROH,JR,CDC
Davis, Samuels	Pvt.	C	Hol.Leg.		SG	/ /		DOD		HOS
Davis, Sylvester	Pvt.	C	12th SCVI		FD	01/29/63	Staunton, VA	DOW	Thornrose C. Staunton, VA	ROH,JR,HFC,TOD
Davis, T.C.	Pvt.	G	3rd SCVIBn	26	BL	12/08/62	Petersburg, VA	DOD		ROH,KEB,PP
Davis, Thomas	Pvt.	B	7th SCVI			/ /	Richmond, VA		Oakwood C.#10 Row A Div A	ROH,OWC,KEB
Davis, Thomas	Pvt.	F	25th SCVI		OG	02/15/65	Pt. Lookout, MD	DIP	C.C. Pt. Lookout, MD	ROH,HAG,P114,E
Davis, Thomas	Pvt.	A	3rd SCVIBn		LS	07/28/64	Deep Bottom, VA	KIA		ROH,JR,KEB
Davis, Thomas	Pvt.	B	2nd SCV			09/15/62		DOD (7th SCVI?)		JR
Davis, Thomas	Pvt.	A	8th SCVI		DN	08/26/62	Mississippi	DOD (Dennis in KEB?)		JR
Davis, Thomas J.	1st Sgt.	K	1st SCVIH		OG	12/22/62	Richmond, VA	DOD		ROH,JR,SA1,JRH
Davis, Thomas Jefferson	Pvt.	C	2nd SCVIRi			06/20/62		DOD (Typhoid)		JR
Davis, Thomas M.	1st Cpl.	B	3rd SCVI		NY	01/15/62	Richmond, VA	DOD (JR=Centreville)		ROH,JR,SA2,ANY
Davis, Turner G.	Pvt.	K	Orr's Ri.	44	AE	05/12/64	Spotsylvania VA	KIA		ROH
Davis, W.A.	Pvt.	C	Ham.Leg.			/ /			Oakwood C.#52 Row A Div B	OWC
Davis, W.E.	Pvt.	C	2nd SCVIRi			05/16/64	Drury's Bluff VA	KIA		JR
Davis, W.H.	Pvt.	I	4th SCVC			05/28/64	Hawe's Shop, VA	KIA		ROH,JR
Davis, W.H.	Pvt.	A	Orr's Ri.			07/09/62	Dill Farm, VA	DOD		JR
Davis, W.M.	Pvt.	B	13th SCVI		SG	06/30/62	Frayser's Farm	KIA (JR=Laurel Hill & 7/16/62)		ROH,JR,CDC,CNM
Davis, W.R.	Pvt.	F	1st SCVIH		BL	09/13/64	Pt. Lookout, MD	DIP		ROH,HAG,SA1
Davis, W.R.	Seaman		Dis. Boat		CN	09/17/64	Pt. Lookout, MD	DIP	C.C. Pt. Lookout, MD	FPH,P6
Davis, W.R.	Pvt.	K	4th SCVC		CN	10/01/64	Peebles' Farm VA	KIA		CLD
Davis, Washington W.	Cpt.	D	26th SCVI		MO	05/20/64	Drury's Bluff VA	KIA (Clay's Farm ?)		ROH,HOM,R48
Davis, Westley K.	Pvt.	E	16th SCVI	28	AN	11/30/64	Franklin, TN	KIA	Macgavock C. Frkln Gv# 14	ROH,16R,PP
Davis, William	Pvt.	C	11th SCVI	22	CN	07/02/62	Hardeeville, SC	DOD		ROH,JR
Davis, William	Pvt.	H	Orr's Ri		MN	04/11/62	Sullivans I., SC	DOD (1862)		JR,CDC,HMC
Davis, William A.	Pvt.	D	27th SCVI	22	CN	08/21/64	Ream's Stn., VA	KIA		ROH,CDC,HAG
Davis, William B.	Pvt.	K	Orr's Ri.	28	AN	04/25/62	Williamsburg, VA	DOD		ROH,JR,CDC
Davis, William C.	1st Lt.	B	Orr's Ri.	29	AE	08/29/62	2nd Manassas, VA	KIA		ROH,JR,CDC,R45
Davis, William Henry	Pvt.	I	4th SCVC	20	WG	05/29/64	Hawes Shop, VA	KIA		CTA,HOW
Davis, William R.	Pvt.	M	P.S.S.	20	SG	05/31/62	7 Pines, VA	KIA		ROH,JR
Davis, William T.	Pvt.	H	18th SCVI	31	YK	09/17/62	Sharpsburg, MD	KIA (JR=Co. K)		JR,YEB
Davis, William T. (P.?)	Pvt.	B	9th SCVIB			11/23/61	Virginia	DOD		JR
Davis, William Z	Pvt.	G	22nd SCVI	20	AN	03/01/62	Columbia, SC	DOD		ROH,PP
Davis, Younger	Pvt.	D	26th SCVI		MO	11/11/62	Secessionville	DOD		JR,HOM
Davis, Zachariah J.	Pvt.	L	2nd SCVIRi	24	AN	03/15/64	Columbia, SC	DOD		ROH,PP
Davison, James H.	Pvt.	A	17th SCVI	24	CR	08/30/62	2nd Manassas, VA	KIA		ROH,JR,HHC,PP
Davison, William A.	Pvt.	A	17th SCVI	33	CR	08/12/62	Richmond, VA	DOD (Typhoid)		ROH,JR,HHC,CB
Dawkins,	Pvt.	E	6th SCVI			05/03/62		KIA		JR
Dawkins, Elisha A.	Cpl.	D	26th SCVI		MO	05/23/64	Petersburg, VA	KIA		HOM,PP
Dawkins, J.E.	Pvt.		18th SCVI		UN	09/17/62	Sharpsburg, MD	DOW	Shepherdstown, VA	ROH,CV
Dawkins, John	Pvt.	H	13th SCVI		LN	12/27/62	Staunton, VA	DOD	Thornrose C. Staunton, VA	ROH,JR,TOD
Dawkins, John	Pvt.	D	17th SCVI		CR	/ /		DOD (Record in H,13th wrong?)		CB
Dawkins, M.T.	Pvt.	G	6th SCVI	26	CR	10/02/61	Germantown, VA	DOD		ROH,HHC,CNM
Dawkins, Thomas	Cpl.		Boyce's LA			09/17/62	Sharpsburg, MD	KIA		ROH,JR,CDC

D

SOUTH CAROLINA DEAD IN CSA SERVICE 1861-1865

NAME	RANK	C	REGIMENT	AGE	DS	DIED	WHERE	WHY	BURIED	SOURCES
Dawkins, W.L.	Pvt.	G	24th SCVI	38	OG	05/16/62	Secessionville	KIA		ROH,JR,CDC,PP
Dawkins, William	Pvt.	D	17th SCVI		CR	/ /		DOD		CB
Dawkins, William B.	Pvt.	E	2nd SCVI		KW	/ /	Richmond, VA	DOD (May, 1862)		H2,SA2,KERB
Dawsey, Daniel	Pvt.	G	10th SCVI		HY	06/23/62	Columbus, MS	DOD	Prob Friendship C. there	RAS,PP
Dawson, Francis	Pvt.	I	1st SCVIR		AN	04/04/64	Raleigh, NC		Oakwood C. Raleigh, NC	TOD,SA1
Dawson, Stephen	Pvt.	I	P.S.S.		PS	01/17/64	Danbridge, TN	KIA		ROH,CDC
Dawson, Thomas	Pvt.	A	23rd SCVI		CN	08/19/64	Petersburg, VA	KIA		ROH
Day, A.	Pvt.	C	4th SCVC		PS	05/28/64	Hawes Shop, VA	KIA		BHC
Day, B.B.	Pvt.	K	22nd SCVI		PS	11/06/62	Columbia, SC	DOD		ROH,PP
Day, Benjamin	Pvt.	H	14th SCV			05/06/64		KIA		UD2
Day, Burnett	Pvt.	D	5th SCRes			12/19/62	Adams Run, SC	DOD		PP
Day, Franklin M.	Pvt.	L	P.S.S.	29	AN	05/08/64	Wilderness, VA	DOW (Wdd 5/6/64)		ROH,JR
Day, J.B.	Pvt.	F	12th SCVI		FD	12/21/63	Richmond, VA	DOD (NI HFC)		ROH
Day, J.T.	Pvt.	C	4th SCVC			05/28/64	Hawe's Shop, VA	KIA		JR
Day, John G.	Pvt.	A	3rd SCVI		CN	11/18/63	At home	DOD (2/29/64 roll=in hospital)		ROH,SA2,KEB
Day, N.	Pvt.	C	4th SCVC			05/28/64	Hawes Shop, VA	DOW		BHC
Day, Nathaniel T.	Pvt.	A	3rd SCVI		LS	11/18/63	Knoxville, TN	KIA		ROH,SA2,KEB,CDC
Day, Peter	Pvt.	H	14th SCVI		BL	01/01/62	Port Royal Ferry	KIA		JR,UD2
Day, Robert	Pvt.	B	19th SCVI		ED	/ /	Atlanta, GA	DOD		HOE
Day, Robert	Pvt.	C	4th SCVC			05/28/64	Hawe's Shop, VA	KIA		JR
Day, William	Pvt.	B	24th SCVI	40	MO	09/22/63	Chickamauga, GA	DOW		ROH,HOM,CDC
Day, Zack	Pvt.	F	12th SCVI		FD	06/27/62	Gaines' Mill, VA	DOW		HFC
Days, Allen	Pvt.	C	4th SCVC		PS	08/15/64	Pt. Lookout, MD	DIP	C.C. Pt. Lookout, MD	ROH,FPH,P6,P113
De Armond, James R.	Pvt.	E	Orr's Ri.	19	PS	06/27/62	Gaines' Mill, VA	KIA		ROH,JR,CDC
DeBar, L.W.	Pvt.	E	14th SCVI			06/01/65		DIP	Cypress Hills N.C.#2568 NY	FPH
DeBruhl, Jesse E.	Pvt.	A	7th SCVIBn	23	KW	05/16/64	Drury's Bluff VA	KIA		ROH,HIC,HAG
DeCaradeauc, Frank	Pvt.	C	1st SCVC	21	CN	12/02/62	Staunton, VA	DOD	St. Lawrence C. Charleston	ROH,JR,MAG,ACL
DeCaradeauc, J. Antoine	Pvt.	C	1st SCVC	16	CN	11/03/62	Richmond, VA	DOD	St. Lawrence C. Charleston	ROH,JR,MAG,ACL
DeGruy, E.A.	Pvt.	A	19th SCVAB		RD	08/29/61	At home	DOD	St.Peter's Ch. Columbia SC	MP
DeHart, Daniel	Pvt.	I	15th SCVI	34	LN	05/31/64	Winchester, VA	DOD		H15,TOD,KEB
DeHart, Joel	Pvt.	I	15th SCVI	24	LN	01/23/63	Richmond, VA	DOD		H15,TOD,KEB
DeHay, R.F.	Pvt.	D	3rd SCVABn		CN	10/07/64	Charleston, SC	DOD	Magnolia Cem. Charleston	ROH,MAG
DeLoach, E.	Pvt.	A	7th SCVI		ED	06/29/62	Savage Stn. VA	KIA		ROH,CDC
DeLoach, J.	Pvt.	E				/ /			Magnolia Cem. Charleston	MAG
DeLoach, J.C.	Pvt.	D	14th SCVI	30	ED	05/06/64	Wilderness, VA	KIA		D14,HOE
DeLoach, James	Pvt.	F	11th SCVI	35	BT	07/08/65	Pt. Lookout, MD	DIP	C.C. Pt. Lookout, MD P6	ROH,FPH,HAG,P114
DeLoach, Nelson	Pvt.	I	25th SCVI		CL	03/04/65	Elmira, NY	DIP	Woodlawn N.C.#1980 Elmira	FPH,P6,P65,HAG
DeLoach, William	Pvt.	F	27th SCVI	23	ED	08/21/64	Weldon RR, VA	KIA	HAG	ROH,JR,HOE,UD3
DeLorme, T.U.	Pvt.	E	P.S.S.		SR	06/15/62	Richmond, VA	DOD		ROH
DeLorne, John Francis	Pvt.	E	P.S.S.			/ /	Manchester, VA	DOD (Typhoid)		JR
DeSaussure, Henry W.	1st Lt.	C	6th SCVI	27	KW	06/30/62	Frayser's Farm	KIA	Quaker Cem. Camden, SC	ROH,HC,JR,WDB,PP
DeSaussure, William D.	Col.		15th SCVI	44	RD	07/02/63	Gettysburg, PA	KIA	1st P.C. Columbia, SC PP	ROH,JR,GDR,WV
DeTreville, Robert T.	Lt.Col.		1st SCVIR		CN	03/16/65	Averysboro, NC	KIA	Chicora C. Harnett Cty. NC	ROH,SA1,WAT,PP
DeVore, James Sheppard	Pvt.	K	15th SCVI	22	ED	10/08/62	Salem, VA	DOD		ROH,JR,KEB
DeVore, John H.	Pvt.	C	19th SCVI		ED	02/13/62	Charleston, SC	DOD		HOE
Deaconte,	Pvt.	K	2nd SCVIRi			07/18/61	1st Manassas, VA	KIA (? 2nd Ri. not at 1st M)		JR
Deal, Francis	Pvt.	F	5th SCVI		YK	06/27/62	Gaines' Mill, VA	KIA		JR,SA3,CB
Deal, Samuel Caldwell	Pvt.	F	2nd SCVI	28	AE	05/21/62	Richmond, VA	DOD	Hollywood Cem.Rchmd. G87	ROH,HC,SA2,KEB
Deal, William M.	Pvt.	I	24th SCVI		ED	12/31/63	Atlanta, GA	DOD	Oakwood Cem. Atlanta, GA	BGA
Dean, A.F.	Pvt.	E	P.S.S.		SR	06/13/62	Richmond, VA	DOD		ROH,JR,CDC
Dean, Benedict	Pvt.	K	14th SCVI		ED	10/15/62	At home	DOD		JR,HOE

SOUTH CAROLINA DEAD IN CSA SERVICE 1861-1865

NAME	RANK	C	REGIMENT	AGE	DS	DIED	WHERE	WHY	BURIED	SOURCES
Dean, Frank	Pvt.	G	7th SCVI		ED	/ /		DOD		HOE
Dean, John	Pvt.	D	18th SCVI		AN	/ /		DOD		ROH
Dean, Samuel		E	Perrin's			/ /	Griffin Hosp	DOD	Spaulding Cnty GA	UD2
Dean, Starling	Pvt.	D	24th SCVI		BT	10/15/63	Tennessee			EJM
Dean, Thaddeus Charles	Sgt.	H	2nd SCVIRi	21	AN	06/30/62	Frayser's Farm	KIA		ROH,JR,CDC
Dean, W. Marion	1st Lt.	C	19th SCVI		ED	09/27/63	Chickamauga, GA	DOW		ROH,HOE,CDC,UD
Deane, E.	Pvt.	G	7th SCVI		ED	/ /	Richmond, VA		Oakwood C.#15 Row 8 Div D	ROH,OWC
Deane, J.W.	Pvt.					/ /			Oakwood C.#112 Row K Div A	OWC
Deane, N.M.	Pvt.	G	5th SCVI			/ /	Richmond, VA		Oakwood C.#173 Row J Div A	ROH,OWC
Deans, Stephen R.	Pvt.	E	1st SCVIG		MN	06/27/62	Richmond, VA	DOD		JR,SA1,PDL,HMC
Deanson, J.R.D.	Pvt.	E	Orr's Ri.		PS	06/27/62	Gaines' Mill, VA	KIA	(JR=2nd sCVIRi)	ROH,JR,CDC
Deas, Aaron	Pvt.	A	23rd SCVI		CD	07/30/64	Crater, Pbg., VA	KIA		ROH,JR,BLM
Deas, Duncan	Pvt.	B	26th SCVI	28	CD	06/16/62	Secessionville	KIA		ROH,JR,PP
Deas, H.	Pvt.	A	1st SCVIH		OG	09/17/62	Sharpsburg, MD	KIA	(Color bearer) UD3	ROH,JR,SA1,JRH
Deas, H. Asa	Pvt.	H	2nd SCVI		LR	12/16/62	Fredericksburg	DOD	(H2=12/22/62)	SA2,LAN,KEB,H2
Deas, J.H.	Sgt.					/ /			Fredericksburg C.C. R6S13	FBG
Deas, James	Pvt.	D	1st SCVIR			04/03/65	New Bern, NC	DOW	Cedar Grove C. Newbern, NC	P1,PP,WAT,SA1
Deas, John	Pvt.	B	26th SCVI	40	CD	08/15/62	At home	DOD		ROH,JR
Deas, John	Pvt.	I	17th SCVI		LR	/ /	Adams Run, SC	DOD	(JR=Joseph)	JR,LAN
Deas, N.	Pvt.	D	8th SCVI		CD	01/01/62	Richmond, VA	DOD	(Typhoid)	JR
Deas, William	Pvt.	D	8th SCVI		CD	10/07/61	Charlottesville	DOW	Univ. Cem. Charlottesville	JR,ACH,KEB
Dease, J.J.	Pvt.	D	4th SCVC			06/12/64	Trevillian Stn.	KIA		ROH
Dease, John	Pvt.	A	14th SCVI	35	DN	11/20/62	Winchester, VA	DOD	Stonewall Cem. Winchester	ROH,JR,WIN
Dease, Nathan	Pvt.	K	6th SCVI	35	CD	02/19/63	Charlottseville	DOD	Univ. Cem. Charlottesville	ROH,3RC,ACH
Deason, A.	Cpl.	K	15th SCVI		AE	12/13/62	Richmond, VA	DOD		ROH,KEB
Deason, Aquilla	Cpl.	K	13th SCVI			09/14/62		DOW		JR
Deason, R.	Pvt.	G	17th SCVI		BL	/ /	John's Island SC	DOD		JR
Deason, Thomas	Pvt.	G	17th SCVI		BL	08/30/62	2nd Manassas, VA	KIA		JR
Decker, J.	Pvt.	A	Tucker's R			03/01/65	Salisbury, NC		Prob Old Lutheran C. there	PP
Deer, William Anderson	Pvt.	C	1st SCVIH	19	BL	05/06/64	Wilderness, VA	KIA		ROH,SA1
Dees, Doe	Pvt.	B	26th SCVI	28	CD	07/03/64	Petersburg, VA	DOD		ROH
Dees, H.C.	Pvt.	G	7th SCVI		ED	07/05/62	Savage Stn., VA	DOW	Hollywood Cem.Rchmd. M445	ROH,HC,KEB,HOE
Dees, N.	Pvt.	C	5th SCRes			03/24/65	Raleigh, NC		Oakwood C. Raleigh, NC	TOD
Dees, N.T.	Pvt.	B	26th SCVI	18	CD	06/15/64	Petersburg, VA	KIA		ROH
Dees, P.S.	Pvt.	B	26th SCVI	19	CD	05/27/62	Charleston, SC	DOD	Magnolia Cem. Charleston	ROH,JR,MAG
Dees, Richard	Pvt.	B	26th SCVI	28	CD	10/17/64	Petersburg, VA	DOD		ROH
Dees, William	Pvt.	G	7th SCV			/ /		KIA		UD2
Deland, Wiley	Pvt.	E	14th SCVI		LS	/ /		DIP		CGS
Delaney, Frank	Pvt.	B	Orr's Ri.	20	AE	12/13/62	Fredericksburg	KIA		ROH
Delaney, J.N.	Pvt.	B	11th SCVI			12/19/62	Richmond, VA	DOD	(May be Delancy, NI HAG)	ROH
Delaney, John H.	Pvt.	B	Orr's Ri.	22	AE	12/22/62	Richmond, VA	DOW	(Wdd @ Fredericksburg)	ROH,JR,CDC
Delaney, John W.	1st Lt.	C	12th SCVI		FD	06/27/62	Gaines' Mill, VA	KIA		ROH,JR,HFC,R47
Dellinger, J.J.	Pvt.	A	18th SCVI			11/08/62			Stonewall C. Winchester VA	WIN
Delrack, C.	Pvt.	D	12th SCVI		RD	/ /	Lynchburg, VA		Lynchburg CSA Cem. #7 R5	BBW
Dempsey, Adam W.	Pvt.	D	3rd SCVABn		CN	11/11/64	Adams Run, SC	DOD		PP
Dendy, Daniel	3rd Sgt.	C	7th SCVC		NY	10/14/64	Baltimore, MD	DOW	Loudon Pk. Cem. C.L.B-54	FPH,PP,P6,ANY
Denis, Joseph Adolph	Pvt.		LafayetteA	20		03/30/64	James Island, SC	DOD		ROH
Denkins, Samuel	Pvt.	F	3rd SCVIBn		RD	01/07/63	Richmond, VA		Hollywood Cem.Rchmd. G87	HC,KEB
Denneau, John	Pvt.	I	14th SCVI			08/23/64	Gravelly Run, VA	KIA		HOL
Dennis, D.I.	Pvt.	K	25th SCVI		WG	05/09/64	Swift Creek, VA	KIA	(? T.J. in HAG)	CTA,HOW
Dennis, Edward Elliott	Pvt.	D	2nd SCVI		SR	12/30/61	Charlottesville	DOD		H2,KEB

D

SOUTH CAROLINA DEAD IN CSA SERVICE 1861-1865

NAME	RANK	C REGIMENT	AGE	DS	DIED	WHERE	WHY	BURIED	SOURCES
Dennis, J.A.	Pvt.	A 8th SCVI		DN	05/12/62		DOD	(Diptheria)	ROH,JR
Dennis, J.E.	Pvt.	K 25th SCVI			07/22/62	James Island, SC	DOD	(Congestive Chill)	JR
Dennis, J.H.	Pvt.	F 9th SCVIB	18	SR	11/12/61	Charlottesville	DOD	Univ. Cem. Charlottesville	ROH,JR,ACH
Dennis, J.R.	Pvt.	SCV			06/16/65	Newport News, VA		Greenlawn C. Newport News	PP
Dennis, J.S.	Pvt.	E 3rd SCVABn		NY	11/05/63	Columbia, SC	DOD	(Palmetto Battalion)	ROH,ANY,PP
Dennis, James	Pvt.	A 8th SCVI		DN	/ /			(Duplicate of J.H. ?)	ROH
Dennis, Jeremiah	Pvt.	H 26th SCVI		SR	05/22/64	Petersburg, VA		Blandford Church Pbg., VA	BLC,PP
Dennis, Jesse A.	Pvt.	C 23rd SCVI		NY	07/30/64	Crater, Pbg., VA	KIA	Prosperity Cem. SC	ROH,JR,NCC,BLM
Dennis, Jesse O.	Pvt.	H 1st SCVIH	22	NY	01/06/64	Knoxville, TN	DIP	(POW in Knoxville)	ROH,SA1,P5
Dennis, Joseph Warren	Pvt.	G 13th SCVI	27	NY	06/22/64	Petersburg, VA	KIA		ROH,ANY
Dennis, Nelson	Pvt.	C 25th SCVI		WG	09/07/63	Bty Wagner, SC	KIA	(NI HAG)	CTA,HOW
Dennis, Sherod R.	Pvt.	C 25th SCVI	24	WG	09/30/63	Bty Wagner, SC	DOW	(JR= S,R, & 9/23/63)	ROH,JR,HOW,HAG
Dennis, W.J.	Pvt.	L 1st SCVIG		CN	07/14/62	Richmond, VA	DOD	(Typhoid)	JR,SA1
Denny, George Witner	Pvt.	E 7th SCVI	24	ED	01/03/62	Warren Spgs., VA	DOD	(Typhoid) KEB	JR,HOE,EDN,UD3
Denny, Pinckney D.	Pvt.	D 19th SCVI	18	ED	06/21/62	Enterprise, MS	DOD		ROH,HOE,UD3,PP
Denny, William J.	2nd Lt.	E 7th SCVI	25	ED	05/08/64	Spotsylvania, VA	KIA	KEB	ROH,JR,HOE,UD3
Denson, Charles	Pvt.	A 13th SCVI		LS	10/31/62	Lynchburg, VA		Lynchburg CSA Cem. #5 R2	JR,BBW
Dent, L.T.	Pvt.	D 12th SCVI		RD	/ /			Charlestown, VA	ROH
Denton, Francis M.	Pvt.	H 4th SCVC		LR	09/02/64	Lincoln Hos., DC	DOW	(Wdd & POW @ Hawe's Shop)	LAN,P6
Deonse, W.G.	Pvt.	Matthews A			04/10/65	High Point, NC		Oakwood Cem. High Point NC	CV
Deracken, Samuel	Pvt.	C Ham.Leg.		MN	05/31/62	7 Pines, VA	KIA		ROH,JR,CDC
Derrer, Marcus	Pvt.	F 17th SCVI	31	YK	05/13/65	City Point, VA	DOW	City Pt. N.C. Hopewell, VA	PP,YEB,TOD
Derrick, D.W.	Pvt.	F P.S.S.		LN	03/25/62	Petersburg, VA	DOD	Blandford Church Pbg., VA	ROH,JR,BLC,PP
Derrick, Frederick E.	Pvt.	I 15th SCVI		LN	08/22/63	Gettysburg, PA	DOW	Magnolia Cem. Charleston	ROH,KEB,P1,P5
Derrick, George C.	Pvt.	E 3rd SCVI		NY	02/24/62	At home	DOD	Wise Fam.Cem. Newberry, SC	ROH,JR,NCC,ANY
Derrick, George Melvin	Pvt.	H 13th SCVI	18	LN	07/18/63	Gettysburg, PA	DOW	Magnolia Cem. Charleston	ROH,JR,GDR,P6
Derrick, Henry F.	2nd Sgt.	C 15th SCVI	29	LN	09/14/62	South Mtn., MD	KIA	TOD	ROH,JR,KEB,H15
Derrick, J.V.	Pvt.	H 13th SCVI		LN	07/24/63	Chester, PA	DOW	(Wdd & left @ Gettysburg)	ROH,CDC,P1
Derrick, Jacob A.	Pvt.	I 15th SCVI	28	LN	12/06/63	Knoxville, TN	DOD		ROH
Derrick, Jacob J.	Pvt.	C 4th ResBn		NY	02/04/65	Columbia, SC	DOD	Wise Fam.Cem. Newberry, SC	ROH,NCC,PP
Derrick, Jacob L.	Sgt.	I 15th SCVI	28	LN	01/02/64	Russelville, TN	DOD	(Pneumonia)	H15,TOD
Derrick, Simeon P.	Pvt.	I 24th SCVI	16	ED	06/25/64	Griffin, GA	DOD		EJM,UD2
Deveat, R.E.	Pvt.	A Ham.Leg.		CN	08/19/61	Culpepper, VA	DOW		JR,CDC
Devine, Frank G.	5th Sgt.	E 2nd SCVI		KW	09/20/63	Chickamauga, GA	KIA		ROH,JR,SA2,HIC
Devinny, Robert Love	Pvt.	H 18th SCVI	19	YK	06/10/64	Drury's Bluff VA	DOW	Blandford Church Pbg., VA	YMD,BLC,PP
Devore, Richard	Pvt.	G 24th SCVI			11/30/64	Franklin, TN	KIA	Williamson Cty. C.C., TN	ROH,WCT,PP
Dew, F.C.	Pvt.	C 26th SCVI		MN	/ /	Church Flats, SC	DOD		HMC
Dew, John W.	Pvt.	D 25th SCVI		MN	05/22/64	Richmond, VA	DOD	Hollywood Cem.Rchmd. I265	ROH,HC,HAG,HMC
Dew, S.W.	Pvt.	H 23rd SCVI		MN	12/12/62	Goldsboro, NC	KIA	(ROH=Fredericksburg)	ROH,JR,HMC,CDC
Dewberry, Samuel Thomas	Pvt.	I 5th SCVI		SG	05/06/64	Wilderness, VA	KIA		ROH,HOS,SA3
Dewitt, John	Pvt.	C 26th SCVI		MN	07/24/64	Petersburg, VA	DOD	Hollywood Cem.Rchmd. V96	ROH,HMC,HC
Dewitt, John	Pvt.	B 3rd SCVC	20	CO	02/02/65	Salkehatchie, SC	KIA		ROH
Dial, B.	Pvt.	D 12th SCVI		RD	08/01/62	Bay Point, SC	DOD		JR
Dial, Jacob	Pvt.	F 21st SCVI		MO	03/19/65	Elmira, NY	DIP	Woodlawn N.C.#1583 Elmira	ROH,FPH,P6,P65
Dibble, Samuel W.	1st Lt.	G 25th SCVI		CN	02/28/65	Washington, DC	DOW	(POW @ Town Ck. 2/20/65)	ROH,WLI,HAG,P120
Dick, James Somers	Pvt.	K 23rd SCVI		SR	07/30/64	Petersburg, VA	KIA		ROH,K23,UD3
Dick, T.M.	Pvt.	E P.S.S.		SR	06/30/62	Frayser's Farm	KIA		ROH,JR,CDC
Dick, William Edward	Pvt.	A 2nd SCVC		SR	/ /	Green Pond, SC	DOD		PP
Dickard, William	Pvt.	F 24th SCVI		AN	/ /		DOD	(1865)	HOL
Dickens, John					/ /			(Richmond effects list)	CDC
Dickens, W.	Pvt.	C 2nd SCV			05/05/62	Richmond, VA	DOD		ROH

D

SOUTH CAROLINA DEAD IN CSA SERVICE 1861-1865

NAME	RANK	C REGIMENT	AGE	DS	DIED	WHERE	WHY	BURIED	SOURCES
Dickenson, James H.	Sgt.	A 25th SCVI	24	CN	/ /	Pt. Lookout, MD	DIP		ROH,HAG
Dickerson, Hiram	Pvt.	B 17th SCVI		FD	08/30/62	2nd Manassas, VA	KIA		JR,UD3
Dickerson, M.	Pvt.	D 4th SCVI			10/27/62	Richmond, VA		Hollywood Cem.Rchmd. B227	HC
Dickerson, P.F.	Sgt.	2nd SCV			07/02/63	Gettysburg, PA	KIA	Magnolia Cem. Charleston	MAG
Dickert, B. Fletcher	Pvt.	H 3rd SCVI		LN	09/20/63	Chickamauga, GA	KIA		ROH,JR,SA2,ANY
Dickert, John Philip	Pvt.	H 13th SCVI	18	NY	07/08/62	Winder Hos Rchmd	DOD	(Typhoid)	JR,ANY
Dickert, Warren	Pvt.	F 20th SCVI		NY	/ /		DOD	(William T. in KEB?)	ANY
Dickey, David S.	Pvt.	A 6th SCVI	21	CR	05/31/62	7 Pines, VA	KIA	Oakwood C.#26 Row K Div B	ROH,OWC,HHC,GL
Dickhardt, J.P.	Pvt.	H 13th SCVI		LN	07/09/62	Richmond, VA			ROH
Dickinson, William M.	Pvt.	D 18th SCVI		AN	12/18/64	Elmira, NY	DIP	Woodlawn N.C.#1066 Elmira	ROH,FPH,P6,P11
Dicks, Augustus	Cpl.	A 1st SCVIG		BL	09/15/62	Warrenton, VA	DOW	(Wdd 2nd M.as Cpl. A. Dix)	JR,SA1,CDC
Dicks, George	Pvt.	G 1st SCV			/ /	High Point, NC		Oakwood C. High Point, NC	TOD
Dicks, J.A.	Pvt.	A 1st SCVIG		BL	05/15/64	Spotsylvania, VA	DOW		ROH,SA1
Dicks, T.M.	Pvt.	E P.S.S.			/ /			Oakwood C.#38, Row A Div C	OWC
Dickson, A.V.	Pvt.	E 2nd SCVIRi			/ /	Lynchburg, VA		Lynchburg CSA Cem.#5 R4	BBW
Dickson, Archibald P.	Pvt.	F 8th SCVI	17	FD	07/21/61	1st Manassas, VA	KIA	(KEB= Dixon, A.P.)	ROH,JR,KEB
Dickson, D.M.	Pvt.	D 20th SCVI			10/27/61	Richmond, VA	DOD		ROH
Dickson, E.V.	Pvt.	I 2nd SCVI			01/12/63	Lynchburg, VA	DOD		SA2
Dickson, J.K.	Pvt.	F Orr's Ri.			05/03/63	Chancellorsville	KIA		ROH,JR
Dickson, James C.	Pvt.	F 8th SCVI	20	FD	12/15/61	Charlottesville	DOD	(JR=Manassas, VA)	ROH,JR,KEB
Dickson, John H.	Pvt.	E 2nd SCVC		SG	08/03/64	Charleston, SC	DOD	Magnolia Cem. Charleston	ROH,MAG,HOS
Dickson, John R.	Pvt.	C Orr's Ri.		PS	12/13/62	Fredericksburg	KIA	(JR=Dixon)	ROH,JR,CDC
Dickson, L.W.	Cpt.	K 22nd SCVI		PS	08/26/62	At home	DOD		ROH,R48,UD2
Dickson, Lewis	Pvt.	B P.S.S.		PS	06/25/62	Richmond, VA	DOD		ROH,JR
Dickson, Samuel W.G.	Pvt.	C 8th SCVI		CN	07/01/63	Gettysburg, PA	KIA		ROH,JR,GDR,KEB
Dickson, Thomas J.	1st Sgt.	D Ham. Leg.		AN	12/18/63	Camp Morton, IN	DIP	Green Lawn C. Indianapolis	FPH,P5,CDC,CV
Dickson, W.H. (N.H.?)	Pvt.	D Orr's Ri.		AN	02/15/63	Lynchburg, VA	DOD		JR,CDC
Dickson, W.J.	Pvt.	F Orr's Ri.			06/23/62		DOD		JR
Dickson, William J.	2nd Lt.	C Orr's Ri.		PS	12/13/62	Fredericksburg	KIA	Spotsylvania C.H. Cem, VA	JR,SCH,R45,CDC
Dierssen,	Pvt.	1st CSEng		CN	01/15/65	Petersburg, VA	ACD	(Drowned in flood)	HOF
Dike, Joseph	Pvt.	2nd SCVIRi			09/28/62	Mt. Jackson, VA	DOW	(Wdd @ Sharpsburg, MD)	ROH,JR,CDC
Dill, Benjamin	Pvt.	E 12th SCVI		GE	/ /	Richmond, VA		Oakwood C.#17 Row R Div C	ROH,OWC
Dill, George	Pvt.	L 6th SCRes		CR	/ /		DOD		HHC
Dill, J. Perry	Pvt.	E 1st SCVIR		GE	06/11/64	Mt. Pleasant, SC	DOD		SA1
Dill, L.C.	Pvt.	D 16th SCVI		GE	11/30/64	Franklin, TN	KIA	Macgavock C. Frkln Gv# 14	ROH,16R,PP
Dill, S.R.	Pvt.	D 16th SCVI			11/30/64	Franklin, TN	KIA	(16R=Sgt. non Casualty)	ROH,16R
Dill. B.C.	Pvt.	E 2nd SCVC		GE	02/13/63	Petersburg, VA	DOD		ROH
Dillard,	Pvt.	G 1st SCV			/ /	Richmond, VA		Oakwood C.#2 Row 7 Div D	ROH,OWC
Dillard, Felix L.	Pvt.	C 13th SCVI		SG	08/07/62	Richmond, VA	DOD	Hollywood Cem.Rchmd. S138	ROH,HC,HOS
Dillard, S.S.	2nd Cpl.	B 13th SCVI		SG	12/27/62		DOD		JR,HOS
Dillard, T.J.	Pvt.	C 13th SCVI		SG	08/13/62	Richmond, VA	DOD	(Typhoid)	JR,HOS
Dillard, Winberry	Pvt.	A Hol.Leg.	30	SG	10/07/62	Lynchburg, VA	DOD	Lynchburg CSA Cem.#2 R2	ROH,JR,CDC,BBW
Dillingham, Samuel	Cpl.	H 24th SCVI			03/31/64	Alexandria, VA	DIP		P6
Dilworth, R.G. (B.G.?)	Pvt.	K 6th SCVI		AN	08/25/64	Ream's Stn., VA	KIA		ROH,JR
Dinan, Cornelius	Pvt.	H 27th SCVI		CN	08/14/64	Elmira, NY	DIP	Woodlawn N.C.#22 Elmira NY	FPH,HAG,P6,P11
Dingle, James H.	Major	Ham.Leg.	38	CN	09/17/62	Sharpsburg, MD	KIA		ROH,JR,CDC,R48
Dinkins, Charles C.	Pvt.	E 6th SCVI		SR	05/31/62	7 Pines, VA	KIA	(CDC= Dunkins)	ROH,JLC,WDB,CD
Dinkle, J.M.	Pvt.	I 5th SCV			05/05/64	Wilderness, VA	KIA	(NI SA3, 5th Cav.?)	JR
Dix, George	Pvt.	G 1st SCV			04/13/65	High Point, NC		Oakwood Cem. High Point NC	CV,WAT
Dixon, Albert O.	Pvt.	E 6th SCVI		SR	08/30/62	2nd Manassas, VA	KIA	(Color Bearer)	ROH,JR,JLC,WDB
Dixon, Bailey S.	Pvt.	G 2nd SCVI		KW	08/08/61	Fairfax, VA	DOD		SA2,HIC,KEB

D

SOUTH CAROLINA DEAD IN CSA SERVICE 1861-1865

NAME	RANK	C REGIMENT	AGE	DS	DIED	WHERE	WHY	BURIED	SOURCES
Dixon, Elias	Pvt.	F 21st SCVI			09/06/62	Charleston, SC	DOD	Magnolia Cem. Charleston	ROH,JR,MAG,HAG
Dixon, F.B.	Pvt.	G 14th SCVI	22	AE	01/27/65	Pt. Lookout, MD	DIP	C.C. Pt. Lookout, MD	ROH,FPH,P113
Dixon, H.	Pvt.	D 20th SCVI		OG	10/14/64	Richmond, VA		Hollywood Cem.Rchmd. V258	ROH,HC
Dixon, Rivers L.	Pvt.	E 6th SCVI		SR	05/31/62	7 Pines, VA	KIA		ROH,JR,JLC,WDB
Dixon, William James	Sgt.	I 6th SCVI		RD	05/06/64	Wilderness, VA	KIA		ROH,JR
Dixon, William N.	Sgt.	H 6th SCVI		FD	05/08/64	Spotsylvania, VA	KIA	(JR=Wilderness 5/5/64)	JR,CDC
Dixon, Zimmerman	Cpl.	E P.S.S.		CL	07/15/62	Richmond, VA	DOW	(Wdd @ Frayser's Fm, 6/30)	ROH,JR,CDC,SA1
Dobbins, G.W.	Pvt.	B 7th SCVC			05/30/64	Old Church, VA	DOW	Dr. Brockenborough's home	ROH,CDC
Dobbins, J.B.	Pvt.	D			10/14/62			Stonewall Cem. Winchester	ROH,WIN
Dobbins, James E.	Pvt.	L Orr's Ri.		AN	05/19/64	Staunton, VA	DOD		ROH,PP
Dobbins, W.P.	Pvt.	H P.S.S.	17	SG	07/06/62	Petersburg, VA	DOD	Blandford Church Pbg., VA	ROH,JR,BLC,PP
Dobey, John L.	Pvt.	K 14th SCVI		ED	07/01/63	Gettysburg, PA	KIA		HOE,GDR
Dobson, A.B.	Pvt.	B 22nd SCVI		SG	/ /				HOS
Dobson, Charles R.	Pvt.	E 11th SCVI	30	BT	01/03/65	Elmira, NY	DIP	Woodlawn N.C.#1343	ROH,FPH,P6,P65
Dobson, E.F.	Lt.				/ /			Rose Hill C. Hagerstown MD	BOD
Dobson, J.C.	Pvt.	D 22nd SCVI		PS	03/06/65	Pt. Lookout, MD	DIP	C.C. Pt. Lookout, MD	FPH,P6,P113
Dobson, J.J.	Pvt.	H 7th SCVI			/ /	Richmond, VA		Oakwood C.#140 Row L Div A	ROH,OWC
Dobson, Jacob	Pvt.	E 11th SCVI	35	BT	06/15/64	Petersburg, VA	KIA		ROH,HAG
Dobson, John S.	Pvt.	E 11th SCVI	32	BT	11/20/64	At sea	DIP	(Xchange to Savannah, GA)	ROH,CDC,HAG,P120
Dobson, W.R.	Pvt.	B 22nd SCVI		SG	05/03/62	Charleston, SC	DOD	(HOS=Crater, Pbg.)	ROH,HOS
Doby, Alfred English	Cpt.	Div. F&S		KW	05/06/64	Wilderness, VA	KIA	Quaker Cem. Camden, SC	ROH,JR,HIC,PP
Doby, Joseph W.	Pvt.	H 7th SCVC		KW	01/29/65	Pt.Lookout, MD	DIP	C.C. Pt. Lookout, MD	ROH,FPH,P6,HIC
Dodd, F.M.	Pvt.	A Orr's Ri.			05/18/62	Virginia	DOD		JR
Dodd, George Washington	Pvt.	K 4th SCVI	20		08/08/61	Culpepper, VA	DOD	Fairview Cem. Culpepper VA	ROH,JR,CGH,SA2
Dodd, N.G.	Pvt.	I 27th SCVI			09/14/63	Columbia, SC	DOD		JR
Dodds, John W.	Pvt.	I 6th SCVI		CR	05/05/62	Williamsburg, VA	DOW	(JR=Ft. Delaware 6/7/62)	JR,WDB,HHC,CB
Dodgen, Josiah	Pvt.	D 19th SCVI	27	ED	/ /	Chattanooga, TN	DOD	(1863)	HOE,UD3
Dodgin, Wiley	Pvt.	G 7th SCVI		ED	/ /		KIA	(Dogin in KEB)	HOE,KEB
Dodson, G.W.	Pvt.	B 2nd SCV			/ /		DOW	Con. Cem. Marietta, GA	CCM,UD2
Dollar, John I.	Pvt.	E 14th SCVI		LS	10/02/61	Camp Butler, SC	DOD	(Measles)	JR,CGS
Dominick, A.B.C.	Pvt.	G 13th SCVI		NY	05/23/64	Jericho Mills VA	KIA		ROH,ANY
Dominick, George Adam	Pvt.	H Hol. Leg.	40	NY	09/07/62	Culpepper, VA	DOW	Prosperity Cem. Newberry	NCC,CGH,ANY,ROH
Dominick, Henry F.	Pvt.	H Hol.Leg.		NY	/ /	Stony Creek, VA	DOD	(Not on NY Monument list)	ANY
Donald, Lewis D.	2nd Sgt.	A 2nd SCVIRi			07/24/62	Richmond, VA	DOW	Oakwood C.#191 Row L Div C	ROH,JRR,OWC
Donald, M.T.E.					/ /			(Rchmd effects list 12/62)	CDC
Donald, Robert	Pvt.	F 7th SCVI	21	ED	/ /	At home	DOD	(Wdd @ Winchester)	HOE,KEB
Donalds, M.E.E.	Pvt.	E 8th SCVI		DN	04/29/62	Richmond, VA	DOD	Oakwood C.#161 Row J Div A	ROH,JR,OWC,KEB
Donaldson, William McC.	3rd Cpl.	A 3rd SCVI		LS	10/13/64	Strasburg, VA	KIA		SA2,KEB
Donan, R.S.	Sgt.				10/28/63	Lookout Valley	KIA		CDC
Dondrich, Pedro	Pvt.	A Tucker's R			02/16/65	Salisbury, NC	DOD	Prob Old Lutheran C. there	PP
Donhelly, M.P.	Sgt.	H Ham.Leg.			08/19/64	Globe Tavern, VA	KIA		JR,CDC
Donn, A.O.	Pvt.	C 1st SCV			06/15/63	Richmond, VA		Hollywood Cem.Rchmd. T243	HC
Donnald, J.C.	Pvt.	F 14th SCVI		LS	08/02/62	Richmond, VA	DOD	(Typhoid, HR=Donnard)	ROH,JR
Donnald, James A.	2nd Sgt.	K 2nd SCVIRi		PS	09/30/64	Ft. Harrison, VA	KIA		ROH
Donnald, John C.	Pvt.	G Orr's Ri.		AE	06/05/64	Richmond, VA	DOW	(Wdd @ Noel Stn.5/23/64)	ROH
Donnally, W.	Pvt.	C 4th SCVC			06/24/64	Petersburg, VA	KIA		JR
Donnard, C.C.	Pvt.	F 14th SCVI		LS	08/10/62	Danville, VA	DOD	(Typhoid)	JR
Donnell, J.	Pvt.	2nd SCVIRi			07/01/62	Malvern Hill, VA	KIA	(JR=6/29/62)	ROH,JR,CDC
Donnelly, Joseph	Pvt.	K 1st SCVIG		CN	12/13/62	Fredericksburg	KIA		ROH,JR,SA1,CDC
Donnelly, Samuel Thomas	Pvt.	A 2nd SCVIRi	19	AE	12/17/63	At home	DOD	Methodiost Ch. Greenwood	ROH,JR,UD3
Donnely, William	Pvt.	C 11th SCVI		CN	06/24/64	Petersburg, VA	KIA		ROH

SOUTH CAROLINA DEAD IN CSA SERVICE 1861-1865

NAME	RANK	C	REGIMENT	AGE	DS	DIED	WHERE	WHY	BURIED	SOURCES
Donoghue, Bernard	Pvt.	D	1st SCVIR	19	CN	02/14/65	Sullivan's I. SC	DOD	St.Lawrence C. Charleston	MAG,RCD,SA1
Donovan, Christopher	Pvt.	F	14th SCVI			08/10/62		DOD		JR
Dooley, J.T.	Pvt.	H	20th SCVI		LN	03/20/65	Pt. Lookout, MD	DIP	(KEB=J.L.)	ROH,KEB
Dooley, James L.	Cpl.	H	20th SCVI		LN	06/15/64		KIA		ROH,KEB
Dooley, William	Pvt.	A	25th SCVI	20	CN	09/15/64	Charleston, SC	DOD		ROH,HAG
Doolitle, Benjamin	Pvt.	K	1st SCVIG		RD	10/30/64	Elmira, NY	DIP	Woodlawn N.C.#746 Elmira	FPH,SA1,P6,P12
Doram, William D.	Pvt.	K	2nd SCVI	25	CO	07/02/62	Savage Stn., VA	DOW	(Wdd 6/29 @ Savage Stn.)	ROH,SA2,KEB
Dorkins, E.G.	Sgt.	D	26th SCVI		MO	05/23/64	Petersburg, VA	DOW	Blandford Church Pbg., VA	ROH,BLC
Dorkins, John T.	Pvt.	D	17th SCVI		CR	08/23/64	Elmira, NY	DIP	Woodlawn N.C.#35 Elmira	ROH,FPH,P6,P65
Dorkins, W.C.	Pvt.	G	17th SCVI		BL	09/04/64	Elmira, NY	DIP	Woodlawn N.C.#229 Elmira	FPH,P6,P65,P12
Dorley, H.N.	Pvt.	K	13th SCVI		LN	07/02/63	Gettysburg, PA	DOW	(ROH=Chancellorsville)	ROH,JR
Dorman, J.R.	Pvt.		5th SCVI			08/05/61	Charlottesville	DOD	Univ. Cem. Charlottesville	ROH,ACH
Dorn, George	Pvt.	K	24th SCVI		ED	07/02/64	Jonesborough, GA	KIA		HOE
Dorn, J.J.	Cpl.	K	15th SCVI		AE	06/27/64	Richmond, VA	KIA	Hollywood Cem.Rchmd. U417	ROH,JR,HC,KEB
Dorn, John	Pvt.	K	24th SCVI		ED	08/07/63	Rome, GA	DOD		HOE
Dorn, Leonard Yancey	Pvt.	B	Ham.Leg.	19	ED	06/24/64	Samaria Ch., VA	KIA		ROH
Dorn, Rufus M.	Pvt.	G	1st SCVIG	20	ED	06/26/64	Spotsylvania, VA	DOW	(Thigh wound)	ROH,SA1,HOE,CD
Dorn, W.	Pvt.	G	24th SCVI		RD	09/01/63	Selma, AL	DOD		EJM
Dorn, W.P.	Pvt.	K	24th SCVI		ED	10/15/63	Dalton, GA	DOD		HOE,PP
Dorning, William	Pvt.	C	12th SCVI		FD	03/15/64	At home	DOD	(Cedar Creek Ri. p126/HFC)	JR,HFC
Dorr, John C.	Pvt.		3rd SCVABn		CN	07/22/62	Charleston, SC	DOD		ROH
Dorr, P.C. (P.N.?)	Pvt.	D	18th SCVI		AN	07/26/62	Charleston, SC	DOD	Magnolia Cem. Charleston	ROH,JR,MAG
Dorritty, Thomas	Pvt.	C	7th SCVIBn	27	RD	06/18/64	Petersburg, VA	KIA	(ROH=Dority)	ROH,HAG
Dorroh, J.A.	Pvt.	G	3rd SCVI	19	LS	12/13/62	Fredericksburg	KIA		ROH,JR,SA2,KEB
Dorroh, J.R.	4th Cpl.	G	3rd SCVI	20	LS	12/13/62	Fredericksburg	KIA		ROH,JR,SA2,KEB
Dorroh, James William	Pvt.	G	3rd SCVI	21	NY	07/04/64	Burkesville, VA	DOW	Bush River B.C. Newb'y Cty	ROH,JR,NCC,SA2
Dorroh, William Pinckney	Pvt.	E	Ham. Leg.	19	NY	07/27/64	Deep Bottom, VA	KIA	Bush River B.C. Newb'y Cty	ROH,NCC,ANY
Dorsey, John A.	Pvt.	A	6th SCVI		CR	/ /	Centreville, VA	DOD	(Calhoun Guards)	HHC,CNM
Dorsey, W.M.	Pvt.	L	Orr's Ri.		AN	05/04/62		DOD		JR,CDC
Dorty, W.J.	Pvt.	I	3rd SCVI			09/20/63	Chickamauga, GA	KIA		JR
Doscher, Eiber F.W.	Pvt.	A	1st SCVIH		OG	11/22/61	At home	DOD		ROH,SA1,EDR
Doster, George S.	Pvt.	A	12th SCVI	42	YK	10/02/63	Ft. Delaware, DE	DIP	Finn's Pt. NJ Nat. Cem.	ROH,FPH,P6,YEB
Dottart, Daniel	Pvt.	I	15th SCVI		LN	05/15/64	Winchester, VA			JR,H15,KEB
Dottart, Joel	Pvt.	I	15th SCVI	23	LN	01/23/63	Richmond, VA	DOD		H15,KEB
Dotterer, James B.	Sgt. Major		24th SCVI	19	CN	06/15/64	Augusta, GA	DOW	Magnolia Cem. Charleston	MAG,CDC
Dotterer, William A.	Cpl.	A	25th SCVI	23	CN	05/16/64	Drury's Bluff VA	KIA	Magnolia Cem. Charleston	ROH,JR,MAG,HAG
Doty, M.J.	Pvt.	A	20th SCVI			01/02/65	Richmond, VA		Hollywood Cem.Rchmd. W434	ROH,HC
Dougal, Charles H.E.	Pvt.	H	15th SCVI	30	RD	07/06/62	Columbia, SC	DOD	Elmwood Cem. Columbia, SC	ROH,JR,MP,TOD,
Dougherty, J.	Pvt.	C	2nd SCVI		RD	08/17/61	Richmond, VA	DOD	(May be "Dodcets" in HC)	ROH,SA2,KEB
Dougherty, J.	Pvt.	A	14th SCVI		DN	01/20/63	Lynchburg, VA	DOD	Lynchburg CSA Cem. #6 R3	JR,BBW
Dougherty, J.A.E.	Sgt.	D	Ham.Leg.			01/08/64	Knoxville, TN	DOW	(In enemy hands)	P1,P5
Dougherty, W.	Pvt.	G	1st SCVIH			04/24/64		DOD	(To Hosp 12/18/63)	SA1
Douglas, A.	Pvt.	G	1st SCV			09/17/62	Sharpsburg, MD	KIA	Rose Hill C. Hagerstown MD	ROH,CDC,WAT
Douglas, Angus	Sgt.	A	23rd SCVI		CD	08/19/64	Petersburg, VA	DOD		ROH,PP
Douglas, Archibald M.	Pvt.	A	4th SCVC		CD	05/28/64	Hawes Shop, VA	KIA		ROH,JR
Douglas, D. Brice	Pvt.	F	25th SCVI	26	OG	12/11/63	Ft. Sumter, SC	ACD	(Magazine Explosion)	ROH,JR,CDC,HAG
Douglas, Davis Scott	Pvt.	F	12th SCVI		FD	07/05/62	Gaines' Mill, VA	DOW	Hollywood Cem.Rchmd. M401	ROH,JR,HC,HFC
Douglas, E.	Pvt.	F	2nd SCVI			09/20/62	Mt. Jackson, VA	DOW		JR
Douglas, Eli C.	Pvt.	H	7th SCVIBn	25	CR	05/16/64	Drury's Bluff VA	KIA		ROH,JR,HAG
Douglas, Gilbert Shaw	Pvt.	E	17th SCVI	28	YK	03/03/62	John's Island SC	DOD	(Typhoid)	ROH,JR,DEM,YEB
Douglas, Henry A.	Pvt.	D	21st SCVI		CD	04/02/65	Elmira, NY	DIP	Woodlawn N.C.#1699	ROH,FPH,P6,P65

SOUTH CAROLINA DEAD IN CSA SERVICE 1861-1865

NAME	RANK	C REGIMENT	AGE	DS	DIED	WHERE	WHY	BURIED	SOURCES
Douglas, Henry A.	Pvt.	D 21st SCVI		CD	04/02/65	Elmira, NY	DIP	Woodlawn N.C.#1699	ROH,FPH,P6,P65
Douglas, Hugh J.	6th Cpl.	G 8th SCVI	25	MO	10/19/64	Cedar Creek, VA	KIA	(UD2=2nd Lt.)	HOM,KEB,UD1,UD2
Douglas, R.	Pvt.	E 1st SCVA			09/13/62	Charleston, SC	DOD	Magnolia Cem. Charleston	ROH,RCD
Douglas, R.	Pvt.	2nd SCVIRi			09/20/62	Sharpsburg, MD	DOW	Sharpsburg C., MD	ROH,CDC
Douglas, S. Wade	Cpt.	B 7th SCVIBn	29	CR	09/09/64	Weldon RR Pbg VA	DOW		ROH,HAG,R46,HHC
Douglas, S.A.	Cpl.	A 17th SCBn.			04/10/65	Thomasville, NC		Thomasville, NC Con. Cem.	CV,PP
Douglas, Thomas	Pvt.	G 1st SCVC	25	AE	04/01/62	Adam's Run, SC	DOD		ROH
Douglas, William	Pvt.	E 7th SCVI		ED	/ /		DOD		HOE,KEB,UD3
Douglass, Alexander C.	Pvt.	G 6th SCVI		FD	09/17/62	Sharpsburg, MD	KIA		JR,WDB,CDC
Douglass, S.S.	Pvt.	C 12th SCVI		FD	06/27/62	Gaines' Mill, VA	DOW		HFC
Douglass, Samuel A.	2nd Cpl.	H 2nd SCVI		LR	05/10/64	Spotsylvania, VA	KIA		ROH,JR,SA2,LAN
Douglass, W.H.	Pvt.	B 3rd SCV			09/09/62	Richmond area		Hollywood Cem.Rchmd. A87	HC
Douglass, W.J.	Sgt.	B 8th SCVI		CD	/ /	Charlottesville		Univ. Cem. Charlottesville	ACH,KEB
Douglass, W.W.	Pvt.	B Orr's Ri.			02/07/65	Elmira, NY	DIP	Woodlawn N.C.#1915 Elmira	FPH,P6,P65,CDC
Douthet, M.P.	Pvt.	D Orr's Ri.		AN	08/09/62	Dill Farms, VA	DOD	(CDC=Douthill, M.F.)	JR
Dove, Hugh G.	Pvt.	I 8th SCVI		MN	08/07/61	1st Manassas, VA	KIA		HMC,KEB
Dove, John W.	Pvt.	I 8th SCVI		MN	11/04/61	Culpepper, VA	DOD	Fairview Cem. Culpepper VA	CGH,HMC,KEB
Dove, Oliver	Pvt.	F 23rd SCVI		CR	08/30/62	2nd Manassas, VA	KIA		ROH,CDC,HHC
Dove, Yancey	Pvt.	I 19th SCVI	46	AE	08/01/64	Griffin, GA	DOW	Stonewall Cem. Griffin, GA	ROH,BGA,UD2
Dover, G. Washington	Pvt.	G 5th SCVI	32	YK	12/25/63	Camp Morton, IN	DIP	Green Lawn C. Indianapolis	FPH,P5,SA3,YEB
Dover, Martin	Pvt.	I 1st SCVIH		MN	12/26/63		DOD		ROH,SA1
Dover, P.H.	Pvt.	B 12th SCVI		UN	09/12/62		DOW	(Prob 2nd Man.)	JR
Dover, Pinckney	Pvt.	B 12th SCVI	24	YK	/ /		DOD	(Dup of Dover, P.H.?)	YEB
Dover, W.E.	Pvt.	F 17th SCVI			/ /	Livingston, MS	DOD		JR
Dover, W.R.	Pvt.	A 12th SCVI	21	YK	08/12/64	Fussell's Mill	KIA		JR,YEB
Dover, William M.	Pvt.	C 17th SCVI	33	YK	08/07/64	Crater, Pbg., VA	DOW		ROH,BLM,YEB,PP
Dow, A.O.	Pvt.	C 1st SCV			06/15/63	Richmond, VA			ROH
Dowdie, J.	Pvt.	G 18th SCVI			07/30/64	Crater, Pbg., VA	KIA		ROH,JR,BLM
Dowdle, James	Pvt.	17th SCVI	18	YK	/ /		DOD		YEB
Dowell, T.	Pvt.	E 1st SCVIR		CN	03/16/65	Averysboro, NC	KIA		ROH
Downey, S.	Pvt.	P.S.S.			/ /	Richmond, VA		Oakwood C.#17 Row H Div G	ROH,OWC
Downey, Thomas	Pvt.			21	LS	05/02/65	Petersburg, VA		Union B. Ch. LS Cty.	LSC
Doyel, E.W.	Pvt.	A 2nd SCVIRi			/ /	Lynchburg, VA		Lynchburg CSA Cem. #4 R5	BBW
Doyle, R.B.	Pvt.	CN Arsenal		CN	10/02/64	Charleston, SC	DOD	Magnolia Cem. Charleston	ROH,RCD,CDC
Dozier, Griffin	Pvt.	H 23rd SCVI		MN	12/13/62	Fredericksburg	KIA	(Goldsboro per HMC)	ROH,HMC,CDC
Dozier, James Valentine	1st Cpl.	I 21st SCVI		MN	07/13/63	Morris Island SC	DOW	NC Beaufort, SC #53-6360	ROH,JR,P5,HMC,PP
Dozier, James W.	Pvt.	D 21st SCVI		CD	10/23/62	Charleston, SC	DOD	Magnolia Cem. Charleston	ROH,JR,MAG
Draft, Michael	Pvt.	B 15th SCMil	55	LN	04/03/65	New Bern, NC	DOW	Cedar Grove C. Newbern, NC	P1,P6,WAT,PP
Drafts, Jacob F.	Pvt.	F 5th SCVC	26	LN	10/20/64	At home		Cedar Grove L.C. Lexington	ROH,TOD
Drake, Ancil A.	Cpl.	K 8th SCVI		MO	12/25/61	Warrenton, VA		(Ansel in KEB)	JR,HOM,KEB
Drake, J.T.	Pvt.	G 2nd Res Bn	17	AN	01/04/65	Columbia, SC	DOD	Elmwood Cem. Columbia, SC	ROH,MP,PP
Dreher, John H.	Pvt.	F 5th SCVC	18	LN	02/23/63	McClellanville	DOD	Macedonia L.C. Little Mtn.	ROH,NCC,LNC,TOD
Drennan, Robert Derlin	Pvt.	G 14th SCVI	35	AE	08/26/64	Ream's Stn., VA	DOW		ROH
Drew, N.	Pvt.	D 10th SCVI		MN	12/31/62	Murfreesboro, TN	KIA		ROH,RAS,CDC
Drew, R.	Pvt.	I 7th SCVI		MN	12/22/62	Richmond, VA	DOD	Hollywood Cem.Rchmd. Q24	ROH,HC
Driggers,	Pvt.	B 24th SCVI		MO	09/21/63	Atlanta, GA		Oakland C. Atlanta R24#3	BGA
Driggers, H.C.	Pvt.	C 11th SCVI		CN	06/06/64	Richmond, VA		Hollywood Cem.Rchmd. U556	ROH,HC
Driggers, Henry	Pvt.	C 11th SCVI		CN	09/01/64	Richmond, VA	DOD	(Dup. of H.C.?)	ROH,HAG
Driggers, Jesse	Pvt.	G 8th SCVI	18	MO	02/12/62	Manassas, VA	DOD	(Pneumonia, UD2=KIA)	JR,HOM,KEB,UD2
Driggers, Joel	Pvt.	C 11th SCVI		CO	05/08/65	Pt. Lookout, MD	DIP	C.C. Pt. Lookout, MD	ROH,P6,FPH,P114
Driggers, John	Pvt.	B 8th SCVI		CD	02/25/65	Camp Chase, OH	DIP	C.C.#1465 Columbus, OH	FPH,P6,P23,KEB

D

SOUTH CAROLINA DEAD IN CSA SERVICE 1861-1865

NAME	RANK	C REGIMENT	AGE	DS	DIED	WHERE	WHY	BURIED	SOURCES
Driggers, John A.	Pvt.	G 23rd SCVI		MO	08/30/62	Richmond, VA	DOD	Hollywood Cem.Rchmd. S44	ROH,HC
Driggers, Matthew C.	Pvt.	B 24th SCVI	43	MO	07/21/63	At home	DOD	(1862)	HOM
Driggers, Philip	Pvt.	E 4th SCVC		MO	/ /	Lee's Mill, VA	KIA		HOM
Driggers, Roberson	Pvt.	C 11th SCVI		CN	06/19/65	Pt. Lookout, MD	DIP	C.C. Pt. Lookout, MD	FPH,P6,P114,HA
Driggers, Robert	Pvt.	B 24th SCVI	33	MO	02/22/64	At home	DOD		ROH
Driggers, Thomas	Pvt.	E 9th SCVIBn		MO	06/24/62	Secessionville	DOW	Magnolia Cem. Charleston	ROH,MAG,HOM
Driggers,Sr., John	Pvt.	F 3rd SCVABn	47	CN	09/13/64	Adam's Run, SC	DOD		ROH,PP
Drinkard, J.P.	Pvt.	H 13th SCVI		LN	07/08/62	Richmond, VA		Hollywood Cem.Rchmd. M378	HC
Drinkard, W.A.	Pvt.	A 2nd SCVIRi		AE	08/20/62	Richmond, VA	DOD	Hollywood Cem.Rchmd. H183	ROH,HC,CDC
Drinkens, H.K.	Pvt.	K 1st SCV			09/19/63	Richmond area		Hollywood Cem.Rchmd. T423	HC
Driver, G.N.	Pvt.	E 4th SCVIBn		AN	05/31/62	7 Pines, VA	KIA		ROH,HOF
Drose, John S.	Pvt.	D 4th SCVC		CN	06/11/64	Trevillian Stn,	KIA		ROH,CDC
Drowdy, W.T.	Pvt.	E 24th SCVI	19	CO	02/01/65	Macon, GA	DOD		ROH
Droze, J.D.	2nd Lt.	A 24th SCVI		CO	07/22/64	Atlanta, GA	DOW	Stonewall Cem. Griffin, GA	ROH,UD2,R48,BG
Drumm, Daniel	Pvt.	H 24th SCVI	27	CR	06/15/64	Griffin, GA	DOD	Stonewall Cem. Griffin, GA	ROH,BGA,HHC,CB
Drummond, J.A.	Pvt.	E 1st SCVIH		BL	11/30/62	Charlottesville	DOW	Univ. Cem. Charlottesville	ROH,SA1,CDC,AC
Drummond, J.W.	Pvt.	F Hol. Leg.		AE	09/25/64		DOD	Oakwood C.#83 Row H Div G	ROH,OWC
Drummond, James	Pvt.	B 14th SCMil		SG	05/21/65	Hart's Island NY	DIP	Cypress Hills N.C.#2471 NY	FPH,P6,P79
Drummond, John F.	Pvt.	C 27th SCVI			08/22/64		DOW		HAG,P12
Drummond, R.A.	Pvt.	K 3rd SCVI	29	SG	12/15/61	Warrenton, VA	DOD	(JRR=Richmond)	ROH,JRR,SA2,HO
Drummond, Warren S.	1st Sgt.	D P.S.S.		SG	11/26/63	Campbell Stn. TN	DOW	(Wdd 11/11/63)	ROH,HOS
DuBose, A.S.	Pvt.	A 14th SCVI		DN	08/06/62	At home	DOD	(Typhoid)(Dup of S.C.?)	JR
DuBose, Alfred C.	Sgt.	B 21st SCVI	22	DN	06/29/64	Petersburg, VA	KIA	Blandford Church Pbg., VA	ROH,BLC,HAG,PP
DuBose, E.P.	Pvt.	A 14th SCVI	22	DN	10/13/61	Camp Butler, SC	DOD	(Measles)	ROH,JRR
DuBose, Edwin C.	1st Lt.	L 1st SCVIG	23	CN	05/03/63	Chancellorsville	KIA	Magnolia Cem. Charleston	ROH,JRR,BOS,SA
DuBose, Gadsden	Pvt.	E 19th SCVI		SR	07/22/64	Atlanta, GA	KIA		ROH
DuBose, Julius J.	Pvt.	A 14th SCVI	23	DN	02/17/62	Pocotaligo, SC	DOD	(JR=McPhersonville)	ROH,JR
DuBose, Robert S.	Pvt.	H 21st SCVI			04/18/62	Georgetown, SC	DOD	(JR=7/31/63)	JR,HAG,PP
DuBose, S.C.	Pvt.	A 14th SCVI	23	DN	03/18/64	At home	DOD		ROH
DuBose, Theodore J.	Pvt.	B 21st SCVI	62	DN	07/10/63	Bty. Wagner, SC	KIA		ROH,CDC,R48
DuBose, William C.	Pvt.	E 7th SCVIBn	46	CN	06/06/64	Cold Harbor, VA	KIA		ROH,JR,HAG
DuBose, William Porcher	1st Lt.Adj	Hol.Leg.		DN	/ /	Sewanee, TN	DOD	Cem. Sewanee, TN	PP
DuBose, Zimmerman J.	Pvt.	K 21st SCVI		DN	07/24/62	At home	DOD		JR,HAG
DuPre, Henry W.	Pvt.	A 25th SCVI	19	CN	09/20/64	Adam's Run, SC	DOD	(PP=SC Artillery)	ROH,PP
DuPre, J.F. (R.F.?)	Pvt.	A P.S.S.		CN	06/30/62	Frayser's Farm	KIA	Oakwood C.#94 Row N Div B	ROH,JR,OWC,CDC
DuPre, John F.	Pvt.	I 1st SCVIG		CN	06/12/62	Richmond, VA	DOD	Oakwood C.#72 Row J Div G	ROH,SA1,OWC
DuPre, W.H.	Pvt.	A 25th SCVI	20	CN	09/20/64	Adam's Run, SC	DOD		ROH
DuPree, S.N.	Pvt.	A 18th SCVI		UN	08/30/62	2nd Manassas, VA	KIA		ROH,JR,CDC
DuRant, James A.	Pvt.	E 2nd SCVI		KW	10/19/61	Charlottesville	DOD		SA2,HIC
Duan, William	Pvt.	H 23rd SCVI		MN	08/05/63	Petersburg, VA	DOD		ROH
Duane, Patrick	Pvt.	H Ham.Leg.		CN	09/12/62	2nd Manassas, VA	DOW		ROH,JR,CDC
Dubard, L.W.	Pvt.	E 14th SCVI			06/01/65	Hart's Island NY	DIP	Cypress Hills N.C. #2568	FPH,P6,P79
Duc, Virgil	2nd Lt.	E 25th SCVI		CN	01/06/65	Charleston, SC	DOD	St. Lawrence C. Charleston	MAG,CDC,HAG
Ducket, Isaac	Pvt.	F 20th SCVI			10/13/64	Strasburg, VA	KIA	(John in ANY & KEB)	ROH,JR,ANY,KEB
Duckett, J.	Pvt.	G 27th SCVI		SG	06/24/64		ACD	(In Camp, JR=KIA)	JR,HOS,HAG
Duckett, James	Pvt.			NY	06/05/64	Cold Harbor, VA	KIA	Lower Duncan's Ck. B.C. NY	NCC,ANY
Duckworth, A.A.	Pvt.	E 16th SCVI	25	AN	09/17/63	Lauderdale, MS	DOD		ROH,16R,PP
Duckworth, J.N.	Pvt.	E 16th SCVI	28	AN	09/20/63	Gainesville, AL	DOD	Gainsville, AL	ROH,16R,TOD
Duckworth, Thomas J.	Pvt.	D 4th SCVI		AN	09/21/61	Germantown, VA	DOD		SA2
Duff, J.J.	Pvt.	K 5th SC Res		CN	10/31/63	Charleston, SC	DOD	Magnolia Cem. Charleston	ROH,MAG
Duffie, J.	Pvt.	F 19th SCVI		ED	02/21/62		DOD		HOE

D

SOUTH CAROLINA DEAD IN CSA SERVICE 1861-1865

NAME	RANK	C REGIMENT	AGE	DS	DIED	WHERE	WHY	BURIED	SOURCES
Duffus, George E.L.	Pvt.	L 1st SCVIG	22	CN	08/30/63	Davids Island NY	DOW	Magnolia Cem. Charleston	ROH,P6,GDR,SA1
Duffus, J.J. Walker	Cpt.	B 23rd SCVI	28	CN	06/17/64	Petersburg, VA	KIA	Magnolia Cem. Charleston	ROH,MAG,R48
Dufort, John L.	Pvt.	E 25th SCVI	40	CN	10/04/64	Charleston, SC	DOD	St. Lawrence C. Charleston	ROH,MAG,RCD
Duke, Abram L.	Pvt.	A 5th SCVC	18	OG	10/22/62	Pocotaligo, SC	KIA	(? Co.C,14th SCVCBn)	ROH
Duke, Benjamin F.	Pvt.	C 25th SCVI	19	WG	05/25/64	Fts. Monroe, VA	DIP	(Wdd & POW, Drury's Bluff)	ROH,HOW,CDC
Duke, C.A.	Pvt.	F Orr's Ri.			09/01/62	Ox Hill, VA	KIA		JR
Duke, H.	Sgt.	F 21st SCVI			08/08/64	Richmond, VA	DOD	Hollywood Cem.Rchmd. V103	ROH,HC
Duke, Samuel H.	2nd Sgt.	B 7th SCVIBn	44	FD	09/28/64	Petersburg, VA	DOD		ROH,HAG,HFC,PP
Duke, William David	3rd Sgt.	K 25th SCVI	23	WG	05/06/64	Pt.Walthall Jct.	KIA		CTA,HOW,HAG
Dukes, A.J.	Pvt.	A 5th SCV		OG	12/15/62	At home	DOD		JR
Dukes, Abraham S.	Pvt.	B 14th SCVCB		OG	10/22/62	Pocotaligo, SC	KIA		ROH,CDC,PP
Dukes, George	Cpl.	D 5th SCVI		OG	05/31/62	7 Pines, VA	KIA		ROH,SA3
Dukes, James P.	Pvt.	C 24th SCVI	24	CO	12/11/63	At home	DOW	(Wdd 9/20/63 @ Ch'ga)	ROH,CDC,DRE
Dukes, William D.	Pvt.	C 25th SCVI		WG	06/15/64	Swift Creek, VA	KIA		ROH,HOW,HAG
Dulin, William	Pvt.	SCVC	16	YK	04/15/63	Warrenton, VA	KIA	(See p129 BHC)	BHC
Dumas, J.H.	Pvt.	B 3rd SCVI		NY	05/15/61	At home	DOD		JR,KEB
Dunaway, Abram	Pvt.	A P.S.S.	18	UN	08/12/64	Deep Bottom, VA	KIA		ROH
Dunaway, Joseph	Cpl.	A P.S.S.	26	UN	10/07/64	Petersburg, VA	DOW		ROH,JR
Dunaway, Stephen	Pvt.	A P.S.S.	23	UN	08/12/64	Deep Bottom, VA	KIA		ROH
Dunbar, James	Pvt.	E 6th SCVI	28	FD	12/25/61	Mt. Jackson, VA	DOD	Mt. Jackson, VA	ROH,SHS,CV,PP
Dunbar, W.W.	Pvt.	E 2nd SCVA		BL	06/03/62	Charleston, SC	DOD		ROH
Duncan, B.					/ /			(Rchmd effects list 12/62)	CDC
Duncan, B.C.	Pvt.	I 7th SCVI		ED	08/30/62	Richmond, VA		Hollywood Cem.Rchmd. S94	ROH,HC
Duncan, Benjamin	Pvt.	F 7th SCVI	18	ED	12/13/62	Fredricksburg VA	KIA		HOE,KEB
Duncan, Benjamin. F.	Pvt.	C Orr's Ri.		PS	05/24/62	Richmond, VA	DOD	Hollywood Cem.Rchmd. J72	ROH,JR,HC,CDC
Duncan, C.H.	Pvt.	C 16th SCVI		GE	11/30/64	Franklin, TN	KIA	Macgavock C. Fr'kln GV#35	16R,WCT,PP
Duncan, Charles	Pvt.	C 16th SCVI		GE	07/26/62	Adams Run, SC	DOD		16R,PP
Duncan, David	Pvt.	G 14th SCVI	38	AE	07/18/62	Gaines' Mill, VA	DOW		ROH,JR,CDC
Duncan, David	Pvt.	B 7th SCVI		AE	11/03/64	Camp Chase, OH	DIP	C.C.#393 Columbus, OH	FPH,KEB,P22
Duncan, G.W.	Pvt.	E 27th SCVI		LS	01/16/64	Ft. Sumter, SC	DOD		ROH
Duncan, George W.	Cpl.	F 7th SCVC			01/14/65	Elmira, NY	DIP	Woodlawn N.C.#1461 Elmira	FPH,P6,P65,P120
Duncan, Hosea A.	Pvt.	M 10th SCVI		HY	06/15/62	Georgetown, SC	DOD	(Date approx)	ROH,RAS
Duncan, Isiah	Pvt.	C Orr's Ri.		PS	07/24/62	Laurel Hill, VA	DOD	(Josiah in CDC)	JR,CDC
Duncan, J. Madison	Pvt.	B 22nd SCVI		SG	08/11/62	Charleston, SC	DOD	Magnolia Cem. Charleston	ROH,JR,MAG
Duncan, J.A.	Pvt.	B 22nd SCVI		SG	07/30/64	Crater, Pbg., VA	KIA		HOS
Duncan, J.C.	Pvt.	Orr's Ri.		GE	07/07/64	Richmond, VA		Hollywood Cem.Rchmd. U565	HC
Duncan, J.C.	Pvt.	I 6th SCVI		CR	/ /	Charlottesville		Univ. Cem. Charlottesville	ACH
Duncan, J.W.M.	Pvt.	G 13th SCVI		NY	12/20/62	Charlottesville	DOW	Univ. Cem. Charlottesville	ROH,ANY,ACH
Duncan, James	Pvt.	B 22nd SCVI		SG	07/30/64	Crater, Pbg., VA	KIA		ROH,BLM
Duncan, Jesse	Pvt.	I 5th SCVI		SG	05/06/64	Wilderness, VA	KIA		HOS
Duncan, Joel	Pvt.	B 22nd SCVI		SG	07/30/64	Crater, Pbg., VA	KIA		BLM,HOS
Duncan, John	Pvt.	I 14th SCVI	34	AE	06/30/64	Fussel's Mill VA	KIA	(HOL= DOD)	ROH,HOL
Duncan, John C.	Pvt.	D 13th SCVI	21	NY	06/24/62	Ashland, VA	DOD	Lower Duncan's Ck.B.C. NY	ROH,JR,NCC,ANY
Duncan, Jordan	Cpl.	H 3rd SCVABn		GE	06/14/63		DOD	(Typhoid)	ROH,JR
Duncan, Judge	Pvt.	B 22nd SCVI		SG	07/30/64	Crater, Pbg., VA	KIA		ROH,BLM
Duncan, Lewis	Pvt.	C 16th SCVI		GE	01/20/63	Charleston, SC	MUR	(A fight on SCRR,16R= DOD)	ROH,16R,CDC
Duncan, M.	Pvt.	E 1st SCV			12/16/62	Richmond, VA		(Co. C in Orr's Ri.?)	ROH
Duncan, Madison	Pvt.	C Orr's Ri.		PS	/ /	Lynchburg, VA	DOD		JR,CDC
Duncan, Miles	Pvt.	I 1st SCVA		PS	06/15/64	Charleston, SC	DOD	Magnolia Cem. Charleston	ROH,MAG,CDC
Duncan, R.J.	Cpl.	B 22nd SCVI		SG	/ /				HOS
Duncan, Reuben	Pvt.	F 7th SCVI	21	ED	/ /	At home	DOD		HOE,KEB

D

SOUTH CAROLINA DEAD IN CSA SERVICE 1861-1865

NAME	RANK	C REGIMENT	AGE	DS	DIED	WHERE	WHY	BURIED	SOURCES
Duncan, Thomas	Pvt.	A P.S.S.			06/30/62	Frayser's Farm	KIA	(Same as Sgt. in Co,K?)	ROH,UD1
Duncan, Thomas Casey	Sgt.	K P.S.S.		SG	06/30/62	Frayser's Farm	KIA		JR,HOS,CDC,CV
Duncan, Thomas W.	Pvt.	G 4th SCVI		GE	02/27/62		DOD	(Typhoid)	JR,SA2
Duncan, W.B.	Pvt.	K 6th SCVC	44	CD	05/17/63	Adams Run, SC	DOD		PP
Duncan, W.J.	Pvt.	B 22nd SCVI		SG	07/30/64	Crater, Pbg., VA	KIA		HOS
Duncan, W.P.	Pvt.	B 7th SCVI			10/15/62		DOD	(JR=Dunkin)	JR,KEB
Duncan, W.W.	Pvt.	B 22nd SCVI		SG	06/25/62	Augusta, GA	DOD		ROH
Duncan, William	Pvt.	F Hol.Leg.	18	AE	02/08/62	Adam's Run, SC	DOD		ROH
Duncan, William F.	Pvt.	I 19th SCVI	22	AE	03/01/62	At home	DOD	(Measles, JR=2/28/62)	ROH,JR
Duncan, William Pinckney	3rd Sgt.	I 19th SCVI	21	AE	10/30/62	At home	DOD	(Diarrhea)	ROH,JR
Dunford, John	Pvt.	G 23rd SCVI		MO	11/18/62	Richmond, VA	DOD	Hollywood Cem.Rchmd. S296	ROH,HC,HOM
Dunham, M.	Pvt.	E 1st SCV			/ /			Oakwood C.#51 Row M Div A	OWC
Dunkin, J.V.	Pvt.	M 7th SCVI		ED	02/09/63	Richmond, VA	DOD		ROH,HOE
Dunkins,	Pvt.	C 6th SCVI			05/03/62	Chancellorsville	KIA		JR
Dunlap, A.S.	Pvt.	C 12th SCVI		FD	10/02/63	Ft. Delaware, DE	DIP	Finn's Pt., NJ Nat. Cem.	ROH,FPH,P6,HFC
Dunlap, David A.	Pvt.	C 4th SCVC		PS	05/11/64	Greensboro, NC	DOD		PP
Dunlap, David C.	Pvt.	G 6th SCVI	27	CR	02/26/62	Centreville, VA	DOD		ROH,HHC
Dunlap, Frank	Pvt.	C 6th SCVI		KW	/ /	Virginia	DOD		HIC
Dunlap, J.S.	Pvt.	E 12th SCVI		LR	09/06/63	Davids Island NY	DIP	Cypress Hills N.C.#841 NY	FPH,P1,P6
Dunlap, J.W.	Pvt.	A 5th SCVI			09/18/64	Richmond, VA		Hollywood Cem.Rchmd. V278	ROH,HC
Dunlap, Jacob	Pvt.	F 24th SCVI		AN	/ /		DOD		HOL
Dunlap, James	Pvt.	C 12th SCVI		FD	06/15/63	Richmond, VA	DOD	(Date approx)	HFC
Dunlap, James Alonzo	Pvt.	H 4th SCVC		LR	06/29/64	Louisa C.H., VA	DOW	(Wdd @ Trevillian Stn.)	LAN
Dunlap, James H.	Cpt.	F 14th SCVI		LS	09/20/62	Shepherdstown VA	KIA	(JR=Lt. & KIA 9/17)	ROH,JR,BOS,R47
Dunlap, John	Pvt.	A 6th SCVI	35	CR	12/15/64	Virginia	DOD	(Wdd @ 7 Pines also)	ROH,HHC
Dunlap, John Julius	Pvt.	C 12th SCVI		FD	09/18/62	Sharpsburg, MD	DOW	Rose Hill C. Hagerstown MD	ROH,JR,BOD
Dunlap, Joseph J.	Pvt.	C 12th SCVI		FD	12/13/62	Fredericksburg	KIA	Fredericksburg C.C. R6 S11	ROH,JR,HFC,FBG
Dunlap, Joseph L.	2nd Lt.	A 5th SCVI		LR	07/09/62	Frayser`s Farm	DOW		JR,SA3,LAN,R46
Dunlap, L.D.	Pvt.	E 19th SCVI		SR	09/30/64	Thomaston, GA		Glenwood C. Thomaston, GA	CVGH,BGA
Dunlap, Lewis J.	Pvt.	E 12th SCVI	30	LR	07/03/63	Gettysburg, PA	KIA	(35 per LAN)	ROH,LAN
Dunlap, Matthew L.	1st Cpl.	H 4th SCVC		LR	06/01/64	Richmond, VA	DOW	(Wdd @ Hawes Shop)	ROH,LAN
Dunlap, Robert A.	Pvt.	A 17th SCVI	40	YK	10/15/64	Savannah, GA	DOD	Laurel Grove C. Savannah	ROH,CB,P120,BG
Dunlap, Robert Nance	4th Sgt.	H 5th SCVI	25	UN	08/24/62	Richmond, VA	DOW	Hollywood Cem.Rchmd. Q204	ROH,JR,HC,SA3
Dunlap, Thomas W.	Pvt.	D 1st SCVC	22	CR	02/24/63	At home	DOD		ROH,HHC
Dunlap, Wesley	Pvt.	F 1st SCMil			02/17/65	Charleston, SC	DOD	Magnolia Cem. Charleston	ROH,MAG
Dunlap, William	Sgt.	3rd SCVI	22	LS	12/21/62	Fredericksburg	DOW	Dunlap F.C. Clinton, SC	LSC
Dunlap, William B.	Pvt.	A 6th SCVI	23	CR	07/30/64	Petersburg, VA	DOW		ROH,GLS,HHC,CB
Dunlap, William T.	Pvt.	H Orr's Ri.	19	AN	06/12/62	Dill Farms, VA	DOD		ROH,JR
Dunn, Alexander	Pvt.	B 24th SCVI		MO	11/15/63	Will's Valley TN	DOD		ROH,HOM
Dunn, D.	Pvt.	E 12th SCVI		LR	07/30/64	Richmond, VA		Hollywood Cem.Rchmd. V292	ROH,HC
Dunn, David	Pvt.	C 12th SCVI		FD	08/07/64	Spotsylvania, VA	DOW	(?Dunn, D. in HC)	JR,HFC
Dunn, Edmund	Pvt.	G 27th SCVI	32	CN	/ /		DOD	3rd P.C. Charleston, SC	MAG,RCD,HAG
Dunn, James	Pvt.	B 19th SCVI	32	ED	10/15/62	Bardstown, KY	DOD		ROH,HOE,PP
Dunn, M.C.	Pvt.	A 1st SCVIG		BL	12/13/62	Fredericksburg	KIA		JR,SA1
Dunn, Richard	Pvt.	B 19th SCVI		ED	/ /	Atlanta, GA	DOD		HOE
Dunn, Silas Y.	Cpl.	A P.S.S.		UN	07/24/62	Richmond, VA	DOW	Hollywood Cem.Rchmd. M13	ROH,JR,HC,SA3
Dunn, T.F.	Pvt.	A 1st SCVIG		BL	07/02/63	Gettysburg, PA	KIA	(JR=Co.C)	ROH,JR,SA1,GDR
Dunn, Thomas	Pvt.	F 21st SCVI		MO	07/28/64	Petersburg, VA	KIA		ROH,HOM,HAG
Dunn, Thomas	Pvt.	B 19th SCVI		ED	01/28/65	Camp Chase, OH	DIP	Con.Cem.#926 Columbus, OH	FPH,P6,P22
Dunn, Thomas H.	Cpt.	C 5th SCVI		UN	05/06/62	Williamsburg, VA	DOW	(Wdd 5/05/62)	JR,SA3,UD1,NHU
Dunn, W.J.	Pvt.	G 2nd SCVI		KW	07/24/63	Richmond, VA	DOD	Hollywood Cem.Rchmd. T165	ROH,SA2,HIC,HC

SOUTH CAROLINA DEAD IN CSA SERVICE 1861-1865

NAME	RANK	C REGIMENT	AGE	DS	DIED	WHERE	WHY	BURIED	SOURCES
Dunn, William	Pvt.	F 21st SCVI		MO	/ /	At home	DOD		HOM,HAG
Dunn, William	Pvt.	C 12th SCVI		FD	11/08/61	Bay Point, SC	DOD		JR
Dunnan, R.L.	Sgt.	A 2nd SCVIRi			10/28/63	Racoon Mtn., TN	KIA		JR
Dunning, Reaves	Pvt.	H 7th SCVIBn	17	RD	02/12/64	Sullivans I., SC	DOD		ROH,HAG
Dunnon, R.L.	Sgt.	A 2nd SCVIRi			10/28/63	Lookout Va., TN	KIA		ROH,CDC
Dunovant, John	Brig. Gen.	SCVC	39	CR	10/01/64	Ft. Harrison, VA	KIA	Dunovant F.C. Chester, SC	ROH,GIG,HHC
Dupriest, John	Pvt.	K P.S.S.			06/30/62	Frayser's Farm	KIA		ROH,JR,CDC
Durant, Andrew S.	Pvt.	K P.S.S.		SG	06/30/64	Richmond, VA	DOD	Hollywood Cem.Rchmd. U641	ROH,HC,HOS
Durant, James Sumter	Cpl.	K 23rd SCVI	29	SR	06/17/64	Petersburg, VA	KIA		ROH,JR,K23,UD3
Durant, John	Pvt.	K P.S.S.		SG	10/07/64	Darbytown Rd. VA	KIA	(JR=DOW 10/8/64)	JR,HOS
Duren, William	Pvt.	C 12th SCVI		FD	06/15/61	Beaufort, SC	DOD	(Date approx)	HFC
Durham, Benjamin	Pvt.	D Orr's Ri.			07/03/63	Davids Island NY	DOW		P1
Durham, E.B.	Pvt.	I 5th SCVI		SG	04/15/62	Orangeburg, SC	DOD	(Pneumonia,HOS=KIA W'ness)	JR,HOS
Durham, G.	Pvt.	B 2nd SCVIRi		PS	/ /				ROH
Durham, George	Pvt.	I Hol.Leg.	33	SG	11/19/64	Richmond, VA	DOW	(Wdd @ Petersburg)	ROH
Durham, J.H.	Pvt.	E 2nd SCVIRi			/ /			Oakwood C.#75 Row G Div C	ROH,OWC
Durham, James P.	Pvt.	A Orr's Ri.		AN	08/04/62	Winder Hos Rchmd	DOD		JR,CDC
Durham, M.A.	Pvt.	D 18th SCVI		AN	06/14/62	Charleston, SC	DOD	Magnolia Cem. Charleston	ROH,JR,MAG
Durisoe, C.L.	1st Sgt.	D 14th SCVI		ED	07/23/63	Davids Island NY	Dow	Cypress Hills N.C.#664 NY	JR,FPH,GDR,P1,P6
Durisoe, G.R.	Pvt.	D 14th SCVI	17	ED	/ /	Petersburg, VA	KIA		D14,HOE
Durn, Perry	Pvt.	F 1st SCVA			07/03/65	Davids Island NY	DIP	Cypress Hills N.C.#3089 NY	FPH,P6
Durr, J.L.	Pvt.	H 11th SCVI		CO	07/15/64	Petersburg, VA	DOD		ROH
Durr, John	Pvt.	H 11th SCVI			08/01/64	Pt. Lookout, MD	DIP	C.C. Pt. Lookout, MD	ROH,FPH,P6,P113
Durr, Peter E.	Pvt.	C 11th SCVI		CO	07/15/64	At home	DOD		ROH,HAG
Durst, George Erasmus	Pvt.	H 7th SCVIBn	22	ED	05/16/64	Drury's Bluff VA	KIA	(ROH= Co. G)	ROH,JR,HAG
Dutart, James Elias	Cpt.	K 2nd SCVI	23	CN	06/21/64	Petersburg, VA	KIA	(CDC= Dutard)	ROH,SA2,KEB,R45
Dutart, John Steele	Sgt.	F 6th SCVC	21	CN	02/09/64	Johns Island, SC	KIA		ROH,CDC,CAG
Dutton, William C.	1st Sgt.	E 2nd SCVI		KW	09/19/62	Sharpsburg, MD	DOW		ROH,JR,SA2,CDN
Dye, J.S.	Cpl.	B 17th SCVI		FD	07/30/64	Petersburg, VA	DOW	Blandford Church Pbg., VA	ROH,JR,BLC,PP
Dye, Major R.	Pvt.	D 17th SCVI	31	CR	08/08/63	Meridian, MS	ACD	(ROH=RR ACD 8/5/63)	ROH,JR,CB
Dye, Singleton	Pvt.	H 6th SCVI	19	FD	08/13/61	Culpepper, VA	DOD	Fairview Cem. Culpepper VA	ROH,JR,CGH,CDC
Dyer, Gerard B.	1st Sgt.	B 2nd SCVI	26	GE	06/01/64	Cold Harbor, VA	KIA		ROH,SA2
Dyer, James M.	Pvt.	B 2nd SCVI	19	GE	09/21/63	Chickamauga, GA	KIA	(KEB= J.N.)	ROH,SA2,KEB
Dyer, John	Pvt.	D 22nd SCVI		PS	07/30/64	Crater, Pbg., VA	KIA		ROH,BLM
Dyer, Nathan	Pvt.	I 5th SCVI		SG	06/21/62	Richmond, VA	DOW	Hollywood Cem.Rchmd. O304	ROH,JR,HC,SA3
Dyer, Wylie E.	Pvt.	F 1st SCVIR		CN	12/28/63	Mt. Pleasant, SC	DOD		SA1
Dyeres, J.B.	Pvt.	L 2nd SCVIRi			08/30/62	2nd Manassas, VA	DOW	Manassas, VA	ROH,JR,CDC
Dykes, H.H.	Pvt.	B 1st SCVA		BL	06/16/62	Secessionville	KIA		ROH,JR,CDC,PP
Dykes, J.R.	Pvt.	H 3rd SCVI		LN	09/28/62		DOW	(Wdd @ Sharpsburg)	JR
Dyson, A.S.	Pvt.	G 21st SCVI		DN	12/23/63	Pt. Lookout, MD	DIP	C.C. Pt. Lookout, MD	ROH,FPH,P5,CDC
Dyson, J.E.	Pvt.	H 5th SCVC	23	CL	11/12/63	Petersburg, VA	DOW	Blandford Church Pbg., VA	ROH,BLC,PP

E

SOUTH CAROLINA DEAD IN CSA SERVICE 1861-1865

NAME	RANK	C	REGIMENT	AGE	DS	DIED	WHERE	WHY	BURIED	SOURCES
Eaddy, Gregory	Pvt.	I	10th SCVI		MN	/ /	Mississippi	DOD		RAS,HMC
Eaddy, John T.	Pvt.	G	15th SCVI	20	WG	07/02/63	Gettysburg, PA	DOW	Magnolia Cem. Charleston	ROH,JR,GDR,HOW
Eaddy, R.C.	Pvt.	G	26th SCVI		DN	07/10/63		DOD		JR
Eaddy, Robert James	Pvt.	D	2nd SCRes	38	WG	/ /		DOD	(1863)	CTA
Eadon, John Legrand	Pvt.	I	23rd SCVI		CL	04/08/65	Fair Gds H. Pbg.	DOW	Near the hospital	P6,HCL,P12
Eadon, John W.	Pvt.	I	23rd SCVI		CL	08/05/62		DOD	(Congestive chill)	JR
Eadon, Legrand	Pvt.	I	23rd SCVI		CL	04/10/65	Petersburg, VA	DOW	(Wdd 4/8/65)	ROH
Eadon, S.L.	Cpl.	I	23rd SCVI		CL	03/25/65	Ft. Steadman, VA	KIA		HCL
Eady, Clark	Pvt.		Supply Trn	30	WG	04/05/65	Richmond area	KIA	(Lost in retreat at end)	ROH
Eagan, D.G.	Sgt.	F	P.S.S.		LN	09/30/64		KIA		JR
Eagan, John S.	Pvt.	H	P.S.S.	32	LN	07/03/63	Gettysburg, PA	DOW	Eagan Family C. Lexington	TOD
Eakin, J.D.	Pvt.	F	Hol.Leg.		AE	03/25/65	Richmond, VA		Hollywood Cem.Rchmd. W651	HC
Eame, Thomas	Pvt.	F	12th SCVI			/ /	Richmond, VA			ROH
Eargle, Alfred Osman	Pvt.	H	13th SCVI	22	LN	08/30/62	2nd Manassas, VA	KIA	(JR=8/24/62)	ROH,JR,ANY,CDC
Eargle, Andrew David	Pvt.	C	20th SCVI	20	LN	09/15/63	Sullivan's I. SC	DOD		ROH,KEB
Eargle, Frederick P.	Pvt.	K	20th SCVI		LN	02/25/62		DOD	Cedar Grove L.C. Leesville	ROH,KEB,TOD
Eargle, Jacob J.	Pvt.	C	20th SCVI	30	LN	11/01/64	Staunton, VA	DOW		ROH,KEB
Eargle, John Henry	Pvt.				LN	/ /	Goldsboro		Goldsboro, NC	NCC
Eargle, Wesley A.	Pvt.	H	13th SCVI	19	LN	05/05/64	Wilderness, VA	KIA		ROH,JR
Earhardt, Clayborn B.W.	3rd Sgt.	C	15th SCVI	39	LN	10/04/63	Richmond, VA	DOD	Hollywood Cem.Rchmd. T624	ROH,HC,KEB,H15
Earkeen, J.M.	Pvt.	G	23rd SCVI		AN	11/16/64	Richmond, VA		(Earskine?)	ROH
Earle, C.E.	1st Lt.	B	4th SCVI		AN	08/07/61	Richmond, VA	ACD	(Fell frm window,Excg.Htl)	ROH,JR,CDC,GMJ
Earle, Wilton Robinson	Pvt.	B	4th SCVI	22	AN	07/28/61	Culpepper, VA	DOW	Earle Fam. Gvyd. Seneca SC	ROH,JR,CGH,CDC
Earnest, T.J.	Pvt.	G	6th SCVC		RD	/ /	Wilson, NC			PP
Earnhart, James B.	Pvt.	K	P.S.S.			05/09/65	Camp Chase, OH	DIP	C.C.#1948 Columbus, OH	FPH,P6,P12
Eason, Julius	Pvt.	D	19th SCVI	22	ED	05/25/64	New Hope Ch., GA	KIA		HOE,UD3
Eason, Russell G.	Pvt.					12/07/62	Charlottesville	DOD	Magnolia Cem. Charleston	MAG
Eason, William	Pvt.		Brook's A	25	CN	07/03/63	Gettysburg, PA	KIA		ROH,JR,GDR,CDC
East, J.H.L.	1st Sgt.	F	3rd SCVI		LS	01/06/65	Richmond area		Hollywood Cem.Rchmd. W235	ROH,HC
East, Wm. Washington	Pvt.	G	P.S.S.	25	LS	06/29/62	At home	DOW	(Wdd. in thigh @ 7 Pines)	ROH,JR,LSC,SA3
Easteds, M.	Pvt.	E	27th SCVI			09/27/62	Frederick, MD	DOW	Rose Hill C. Hagerstown MD	ROH,FPH,BOD
Easter, M.N. (M.B.?)	Pvt.	I	9th SCVIB		UN	10/07/61	Charlottesville	DOD	(ROH=Richmond)	ROH,JR
Easterby, George	Sgt.	D	23rd SCVI		CN	08/30/62	2nd Manassas, VA	KIA		ROH,JR,CDC
Easterby, Washington	Pvt.	E	1st SCVIBn		CN	09/01/63	Columbia, SC	DOD		JR
Easterling, A. Jackson	Pvt.	F	21st SCVI		MO	05/26/65	Elmira, NY	DIP	Woodlawn N.C. #2917 Elmira	ROH,FPH,HAG,P6
Easterling, Alfred R.	Cpl.	G	8th SCVI	25	MO	04/03/62	Richmond, VA	DOD	Oakwood C.#9 Row F Div A	ROH,JR,UD1,OWC
Easterling, Andrew B.	2nd Sgt.	F	21st SCVI		MO	/ /	Washington, DC	DOW	(POW 8/21/64 Weldon RR)	ROH,P1,P5,HAG
Easterling, Edward	Pvt.	G	11th SCVI		CO	09/05/64	Richmond, VA	DOD		ROH
Easterling, Emory A.	Sgt.	H	11th SCVI		OG	/ /	Petersburg, VA	KIA		ROH,HAG
Easterling, Enos	Pvt.	H	1st SCVIG		CN	09/15/62	(Prob Warrenton)	DOW	(Wdd @ 2nd Manassas)	ROH,SA1,CDC
Easterling, Harris R.	Pvt.	F	21st SCVI		MO	05/09/64	Chester, SC	DOD	Paul's Cem. Chester, SC	ROH,CCP,HOM,HA
Easterling, Henry	Pvt.	I	1st SCVIH		MN	10/02/64	Ft. Harrison, VA	KIA		SA1,HMC
Easterling, J.T.	Pvt.	H	Orr's Ri.			06/27/62	Gaines' Mill, VA	KIA		JR
Easterling, Jesse A.	3rd Sgt.	F	21st SCVI		MO	07/10/63	Morris Island SC	DOW		ROH,JR,HOM,HAG
Easterling, Joel A.	Pvt.	F	21st SCVI		MO	02/15/62	Georgetown, SC	DOD		ROH,JR,HOM,HAG
Easterling, John A.	Pvt.	F	21st SCVI		MO	/ /		DOD		HOM,HAG
Easterling, John T.	Cpl.	B	24th SCVI		MO	11/30/64	Franklin, TN	KIA	Macgavock C. Frkln Gv# 5	ROH,HOM,CDC,PP
Easterling, Josiah K.	Cpl.	G	8th SCVI	20	MO	07/02/63	Gettysburg, PA	KIA	UD1	ROH,JR,GDR,HOM
Easterling, Nelson A.	1st Lt.	F	21st SCVI	30	MO	12/03/64	Ft. Delaware, DE	DIP	Finn's Pt., NJ Nat. Cem.	ROH,FPH,P5,P42
Easters, Elijah	Pvt.	D	5th SCVI		UN	10/13/64	Ft. Harrison, VA	KIA	Richmond, VA	ROH,SA3
Easters, J.W.	Pvt.	C	18th SCVI		UN	02/22/63	Wilmington, NC	DOD		ROH,JR

E

SOUTH CAROLINA DEAD IN CSA SERVICE 1861-1865

NAME	RANK	C REGIMENT	AGE	DS	DIED	WHERE	WHY	BURIED	SOURCES
Eastler, Alger	Pvt.	B 7th SCVIBn	36	FD	03/21/64	At home		(Eugene,Adgena?)	ROH,HOF,HAG
Eastridge, John W.	Pvt.	E 22th SCVI		LR	02/03/65	Elmira, NY	DIP	Woodlawn N.C.#1890 Elmira	JR,FPH,P6,P65
Eastridge, Minor	Pvt.	E 22nd SCVI		LR	09/14/62	South Mtn., MD	DOW	(LAN=only Wdd)	JR,LAN
Eastridge, S.	Pvt.	G 1st SCVA			04/02/65	High Point, NC		Oakwood C. High Point, NC	CV,WAT,TOD
Eaves, A.V.	Pvt.	A 1st SCVIH		BL	08/30/62	2nd Manassas, VA	DOW	(SA1=Wdd & Discharged)	ROH,JR,SA1,CDC
Eaves, Ervin H.	Pvt.		18	BL	08/14/61	Summerville, SC	DOD	(Twin of Furman Eaves)	CNM
Eaves, Furman J.	Pvt.		18	BL	09/16/61	Coles Island, SC	DOD	(Twin of Ervin Eaves)	CNM
Eaves, Jefferson C.	Pvt.	B 2nd SCVA		BL	06/23/62	Secessionville	DOW	Magnolia Cem. Charleston	ROH,MAG,PP
Eaves, Joseph Franklin	Pvt.	L 1st SCVIG	20	CN	06/14/62	Richmond, VA	DOD	(JR=6/12/63)	JR,CDC
Eavesleigh, Henry	Pvt.	Ham.leg.		SR	/ /	Richmond, VA			ROH
Echols, John.	Pvt.	I 1st SCVA			11/06/63	Pt. Lookout, MD	DIP	C.C. Pt. Lookout, MD	ROH,FPH,P5,CDC
Eden, John	Cpl.	B 23rd SCVI	27	CN	06/15/64		DOD		ROH
Eden, John A.	Pvt.	B 23rd SCVI	34	CN	11/24/64	At home	DOD		ROH
Edens, H.L.		D 3rd SCRes		MO	/ /	Raleigh, NC			HOM
Edens, J.H.	Pvt.	H 7th SCVC		MO	01/07/65	Pt. Lookout, MD	DIP	C.C. Pt. Lookout, MD	ROH
Edens, Thomas H.	Pvt.	K 8th SCVI		MO	12/09/63	Beans Station TN	KIA		HOM,KEB
Edens, W.J.					/ /	Richmond, VA		(Richmond effects list)	CDC
Edge, Hamilton	Pvt.	D 25th SCVI		MN	/ /		DOD		HMC,HAG
Edgerton, Samuel Fields	Pvt.	D 1st SCVIBn		CN	06/17/62	Secessionville	DOW	Magnolia Cem. Charleston	ROH,JR,PP,HAG
Edings, John	Pvt.	K 5th SCVI		CO	/ /	Yorktown, VA	DOD	(1862)	SA3
Edins, William	Pvt.	B 2nd SCVIRi		PS	/ /				ROH
Edmond, J.	Pvt.	E		CN	/ /	Gordonsville, VA			ROH
Edmondson, Edward	Pvt.	A 24th SCVI	28	CN	12/03/64	Camp Douglas, IL	DIP	Oak Woods Cem. Chicago, IL	ROH,FPH,P5,P53
Edmunds, S.F.	1st Sgt.	C 7th SCVI	22	AE	10/19/64	Cedar Creek, VA	KIA	(Also Wdd. @ Sharpsburg)	ROH,JR,KEB
Edmunds, Thomas J.	Pvt.	C 7th SCVI	19	AE	06/15/63	Petersburg, VA	DOD		ROH,KEB
Edmunds, Whitfield F.	Pvt.	C 7th SCVI	17	AE	11/14/61	Charlottesville	DOD	Edmonds B.G. McCormick SC	ROH,JR,KEB,MCC
Edwards, A.D.H.	Pvt.	A 2nd SCVIRi			08/09/62	Richmond, VA	DOW	(JR=Co. E)	ROH,JR
Edwards, A.H.	Pvt.	B 18th SCVI		UN	08/07/62	Charleston, SC	DOD		JR
Edwards, Alexander	Pvt.	D 21st SCVI		CD	06/15/65	Elmira, NY	DIP	(POW @ Morris Island SC)	ROH,HAG,P120
Edwards, Benjamin	Pvt.	A 18th SCVI		UN	07/30/64	Crater, Pbg., VA	KIA		JR
Edwards, E. Harleston	Midshipmn	CSN	19	CN	08/29/63	Mobile, AL	DOD		ROH
Edwards, Elisha	Pvt.	H 3rd SCVABn		GE	/ /				ROH
Edwards, Franklin	Pvt.	D 21st SCVI		CD	06/15/64	At home		(HHC=KIA in Georgia)	ROH,HAG,HHC
Edwards, H.M. DeSaussure	2nd Lt.	K 2nd SCVI		CO	07/02/63	Gettysburg, PA	KIA	KEB	ROH,JR,SA2,GDR
Edwards, Isaac	Pvt.	A 18th SCVI	32	UN	07/30/64	Crater, Pbg., VA	KIA		ROH,JR,BLM
Edwards, John	Pvt.	G 14th SCVI	23	AE	06/10/62	Richmond, VA	DOD	(Typhoid)	ROH,JR
Edwards, John	Pvt.	C 10th SCVI		HY	/ /	Okolona, MS	DOD	(RAS=Saltillo, MS)	RAS,PP,TOD
Edwards, John	Pvt.	E 14th SCVI		LS	05/06/64	Wilderness, VA	KIA		CGS
Edwards, John C.	Pvt.	B 1st SCVIBn		SG	07/18/63	Bty Wagner, SC	KIA	Magnolia Cem. Charleston	MAG,HOS,HAG
Edwards, John H.	Pvt.	D 21st SCVI		CD	04/02/65	Boydton Plk.Rd.	KIA		ROH,HAG
Edwards, John Jones	3rd Lt.	B 1st SCVIBn		CN	06/16/62	Secessionville	KIA	Magnolia Cem. Charleston	ROH,JR,PP,HAG
Edwards, Jonas	Pvt.	E Hol.Leg.	28	LS	06/06/62	Adam's Run, SC	DOD		ROH,HOS,PP
Edwards, Joseph W.	Pvt.	B 18th SCVI	19	UN	08/07/62		DOD		ROH
Edwards, Lacey L.	Pvt.	G 3rd SCVI	21	LS	06/29/62	Savage Stn., VA	KIA		ROH,JR,SA2,KEB
Edwards, Mack Bennett	Pvt.	A 18th SCVI	26	UN	07/30/64	Crater, Pbg., VA	KIA	(A.B. in BLM)	ROH,BLM
Edwards, Matthew H.	Pvt.	H 23rd SCVI		MN	08/30/62	2nd Manassas, VA	KIA		ROH,HMC,CDC
Edwards, Newman	Pvt.	G 1st SCVIBn		SG	08/24/63	Bty. Wagner, SC	KIA		ROH,JR,CDC,R45
Edwards, Oliver Evans	Col.	13th SCVI	44	SG	06/21/63	Goldsboro, NC	DOW	(Wdd @ Chancelorsville)	ROH,JR,LC,BOS
Edwards, Owen	Pvt.	K 1st SCVIH		OG	05/06/64	Wilderness, VA	KIA		SA1
Edwards, Scenas B.	Pvt.	H 7th SCVC		KW	/ /		KIA		HIC
Edwards, W.P.	Pvt.	G 1st SCVIBn		CN	08/24/63	Bty. Wagner, SC	KIA		ROH,CDC

SOUTH CAROLINA DEAD IN CSA SERVICE 1861-1865

NAME	RANK	C REGIMENT	AGE	DS	DIED	WHERE	WHY	BURIED	SOURCES
Egleson, H.	Pvt.	K 10th SCVI		CN	/ /		DOD		RAS
Egleston, George	Pvt.			CN	08/11/63	Bty. Wagner, SC	KIA		ROH
Ehlers, George	Cpl.	A 15th SCVI		RD	09/20/63	Chickamauga, GA	KIA	(JR=9/23/63)	ROH,JR.KEB
Eichelberger, George A.	Pvt.	H 13th SCVI		LN	02/22/62	White Hall, SC	DOD	Eichelberger Gvyd. Newb'y	JR,NCC
Eichelberger, William T.	Pvt.	H 13th SCVI		LN	06/01/62	Williamsburg, VA		Eichelberger C. Newberry	NCC
Eidson, Edward	Pvt.	A 7th SCVI		ED	09/20/63	Chickamauga, GA	KIA		ROH
Eidson, John	Pvt.	A 19th SCVI	28	ED	/ /	Chattanooga, TN	DOD		HOE,UD3
Eidson, Rowland	Cpl.	D 19th SCVI	26	ED	07/28/64	Atlanta, GA	KIA		HOE,UD3
Eison, D.C.	Pvt.	K 5th SCVC		UN	03/19/65	Bentonville, NC	KIA		CV
Eison, James	Pvt.	I Ham.Leg.		UN	01/07/65	Elmira, NY	DIP	Woodlawn N.C. #1503 Elmira	ROH,FPH,P6
Elder, John W.	Pvt.	C 13th SCVI		SG	01/09/62	Richmond, VA	DOD	Hollywood Cem.Rchmd. O136	ROH,JR,HC,HOS
Elder, M.V.	Pvt.	I 9th SCVIB			10/15/61	Richmond area	DOD	Hollywood Cem.Rchmd. F189	ROH,HC
Elder, Robert	Pvt.	F 12th SCVI		FD	10/11/62	(Prob Warrenton)	DOW	(Wdd @ 2nd Man.)	JR
Elder, Samuel	Pvt.	B Hol.Leg.	28	SG	06/22/62	Adam's Run, SC	DOD		ROH,HOS,PP
Elder, W.	Pvt.	C 7th SCVI			/ /	Charlotte, NC		(Elkins?)	ROH
Eldraff, Edward	Pvt.	A 7th SCVI			09/20/63	Chickamauga, GA	KIA	(JR=Eldran & Co.E))	JR,CDC
Eldridge, H.	Pvt.	H 6th SCVI			/ /	Richmond, VA		Oakwood C.#7 Row A Div A	ROH,OWC
Eldridge, W.H.	Pvt.	A 6th SCVI		CR	06/22/64	Richmond, VA		Hollywood Cem.Rchmd. U216	HC
Eleck,	Lt.	D Hol.Leg.			08/30/62	2nd Manassas, VA	KIA		JR
Elfe, George	Pvt.	18th SCVAB		CN	05/01/65	Salisbury, NC	DOD	(Returning after SUR)	ROH
Elfe, Robert Edward	Pvt.	18th SCVAB		CN	05/01/65	Salisbury, NC	DOD	(Returning after SUR)	ROH
Elfe, William W.C.	Pvt.	A 18th SCVAB		CN	03/16/65	Averysboro, NC	KIA		ROH,WAT,PP
Elford, F.J.	Pvt.	Ferguson's			07/24/63	Columbia, SC		Elmwood Cem. Columbia, SC	MP,PP
Elford, Orville	Pvt.				10/31/63	Ft. Sumter, SC		Magnolia Cem. Charleston	MAG
Elford, Thomas G.	Pvt.				07/24/63	Columbia, SC			PP
Elgin, J.A.	Pvt.	G Orr's Ri.		AE	07/28/62	Frayser's Farm	KIA		ROH
Elgin, Meredith	Pvt.	I 19th SCVI	22	AE	06/19/62	Lauderdale, MS	DOD	(2nd PP entry=Enterprise)	ROH,PP
Elgin, Thomas G.	Pvt.	K 2nd SCVIRi	35	AE	08/30/62	2nd Manassas, VA	DOW	(Leg shot off)	ROH,R45
Elkes, J.W.	Sgt.	E 26th SCVI		HY	07/30/64	Richmond, VA	KIA		ROH
Elkin, Thomas	Pvt.	K 2nd SCVIRi			09/15/62	Warrenton, VA	DOW	(Wdd 2nd Man)	ROH
Elkin, William Fletcher	Pvt.	H 7th SCVIBn	36	FD	05/16/64	Drury's Bluff VA	KIA		ROH,JR
Elkins, Archibald K.	Pvt.	E 2nd SCVI	27	KW	06/14/62	Richmond	DOD		ROH,SA2
Elkins, B.A.L.	Pvt.	5th SCVC			/ /	Gordonsville, VA			ROH
Elkins, E.	Pvt.	E 2nd SCVI		KW	/ /	Richmond, VA	DOD		HIC,KEB
Elkins, M.C.	2nd Sgt.	G 14th SCVI	25	AE	07/28/64	Deep Bottom, VA	KIA		ROH,JR
Elkins, William	Pvt.	I 5th SCVI		YK	05/20/65	Newport News, VA	DIP	Greenlawn C. Newport News	P6,SA3,PP
Elledge, J.F.	Pvt.	C 14th SCVI		LS	01/12/62	McPhersonville	DOD	(Typhoid)	JR
Ellen, Elijah J.	Pvt.	I 8th SCVI		MN	09/05/61	Richmond, VA	DOD	Hollywood Cem.Rchmd. G120	ROH,JR,HC,HMC
Ellen, William B.	Pvt.	B 24th SCVI		MO	/ /	At home	DOD		HOM
Ellenburg, Martin	Pvt.	H 7th SCVIBn	30	ED	05/16/64	Drury's Bluff VA	KIA		ROH,JR,HAG
Ellenburg, Martin	Pvt.	3rd SCRes		PS	12/16/62	SC	DOD		ROH
Ellenburg, T.J.	Pvt.	A 22nd SCVI		PS	06/27/62	Charleston, SC	DOD	Magnolia Cem. Charleston	ROH,MAG
Ellerbe, A. Cooper	Pvt.	G 21st SCVI		CD	01/15/65	Ft. Fisher, NC	KIA		PP,HAG
Ellerbe, Hossack	Pvt.	G 21st SCVI	35	CD	06/18/64	Petersburg, VA	KIA		ROH,JR,CDC,HAG
Ellerbe, Hossack F.	Pvt.	A 4th SCVC	20	CD	02/17/65	Columbia, SC	ACD	(Demolition of RR depot)	ROH,PP
Ellerbe, W.H.	Pvt.	A 6th SCVI			06/22/64	Richmond, VA			ROH
Ellford, Thomas G.	Pvt.	1st SCVA			07/24/63	Columbia, SC		(Contusion)	ROH
Elliott, E.H.	Pvt.	B P.S.S.		PS	05/12/64	Spotsylvania, VA	KIA		ROH,JR
Elliott, Franklin	Pvt.	F 1st SCVIG	21	HY	05/12/64	Spotsylvania, VA	KIA	TOD	ROH,JR,SA1,PDL
Elliott, George H.	2nd Lt.	G 25th SCVI	40	OG	05/16/64	Drury's Bluff VA	KIA		ROH,JR,HAG,EDR
Elliott, J.E.	Pvt.	K 22nd SCVI		PS	03/11/63	At home	DOD		ROH

SOUTH CAROLINA DEAD IN CSA SERVICE 1861-1865

NAME	RANK	C REGIMENT	AGE	DS	DIED	WHERE	WHY	BURIED	SOURCES
Elliott, J.L.	Pvt.	B P.S.S.		PS	11/28/63	LaGrange, GA	DOW	Con. Cem. LaGrange, GA	ROH,JR,TOD
Elliott, J.M.	Pvt.	D 6th SCVI			12/20/61	Dranesville, VA	KIA		ROH,JR
Elliott, John F.A.	Cpt.	H 21st SCVI	53	DN	01/27/63	Morris Island SC	DOD		ROH,JR,HAG,R48
Elliott, Levi	Pvt.	F 1st SCVIG	27	HY	09/25/64	At home	DOD		SA1,PDL,TOD
Elliott, Ralph Emmes	Cpt.	I 2nd SCVI	30	BT	06/05/64	Richmond, VA	DOW	Hollywood Cem.Rchmd. X155	ROH,JR,HC,SA2
Elliott, Robert P.	Pvt.	F 1st SCVIG		HY	04/06/63	Richmond, VA	DOD	Oakwood C.#1 Row 4 Div D	ROH,SA1,PDL,OWC
Elliott, W.J.	Pvt.	K 12th SCVI		PS	07/03/63	Gettysburg, PA	KIA		JR
Elliott, W.P.	1st Sgt.				12/17/62		KIA	(Kinston, NC?)	JR
Elliott, W.S.	Cpt.	17th SCMil			/ /		DOD	Magnolia Cem. Charleston	MAG
Elliott, W.T.	Pvt.	B P.S.S.			05/12/64		KIA		JR
Elliotte, S.S.	Pvt.	K 26th SCVI	30	HY	08/28/63	Savannah, GA	DOD	Laurel Grove C. Savannah	ROH,JR,BGA
Ellis, Archibald	Pvt.	E 21st SCVI		CD	05/06/64	Walthal Jctn. VA	KIA		CDC,HAG
Ellis, Charles	Pvt.	I 3rd SCVABn			03/23/62	Ft. Sumter, SC	KIA	Magnolia CEm. Charleston	MAG,RCD
Ellis, D.W.	Pvt.	G 6th SCVI		FD	08/30/62	2nd Manassas, VA	KIA		JR,CDC
Ellis, Ellie S.	Pvt.	C 25th SCVI	26	WG	05/17/65	Elmira, NY	DIP	Woodlawn N.C.#2953 Elmira	FPH,P6,P65,HOW
Ellis, George W.	Pvt.	D 2nd SCVI			02/25/62	Manassas, VA	DOD	(Pneumonia)	H2
Ellis, Henry H.	Pvt.	E 6th SCVI		DN	05/23/65	Pt. Lookout, MD	DIP	C.C. Pt. Lookout, MD	ROH,FPH,P6,JLC
Ellis, J.M.	Pvt.	M 7th SCVC			08/17/64	Pt. Lookout, MD	DIP	C.C. Pt. Lookout, MD	P113,FPH
Ellis, J.T.	Pvt.	E P.S.S.			/ /		DOD		JR
Ellis, James R.	Sgt.	G Orr's Ri.		AE	08/29/62	2nd Manassas, VA	KIA		ROH,JR,CDC
Ellis, Jesse B.	Pvt.	H 26th SCVI		DN	07/15/63	Jackson, MS	DOW		ROH,JR,CDC,PP
Ellis, Jesse C.	Cpl.	A 1st SCVC		AE	06/15/62	Wadmalaw Isl. SC	DOD		ROH
Ellis, N.A.	Pvt.	G 12th SCVI		PS	02/21/64	Richmond, VA	DOD	Hollywood Cem.Rchmd. D46	ROH,JR,HC
Ellis, Robert E.					/ /	Richmond, VA		(Richmond effects list)	CDC
Ellis, Robert M.	Pvt.	G Orr's Ri.		AE	07/14/62	Richmond, VA	DOD	(JR=7/19/62)	ROH,JR
Ellis, Samuel	Pvt.	B 23rd SCVI	49	CN	01/24/65	Elmira, NY	DIP	Woodlawn N.C.#1619 Elmira	ROH,FPH,P6,P65
Ellis, W.	Pvt.	I 1st SCVA			10/25/63	Charleston, SC	DOD	Magnolia Cem. Charleston	ROH,MAG
Ellis, W. Kendrick	Pvt.	E 12th SCVI		LR	01/01/63		DOD	(? W.K. E,22nd @ Crater)	LAN
Ellis, W.K.	Pvt.	E 22nd SCVI			07/30/64	Crater, Pbg., VA	KIA		BLM
Ellis, Wesley W.	Pvt.	B 21st SCVI		DN	03/06/65	Elmira, NY	DIP	Woodlawn N.C.#1961 Elmira	ROH,FPH,P6,P65
Ellis, William	Pvt.	F 7th SCVI		ED	/ /	At home	DOD	(Wdd @ Pbg.)	HOE
Ellis, William	Pvt.	C 12th SCVI		FD	07/27/63	At home	DOD		JR,HFC
Ellis, William D.	Pvt.	M 10th SCVI		HY	/ /		DOD		RAS,P39
Ellis, William M.	Pvt.	G Orr's Ri.		AE	07/14/62	Richmond, VA	DOD		ROH,JR,CDC
Ellison, A.M.	Pvt.	D 18th SCVI		AN	07/27/64	Petersburg, VA	KIA		ROH
Ellison, James	Pvt.	E Ham.Leg.			01/08/65	Elmira, NY	DIP	Woodlawn N.C.#1503 Elmira	FPH,P65,P120,P12
Ellison, Jasper Wheaton	Pvt.	H 13th SCVI	22	LN	05/20/62	Ashland Stn. VA	DOD	(Typhoid)	ROH,JR
Ellison, Joel	Pvt.	K 18th SCVI			/ /	Petersburg, VA			ROH
Ellison, William Adger	Pvt.	G 6th SCVI	21	FD	05/31/62	7 Pines, VA	KIA	Presby. Ch. Winnsboro, SC	ROH,JR,WDB,PP
Ellisor, Charlton Gary	Pvt.	H 3rd SCVI	24	LN	04/19/62	Richmond, VA	DOD	(JR=4/20/62)	ROH,JR,SA2
Ellisor, Warren Preston	Pvt.	D 13th SCVI	20	NY	07/01/63	Gettysburg, PA	KIA		ROH,JR,ANY
Elmore, D.W.	Pvt.	C 26th SCVI			05/30/63	Charleston, SC	DOD	Magnolia Cem. Charleston	ROH,MAG
Elmore, Ellis	Pvt.	H 21st SCVI			05/14/65	Pt. Lookout, MD	DIP	C.C. Pt. Lookout, MD	ROH,FPH,P6,P113
Elmore, J.E.	Pvt.	3rd SCVAB			/ /	Lynchburg, VA		Lynchburg CSA Cem. #9 R3	BBW
Elmore, M.L.	Pvt.	A 3rd SCVI		SG	12/13/62	Fredericksburg	KIA		ROH,JR,SA2,KEB
Elmore, Providence	Pvt.	K 2nd SCVIRi	35	AE	05/08/62	Adam's Run, SC	DOD		ROH,PP
Elmore, William	Pvt.	C 17th SCVI		YK	07/30/64	Crater @ Pbg.	KIA		ROH,JR
Elmore, William J.	Pvt.	E 1st SCVIG		MN	07/10/62	Richmond, VA	DOD	(Typhoid)	ROH,JR,HMC,SA1
Elrod, D.S.	Pvt.	F 24th SCVI		AN	/ /		DOD	(1865)	HOL
Elrod, E.B.	Pvt.	D 18th SCVI		AN	07/22/62	Charleston, SC	DOD		ROH,JR
Elrod, E.E.	Pvt.	Ferguson's			05/12/64	Dalton, GA			PP

E

SOUTH CAROLINA DEAD IN CSA SERVICE 1861-1865

NAME	RANK	C REGIMENT	AGE	DS	DIED	WHERE	WHY	BURIED	SOURCES
Elrod, Grief	Pvt.	L Orr's Ri.		AN	05/15/63	Richmond, VA	DOD		JR
Elrod, Hadley					/ /	Richmond, VA		(Richmond effects list)	CDC
Elrod, Isaac M.	Pvt.	D 18th SCVI		AN	07/12/62	Columbia, SC	DOD		ROH,JR,PP
Elrod, S.S.	Cpl.	D 18th SCVI		AN	02/11/62	Charleston, SC	DOD		ROH,JR
Elrod, T.H.	Pvt.	D 18th SCVI		AN	10/15/62	Winchester, VA	DOD		ROH,JR
Elsmore, Allen	Pvt.	A 19th SCVI	22	ED	07/22/64	Atlanta, GA	KIA		ROH,JR,HOE,UD3
Elvin, H.H.	Pvt.	P.S.S.			05/23/63	Washington, DC	DIP	(Wdd & POW @ Wmsbg, VA)	ROH,CDC
Elvington, David R.	Pvt.	E 1st SCVIG		MN	07/31/64	Deep Bottom, VA	DOW	(POW in enemy hands)	HMC,SA1,P12
Elvington, Dennis	Pvt.	I 8th SCVI		MN	02/02/62	Culpepper, VA	DOD	Fairview Cem. Culpepper VA	JR,CGH,HMC,KEB
Elvington, Joel	Pvt.	C 26th SCVI		MN	/ /	Savannah, GA			HMC
Elvington, John H.	Pvt.	E 1st SCVIG		MN	08/29/62	2nd Manassas, VA	DOW		SA1,HMC,CDC
Elvington, Nathan T.	Pvt.	E 1st SCVIG		MN	08/10/64	Elmira, NY	DIP	(POW in enemy hands)	HMC,SA1,P120
Elvington, Owen	Pvt.	E 1st SCVIG		MN	03/15/63		DOD	(Place & date UK in SA1)	SA1,HMC
Emanuel, Edwin C.	2nd Sgt.	A 10th SCVI	26	GN	06/19/62	Oxford, MS	DOD	(PP=Okolona, MS) PP	ROH,JRR,RAS,GR
Emanuel, Washington	Pvt.	A 10th SCVI	20	WG	07/28/64	Macon, GA	DOW	(Wdd @ Atlanta 7/22/64)	ROH,RAS,GRG,HO
Emerson, J.	Pvt.	A 14th SCVI		DN	08/03/62	Richmond, VA			ROH
Emerson, Jeptha H.	Cpl.	I P.S.S.		PS	06/30/62	Frayser's Farm	KIA		ROH,JR,CDC
Emerson, Jesse N.	1st Cpl.	L 2nd SCVIRi	33	AN	09/01/62	2nd Manassas, VA	DOW		ROH,CDC
Emerson, Jesse N.	Pvt.	J 4th SCVI		AN	02/15/62		DOD		SA2
Emory, John	Pvt.	17th SCVI		RD	11/27/62	Richmond, VA			ROH
English, Franklin	Pvt.	C 6th SCVI		RD	12/20/61	Dranesville, VA	KIA	1st Presby. Ch. Columbia	ROH,JR,PP,R46
English, John	Pvt.	C 23rd SCVI			05/18/65	Pt. Lookout, MD	DIP	C.C. Pt. Lookout, MD	FPH,P6,P114
English, Welcome	Pvt.	D 26th SCVI		MO	07/15/64	Petersburg, VA	KIA	(Date approx 6/17-7/27)	ROH,HOM,CDC
English, William	Pvt.	K 8th SCVI		MO	/ /	Culpepper, VA	DOD		HOM,KEB
Enloe, Isaac N.	1st Sgt.	G 18th SCVI	23	YK	05/16/64	Clay's Farm, VA	KIA	(JR=5/20/64)	ROH,JR,YMD,SA3
Enloe, Thomas A.	Pvt.	G 18th SCVI	21	YK	05/05/64	Pt. Lookout, MD	DOW	C.C. Pt. Lookout, MD	FPH,P5,YEB,P12
Enlow, H.F.	Pvt.	D 13th SCVI			06/29/63	Richmond, VA	DOD	(Prob Henry Frank DOW)	ROH
Enlow, Henry Frank	Pvt.	D 13th SCVI	28	NY	05/04/63	Chancellorsville	KIA		ROH,ANY
Enlow, J. Belton	Pvt.	H 3rd SCVI		LN	09/17/62	Sharpsburg, MD	KIA	(MIA in 1st reports)	SA2,ANY,CDC,KE
Entriken, H.G.	Pvt.	F 3rd SCVI		PS	12/26/62	Manchester, VA	DOD		ROH,JR,SA2
Eppes, Robert A.	Pvt.	E 17th SCVI	19	YK	08/07/62	Richmond, VA	DOD		ROH,JR,YEB
Eppes, William	Pvt.			YK	/ /	Gettysburg, PA			ROH
Eppes, William H.	Pvt.	D 3rd SCVIBn	18	LS	05/06/64	Wilderness, VA	KIA	UD3	ROH,JR,RHL,KEB
Epps, H.	Pvt.	E 17th SCVI		YK	07/31/62	Richmond, VA		Hollywood Cem.Rchmd. H45	HC
Epting, David Wesley	Pvt.	I 15th SCVI	20	LN	07/06/62	Columbia, SC	DOD	Macedonia L.C. Prosperity	ROH,JR,LNC,PP
Epting, Earl W. Baylis	Pvt.	I 15th SCVI	19	LN	10/09/61	At home	DOD	Macedonia C. Prosperity SC	TOD
Epting, George Adams	Cpl.	H 13th SCVI	24	LN	07/09/62	Lynchburg, VA	DOD	Epting F.C. Little Mtn. SC	ROH,JR,LNC
Epting, H.M.	Pvt.	E 4th SC Res		NY	02/06/65	Columbia, SC	DOD		ROH,ANY,PP
Epting, J.M.	Pvt.	H 13th SCVI		LN	01/07/64	Pt. Lookout, MD	DIP	C.C. Pt. Lookout, MD	ROH,FPH,P5,CDC
Epting, J.W.	Pvt.	I 5th SCVI		SG	09/02/64	Richmond, VA	DOW	Hollywood Cem.Rchmd. V174	ROH,HC,HOS,SA3
Epting, James Hilliard	Pvt.	C 20th SCVI	26	LN	09/13/63	Mt. Pleasant, SC	DOD	(Wdd,Morris Isl.= Hosp'l)	ROH,KEB
Epting, John A.	Pvt.	H 13th SCVI	16	LN	08/28/62	2nd Manassas, VA	KIA	(JR=8/29/62)	ROH,JR,CDC
Epting, Melvin	Pvt.			LN	/ /				ROH
Epting, T.R.	Pvt.	H 13th SCVI		LN	/ /			Oakwood C.#65 Row L Div C	OWC
Epting, William Robert	Pvt.	H 13th SCVI	20	LN	06/26/64	Cold Harbor, VA	DOW	(JR=7/16/62)	ROH,JR
Erskin, John C.	Pvt.	B 37th VAVCB	31	GE	02/01/65	Camp Chase, OH	DIP	Con.Cem.#1001 Columbus, OH	37V,FPH
Erskine, William P.	Pvt.	L 2nd SCVIRi	29	AN	06/29/62	7 Pines, VA	KIA		ROH,JR,CDC
Ervin, H.J.	Pvt.			WG	/ /		KIA		HOW
Ervin, Henry	Pvt.	I 5th SCVI		SG	/ /	At home	DOD		HOS
Ervin, J.R.	Pvt.	A 8th SCVI	39	DN	07/28/64	Deep Bottom, VA	KIA		ROH,KEB
Ervin, James	Pvt.	H 1st SCVC	27	YK	/ /		DOD		YEB

SOUTH CAROLINA DEAD IN CSA SERVICE 1861-1865

NAME	RANK	C REGIMENT	AGE	DS	DIED	WHERE	WHY	BURIED	SOURCES
Erwin, Adolphus S.	Pvt.	K Hol.Leg.			10/29/64	Elmira, NY	DIP	Woodlawn N.C.#731 Elmira	FPH,P5,P65,P113
Erwin, Ephraim A.	1st Lt.	A 1st SCVIR		CN	09/07/63	Sullivan's I. SC	KIA		ROH,SA2,DOC,CDC
Erwin, Francis Augustus	Cpt.	H 12th SCVI	20	YK	09/17/62	Sharpsburg, MD	KIA	(ROH=2nd Man.)	ROH,JR,CWC,YEB
Erwin, H.H.	Pvt.	G P.S.S.			05/23/62	Washington, DC	DOD	(Measles as POW)	JR
Erwin, W.R.	Pvt.	G P.S.S.			01/17/64	Danbridge, TN	DOW	(JR=H.R.)	ROH,JR,CDC,UD3
Erwin, William A.	Pvt.	C 17th SCVI			08/27/62	Lynchburg, VA	DOW	Lynchburg CSA Cem. #3 R1	ROH,JR,CDC,CB
Erwin, William A.	Pvt.	F 13th SCVI		SG	12/13/62	Fredericksburg	DOW	Univ. Cem. Charlottesville	HOS,ACH
Eskew, A.N.	Pvt.	F 2nd SCVIRi		AN	08/30/62	2nd Manassas, VA	DOW	CSA Cem. Manassas, VA	ROH,CDC
Ester, N.	Pvt.	G 9th SCVIB			10/09/61			Hollywood Cem.Rchmd. F40	HC
Esters, William	Pvt.	D 5th SCVI		UN	06/18/62	Cliffburn Hos DC	DOW		JR,SA3,P6
Estes, A.C.	Pvt.	D 18th SCVI		AN	08/06/64	Richmond, VA	DOD	Hollywood Cem.Rchmd. V6	ROH,HC
Estes, J.G.J.	Pvt.	A 12th SCVI	28	UN	06/27/62	Gaines' Mill, VA	KIA		ROH,JR,YEB,CNM
Estes, J.J.	Pvt.	D 18th SCVI		AN	05/21/64	Virginia	DOW		ROH
Estes, James E.	Pvt.	E Ham.Leg.	23	GE	11/16/62	Staunton, VA	DOD	Thornrose C. Staunton, VA	ROH,PP,UD3
Estes, Johnson D.	Pvt.	E 5th SCVI	24	CR	07/27/62	Gaines' Mill, VA	KIA	(JR=Co. D)	ROH,JR,SA3,HHC
Estes, McIver	Pvt.	F 18th SCVI			08/29/62	Virginia	DOD		JR
Estes, Wylie Carlisle	Pvt.	B 7th SCVIBn	18	CR	03/21/64	At home	DOD		ROH,HAG,HHC
Estill, Thomas	Pvt.	8th SCVI		CN	07/28/61	Charlottesville	DOW	(Wdd @ 1st Man)	ROH
Estin, A.M.					/ /	Richmond, VA		(Richmond effects list)	CDC
Etheridge, Guildford	Pvt.	B 14th SCVI	25	ED	07/03/63	Davids Island NY	DOW	(Wdd @ Gettysburg)	JR,HOE,UD3
Etheridge, R.G.	Pvt.	A 21st SCVI		GN	04/15/63	Morris Island SC	DOD		ROH, JR
Etheridge, W.	Pvt.	E 7th SCVI		NY	01/01/61	Richmond, VA	DOD	St.Marks L.C. Prosperity	NCC,KEB
Etheridge, W.	Pvt.	A 21st SCVI		CN	03/10/63	Morris Island SC	DOD		JR
Etheridge, William	Pvt.	E 7th SCVI			07/29/61	Charlottesville	DOW	Univ. Cem. Charlottesville	ROH,KEB,ACH
Ethridge, Noah	Pvt.	E 7th SCVI		ED	11/30/61		DOD		JR,HOE,KEB
Ethridge, William H.	Pvt.	D 19th SCVI		ED	02/24/62		DOD	(Typhoid Pneumonia)	JR
Eubank, John	Pvt.	C 1st SCVC	22	BL	02/15/65	Cheraw, SC	DOD		ROH
Eubanks, Charner	Pvt.	B 15th SCVI		UN	/ /		DOW	Fredericksburg C.C. R6S13	JR,FBG,KEB
Eubanks, Darley	Pvt.	H 14th SCVI	18	BL	01/01/62	Port Royal Ferry	KIA	UD2	ROH,JR,PP,CNM
Eubanks, George	Pvt.	C 5th SCVI			06/16/63	Petersburg, VA	ACD	(Drowned in Appomattox R.)	JR,SA3
Eubanks, Isaac	Pvt.	H 14th SCVI		BL	04/18/62	At home	DOD	(Erysipelas)	JR,UD2
Eubanks, Isaac (W.J.?)	Pvt.	I Hol.Leg.		SG	/ /	At home	DOD	(POW @ Stoney Ck & xchd)	HOS
Eubanks, J.L.	Pvt.	H 14th SCVI		BL	06/27/62	Gaines' Mill, VA	KIA		JR,CNM
Eubanks, Jason	Cpl.	H 14th SCVI		BL	01/01/62	Port Royal Ferry	KIA	UD2	ROH,JR,PP,CNM
Eubanks, Julius	Pvt.	H 14th SCV			/ /		KIA	(6/ /62)	UD2
Eubanks, T.	Pvt.	B 15th SCVI		UN	05/06/63	Chancellorsville	DOW	(Wilbanks, T. in KEB?)	CDC
Eubanks, Thomas J.	Sgt.	I Hol.Leg.		SG	08/30/62	Warrenton, VA	DOW	(Wwd @ 2nd Man.)	HOS
Eure, W.E. (or E.W. ?)	Sgt.	H 15th SCVI			07/02/63	Gettysburg, PA	KIA	Magnolia Cem. Charleston	MAG
Evander, Joseph	Pvt.	L 21st SCVI			04/07/64	Petersburg, VA	DOW	Blandford Church Pbg., VA	ROH,BLC
Evans, A.Oliver	Pvt.	C 16th SCVI		GE	11/30/64	Franklin, TN	KIA	Macgavock C. Fr'kln GV#34	16R,WCT
Evans, Andrew Moore	Pvt.	K P.S.S.	34	SG	03/01/62	At home	DOW	Nazareth P.C. SG County	HOS,GEE
Evans, B.F.	Sgt.	B 8th SCVI	22	CD	07/28/64	Deep Bottom, VA	KIA		ROH,KEB
Evans, Barnwell	Pvt.	K 6th SCVI	24	CL	11/11/62	Lynchburg, VA	DOD	Lynchburg CSA Cem. #6 R3	ROH,SRC,BBW
Evans, C.T.C.	Pvt.	K 6th SCVC			/ /	Savannah, GA	DOD	Laurel Grove C. Savannah	P65,P114,BGA
Evans, C.W.	Pvt.	I 25th SCVI		CL	08/03/64	Richmond, VA		Hollywood Cem.Rchmd. V581	HC,ROH,HAG
Evans, D.E.	Pvt.	L 1st SCVIG		CL	05/06/64	Lynchburg, VA	DOD		SA1
Evans, Daniel	Pvt.	B 22nd SCVI		SG	06/23/62	Columbia, SC	DOD	(HOS says Crater, Pbg.)	ROH,HOS
Evans, Daniel A.	Pvt.	E 2nd SCVI		KW	05/16/62	Richmond, VA	DOD	Hollywood Cem.Rchmd. G161	ROH,HC,SA2,KEB
Evans, G.H. (J.H.?)	Pvt.	I 25th SCVI			07/21/65	Elmira, NY	DIP	Woodlawn N.C.#2866 Elmira	FPH,HAG
Evans, George	Pvt.	E 2nd SCVI		KW	07/01/62	Malvern Hill, VA	KIA		HIC,SA2,CDC,KEB
Evans, George L.	Cpl.	D 5th SCVI	20	UN	06/27/62	Gaines' Mill, VA	KIA	Hurricane B.C. Lawrens Cty	JR,NCC,SA3,UNC

SOUTH CAROLINA DEAD IN CSA SERVICE 1861-1865

NAME	RANK	C	REGIMENT	AGE	DS	DIED	WHERE	WHY	BURIED	SOURCES
Evans, Hilliard	Pvt.	C	7th SCVIBn	23	RD	11/12/63	Adam's Run, SC	DOD	(James ? in HAG)	ROH,PP
Evans, J.F.	Pvt.	L	1st SCVIG		BL	07/13/62	Richmond, VA	DOD		SA1
Evans, J.M.	Pvt.	C	2nd SCVIRi			09/30/64	Ft. Harrison, VA	KIA		ROH,JR
Evans, J.M.	Pvt.	F	24th SCVI		AE	/ /		DOD	(1865)	HOL
Evans, J.O.	Pvt.	F	24th SCVI		AN	/ /		DOD	(1865)	HOL
Evans, J.T.R.	Pvt.	H	26th SCVI		SR	06/28/63		DOD		JR
Evans, J.W.	Pvt.	I	25th SCVI			07/09/64	Petersburg, VA	DOW		ROH
Evans, James R.	1st Lt.		Chfld L.A.		CD	09/01/63	Petersburg, VA	DOD		ROH,R44
Evans, Jay	Pvt.	L	21st SCVI		CD	09/09/64	Davids Island NY	DOW	Cypress Hills N.C.#1841 NY	FPH,P1,P5,P12
Evans, John G.	2nd Lt.	F	25th SCVI	30	OG	08/21/64	Ream's Stn., VA	KIA	(Weldon RR)	ROH,HAG,R48
Evans, Joseph W.	Pvt.	I	25th SCVI		CL	07/08/64	Richmond, VA	DOW	Hollywood Cem.Rchmd. U332	HC,CDC,HAG
Evans, M.Z. (M.Y.?)	Pvt.	L	Orr's Ri.		AN	09/06/62		DOW		JR,CDC
Evans, Mitchell	Pvt.	E	25th SCVI		CN	09/10/64	McClellan H Phil	DOW	Phila. N.C.#271 OFS, PA	FPH,P6,P12
Evans, Moses	Pvt.	B	22nd SCVI		SG	07/30/64	Crater, Pbg., VA	KIA		BLM,HOS
Evans, N.	Pvt.	F	10th SCVI		MN	/ /	Mississippi	DOD		RAS,HMC
Evans, Nelson	Pvt.	H	Orr's Ri		MN	05/12/64	Spotsylvania, VA	KIA		HMC
Evans, Oliver	Pvt.	A	Hol.Leg.	18	SG	03/20/63	Wilmington, NC	DOD		ROH
Evans, Oliver	Pvt.	C	16th SCVI		GE	11/30/64	Franklin, TN	KIA	(16R=Nashville)	16R,PP
Evans, Richard M.	Cpl.	F	25th SCVI	28	OG	06/02/65	Elmira, NY	DIP	Woodlawn N.C.#2903	ROH,FPH,P6,P65
Evans, Simpson	Pvt.	G	14th SCVI	35	AE	01/14/63	Richmond, VA(Fbg	DOW	Hollywood Cem.Rchmd. D29	ROH,HC
Evans, Thomas H.	Pvt.	G	14th SCVI		AE	08/22/62	Richmond, VA	DOD	Hollywood Cem.Rchmd. C164	ROH,HC,CDC
Evans, Thomas J.	Pvt.	E	6th SCVI		CR	/ /	Richmond, VA	DOD	(Richmond effects list)	HHC,CDC
Evans, W.B.	Pvt.	I	25th SCVI		CL	02/01/63	At home	DOD	(Measles, NI HAG)	JR
Evans, W.J.	Pvt.	C	2nd SCVIRi			09/17/62	Sharpsburg, MD	KIA		ROH
Evans, William S.	Pvt.		2nd SCV			03/01/65	Raleigh, NC		Oakwood C. Raleigh, NC	TOD
Evart, G.F.S.	Pvt.	B	2nd SCV			/ /	Charlottesville		Univ. Cem. Charlottesville	ACH
Evatt, Ben Franklin	Pvt.	G	22nd SCVI	40	PS	07/30/64	Crater, Pbg., VA	KIA		ROH,BLM
Eveleigh, W.R.	Cpl.	G	Ham.Leg.		DN	06/13/64	Riddle's Shop VA	KIA	(JR=W.B.)	ROH,JR
Everett, E.F.	Pvt.	E	2nd SCVIRi		PS	11/20/63	Bridgeport, AL	DIP	(POW @ Shell Mound)	ROH,CDC,P2
Everitte, William	Pvt.	H	9th SCVIB			03/21/61	Richmond, VA	DOD		JR,CNM
Everly, H.	Pvt.		Ham.Leg.			/ /			Oakwood C.#117 Row K Div A	OWC
Evers, W.H.	Pvt.		9th SCVIB			/ /	Manassas, VA		CSA Cem. Manassas, VA	CV
Evins, Andrew M.	Pvt.	K	P.S.S.		OG	/ /		DOD		JR,SA3
Ewart, D.R.	Asst Surg		CS Chicora			10/21/64	Charleston, SC	DOD		CDC
Ewart, David Edmunds	Surgeon		3rd SCVI		NY	10/11/64	Newberry, SC		Rosemont Cem. Newberry, SC	NCC,SA2
Ewart, Robert E.L.	1st Sgt.	K	P.S.S.		SG	11/21/61	Warm Springs, VA	DOD		HOS,SA3,CNM
Exum, James J.	1st Lt.	G	Ham.Leg.	25	SR	09/17/62	Sharpsburg, MD	KIA	(CDC= Cpt.)	ROH,JR,CDC,R48
Exum, Joseph W.	Cpl.	G	Ham.Leg.	19	SR	09/18/62	At home	DOD		ROH,JR
Ezell, William	Pvt.	E	13th SCVI		SG	05/12/64	Spottsylvania VA	KIA		ROH,HOS
Ezell, Zebean	Pvt.	E	13th SCVI		SG	07/13/63	Williamsport, MD	DOW	(ROH says Gettysburg)	ROH,HOS

F

SOUTH CAROLINA DEAD IN CSA SERVICE 1861-1865

NAME	RANK	C REGIMENT	AGE	DS	DIED	WHERE	WHY	BURIED	SOURCES
Fagin, Peter	Pvt.	F 7th SCVI	29	ED	/ /	Richmond, VA	DOD		HOE
Fail, John	Pvt.	G 2nd SCVI	18	LR	10/27/62	Winchester, VA	DOD		ROH,SA2
Fail, John	Pvt.	I 12th SCVI	17	LR	09/17/62	Sharpsburg, MD	KIA		LAN
Fail, Marion N.	Cpl.	I 17th SCVI	25	LR	09/15/62	Richmond, VA	DOD	Hollywood Cem.Rchmd. H176	ROH,JR.HC,LAN
Fail, Samuel	Pvt.	D 1st SCVIH	24	LR	11/02/64	Richmond, VA	DOD	Hollywood Cem.Rchmd. W440	ROH,HC,SA1
Fair, George A.	Pvt.	E 3rd SCVI		NY	10/15/62	Culpepper, VA	DOD	(JR=Staunton, VA)	ROH,JR,SA2,ANY
Fair, George S.	Pvt.	B 20th SCVI		OG	06/20/64	Petersburg, VA	DOW	(Left leg amputated)	ROH,CDC
Fair, Robert Pearson	Pvt.	E 3rd SCVI		NY	10/15/61	Columbia, SC	DOD	(SA2= DIS Sept/61 unfit)	ROH,JR,SA2
Fair, Warren Benjamin	Sgt.	A 7th SCVI	21	ED	09/17/62	Sharpsburg, MD	KIA	(JR=Maryland Hts.)	ROH,JR,EDN
Fairbairn, J. Drayton	Pvt.	G 3rd SCVI	20	LS	08/24/61	Culpepper, VA	DOD	Fairview Cem. Culpepper VA	ROH,JR,CGH,SA2
Fairbairn, John A.	3rd Sgt.	G 3rd SCVI	23	LS	07/02/63	Gettysburg, PA	KIA		ROH,JR,GDR,SA2
Faircloth, Daniel	Pvt.	B 10th SCVI		HY	/ /	Atlanta, GA	KIA	(On picket post)	RAS
Fairey, George W.B.	Pvt.	G 25th SCVI		OG	05/16/64	Drury's Bluff VA	KIA		ROH,CV,CDC,HAG
Fairlee, George Milton	Cpt.	H Orr's Ri.		MN	06/01/62	Guinea Stn., VA	DOD	(Born in NC)	ROH,JR,HMC,R48
Fairley, William H.	Pvt.	K 4th SCVC	27	CN	06/11/64	Trevillion Stn.	KIA	St Philips Ch. Charleston	ROH,JR,RCD,CLD
Fajen, H.	Pvt.	A German Art		CN	02/07/64	Toogadoo, SC	KIA	Bethany Cem.,Charleston	MAG
Fallow, A.	Pvt.	F P.S.S.		LN	06/30/62	Frayser's Farm	KIA	(JR=Co.E)	ROH,JR,CDC
Falls, Eli W.	Pvt.	F 5th SCVI	50	YK	10/07/64	Darbytown Rd. VA	KIA		SA3,YEB,CB
Fan, C.	Pvt.	E 1st SCV			/ /	Ft. Delaware, DE	DIP	Finn's Pt., NJ Nat. Cem.	CV
Fanning, D.B.	Pvt.	Hart's Bty			/ /	Petersburg, VA			CNM
Fanning, James H.	1st Lt.	K 1st SCVIH		OG	12/15/62	Fredericksburg	DOD		ROH,SA1,R45
Fanny, F.M.	Pvt.	B 15th SCVI		UN	12/08/64	Pt. Lookout, MD	DIP		ROH
Fanon, P.D.	Pvt.	F 14th SCVI			07/01/62	Richmond, VA	DOD	(Typhoid Fever)	JR
Fant, C.M.	Pvt.	C 4th SCVC			03/20/65	Elmira, NY	DIP	(POW @ Hawes Shop, VA)	P65,P12
Fant, Ephraim Hodgins	Pvt.	B 17th SCVI		CR	11/10/64	Petersburg, VA	KIA	(JR=DOW Culpepper)	ROH,JR,HHC
Fant, H. English	Pvt.	I 14th SCVI			06/27/62	Gaines' Mill, VA	KIA		JR
Fant, H.H.	Pvt.	I 1st SCVIR		AN	08/10/62	Camp Evans, SC	DOD		SA1
Fare, S.A. (Farr?)	Pvt.	B 11th SCVI		CO	/ /	Richmond, VA		Oakwood C.#5,Row L,Div F	ROH,OWC
Faris, Harvey	Pvt.	H 18th SCVI	34	YK	/ /	At home	DOW	(1865)	YEB
Faris, J.S.Q.	Pvt.	A 12th SCVI	18	YK	11/22/62	Mt. Jackson, VA	DOD	(PP=11/09/62)	JR,PP,YEB
Faris, James M.	Pvt.	E 17th SCVI	29	YK	09/17/62	Sharpsburg, MD	KIA	Rose Hill C. Hagerstown MD	ROH,CDC,BOD,YE
Faris, John	Pvt.	B 6th SCVI		YK	12/20/61		DOW		ROH
Faris, John N.	4th Sgt.	H 6th SCVI		YK	12/25/61	Centreville, VA	DOW	(Wdd @ Dranesville, VA)	ROH,CDC,YEB
Faris, Josiah	Pvt.			YK	01/09/65		DOD		ROH
Faris, Samuel W.R.	Pvt.	A 12th SCVI	19	YK	12/14/61	Pocotaligo, SC	DOD		YEB
Farley, William D.	Cpt.	Cav.DivF&S	27	LS	06/09/63	Brandy Stn., VA	DOW	Fairview Cem. Culpepper VA	ROH,BHC,RHL,UD
Farmer, E.J.	Pvt.	D 7th SCVIBn	22	KW	04/08/62	Adams Run, SC	DOD	PP	ROH,JR,HIC,HAG
Farmer, Elias	Pvt.	F 13th SCVI		SG	07/08/62	Richmond, VA	DOD	Hollywood Cem.Rchmd. M246	ROH,JR,HC,HOS
Farmer, Ervin	Cpl.	I 17th SCVI	31	LR	07/14/63	Montgomery, AL	DOD	(LAN says Boonsboro)	ROH,LAN
Farmer, Gaddis	Pvt.	D Ham.Leg.			10/28/63	Lookout Valley	DOW		CDC
Farmer, J.A.	Pvt.	D 7th SCVIBn		KW	02/04/62	Charleston, SC	DOD	Magnolia Cem. Charleston	ROH,JR,HIC,HAG
Farmer, J.L.	Pvt.	D 1st SCV			06/04/65	Hart's Island NY	DIP	Cypress Hills N.C.#2941 NY	FPH,P6,P79,P12
Farmer, James A.	Pvt.	G 22nd SCVI	35	AN	09/18/63	Savannah, GA	DOD	Laurel Grove C. Savannah	ROH,BGA
Farmer, James F.	Pvt.	F Ham.Leg.		GE	06/15/61	Brentsville, VA	DOD		ROH
Farmer, James R.	Pvt.	D 18th SCVI		AN	07/30/64	Crater, Pbg., VA	KIA	(PP=John R. 7/2/64)	ROH,BLM,PP
Farmer, Jasper	Pvt.	B 27th SCVI			05/02/65	Pt. Lookout, MD	DIP	C.C. Pt. Lookout, MD	FPH,P6,P114
Farmer, John	Pvt.	E 18th SCVI	19	SG	11/27/62	Charleston, SC	DOD	(HOS/JR=Staunton/Winchstr)	ROH,JR,HOS
Farmer, John	Pvt.	H 6th SCVC	40	GE	11/15/64	Petersburg, VA	DOW	Blandford Church Pbg., VA	ROH,BLC,PP
Farmer, Josiah	Pvt.	G 22nd SCVI	37	AE	07/30/64	Crater, Pbg., VA	KIA		ROH,BLM
Farmer, Minor	Cpl.	I 17th SCVI		LR	09/09/62	Richmond, VA	DOD	Hollywood Cem.Rchmd. H146	ROH,JR,HC,LAN
Farmer, Pinckney	Pvt.	E 1st SCVIR			09/08/63	Ft. Moultrie, SC	KIA		ROH,SA1,CDC

SOUTH CAROLINA DEAD IN CSA SERVICE 1861-1865

NAME	RANK	C REGIMENT	AGE	DS	DIED	WHERE	WHY	BURIED	SOURCES
Farmer, Robert	Pvt.	H 1st SCVIH		SG	12/15/63	Knoxville, TN	DOD	(Straggled from march)	SA1,HOS
Farmer, T.	Pvt.	F 2nd SCVIRi		PS	06/27/62	Gaines' Mill, VA	KIA		ROH,JR,CDC
Farmer, W.P.	Pvt.	D 16th SCVI		GE	/ /	Atlanta, GA	DOD	(1864)	16R
Farmer, William	Pvt.	E 12th SCVI	24	LR	07/16/62	At home	DOD		ROH,LAN
Farmer, William F.	Pvt.	PeeDee LA		DN	04/15/62	Fredericksburg	DOD	(Date approx)	ROH,PDL
Farr, A.H.	Sgt.	C 19th SCVCB	39	BT	10/26/64	Georgetown, SC	DOD		PP
Farr, A.J.	Pvt.	I 27th SCVI			06/23/62		DOD		JR
Farr, J.D.	Pvt.	B 37th VAVCB		GE	08/31/64	Old Town, VA	KIA		37V
Farr, James A.	Pvt.	A 16th SCVI		GE	/ /	Charleston, SC	DOD		16R
Farr, N.	Pvt.	H 15th SCVI		UN	/ /	Gordonsville, VA			ROH,KEB
Farr, Richard T.	3rd Sgt.	H 5th SCVI	34	UN	06/30/62	Frayser's Farm	KIA		ROH,JR,SA3
Farr, Thomas F.	1st Sgt.	B 11th SCVI		CO	06/15/64	Drury's Bluff VA	DOW	(Wdd 5/16/64)	ROH,HAG
Farr, William P.	Cpt.	H 15th SCVI	22	UN	09/14/62	South Mtn., MD	KIA		ROH,KEB,UD3
Farrant, W.F.	Pvt.	A 13th SCVI		LS	07/08/62			Hollywood Cem.Rchmd. O39	HC
Farrar, F.	Pvt.	H 1st SC Mil		CN	02/19/65	Charleston, SC	DOD	Magnolia Cem. Charleston	ROH,MAG
Farrar, W. Thomas	Cpl.	F 6th SCVI	26	CR	09/30/64	Ft. Harrison, VA	KIA	(Also Slight Wd.@ 7Pines)	ROH,HHC
Farrel, Joseph	Pvt.	Tucker's R			01/19/65	Salisbury, NC	DOD		PP
Farrell, George Hare	Pvt.		23	YK	05/06/64	Wilderness, VA	DOW	Fredericksburg C.C. R1S11	YMD,FBG
Farrell, James S. (L.?)	Pvt.	I 12th SCVI		LR	06/25/64	Richmond, VA	DOD	Hollywood Cem.Rchmd. U144	ROH,HC,LAN
Farris, Doctor	Pvt.	G 12th SCVI		PS	/ /	Lynchburg, VA		Lynchburg CSA Cem. #5 R2	BBW
Farris, J.M.	Pvt.	G 17th SCVI			09/17/62	Sharpsburg, MD	KIA		JR
Farris, James	Pvt.	Kanapaux's	17	YK	/ /	Gibsonville, SC	DOD		YEB
Farris, O.A.	Pvt.	G 18th SCVI		BT	01/07/65	Richmond, VA	DOD	Hollywood Cem.Rchmd. W126	ROH,HC
Farris, S.R.W.	Pvt.	A 12th SCVI			12/15/61		DOD		JR
Faulk, James L.	Pvt.	L 7th SCVI		HY	07/02/63	Gettysburg, PA	KIA		ROH,CDC,KEB,GDR
Faulk, Joseph E.	Pvt.	L 7th SCVI		HY	08/13/64	Pt. Lookout, MD	DIP	C.C. Pt. Lookout, MD	ROH,FPH,P5,P113
Faulk, William	Pvt.	C 14th SCVI		LS	04/20/63	At home	DOD	(Pneumonia)	JR
Faulkenberry, Joseph W.	Pvt.	G 2nd SCVI		KW	01/18/65	Pt. Lookout, MD	DIP	C.C. Pt. Lookout, MD P6	FPH,SA2,HIC,P113
Faulkenberry, Wylie J.	Pvt.	G 2nd SCVI		KW	07/01/61	Charottesville	DOD	Univ. Cem. Charlottesville	SA2,HIC,ACH
Faulkenbury, J.C.	Pvt.	E 12th SCVI	23	LR	08/24/62	Richmond, VA	DOD		ROH,JR,LAN
Faulkenbury, James R.	3rd Lt.	E 12th SCVI	23	LR	05/12/64	Spotsylvania, VA	KIA	(Bloody Angle) BOS	ROH,JR,HCD,LAN
Faulkenbury, William S.	Pvt.	E 12th SCVI	28	LR	03/15/65	Petersburg, VA	KIA	(LAN=Age 35)	ROH,LAN
Faulkner, Samuel J.	Pvt.	H 6th SCVI	30	YK	08/05/61	Culpepper, VA	DOD	Fairview Cem. Culpepper VA	ROH,JR,CGH,YEB
Faulkner, William L.	Cpl.	I 17th SCVI		LR	09/17/64	Elmira, NY	DIP	Woodlawn N.C.#309 Elmira	FPH,P5,P65,LAN
Faulkner, William H.	1st Lt.	I 17th SCVI		LR	10/30/62			DOW (Wdd @ Shpsbg or 2nd Man.)	LAN,R47
Faun, D.M.	Pvt.	10th SCVI			/ /		DIP	Danville, KY National Cem.	CV
Faunt, C.M.	Pvt.	C 4th SCVC			03/20/65	Elmira, NY	DIP	Woodlawn N.C.#1574 Elmira	FPH,P6
Faunt, E	Pvt.	C 1st SCVI			06/27/62	Fraysers Farm VA	KIA		JR
Faust, Jasper J.	Pvt.	B 7th SCVIBn	18	FD	11/11/63	Charleston, SC	DOD	Magnolia Cem. Charleston	ROH,JR,MAG,HFC
Faust, Sumpter	Pvt.	C 24th SCVI			12/07/63	Nashville, TN	DIP	Nashville Cem. #5787	P2,P6,P12
Fayger,	Pvt.	E 1st SCV			08/30/63	Charleston, SC	DOD	Magnolia Cem. Charleston	ROH,MAG
Feagan, E.J.	4th Sgt.	F 21st SCVI		MO	06/04/64	Cold Harbor, VA	KIA		ROH,HAG
Feagans, Edmond	Pvt.	F 13th SCVI		SG	07/15/64	Petersburg, VA	KIA	(Day approx)	HOS
Feagin, James Alfred	Pvt.	C 25th SCVI	24	WG	05/09/64	Swift Creek, VA	KIA	(ROH=Drury's Bluff)	ROH,CTA,HAG,HOW
Feagle, George	Pvt.	I 15th SCVI	33	NY	06/27/64	Pt. Lookout, MD	DIP	C.C. Pt. Lookout, MD H15	ROH,FPH,ANY,KEB
Feard, James	Pvt.	K 9th SCVIB			10/11/61	Virginia	DOD	(Freak, J.A.?)	JR
Feaster, A.C.	Pvt.	6th SCVI			10/25/62		DOW		JR
Feaster, F.J.	Pvt.	6th SCVC			08/11/64	Trevillian Stn.	KIA		JR
Feaster, Lorenzo	Lt.	D 9th SCVI			01/29/61		DOD		JR
Feaster, Lorenzo F.	Cpl.	F 19th SCVI		OG	06/30/62	Tupelo, MS	DOD	(PP=Enterprise, MS)	ROH,PP
Feaster, Nathan A.	1st Sgt.	F 1st SCVIH		GE	09/17/62	Sharpsburg, MD	KIA		ROH,SA1,CGS

SOUTH CAROLINA DEAD IN CSA SERVICE 1861-1865

NAME	RANK	C	REGIMENT	AGE	DS	DIED	WHERE	WHY	BURIED	SOURCES
Featherston, E.B.	Pvt.	C	P.S.S.		FD	06/07/62	Richmond, VA	DOD	Oakwood C. #20 Row J Div E	ROH,JR,OWC,GMJ
Featherston, T.C.	Pvt.	C	P.S.S.		FD			DIP	(NI FPH)	GMJ
Feehan, F.P.	1st Sgt.	A	24th SCVI	22	CN	05/14/63	Jackson, MS	KIA		ROH,JR,CDC,PP
Felder, D.B.	Pvt.	I	11th SCVI			05/09/64	Swift Creek, VA	KIA		JR
Felder, Daniel R.	Pvt.	A	5th SCVC	35	OG	08/23/64	Gravelly Run, VA	KIA		ROH,JR,CDC
Felder, David A.	2nd Sgt.	B	1st SCVIG	18	OG	05/23/64	Jericho Ford, VA	KIA		ROH,SA1,ANY
Felder, H. James D.	Pvt.		Ham.Leg.	24	OG	08/30/62	Warrenton, VA	DOW	(Wdd 2nd Man.)	ROH,CDC
Felder, J.J.	Pvt.		Ham.Leg.			08/30/62	2nd Manassas, VA	KIA		ROH
Felder, John H.	1st Lt.	A	1st SCVIH		OG	08/16/61	At home	DOD		ROH,HAG,EDR
Felder, Olin J.	Pvt.	F	25th SCVI	19	OG	09/30/65		DOW	(Wdd 6/2/64,Cold Harbor)	ROH,EDR,HAG
Felder, P.A.	Pvt.	A	5th SCVC	28	OG	06/28/64	Drury's Bluff VA	DOW		ROH
Felder, Pelham L.	Pvt.	D	1st SCVIH		OG	11/18/61	At home	DOD		SA1
Felder, Samuel J.	Pvt.	A	1st SCVIH		OG	/ /	At home	DOD	(1861)	EDR
Felder, W.E.	Pvt.	D	2nd SCVI		SR	07/02/63	Gettysburg, PA	KIA	Magnolia Cem. Charleston	ROH,JR,SA2,GDR
Felkel, Obidiah B.	Pvt.	A	5th SCVC	18	OG	10/27/64	Burgess' Mill VA	KIA	(JR=White Oak Road)	ROH,JR,CDC
Fell, J. Thomas	Pvt.	H	19th SCVI	30	AE	07/01/62	Lauderdale, MS	DOD		ROH,PP
Fellen, Edward N. James	Cpt.		Drayton's			09/17/62	Sharpsburg, MD	KIA	(B.G.Drayton's staff)	JR
Fellers, Hiram A.	Pvt.	A	22nd SCVI	33	ED	10/06/64	Richmond, VA	DOD		ROH
Fellers, J. Pressley	Pvt.	C	3rd SCVI		NY	09/20/63	Chickamauga, GA	KIA		ROH,JR,SA2,ANY
Fellers, J.H.	Pvt.	A	4th SCRes		NY	/ /	SC Coast	DOD		ANY
Fellers, W.L.	Pvt.	G	13th SCVI		NY	09/01/62	Richmond, VA	DOD		ROH,JR,ANY
Fellers, Wm. Lawson	Pvt.	G	13th SCVI		NY	10/29/63	Chickamauga, GA	DOW	(? Dup DOD Rchmd)	JR
Felner, D.A.	Pvt.	B	7th SCVC			05/02/65	Pt. Lookout, MD	DIP		ROH
Felt, A.H.	Pvt.		2nd SCVIRi		AE	07/16/62	Richmond, VA	DOD	Hollywood Cem.Rchmd. H38	ROH,HC
Felton, Amanah	1st Lt.	C	P.S.S.		AN	06/14/62	7 Pines, VA	DOW		ROH,R48
Felts, H.J.	Pvt.	E	17th SCVI			09/14/62	South Mtn., MD	KIA		JR
Felts, H.S.						/ /	Richmond, VA		(Richmond effects list)	CDC
Felts, Hilliard	Pvt.	B	6th SCVI		YK	09/17/62	Sharpsburg, MD	KIA		ROH
Felts, J.W.	Pvt.	G	P.S.S.	19	YK	03/16/63	Petersburg, VA	DOD	(JR=Pneumonia & 3/26/63)	ROH,JR,PP,UD2
Felts, John A.	Pvt.	F	3rd SCVI	36	LS	12/13/62	Fredericksburg	KIA	Beaverdam B.C. Laurens Cty	ROH,JR,SA2,LSC
Felts, W.J.	Pvt.	E	17th SCVI	28	YK	10/24/63	Richmond, VA	DOD		ROH
Fender, T.D.	Pvt.	G	1st SCVIH		BL	02/09/65	Ft. Harrison, VA	DOW	Hollywood Cem.Rchmd. W57	ROH,HC,SA1
Fenders, William	Pvt.					/ /			Fredericksburg C.C. R4S11	FBG
Fendley, G.W.	Cpl.	H	P.S.S.			09/17/62	Sharpsburg, MD	KIA		ROH,JR,CDC
Fendley, Joshua D.	Cpl.	B	Hol.Leg.	18	SG	11/21/64	Petersburg, VA	KIA	(HOS=11/12/64 Fenley?)	ROH,HOS
Fengan, E.J.	Sgt.	H	4th SCV			06/15/64	Petersburg, VA	KIA		JR
Fenley, Daniel D.	Pvt.	E	15th SCVI	22	FD	09/20/63	Chickamauga, GA	DOW	Con. Cem. Marietta, GA	ROH,JR,KEB,CCM
Fenn, W.W.	Pvt.	G	18th SCVI			09/07/64	Petersburg, VA	KIA		ROH
Fennel, Arthur	Pvt.	F	11th SCVI	18	BT	02/19/64	James Island, SC	DOD		ROH,HAG
Fennel, Frederick	Pvt.	I	P.S.S.			05/06/64	Wilderness, VA	KIA		ROH
Fennel, Henry L.	Pvt.	G	22nd SCVI	28	PS	08/04/64	Richmond, VA	DOD	Hollywood Cem.Rchmd. V166	ROH,HC
Fennell, S.A.	Pvt.	E	17th SCVI		YK	/ /	2nd Manassas, VA	DOW	(Farrall,Fewell?)	JR
Fennell, William H.	Pvt.	F	11th SCVI		BT	05/15/64	City Point, VA		City Pt. N.C. Hopewell, VA	PP,HAG,TOD
Fennell, William M.	Pvt.	G	22nd SCVI		AN	09/06/64	Elmira, NY	DIP	Woodlawn N.C.#221 Elmira	FPH,BLM,P5,P12
Fenters, Daniel F.	Pvt.	E	10th SCVI		GN	09/20/63	Chickamauga, GA	KIA	(PP=DOD Okolona, MS) PP	ROH,RAS,HOW,FL
Fenters, J.C.	Pvt.	E	10th SCVI		WG	/ /	Shelbyville, TN	DOD	(HOW=Venters)	FLR,HOW,RAS
Fenters, John J.	Pvt.	E	10th SCVI	27	WG	/ /	Corinth, MS	DOD	(1862, ROH=Venters)	HOW,ROH,RAS
Fenters, L.W.	Pvt.	E	10th SCVI		WG	/ /	South Island, SC	DOD	(1861, Venters ?)	HOW,RAS
Fenters, Nathaniel	Pvt.				WG	09/20/63	Chickamauga, GA	KIA		HOW
Fenters, Thomas J.	Pvt.	A	21st SCVI		GN	/ /	(POW 6/24/64)	DIP		ROH,HAG,P120
Fentrell, Samuel	Pvt.	C	7th SCVIBn	20	RD	10/22/62	Pocotaligo, SC	KIA	(HAG=Futril)	ROH,HAG

SOUTH CAROLINA DEAD IN CSA SERVICE 1861-1865

NAME	RANK	C REGIMENT	AGE	DS	DIED	WHERE	WHY	BURIED	SOURCES
Ferale, Charles	Pvt.	E 24th SCVI	10	CO	08/20/63	Mississippi	DOD		ROH
Ferdon, William B.			24	WG	/ /		DOD	(1862)	CTA,HOW
Ferguson, Andrew R.	Pvt.	I 14th SCVI	19	AE	04/17/63	Fredericksburg	DOD	(HOL/JR=Staunton/Gordnvle)	ROH,JR,HOL
Ferguson, Charles P.	Pvt.	SC Res.		CO	06/15/64		DOD		ROH
Ferguson, Elisha A.	Pvt.	H 4th SCVI	26	PS	08/18/61	Culpepper, VA	DOW	Secona B.C. Pickens SC	CGH,PCS,SA2,UD2
Ferguson, G. Isham	Pvt.	D 6th SCVI		CR	08/30/62	2nd Manassas, VA	KIA		ROH,JR,WDB,CDC
Ferguson, George S.	Sgt.	A 17th SCVI	32	CR	01/05/65	Elmira, NY	DIP	Woodlawn N.C.#1257 Elmira	ROH,FPH,P6,HHC
Ferguson, George Willis	Pvt.	E 11th SCVI	30	BT	06/25/64	Petersburg, VA	DOW	(Wdd 6/24/64)	ROH,JR,HAG
Ferguson, J.A.	Pvt.	F 14th SCVI			08/14/62	Richmond, VA	DOW		JR
Ferguson, J.B.	Pvt.	A 17th SCVI			12/13/62	At home	DOD		JR
Ferguson, J.C.	2nd Sgt.	A 6th SCVI		CR	05/06/64	Wilderness, VA	KIA	(LAN= 5th, dup of J.P.?)	ROH,JR,GLS,HHC
Ferguson, J.P.	3rd Cpl.	G 5th SCVI		YK	05/06/64	Wilderness, VA	KIA		ROH,JR,SA3
Ferguson, James	Pvt.	E 6th SCVI			07/08/62	Charlottesville	DOD	Univ. Cem. Charlottesville	JR,ACH,HHC
Ferguson, James	Pvt.	G 17th SCVI			/ /	Adams Run, SC	DOD		JR
Ferguson, John J.	Pvt.	A 17th SCVI	33	CR	02/19/62	At home	DOD	(Measles)	ROH,HHC,CB
Ferguson, Joseph B.	Sgt.	Ham.Leg.		CN	06/15/62		DOD		ROH
Ferguson, Joseph S.	Pvt.	Marion L.A	20	MN	07/15/63	Bty. Marshall SC	DOD	St.Phillips C. Charleston	ROH,MAG
Ferguson, Judge H.	Pvt.	E 6th SCVC			08/01/64	City Point, VA	DOW	City Pt. N.C. Hopewell, VA	PP,TOD,P12
Ferguson, Marion	Pvt.	B 4th SCVC		CR	/ /		DOD		CB,HHC
Ferguson, R.	Pvt.	I			/ /	Gordonsville, VA			ROH
Ferguson, Richard C.	Pvt.	B 1st SCVC	30	LS	12/19/62	Richmond, VA	DOD	(Smallpox)	ROH,JR,NCC
Ferguson, W.J.	Pvt.	B 15th ACVAB		CR	04/04/64	Charleston, SC	DOD	Magnolia Cem. Charleston	ROH,MAG,CDC
Ferguson, Wilburn C.	Pvt.	B 12th SCVI	19	YK	/ /		DOD	(1862)	YEB
Ferguson, William Nolan	Pvt.	A 17th SCVI	19	CR	10/17/62	Richmond, VA	DOD		ROH,JR,HHC,CB
Ferrell, Benjamin F.	Pvt.	G 15th SCVI	22	WG	12/08/61	Hardeeville, SC	DOD	(KEB=Ferrel, F.)	ROH,JR,HOW,KEB
Ferrell, Charles E.	Pvt.	E 24th SCVI			09/22/63	Camp Morton, IN	DIP	Green Lawn C. Indianapolis	ROH,P5,FPH,CV
Ferrell, Henry C.	Pvt.	A Ham.Leg.	18	CN	10/28/63	Lookout Valley	DOW		ROH,CDC,WLI
Ferrell, J.B.	Pvt.	D 5th SCVI			11/26/63	Bridgeport, AL	DOW	(In enemy hands,NI SA3)	ROH,CDC
Ferris, T.	Pvt.	D 5th SCVI		YK	01/09/63	At home	DOD		JR,SA3
Fersner, Francis M.	Pvt.	F 25th SCVI		OG	06/11/64	Petersburg, VA	DOD	Blandford Church Pbg., VA	ROH,BLC,PP,EDR
Fersner, Lawrence W.	Cpl.	F 25th SCVI	20	OG	01/01/65	Raleigh, NC	DOD		ROH,HAG,EDR
Fertic, Boyd	Pvt.	F 25th SCVI	20	OG	08/04/63	Bty. Wagner, SC	KIA	(On a night raid)	ROH,HAG,EDR,R48
Fertic, Charles	Pvt.	F 25th SCVI	21	OG	08/22/64	Alexandria, VA	DOW	Christ Ch. Alexandria, VA	ROH,CV,HAG,EDR
Fertic, George	Pvt.	F 25th SCVI		OG	08/02/63	Columbia, SC	DOD	(Measles)	JR,HAG
Fertic, Joseph	Pvt.	F 25th SCVI		OG	/ /				ROH,HAG,EDR
Fester, W.C.	Pvt.	B 17th SCVI			06/26/63	Petersburg, VA	DOD		ROH
Fesyhenson, W.	Pvt.	A 24th SCVI			06/21/64	Med Col. Atlanta		Oakland C. Atlanta R56#6	BGA
Fetner, David A.	Pvt.	D 7th SCVC			05/03/65	Pt. Lookout, MD	DIP	C.C. Pt. Lookout, MD	FPH,P6,P12
Fetner, W.D.	Pvt.	E 12th SCVI		RD	07/11/64	Richmond, VA	DOW	Hollywood Cem.Rchmd.U342	ROH,JR,HC,P12
Few, W. Manning	Sgt.	D 16th SCVI		GE	11/30/64	Franklin, TN	KIA		16R
Fewell, Benjamin F.	Pvt.	H 5th SCVI		YK	01/16/62	Richmond, VA	DOD		ROH,JR,SA3
Fewell, John Alexander	4th Cpl.	E 17th SCVI	19	YK	08/29/62	2nd Manassas, VA	KIA		ROH,DEM
Fewell, William Alex.	Pvt.	G P.S.S.	19	YK	06/24/62	Fts. Monroe, VA	DOW	(Wdd @ 7Pines) CNM	ROH,JR,YMD,YEB
Field, J.H.	Pvt.	K 6th SCVC			06/11/64	Trevillion Stn.	KIA		ROH,JR
Fielding, J.B.	Pvt.	D Ham.Leg.			06/11/65	Pt. Lookout, MD	DIP	C.C. Pt. Lookout, MD	FPH,P6,P114,P12
Fielding, William Henry	2nd Cpl.	D 4th SCVI		AN	10/28/62	Richmond, VA	DOD		ROH,SA2
Fields, Calvin	Pvt.	A 14th SCVI	29	DN	11/03/61	At home	DOD	(JR=Measles 12/1/61)	ROH,JR
Fields, Elijah	Pvt.	C 6th SCVI		DN	/ /		KIA		HIC
Fields, Joseph D.	Pvt.	K 11th SCVI	35	BL	02/03/64	James Island, SC	DOD		ROH,HAG
Fields, P.C.	Pvt.	A 14th SCVI	30	DN	07/08/63	Gettysburg, PA	DOW		ROH,JR
Fields, Peter	Pvt.	B 24th SCVI	20	MO	11/15/64	Georgia	DOD	(HOM=died at home)	ROH,HOM

SOUTH CAROLINA DEAD IN CSA SERVICE 1861-1865

NAME	RANK	C REGIMENT	AGE	DS	DIED	WHERE	WHY	BURIED	SOURCES
Fields, Samuel	Pvt.	G Orr's Ri.		AE	06/27/62	Gaines' Mill, VA	KIA		ROH,JR,CV,CDC
Fife, James E.	Pvt.	G 6th SCVI		FD	08/30/62	2nd Manassas, VA	KIA		ROH,JR,WDB,CDC
Fikes, Jerrod A.	Pvt.	K 20th SCVI		LN	10/27/64	Staunton, VA	DOW	(Wdd @ Cedar Creek)	ROH,KEB,PP
Filton, J.B.	Pvt.	H 6th SCVI		FD	06/25/64	Richmond, VA		Hollywood Cem.Rchmd. U394	HC
Filyaw, J.J.	Pvt.		38	WG	/ /		DOD	(1863)	RAS,CTA,HOW
Finch, James A.	Pvt.	G 6th SCVI		FD	08/30/62	2nd Manassas, VA	DOW		ROH,WDB,CDC
Finch, John M.	Pvt.	I 13th SCVI	21	SG	08/15/62	Warrenton, VA	DOD		ROH
Finch, John P.	Pvt.	A Hol.Leg.		SG	05/19/65	Pt. Lookout, MD	DIP	C.C. Pt. Lookout, MD	FPH,HOS,P114,P
Finch, Miles A.	Pvt.	A Hol.Leg.	21	SG	07/22/62	Orangeburg, SC	DOD		ROH,HOS
Finch, Robert A.	Pvt.	B 16th SCVI		GE	11/30/64	Franklin, TN	KIA		ROH,16R,PP
Finch, William	Pvt.	A 1st SCResB			/ /	Coosawatchie, SC	KIA		UD3
Fincher, Silas A.	Pvt.	E 22nd SCVI		LR	04/07/65	Jackson H. Rchmd	DOD	Hollywood Cem.Rchmd. U642	HC,LAN,P6,P12
Fincher, Timothy W.	Pvt.	E Orr's Ri.	22	PS	05/03/63	Chancellorsville	KIA	(JR=DOD 3/21 @ Guinea Stn)	ROH,JR,CDC
Finerty, James	Pvt.	D 1st SCVIR			08/05/63	Petersburg, VA	DOD	(POW 5/21/63 CN harbor?)	ROH,SA1
Finger, D.E.	Pvt.	F 5th SCVI		SG	11/11/61	Virginia	DOD	(JR=C, P.S.S.)	ROH,JR,SA3
Fink, George	Pvt.	H P.S.S.		CN	/ /	MD			ROH
Finklea, Hugh	Pvt.	H Orr's Ri.		MN	05/24/62	At home	DOD	(CDC=Finklea,Hardy)	JR,HMC,CDC
Finley, C.	Pvt.	E 12th SCVI		LR	/ /	Richmond, VA		Oakwood C.#80,Row K,Div B	ROH,OWC
Finley, Elisha	Pvt.	G 1st SCVC	47	AE	04/20/63	Farmville, VA	DOD		ROH
Finley, Joseph H.	Cpl.	C Orr's Ri.			11/02/64	Richmond, VA	DOW	Hollywood Cem.Rchmd. W379	ROH,HC
Finley, S.D.	Pvt.	B Hol.Leg.			11/21/64			Hollywood Cem.Rchmd. W437	HC
Finley, Sidney J.	Pvt.	B 3rd SCVIBn		LS	02/08/65	Pt. Lookout, MD	DIP	C.C. Pt. Lookout, MD	FPH,KEB,P6,P11
Finley, Thomas W.	Pvt.	C Orr's Ri.	27	PS	07/24/63	Richmond, VA	DOD	(Typhoid)	ROH,JR
Finley, William	Pvt.	G 14th SCVI	25	AE	05/06/65	Ft. Delaware, DE	DIP	Finn's Pt., NJ Nat. Cem.	ROH,FPH,P6,P42
Finley, Zachariah E.	Pvt.	C Orr's Ri.	19	PS	06/24/63	Virginia	DOD	(JR=Measles 6/4/62)	ROH,JR
Fipps, John L.	Pvt.	F 1st SCVIG		HY	07/11/62	Gaines' Mill, VA	DOW	(JR=7/9/62)	ROH,JR,SA1,PDL
Fipps, Thomas P.	Pvt.	F 1st SCVIG		HY	09/17/62	Sharpsburg, MD	KIA	(JR=DOW 9/11 2nd Man.)	JR,SA1,PDL
Fishbeck, William	Pvt.	G 3rd SCVC		CN	07/03/63	Pocotaligo, SC	ACD	(Drowned)	ROH
Fisher, Charles A.	3rd Lt.	D 15th SCVI	28	KW	09/22/62	Sharpsburg, MD	DOW	(Also wdd @ 2nd M)	ROH,HIC,KEB,R4
Fisher, Henry Newton	Pvt.	D 16th SCVI		GE	/ /		DOD	(Prob died Louisville,KY)	16R,P39
Fisher, J.M.	Pvt.	I Ham.Leg.			05/03/63	Jackson H. Rchmd	DOD	Hollywood Cem. Rchmd	P6
Fisher, T.M.	Pvt.	Hol.Leg.		AE	03/05/65	Richmond, VA	DOD	Hollywood Cem.Rchmd. W462	ROH,HC
Fisher, Wilburn	Pvt.	H 24th SCVI		CR	/ /	Georgia			HHC
Fitch, B.F.	Pvt.	B 27th SCVI			06/24/64	Petersburg, VA	KIA		ROH,CDC
Fitch, R.G.	Pvt.	G 24th SCVI		RD	09/04/64	Kenesaw Mtn., GA	KIA	On the battlefield	BIG
Fitcher, James	Pvt.	A 24th SCVI	32		08/15/63	SCRR	ACD	(Dtld to Cameron Foundry)	EJM
Fitchett, Jonathan	1st Lt.	F 5th SCVI		YK	07/12/62	Richmond, VA	DOW	(Wdd @ Frayser's Fm 6/30)	ROH,JR,SA3,YEB
Fitts, Benjamin P.	Sgt.	F 3rd SCVC	26	BT	/ /	At home	DOD		ROH
Fitts, John A.	2nd Sgt.	E 11th SCVI	33	BT	11/14/64	Savannah, GA	DOD	(DIS Contracted in prison)	ROH,CDC,HAG
Fitts, Richard	Pvt.	F 3rd SCVC	18	BT	/ /		DOD		ROH
Fitts, William Forester	Pvt.	F 3rd SCVC	23	BT	05/31/64	At home	DOD		ROH
Fitzgerald, James B.	Pvt.	I 5th SCVI			07/08/62	Richmond, VA	DOD	(JR=DOW)	JR,SA3
Fitzgerald, Patrick	Pvt.	F 1st SCVIR		CN	09/15/64	Charleston, SC	DOD		SA1
Fitzgerald, W.F.	Pvt.	F Orr's Ri.		PS	05/15/62		DOD		JR,CDC
Fitzpatrick, John	Pvt.	K 1st SCVIG		CN	01/01/63	Lynchburg, VA	DOD	Lynchburg CSA Cem. #5R4	JR,SA1,BBW
Flack, Jacob	Pvt.	A 12th SCVI	33	YK	07/17/62	Gaines' Mill, VA	DOW	(Richmond effects list)	JR,YEB,CNM,CDC
Fladger, Charles J.	Cpt.	E 23rd SCVI		MN	/ /	At home	MUR	(Killed by a deserter)	HMC
Fladger, Hugh	Pvt.	H Orr's Ri.		MN	/ /	VA	DOD	(1862)	HMC,CDC
Fladger, James	Pvt.	H Orr's Ri.		MN	05/31/62	Richmond, VA	DOD		JR
Flager, J.M.	Pvt.	K 9th SCVIB		LN	/ /	Richmond, VA		Oakwood C.#56,Row L,DivG	OWC
Flagg, Charles E.B.	Pvt.	A 4th SCVC		CN	05/30/64	Cold Harbor, VA	KIA		ROH

F

SOUTH CAROLINA DEAD IN CSA SERVICE 1861-1865

NAME	RANK	C REGIMENT	AGE	DS	DIED	WHERE	WHY	BURIED	SOURCES
Flagler, Andrew P.	Pvt.	G 15th SCVI	46	WG	10/15/62	Staunton, VA	DOD	Thornrose C. Staunton, VA	ROH,JR,HOW,TOD
Flagler, Samuel M.	Pvt.	K 6th SCVI	20	WG	10/02/64	Ft. Harrison, VA	DOW	(HOW=9/28/64)	ROH,CTA,HOW,3RC
Flake, J.R.	Pvt.	K 1st SCVIH		OG	01/25/63	Richmond, VA	DOD	Oakwood C.#15,Row A,Div E	ROH,SA1,OWC
Flake, J.T.	Pvt.	K 1st SCVIH		OG	08/30/62	2nd Manassas, VA	KIA	(JR=8/29/62)	ROH,JR,SA1,CDC
Flanigan, J.F.	Cpl.	A P.S.S.			09/17/62	Sharpsburg, MD	KIA		ROH,JR
Fleetwood, Thomas W.	Pvt.	L 1st SCVIG		CN	08/29/62	2nd Manassas, VA	KIA		ROH,JR,SA1,CDC
Fleming, David George	Col.	22nd SCVI	32	RD	07/30/64	Crater, Pbg., VA	KIA	In Crater, Petersburg, VA	ROH,SCA,KEB,BLM
Fleming, E.W.	Pvt.	D 7th SCVI			/ /	Charlottesville		Univ. Cem. Charlottesville	ACH
Fleming, Ely A.	Pvt.	C 9th SCVIB	24	CL	08/29/61	Germantown, VA	DOD		ROH,JR
Fleming, Harvey L.B.	Pvt.	I 25th SCVI		CL	09/25/64	Alexandria, VA	DOW	Christ Ch. Alexandria, VA	CV,HAG,P1,P5,P12
Fleming, James B.	Pvt.	I 12th SCVI		LR	07/01/63	Gettysburg, PA	KIA	(JR=January)	JR,LAN
Fleming, S.W.	Pvt.	I 25th SCVI			04/26/65	Elmira, NY	DIP	Woodlawn N.C.#1423 Elmira	FPH,P6,P65,HAG
Fleming, T.B.	Cpl.	I 25th SCVI		WG	05/01/65	Raleigh, NC	DOD	Oakwood C. Raleigh, NC	CTA,HOW,WAT,TOD
Fleming, W.H.	Cpl.	D 5th SCVC	17	CN	08/15/61	Charleston, SC	DOD		ROH,WLI
Fleming, Warren	Pvt.	F 24th SCVI		AN	/ /		DOD	(1865)	HOL
Flemming, Gainum	Pvt.	B Hol.Leg.	22	SG	08/30/62	2nd Manassas, VA	KIA		ROH,HOS
Flemming, Gaston	Pvt.	B Hol.Leg.	28	SG	08/30/62	2nd Manassas, VA	DOW	(HOS=DOW Warrenton, VA)	ROH,HOS
Flemming, George	Pvt.	F 24th SCVI		AN	/ /		DOD	(1865)	HOL
Flemming, H.T.	Pvt.	I 25th SCVI		CL	01/15/63	At home	DOD	(Pneumonia)	JR,HAG
Flemming, R.J.	Pvt.	D 18th SCVI		AN	07/20/64	Richmond, VA	DOW	Hollywood Cem.Rchmd. U248	ROH,HC
Flemming, Tilman	Pvt.	B Hol. Leg.	22	SG	03/15/63	Wilmington, NC	DOD		ROH,HOS
Fletcher, David G.	Pvt.	D 15th SCVI		KW	/ /		KIA	(HIC=MIA @ Boonsboro)	JR,KEB,HIC
Fletcher, J.	Pvt.	1st SCV			07/14/62			Hollywood Cem.Rchmd. O75	HC
Fletcher, J.D.	Pvt.	G 8th SCVI		MO	08/08/62	(HOM=survived)		Hollywood Cem.Rchmd. K129	HC,KEB
Fletcher, Nicholas	Pvt.	B 24th SCVI	36	MO	11/19/62	Secessionville	DOD		ROH,HOM
Flinn, John B.	Pvt.	G Orr's Ri.		AE	09/12/62	Richmond, VA	DOD	(Howard Grove Hospital)	ROH,JR,CDC
Flinn, Marion	Pvt.	G Orr's Ri.		AE	11/24/63	Pt. Lookout, MD	DIP	C.C. Pt. Lookout, MD P5	ROH,FPH,CDC,P113
Flowers, Andrew	Pvt.	B 21st SCVI		DN	03/29/65	Elmira, NY	DIP	Woodlawn N.C.#2498 Elmira	ROH,FPH,P6,P120
Flowers, Bennett A.	Pvt.	L 10th SCVI	22	MN	05/15/64	Resaca, GA	DOW		ROH,RAS,HMC,CDC
Flowers, Burnett	Pvt.	G 10th SCVI			09/19/63	Fair Gds Atlanta		Oakland Cem. Atlanta R23#2	BGA
Flowers, E.A.	Pvt.	H 10th SCVI		WG	/ /		DOD		RAS,HOW
Flowers, G.S.	Pvt.	D 10th SCVI		MN	09/20/63	Chickamauga, GA	KIA		ROH,RAS,HMC,CDC
Flowers, Henry	Pvt.	F 4th SCVC	33	MN	09/22/64	Elmira, NY	DIP	Woodlawn N.C.#479 Elmira	ROH,FPH,HMC,P65
Flowers, J. Nicholas	Pvt.	C 26th SCVI		MN	06/15/64	Petersburg, VA	KIA		ROH,HMC,CDC
Flowers, J.A.	Pvt.	F 4th SCVC		MN	03/15/65	Elmira, NY	DIP	Woodlawn N.C.#1660 Elmira	FPH,HMC,P65,P120
Flowers, J.B.	Pvt.	H 10th SCVI		WG	06/15/61		DOD	(Date approx)	RAS,HOW
Flowers, James J.	Pvt.	E 1st SCVIG	35	MN	12/17/63	At home	DOD		ROH,SA1,PDL,HMC
Flowers, Joel A.	Pvt.	F 4th SCVC	23	MN	03/15/65	Elmira, NY	DIP	Woodlawn N.C.#1660 Elmira	ROH,FPH
Flowers, Nathan	Pvt.	L 10th SCVI	34	MN	01/15/65	Rock Island, IL	DIP	C.C.#1780 Rock Island, IL	ROH,FPH,P6,RAS
Flowers, Peter Morgan	Pvt.	D 5th SCVI	20	UN	03/09/63	Petersburg, VA	DOD	(PP=NY District)	ROH,JR,SA3,PP
Flowers, S.	Pvt.	2 10th SCVI			09/20/63	Chickamauga, GA	KIA		CDC
Floyd, A.P.	Pvt.	F 1st SCVIG		HY	12/14/61	Suffolk, VA	DOD	(Camp Huger)(JR=12/4/61)	JR,SA1,PDL
Floyd, B. (M.?)	Pvt.	B 11th SCVI		CO	10/06/64	Richmond, VA		Hollywood Cem.Rchmd. V401	HC
Floyd, D.	Pvt.	I 7th SCVI		ED	/ /	Richmond, VA		Oakwood C.#32,Row 31,Div D	ROH,OWC
Floyd, Enoch B.	Sgt.	A Hol.Leg.	28	SG	08/14/62	Richmond, VA	DOD		ROH
Floyd, Everett	Pvt.	B 11th SCVI			05/05/65	Pt. Lookout, MD	DIP	C.C. Pt. Lookout, MD	ROH,FPH,P6,P115
Floyd, Francis	Pvt.	C 10th SCVI		HY	04/15/62	Mobile, AL	DOD		ROH,RAS,CDC
Floyd, Giles	Pvt.	F 1st SCVIG		HY	08/12/62	Richmond, VA	DOD		JR,SA1,PDL
Floyd, J.	Pvt.	H 5th SCVC			/ /	Richmond, VA		Oakwood C.#102,Row L,Div A	ROH,OWC,CDC
Floyd, J.C.	2nd Lt.	H 26th SCVI		SR	07/08/63	Jackson, MS	DOD	(JR=7/8/62)	JR,R48
Floyd, J.G.	Pvt.	A P.S.S.			/ /		DOD		JR

114

SOUTH CAROLINA DEAD IN CSA SERVICE 1861-1865

NAME	RANK	C	REGIMENT	AGE	DS	DIED	WHERE	WHY	BURIED	SOURCES
Floyd, J.J.	Pvt.	H	P.S.S.		SG	06/30/62	Frayser's Farm	KIA		ROH,JR,CDC
Floyd, J.L.	Pvt.	C	10th SCVI		HY	/ /	Gainesville, AL	DOD	Gainesville, AL	RAS,TOD
Floyd, J.M.	Pvt.	D	3rd SCVI		SG	06/06/64	Rapidan R., VA	DOW	Hollywood Cem.Rchmd. U43	ROH,HC,SA2
Floyd, Jesse	Pvt.			48	WG	11/25/63	Missionary Ridge	KIA		CTA,HOW
Floyd, John F.	Pvt.	A	Hol.Leg.	19	SG	09/02/62	Manassas, VA	DOW	(Wdd 8/30/64)	ROH,HOS
Floyd, John N.	Pvt.	A	15th SCVAB		YK	12/07/61	Charleston, SC	DOD	Magnolia Cem. Charleston	ROH,MAG
Floyd, John P.	Pvt.	I	26th SCVI	20	WG	07/02/63	Gettysburg, PA	KIA		CTA,HOW
Floyd, John P.						/ /			(Rchmd effects list 12/62)	CDC
Floyd, John R.	Pvt.	E	16th SCVI		GE	/ /	Rome, GA (1863)	DOD	Myrtle Hill Cem. Rome, GA	ROH,16R,BGA
Floyd, Joseph	Pvt.	K	6th SCVI	35		/ /	Frederick, MD	DOD		ROH
Floyd, Joseph Cotesworth	2nd Lt.	H	26th SCVI		SR	07/08/63	Jackson, MS			PP
Floyd, Joseph P.	Pvt.	F	1st SCVIG		HY	07/06/62	Gaines' Mill, VA	DOW	(JR=7/5/62)	JR,SA1,PDL
Floyd, L.P.	Pvt.	H	10th SCVI		WG	07/07/62	Columbus, MS	DOD	Friendship C. Columbus, MS	RAS,HOW,PP
Floyd, Marshall	Pvt.	G	1st SCVIG			12/17/63	Richmond, VA	DOD		ROH,SA1
Floyd, Mathew	Pvt.	E	P.S.S.		CL	11/19/63	Knoxville, TN	DOW		ROH,JR
Floyd, Miles	Pvt.	B	13th SCVI		SG	/ /	Gordonsville, VA		(Dup of same in B, 11th?)	ROH,HOS
Floyd, Miles	Pvt.	B	11th SCVI		CO	09/06/64	Richmond, VA	DOD	(? POW Exchd 9/18/64)	ROH,HAG,P113
Floyd, Pleasant	Pvt.	F	1st SCVIG		HY	09/04/62	(Prob Warrenton)	DOW	(Wdd @ 2nd Man)	JR,SA1,PDL,CDC
Floyd, R.	Pvt.		Macbeth LA		CN	/ /	Lynchburg, VA	DOD	Lynchburg CSA Cem. #1 R2	BBW
Floyd, Thomas V.	Pvt.		5th SCVC			12/02/64	Danville, VA	DOD		ROH
Fludd, D.	Pvt.	E	18th Bn A		CO	09/01/62	Charleston, SC	DOD	Magnolia Cem. Charleston	ROH,MAG
Flynn, Charles E.	Sgt.	G	24th SCVI	21	RD	09/20/63	Chickamauga, GA	KIA	St. Peter's C. Columbia SC	ROH,JR,MP,CDC,
Flynn, John	Pvt.	C	27th SCVI			08/15/64	Elmira, NY	DIP	Woodlawn N.C.#20 Elmira	FPH,P5,P65,HAG
Fobbs, J.	Pvt.					/ /	Richmond, VA		Owkwood C.#4, Row 47, Div D	OWC
Fogartie, Jr., Edward	Pvt.	A	18th SCVAB		CN	08/26/62	Charleston, SC	DOD	2nd P.C.(Flynn's) Chastn.	JR,MAG,CDC
Fogle, G. Jefferson	Pvt.	C	1st SCVIH		OG	05/08/62	Orangeburg, SC	ACD	(Slipped boarding train)	CNM
Fogle, Gabriel H.	Pvt.	I	2nd SCVA	19	OG	05/03/65	Pt. Lookout, MD	DIP	C.C. Pt. Lookout, MD	ROH,FPH,P6,P11
Fogle, Gabriel J.	Pvt.	B	1st SCVIH	38	OG	03/21/63	Petersburg, VA	DOD	Blandford Church Pbg., VA	ROH,SA1,BLC,PP
Fogle, J.G.	Pvt.	F	2nd SCVA	10	OG	06/15/62	Orangeburg, SC	ACD		ROH,R44
Fogle, W.J.	Citizen		Orangeburg		OG	06/02/65	Hart's Island NY	DIP	(Prob. in Cypress Hills)	P12,P79
Fogle, William J.	Pvt.	F	25th SCVI	22	OG	03/16/65	Elmira, NY	DIP	Woodlawn N.C.#1679 Elmira	ROH,FPH,P6,HAG
Folk, S. Henry	Pvt.	C	3rd SCVI		NY	10/15/64		DOW	(Wdd @ Cedar Creek, VA)	ROH,ANY,KEB,SA
Follin, S.V.	Pvt.	B	18th SCVI		UN	08/12/62	Charleston, SC	DOD		JR
Folsom, J.B.	Pvt.	E	9th SCVIB			02/20/62	Richmond, VA	DOD		JR
Folsom, Stephen Thomas	Cpl.	F	7th SCVIBn		KW	10/22/62	Pocotaligo, SC	KIA		PP ROH,JR,HIC,HAG
Fontaine,	Surgeon		SC Brigade			10/01/64	Ft. Harrison, VA	KIA		MDM
Fooshe, James A.	Pvt.	A	3rd SCVIBn		LS	07/02/63	Gettysburg, PA	KIA		GDR,KEB
Footman, Richard M.	Pvt.	K	6th SCVI	22	WG	06/30/62	7 Pines, VA	DOW	(POW @ Fts. Monroe)	ROH,HOW,CTA,3R
Footon, G.J.	Pvt.	H	1st SCV			/ /	Richmond, VA		Owkwood C.#112, Row D, Div C	OWC
Fora, J.B.	Pvt.	C	12th SCVI		FD	07/25/62	Richmond, VA			ROH
Fora, J.R.	Pvt.	E	7th SCVI			10/24/64	Richmond, VA			ROH
Force, Phillip H.	3rd Sgt.	L	1st SCVIG	20	CN	05/12/64	Spotsylvania, VA	KIA		ROH,JR,SA1,BBC
Ford, A. Wilson	Cpl.	L	P.S.S.	20	AN	07/15/62	Winchester, VA	DOW	(Wdd @ 7P, RR=KIA 5/31)	ROH,JR,CDC
Ford, Charles P.	Pvt.	E	1st SCVIG		MN	10/07/63	Ft. Delaware, DE	DIP	Finn's Pt., NJ Nat. Cem.	ROH,FPH,P5,SA1
Ford, George W.	Pvt.	E	1st SCVIG		MN	11/29/63	Ft. Delaware, DE	DIP	Finn's Pt., NJ Nat. Cem.	ROH,FPH,P5,SA1
Ford, George W.	Pvt.	F	23rd SCVI		CR	10/28/62	Mt. Jackson, VA	DOD	Mt. Jackson, VA	ROH,CV,CDC,PP
Ford, H.	Pvt.		12th SCVI			06/20/62			Hollywood Cem.Rchmd. O224	HC
Ford, J.F.	Pvt.	C	6th SCVI		KW	/ /	VA	DOD		HIC
Ford, J.F.	Pvt.	E	9th SCVIB			10/27/61	Richmond, VA	DOD	(Typhoid)	JR
Ford, J.H.	Pvt.	F	1st SCVI			/ /				ROH
Ford, J.J.	Pvt.	G	9th SCVIB			/ /	Charlottesville		Univ. Cem. Charlottesville	ACH

SOUTH CAROLINA DEAD IN CSA SERVICE 1861-1865

NAME	RANK	C REGIMENT	AGE	DS	DIED	WHERE	WHY	BURIED	SOURCES
Ford, J.L.	Pvt.	G 14th SCVI	25	AE	04/04/63	Richmond, VA	DOD	Hollywood Cem.Rchmd. T144	ROH,JR,HC
Ford, J.W.	Pvt.	A 6th SCVI		CR	/ /	Virginia	DOD	(1861)	GLS,CB
Ford, Steven	Pvt.	H 14th SCV		BL	/ /	On furlough		(1863)	UD2
Ford, William	Pvt.	A 6th SCVI		CR	10/15/61	Charlottesville	DOD	Univ. Cem. Charlottesville	ROH,ACH,GLS,HHC
Ford, William	Pvt.	B 22nd SCVI		SG	07/30/64	Crater, Pbg., VA	KIA		BLM,HOS
Fore, Alfred	5th Sgt.	H 23rd SCVI		MN	09/02/64	White Sulpher Sg	DOD		ROH,HMC,PP
Foreman, Jacob J.	Pvt.	K 1st SCVC	18	ED	/ /	Virginia	KIA		ROH
Forest, J.A.	Pvt.	13th SCVI			05/14/62	Richmond, VA	DOD	(Dup of Thomas A.?)	ROH
Forest, Thomas A.	Pvt.	F 13th SCVI		SG	/ /	Richmond, VA	KIA		HOS,CDC
Forester, Henry F.	Pvt.	B 1st SCVIR		GE	03/16/65	Averysboro, NC	KIA		ROH,SA1,WAT,PP
Forester, Isaac	Pvt.	I 16th SCVI		GE	11/30/64	Franklin, TN	KIA	Macgavock C. Frkln Gv# 42	ROH,16R,WCT,PP
Forester, John	Pvt.	I 16th SCVI		GE	03/19/65	Camp Morton, IN	DIP	Green Lawn C. Indianapolis	FPH,CV,P6,P12
Former, W.F.	Pvt.	H 2nd SCV		.	09/17/62	Richmond, VA			ROH
Forrest, Joseph C	Pvt.	F 13th SCVI		SG	05/12/64	Spotsylvania, VA	KIA		JR,HOS,SCH
Forrest, Thomas A.					/ /			(Rchmd effects list 12/62)	CDC
Forrester, W.L.	Pvt.	I 16th SCVI		GE	11/30/64	LaGrange, GA	DOW	Con. Cem. LaGrange, GA	16R,TOD
Forsythe, W.D.	Pvt.	L Orr's Ri.			10/01/63	Orange C.H., VA	DOD		JR
Fort, Edward	Pvt.	Pal. LA		ED	03/03/63	Richmond, VA	DOD	(Pneumonia)	JR,SOB
Fort, J. Edward	Pvt.	F 8th SCVI	22	DN	07/08/61	Germantown, VA	DOD		ROH,JR,KEB
Fort, Wiley	Pvt.	D 4th SCVC		CN	07/20/63		DOD	(Typhoid)	ROH,JR
Fortman, R.M.	Pvt.	K 6th SCVI			06/30/62	Fts. Monroe, VA	DOW	(Wdd & POW @ 7Pines)	ROH,CDC
Foster,	Sgt.	23rd SCVI			/ /				ROH,CDC
Foster, A.A.	Pvt.	D 18th SCVI			01/22/63	Staunton, VA	DOW		ROH,JR
Foster, A.P.	Pvt.	K 5th SCVI		SG	05/08/62	Richmond, VA	DOD	Hollywood Cem.Rchmd. F100	ROH,HC,SA3,CDC
Foster, Abner J.	Pvt.	D P.S.S.		SG	04/27/65	Pt. Lookout, MD	DOD	C.C. Pt. Lookout, MD	ROH,FPH,HOS,P6
Foster, Adolphus B.	Pvt.	M P.S.S.	17	UN	06/30/62	Frayser's Farm	KIA	El Bethel Ch. Union Cty.	ROH,JR,CDC,UNC
Foster, Asa M.	Pvt.	K P.S.S.		SG	06/30/62	Frayser's Farm	KIA	(JR=6/29/62)	ROH,JR,HOS,CDC
Foster, Berryman H.	Pvt.	B 27th SCVI		CN	05/26/64	Petersburg, VA		Blandford Church Pbg., VA	BLC,PP
Foster, Charles Bernard	Pvt.	D 27th SCVI	21	CN	09/17/64	Alexandria, VA	DOW	(Wdd & POW 8/21/64)	ROH,HAG,P1,P5
Foster, Dean	Pvt.	H 22nd SCVI			03/04/65	Elmira, NY	DIP	Woodlawn N.C.#2420 Elmira	FPH,P6,P65,P120
Foster, Francis M.	Pvt.	F 5th SCVI	33	YK	10/28/63	Lookout Valley	DOW	(CDC= F.H.)	SA3,CDC,YEB,CB
Foster, H.H.	Pvt.	D 18th SCVI		AN	01/20/63	Staunton, VA		Thornrose C. Staunton, VA	TOD
Foster, Henry M.	3rd Cpl.	H 5th SCVI		UN	08/30/62	2nd Manassas, VA	KIA	Gilead Cem. Union Cty. SC	ROH,JR,SA3,NHU
Foster, J.A.	Pvt.	A 3rd SCVIBn		LS	07/02/63	Gettysburg, PA	KIA	(Fooshe?)	ROH,CDC
Foster, J.J.	Pvt.	K 27th SCVI		DN	10/15/63		DOD		JR,HAG
Foster, J.S.	Pvt.	H 1st SC			/ /	Richmond, VA			ROH
Foster, James	Pvt.	F 22nd SCVI		PS	09/15/62	Culpepper, VA	DOW	Fairview Cem. Culpepper VA	CGH
Foster, James Anthony	Cpl.	K 3rd SCVI	21	SG	09/13/62	Md. Heights, MD	KIA	(Bio in HOS) HOS	ROH,JR,SA2,KEB
Foster, James J.	2nd Lt.	A Hol.Leg.		SG	03/29/65	Hatcher's Run VA	KIA		HOS
Foster, Jess	Pvt.	L P.S.S.			/ /		DOW		JR
Foster, John	Pvt.	I 3rd SCVI		LS	11/16/63	Knoxville, TN	KIA	(?P39=POW Xchd 1/24/64)	ROH,KEB
Foster, John A.	Pvt.	D P.S.S.		SG	06/30/62	Frayser's Farm	KIA		HOS
Foster, John J.	Cpl.	D P.S.S.		SG	06/21/62	7 Pines, VA	DOW		ROH,JR,HOS,CDC
Foster, John W.	3rd Lt.	F 18th SCVI	42	UN	07/30/64	Crater, Pbg., VA	KIA		ROH,BLM,R47
Foster, Joseph H.	Pvt.	D P.S.S.		SG	05/15/63	Cassville, VA	KIA	(Severe head Wd @ 7Pines)	ROH,JR,HOS
Foster, L. Perrin	Cpt.	K 3rd SCVI		SG	12/13/62	Fredericksburg	KIA	Family Gvyd. Spartanburg	ROH,JR,SA2,HOS
Foster, L.J.W.	Pvt.	F 18th SCVI			07/30/64	Petersburg, VA	KIA		JR
Foster, L.S.	Pvt.	H 5th SCVI	25	UN	/ /		DOD		ROH,SA3
Foster, Leonard					/ /				ROH
Foster, Simpson	Pvt.	D 8th SCVI		CD	09/13/62	Maryland Hts. MD	KIA		JR,KEB
Foster, Thomas J.	Pvt.	D P.S.S.		SG	06/30/62	Frayser's Farm	KIA		ROH,JRR,HOS,CDC

SOUTH CAROLINA DEAD IN CSA SERVICE 1861-1865

NAME	RANK	C REGIMENT	AGE	DS	DIED	WHERE	WHY	BURIED	SOURCES
Foster, William	Pvt.				/ /	Richmond, VA		Oakwood C.#25,Row K,Div B	OWC
Foster, William A.	Pvt.	D P.S.S.		SG	09/14/62	South Mtn., MD	DOW	(CDC=W.D., JRR=W.J.)	ROH,JRR,HOS,CD
Foster, William G.	Pvt.	F 18th SCVI		YK	09/09/62	Richmond, VA	DOD	Oakwood C.#65,Row F,Div B	ROH,JRR,OWC
Foulkes, Alexander M.	Pvt.	F 6th SCVI	29	CR	01/10/64	Morristown, TN	DOD		ROH,HHC
Fountain, Alexander G.	Pvt.	E 6th SCVI		DN	11/21/62	Culpepper, VA	DOD	(Wdd @ Frayser's Farm)	JR,JLC
Fountain, G.W.	Pvt.	C 26th SCVI			06/20/63		DOD		JR
Fountain, J.A.	Pvt.	E Orr's Ri.			/ /	Lynchburg, VA		Lynchburg CSA Cem. #9R1	BBW
Fountain, James	Pvt.	F Orr's Ri.		PS	08/09/63	Lynchburg, VA	DOD		JR,CDC
Fountain, William A.	2nd Sgt.	B 21st SCVI		DN	08/02/63	Morris Island SC	DOW	Louther's Hill, SC	JR,R48,HAG
Fourcher, C.	Pvt.	D 1st SCVIBn		CN	08/28/63	Charleston, SC	DOD	Magnolia Cem. Charleston	RCD
Fourcher, J. Henry	Pvt.	D 27th SCVI	37	LS	08/28/63	Charleston, SC	DOD	Magnolia Cem. Charleston	ROH,JR,MAG,HAG
Foushe, Benjamin	Pvt.	F 2nd SCVI	20	AE	07/01/62	Malvern Hill, VA	KIA		ROH,KEB
Foushe, John W.	Pvt.	F 2nd SCVI	23	AE	07/22/63	Gettysburg, PA	DOW	Magnolia Cem. Charleston	ROH,JR,GDR,SA2
Fowler, A.M.	Pvt.	K 26th SCVI	24	HY	12/21/63	Charleston, SC	DOD		ROH,JR
Fowler, B.	Pvt.	C 10th SCVI		HY	/ /		DOD		RAS
Fowler, B.F.	Pvt.	F 15th SCVI		UN	01/10/63	Richmond, VA	DOD		ROH,JR,KEB
Fowler, C.C.	Pvt.	C 2nd SCVA			/ /	Richmond, VA		Oakwood C.#7, Row K, Div B	ROH,OWC
Fowler, Charles N.	Pvt.	D Hol.Leg.		BL	06/07/62	Adams Run, SC	DOD		PP
Fowler, D.P.	Pvt.	K 26th SCVI	25	HY	03/04/62	Camp Lookout, SC	DOD		ROH,JR
Fowler, Daniel M.	Pvt.	F 1st SCVIG	24	HY	12/27/63	Ft. Delaware, DE	DIP	Finn's Pt., NJ Nat. Cem.	ROH,FPH,SA1,PD
Fowler, Eber	Pvt.	H 1st SCVIH		SG	01/24/63	Lynchburg, VA	DOD		ROH,SA1,HOS
Fowler, Elias	Pvt.	H 1st SCVIH		SG	12/15/62		DOD	(Day appr., to Hos 12/1/62)	SA1,HOS
Fowler, F.	Sgt.				10/16/61	Columbia, SC	DOD		ROH
Fowler, G.	Pvt.	C 10th SCVI		HY	/ /		DOD		RAS
Fowler, G.B.	Pvt.	H 15th SCVI		UN	/ /		DOD		JR,KEB
Fowler, G.K.	Pvt.	B 18th SCVI			07/30/62		DOW		JR
Fowler, George R.	Pvt.	I 16th SCVI		GE	12/16/63	St. Louis, MO	DIP	(Chronic Diarrhea)	P12
Fowler, H.C.	Pvt.	A 6th SCVI		CR	05/15/62	Virginia	DOW		CB,HHC
Fowler, Henry D.	Pvt.	I 1st SCVIG			06/30/62	Richmond, VA	DOD		ROH,SA1
Fowler, Hosea	Pvt.	K 27th SCVI			02/03/65	Elmira, NY	DIP	Woodlawn N.C.#1750 Elmira	FPH,P6,P65,HAG
Fowler, I.	Pvt.	C 10th SCVI		HY	/ /		DOD	(CEN=Isaac, 21 in 1860)	RAS
Fowler, J.	Pvt.	H 1st SCVI			/ /	Lynchburg, VA		Lynchburg CSA Cem. #5 R1	BBW
Fowler, J.E.	Pvt.	E Ham.Leg.			08/30/62	2nd Manassas, VA	KIA		JR
Fowler, J.J.	Pvt.	E Ham.Leg.			09/30/62	Warrenton, VA	DOW	(Wdd 2nd Man)	ROH
Fowler, J.W.	Pvt.	B 18th SCVI			09/30/62	Warrenton, VA	DOW	(Wdd 2nd Man)	ROH
Fowler, J.W.	Sgt.	E Ham.Leg.			12/30/61		DOD	(Pneumonia)	JR
Fowler, James	Pvt.	L Orr's Ri.		AN	09/03/64	Weldon RR, VA	KIA		JR,CDC
Fowler, James	Pvt.	B 26th SCVI			09/16/62	Warrenton, VA	DOW	(Wdd @ 2nd Man.)	JR
Fowler, James F.	Pvt.	D 27th SCVI	18	LS	07/01/64	Petersburg, VA	DOW	(Wdd 6/22/64)	ROH,HAG,CDC
Fowler, James H.	Cpl.	B 18th SCVI		UN	07/30/64	Crater, Pbg., VA	KIA	Gilead B.C, Union, SC	ROH,BLM,UD3
Fowler, James J.	Pvt.	C 10th SCVI		HY	/ /	Okolona, MS	DOD		RAS,PP
Fowler, James L.	Pvt.	F 24th SCVI		AN	/ /		DOD	(1865)	HOL
Fowler, Jerry F.	Pvt.	D 16th SCVI		GE	07/11/62	Adams Run, SC	DOD		16R,PP
Fowler, John	Pvt.	F 18th SCVI		YK	05/25/65	Newport News, VA	DIP	Greenlawn C. Newport News	PP,P12
Fowler, John L.	Pvt.	H 1st SCVIH		SG	07/14/63	Richmond, VA	DOD	Oakwood C.#10,Row 41,Div D	ROH,SA1,OWC
Fowler, John W.	Cpl.	B 1st SCVIR			11/30/61		DOD		SA1
Fowler, L.D.	Pvt.	C 2nd SCVIRi			06/27/62	Gaines' Mill, VA	KIA		ROH,JR
Fowler, Lawson	Pvt.	K 26th SCVI	18	HY	08/03/62	Secessionville	DOD		ROH,JR
Fowler, Matthew	Pvt.	F 1st SCVIG	33	HY	12/12/62	Lynchburg, VA	DOD	Lynchburg CSA Cem. #3 R5	SA1,PDL,BBW
Fowler, Newton F.	Pvt.	F 18th SCVI			08/31/64	Elmira, NY	DIP	Woodlawn N.C.#93 Elmira	FPH,P5,P65,P12
Fowler, P.O.	Pvt.	F 3rd SCVI		LS	12/09/62	Richmond, VA	DOD	(Wdd & POW @ Shpsbg)	ROH,JR,SA2,KEB

F

SOUTH CAROLINA DEAD IN CSA SERVICE 1861-1865

NAME	RANK	C REGIMENT	AGE	DS	DIED	WHERE	WHY	BURIED	SOURCES
Fowler, Peter	Pvt.	K 26th SCVI	33	HY	09/06/64	Petersburg, VA	KIA		ROH
Fowler, R.	Pvt.	D 16th SCVI		GE	07/22/64	Atlanta, GA	KIA		ROH
Fowler, R.	Pvt.	C 10th SCVI		HY	/ /		DOD		RAS
Fowler, R.H.	Pvt.	E Ham.Leg.			05/31/62	Fair Oaks, VA	KIA	(RR=7 Pines)	ROH,JR,CDC
Fowler, R.M.	Sgt.	F 15th SCVI		UN	05/05/64	Wilderness, VA	KIA	(UD2=Spotsylvania)	JR,KEB,UD2
Fowler, Reilly	Pvt.	I 16th SCVI		GE	11/25/64	Missionary Rdge.	KIA		16R
Fowler, S. Waddy	Pvt.	B Orr's Ri.	19	AE	12/16/61	Adam's Run, SC	DOD	(JR=Typhoid & in Co. G)	ROH,JR,CDC,PP
Fowler, S.H.	Pvt.	B 18th SCVI			06/11/64	Trevillian Stn.	KIA		JR
Fowler, T.R.	Pvt.	H 3rd SCVI			07/21/61	1st Manassas, VA	KIA		JR
Fowler, Thomas M.	Pvt.	C 13th SCVI		SG	07/15/63	NC	DOW	(Wdd @ 2nd Man)	ROH,HOS,CDC
Fowler, Thomas W.	Sgt.	B 1st SCVC	30	SG	10/16/61	Columbia, SC	DOD		ROH,PP
Fowler, Thomas W.	Pvt.	E 5th SCVI	27	UN	07/21/61	1st Manassas, VA	KIA	Gilead B.C. Union Cty., SC	JR,SA3,UNC,NHU
Fowler, Thompson	Pvt.	H 15th SCVI		UN	/ /		DOD		JR,KEB
Fowler, W.	Pvt.	F 15th SCVI			/ /		DOD		JR
Fowler, W. Allen	Pvt.	D 2nd SCVI			06/01/64	Virginia	KIA		SA2
Fowler, W. Simpson	Pvt.	H 1st SCVIH		SG	11/15/62		DOD	(Day approx, to Hos 11/4)	SA1,HOS
Fowler, W.W.	Pvt.	D 27th SCVI	32	LS	07/20/63	Bty. Wagner, SC	DOW		ROH,JR,HAG
Fowler, William	Cpl.	K 26th SCVI		HY	06/27/64	At home	DOW	(Wdd @ Petersburg)	ROH
Fowler, William	Pvt.	1st CSEng		SG	01/15/65	Petersburg, VA	ACD	(Drowned in flood)	HOF
Fowler, William R.	Pvt.	E 18th SCVI	45	SG	04/23/65	Pt. Lookout, MD	DIP	C.C. Pt. Lookout, MD	ROH,FPH,P6,P114
Fox, Henry	Pvt.	K 10th SCVI		CN	/ /		DOD		RAS
Fox, J.R.	Pvt.	E 7th SCVC	19	ED	/ /	At home	DOD		ANY,HOE,UD2
Fox, James	Pvt.	H 7th SCVIBn		ED	03/19/65	Bentonville, NC	KIA		ROH,HAG,PP
Fox, W.	Pvt.				/ /	Richmond, VA		Oakwood C.#20,RowN,Div A	OWC
Fox, William	Sgt.	E 1st SCVIG			07/30/63	Davids Island NY	DOW	(Wdd @ Gettysburg)	ROH,CDC,P1
Foxworth, A.C.	Pvt.	B 18th SCVAB		MN	06/02/63	Charleston, SC	DOD	Magnolia Cem. Charleston	ROH,MAG
Foxworth, Charles J.	Pvt.	F 4th SCVC		MN	06/18/64	Armory Sq. H. DC	DOW	(Wdd & POW @ Hawe's Shop)	HMC,P6
Foxworth, Eli	Pvt.	I 21st SCVI		MN	02/02/62	At home	DOD	(? Dup of Erwin)	JR
Foxworth, Ervin J.	Pvt.	I 21st SCVI		MN	02/11/62	At home	DOD		JR,HMC,HAG
Foxworth, Joseph B.	Pvt.	I 21st SCVI		MN	05/16/64	Drury's Bluff VA	KIA		ROH,HMC,HAG
Foxworth, R.W.	Cpl.	F 10th SCVI		MN	/ /	Tupelo, MS	DOD		RAS,HMC
Foxworth, T.	Pvt.	F 4th SCVC		MN	/ /	Pocotaligo, SC	DOD	(1862)	HMC
Foxworth, W.K.	Pvt.	D 25th SCVI		MN	08/26/64	City Pt. Hos.	DOW	(color bearer,Wdd Weld RR)	HMC,HAG,P12
Foy, J.R.	Pvt.	E 7th SCVI		ED	10/02/64			Hollywood Cem.Rchmd. E49	HC
Foy, John	Sgt.	A 22nd SCVI			07/01/63	Petersburg, VA	DOW	(Wdd 6/18)	ROH
Frady, William	Pvt.	G 12th SCVI			07/01/63	Gettysburg, PA	KIA		JR
Fralic, William Joseph	Sgt.	F 25th SCVI	21	OG	09/10/64	Alexandria, VA	DOW	Christ Ch., Alexandria, VA	ROH,HAG,CV,P1,P6
Fralix, David S.	Pvt.	K 11th SCVI	23	CO	10/10/63	Charleston, SC	DOD		ROH,JR,HAG
Francis, Henry	Pvt.	B 3rd SCVC	49	CO	01/02/64	McPhersonville	DOD		ROH
Franklin,	Pvt.	K 24th SCVI			09/24/63	Chickamauga, GA	DOW		JR
Franklin, Avery	Pvt.	A 22nd SCVI			12/07/64	Pt. Lookout, MD	DIP	C.C. Pt. Lookout, MD	ROH,FPH,P6,P113
Franklin, James N.	Pvt.	F 3rd SCVI		NY	11/14/62			Little River P.C. NY	NCC,KEB
Franklin, John	Pvt.	C 19th SCVI		ED	06/28/62	Enterprise, MS	DOD		HOE,PP,UD3
Franklin, Marshall	Pvt.	A 19th SCVI	29	ED	/ /		DOD		HOE
Franklin, R.L.	Pvt.	K 13th SCVI			06/23/65	Hart's Island NY	DIP	Cypress Hills N.C.#3051 NY	FPH,P6,P12,P79
Franklin, T.T.	Sgt.				/ /			Fredericksburg C.C. R6S13	FBG
Franklin, Thomas	Pvt.	B 19th SCVI		ED	09/20/63	Chickamauga, GA	KIA	(10th Co. 10/19 Consol.)	ROH,JR,HOE,CDC
Franklin, Thomas	Pvt.	D 5th SCVC			07/20/63		DOD	(Typhoid)	JR
Franklin, W.R.	Pvt.	B 1st SCVIG		NY	11/15/62	Richmond, VA	DOD	Oakwood C.#35,Row L,Div C	ROH,SA1,ANY,OWC
Franklin, William M.	Pvt.	H 7th SCVIBn	29	AE	12/24/64	Richmond, VA	DOW	Hollywood Cem.Rchmd. W596	ROH,HC,HAG
Franklin, William T.	Pvt.	G 3rd SCVI		LS	09/17/62	Sharpsburg, MD	DIP	Rose Hill C. Hagerstown MD	ROH,JR,SA2,BOD

SOUTH CAROLINA DEAD IN CSA SERVICE 1861-1865

NAME	RANK	C REGIMENT	AGE	DS	DIED	WHERE	WHY	BURIED	SOURCES
Franks, Beverly T.	2nd Cpl.	G 3rd SCVI	21	LS	07/09/64	At home	DOD		ROH,SA2,KEB
Franks, Frederick P.	Pvt.	I 14th SCVI	24	AE	06/30/64	Richmond, VA	DOD	(HOL=Francis P.)	ROH,HOL
Franks, Henry	1st Sgt.	G 24th SCVI	23	RD	09/20/63	Chickamauga, GA	KIA		ROH,CDC
Franks, James W.W.	Pvt.	E 3rd SCVIBn		LS	11/18/62	Mt. Jackson, VA	DOW	Mt. Jackson, VA RHL	ROH,UD3,PP,SHS
Franks, John W.	Cpl.	K 7th SCVI	32	LS	09/17/62	Sharpsburg, MD	KIA	(RHL= Md. Heights)	ROH,JR,RHL,UD3
Franks, W.H.	2nd Sgt.	E 14th SCVI		LS	07/02/62	Gaines' Mill, VA	DOW	(JR=Co.E, 1st SCV)	ROH,JR
Fraser, A.C.	Pvt.	G 6th SCVI		FD	05/31/62	7 Pines, VA	DOW		WDB
Fraser, Charles	Pvt.	B 21st SCVI	18	DN	06/16/64	Petersburg, VA	KIA	(HAG= Frazier)	ROH,JR,HAG,CDC
Fraser, Daniel J.	Cpl.	B 7th SCVIBn		FD	09/10/64	Alexandria, VA	DOW	Christ Ch. Alexandria, VA	JR,P1,P6,HAG,C
Fraser, Elias Lynch	Pvt.	I 12th SCVI	17	LR	09/17/62	Sharpsburg, MD	DOW	Rose Hill C. Hagerstown MD	ROH,JR,LAN,BOD
Fraser, John	Pvt.	B 21st SCVI	28	DN	09/16/64	Petersburg, VA	MIA	(HAG= Frazier)	ROH,HAG
Fraser, John	Pvt.	E 4th SCVC		MO	/ /	Hawes Shop, VA	KIA		HOM
Fraser, John B.	Lt.	Arsenal			03/19/63	Charleston, SC	DOD		ROH
Fraser, Simon Lovat	Pvt.	F 9th SCVIB	26	LR	08/21/61	Germantown, VA	DOD		ROH,JR,LAN
Fraser, William B.	Pvt.	B 21st SCVI	30	DN	09/15/64	At home	DOD	(HAG- Frazier)	ROH,HAG
Frasher, J.J.					/ /	AthensGA Armory	DOD		UD2
Frazer,Jr., Phineas F.	Pvt.	A 15th SCVI		RD	03/28/62	Beaufort, SC	ACD	(Fall from a wagon)	ROH,JR,KEB
Freak, J.A.	Pvt.	D 9th SCVIB		SR	/ /			Stonewall Cem. Winchester	WIN
Frederick, Charles	Pvt.	D 27th SCVI	17	CN	06/16/64	Hare's Hill, VA	KIA	(KIA with Cpt.Hopkins)	CDC
Frederick, James	Pvt.	K 12th SCVI		PS	/ /	Martinsburg, WV		Greenhill C. Martinsburg	PP
Fredericks, J.W.	Pvt.			PS	/ /			Fredericksburg C.C. R6S13	FBG
Fredericks, W.	Pvt.	C Orr's Ri.		PS	05/03/63	Chancellorsville	KIA	(May be J.W.buried in Fbg)	ROH,JR
Free, A.J.	Pvt.	2nd SCVA			06/02/63	Charleston, SC	DOD	Magnolia Cem. Charleston	ROH,MAG
Free, George W.	Pvt.	K 14th SCVI		ED	07/03/63	Gettysburg, PA	KIA		JR,GDR,UD2
Freeman,	Pvt.	23rd SCVI			/ /				ROH,CDC
Freeman, Albert	Pvt.	E 11th SCVI			06/18/64	Petersburg, VA	KIA		JR
Freeman, B.R.	Cpl.	H 17th SCVI	19	RD	11/10/64	Petersburg, VA	KIA		ROH,PP
Freeman, Benjamin	Pvt.	E 13th SCVI			10/12/62	Mt. Jackson, VA	DOD	(Typhoid)	ROH,JR,CV,SHS,
Freeman, Benjamin	Pvt.	F 11th SCVI	23	BT	05/09/64	Swift Creek, VA	KIA		ROH,HAG
Freeman, Benjamin	Pvt.	I Hol.Leg.		SG	/ /	Virginia	DOD		HOS
Freeman, Benjamin F.	Pvt.	E 4th SCVC		MO	06/18/64	Washington, DC	DOW	(Wdd & POW @ Hawe's Shop)	HOM,P5,P12
Freeman, C.M.	Pvt.	B 5th SCVC		CN	08/15/63	Kennansville, SC	DOD		ROH,MDM
Freeman, E.	Pvt.	D 24th SCVI			/ /			Milner, GA	CKB
Freeman, Enoch	Pvt.	C 12th SCVI		FD	04/01/62	McPhersonville	DOD		JR,HFC
Freeman, George	Pvt.	D 25th SCVI		MN	02/25/65	Elmira, NY	DIP	Woodlawn N.C.#2270 Elmira	FPH,P6,P65,P12
Freeman, Isaac	Pvt.	C 2nd SCVI		RD	08/08/64	Richmond, VA	DOD	Hollywood Cem.Rchmd. V568	ROH,HC,SA2
Freeman, John	Pvt.	E 21st SCVI		CD	06/21/64	Fts. Monroe, VA	DOW	N.C. Hampton, VA	ROH,P12
Freeman, J.A. (Albert?)	Pvt.	E 11th SCVI		BT	06/18/64	Petersburg, VA	KIA	(Sniped on picket)	ROH
Freeman, J.B.	Pvt.	E 10th SCVI		WG	06/12/62	Mississippi	DOD	(Typhoid)	JR,RAS,HOW
Freeman, J.T.	Pvt.	G 19th SCVI		AE	02/12/62		DOD		HOL
Freeman, James	Pvt.	L 8th SCVI		MN	05/12/64	Spotsylvania, VA	KIA		JR
Freeman, James A.	Cpl.	C 16th SCVI		GE	06/24/64	At home	DOD		16R,PP
Freeman, James E.	Pvt.	D 24th SCVI	24	BT	07/30/64	Kenesaw Mtn., GA	DOW		EJM
Freeman, James N.	Pvt.	D 2nd SCVA			01/12/64	Adams Run, SC	DOD		ROH,PP
Freeman, John	Pvt.	C 12th SCVI		FD	06/15/63	Guinea Stn., VA	DOD	(Date approx)	HFC
Freeman, John	Pvt.	K 1st SCVIR		MO	06/07/65	Hart's Island NY	DIP	Cypress Hills N.C. #2952	Fph,P6,SA1,P79
Freeman, Joseph W.	Pvt.	I 8th SCVI		MN	05/12/64	Spotsylvania, VA	KIA		SCH,HMC,KEB
Freeman, L.T.	Pvt.	H 2nd SCVIRi			05/15/64	Virginia	KIA		ROH,JR
Freeman, Lorenzo D.	Pvt.	G 23rd SCVI		MO	08/30/62	2nd Manassas, VA	KIA	(JR=28th SCVI)	JR,HOM
Freeman, Middleton	Pvt.	G Orr's Ri.		AE	06/17/62	Gaines' Mill, VA	DOW		ROH,JR,CDC
Freeman, N.	Pvt.	B 7th SCVI			09/17/62	Sharpsburg, MD	KIA		ROH,JR

F

SOUTH CAROLINA DEAD IN CSA SERVICE 1861-1865

NAME	RANK	C REGIMENT	AGE	DS	DIED	WHERE	WHY	BURIED	SOURCES
Freeman, Owen Clinton	Sgt.	Pee Dee L.			01/16/62		DOD	(Cooper's Company)	JR
Freeman, Robert	Pvt.	D 25th SCVI		MN	05/16/64	Drury's Bluff VA	KIA	(Swift Creek ?)	ROH,JR,HMC,HAG
Freeman, Robert	Pvt.	C 12th SCVI		FD	06/15/64	Richmond, VA	DOD	(Date approx)	HFC
Freeman, W.B.	Pvt.	F 11th SCVI			05/09/64	Swift Creek, VA	KIA		JR
Freeman, William	Pvt.	C 2nd SCVI		RD	07/02/63	Gettysburg, PA	KIA		KEB ROH,JR,GDR,SA2
Freeman, William	Pvt.	C 12th SCVI		FD	06/15/63	Guinea Stn., VA	DOD	(Date approx)	HFC
Freeman, William D.	Pvt.	L 2nd SCVIRi	30	AN	10/16/62	At home	DOD		ROH
French, Henry	1st Sgt.	G 24th SCVI			09/24/63	Chickamauga, GA	DOW		JR
French, J.J.	Pvt.	L Orr's Ri.		AN	07/27/62	Camp Jackson, VA	DOD		JR,CDC
French, John D.	Pvt.	F 13th SCVI			01/15/62	Camp Pemberton	DOD	(Typhoid)	JR
Freshly, George W.	Pvt.	C 20th SCVI	23	LN	06/12/64	Gaines' Mill, VA	KIA	(JR=6/11/62)	ROH,JR,CDC,KEB
Freshly, James P.	Pvt.	H 13th SCVI		LN	07/01/63	Gettysburg, PA	KIA		ROH
Freshwater, John H.	Sgt.	B 11th SCVI		CO	04/07/63	Columbia, SC	DOD	(PP=6/16/63)	JR,HAG,PP
Frey, James W.	Pvt.	K 20th SCVI		LN	06/01/64	Cold Harbor, VA	KIA		ROH,KEB
Frick, Elias D.	Pvt.	C 20th SCVI	30	LN	02/21/65	Pt. Lookout, MD	DIP	C.C. Pt. Lookout, MD P6	ROH,FPH,KEB,P114
Frick, John	Pvt.	C 2nd SCVIRi		PS	12/15/63	Pt. Lookout, MD	DIP		ROH,CDC
Fricks, Abraham J.	1st Sgt.	I 15th SCVI	40	LN	07/27/64	Wilderness, VA	DOW	(Wdd 5/12/64)	ROH,H15,KEB,TOD
Fricks, J.H.	Lt.	C Orr's Ri.		PS	05/03/63	Chancellorsville	KIA		ROH,JR,BOS,R45
Fricks, John D.	Pvt.	C Orr's Ri.	19	PS	08/31/63	Baltimore, MD	DIP	Loudon Pk. Cem.A-14 Balto.	ROH,JR,FPH,PP,P6
Fricks, W.D.S.	Pvt.	I 2nd SCVI			05/08/64	Wilderness, VA	KIA		ROH,JR,SA2
Friday, J.E.	Pvt.	I 22nd SCVI		LN	12/29/64	Petersburg, VA	KIA		ROH
Friday, Samuel David	Pvt.	C 2nd SCVC		RD	08/07/64	Adams Run, SC	DOD		PP
Fridel, Job M.	Pvt.	C 15th SCVI	16	LN	10/15/61	Columbia, SC	DOD	Shiloh M.C. Gilbert, SC	ROH,JR,LNC,KEB
Friedeburg, Joseph F.	2nd Lt.	F 3rd SCVIBn	39	RD	09/18/62	Maryland Hts. MD	DOW	(Wdd 9/14/62) PP	ROH,JR,KEB,R45
Frierson, Augustus C.	Pvt.	K 4th SCVC	19	SR	07/30/64	Pt. Lookout, MD	DIP	C.C. Pt. Lookout, MD P6	ROH,FPH,CLD,P115
Frierson, John	Pvt.	Hol.Leg.			04/08/63	Richmond, VA	DOD	Hollywood Cem.Rchmd. T221	ROH,HC
Frierson, T. Rush	2nd Lt.	D 9th SCVIB		SR	11/28/61	Manchester, VA	DOD	(JR=J. Rush & Co.G)	JR,R46
Frierson, T.K.	Lt.	E P.S.S.			/ /		DOD		JR
Frieze, Franz J.	Pvt.	G 25th SCVI		OG	08/21/64	Weldon RR Pbg VA	KIA		ROH,HAG
Fripp, George W.			30	BT	02/05/62	Boyd's Landing	KIA	(Cpt. Nowell's Co.)	ROH,CDC
Fripp, J. Edmund	Pvt.	Beaufort A	27	BT	10/22/62	Pocotaligo, SC	KIA		ROH,CDC,PP
Fripp, J.T.E.	Pvt.	D 5th SCVC	41	BT	06/13/63	Green Pond, SC	DOW	(On sick leave, as guide)	ROH,R43
Fripp, Thomas B.	Pvt.	H 3rd SCVC	34	BT	10/22/62	Pocotaligo, SC	KIA		ROH,CDC
Frith, John	Pvt.	H 19th SCVI	25	AE	06/15/62	At home	DOD		ROH
Frost, Campbell R.	Cpt.	D 7th SCVC	31	RD	05/30/64	Old Church, VA	KIA		ROH,JR,CDC,R47
Frost, Edward Downes	Cpt.	S 15th SCVAB	30	CN	12/11/63	Ft. Sumter, SC	ACD	St.Michael's C. Charleston	ROH,MAG,DOC,CDC
Frost, Eli	Pvt.	C 3rd SCVI		NY	09/23/63	Chickamauga, GA	DOW	Con. Cem. Marietta, GA	ROH,JR,SA2,KEB
Frost, Eli	Pvt.	H 3rd SCVI		LN	06/29/62	Savage Stn., VA	KIA		SA2,ANY,KEB
Frost, Henry	pvt.	G 5th SCVC			09/24/64	Harewood Hos. DC	DOW		P5,P6,P12
Frost, Snow	Pvt.	K Orr's Ri.			01/02/63	Fredericksburg	DOW		JR
Fry, J. Marion	Pvt.	A 6th SCVI	22	CR	05/31/62	7 Pines, VA	KIA	HHC,CB	ROH,JR,GLS,WDB
Fry, John M.	Pvt.	G 1st SCVIG		LN	09/01/64	Columbia, SC	DOD		ROH,SA1,HOE,PP
Fry, John Martin	Pvt.	20th SCVI	40	LN	06/15/63	Columbia, SC	DOW		ROH
Fry, Joseph Tyler	Pvt.	H 20th SCVI	18	LN	03/19/65	Pt. Lookout, MD	DIP	C.C. Pt. Lookout, MD	ROH,FPH,KEB,P6
Fry, Thomas Albert	Pvt.	H 20th SCVI	18	LN	08/13/62	Columbia, SC	DOD		ROH,KEB,PP
Fryer, C.W.	Pvt.	C 11th SCVI		CN	06/24/64	Petersburg, VA	KIA	(Wesley or William)	ROH,HAG
Fryer, Robert A.	Pvt.	C 11th SCVI		CN	08/21/64	Weldon RR Pbg VA	KIA		ROH,HAG
Fryer, S.J.	Pvt.	C 11th SCVI		CN	10/07/64	Darbytown Rd Pbg	KIA	(S. James ?)	ROH,HAG
Fryer, W.T.	Pvt.	C 11th SCVI		CN	06/24/64	Petersburg, VA	KIA	(Wesley or William)	ROH,JR,HAG
Fuan, D.M.	Pvt.	K 10th SCVI			09/28/62	Danville, KY	DIP	Danville Cem. C.L. KY	ROH,FPH
Fudge, A.B.	Pvt.	G 17th SCVI		BL	01/06/65	Petersburg, VA	KIA	Blandford Church Pbg., VA	ROH,BLC

SOUTH CAROLINA DEAD IN CSA SERVICE 1861-1865

NAME	RANK	C REGIMENT	AGE	DS	DIED	WHERE	WHY	BURIED	SOURCES
Fulgham, J.J.	Pvt.	G 10th SCVI		KW	09/20/63	Chickamauga, GA	KIA	(CDC= Cpl. Co. A)	ROH,JR,RAS,CDC
Fullem, J.S.	Cpl.	F 1st SCVIR		NC	06/15/63	Ft. Moultrie, SC	DOD	Magnolia Cem. Charleston	ROH,MAG,SA1
Fuller, Adolphus A.	1st Lt.	B 3rd SCVIBn			07/16/63	Gettysburg, PA	DOW	Magnolia Cem. CN P1	ROH,JR,KEB,GDR
Fuller, Edward P.	Pvt.	B 3rd SCVIBn			07/03/63	Gettysburg, PA	KIA		ROH,JR,GDR,KEB
Fuller, Henry L.	2nd Lt.	D 13th SCVI	26	NY	05/09/63	Chancellorsville	DOW	R47	ROH,JR,BOS,ANY
Fuller, James	Pvt.	C 14th SCVI			12/20/61	Coosawatchie, SC	DOD		JR
Fuller, James M.	Pvt.	F 3rd SCVI			12/13/62	Fredericksburg	KIA	(KEB= J.N.)	ROH,JR,SA2,KEB
Fuller, P.A.	Pvt.	B 3rd SCVIBn		LS	09/14/62	Maryland Hts. MD	DOW		JR,KEB
Fuller, P.H.	Cpl.	F 3rd SCVI		LS	12/13/62	Fredericksburg	KIA		ROH
Fuller, Patrick McD.	Pvt.	F 2nd SCVI	21	AE	10/05/64	Charlottesville	DOW	(Wdd @ Wilderness 5/6/64)	ROH,SA2,KEB
Fuller, Robert	Pvt.	H 7th SCVC			10/19/64	Elmira, NY	DIP	Woodlawn N.C.#533 Elmira	FPH,P120,P12
Fuller, Taylor	Pvt.	H 1st SCVIR		CN	02/23/64	Mt. Pleasant, SC	DOD		SA1
Fuller, W.H.	Cpl.	F 3rd SCVI		LS	01/03/62	Centreville, VA	DOD	(Pneumonia)	ROH,JR,SA2,KEB
Fuller, William Thomas	3rd Lt.	F 4th SCVI	26	GE	07/25/61	Culpepper, VA	DOW	Fairview Cem. Culpepper VA	ROH,JR,CGH,SA2
Fuller,Jr., Edmund N.	Lt.	F&S Draytn		CN	09/17/62	Sharpsburg, MD	KIA		ROH,CDC,WLI
Fullers, H.A.	Pvt.	A 22nd SCVI			10/09/64			Hollywood Cem.Rchmd. V339	HC
Fullerton, George F.	Pvt.	E 2nd SCVI		KW	08/07/61	Culpepper, VA	DOD	Fairview C. Culpepper, VA	ROH,JR,CGH,SA2
Fullerton, George W.	Cpt.	F Orr's Ri.	30	PS	05/12/64	Spotsylvania, VA	KIA		ROH,CGS,BOS,R4
Fulman, W.C.	Pvt.	I 3rd SCVI			08/14/63	Gettysburg, PA	DOW		ROH,CDC,P1
Fulmer, George W.	Pvt.	H 3rd SCVI		LN	12/13/62	Richmond, VA	DOD	(ROH=George M.)	ROH,JR,KEB
Fulmer, J.	Pvt.				10/27/62	Richmond, VA		Oakwood C.#17,Row P,Div B	ROH,OWC
Fulmer, John A.	Pvt.	C 6th SCVC			04/05/65	Pt. Lookout, MD	DIP	C.C. Pt. Lookout, MD	FPH,P6,P114,P1
Fulmer, John Hezekiah	2nd Lt.	I 15th SCVI	32	LN	10/29/63	At Home	DOW	Macedonia L.C. LN Cty.	JR,UNC,TOD,KEB
Fulmer, John W.	Pvt.	C 20th SCVI	18	LN	07/30/62	Sullivans I., SC	DOD	(J,F, in KEB?)	ROH
Fulmer, W.F.	Pvt.	C 20th SCVI			07/31/64	Richmond, VA		(ROH=W.T.)	ROH,KEB
Fulmer, William E.C.	Pvt.	F 3rd SCVIBn	20	RD	08/14/63	Gettysburg, PA	DOW	Magnolia Cem. Charleston	ROH,MAG,P5,KEB
Fulmer, William W.	2nd Lt.	C 15th SCVI	26	LN	10/20/61	Columbia, SC	DOD	TOD,PP	ROH,JR,KEB,R47
Fulton, James	Pvt.	F 17th SCVI	41	YK	02/10/64	Petersburg, VA	KIA	Blandford Church Pbg., VA	ROH,BLC,PP,CB
Fulton, Thomas M.	1st Sgt.	G 15th SCVI	23	WG	/ /		DOD	(1861)(JR=Lt.)	JR,CTA,HOW,KEB
Funchess, John E.	Pvt.	A 5th SCVC		OG	06/26/63	Culpepper, VA	DOD	(JR=6/29/63)	ROH,JR
Funderback, William	Pvt.	K 6th SCVC	38	LR	06/12/64	Trevillion Stn.	KIA	(JR=6/11/64)	ROH,JR
Funderburgh, Archibald	Pvt.	B 6th SCVC		ED	07/15/63	Jacksonboro, SC	DOD		ROH,HOE,UD3
Funderburk, Albert	Pvt.	F 5th BnRes		CD	12/28/64	Florence, SC	DOD		ROH,PP
Funderburk, F.M.	Pvt.	C 1st SCVIR		CD	07/23/62	Adams Run, SC	DOD		ROH,SA1
Funderburk, John	Pvt.	K 1st SCVIR		LR	11/20/63		KIA	(Shell explosion)	SA1
Funderburk, John B.	Pvt.	B 8th SCVI	20	CD	10/03/61	Culpepper, VA	DOD	Fairview Cem. Culpepper VA	ROH,JR,CGH,KEB
Funderburk, Joseph C.	Pvt.	H 2nd SCVI		LR	07/28/62	McClaw's Div.Inf	DOD	(Near Richmond)	H2,SA2,KEB
Funderburk, L.N.	Pvt.	E 22nd SCVI		LR	05/26/65	Elmira, NY	DIP	Woodlawn N.C.#2921 Elmira	FPH,LAN,P65,P1
Funderburk, W.W.	Sgt.	E 22nd SCVI		LR	07/30/64	Crater, Pbg., VA	KIA		JR,BLM,LAN
Funding, J.W.					/ /	Richmond, VA		(Richmond effects list)	CDC
Furgerson, Burrell					/ /	Richmond, VA		(Richmond effects list)	CDC
Furnance, Thomas	Pvt.	F Foreign Bn			12/15/64	Columbia, SC		Elmwood Cem. Columbia SC	MP
Furness, Mathew	Pvt.	H 7th SCVIBn		ED	09/12/63	Charleston, SC	DOD	Magnolia Cem. Charleston	JR,MAG,HAG
Furse, G.C.	Pvt.	8th BnRes			10/08/64	Charleston, SC	DOD	Magnolia Cem. Charleston	ROH,MAG,CDC
Furse, J.J.	Pvt.	K 1st SC MR		BT	01/15/62		DOD	(Red Oak Rangers)	CNM
Furt, William	Pvt.	Brooks GA		CN	/ /	Lynchburg, VA	DOD	(1st in K,2nd SCVI d:1865)	H2,Sa2,KEB
Furtic, George	Pvt.	F 25th SCVI	24	OG	08/02/62	Columbia, SC	DOD		ROH,HAH
Furtick, Charles	Pvt.	B 1st SCVIH		OG	12/20/62	Lynchburg, VA	DOD	Lynchburg CSA Cem. #4 R4	ROH,SA1,BBW
Futch, David	Pvt.	G 17th SCVI	38	BL	01/08/65	Petersburg, VA			PP
Futril, Samuel	Pvt.	C 7th SCVIBn		RD	10/22/62	Pocotaligo, SC	KIA		JR,HAG,R46,PP

121

G

SOUTH CAROLINA DEAD IN CSA SERVICE 1861-1865

NAME	RANK	C REGIMENT	AGE	DS	DIED	WHERE	WHY	BURIED	SOURCES
Gabb, J.M.	Pvt.	G 6th SCVI			08/23/64	Ream's Stn., VA	KIA		JR
Gable, Emaniah Milton	Pvt.	L P.S.S.	28	AN	07/23/62	Gaines' Mill, VA	DOW		ROH
Gable, Henry David	Pvt.	C 4th SCVI	19	AN	01/08/62	Manassas, VA	DOD	(To hosp 12/19/61)	ROH,SA2
Gable, John Martin	Pvt.	G 6th SCVC	19	AN	08/23/64	Ream's Stn., VA	KIA		ROH
Gabriel, David	Pvt.	I P.S.S.			/ /		DOD		JR
Gadberry, James M.	Colonel	18th SCVI	44	UN	08/30/62	2nd Manassas, VA	KIA	Unionville P.C. Union Cty.	ROH,JR,NHU,CDC
Gaddy, Levi	3rd Cpl.	H Orr's Ri.		MN	01/14/63	Richmond, VA	DOW	(Wdd @ Fbg)	JR,HMC,CDC
Gaddy, William D.	Pvt.	I 8th SCVI		MN	12/09/61	Richmond, VA	DOD	(Pneumonia)	JR,HMC,KEB
Gadsden, Christopher E.	1st Sgt.	B 7th SCVIBn	32	FD	06/15/63	Richmond, VA	DOD	(ROH=Co.G)	ROH,HAG
Gadsden, Thomas Screven	Pvt.	I 2nd SCVI			07/02/63	Gettysburg, PA	KIA	Magnolia Cem. CN WV	ROH,JR,GDR,SA2
Gadsden,Jr., Thomas N.	Pvt.	B 25th SCVI	18	CN	06/16/62	Secessionville	KIA	Magnolia Cem. Charleston	ROH,JR,HAG,PP
Gailey, Albert	2nd Lt.	F 24th SCVI		AN	11/30/64	Franklin, TN	DOW	Franklin C. C.985 #31	HOL,R48,PP
Gaillard, C. David	Pvt.	B P.S.S.		AN	10/07/64	Darbytown Rd. VA	KIA	(JR=Co. C & Aller's Farm)	JR,CCB,GMJ
Gaillard, Franklin	Lt. Col.	2nd SCVI	35	RD	05/06/64	Wilderness, VA	KIA		ROH,JR,SA2,KEB
Gaillard, Thomas Edmund	Sgt.	I 2nd SCVI		FD	08/12/63	Gettysburg, PA	DOW	Magnolia Cem. Charleston	ROH,GDR,SA2,P1
Gaines, E.A.	Pvt.	F 14th SCVI		LS	09/20/62	Shepherdstown VA	KIA		JR
Gaines, Edmond Pendleton	Pvt.	C 13th SCVI		PS	07/28/62	Frayser's Farm	KIA	(JR=1864)	ROH,JR,HOS,UD1
Gaines, Edwin D..D.	Pvt.	B 2nd SCVIRi		PS	05/15/62	Adams Run, SC	DOD	Mt. Zion U.M.C. Central SC	PCS,PP
Gaines, G.W.	Pvt.	F 1st SCV			/ /	Richmond, VA		Oakwood C.#29,Row F,Div E	ROH,OWC
Gaines, Henry	Pvt.	L P.S.S.			/ /		DOD		JR
Gaines, J.H.	Pvt.	H P.S.S,			07/22/64	Petersburg, VA	KIA		JR
Gaines, J.P.	Pvt.	A 22nd SCVI			02/12/65	Pt. Lookout, MD	DIP	C.C. Pt. Lookout, MD	ROH,FPH,P6,P11
Gaines, Jesse W.	Pvt.	C 13th SCVI		SG	10/18/64	Jones Farm, VA	DOW	Hollywood Cem.Rchmd. I27	ROH,HC,HOS
Gaines, John	Pvt.	A Orr's Ri.			07/13/62	Winder H. Rchmd	DOD		JR
Gaines, John H.	Pvt.	K Orr's Ri.	24	AE	06/27/62	Gaines' Mill, VA	KIA		ROH,JR,CDC
Gaines, John T.	Pvt.	K Orr's Ri.		AN	05/03/63	Chancellorsville	KIA		JR
Gaines, L.P.	Pvt.	1st SCVC	24		01/27/63	Strasburg, VA	DOD		ROH
Gaines, Pressley	Pvt.	G 1st SCVC	30	AE	01/15/63	Stevensburg, VA	DOD		ROH
Gaines, T.W.	Pvt.		20		02/14/63	Strasburg, VA	DOD		ROH
Gaines, Tandy	Pvt.	G 1st SCVC	28	AE	01/15/63	Stevensburg, VA	DOD	(T.W.?)	ROH
Gaines, Thomas J.	Cpl.	I Hol.Leg.		SG	/ /	Elmira, NY	DIP		HOS
Gainey, Evander	Pvt.	G 21st SCVI	20	DN	06/16/62	Georgetown, SC	DOD	(JR=Co.C, PP=Co. E))	ROH,JR,HAG,PP
Gainey, George W.	Pvt.	E 21st SCVI		CD	09/04/64	Elmira, NY	DIP	Woodlawn N.C.#74 Elmira	FPH,HAG,P5,P12
Gainey, Ira	Pvt.	L 1st SCVIG		CD	03/24/64	Staunton, VA	DOD		SA1,PP
Gainey, Isaiah	Pvt.	M 8th SCVI	27	DN	02/13/62	Richmond, VA	DOD	(Pneumonia)	ROH,JR,KEB
Gainey, J. Matthew	Pvt.	C 1st SCVIR			12/06/64	Charleston, SC	DOW	Magnolia Cem. Charleston	ROH,MAG,SA1
Gainey, Peter	Pvt.	M 8th SCVI		DN	/ /	Richmond, VA		Oakwood C.#3, Row S,Div D	OWC,KEB
Gainey, Wiley	Pvt.	E 6th SCVI	30	DN	05/06/64	Wilderness, VA	KIA	(Also Wdd @ 7Pines)	ROH,JR,JLC
Gainey, William Green	Pvt.	E 21st SCVI		DN	06/15/64	Petersburg, VA	KIA		ROH,HAG
Gaison, W.W.	Pvt.	C 8th SCVI		CD	/ /	Farmville, VA			ROH
Gale, Henry A.	Cpl.	C 8th SCVI		CD	12/14/63	Bean's Stn., TN	KIA	(KEB= Sgt. Gayle, H.A.)	ROH,KEB
Gales, H.	Pvt.	F 11th SCVI			01/01/62	Wordsville, SC	DOD	(Prob 9th SCVIH)	JR
Gales, R.	Pvt.	E 13th SCVI		SG	06/03/62	Richmond, VA		Hollywood Cem.Rchmd. M12	ROH,HC
Gallagher, Samuel A.	Pvt.	I 17th SCVI			11/29/62	Tarboro, NC	DOD	(Typhoid)	JR
Gallin, J.H.	Pvt.	A 3rd SCVABn		GE	08/15/63	Morris Island SC	KIA		ROH
Gallman, D. Frederick	1st Cpl.	C 3rd SCVI		NY	09/17/62	Sharpsburg, MD	KIA	(Pvt. in NCC) KEB	ROH,JR,SA2,ANY
Gallman, Daniel T.	Sgt.Major	18th SCVI		UN	08/30/62	2nd Manassas, VA	KIA	Manassas, VA Cem.	ROH,CDC
Gallman, Gerrimar	Pvt.	15th SCVI		UN	/ /		KIA		UD3
Gallman, Henry G.G.	Pvt.	C 3rd SCVI		NY	09/17/62	Sharpsburg, MD	DOW	Rose Hill C. Hagerstown MD	ROH,JR,SA2,ANY
Gallman, J.L.	Pvt.	H 5th SCVI		UN	08/16/64	Petersburg, VA	KIA		JR
Gallman, James H.	Pvt.	H 5th SCVI		UN	05/31/62	7 Pines, VA	KIA		JR,SA3,NHU,UD1

G

SOUTH CAROLINA DEAD IN CSA SERVICE 1861-1865

NAME	RANK	C REGIMENT	AGE	DS	DIED	WHERE	WHY	BURIED	SOURCES
Gallman, John W.	Cpl.	H 5th SCVI		UN	06/30/62	Frayser's Farm	KIA		ROH,JR,SA3
Gallman, John Z.	Pvt.	H 5th SCVI		UN	06/30/62	Frayser's Farm	KIA	Gallman Fam.Cem. Union Cty	JR,SA3,UNC
Gallman, L.G.	Pvt.	K 1st SCVIG		UN	05/06/64	Wilderness, VA	KIA	(JR=K, 5th SCVI)	ROH,JRR,SA1,CDC
Gallman, O.N.	Pvt.	C 4th SCV			03/29/65	High Point, NC		Oakwood C. High Point, NC	CV,WAT,TOD
Gallman, William G.	Pvt.	E 5th SCVI		UN	09/03/61	Germantown, VA	DOD	(Body returned to SC)	SA3,UD1
Gallop, M.W.	Pvt.	B 3rd SCV			04/22/62	Richmond, VA		Oakwood C.#91,Row J,Div A	ROH,OWC
Galloway, Calvin M.	Cpl.	G Orr's Ri.		AE	05/12/64	Spotsylvania, VA	KIA		ROH
Galloway, Emory	Pvt.	B 21st SCVI		DN	/ /	Richmond, VA		Oakwood C.#22,Row B,Div G	ROH,OWC,HAG
Galloway, John	Pvt.	B 14th SCVI		ED	/ /	Richmond, VA		Oakwood C.#52,Row S,Div C	ROH,OWC,CDC
Galloway, John	Pvt.	B 3rd SCVI		NY	11/18/63	Knoxville, TN	KIA		SA2,ANY,CDC,KEB
Galloway, John	Pvt.	A 12th SCVI	24	YK	07/06/63	Gettysburg, PA	DOW		JR,YEB
Galloway, John	Pvt.	H 14th SCV			/ /			(In Hos. Jan., 1863)	UD2
Galloway, L.C.	Pvt.	H 21st SCVI		DN	04/25/65	Elmira, NY	DIP	Woodlawn N.C.#1417 Elmira	FPH,P5,P65,HAG
Galloway, Peter	Pvt.	H 14th SCV			/ /			(In Hos. Feb., 1862)	UD2
Galloway, Pipkin	Pvt.	H 21st SCVI		DN	03/07/65	Elmira, NY	DIP	Woodlawn N.C.#2397 Elmira	FPH,P5,P65,HAG
Galloway, Ross	Pvt.	A 12th SCVI	24	YK	03/25/65	Petersburg, VA	KIA		YEB
Galloway, T.C.	Pvt.	B 21st SCVI		DN	/ /	Richmond, VA			ROH
Galloway, Thomas	Pvt.	H 21st SCVI		CD	08/06/64	Petersburg, VA	KIA		ROH,PP,HAG
Galloway, W.M.	Pvt.	C Orr's Ri.		PS	06/27/62	Gaines' Mill, VA	KIA		ROH,JR,CDC
Galloway, William A.	Pvt.	A 12th SCVI	25	YK	12/08/62	At home	DOD		JR,YEB
Galman, D.F.	Pvt.	F 18th SCVI		YK	08/30/62	2nd Manassas, VA	KIA	(Sgt.Maj. Gallman?)	JR
Galvin, G.S.	Lt.	D 2nd SCResB			04/13/65	Thomasville, NC		Con. Cem. Thomasville, NC	CV
Gamball, W.	Pvt.	K Orr's Ri.		AN	06/10/62	Richmond, VA		Hollywood Cem.Rchmd. P164	HC,CDC
Gamble, A.M.	Pvt.	K 6th SCVI		WG	/ /	7 Pines, VA	KIA		HOW,3RC
Gamble, J.N.					/ /	Richmond, VA		(Richmond effects list)	CDC
Gamble, James J.	Pvt.	K 6th SCVI	17	WG	05/31/62	7 Pines, VA	KIA	(D,9th SCVI in CTA)	ROH,HOW,CTA
Gamble, Thomas E.	Pvt.	I 25th SCVI		CN	04/07/65	Elmira, NY	DIP	Woodlawn N.C.#2645	FPH,P5,P65,HAG
Gamble, W.J.	Pvt.	I 4th SCVC	25	WG	09/15/63	McPhersonville	DOD		JR
Gamble, William G.	Pvt.	A 10th SCVI		GN	03/19/65	Bentonville, NC	KIA	(Wdd twice before)	GRG,RAS,HOW
Gambrell, Enoch B.	Pvt.	K Orr's Ri.	20	AN	07/10/62	Dill Farm, VA	DOD		ROH,JR,CDC
Gambrell, Enos	Pvt.	E 16th SCVI	53	LS	07/10/63	Jackson, MS	KIA		16R,PP
Gambrell, H.R.	Pvt.	K Orr's Ri.	47	AN	09/17/62	Sharpsburg, MD	KIA		ROH
Gambrell, J.E.	Pvt.	K Orr's Ri.		AN	05/03/63	Chancellorsville	KIA		JR
Gambrell, J.H.	Pvt.	D 18th SCVI		AN	06/11/62	Charleston, SC	DOD	(JR=7/16/62)	ROH,JR
Gambrell, John R.	Pvt.	K Orr's Ri.	20	AN	12/13/62	Fredericksburg	KIA	Spotsylvania C.H. Cem. VA	ROH,JR,CDC,SCH
Gambrell, W.J.	Pvt.	K Orr's Ri.		AN	10/09/62	Staunton, VA	DOD		JR
Gambrell, William A.	Pvt.	K Orr's Ri.	34	AN	07/12/62	Richmond, VA	DOD	(JR=KIA 6/27/62)	ROH,JR,CDC
Gambril, N.T.	Pvt.	Orr's Ri.			10/24/64	Richmond, VA			ROH
Gambril, William	Pvt.	K Orr's Ri.	21	AN	07/05/62	Dill Farm, VA	DOD	(JR=6/18/62)	ROH,JR
Gambrill, M.A.	Pvt.	K Orr's Ri.		AN	06/27/62	Gaines' Mill, VA	KIA	(Dup Wm.A?)	ROH,JR,CDC
Gambrill, William N.	Pvt.	L Orr's Ri.	22	AN	06/27/62	Gaines' Mill, VA	KIA		ROH,CDC
Gamell, William	Pvt.	K 6th SCVC			06/11/64	Trevillian Stn.	KIA		ROH,JR
Gamron, F.	Pvt.	D 5th SCV			06/10/64	Ins. H. Atlanta		Oakland C. Atlanta R39#7	BGA
Gandy, Darius F.	1st Lt.	G 9th SCVIB	20	DN	11/18/61	Warrenton, VA	DOD	(R46=RES 11/18/61)	ROH,JLC,R46
Gandy, J.J.	Pvt.	A 21st SCVI		CN	/ /			(Goude ?)	JR
Gandy, James	Pvt.	B 21st SCVI		DN	03/20/62	Georgetown, SC	DOD	(Co, A? Goude?)	ROH,JR,PP
Gandy, Julius	Pvt.	E 6th SCVI	18	DN	09/30/64	Ft. Harrison, VA	KIA		ROH,JLC
Gannon, A.H.	Pvt.	H 3rd SCVC		CN	09/21/64	Richmond, VA		Hollywood Cem.Rchmd. V545	HC
Gant, J.A.	Pvt.	E 2nd SCVIRi			05/06/64	Wilderness, VA	KIA	(JR=DOD 1863)	ROH,JR
Gant, W.A.	Pvt.	I 17th SCVI		LR	07/15/64	Petersburg, VA	DOW	(Wdd 7/1/64)	ROH,LAN
Gantey, R.E.	Pvt.	A 7th SCVI			10/27/62	Winchester, VA		Stonewall C. Winchester VA	ROH,WIN,P12

SOUTH CAROLINA DEAD IN CSA SERVICE 1861-1865

NAME	RANK	C REGIMENT	AGE	DS	DIED	WHERE	WHY	BURIED	SOURCES
Gantt, Elisha	Pvt.	K 9th SCVIB			08/27/61	Germantown, VA	DOD		JR
Gantt, J.	Pvt.	H 5th SCV			08/12/64	Richmond, VA			ROH
Gantt, Jackson	Pvt.	D 1st SCVIH		LR	07/11/62	Richmond, VA	DOD	Hollywood Cem.Rchmd, M195	HC,LAN
Gantt, Jerard H.	Pvt.	K 9th SCVIB			10/23/61	Pleasant Val.Hos	DOD	(Note says F,P.S.S.)	JR
Gantt, L.E.	Sgt. Major	11th SCVI	24	BL	06/30/64	Petersburg, VA	KIA	(JR=6/21/64)	ROH,JR,HAG
Gantt, R.R.	Pvt.	C 2nd SCVI		UN	09/17/62	Sharpsburg, MD	KIA		ROH,SA2
Gantt, William	Pvt.	K 9th SCVIB			10/23/61	Germantown, VA	DOD		JR
Garden, Alister	Sgt.	Palm. LA	19	SR	05/25/63	At home	DOW	(Wdd @ Suffolk)	JR,SOB
Gardner, A.F.	Pvt.	I 6th SCVC			06/24/64	Ladd's Shop, VA	KIA	(JR=Nance's Shop 6/22/64)	ROH,JR
Gardner, Alfred	Pvt.	E 12th SCVI	23	LR	/ /	At home	DOD	(1864)	LAN
Gardner, C.L.	Pvt.	G 7th SCVIBn	37	KW	05/16/64	Drury's Bluff VA	KIA	H2	ROH,JR,HIC,HAG
Gardner, Casper N.	1st Cpl.	G 1st SCVIG		ED	08/29/62	2nd Manassas, VA	KIA	(Gardiner ?)	ROH,SA1,HOE,CD
Gardner, Charles A.	Pvt.	A 1st SCVIG	20	BL	08/15/62	Richmond, VA	DOW	(Wdd @ Gaines' Mill)	ROH,JR,SA1
Gardner, D.F.	Pvt.	E 12th SCVI		LR	05/12/64	Spotsylvania, VA	KIA		LAN
Gardner, Daniel	Pvt.	L 21st SCVI	32	MN	06/15/64	Petersburg, PA	KIA		ROH,HMC,HAG
Gardner, Elijah T.	4th Sgt.	E 2nd SCVI		KW	05/12/64	Spotsylvania, VA	KIA	Spotsylvania C.H., VA	ROH,JR,SCH,SA2
Gardner, Evander M.	2nd Lt.	A 8th SCVI	29	DN	11/15/62	Sharpsburg, MD	DOW		ROH,JR,KEB,R46
Gardner, F.M.	Pvt.	E 12th SCVI	17	LR	07/23/63	Davids Island NY	DOW	Cypress Hills N.C.#668 NY	ROH,JR,FPH,LAN
Gardner, G.W.	Pvt.	M P.S.S.		DN	04/01/63	Jerusalem, VA	DOD		JR
Gardner, H.N.	Pvt.	G 7th SCVIBn		KW	04/27/65	Charlotte, NC			PP.HAG
Gardner, H.W.	Pvt.	C 1st SCV			11/15/64	Baltimore, MD	DIP	Loudon Park C. Balto., MD	CV
Gardner, J.C.	Pvt.	H 7th SCVI			01/30/65	Richmond, VA	DOD	Hollywood Cem.Rchmd. W2	HC,CDC
Gardner, J.M.	Pvt.	G 14th SCVI		AE	06/10/63	Richmond, VA	DOD	(Pneumonia)	JR
Gardner, J.W.	Pvt.	F 7th SCVI			10/30/62	Richmond, VA	DOD	Hollywood Cem.Rchmd. C68	ROH,HC
Gardner, J.W.	Pvt.	E 21st SCVI		CD	05/08/63		DOD		JR
Gardner, James B.	1st. Lt.	G 1st SCVIBn		CN	09/10/63	Bty. Wagner, SC	DOW	Magnolia Cem. Charleston	ROH,JR,WLI,R48
Gardner, James D.	Pvt.	E 8th SCVI		DN	07/05/62	Richmond, VA	DOW		ROH,JR,KEB
Gardner, James L.	Sgt.	D 15th SCVI		KW	07/31/64	City Point, VA	DOW	City Pt. N.C. Hopewell, VA	PP,KEB,TOD,P12
Gardner, John	Pvt.	H 14th SCV			/ /			(In Hos. May, 1863)	UD2
Gardner, Milton R.	Pvt.	E 12th SCVI	19	LR	09/17/62	Sharpsburg, MD	KIA		ROH,JR,LAN
Gardner, Peter T.	Pvt.	A 8th SCVI		DN	06/15/61	Culpepper, VA		(ROH=Peter F.)	ROH,KEB
Gardner, R.J.	Pvt.	D 7th SCVIBn	30	KW	11/03/63	At home	DOD	(HIC says Pbg)	ROH,JR,HIC,HAG
Gardner, Robert C.	Pvt.	G 2nd SCVI		KW	11/13/61	Orange C.H., VA	DOW	(1st Manassas)	SA2,HIC,KEB
Gardner, Samuel	Pvt.	H 15th SCVI		UN	/ /		DOD	(Garner?)	JR
Gardner, Timothy B.	Cpl.	E 2nd SCVI		KW	07/19/63	Staunton, VA	DOW	Thornrose C. Staunton, VA	ROH,GDR,SA2,TO
Gardner, W. Columbus	Pvt.	I 17th SCVI		LR	07/30/64	Crater, Pbg., VA	KIA		ROH,JR,BLM
Gardner, W. Tyler	Pvt.	K 15th SCVI	21	ED	09/23/62	Leestown, VA	DOD	(Typhoid)	JR
Gardner, W.J.	Pvt.	D 4th SCVC		CN	05/15/62		DOD		ROH
Gardner, W.L.	Pvt.	A 12th SCVI	25	YK	05/12/64	Spotsylvania, VA	KIA		YEB
Gardner, William	Pvt.	D 5th SCVI			04/24/62		DOD		JR
Gardner, William W.	Pvt.	H 2nd SCVI		LR	12/27/61	Manchester, VA	DOD		SA2,LAN,KEB,H2
Gardner. J.M.	Pvt.	K 14th SCVI		AE	/ /	Richmond, VA		Oakwood C.#11,Row 35,Div D	ROH,OWC
Garett, S.L.	Pvt.	F 2nd SCVIRi			06/19/64	Petersburg, VA	KIA		JR
Garland, Edward	Pvt.	F 7th SCVC		HY	05/31/65	Pt. Lookout, MD	DIP	C.C. Pt. Lookout, MD	FPH,P6,JES,P12
Garland, Robert	Pvt.	A 1st SCVIR		CD	04/16/61		DOD	(Regimental hospital)	SA1
Garland, William H.	Sgt.	M 8th SCVI		DN	07/02/63	Gettysburg, PA	KIA	(JR=Co.E)	ROH,JR,GDR,KEB
Garlington, B.C.	Lt. Col.	3rd SCVI	26	LS	06/29/62	Savage Stn., VA	KIA	UD3	ROH,JR,SA2,RHL
Garlington, Henry L.	1st Lt.	A 3rd SCVI		LS	05/10/64	Wilderness, VA	DOW	(Wdd 5/6/64) UD3	SA2,JR,RHL,KEB
Garlington, John D.	Sgt. Major	G 3rd SCVI		LS	06/29/62	Savage Stn., VA	KIA	(JR=Co.F) UD3	ROH,JR,SA2,RHL
Garlington,Jr., John	3rd Sgt.	A 3rd SCVI	22	LS	12/13/62	Fredericksburg	KIA	UD3,PP	ROH,JR,SA2,RHL
Garmany, William H.	Pvt.	B 2nd SCVI	21	GE	10/17/64	Cedar Creek, VA	KIA		ROH,KEB,SA2

G

SOUTH CAROLINA DEAD IN CSA SERVICE 1861-1865

NAME	RANK	C REGIMENT	AGE	DS	DIED	WHERE	WHY	BURIED	SOURCES
Garner, Alexander	Pvt.	B 21st SCVI		DN	10/14/64	Pt. Lookout, MD	DIP	(POW Morris I. 7/10/63)	P114,HAG
Garner, Enos	Pvt.	C 23rd SCVI		CN	/ /	Petersburg, VA	KIA		ROH
Garner, G.W.	Pvt.	C 25th SCVI		WG	03/20/65	Richmond, VA			ROH
Garner, James	Pvt.	I 1st SCVIH		MN	07/16/62	Secessionville	DOD		ROH,SA1
Garner, John	Pvt.	K 7th SCVC			/ /	Virginia	DOD		HIC
Garner, L.	Pvt.	H 15th SCVI		UN	/ /	Richmond, VA		Oakwood C.#49,Row A,Div E	ROH,OWC,KEB
Garner, Richard A.	Pvt.	B 21st SCVI	21	DN	06/07/64	Richmond, VA	KIA		ROH
Garner, Thomas	2nd Cpl.	C 2nd SCVI		RD	08/15/61	Fairfax, VA	DOD	(H2=Co. B, d: Flint Hill)	ROH,SA2,KEB,H2
Garner, Thomas	Pvt.	12th SCVI			06/12/65	Richmond, VA			ROH
Garner, W.E.	Pvt.	H 15th SCVI		UN	07/15/64	Petersburg, VA	KIA	(JR=June)	ROH,JR,KEB
Garner, W.F.	Pvt.	H 15th SCVI		UN	/ /		DOD	(JR=Gardner)	JR
Garner, William	Pvt.	A 14th SCVI	24	DN	09/20/62	Oxford, VA	DOW	(JR=Wdd @ Shepherdstown)	ROH,JR
Garner, William H.	Pvt.	C 2nd SCVI		RD	08/15/61	Fairfax, VA	DOD	(H2=Co.B, d: Flint Hill)	ROH,SA2,KEB,H2
Garnett, L.J.	Pvt.	C Orr's Ri.			12/13/62	Fredericksburg	KIA		JR
Garold, S.	Pvt.	A 26th SCVI		HY	08/02/64	Petersburg, VA	DOW	Blandford Church Pbg., VA	ROH,BLC
Garone, S.	Pvt.	C 7th SCVC			/ /	Gordonsville, VA			ROH
Garrett, A.F.	Pvt.	H 12th SCVI		YK	04/18/65	Pt. Lookout, MD	DIP		ROH
Garrett, D.	Pvt.	B 2nd SCVIRi			/ /	Richmond, VA			ROH
Garrett, David	Pvt.	C Hol.Leg.		NY	03/09/62	Adams Run, SC	DOD	(Not on NY Monument list)	ANY
Garrett, E.B.	Pvt.	D 27th SCVI	38	LS	02/12/65	Pt. Lookout, MD	DIP	C.C. Pt. Lookout, MD	ROH,FPH,P113
Garrett, H.M.	Pvt.	G 3rd SCVI		LS	09/23/63	Chickamauga, GA	DOW	Con. Cem. Marietta, GA CCM	ROH,JR,SA2,KEB
Garrett, Holen	Pvt.	E 3rd SCVIBn		LS	09/20/63	Chickamauga, GA	KIA		ROH
Garrett, J.A.	Pvt.	E 14th SCVI		LS	09/19/62	Lynchburg, VA	DOW	Lynchburg CSA Cem. #5 R2	CGS,BBW
Garrett, J.H.	Pvt.	E 14th SCVI		LS	09/20/62	Shepherdstown VA	KIA		CGS
Garrett, John	Pvt.	E 3rd SCVIBn	41	LS	10/15/64	Lynchburg, VA	DOD	Durbin Creek B.C. GE Cty.	ROH,GEC,LSC
Garrett, John A.	Pvt.	G 22nd SCVI	27	AN	07/30/64	Crater, Pbg., VA	KIA		ROH,BLM
Garrett, John W.	Pvt.	C Hol.Leg.		SG	/ /	Adams Run, SC	DOD		HOS
Garrett, Nelson A.	Pvt.	B 16th SCVI		GE	08/02/62	Camp Leesburg	DOD	(Near Adams Run ?)	16R,PP
Garrett, P.G.	Pvt.	F Ham. Leg.		GE	06/15/61	Brentsville, VA	DOD		ROH
Garrett, Stephen	Pvt.	F 1st SCVIH		GE	11/06/63	Pt. Lookout, MD	DIP	C.C. Pt. Lookout, MD	ROH,SA1,JRH,P12
Garrett, T.B.	Pvt.	D 27th SCVI	16	LS	08/05/64		DOD	Robertson F.C. Graycourt	ROH,LSC
Garrett, William	Pvt.	E 13th SCVI		SG	05/18/62	Richmond, VA	DOD	Hollywood Cem.Rchmd. F119	JR,HC,HOS
Garrett, William B.	Pvt.	D 18th SCVI		AN	10/14/64	Baltimore, MD	DOW	Loudon Pk. Cem.B-40 Balto.	ROH,FPH,PP,P1
Garrett, William G.	Pvt.	G 22nd SCVI	20	AN	07/18/64	Petersburg, VA	KIA		ROH
Garrett, William H.	Pvt.	G 3rd SCVI			09/27/63	Chickamauga, GA	DOW	(Dup of H.M.?)	ROH
Garrette, J.M.	Pvt.	I 16th SCVI		GE	08/10/63	Lauderdale Ss MS	DOD		PP
Garrette, Madison R.	Pvt.	I 16th SCVI	38	GE	09/30/64	Forsyth, GA	DOD	New Harmony B.C. GE Cty.CD	16R,CKB,GEC,LSC
Garrick, H.	Pvt.	A 8th SCRes		CN	02/04/65	Columbia, SC	DOD	Elmwood Cem., Columbia, SC	ROH,MP,PP
Garrick, John M.	Pvt.	H Ham.Leg.			03/23/64	Nashville, TN	DOW	(Wdd & POW @ Lookout Mtn.)	CDC,P2,P5
Garris, Calvin	Pvt.	E 24th SCVI	32	CO	11/30/64	Franklin, TN	KIA	Williamson Cty Con. Cem.TN	ROH,WCT,PP
Garris, James	Pvt.	F P.S.S.			/ /		KIA		JR
Garris, John	Pvt.	E 24th SCVI		CO	12/15/63	Cassville, GA	DOD		ROH
Garris, Joseph H.	Pvt.	F 1st SCVIG		CN	10/09/61	Richmond, VA	DOD	Hollywood Cem.Rchmd. F153	ROH,JR,HC,SA1
Garris, William J.	2nd Lt.	G 8th SCVIBn	50	HY	03/20/62	Georgetown, SC	DOD	(Unit later K, 26th SCVI)	ROH,JR,R48,PP
Garrison, Henry D.	3rd Cpl.	B 16th SCVI		GE	11/30/64	Franklin, TN	KIA		ROH,16R,PP
Garrison, Isaac A.	Pvt.	H 18th SCVI	19	YK	01/31/62	At home	DOD		JR,DEM
Garrison, J.V.	Pvt.	B 5th SCVI		YK	09/30/64	Chaffin's Fm. VA	KIA		ROH,SA3
Garrison, John A.	4th Cpl.	B 16th SCVI		GE	11/30/64	Franklin, TN	KIA	(W. on some rolls)	ROH,16R
Garrison, John N.	Pvt.	E 17th SCVI	27	YK	01/18/64	At home	DOD	(Typhoid)	ROH,JR
Garrison, John W.	Pvt.	B 16th SCVI		GE	11/30/64	Franklin, TN	KIA		16R,PP
Garrison, S.C.	Pvt.	E 17th SCVI	22	YK	08/06/64	At home	DOD		ROH

SOUTH CAROLINA DEAD IN CSA SERVICE 1861-1865

G

NAME	RANK	C	REGIMENT	AGE	DS	DIED	WHERE	WHY	BURIED	SOURCES
Garry, John	Pvt.	D	1st SCV			03/26/64	Staunton, VA			ROH
Gartman, H.S.	Pvt.	K	13th SCVI		LS	10/06/64	Richmond, VA			ROH
Garvin, G.S.	Lt.		SCV			04/13/65	Thomasville, NC		Con. Cem. Thomassville, NC	PP
Garvin, J.T.	Pvt.	B	2nd SCVIRi		PS	09/17/62	Sharpsburg, MD	KIA		JR
Garvin, James L.	Pvt.	K	17th SCVI	39	YK	11/13/64	Petersburg, VA	DOW	Blandford Church Pbg., VA	ROH,BLC,PP
Garvin, L.A.	1st Lt.	G	12th SCVI		PS	05/05/64	Wilderness, VA	KIA		ROH,JR,BOS,R47
Garvin, T.F.	Pvt.	B	2nd SCVIRi		PS	09/17/62	Sharpsburg, MD	DOW	Shepherdstown WV C.C.	ROH,CV,CDC,R45
Garvin, Wilson	Pvt.	F	11th SCVI	24	BT	03/12/62	Gillisonville SC	DOD	(JR=1/25/62)	ROH,JR,HAG
Garvin,Jr., J.J.	Pvt.	F	17th SCVI	18	YK	07/25/64	At home	DOD		YMD,YEB
Gary,	Pvt.					04/30/64	Columbia, SC		Gary Fam. Gvyd. Laurens SC	NCC
Gary, D. (Gable?)	Pvt.	C	4th SCVI		AN	/ /	Richmond, VA		Oakwood C.#122,Row C,Div D	ROH,OWC
Gary, D.T.	Cpl.			27	LS	04/01/61	Columbia, SC	DOD		ROH
Gary, D.W.	Pvt.	F	Ham.Leg.		GE	06/15/61	Brentsville, VA	DOD		ROH
Gary, Duff E.	Pvt.	A	3rd SCVI	23	LS	04/30/61	Columbia, SC	DOD	Gary Burial Gds. LS Cty.	ROH,JR,LSC,KEB
Gary, J.	Pvt.	A	5th SCVI			09/18/64	Richmond, VA		Hollywood Cem.Rchmd. V143	HC
Gary, J.P.	Pvt.		Ham.Leg.			/ /	Richmond, VA		Oakwood C.#26,Row J,Div B	OWC
Gary, James A.	Pvt.	G	Ham.Leg.		SR	05/28/65	Newport News, VA		Greenlawn C. Newport News	PP
Gary, Jesse	Pvt.	B	3rd SCVI		NY	09/17/62	Sharpsburg, MD	DOW	Rose Hill C. Hagerstown MD	ROH,JR,SA2,BOD
Gary, John C.	3rd Cpl.	B	3rd SCVI		NY	/ /	At home	DOD		ANY,KEB,SA2
Gary, John H.	Cpt.	A	15th SCVIB			08/17/63	Bty. Wagner, SC	DOW	(Wdd 8/12/63) UD1	ROH,HAG,CDC,R4
Gary, Samuel Jefferson	Pvt.	D	Ham.Leg.		PS	06/07/62	Richmond, VA	DOW	(Wdd 7 Pines, CNM=H,18th)	ROH,GRS,CNM
Gary, Thomas N.	Lt.				PS	07/02/65	Charleston, SC		Keeowee, SC	PCS
Gary, William G.	Pvt.	I	16th SCVI		GE	07/23/64	Atlanta, GA	KIA		ROH,16R
Gaskin, John	Pvt.	G	2nd SCVI		KW	07/02/63	Gettysburg, PA	KIA		ROH,JR,SA2,KEB
Gaskin, Ransom	Pvt.	D	7th SCVIBn	31	KW	07/11/63	Bty. Wagner, SC	KIA		ROH,JR,HIC,HAG
Gaskins, A.M.	Pvt.	G	15th SCVI	20	WG	05/06/64	Wilderness, VA	KIA	Fredericksburg C.C. R6S13	ROH,JR,FBG,HOW
Gaskins, G.W.	Pvt.	G	7th SCVIBn	22	KW	05/16/64	Drury's Bluff VA	KIA		ROH,JR,HIC,HAG
Gaskins, J.J.	Pvt.	G	15th SCVI		WG	/ /		DOD		JR,KEB
Gaskins, T.J.	Pvt.				WG	/ /		DOD	(1861)	HOW
Gaskins, Thomas	Pvt.	K	1st SCVIG		CN	06/27/62	Gaines' Mill, VA	KIA		ROH,JR,SA1
Gasque, Alexander	Pvt.	M	10th SCVI		HY	/ /	Tazewell, KY	DOD	(Left behind)	RAS
Gasque, C. Marion	2nd Sgt.	I	21st SCVI		MN	05/22/64	Drury's Bluff VA	DOW	(Wdd 5/20,wdd @ Morris I.)	ROH,HMC,HAG
Gasque, Eli	Pvt.	D	10th SCVI		MN	09/28/62	In camp	DOD	(JR=Co.E, 21st SCVI)	JR,RAS,HMC
Gasque, Erwin A.	Pvt.	I	21st SCVI	18	MN	06/05/64	Cold Harbor, VA	KIA		ROH,JR,HMC,HAG
Gasque, G.W.	Pvt.	A	2nd SCVI		RD	03/15/64	At home	DOW	(Wdd @ Sharpsburg)	SA2,KEB
Gasque, Henry	Pvt.	L	21st SCVI	17	MN	09/26/62	Charleston, SC	DOD	(JR=Co.E & 9/29/63)	ROH,JR,HMC,HAG
Gasque, J.H.	Pvt.	C	2nd SC Mil		MN	02/17/65	Columbia, SC	DOD		ROH,PP
Gasque, Samuel	Pvt.	A	26th SCVI	25	HY	06/05/62	Charleston, SC	DOD		ROH,JR
Gasque, Samuel Oliver	Pvt.	L	21st SCVI	24	MN	03/28/65	Elmira, NY	DIP	Woodlawn N.C.#2503 Elmira	ROH,FPH,P5,HAG
Gasque, Thomas	Pvt.	H	Orr's Ri.		MN	09/11/62	Washington, DC	DOW	Congressional Cem. 64R85CC	JR,FPH,HMC,PP
Gassaway, A.J.	Pvt.				PS	/ /	Richmond, VA		Oakwood C.#19,Row N,Div C	OWC
Gassaway, Benjamin F.	Pvt.	G	Orr's Ri.		AE	07/09/62	Winder H. Rchmd	DOW	(Wdd @ Gaines' Mill 6/27)	ROH,JR,CDC
Gassaway, Charles	Pvt.	A	P.S.S.			/ /		KIA		JR
Gassaway, W.W.	Pvt.	F	Orr's Ri.		PS	09/26/63	Camp Gregg, VA	DOD	(Fredericksburg)	JR,CDC
Gassaway, William	Pvt.	G	19th SCVI		AE	/ /	Corinth, MS	DOD		HOL
Gaston, Alexander Wylie	Pvt.	A	6th SCVI	22	CR	11/15/63	LaGrange, GA	DOD	Con. Cem. LaGrange, GA	ROH,GLS,HHC,TO
Gaston, Isaac N.	Pvt.	F	6th SCVI			/ /				CB
Gaston, James H.	Pvt.	B	13th SCVI		SG	08/29/62	2nd Manassas, VA	KIA	JR=W.H. & DOW 9/5/62)	HOS,JR
Gaston, Joel R. Poinsett	Pvt.			18		05/05/65	Salisbury, NC	DOD	(Measles)	UD3
Gaston, John Harrison	Pvt.	A	6th SCVI	26	CR	06/17/62	7 Pines, VA	DOW	Oakwood C.#65,Row O,Div B	ROH,OWC,HHC,GL
Gaston, John J.	Pvt.	K	18th SCVI	22	YK	06/04/62	At home	DOD	Buffalo B.C. Cherokee, SC	ROH,JR,TCC

G

SOUTH CAROLINA DEAD IN CSA SERVICE 1861-1865

NAME	RANK	C	REGIMENT	AGE	DS	DIED	WHERE	WHY	BURIED	SOURCES
Gaston, Joseph Lucius	Cpt.	F	6th SCVI	32	CR	05/31/62	7 Pines, VA	KIA (JR=Co.E)	HHC	ROH,JR,HCD,WDB
Gaston, Robert L.	Pvt.	K	18th SCVI	20	YK	02/15/62	Charleston, SC	DOD	Buffalo B.C. Cherokee Cty.	ROH,JR,TCC
Gaston, W.H.	Cpl.	F	Orr's Ri.		PS	09/10/62	2nd Manassas, VA	DOW (JR=W.J.)		JR
Gaston, William H.	Pvt.	F	6th SCVI		CR	05/31/62	7 Pines, VA	KIA		JR,WDB,CDC,HHC
Gatch, Charles W.	Pvt.	B	3rd SCVC	19	CO	01/20/65	Ferguson's Br.SC	KIA		ROH
Gates, Charles			CS Navy			01/31/65	Richmond, VA			ROH
Gates, Daniel	Pvt.	F	11th SCVI	32	BT	02/15/62	Hardeeville, SC	DOD		ROH
Gates, J.T.G.	Pvt.	A	5th SCVC	19	OG	06/12/64	Trevillian Stn.	KIA (JR=6/11/64)		ROH,JR,CDC
Gates, L.	Pvt.	F	7th SCVI		ED	07/14/64	Richmond, VA		Hollywood Cem.Rchmd. U153	ROH,HC
Gates, R.	Pvt.	E	13th SCVI		SG	06/30/62	Frayser's Farm	KIA		ROH
Gates, William	Pvt.		3rd SCVABn			07/28/62	Charleston, SC	DOD	Magnolia Cem. Charleston	ROH,JR,MAG
Gatlin, J.B.	Sgt.	D	8th SCVI		CD	08/29/62	Richmond, VA	DOD (Typhoid)		JR,KEB
Gattin, Richard	Pvt.	I	18th SCVI	34	DN	02/04/62	Richmond, VA	DOD		ROH,JR
Gaulden, William	Pvt.	H	12th SCVI	21	YK	02/03/62	At home	DOD		JR,DEM,CWC
Gaunt, A.R.	Pvt.	I	17th SCVI		LR	07/30/64	Crater, Pbg., VA	KIA		BLM
Gaunt, J.P.	Pvt.	F	P.S.S.			/ /		DOD		JR
Gaunter, Joseph			CS Navy			04/16/65	Richmond, VA			ROH
Gauntt, Thomas J.	Pvt.	F	20th SCVI		NY	10/19/64	Fisher's Hill VA	KIA (KEB=Gaunt, Jeff)		NCC,ANY,KEB
Gause, J.W.	Pvt.	G	10th SCVI		HY	/ /		DOD		RAS
Gause, M.F.	Sgt.	G	10th SCVI		HY	11/15/63	Chattanooga, TN	DOD (Date approx)		RAS
Gausey, James	Pvt.	F	P.S.S.		LN	05/31/62	7 Pines, VA	KIA		JR,CDC
Gay, C. Butler	Pvt.	G	7th SCVIBn	17	KW	05/19/64	Drury's Bluff VA	DOW		ROH,HIC,HAG
Gay, P.W.	Pvt.	F	21st SCVI		MO	02/15/65	Pt. Lookout, MD	DIP	C.C. Pt. Lookout, MD	ROH,FPH,P5,HAG
Gayle, James Robert	Sgt.	E	7th SCVIBn		SR	10/28/64	At home	DOD		ROH
Geary, James	Pvt.	G	Ham.Leg.			05/25/65	Newport News, VA	DIP	Newport News Cem. #67	P6
Geddings, Abraham W.	Pvt.	E	1st SCVIR		CN	09/08/63	Ft. Moultrie, SC	KIA (Ammo chest explosion)		ROH,SA1,CDC
Gee, A.J.	Pvt.	H	P.S.S.		SG	07/19/64	Richmond, VA	DOD	Hollywood Cem.Rchmd. U473	ROH,JR,HC,HOS
Gee, L.N.	Pvt.	K	Orr's Ri.		SG	/ /	Richmond, VA		Oakwood C.#106,Row N,Div B	ROH,OWC
Gee, Peterson M.	Pvt.	B	15th SCVI		UN	/ /		DOD		JR,KEB
Gee, Samuel	Pvt.	E	8th SCVI		CL	07/02/63	Gettysburg, VA	KIA		ROH,JR,CDC,GDR
Gee, Spirus W.	1st Cpl.		PeeDee LA		DN	07/02/63	Gettysburg, PA	KIA		PDL,GDR
Geer, J.M.	Pvt.	K	Orr's Ri.		AN	02/03/63	Richmond, VA	DOD		JR
Geer, Levi N.	4th Sgt.	K	Orr's Ri.	33	AN	07/17/62	Richmond, VA	DOD (JR=6/17/62)		ROH,JR,CDC
Geer, W.F.	Pvt.	K	Orr's Ri.		AN	06/24/62	Richmond, VA	DOD		JR
Geiger, G. Martin	Pvt.	C	20th SCVI	24	LN	07/15/62	At home	DOD		ROH,KEB
Geiger, Jacob G.	Pvt.	A	15th SCVI		LN	06/15/65	(On Rd.home/POW)	DOD	Sandy Run Luth. Church LN	ROH,KEB,LGS
Geiger, Jesse	Pvt.	C	20th SCVI	32	LN	08/14/62	At home	DOD		ROH,KEB
Geiger, Joseph	Pvt.	E	7th SCVI		ED	/ /		DOD		HOE,KEB,UD3
Geiger, W.D.	Pvt.	H	3rd SCVI		LN	12/13/62	Fredericksburg	KIA		ROH,JR,KEB,SA2
Gelling, George Brown	2nd Lt.	C	27th SCVI	28	CN	06/16/64	Hare's Hill, VA	KIA 1st P.C.(Scotch) Charlstn.		JR
Gelmer, John W.	Pvt.	A	2nd SCVIRi		AE	06/29/62	Savage Stn., VA	KIA (JR=Gaines' Mill 6/27/62)		ROH,JR,CDC,CNM
Gemmell, William	Pvt.	K	6th SCVC	40	CD	06/12/64	Trevillian Stn.	KIA		ROH
Genobles, Hiram	Pvt.	C	13th SCVI		SG	07/13/62	Richmond, VA	DOD (Typhoid)		ROH,JR
Genobles, Rufus B.	Pvt.	G	20th SCVI		SR	09/08/64	Elmira, NY	DIP	Woodlawn N.C.#215 Elmira	FPH,P5,P120,P113
Gent, Jackson	Pvt.	D	1st SCVIH		LR	02/15/63	Richmond, VA	DOD (Date Approx)		SA1
Gentry, D.O.	Pvt.	F	24th SCVI		AN	09/20/63	Chickamauga, GA	KIA		ROH,JR,HOL,CDC
Gentry, James M.	Pvt.	L	Orr's Ri.		AN	06/29/62	Gaines' Mill, VA	DOW		JR,CDC
Gentry, John L.	4th Sgt.	K	3rd SCVI		SG	06/29/62	Savage Stn., VA	KIA		ROH,JR,SA2,KEB
Gentry, M.B.	Pvt.	K	7th SCVI		ED	07/02/63	Gettysburg, PA	KIA		ROH,CDC,GDR
Gentry, Patrick C.	Pvt.	A	Hol.Leg.	19	SG	11/14/62	Harrisonburg, VA	DOW (PP=11/17/62)		ROH,JR,HOS,PP
Gentry, William	Pvt.	C	4th Res Bn			10/25/64	Charleston, SC	DOD	Magnolia Cem. Charleston	ROH,MAG,CDC

SOUTH CAROLINA DEAD IN CSA SERVICE 1861-1865

NAME	RANK	C REGIMENT	AGE	DS	DIED	WHERE	WHY	BURIED	SOURCES
Gentry, William	Pvt.	D 19th SCVI	28	ED	11/30/64	Franklin, TN	KIA		HOE,UD3
George, Alexander B.	Pvt.	K 11th SCVI		CO	12/27/61	Hardeeville, SC	DOD		ROH,JR,HAG
George, B.F.	Pvt.	B 18th SCVI	25	UN	07/30/64	Petersburg, VA	KIA		ROH
George, David	Pvt.			LN	/ /				ROH
George, E.J.	Pvt.				07/11/64			Magnolia Cem. Charleston	MAG
George, J. Willis	Pvt.	F Orr's Ri.		PS	05/04/63	Richmond, VA	dod	Oakwood C.#25,Row 25,Div D	ROH,JR,OWC
George, Jacob L.	Pvt.	E 24th SCVI	25	CO	12/24/64	Camp Douglas, IL	DIP	Oak Woods Cem., Chicago IL	ROH,FPH,P5,CDC
George, James	Pvt.	C 24th SCVI		CO	09/20/63	Chickamauga, GA	KIA		ROH,JR,CDC,TEB
George, James C.	Pvt.	C 3rd SCVI	28	LN	10/15/63	Missionary Ridge	MUR	(See page 291, KEB)	ROH,KEB,SA2
George, Jefferson	Pvt.	I 13th SCVI	34	SG	08/29/62	2nd Manassas, VA	KIA	(JR=DOW 7/10/62)	ROH,JR,HOS
George, Richard	Pvt.	E 24th SCVI	21	CO	10/23/63	Ins. H. Atlanta	DOW	Oakland C. Atlanta R13#3	ROH,BGA
George, Thomas	Pvt.		18	LN	/ /	Warrenton, VA	DOW	(Wdd @ 2nd Manassas)	CDC
George, W.J.	Pvt.	H 23rd SCVI		MN	/ /	Virginia	DOD	(Left sick, presumed dead)	HMC
George, William	Pvt.	B 18th SCVI	24	UN	07/09/62	Charleston, SC	DOD	El Bethel Cem. Union Cty.	ROH,JR,UNC
Gerald, Berry	Pvt.	7th SCVI			07/13/61	Richmond, VA	DOD	Hollywood Cem.Rchmd. K108	ROH,HC
Gerald, C.A.	Pvt.	K 26th SCVI			/ /	Richmond, VA		Oakwood C.#78,Row C,Div G	OWC
Gerald, M.	Pvt.	K 15th SCVI			/ /		DOW		JR
Gerald, Reuben L.	1st Sgt.	E 2nd SCVI		KW	09/20/63	Chickamauga, GA	KIA		ROH,JR,SA2,HIC
Gerald, S.W.	Pvt.	D 10th SCVI		MN	/ /	Holly Springs MS	DOD		RAS,HMC,PP
Gerald, W.H.	Pvt.	B 10th SCVI		HY	/ /		DOD		RAS
Gerald, William	Sgt.	D 1st SCVC		CR	07/03/63	Gettysburg, PA	KIA		HHC
Gerken, Benjamin R.	Pvt.	I 1st SCVIG		CN	07/03/62	Gaines' Mill, VA	DOW		SA1
German, E.	Pvt.	I 22nd SCVI		OG	09/14/62	South Mtn., MD	KIA		ROH
German, William	Pvt.	F 7th SCVI	23	ED	04/15/63	Richmond, VA	DOD	(Wdd @ Sharpsburg)	ROH,HOE,KEB
Gernigham, Daniel F.	Pvt.	D 7th SCV	22		08/12/62	Petersburg, VA			PP
Gerrald, Henry	Pvt.	K 26th SCVI		HY	02/21/65	Greensboro, NC			PP
Gerrald, Levi	Pvt.	B 18th SCVAB		CN	08/15/63	Bty. Wagner, SC	DOW	(Wdd 8/11/63)	ROH,CDC
Gerrald, S.	Pvt.	K 26th SCVI	25	HY	08/02/64	Petersburg, VA			PP
Gerrick, Joseph	Pvt.	H 6th SCVI		OG	/ /	Richmond, VA			ROH
Getsinger, Benjamin R.	Pvt.	I 1st SCVIG		CN	11/16/63	Charleston, SC	DOD	1st Baptist C. Charleston	SA1,MAG
Getstrap, L.T.	Pvt.	G 6th SCVI			/ /			Kitrell Spgs, NC Con. Cem.	WAT
Gettis, F.	Pvt.	D Orr's Ri.		AN	06/20/62		DOD		ROH
Gettys, Ebenezer	Pvt.	H 12th SCVI	42	YK	06/02/64	Richmond, VA	DOW	(Wdd 5/12/64)	ROH,CWC,YEB
Gholson, James D.	Pvt.	F 25th SSCVI		OG	01/16/65	Ft. Fisher, NC	DOW	(HAG=Golson)	ROH,HAG
Gholson, James P.	Pvt.	I 2nd SCVA		OG	01/22/65	Moorehead City	DOD	(EDR=Golson)	ROH,EDR
Gholson, John W.	Pvt.	I 2nd SCVA	32	OG	04/22/65	Greensboro, NC	DOD	(EDR=Golson)	ROH,EDR
Gibbes, Benjamin Taylor	2nd Lt.	D 16th SCVI	17	GE	03/14/64	Columbia, SC	DOD	Trinity Ch. Columbia, SC	ROH,MP,16R,PP
Gibbes, Isaac Ball	Pvt.	B 25th SCVI	24	CN	08/21/64	Weldon RR Pbg.VA	DOW	St. Philips Ch. Charleston	ROH,RCD,WLI,HA
Gibbes, William Allston	Cpt.	D 16th SCVI		GE	/ /	Marietta, GA	DOD	(1863)	16R
Gibbons, John D.					06/15/64				ROH
Gibbons, Thomas H.	Pvt.	K 6th SCVI	28	WG	01/05/64	Nashville, TN	DIP	(Wdd & POW @ L.O. Mtn, GA)	ROH,P12,HOW,3R
Gibbs, George F.	Pvt.	Gregg's LA			04/12/65	Hart's Island SC	DIP	Cypress Hills N.C.#2503 NY	FPH,P79
Gibson,	Pvt.	B 2nd SCVC			08/01/63	Culpepper, VA	KIA		AOA
Gibson, Aaron C.	Pvt.	F 26th SCVI			04/28/65	Pt. Lookout, MD	DIP		ROH,P12,P114
Gibson, Absalom	4th Cpl.	E Orr's Ri.	22	PS	06/22/64	Wilcox Farm, VA	KIA		ROH
Gibson, Allen	Pvt.			LN	/ /				ROH
Gibson, Allen	Pvt.	D 8th SCVI		CD	06/16/61	At home	DOD	(Typhoid)	JR,KEB
Gibson, Andrew H.	Pvt.	F 21st SCVI		MO	05/16/64	Drury's Bluff VA	KIA		ROH,JR,HOM,HAG
Gibson, D.B.	Pvt.	D 16th SCVI		GE	07/19/62	Adams Run, SC	DOD	(Daniel R.?)	PP
Gibson, D.C.	Pvt.	C 9th SCVIH		CO	09/15/61	Hilton Head, SC	DOD	(PP=D.O.)	ROH,PP
Gibson, E.	Pvt.	K 13th SCVI		LN	06/17/62	Richmond, VA	DOD		ROH

G

SOUTH CAROLINA DEAD IN CSA SERVICE 1861-1865

NAME	RANK	C REGIMENT	AGE	DS	DIED	WHERE	WHY	BURIED	SOURCES
Gibson, Elias	Pvt.	I 5th SCRes	36	AE	01/04/63	Jacksonboro, SC	DOD		ROH
Gibson, Franklin A.	Cpl.	A 15th SCVI		RD	06/18/64	Petersburg, VA	KIA	Elmwood Cem. Columbia, SC	MP,ROH,KEB,PP
Gibson, Hosiah	Pvt.	B 2nd SCVI	23	GE	08/15/61	Gordonsville, VA	DOD		ROH
Gibson, J.H.	Pvt.	I P.S.S.			/ /		DOD		JR
Gibson, J.M.	1st Cpl.	F 21st SCVI		MO	05/09/64	Swift Creek, VA	KIA		ROH,HOM,HAG
Gibson, J.M.	Pvt.	D 21st SCVI			05/09/64	Swift Creek, VA	KIA		JR
Gibson, J.W.	Pvt.	I 1st SCVA		OG	06/16/62	Secessionville	KIA		ROH,JR,CDC,PP
Gibson, James	Pvt.	I 4th SCVI		PS	02/21/62	Virginia	DOD		ROH,SA2
Gibson, James Allen	Pvt.	H 3rd SCVI		LN	11/18/63	Knoxville, TN	KIA		ROH,SA2,KEB
Gibson, James H.	Pvt.	D 17th SCVI	30	CR	06/18/63	Jackson, MS	DOW		ROH,JR,HHC,CB
Gibson, John F.	Pvt.	D 26th SCVI		MO	09/15/64	Petersburg, VA	DOW (Wdd 8/26/64)		ROH,HOM
Gibson, John R.	Pvt.	B 4th SCVC		CR	06/11/64	Trevillian Stn.	KIA		ROH,CDC,HHC,CB
Gibson, John S.	Pvt.	L 21st SCVI	19	MN	05/10/65	Pt. Lookout, MD	DIP	C.C. Pt. Lookout, MD	ROH,FPH,P6,HAG
Gibson, Josephus W.	Pvt.	B 2nd SCVI		GE	09/16/61	Culpepper, VA	DOD	Fairview Cem. Culpepper VA	ROH,SA2,KEB
Gibson, Meredith	Pvt.	B 3rd SCVI		NY	10/06/63	Chickamauga, GA	DOW	Con. Cem. Marietta, GA	ROH,JR,SA2,ANY
Gibson, Nathan W.	Pvt.	F 26th SCVI		CD	04/29/65	Pt. Lookout, MD	DIP	C.C. Pt. Lookout, MD	FPH,P6,P114
Gibson, O.L.	Pvt.	B 11th SCVI		CO	01/15/62	South Carolina	DOD		ROH,HAG
Gibson, Oscar E.	Pvt.	L 21st SCVI		MN	06/02/66	At home	DOW (Wdd & POW @ Ft. Fisher)		ROH,HMC,HAG,P114
Gibson, P.F. (P.T.?)	Pvt.	H 26th SCVI		SR	08/11/63	Mobile, AL	DOD	Magnolia Cem. Mobile, AL	JR,TOD
Gibson, Robert W.	Pvt.	L 21st SCVI	23	MN	10/17/64	Baltimore, MD	DOW	Loudon Pk. C. A-24 Balto.	ROH,FPH,P1,HAG
Gibson, S.D.	Pvt.	C 7th SCVIBn	54	KW	11/11/63	Charleston, SC	DOD	Magnolia Cem. Charleston	ROH,MAG,HAG
Gibson, Samuel K.	Pvt.	B 2nd SCVI	25	GE	08/15/61	Orange C.H., VA	DOD		ROH,SA2,KEB
Gibson, Thomas	Pvt.	E Orr's Ri.	24	PS	03/01/62	Sullivans I., SC	DOD		ROH
Gibson, W.S.	Pvt.	Ham.Leg.			07/06/64	Richmond, VA		Hollywood Cem.Rchmd. U196	ROH,HC
Gibson, Walter Ewing	Pvt.	A 25th SCVI		CN	10/31/63	Ft. Sumter, SC	KIA	St.Phillips Ch. Charleston	ROH,JR,DOC,HAG
Gibson, Wiley	Pvt.	I 2nd SCVA.	35	OG	06/16/62	Secessionville	KIA (Prob Gibson, W.)		ROH
Gibson, William	Cpl.	I 5th SCRes	47	AE	12/04/62	At home	DOD		ROH
Gibson, William	Pvt.	M 7th SCVI		ED	09/20/63	Chickamauga, GA	KIA	Con. Cem. Marietta, GA	ROH,JR,CCM,HOE
Gibson, William L.	Pvt.	G 8th SCVI		MO	10/11/61	Richmond, VA	DOD	Oakwood C.#87,Row A,Div A	ROH,JR,HOM,OWC
Gibson, William W.	Pvt.	B 3rd SCVI		NY	05/06/64	Wilderness, VA	KIA		ROH,JR,SA2,ANY
Gibson, Y.W.	Pvt.	A Orr's Ri.		AN	04/06/62	Pickens, SC	MUR		JR
Gilbert, Gibson	Pvt.	E 13th SCVI		SG	09/15/62	At home	DOD (Typhoid)		JR
Gilbert, H.	Pvt.	I 7th SCVI		ED	10/09/62	Brucetown, VA		Stonewall Cem. Winchester	WIN
Gilbert, H.E.	Pvt.	D 3rd SCVI		SG	09/13/62	Maryland Hts. MD	KIA		ROH,JR,SA2,CDC
Gilbert, J.E.T.	1st Sgt.	Wash. Arty			01/15/63	Culpepper, VA	ACD (Accidentaly shot in camp)		JR
Gilbert, John	Pvt.	K 2nd SCVIRi	18	AN	11/08/62	Winchester, VA	DOD	Stonewall Cem. Winchester	ROH,WIN
Gilbert, P.M.	Pvt.	K 5th SCVI		SG	05/10/62	Richmond, VA	DOD	Oakwood C.#103,Row K,Div A	ROH,JR,SA3,OWC
Gilbert, R.W.	Sgt.	K 22nd SCVI		PS	07/21/62	At home	DOD		ROH,JR
Gilbert, Reuben H.	Pvt.	K 2nd SCVIRi	17	AN	12/28/62	Richmond, VA	DOD		ROH
Gilbert, William	Pvt.	H Orr's Ri.		MN	05/06/64	Wilderness, VA	KIA		ROH,JR,HMC
Gilbert, Zebean	Pvt.	E 13th SCVI		SG	09/26/61		DOD		HOS
Gilder, Gifford A.	Pvt.	B 14th SCVI	18	ED	08/02/63	Davids Island NY	DOW	Cypress Hills N.C.#731 NY	ROH,JR,FPH,P1,P6
Giles, Andrew J.	Sgt.	B 6th SCVC		ED	07/01/64	Charlottesville	DOW	Univ. Cem. Charlottesville	ROH,HOE,ACH,UD3
Giles, John B.	Pvt.	L 10th SCVI		MN	04/23/63	Rome, GA	DOD	Myrtle Hill Cem. Rome, GA	ROH,JR,RAS,BGA
Giles, J.R.R.	Colonel	5th SCVI	24	UN	05/31/62	7 Pines, VA	KIA		ROH,SA3,NHU,UD1
Giles, Leonard D.	Pvt.	I 14th SCVI	30	AE	06/15/64	Camp Douglas, IL	DIP		ROH,HOL
Giles, Robert	Pvt.	E 13th SCVI		SG	06/26/62	Winder H. Rchmd	DOD (Typhoid)		JR
Giles, Thomas	Pvt.	C 5th SCVI		SG	08/18/61	Charlottesville	DOD	Univ. Cem. Charlottesville	SA3,ACH
Giles, W.H.	2nd Lt.	L 10th SCVI		MN	07/28/64	Atlanta, GA	KIA		ROH,RAS
Gilhooly, P.	Pvt.	B 1st SCVIBn		CN	06/16/62	Secessionville	DOW		ROH,CDC,PP
Gill, C.	Pvt.	1st SCVC			01/09/65	Charleston, SC	DOD	Magnolia Cem. Charleston	ROH,MAG

SOUTH CAROLINA DEAD IN CSA SERVICE 1861-1865

G

NAME	RANK	C	REGIMENT	AGE	DS	DIED	WHERE	WHY	BURIED	SOURCES
Gill, Charles	Pvt.	I	1st SCVC	30	CO	02/15/64	Columbia, SC	DOD		ROH
Gill, G.W.	Pvt.		20th SCVI			/ /			Charlestown, W.VA	ROH
Gill, J.W.	Pvt.	K	1st SCVIR		CN	12/09/63		DOD		SA1
Gill, S.H.	Pvt.	C	27th SCVI	27	YK	04/15/63	Bermuda Hundred	DOD	(HAG=E.H.)	JR,HAG,YEB
Gill, Samuel K.	Pvt.		SC Arty		YK	/ /	Charleston, SC	DOD		YEB
Gill, W.	Pvt.	A	5th SCVI		LR	12/07/62	Lynchburg, VA	DOD	Lynchburg CSA Cem. #10 R3	SA3,LAN,BBW
Gillam, James M.	Pvt.	F	2nd SCVI	26	AE	10/15/64	Cedar Creek, VA	MIA	(MIA, assumed dead)	ROH,KEB,SA2
Gillam, Newton F.	1st Sgt.	G	Hol.Leg.	18	NY	12/14/62	Kinston, NC	KIA	(ANY= Pvt.)	ROH,ANY,PP
Gillard, C.L.	Pvt.		2nd SCResB			01/03/64				PP
Gillebeau, Peter D.	Pvt.	C	7th SCVI		AE	06/17/63	Gordonsville, VA	DOD	Gordonsville, VA C.C.	ROH,KEB,GOR
Gillespie, A.	Pvt.	E	20th SCVI		AE	12/25/64	Richmond, VA		Hollywood Cem.Rchmd. W249	ROH,HC,KEB
Gillespie, B.J.	Pvt.	G	P.S.S.	17	YK	10/01/62	Culpepper, VA	DOD	Fairview Cem. Culpepper VA	JR,CGH,YEB
Gillespie, M.	Pvt.	B	Ham.Leg.			08/30/62	2nd Manassas, VA	KIA		ROH,JR,CDC
Gillespie, Samuel	Pvt.	G	8th SCV		MO	/ /	At home		(DIS 1861, S.J. in KEB?)	UD2
Gillespie, Thomas J.	Pvt.	H	24th SCVI	27	CR	03/26/63	McPhersonville	DOD		ROH,HHC,CB
Gillespie, W.L.	Pvt.	C	1st SCVC			06/24/64	Richmond, VA		Hollywood Cem.Rchmd. U326	HC
Gilliam, J.J.	Pvt.	G	1st SCVIH		BL	11/15/62	Richmond, VA	DOD	Oakwood C.#99,Row L,Div B	ROH,SA1,OWC
Gilliam, Robert W.	3rd Lt.	K	5th SCVC	36	UN	07/30/64	Malone Farm, VA	KIA	Fishdam C. Santuc, SC	ROH,UNC,R43,UD
Gilliam, Tignal	Pvt.	I	17th SCVI			09/17/62	Sharpsburg, MD	KIA	(JR=South Mtn. 9/14/62)	JR,LAN
Gilliland, Abner	Pvt.	C	18th SCVI	37	UN	06/23/65	Davids Island NY	DIP	Cypress Hills N.C.#3042 NY	ROH,FPH,P12
Gilliland, E.E.	Pvt.	D	5th SCVC		CN	/ /		DOD		ROH
Gilliland, Edward B.	Pvt.	B	25th SCVI	21	CN	06/18/64	Washington, GA	ACD	2nd P.C.(Flynn's) Cha'ston	ROH,MAG,HAG,WL
Gilliland, William M.	Pvt.	E	3rd SCVIBn		LS	03/24/65	Ft. Delaware, DE	DIP	(Reported buried in MD)	ROH,FPH,P5,GEC
Gillis, Joseph	Pvt.	A	24th SCVI	28	CN	08/05/64	Atlanta, GA	KIA		EJM
Gillroach, P.	Pvt.	B	1st SCVIBn			06/24/62	Secessionville	DOW		JR
Gillstrap, Elias	Sgt.	F	22nd SCVI		PS	08/27/64	(Wdd @ Crater)	DOW	Hollywood Cem.Rchmd. V291	ROH,JR,HC,BLM
Gillstrap, L.J.	Pvt.	G	6th SCVC	30	PS	09/27/64	Kitrell Spgs. NC	DOW	Kitrell Spgs., NC Con.Cem.	ROH,JR,CV,PP
Gilmer, Crawford L.	Pvt.	E	4th SCVIBn	22	AN	07/03/62	7 Pines, VA	DOW		ROH,SA2
Gilmer, H.M.	Pvt.	B	8th SCVI			/ /	Chattanooga, TN	DOD	City C. Chattanooga, TN	TOD
Gilmer, Robert	Pvt.		1st SC Mil			01/07/65	Charleston, SC	DOD	Magnolia Cem. Charleston	ROH,MAG
Gilmer, Robert H.	Pvt.	A	2nd SCVIRi			08/30/62	2nd Manassas, VA	KIA		ROH,JR,CDC
Gilmer, Robert P.	Pvt.	F	2nd SCVI		AN	/ /	Culpepper, VA	DOD	(SA2= DIS unfit 4/16/63)	H2,SA2,KEB
Gilmer, S.	Pvt.	F	Hol.Leg.		AE	08/31/62	2nd Manassas, VA	DOW		ROH,JR
Gilmer, William J.G.	Pvt.	F	2nd SCVI		AE	03/01/65	Camp Chase, OH	DIP	C.C.#1683 Columbus, OH	ROH,FPH,P6,SA2
Gilmore, E.J.	Pvt.	D	12th SCVI		RD	06/16/63	Richmond, VA	DOW	Oakwood C.#149,Row L,Div A	ROH,JR,OWC
Gilmore, J.J.	Pvt.	G	18th SCVI		UN	04/06/62	Charleston, SC	DOD		JR
Gilmore, John W.	Pvt.	B	7th SCVI		AE	06/29/62	Gaines' Mill, VA	DOW		JR,KEB
Gilmore, Wheeler	Pvt.	E	4th SCVIBn		AN	/ /	7 Pines, VA	DOW	(? C.L. Gilmer)	HOF
Gilreath, Lawrence P.	Pvt.	B	2nd SCVI	23	GE	10/02/63	Gettysburg, PA	DOW	Springwood Cem. GE Cty.	ROH,JR,GDR,SA2
Gilreath, S.C.	Pvt.	G	16th SCVI		GE	07/22/64	Atlanta, GA	KIA		ROH
Gilstrap, J.W.	Pvt.	I	P.S.S.			/ /		KIA		JR
Gilstrap, John	Pvt.	I	P.S.S.		PS	05/31/62	7 Pines, VA	KIA		ROH
Ginn, Andrew C.	Pvt.	E	11th SCVI	21	BT	06/19/64	Petersburg, VA	KIA	(ROH=Grines, A.C.)	ROH,HAG
Ginn, J.G.	Pvt.		Ward's LA	26	GN	09/01/63	Georgetown, SC	DOD		PP,CDC
Ginn, S.A.	Pvt.	G	11th SCVI		CN	08/23/64	Ream's Stn., VA	KIA		JR
Ginnings, W.	Pvt.	H	Orr's Ri.		SG	10/28/63	Lookout Valley	KIA		ROH
Gissendanner, James D.	Pvt.	A	5th SCVC	30	OG	06/12/64	Trevillian Stn.	KIA	(ROH=Gessundammer)	ROH,JR,CDC
Gist, Gabriel G.	Pvt.	G	15th SCVI		WG	07/02/63	Gettysburg, PA	KIA	(HOW= J.G.) KEB	ROH,JR,HOW,GDR
Gist, James D.	Cpt.		ADC/G.Gist	30	UN	08/24/63	Morton, MS	DOD	Fairforest P.C. Union Cty.	ROH,JR,UNC,SRG
Gist, States Rights	Brig. Gen.			33	UN	11/30/64	Franklin, TN	KIA	Trinity Ch. Columbia, SC	ROH,MP,PP
Gist, William M.	Major		15th SCVI	23	UN	11/18/63	Knoxville, TN	KIA		ROH,KEB

G

SOUTH CAROLINA DEAD IN CSA SERVICE 1861-1865

NAME	RANK	C	REGIMENT	AGE	DS	DIED	WHERE	WHY	BURIED	SOURCES
Gitsinger, Benjamin R.	Pvt.	1	1st SCV		CN	11/16/63		DOD	1st B.C. Charleston, SC	RCD
Givens, Francis	Pvt.	G	5th SCV		YK	07/05/62	Columbia, SC	DOD		JR,YEB
Givin, Josiah	Pvt.	G	27th SCVI		SG	/ /	Pt. Lookout, MD	DIP	(POW Weldon RR)	HOS,HAG,P125
Gladden, A. Jesse	Pvt.	G	6th SCVI	27	CR	10/09/61	Fairfax Stn., VA	DOD	(HHC=W.E.)	ROH,HHC
Gladden, J. Edward	Pvt.	B	4th SCVC		CR	03/12/65	North Carolina	DOD	(On way home from Appomtx)	CB,HMC
Gladden, Lee T.	Pvt.	F	3rd SCVIBn	35	RD	09/28/62	Winchester, VA			ROH,KEB
Gladden, Silas	Pvt.	B	7th SCVIBn		FD	02/15/65	Elmira, NY	DIP	Woodlawn N.C.#2176 Elmira	FPH,HAG,P1,P5
Gladden, T.C.	Cpl.	C	17th SCVI		YK	09/14/62	South Mtn., MD	KIA		JR
Gladden, T.L.	Pvt.	B	4th SCV		CR	06/13/64	Charlottesville	DOW	Univ. Cem. Charlottesville	ACH,CB
Gladden, W.A.	Pvt.	E	15th SCVI		FD	11/11/64	Camp Chase, OH	DIP	C.C.#449 Columbus, OH	FPH,P23,KEB
Gladden, William T.	Pvt.	D	17th SCVI		CR	07/14/65	At home	DOD	(Scurvy from Elmira)	ROH,P65
Gladding, T.	Pvt.	E	15th SCVI		FD	07/03/63	Gettysburg, PA	KIA	Gettysburg, PA	WV
Gladney, Amos J.	Pvt.	E	15th SCVI	17	FD	07/02/63	Gettysburg, PA	KIA		ROH,JR,GDR,KEB
Gladney, J.W.	1st Lt.	G	3rd SCVIBn		FD	06/24/62		DOD		KEB,R45
Gladney, John R.	Pvt.	E	15th SCVI	21	FD	06/25/62	Summerville, SC	DOD		ROH,JR,KEB
Gladney, Samuel	Cpl.	E	15th SCVI	27	FD	11/08/64	Strasburg, VA	DOW	(Wdd 10/16-18,also Gbg.)	ROH,KEB,PP
Glanton, Charles R.	Pvt.	B	6th SCVC		ED	10/22/64	Richmond, VA	DOD	Hollywood Cem.Rchmd. I88	ROH,HC,HOE,UD3
Glanton, Lewis	Pvt.	B	6th SCVC		ED	01/15/64	At home	DOD		ROH,HOE,UD3
Glanton, Patrick H.	Pvt.	I	24th SCVI		ED	12/14/63	At home	DOD		EJM
Glasgow, J.N.	Pvt.	G	14th SCVI	30	AE	06/13/65	Davids Island NY	DIP	Cypress Hills N.C.#2998 NY	ROH,FPH,P6,P79
Glasgow, John William	Pvt.	D	13th SCVI	20	NY	10/23/62	Mt. Jackson, VA	DOD	Mt. Jackson, VA	ROH,JR,ANY,PP
Glatter, E.D.	Pvt.	C	Orr's Ri.		PS	06/17/62	Richmond, VA	KIA		JR
Glaze, James	Pvt.	C	2nd SCVI		RD	01/07/63		DOD		ROH,SA2
Glaze, John	Pvt.	C	2nd SCVI		RD	10/01/63	Chickamauga, GA	DOW		ROH,JR,SA2,KEB
Glaze, John L.	Pvt.	A	5th SCVC		OG	07/22/62	McPhersonville	DOD	(Typhoid)	ROH,JR
Glaze, John M.	Pvt.	A	5th SCVC	40	OG	09/15/62	Charleston, SC	DOD		ROH
Glaze, R.M.	Sgt.	A	5th SCVC	40	OG	06/11/64	Trevillian Stn.	KIA	(UD4=Richard L.)	ROH,JR,ETW,UD4
Glaze, Richard	Pvt.	K	24th SCVI		ED	08/04/63	Lauderdale, MS	DOD		HOE,BIG,PP
Glaze, William	Sgt.	K	19th SCVI	23	ED	05/18/65	Franklin, TN	DOW	(P12=Co.H)	HOE,CDC,P12
Gleason, Joel H.	2nd Lt.	C	P.S.S.		AN	06/30/62	Frayser's Farm	DOW	(In enemy hands)	JR,R47,GMJ
Gleaton, John	Pvt.			18	OG	06/15/62		MIA		ROH
Gleaton, W.W.	Cpl.	I	5th SCVC		OG	05/16/64	Drury's Bluff VA	KIA		ROH,JR,JMB
Glenn, B.F.	1st Lt.	F	2nd SCVIRi			09/06/62		DOD		R45
Glenn, Daniel E.	1st Sgt.	A	18th SCVI		UN	09/14/62	South Mtn., MD	KIA		JR
Glenn, G.T.	Pvt.	D	Orr's Ri.		AN	06/19/62	Virginia	DOD		JR
Glenn, James H.	Pvt.	H	18th SCVI		YK	06/08/65	Farmville, VA	DOW	Farmville US Hos. Gvyd.	P6,YEB,SA3,P12
Glenn, John D.	Pvt.	D	1st SCVIH		LR	04/06/63	Lynchburg, VA	DOD	Lynchburg CSA Cem. #3 R1	ROH,SA1,LAN,BBW
Glenn, John M.	Pvt.	H	18th SCVI	24	YK	02/05/65	Hatcher's Run VA	KIA		YEB
Glenn, Judge	Pvt.	B	1st SCVC	40	LS	06/15/61	Columbia, SC	DOD	Bramlett M.C. Laurens Cty.	ROH,LSC
Glenn, Michael	Pvt.	C	27th SCVI		CN	01/31/65	Elmira, NY	DIP	Woodlawn N.C.#1772 Elmira	FPH,HAG,P5,P120
Glenn, Robert J.	Pvt.	C	4th SCVC	34	PS	10/27/64	Burgess Mill, VA	KIA		ROH,JR,CDC
Glenn, Samuel L.	Pvt.	H	5th SCVI	21	YK	02/21/62	Centreville, VA	DOD	(JR=Co.B & 7/1/61) UD2	ROH,JR,SA2,YEB
Glenn, William C.	Pvt.	D	5th SCVI		UN	06/15/62	Lynchburg, VA	DOD		SA3
Glenn, William H.	Pvt.	F	20th SCVI		NY	06/18/64	Petersburg, VA	KIA	(William E. on monument)	ROH,JR,ANY,KEB
Glenn, William R.	5th Sgt.	H	5th SCVI	28	YK	12/26/61	Culpepper, VA	DOD	Fairview Cem. Culpepper VA	JR,CGH,SA3,YEB
Glisson, E.B.	Cpl.	F	10th SCVI	35	MN	09/20/63	Chickamauga, GA	KIA		ROH,RAS,CGW,HMC
Glover, George	Pvt.	H	24th SCVI		CR	07/22/64	Atlanta, GA	KIA		ROH,JR,HHC,CB
Glover, John R.	Pvt.	C	1st SCVIG		RD	05/20/65	Hart's Island NY	DIP	Cypress Hills N.C.#2838 NY	FPH,P6,SA1,P79
Glover, John V.	Major		25th SCVI	29	OG	06/19/64	Cold Harbor, VA	DOW	(See p263,HAG)	ROH,HAG,EDR,R48
Glover, Leslie	1st Lt.	G	1st SCVIR	22	OG	03/16/65	Averysboro, NC	KIA	PP	ROH,WLI,SA1,WAT
Glover, Madison	Pvt.	B	Ham.Leg.			08/30/62	2nd Manassas, VA	KIA		JR

SOUTH CAROLINA DEAD IN CSA SERVICE 1861-1865

NAME	RANK	C REGIMENT	AGE	DS	DIED	WHERE	WHY	BURIED	SOURCES
Glover, Robert J.	Pvt.	H 7th SCVI	21	ED	09/22/62	Maryland Hts. MD	DOW	(JR=10/18)	ROH,JR
Glover, S.L.	Colonel	SC QM Gen.		OG	05/27/62	At home	DOD		ROH
Glover, Thomas Jamison	Colonel	1st SCVIH	32	OG	08/31/62	2nd Manassas, VA	DOW		ROH,JR,SA1
Glover, Thomas Wiley	Pvt.	I 2nd SCVC	19	ED	05/13/65	Charlotte, NC	DOD	(HOE=Bacon Hall,VA)	ROH,HOE
Glover, William Edwin	2nd Lt.	B 23rd SCVI		CN	07/30/62	Orangeburg, SC	DOD	(JR=8/14/62)	ROH,JR,WLI,R48
Glymph, F.J.	Pvt.	F 1st SCVIH		NY	12/15/63		DOD	(To Hosp 11/1/63)	SA1
Glymph, L. Pinckney	4th Cpl.	E 3rd SCVI		NY	11/13/63	Knoxville, TN	DOW		ROH,ANY,SA2,KE
Gober, J.A.	Pvt.	I 1st SCVIR		GA	04/21/62		DOD		SA1
Godbold, David	3rd Sgt.	H 8th SCVI		MN	11/15/61	Richmond, VA	DOD	(Measles)	JR,HMC,KEB,MAG
Goddard, Peter Cuttino.	Pvt.	RutledgeMR			05/29/62	Garners, SC	KIA	Magnolia Cem. Charleston	JR
Godfrey, James W.	Pvt.	H 11th SCVI		CN	11/09/61	Savannah, GA	ACD	(ACD stab wd in thigh)	ROH,JR,HAG
Godfrey, John W.	Pvt.	C Hol.Leg.		SG	04/02/65	Pt. Lookout, MD	DIP	C.C. Pt. Lookout, MD	FPH,HOS,P6,P11
Godfrey, R.	Pvt.	I 2nd SCVI			09/20/63	Chickamauga, GA	KIA		ROH,JR,SA2,CDC
Godfrey, Samuel	Pvt.	I 1st SCVIG		LS	07/19/62	Richmond, VA	DOD	(JR=13th SCVI)	JR,SA1
Godfrey, W.M.	Pvt.	E Ham.Leg.			12/15/62	Fredericksburg	DOW		JR
Godfrey, William H.	Pvt.	H 1st SCVIG		CN	06/15/64	Richmond, VA	MIA	(Prsmd POW & dead, NI FPH)	ROH,SA1
Godley, Henry D.	Pvt.	H 1st SCVIG		CO	12/15/62	Warrenton, VA	DOW	(Wdd @ 2nd Man)	ROH,SA1,CDC
Godley, J.B.	Pvt.	K 11th SCVI	33	CO	10/24/63	At home	DOD		ROH,JR,HAG
Godwin, D.A.D.	Pvt.	H 10th SCVI		WG	/ /		DOD		RAS
Godwin, Joseph B.	Pvt.	E 10th SCVI		WG	06/07/62	Holly Springs MS	DOD		JR,RAS,HOW
Godwin, S.F.R.	2nd Cpl.	H 10th SCVI	20	WG	01/07/63	Murfreesboro, TN	DOW		ROH,RAS,CTA,P1
Godwin, W.	Pvt.	K 10th SCVI		CN	/ /		DOD		RAS
Godwin, W. Robert	Cpl.	A 7th SCVC	22	WG	08/16/64	Fussel's Mill VA	KIA		ROH,HOW,CDC
Goethe, Andrew J.	Pvt.	H 1st SCVIG	23	BT	08/29/62	2nd Manassas, VA	KIA		ROH,JR,SA1
Goetjen, John D.	Sgt.	A German A.	22	CN	07/24/63	McClellanville	DOD	St.Lawrence C. Charleston	ROH,MAG
Goff, J.E.	Pvt.	F P.S.S.			03/23/64		DOD		ROH,JR
Goff, James	Pvt.	H Orr's Ri.		MN	05/12/64	Spotsylvania, VA	KIA		HMC
Goff, Joseph	Pvt.	F 10th SCVI		HY	07/22/64	Atlanta, GA	DOW	(Left elbow resected)	RAS,CDC
Goff, Joseph	Pvt.	E 7th SCVI		ED	/ /		DOD		HOE
Goforth, J. Preston	Pvt.	K 27th SCVI	19	SG	07/16/64	Petersburg, VA	DOD	Blandford Church Pbg., VA	ROH,BLC,HAG,PP
Goforth, John H.	Pvt.	F 17th SCVI	25	YK	02/26/62	At home	DOD	Mt. Paran B.C. Cherokee SC	JR,TCC,CB
Goforth, William B.	Pvt.	M P.S.S.		SG	01/17/64	Dandridge F'm TN	KIA		ROH,JR,CDC
Goggans, W. Davidson	Lt.(Adj.)	13th SCVI	25	NY	08/29/62	2nd Manassas, VA	KIA	Reeder/Goggans F.C. NY CTY	ROH,JR,NCC,ANY
Goggans, William Tandy	Pvt.	B 1st SCVIG	34	NY	08/29/62	2nd Manassas, VA	KIA	(JR=Co.A & 8/30/62)	ROH,JR,SA1,ANY
Goin, James	Pvt.	I Hol.Leg.		SG	09/10/62	Richmond, VA	DOD	(HOS=DIP Elmira)	ROH,HOS
Goin, Thomas R.	Pvt.	I Hol.Leg.		SG	10/10/62	Weldon, NC	DOD	(PP=10/12/62)	ROH,PP
Goin, W.N.	Pvt.	L 5th SCVI		SG	04/13/62	Richmond, VA	DOD	Oakwood C.#70,Row H,Div A	ROH,JR,OWC
Going,	Sgt.	H 15th SCVI		UN	/ /		KIA		UD3
Going, Elisha P.	1st Sgt.	H 5th SCVI		UN	08/16/64	Fussell's Mill	KIA		ROH,JR,SA3
Going, James M.	Pvt.	E 5th SCVI	20	UN	08/19/61	Charlottesville	DOD	Univ. Cem. Charlottesville	ROH,SA3,ACH,UD
Goings, E.B.	Pvt.	A 3rd SCVI		SG	09/17/62	Sharpsburg, MD	DOW	Rose Hill C. Hagerstown MD	ROH,JR,BOD,SA2
Goins, Ainsley	Pvt.	C 7th SCVIBn	24	RD	06/19/64	Petersburg, VA	KIA	(JR=Aubrey)	ROH,JR,HAG
Golden, G.W.	Pvt.	D 12th SCVI		RD	08/01/64		DOD		JR
Golden, O.P.	Pvt.	G 1st SCVIH		BL	10/11/63	Chattanooga, TN	DOW	(Wdd 9/23/63)	ROH,SA1
Golden, W.H.	Pvt.	E Orr's Ri.		AN	03/12/65	Richmond, VA		Hollywood Cem.Rchmd. W130	ROH,HC
Golden, William	Pvt.	H 18th SCVI	21	YK	/ /		DOD		YEB
Golding, J. Washington	Pvt.	B 1st SCVIG	24	NY	08/29/62	Richmond, VA	DOD		ROH,SA1,ANY
Golding, James W.	Pvt.	B 3rd SCVI		NY	02/15/64	New Market, TN	DOD		ROH,SA1,ANY,KE
Golding, John J.	Cpl.	A 3rd SCVIBn		LS	07/17/63	Gettysburg, PA	DOW	(JR=Died after amputation)	ROH,JR,GDR,P1
Golding, Richard W.	Pvt.	F 3rd SCVABn	36	CN	10/08/63	Adams Run, SC	DOD		ROH,PP
Goldman, John M.	Pvt.	K 14th SCVI		ED	06/27/62	Gaines' Mill, VA	KIA	(EDN=Goleman)	ROH,JR,HOE,EDN

G

SOUTH CAROLINA DEAD IN CSA SERVICE 1861-1865

NAME	RANK	C REGIMENT	AGE	DS	DIED	WHERE	WHY	BURIED	SOURCES
Goldsmith, Isaac P.	Pvt.	G 5th SCVC	24	CN	08/12/62	Charleston, SC	DOD	Beth Elohim Charleston, SC	ROH,MAG,RCD
Goldsmith, Mikell M.	Lt.	CN Prov.Gd	17	CN	08/30/64	Macon, GA	ACD	Beth Elohim Charleston, SC	ROH,MAG,CDC,RCD
Goldsmith, William Henry	Pvt.	A 16th SCVI	22	GE	06/22/64	Kenesaw Mtn., GA	KIA	Clear Springs B.C. GE Cty.	ROH,16R,GEC,SA2
Golightley, David T.	Pvt.	F 13th SCVI		SG	09/01/62	Ox Hill, VA	KIA		JR
Golightley, F.	Pvt.	K 5th SCV			/ /		DOD		JR
Golightly, Christopher	Pvt.	K 5th SCVI		SG	09/17/62	Sharpsburg, MD	KIA	Rose hill C. Hagerstown MD	ROH,JR,SA3,BOD
Golightly, J.F.	Pvt.	C 5th SCVI		SG	11/14/61	Manassas, VA	DOD		SA3
Golightly, Jacob R.	Pvt.	D P.S.S.		SG	11/27/63	Marietta, GA	DOD	C. C. Marietta, GA UD2	ROH,JR,CCM,BGA
Golightly, Thomas	Pvt.	F 13th SCVI		SG	09/01/62	Ox Hill, VA	KIA		ROH,HOS
Golightly, William B.	Pvt.	F 13th SCVI		SG	07/13/62	Winder H. Rchmd	DOD	Hollywood Cem.Rchmd. C163	ROH,JR,HC,HOS
Golightly, Z. Dow	Pvt.	D P.S.S.		SG	05/05/62	Williamsburg, VA	KIA		ROH,JR,HOS,CDC
Golland, J. Cuttino	Pvt.	G 7th SCVC		GN	05/28/63	Virginia	KIA	(As courier after battle)	ROH
Golson, James D,	Pvt.	F 25th SCVI		OG	03/10/65	Morehead City NC	DOW	Hospital Gvyd.	P6,PP,HAG
Good, Samuel W.	Cpt.	G 18th SCVI	32	YK	09/30/64	Ft. Harrison, VA	KIA	(ROH=Ft. Steadman)	ROH,YEB
Goode, John	Pvt.	I 2nd SCVC		ED	12/29/64	Wilmington, NC	KIA	(HOE=DOW Johns Isl.)	ROH,HOE
Gooden, Henry	Pvt.	C 2nd SCVI		UN	12/29/62	Fredericksburg	DOW	(On Rchmd effects list)	ROH,SA2,CDC
Goodeth, T.E.	Pvt.	F 4th SCVIBn			07/08/62	Richmond, VA		Oakwood C.#24,Row N,Div C	ROH,OWC
Gooding, Perry	Pvt.	F 11th SCVI	28	BT	05/16/64	Fts. Monroe, VA	DOW	Prob N.C. Hampton, VA	ROH,HAG,P12
Gooding, Richard	Pvt.	D 11th SCVI	38	BT	06/05/64	Drury's Bluff VA	DOW	(Goodwin, R. in OWC?)	ROH,HAG
Gooding, Thomas	Pvt.	D 11th SCVI		BT	04/23/65	Hart's Island NY	DIP	Cypress Hills N.C.#2589 NY	FPH,P6,P12,P79
Goodlett, F. Marion	Pvt.	B 2nd SCVI	21	GE	06/01/64	Cold Harbor, VA	KIA		ROH,SA2,KEB
Goodlett, John Young	Pvt.	B 2nd SCVI	25	GE	08/10/61	Orange C.H., VA	DOD		ROH,SA2,KEB,H2
Goodlett, L. Alexander	2nd Lt.	F 4th SCVI		GE	11/11/61	Richmond, VA	DOD		SA2,R46
Goodlett, Thomas	Pvt.	K 16th SCVI		GE	06/15/64	Pine Mtn., GA	KIA	(JRR=Petersburg)	ROH,JR
Goodman, H.	Pvt.	C 2nd SCVIRi			/ /	Richmond, VA		Oakwood C.#85,Row N,Div A	ROH,OWC
Goodman, S.L.	Pvt.	E 19th SCVI		SR	04/22/63	Shelbyville, TN	DOD	Willowmount C. Shelbyville	PP,TOD
Goodson, Basley	Pvt.	B 2nd SCVIRi			/ /	Lynchburg, VA		Lynchburg CSA Cem. #9 R2	BBW
Goodson, C.	Pvt.	M 8th SCVI		DN	07/10/62	Richmond, VA	DOD	(Measles)	JR,CDC
Goodson, James	Pvt.	A 8th SCVI	45	DN	04/25/62	Charlottesville	DOD	Univ. Cem. Charlottesville	ROH,ACH,CDC
Goodson, Laban	Pvt.	E 6th SCVI		DN	10/01/62	Winchester, VA	DOD	Stonewall Cem. Winchester	ROH,WIN,JLC
Goodson, N.	Pvt.	PeeDee LA		DN	/ /				ROH
Goodson, Robert	Pvt.	M 8th SCVI	27	DN	06/15/62	Richmond, VA	DOD	(Measles)	ROH,JR,KEB,CDC
Goodson, Thomas	Pvt.	H 25th SCVI	33	DN	04/26/63	Timmonsville, SC	DOD	(JR=CN & 5/13/63)	ROH,JR
Goodson, Uzzell	Sgt.	E 6th SCVI		DN	12/28/63	Camp Morton, IN	DIP	Green Lawn C. Indianapolis	ROH,FPH,P5,JLC
Goodson, Wiley	Pvt.	K 23rd SCVI		DN	09/15/64	Petersburg, VA	KIA		ROH,K23,UD3
Goodson, William	Pvt.	B 21st SCVI		DN	09/26/64	Elmira, NY	DIP	(POW 6/18/64@PBG)	ROH,P5,P65,P120
Goodwin, A.J.	Pvt.	K 13th SCVI		LN	08/15/64	Ft. Delaware, DE	DIP	Finn's Pt., NJ Nat. Cem.	ROH,FPH,P5,P41
Goodwin, Alexander	Pvt.	D 21st SCVI		CD	10/15/64	Pt. Lookout, MD	DIP	C.C. Pt. Lookout, MD	ROH,FPH,P6,P120
Goodwin, Henry	Pvt.	I 16th SCVI		GE	/ /	Georgia	DOD		16R
Goodwin, J. Franklin	Pvt.	I 16th SCVI		GE	09/23/63	At home	DOD		16R,PP
Goodwin, J.A.	Pvt.	G 14th SCVI	18	AE	06/27/62	Gaines' Mill, VA	KIA		ROH,JR,CNM
Goodwin, J.M.	Pvt.	F 14th SCVI		LS	12/18/62	At home	DOD	(Pneumonia)	JR
Goodwin, John	Pvt.	I 6th SCVI		CR	/ /		KIA		CB,HHC
Goodwin, R.	Pvt.	D 11th SCVI		CO	/ /	Richmond, VA		Oakwood C.#96,Row C,Div G	ROH,OWC
Goodwin, S.R.	4th Cpl.	I 3rd SCVI		LS	09/20/63	Chickamauga, GA	KIA		ROH,JR,SA2
Goodwin, W.R.	Cpl.	A 7th SCVC		GN	08/18/64	Globe Tavern, VA	KIA		JR,CDC
Goodwyn, E. Middleton	2nd Lt.	C 2nd SCVI		RD	10/05/62	Martinsburg, VA	DOW	Trinity Ch. Columbia, SC	ROH,SA2,R45,PP
Goodyear,	Pvt.	C 26th SCVI		MN	/ /	Petersburg, VA	DOW		HMC
Goodyear, John Emory	Pvt.	E 1st SCVIG		MN	08/25/63	Ft. Delaware, DE	DIP	Finn's Pt., NJ Nat. Cem.	ROH,FPH,P5,PDL
Googe, Brantley W.	Cpl.	F 24th SCVI		AN	08/28/63	Lauderdale, MS	DOD		EJM,PP
Goralist, J.B.	Pvt.			LN	08/06/64	Petersburg, VA		Blandford Church Pbg., VA	BLC

SOUTH CAROLINA DEAD IN CSA SERVICE 1861-1865

NAME	RANK	C REGIMENT	AGE	DS	DIED	WHERE	WHY	BURIED	SOURCES
Gordon, A.	Pvt.	C 14th SCVI		LS	06/18/62	Lynchburg, VA	DOD	Lynchburg CSA Cem, #5 R4	ROH,JR,CDC,BBW
Gordon, A.M.	Pvt.	F 7th SCVI			12/31/64	Pt. Lookout, MD	DIP	(7th Cav?)	ROH
Gordon, Allison	Pvt.	E 21st SCVI		CD	06/24/64	Petersburg, VA	KIA		UD3
Gordon, Charlton Henry	Pvt.	G 15th SCVI	25	WG	07/18/64	Ft. Delaware, DE	DIP	Finn's Pt., NJ Nat. Cem.	ROH,FPH,P6,KEB
Gordon, D. Morgan	Pvt.	I 3rd SCVI		LS	10/12/62	Maryland Hts. MD	DOW	(ANY= C, 7th SCVC,?NI Va.)	ANY,SA2
Gordon, J.T.	2nd Lt.	G 14th SCVI	27	ED	07/01/63	Gettysburg, PA	DOW		HOE
Gordon, James T.	Pvt.	C 24th SCVI	40	CO	/ /	Dalton, GA	KIA	(Lost enroute to Atlanta)	EJM
Gordon, John B.	Pvt.	G Orr's Ri.		AE	08/27/62	Richmond, VA	DOD	(JR=Livingston, VA)	ROH,JR,CDC
Gordon, John Thomas	Pvt.	C 4th SCVI		AN	/ /	Richmond, VA '61	DOD	Oakwood C.#119,Row L,Div C	OWC,SA2
Gordon, P.T.	Pvt.	E 4th SCV			/ /	Richmond, VA			ROH
Gordon, R.	Pvt.	8th SCVI			06/02/62	Richmond, VA			ROH
Gordon, Robert A.	Pvt.	G Orr's Ri.		AE	07/02/62	Gaines' Mill, VA	DOW		ROH,JR,CV,CDC
Gordon, T.	Pvt.	F 5th SCV			05/26/64	Richmond, VA			ROH
Gordon, William	Pvt.	conscript			10/31/64	Charleston, SC	DOD	Magnolia Cem. Charleston	MAG
Gordon, William B.	Cpt.	K 25th SCVI	31	WG	08/21/64	Weldon RR, VA	DOW	(Died in enemy hands)	ROH,HAG,HOW
Gordon, William J.	Pvt.	B 26th SCVI			12/29/64	Pt. Lookout, MD	DIP	(NI FPH)	ROH
Gore, Edward James	3rd Cpl.	F 1st SCVIG		HY	09/15/62		DOW	(Wdd @ 2nd M. dth date ap)	SA1,PDL,CDC
Gore, G.	Pvt.	F 4th SCV			/ /	Richmond, VA		Oakwood C.#20,Row 29,Div D	ROH,OWC
Gore, G.H.H.	Pvt.	I 1st SCV			/ /	Richmond, VA		Oakwood C.#6,Row 36,Div D	ROH,OWC
Gore, Joshua	Pvt.	F 14th SCVI		LS	05/12/63	Richmond, VA	DOW	Oakwood C.#24,Row 27,Div D	ROH,JR,OWC
Gore, S.F.	Pvt.	L 7th SCVI		HY	/ /	Charlottesville		Univ. Cem. Charlottesville	KEB,ACH
Gorman, Charles	Pvt.	A 8th SCVI		DN	02/27/61	Charlottesville	DOD	Univ. Cem. Charlottesville	ROH,JR,KEB,ACH
Gortney, James M.	Pvt.	F 24th SCVI	18	AN	05/14/63	Jackson, MS	KIA		ROH,JR,HOL,PP
Gosling, G.W.	Pvt.	H 22nd SCVI			05/15/65	Elmira, NY	DIP	Woodlawn N.C.#2806 Elmira	FPH,P6,P65,P12
Gosnell, A.J.	Sgt.	D 16th SCVI		GE	/ /	GA	DOD		16R
Gosnell, C.	Pvt.				/ /			Rose Hill C. Hagerstown MD	BOD
Gosnell, M.C.	Sgt.	D 16th SCVI		GE	04/24/64	Med.Col. Atlanta		Oakwood Cem. Atlanta R6#12	16R,BGA
Gosnell, Thomas C.	Pvt.	D 16th SCVI		GE	/ /	Adams Run, SC	DOD		16R
Goss, John Wesley	Lt. Col.	P.S.S.	45	UN	/ /		DOW	Presbyterian C. Union, SC	ROH,LC
Goss, R.H.	Pvt.	A 1st SCVIG		BL	05/30/64	Spotsylvania, VA	DOW		ROH,JR,SA1,CDC
Gossett, Abraham	Pvt.	D 19th SCVI		ED	06/24/62	Lauderdale Ss MS	DOD		PP
Gossett, Alfred C.	Pvt.	I 13th SCVI	20	SG	11/13/62	Richmond, VA	DOD		ROH,HOS
Gossett, E.M.	Pvt.	I 13th SCVI	31	SG	07/08/62	Richmond, VA	DOD	Hollywood Cem.Rchmd. M142	ROH,JR,HC,HOS
Gossett, James	Pvt.	C Hol.Leg.	30	SG	08/23/62	Rappahannock Stn	KIA	(HOS=Joseph,JR=2nd M 8/30)	ROH,JR,HOS
Gossett, R.W.P.	Pvt.	I 13th SCVI	35	SG	08/29/62	2nd Manassas, VA	KIA		ROH,JR,HOS,CDC
Gossett, T.G.	Pvt.	B 15th SCVI		UN	05/03/63	Chancellorsville	KIA		ROH,JR,KEB
Gossett, W.M.	Pvt.	E 13th SCVI		SG	/ /	Petersburg, VA	KIA		HOS
Goude, J.I.	Pvt.	A 21st SCVI		GN	02/10/62	Georgetown, SC	DOD	(HAG=John/Joseph,JR=Gowdy)	ROH,JR,HAG
Goudelock, George O.	Pvt.	C 5th SCVI	18	SG	06/22/64	Petersburg, VA	KIA		ROH,SA3
Goudelock, John A.	Pvt.	G 5th SCVI		SG	08/04/61	Charlottesville	DOD	(Measles, JR=Adam J.)	JR,SA3
Goudelock, Nicholas C.	Pvt.	A 12th SCVI	30	UN	09/26/61	Columbia, SC	DOD	Goudelock Fam. Cem. Union	ROH,JR,UNC,YEB
Goudelock, Samuel E.	Pvt.		32	SG	12/18/63	Atlanta, GA	DOW	(Wdd Mission Rdg.11/25/64)	ROH,UNC
Goza, Elijah A.	Pvt.	E 7th SCVIBn	34	CR	04/15/64	At home	DOD		ROH,HAG,HHC
Goza, N.A.	Pvt.	Wood's Co.			01/20/65	(Reserves?)		Magnolia Cem. Charleston	MAG
Goza, Robert	Pvt.	C 12th SCVI		FD	07/15/62	Richmond, VA	DOD	(Date approx)	JR,HFC
Gracey, George	Pvt.	B 9th SCVIB			01/12/62	Centreville, VA	DOD		JR
Gradick, Fletcher C.	Pvt.	G 7th SCVI		RD	Q8/07/61	Flint Hill, VA	DOD	Fairview Cem. Culpepper VA	ROH,JR,CGH,UD3
Gradick, J.B.	Pvt.		22	LN	08/06/64	Petersburg, VA	DOW		PP
Gradon, John	Pvt.	E 16th SCVI	30	LS	07/22/64	Atlanta, GA	KIA		ROH
Grady, Edward	Pvt.	B 25th SCVI	22	CN	06/04/64	Cold Harbor, VA	KIA	(Sniped on picket)	ROH,JR,CDC,WLI
Grady, J.B.	Pvt.	I 7th SCVI		ED	06/29/64	Richmond, VA		Hollywood Cem.Rchmd. U506	ROH,HC

G

SOUTH CAROLINA DEAD IN CSA SERVICE 1861-1865

NAME	RANK	C REGIMENT	AGE	DS	DIED	WHERE	WHY	BURIED	SOURCES
Graffts, Charles N.	Sgt.	D 21st SCVI		CD	06/17/63	Hart's Island NY	DIP	Cypress Hills N.C. #3021	ROH,FPH,P6,HAG
Graham, A.	Pvt.	D 3rd SCVIBn		LS	02/12/62	Adams Run, SC	DOD		PP,KEB
Graham, B.	Pvt.	G 5th SCV			/ /	Richmond, VA		Oakwood C.#6,Row K,Div B	OWC
Graham, C. Newton	Pvt.	G Orr's Ri.		AE	07/03/62	Dill's Farm, VA	DOD		ROH,JR,CDC
Graham, Dempsey	Pvt.	E 2nd SCVI		KW	01/01/64	Rogersville, TN	DOW	(Wdd 12/14/63 @ Bean's St)	SA2,KEB,H2
Graham, Dougal	Pvt.	I 1st SCVIH		MN	11/15/62	At home	DOD	(HMC= MIA @ Sharpsburg)	ROH,SA1,HMC
Graham, E.	Pvt.	K 8th SCVI		MO	/ /	Culpepper, VA		(1863)	HOM,KEB
Graham, Eldridge	Pvt.	D 25th SCVI		MN	09/04/63	Bty. Wagner, SC	KIA		ROH,JR,HAG,HMC
Graham, Evander M.	2nd Sgt.	K 6th SCVI	22	WG	01/29/64	At home	DOW	(Wdd Loudon, TN)	ROH,3RC
Graham, G.W.	Pvt.	H 10th SCVI		WG	05/15/62	Macon, MS	DOD		RAS,HOW,PP
Graham, George C.	Pvt.	L 1st SCVIG		CN	06/27/62	Gaines' Mill, VA	KIA		ROH,JR,SA1,WLI
Graham, H.C.	Pvt.	B 7th SCVI	19	AE	07/22/62	Savage Stn., VA	DOW	(KEB=E.C., CNM=A.C.)	ROH,KEB,CNM
Graham, H.L.F.	Pvt.	I 26th SCVI		WG	09/24/64	Richmond, VA		Hollywood Cem.Rchmd. U506	ROH,HC
Graham, Henry C.	Pvt.	G 8th SCVI	24	MO	01/11/62	Manassas, VA	DOD		HOM,JR,KEB,UD2
Graham, J.G.	Pvt.	G 10th SCVI		HY	/ /		DOD		RAS
Graham, J.L.	Sgt.	C 10th SCVI		HY	05/14/64	Resaca, GA	KIA	(JR=5/15/64)	ROH,JR,RAS,CDC
Graham, J.M.	Pvt.	G 2nd Res Bn		AN	01/06/65	Columbia, SC	DOD	Elmwood Cem. Columbia, SC	ROH,MP,PP
Graham, Jackson	Pvt.	G 2nd SCVI	19	KW	07/16/61	Culpepper, VA	DOD	Fairview Cem. Culpepper VA	CGH,SA2,HIC,KEB
Graham, James	Pvt.	F 5th SCVI			08/12/62	Richmond, VA			ROH
Graham, James	Pvt.	D 25th SCVI		MN	02/01/65	Elmira, NY	DIP	Woodlawn N.C.#1887 Elmira	FPH,P5,HMC,HAG
Graham, Jesse	Pvt.	K 14th SCVI		ED	07/23/62	Gaines' Mill, VA	DOW		JR
Graham, John	Pvt.	G 26th SCVI		DN	07/09/63		DOD		JR
Graham, John A.	Pvt.			WG	09/20/63	Chickamauga, GA	KIA		HOW
Graham, John B.	Pvt.	G Orr's Ri.	24	AE	07/21/62	Laurel Hill, VA	DOD		ROH,JR,CDC
Graham, John C.	Sgt.	C 18th SCVI	25	UN	09/01/62	(Prob Warrenton)	DOW	(Wdd 2nd Man)	ROH,JR
Graham, John R.A.	Pvt.	D 2nd SCVI		SR	11/24/63	Knoxville, TN	DOW	(Near Loudon, TN)	ROH,SA2,KEB,H2
Graham, Joseph C.	Cpl.	C Ham.Leg.	39	PS	07/31/64	Richmond, VA		Hollywood Cem.Rchmd. V690	HC,ROH,PP
Graham, Nathaniel	Pvt.	B 15th SCMil	40	MO	04/04/65	Newbern, NC	DIP	Cedar Grove C. Newbern, NC	P6,WAT,PP,P12
Graham, Thomas J.	Pvt.	K 26th SCVI	38	HY	09/27/62	Charleston, SC	ACD	(At C & S RR Depot)	ROH,JR
Graham, W.	Pvt.	I 26th SCVI		WG	09/13/64	Petersburg, VA	KIA	(PP=9/29/64)	ROH,PP
Graham, W.J.	Cpl.	B 10th SCVI			/ /	Chattanooga, TN	DOD	(HY?)	RAS
Graham, W.J. (M.J.?)	Pvt.	K 14th SCVI		ED	07/08/62	Gaines' Mill, VA	DOW		JR,HOE
Graham, William R.	1st Lt.	M 10th SCVI		HY	/ /		DOD	(Not reelected '62)	RAS
Grain, J. (Graham?)	Pvt.				/ /	Richmond, VA		Oakwood C.#93,Row J,Div B	OWC
Grainger, Franklin	Pvt.	F 1st SCVIG		HY	08/02/62	Richmond, VA	DOD		ROH,JR,SA1,PDL
Grainger, H.J.	Pvt.	K 26th SCVI	36	HY	09/09/63	Lauderdale, MS	DOW	(Wdd @ Jackson 7/12/63)	ROH,JR,CDC,PP
Grainger, James A.	Pvt.	K 2nd SCVI		CN	10/04/62	Lynchburg, VA	DOD	Lynchburg CSA Cem. #7 R4	ROH,JR,SA2,BBW
Grainger, William	4th Cpl.	F 1st SCVIG		HY	05/15/63	Richmond, VA	DOW	Hollywood Cem.Rchmd. T91	ROH,HC,PDL,SA1
Grambling, A.M.	Cpl.	B 20th SCVI		OG	03/19/65	Pt. Lookout, MD	DIP	C.C. Pt. Lookout, MD	ROH,FPH,P6,P114
Grambling, Michael W..	1st Sgt.	F 25th SCVI	32	OG	01/15/65	Ft. Fisher, NC	KIA	(HAG=Gramling)	ROH,HAG,EDR,PP
Grammell, F.B.	Pvt.	H 22nd SCVI			07/30/64	Crater, Pbg., VA	KIA		BLM
Graner, John	Pvt.	H Orr's Ri.		MN	05/12/64	Spotsylvania, VA	KIA		HMC
Grant, A.A.	Pvt.	D 27th SCVI	18	LS	02/20/65	Town Creek, NC	KIA		ROH,HAG
Grant, Barnabas	Pvt.	E 4th SCVC		MO	01/31/65	Elmira, NY	DIP	Woodlawn N.C.#1778 Elmira	FPH,P5,HOM,P120
Grant, Francis E.	Sgt.	I 11th SCVI	23	OG	10/22/62	Pocotaligo, SC	KIA		ROH,CDC,PP
Grant, G.W.	Pvt.	D Orr's Ri.		AN	01/14/62	Richmond, VA	DOW	Oakwood C.#51,Row B,Div E	ROH,JR,OWC,CDC
Grant, H.B.	Pvt.	D Orr's Ri.		AN	06/27/62	Gaines' Mill, VA	KIA	(Later Rpt= Savage Stn.)	ROH,JR,CDC,CNM
Grant, J.W.	Pvt.	G 14th SCVI		AE	/ /	(OWC=19th SCVI)		Oakwood C.#30,Row K,Div C	ROH,OWC,CDC
Grant, J.W.	Sgt.	B 2nd SCVIRi		PS	/ /				ROH
Grant, Jasper J.	Pvt.	I 14th SCVI	20	AE	06/27/62	Gaines' Mill, VA	KIA		ROH,JR,HOL,CNM
Grant, John	Pvt.	D 21st SCVI		CD	06/15/64	Richmond, VA	DOD		ROH,HAG

SOUTH CAROLINA DEAD IN CSA SERVICE 1861-1865

NAME	RANK	C REGIMENT	AGE	DS	DIED	WHERE	WHY	BURIED	SOURCES
Grant, John S.	Pvt.	F 2nd SCVI	21	AE	06/30/64	Richmond, VA	DOW	Hollywood Cem. Rchmd. U299	ROH,HC,SA2,KEB
Grant, Neely	Pvt.	H 1st SCVIG		CN	09/15/62	Warrenton, VA	DOW	(Wdd @ 2nd Man.)	ROH,SA1,CDC
Grant, Perry	Pvt.	L Orr's Ri.			06/29/62	Dill Farm, VA	DOD		ROH,JR,CDC
Grant, Robert A.	Pvt.	I 14th SCVI	18	AE	10/18/62	Lynchburg, VA	DOW	Lynchburg CSA Cem. #2 R2	ROH,JR,HOL,BBW
Grant, T.J.	Pvt.				08/31/64	Pt. Lookout, MD	DIP	C.C. Pt. Lookout, MD	ROH
Grant, Willam M.	Pvt.	E Orr's Ri.	24	PS	02/04/62	Sullivans I., SC	ACD	(ROH=Wade M.)	ROH,CDC
Grant, William	Pvt.	9th SCVIB			10/24/62	Richmond, VA	DOD	Hollywood Cem.Rchmd. B146	ROH,HC
Granter, J.	Pvt.	A 21st SCVI			06/05/64	Petersburg, VA	ACD		ROH
Grantham, Elias	Pvt.	I 18th SCVI	18	DN	08/30/62	2nd Manassas, VA	KIA		ROH,JR,CDC
Grantham, John Z.	Pvt.	B 21st SCVI		DN	/ /				ROH
Grantham, R.W.	Pvt.	H 21st SCVI		DN	03/05/65	Elmira, NY	DIP	Woodlawn N.C.#2398 Elmira	FPH,P5,P65,HAG
Gravely,	Sgt.	B P.S.S.		PS	/ /	Richmond, VA			ROH
Gravely, J.D.	Pvt.	A P.S.S.			/ /		KIA		JR
Gravely, James C.	Pvt.	B P.S.S.		PS	09/20/62		DOW	(Wdd @ Shpsbg)	ROH
Gravely, John	Pvt.	3rd SC Res		PS	12/25/62	SC	DOD		ROH
Gravely, Joseph	Pvt.	F 22nd SCVI		PS	07/30/64	Petersburg, VA	KIA	Blandford Church Pbg., VA	ROH,JRR,BLC
Graver, P.	Pvt.	K 12th SCVI		CN	07/16/62	Richmond, VA		Hollywood Cem.Rchmd. M4	ROH,HC
Gravery, J. (Gravely)					/ /	Richmond, VA		(Richmond effects list)	CDC
Graves, B.M.	Pvt.	C 25th SCVI			01/18/64	Petersburg, VA	KIA		JR
Graves, Bennett					/ /			(Rchmd effects list 12/62)	CDC
Graves, Burnett	Pvt.	I 22nd SCVI		OG	/ /	Richmond, VA		Oakwood C.#40,row H,Div A	ROH,OWC,CDC
Graves, George	Pvt.	H Orr's Ri.		MN	10/09/61	Mars Bluff, SC	ACD	(Railroad accident)	HMC,JR
Graves, J.C.	Pvt.	A 13th SCVI		LS	07/06/62	Richmond, VA	DOD	Hollywood Cem.Rchmd. M139	ROH,JR,HC
Graves, John	Pvt.	G 21st SCVI		CD	02/15/62		DOD		JR,HAG
Graves, Thomas	Pvt.	C 8th SCVI		CD	10/19/62	Winchester, VA	DOD		JR
Graves, W.B.	Pvt.	D 27th SCVI	21	LS	08/09/63		DOD	(Typhoid)	ROH,JR,HAG
Graves, W.M.	Pvt.	D 25th SCVI		MN	06/30/64	Petersburg, VA	DOW	(Wdd 6/29)	ROH,HMC,HAG
Graves, W.W.	Pvt.	D 27th SCVI	39	LS	07/16/63		DOD	(Typhoid)	ROH,JR,HAG
Gray, Alfred	Pvt.	H 10th SCVI		WG	/ /	Chattanooga, TN	DOD	City C. Chattanooga, TN	RAS,HOW,TOD
Gray, Alfred	Pvt.	B 25th SCVI	24	CN	09/01/64	Alexandria, VA	DOW	Unitarian C. Charleston SC	ROH,MAG,P1,P6
Gray, Daniel H.	Pvt.	B 9th SCVIB			09/10/61	Germantown, VA	DOD	(JR=09/01/61)	ROH,JR
Gray, Henry D.	Pvt.	G Orr's Ri.		AE	07/03/63	Gettysburg, PA	KIA		ROH,JR,CDC
Gray, J.H.	Pvt.	K 22nd SCVI		PS	07/30/64	Crater, Pbg., VA	KIA		BLM
Gray, J.S.	Pvt.	K 22nd SCVI		PS	07/30/64	Crater, Pbg., VA	KIA		BLM
Gray, John	Pvt.	C 2nd SCVA			06/03/64	Charleston, SC	DOD	Magnolia Cem. Charleston	ROH,MAG
Gray, John T.	Pvt.	F 2nd SCVIRi	27	AN	03/08/63	Petersburg, VA			PP
Gray, Joseph	Pvt.	C 1st SCVIH		BL	/ /	Tennessee	DOD	(To hosp 9/18/63)	SA1
Gray, N.	Pvt.	H 10th SCVI		WG	06/25/64	New Hope, GA	KIA		ROH,RAS
Gray, R.A.	Pvt.	A 8th SCVI	22	DN	07/02/62	Malvern Hill, VA	KIA		ROH,KEB
Gray, W.	Pvt.	H 10th SCVI		WG	06/15/64	Med.Col. Atlanta		Oakland C. Atlanta R46#8	BGA
Gray, W.P.	Pvt.	H 6th SCVI		FD	05/31/62	7 Pines, VA	KIA		WDB
Gray, W.S.	Cpl.	F 3rd SCVI		LS	12/13/62	Fredericksburg	KIA		ROH,JR,SA2
Gray, William	Pvt.	B 9th SCVIB		RD	10/09/61	Richmond, VA	DOD	Hollywood Cem.Rchmd. F42	ROH,JR,HC,CDC
Gray, William	Pvt.	G 19th SCVI		AE	06/12/62		DOD		HOL
Gray, William Henry	Pvt.	C 19th SCVI	19	ED	09/20/63	Chickamauga, GA	KIA		ROH,JR,HOE,UD3
Graydon, John	Pvt.	E 16th SCVI		GE	07/22/64	Decatur, GA	KIA	West Point Troup Cty., GA	16R,UD2
Grayham, George	Pvt.	SCVA			/ /	(Fed Deserter)	DOD	Magnolia Cem. Charleston	RCD
Grayton, John	Pvt.	I 16th SCVI		GE	11/24/63	Lookout Mtn. TN	KIA		16R
Green,	Lt.	I SCVI			10/09/62	Brucetown, VA		Stonewall Cem. Winchester	WIN
Green, A.	Pvt.	D 4th SCVIBn			05/31/62	Philadelphia, PA	DIP		ROH
Green, B.	Cpl.	C 23rd SCVI		CN	06/17/64	Petersburg, VA	KIA	(JR=July)	ROH,JR,CDC

G

SOUTH CAROLINA DEAD IN CSA SERVICE 1861-1865

NAME	RANK	C REGIMENT	AGE	DS	DIED	WHERE	WHY	BURIED	SOURCES
Green, B.F.	Pvt.	H 15th SCVI			11/01/62	Staunton, VA		Thornrose C. Staunton, VA	TOD
Green, E.	Pvt.	C 23rd SCVI		CN	05/04/65	Elmira, NY	DIP	Woodlawn N.C.#2760 Elmira	FPH,P6
Green, Ellison J.	Pvt.	B 13th SCVI		SG	01/16/63	Buena Vista, SC	DOD	(Consumption)	JR,HOS
Green, Emory	Pvt.	F 16th SCVI		GE	/ /	At home	DOD	(1861)	16R
Green, G. Nelson	Pvt.	F 16th SCVI		GE	11/16/63	Marietta, GA	DOD	Con. Cem. Marietta, GA	16R,BGA,CCM
Green, George G.	Pvt.	B 24th SCVI		MO	05/06/65	Wadesboro, NC	DOD	(SUR @ Greensboro)	ROH,HOM,GSR
Green, H.A.	Pvt.	D P.S.S.		SG	10/07/64	Darbytown Rd. VA	KIA	(Left on field,Attlees Fm)	ROH,HOS
Green, H.R.B.	Pvt.	C 16th SCVI		GE	06/01/64	New Hope Church	KIA	(JR=Marietta 6/20/64)	ROH,JR,16R
Green, Hansford	Pvt.	D Hol.Leg.	40	BL	09/14/62	South Mtn., MD	KIA		ROH
Green, Irving	Pvt.	1st SCVC			/ /	Richmond, VA		Oakwood C.#95,Row F,Div G	ROH,OWC
Green, J. Alexander	Pvt.	B 22nd SCVI		SG	05/21/65	Elmira, NY	DIP	Woodlawn N.C.#2936 Elmira	FPH,P6,P65,P120
Green, J.A.	Pvt.	H Orr's Ri.			10/09/62	Staunton, VA	DOD		JR
Green, J.D.	Pvt.	C 16th SCVI		GE	11/30/64	Franklin, TN	KIA	(May be Dup of James M.)	PP
Green, J.E.	Pvt.	B 22nd SCVI		SG	07/30/64	Crater, Pbg., VA	KIA		BLM
Green, J.J.	Pvt.	B 13th SCVI		SG	09/05/62		DOW		JR
Green, J.M.	Pvt.	C 16th SCVI		GE	11/30/64	Franklin, TN	KIA	Macgavock C. Frkln Gv# 44	ROH,16R,WCT
Green, J.W.	Pvt.	C 1st SCVA			03/26/64	Raleigh, NC		Oakwood C. Raleigh, NC	TOD
Green, Jackson	Pvt.	D Hol.Leg.	39		12/30/64	Petersburg, VA	KIA	Blandford Church Pbg., VA	ROH,BLC,PP
Green, James	Pvt.	B 22nd SCVI		SG	07/30/64	Crater, Pbg., VA	KIA		ROH,BLM
Green, James A.	Pvt.	K Orr's Ri.	22	AN	09/20/63	Staunton, VA	DOD	Thornrose C. Staunton, VA	ROH,PP
Green, James Hardy	Pvt.	G 2nd Bn Res		AN	/ /	At home	DOD		ROH
Green, James M.	Pvt.	C 16th SCVI		GE	11/30/64	Franklin, TN	KIA	Macgavock C. Fr'kln GV#44	16R
Green, Jeremiah	Pvt.	C 22nd SCVI	27	SG	06/15/65	On way home	DOD	(? Greer, J.M. in AR)	ROH
Green, John	Pvt.	B 19th SCVI	27	ED	11/25/63	Missionary Ridge	KIA		ROH,HOE
Green, John C.	Pvt.	2nd SCVC		GE	10/09/63	James City, VA	KIA		ROH
Green, John L.	Pvt.	E 26th SCVI			08/05/63	Shubuta, MS	DOD		PP
Green, Johnson	Pvt.	D Hol.Leg.	33	BL	05/15/62	Charleston, SC	DOD		ROH
Green, Joseph	Pvt.	G P.S.S.	35	YK	/ /		DOD		YEB
Green, Lewis Vandiver	Pvt.	D Ham.Leg.	27	AN	06/21/62	7 Pines, VA	DOW	Nat. Cem. Hampton, VA	ROH,GRS,PP,TOD
Green, Nance J.	Pvt.	B 13th SCVI		SG	07/09/62	Richmond, VA			ROH
Green, P.C.	Pvt.	B 22nd SCVI		ED	07/29/62	Ft. Johnson, SC	DOD		ROH
Green, Plowden W.	3rd Lt.	F 7th SCVC	32	HY	02/05/65	Richmond, VA	DOD	(Typhoid fever)	ROH,JES,CEN
Green, Richard H.	Pvt.	C 16th SCVI	20	GE	06/28/64	Kenesaw Mtn., GA	KIA		ROH
Green, Samuel	Pvt.				04/09/65	Averysboro, NC	DOW	Averysboro Cem. NC	GEC
Green, T.	Pvt.	H 13th SCVI		LN	07/09/62	Richmond, VA		Hollywood Cem.Rchmd. C101	HC
Green, Thomas	Pvt.	D Ham.Leg.	56	AN	05/31/62	7 Pines, VA	KIA		ROH,GRS
Green, Thomas	Pvt.	B 7th SCVC			08/15/64	Richmond, VA			ROH
Green, Thomas	Pvt.	H			08/05/63	Mississippi	DOD	(JR=21st SCVI)	JR
Green, Thomas J.	Pvt.	H 26th SCVI			08/06/63		DOD		JR
Green, William	Pvt.	C 16th SCVI		GE	/ /	Adams Run, SC	DOD		16R
Green, William F.	Cpl.	K 18th SCVI	38	SG	07/30/64	Crater, Pbg., VA	KIA		ROH,JR,BLM
Green, William Henry			28	ED	/ /	Virginia	DOD		ROH
Green, William J.	2nd Lt.	B 24th SCVI	23	MO	07/20/64	Peachtree Ck. GA	KIA	(JR=White Oak Rd.)	ROH,JR,HOM,R48
Green, William J.	Pvt.	B 13th SCVI		SG	05/15/64	Spotsylvania, VA	KIA		ROH,JR,HOS
Green, William R.	Pvt.	D 16th SCVI		GE	04/05/63	Adams Run, SC	DOD	(16R=Kingston, GA)	16R,PP
Green, William Thomas	Pvt.	H 3rd SCVI	21	LN	07/02/63	Gettysburg, PA	KIA		ROH,JR,SA2,KEB
Green,Jr., William Glenn	Pvt.	I 2nd SCVI		CN	06/01/64	Beulah Church VA	KIA	(JR=5/30/64)	ROH,JR,SA2,KEB
Greenburg, Martin	Pvt.	B 1st SCVA	47	AE	05/04/65	Newbern, NC	DIP	Cedar Grove C. Newbern, NC	P1,P6,WAT,PP
Greer, Frank B.	Sgt.	H 15th SCVI	24	UN	10/30/62	Staunton, VA	DOD		ROH,JR,CV,KEB
Greer, John	Pvt.	I 16th SCVI		GE	11/25/63	Missionary Rdge.	KIA		16R
Greer, Richard Walsh	2nd Lt.	B 25th SCVI	27	CN	06/16/62	Secessionville	KIA	1st P.C.(Scotch) Chastn SC	ROH,JR,PP,LED

SOUTH CAROLINA DEAD IN CSA SERVICE 1861-1865

NAME	RANK	C	REGIMENT	AGE	DS	DIED	WHERE	WHY	BURIED	SOURCES
Greer, Robert P.	Pvt.	F	16th SCVI		GE	/ /	Rome, GA	DOD	Myrtle Hill Cem. Rome, GA	ROH,16R,RCD
Greer, William H.	Pvt.	F	Pal. Bn.LA	22	NY	08/31/64	Charleston, SC	DOD	Magnolia Cem. Charleston	ROH,MAG
Gregg, H.D.	Pvt.	B	21st SCVI			11/13/64	Richmond, VA			ROH
Gregg, H.W.	Pvt.	C	1st SCVIR			/ /			Con.Cem. Marietta, GA	SA1,CCM
Gregg, Henry Junius	Pvt.	I	7th SCVC	18	SR	04/14/65	Farmville, VA	DOW	(Wdd 4/8 @ Appomatox)	ROH,AR,P6,P12
Gregg, John B.	2nd Lt.	F	7th SCVI	23	ED	12/01/61	Charlottesville	DOD	Magnolia Cem. Charleston	ROH,JR,MAG,P46
Gregg, John W.	Sgt.	H	8th SCVI		MN	05/09/65	Camp Chase, OH	DIP	Con.Cem.#1947 Columbus, OH	FPH,P6,P12,KEB
Gregg, Maxcy	Brig. Gen.			47	RD	12/15/62	Fredericksburg	DOW	Elmwood Cem. Columbia, SC	ROH,JR,MP,PP
Gregg, McFadden	1st Sgt.	H	8th SCVI		MN	11/29/63	Knoxville, TN	KIA		HMC,KEB
Gregg, W.W.	Pvt.	I	21st SCVI		MN	/ /	Richmond, VA		Oakwood C.#47,Row K,Div G	ROH,OWC
Gregg, William Carter	Pvt.	K	23rd SCVI	24	SR	03/25/65	Ft. Steadman, VA	KIA		ROH,K23,UD3
Gregg, William W.	3rd Sgt.	E	1st SCVIG		MN	06/27/62	Gaines' Mill, VA	KIA	(Color Bearer)	JR,SA1,PDL,HMC
Gregory, A.	Pvt.	H	15th SCVI		UN	/ /		DOD		JR
Gregory, Ansel	Pvt.	H	1st SCVIH		SG	/ /		DOD	(Present on roll 2/28/65)	SA1,HOS
Gregory, Charles A.	Pvt.	B	7th SCVC			10/07/64	(Wdd Darbytown R	DOW	Oakwood C.#16,Row H,Div G	ROH,OWC
Gregory, D.J.	Pvt.	D	1st SCV		LR	10/08/62	Winchester, VA	DOD		ROH,LAN
Gregory, E.H.	Pvt.	A	P.S.S.			/ /		DOD		JR
Gregory, H.H.	Sgt.	L	7th SCVI		HY	06/29/62	Savage Stn., VA	KIA	(KEB=T.H.,CNM=H.A.)	ROH,JR,CNM,KEB
Gregory, Harvey S.	Pvt.	A	18th SCVI	20	UN	08/30/62	2nd Manassas, VA	KIA	Gregory Fam. Cem. Union	ROH,JR,CDC,UNC
Gregory, Isaac F.	3rd Sgt.	D	5th SCVI		UN	05/06/64	Wilderness, VA	KIA		ROH,JR,SA3
Gregory, J.C.	Pvt.	E	7th SCVC	30	UN	04/08/65	Appomatox, VA	DOD		ANY
Gregory, J.E. Thomas	Pvt.	E	5th SCVI	21	UN	12/12/61	Centreville, VA	DOD	Mt. Tabor Cem. Union Cty.	SA3,UNC,UD1
Gregory, John	Pvt.	A	18th SCVI		UN	12/09/64	Elmira, NY	DIP	Woodlawn N.C.#1164 Elmira	JR,FPH,P12,P66
Gregory, John J.	Sgt.	H	7th SCVIBn		RD	05/17/64	Drury's Bluff VA	DOW		ROH,HAG
Gregory, Nathaniel B.	Pvt.	D	1st SCVIH	16	LR	09/18/63	Petersburg, VA	DOD	(Body moved home) PP	ROH,SA1,LAN,BL
Gregory, R.F. (P.B.?)	Pvt.	F	18th SCVI			09/12/62	Lynchburg, VA	DOD	Lynchburg CSA Cem. #6R2	ROH,JR,CDC,BBW
Gregory, R.H.	Pvt.	A	5th SCV			06/01/62	Richmond, VA			ROH
Gregory, Samuel.	Pvt.	H	5th SCVI		UN	06/30/62	Frayser's Farm	DOW	Oakwood C.#127,Row L,Div C	ROH,JR,SA3,OWC
Gregory, Spencer	Pvt.	K	2nd SCVIRi	45	AN	03/15/64		DOD		ROH
Gregory, Thomas	Pvt.	B	18th SCVI		UN	02/15/62	Newberry, SC	DOD		JR
Gregory, Thomas	Pvt.					/ /	Camp Gurin,Chstn	DOD	Measles (Jan or Feb 1862)	UD2
Gregory, W.	Pvt.	A	3rd SCVC		LS	03/31/65	Kittrell Spgs.NC	DOD	Kittrell Springs, NC C.C.	CV,WAT
Gregory, Wesley	Pvt.	B	18th SCVI		UN	08/30/62	2nd Manassas, VA	KIA		ROH,JR,CDC
Gregory, William	Pvt.	D	7th SCVI			07/03/64	Richmond, VA			ROH
Gregory, William	Pvt.	C	7th SCVIBn	45	UN	07/01/64	Cold Harbor, VA	KIA		ROH,UNC
Gregory, Willis T.	Pvt.	H	2nd SCVI		LR	08/12/61	Richmond, VA	DOD	(Typhoid)	ROH,JR,SA2,LAN
Grenoble, H.	Pvt.	I	13th SCVI		SG	07/14/62	Richmond, VA			ROH
Gresham, H.B.	Pvt.	D	13th SCVI		GE	07/01/62	Richmond, VA		Hollywood Cem.Rchmd. M52	HC
Gressett, Tatum	Cpl.	C	24th SCVI	29	CO	05/22/64	Calhoun, GA	DOW	(Wdd Pine Mtn.5/16/64)	ROH,DRE
Gretten, R.	Pvt.	F	6th SCVI		CR	09/17/62	Sharpsburg, MD	KIA		ROH
Greven, J.M.	Pvt.	A	12th SCVI		YK	06/08/62	Richmond, VA		Hollywood Cem.Rchmd. P45	HC
Grey, John T.	Pvt.	F	2nd SCVIRi		AN	03/08/63	Petersburg, VA	DOD	Blandsford Church Pbg., VA	BLC
Grey, R.L.	Pvt.		Culpeppers			05/04/65	New Orleans, LA	DIP	Monument Cem. 66 SQ.69	P3,P6
Grice, Ambrose B.	Pvt.	D	14th SCVI	16	ED	10/19/62	White Sulpher Sp	DOD	(Phrenitis)	JR,D14,HOE,EDN
Grice, Benjamin	Pvt.	A	19th SCVI	23	ED	/ /	Charleston, SC	DOD		HOE,UD3
Grice, Ephraim G.	Pvt.	F	21st SCVI		MO	01/15/65	Ft. Fisher, NC	KIA		PP,HAG
Grice, Henry	Pvt.	A	19th SCVI	21	ED	12/31/62	Murfreesboro, TN	DOW		HOE,UD3
Grice, John E.	5th Cpl.	B	14th SCVI	18	ED	11/06/64	Pt. Lookout, MD	DIP	C.C. Pt. Lookout, MD	ROH,FPH,P5,UD3
Gridley, Edward	Pvt.	A	16th SCVI		GE	06/29/64	Kennesaw Mtn. GA	DOW		ROH,16R
Grier, Edward Henry	Pvt.	H	12th SCVI	18	YK	02/05/63	At home	DOD	Bethesda Ch. York, SC	RCD,JR,CWC,YEB
Grier, J. Livingston	Pvt.	G	Orr's Ri.		AE	06/27/62	Gaines' Mill, VA	KIA	Due West, SC	ROH,JR,CV

G

SOUTH CAROLINA DEAD IN CSA SERVICE 1861-1865

NAME	RANK	C REGIMENT	AGE	DS	DIED	WHERE	WHY	BURIED	SOURCES
Grier, J.G.	Pvt.	G Orr's Ri.		AE	06/27/62	Gaines' Mill, VA	KIA	(Dup J. Livingston?)	ROH,JR,CDC
Grier, L.C.	Pvt.	A 21st SCVI		GN	/ /		DIP	(POW 6/16/64, T.C. ?)	ROH
Grier, W.S.	Pvt.	A 21st SCVI		GN	03/12/65	Elmira, NY	DIP	Woodlawn N.C.#1852 Elmira	ROH,FPH,P5,P65
Griffin, A. Brown	Pvt.	F 25th SCVI	24	OG	05/06/65	Elmira, NY	DIP	Woodlawn N.C.#2765 Elmira	ROH,FPH,P6,HAG
Griffin, A.B.	Pvt.	B 5th SCVI			09/30/62	Frederick, MD	DOW	Frederick, MD Cem.	P6
Griffin, A.C.	Pvt.	B 5th SCVI			09/30/62	Frederick, MD	DIP	Mt.Olivet Cem. C.S.#66	ROH,FPH,P1,BOD
Griffin, Drewry	Pvt.	I 13th SCVI	21	SG	08/15/62		DOD		ROH,HOS
Griffin, G.E.	Pvt.	K 15th SCVI			/ /		DOD		JR
Griffin, George White	Pvt.	G 2nd SCVC	20	AE	10/16/62	Charlottesville	ACD	(Killed in RR accident)	ROH,H2,SA2
Griffin, H.T.	Sgt.	C 4th SCVC			07/04/64	Richmond, VA	DOW	Hollywood Cem.Rchmd. U30	ROH,HC
Griffin, Henry J.F.	Pvt.	F 25th SCVI	25	OG	05/16/65	Elmira, NY	DIP	Woodlawn N.C.#2963 Elmira	ROH,FPH,P6,HAG
Griffin, J.R.	Pvt.	G 1st SCVI			09/01/62	Richmond, VA		Hollywood Cem.Rchmd. A1	HC
Griffin, Jackson	Pvt.	B 7th SCVI		AE	10/15/61		DOD		JR
Griffin, James	Pvt.	F 4th SCVC		MN	/ /	Virginia	DOD		HMC
Griffin, James	Pvt.	D 12th SCVI		RD	05/31/64		KIA		JR
Griffin, Joel	Pvt.	B Arty Bn			12/25/61	Charleston, SC	DOD	Magnolia Cem. Charleston	ROH,MAG
Griffin, Joel J.	Pvt.	C 9th SCVIBn	31	HY	03/27/62	Georgetown, SC	DOD	(JR=DOW MS 4/9/63)	ROH,JR,PP
Griffin, John L.	Pvt.	I 13th SCVI		SG	08/05/62	Richmond, VA	DOD	Hollywood Cem.Rchmd. H169	ROH,HC,HOS
Griffin, John M.	Pvt.	B 13th SCVI		SG	01/18/63	At home	DOD	(Typhoid)	JR,HOS
Griffin, John S.	Pvt.	C Hol. Leg.	25	SG	08/14/62	Richmond, VA	DOD	Hollywood Cem.Rchmd. Q130	ROH,HC,HOS
Griffin, John W.	Pvt.	B 24th SCVI		MO	07/15/63	Brandon, MS	DOD		ROH,HOM,PP
Griffin, Joseph D.	Pvt.	F 23rd SCVI		CR	09/17/62	Warrenton, VA	DOW	(Wdd 2nd Man)	ROH,JR,CDC,HHC
Griffin, Joseph W.	1st Sgt.	G 7th SCVI	22	ED	01/17/62	Centreville, VA	DOD	(Typhoid)	JR,HOE,EDN,UD2
Griffin, Landrum	Pvt.	I 13th SCVI	19	SG	07/15/62		DOD	(Typhoid)	ROH,JR
Griffin, Larkin A.	2nd Sgt.	B Orr's Ri.	19	AE	06/08/64	Washington, DC	DOW	(CDC=Co. G, Wdd @ Spotva)	ROH,CDC,P5,P12
Griffin, N.	Pvt.	D 23rd SCVI		CN	08/30/62	2nd Manassas, VA	KIA		ROH,JR,CDC
Griffin, N.L.	Pvt.	I 2nd SCVC		ED	/ /	Pohick Church VA	DOW		HOE
Griffin, N.T.	Pvt.	B 3rd SCVIBn			/ /	MD		Rose Hill C. Hagerstown MD	ROH,BOD
Griffin, Robert C.	Cpl.	F 5th SCVI		YK	09/17/62	Sharpsburg, MD	KIA	Rose Hill C. Hagerstown MD	ROH,CDC,SA3,BOD
Griffin, Robert Y.H.	Cpt.	C 4th SCVIBn	28	PS	07/11/62	7 Pines, VA	DOW	Hagood Fam.Cem. Pickens SC	ROH,PCS
Griffin, Silas	Pvt.	C 14th SCMil	52	OG	06/04/65	Hart's Island NY	DIP	Cypress Hills N.C.#2935 NY	ROH,FPH,P6,P79
Griffin, Stephen H.	Pvt.	F 4th SCVC		MN	07/31/64	Raleigh, NC	DOD	Oakwood C. Raleigh, NC	HMC,TOD
Griffin, T.B.	Pvt.	K 27th SCVI	18	SG	08/17/64	Petersburg, VA	DOW	Blandford Church Pbg., VA	ROH,BLC,HAG,PP
Griffin, Thomas	Pvt.	F 15th SCVI		SG	11/06/62	Winchester, VA	DOD	Stonewall Cem. Winchester	ROH,WIN,HOS,KEB
Griffin, William B.	Pvt.	B 3rd SCVI		NY	11/15/61	Charlottesville	DOD		ROH,JR,ANY,KEB
Griffin, William Dunlap	4th Sgt.	A 3rd SCVI		LS	12/21/62	Richmond, VA	DOW	(Wdd Fbg 12/13)(NI SA2)	ROH,JR,ANY,SA2
Griffis, George A.	Pvt.		26	CO	01/17/63	Hardeeville, SC	DOD	Sheider/Rayso/Risher F.C.	CUC
Griffith, Anderson	Pvt.	K 2nd SCVI		GE	03/13/63	Gordonsville, VA	DOD	Gordonsville, VA C.C.	ROH,SA2,GOR
Griffith, Benjamin F.	Pvt.	B 16th SCVI		GE	03/26/63	Adams Run, SC	DOD		PP
Griffith, Elias P.	Pvt.	E 8th SCVI		DN	07/23/61	Winchester, VA	DOD	(Typhoid)	JR
Griffith, George	Pvt.	Ham.Leg.		AE	10/14/62	Centreville, VA	ACD	(RR, derailed by cow)	ROH,CDC
Griffith, George W.	Pvt.	C 3rd SCVI		NY	07/02/63	Gettysburg, PA	KIA		ROH,JR,GDR,SA2
Griffith, Henry	Pvt.	H Hol.Leg.	29	NY	12/15/63	At home	DOD		ROH,ANY
Griffith, J.C.	Pvt.	G 13th SCVI		NY	05/28/62	Winder H. Rchmd	DOD	(Typhoid)	ROH,JR,ANY
Griffith, J.L.	Pvt.	C 1st SCVIR		LR	03/09/64	Charleston, SC	DOW	Magnolia Cem. Charleston	ROH,MAG,CDC,SA1
Griffith, James	Pvt.	E 24th SCVI	36	CO	03/21/65	Camp Chase, OH	DIP	C.C.#1724 Columbus, OH	ROH,FPH,P6,P12
Griffith, John A.	Pvt.	K 6th SCVI			02/17/62	Centreville, VA	DOD	(Typhoid)	JR
Griffith, Lemuel	Pvt.	B 16th SCVI		GE	07/16/64	Atlanta, GA	KIA		ROH
Griffith, R.	Pvt.	E 14th SCVI		LS	06/17/62	Richmond, VA	DOD		ROH
Griffith, R. Flynn	Pvt.	B 16th SCVI		GE	08/16/64	Atlanta, GA	KIA		ROH,16R
Griffith, Sanders F.	Pvt.	F 2nd SCVA		CN	07/13/64	Charleston, SC	DOW	Magnolia Cem. Charleston	ROH,MAG,CDC

SOUTH CAROLINA DEAD IN CSA SERVICE 1861-1865

NAME	RANK	C REGIMENT	AGE	DS	DIED	WHERE	WHY	BURIED	SOURCES
Grigg, A.D.	Pvt.	B 21st SCVI			11/13/64	Richmond, VA		Hollywood Cem.Rchmd. W593	HC
Griggs, Clement	Pvt.	G 21st SCVI		CD	01/29/63		DOD		JR,HAG
Griggs, D.W.	Pvt.	A 21st SCVI		CN	07/18/63	James Island, SC	DOD		JR
Griggs, Martin	Pvt.	A 21st SCVI		GN	/ /	Morris Island SC	DOD	(1863)	FLR,HAG
Grimball, William H.	1st Lt.	E 1st SCVA	27	CN	07/27/64	James Island, SC	DOD	Magnolia Cem. Charleston	ROH,JR,SCA,R44
Grimballs, Robert	Pvt.	H 16th SCVI		GE	01/07/64	Lookout Mtn., GA	DOD	(Prob @ Dalton, GA)	16R,PP
Grimes, Allen	Pvt.	B 2nd SCVIRi		PS	/ /				ROH
Grimes, George Martin	Cpt.	G 1st SCVIH		BL	09/30/64	Ft. Harrison, VA	KIA		ROH,SA1
Grimes, J.W.	3rd Sgt.	B 2nd SCVIRi		PS	/ /				ROH
Grimsley, Wesley E.	Cpl.	D 21st SCVI		CD	03/20/62	Georgetown, SC	DOD	(JR=Adams Run, SC)	ROH,JR,HAG,PP
Grindley, Joseph	Pvt.	F 22nd SCVI		PS	07/30/64	Crater, Pbg., VA	KIA		BLM
Griner, Jesse W.	Sgt.	F 11th SCVI		BT	06/17/64	Fts. Monroe,VA	DOW	(Wdd @ Swift Creek 5/9/64)	ROH,HAG,P12
Griner, Raford	Pvt.	F 11th SCVI	24	BT	08/27/64	Gillisonville SC	DOD	(HAG=Ralph)	ROH,HAG
Grisham, Hugh B.	Pvt.	B 13th SCVI		SG	07/01/62	Richmond, VA	DOD	(Winder Hospital)	ROH,HOS
Grissett, J.	Pvt.	C 24th SCVI		CO	05/23/64	Fair Gds Atlanta		Oakland Cem. Atlanta R15#4	BGA
Griswold, S.	Surgeon				/ /			Magnolia Cem. Charleston	MAG
Grizzard, John W.	Pvt.	K 8th SCVI		MO	/ /	Rome, GA		Myrtle Hill Cem. Rome, GA	ROH,HOM,KEB,BG
Groce, Henry L.	Sgt.	C 16th SCVI		GE	08/25/62	Adams Run, SC	DOD	(Congestive Chill)	JR,16R,PP
Grogan, Henry	Pvt.	C 16th SCVI		GE	11/30/64	Franklin, TN	DOW	Macgavock C. Fr'kln, Gv#21	16R,WCT
Grogan, James Henry	Pvt.	F 16th SCVI		GE	02/23/65	Nashville, TN	DOW	(Wdd & POW @ Franklin)	16R,P3,P5,PP
Grogan, Thomas R.	Pvt.	B 2nd SCVI		GE	10/15/62	Winchester, VA	ACD		ROH,SA2,KEB
Groom, John	Pvt.	6th SCVI		AN	08/29/62	Lynchburg, VA	DOD	(H2-1st in F,2nd SCVI)	H2
Groomes, Shecut	Pvt.	D 5th SCVC	23	CN	06/11/64	Trevillian Stn.	KIA		ROH,JR,CDC
Grooms, Alpheus	Pvt.	D 2nd SCVI		SR	07/16/61	Richmond, VA	DOD	Hollywood Cem.Rchmd. V690	ROH,HC,KEB,SA2
Grooms, E.	Pvt.	K 8th SCVI		MO	/ /	Culpepper, VA		(1861,KEB=Groomes, F.)	HOM,KEB
Grooms, Evander	Pvt.	D 26th SCVI		MO	/ /	Petersburg, VA	KIA		HOM
Grooms, N. Wesley	Pvt.	C 11th SCVI		CN	05/26/64	Bermuda Hundred	KIA		ROH,HAG
Grophr,	Lt.				/ /			Fredericksburg C.C. R9S12	FBG
Gross, Alfred H.	Pvt.	K 20th SCVI		LN	06/15/65		ACD		ROH,KEB
Gross, John G.	Pvt.	B 15th SCVI		UN	12/07/64	Elmira, NY	DIP	Woodlawn N.C.#1186 Elmira	FPH,KEB,P5,P12
Grott, H.W.	Pvt.	19th SCVI			/ /	Murfreesboro, TN		Evergreen C. Murfreesboro	TOD
Grouter, John	Pvt.	A 21st SCVI	36	GN	06/07/64	(Fatal burns)	ACD	Oakwood C.#8,Row O,Div F	ROH,OWC,HAG,CD
Groves, Allan L.	Pvt.	B 3rd SCVC	41	CO	02/04/64	At home	DOD		ROH
Grubbs, Alfred	Pvt.	H 6th SCVI	19	FD	05/31/62	7 Pines, VA	DOW		ROH,CDC
Grubbs, John L.	Pvt.	D 2nd SCVIRi		PS	10/28/63	Lookout Valley	KIA	In the field, Lookout Mtn.	ROH,JR,CDC,UD2
Grubbs, N.T.	Pvt.	I Orr's Ri.		PS	05/20/64	Richmond, VA		Hollywood Cem.Rchmd. E4	HC
Grubbs, R.W.					/ /	Warrenton Hosp.	DOW	(after 2nd Manassas)	UD2
Grubbs, Richard L.	Lt.	C 2nd SCVIRi		PS	06/30/62	Richmond, VA	DOD	Oakwood C.#28, Row D,Div C	ROH,OWC,R45
Grubbs, Richard L.	Pvt.	K Orr's Ri.	19	AN	07/18/62		DOD	(JR=6/20/62)	ROH,JR,CDC
Grubbs, Richard W.	Pvt.	D 2nd SCVIRi		PS	09/20/62	Warrenton, VA	DOW	(Wdd 2nd Man)	ROH,CDC
Grubbs, Robert W.	Pvt.	K 4th SCVIBn			09/20/62	(Prob Warrenton)	DOW	(Wdd @ 2nd Manassas)	JR
Grubbs, Thomas	Pvt.	C 1st SCVA			06/15/65	Pt. Lookout, MD	DIP	C.C. Pt. Lookout, MD	FPH,P6,P114
Grubbs, William L.	Pvt.	K 2nd SCVI		BL	11/14/62	Danville, VA	DOD		H2,SA2,KEB
Gruber, P.	Pvt.	H 12th SCVI	30	PS	07/15/62	Richmond, VA	DOD	(On Richmond effects list)	ROH,JR,CDC
Grumbles, R.P.	Pvt.	G 3rd SCVI		LS	09/13/62	Maryland Hts. MD	KIA		ROH,JR,SA2,KEB
Gubell, E.M.	Pvt.	L P.S.S.			/ /		DOW		JR
Guerard, Jacob John	1st Lt.	C 11th SCVI		CN	09/14/64	Ft. Delaware, DE	DIP	St. Philips Ch. Charleston	ROH,FPH,P5,HAG
Guerry, LeGrand P.	Pvt.	Harts Bty	19	CN	11/02/64	Petersburg, VA	DOW	(Wdd 10/27/64)	ROH,CNM
Guess, Burgess M.	Pvt.	C 25th SCVI	40	WG	05/16/64	Drury's Bluff VA	KIA		CTA,HOW,HAG
Guess, J.A.	Pvt.			WG	/ /		DOD	(1864)	HOW
Guggisy, D.F.	Pvt.	D 1st SCVI			10/14/62			Stonewall Cem. Winchester	WIN

G

SOUTH CAROLINA DEAD IN CSA SERVICE 1861-1865

NAME	RANK	C REGIMENT	AGE	DS	DIED	WHERE	WHY	BURIED	SOURCES
Guise, Amos Bartley	Cpl.	H 3rd SCVI	24	LN	11/21/61	Warren Sprgs. VA	DOD		ROH,JR,CDC,KEB
Guiton, A.	Pvt.	G 18th SCVI		UN	05/20/64	Clay's Farm, VA	KIA		ROH,JR
Gulledge, Alexander	Pvt.	M 8th SCVI	24	DN	05/15/62	Richmond, VA	DOD (JR=DOD in SC)		ROH,JR,KEB
Gulledge, Alfred	Pvt.	B 26th SCVI	30	CD	10/07/63		DOD		ROH
Gulledge, John	Pvt.	C Hol.Leg.	28	SG	02/06/62	Adams Run, SC	DOD (PP=6/4/62)		ROH,HOS,PP
Gulledge, John	Pvt.	D 21st SCVI		CD	06/15/63	At home	DOW (Wdd in knee 5/16/64)		ROH,CDC
Gundy, C.M.	Pvt.				/ /	Richmond, VA		Oakwood C.#9, Row E, Div C	OWC
Gunn, C.G.	Pvt.	I 15th SCVI		LN	04/04/64	Richmond, VA		Hollywood Cem.Rchmd. I115	HC
Gunn, Felix	Pvt.	I 1st SCVIG		CN	10/15/62	Warrenton, VA	DOW (Wdd @ 2nd Man)		SA1,CDC
Gunn, James	Pvt.	G P.S.S.	36	YK	02/15/64		DOW (ROH=DOD)		ROH,YEB
Gunn, Jesse M.	Pvt.	A 12th SCVI	32	YK	06/08/62	Richmond, VA	DOD		ROH,JR,YEB
Gunnells, William M.	Pvt.	E 16th SCVI	19	GE	09/30/64	Franklin, TN	KIA	Macgavock C. Frkln Gv#1	ROH,16R,PP
Gunter, Felix	Pvt.	I 20th SCVI		LN	06/01/64	Beulah Church VA	KIA		ROH,KEB
Gunter, G.	Pvt.	D 16th SCVI		GE	02/01/65	Camp Douglas, IL	DIP	Oak Woods Cem. Chicago, IL	FPH,P6
Gunter, G.N.	Pvt.	I SCVA Bn			03/23/62	Ft. Sumter, SC		Magnolia Cem. Charleston	MAG
Gunter, Henry J.	Pvt.	F 10th SCVI		MN	07/22/64	Atlanta, GA	DOW		RAS,HMC,CDC
Gunter, Hugh	Pvt.	I 26th SCVI		WG	05/20/64	Drury's Bluff VA	DOW		ROH,CTA,HOW
Gunter, J.L.	Pvt.	F P.S.S.			06/20/64	Petersburg, VA	KIA	Blandford Church Pbg., VA	ROH,JR,BLC
Gunter, James H.	Pvt.	I 19th SCVI	17	AE	06/27/64	Marietta, GA	KIA (Sniped on picket)		ROH
Gunter, Leander	Sgt.	I 20th SCVI		LN	10/13/64	Strasburg, VA	KIA (KEB=Gunter, Levi)		ROH,JR,KEB
Gunter, Stancil	Pvt.	I 20th SCVI		LN	09/15/63	Mt. Pleasant, SC	DOD		ROH,KEB
Gunter, W.J.	Pvt.	H 7th SCVI		ED	12/27/64	Pt. Lookout, MD	DIP	C.C. Pt. Lookout, MD	ROH,FPH,P5,P114
Gunter, William D.	Pvt.	I 21st SCVI		MN	05/09/64	Pt. Walthall, VA	DOW	Blandford Church Pbg., VA	ROH,HMC,BLC,PP
Gurgamus, J.F.	Pvt.		29	WG	/ /		DOD (1861)		CTA,HOW
Guyton, J.	Cpl.	D 12th SCVI		RD	05/06/64	Wilderness, VA	KIA		JR
Gwin, Richard A.	3rd Sgt.	F 1st SCVIH		GE	06/27/64	Kennesaw Mtn. GA	KIA (Tfd frm B, 2nd SCVI)		H2,SA2,SA1,KEB
Gwin, T.J.	Pvt.	E 14th SCVI		LS	/ /	Petersburg, VA	KIA		CGS
Gwinn, Henry J.	Pvt.	G P.S.S.	21	YK	07/22/64	Petersburg, PA	KIA		ROH,YEB
Gwinn, Holly M.	Pvt.	A 12th SCVI	26	YK	/ /	At home	DOW		YEB
Gwinn, Jefferson	Pvt.	K 3rd SCVI		SG	03/19/65	Bentonville, NC	KIA		HOS,KEB
Gwinn, Lewis H.	Pvt.	E Hol.Leg.	22	SG	06/14/62	Adams Run, SC	DOD		ROH,HOS
Gwinn, W. Frank	Pvt.	C Hol.Leg.		SG	/ /	Florence, SC	ACD (RR Acd, Company drummer)		HOS

SOUTH CAROLINA DEAD IN CSA SERVICE 1861-1865

NAME	RANK	C	REGIMENT	AGE	DS	DIED	WHERE	WHY	BURIED	SOURCES
Hackel, Thomas Lipscomb	Pvt.	C	6th SCVC	19	AE	07/23/64	Ream's Stn., VA	KIA		ROH
Hackett, F.	Pvt.	D				06/15/62	Richmond, VA		Oakwood C.#63, Row K, Div B	ROH, OWC
Hackett, J.L.	Pvt.	C	6th SCVC			08/23/64	Ream's Stn., VA	KIA	(JR=T.L.)	ROH, JR
Hackett, John W.	Pvt.	G	22nd SCVI	30	AN	04/15/64	Summerville, SC	DOD	(BLM=KIA @ Crater)	ROH
Hackett, Robert	Pvt.	G	22nd SCVI	22	AN	07/30/64	Crater, Pbg., VA	KIA		ROH
Hackett, William K.	Pvt.	G	P.S.S.	26	YK	06/07/62	Fts. Monroe, VA	DOW	(Prob. Wdd @ 7 Pines)	ROH, JR, YEB, CDC
Hacknah, William	Pvt.	H	13th SCVI		LN	/ /	Richmond, VA		Oakwood C.#15, Row H, Div B	ROH, OWC
Hackon, John	Pvt.					/ /			Fredericksburg C.C. R4S11	FBG
Hadden, John C.	Pvt.	B	13th SCVI		SG	07/14/62	Richmond, VA	DOD	(Typhoid)	ROH, HOS
Hadden, L.C.	Pvt.					08/19/64	Petersburg, VA	DOW	Blandford Church Pbg., VA	BLC
Hadden, William M.	Lt. Col.		Orr's Ri.	35	PS	07/28/64	Deep Bottom, VA	KIA		ROH, JR, BOS, LC
Haddon, A.F.	Pvt.	G	Orr's Ri.		AE	02/10/65	Pt. Lookout, MD	DIP	C.C. Pt. Lookout, MD	ROH, FPH, P6, P11
Haddon, David P.	Pvt.	G	Orr's Ri.		AE	08/29/62	2nd Manassas, VA	KIA		ROH, JR, CDC
Haddon, John Davis	Pvt.	H	2nd SCVA	20	AN	05/10/65	Greensboro, NC	DOD	(Courier, Gen. Tagliafero)	ROH, PP
Haddon, Lafayette W.	Pvt.	G	Orr's Ri.	27	AE	02/16/62	Sullivans Isl. SC	DOD	Due West A.R.P.	ROH, CAE
Haddon, W.L.	Pvt.	G	Orr's Ri.		AE	07/12/62	Gaines' Mill, VA	DOW		JR, CDC
Hading,						/ /	Richmond, VA		Oakwood C.#62, Row H, Div B	OWC
Hadwin, John	Pvt.	F	3rd SCVC			05/18/65	Ft. Delaware, DE	DIP	Finn's Pt., NJ Nat. Cem.	ROH, FPH, P6, P12
Haffner, Ephraim	Pvt.	A	12th SCVI	30	YK	/ /	Farmville, VA	DOD		YEB
Hafner, J.A.	Pvt.	K	1st SCVC			10/02/64	Charleston, SC	DOD		ROH
Hagan, W.T.	Pvt.		5th SCVI			/ /	Richmond, VA		Oakwood C.#51, Row R, Div C	OWC, CDC
Hagens, J.H.	Pvt.		Hart's Bty			01/15/63	Richmond, VA		(Day approximate)	CDC
Hagerty, J.F.	Pvt.	G	18th SCVI	48		08/28/64	Petersburg, VA	KIA		ROH, PP
Hagerty, M.	Pvt.	A				/ /	Richmond, VA		Oakwood C.#40, Row G, Div B	ROH, OWC
Haggerty, Thomas	Pvt.	K	1st SCVIG		CN	06/27/62	Gaines' Mill, VA	KIA		ROH, JR, SA1
Hagins, Calvin G.	Pvt.	B	12th SCVI	19	YK	/ /	Richmond, VA	DOD	(1862)	YEB
Hagins, John J.	Pvt.	B	12th SCVI	21	YK	08/15/62	Richmond, VA	DOD	(YEB=Pocotaligo)	ROH, JR, YEB
Hagins, Wyatt	Pvt.	B	12th SCVI	24	YK	02/15/62	Charleston, SC	DOD	(YEB=DOW)	JR, YEB
Haglar, J.P.	Pvt.	K	10th SCVI		CN	/ /	Okolona, MS	DOD		PP
Haglar, Littleton	Pvt.	E	22nd SCVI		LR	12/13/62	Kinston, NC	DOW	(LAN=Heigler)	ROH, CDC, LAN, PP
Hagood, George M.	Pvt.	B	7th SCVIBn	39	FD	07/15/64	Petersburg, VA	KIA	(HOF= G.W., JR=Wdd 6/18)	ROH, JR, HAG, HOF
Hagood, H.W.	Cpl.	I	Hol.Leg.	33	SG	11/18/64	Winnsboro, SC	DOD		ROH
Hagood, Jesse M.	Pvt.	F	7th SCVIBn	17	FD	09/19/64	Elmira, NY	DIP	Woodlawn N.C.#500 Elmira	ROH, HIC, FPH, P6
Hagood, Robert M.	Pvt.	B	21st SCVI		DN	05/16/64	Drury's Bluff VA	KIA		ROH, JR, CDC, HAG
Hahn, John C.	Sgt.		Bachman's		CN	09/17/62	Sharpsburg, MD	KIA		ROH, CDC
Haigler, Frank M.	Pvt.	F	25th SCVI		OG	06/15/64	Petersburg, VA	KIA	(Shot by sniper)	ROH, HAG, EDR
Haigler, Joshua	Pvt.	A	14th SCVI		DN	03/15/65	Fayetteville, NC	DIP		ROH
Haile, G.W.	Pvt.	G	2nd SCVI		KW	10/15/62	(As Harle, J.M.)	DOD	Stonewall Cem. Winchester	WIN, SA2, KEB
Haile, James S.	Pvt.	E	12th SCVI	45	LR	06/15/62		DOD		LAN
Hain, S.R.	Pvt.	K	17th SCVI			/ /	2nd Manassas, VA	DOW		JR
Haines, L.	Pvt.				WG	/ /		DOD	(1862)	CTA, HOW
Haines, S.E.	Pvt.	K	P.S.S.			06/02/62	Fts. Monroe, VA	DOW	(Wdd 7 Pines or Wlmsbg.)	ROH, CDC, CNM
Haines, W.D.	Pvt.	I	22nd SCVI		OG	/ /	Richmond, VA		Oakwood C.#58, Row H, Div G	ROH, OWC
Haines, W.L.	Pvt.	B	27th SCVI		CN	05/16/64	Drury's Bluff VA	KIA		JR
Hainey, Benjamin	Pvt.	D	21st SCVI	37	CD	04/16/62	Georgetown, SC	DOD	(PP=3/24/62)	ROH, JR, HAG, PP
Hainey, M.	Cpl.	K	19th SCVI		ED	11/30/64	Franklin, TN	KIA		ROH, HOE
Hains, W.J.	Pvt.	D	Orr's Ri.			07/17/63	Petersburg, VA	DOD		ROH
Hair, Calvin	Pvt.	E	22nd SCVI	38	LR	12/21/62	Petersburg, VA	DOD	Blandford Church Pbg., VA	ROH, BLC, LAN, PP
Hair, E.K.	Pvt.	I	5th SCVC		BL	/ /	Richmond, VA		Oakwood C.#53, Row D, Div G	ROH, OWC
Hair, J.H.	Pvt.	K	17th SCVI			/ /	Danville, VA	DOD		JR
Hair, J.W.	Pvt.	I	Inglis LA		DN	04/08/64	At home	DOD	(Society Hill, SC)	ROH

SOUTH CAROLINA DEAD IN CSA SERVICE 1861-1865

NAME	RANK	C REGIMENT	AGE	DS	DIED	WHERE	WHY	BURIED	SOURCES
Hair, W. Jennings	Pvt.	A 1st SCVIG		BL	09/14/63	Davids Island NY	DIP	Cypress Hills N.C.#858 NY	FPH,GDR,SA1,P1
Hairston, Thomas B.	Pvt.		40	LS	07/30/64	Petersburg, VA	KIA	Leesville S.M.C. LS Cty.	LSC
Haithcock, Hopkins	Pvt.	C 7th SCVIBn	33	RD	07/16/64	Richmond, VA	DOD		ROH,HAG
Halbert, F.M.	Pvt.	K 22nd SCVI		PS	09/07/62	Richmond, VA		Hollywood Cem.Rchmd. A71	HC
Hale, George	Pvt.	D Hol.Leg.	25	BL	12/06/64	Petersburg, VA	KIA		ROH
Hale, H.A.	Pvt.				/ /	Petersburg, VA		Blandford Church Pbg., VA	BLC
Hale, James Wesley	Pvt.	C 4th SCVI		AN	10/27/61	Culpepper, VA	DOD	Fairview Cem. Culpepper VA	CGH,SA2,HOF
Hale, R.O.	Pvt.	K 13th SCVI		LN	06/17/62			Richmond, VA	ROH
Hale, T.F.	Cpl.	D Hol.Leg.		BL	08/10/62	Richmond, VA	DOD		ROH
Haley, Ferdinand B.	Pvt.	E 7th SCVIBn	48	SR	04/28/62	Adams Run, SC	DOD	(JR=4/24/62)	ROH,JR,HAG,PP
Haley, H.V.	Cpl.	I 25th SCVI		CL	03/17/65	Elmira, NY	DIP	Woodlawn N.C.#1821 Elmira	FPH,HAG,P65
Haley, O.B.	Pvt.	D Orr's Ri.			12/10/62	Richmond, VA	DOD	(On Rchmd effects list)	ROH,CDC
Halfacre, Frederick	Pvt.	D 13th SCVI	18	NY	12/17/61	Coosawatchie, SC	DOD	Clayton M.U.Ch. Newb'y Cty	ROH,JR,NCC,ANY
Halfacre, John	Pvt.	D 13th SCVI	21	NY	08/29/62	2nd Manassas, VA	KIA	Clayton M.U.Ch. Newb'y Cty	ROH,JR,NCC,ANY
Halfield, C.W.	Pvt.	E 1st SCVI			/ /	Richmond, VA		Oakwood C.#110,Row N,Div C	OWC
Halford, James M.	Pvt.	E 8th SCVI		DN	04/15/62	Richmond, VA	DOD	(Pneumonia)	JR
Halk, Barton.	Pvt.	E 14th SCVI		LS	08/30/62	2nd Manassas, VA	KIA		ROH,CGS,CDC
Halk, J.T.	Pvt.	E 14th SCVI		LS	/ /	Richmond, VA	DOD	(Mt. Jackson Hospital)	CGS
Hall, A.M.	Pvt.	F 24th SCVI		AN	11/15/63		DOD		HOL
Hall, Alexander	Pvt.	D 11th SCVI		CO	04/02/65	Elmira, NY	DIP		P65
Hall, Andrew O.N.	Sgt.	C P.S.S.	25	AN	06/17/64	Bermuda Hundred	KIA	(JR=Lookout Valley,1863)	ROH,JR,GMJ
Hall, Angus	Pvt.	A 1st SCVIR			10/06/63		DOD		SA1
Hall, B.F.	Pvt.	D 3rd SCResB			01/08/65	Columbia, SC			PP
Hall, Benjamin	Pvt.			YK	/ /			(Died in service)	YEB
Hall, Daniel	Pvt.	G 21st SCVI		CD	02/24/65	Elmira, NY	DIP	Woodlawn N.C.#2281 Elmira	FPH,HAG,P6,P65
Hall, Darling P.	5th Sgt.	E 1st SCVIH		BL	10/28/63	Lookout Valley	KIA	(JR=Racoon Mtn.)	ROH,JR,SA1,CDC
Hall, David	Pvt.	K Orr's Ri.	28	AN	08/29/62	2nd Manassas, VA	KIA	(ROH=8/30/62)	ROH,JR
Hall, David	Pvt.	E Orr's Ri.	26	PS	08/30/62	2nd Manassas, VA	KIA		ROH
Hall, David	Pvt.	M 8th SCVI		DN	07/05/62	Richmond, VA	DOD		JR
Hall, Davis	Pvt.	F 24th SCVI		AN	/ /	Yazoo City, MS	DOD	(Left behind sick)	EJM
Hall, E.S.	Pvt.	D Orr's Ri.		AN	09/01/62	Ox Hill, VA	KIA	On the field	JR
Hall, Edward G.	Pvt.	D 11th SCVI	35	BT	05/30/64	Fts. Monroe, VA	DOW	(POW @ Swift Creek 5/9/64)	ROH,HAG
Hall, Edwin M.	Cpl.	L P.S.S.	22	PS	06/15/63	Lynchburg, VA	DOD	Lynchburg CSA Cem. #10 R2	ROH,JR,BBW
Hall, Ellis	Pvt.	G 16th SCVI		GE	11/30/64	Franklin, TN	KIA	Macgavock C. Frkln Gv#20	ROH,16R,WCT,PP
Hall, F.G.	Pvt.	C Orr's Ri.		PS	06/29/62	Gaines' Mill, VA	DOW		JR
Hall, Francis M.	Pvt.	E Orr's Ri.	22	AN	09/13/62	Warrenton, VA	DOW	(Wdd @ 2nd Man)	ROH,CDC
Hall, Francis Marion	Pvt.	A 7th SCVIBn	28	KW	06/15/64		ACD	(Acd discharge of own gun)	ROH,HIC,HAG
Hall, George	Pvt.	F 13th SCVI		SG	05/03/63	Chancellorsville	KIA		HOS
Hall, George L.	Cpl.	B 19th SCVI		ED	/ /		ACD	(Shot accidentaly)	HOE
Hall, Hezekiah	Pvt.	G 19th SCVI		AE	06/15/64	Atlanta, GA	KIA		ROH,HOL
Hall, Isaac	4th Cpl.	K 21st SCVI		DN	01/09/64	Pt. Lookout, MD	DIP	C.C. Pt. Lookout, MD	FPH,HAG,P5,P113
Hall, J.	Pvt.	A 7th SCVIBn		KW	11/01/62	At home	DOD		JR,HAG
Hall, J.M.	Pvt.	F 2nd SCVIRi			05/15/64	Virginia	KIA	(JR=T.M.)	ROH,JR
Hall, James	Pvt.	D 2nd SCVI			12/14/63	Pt. Lookout, MD	DIP	C.C. Pt. Lookout, MD	ROH,FPH,SA2,P113
Hall, James	Pvt.	F 7th SCVIBn	22	CD	10/22/62	Pocotaligo, SC	KIA		ROH,HIC,HAG,R46
Hall, James A.	Pvt.	I 14th SCVI		AE	10/02/62	Farmville, VA	DOD	(JR=Lynchburg)	ROH,JR
Hall, James H.	Pvt.	F 13th SCVI		SG	07/21/62	Richmond, VA	DOD	Hollywood Cem.Rchmd. M149	ROH,JR,HC,HOS
Hall, James H.	Pvt.	K 21st SCVI		DN	08/29/65	Elmira, NY	DIP	Woodlawn N.C.#2857 Elmira	FPH,HAG,P6,P12
Hall, James Major	Pvt.	F 6th SCVI	20	YK	05/04/62	Manchester, VA	DOD	(Typhoid, JR=6/11/62)	ROH,JR
Hall, John E.	Pvt.	F 13th SCVI		SG	07/10/62	Richmond, VA	DOD	Hollywood Cem.Rchmd. M57	ROH,JR,HC,HOS
Hall, John H.	Pvt.	A 25th SCVI	17	CN	05/15/64	Drury's Bluff VA	KIA	(Sniper)	ROH,JR,HAG,WLI

SOUTH CAROLINA DEAD IN CSA SERVICE 1861-1865

NAME	RANK	C REGIMENT	AGE	DS	DIED	WHERE	WHY	BURIED	SOURCES
Hall, John James	Pvt.	A 7th SCVIBn	33	KW	06/03/64	Cold Harbor, VA	KIA		ROH,JR,HAG,HIC
Hall, John M.	1st Lt.	F 24th SCVI		AN	08/30/63	Macon, GA	DOD	Prob Rose Hill C. Macon GA	JR,HOL,R48
Hall, Joseph	Pvt.	F 7th SCVIBn	27	CD	05/16/64	Drury's Bluff VA	KIA	(James E. of KW in HIC)	ROH,HIC,HAG
Hall, L. McCullough	Pvt.	A 7th SCVIBn	29	CD	02/16/62	Adams Run, SC	DOD	PP	ROH,JR,HAG,HIC
Hall, L.J.	Pvt.	I 14th SCVI		AE	10/06/62	Lynchburg, VA	DOD	Lynchburg CSA Cem. #6 R10	ROH,CDC,BBW
Hall, M.H.	1st Sgt.	F 24th SCVI		AN	05/14/64		DIP	(POW 11/63)	HOL
Hall, M.M.	Pvt.	E 19th SCVI		SR	04/02/63	Shelbyville, TN	DOD	Willowmount C. Shelbyville	PP,TOD
Hall, Major T.	Pvt.	5th SCVI	20	YK	06/05/62	Manchester, VA	DOD	(YEB=KIA)	YMD,YEB
Hall, Milledge	Pvt.	K 14th SCVI		ED	/ /		DOD		HOE
Hall, P.H.	Pvt.	G 11th SCVI			/ /	Richmond, VA		Oakwood C.#23, Row K, Div C	ROH,OWC
Hall, Pennel P.	Pvt.	K 12th SCVI	36	PS	08/09/63	Davids Island NY	DOW	Cypress Hills N.C. #745 NY	ROH,JR,FPH,P1,
Hall, R.E.	Pvt.	I 1st SCVA			09/15/63	Ft. Johnson, SC	KIA		R44
Hall, Samuel R.	Pvt.	G 25th SCVI	22	OG	06/16/64	Petersburg, VA	KIA		ROH,HAG
Hall, Sylvanus	Pvt.	G 25th SCVI		OG	06/15/64	Petersburg, VA	DOW	(In enemy hands)	ROH,CDC,HAG
Hall, T.J.	Pvt.	A 1st SCVIG		BL	07/03/63	Gettysburg, PA	DOW	(Left arm Amp.@ shoulder)	GDR,SA1,CDC
Hall, Thomas H.	Pvt.	G 1st SCVIG		ED	07/05/62	Richmond, VA	DOD	(Typhoid, JR=8/5/62)	ROH,JR,SA1,HOE
Hall, W.C.	Pvt.	F 24th SCVI	22	AN	05/14/63	Jackson, MS	KIA		ROH,JR,HOL,PP
Hall, Wesley	Pvt.	E 1st SCVIR		LR	09/08/63	Ft. Moultrie, SC	KIA	(Ammo chest explosion)	SA1,CDC
Hall, Whitner	Pvt.	F 24th SCVI		AN	05/14/63	Jackson, MS	KIA	(?DOD Columbia 8/28/62)	HOL,PP
Hall, William B.	Pvt.	K 5th SCVI		SG	07/01/64	Petersburg, VA	KIA		ROH,SA3,HOS,WA
Hall, William D.	Pvt.	H Ham.Leg.		OG	11/26/63	Camp Morton, IN	DIP	Green Lawn C. Indianapolis	ROH,FPH,P5,CV
Hallams, Clark	Pvt.	D Ham.Leg.		AN	07/21/61	1st Manassas, VA	KIA		GRS
Hallbrocks, W.	Pvt.	H 12th SCVI			08/29/62	2nd Manassas, VA	KIA		JR
Hallford, William	Pvt.	K 25th SCVI		WG	05/16/64	Drury's Bluff VA	KIA		CTA,HOW
Halliburton, John J.	Pvt.	M 8th SCVI	20	DN	09/05/63	Davids Island NY	DOW	Cypress Hills N.C. #842 NY	ROH,FPH,P1,KEB
Halliburton, Robert	Sgt.	M 8th SCVI		DN	11/29/63	Knoxville, TN	KIA		ROH,KEB
Hallman, G.R.	Pvt.	F P.S.S.			05/01/64	Lynchburg, VA	DOD	Lynchburg CSA Cem. #9 R3	ROH,JR,BBW
Hallman, Henry	Pvt.	F 19th SCVI	30	ED	06/14/62	Enterprise, MS	DOD		ROH,HOE,PP
Hallman, J.M.	Pvt.	C 15th SCVI		LN	06/30/64	TN	DOW	(In enemy hands)	ROH
Hallman, L.	Pvt.	F P.S.S.			/ /		DOD		JR
Hallman, L.L.	Pvt.	B 1st SCVA			09/18/62	Columbia, SC	DOD		ROH
Hallman, Levi	Pvt.	K 9th SCVIB			08/20/61	Germantown, VA	DOD		JR
Hallman, M.W.	Pvt.	K 13th SCVI		LN	11/11/63	Virginia			ROH
Hallman, Martin Luther	Pvt.	K 20th SCVI		LN	07/05/63	Charleston, SC	DOD	Magnolia Cem. Charleston	ROH,JR,MAG,KEB
Hallman, W.W.	Pvt.	K 13th SCVI		LN	/ /	Winchester, VA		Stonewall C. Winchester VA	ROH,WIN,P12
Hallman, William W.	Pvt.	I 15th SCVI	25	LN	09/14/62	South Mtn., MD	KIA	(KEB=Holman)	ROH,JR,KEB,TOD
Halloway, Hix	Pvt.	G 7th SCV			/ /		SOW		UD2
Haltiwanger, J. George	Pvt.	C 20th SCVI	21	LN	11/15/64	Mt. Jackson, VA	DOW	(Wdd 10/19,PP=George I.)	ROH,KEB,PP
Haltiwanger, John J.	Pvt.	C 20th SCVI	19	LN	02/04/65	Charleston, SC	DOD	Magnolia Cem. Charleston	ROH,MAG,KEB
Haltiwanger, Richard H.	2nd Lt.	E 3rd SCVI		LN	07/06/63	Gettysburg, PA	DOW	(JR=Robert Henry)	ROH,JR,GDR,SA2
Halverson, Joseph	Pvt.	A 24th SCVI	18	CN	05/14/63	Jackson, MS	KIA		ROH,JR,CDC,PP
Ham, Charles W.	Pvt.	I 21st SCVI		MN	04/25/63	Georgetown, SC	DOD		JR,HMC,HAG,PP
Ham, H.W.	Pvt.	E 8th SCVI		DN	07/02/63	Gettysburg, PA	KIA	(KEB=Hane, H.W.)	ROH,JR,KEB
Ham, J.A.	Pvt.	A 14th SCVI	30	DN	05/03/62	McPhersonville	DOD	(Typhoid, JR=4/10/62)	ROH,JR
Ham, John	Pvt.	B 7th SCVC			03/06/65	Pt. Lookout, MD	DIP	C.C. Pt. Lookout, MD	FPH,P6,P113
Hambre, James F.	Pvt.	B 18th SCVI		UN	/ /	Lynchburg, VA		Lynchburg CSA Cem.#7 R1	BBW
Hambree, A.D.	Pvt.	D Orr's Ri.		AN	07/15/62	Huguenot Spgs VA	DOD		JR
Hambrick, George W.	3rd Sgt.	C 17th SCVI	31	YK	08/30/62	2nd Manassas, VA	KIA		ROH,JR,YEB
Hambright, J.M.	Pvt.	G P.S.S.			11/14/63	Inst H. Atlanta	DOD	Oakwood C. Atlanta R24#5	ROH,JR,BGA
Hambright, James K.	Pvt.		29	YK	/ /		KIA	(Buried in the field)	TCC
Hamby, A.B.H.	Pvt.	C 27th SCVI			08/19/64	Pt. Lookout, MD	DIP	C.C. Pt. Lookout, MD	FPH,CDC,P5,P11

SOUTH CAROLINA DEAD IN CSA SERVICE 1861-1865

NAME	RANK	C REGIMENT	AGE	DS	DIED	WHERE	WHY	BURIED	SOURCES
Hamby, James A.	Pvt.	B 16th SCVI		GE	12/15/64	Nashville, TN	KIA		16R
Hamby, James H.	Pvt.	G 12th SCVI		PS	07/27/62	Richmond, VA	DOD	Hollywood Cem.Rchmd. Q196	ROH,JR,HC
Hamby, James H.	Pvt.	K 3rd SCVI	24	SG	12/11/62	Warrenton, VA	DOD		ROH,SA2,HOS
Hamby, William J.	Pvt.	B 16th SCVI		GE	03/20/65	Nashville, TN	DOW	Nashville City C.#12633	16R,P4,P6
Hamby, William P.	Pvt.	C 22nd SCVI		SG	10/27/62	(HOS=Hamley)	DOW	Mt.Olivet C. Frederick, MD	ROH,FPH,HOS,BOD
Hamel, A.	Pvt.	H 18th SCVI		YK	07/30/64	Crater, Pbg., VA	KIA		ROH,JR,BLM
Hamer, Abner C.	Pvt.	F 21st SCVI		MO	06/18/64	Petersburg, VA	DOW	(POW, died in enemy hands)	ROH,HOM,HAG
Hamer, Charles H.	Pvt.	F 21st SCVI		MO	02/06/65	Elmira, NY	DIP	Woodlawn N.C.#1919 Elmira	ROH,FPH,P6,P65
Hamer, James C.	Pvt.	F 21st SCVI		MO	03/02/65	Elmira, NY	DIP	Woodlawn N.C.#2022 Elmira	FPH,P6,P65,HOM
Hamer, Thomas C.	Pvt.	F 21st SCVI		MO	06/15/64	At home	DOD		ROH,HOM,HAG
Hames, A. Jackson	Sgt.	H 15th SCVI		UN	07/05/63	Gettysburg, PA	DOW	(KEB=Pvt.)	ROH,JR,GDR,KEB
Hames, Charles A.	Sgt.	B 18th SCVI	28	UN	08/30/62	2nd Manassas, VA	KIA	Gilead Cem. Union Cty, SC	ROH,JR,UD3
Hames, Gadbury	Pvt.	G 27th SCVI		UN	04/09/65	Pt. Lookout, MD	DIP	C.C. Pt. Lookout, MD	FPH,P6,P114,HAG
Hames, Isaac A.	Pvt.	H 5th SCVI		UN	03/21/63	Winchester, VA	DOD		JR,SA3
Hames, John E.	Cpt.	B 18th SCVI	26	UN	08/30/62	2nd Manassas, VA	KIA	Gilead Cem. Union Cty. SC	ROH,JR,NHU,UD3
Hames, L.A.	Pvt.	F 15th SCVI		UN	07/02/63	Gettysburg, PA	KIA		ROH,JR,GDR,KEB
Hames, L.B.	Pvt.	B 27th SCVI	39	UN	04/04/65	Pt. Lookout, MD	DIP	C.C. Pt. Lookout, MD	ROH,FPH,P6,P113
Hames, W.H.	Pvt.	B 9th SCVI		UN	/ /	Richmond, VA		Oakwood C.#7,Row K,Div A	ROH,OWC
Hames, Zelos H.	Pvt.	H 15th SCVI		UN	11/11/64	Baltimore, MD	DIP	Loudon Pk. Cem. B-94 Balto	FPH,P1,P5,PP
Hamett, Horace Calhoun	2nd Cpl.	L 1st SCVIG		CN	01/24/63	Richmond, VA	DOD	(Lung Inflammation)	ROH,JR,SA1
Hamett, J.	Pvt.	E 16th SCVI		GE	07/26/64	Barnesville, GA	DOD	(NI 16R, Hammett Co.F?)	ROH
Hamilton, A.H.	Pvt.	D Ham.Leg.		AN	/ /	At home	DOD	(ROH=Winchester, VA)	ROH,GRS
Hamilton, David A.	Pvt.	D Ham.Leg.		PS	08/11/61	Brentsville, VA	DOD	(Measles)	JR,GRS
Hamilton, David G.	Pvt.	E 15th SCVI	33	FD	07/12/63		DOW	(Wdd @ Gtysbg 7/2/63)	ROH,JR,KEB
Hamilton, E.W.	Pvt.	A 16th SCVI		GE	01/06/65	Camp Chase, OH	DIP	C.C.#1065 Columbus, OH	FPH,P6,P12,P23
Hamilton, Eli C.	Cpl.	H 24th SCVI	22	CR	07/04/62	Columbia, SC	DOD		ROH,HHC,CB,PP
Hamilton, James A.W.	1st Lt.	Beaufort A		BT	11/04/64	Charleston, SC	DOD	Magnolia Cem. Charleston	ROH,MAG,R47,PP
Hamilton, James H.	2nd Lt.	H 24th SCVI		CR	08/27/62	Columbia, SC	DOD		R48,HHC,PP
Hamilton, John S.	Pvt.	A 17th SCVI	22	CR	06/23/62	At home	DOD	(HHC=Charleston)	ROH,JR,HHC,CB
Hamilton, Paul	Cpt.(ADC)	S.D. Lee S	21	BT	12/29/62	Vicksburg, MS	KIA	(Xpl of caison)	ROH,JR,CDC
Hamilton, Pleasant	Pvt.	K 24th SCVI	37	ED	10/16/63	Atlanta, GA	DOD		ROH,HOE
Hamilton, Theodore	Pvt.	A 24th SCVI		CN	/ /	Camp Chase, OH	DIP		ROH
Hamilton, Thomas	2nd Lt.	E 11th SCVI	35	BT	06/18/64	Petersburg, VA	KIA		ROH,HAG,R47
Hamilton, Thomas J.	Pvt.	K 7th SCVI		ED	08/28/61	Culpepper, VA	DOD	Fairview Cem. Culpepper VA	JR,CGH,CDC
Hamilton, Tristram	Pvt.	I 1st SCVIH		MN	06/12/62	Charleston, SC	DOD	Magnolia Cem. Charleston	MAG,HMC,HAG,JRH
Hamilton, W.H.	Pvt.	L 7th SCVI			08/11/61	Richmond, VA		Hollywood Cem.Rchmd. K11	ROH,HC,KEB
Hamilton, W.R.	Pvt.	B Orr's Ri.		AE	05/09/63	Chancellorsville	DOW		JR
Hamilton, Warren	Pvt.	D Ham.Leg.			06/15/62	Ashland, VA	DOD		GRS
Hamilton, William	Pvt.	F 23rd SCVI		CR	06/15/64	Petersburg, VA	KIA	(HHC=Cowpens)	ROH,HHC
Hamilton, William M.	Pvt.	K 15th SCVI		AE	07/02/63	Gettysburg, PA	KIA		ROH,JR,GDR,KEB
Hamilton, William M.	Pvt.	C 19th SCVI	41	ED	01/23/65	Camp Chase, OH	DIP	C.C.#847 Columbus, OH	ROH,FPH,P6,UD3
Hamilton, William McE.	Pvt.	H 6th SCVI	21	YK	05/20/62	Gaines' Mill, VA	DOW	(CDC=DOW@Dranesvl 12/25/61	ROH,CDC,YEB
Hamiter, David	Pvt.	H 3rd SCVI		LN	03/06/62	Richmond, VA	DOD	(SA2=to hospital 8/15/62)	ROH,JR,SA2
Hamiter, James H.	Pvt.	H 3rd SCVI		LN	04/01/62	Manassas, VA	DOD		JR,SA2,KEB
Hamm, Thomas P.	Pvt.	A Hol.Leg.		SG	12/13/62	Kinston, NC	KIA	(PP=12/14/62)	HOS,PP
Hammer, Joseph	Pvt.	C 15th SCVAB		CN	08/27/63	Charleston, SC	DOD	Magnolia Cem. Charleston	ROH,JR,MAG,CDC
Hammet, J.B.N.	Pvt.	B 1st SCVIBn		CN	06/16/62	Secessionville	KIA		ROH,JR,CDC,PP
Hammet, W.J.N.	Sgt.	C Ham.Leg.		CL	06/01/62	7 Pines, VA	DOW		ROH,JR,CDC
Hammett, C.V.	Cpl.	B Hol.Leg.	21	SG	08/26/62	Richmond, VA	DOD	Hollywood Cem.Rchmd. H12	ROH,HC,HOS
Hammett, Gideon	Pvt.	F 16th SCVI		GE	06/28/64		DOD	(Pneumonia)	16R,CDC
Hammett, Samuel	Pvt.	L Orr's Ri.		AN	07/15/62	Richmond, VA	DOD		JR,CDC

SOUTH CAROLINA DEAD IN CSA SERVICE 1861-1865

NAME	RANK	C	REGIMENT	AGE	DS	DIED	WHERE	WHY	BURIED	SOURCES
Hammett, W.P.	Pvt.	K	5th SCVI		SG	07/01/64	Petersburg, VA	KIA		SA3,HOS,WAT
Hammett, W.T.	Pvt.	I	13th SCVI	22	SG	07/15/62	Laurel Hill, VA	DOD	(Typhoid)	ROH,JR,HOS
Hammett, William D.	Pvt.	K	P.S.S.		SG	/ /		DIP		HOS
Hammond,	Sgt.		3rd SCVABn			12/11/63	Ft. Sumter, SC	ACD	(Magazine explosion)	ROH,CDC
Hammond, A.J.	Pvt.	D	Ham.Leg.		AN	/ /	Culpepper, VA	DOD		GRS
Hammond, Benjamin F.	Pvt.	D	Orr's Ri.	22	AN	05/23/64	Lynchburg, VA	DOW	Lynchburg CSA Cem. #10 R4	ROH,BBW
Hammond, C.D.	Pvt.	D	12th SCVI		RD	06/14/64	Richmond, VA	DOW	(Gunshot in right knee)	ROH,JR,P12
Hammond, Charles	Pvt.	A	7th SCVI			07/02/63	Gettysburg, PA	KIA		ROH,JR,GDR
Hammond, Charles L.	Pvt.		Brooks G.A		CN	06/30/62	Frayer's Farm VA	KIA	(Orig. in Co. K,2nd SCVI)	ROH,JR,SA2,CNM
Hammond, Christian V.	Pvt.	B	Orr's Ri.		AE	07/02/63	Gettysburg, PA	KIA		GDR,CDC,WV
Hammond, Frederick G.W.	2nd Lt.	H	25th SCVI	24	CN	05/09/64	Swift Creek, VA	DOW		ROH,HAG,CV,R48
Hammond, H.S.	Pvt.	C	P.S.S.		AN	08/30/62	2nd Manassas, VA	KIA	Manassas CSA Cem. VA	ROH,JR,CDC,GMJ
Hammond, J.F.	Pvt.	A	2nd SCVIRi		AE	03/10/63	Petersburg, VA			PP
Hammond, J.R.	Pvt.	K	7th SCVI		ED	10/30/64	Staunton, VA			ROH,PP
Hammond, J.W.	Pvt.	H	23rd SCVI		MN	07/04/62	Richmond, VA			ROH
Hammond, Jesse	Pvt.	D	12th SCVI		RD	08/02/62	Richmond, VA	DOD	Hollywood Cem.Rchmd. H105	ROH,JR,HC
Hammond, M.	Pvt.	H	6th SCVI		FD	/ /		KIA	Spotsylvania C.H., VA	SCH
Hammond, S.	Pvt.		4th Res Bn			09/25/64	Charleston, SC	DOD	Magnolia Cem. Charleston	ROH,MAG
Hammond, Samuel Leroy	Cpt.	H	25th SCVI		CN	05/09/64	Swift Creek, VA	KIA	(R48=5/12/64)	ROH,HAG,CV,R48
Hammond, William H.	Cpl.	B	Orr's Ri.		AE	/ /	Laurens, SC		Lawrens Cemetery, SC	PP,CDC
Hammond, William W.	Pvt.	K	13th SCVI		LN	09/01/62	Ox Hill, VA	KIA	In the field	ROH,JR
Hampton, C.J.	Pvt.	G	5th SCVI		YK	12/27/62	Manchester, VA	DOD		ROH,JR,SA3
Hampton, Frank	Lt. Col.		2nd SCVC		RD	06/09/63	Brandy Stn., VA	KIA	Trinity Ch. Columbia, SC	JR,MP,CDC,PP
Hampton, James	Pvt.	K	16th SCVI		GE	07/22/64	Atlanta, GA	KIA		16R
Hampton, M.A.	Pvt.	G	10th SCVI		HY	/ /		DOD		RAS
Hampton, Thomas	Pvt.	H	8th SCVI		MN	07/03/63	Gettysburg, PA	DOW	Magnolia Cem. Charleston	JR,GDR,HMC,KEB
Hampton, Thomas Preston	Lt. (ADC)		W.Hampton	21	RD	10/27/64	Burgess' Mill VA	KIA	Trinity Ch. Columbia, SC	ROH,JR,MP,CSO,
Hampton, W. (Hamilton?)	Pvt.		1st SCV			08/23/61	Richmond, VA		Hollywood Cem.Rchmd. K30	HC
Hamrick, Henry	Pvt.	E	1st SCVA			05/11/65	Charlotte, NC			PP
Hance, Theodore Stanley	Pvt.	A	3rd SCVI	18	LS	09/20/63	Chickamauga, GA	KIA	UD3	ROH,JR,SA2,RHL
Hance, William Wood	Cpt.	A	3rd SCVI		LS	01/07/63	Richmond, VA	DOW	(Amptd leg, Wdd @ Fbg) UD3	ROH,JR,SA2,RHL
Hanckel, James Stuart	Pvt.	I	2nd SCVI		CN	09/25/62	Sharpsburg, MD	DOW		SA2,CDC,KEB
Hancock, F.J.	Pvt.	H	20th SCVI		LN	/ /	Mt. Jackson, VA	DOD	Mt. Jackson, VA	SHS,CV
Hancock, George W.	Pvt.	E	5th SCVI		CR	06/20/62	7 Pines, VA	DOW	(Wdd 5/31/62)	JR,SA3
Hancock, J. Paddy	Pvt.	H	4th SCVC		LR	05/28/64	Hawes Shop, VA	KIA		LAN
Hancock, J.D.	Pvt.	B	9th SCVIBn			07/14/62		DOD	(JR=26th SCVI)	JR
Hancock, J.T.	Pvt.	B	8th SCVI		CD	/ /	(Wilderness?)		Spotsylvania C.H., VA	SCH,KEB
Hancock, John	Pvt.	A	14th SCVI	27	DN	06/27/62	Gaines' Mill, VA	KIA		ROH,CNM
Hancock, John H.	Pvt.	H	6th SCVC	42	CD	08/02/63	Adams Run, SC	DOD		PP
Hancock, Pascal	Pvt.	C	10th SCVI		HY	12/31/62	Murfreesboro, TN	KIA		ROH,JR,RAS,CDC
Hancock, Thomas A.	Pvt.	A	20th SCVI		PS	08/29/64	Mt. Jackson, VA		Mt. Jackson, VA	PP
Hand, W.H.	Color Sgt.	H	12th SCVI	26	YK	07/01/63	Gettysburg, PA	KIA		JR,GDR,YEB,CWC
Handback, Mel	Pvt.	E	3rd SCVIBn		LS	07/02/63	Gettysburg, PA	KIA	(JR= Hamback)	JR,GDR,CDC,KEB
Hane, C.G.	Pvt.	F	18th SCVI		YK	10/12/62	Virginia	DOD		JR
Hanes, Robert	Pvt.	D	P.S.S.		SG	04/11/63	Blackwater, VA	DOD		ROH,HOS
Haney, C.G.	Pvt.	F	18th SCVI		YK	10/10/62	Richmond, VA	DOD	Hollywood Cem.Rchmd. A8	ROH,HC
Haney, E.G.	Pvt.					/ /	VA		(Rchmd.effects list 1/63)	CDC
Haney, J.R.	Pvt.	D	Orr's Ri.		AN	/ /	Richmond, VA		Oakwood C.#65,Row R,Div C	ROH,OWC,CDC
Haney, Joseph	Pvt.	H	2nd SCV			/ /	Richmond, VA		(2nd SCVIRi or SCVC?)	ROH
Haney, Wilson P.	3rd Sgt.	K	19th SCVI	40	ED	04/24/62	Enterprise, MS	ACD	(M & O RR accident)	ROH,JR,HOE,PP
Hankins, F.	Pvt.	B	1st SC Res			/ /	Columbia, SC		Elmwood Cem. Columbia, SC	MP,PP

H

SOUTH CAROLINA DEAD IN CSA SERVICE 1861-1865

NAME	RANK	C REGIMENT	AGE	DS	DIED	WHERE	WHY	BURIED	SOURCES
Hanks, James A.	Pvt.	K Orr's Ri.	22	AN	06/27/62	Gaines' Mill, VA	KIA		ROH
Hanks, Jesse	Pvt.	19th SCV	18	AN	09/17/63	At home	DOD		ROH
Hanks, Luke	Sgt.	E 20th SCVI	35	AN	07/14/63	Bty. Wagner, SC	DOW	Ebenezer B.C. Belton, SC	ROH,ANC,CDC,KEB
Hanna, D. Pinckney	Pvt.	I 10th SCVI	25	MN	09/17/62	Tompkinsville KY	DOD		ROH,HMC,RAS
Hanna, G.W.T.	Pvt.	G 15th SCVI	22	WG	09/09/62	Richmond, VA			ROH,JR,KEB,HOW
Hanna, James R.	Pvt.	I 10th SCVI	30	MN	06/15/61	South Island, SC	DOD		ROH,RAS,HMC
Hanna, Julius Jessie D.	Pvt.	G 15th SCVI	25	WG	/ /	Richmond, VA			CTA,HOW,KEB
Hanna, Robert	Pvt.	G 15th SCVI	20	WG	/ /			(Age 19 in 1861)	CTA,HOW,KEB
Hanna, Robert C.	Pvt.	K 17th SCVI	27	YK	03/10/62	Charleston, SC	DOD	Bethesda Ch. YK Cty.	RCD,YEB
Hanna, William Thomas	Pvt.		23	YK	04/14/61	At home	DOD		YMD
Hansel, William	Pvt.	G 12th SCVI		PS	07/02/63	Gettysburg, VA	KIA		JR
Hansell, A.	Pvt.			GE	08/20/64	Petersburg, VA	DOW	Blandford Church Pbg., VA	BLC,PP
Hanson, P.B.	Pvt.	I 2nd SCVC		ED	/ /	At home	DOD	Magnolia Cem. Augusta, GA	HOE,BGA
Hanvey, James	Pvt.	H 19th SCVI	44	AE	10/10/62	KY	DOD		ROH
Happoldt, C.D.	Pvt.	Brooks GA		CN	06/15/62		DOD		ROH
Happoldt, D.H.	Pvt.	Brooks GA		CN	/ /		DOD		JR
Happoldt, David	Pvt.	K 2nd SCVI		CN	03/14/62	At home	DOD	(On furlough)	SA2
Harb, Alfred	Pvt.	19th SCVI	18	ED	11/15/64	Shelbyville, TN	KIA		ROH
Harbin, C.N.	Pvt.	H 2nd SC Res			04/15/65	Dingle's Mill SC	DOW	(Wdd 4/10/65)	ROH,HSR
Harbin, Edward	Pvt.	F 16th SCVI		GE	01/20/63	Charleston, SC	DOD		ROH,16R
Harbin, Elias N.	Pvt.	K 2nd SCVC	17	PS	04/18/65	Summerville, SC	DOW	(Wdd in Skirmish 4/9/65)	ROH
Harbin, J.B.	Pvt.	E 2nd SCVIRi		PS	/ /	Charlottesville		Univ. Cem. Charlottesville	ACH
Harbin, Nathaniel W.	Cpt.	B P.S.S.		AN	09/17/62	Sharpsburg, MD	KIA		ROH,JR,CDC,R48
Harbin, Sevier	Pvt.	E 1st SCVIR		PS	06/12/64	Mt. Pleasant, SC	DOD		SA1
Hard, John S.	Major	7th SCVI	20	ED	09/20/63	Chickamauga, GA	KIA	LC	ROH,JR,HOE,UD3
Hardee, Cornelius	Pvt.	A 26th SCVI	17	HY	04/08/62	Waccamaw Neck SC	DOD		ROH,JR
Hardee, I.O.D.	Pvt.	M 10th SCVI		HY	/ /	Okolona, MS	DOD	(1862)	RAS,PP,TOD
Hardee, Isaac	Pvt.	F 1st SCVIG		HY	12/17/62	Lynchburg, VA	DOW	Lynchburg CSA Cem. #9 R1	SA1,PDL,BBW
Hardee, Isaac B.	1st Cpl.	F 1st SCVIG		HY	07/04/62	Lynchburg, VA	DOD	Lynchburg CSA Cem. #4 R5	SA1,BBW
Hardee, Isaac B.	Sgt.	M 10th SCVI		HY	06/15/63	Barbourville, KY	DOD		RAS
Hardee, J.J.	Pvt.	C 10th SCVI		HY	/ /	Gainesville, AL	DOD	Gainesville, AL	RAS
Hardee, Joel	Pvt.	F 1st SCVIG		HY	09/21/63	Ft. Delaware, DE	DIP	Finn's Pt. NJ Nat. Cem.	ROH,FPH,P5,SA1
Hardee, M.	Pvt.	C 10th SCVI		HY	/ /		DIP		RAS
Hardee, R.C.	Pvt.	G 10th SCVI		HY	10/23/62	Danville, KY	DIP	Con. Lot #50 Danville, KY	FPH,RAS,CV
Harden, Obediah	Cpt.	E 6th SCVI	34	CR	01/01/62	Dranesville, VA	DOW	Bushy Creek Ch. Chester Cy	ROH,UNC,R46,HHC
Harden, Thomas Cornwell	Pvt.	E 6th SCVI	21	CR	12/20/61	Dranesville, VA	KIA	Calvary Ch. Chester Cty.	ROH,CDC,R46
Harden, W.W.	Pvt.	Brooks GA			05/03/63	Chancellorsville	KIA	(Co.A, Alexander's L.A.)	JR
Hardin, Abraham	1st Cpl.	B 5th SCVI		YK	04/20/62	Richmond, VA	DOD	Hollywood Cem.Rchmd. B81	ROH,JR,HC,SA3
Hardin, George	4th Cpl.	G 5th SCVI		YK	12/05/63	Middle Ckeek, TN	DOW	(In enemy hands)	P1,P5,SA3,CB
Hardin, James	Pvt.	H 2nd SCVIRi			06/30/62		DOD	(Measles, Harbin, J.B.?)	JR
Hardin, John A.	Pvt.	F 5th SCVI	66	YK	/ /	Yorktown, VA	DOD		YEB
Hardin, Samuel	Pvt.	C 2nd SCVIRi		PS	/ /	Lynchburg, VA		Lynchburg CSA Cem.#3 R3	BBW
Harding,	Cpl.	I 7th SCVI			07/02/63	Gettysburg, PA	KIA		JR
Hardwick, A. Stanley	1st Cpl.	G 18th SCVI	43	YK	07/30/64	Crater, Pbg., VA	KIA		JR,BLM,YEB,HHC
Hardwick, A.M.	Pvt.	C 10th SCVI		HY	12/31/62	Murfreesboro, TN	KIA		ROH,RAS,CDC
Hardwick, J.C.	Pvt.	E 26th SCVI			06/28/62		DOD		JR
Hardwick, J.W.	Pvt.	A 9th SCVIBn		HY	06/29/62	Charleston, SC		Magnolia Cem. Charleston	MAG
Hardwick, James	Pvt.	E 26th SCVI		HY	05/15/62	Rikersville, SC	DOD	(ROH=Harwick)	ROH
Hardwick, N.	Pvt.	E 26th SCVI			03/08/62		DOD		JR
Hardwick, S.M.	Pvt.	D 7th SCVI			/ /	Lynchburg, VA		Lynchburg CSA Cem. #6 R1	BBW
Hardwick, Valentine	Pvt.	E 11th SCVIB	22	HY	04/15/62	Camp Lookout, SC	DOD		ROH

148

SOUTH CAROLINA DEAD IN CSA SERVICE 1861-1865

NAME	RANK	C REGIMENT	AGE	DS	DIED	WHERE	WHY	BURIED	SOURCES
Hardwick, W.B.	Pvt.	E 10th SCVI		HY	06/15/62	Rome, GA	DOD	(RAS=Hardick)	ROH,RAS,CTA,HO
Hardwick, W.S.	Pvt.			WG	/ /		DOD	(1863)	CTA,HOW
Hardy, E.W.F.	Pvt.	I 14th SCVI		AE	/ /	Richmond, VA		(1862)	HOL
Hardy, J.	Pvt.	G Ham.Leg.		SR	12/04/64	Richmond, VA			ROH
Hardy, James Haywood	4th Sgt.	D 5th SCVI	25	NY	05/25/64	At home	DOD		ROH,SA3,ANY
Hardy, W.J.	Pvt.	E Orr's Ri.		PS	05/03/63	Chancellorsville	KIA	(Prob Harbin, W.J. Co.E)	ROH,JR
Hardy, Wilbur	Pvt.	F 24th SCVI		AN	07/22/64	Atlanta, GA	KIA		HOL
Hardy, William H.	Vol. Aide	2nd SCVI			07/21/61	1st Manassas, VA	KIA		ROH
Hare, Caleb	Pvt.	B 14th SCVI	17	ED	05/05/63	Chancellorsville	DOW		JR,HOE,UD3
Hare, E.R.	Cpl.	I 5th SCVC		BL	06/15/64	Hawe's Shop, VA	DOW		ROH
Hare, J.H.	Pvt.	Inglis LA		DN	/ /				ROH
Hare, Thomas D.	Pvt.	A 1st SCVIR		CD	01/11/64	Pt. Lookout, MD	DIP	C.C. Pt. Lookout, MD	ROH,FPH,P1,SA1
Hare, William J.	Pvt.	I 12th SCVI		LR	08/29/62	2nd Manassas, VA	KIA		JR,LAN
Harget, Eli	Pvt.			LR	/ /	NC	DOD		ROH
Hargit, Andrew	Pvt.	B 14th SCVI	25	ED	07/28/64	Deep Bottom VA	KIA	(UD3=Hargrove)	HOE,UD3
Hargrove, Isaac H.	Pvt.	I 1st SCVIH		MN	02/04/64	Dandridge, TN	DOW	(HMC =KIA 1/17/64)	ROH,SA1,HMC
Hargrove, N.N.	Pvt.	E 23rd SCVI		MN	09/17/62	Sharpsburg, MD	KIA	(? HMC=living in 1901)	ROH,JR,CDC,HMC
Hargrove, Wiley S.	Pvt.	H 16th SCVI		GE	06/18/62	Adams Run, SC	DOD		PP
Hargrove, William H.	Pvt.	D 25th SCVI		MN	09/14/62	James Island, SC	DOD	(Typhoid, JR= John's I.)	JR,HMC,HAG
Harken, H.	Pvt.	B 1st SCVA		CN	11/07/61	Port Royal, SC	KIA	(German Artillery)	ROH,JR,CDC
Harkness, R.H.	Pvt.	I 14th SCVI		AE	07/07/62	Richmond, VA	DOW	(JR=DOD Guinea St.5/22/63)	JR,HOL
Harkness, William H.	Pvt.	B 7th SCVI	17	AE	12/13/62	Fredericksburg	KIA	(W.B. in Co. D?)	ROH,JR
Harlan, Henry	Pvt.	K 5th SCV			05/02/63	Petersburg, VA	DOD	(Typhoid)	JR
Harlee, James	Pvt.	Brooks GA			05/03/63	Chancellorsville	KIA		JR
Harlee, Robert Armstrong	4th Sgt.	I 8th SCVI	19	DN	02/28/62	Manassas, VA	DOD	Hopewell P.C. Florence, SC	ROH,JR,TOD,KEB
Harleston, Francis Huger	Cpt.	D 1st SCVA	24	CN	11/24/63	Ft. Sumter, SC	KIA	(See p:178 DOC)	ROH,SCA,DOC,R4
Harley, John E.	Pvt.	C 1st SCVIH			05/26/64	Hanover Jctn. VA	KIA	Mrs. Huff's Yard, Hanover	WAT,SA1
Harley, Joseph M.	Pvt.	D 5th SCVC	24	CO	03/18/65	Deep River, NC	ACD	(Drowned in line of duty)	ROH,H2,SA2
Harley, Richard W.	Pvt.	SCVC	21	BL	12/07/61	Manassas, VA	DOD	(CNM issue of 3/27/62)	ROH,CNM
Harley, T.J.	Pvt.	F 6th SCVC		SR	/ /	(Frm Elmira/Xch)	DIP	(AWOL frm Co.D 2nd SCVI)	SA2,P120,P65
Harley, Virgil	5th Sgt.	A 1st SCVIG	21	BL	07/05/62	Gaines' Mill, VA	DOW		ROH,JR,SA1,CDC
Harling, F.L.	2nd Cpl.	K 14th SCVI		ED	12/13/62	Fredericksburg	KIA		HOE
Harling, James	Pvt.	K 14th SCVI		ED	/ /		DOD		HOE
Harling, Joseph	Pvt.	K 14th SCVI		ED	02/01/63	Richmond, VA	DOD		JR,HOE
Harling, Newton C.	2nd Sgt.	C 19th SCVI		ED	09/20/63	Chickamauga, GA	KIA		ROH,JR,HOE,UD3
Harling, Thomas	2nd Cpl.	I 7th SCVI		ED	07/02/63	Gettysburg, PA	KIA		ROH,GDR,CDC,HO
Harman, C.E.	Pvt.	K 13th SCVI		LN	10/24/64	Richmond, VA			ROH
Harman, Eliphus	Pvt.	K 3rd SCVI		LS	09/17/62	Sharpsburg, MD	KIA	Sharpsburg, MD	ROH,JR,SA2,CDC
Harman, George W.	Pvt.	K 13th SCVI		LN	06/06/62	Richmond, VA	DOD		ROH
Harman, J.	Pvt.	K 2nd SCVIRi			09/18/62	Sharpsburg, MD	DOW	(JR= DOW @ Mt. Jackson VA)	ROH,JR
Harman, J.M.	Pvt.	F 25th SCVI		OG	02/02/63	Wilmington, NC	DOD	(Huffman ?)	ROH
Harman, Milledge B.	Pvt.	K 20th SCVI		LN	08/11/63		DOD		ROH,KEB
Harman, S.A.	Pvt.	K 13th SCVI		LN	08/08/62	Danville, VA	DOD		ROH
Harmes, George	Pvt.	B 25th SCVI			/ /				ROH
Harmon, Andrew	Pvt.	I 13th SCVI	24	SG	08/15/62		DOD		ROH
Harmon, Elisha	Pvt.	B 26th SCVI			03/06/65	Douglas Hos., DC	DOD	(Bronchitus, Coloured Man)	P6
Harmon, Franklin J.	2nd Lt.	K 20th SCVI		LN	09/12/63	Charleston, SC	KIA		R48,KEB
Harmon, Hugh T.	Pvt.	B 3rd SCVI		NY	07/23/64	Camp Chase, OH	DIP	C.C.#188 Columbus, OH	ROH,FPH,SA2,P6
Harmon, James	Pvt.	K 3rd SCVI		SG	09/20/63	Chickamauga, GA	DOW	Con. Cem. Marietta, GA	ROH,HOS,SA2,CC
Harmon, John F.	Pvt.	C 13th SCVI		SG	08/29/62	2nd Manassas, VA	KIA		ROH,JR,HOS,CDC
Harmon, John W.P.	Pvt.	D 13th SCVI	25	NY	08/29/62	2nd Manassas, VA	KIA		ROH,JR,ANY,CDC

SOUTH CAROLINA DEAD IN CSA SERVICE 1861-1865

NAME	RANK	C REGIMENT	AGE	DS	DIED	WHERE	WHY	BURIED	SOURCES
Harmon, Samuel	Cpl.	I 13th SCVI	27	SG	07/28/63	Chester, PA	DIP	Magnolia Cem. Charleston	ROH,MAG,P1,P6
Harmon, Samuel A.	Pvt.	K 13th SCVI			08/08/62	Danville, VA	DOD	(Typhoid)	JR
Harmon, Thomas S.	Pvt.	F 3rd SCVABn	50	CN	06/18/62	James Island, SC	DOD		ROH
Harmon, William K.D.	Pvt.	D 13th SCVI	25	NY	05/12/64	Spotsylvania, VA	KIA	(ANY= 2nd SCVI,NI SA2)	ROH,JR,ANY
Harmon, William Simpson	Sgt.	H Hol.Leg.		NY	05/13/65	Pt. Lookout, MD	DIP	Zion U.M.C. Prosperity SC	ROH,FPH,NCC,P6
Harner, J.M.	Pvt.	K 6th SCVI		GE	03/17/62	White Sulpher Ss	DOD		ROH
Harp, David	Pvt.	B 3rd SCVI	21	NY	09/04/61	Culpepper, VA	DOD	Fairview Cem. Culpepper VA	ROH,JR,CGH,ANY
Harp, James	Pvt.	Pal. LA		CD	10/13/64	Darbytown Rd. VA	DOW		SOB
Harper, Benjamin	Pvt.	A 26th SCVI	32	HY	02/15/62	Waccamaw Neck SC	DOD	(JR & PP=3/19/63)	ROH,JR,PP
Harper, John	Pvt.	L 1st SCVIG		SG	06/08/64	On way home	DOW	(Wdd @ Spotsylvania, VA)	SA1,HOS
Harper, M.R.	Pvt.	K Orr's Ri.		AN	07/10/62	Richmond, VA		Hollywood Cem.Rchmd. M313	ROH,HC
Harper, Martin F.	Pvt.	K Orr's Ri.	19	AN	07/25/62		DOD	(Dup of M.R.?)	ROH
Harper, Mason J.	2nd Sgt.	K Orr's Ri.	27	AN	12/19/61		DOD		ROH,JR,CDC
Harper, R.L.	Pvt.	I 12th SCVI		LR	/ /		DOD	(? dup of R.S. ?)	LAN
Harper, R.S.	Pvt.	I 12th SCVI		LR	10/15/62	Jordan Sprgs, VA	DOD	(Camp Barnes)	LAN
Harper, S.L.	Pvt.	I 1st SCVA			07/17/63	Charleston, SC	DOD	Magnolia Cem. Charleston	ROH,MAG
Harper, William A.	Pvt.	L 1st SCVIG	20	SG	02/24/64	Orange C.H., VA	DOD		ROH,SA1
Harral, Donald	Sgt.	F 8th SCVI			07/03/63	Gettysburg, PA	DOW		JR
Harral, James L.	Pvt.	K Orr's Ri.			07/17/62	Manchester, VA	DOD		JR
Harrall, Ephraim	Pvt.	H 8th SCVI		MN	/ /	Virginia	DOD	(1861)	HMC,KEB
Harrall, James	Pvt.	D 15th SCVI		KW	/ /	irginia	DOD	(1862)	JR,HIC,KEB
Harrall, John	Pvt.	D 15th SCVI		KW	/ /	At home	DOD	(1862)	JR,HIC,KEB
Harrall, N.W.	Pvt.	H 8th SCVI		MN	12/07/61	Charlottesville	DOD	(Pneumonia)	JR,HMC,KEB
Harrall, W.T.	Pvt.	H 8th SCVI		MN	09/14/62	Maryland Hts. MD	KIA	(JR=DOW 9/28/62)	JR,HMC,KEB
Harrell, Amos	Pvt.				/ /	Virginia		(Rchmd effects list 1/63)	CDC
Harrell, James A.	Pvt.	F 1st SCVIG		HY	10/11/61	Suffolk, VA	DOD	(SA1=Harrall, J.J.)	JR,SA1
Harrell, Joel E.	Pvt.	B 21st SCVI		DN	05/16/64	Drury's Bluff VA	DOW	(PP=KIA @ Ft. Fisher)	ROH,HAG,PP
Harrell, John W.	1st Lt.	A 14th SCVI	28	DN	02/13/65	Petersburg, VA	DOD		ROH,R47
Harrell, L.	Pvt.	H 5th SCV			/ /	Charlottesville		Univ. Cem. Charlottesville	ACH
Harrell, Leonard B.	Sgt.	F 8th SCVI	18	DN	07/03/63	Gettysburg, PA	DOW		ROH,JR,GDR,KEB
Harrell, M.W.	Pvt.	D 10th SCVI		MN	07/22/64	Atlanta, GA	DOW	(Also Wdd @ Chickamauga)	RAS,HMC,CDC
Harrelson, George W.	Pvt.	L 10th SCVI		MN	06/21/62	Winona, MS	DOD	(Pneumonia)	JR,RAS,PP,TOD
Harrelson, George W.	Pvt.	K 26th SCVI	17	HY	07/14/63	Jackson, MS	KIA	(PP=D, 18th SCVI)	ROH,CDC,PP
Harrelson, John B.	Pvt.	H 23rd SCVI		MN	08/30/62	2nd Manassas VA	KIA		ROH,HMC,CDC
Harrelson, John L.	Pvt.	L 21st SCVI	39	MN	07/10/63	Bty. Wagner, SC	KIA		ROH,JL,HMC,HAG
Harrelson, John W.	Pvt.	B Orr's Ri.		AE	07/10/62	Manchester, VA	DOD		JR,CDC
Harrelson, M. Jackson	Pvt.	I 8th SCVI		MN	/ /	Cold Harbor, VA	KIA	(1862 or 1864?)	HMC,KEB
Harrelson, S.F.	2nd Sgt.	K 26th SCVI		HY	06/26/62	Charleston, SC	DOD		ROH,JR
Harrelson, S.T.	Pvt.	9th SCVIBn		CN	06/27/62	Charleston, SC		Magnolia Cem. Charleston	ROH,MAG
Harrelson, Timothy	Pvt.	L 21st SCVI	27	MN	05/10/64	Petersburg, VA	DOW	(Wdd @ Walthall Jctn)	ROH,HMC,HAG,PP
Harricutt, G.W.	Pvt.	G			07/10/63	Gettysburg, PA	DOW	(ROH=21st but not @ Gbg.)	ROH,CDC,P12
Harrin, J. Joseph	Pvt.	C Ham.Leg.			01/31/62	Oraquan, VA	DOD	(Typhoid)	JR
Harrington, D.W.	2nd Lt.	E P.S.S.		SR	06/30/62	Frayser's Fm. VA	KIA		JR,R48
Harrington, J.R.	Pvt.	I 25th SCVI			07/01/64	Raleigh, NC		Oakwood C. Raleigh, NC	TOD
Harris, A.H.	Pvt.	A 18th SCVI		UN	07/30/64	Crater, Pbg., VA	KIA		ROH,JR,BLM
Harris, Anderson	Pvt.	K 18th SCVI		SG	09/10/63	At home	DOD		JR
Harris, B.C.	Pvt.	C 5th SCVI	28	UN	04/18/63	Blackwater, VA	KIA		ROH,JR,SA3
Harris, Benjamin	Pvt.	A 22nd SCVI		ED	06/16/62	Secessionville	KIA		ROH,JR,CDC,PP
Harris, C.B.	Pvt.	H 4th SCVI		AN	02/01/62	Charlottesville	DOD		ROH,SA2,CDC
Harris, Charles	Pvt.	F 18th SCVI			10/12/62	Virginia	DOD		JR
Harris, D.H.	Pvt.	C 2nd SCVIRi			/ /	Richmond, VA		Oakwood C.#57,Row M,Div C	OWC

SOUTH CAROLINA DEAD IN CSA SERVICE 1861-1865

NAME	RANK	C REGIMENT	AGE	DS	DIED	WHERE	WHY	BURIED	SOURCES
Harris, E.J.	Pvt.	D 6th Bn Res			06/03/65	Davids Island NY	DIP	Cypress Hills N.C.#2936 NY	FPH,P6,P12,P79
Harris, Edward	Pvt.	A 18th SCVI		UN	07/30/64	Crater, Pbg., VA	KIA		ROH,BLM
Harris, Edward	Pvt.	D 6th ResBn		ED	03/19/65	Bentonville, NC	KIA		UD1
Harris, Franklin	Pvt.	I 3rd SCVI		LS	04/03/63	Fredericksburg	DOD	Spotsylvania C.H., VA	ROH,JR,SCH,SA2
Harris, George T.	Pvt.	H 2nd SCVI		LR	12/25/61	Richmond, VA	DOD	Oakwood C.#34,Row O,Div C	SA2,OWC,LAN,H2
Harris, Isham S.	Pvt.			YK	11/25/63	Missionary Rdge.	KIA	(Prob 24th SCVI)	ROH
Harris, J.L.	Cpl.	M 7th SCVI			05/06/64	Wilderness, VA	KIA		JR
Harris, J.M.	Pvt.	A 18th SCVI	31	UN	03/29/65	Burgess' Mill VA	KIA		ROH
Harris, J.R.	Pvt.	K 10th SCVI		CN	/ /		DOD		RAS
Harris, James	Pvt.	B 15th SCVAB			07/27/63	Bty. Wagner, SC	KIA		ROH,CDC
Harris, James G.	1st Sgt.	C Hol.Leg.	23	SG	08/30/62	2nd Manassas, VA	KIA		ROH,JR,HOS
Harris, James H.	Pvt.	E 22nd SCVI	28	LR	08/01/64	Crater, Pbg., VA	DOW	Blandford Church Pbg., VA	ROH,BLM,BLC,PP
Harris, John	Pvt.	D Orr's Ri.	24	AN	12/13/62	Fredericksburg	KIA	(CDC=Joseph)	ROH
Harris, John	Pvt.	C 2nd SCVIRi			09/30/64	Ft. Harrison, VA	KIA		ROH,JR
Harris, John	Pvt.	H 12th SCVI		YK	08/15/64		DOD		CWC
Harris, John A.	Pvt.	D Orr's Ri.		AN	01/09/63	Fredericksburg	DOW		ROH,JR
Harris, John B.	1st Lt.	C 19th SCVI		ED	04/15/63		DOD		HOE
Harris, John R.	2nd Cpl.	E 3rd SCVI		NY	09/17/62	Sharpsburg, MD	KIA	Rose Hill C. Hagerstown MD	ROH,JR,NCC,BOD
Harris, John W.	Pvt.	H 7th SCVIBn	21	RD	05/16/64	Drury's Bluff VA	KIA		ROH,JR,HAG
Harris, Joseph Milton	Pvt.	G 2nd SCVIRi	18	AN	12/19/63	Strawberry Pl TN	DOD		ROH
Harris, Leonidas S.	Pvt.	G P.S.S.	20	YK	08/14/64	Chaffin's Farm	KIA	(JR=8/4/64)	ROH,JR,UD2,YEB
Harris, Marcus D.	Pvt.	A 13th SCVI		LS	08/07/62	Richmond, VA	DOW	Hollywood Cem.Rchmd. Q86	ROH,JR,HC
Harris, Martin	Pvt.	K Hol.Leg.			05/24/65	Pt. Lookout, MD	DIP	C.C. Pt. Lookout, MD	FPH,P6,P12,P11
Harris, R.	Cpl.	L 7th SCVI		HY	09/17/62	Sharpsburg. MD	KIA		JR
Harris, Rice H.	Pvt.	M P.S.S.	32	SG	05/31/62	7 Pines, VA	KIA	(TFD frm G, 5th SCVI)	ROH,JR,HOS,CDC
Harris, Richard S.	4th Sgt.	D 5th SCVI		UN	05/15/64	Wilderness, VA	DOW	(Wdd 5/6/64)	SA3
Harris, Robert	Pvt.	B 16th SCVI		GE	11/30/64	Franklin, TN	KIA		16R
Harris, Robert T.	Pvt.	G 3rd SCVI	24	LS	02/15/62	Charlottesville	DOD	Dials Meth. Ch. GE County	ROH,JR,GEC,KEB
Harris, S. (T. ?)	Pvt.	H 13th SCVI		LN	/ /	Richmond, VA		Oakwood C.#87,Row B,Div G	ROH,OWC
Harris, Samuel N.	Cpl.	D 3rd SCVIBn	19	AE	05/08/64	Spotsylvania, VA	KIA	Spotsylvania C.H., VA	ROH,JR,SCH,KEB
Harris, Smith	Pvt.	I 9th SCVIB	35	SG	10/15/61	Germantown, VA	DOD		ROH,HOS
Harris, T.	Pvt.	SCVI			07/30/62	Richmond, VA		Hollywood Cem.Rchmd. Q28	HC
Harris, T.	Pvt.	B 3rd SCVI			08/07/62	Richmond, VA		Hollywood Cem.Rchmd. C143	HC,
Harris, T.J.	Pvt.	A 14th SCVI	17	DN	01/28/65	Richmond, VA	DOD	Hollywood Cem.Rchmd. W5	ROH,HC,CDC
Harris, Thomas	Pvt.	K Hol.Leg.	39		11/10/64	Richmond, VA	DOD		ROH
Harris, Thomas	Pvt.	F 2nd SCVI	44	AE	05/06/64	Wilderness, VA	KIA		ROH,JR,SA2,KEB
Harris, Thomas	Sgt.	K 18th SCVI			05/20/64	Clay's Farm, VA	KIA		ROH,JR
Harris, Thomas J.	Pvt.	E 2nd SCVA			04/28/65	Pt. Lookout, MD	DIP	C.C. Pt. lookout, MD	ROH,FPH,P6,P11
Harris, Thomas J.	2nd Cpl.	E 3rd SCVI		NY	10/25/62	Winchester, VA	DOD		ROH,JR,SA2,ANY
Harris, W.	Pvt.	B 18th SCVI			09/14/63	South Mtn., MD	KIA		JR
Harris, W.B. (W.M.?)	Pvt.	B 7th SCVI			02/15/65	Charleston, SC	DOD	Magnolia Cem. Charleston	ROH,MAG
Harris, W.E.	Pvt.	McBeth LA	19	UN	07/30/64	Crater, Pbg, VA	KIA		ROH
Harris, William	Pvt.	K Hol.Leg.	27		09/05/62	Staunton, VA	DOW	(Wdd Rappahanock Bridge)	ROH
Harris, William Edward	Pvt.	A 18th SCVI			07/30/64	Crater Pbg., VA	KIA		JR
Harris, William L.	Pvt.	B 27th SCVI		CN	05/16/64	Drury's Bluff VA	KIA	(JR=8/6/64)	ROH,JR,CDC,HAG
Harris, William P.	Pvt.	K Hol.Leg.			09/20/62	Warrenton, VA	DOW	(Wdd and Man)	ROH
Harris, William P.	Sgt.	B P.S.S.	20	PS	05/30/62	7 Pines, VA	KIA		ROH,JR
Harrison, Abraham T.	Cpt.	D 16th SCVI		GE	09/07/63		DOD		16R
Harrison, Andrew M.	Pvt.	D 16th SCVI		GE	/ /	Atlanta, GA	DOD	(1864)	16R
Harrison, F.	Pvt.	C 11th SCVI			04/07/63	Hardeeville, SC	DOD		JR
Harrison, F.B.	Pvt.	F 22nd SCVI			07/30/64	Crater, Pbg, VA	KIA		BLM

H

SOUTH CAROLINA DEAD IN CSA SERVICE 1861-1865

NAME	RANK	C	REGIMENT	AGE	DS	DIED	WHERE	WHY	BURIED	SOURCES
Harrison, F.M.	Cpt.	D	16th SCVI		GE	12/15/63	Brownville, MS	DOD		16R
Harrison, J. Edmonds	Pvt.	B	7th SCVIBn	18	FD	05/16/64	Drury's Bluff VA	KIA		ROH,JR,HAG
Harrison, J.E.	Pvt.	D	16th SCVI			04/12/64	Inst. H. Atlanta		Oakland C. Atlanta R10#16	BGA
Harrison, J.H.	Pvt.	D	16th SCVI		GE	/ /	Adams Run, SC	DOD	(1863)	16R
Harrison, J.L.	Pvt.	E	Ham.Leg.		GE	09/04/63	GE			ROH
Harrison, J.W.	Pvt.	K	24th SCVI			09/09/63	Empire H.Atlanta		Oakland C. Atlanta R20#2	BGA
Harrison, James Anthony	Pvt.		PeeDee LA	32	LS	12/13/62	Fredericksburg	KIA	Fairview P.C., GE County	ROH,PDL,GEC,UD3
Harrison, James Mitchell	2nd Lt.	H	22rd SCVI	23	GE	07/30/64	Crater, Pbg., VA	KIA		ROH,JR,BLM
Harrison, John	Pvt.	D	14th SCVI	22	ED	07/06/62	Gaines' Mill, VA	DOW		ROH,JR,D14,EDN
Harrison, John	Pvt.	H	12th SCVI		YK	12/15/61		DOD		CWC
Harrison, John A.	Pvt.	C	P.S.S.			10/28/63	Lookout Valley	KIA	(JR=10/21/63)	ROH,JR,CDC,GMJ
Harrison, John J.	Major		11th SCVI		CO	10/22/62	Coosahatchie, SC	KIA	(PP=Pocotaligo) PP	ROH,LC,MDM,SSO
Harrison, Pickney McD.	Pvt.		PeeDee LA	29	LS	12/13/62	Fredericksburg	KIA	Fairview P.C. LS Cty. SC	ROH,PDL,UD3,RHL
Harrison, Reuben	Pvt.	D	16th SCVI		GE	06/28/64	Mobile, AL	DOD	(PP=At home)	16R,PP
Harrison, Richard R.	Pvt.	C	1st SCVIH	27	BL	12/17/62	Richmond, VA	DOD	(Rchmd effects list 1/63)	ROH,SA1,CDC
Harrison, Robert	Pvt.	E	24th SCVI	40	CO	08/31/62	Secessionville	DOD		ROH
Harrison, Robert	Pvt.	H	7th SCVIBn		FD	05/16/64	Drury's Bluff VA	KIA	(JR=Harris)	ROH,JR,HAG
Harrison, Robert	Sgt.	K	6th SCVI			12/20/61	Dranesville, VA	KIA		JR
Harrison, T.	Pvt.	H	14th SCVI		BL	06/27/62	Richmond, VA			ROH
Harrison, Thomas J.	Sgt.	A	10th SCVI		GN	12/28/62	Murfreesboro, TN	KIA		ROH,JR,GRG,RAS
Harrison, W.M.	Pvt.	D	16th SCVI		GE	/ /	At home	DOD	(1864)	16R
Harrison, William	Pvt.	K	24th SCVI		ED	07/20/63	Atlanta, GA	DOD	Oakland Cem. Atlanta	HOE,CVG
Harrison, William	Pvt.	I	5th SCVI			11/28/63	Bridgeport, AL	DOW		P6
Harrison, Wilson S.	Pvt.	K	1st SCVA	44	CD	04/14/65	Pt. Lookout, MD	DIP	C.C. Pt. Lookout, MD	ROH,FPH,P6,P114
Harristen, T.B.	Pvt.	F	22nd SCVI		PS	07/30/64	Crater Pbg., VA	KIA		JR
Harrod, William P.	Pvt.	C	1st SCVIH	21	BL	05/06/64	Wilderness, VA	KIA	(Also Wdd.@ Loudon Stn.)	ROH,SA1
Harroldson,	Cpl.	L	7th SCVI		HY	09/17/62	Sharpsburg, MD	KIA	(JR=MD Hts. 9/13/62)	ROH,JR
Harroldson, Edward F.	Pvt.	B	Orr's Ri.			06/23/65	Pt. Lookout, MD	DIP	C.C. Pt. Lookout, MD	FPH,P6,P114
Harroll, D.	Pvt.	D	6th SCVI		CR	06/02/62	Lynchburg, VA	DOD	Lynchburg CSA Cem.#4 R1	ROH,JR,CDC
Harroll, James	Pvt.	K	7th SCVI			05/15/64		KIA		JR
Harshaw, Robert	Pvt.	G	P.S.S.	30	YK	/ /	Farmville, VA	DOD		YEB
Hart, Alfred	3rd Cpl.	C	19th SCVI	19	ED	04/19/63	Shelbyville, TN	DOD	Little Stevens Ck.B.Ch. ED	HOE,EDN,UD3
Hart, Harvey H.	Pvt.	H	12th SCVI		YK	08/13/64		DOD	(CWC=Heart)	CWC,YEB
Hart, J. Hartwell	Pvt.	I	6th SCVC	27	DN	07/08/64	Gordonsville, VA	DOW	(Wdd. @ Trevillian Stn.)	ROH
Hart, J.M.	Pvt.	H	22nd SCVI			11/19/64	Savannah, GA	DOD	Laurel Grove C. Savannah	ROH,P114,BGA
Hart, James	Pvt.	K	16th SCVI			06/18/62	Adams Run, SC	DOD		JR
Hart, John	Pvt.	D	16th SCVI		GE	06/15/62	At home	DOD		16R,PP
Hart, John	Pvt.	H	12th SCVI		YK	06/15/63		DOD	(CWC=Heart)	CWC,YEB
Hart, John L.	1st Lt.	B	21st SCVI		DN	05/09/64	Swift Creek, VA	KIA		ROH,JR,DAR,HAG
Hart, Leroy	Pvt.	H	12th SCVI			05/06/64	Wilderness, VA	KIA		JR
Hart, Thomas C.	Sgt.	G	27th SCVI		SG	12/17/64	Pt. Lookout, MD	DIP	C.C. Pt. Lookout, MD	ROH,FPH,P6,P113
Hart, William D.	2nd Lt.	F	15th SCVI		UN	07/02/63	Gettysburg, PA	KIA		ROH,JR,GDR,KEB
Hartford, George T.	Cpl.	F	18th SCVI	21	UN	07/24/64	Petersburg, VA	KIA	Blandford Church Pbg., VA	ROH,BLC,PP
Harthorne, J.T.	Pvt.	F	Hol. Leg.	20	AE	09/11/62		DOD		ROH
Hartin, J.A.	Pvt.	H	15th SCVI			/ /	Farmville, VA	DOD	(JR= G, 17th SCVI)	ROH,JR
Hartley, Gabriel	Pvt.	H	1st SCVIH		LN	12/06/62	Winchester, VA	DOD	Stonewall C. Winchester VA	ROH,WIN,SA1
Hartley, J.B.	Pvt.	F	P.S.S.			03/15/64		DOD		ROH,JR
Hartley, Jeremiah	Pvt.	F	1st SCVIH		GE	11/15/62		DOD	(Died of Rubella)	ROH,SA1,JRH,HAG
Hartley, John J. (L.?)	Pvt.	K	20th SCVI		LN	10/14/64	Strasburg, VA	DOW	(Hartwell in KEB ?)	ROH,JR,CDC
Hartley, Joseph L.	Pvt.	C	15th SCVI	25	LN	06/12/64	Cold Harbor, VA	DOW	Hollywood Cem.Rchmd. U364	ROH,JR,HC,KEB
Hartley, William B.	Cpl.	F	19th SCVI	22	LN	06/03/62	Okolona, MS	DOD		ROH,PP,TOD

SOUTH CAROLINA DEAD IN CSA SERVICE 1861-1865

NAME	RANK	C REGIMENT	AGE	DS	DIED	WHERE	WHY	BURIED	SOURCES
Hartley, Willis	Pvt.	I 20th SCVI		LN	11/13/64	Staunton, VA		(HOE=F, 19th)	ROH,KEB
Hartman, G.B.	Pvt.	I 15th SCVI		LN	09/17/62	Sharpsburg, MD	KIA		ROH,H15,TOD
Hartman, H.C.N.	Pvt.	G 13th SCVI		NY	/ /	At home	DOD		ROH,ANY
Hartman, J. Martin	Pvt.	H Hol.Leg.	24	NY	01/12/63	Goldsboro, NC	DOW	(Wdd @ Kinston,JR=Fdrksbg)	ROH,JR,ANY
Hartman, S.O.	Pvt.	H 3rd SCVI		LN	12/15/62	Fredericksburg	DOW		JR,SA2,KEB
Hartness, A. Davis	Sgt.	C 17th SCVI	41	YK	08/13/64	Crater, Pbg., VA	DOW	Blandford Church Pbg., VA	BLM,BLC,YEB,PP
Hartness, John R.	Pvt.	C 17th SCVI	22	YK	03/20/65	Elmira, NY	DIP	Woodlawn N.C.#1570 Elmira	FPH,P6,P65,YEB
Hartwell, Thomas	Pvt.	A 12th SCVCB		DN	10/25/62	georgetown, SC	DOD		ROH,DOD
Hartzog, C.C.	Pvt.	I 5th SCVC			06/15/64	Price's Farm, VA	DOW	(Wdd 5/28/64)	ROH,JR,CDC
Hartzog, G.L.	Pvt.	K 1st SCVIH		BL	10/08/61		DOD		SA1
Hartzog, Israel P.	Pvt.	D 19th SCVI	27	ED	09/20/63	Chickamauga, GA	KIA	(#7 Co. 10/19th Consol)	ROH,JR,HOE,UD3
Hartzog, J.B.	Pvt.	A 1st SCVIH		BL	09/06/62	At home	DOW	(Wdd @ 2nd Man 8/30/62)	SA1,CDC,UD3
Hartzog, Nicholas	Pvt.	5th SCVC			05/28/64		DOW		JMB
Hartzog, W.W.	Pvt.	A 1st SCVIH		BL	09/23/62	At home	DOW	(Wdd @ 2nd Man 8/30/62)	JR,SA1,CDC,UD3
Hartzog, Wyatte J.	Pvt.		29		06/22/62	Pocotaligo, SC	DOD		CNM
Harvel, John	Pvt.	G 8th SCVI		MO	10/22/63	Fair Gds Atlanta	DOW	Oakland C. Atlanta R11#9	JR,HOM,UD2,BGA
Harvely, James	Pvt.	H 7th SCVIBn	26	ED	05/19/64	Drury's Bluff VA	KIA		ROH,HAG
Harvey, A.G.	Pvt.	B 27th SCVI		CN	/ /				ROH
Harvey, A.J.	Pvt.	G 17th SCVI		BL	03/25/65	Unknown	DIP	Cypress Hills N.C.#2411 NY	FPH
Harvey, Columbus	Pvt.	B Hol.Leg.	18	SG	07/23/63	Macon, GA	DOD		ROH
Harvey, F.	Pvt.	H 15th SCVI			/ /		DOD	(Haney?)	JR
Harvey, G.W.	Pvt.	D 22nd SCVI		PS	04/01/65	Pt. Lookout, MD	DIP	C.C. Pt. Lookout, MD	FPH,P6,P12,P11
Harvey, J.D.	Pvt.	K P.S.S.			/ /		DOD		JR
Harvey, J.T.	Pvt.	1st SCV			/ /	Richmond, VA		Oakwood C.#12,Row R,Div C	OWC
Harvey, James W.	Cpl.	D 16th SCVI		GE	07/20/64	Peachtree Ck. GA	KIA		16R
Harvey, Joseph	Pvt.	B Hol.Leg.	19	SG	08/23/62	Rappahanock Stn.	KIA	(JR=7/30/62)	ROH,JR,HOS
Harvey, Morgan	Pvt.	B Hol.Leg.	23	SG	08/30/62	2nd Manassas, VA	KIA		ROH,HOS
Harvey, T.B.	Pvt.	K 14th SCVI		ED	/ /		DOW		HOE
Harvey, W.J.	Pvt.	A 1st SCVIH			10/19/64	Richmond, VA	DOW	Hollywood Cem.Rchmd. I30	ROH,HC,SA1,UD3
Harvey, William	Pvt.	A 5th SCVI		UN	07/27/61	Charlottesville	DOD	Univ. C. Charlottesville	ROH,SA3,ACH
Harvey, William	Pvt.	I 5th SCVI		SG	05/31/62	7 Pines, VA	DOW		JR,SA3
Harvey, William A.	2nd Lt.	E 7th SCVIBn		FD	06/18/64	Hare's Hill, VA	KIA		JR,HAG,R46
Haselden, Hugh G.	Pvt.	F 4th SCVC		MN	01/06/65	Elmira, NY	DIP	Woodlawn N.C.#1243 Elmira	JR,FPH,P6,HMC
Haselden, John J.	Pvt.	G 15th SCVI	22	WG	11/15/61	Hardeesville, SC	DOD		JR,ROH,HOW,KEB
Haselden, Samuel T.	Cpl.	B Pioneer Cp	30	WG	04/14/65	Richmond, VA	DOD		ROH
Haseltine, Edward E.	Pvt.	D 27th SCVI	27	CN	10/31/62	Charleston, SC	DOD	Magnolia Cem. Charleston	ROH,JR,MAG
Haselwood, Hosey H.	Pvt.	B 15th SCVI		UN	04/29/64	Columbia, SC	DOD		ROH,PP
Haselwood, Thomas J.	Pvt.	B 15th SCVI		UN	/ /		DOD		JR
Haskell, William T.	Cpt.	H 1st SCVIG	26	AE	07/02/63	Gettysburg, PA	KIA	Trinity E.C. Abbeville, SC	ROH,JR,GDR,CGS
Haskell,Jr., Charles T.	Cpt.	D 1st SCVIR	28	AE	07/10/63	Morris Island SC	KIA	Trinity E.C. Abbeville, SC	ROH,JR,SA1,DOC
Haskins, Miles	Pvt.	B 22nd SCVI		SG	03/03/63	Kalorama Hos. DC	DIP		HOS,P12
Hastings, James W.	Pvt.	G 1st SCVIG		ED	07/01/62	Richmond, VA	DOD		JR,SA1,HOE
Hastings, R.N.	2nd Lt.	B 22nd SCVI	23	SG	08/10/63	Savannah, GA	DOD	Ebenezer M.C. SG Cty. SC	ROH,HOS,R48
Hatch, J.G.	Pvt.				/ /	Richmond, VA		Oakwood C.#40,Row R,Div C	OWC
Hatch, Joseph	Pvt.	C 10th SCVI			02/01/64	Cassville, GA			ROH
Hatchel, A.J.	Pvt.	H 10th SCVI		WG	05/04/62	Mississippi	DOD	(1863)	RAS,HOW
Hatchel, J.N.	Pvt.	H 10th SCVI		WG	/ /		DOD	(1863)	RAS,HOW
Hatchel, Jasper	Pvt.	H 10th SCVI		WG	01/15/62		DOD	(Date approx)	RAS,HOW
Hatchel, R.N.	Pvt.	Culpeppers			11/13/64	New Orleans, LA	DIP		P3
Hatchel, T.H.	Pvt.	H 10th SCVI		WG	06/15/62		DOD	(Date approx)	RAS,HOW
Hatchell, H.	Pvt.	E 3rd SCVABn		DN	08/05/62	Charleston, SC	DOD	Magnolia Cem. Charleston	ROH,MAG

H

SOUTH CAROLINA DEAD IN CSA SERVICE 1861-1865

NAME	RANK	C REGIMENT	AGE	DS	DIED	WHERE	WHY	BURIED	SOURCES
Hatchell, R.L.	Pvt.	E 8th SCVI		DN	/ /	Richmond, VA		Oakwood C.#74,Row E,Div A	ROH,OWC,KEB
Hatchell, William H.	Pvt.	D 21st SCVI		DN	06/29/65	Elmira, NY	DIP	Woodlawn N.C.#2826 Elmira	ROH,FPH,HAG,P65
Hatcher, Aaron	Pvt.	D 26th SCVI		MO	/ /	At home	DOD		HOM
Hatcher, Benjamin T.	Pvt.	E 2nd SCVA	23	ED	07/10/64	At home	DOD		ROH
Hatcher, Edward	Pvt.	K 1st SCVA			10/20/63	Charleston, SC		Magnolia Cem. Charleston	ROH,MAG
Hatcher, John	Pvt.	D 14th SCVI	28	ED	01/10/63	Fredericksburg	DOD	(Pneumonia)	ROH,JR,D14,HOE
Hatcher, John G.	Pvt.	B 19th SCVI	18	ED	09/20/63	Chickamauga, GA	KIA	Hatcher Fam.C. Trenton, SC	ROH,JR,HOE,EDN
Hatchett, William	Pvt.	A Hol.Leg.	42	SG	05/24/64	Stony Creek, VA	DOD		ROH,HOS
Hatfield, C.W.	Pvt.	E P.S.S.		SR	07/23/62	Gaines' Mill, VA	DOW		ROH,JR
Hatfield, James W.	Pvt.	E 7th SCVIBn		SR	04/29/65	Elmira, NY	DIP	Woodlawn N.C.#2730 Elmira	JR,FPH,HAG,P6
Hathaway, T.P.	Pvt.	Santee LA		CN	03/08/65	Ft. Delaware, DE	DIP	Finn's Pt., NJ Nat. Cem.	ROH,FPH,P6,P41
Hattaway, John	Pvt.	A 21st SCVI		CN	06/15/62	Georgetown, SC	DOD		ROH
Hatton, F.D.	Pvt.	B Ham.Leg.		NY	09/09/61	Virginia	DOD	(Typhoid)	JR,ANY
Hatton, J. Robert	Pvt.	A 13th SCVI			10/13/61	Lightwood Knot	DOD	Measles	JR
Hatton, James Ivey	Pvt.	B Ham.Leg.		NY	09/21/61	At home	DOD	(Typhoid, Surgeon's Asst.)	JR,ANY
Hatton, William H.	Pvt.	E 3rd SCVI		NY	09/17/64	James River, VA	KIA	Stonewall Cem. Winchester	ROH,WIN,ANY,SA2
Hatton, William M.	1st Lt.	G Hol. Leg.	33	NY	08/30/62	2nd Manassas, VA	KIA	Head Spgs. C. Newberry Cty	ROH,JR,NCC,ANY
Hatz, H.	Pvt.	E 5th SCVC			11/16/63	Knoxville, TN	KIA		ROH
Hauscheldt, Peter F.	Pvt.	I 1st SCVIG	34	CN	06/08/64		DOD	St. John's Ch. Charleston	CDC
Havener, J.P.	Pvt.	K 3rd SCVI	21	SG	07/26/62	Malvern Hill, VA	DOW	(ROH & HOS=Savage Stn)	ROH,JR,SA2,HOS
Havird, Daniel	Pvt.	D 19th SCVI	22	ED	01/25/62	Charleston, SC	DOD	(Exhaustion on march)	JR,HOE,UD3
Havird, Franklin J.	Pvt.	D 19th SCVI	20	ED	01/15/62	Charleston, SC	DOD	(Brain fever)	JR,HOE,UD3
Hawk, R.B.	Pvt.	E 14th SCVI			08/29/62	2nd Manassas, VA	KIA		JR
Hawkins, Augustus	Pvt.	C 7th SCVIBn	20	RD	01/30/63	Wilmington, NC	DOD		ROH,JR
Hawkins, D.J.M.	Pvt.	B 18th SCVI	24	UN	03/29/65		DOD	Hawkins Fam. Cem. UN Cty.	UNC
Hawkins, F.	Pvt.	B 1st SC Res		RD	02/11/65	Columbia, SC			ROH,PP
Hawkins, G.A.	Pvt.	C 1st SCVIR		GE	07/09/62	Camp Evans, SC	DOD	(ROH=DOW @ Averysboro)	ROH,SA1
Hawkins, H.	Pvt.	F 10th SCVI		MN	/ /		DOD		RAS
Hawkins, Isaac	Pvt.	D 18th SCVI		AN	07/11/63	Jackson, MS	KIA		ROH,JR,PP
Hawkins, J. Caldwell	Pvt.	K P.S.S.		SG	06/15/62	7 Pines, VA	DOW		JR,HOS
Hawkins, J. Ransom	Pvt.	F 16th SCVI		GE	/ /		ACD	(RR collision, SUR Gbo.?)	16R
Hawkins, J.A.	Pvt.	K Orr's Ri.		AN	06/27/62	Gaines' Mill, VA	KIA		ROH,JR,CDC
Hawkins, J.B.	Pvt.	H 16th SCVI		GE	06/20/64	Fair G. Atlanta		Oakland C. Atlanta R53#1	BGA
Hawkins, J.J.	Pvt.	E 14th SCVI		LS	11/04/62	Winchester, VA		Stonewall Cem. Winchester	ROH,WIN
Hawkins, J.P.T.	Pvt.	B 18th SCVI	30	UN	10/18/63	Winchester, VA	DOD	Stonewall Cem. Winchester	ROH,JR,WIN
Hawkins, Jabez B.	Pvt.	C P.S.S.		GE	10/28/63	Lookout Valley	KIA	(JR=Racoon Mtn.)	ROH,JR,CDC,GMJ
Hawkins, James	Pvt.	C 16th SCVI		GE	08/31/64	Jonesboro, GA	KIA		16R
Hawkins, James Franklin	Pvt.	B 18th SCVI	22	UN	05/27/62	On the SC coast	DOD	Hawkins Fam. C. UN Cty. SC	ROH,JR,UNC
Hawkins, James M.	Pvt.	K 16th SCVI		GE	12/03/63	Rock Island, IL	DIP	C.C.#106 Rock Island, IL	FPH,P5,P39,16R
Hawkins, Jeremiah C.	2nd Lt.	F 4th SCVI	35	GE	08/19/61	Culpepper, VA	DOW	Fairview Cem. Culpepper VA	ROH,CGH,SA2,CDC
Hawkins, Jesse	3rd Lt.	F 16th SCVI		GE	11/30/64	Franklin, TN	KIA		ROH,16R,CDC,PP
Hawkins, John	Pvt.	A 18th SCVI	39	UN	05/25/62	At home	DOD	(A, 16th SCVI?)	ROH
Hawkins, Jonathan H.	1st Sgt.	B 18th SCVI	21	UN	06/25/64	Petersburg, VA	KIA	Hawkins Fam. C. UN Cty. SC	ROH,UNC
Hawkins, Joseph	2nd Cpl.	F 1st SCVIH		GE	03/28/64	Virginia	DOD		SA1
Hawkins, Joseph Marion	Pvt.	B 18th SCVI	23	UN	03/29/65	Burgess' Mill VA	KIA		ROH
Hawkins, Michael	Pvt.	C 5th SCVI		SG	08/05/61	Orange C.H., VA	DOD		SA3
Hawkins, P.	Pvt.	D 12th SCVI			08/29/62	2nd Manassas, VA	KIA		JR
Hawkins, P.W.	Pvt.	F 2nd SCVIRi			02/19/65	Richmond, VA		Hollywood Cem.Rchmd. W54	ROH,HC
Hawkins, S.	Cpl.	H 22nd SCVI		GE	07/30/64	Crater, Pbg., VA	KIA		JR,BLM
Hawkins, S.P.	Pvt.	G 13th SCVI		NY	05/05/65		KIA	(On retreat from Pbg)	ROH,ANY
Hawkins, T.	Pvt.	B 1st SC Res		GE	02/11/65	Columbia, SC	DOD		ROH

SOUTH CAROLINA DEAD IN CSA SERVICE 1861-1865

NAME	RANK	C REGIMENT	AGE	DS	DIED	WHERE	WHY	BURIED	SOURCES
Hawkins, Thomas	Pvt.	E 2nd SCVIRi		PS	/ /	Lynchburg, VA		Lynchburg CSA Cem. #4 R4	BBW
Hawkins, W.G.	Pvt.	C 1st SCSSBn		CN	08/18/63		DOD	(JR & ROH=G, 27th SCVI)	ROH,JR
Hawkins, William C.	Pvt.	D 16th SCVI		GE	/ /	Atlanta, GA	DOD	(? W.C.SUR @ Gbo)	16R
Hawkins, William H.	Pvt.	B 18th SCVI	30	UN	10/04/64	Burkeville, VA	DOD		ROH
Hawkins, William J.	Sgt.	L 2nd SCVIRi	24	AN	02/15/64	Richmond, VA	DOD		ROH
Hawkins, Zion	Pvt.	F 16th SCVI		GE	03/08/62	At home	DOD	(Measles)	JR,PP
Hawle, M.	Cpl.	C Ham.Leg.			06/05/62	Richmond, VA		Hollywood Cem.Rchmd. O9	HC
Hawthman, H.S.	Pvt.	K 13th SCVI		LN	10/05/64	Richmond, VA		Hollywood Cem.Rchmd. V550	HC
Hawthorn,	Pvt.	B Orr's Ri.	27	AE	05/12/64	Spotsylvania, VA	KIA		ROH
Hawthorn, Jasper N.	1st Lt.	I P.S.S.	33	PS	06/30/62	Frayser's Farm	KIA		ROH,JR,CDC,R48
Hawthorn, M.C.	Pvt.	F 12th SCVI		FD	06/15/64	Petersburg, VA	KIA	(Wdd. 3 times)	HFC
Hawthorn, M.F.	Sgt.				09/30/64	Jones' Farm, VA	KIA		LSS
Hawthorne, Robert H.	Cpt.	F Orr's Ri.	30	PS	06/27/62	Gaines' Mill, VA	KIA	Terrell/Perry Gvyd Oconee	ROH,JR,OCS,CDC
Hawthorne, Thomas M.	Pvt.	G Orr's Ri.		AE	03/16/64	Pt. Lookout, MD	DIP	C.C. Pt. Lookout, MD	ROH,FPH,P5,CDC
Hay, George J.	Pvt.	G 9th SCVIB		DN	03/15/62	Charlottesville	DOD	Univ. C. Charlottesville	ROH,JLC,ACH
Hay, T.	Pvt.	Rhetts Bty			07/02/63	Gettysburg, PA	KIA	Magnolia Cem. Charleston	MAG
Hay, W.A.R.	4th Sgt.	B 1st SCVIH		OG	09/30/64	Ft. Harrison, VA	KIA		SA1
Hayes, A.B.	Pvt.	D Orr's Ri.		AN	12/28/62	Staunton, VA		Thornrose C. Staunton, VA	ROH,CDC,TOD
Hayes, Allen A.	Pvt.	C 8th SCVI		CD	09/27/64	Cheraw, SC	DOW	(Wdd @ Rchmd 4/24/64)	ROH,KEB
Hayes, Arthur W.N.	Pvt.	K 20th SCVI		LN	07/20/63	Morris Island SC	KIA		ROH,KEB,CDC
Hayes, C.E.	Pvt.	D 2nd SCVI			04/11/63		DOD		H2,SA2
Hayes, J.C.	Pvt.	K 22nd SCVI		PS	03/06/63	Columbia, SC	DOD		ROH
Hayes, James H.	3rd Lt.	C 1st SCVIH		BL	10/01/64	Richmond	DOW	Oakwood C.#108,Row M,Div A	ROH,SA1,OWC
Hayes, Joseph	Pvt.	D 15th SCVI		KW	06/17/64	Richmond, VA	DOW	Hollywood Cem.Rchmd. U52	ROH,HC,KEB,HIC
Hayes, Peter J.	Pvt.	G 14th SCVI	25	AE	02/13/63	Fredericksburg	DOD	Fredericksburg C.C. R9S14	ROH,JR,FBG
Hayes, Robert		5th SCVC		LN	05/16/64	Drury's Bluff VA	KIA		JMA
Hayes, William W.	Pvt.	L 1st SCVIG		CN	08/29/62	2nd Manassas, VA	KIA		ROH,JR,SA1,CDC
Hayne, Edmund Shubrick	3rd Cpl.	L 1st SCVIG	18	CN	06/30/62	Gaines' Mill, VA	DOW	Magnolia Cem. Charleston	ROH,JR,SA1,RCD
Haynes, John W.	Pvt.	K P.S.S.			/ /		KIA		JR
Haynes, W. Simpson	Pvt.	K P.S.S.		SG	05/31/62	7 Pines, VA	KIA		JR,HOS
Haynesworth, John R.	2nd Lt.	C Ham.Leg.		CL	07/21/61	1st Manassas, VA	KIA		R48
Haynie, John R.	Pvt.	D Orr's Ri.		AN	07/14/62	Gaines' Mill, VA	DOW		JR
Haynie, Stephen P.	2nd Lt.	E 4th SCVIBn		AN	07/10/62	Malvern Hill, VA	DOW		JR,HOF,SA2,R47
Hays, A.B.	Pvt.	L Orr's Ri.		AN	/ /	Richmond, VA		Oakwood C.#108,Row M,Div A	ROH,OWC
Hays, A.T.	2nd Lt.	C 26th SCVI		MN	07/30/64	Petersburg, VA	KIA		HMC,R48
Hays, Allen	Pvt.	C 26th SCVI		MN	07/15/64	Petersburg, VA	KIA	(Date app.btwn 6/17-7/2)	HMC,CDC
Hays, Benjamin	Pvt.	C 12th SCVI		FD	02/14/63		DOD		ROH
Hays, Benjamin T.	Pvt.	B 37th VAVCB	34	AN	10/16/64	Staunton, VA	DOW		37V,PP
Hays, C.F.	Pvt.	D 25th SCVI		MN	03/23/65	Elmira, NY	DIP	Woodlawn N.C.#1515 Elmira	FPH,HMC,P6,P65
Hays, D.H.	Pvt.	E 23rd SCVI		MN	07/13/64	Petersburg, VA	KIA		ROH,HMC
Hays, Daniel S.	Pvt.	C 26th SCVI		MN	/ /	Deep Bottom, VA	KIA	(In enemy hands)	HMC
Hays, Erastus W.	Pvt.	D 25th SCVI		MN	09/11/64	Alexandria, VA	DOW	Christ Ch. Alexandria, VA	ROH,HMC,HAG,P1
Hays, Jesse R.	Pvt.	E 1st SCVIG		MN	05/03/63	Chancellorsville	KIA		ROH,SA1,HMC
Hays, John	Pvt.	C 12th SCVI		FD	01/13/63	Guinea Stn., VA	DOD		JR,HFC
Hays, John J.	Pvt.	F 17th SCVI	19	YK	08/30/62	Virginia	DOD		JR,YEB
Hays, L.B.	Pvt.	F 4th SCVC		MN	/ /	At home	DOD	(1864)	HMC
Hays, N.	Pvt.	E 23rd SCVI		MN	08/01/64				HMC
Hays, R.	Pvt.	C 12th SCVI		FD	02/16/63	Guinea Stn., VA	DOD		JR
Hays, R.H.	Pvt.	D 25th SCVI		MN	11/27/63	James Island, SC	KIA		ROH,JR,HMC,HAG
Hays, Robert	Pvt.	D P.S.S.			/ /		DOD		JR
Hays, Robert H.	Pvt.	5th SCVC	36	BL	05/16/64	Drury's Bluff VA	KIA		ROH,JR

SOUTH CAROLINA DEAD IN CSA SERVICE 1861-1865

NAME	RANK	C REGIMENT	AGE	DS	DIED	WHERE	WHY	BURIED	SOURCES
Hays, T.S.	Pvt.	C 2nd SCVI		UN	12/18/62		DOD	(ROH = Robert)	ROH,SA2
Hays, Thomas	Pvt.	H 1st SCVA			05/15/64	Charleston, SC	DOD		ROH,CDC
Hays, W.C.	Pvt.	D 25th SCVI		MN	08/03/62	James Island, SC	DOD	(HMC=KIA)	JR,HMC
Hays, W.M.	Pvt.	D 25th SCVI		MN	/ /	Virginia			HMC
Haywood, Isham	Pvt.	F 21st SCVI	18	MO	07/10/63	Morris Island SC	KIA	(HOM=Heyward)	ROH,JR,HOM,R48
Haywood, John	Pvt.	L 21st SCVI	30	MN	09/15/64	Virginia	DOD		ROH,HAG,HMC
Haywood, William	Pvt.	F 21st SCVI		MO	08/21/63	Pt. Lookout, MD	DIP	NC Beaufort, SC #53-6321	ROH,HAG,HOM,PP
Hazleton, F.	Pvt.	B 1st CS Eng			/ /	Richmond, VA		Oakwood C.#116,Row M,Div G	OWC
Head, John P.	Pvt.	E 13th SCVI		SG	05/14/62	Richmond, VA	DOD	Hollywood Cem.Rchmd. F122	ROH,JR,HC,HOS
Head, Miles	Pvt.	B 2nd SCVIRi		PS	/ /				ROH
Head, Robinson	Pvt.	C 1st SCVIR		CD	03/20/65	Averysboro, NC	DOW		ROH,SA1,WAT,PP
Head, William H.	Pvt.	K 12th SCVI		PS	07/02/63	Gettysburg, PA	KIA		GDR
Headon, R.	Pvt.	K Orr's Ri.		AN	06/27/62	Gaines' Mill, VA	KIA		ROH,CDC
Healer, James B.	Pvt.	F 17th SCVI		YK	09/11/64	Elmira, NY	DIP		P5,P12,P65,P120
Healey, G.B.	Pvt.	F 1st SCVA		CN	05/08/65	Pt. Lookout, MD	DIP		ROH
Heape, John J.	Pvt.	K 11th SCVI	35	CO	12/19/64	At home	DOD		ROH,HAG
Heape, Wheeler	Pvt.	F 11th SCVI	19	BT	04/13/64	Lake City, FL	DOD		ROH,PP
Hearl, Jeremiah	Cpl.	E 26th SCVI		HY	07/15/64	Petersburg, VA	KIA	(Date appr. 6/17-7/27)	ROH,CDC
Hearn, N. Mahon	Pvt.	K 14th SCVI		ED	08/30/62	2nd Manassas, VA	KIA		ROH,JR,HOE,CDC
Hearon, George W.	Cpl.	F 8th SCVI		DN	08/21/61	Culpepper, VA	DOD	Fairview Cem. Culpepper VA	JR,CGH
Hearon, Joseph N.	Pvt.	H 21st SCVI		DN	07/10/63	Bty. Wagner, SC	KIA		ROH,JR,CDC,HAG
Heath, A. Jackson	Pvt.	A 1st SCVIG		BL	06/27/62	Gaines' Mill, VA	KIA		JR,SA1
Heath, Andrew M.	Pvt.	B 21st SCVI		DN	11/06/64	Philadelphia, PA	DOW	Nat. Cem.#109 OFS Phila.PA	ROH,FPH,P6,HAG
Heath, George L.	Pvt.	A 9th SCVIB		LR	11/19/61	Richmond, VA	DOD	Hollywood Cem.Rchmd. B253	JR,HC,LAN
Heath, Jeff T.	Pvt.	H 14th SCVI		BL	06/27/62	Gaines' Mill, VA	KIA	Oakwood C.#105,Row N,Div C	ROH,JR,OWC,UD2
Heath, John A. (J.C.?)	Pvt.	PeeDee LA		DN	06/15/65	Columbia, SC	DOD		ROH
Heath, Lee G.	Pvt.	B 6th SCVI	45	YK	/ /		DOD		YEB
Heath, William D.	Pvt.	I 17th SCVI		LR	08/30/62	2nd Manassas, VA	DOW		LAN
Heaton, A.S.	Pvt.	D Orr's Ri.		AN	01/23/62	At home	DOD		JR
Heaton, Absalom C.	Pvt.	K 2nd SCVIRi	40	PS	06/30/62	Frayser's Farm	KIA		ROH,JR,CDC
Heaton, Charles T.	Pvt.	H 11th SCVI		CO	12/05/64	Pt. Lookout, MD	DIP	C.C. Pt. Lookout, MD	ROH,FPH,P5,HAG
Heaton, George	Pvt.	C 24th SCVI	34	CO	01/14/64	Kingston, TN	DOD		DRE,EJM
Heaton, Joseph C.	Pvt.	B 37th VAVCB	32	PS	11/15/63	Virginia	DOW		37V
Heaton, Peter L.	Pvt.	H 11th SCVI		CO	06/01/64	Drury's Bluff VA	DOW	(Wdd 5/16/64)	ROH,HAG
Heaton, William	Pvt.	H 24th SCVI	25	CO	03/02/62	Charleston, SC	DOD		ROH,DRE,EJM
Heaton, William M.	Pvt.	F 24th SCVI	22	AN	07/20/64	Peachtree Ck. GA	KIA	(JR=7/22/64)	ROH,JR,HOL,CDC
Heavill, R.	Pvt.	C 5th SCVI			05/31/62	7 Pines, VA	KIA		ROH
Heckle, Andrew J.	Pvt.	F 25th SCVI		OG	02/09/65	Elmira, NY	DIP	Woodlawn N.C.#1951 Elmira	ROH,FPH,HAG,P65
Hedden, Elisha	Pvt.	A 20th SCVI		CO	07/21/64	Charleston, SC	DOD	Magnolia Cem. Charleston	ROH,MAG
Hedge, James	Pvt.	C Orr's Ri.		DN	06/15/62	Richmond, VA			ROH
Hedricks, E.G.	Pvt.	F 1st SC Res		YK	02/02/65	Columbia, SC	DOD	Elmwood Cem. Columbia, SC	ROH,MP
Heffner, Ephraim	Cpl.	A 12th SCVI	35	YK	06/23/63	Farmville, VA	DOD	(JR=Cpt., YEB=Haffner)	JR,YEB
Hefley, Thomas	Pvt.	B 4th SCVC		CR	05/30/64	Washington, DC	DOW	(Wdd @ Cold Harbor)	CB
Hegan, W.S.					/ /			(Rchmd effects list 12/62)	CDC
Heines, Y.	Pvt.	D 5th SCVI		UN	02/17/63	Richmond, VA	DOD	(Pneumonia)	JR,SA3
Heisenbottel, H.W.	Pvt.	A 10th SCVI		GN	/ /		DOD		GRG,RAS
Hellams, Robert V.	Pvt.	G 3rd SCVI	22	LS	12/13/62	Fredericksburg	KIA	Dials M.C. LS County KEB	ROH,JR,SA2,LSC
Hellams, W. Rapley	Pvt.	G 3rd SCVI	21	LS	04/22/62	Williamsburg, VA	DOD		ROH,SA2,KEB
Hellins, O.H.	Pvt.	H 2nd SCVIRi			/ /	Richmond, VA			ROH
Hellman, H.T.	Pvt.	C 14th SCVI		LS	10/20/62	Chester, SC	DOD	(Smallpox)	JR
Helmes, Amos	Pvt.	C 1st SCVIR		CN	11/16/63	Ft. Sumter, SC	KIA		SA1,R45

156

SOUTH CAROLINA DEAD IN CSA SERVICE 1861-1865

NAME	RANK	C REGIMENT	AGE	DS	DIED	WHERE	WHY	BURIED	SOURCES
Helton, Tilman	Pvt.	H 2nd SCVIRi	22	LR	05/31/62	7 Pines, VA	KIA		ROH
Hembree, Chambers	Pvt.	A Hol. Leg.		SG	03/25/65	Ft. Steadman, VA	KIA		HOS
Hembree, Elias B.	Pvt.	K 2nd SCVIRi	26	AN	05/15/62	Adams Run, SC	DOD		ROH,PP
Hembree, Erwin	Pvt.	B 15th SCVI		SG	/ /	Richmond, VA	DOD		JR,HOS,KEB
Hembree, Frank	Pvt.	E 18th SCVI		SG	/ /	Petersburg, VA	DOD		HOS
Hembree, J.G.	Pvt.	B 1st SCVIR		AN	03/16/65	Averysboro, NC	KIA		ROH,SA1,WAT,PP
Hembree, Robert	Pvt.	I 13th SCVI	23	SG	10/11/62	Lynchburg, VA	DOD	Lynchburg CSA C. #8 R1	ROH,JR,CDC,BBW
Hembree, Thomas H.	Pvt.	E 18th SCVI	19	SG	08/27/62	Rappahanock Stn.	DOW	(Wdd @ Gaine's Mill)	ROH,JR,HOS,CDC
Heming, E.A.	Pvt.	C 9th SCVIB			08/29/61	Germantown, VA	DOD		JR
Hemphill, James J.	Pvt.	F 5th SCVI.	18	YK	08/05/61	Charlottesville	DOD	(ROH= Orr's Ri) UD2	ROH,JR,SA3,YEB
Hemphill, Robert B.	Pvt.	F 6th SCVI	21	CR	06/18/62	7 Pines, VA	DOW		ROH,JR,HHC,WDB
Hemphill, Robert L.	Pvt.	G P.S.S.	19	YK	05/04/62	Williamsburg, VA	KIA	(CDC=R.M.) UD2	ROH,JR,CDC,YEB
Hempire, S.	Pvt.	P.S.S.			11/15/62	Gordonsville, VA		(Perhaps Ham.Leg.)	GOR
Henagan, John Williford	Col.	8th SCVI	43	MO	04/26/65	Johnson's Isl.OH	DIP	C.C.#177 Sandusky, OH	FPH,LC,HOM,CV
Hencken, G.	Pvt.	B German A		CN	/ /			St.Lawrence C. Charleston	MAG
Hencken, John M.	1st Lt.	K 12th SCVI	46	PS	05/12/65	Johnson's Is. OH	DIP	C.C.#178 Sandusky, OH	ROH,FPH,P5,P6
Henderson, Ambrose	Pvt.	E 13th SCVI		SG	12/21/61	Charleston, SC	DOD	Magnolia Cem. Charleston	ROH,JR,MAG,HOS
Henderson, Andrew	Pvt.	H 22nd SCVI		GE	12/26/64	Elmira, NY	DIP	Woodlawn N.C.#1292 Elmira	FPH,P5,P65,P12
Henderson, B.C.	Pvt.	H 12th SCVI		YK	/ /	Richmond, VA			ROH
Henderson, C.T.	Pvt.	C 14th SCVI		LS	08/17/62	Richmond, VA	DOD	Oakwood C.#82,Row P,Div B	ROH,JR,OWC
Henderson, Calvin F.	Pvt.	F 13th SCVI		SG	07/01/64	Richmond, VA		Hollywood Cem.Rchmd. U285	ROH,HC,HOS
Henderson, David A.	Pvt.	C 6th SCVI		FD	09/05/61	Germantown, VA	DOD	(Measles)	JR
Henderson, Eli	Pvt.	B 16th SCVI		GE	04/06/65	Nashville, TN	DIP	Nashville City Cem.	16R,P3,P6
Henderson, J.H.	Cpl.	C 14th SCVI			07/31/62	Richmond, VA	DOD	(Brain Fever)	JR
Henderson, J.J.	Pvt.	F Orr's Ri.		PS	06/27/62	Gaines' Mill, VA	KIA		ROH,JR,CDC
Henderson, James	Pvt.	D 7th SCVIBn	30	KW	06/23/64	Petersburg, VA	DOW	Blandford Church Pbg, VA	ROH,HIC,BLC,PP
Henderson, James C.	Pvt.	I 7th SCVI	24	ED	12/01/61	Culpepper, VA	DOD	Fairview Cem. Culpepper VA	JR,CGH,EDN,HOE
Henderson, James E.	Pvt.	B 7th SCVI		ED	06/15/63	Gordonsville, VA			ROH,HOE,KEB
Henderson, James F.	Pvt.	E 6th SCVC	19	LS	07/28/64	Richmond, VA		Hollywood Cem.Rchmd. V42	ROH,HC,LSC
Henderson, James M.	Pvt.	F 2nd SCVI	20	AE	06/01/63	Richmond, VA	DOW	Hollywood Cem.Rchmd. T323	ROH,HC,SA2
Henderson, James S.	Pvt.	M P.S.S.	19	SG	05/06/64	Wilderness, VA	KIA		ROH,JR,CDC
Henderson, James W.	Pvt.	A Wright's B			02/25/62	Charleston, SC	DOD	(White's Bn.?)	JR
Henderson, John Trapp	Pvt.	F 2nd SCVI	26	AE	06/08/62	Winchester, VA	DOD	(Typhoid, JR=6/8/64)	ROH,JR,SA2,UD2
Henderson, L.	Pvt.	K 18th SCVI		SG	09/15/62	At home	DOD		JR
Henderson, Louis	Pvt.	E 13th SCVI		SG	05/12/62	Richmond, VA	DOD	(Typhoid)	JR,HOS
Henderson, M.M.	Pvt.	F 27th SCVI			01/19/65	Richmond, VA		Hollywood Cem.Rchmd. W295	HC
Henderson, Marion J.	Pvt.	G 3rd SCVABn			07/17/63	Columbia, SC	DOD	(Fever @ College Hospital)	ROH,JR,PP
Henderson, Martin W.	1st Lt.	C 3rd SCVIBn		LS	09/13/62	Maryland Hts. MD	KIA		KEB,R45
Henderson, Ransom S.	Pvt.	I Hol.Leg.	21	SG	05/19/62	Adams Run, SC	DOD	(HOS=DOW Savannah, GA)	ROH,HOS,PP
Henderson, Spencer	Pvt.	K 5th SCVI			12/18/62		DOD		JR,SA3
Henderson, Starlin E.	Pvt.	E 16th SCVI	43	LS	11/30/64	Franklin, TN	KIA	Macgavock C. Frkln Gv#4	ROH,16R,PP
Henderson, Thomas W.	Pvt.	D 5th SCVI		NY	06/27/62	Gaines' Mill, VA	KIA	Hollywood Cem.Rchmd. O53	ROH,JR,HC,ANY
Henderson, W.B.	Pvt.	I Ham.Leg.			10/28/63	Lookout Valley	DOW		CDC
Henderson, W.C.	Pvt.	H 2nd SCVIRi			06/30/62	Richmond, VA	KIA		JR
Henderson, W.M.	Pvt.	D 7th SCVIBn	37	KW	07/07/64	Petersburg, VA	KIA		ROH,HIC,HAG
Henderson, W.P.	Musician	C 14th SCVI		LS	06/30/62	Frayser's Farm	KIA		ROH,JR
Henderson, William	Pvt.	E 13th SCVI		SG	05/03/63	Chancellorsville	KIA	(JR=DOD @ home)	ROH,JR,HOS
Henderson, William H.	Pvt.	C 14th SCVI		LS	05/23/64	Richmond, VA		Hollywood Cem.Rchmd. I234	ROH,HC
Henderson, William H.	Pvt.	H 18th SCVIB		YK	07/11/64	Kitrell Spgs. NC		Kitrell Springs, NC	PP
Henderson, William P.	Pvt.	I Orr's Ri.			11/20/63	Bridgeport, AL	DOW	(POW Wdd @ Shell Mound)	ROH,CDC,P2,P12
Henderson, William R.	Pvt.	B 1st SCVC	38	SG	06/15/64	Summerville, SC	DOD	(HOS=DOW)	ROH,HOS

SOUTH CAROLINA DEAD IN CSA SERVICE 1861-1865

NAME	RANK	C	REGIMENT	AGE	DS	DIED	WHERE	WHY	BURIED	SOURCES
Hendrick, J.M.	Sgt.	G	Hol.Leg.	33	NY	07/05/62	At home	DOD	(ANY=J.N., KIA 2nd M.)	ROH
Hendricks, C.J. (E.G.?)	Pvt.	F	2nd SCResB			02/02/65	Columbia, SC		Elmwood C. Columbia, SC	PP
Hendricks, G. Pinckney	4th Cpl.	G	Hol.Leg.		NY	06/15/64	Petersburg, VA	KIA	(Date approx)	ROH,ANY
Hendricks, G.A.	Cpt.	E	2nd SCVIRi		PS	12/19/64	Richmond, VA		Hollywood Cem.Rchmd. W439	HC,R45
Hendricks, G.M.	Sgt.	C	17th SCVI		YK	08/30/62	2nd Manassas, VA	KIA		JR
Hendricks, G.S.	Lt.	E	27th SCVI			05/20/64	Drury's Bluff VA	KIA	(HAG=Pvt.)	ROH,JR,HAG,CDC
Hendricks, George W.	Pvt.	C	15th SCVI	26	LN	08/09/62	Richmond, VA	DOD	Hollywood Cem.Rchmd. Q209	ROH,JR,HC,H15
Hendricks, H.G.	Cpl.	D	8th SCVI		CD	12/05/61	Charlottesville	DOD		JR
Hendricks, J.	Pvt.	F	26th SCVI			07/27/63	Petersburg, VA	DOW		ROH
Hendricks, J.H.	Pvt.	C	12th SCVI			07/29/63	Chester, PA	DOW	#82 Chester Gv. Yd.	P6
Hendricks, James Allen	Pvt.		Brooks GA			06/30/62	Frayser's Farm	KIA	H2	ROH,JR,CNM,SA2
Hendricks, James Ross	Pvt.	E	7th SCVIBn	36	FD	08/17/64	Petersburg, VA	DOD		ROH,HAG
Hendricks, Jesse S.	Pvt.	C	12th SCVI		FD	07/29/63	Chester, PA	DIP	Magnolia Cem. Charleston	FPH,MAG,GDR,P1
Hendricks, John L.	Sgt.	D	8th SCVI		CD	09/20/63	Chickamauga, GA	DOW	Con. Cem. Marietta, GA	ROH,JR,CCM,KEB
Hendricks, John P.	Pvt.	F	26th SCVI			02/28/62		DOD		JR
Hendricks, L.	Sgt.	E	20th SCVI		PS	12/28/62	Lynchburg, VA	DOD	Crossroads B.C. Table Rock	PCS
Hendricks, Milton M.	Pvt.	H	4th SCVI		PS	02/22/62		DOD		SA2
Hendricks, N.B.	Pvt.	C	22nd SCVI	41	SG	03/28/65	Elmira, NY	DIP	Woodlawn N.C.#2487 Elmira	ROH,FPH,P6,P120
Hendricks, S.W.	Pvt.	M	8th SCVI		DN	05/04/62	Manchester, VA	DOD	(Pneumonia)	JR
Hendricks, T.M.	Pvt.	K	27th SCVI		CN	11/14/64	Elmira, NY	DIP	Woodlawn N.C.#817 Elmira	FPH,HAG,P65,P120
Hendricks, W.W.	Pvt.	C	22nd SCVI	43	LN	10/27/64	Pt. Lookout, MD	DIP	C.C. Pt. Lookout, MD	ROH,FPH,P5,P65
Hendricks, William Clark	3rd Cpl.	G	22nd SCVI	27	AN	07/30/64	Crater, Pbg., VA	KIA	(Buried alive in crater)	ROH,BLM,CB
Hendricks, William F.	Pvt.	F	26th SCVI			06/01/65	Petersburg, VA	KIA	Blandford Church Pbg., VA	ROH,BLC,PP
Hendrix,	Pvt.	I	8th SCVI			09/15/63	Ringgold, GA	KIA		JR
Hendrix, F.M.	Pvt.	F	5th SCVC	22	LN	05/30/64	Old Church, VA	KIA	(JR=6/2/64)	ROH,JR,CDC
Hendrix, Fields E.	Pvt.	B	37th VAVCB		PS	06/16/64	Virginia	KIA		37V
Hendrix, George W.L.	Pvt.	C	12th SCVI		FD	08/17/64	Petersburg, VA	DOW	(Wdd 8/16/64, JR=Co.B)	ROH,JR,HFC
Hendrix, Henry	4th Sgt.	G	Hol.Leg.		NY	08/29/62	2nd Manassas, VA	DOW		ANY
Hendrix, J. Patrick	Pvt.	C	15th SCVI	22	LN	05/29/63	Fredericksburg	ACD		ROH,KEB,H15,TOD
Hendrix, J.E.	Pvt.	B	7th SCVC			06/15/64		KIA	(Day estimated)	JR
Hendrix, John Elias	2nd Cpl.	C	3rd SCVI	31	NY	05/23/64	N. Anna River VA	DOW		ROH,JR,ANY,KEB
Hendrix, John N.	Pvt.	G	Hol.Leg.			08/29/62	2nd Manassas, VA		KIA	ANY
Hendrix, M.S.	Pvt.	D	6th SCVC		LN	06/11/64	Trevillian Stn.	KIA		ROH,JR,JMB
Henegan, James Hamilton	Cpt.	H	Orr's Ri.		MO	06/27/62	Gaines' Mill, VA	KIA	(JR=DOW 6/28/52)	JR,HMC,CDC,R48
Henley, C.C.	Pvt.	C	14th SCVI			06/19/65	Hart's Island NY	DIP	(Prob Cypress Hills N.C.)	P6,P12
Henley, C.M.	Pvt.	I	13th SCVI		SG	09/15/62	Lynchburg, VA	DOD	(Typhoid)	JR
Henley, Charles	Pvt.		1st SCV	24	BT	/ /	Robertville, SC	DOD		ROH
Henley, E.McD.	Pvt.	I	13th SCVI	21	SG	09/19/63	(OWC= Co.D)		Oakwood C.#47,Row F,Div B	ROH,OWC,HOS
Hennies, William	Pvt.	A	2nd SCVI		RD	12/15/61	Centreville, VA	DOD		ROH,SA2,KEB
Henning, George W.	Pvt.	B	15th SCVAB			06/17/65	Pt. Lookout, MD	DIP	C.C. Pt. Lookout, MD	FPH,P6,P12,P114
Henning, M.D.						01/31/65	Columbia, SC		Elmwood Cem. Columbia, SC	MP,PP
Henning, Norman P.	Pvt.	A	16th SCVI	20	GE	03/20/65	Bentonville, NC	KIA	(ROH=B,2nd SCVI)	ROH,16R,WAT,PP
Henning, Norman P.	Pvt.	B	2nd SCVI		GE	03/19/65	Bentonville, NC	KIA		H2,SA2,KEB
Henning, William Alston	2nd Lt.	A	Ham.Leg.	29	GN	11/18/63	Campbell Stn. TN	DOW		ROH,CDC,WLI,R48
Henry, B.P.R.	Pvt.	A	12th SCVI	19	YK	07/08/62	Gaines' Mill, VA	DOW	Hollywood Cem.Rchmd. Q77	ROH,JR,HC,YEB
Henry, Dablen L.	Pvt.	I	3rd SCVI	41	LS	03/20/64	Lynchburg, VA	DOW	Henry Fam. C. Madden's Stn	ROH,LSC
Henry, George Rainey	Pvt.	I	6th SCVI	34	CR	04/06/63	At home	DOD		ROH,HHC,CB
Henry, I.F.	Pvt.	G	3rd SCVI	20	LS	07/13/62	Manchester, VA	DOW	(JR=2nd SCVI)	ROH,JR,KEB,SA2
Henry, J.M.	Pvt.	H	12th SCVI	18	YK	09/17/62	Sharpsburg, MD	KIA	(JR=DOW 9/27/62,YEB=J.N.)	JR,CWC,YEB
Henry, J.R.J.	Sgt.	C	1st SCVIBn		CN	06/16/62	Secessionville	KIA	(PP=Robert J. Co.F)	JR,PP
Henry, James W.	Pvt.	F	5th SCVI	21	YK	07/19/62	7 Pines, VA	DOW	Hollywood Cem.Rchmd. C124	ROH,JR,HC,SA3,CB

SOUTH CAROLINA DEAD IN CSA SERVICE 1861-1865

NAME	RANK	C REGIMENT	AGE	DS	DIED	WHERE	WHY	BURIED	SOURCES
Henry, John	Pvt.	B 6th SCVI		YK	06/15/64	At home	DOD		ROH
Henry, John E.	3rd Sgt.	I 3rd SCVI		LS	11/30/61	Charlottesville	DOD	(Pneumonia)	JR,KEB,SA2
Henry, R.S.	Sgt.	F 1st SCVIBn		CN	06/16/62	Secessionville	kia	Magnolia Cem. Charleston	MAG,ROH,CDC
Henry, S.P.	Pvt.	G 3rd SCVI	25	LS	10/25/62	Staunton, VA	DOW	Thornrose C. Staunton, VA	ROH,JR,SA2,TOD
Henry, Samuel	Pvt.	F 1st SCVIR		TN	06/07/61	Sullivans I., SC	DOD		SA1
Henry, Thomas Dixon	Pvt.	B 6th SCVI		YK	06/15/62		DOD		ROH
Herbert, J.D.	Pvt.	K 22nd SCVI		PS	07/30/64	Crater, Pbg., VA	KIA		BLM
Herbert, J.H. (T.H.?)	Pvt.				/ /	Virginia		(Rchmd effects list 1/63)	CDC
Herkeimer, Charles	Pvt.	A Orr's Ri.		AN	09/17/62	Sharpsburg, MD	KIA		JR
Herlong,	Pvt.	B 1st SCV			02/03/63		DOD	(Typhoid Pneumonia)	JR
Herman, C.A.	Pvt.	K 13th SCVI		LN	10/20/64	Richmond, VA		Hollywood Cem.Rchmd. I89	HC
Herndon, Dillard J.	Pvt.	C P.S.S.		AN	06/30/62	Frayser's Farm	KIA		ROH,JR,SA2,GMJ
Herndon, G.W.	Pvt.	E 24th SCVI	35	CO	06/01/64	At home	DOD		ROH
Herndon, James E.	Pvt.	E 24th SCVI	22	CO	09/20/63	Chickamauga, GA	KIA		ROH,CDC
Herndon, W. Claude	Cpl.	C P.S.S.		AN	10/28/63	Lookout Valley	DOW	(JR=DOW 12/30/63)	ROH,JR,SA2,GMJ
Herren, Stephen	Pvt.	D 10th SCVI		MN	01/27/65	Camp Chase, OH	DIP	C.C.#905 Columbus, OH	FPH,P6,P12,P23
Herrin, Allison W.	Pvt.	I 21st SCVI		MN	01/26/63	Morris Island SC	DOD	(Typhoid)	JR,HMC,HAG
Herrin, David F.	Pvt.	I 21st SCVI		MN	04/25/63	Georgetown, SC	DOD	(JR=4/19/62)	JR,HMC,HAG,PP
Herrin, J.P.	Pvt.	D 10th SCVI		MN	/ /	Holly Springs MS	DOD		RAS,HMC,PP
Herrin, Jesse J.	Pvt.	A 19th SCVI	28	ED	06/17/62	Enterprise, MS	DOD	(PP=Jeremiah J.)	HOE,EDN,PP,UD3
Herrin, W.P.	Pvt.	D 10th SCVI		MN	/ /		DOD		RAS,HMC
Herring, Daniel M.	Pvt.	C 26th SCVI		MN	/ /	Charleston, SC			HMC
Herring, David W.	Pvt.	A 26th SCVI	37	HY	07/15/65	At home	DOD		ROH
Herring, Ebby B.	Pvt.	L 8th SCVI		MN	09/28/62	At home	DOD	(Pneumonia)	JR,HMC,KEB
Herring, Elijah	Pvt.	I 1st SCVIR		AN	06/03/63		DOD		SA1
Herring, James	Pvt.	C 26th SCVI		MN	/ /	Petersburg, VA	KIA		HMC
Herring, John C.	2nd Cpl.	D 25th SCVI		MN	/ /	Weldon RR, VA	KIA	(? 8/19-21/64 Globe Tavn.)	HMC,HAG
Herring, McSwain	Pvt.	C 26th SCVI		MN	06/30/63	Jackson, MS	DOD		JR,HMC
Herron, A.B.	Pvt.	K 12th SCVI	30	PS	01/20/62	McPhersonville	DOD		ROH
Herron, Alfred	Pvt.	E Orr's Ri.	40	PS	06/11/62	Dill Spgs., VA	DOD		ROH
Herron, E.E.	Pvt.	F 24th SCVI	40	AN	09/09/63	Rome, GA	DOD		ROH,HOL
Herron, G. Washington	Cpl.	F 8th SCVI		DN	08/21/61	Culpepper, VA	DOD	(KEB=Hearon,JR=DOW)	ROH,JR,CDC,KEB
Herron, George S.	Pvt.	F 7th SCVIBn		SR	09/18/64	Alexandria, VA	DOW	Christ Ch. Alexandria, VA	CV,P1,P5,P12
Herron, J.N.	Pvt.	H 21st SCVI			07/10/63	Morris Island SC	KIA		JR
Herron, Samuel S.	Pvt.	F 7th SCVIBn		LN	/ /		KIA		HIC
Herron, V.M.	Pvt.	F 24th SCVI		AN	10/10/62	Noonan, GA	DOD		HOL
Hersey, George R.	Pvt.	F 1st SCVA		LR	05/09/65	Pt. Lookout, MD	DIP	C.C. Pt. Lookout, MD	FPH,P6,P12,P11
Hersey, Peter	Pvt.	I 17th SCVI		LR	08/30/62	2nd Manassas, VA	KIA		ROH,JR,LAN
Hess, Jacob	Pvt.			CO	07/11/64	Petersburg, VA		Blandford Church Pbg., VA	BLC
Hess, W.D.	Pvt.	C Orr's Ri.			07/10/62	Dill Farm, VA	DOD		JR
Hester, James	Pvt.	K 16th SCVI		GE	06/18/62	Adams Run, SSC	DOD		16R,PP
Hester, James Lewis	2nd Lt.	B 19th SCVI		ED	12/15/64	Nashville, TN	KIA		ROH,HOE
Hester, Robert	Pvt.	G 16th SCVI		GE	08/06/64	Macon, GA	DOD	Rose Hill Cem. Macon, GA	16R,BGA,PP
Hester, Samuel J.	Pvt.	A Orr's Ri.		AN	10/23/62	Winchester, VA	DOD		JR
Hester, William	Pvt.	G 16th SCVI		PS	06/15/64	Macon, GA	DOD		PCS,16R,PP
Hetherington, Foley	Pvt.	E 5th SCVI	25	YK	08/09/62	Gaines' Mill, VA	DOW	(Wdd 6/27, YEB=At home)	JR,SA3,YEB
Hetherington, James E.	Pvt.	F 17th SCVI	31	YK	08/30/62	2nd Manassas, VA	KIA		JR,YEB
Heustiss, George W.	Pvt.	F 21st SCVI		MO	03/09/65	Elmira, NY	DIP	Woodlawn N.C.#2515 Elmira	ROH,HOM,HAG,P6
Hewin, W.D.	Pvt.	F 2nd SCVIRi			09/30/64	Ft. Harrison, VA	KIA		JR
Hewitt, T.G.	Cpl.	G 26th SCVI		DN	05/20/64	Clay's Farm, VA	KIA		ROH
Hewitt, William E.	Cpt.	F 4th SCVC	27	MN	06/22/64	Lincoln Hos, DC	DOW	Soldiers Gvyd,DC UD3	ROH,JR,HMC,P6

159

SOUTH CAROLINA DEAD IN CSA SERVICE 1861-1865

NAME	RANK	C REGIMENT	AGE	DS	DIED	WHERE	WHY	BURIED	SOURCES
Heyward, Edward B.	Pvt.	Marion Art	24	CN	12/16/64	Church Flats, SC	DOD	St.Philips C. Charleston	ROH,MAG,RCD
Heyward, James	Pvt.	A 21st SCVI		GN	08/21/64	Globe Tavern, VA	KIA		ROH,FLR,HAG
Heyward, Joseph	Cpt.	A.A.G. CSA	32	CN	11/07/62	Greenville, SC	DOD	St. Philips C. Charleston	ROH,RCD,PP
Heyward, Nathaniel	Pvt.	L 1st SCVIG	19	CN	08/29/62	2nd Manassas, VA	KIA	St. Philips C. Charleston	ROH,JR,SA1,CDC
Heyward, W.M.	Pvt.				08/21/63	Hilton Head, SC	DIP	(Typhoid, SC soldier?)	P10
Heyward, William Cruger	Colonel	9th SCVIH		CO	09/19/63	Charleston, SC	DOD	St.Michaels Ch. Charleston	MAG,HAG,RCD
Hickhart, J.C.	Pvt.	I 15th SCVI		LN	/ /	Gordonsville, VA			ROH
Hicklin, Joseph H.	Pvt.	A 6th SCVI	27	CR	10/25/62	Frederick, MD	DOD	Mt. Olivet Cem.#142 CB	ROH,FPH,GLS,BOD
Hickman, Joe	Pvt.	E 8th SCVI		DN	12/15/61	Richmond, VA	DOD	(Hickson ?)	JR
Hicks, A.					/ /	Petersburg, VA			ROH
Hicks, C.R.	Pvt.	L P.S.S.		AN	05/31/62	7 Pines, VA	DOW	(CNM=Hix)	JR,CNM
Hicks, E.C.	Pvt.	C 2nd SCV			/ /	Marietta, GA		Con. Cem. Marietta, GA	CCM
Hicks, George W.	Pvt.	I 26th SCVI	23	WG	/ /	Petersburg, VA	KIA		CTA,HOW
Hicks, J.	Pvt.	B 1st SC Res			03/25/65	Columbia, SC	DOD	Elmwood Cem. Columbia, SC	ROH,MP,PP
Hicks, John	Pvt.	B 7th SCVC		CN	06/13/64	Richmond, VA	DOW	Oakwood C.#8,Row B,Div G	OWC,JES
Hicks, John	Pvt.	D 9th SCVIBn			07/18/62	Charleston, SC		Magnolia Cem. Charleston	MAG
Hicks, L.N.	Pvt.	E 8th SCVI		DN	04/23/62	Richmond, VA	DOD	(Pneumonia)	JR
Hicks, N.C.	Cpl.	I 10th SCVI		MN	/ /	KY	DOD		RAS,HMC
Hicks, T.	Pvt.	H 12th SCVI		YK	06/15/62	Richmond, VA		Hollywood Cem. Rchmd. P38	HC
Hickson, J.E.B.	Pvt.	F 26th SCVI	17		07/08/62	Charleston, SC	DOD	Magnolia Cem. Charleston	ROH,MAG,PP
Hickson, M.J.E.	Pvt.	E 10th SCVI		GN	/ /	MS	DOD	(Hixon in RAS)	RAS
Hickson, R.G.	Pvt.	K 17th SCVI		YK	08/30/64	Petersburg, VA	KIA		ROH
Hickson, W.L.	Pvt.	H 26th SCVI		SR	10/06/64	Elmira, NY	DIP	Woodlawn N.C.#584 Elmira	FPH,P5,P65,P120
Hide, R.H.	Sgt.	G Orr's Ri.		AE	12/09/63	Pt. Lookout, MD	DIP	C.C. Pt. lookout, MD	ROH,FPH,CDC,P113
Hiers, G.A.	Pvt.	H 17th SCVI		BL	07/30/64	Petersburg, VA	KIA		ROH
Hiers, George S.	4th Cpl.	K 2nd SCVI		BL	01/10/63	Richmond, VA	DOD		SA2,KEB
Hiers, Jacob	Cpl.	K 11th SCVI	28	CO	06/20/64	Petersburg, VA	DOD		ROH,HAG
Hiers, W.E.	Pvt.	B 19th SCVCB		BT	02/25/65	Columbia, SC	DOD		ROH,PP
Hiers, William J.	Pvt.	K 11th SCVI	22	CO	03/22/65	Pt. Lookout, MD	DIP	C.C. Pt. Lookout, MD	ROH,FPH,HAG,P6
Hiett, William H.	Pvt.	K Orr's Ri.	23	GE	08/15/62		DOD		ROH
Hifley, Thomas	Pvt.	D 4th SCVC		CN	07/14/64	Washington, DC	DOW	(Nesley ?)	P5,P12
Higgin, C.J.	Pvt.	B 12th SCVI		YK	08/04/62	Richmond, VA			ROH
Higginbottom, J.C.					/ /			Spotsylvania C.H., VA	SCH
Higgins,	Pvt.	7th SCVC			/ /	Pt. Lookout, MD	DIP		MJL
Higgins, H.	Pvt.	H 2nd SCVIRi		AE	12/18/62	Richmond, VA	DOD		ROH
Higgins, J.H.	Pvt.	E 1st SCV			06/20/63	Richmond, VA		Hollywood Cem.Rchmd, T465	HC
Higgins, James H.	Pvt.	H 1st SCVIR		GE	07/12/62	Camp Evans, SC	DOD		SA1
Higgins, R.J.	Pvt.	G 3rd SCVI	25	LS	06/29/62	Savage Stn., VA	KIA		ROH,JR,SA2,KEB
Higgins, Sanders Burton	Pvt.	B 1st SCVIG	22	NY	06/27/62	Gaines' Mill, VA	KIA	Rosemont Cem. Newberry, SC	ROH,JR,NCC,ANY
Higgins, Theodore	Pvt.	A 16th SCVI		GE	/ /	At home	DOD	(on active duty ?)	16R
Higgins, William W.	1st Lt.	G Orr's Ri.		AE	12/13/62	Fredericksburg	KIA	(JR=3rd SCVI)	ROH,JR,CDC,R45
High, Benjamin F.	Pvt.	L 1st SCVIG		CN	06/27/62	Gaines' Mill, VA	KIA		ROH,JR,SA1
Hightower, James F.	3rd Cpl.	F 4th SCVI	22	GE	11/23/61	Culpepper, VA	DOD	Fairview Cem. Culpepper VA	CGH,SA2
Hilberth, E.	Pvt.	H 14th SCVI		BL	/ /	Richmond, VA		Oakwood C.#56,Row B,Div G	OWC
Hilburn, J. Ebenezer	Pvt.	E 5th SC Res	45		12/25/62	Adams Run, SC	DOD		PP
Hill,	Pvt.	1st CS Eng		AN	01/15/65	Petersburg, VA	ACD	(Drowned in flood)	HOF
Hill, Alfred	Pvt.	A Hol.Leg.		SG	03/29/65	Hatcher's Run VA	DOW		HOS
Hill, Asaph	Pvt.	F 1st SCVC		PS	03/21/62	Adams Run, SC	DOD		PP
Hill, B.M. (R.M.?)	Pvt.	E 8th SCVI		DN	05/03/62	Petersburg, VA	DOD	(Pneumonia)	JR
Hill, Bailis E.	Cpl.	E 18th SCVI	28	SG	05/20/64	Clay's Farm, VA	KIA		ROH,JR,HOS
Hill, C.E.	Pvt.	B 17th SCVI		FD	/ /	Richmond, VA	DOD	(Edward C,?)	JR

SOUTH CAROLINA DEAD IN CSA SERVICE 1861-1865

NAME	RANK	C	REGIMENT	AGE	DS	DIED	WHERE	WHY	BURIED	SOURCES
Hill, Calvin	Pvt.	A	Hol.Leg.	18	SG	08/20/62	Richmond, VA	DOD	Oakwood C.#80,Row A,Div C	ROH,OWC,HOS
Hill, D.	Pvt.	H	11th SCVI		CO	08/20/61	Hilton Head, SC	DOD	(Ft. Walker)	ROH,JR
Hill, D.F.	Major		24th SCVI		AN	09/01/64	Jonesborough, GA	KIA	Lovejoy's Stn, Clayton Cty	ROH,HOL,UD2
Hill, David C.	Pvt.	A	5th SCVC		CO	03/10/65	Fayetteville, NC	KIA	(Chg.on Kilpatrick's camp)	ROH,PP
Hill, David S.	Pvt.	H	9th SCVIH		CO	09/01/61	Hilton Head, SC	DOD		ROH,HAG,PP
Hill, E.F.	Pvt.		Ham.Leg.			/ /	Virginia	DOD		ROH,CDC
Hill, Edward	Pvt.		Gregg's By		MN	/ /	At home	MUR	(Shot as DES by locals)	HMC
Hill, Eli	Pvt.	B	21st SCVI		DN	05/22/65	Elmira, NY	DIP	Woodlawn N.C.#2744 Elmira	FPH,P6,P12,P65
Hill, Elliott E.	Pvt.		Palm. LA		RD	05/01/63	Suffolk, VA	DOD	(Typhoid)	JR,SOB
Hill, F.M.	Pvt.	A	5th SCVI		CR	03/18/63	Blackwater, VA	DOD	(JR=Jerusalem Hos.)	JR,SA3,LAN
Hill, Frank	Pvt.	K	1st SCVIR		CN	11/20/63	Ft. Sumter, SC	KIA	(Shell explosion)	SA1
Hill, Henry	Pvt.	A	Hol.Leg.		SG	12/14/62	Kinston, NC	DOW		HOS
Hill, Henry Marion	Pvt.	E	14th SCVI		LS	08/27/62	Richmond, VA	DOD	Hollywood Cem.Rchmd. H110	ROH,JR,HC,CGS
Hill, J.	Cpl.	G	26th SCVI		DN	08/05/64	Richmond, VA		Hollywood Cem.Rchmd. W99	HC
Hill, J. Quincy	Pvt.	E	6th SCVI		DN	08/15/62	Gaines' Mill, VA	DOW	Oakwood C.#111,Row L,DivC	ROH,JLC,OWC
Hill, J.B.	Pvt.	E	14th SCVI			07/25/62	Richmond, VA	DOD	(Measles)	JR
Hill, J.C.	Cpl.	C	26th SCVI		MN	05/03/65	Richmond, VA	DOW	Hollywood Cem. #98 Rchmd.	ROH,P6
Hill, J.H.	Pvt.	C	Orr's Ri.		PS	04/28/65	Hart's Island NY	DIP	Cypress Hills N.C.#2647 NY	FPH,P6,P79
Hill, J.V.	Pvt.					/ /	Virginia		(Rchmd effects list 1/63)	CDC
Hill, James	Pvt.	E	8th SCVI		DN	12/15/61	Richmond, VA	DOD		JR
Hill, James B.	Pvt.				GE	10/15/64	At home	DOD		ROH
Hill, James C.	3rd Lt.	F	3rd SCVI		LS	12/13/62	Fredericksburg	KIA	Hill Fam.C. Cross Hill, SC	ROH,JR,SA2,LSC
Hill, James J.	Pvt.	I	18th SCVI	25	DN	10/14/64	Elmira, NY	DIP	Woodlawn N.C.#704 Elmira	ROH,FPH,P65,P1
Hill, James S.	Pvt.	H	6th SCVI		FD	06/30/62	Frayser's Fm. VA	KIA	Oakwood C.#5,Row C,Div A	ROH,OWC,WDB,HF
Hill, Jeremiah	Pvt.	A	Hol.Leg.	24	SG	08/30/62	2nd Manassas, VA	KIA		ROH,JR,HOS
Hill, Jerry	Pvt.	E	14th SCVI		LS	/ /		DOD		CGS
Hill, John	Pvt.	G	7th SCVIBn	20	KW	06/29/64	Richmond, VA	DOW	Oakwood C.#33,Row N,Div C	ROH,HIC,OWC,HA
Hill, John	Pvt.	C	18th SCVI		UN	05/05/62	Charleston, SC	DOD		ROH,JR
Hill, John W.	Pvt.	C	7th SCVI	21	AE	09/13/62	Maryland Hts. MD	KIA		ROH,JR,CDC
Hill, Nathaniel	Pvt.	E	5th SCVI		YK	05/05/62	Williamsburg, VA	KIA		UD3 ROH,JR,SA3,YEB
Hill, Nicholas	Cpl.	A	3rd SCVIBn		LS	08/30/63	Gettysburg, PA	DOW	Magnolia Cem. charleston	JR,MAG,GDR,KEB
Hill, P.S.	Pvt.	H	6th SCVI		FD	06/30/62	7 Pines, VA	KIA		ROH
Hill, P.T.	Pvt.	E	14th SCVI		LS	07/27/62	Richmond, VA			ROH
Hill, Peter	Pvt.	B	3rd SCVIBn		LS	07/03/63	Gettysburg, PA	KIA	Magnolia Cem. Charleston	ROH,MAG,CDC,KE
Hill, R.A.	Pvt.	F	1st SCVIR		PS	03/21/62	Adams Run, SC	DOD	Crossroads B.C. Table Rock	PCS
Hill, Samuel	Pvt.	C	SC Militia			03/05/65	Columbia, SC		Elmwood Cem. Columbia, SC	ROH,MP,PP
Hill, T.F.C.	3rd Sgt.	D	3rd SCVI		SG	07/01/62	Malvern Hill, VA	DOW	(Died in enemy hands)	JR,SA2,HOS,KEB
Hill, T.W.	Pvt.	H	4th SCVI		GE	12/25/61	Manchester, VA	DOD		SA2
Hill, Thomas	Pvt.	A	Hol.Leg.	26	SG	09/27/62	At home	DOD		ROH,HOS
Hill, Thomas	Pvt.	E	7th SCVC	27	LS	04/07/65	Pt. Lookout, MD	DIP	C.C. Pt. Lookout, MD	ROH,FPH,P6,P11
Hill, Thomas	Pvt.	K	15th SCVI		AE	09/17/62	Sharpsburg, MD	KIA		ROH,JR,KEB
Hill, Thomas T.	Cpl.	A	7th SCVI		ED	06/29/62	Savage Stn., VA	KIA		ROH,CDC,KEB,CN
Hill, W.A.	Pvt.	E	14th SCVI		LS	08/08/62	Richmond, VA	DOD		ROH,CGS,CDC
Hill, W.C.	Pvt.	D	7th SCVI			/ /	Lynchburg, VA		Lynchburg CSA Cem.#62 R2	BBW
Hill, W.E.	Pvt.	A	1st SCVIH		BL	09/25/62	Boonsboro, MD	DOD	Rose Hill C. Hagerstown MD	ROH,SA1,BOD
Hill, William	Pvt.	I	12th SCVI		LR	/ /	Richmond, VA	DOD		LAN
Hill, William	3rd Sgt.	C	2nd SCVI		RD	/ /	Chattanooga F.H.	DOW	(Wdd/POW @ Loudon,TN '63)	LAN,SA2,KEB,P1
Hill, William A.	Pvt.	I	18th SCVI	20	DN	07/30/64	Crater, Pbg., VA	KIA		ROH,JR,BLM
Hill, William A.	Pvt.	E	12th SCVI	29	LR	09/02/62	Richmond, VA	DOD	Hollywood Cem.Rchmd. S124	ROH,JR,HC,LAN
Hill, William Aaron	Pvt.	E	14th SCVI			06/07/62	Richmond, VA	DOD	(Measles)	JR
Hill, William W.	Pvt.		9th SCVIB	22	OG	/ /	Virginia			ROH

H

SOUTH CAROLINA DEAD IN CSA SERVICE 1861-1865

NAME	RANK	C REGIMENT	AGE	DS	DIED	WHERE	WHY	BURIED	SOURCES
Hillard,	Pvt.	L P.S.S.			/ /		DOW		JR
Hiller, Paul J.	Pvt.	C 20th SCVI	22	LN	10/19/64	Cedar Creek, VA	KIA	Stonewall Cem. Winchester	ROH,WIN,KEB
Hiller, Samuel	Pvt.	C 20th SCVI	35	LN	08/15/64	At home	DOD		ROH,KEB
Hillhouse, James Wadell	3rd Sgt.	K 4th SCVI		AN	07/22/61	Manassas, VA	ACD	(Explosion of dud? shell)	ROH,JR,SA2,UD2
Hillhouse, Samuel P.	2nd Sgt.	L 2nd SCVIRi	47	AN	12/15/62	Lynchburg, VA	DOD	Lynchburg CSA Cem. #9 R1	ROH,BBW
Hilton, C.J.	Pvt.	E 12th SCVI	23	LR	06/27/62	Gaines' Mill, VA	KIA		ROH,LAN
Hilton, George P.	Pvt.	A 4th SCVC	18	CD	05/28/64	Hawes Shop, VA	KIA		ROH,JR
Hilton, J. Leander	Pvt.	E 12th SCVI	17	LR	06/27/62	Gaines Mill, VA	DOW		ROH,JR,LAN,CNM
Hilton, Jesse	Pvt.	G 5th SCVC		LN	05/28/64	Price's Farm, VA	KIA		ROH,CDC
Hilton, M.D.	Pvt.	C 1st SCVIR		CN	09/08/63	Ft. Moultrie, SC	KIA		ROH,SA1,CDC
Hilton, O.T.	Pvt.	E 12th SCVI	20	LR	06/27/62	Gaines' Mill, VA	KIA		ROH,JR,LAN,CNM
Hilton, R. Terrell	4th Cpl.	H 2nd SCVI	34	LR	07/27/62	Gaines' Mill, VA	DOW	(H2=Savage Stn.)	ROH,JR,LAN,SA2
Hilton, Richard	4th Sgt.	E 12th SCVI	25	LR	05/12/64	Spotsylvania, VA	KIA		ROH,JR,LAN
Hilton, Samuel	Pvt.	E 12th SCVI		LR	06/28/62	Gaines' Mill, VA	DOW		JR
Hilton, T.F.	Pvt.	D 1st SCVIH		LR	03/01/64	Rock Island, IL	DIP	C.C.#678 Rock Island, IL	FPH,LAN,SA1
Hilton, Terrell	4th Sgt.	E 12th SCVI	34	LR	06/27/62	Gaines' Mill, VA	KIA		CNM,LAN
Hinde, John	Pvt.	I Ham.Leg.			07/26/64	Nashville, TN	DOW	(POW @ Lookout Mtn.)	P2,P12
Hindman, A.J.	Pvt.	E 5th SCVI		UN	05/31/62	7 Pines, VA	KIA		JR,SA3
Hindman, Bailis E.	Pvt.	E 18th SCVI	20	SG	05/20/62	Charleston, SC	DOD	(Brain Fever)	ROH,JR,HOS
Hindman, Jonathon F.	Pvt.	K Orr's Ri.	35	AN	05/12/64	Spotsylvania, VA	KIA	(CDC=Hynman)	ROH,CDC
Hindman, Samuel	Pvt.	C 2nd SCVIRi		PS	11/15/62		DOD		ROH
Hinds, H.N.	Pvt.	F 10th SCVI		MN	/ /	At home	DOD		ROH,RAS
Hinds, S.O.	Pvt.	F 10th SCVI		MN	07/16/62	Columbus, MS	DOD	Friendship C, Columbus, MS	JR,RAS,HMC,PP
Hines, J.L. Berry	Pvt.	E 13th SCVI		SG	06/25/62	Richmond, VA	DOD	Hollywood Cem.Rchmd. Q250	ROH,JR,HC,HOS
Hines, John	Pvt.	C 27th SCVI		CN	04/08/65	Pt. Lookout, MD	DIP	(P65=Released 5/17/65)	ROH,HAG,P65,P120
Hines, Joseph		CSN			04/24/65	Richmond, VA			ROH
Hines, L.A.	Pvt.	H 1st SCVIH		SG	10/15/64	Ft. Harrison, VA	DOW	Hollywood Cem.Rchmd. V641	ROH,HC,SA1
Hinkle, Elias	Pvt.	A 2nd SCVI		PS	02/01/64	Richmond, VA	DOD	Oakwood C.#10,Row 49,Div D	ROH,SA2,OWC,KEB
Hinkle, John C.	Pvt.	I Ham.Leg.			07/26/64	Nashville, TN	DOW	Nashville City C. #8829	CDC,P3,P6
Hinson, Bradley A.	Pvt.	Palm. LA		CD	05/09/63	Manchester, VA	MUR	(Stabbed with a knife)	JR,SOB
Hinson, Elijah	Pvt.	H 2nd SCVI		LR	07/17/63	Gettysburg, PA	DOW	Gettysburg, PA P1	ROH,JR,GDR,SA2
Hinson, Evander D.	Pvt.	B 24th SCVI		MO	06/17/64	At home	DOD	(ROH=E.A.)	ROH,HOM
Hinson, J.M.	Pvt.	I 3rd SCV			08/30/62	Wilmington, NC	DOD		JR
Hinson, James G.	Pvt.	A 12th SCVCB		CD	09/28/62	Georgetown, SC	DOD		ROH,PP
Hinson, John	Pvt.	A 21st SCVI		CN	05/18/65	Elmira, NY	DIP	Woodlawn N.C.#2947 Elmira	FPH,HAG,P6,P65
Hinson, Joseph	Pvt.	I 17th SCVI		LR	/ /	Wilmington, NC	DOD		LAN
Hinson, Joshua	Pvt.	C 6th SCVI		KW	/ /		DOD		HIC
Hinson, O.P.	Pvt.	D 16th SCVI		GE	08/19/64	Atlanta, GA	KIA		ROH,16R
Hinson, Stiles M.	Pvt.	B 7th SCVC	28	CN	08/14/64	Richmond, VA	DOW	(Body taken home)	ROH,CDC,JES
Hinson, William	Pvt.	A 21st SCVI		CN	02/16/62	Georgetown, SC	DOD		JR
Hinson,Jr., John	Pvt.	D 15th SCVI		KW	/ /	Columbia, SC	DOD	(1862)	JR,HIC,KEB
Hinson,Jr., Marion R.	3rd Lt.	H 2nd SCVI		LR	07/03/63	Gettysburg, PA	DOW	Gettysburg, PA WV	ROH,JR,GDR,SA2
Hinton, A.	Pvt.	B 7th SCVI		AE	09/20/63	Chickamauga, GA	DOW		ROH,JR,CDC,KEB
Hinton, James A.	Pvt.	G 22nd SCVI	36	PS	07/30/64	Crater, Pbg., VA	KIA		ROH,BLM
Hinton, Jesse W.	Pvt.	I 8th SCVI		MN	/ /	Virginia	DOD	(1861)	HMC,KEB
Hinton, John A.	Pvt.	I 19th SCVI	30	AE	04/20/64	Cassville, GA	DOD		ROH
Hinton, Thomas	Pvt.	H 3rd SCVI		LN	10/28/62	Staunton, VA	DOD	Thornrose C. Staunton, VA	ROH,JR,SA2,TOD
Hinton, Vachel	Pvt.	F Hol.Leg.	21	AE	10/24/62	Staunton, VA	DOD	Thornrose C. Staunton, VA	ROH,PP
Hiott, Charles W.	Pvt.	B 3rd SCVC	30	CO	12/18/62	At home	DOD		ROH
Hiott, Hansford	Pvt.	B 3rd SCVC	17	CO	09/04/64	Pocotaligo, SC	ACD	(Fall from horse)	ROH
Hiott, Lawrence P.	Pvt.	I 11th SCVI		CO	10/24/64	Elmira, NY	DIP	Woodlawn N.C.#850 Elmira	FPH,HAG,P65,P120

SOUTH CAROLINA DEAD IN CSA SERVICE 1861-1865

NAME	RANK	C	REGIMENT	AGE	DS	DIED	WHERE	WHY	BURIED	SOURCES
Hiott, N.F.	Pvt.	I	11th SCVI		CO	05/19/64	Bermuda Hundred	KIA		ROH,HAG
Hiott, William	Pvt.	B	3rd SCVC	38	CO	08/02/64	Pocotaligo, SC	ACD	(By own gun)	ROH,R43
Hip, Riley F.	Pvt.	F	4th SCVI		GE	07/21/61	1st Manassas, VA	KIA		ROH,SA2
Hipp, A.	Pvt.	I	3rd SCVI			09/01/61	Richmond, VA	DOD		JR
Hipp, Andrew J.	Pvt.	D	13th SCVI	17	NY	12/17/61	Cmp Pemberton SC	DOD		ROH
Hipp, Elijah	Pvt.	G	Hol.Leg.	36	NY	08/30/62	2nd Manassas, VA	DOW		ROH,ANY
Hipp, Elijah	Pvt.	D	13th SCVI	30	NY	/ /	SC Coast	DOD		ANY
Hipp, George Anderson	Pvt.			25	LS	09/12/61	Richmond, VA	DOD	Hurricane B.C. LS Cty.	LSC
Hipp, H.	Pvt.	F	14th SCVI		LS	01/29/63	Richmond, VA			ROH
Hipp, J.M.	Pvt.	H	3rd SCVI		LN	10/21/61	Front Royal, VA	DOD	Prospect Hill C. Frt.Royal	JR,SA2,KEB,TOD
Hipp, John S.	Pvt.	F	14th SCVI	32	LS	01/01/64	Richmond, VA	DOD	Hurricane B.C. Laurens SC	JR,NCC,LSC
Hipp, S. Asbury	Pvt.	D	13th SCVI	23	NY	01/05/62	SC Coast	DOD	(Typhoid Dysentery)	JR,ANY
Hipp, W. Walter	Pvt.	H	3rd SCVI		LN	06/28/61	Manassas, VA	DOD	KEB	ROH,JR,SA2,ANY
Hise, C.E.	Pvt.	E	3rd SCV			12/13/62	Fredericksburg	KIA		JR
Hitch, Young H.E.	Pvt.	I	16th SCVI		GE	06/19/64	Marietta, GA	KIA	(16R=Kennesaw Mt.)	ROH,JR,16R
Hitchcock, F.H.	Pvt.	C	7th SCVIBn		RD	08/04/64			Hollywood Cem.Rchmd. V358	HC,HAG
Hite, N.W.	Pvt.	C	15th SCVI		LN	/ /		DOD		JR
Hite, Noah W.	Pvt.	C	15th SCVI	18	LN	06/24/62	Summerville, SC	DOD		H15,KEB,TOD
Hitt, Benjamin	Pvt.	F	3rd SCVI		LS	06/29/62	Savage Stn., VA	KIA		ROH,JR,KEB,SA2
Hitt, Ellis S.	Pvt.	F	3rd SCVI			08/29/62	Manchester, VA	DOW		ROH,JR,SA2,KEB
Hitt, Franklin	Pvt.	G	16th SCVI		GE	/ /	Georgia	DOD		16R
Hitt, H.A.	Pvt.	A	13th SCVI		LS	07/01/63	Virginia	DOD		JR
Hitt, H.P.	Pvt.	B	3rd SCVIBn		LS	11/07/62	(KEB=H.L.)		Stonewall Cem. Winchester	ROH,WIN,KEB
Hitt, J.S.	Pvt.	F	14th SCVI		LS	07/01/62	Richmond, VA	DOD		JR
Hitt, Marshall	Pvt.	G	16th SCVI		GE	/ /	GA	DOD		16R
Hitt, Reuben	Pvt.	A	13th SCVI		LS	05/28/61		DOD	(Measles)	JR
Hitt, Robert	Pvt.	B	3rd SCVIBn		LS	05/08/64	Spottsylvania VA	KIA	(JR=Hill)	ROH,JR,KEB,R45
Hix, Clarence Eugene	Pvt.	A	3rd SCVI	18	LS	12/13/62	Fredericksburg	KIA	Mem. Mrkr in Laurens C.	JR,SA2,RHL,PP
Hix, John	Pvt.	B	26th SCVI	26	CD	07/15/62	Charleston, SC	DOD	(JR=7/17/62)	ROH,JR
Hix, John S.	Pvt.	B	13th SCVI		SG	07/28/62	Richmond, VA	DOD	(Typhoid)	ROH,JR
Hix, Thomas B.	Pvt.	A	26th SCVI	23	HY	06/27/64	Petersburg, VA	DOW		ROH
Hix, W.S.	Pvt.	F	6th SCVC	38	CN	10/27/64	Burgess Mills VA	KIA	(CDC=Hix, M.F.)	CDC,CAG
Hixon, M.J.E.	Pvt.				WG	/ /		DOD	(1863)	CTA,HOW
Hoagland, Charles	Pvt.	G	24th SCVI	35	RD	04/19/62	At home	DOD		EJM,PP
Hobbes, John A.	Pvt.	B	7th SCVIBn		LN	03/20/65	Bentonville, NC	KIA		ROH,WAT,HAG,PP
Hobbs, Isaac	Pvt.	C	Orr's Ri.		PS	08/15/62	Gaines' Mill, VA	DOW		JR,CDC
Hobbs, W.G.	Pvt.	K	12th SCVI		PS	09/18/63	Ft. Delaware, DE	DIP	Finn's Pt., NJ Nat. Cem.	ROH,FPH,P6,CDC
Hobbs, William E.	Sgt.	K	24th SCVI		ED	08/09/64	Atlanta, GA	KIA	Forsyth, GA	HOE,CKB
Hobby, J.A.	Pvt.	G	3rd SCVI		SG	12/26/62	Richmond, VA	DOD	Hollywood Cem.Rchmd.Q20 HC	ROH,JR,SA2,HOS
Hoberg, A.	Pvt.	A	German Art		CN	11/07/61	Port Royal, SC	KIA		ROH,JR,CDC
Hockaday. B.	Pvt.	A	SCV		CN	03/05/65	Elmira, NY	DIP	Woodlawn N.C.#1966 Elmira	FPH
Hodel, H.V.	Pvt.	C	Orr's Ri.		PS	/ /	Mt. Jackson, VA	DOD	Mt. Jackson, VA	ROH,SHS,CV
Hoden, C.	Pvt.	F	2nd SCV			11/09/62	Staunton, VA		Thornrose C. Staunton, VA	TOD
Hoden, C.	Pvt.	F	2nd SCV			11/09/62	Staunton, VA		Thornrose C. Staunton, VA	TOD
Hodge, A.J.	Pvt.	C	21st SCVI		CL	07/10/62	Charleston, SC		Magnolia Cem. Charleston	JR,MAG,HAG
Hodge, Charles	Pvt.	H	Orr's Ri.		MN	/ /		DOD	(1863)	HMC,CDC
Hodge, Isaac B.	Pvt.	D	2nd SCVI		SR	07/02/63	Gettysburg, PA	KIA		GDR,SA2,KEB
Hodge, J.C.	Pvt.	E	15th SCVI		FD	/ /	Lynchburg, VA		Lynchburg CSA Cem.#5 R2	KEB,BBW
Hodge, James D.	Pvt.	I	25th SCVI		CL	04/10/65	Elmira, NY	DIP	Woodlawn NN.C.#2606 Elmira	FPH,HAG,P6,P65
Hodge, John William	1st Sgt.	D	2nd SCVI		SR	05/02/64	Virginia	KIA		SA2,KEB,H2
Hodge, Peter H.	Pvt.	I	18th SCVI	24	DN	08/30/62	2nd Manassas, VA	KIA		ROH,JR,CDC

H

SOUTH CAROLINA DEAD IN CSA SERVICE 1861-1865

NAME	RANK	C	REGIMENT	AGE	DS	DIED	WHERE	WHY	BURIED	SOURCES
Hodge, R. Bunyan	Pvt.	E	15th SCVI	23	FD	04/30/63	Staunton, VA	DOD	Thornrose C. Staunton, VA	ROH,JR,KEB,TOD
Hodge, R.J.	Sgt.	I	23rd SCVI		CL	06/15/65	Fair Gds Pbg. VA	DOW	Graveyard near Hospital	ROH,HCL,P6
Hodge, Samuel N.	Pvt.	I	25th SCVI		CL	02/11/65	Elmira, NY	DIP	Woodlawn N.C.#2175 Elmira	FPH,HAG,P6,P65
Hodge, T.G.	Pvt.	I	25th SCVI		CL	02/01/62	At home	DOD	(Measles)	JR
Hodge, T.W.	Pvt.	A	12th SCVI		YK	03/02/62	Richmond, VA	DOD	Hollywood Cem. Rchmd. C29	HC
Hodge, William	Pvt.	H	11th SCVIB		WG	01/14/62	At home	DOD	(HOW=K,25th SCVI)	JR,CTA,HOW
Hodge, William H.	2nd Cpl.	K	21st SCVI		DN	03/07/65	Elmira, NY	DIP	Woodlawn N.C.#2392 Elmira	FPH,HAG,P6,P65
Hodges, A.	Pvt.	A	2nd SCVIRi			11/02/62	Richmond, VA	DOD		ROH
Hodges, C.A. (E.A.?)	Pvt.	B	Orr's Ri.		AE	04/04/62	Adam's Run, SC	DOD		JR
Hodges, C.R.	Pvt.	B	7th SCVI		AE	07/06/62	Savage Stn., VA	DOW		JR,KEB,CNM
Hodges, Emory Archibald	Pvt.	B	Orr's Ri.	26	AE	08/25/62	Adams Run, SC	DOD	(PP=4/25/62)	JR,CDC,PP
Hodges, J.T.	Pvt.	G	9th SCVIBn	25	HY	03/12/62	Georgetown, SC	DOD	(ROH=J.L.)	ROH,JR,PP
Hodges, James R.	2nd Lt.	B	7th SCVI		AE	09/17/62	Sharpsburg, MD	KIA		ROH,JR,KEB,R46
Hodges, John B.	Pvt.	E	1st SCVIG		MN	05/12/64	Spotsylvania, VA	KIA		ROH,JR,CDC,HMC
Hodges, John D.	Pvt.	E	1st SCVIG		MN	07/04/63	Gettysburg, PA	DOW	(?P40=John B. POW @ Gbg)	GDR,SA1,PDL
Hodges, John H.	Pvt.	B	24th SCVI	25	MO	06/15/64	Atlanta, GA	DOD	Oakland C. Atlanta R18#4	ROH,HOM,BGA
Hodges, William C.C.	2nd Lt.	B	7th SCVI		AE	07/02/63	Gettysburg, VA	KIA	KEB	ROH,JR,GDR,R46
Hodgins, William B.	Pvt.	C	Orr's Ri.		PS	09/20/64	Elmira, NY	DIP	Woodlawn N.C.#325 Elmira	FPH,CDC,P65,P113
Hoepke, Henry	Pvt.		Ham.Leg.		CN	09/17/62	Sharpsburg, MD	KIA		ROH
Hoffendon, Thomas	Pvt.	I	1st SCVIG		CN	08/29/62	2nd Manassas, VA	KIA		ROH,JR,SA1,CDC
Hoffman, George	Pvt.		SCVI	51	OG	/ /	Virginia	DOD	(1864)	ROH
Hoffman, Jacob M.	Pvt.	K	10th SCVI		CN	11/30/64	Franklin, TN	KIA		ROH,RAS,BIG,PP
Hoffman, Samuel W.	Pvt.	H	6th SCVI	23	YK	12/20/61	Dranesville, VA	KIA	(YEB=Huffman)	ROH,JR,YEB,R46
Hogan, Emanuel J.	Pvt.			16	CN	03/15/64	Charleston, SC	ACD	(Explosion @ Arsenal)	ROH
Hogan, John H.	Pvt.	G	1st SCVC	36	AE	05/01/64	Columbia, SC	DOD	(PP=5/12/64)	ROH,PP
Hogan, Patrick J.	Pvt.	H	27th SCVI		CN	06/19/64	Petersburg, VA	KIA	(Hagan in ROH)	ROH,HAG
Hogan, W.H.	Pvt.				YK	08/07/64	Petersburg, VA		Blandford Church Pbg., VA	BLC
Hogan, W.S.	5th Sgt.	D	5th SCVI		UN	07/17/62	Gaines' Mill, VA	DOW		ROH,JR,SA3
Hogan, Wyatt	Pvt.	F	5th SCRes	48		12/09/62	Adams Run, SC	DOD		PP
Hogg, J.C.	1st Sgt.	A	1st SCVIG		BL	08/16/64	Fussel's Mill VA	KIA	(JR=Deep Bottom)	ROH,JR,SA1,CDC
Hogg, R.B.	2nd Lt.	C	1st SCVIH		BL	12/20/62	Richmond, VA	DOD		ROH,SA1,JRH
Hogg, Thomas D.	Pvt.	G	Hol. Leg.	36	NY	08/30/62	2nd Manassas, VA	KIA		ROH,ANY
Hoggers, J.	Pvt.		25th SCVI			/ /	Richmond, VA		Oakwood C.#51, Row K, Div G	ROH,OWC
Hogshead, W.R.	2nd Lt.	K	12th SCVI	32	PS	05/12/64	Spotsylvania, VA	KIA		ROH,R47
Hogue, William H.	Pvt.	E	17th SCVI	26	YK	08/07/64	Petersburg, VA	ACD	(Falling of trench wall)	ROH,YMD,YEB,PP
Hoke, James	Cpl.	A	17th SCVI		CR	07/30/64	Crater, Pbg. VA	KIA	(See pg 170 LSS)	ROH,JR,LSS
Hoke, William A.	Pvt.	A	17th SCVI	32	CR	07/30/64	Crater, Pbg. VA	KIA	Hopewell B.C. Chester, SC	ROH,KEB,HHC,CB
Holbrooks, William	Pvt.	K	12th SCVI	25	PS	08/29/62	2nd Manassas, VA	KIA		ROH,JR
Holcomb, Andrew J.	Pvt.	E	3rd SCVIBn	30	LS	05/31/62	Adams Run, SC	DOD		ROH,KEB,PP
Holcomb, D.N.	Pvt.	C	4th SCVC		PS	06/11/64	Trevillian Stn.	KIA		ROH,JR,CDC
Holcomb, J.	Pvt.	K	16th SCVI		GE	06/29/64	Kenesaw Mtn., GA	KIA		ROH
Holcomb, J.S.	Pvt.	K	Ham.Leg.			01/17/64	Danbridge, TN	KIA		ROH,CDC
Holcomb, Jesse	Pvt.	H	16th SCVI		GE	07/08/64	At home	DOD		16R,PP
Holcomb, Lovejoy	Pvt.		6th SCVC		AE	/ /		DOD	Houston Cem. Mt. Carmel SC	MCC
Holcomb, W.L.	Pvt.	H	12th SCVI	23	YK	05/15/62		DOD		CWC,YEB
Holcombe, H.H.	Pvt.	H	3rd SCVABn		GE	/ /				ROH
Holcombe, Hosea K.	Pvt.	I	16th SCVI		GE	06/22/64	Kennesaw Mtn. GA	KIA	Con. Cem. Marietta, GA	16R,CCM
Holcombe, P.F.	Pvt.	F	1st SCVIH		GE	01/09/65	(OWC=I,4th SCVI)	DOD	Oakwood C.#26, Row J, Div G	ROH,OWC,SA1
Holden,	Pvt.	D	19th SCVI	18	CR	11/30/64	Franklin, TN	KIA		HOE,UD3
Holder, J.	Pvt.	G	7th SCVC		CN	/ /	At sea for Xchg	DIP	(CDC= Holden)	CDC,P114
Holkins, B.P.	Pvt.	A	P.S.S.			06/29/62	Richmond, VA	KIA		JR

SOUTH CAROLINA DEAD IN CSA SERVICE 1861-1865

NAME	RANK	C REGIMENT	AGE	DS	DIED	WHERE	WHY	BURIED	SOURCES
Hollan, J.	Pvt.	H 15th SCVI		UN	10/13/64	Strasburg, VA	KIA		ROH
Holland,	Sgt.	F 2nd SCVC		GE	06/21/63	Upperville, VA	KIA	Ivy Hill C.Upperville, VA	ROH,JR
Holland, Andrew J.	Pvt.	B 2nd SCVI	27	GE	11/21/62	Staunton, VA	DOD	Thornrose C. Staunton, VA	ROH,SA2,KEB,TO
Holland, G.R.	Pvt.	B 1st SCVC	28	LS	06/15/65	At home	DOD		ROH
Holland, George W.	3rd Lt.	D Hol.Leg.	25	BL	08/30/62	2nd Manassas, VA	KIA	(JR= 1st Sgt. Co.C)	ROH,JR,SAS
Holland, J.B.	Pvt.	E 19th SCVI			/ /	Chattanooga, TN		City C. Chattanooga, TN	TOD
Holland, J.D.					/ /	Virginia		(Rchmd effects list 1/63)	CDC
Holland, J.H.	Cpl.	L Orr's Ri.		AN	02/21/65	Ft. Delaware, DE	DIP	Finn's Pt., NJ Nat. Cem.	ROH,FPH,P5,P41
Holland, J.R.	Pvt.	I 3rd SCVI		LS	05/06/64	Wilderness, VA	KIA		ROH,SA2,KEB
Holland, J.S.	Pvt.	H 8th SCVI		MN	10/13/64	Cedar Creek, VA	KIA		HMC,KEB
Holland, J.W.		CSN			11/18/64	Richmond, VA			ROH
Holland, John	Pvt.	G 3rd SCVABn	26	KW	05/12/63	Columbia, SC	DOD	Antioch Ch. Kershaw Cty.	ROH,CDC,HIC,PP
Holland, John C.	Pvt.	G 7th SCVIBn	21	KW	05/16/64	Drury's Bluff VA	KIA		ROH,JR,HIC,HAG
Holland, John G.A.	Pvt.	I 3rd SCVI	24	YK	07/02/62	Savage Stn., VA	DOW	(JR=Gaines' Mill)	ROH,JR,SA2,YMD
Holland, John P.	Pvt.	A 1st SCVIG		BL	05/06/64	Wilderness, VA	DOW	(Head wound)	SA1,CDC
Holland, Joseph T.	Pvt.	A 1st SCVIG		BL	08/11/62	Richmond, VA	DOD	(Typhoid, JR=Co.B)	JR,SA1
Holland, P.A.	Pvt.	D 18th SCVI		AN	06/06/62	Charleston, SC	DOD	Magnolia Cem. Charleston	ROH,JR,MAG
Holland, R.	Pvt.	F Ham.Leg.		GE	06/01/62	7 Pines, VA	DOW		ROH,JR,CDC
Holland, Robert T.	Pvt.	B 4th SCVC		CR	06/11/64	Trevillian Stn.	KIA		SA2,ROH,HHC,CB,GMJ
Holland, Robert M.	Pvt.			PS	05/18/62	Adams Run, SC	DOD		OCS
Holland, Thomas Rease	Pvt.	F 7th SCVIBn	27	KW	08/27/64	Richmond, VA	DOD	Hollywood Cem.Rchmd. V673	ROH,HC,HAG
Holland, William M.	Pvt.	J 4th SCVI		AN	10/01/61	Germantown, VA	DOD	(JR=L, P.S.S.)	ROH,JR,SA2
Holley, Alexander T.	Pvt.	H 6th SCVI	18	FD	05/31/62	7 Pines, VA	DOW		ROH,WDB,CDC
Holley, Jasper	Pvt.	G 1st SCVIG		ED	08/29/62	2nd Manassas, VA	KIA		ROH,JR,SA1,HOE
Holley, Joel	Pvt.	G 2nd SCVI		KW	12/14/63	Bean's Stn., TN	KIA		SA2,KEB,HIC
Holley, John Bunyan	Pvt.	H 6th SCVI		FD	06/28/64	SC	DOD		ROH
Holley, John C.	Cpt.	E 17th SCVI	46	YK	06/18/62	James Island, SC	DOD	(JR=Johns I., Brain fever)	JR,DEM,R47,YEB
Holley, T. Willingham	1st Lt.	K 1st SCVC		CR	10/04/64	Charleston, SC	DOD	(Yellow fever)	ROH,JR,HHC,R43
Holley, W.	Pvt.	H 1st SCV			09/15/62	Warrenton, VA	DOW	(Wdd 2nd Man.)	ROH
Holliday,	Sgt.	F 2nd SCVC			06/21/63	Upperville, VA	KIA		BHC
Holliday, J.S.	Pvt.	14th SCVI			/ /	Richmond, VA		Oakwood C.#59,Row B,Div G	ROH,OWC
Holliday, Joseph	Pvt.	I 7th SCVI		ED	09/15/62	Richmond, VA	DOD		ROH
Holliday, S.B.	Pvt.	A 10th SCVI		GN	/ /		DOD		GRG,RAS
Holliday, Thomas	Pvt.	K 24th SCVI		ED	05/14/64	Dalton, GA	DOD	(Sent to Hos,lost since)	ROH,HOE
Holliday, Thomas	Pvt.	I 4th SCVC		WG	08/14/63	Georgetown, SC	DOD		JR,PP
Holliday, W.M.	Pvt.	I 24th SCVI	18	ED	07/22/64	Atlanta, GA	KIA		EJM
Holliday, William J.	Pvt.	I 24th SCVI	28	ED	03/12/65	Nashville, TN	DOW	Nashville City C. #12592)	ROH,P6
Hollingfield, Jacob	Pvt.	G 1st SCVIR		TN	05/08/65	Davids Island NY	DIP	Cypress Hills N.C.#2735 NY	FPH,P6,SA1,P79
Hollingsworth,	Pvt.	3rd SCVIBn		LS	09/14/62	Maryland Hts. MD	KIA		JR
Hollingsworth, B. Frank	Pvt.	I 3rd SCVI		LS	06/29/62	Savage Stn., VA	KIA	(Jr., J.B. in ROH)	ROH,JR,,KEB
Hollingsworth, Benjamin	Pvt.	B 15th SCVI		SG	08/30/62	2nd Manassas, VA	KIA		ROH,JR,,KEB
Hollingsworth, E.	Pvt.	E 2nd SCVIRi		PS	/ /	Richmond, VA			ROH
Hollingsworth, James	3rd Lt.	A 3rd SCVI	32	LS	12/13/62	Fredericksburg	KIA	Laurens Cem., SC PP	ROH,JR,SA2,RHL
Hollingsworth, James M.	Pvt.	H 7th SCVIBn		ED	11/23/64	Darbytown Rd. VA	DOW	(Wdd 10/27/64)	ROH,HAG
Hollingsworth, John A.	Pvt.	G 7th SCVI		ED	01/08/63	Richmond, VA	DOD	(UD2=KIA)	ROH,HOE,KEB,UD
Hollins, George N.	Engineer	CS Chicora			/ /			Magnolia Cem. Charleston	MAG
Hollins, W.H.	Pvt.	7th SCVI			/ /	Richmond, VA		Oakwood C.#118,Row B,Div A	ROH,OWC
Hollis, Charles	Pvt.	A 2nd SCVI		FD	02/15/62	Manassas, VA	DOD		ROH,SA2,KEB,HF
Hollis, D.W.	Pvt.	G 6th SCVI		FD	08/30/62	2nd Manassas, VA	KIA		WDB
Hollis, Hugh	4th Cpl.	E 5th SCVI	34	YK	11/16/63	Campbell's Stn.	KIA		UD3,SA3,YEB
Hollis, Moses	Pvt.	A 2nd SCVI		FD	06/29/62	Savage Stn., VA	KIA		ROH,JR,SA2,HFC

H

SOUTH CAROLINA DEAD IN CSA SERVICE 1861-1865

NAME	RANK	C REGIMENT	AGE	DS	DIED	WHERE	WHY	BURIED	SOURCES
Hollister, Andrew	Pvt.	I 1st SCVAR		CN	08/22/62	Charleston, SC	DOD	Magnolia Cem. Charleston	ROH,RCD
Holloway, Douglas	Pvt.	I 2nd SCVC		ED	/ /	At home	DOD		HOE
Holloway, Henry W.	1st Cpl.	G 1st SCVIG		ED	07/28/64	Deep Bottom, VA	MIA	(Died in enemy hands)	SA1,HOE
Holloway, J. Simpson	Pvt.	H 7th SCVIBn	22	ED	07/11/63	Bty. Wagner, SC	KIA		ROH,JR,HAG
Holloway, James A.	Pvt.	L Orr's Ri.		AN	06/27/62	Gaines' Mill, VA	KIA		JR,CDC
Holloway, R. Hix	Pvt.	G 7th SCVI	28	ED	05/30/62	Richmond, VA	DOD		HOE,EDN,KEB
Holloway, Thomas	Pvt.	G 24th SCVI	40		12/26/63	Rock Island, IL	DIP		EJM
Holloway, William	Pvt.	C 24th SCVI		CO	01/16/64	Rock Island, IL	DIP	C.C.#204 Rock Island, IL	FPH,P5
Holloway, William C.	Pvt.	H 7th SCVIBn	17	ED	05/16/64	Drury's Bluff VA	KIA		ROH,JR,HAG
Holloway,Jr., Wiley H.	Pvt.	G 1st SCVIG		ED	09/09/62	Warrenton, VA	DOW	(Wdd @ 2nd Man)	JR,SA1,HOE,CDC
Holly, Peter	Pvt.	I 8th SCVI		MN	06/15/64		KIA		JR
Holly, William	Pvt.	H 5th SCVI		UN	/ /		DOD	(Died before 6/30/63)	JR,SA3
Holly, William	Pvt.	H 22nd SCVI		GE	07/08/64	Kitrell Spgs. NC		C.C. Kitrell Springs, NC	PP
Holman, Calvin	Pvt.	F 19th SCVI		ED	01/16/65	Camp Douglas, IL	DIP	Oak Woods Cem. Chicago, IL	ROH,FPH,P5,CDC
Holman, Daniel P.	Pvt.	C 15th SCVI	21	LN	03/03/65	Camp Chase, OH	DIP	C.C.#1529 Columbus, OH	ROH,FPH,PP,P1
Holman, J.F.					/ /	Virginia		(Rchmd effects list 1/63)	CDC
Holman, Jesse	2nd Lt.	B 15th SCMil			05/21/65	Newbern, NC	DIP	Cedar Grove C. Newbern, NC	WAT,PP,P6,P5
Holman, T.B.	Pvt.	A Ham.Leg.		CN	/ /	Richmond, VA		Oakwood C.#122,Row J,Div A	ROH,OWC
Holme,	Pvt.				07/10/62	Richmond, VA		Hollywood Cem.Rchmd. M358	HC
Holmes, Amos S.	Pvt.	B 13th SCVI		SG	05/03/63	Chancellorsville	KIA		ROH,JR,HOS
Holmes, Benjamin	3rd Cpl.	Ward's LA	41		07/03/62	Georgetown, SC	DOD		PP
Holmes, James C.	Pvt.	A 2nd SCVI		CN	06/30/62	Manchester, VA	DOW	(H2=Wdd @ Savage Stn.)	ROH,SA2,CDC,H2
Holmes, Philip Gadsden	Pvt.	L 1st SCVIG		CN	06/27/62	Gaines' Mill, VA	KIA	Magnolia Cem. Charleston	JR,MAG,SA1,CV
Holmes, R.S.	Pvt.	10th SCV			/ /		SOW	Near Atlanta Ferry Road	UD2
Holmes, Randolph Scott	Pvt.	G 10th SCVI	22	HY	07/22/64	Atlanta, GA	KIA	Leonard place,Ferry Rd. GA	ROH,RAS,CDC,TOD
Holmes, Robert Little	Pvt.	L 1st SCVIG		CN	01/07/61	Castle Pinckney	ACD	Magnolia Cem. Charleston	JR,ROH,MAG,CV
Holmes, Thomas G.	Pvt.	K 4th SCVC		CN	05/28/64	Hawes Shop, VA	KIA		CLD,CV
Holmes, W.C.	Pvt.	C 4th SCVI		AN	07/18/62	Richmond, VA		Hollywood Cem.Rchmd. M372	HC
Holmes, W.W.	Pvt.	B			07/27/64	Richmond, VA			ROH,P12
Holsenbach, Henry H.	Pvt.	K 15th SCVI		AE	11/12/62	Richmond, VA	DOD	Hollywood Cem.Rchmd. S264	ROH,JR,HC,KEB
Holstein, Hiram L.	3rd Lt.	F 19th SCVI	37	ED	06/14/62	At home	DOD	(Left wife & 8 children)	ROH,HOE,EDN,R47
Holstein, Joseph A.	Pvt.	G 25th SCVI		ED	03/07/65	Elmira, NY	DIP	Woodlawn N.C.#2381 Elmira	ROH,FPH,EDR,P65
Holt, James P.	Pvt.	K P.S.S.		SG	06/30/62	Frayser's Farm	KIA		ROH,JR,CDC
Holt, John	Pvt.	F 2nd SCVIRi	50	AE	06/25/64	Wilderness, VA	DOW		ROH
Holt, John C.	Pvt.	K P.S.S.		SG	09/18/62	2nd Manassas, VA	DOW	(PP=Weldon, NC 6/22/63)	JR,HOS,CDC,PP
Holt, John H.	Pvt.	F 2nd SCVI			06/29/64	Liberty G.H., VA	DOW	(Pbg./Rchmd lines)	H2
Holt, Joseph T.	Cpl.	K P.S.S.		SG	06/30/62	Frayser's Farm	KIA		HOS
Holton, George	Pvt.	A 4th SCVC		CD	05/28/64	Hawes Shop, VA	KIA		ROH
Holtzclaw, George H.	Pvt.	C 22nd SCVI		SG	05/09/65	Newport News, VA	DIP	Greenlawn C.Newport News	ROH,PP,P6,P12
Holtzclaw, J. Frank	Pvt.	F 16th SCVI		GE	07/22/64	Decatur, GA	KIA		16R
Holtzclaw, J.P.	Pvt.	C 22nd SCVI	22	SG	06/26/65	Petersburg, VA	DOD	Graveyard near Fair Gds.	ROH,P6,P12
Holwell, J.A.	Pvt.	L Orr's Ri.		AN	06/27/62	Gaines' Mill, VA	KIA	(CDC=Holloway)	ROH,CDC
Homander, James	Pvt.	A 14th SCVI		DN	06/28/63	Petersburg, VA	DOD		ROH
Home, J.H.	Pvt.	H 14th SCVI		BL	07/05/62	Richmond, VA			ROH
Honea, R.S.	Pvt.	F Orr's Ri.		PS	/ /	Richmond, VA		Oakwood C.#83,Row G,Div G	ROH,OWC,CDC
Honey, G.W.	Pvt.	D 27th SCVI		CN	03/31/65	Pt. Lookout, MD	DIP		ROH
Honey, John	Pvt.	H 6th SCVI		YK	01/09/62	Manassas, VA	DOW	(Wdd @ Dranesville)	ROH
Honey, Stephen Decatur	Pvt.	G 2nd SCVI	27	KW	08/08/61	Culpepper, VA	DOD	Fairview Cem. Culpepper VA	ROH,JR,CGH,SA2
Honeycutt, John T.	Cpl.	C Orr's Ri.		PS	09/24/64	Elmira, NY	DIP	Woodlawn N.C.#471 Elmira	FPH,CDC,P65,P113
Hood,	Pvt.	H 2nd SCVC		RD	06/21/63	Upperville, VA	KIA	(BHC= Sgt. Co.C)	ROH,BHC
Hood,	Pvt.	F 2nd SCVC			07/02/63	Gettysburg, PA	KIA		JR

SOUTH CAROLINA DEAD IN CSA SERVICE 1861-1865

NAME	RANK	C	REGIMENT	AGE	DS	DIED	WHERE	WHY	BURIED	SOURCES
Hood, Andrew J.	Pvt.	A	6th SCVC		CR	06/21/63	Upperville, VA	KIA	Ivy Hill C. Upperville, VA	CRM,HHC,HSF
Hood, Benjamin	Pvt.	C	12th SCVI		FD	06/25/62	Richmond, VA	DOD	Hollywood Cem.Rchmd. 0299	ROH,JR,HC,HFC
Hood, Charles W.A.J.	Pvt.	E	5th SCVI	26	YK	09/17/62	Sharpsburg, MD	KIA	(YEB=South Mtn., MD)	ROH,JR,SA3,YEB
Hood, D.H.	Pvt.	K	10th SCVI		CN	/ /		DOD		RAS
Hood, Enoch	Pvt.	A	20th SCVI		PS	06/24/64	Petersburg, VA	KIA	(JR=6/18/64)	ROH,JR,CDC
Hood, Hugh	Pvt.				CR	/ /	Corinth, MS	KIA		HHC
Hood, Isaiah J.	Pvt.	B	7th SCVIBn	36	FD	10/13/64	At home			ROH,HAG,HFC
Hood, J.E.	Pvt.	K	10th SCVI		CN	/ /		DOD		RAS
Hood, James	Pvt.	G	SCVI			03/28/65	Elmira, NY	DIP	Woodlawn N.C.#2509 Elmira	FPH
Hood, John J.	Pvt.	G	23rd SCVI		MO	08/24/62	Lynchburg, VA	DOD	Lynchburg CSA Cem.#10 R3	ROH,JR,HOM,BBW
Hood, W.	Pvt.	H	16th SCVI		GE	05/14/64	Resaca, GA	KIA		16R
Hood, Wellington	Pvt.	G	23rd SCVI		MO	/ /	2nd Manassas, VA	KIA		HOM
Hood, William H.	Cpl.	H	16th SCVI		GE	07/01/64	Atlanta, GA		(Or Macon Dup ? NI 16R)	PP
Hook, J.G.	Pvt.	H	20th SCVI		LN	08/23/64	Winchester, VA		Stonewall Cem. Winchester	ROH,WIN,KEB,P1
Hook, John P.	Pvt.	K	9th SCVIB		LN	09/16/61	Germantown, VA	DOD	(JR=P.S.S.)	ROH,JR
Hook, Joseph	Pvt.	D	15th SCMil		KW	04/05/65	New Bern, NC	DOW	Cedar Grove C. Newbern NC	ROH,P1,P6,WAT,
Hook, Lawrence L.	Pvt.	G	25th SCVI	41	OG	06/15/64	At home	DOD		ROH,HAG,EDR
Hook, M.M.	Pvt.	H	20th SCVI		LN	06/23/64	Petersburg, VA	KIA		ROH,JR,CDC,KEB
Hook, Samuel P.	Pvt.	G	25th SCVI	30	OG	03/08/65	Elmira, NY	DIP	Woodlawn N.C.#2374 Elmira	ROH,FPH,EDR,P6
Hooker, David H.	Pvt.	B	1st SCVIH		CN	05/06/64	Wilderness, VA	DOW	Spotsylvania C.H., VA	SCH,SA1
Hooker, F.F.M.	Pvt.	B	1st SCVIH		CN	05/12/64	Spotsylvania, VA	DOW	Spotsylvania C.H., VA	SCH,SA1
Hooker, G.W.	Pvt.	D	20th SCVI		LS	10/13/64	Strasburg, VA	DOW		ROH,JR,CDC,KEB
Hoole, Axalla J.	Lt. Col.		8th SCVI	40	DN	09/20/63	Chickamauga, GA	KIA	Brunson Graveyard, DN Cty.	ROH,JR,KEB,TRR
Hoop, J.	Pvt.	C	7th SCV			/ /	Richmond, VA		Oakwood C.#33,Row N,Div C	OWC
Hoopaugh, John L.	Pvt.	H	6th SCVI		FD	02/18/62	Centreville, VA	DOD		ROH,HFC
Hooten, Samuel	Pvt.	A	14th SCVI		DN	02/23/62		DOD	(Brain inflamation)	JR
Hoover, Henry A.	Pvt.	I	2nd SCVA	23	OG	06/16/62	Secessionville	KIA		ROH,PP
Hoover, J.	Pvt.	I	1st SCVA		OG	06/16/62	Secessionville	KIA		ROH,JR,CDC
Hoover, James J.	4th Cpl.	C	1st SCVIH	21	BL	05/06/64	Wilderness, VA	KIA	Fredericksburg C.C. R6S13	ROH,SA1,FBG,JR
Hope, Davis McDonough	Pvt.	G	P.S.S.	24	YK	10/10/64	Richmond, VA	DOW	(Wdd @ Chaffins Farm 9/30)	YMD,YEB,SA3
Hope, J. Meek	Cpl	F	17th SCVI	23	YK	05/06/64	Florence, SC	DOD	Smyrna Ch. York, SC	ROH,YMD,YEB,PP
Hope, Mack	Pvt.	F	17th SCVI		YK	07/30/64	Crater, Pbg., VA	KIA		BLM
Hopkins, B.P.	Pvt.	A	P.S.S.		UN	06/29/62	Savage Stn., VA	KIA		ROH,CDC,CNM
Hopkins, David T.	Pvt.	I	4th SCVI		AN	02/19/62	Centreville, VA	DOD	(JR=P.S.S.)	JR,CCR,SA2
Hopkins, J. Ward	Cpt.	D	27th SCVI	32	CN	06/16/64	Hare's Hill, VA	KIA	1st P.C.(Scotch) Charlstn.	ROH,JR,UD1,SMC
Hopkins, J.H.	Pvt.	B	22nd SCVI		SG	06/24/65	Newport News, VA	DIP	Greenlawn C. Newport News	PP,P12
Hopkins, Lucius	Pvt.	F	7th SCVIBn	18	KW	06/27/64	Petersburg, VA	DOW		ROH,HIC,HAG
Hopkins, W.T.	Pvt.	F	2nd SC Res		PS	01/04/65	Columbia, SC	DOD	Elmwood Cem. Columbia, SC	ROH,MP,PP
Hopkins, William	Pvt.	A	1st SCVIR	21	LR	03/14/62	Sullivans I., SC	DOD		ROH,SA1
Hopper, C.J.	Pvt.	C	17th SCVI		YK	/ /	Charlottesville	DOD	Univ. Cem. Charlottesville	JR,ACH
Hopson, R.R.	Pvt.		1st SCV			/ /	Richmond, VA		Oakwood C.#57,Row M,Div A	ROH,OWC
Hore, W.P.	Pvt.	A	17th SCVI		CR	07/30/64	Crater, Pbg., VA	KIA		BLM
Horlbeck, Elias B.M.D.	Pvt.	A	9th SCVIB	21	CN	09/12/61	Germantown, VA	DOD		ROH,JR,LAN
Horlbeck, J. Moultrie	Pvt.					/ /			Magnolia Cem. Charleston	MAG
Horn, Benson	Pvt.	C	5th SCVI			10/28/63	Lookout Valley	KIA		ROH,CDC
Horn, Bud	Pvt.	C	19th SCVI		ED	06/15/62	Enterprise, MS	DOD		HOE,UD3
Horn, Elijah	Pvt.	B	19th SCVI		ED	06/08/63	Rome, GA	DOD	Myrtle Hill C. Rome, GA	ROH,HOE,BGA
Horn, Felix	Pvt.	B	18th SCVI		UN	08/30/62	2nd Manassas, VA	KIA	Mannassas CSA Cem.	ROH,JR,CDC
Horn, J.	Pvt.	D	8th SCVI		CD	06/19/62	Richmond, VA	DOD	Hollywood Cem.Rchmd. 0213	JR,HC,KEB
Horn, J.A.	Pvt.	E	14th SCMil		LS	04/28/65	Hart's Island NY	DIP	Cypress Hills N.C. #2640	FPH,P6,P79
Horn, J.M.	Pvt.	L	10th SCVI		MN	/ /		DOD		RAS,HMC

H

SOUTH CAROLINA DEAD IN CSA SERVICE 1861-1865

NAME	RANK	C REGIMENT	AGE	DS	DIED	WHERE	WHY	BURIED	SOURCES
Horn, John	Pvt.	B 19th SCVI	25	ED	08/01/62	Lauderdale Ss MS	DOD	Probably in UK C.C. there	ROH,HOE,PP
Horn, John W.	Pvt.	K 23rd SCVI	43	SR	04/02/65	Petersburg, VA	DOW	(Wdd 4/1/65)	ROH,K23,UD3
Horn, L. Simpson	Pvt.	C 19th SCVI		ED	09/20/63	Chickamauga, GA	KIA		HOE,CDC,UD3
Horn, R.A.	Pvt.	I 22nd SCVI		OG	02/14/65	Richmond, VA			ROH
Horn, Samuel	Pvt.	B 19th SCVI	18	ED	03/18/65	Bentonville, NC	KIA		ROH,HOE
Horn, William	Pvt.	F 26th SCVI			06/15/64	Petersburg, VA	KIA	(Date ? Between 6/17-7/27)	ROH,CDC
Horn, William G.	Pvt.	B 19th SCVI		ED	09/20/63	Chickamauga, GA	KIA	(10th Co. 10/19 Consol.)	ROH,JR,HOE,CDC
Horn, William Pinckney	Pvt.	McQueen LA	25	MN	08/18/64	Davis Farm, VA	KIA	(PP=Pbg. 9/6/64)	HMC,CDC,PP
Horne, John P.	Pvt.	H 7th SCVI	24	ED	06/29/62	Savage Stn., VA	KIA		ROH,CDC,EDN,CNM
Horne, P.	Pvt.	B 7th SCVI			09/24/65	Chickamauga, GA	DOW		JR
Horne, William	Cpl.	H Orr's Ri.			07/28/62	Frayser's Farm	KIA	(HMC=Died at home)	ROH,JR,CDC,HMC
Horney, John	Pvt.	SCVC		YK	/ /		DOD	(Prob Dup of Honey, John)	YEB
Hornsby, Jesse	Pvt.	F 7th SCVIBn		KW	07/14/64	Petersburg, VA	DOD	Blandford Church Pbg., VA	HIC,BLC,HAG,PP
Hornsby, S. Wyatt	Pvt.	D 15th SCVI		KW	05/06/64	Wilderness, VA	DOW	Fredericksburg C.C. R6S13	JR,FBG,HIC,KEB
Hornsby, Samuel	Pvt.	D 15th SCVI		KW	09/17/62	Sharpsburg, MD	DOW		JR,HIC,KEB
Horsey, J.H.W.	Pvt.	K 1st SCVIH		OG	08/30/62	2nd Manassas, VA	KIA		ROH,JR,SA1,JRH
Horton, Albert E.	Pvt.	A 1st SCVIR		LR	03/19/65	Bentonville, NC	KIA	PP	ROH,SA1,LAN,WAT
Horton, Benjamin	Pvt.	F 11th SCVI	28	BT	10/28/63	Charleston, SC	DOD		ROH,JR,HAG
Horton, Doniver A.	Pvt.	D 1st SCVIH		LR	09/30/64	Ft. Harrison, VA	KIA		SA1,LAN
Horton, E.H.	Pvt.	C 5th SCVI		SG	11/14/61	Manassas, VA	DOD		SA3
Horton, George W.	Pvt.	A 13th SCVI		LS	08/30/62	2nd Manassas, VA	KIA	(JR=8/29/62)	ROH,JR,CDC
Horton, H.E.	Pvt.	E 11th SCVI		BT	06/27/64	Petersburg, VA	KIA		JR,HAG
Horton, Henry C.	Cpl.	D 24th SCVI	36	BT	09/13/64	Lauderdale Ss MS	DOD	Prob in C.C.unknowns there	ROH,PP
Horton, J. Franklin	Pvt.	G 18th SCVI	31	UN	08/30/62	2nd Manassas, VA	KIA		JR,CDC,YEB
Horton, J.J.	Pvt.	H 2nd SCVI		LR	12/15/61		DOD	(Date approximate)	SA2,LAN
Horton, James Erwin	2nd Lt.	F 7th SCVIBn	27	KW	11/01/62	Adams Run, SC	DOD	(JR=Died at home)	ROH,JR,HIC,R46
Horton, James T.	Pvt.	H 2nd SCVI		LR	07/15/63	At home	DOD		SA2,LAN,H2
Horton, James Wyatt	Pvt.	F 7th SCVIBn	29	KW	09/07/63	Bty. Marshall SC	DOD		ROH,JR,HAG,HIC
Horton, Jesse	Pvt.	G 5th SCVC			07/28/64	Richmond, VA	KIA	(JR=Fraser's Farm)	JR
Horton, Joel A.	Pvt.	K P.S.S.		SG	/ /		DOD		JR,HOS
Horton, Lewis	Pvt.	K Hol.Leg.			03/03/65	Baltimore, MD	DIP	Loudon Pk. C. Baltimore MD	FPH,P120,PP
Horton, R.F.	Pvt.	E 11th SCVI		BT	06/27/64	Petersburg, VA	KIA		JR,HAG
Horton, Ransom	Pvt.	F 7th SCVIBn		KW	07/15/64	Petersburg, VA	KIA	(HAG= Ramsour)	JR,HIC,HAG
Horton, Samuel D.	Pvt.	C 7th SCVIBn		RD	07/12/64	Petersburg, VA	KIA		ROH,HAG
Horton, T.F.	Pvt.	F 1st SCVIH			08/30/62	2nd Manassas, VA	KIA		ROH
Horton, W.C.	Pvt.	H 2nd SCVI		LR	07/04/63	Gettysburg, PA	DOW	Gettysburg, PA KEB	ROH,GDR,SA2,LAN
Houck, Daniel D.S.	Cpl.	F 25th SCVI	26	OG	08/06/64	Pt. Lookout, MD	DIP	C.C. Pt. Lookout, MD	ROH,FPH,HAG,P113
Hough, Amos	Pvt.	E 22nd SCVI	18	CD	02/02/65	Petersburg, VA	KIA		ROH,PP
Hough, Christian C.	Pvt.		21	CN	09/09/62	Richmond, VA	DOD		ROH
Hough, J.C.	Pvt.	A 8th SCVI		DN	/ /	Richmond, VA		Oakwood C.#15,Row C,Div A	OWC
Hough, J.E.	Pvt.	D 8th SCVI		CD	12/09/61	Richmond, VA	DOD	(Typhoid)	JR,KEB
Hough, J.T.	Pvt.	D 8th SCVI	22	CD	01/01/62	Charlottesville	DOD		ROH,KEB
Hough, John T.B.	Pvt.	E 1st SCVIR		LR	07/20/63	Ft. Moultrie, SC	DOD		SA1,LAN
Hough, N.J.	Pvt.	H 2nd SCVI		LR	01/15/62		DOD	(KEB=M.J.)	SA2,LAN,KEB
Hough, Nathaniel	4th Cpl.	G 2nd SCVI		KW	04/24/65	Newbern, NC	DOW	Cedar Grove C. Newbern NC	KEB,P6,WAT,PP
Hough, William	Cpl.	C 6th SCVI		KW	06/30/62	Frayser's Farm	DOW		HIC,WDB
Hough, William Thomas	Pvt.	1st SCV		CD	07/02/62	Ft. Moultrie, SC	DOD		ROH
House, D.M.	Sgt.	F 23rd SCVI		CR	11/15/63	Charleston, SC	DOD	Magnolia Cem. Charleston	ROH,MAG
House, George A.	Pvt.	K 21st SCVI		DN	01/15/65	Ft. Fisher, NC	KIA		PP,HAG
Houston, E.	Pvt.			WG	/ /		DOD	(1863)	CTA,HOW
Houston, W.G. (W.Y. ?)	Pvt.	G 3rd SCV			/ /	Richmond, VA		Oakwood C.#26,Row A,Div E	ROH,OWC

SOUTH CAROLINA DEAD IN CSA SERVICE 1861-1865

NAME	RANK	C REGIMENT	AGE	DS	DIED	WHERE	WHY	BURIED	SOURCES
Howard, Alexander	Pvt.	H 20th SCVI		LN	01/19/65	At home	DOD		ROH,KEB
Howard, Daniel	Pvt.	C 1st SCVIBn	25	CN	06/16/62	Secessionville	KIA		JR,HAG,PP
Howard, Edmund K.	Pvt.	A 10th SCVI	19	GN	01/29/64	Cassville, GA	DOD		ROH,JR,GRG,RAS
Howard, F.M.	Pvt.	E 10th SCVI		WG	/ /	MS	DOD		RAS,HOW
Howard, George McDuffie	Pvt.	C 4th SCVI		AN	12/25/61	Warrenton, VA	DOD		SA2
Howard, George W.	Pvt.	H 25th SCVI		CN	05/07/64	Port Walthall Jn	DOW	Blandford Church Pbg., VA	ROH,JR,BLC,PP
Howard, Isom	Pvt.	H 14th SCVI		BL	07/01/63	Gettysburg, PA	KIA		JR,UD2
Howard, J.D.	Pvt.	E Ham.Leg.		GE	12/12/62	Staunton, VA	DOD		ROH
Howard, J.F.	Pvt.	D Ham.Leg.		AN	07/28/64	Riddle's Shop VA	KIA	Oakwood C.#78,Row A,Div G	ROH,GRS,OWC
Howard, James W.	Pvt.	A 19th SCVI	17	ED	09/20/63	Chickamauga, GA	KIA	(10th Co. 10/19 Cosol)	ROH,JR,HOE,UD3
Howard, Jasper	Pvt.	K 19th SCVI	25	ED	12/31/62	Murfreesboro, TN	KIA		ROH,JR,HOE
Howard, John L.	Pvt.	I 17th SCVI		LR	03/16/65	Elmira, NY	DIP	Woodlawn N.C.#1705 Elmira	FPH,LAN,P65,P1
Howard, Joseph	Pvt.	A 21st SCVI		CN	09/28/64	Elmira, NY	DIP	Woodlawn N.C.#394 Elmira	FPH,CDC,P5,P65
Howard, Joseph A.	Pvt.	A 21st SCVI		GN	/ /	Charleston, SC	DOD	(1863)	FLR,HAG
Howard, Julius	Cpl.	A 19th SCVI	20	ED	05/29/62	Okolona, MS	DOD	(1862)	HOE,PP,UD3
Howard, M.D.L.	Pvt.	D Ham.Leg.		AN	05/31/62	7 Pines, VA	KIA		GRS
Howard, N.	Pvt.	B 1st SCV			08/19/64	Richmond, VA			ROH
Howard, N.H.	Pvt.	H 25th SCVI		CN	06/03/63	At home	DOD		JR
Howard, R.P.	Pvt.	K 2nd SCVI		CN	12/13/62	Fredericksburg	KIA		ROH,JR,SA2,KEB
Howard, Thomas	Pvt.	B 16th SCVI		GE	11/30/64	Franklin, TN	KIA	(16R=Jonesboro)	ROH,16R
Howard, W.J.	Pvt.	A 10th SCVI		GN	/ /		DOD		GRG,RAS
Howard, W.P.	Pvt.	A 2nd SCVI		RD	12/15/63		DOD	(Date approximate)	SA2,KEB
Howard, William	Pvt.	A 19th SCVI	40	ED	/ /		DOD		HOE,UD3
Howard, Young	Cpl.	I 16th SCVI		GE	07/22/64	Atlanta, GA	KIA	(ROH=Sgt. 8/24/64)	ROH,16R
Howe, Benjamin F.	Pvt.	B 13th SCVI		SG	06/27/62	Gaines' Mill, VA	DOW	(JR=Frayser's Farm)	ROH,JR,HOS
Howe, James L.	3rd Sgt.	K 17th SCVI	21	YK	07/30/64	Crater, Pbg., VA	KIA		ROH,JR,BLM,YEB
Howe, John J.	1st Sgt.	G 18th SCVI	25	YK	09/01/62	Martin's Lane VA	DOD	(Lung hemourage)	JR,YEB
Howe, John T.	Pvt.	G 18th SCVI	23	UN	09/24/64	Elmira, NY	DIP	Woodlawn N.C.#459 Elmira	FPH,P5,P65,YEB
Howe, Joseph L.	4th Sgt.	F 5th SCVI	22	YK	07/02/62	Frayser`s Farm	DOW	(Wdd 6/30/62, YEB=James)	JR,SA3,YEB,CB
Howe, Nathaniel L.	Pvt.	B 22nd SCVI		SG	11/23/64	Elmira, NY	DIP	Woodlawn N.C.#930 Elmira	FPH,HOS,P65,P1
Howe, S. (Howell?)	Pvt.	B 7th SCV			11/15/64	City Point, VA	DOW	City Pt. N.C. Hopewell, VA	PP,TOD
Howe, Sylvester V.	Pvt.	I 13th SCVI		SG	12/24/61	Instruction camp	DOD		JR
Howe, Thomas A.	Pvt.	H 18th SCVI	27	YK	01/13/62	Danville, VA	DOD	(YEB=Winchester)	JR,YEB
Howe, William	1st Sgt.	C 2nd SCVI	20	RD	02/02/62	Centreville, VA	DOD		ROH,SA2,KEB,PP
Howell, D.A.	Pvt.	F P.S.S.		LN	06/27/62	Gaines' Mill, VA	KIA	(JR=D.E.)	ROH,JR,CDC
Howell, Enoch	Cpl.	D 16th SCVI		GE	07/20/64	Peachtree Crk GA	KIA		ROH,16R
Howell, F.E.	Sgt.	H 11th SCVI		CO	06/24/64	Petersburg, VA	KIA	(JR=6/18/64)	ROH,JR,HAG
Howell, George W.	Cpl.	D P.S.S.		SG	09/02/62	2nd Manassas, VA	DOW		ROH,JR,HOS,CDC
Howell, Henry R.	Citizen	Lydia, SC		DN	04/25/65	Hart's Island NY	DIP	Cypress Hills N.C. #2602	FPH,P6,P79
Howell, Ira	Pvt.	F Orr's Ri.		PS	07/21/62	Richmond, VA	DOW	(JR=P.S.S.)	ROH,JR
Howell, James M.	Pvt.	A 16th SCVI		GE	09/07/64	Lovejoy, GA	KIA	Academy lot, Jonesboro, GA	16R,UD2
Howell, John P.	Pvt.	D P.S.S.		SG	11/16/63	Campbells Stn TN	KIA	(JR=6/19/63)	ROH,JR,HOS
Howell, M.	Pvt.	H 12th SCVI		YK	/ /		DOW	(In enemy hands)	JR
Howell, M.P.L.	Pvt.	F 24th SCVI		AN	11/22/63	Newman, GA	DOD	Oak Hill C. Newman, GA	HOL,BGA
Howell, Madison F.	Pvt.	F 5th SCVI	19	UN	08/03/61	Charlottesville	DOD	Univ. Cem. Charlottesville	ROH,JR,SA3,ACH
Howell, N.A.	Pvt.	G 10th SCVI		HY	/ /		DOD		RAS
Howell, Richard A.	Pvt.	D P.S.S.		SG	05/17/63	Carrsville, VA	DOW	(Wdd 5/12/63)	ROH,JR,HOS
Howell, W.	Pvt.	F 13th SCVI		SG	/ /	Petersburg, VA	KIA		ROH
Howell, William J.	Pvt.	A 3rd SCVABn		GE	08/06/62	At home	DOD	(PP=8/7/62)	JR,PP
Howell, William W.	Pvt.	F 18th SCVI	18	UN	08/31/64	Petersburg, VA	DOD	(PP=9/1/64)	ROH,PP
Howerton, Joseph F.	Pvt.	D P.S.S.		SG	02/20/65	Columbia, SC			PP

SOUTH CAROLINA DEAD IN CSA SERVICE 1861-1865

NAME	RANK	C REGIMENT	AGE	DS	DIED	WHERE	WHY	BURIED	SOURCES
Howle, Thomas E.	Cpt.	M 8th SCVI		DN	09/17/62	Sharpsburg, MD	KIA	(JR=MD Hts.)	ROH,JR,TRR,R46
Hoy, Joseph B.	2nd Lt.	E 15th SCVI	21	FD	09/14/62	South Mtn., MD	KIA		ROH,JR,R47,HOF
Hoyle, William	Pvt.	G Hol.Leg.		FD	/ /		DOD		ANY
Hoys, A.S.	Pvt.	1st SCV			07/03/62	Richmond, VA		Hollywood Cem.Rchmd. M219	HC
Hubbard, E.G.	Pvt.	G 23rd SCVI		MO	/ /	Mississippi	DOD		HOM
Hubbard, J.B.	Pvt.	B 12th SCVI		YK	02/22/65	Richmond, VA			ROH
Hubbard, W.H.	Pvt.	K 22nd SCVI		PS	07/30/64	Crater, Pbg., VA	KIA		BLM
Hubbs, Freedom J.	Pvt.	C 1st SCVIG		RD	05/12/64	Spotsylvania, VA	KIA		ROH,SA1,CDC
Huchens, J.S.	Pvt.	D 2nd SCV			/ /	Charlottesville		Univ. Cem. Charlottesville	ACH
Huchinson, H.	Pvt.	G 6th SCVC		RD	01/08/65	Pt. Lookout, MD	DIP		ROH
Huckabee, Philip	Pvt.	B 15th SCVI		SG	05/03/63	Chancellorsville	KIA	Fredericksburg C.C. R6S13	FBG,HOS,KEB
Huckabee, William P.	Pvt.	B 15th SCVI		SG	09/14/62	South Mtn., MD	KIA		ROH,JR,HOS,KEB
Huckaby, Richard	Pvt.	C 18th SCVI	40	UN	06/15/64	Summerville, SC	DOD		ROH
Huckins, Elbert	Pvt.	L 2nd SCVIRi	17	AN	06/27/62	Gaines' Mill, VA	KIA		ROH
Hucks, Isaiah	Pvt.	E 26th SCVI	25	HY	/ /	At home	DOD		ROH
Hucks, J.B.	Pvt.	A 26th SCVI		HY	08/15/63	Petersburg, VA	DOW	(Wdd 7/27/63)	ROH,CDC
Huddleston, James	Pvt.	H 18th SCVI		YK	07/30/64	Crater, Pbg., VA	KIA		ROH,JR,BLM
Hudgens, A.		CSN			08/14/64	Pt. Lookout, MD	DIP		ROH
Hudgens, Abner L.	Pvt.	I 19th SCVI	23	AN	/ /		DOD		ROH
Hudgens, Cunningham	Pvt.	C 3rd SCVIBn		LS	11/08/64	Baltimore, MD	DOW	Loudon Pk. C.B-52 Balto.MD	FPH,KEB,PP,P1,P6
Hudgens, W.L.	Cpt.	C 3rd SCVIBn		LS	07/02/62	Richmond, VA	DOD	(UD3=Charleston)	KEB,R45,UD3
Hudgens, William H.	Pvt.	A 3rd SCVI	19	LS	11/18/63	Knoxville, TN	KIA	UD3	ROH,SA2,KEB,RHL
Hudson, A.B.	Pvt.	E 24th SCVI	30	CO	08/10/64	Atlanta, GA	KIA		ROH
Hudson, B.C.	Pvt.	E 24th SCVI	31	CO	12/20/62	Ft. Delaware, DE	DIP		ROH
Hudson, Burrell C.	Pvt.	F 12th SCVI		FD	07/09/62	Richmond, VA	DOD	(Rchmd effects list)	JR,HFC,CDC
Hudson, D.L.	Cpl.	C 11th SCVI		CO	05/09/64	Swift Creek, VA	KIA		ROH
Hudson, D.W.	Pvt.	F 16th SCVI		GE	11/30/64	Franklin, TN	KIA		16R
Hudson, David	Pvt.	A 6th SCVI		CR	12/15/61	Charlottesville	DOD	Univ. Cem. Charlottesville	ACH,GLS,HHC,CB
Hudson, E.G.	Sgt.	C Orr's Ri.		PS	02/26/65	Elmira, NY	DIP	Woodlawn N.C.#2286 Elmira	FPH,P65,P66
Hudson, George	Pvt.	G 7th SCV			/ /		DOD		UD2
Hudson, Henry	Pvt.	4th SCVC	32	YK	/ /	Charleston, SC	DOD		YEB
Hudson, J.C.					/ /	Virginia		(Rchmd effects list 1/63)	CDC
Hudson, J.H.	Pvt.	B 2nd SCVIRi		PS	/ /				ROH
Hudson, J.M.	Pvt.	M P.S.S.		SG	/ /	Staunton, VA		Thornrose C. Staunton, VA	PP
Hudson, James O.	Pvt.	G 15th SCVI		WG	09/14/62	South Mtn., MD	KIA	(JR=J.E.)	ROH,JR,KEB,CDC
Hudson, Jesse D.	Pvt.	D 6th SCVI	22	DN	06/25/62	Richmond, VA	DOD	1st B.C. Hartsville, SC	ROH,JLC,PP
Hudson, John L.	Pvt.	H 3rd SCVABn		GE	09/19/63	Charleston, SC	DOD	Magnolia Cem. Charleston	ROH,MAG,PP
Hudson, L.M.	1st Cpl.	B 22nd SCVI		SG	07/30/64	Crater Pbg., VA	KIA		HOS,BLM
Hudson, M.M.	Pvt.	F 23rd SCVI		CR	01/04/65	Richmond, VA			ROH
Hudson, P.	Pvt.	C 6th SCVI			/ /	Richmond, VA			ROH
Hudson, Pleasant W.	Pvt.	F 16th SCVI		GE	/ /	Pulaski, TN	DOD	(In enemy hands)	16R
Hudson, Robert A.	2nd Lt.	G 21st SCVI	21	DN	07/11/64	Cold Harbor, VA	KIA	1st B.C. Hartsville, SC	ROH,HAG,R48,PP
Hudson, T.F.	Pvt.	I 6th SCVI		CR	/ /		DOD		CB,HHC
Hudson, Thomas H.	Pvt.	E 6th SCVI	24	DN	05/31/62	7 Pines, VA	KIA		ROH,JR,JLC,WDB
Hudson, Tillman J.	Cpl.	C 11th SCVI	22	CO	06/24/64	Petersburg, VA	KIA	(PP=7/12/64)	ROH,PP
Hudson, W.A.	Pvt.	B 2nd SCVI		PS	09/09/64	Elmira, NY	DIP	Woodlawn N.C.#202 Elmira	FPH,KEB,P65,P120
Hudson, Waddy Thompson	1st Sgt.	A 16th SCVI	24	GE	11/30/64	Franklin, TN	KIA		ROH,16R,PP
Huey, A.M.	Cpl.	B 7th SCVIBn	25	FD	02/14/62	At home	DOD	(JR=2/17/62)	ROH,JR,HFC,HAG
Huff, D.M.	Pvt.	A 19th SCVI	17	OG	/ /	Cheraw, SC			ROH
Huff, D.W.	Pvt.	B 20th SCVI	29	OG	06/18/63	Sullivans I., SC	DOD		ROH
Huff, G.W.	Pvt.	B 20th SCVI	28	OG	10/13/64	Strasburg, VA	KIA		ROH,JR,KEB,CDC

SOUTH CAROLINA DEAD IN CSA SERVICE 1861-1865

NAME	RANK	C	REGIMENT	AGE	DS	DIED	WHERE	WHY	BURIED	SOURCES
Huff, J.R.	2nd Lt.	E	Ham.Leg.		GE	06/20/64	Richmond, VA		Hollywood Cem.Rchmd. U217	ROH,HC,R48
Huff, Jabery	Pvt.	C	18th SCVI	40	UN	03/29/65	Petersburg, VA	KIA		ROH
Huff, John	Pvt.	B	15th SCVI		SG	/ /	Richmond, VA	DOD		HOS,JR,KEB
Huff, Philip W.	Pvt.	B	2nd SCVI	20	GE	02/07/64	Ft. Delaware, NJ	DIP	Finn's Pt., NJ Nat. Cem.	ROH,FPH,P5,KEB
Huffman, Andrew	Pvt.	F	25th SCVI	26	OG	04/06/65	Elmira, NY	DIP	Woodlawn N.C.#2641 Elmira	ROH,FPH,P6,P65
Huffman, John	Pvt.	F	25th SCVI	36	OG	06/16/64	Petersburg, VA	DOD	Blandford Church Pbg., VA	ROH,BLC,PP,EDR
Huffman, P.M.	Pvt.	A	5th SCVC	35	OG	06/15/64	Trevillian Stn.	DOW		ROH
Huffman, W.R. (W.H.?)	Pvt.	F	25th SCVI		OG	09/14/64	Pt. Lookout, MD	DIP	C.C. Pt. Lookout, MD	ROH,FPH,HAG,P1
Huger, Cleland Kinloch	2nd Lt.	E	1st SCVA	20	CN	02/26/64	Charleston, SC	DOD	Magnolia Cem. Charleston	MAG,SCA,R44
Huger, Joseph Proctor	Pvt.		Signal Cp.	19	CN	03/15/64	Ft. Sumter, SC	KIA	Huegenont Ch. Charleston	ROH,MAG,CGW
Huger, Stephen Proctor	Cpt.		ADC Gen. S	21	CN	01/25/63	Corinth, MS	DOD	Huegenont Ch. Charleston	ROH,MAG,RCD
Huger, Thomas B.	Lt.		CS McRae		CN	04/24/62	New Orleans	DOW	Magnolia Cem. Charleston	ROH,CDC,CNM
Huger,Jr., Daniel E.	Cpt.		Insp. Gen.	24	CN	09/20/63	Chickamauga, GA	KIA	Huegenont Ch. Charleston	ROH,MAG,CGW,RC
Huggins,	Pvt.	C	8th SCVI		CD	07/05/62	Richmond, VA	DOD	(Typhoid)	JR
Huggins, A. Harrison	Pvt.	L	10th SCVI		MN	06/25/62	Goodman, MS	DOD		RAS,HMC,PP
Huggins, B.	Pvt.	G	20th SCVI		SR	11/19/64	Staunton, VA		(KEB= Willie)	ROH,KEB
Huggins, C.J. (Hagins?)	Pvt.	B	12th SCVI		YK	08/04/62	Richmond, VA	DOD	Hollywood Cem.Rchmd. Q142	JR,HC
Huggins, Christopher	4th Sgt.	L	21st SCVI	33	MN	06/15/64	At home	DOD	(POW @ Morris I.)	ROH,HMC,HAG,P2
Huggins, Christopher C.	Pvt.	E	1st SCVIG		MN	07/24/62	Richmond, VA	DOD	(Richmond effects list)	ROH,JR,SA1,CDC
Huggins, Daniel W.	Pvt.	G	7th SCVIBn		RD	09/13/62	Columbia, SC	DOD		ROH,PP
Huggins, F.	Pvt.	F	8th SCVI		DN	07/15/61	Charlottesville	DOD	(Typhoid)	JR
Huggins, Frank A.	Pvt.	K	7th SCVC		KW	/ /		KIA		HIC
Huggins, G.W.	Cpl.	H	10th SCVI		WG	07/22/64	Atlanta, GA	KIA		RAS,HOW
Huggins, J.M.	Pvt.	M	P.S.S.			/ /		DOD		JR
Huggins, Jasper A.	Pvt.	E	1st SCVIG		MN	06/21/63	Richmond, VA	DOW	(Wdd @ Chancelorsville)	ROH,SA1,PDL,HM
Huggins, John C.	Cpl.	E	21st SCVI	30	CD	05/07/64	Port Walthall Jn	KIA		ROH,JR,CDC,HAG
Huggins, Neal C.	Pvt.	L	10th SCVI		MN	01/22/65	Nashville, TN	DOW	(In enemy hands)	RAS,HMC,P3,P5
Huggins, Neal C.	Pvt.		McQueen LA		MN	08/18/64	Davis Farm, VA	KIA		HMC,CDC
Huggins, S.M.	Pvt.	A	14th SCVI	17	DN	07/21/65	At home	DOD		ROH
Huggins, W.J.	Pvt.	I	21st SCVI		MN	09/25/64	Elmira, NY	DIP	Woodlawn N.C.#385 Elmira	FPH,P5,P65,P12
Huggins, Wesley	Pvt.	L	21st SCVI		MN	01/15/65	Ft. Fisher, NC	KIA		HMC,HAG,PP
Huggins, William D.	Pvt.	L	21st SCVI		MN	/ /		KIA	(1864)	HMC,HAG
Hughes, D.K.	Pvt.	F	Orr's Ri.		PS	07/03/62	Gaines' Mill, VA	DOW		JR
Hughes, F. Porcher	Sgt. Major	A	Ham.Leg.		CN	10/14/64	Richmond, VA	KIA		ROH,WLI
Hughes, G.P.	Pvt.	I	2nd SCVIRi	22	OG	06/28/62	James Island, SC	DOD		ROH
Hughes, Hampton	Pvt.	C	16th SCVI		GE	03/15/62		DOD	(Measles)	JR
Hughes, Henry	Pvt.	B	1st SCVA			04/19/65	Pt. Lookout, MD	DIP	C.C. Pt. Lookout, MD	ROH,FPH,P6,P11
Hughes, Henry M.	Pvt.	A	1st SCVIBn		CN	09/04/63	Bty. Wagner, SC	DOW		JR,HAG
Hughes, Horlan	Pvt.	K	5th SCVI	34	SG	05/02/63	Petersburg, VA	DOD	Blandford Church Pbg., VA	ROH,SA3,BLC,PP
Hughes, J.	Pvt.	G	2nd SCVIRi			/ /	Richmond, VA			ROH
Hughes, J.C.	Pvt.	C	22nd SCVI	44	SG	10/15/62	At home	DOW	(Date app. Wdd @ S.Mtn.MD)	ROH,HOS
Hughes, J.H.	Pvt.	B	3rd SCVIBn		LS	09/20/63	Ft. Delaware, DE	DIP	Finn's Pt., NJ Nat. Cem.	FPH,P5,P40,KEB
Hughes, J.H.	Pvt.	C	2nd SCVC		SG	09/18/63	Ft. Delaware, DE	DIP	Finn's Pt., NJ Nat. Cem.	ROH,FPH,P5,P47
Hughes, J.W.	Pvt.	H	17th SCVI			08/30/62	Danville, VA	DOD		JR
Hughes, John	Pvt.	I	1st SCVIG			05/23/65	Hart's Island NY	DIP	Cypress Hills N.C. #2898	CGS,FPH,P6,P79
Hughes, John B.	Pvt.	K	2nd SCVIRi	18	PS	08/16/64	Fussell's Mill	KIA	(JR=8/12/64)	ROH,JR,CDC
Hughes, Joseph S.	Pvt.	C	19th SCVCB		ED	04/25/65	Pt. Lookout, MD	DIP	C.C. Pt. Lookout, MD	ROH,FPH,P6,P11
Hughes, N.W.	Pvt.	D	2nd SCVI		SR	12/13/62	Fredericksburg	KIA		ROH,SA2,H2
Hughes, Nathaniel	Pvt.	B	11th SCVI		CO	02/06/64	Charleston, SC	DOD	Magnolia Cem. Charleston	ROH,MAG
Hughes, Pinckney	Pvt.	H	16th SCVI		GE	/ /	At home	DOD	(On active duty ?)	16R
Hughes, Robert	Pvt.	C	22nd SCVI		SG	01/15/64	Charleston, SC	DOD		ROH

H

SOUTH CAROLINA DEAD IN CSA SERVICE 1861-1865

NAME	RANK	C REGIMENT	AGE	DS	DIED	WHERE	WHY	BURIED	SOURCES
Hughes, S.D.	Pvt.	E 14th SCVI		LS	02/16/64	Pt. Lookout, MD	DOW	C.C. Pt. Lookout, MD	ROH,FPH,CGS,P1
Hughes, T.J.	Pvt.	D 2nd SC Res	40	WG	/ /		DOD	(1864)	CTA,HOW
Hughes, Thomas	Pvt.	E 14th SCVI		LS	05/05/63	Chancellorsville	KIA	(CGS=Wilderness, 1864)	ROH,CGS
Hughes, Thomas H.	Pvt.	B 15th SCVI		SG	08/30/62	2nd Manassas, VA	KIA		ROH,JR,HOS,KEB
Hughes, Timothy H.	Pvt.	K 12th SCVI	24	PS	09/15/62	Warrenton, VA	DOW	(Wdd @ 2nd Man.)	ROH,JR
Hughes, W.	Pvt.		48	ED	01/07/64	Petersburg, VA	DOW	Blandford Church Pbg., VA	BLC,PP
Hughes, W.C.	Pvt.	F Orr's Ri.		PS	04/30/63	Richmond, VA	DOD	(Probably Cpl. W.J.)	ROH,JR
Hughes, Wesley Addison	Pvt.	A 19th SCVI	22	AE	06/20/62	Okolona, MS	DOD		ROH,PP,TOD
Hughes, William	Pvt.	H Ham.Leg.	25	OG	06/15/64	VA	DOD		ROH
Hughes, William	Pvt.	H 16th SCVI		GE	08/05/64	At home	DOD		16R,PP
Hughes, William	Pvt.	K 10th SCVI		CN	05/31/62	Canton, MS	DOD	Con.Cem. Canton, MS Gv#255	RAS,PP,TOD
Hughes, William B.	Sgt.	A 22nd SCVI		ED	09/14/62	South Mtn., MD	KIA		ROH,PP
Hughes, William F.	Pvt.	K 1st SCVIH		OG	10/25/62	Warrenton, VA	DOW	(Wdd @ 2nd Man.)	ROH,SA1
Hughes, William H.	Pvt.	A Ham.Leg.	25	CN	08/03/64	Greenville, SC	DOD	Magnolia Cem. Charleston	ROH,MAG,WLI
Hughes, William T.	Pvt.	E 13th SCVI		SG	11/26/61			DOD (JR=Co.B)	JR,HOS
Hughey, Frederick T.	Pvt.	F 2nd SCVI		AE	10/19/64	Cedar Creek, VA	DOW	(In enemy hands)	ROH,KEB,SA2
Hughey, James Edward	Pvt.	F 2nd SCVI	21	AE	03/08/62	Richmond, VA	DOD	(H2=Culpepper, VA)	ROH,SA2,KEB,H2
Hughey, James Samuel	Pvt.	6th SCVC	18	AE	07/22/64	Trevillian Stn.	KIA		ROH
Hughey, Nimrod M.	Pvt.	F 2nd SCVI		AE	09/17/62	Sharpsburg, MD	KIA	Rose Hill C. Hagerstown MD	ROH,JR,SA2,BOD
Hughey, W.M.	Pvt.	A 1st SCVC		AE	11/05/64	James Island, SC	DOD		ROH
Hughey, William M.	2nd Sgt.	C 5th SCVI		SG	12/14/61	Lynchburg, VA	DOD	Lynchburg CSA Cem.#8 R4	SA3,BBW
Hughston, Elisha W.R.	Pvt.	K P.S.S.		SG	05/31/62	7 Pines, VA	KIA		JR,HOS
Hughston, George R.	Pvt.	K P.S.S.		SG	05/31/62	7 Pines, VA	KIA	(CNM=George F.)	JR,HOS,CDC,CNM
Huiett, Joseph R.	4th Sgt.	B 14th SCVI	20	ED	06/30/62	Frayser's Farm	DOW	Hulett Fam. Cem. ED Cty.	ROH,JR,UD3,EDN
Huin, W.D.	Pvt.	E 2nd SCVIRi		PS	10/03/64	Richmond, VA			ROH
Hull, S.J.	Lt.				/ /			Magnolia Cem. Charleston	MAG
Hull, Samuel	Pvt.	E 11th SCVI		BT	03/18/65	Elmira, NY	DIP	Woodlawn N.C.#1723 Elmira	FPH,HAG,P65,P120
Hull, William H.	Pvt.	D 11th SCVI		BT	05/16/64	Fts. Monroe, VA	DOW	Probably N.C. Hampton, VA	ROH,HAG,P12
Humphrey, M.C.	Pvt.	C 7th SCVI			02/05/63	Richmond, VA			ROH
Humphrey, Moses B.	Cpl.	F 6th SCVC	25	CL	04/30/65	Charlotte, NC	DOW		R43,CAG
Humphrey, S.R.	Pvt.	C Ham.Leg.		CL	08/30/62	2nd Manassas, VA	KIA		ROH,JR,CDC
Humphreys, F.M.	Sgt.	A P.S.S.		UN	06/19/64	Petersburg, VA	KIA		ROH
Humphreys, J.S.	Pvt.	H 6th SCVI		FD	/ /	Lynchburg, VA		Lynchburg CSA Cem. #7 R3	BBW
Humphreys, Simpson	Pvt.	H P.S.S.		SG	/ /	Gordonsville, VA	DOD	(HOS=Martinsburg, VA)	ROH,JR,HOS
Humphries, Elias J.	Pvt.	G Orr's Ri.	22	AE	07/29/62	Gaines' Mill, VA	DOW	(JR=7/12/62)	ROH,JR,CDC
Humphries, George W.	Pvt.	A 18th SCVI		UN	07/30/64	Crater, Pbg., VA	KIA		ROH,JR,BLM
Humphries, Jackson	Sgt.	K 18th SCVI	35	SG	01/01/64	Camp Morton, IN	DIP	Green Lawn C. Indianapolis	ROH,FPH,CV,P5
Humphries, John B.	2nd Cpl.	E 5th SCVI		CR	10/28/63	Lookout Valley	KIA	UD3	ROH,JR,SA3,HHC
Humphries, R.	Pvt.	A P.S.S.			06/19/64	Petersburg, VA	DOW		JR
Humphries, W.L.	Pvt.	E 27th SCVI			10/01/64	Elmira, NY	DIP	Woodlawn N.C.#404 Elmira	FPH,HAG,P65,P120
Hungerpiler, J.S.	Pvt.	H Ham.Leg.		RD	09/20/62	Warrenton, VA	DOW	(Wdd 2nd Man)	ROH
Hungerpiler, C.	Pvt.	I 3rd SCVI		LS	07/02/63	Gettysburg, PA	KIA		ROH,JR,GDR,SA2
Hungerpiler, J.J.	Pvt.	G 27th SCVI		CN	02/13/65	Elmira, NY	DIP	Woodlawn N.C.#2068 Elmira	FPH,HAG,P65,P120
Hungerpiler, Lewis	Pvt.	B 20th SCVI	33	OG	06/02/64	Cold Harbor, VA	KIA		ROH,KEB
Hunnicutt, Andrew Y.	Pvt.	E Orr's Ri.	18	PS	06/27/62	Gaines' Mill, VA	KIA		ROH,JR,CDC
Hunnicutt, Giles M.	Pvt.	E Orr's Ri.	28	PS	07/04/63	Gettysburg, PA	DOD		ROH,CDC
Hunnicutt, J.	Cpt.	12th SCVI			07/01/63	Gettysburg, PA	KIA		CGS
Hunnicutt, J.B.	Pvt.	G 12th SCVI		PS	06/27/64	Richmond, VA	DOW	Hollywood Cem.Rchmd. U659	JR,HC,CDC
Hunnicutt, J.R.	2nd Lt.	G 12th SCVI		PS	08/29/62	2nd Manassas, VA	KIA		ROH,JR,R47
Hunnicutt, L.M.	Pvt.	F Orr's Ri.		PS	09/28/64	Richmond, VA		Hollywood Cem.Rchmd. V547	ROH,HC,CDC
Hunnicutt, Milton Reese	Pvt.	E 4th SCVI	17	PS	07/21/61	1st Manassas, VA	KIA	Hopewell B.C. Seneca, SC	ROH,JR,OCS,SA2

SOUTH CAROLINA DEAD IN CSA SERVICE 1861-1865

NAME	RANK	C REGIMENT	AGE	DS	DIED	WHERE	WHY	BURIED	SOURCES
Hunsinger, F.	Pvt.	G 24th SCVI	33		09/20/63	Chickamauga, GA	KIA		ROH,JR,CDC
Hunsucker, Frank C.	Cpl.	H 7th SCVIBn	34	CR	05/16/64	Drury's Bluff VA	KIA		ROH,JR,HAG
Hunsucker, Martin C.	Cpl.	I 6th SCVI		CR	09/30/64	Chaffin's Farm	KIA		ROH,HHC,CB
Hunt, Columbus M.	Pvt.	E 15th SCVI	20	FD	12/01/61	Savannah, GA	DOW	(Wdd @ Hilton Head 11/7)	ROH,JR,PP,HFC
Hunt, Elijah	Pvt.	24th SCVI					DIP	(POW @ Kenesaw Mtn.,lost)	EJM
Hunt, George	Pvt.	B 1st SCSSBn		ED	07/20/63		DOD		JR
Hunt, Giles	Pvt.	A 6th SCVIBn		MN	08/13/62		DOD		JR
Hunt, Harleston H.	5th Sgt.	H 4th SCVI		PS	08/24/61	Germantown, VA	DOD		SA2
Hunt, James	Pvt.	E 6th SCVI		CR	/ /	Manchester, VA			HHC
Hunt, James E.	Pvt.	L 8th SCVI		MN	/ /	Virginia			HMC,KEB
Hunt, James F.	Sgt.	C 16th SCVI		GE	11/30/64	Franklin, TN	KIA	Macgavock C. Frkln Gv#16	ROH,16R,WCT,PP
Hunt, John H.	Pvt.	K 6th SCVI		GE	08/21/61	Fairfax, VA	DOD		ROH
Hunt, Joseph L.	Pvt.	G 24th SCVI			06/12/62	Secessionville	DOW	(JR=7/13/62)	JR,CDC,PP
Hunt, L.S.	Pvt.	E 3rd SCVIBn		LS	05/26/65	Pt. Lookout, MD	DIP	C.C. Pt. Lookout, MD	FPH,KEB,P6,P11
Hunt, P.O.	Pvt.	D 11th SCVIB		CL	05/16/62	Charleston, SC	DOD	Magnolia Cem. Charleston	ROH,JR,MAG,HAG
Hunt, Robert	Pvt.	G 4th SCVI		GE	08/24/61	Germantown, VA	DOD	(HOF= Hunt, Co.I)	HOF,SA2
Hunt, W.B.	Pvt.	C 16th SCVI		GE	/ /	Dalton, GA	DOD		16R
Hunt, W.W.	Pvt.	H 6th SCVI		FD	05/31/62	7 Pines, VA	KIA		WDB,HFC
Hunt, William Pickens	1st Lt.	K 6th SCVC		AN	08/23/64	Graveley Run, VA	KIA	Carmel P.C. Liberty, SC	JR,PCS,SA2,R43
Hunter, A.A.	Pvt.	D 15th SCVI		KW	08/07/64		DOD	Magnolia CEm. Charleston	JR,MAG,KEB
Hunter, D.L.	Pvt.	D 1st SCVA		CN	12/20/61	Charleston, SC	DOD	Magnolia Cem. Charleston	ROH,MAG
Hunter, David T.	Pvt.	D 1st SCVIR		CN	12/18/61	SC	DOD		SA1
Hunter, H.N.	2nd Lt.	F 14th SCVI		LS	05/12/64	Spotsylvania, VA	KIA	(JR=Co.K)	JR,R47
Hunter, J.	Lt.	B 3rd SCV			05/15/64		DOW		JR
Hunter, J.	Pvt.	F 4th SCVC			05/30/64	Old Church, VA	KIA		JR
Hunter, Jacob	Pvt.	B 15th SCVAB			04/17/65	Pt. Lookout, MD	DIP	C.C. Pt. Lookout, MD	ROH,FPH,P6,P11
Hunter, James M.	Cpl.	F 4th SCVC		MN	05/30/64	Hawes Shop, VA	KIA		ROH,JR,HMC
Hunter, James P.	Pvt.	B 1st SCVIG	18	NY	05/03/63	Chancellorsville	KIA	Old Tranquil M.C. Newby Cy	ROH,NCC,ANY,SA
Hunter, James T.	Pvt.	2nd SC Res	46	NY	09/27/64	Charleston, SC	DOD		ROH,ANY
Hunter, John	Pvt.	G 22nd SCVI	45	AN	07/07/63	Farmville, VA	DOD		ROH
Hunter, M.L.	Pvt.	I 3rd SCVI		LS	06/01/64	Cold Harbor, VA	KIA		ROH,JR,SA2
Hunter, P.S.	Pvt.	B 1st SCVIG	23	NY	06/27/62	Gaines' Mill, VA	KIA	(Rchmd effects list) CDC	ROH,JR,ANY,SA1
Hunter, Samuel M.	Pvt.	E 14th SCVI		LS	/ /		DOD		CGS
Hunter, Thomas F.	1st Lt.	D 13th SCVI	27	NY	06/10/63	Chancellorsville	DOW		ROH,ANY,R47
Hunter, W.T.	Pvt.	B 15th SCVAB			09/20/63	Bty. Wagner, SC	DOW		JR
Hunter, William	Pvt.	G 22nd SCVI	41	AN	07/30/64	Crater, Pbg., VA	KIA		ROH,BLM
Hunter, William J.	Pvt.	D 13th SCVI	25	NY	05/12/64	Spotsylvania, VA	KIA		ROH,ANY
Hunter, William P.	2nd Lt.	B 3rd SCVI	27	NY	05/06/64	Wilderness, VA	KIA		ROH,JR,ANY,SA2
Hunter, William R.	Pvt.	B 26th SCVI	21	CD	07/01/64	Petersburg, VA	KIA		ROH,CDC
Hurburt, D.T.	Pvt.	K 1st SCVC	30	PS	09/25/64	Charleston, SC	DOD	Magnolia Cem. Charleston	ROH,MAG
Hurburt, J.D.	Pvt.	K 22nd SCVI		PS	09/17/62	Sharpsburg, MD	KIA		ROH
Hurburt, J.M.	Pvt.	K 22nd SCVI		PS	09/07/62	Richmond, VA	DOD		ROH
Hurd, Thomas	Pvt.	5th SCVC			/ /	Gordonsville, VA			ROH
Hurley, C.C.	Pvt.	C 14th SCVI		LS	06/19/65	Hart's Island NY	DIP	Cypress Hills N.C.#3029 NY	FPH,P79
Hurley, Charles	Pvt.	H 1st SCVIG		BT	09/15/64	At home	DOD	(DIS 8/29/62 lost arm)	ROH,SA1
Hurley, J.R.	Pvt.	7th SCV			05/27/64	Richmond, VA		Hollywood Cem.Rchmd. I26	HC
Hurlong, J.A.	Pvt.	B 1st SCVIH		OG	02/03/63	Lynchburg, VA	DOD		ROH,SA1
Hurst, Isaac	Pvt.	4th SCVI	27	CD	05/15/64	At home	DOD		ROH
Hurst, Isaac	Pvt.	B 9th SCVIBn			06/25/62	Secessionville	DOW		JR
Hurst, Isaac F.	Pvt.	A 12th SCVCB		CD	10/04/62	Georgetown, SC	DOD		ROH,PP
Hurst, Jacob C.	Pvt.	A 4th SCVC		CD	06/15/64		DOD		ROH

SOUTH CAROLINA DEAD IN CSA SERVICE 1861-1865

NAME	RANK	C	REGIMENT	AGE	DS	DIED	WHERE	WHY	BURIED	SOURCES
Hurst, James M. (A.?)	2nd Sgt.	A	1st SCVIBn	22	CN	07/26/63	Beaufort, SC	DOW	St.Mary's R.C. Charleston	MAG,RCD,P10,PP
Hurst, Leander	2nd Lt.	C	8th SCVI		CD	07/01/62	Malvern Hill, VA	KIA	(JR=7/12/62)	ROH,JR,KEB,R46
Hurst, S.H.	Pvt.		4th SCVC			/ /	Gordonsville, VA			ROH
Hurston, A.L.	Pvt.	L	Orr's Ri.			/ /	Marietta, GA		Con.Cem. Marietta, GA	CCM,CDC
Hurt, James	Pvt.	G	6th SCVI		PS	11/22/61	Richmond, VA		Hollywood Cem.Rchmd. B329	HC
Hurt, Kindred	Pvt.	C	1st SCVIG		PS	12/08/64	Elmira, NY	DIP	Woodlawn N.C.#1189 Elmira	FPH,SA1,P65,P120
Hurt, Luke	Pvt.	B	8th SCVI		CD	11/19/62	Richmond, VA	DOD	Hollywood Cem.Rchmd. S302	ROH,JR,HC
Hurtt, Abram F.	Pvt.	A	19th SCVI	40	ED	07/22/64	Atlanta, GA	KIA		HOE,UD3
Huskey, Richard	Pvt.	I	5th SCVI	40	SG	10/05/64	Richmond, VA	DOD	Hollywood Cem.Rchmd. V600	ROH,HC,SA3
Huskison, M.H.	Pvt.	L	Orr's Ri.		AN	06/27/62	Sullivans I., SC	DOD		JR,CDC
Husky, James P.	Pvt.	A	13th SCVI		LS	07/03/63	Gettysburg, PA	KIA	Gettysburg, PA	ROH,JR,GDR,CDC
Husky, W.H.	1st Cpl.	I	3rd SCVI		LS	01/20/64	Knoxville, TN	DOW		ROH,SA2,ANY,KEB
Hussey, John L.	Pvt.	E	1st SCVC		OG	07/02/63	Gettysburg, PA	KIA		ROH,JR
Hussey, W.J. (HC=Hizi)	Pvt.	H	11th SCVI		CO	03/05/65	Richmond, VA		Hollywood Cem.Rchmd. W672	HC,HAG
Hustin, J.R.	Pvt.	K	7th SCVI		ED	05/26/64	Richmond, VA			ROH
Hutcherson, N.P.	Pvt.	F	10th SCVI		MN	/ /	At home	DOD	(Not a casualty in RAS)	HMC,RAS
Hutchins, Hampton	Pvt.	D	16th SCVI		GE	12/02/61	At home	DOD		PP
Hutchins, J.C.	Pvt.	I	19th SCVI		AN	09/15/63	Ray's H. Atlanta		Oakland C. Atlanta R21#10	BGA,CVG
Hutchins, W.R.	Pvt.	D	1st SCV			11/04/62			Stonewall C. Winchester VA	WIN
Hutchins, William	Pvt.		15th SCMil			04/12/65	New Bern, NC	DOW	Cedar Grove C. Newbern NC	P1,P6,WAT,PP
Hutchinson, B.F.	Pvt.	D	7th SCVI			10/13/64	Strasburg, VA	KIA		ROH,KEB
Hutchinson, D.	Pvt.	E	3rd SCVABn			/ /	Bty. Wagner, SC	DOW		CDC
Hutchinson, Elbert	Pvt.	L	2nd SCVIRi			06/29/62	Savage Stn., VA	KIA	(JR=Gaines' Mill)	ROH,JR,CDC,CNM
Hutchinson, Fletcher	Pvt.	I	2nd SCVC		ED	12/29/64	Wilmington, NC	KIA		ROH
Hutchinson, G.W.	Pvt.	I	18th SCVI	32	DN	09/07/62	Richmond, VA	DOD	Hollywood Cem.Rchmd. A70	ROH,JR,HC
Hutchinson, George	Pvt.	H	8th SCVI		MN	07/02/63	Gettysburg, PA	MIA		ROH,KEB
Hutchinson, H.	Pvt.	G	6th SCVC			01/09/65	Pt. Lookout, MD	DIP	C.C. Pt. Lookout, MD	FPH,P5,P12,P120
Hutchinson, J.A.	1st Sgt.	F	24th SCVI	27	AN	05/14/63	Jackson, MS	DOW		ROH,JR,HOL,PP
Hutchinson, J.L.	Pvt.	B	1st SCEng			06/13/64	Richmond, VA	DOD	(Cardiac & Dysentery)	ROH,P12
Hutchinson, J.W.						/ /	Virginia		(Rchmd effects list 1/63)	CDC
Hutchinson, James B.	Pvt.	E	15th SCVI	30	FD	06/24/64	Petersburg, VA	KIA		ROH,JR,KEB
Hutchinson, James L.	Pvt.	I	14th SCVI	24	AE	02/04/63	Fredericksburg	DOD	Fredericksburg C.C. R1S11	ROH,JR,FBG,HOL
Hutchinson, John H.	Sgt.	A	15th SCVI		RD	12/13/62	Fredericksburg	KIA		ROH,JR,CDC,KEB
Hutchinson, John Pope	Pvt.	E	15th SCVI	32	FD	08/01/62	Chapin's Farm VA	DOD	(JR=7/31, Chafin's 1864?)	ROH,JR,KEB
Hutchinson, John W.	Pvt.	F	2nd SCVI	34	AE	05/06/64	Wilderness, VA	KIA		ROH,JR,SA2,KEB
Hutchinson, Milton T.	1st Lt.	I	14th SCVI		AE	07/28/64	Deep Bottom, VA	KIA	(JR=7/20)	ROH,JR,BOS,R47
Hutchinson, W.C.	Pvt.	H	8th SCVI		MN	01/15/62	Charlottesville	DOD	Univ. Cem. Charlottesville	JR,HMC,KEB,ACH
Hutchinson, W.K.	Pvt.	D	P.S.S.		SG	06/15/62	Winchester, VA	DOD		ROH,HOS
Hutchinson, Wm. Soule	Pvt.	F	2nd SCVI	17	AE	06/29/62	Savage Stn., VA	KIA		ROH,SA2,KEB,H2
Hutchison, John	Pvt.	I	10th SCVI		MN	/ /	Kentucky	DOD		RAS,HMC
Hutson, Robert G.	Pvt.	G	11th SCVI		CO	07/09/64	Petersburg, VA	KIA	Blandford Church Pbg., VA	ROH,BLC,PP
Hutson, Scharner	Pvt.	A	6th SCVI		CR	06/30/62	Fraysers Farm VA	KIA		HHC
Hutson, Tilman E.	Cpl.	C	11th SCVI	22	CO	07/12/64	Petersburg, VA	DOW	Blandford Church Pbg., VA	ROH,CDC,BLC
Hutson, W.	Pvt.	F	11th SCVI	18	CO	06/10/64	Virginia	KIA		ROH,HAG
Hutson, William R.	Pvt.	G	11th SCVI		CO	03/17/64		DOD		ROH,HAG
Hutto, Andrew	Pvt.	D	15th SCMil	16	KW	04/15/65	New Bern, NC	DIP	Cedar Grove C. Newbern NC	P1,P6,WAT,PP
Hutto, Charles	Pvt.	F	17th SCVI		YK	06/23/65	NYC Transit Hos.	DIP	Cypress Hills N.C.#3041 NY	FPH,P12
Hutto, F.J.	Pvt.	C	1st SCV			05/15/64		DOW		JR
Hutto, Gideon	Pvt.	H	17th SCVI		BL	07/01/64	Petersburg, VA	KIA	(JR=Co.I)	ROH,JR
Hutto, Govan	Pvt.	K	9th SCVIB		LN	09/12/61	Germantown, VA	DOD		ROH,JR
Hutto, Jacob	Pvt.	C	24th SCVI	43	CO	09/20/63	Chickamauga, GA	KIA		ROH,JR,CDC,DRE

SOUTH CAROLINA DEAD IN CSA SERVICE 1861-1865

NAME	RANK	C	REGIMENT	AGE	DS	DIED	WHERE	WHY	BURIED	SOURCES
Hutto, James	Pvt.	K	13th SCVI		LN	10/09/61	Columbia, SC	DOD	(JR=Congestive chill 10/19	ROH,JR,PP
Hutto, John M.	Pvt.	A	14th SCMil		LN	04/27/65	Hart's Island NY	DIP	Cypress Hills N.C.#2620 NY	FPH,P6
Hutto, N.	Lt.	C	8th Res.Bn		RD	10/14/64	Charleston, SC	DOD	Magnolia Cem. Charleston	ROH,MAG,CDC
Hutto, R.S.	Pvt.	K	1st SCVIH		OG	06/30/63	Richmond, VA	DOD		SA1
Hutto, W.D.	Cpl.	D	8th SCResB			/ /	Columbia, SC	DOD	Elmwood Cem. Columbia, SC	MP,PP
Hutto, William C.	Pvt.	H	Ham.Leg.		OG	10/28/63	Lookout Valley	DOW		ROH,CDC
Hutto, William J.	1st Sgt.	K	17th SCVI	19	BL	12/22/62	At home	DOD		ROH,JR
Hux, Thomas B.	Pvt.	A	26th SCVI	28	HY	06/15/64	Petersburg, VA	KIA		ROH
Hux, W.G.	Pvt.	K	10th SCVI		CN	08/15/64	Griffin, GA	DOW	Stonewall Cem. Griffin, GA	RAS,BGA,UD2
Hyatt, Calvin	Pvt.	A	6th SCVI		CR	/ /	Virginia	KIA	(1864)	HHC
Hyatt, David	Pvt.	I	1st SCVIH		MN	09/14/62	South Mtn., MD	MIA		SA1,HMC,CDC
Hyatt, F.	Pvt.	I	11th SCVI		CO	06/25/65	Charleston, SC	DOD	Magnolia Cem. Charleston	ROH,MAG
Hyatt, George B.	Pvt.	C	5th SCVI		CR	06/19/62	Richmond, VA	DOD	(JR=G.E. & Co.E)	ROH,JR,SA3,HHC
Hyatt, Isaac	Pvt.	E	23rd SCVI			08/30/62	2nd Manassas, VA	KIA	(JR=28th SC)	JR
Hyatt, J.M.	Pvt.	C	24th SCVI	30	CO	06/26/64	Atlanta, GA	DOD		EJM
Hyatt, James R.	Pvt.	H	23rd SCVI		MN	08/30/62	2nd Manassas, VA	KIA		ROH,JR,HMC,CDC
Hyatt, Joseph	Pvt.		24th SCVI			/ /	Secessionville	DOW		JR
Hyatt, Lawrence	Pvt.	I	17th SCVI			10/26/64	Elmira, NY	DIP		P5
Hyatt, Mellard	Pvt.	C	24th SCVI	30	CO	07/03/64	Kenesaw Mtn., GA	DOW	(Severe head wound)	ROH,CDC,DRE
Hyatt, Thomas R.	Pvt.	H	23rd SCVI		MN	/ /	(VA, 1862)	DOD	(Left behind on march)	ROH,HMC
Hyatt, William K.	Pvt.	I	1st SCVIH		MN	11/15/62	Charleston	DOD	(HMC=James K.)	SA1,HMC
Hyde, J.W.	Cpl.	K	22nd SCVI		PS	07/30/64	Crater, Pbg., VA	KIA		BLM
Hyde, James	Pvt.	B	16th SCVI		GE	/ /	At home	DOD	(1863)	16R
Hyde, James H.	Pvt.	I	16th SCVI		GE	02/15/64	At home	DOD		16R,PP
Hyde, R.H.	Sgt.	C	Orr's Ri.		PS	12/08/63		DOD		JR
Hyde, Samuel Tupper	Pvt.	D	1st SCVIBn	17	CN	07/18/63	Bty. Wagner, SC	KIA	1st Baptist C. Charleston	ROH,MAG,CDC,HA
Hyde, William	Pvt.	H	1st SCVA			08/14/62	Charleston, SC	DOD	Magnolia Cem. Charleston	ROH,MAG
Hyde, William	Pvt.	C	Orr's Ri.		PS	07/14/63	Falling Waters	KIA		JR,CDC
Hyman, C.J. (C.E. ?)	Pvt.	H	8th SCVI		MN	09/20/61	Richmond, VA	DOD	Hollywood Cem.Rchmd. G208	ROH,JR,HC,HMC
Hyman, J.E. (C.?)	Pvt.	H	25th SCVI		CN	08/07/64	Petersburg, VA			PP
Hyman, T.	Pvt.				WG	/ /		KIA		HOW
Hyman, William	Pvt.	F	10th SCVI		MN	/ /		DOD	(Not a casualty in RAS)	HMC,RAS
Hynch, Thomas	Pvt.	E	1st SCVA			08/25/63	Columbia, SC	DOD	(Lynch?)	PP

SOUTH CAROLINA DEAD IN CSA SERVICE 1861-1865

NAME	RANK	C REGIMENT	AGE	DS	DIED	WHERE	WHY	BURIED	SOURCES
Ihley, L.	Pvt.	G 17th SCVI		BL	/ /	At home	DOD		JR
Imers, J.N.	Pvt.	A 4th SCVC		CD	07/15/64	Ladd's Store, VA	DOW	(Wdd 6/24/64,JR=6/12/64))	ROH,JR,P12,P79
Inabinet, Archibald	Pvt.	A 1st SCMil			05/29/65	Hart's Island NY	DIP	Cypress Hills N.C.#2918 NY	FPH,P5
Inabinet, Francis S.	Pvt.	G 25th SCVI		OG	05/20/64	Richmond, VA	DOW	(Wdd Drury's Bluff 5/16)	ROH,JR,CV,HAG
Inabinet, James V.	1st Lt.	K 1st SCVIH		LN	08/05/64	Petersburg, VA	DOW	(Wdd 6/24/64)	ROH,SA1,R45
Inabinet, John	Pvt.	E 7th SCVI		ED	/ /		DOD		HOE,UD3
Inabinet, John W.	Pvt.	M 7th SCVI	23	ED	09/03/62	Petersburg, VA			ROH,HOE,PP
Inabinet, Peter D.P.	Pvt.	K 1st SCVIH		OG	07/30/62		DOD	(JRH= 7/12/62)	ROH,SA1,JRH
Inabinet, Samuel A.	Pvt.	F 25th SCVI	27	OG	06/03/64	Cold Harbor, VA	KIA		ROH,JR
Inabinet, Samuel D.	Pvt.	Hart's LA			06/12/64	Trevillian Stn.	DOW	(Thigh amputated)	CDC,CNM
Inack, (Irick?)	Pvt.	F 1st SCV			07/06/62	Richmond, VA		Hollywood Cem.Rchmd. M158	HC
Infinger, Absolom	Pvt.	G 11th SCVI		CO	05/16/64	Drury's Bluff VA	KIA		ROH
Infinger, Henry L.	Pvt.	3rd SCVABn	22	CO	05/21/62	Charleston, SC	DOD		ROH
Ingalls, David	Pvt.	D 13th SCVI		NY	07/20/63	Baltimore, MD	DIP	Loudon Pk. C. A-82 Balto.	FPH,PP
Inge, J.S.	Cpl.	B Orr's Ri.		AE	/ /	Petersburg, VA			ROH
Ingley, D.C.	Pvt.	G 13th SCVI			09/18/62	Sharpsburg, MD	DOW		JR
Inglis, William C.	Cpl.	C 8th SCVI		CD	10/18/61	Richmond, VA	DOD	(Typhoid, JR=Adjutant)	ROH,KEB,JR
Ingraham, A.	Pvt.	K 17th SCVI			/ /	Wadmallaw, SC	DOD		JR
Ingraham, William G.	2nd Lt.	A 23rd SCVI		CN	03/01/63				R48
Ingram, John N.	3rd Sgt.	H 2nd SCVI		LR	01/17/62		DOD		SA2,LAN,KEB
Ingram, Lovick F.	Pvt.	B 4th SCVC		CR	08/25/64	Petersburg, VA	DOW	(CB=Richmond)	ROH,CB
Ingram, Moody	Pvt.	F 7th SCVIBn	37	CD	07/06/64		DOD		ROH,HIC,HAG
Inkles, Richard	Pvt.	H 21st SCVI		DN	10/28/63	Charleston, SC	DOD	Magnolia Cem. Charleston	ROH,MAG,HAG,JR
Inman, J.C.	2nd Lt.	M 10th SCVI		HY	07/22/64	Atlanta, GA	KIA	(CDC=MIA)	ROH,RAS,CDC
Inverds, C.A.	Pvt.	H 7th SCVI			11/22/62			Stonewall C. Winchester VA	WIN
Irby, C.G.	Cpl.	D Ham.Leg.		AN	/ /	Morristown, TN	DOD		GRS
Irby, G.W.	Pvt.	B 6th SCVI			07/09/62	Richmond, VA		Hollywood Cem.Rchmd. O26	HC
Irby, W. (Ivey, W.?)	Pvt.	H 15th SCVI		UN	/ /	Richmond, VA		Oakwood C.#83,Row N,Div A	OWC
Irby, Waddy Thompson	Pvt.	D 3rd SCVIBn	25	LS	09/14/62	South Mtn., MD	DOW	Mem. Mrkr. in Laurens Cem.	ROH,RHL,PP,UD3
Ireland, F.S.	Pvt.	G 25th SCVI		OG	05/23/64	Richmond, VA		Hollywood Cem.Rchmd. I131	HC
Irick, William M.	Pvt.	E 5th SCVC	40	OG	01/29/65	Pt. Lookout, MD	DIP	C.C. Pt. Lookout, MD	ROH,FPH,P5,P11
Irvin,	Pvt.	G 1st SCVIH			05/05/64	Wilderness, VA	DOW		CDC
Irvin, A.P. (A.S.?)	Pvt.	K Hol.Leg.			10/29/64	Elmira, NY	DIP		P5,P66
Irvin, David C.	Pvt.	G 22nd SCVI	35	AN	09/15/62	Salem, VA	DOD		ROH
Irvin, H.	Pvt.	E 1st SC			05/30/63	LaGrange, AL			P12
Irvin, James	Pvt.	K Orr's Ri.	23	AE	12/13/62	Fredericksburg	KIA		ROH
Irvin, John Calhoun	Pvt.	B Orr's Ri.	22	AE	12/13/62	Fredericksburg	KIA	(JR=3rd SCV)	ROH,CDC,JR
Irwin, Ephraim	Lt.	SCVA	24	BL	08/15/63	Ft. Moultrie, SC			ROH
Irwin, James R.	Pvt.	L 8th SCVI		DN	07/27/64	Deep Bottom, VA	KIA	(KEB=1.R.)	HMC,KEB
Irwin, W.J.	Pvt.	B Ham.Leg.		CR	08/28/64	Elmira, NY	DIP	Woodlawn N.C.#49 Elmira	FPH,P5,P65,HHC
Isaacs, W. Zachary	Sgt.	G 11th SCVI		CO	05/09/64	Swift Creek, VA	KIA		ROH,HAG,JR
Isbell,	Pvt.	D 2nd SCV			01/26/63	Richmond, VA		(Walter Co. C,2nd SCVI?)	ROH
Isbell, Benjamin F.	Pvt.	E 4th SCVC		MO	08/08/64	Weldon, NC			PP
Isbell, H. Lawrence	1st Lt.	B 7th SCVIBn	38	FD	08/26/64	City Point, VA	DOW	(Wdd Weldon RR 8/21 & POW)	ROH,HAG,P5,HFC
Isbell, Walter D.	2nd Sgt.	C 2nd SCVI	27	FD	07/16/63	Gettysburg, PA	DOW	Magnolia Cem. Charleston	ROH,JR,P1,GDR
Isbell, William J. (L.?)	Pvt.	B P.S.S.		PS	06/30/62	Frayser's Farm	KIA		ROH,JR,CDC,UD2
Isgett, J.E.	Pvt.	B 21st SCVI		DN	/ /				ROH
Isgett, J.W.	Pvt.	D 2nd SCVA		DN	03/15/63	At home	DOD	(Inglis L.A.)	ROH
Isom, J.W.	Pvt.	F 1st SCVIG		RD	07/04/64	Ft. Delaware, DE	DIP	Finn's Pt. NJ Nat. Cem.	ROH,FPH,P5,SA1
Isom, M.C.	Pvt.	A P.S.S.			/ /		DOD		JR
Itgen, F.	Pvt.	B 1st SCVA		CN	11/07/61	Port Royal, SC	KIA	(German Artillery)	ROH,CDC,JR

I

SOUTH CAROLINA DEAD IN CSA SERVICE 1861-1865

NAME	RANK	C REGIMENT	AGE	DS	DIED	WHERE	WHY	BURIED	SOURCES
Ittner, John	Pvt.	E 25th SCVI		CN	09/07/63	Bty. Wagner, SC	KIA	(JR=10/5/63)	ROH,CDC,HAG,JR
Ives, James Matthew	Pvt.	E 7th SCVIBn	19	SR	07/10/63	Morris Island SC	KIA		ROH,HAG,JR
Ives, William Thomas	Pvt.	E 7th SCVIBn	29	SR	03/28/63	Adams Run, SC	DOD	PP	ROH,JR,DOD,HAG
Ivey, Berry	Pvt.	E 1st SCVIG		MN	09/03/64	Richmond, VA	DOW	Hollywood Cem.Rchmd. V490	ROH,HC,PDL,SA1
Ivey, Calvin	Pvt.	A 18th SCVI			06/13/62	Charleston, SC	DOD		JR
Ivey, H.	Pvt.	A 18th SCVI		UN	07/30/64	Crater, Pbg., VA	KIA		ROH,BLM,JR
Ivey, Isaac	Cpl.	D 12th SCVI		RD	07/22/64	Richmond, VA	DOW	Hollywood Cem.Rchmd. V307	ROH,HC,JR
Ivey, J.	Pvt.	K 15th SCVI		AE	08/10/64	Petersburg, VA	KIA	(KEB= Ivy, T.)	ROH,KEB
Ivey, J.W.	Pvt.	B 7th SCVI			07/09/62	Richmond, VA			ROH
Ivey, James	Pvt.			SR	06/15/63	At home	DOD		ROH
Ivey, John	Pvt.	E 3rd SCVABn		SR	07/18/62	Charleston, SC	DOD	Magnolia Cem. Charleston	ROH,MAG
Ivey, Robert	Pvt.	H 15th SCVI		UN	/ /		DOD		JR,KEB
Ivey, Samuel J.	Pvt.	Ham.Leg. A			06/20/62	White House, VA	KIA		ROH
Ivey, Wiley	Pvt.	H 15th SCVI		UN	/ /		DOD		JR,KEB
Ivey, William	Pvt.	H 15th SCVI		UN	/ /	Richmond, VA	DOD		ROH,JR,KEB
Ivy, H.M.	Cpl.	G 23rd SCVI		MO	08/30/62	2nd Manassas, VA	DOW	(JR=H.L. & 28th SC)	JR,HOM,CDC
Ivy, Joel	Pvt.	A 14th SCVI	30	SR	12/11/63	At home	DOD	(JR=3/28/62)	ROH,JR
Ivy, W.J.					/ /			(Rchmd effects list 12/62)	CDC
Ivy, William	Pvt.	B 6th SCVI		LR	07/10/62	Richmond, VA	ACD		ROH,LAN

SOUTH CAROLINA DEAD IN CSA SERVICE 1861-1865

NAME	RANK	C	REGIMENT	AGE	DS	DIED	WHERE	WHY	BURIED	SOURCES
J...., N.	Pvt.					/ /	(Johnson, N.M.?)		Fredericksburg C.C. R6S11	FBG
J....., W.	Pvt.					/ /	(Jordan, Wm.?)		Fredericksburg N.C. R1S11	FBG
Jabbert, John	Pvt.	I	3rd SCMil		LR	02/17/65	Columbia, SC	DOD		ROH,PP
Jacks, T. Isaac	Pvt.	I	3rd SCVI		LS	08/20/61	Richmond, VA	DOD		SA2,JR,KEB
Jackson, Alfred	Pvt.		Chstfld LA		CD	11/09/64	Kinston, NC	EXC	(Shot as a deserter)	R44
Jackson, Allen	1st Cpl.	I	2nd SCVI	25	CN	01/09/63	Richmond, VA	DOW	Magnolia Cem. Charleston	ROH,MAG,SA2,KE
Jackson, Andrew H.	Pvt.	A	12th SCVI	18	YK	08/29/62	2nd Manassas, VA	KIA		ROH,JR,CDC,YEB
Jackson, Benjamin N.	Pvt.	A	12th SCVI	18	YK	08/29/62	2nd Manassas, VA	KIA		ROH,JR,CDC,YEB
Jackson, D.R.	Pvt.	E	17th SCVI	36	YK	11/30/62	Richmond, VA	DOD		ROH,JR
Jackson, David	Sgt.	A	12th SCVI	31	YK	08/29/62	2nd Manassas, VA	KIA		ROH,JR,CDC,YEB
Jackson, David F.	Pvt.	I	Hol.Leg.	25	SG	01/15/63	Goldsboro, NC	DOD	Prob Willowdale C. G'boro	ROH,HOS,PP
Jackson, David Henry	Cpl.	G	P.S.S.	24	YK	05/09/63	Petersburg, VA	DOD	Blandford Church Pbg., VA	JR,BLC,YEB,PP
Jackson, E. Bellinger	Pvt.	A	5th SCVC		OG	09/27/63	Columbia, SC	DOD	(Ladies' Hospital)	ROH,JR,PP
Jackson, Ellis T.	Sgt.	I	Hol.Leg.	28	SG	09/22/62	Warrenton, VA	DOW	(Wdd 2nd Man)	ROH,HOS
Jackson, Enos	Pvt.	G	8th SCVI	16	MO	/ /			(1864)	HOM,KEB,UD2
Jackson, F.B.	Pvt.	B	1st SCVC		SG	08/02/63	Gettysburg, PA	DIP	(Typhoid Fever)	ROH,CDC,P1,P12
Jackson, H.H.	Pvt.	F	P.S.S.			/ /		DOW		JR
Jackson, H.K.	Pvt.	H	19th SCVI	36	AE	04/20/65	At home	DOD		ROH
Jackson, H.M.	Pvt.	F	P.S.S.		LN	06/02/62	Fts. Monroe, VA	DOW	(Wdd @ Wmbg. or 7 Pines)	ROH,JR,CNM
Jackson, Henry H.	1st Sgt.	D	8th SCVI		CD	05/03/62	Williamsburg, VA	KIA		JR,KEB
Jackson, J. Alexander	Pvt.	B	1st SCVC.	32	SG	04/24/64	Pt. Lookout, MD	DIP	C.C. Pt. Lookout, MD	ROH,FPH,HOS,P5
Jackson, James	Pvt.	I	Hol.Leg.	26	SG	07/15/63	Spartanburg, SC	DOD		ROH
Jackson, James A.	Pvt.	E	Orr's Ri.	22	PS	11/01/62	Lynchburg, VA	DOW	(JR=KIA @ Charlottesville)	ROH,JR,CDC
Jackson, James S.	Pvt.	K	13th SCVI		LN	09/12/62	Virginia	DOD	(JR=8/29/62)	ROH,JR
Jackson, John	Pvt.					08/11/62	Charleston area		Magnolia Cem. Charleston	RCD
Jackson, John C.	Pvt.	K	8th SCVI		MO	10/20/64	Camp Chase, OH	DIP	C.C.#341 Columbus OH	FPH,P6,KEB,P22
Jackson, John F.	Pvt.	K	19th SCVI			07/01/62	Enterprise, MS	DOD	Prob on Enterprise,MS C.C.	JR,PP
Jackson, John O.	Pvt.		P.S.S.	37	YK	06/06/64	Richmond, VA	DOD	Hollywood Cem.Rchmd. U408	ROH,HC,YMD,YEB
Jackson, John T.	Pvt.	I	1st SCVIH		MN	01/20/65	At home	DOD		SA1,HMC
Jackson, Joseph C.	Pvt.	E	4th SCVC		MO	08/12/64	Elmira, NY	DIP	Woodlawn N.C.#133 Elmira	FPH,P120,P65,H
Jackson, Joseph L.	Pvt.	G	18th SCVI	21	YK	08/30/62	2nd Manassas, VA	KIA		ROH,JR,CDC,YEB
Jackson, Middleton	Pvt.	K	10th SCVI		CN	05/31/62	Enterprise, MS	DOD	Prob in unknown C.C. there	RAS,PP
Jackson, Oliver S.	Pvt.	C	24th SCVI	30	CO	05/21/62	James Island SC	DOD	Magnolia Cem. Charleston	ROH,MAG,EJM
Jackson, Parks A.	Pvt.	G	18th SCVI	22	YK	05/20/64	Clay's Farm, VA	DOW	Beersheba P.C. Yk County	ROH,JR,YMD,YEB
Jackson, R.C.	Pvt.					06/01/62	Fts. Monroe, VA	DOW	(Probably 7 Pines)	CDC,CNM
Jackson, R.D.	1st Sgt.	D	8th SCVI		CD	12/04/61	Richmond, VA	DOD	(Typhoid)	JR
Jackson, Ransom	Pvt.	C	6th SCVI		KW	/ /	Virginia	DOD		HIC
Jackson, Robert	Pvt.	B	1st SCVC	30	SG	07/15/63	Gettysburg, PA	DOW	(DOW in enemy hands @ Gbg)	ROH,HOS
Jackson, Robert A.	2nd Lt.	G	18th SCVI	27	YK	07/14/64	Petersburg, VA	KIA	(JR=7/30/64)	ROH,JR,YMD,YEB
Jackson, Robert M.	Pvt.	C	18th SCVI		YK	07/30/64	Crater, Pbg. VA	KIA		ROH,JR,BLM
Jackson, S.						/ /	Columbia, SC		Elmwood Cem. Columbia, SC	MP,PP
Jackson, Samuel	Pvt.	E	1st SCVIH		BL	02/09/64	At home	DOD		ROH,SA1,JRH
Jackson, Selkirk	Pvt.	H	23rd SCVI		MN	/ /	Petersburg, VA	KIA	(1864)	HMC
Jackson, T.H.	Pvt.		13th SCVI		LN	07/05/62	Richmond, VA		Hollywood Cem.Rchmd. M205	HC
Jackson, T.J.	Pvt.	D	12th SCVI		RD	05/06/64	Wilderness, VA	KIA		JR
Jackson, Thomas J.	Pvt.	H	6th SCVI	28	RD	10/04/64	City Pt., VA	DOW	Prob. N.C. Hopewell, VA	ROH,P12
Jackson, Warren A.	Pvt.	I	1st SCVIH		MN	09/05/64	At home	DOD		SA1,HMC
Jackson, William	Pvt.	K	10th SCVI		CN	06/10/62	Canton, MS	DOD		RAS,PP
Jackson, William	Pvt.	I	12th SCVI		LR	05/27/64	Virginia	KIA		LAN
Jackson, William B.	Pvt.	A	12th SCVI	20	YK	07/07/63	Gettysburg, PA	DOW		JR,YEB
Jacobs, A. Jackson	Pvt.	A	21st SCVI		GN	11/01/64	Elmira, NY	DIP	Woodlawn N.C.#756 Elmira	ROH,JR,FPH,P65

J

SOUTH CAROLINA DEAD IN CSA SERVICE 1861-1865

NAME	RANK	C REGIMENT	AGE	DS	DIED	WHERE	WHY	BURIED	SOURCES
Jacobs, Archie	Pvt.	D 26th SCVI		MO	/ /	Petersburg, VA			HOM
Jacobs, B.L.	Pvt.	F 21st SCVI		MO	/ /		DOD		HOM,HAG
Jacobs, Isaiah	2nd Lt.	D 2nd SCVI		SR	09/24/63	Chickamauga, GA	DOW		ROH,JR,SA2,KEB
Jacobs, J.J.	Pvt.	B 10th SCVI		HY	11/30/64	Franklin, TN	KIA		RAS
Jacobs, James S.	Pvt.	A 21st SCVI		GN	10/04/64	Charleston, SC	DOD	Magnolia Cem. Charleston	ROH,MAG,HAG
Jacobs, Joseph	Pvt.	C 20th SCVI	33	LN	08/28/64	New Market Hts.	DOW	City Pt. N.C. Hopewell, VA	ROH,TOD,KEB,PP
Jacobs, Leonard F.	Cpl.	A 26th SCVI	31	HY	06/15/63	Jackson, MS	DOD		ROH,PP
Jacobs, N.L.	Pvt.	A 21st SCVI		GN	06/16/64	Petersburg, VA	KIA		ROH,LOR,HAG,CDC
Jacobs, Thomas Pressley	Pvt.	E 14th SCVI	20	LS	07/01/63	Gettysburg, PA	KIA		UD3 ROH,JR,CGS,RHL
Jacobs, Y.	Pvt.	D 12th SCVI		RD	09/17/62	Sharpsburg, MD	KIA		JR
Jacobs,, John Elijah	Pvt.	I 15th SCVI	28	LN	06/20/64	Richmond, VA	DOW	(Wdd.@ Spotsylvania)	ROH,KEB,LNC,H15
Jacques, Robert	Pvt.	G 4th SCVC	32	CO	08/09/63	Fields Pt., SC	ACD	(Camp on Combahee River)	ROH,SSO,PP
Jager, John	Pvt.	D 5th SCVC	29	CN	04/20/63	Green Pond, SC	DOD		ROH,PP
Jaggers, John H.	Pvt.	I 6th SCVI		CR	09/30/64	Chaffin's Farm	KIA	(+ Slight Wd. @ 7 Pines)	ROH,CDC,CB
Jamerson, W.	Pvt.	SCV			/ /	Murfreesboro, TN		Evergreen C. Murfreesboro	TOD
James, A.	Pvt.	C 10th SCVI		HY	10/01/62	Atlanta, GA	DOD	Oakland Cem. Atlanta R5#46	RAS,BGA,CVGH
James, A.F.	Cpl.	B 13th SCVI		SG	10/22/64	Pt. Lookout, MD	DIP	C.C. Pt. Lookout, MD	FPH,P6,HOS,P114
James, David A.	Pvt.	F 12th SCVI		FD	/ /	White House, VA	KIA		ROH,HFC
James, E.A.	Pvt.	F 14th SCVI			09/17/62	Sharpsburg, MD	KIA		JR
James, G.M. (G.W.?)					/ /			(Rchmd effects list 12/62)	CDC
James, Gamaliel W.	Cpl.	K 3rd SCVI		SG	07/15/62	Malvern Hill, VA	DOW		ROH,SA2,HOS,KEB
James, George	Pvt.	F 16th SCVI		GE	/ /	Charleston, SC	DOD		16R
James, George	Pvt.	H 10th SCVI		WG	06/15/61	South Island, SC	DOD	(Date approx)	RAS
James, George Sholter	Lt. Col.	3rd SCVIBn	40	LS	09/14/62	South Mtn., MD	KIA	In the field	UD3 ROH,LC,BOD,RHL
James, Griffin J.	Pvt.	E 1st SCVIR		GE	09/08/63	Ft. Moultrie, SC	KIA	(Ammo chest explosion)	ROH,SA1,CDC
James, J.	Pvt.	C 2nd SCV			/ /	Richmond, VA			ROH
James, J.A.	Pvt.	F 22nd SCVI		PS	/ /	Petersburg, VA			ROH
James, J.B. (P.B.?)	Pvt.	B 13th SCVI		SG	07/10/62	Richmond, VA	DOd	(Typhoid)	ROH,JR
James, John F.	Pvt.	A 27th SCVI	19	CN	07/04/64	Petersburg, VA	DOW	(Wdd 6/16/64, leg Amptd.)	ROH,CDC
James, John L.	Pvt.	A P.S.S.			/ /		DOW	(Rchmd effects list)	JR,CDC
James, John M.	Pvt.	A 26th SCVI	22	HY	12/15/61	Waccamaw Neck SC	DOD		ROH
James, Joseph	Pvt.	A 15th SCVI		RD	07/06/64	Richmond, VA		Hollywood Cem.Rchmd. U150	ROH,HC,KEB
James, Laban	Pvt.	E 5th SCVI	27	YK	05/06/64	Wilderness, VA	KIA		YEB
James, Lawrence A.	Pvt.	I 1st SCVIG		UN	07/12/64	At home	DOD		SA1
James, Leonard	Pvt.	L 7th SCVI		HY	05/06/64	Wilderness, VA	KIA		JR
James, M.N.	Pvt.	A 1st SCV			06/08/62	Richmond, VA			ROH
James, Robert E.	1st Sgt.	F 8th SCVI	28	DN	05/10/62	Richmond, VA	DOD	(Typhoid)	ROH,JR,KEB
James, Robert Preston	Pvt.	H Orr's Ri.		MN	06/27/62	Gaines' Mill, VA	KIA		ROH,JR,HMC,CDC
James, Simpson T.	Pvt.	E 1st SCVIG		MN	08/07/62	Charlottesville	DOD	Univ. Cem. Charlottesville	JR,HMC,SA1,ACH
James, T. (F.?)	Pvt.	G 27th SCVI		CN	08/21/64	City Point, VA	DOW	City Pt. N.C. Hopewell, VA	PP,TOD
James, W.D.	Pvt.	C 10th SCVI		HY	/ /		DOD		RAS
James, William J.	Pvt.	E 1st SCVIG		MN	08/29/62	2nd Manassas, VA	KIA		ROH,JR,SA1,HMC
James, William W.	Pvt.	A 18th SCVI		UN	04/28/64	Madison, FL	DOD		ROH,PP,UD4
James, Zion	Pvt.	I 3rd SCVI		LS	09/20/63	Chickamauga, GA	KIA	Con. Cem. Marietta, GA	ROH,JR,SA2,CCM
Jameson, Andrew Ralph	Pvt.	G 5th SCVC	28	BT	01/26/65	CO District	DIP	(Xchd POW/Elmira, sick)	ROH,P120
Jamieson, George	Pvt.	G 6th SCVI		CR	09/30/64	Chaffin's Farm	KIA		ROH
Jamieson, W.T.	Pvt.	A Orr's Ri.		CR	06/14/62	Lynchburg, VA	DOD	Lynchburg CSA Cem.#1 R1	ROH,JR,CDC,BBW
Jamieson, William T.	Pvt.	G 18th SCVI		CR	07/30/64	Crater, Pbg., VA	KIA		ROH,JR,BLM,HHC
Jamison, A. Lovet	Pvt.	B 7th SCVIBn	24	FD	05/16/64	Drury's Bluff VA	KIA		ROH,JR,HAG,HFC
Jamison, Carroll	Pvt.	B 37th VAVCB			/ /	Tennessee	DOD		UD1
Jamison, J. Taylor	Pvt.	E 2nd SCVIRi		PS	08/02/64	Columbia, SC	DOD		ROH,PP

SOUTH CAROLINA DEAD IN CSA SERVICE 1861-1865

NAME	RANK	C REGIMENT	AGE	DS	DIED	WHERE	WHY	BURIED	SOURCES
Jamison, Thomas	Pvt.	A P.S.S.			/ /		DOD		JR
Jandon, Benjamin J.	Pvt.	D 3rd SCVC	47	BT	/ /	Lawtonville, SC	DOD		ROH
Jandon, James J.	Pvt.	E 3rd SCVC		BT	02/25/65	Columbia, SC	DOD		ROH,PP
Janes, Silas	Pvt.	C 2nd SCVIRi			11/29/63	Columbia, SC	DOD		ROH
Janican, John	Pvt.	14th SCVI			06/03/63	Richmond, VA			ROH
Jannergan, W.C.	Pvt.	E 8th SCVI		DN	08/08/62	Lynchburg, VA	DOD	Lynchburg CSA Cem.#3 R2	ROH,JR,CDC,BBW
Jarrall, J.J.	Pvt.	F 10th SCVI		MN	/ /		DOD		RAS,HMC
Jarrell, Robert	Pvt.	E 11th SCVI		BT	06/15/64	Petersburg, VA	KIA		JR,HAG
Jarrett, J. Allston	2nd Lt.	I 21st SCVI		DN	06/02/63	Charleston, SC	DOD	(JR=6/22/62)	JR,HMC,HAG,R48
Jarrett, James	Pvt.	L Orr's Ri.		AN	09/15/62	Richmond, VA	DOD		JR
Jarvis, G.W.	Pvt.	C 13th SCVI		SG	10/19/64	Richmond, VA			ROH
Jarvis, James S.	Pvt.	A 4th SCVC		CD	05/30/64	Old Church, VA	KIA		JR
Jarvis, P.	Pvt.	E 3rd SCVI			09/20/62	Richmond, VA		Hollywood Cem.Rchmd. H81	HC
Jasper, Amy W.	Pvt.	L 10th SCVI		MN	12/31/62	Murfreesboro, TN	KIA		RAS,HMC
Jaudon, A.M.	Pvt.	A 10th SCVI		GN	06/15/62		DOD (Typhoid)		JR,GRG,RAS
Jaunt, J.A.	Pvt.	K 1st SCVIR		LR	01/12/65		DOD (On rolls 12/31/64)		ROH,SA1,LAN
Jay, H.	Pvt.	G 7th SCVI		ED	09/20/63	Chickamauga, GA	KIA	Con. Cem. Marietta, GA	ROH,JR,UD2,CCM
Jay, Samuel J.	Pvt.	Ham.Leg. A		SR	10/15/64	White House, VA	KIA		ROH
Jay, William	1st Lt.	H 19th SCVI	32	AE	11/30/64	Franklin, TN	KIA	Williamson Cty Con. Cem.TN	ROH,WCT,R47,PP
Jayroe, Andrew M.	Pvt.	D 2nd SC Res	43	WG	/ /		DOD		CTA
Jayroe, John William	3rd Cpl.	C 25th SCVI	21	WG	05/30/64	Fts. Monroe, VA	DOW (Wdd., POW @ Drury's Bluff)		ROH,CTA,P6,HAG
Jefcoat, M.M.	Pvt.	G 1st SCVIH		BL	06/20/64	Petersburg, VA	KIA		SA1
Jeffcoat, Daniel	Pvt.	I 6th SCVI		CR	/ /		DOD		CB,HHC
Jeffcoat, Bartos J.P.	Pvt.	B 7th SCVC		CN	/ /	At sea	DIP (To Exchg in Savannah)		CDC,P113
Jefferies, Andrew	Pvt.	F 17th SCVI	21	YK	/ /	Petersburg, VA	DOW		YEB
Jeffers, B.	Pvt.	C 27th SCVI		CN	03/20/65	Richmond, VA		Hollywood Cem.Rchmd. W603	HC,HAG
Jeffers, Lewis	Pvt.	E 2nd SCVI		KW	/ /	Richmond, VA	DOD (1862)		ROH,SA2,HIC,KE
Jefferson, Jacob Forbes	Pvt.	C 4th SCVI			01/20/62	Virginia	DOD (?SA2=Reenlisted 2/7/62)		JR,SA2
Jefferson, T.	Pvt.				01/23/63	Richmond, VA			ROH
Jefferys, Foster G.	Pvt.	G P.S.S.	21	YK	07/06/63	At home	DOD (YEB=I, 5th SCVI)		JR,YMD,YEB
Jeffords, G.R.P.	Pvt.	K 21st SCVI		DN	05/16/64	Drury's Bluff VA	KIA		ROH,JR,CDC
Jeffords, Robert J.	Lt.Col.	5th SCVC		CN	10/27/64	Burgess Mill, VA	KIA	Magnolia Cem. Charleston	JR,RCD,LC,BHC
Jeffords, Thomas Jones	Pvt.	E 11th SCVI	40	CN	07/15/64	Petersburg, VA	KIA		ROH,HAG,CDC
Jencks, W.P. (M.P.?)	Pvt.	F 8th SCVI		DN	06/18/62	Richmond, VA		Hollywood Cem.Rchmd. O150	ROH,HC
Jenkins, B.R.	Pvt.	D 9th SCVIBn			06/08/62	Charleston, SC	DOD	Magnolia Cem. Charleston	JR,MAG
Jenkins, Benjamin O.	Pvt.	G 18th SCVI	28	YK	04/21/65	Elmira, NY	DIP	Woodlawn N.C.#1388 Elmira	HC,FPH,P6,YEB
Jenkins, I.R.M.	Pvt.	H 6th SCVC			11/11/64	Charleston, SC	DOD	Magnolia Cem. Charleston	ROH,MAG
Jenkins, J.A.	Pvt.	C 1st SCVIH		BL	10/28/63	Lookout Valley	KIA (Reported MIA)		CDC,SA1,JRH
Jenkins, J.B.	Pvt.	B 12th SCVI		YK	09/15/62		DOD		JR
Jenkins, J.B.M.	Pvt.	F 5th SCVC		LN	/ /	Richmond, VA			ROH
Jenkins, John	Pvt.	G 14th SCVI			06/01/64		DOW		JR
Jenkins, John D.	Pvt.	G P.S.S.			/ /		DOD		JR
Jenkins, John J. LaRoche	Pvt.	I 3rd SCVC	20	CN	10/12/62	Johns Island, SC	DOD		ROH
Jenkins, John M.	Pvt.	K 12th SCVI		PS	09/30/64	Jones' Farm, VA	KIA		JR,ROH
Jenkins, John M.R.	Pvt.	H 6th SCVI	18	YK	/ /	Virginia	DOD (After reorganization)		YEB
Jenkins, Lewis W.	Pvt.	G 25th SCVI	21	OG	05/27/64	Pt. Walthal Jct.	DOW (Body returned home/BLC)		ROH,JR,PP,BLC
Jenkins, M. (Jenks, M.?)	Pvt.	M 8th SCVI		DN	/ /	Richmond, VA		Oakwood C.#31,Row 25,Div D	ROH,OWC
Jenkins, Micah	Bgd. Gen.		30	YK	05/06/64	Wilderness, VA	KIA	Magnolia Cem. Charleston	JR,ROH,CDC,YEB
Jenkins, Thomas	Pvt.	A Ham.Leg.		CN	/ /	TN	KIA		ROH,WLI
Jenkins, W.	Pvt.	K 12th SCVI		PS	09/17/62	Sharpsburg, MD	KIA		JR
Jenkins, W.K.	Pvt.	F 3rd SCVC		BT	03/01/65	Ft. Delaware, DE	DIP	Finn's Pt. NJ Nat. Cem.	ROH,FPH,P6,P41

J

SOUTH CAROLINA DEAD IN CSA SERVICE 1861-1865

NAME	RANK	C REGIMENT	AGE	DS	DIED	WHERE	WHY	BURIED	SOURCES
Jenkins, W.W.	Sgt.	I 6th SCVC		CD	06/24/64	Ladd's Store, VA	KIA		JR
Jenkins, W.W.	Pvt.	D 2nd SCVI		SR	/ /		KIA	(? SA2=DIS before 5/1/62)	H2,SA2,KEB
Jenkins, Wesley				GE	07/03/64	At home	DOD	(DIS unfit @ Atlanta)	ROH
Jenkins, William H.H.	Pvt.	F Orr's Ri.	23	PS	06/28/65	Charleston, SC	DIP	(Scurvy from prison)	CDC,P113,UD1,UD3
Jenkins, William J.	Pvt.	B 17th SCVI		FD	09/14/62	South Mtn., VA	KIA		JR,HFC,UD3
Jenkins, William P.	Pvt.	D 5th SCVI		UN	06/27/62	Gaines' Mill, VA	KIA		JR,SA3
Jenkins, Zebulon	Pvt.	C 14th SCVI		LS	01/20/63		DOW		JR
Jenkinson, William Eli	Pvt.	H 5th SCVC	38	CL	11/02/63	At home	DOD		ROH
Jennerrett, W.J.	Pvt.	E 14th SCVI		LS	09/08/62	Frederick, MD	DOD	(RHL= Generett 3rd SCVI)	CGS,RHL,UD3
Jennett, W.B.	Pvt.	L 7th SCVI		HY	/ /	Charlottesville		Univ. Cem. Charlottesville	ACH
Jennings, A.	Pvt.	A 3rd SCVI		SG	05/25/64	Richmond, VA	DOW	Hollywood Cem.Rchmd. I40	ROH,HC,SA2,KEB
Jennings, B. Coke	Pvt.	A 18th SCVI		UN	08/20/64	Petersburg, VA	KIA		JR,ROH
Jennings, C. Willis	Pvt.	C 5th SCVI			12/18/63	Nashville, TN	DOW	Nashville City C. #5830	ROH,P2,P6,P12
Jennings, Elias	Pvt.	B 15th SCVI		UN	/ /		DOD		JR,KEB
Jennings, H.B.	1st Sgt.	G 1st SCVIH		BL	12/20/62		DOD		ROH,SA1,JRH
Jennings, Henry P.G.	Pvt.	Ham. Leg.	20	OG	04/13/62	Richmond, VA	DOD		ROH
Jennings, J.B.	Pvt.	G 1st SCV			/ /	Richmond, VA		Oakwood C.#65,Row N,Div A	ROH,OWC
Jennings, J.J.	Pvt.	E P.S.S.		SR	09/29/64	Ft. Harrison, VA	KIA	(JR=6/19/64)	ROH,JR
Jennings, James	Pvt.	B 17th SCVI		FD	/ /	At home	DOD		JR
Jennings, James C.	Pvt.	C 5th SCVI	26	OG	09/30/64	Petersburg, VA	DOW	(Wdd 6/22/64)	ROH,SA3,PP
Jennings, Jesse	3rd Cpl.	B 14th SCVI	21	ED	06/07/62	Lynchburg, VA	DOD	Lynchburg CSA Cem.#7 R5	ROH,JR,UD3,BBW
Jennings, John A.	Pvt.	B 2nd SCVI	28	GE	07/02/63	Gettysburg, PA	KIA	(KEB= Cpl.)	ROH,JR,SA2,GDR
Jennings, Matthew W.	Pvt.	B 14th SCVI	17	ED	03/11/62	Ft. Lafayette NY	DIP	Cypress Hills N.C. Gv4451	JR,UD4,FPH,P85
Jennings, R.	Pvt.	B 11th SCVI		CO	09/11/62	At home	DOD		ROH,JR
Jennings, R.	Pvt.	A 3rd SCVI		SG	08/06/64		DOD		SA2,KEB
Jennings, Robert	Pvt.	K 23rd SCVI		SR	/ /	Weldon, NC		(1863)	ROH
Jennings, Sanford D.	Sgt.	B P.S.S.		SR	06/19/64	Petersburg, VA	KIA		ROH,JR
Jennings, T.J.	Pvt.	I 2nd SCVA	23	OG	06/21/63		DOD	(A.J. Co.F?)	ROH
Jennings, W.	Pvt.	D 5th SCVI			05/31/62	7 Pines, VA	KIA		JR
Jenrette, Wilson	Pvt.	B 18th SCVAB		CN	04/15/65	Pt. Lookout, MD	DIP	(P114=Rlsd 3/28/65)	TOD,P114
Jernigan, D.M.	Pvt.	G 7th SCVI		OG	08/12/62	Petersburg, VA	DOD	Blandford Church Pbg., VA	ROH,BLC
Jernigan, Joseph	Pvt.	K 1st SCVIH		OG	10/04/62	Frederick, MD	DOD	Mt. Olivet C.#82 Frederick	ROH,FPH,BOD,JRH
Jerome, Henry	Pvt.	A 17th SCVI		CR	05/02/64	Charleston, SC	EXC	(For desertion)	ROH,HHC,CB
Jerrett, W.F.	Pvt.	E 14th SCVI		LS	02/10/64		DOD	(Pneumonia)	JR
Jerrold, William G.	1st Sgt.	D 1st SCVC	28	NC	07/03/63	Gettysburg, PA	KIA		ROH,HHC
Jerry, Eli	Pvt.	F 26th SCVI			06/26/62		DOD		JR
Jervey, Gabriel C.	Pvt.	A Ham. Leg.	54	CN	07/29/61	Culpepper, VA	DOW	(Wdd 1st Man)	ROH,JR,CDC,WLI
Jervey, J.S.	Sgt.	B 23rd SCVI		CN	06/20/64	Petersburg, VA	DOW	(Wdd & POW 6/17/64)	P5
Jervey, James C.	Sgt.	B 23rd SCVI	21	CN	06/20/64	Petersburg, VA	KIA		ROH,RCD,P5
Jervey, William Capers	Pvt.	A 25th SCVI	26	CN	07/18/64	Petersburg, VA	KIA		ROH,WLI,RCD,HAG
Jeter, J.	Pvt.	A Alexanders			05/03/63	Chancellorsville	KIA		JR
Jeter, S.A.	Pvt.				06/27/64		DOW		JR
Jeter, W.L.	Pvt.	A 25th SCVI		CN	05/09/64	Pt. Walthal Jct.	KIA		ROH,JR,CDC
Jetter, Irenius P.	Pvt.	D 5th SCVI		UN	05/31/62	7 Pines, VA	DOW	(JR=6/6/62)	JR,SA3,CDC
Jewell, Edward	Pvt.	F 1st SCVIH		GE	01/11/64		DOD		ROH,SA1,JRH
Jinks, E.W.	Pvt.	E 2nd SCVI	17	KW	07/28/61	Culpepper, VA	DOD	Fairview Cem. Culpepper VA	ROH,JR,CGH,SA2
Jinks, George W.	Pvt.	M 8th SCVI	25	PS	06/15/62	Richmond, VA	DOD	(JR=Pneumonia @ Ch'ville)	ROH,JR,KEB
Jinks, Mark	Pvt.	M 8th SCVI	25	DN	05/15/62	Richmond, VA	DOD		ROH,JR,KEB
Jinks, Thomas	Pvt.	M 8th SCVI		DN	/ /	Richmond, VA	DOD	(Pneumonia, KEB=Jenks)	JR,KEB
Joanes, E.A.	Pvt.	12th SCVI			/ /			Charlestown, VA	ROH
Johns, A.P.	Sgt.	K 11th SCVI	23	CO	06/21/64	Petersburg, VA	KIA	(JR=6/23/64)	ROH,JR,HAG

SOUTH CAROLINA DEAD IN CSA SERVICE 1861-1865

NAME	RANK	C REGIMENT	AGE	DS	DIED	WHERE	WHY	BURIED	SOURCES
Johns, D.R.	Pvt.	G 21st SCVI		CD	10/29/63		DOD		JR,HAG
Johns, Daniel	Pvt.				/ /	Camp Gurin, Chstn	DOD	Measles (Jan or Feb 1862)	UD2
Johns, Elias H.	Pvt.	B P.S.S.		PS	01/21/64	Morristown, TN	DOW	(Wdd Dandridge,TN)	ROH,JR
Johns, James A.	Pvt.	E 15th SCVI	19	FD	10/19/64	Winchester, VA	KIA	Stonewall C. Winchester VA	ROH,WIN,KEB
Johns, James A.	Pvt.	E 15th SCVI	17	FD	11/26/64	Maybington, SC	DOD		ROH,KEB
Johns, John B.	Pvt.	F Orr's Ri.		PS	/ /	Lynchburg, VA		Lynchburg CSA Cem. #6R4	BBW,CDC
Johns, R.T.	Pvt.	6th SCVI			12/20/61	Dranesville, VA	KIA		CDC
Johns, William	Pvt.	G 3rd SCVIBn		BL	/ /	Richmond, VA		Oakwood C.#38,Row B,Div B	ROH,OWC,KEB
Johns, William	1st Lt.	K 11th SCVI	25	CO	05/05/65	NC	KIA		ROH,HAG
Johnson,	Pvt.	A 13th SCVI		LS	06/09/62	Richmond, VA		Hollywood Cem.Rchmd. M266	HC
Johnson, A.	Pvt.	A 4th SC Mil			02/17/65	Charleston, SC	DOD	Magnolia Cem. Charleston	ROH,MAG
Johnson, A. Jackson	Pvt.	C 9th SCVIB	20	CL	08/15/61	Germantown, VA	DOD		ROH
Johnson, A.H.	Pvt.	A 1st SCVIR		CD	12/14/64	Pt. Lookout, MD	DIP	C.C. Pt. Lookout, MD	ROH,FPH,SA1,P6
Johnson, Alexander	Pvt.	A 23rd SCVI		CD	/ /	At home	DOD		ROH
Johnson, Amos	Pvt.	H 7th SCVC		KW	/ /	At sea	DIP	(To exchg in Savannah)	CDC,P114
Johnson, Anderson C.	2nd Sgt.	C 22nd SCVI	22	SG	10/21/64	Elmira, NY	DIP	Woodlawn N.C.#523 Elmira	ROH,FPH,P6,P65
Johnson, B.	Pvt.	C 11th SCVI		CN	11/08/62	Richmond, VA		Hollywood Cem.Rchmd. C5	HC
Johnson, Barney	Pvt.	D 25th SCVI		MN	05/16/64	Drury's Bluff VA	KIA		ROH,JR,HMC,HAG
Johnson, Benjamin J.	Lt. Col.	Ham.Leg.	45	BT	07/21/61	1st Manassas, VA	KIA	Magnolia Cem. Charleston	ROH,JR,WLI,AOA
Johnson, Blaney H.	Pvt.	M P.S.S.	32	WG	08/30/62	2nd Manassas, VA	KIA		ROH,JR,CTA,CDC
Johnson, C.	Pvt.	F P.S.S.		LN	06/27/62	Gaines' Mill, VA	KIA		ROH,CDC
Johnson, Cecil	Pvt.	B 2nd SCVC		BT	06/21/63	Upperville, VA	KIA		ROH,JR,BHC,AOA
Johnson, Charles B.	1st Sgt.	A 4th SCVC		CD	12/06/64		KIA		ROH
Johnson, Charles E.	Pvt.	C 1st SCVIH		BL	11/15/62		DOD		ROH,SA1,HAG,JR
Johnson, D. Benjamin	Pvt.	A 2nd SCVI		RD	05/12/63	Richmond, VA	DOD	Hollywood Cem.Rchmd. T231	ROH,HC,SA2,KEB
Johnson, D. Wade	1st Lt.	H 7th SCVI			08/27/64	Charlestown, VA	DOW	(Asst Adj. F&S)	ROH,R46
Johnson, D.B.	Pvt.	K 14th SCVI		ED	05/02/64	Richmond, VA	DOD	Hollywood Cem.Rchmd. I230	ROH,HC,HOE
Johnson, Daniel	Pvt.	D P.S.S.		SG	/ /	At home	DOD	(HOS=1863)	ROH,HOS
Johnson, Daniel	Pvt.	G 8th SCVI		MO	10/12/61	Orange C.H., VA	DOD	(JR= David, Dd.of Typhoid)	JR,HOM,KEB,UD2
Johnson, Daniel S.	Sgt.	C 10th SCVI		HY	07/22/64	Atlanta, GA	DOW	Milner, GA	RAS,CKB,BGA
Johnson, David	Pvt.	E 13th SCVI		SG	07/11/62	Richmond, VA	DOD	(JR=Typhoid 6/28/62)	ROH,JR,HOS
Johnson, David C.	Pvt.	F 13th SCVI		SG	07/09/62	Richmond, VA	DOD	(Typhoid, Winder Hos.)	ROH,JR
Johnson, David Q.	Pvt.	F 2nd SCVI	20	AN	09/20/64	Winchester, VA	DOW	(ROH=David R., 2nd SCVIRi)	ROH,H2,SA2,KEB
Johnson, David T.	Pvt.	H 2nd SCVI		LR	12/12/62	Richmond, VA	DOD		SA2,LAN,KEB,H2
Johnson, Edward H.	Pvt.	G 15th SCVI	24	WG	05/24/63	Chancellorsville	DOW	(Probably Wdd 5/1)	CTA,KEB
Johnson, Elbert P.	2nd Sgt.	B 13th SCVI		SG	07/07/62	Richmond, VA	DOD		JR,HOS
Johnson, Elias E.	Pvt.	F 1st SCVIH		GE	06/21/62	At home	DOD		ROH,SA1,JRH
Johnson, Elijah M.	5th Sgt.	K 2nd SCVIRi	25	AN	12/01/63	Campbell Stn. TN	DOW	(Wdd 11/16/63)	ROH
Johnson, Enoch	Sgt.	K 13th SCVI		LN	05/22/64	Jericho Ford VA	KIA		ROH,JR
Johnson, Ezekiel	Pvt.	F 7th SCVI	23	ED	/ /	Fredericksburg	DOD	Spotsylvania C.H., VA	SCH,HOE,KEB
Johnson, F.	Pvt.	H 16th SCVI		GE	06/15/64	At home	DOD		PP
Johnson, Frank	Pvt.	E 1st SCVIG		MN	12/15/62	Richmond, VA	DOD	Hollywood Cem.Rchmd. M473	ROH,JR,HC,SA1
Johnson, Franklin A.	Cpl.	F 10th SCVI	25	MN	/ /	Tupelo, MS	DOD		ROH,RAS,HMC
Johnson, Franklin P.	Pvt.	F 2nd SCVI	22	AE	09/17/62	Sharpsburg, MD	KIA	(JR=DOW 9/1/62)	ROH,JR,SA2,KEB
Johnson, G.W.	Pvt.	A P.S.S.		UN	06/29/62	Savage Stn., VA	KIA		ROH,JR,CDC,CNM
Johnson, G.W.	Pvt.	K 7th SCVI		ED	10/01/61	Culpepper, VA	DOD	Fairview Cem. Culpepper VA	CGH
Johnson, G.W.	Pvt.	E 10th SCVI		WG	/ /	MS	DOD	(May be Dup of Gilbert)	RAS
Johnson, Gilbert	Pvt.	E 10th SCVI		WG	/ /	MS	DOD	(1863)	RAS,HOW
Johnson, H.D.	Pvt.	A 13th SCVI		LS	07/02/63	Gettysburg, PA	DOW	(JR=Johnston, 8/15/63)	JR,CDC
Johnson, H.S.	Pvt.	F 3rd SCVI		LS	11/12/62	Lynchburg, VA	DOD	Lynchburg CSA Cem. #1R1	JR,SA2,KEB,BBW
Johnson, Harmon	Sgt.	C 10th SCVI	21	HY	01/30/63	Murfreesboro, TN	DOW		RAS,TOD,P12

J

SOUTH CAROLINA DEAD IN CSA SERVICE 1861-1865

NAME	RANK	C REGIMENT	AGE	DS	DIED	WHERE	WHY	BURIED	SOURCES
Johnson, Harvey W.	Pvt.	G 22nd SCVI	23	AN	07/30/64	Crater, Pbg., VA	KIA		ROH,BLM
Johnson, Henry	Pvt.	E 21st SCVI		CD	05/06/64	Pt. Walthall Jn.	DOW	(Severe head wound)	CDC,UD3
Johnson, Henry M.	Pvt.	D 13th SCVI	22	NY	11/16/62	Richmond, VA	DOW	(JR=Wdd. @ 2nd Man.)	JR,ANY
Johnson, Hugh W.	Pvt.	K 6th SCVI	30	CL	09/17/62	Sharpsburg, MD	KIA	Rose Hill C. Hagerstown MD	ROH,JR,HOW,BOD
Johnson, Isaac	Pvt.	E 24th SCVI	29	CO	09/20/63	Chickamauga, GA	KIA		ROH,CDC
Johnson, Isaac	Pvt.	B 24th SCVI	24	MO	07/20/64	Peach Tree Ck.GA	KIA		ROH,JR,CDC
Johnson, J.	Pvt.	F 1st SCVA			06/20/64	Charleston, SC	DOW	Magnolia Cem. Charleston	ROH,MAG,CDC
Johnson, J.	Pvt.	I 3rd SCVABn		GE	02/20/64	At home	DOD		PP
Johnson, J. Bird	Pvt.	C 25th SCVI	21	WG	04/08/65	Pt. Lookout, MD	DIP	C.C. Pt. Lookout, MD	FPH,P6,HAG,P114
Johnson, J.B.	Pvt.	E 12th SCVI		PS	06/17/64	Staunton, VA			ROH,PP
Johnson, J.C.	Pvt.	H 24th SCVI		CR	/ /		DOD		CB,HHC
Johnson, J.F.	2nd Cpl.	E 1st SCVIH		CN	05/15/64	Lynchburg, VA	DOW	Lynchburg CSA Cem. #2R5	SA1,BBW
Johnson, J.H.	Pvt.	E Ham.Leg.		GE	05/10/65	Pt. Lookout, MD	DIP	C.C. Pt. Lookout, MD	FPH,P6,P12
Johnson, J.M.	Pvt.	H SCVI			/ /	Richmond, VA		Oakwood C.#78, Row L, Div B	OWC
Johnson, J.W.P.	Pvt.	K 2nd SCV	19	AN	03/10/64	Bristol, TN	DOD		ROH
Johnson, James	Pvt.	I 2nd SCVA	30	OG	06/15/65	At home	DOD		ROH
Johnson, James	Pvt.	A 7th SCVI			07/02/63	Gettysburg, PA	KIA		ROH,JR,GDR,CDC
Johnson, James	Pvt.	E 13th SCVI		SG	05/06/63	Chancellorsville	KIA		ROH,HOS
Johnson, James	Pvt.	A Tucker's R			02/17/65	Salisbury, NC	DOD	Prob Old Lutheran C. there	PP
Johnson, James D.	Pvt.	H 2nd SCVI		LR	07/27/62	Richmond, VA	DOW	Hollywood Cem.Rchmd. L131	ROH,HC,SA2,LAN
Johnson, James H.	Pvt.	(Arty)		CD	03/22/62	Portsmouth, VA	DOD		ROH
Johnson, James H.	Pvt.	E Orr's Ri.		PS	07/26/62	Gaines' Mill, VA	DOW		JR,CDC
Johnson, James J.	Pvt.	G Hol.Leg.	28	NY	08/04/63	Meridian, MS	DOD	Prob in Rose Hill C. There	ROH,PP
Johnson, James L.	Pvt.	C 22nd SCVI		SG	03/14/62	Charleston, SC	DOD		ROH,HOS
Johnson, James M.	Pvt.	E 10th SCVI	32	WG	11/23/63	Chattanooga, TN	KIA	(P3=POW Xchgd 5/23/65)	CTA,ROH,HOW,CDC
Johnson, James T.	1st Cpl.	K 2nd SCV	34	AN	09/15/64	Richmond, VA	DOD	Hollywood Cem.Rchmd. V342	ROH,HC
Johnson, James T.	Pvt.	B 21st SCVI		DN	10/15/63		DOD		JR
Johnson, John	Pvt.	B 26th SCVI	19	CD	08/07/64	Richmond, VA	DOD		ROH
Johnson, John	Pvt.	B 20th SCVI	28	OG	06/15/63	Charleston, SC	ACD		ROH
Johnson, John	Pvt.	D Hol.Leg.	19	BL	12/14/62	Kinston, NC	KIA		ROH,PP
Johnson, John	Pvt.	H 5th SCVI		UN	06/30/62	Frayser`s Farm	KIA	(JR=John A. Co.A)	JR,SA3
Johnson, John A.	Pvt.	E 3rd SCVI		NY	08/15/61	Charlottesville	DOD		JR,ROH,SA2,ANY
Johnson, John Calvin	Pvt.	C Hol.Leg.	18	UN	11/05/63	Bottom's Bridge	DOD	(Probably 2nd SCVC)	ROH
Johnson, John J.	Pvt.	I 25th SCVI		CL	02/16/65	Elmira, NY	DIP	Woodlawn N.C.#2210 Elmira	FPH,P6,HAG,P65
Johnson, John J. (A.?)	Pvt.	F 11th SCVI	27	BT	02/02/62	Hardeeville, SC	DOD	(JR=2/12/62)	ROH,JR,HAG
Johnson, John W.	Pvt.	F 20th SCVI	19	LS	07/27/64	Petersburg, VA	KIA	Blandford Church Pbg., VA	ROH,BLC,PP
Johnson, John Westley	Pvt.	F 2nd SCVI	26	AE	09/20/63	Chickamauga, GA	KIA		ROH,JR,SA2,JLC
Johnson, Joseph	Sgt.	E 3rd SCVC		BT	06/15/65	Walterboro, SC	DOD		ROH
Johnson, Joseph J. (P.?)	Pvt.	E Hol.Leg.		SG	11/05/64	Petersburg, VA	KIA	(ROH=Joseph P.)	ROH,HOS
Johnson, Joseph P.	Cpl.	E 12th SCVI	19	LR	05/05/64	Wilderness, VA	KIA		ROH,LAN
Johnson, L.W.	Pvt.	7th SCVI			10/27/64	Petersburg, VA	KIA		ROH
Johnson, Levi	Pvt.	F P.S.S.			/ /		KIA		JR
Johnson, M. Pinckney	Pvt.	I 25th SCVI		CL	03/23/65	Elmira, NY	DIP	Woodlawn N.C.#2443 Elmira	FPH,P6,HAG,P65
Johnson, Murdoch D.	Pvt.	A 1st SCVIR			05/24/65	Hart's Island NY	DIP	Cypress Hills N.C.#2873 NY	FPH,P6,P12,P79
Johnson, M.H.	Pvt.	C Orr's Ri.		PS	06/27/62	Gaines' Mill, VA	KIA		ROH,JR,CDC
Johnson, Michael M.	Pvt.	K SC Mtd Reg		BT	01/23/61		DOD	(Martin's Co.)	JR
Johnson, Nathaniel M.	Pvt.			WG	05/12/64	Spotsylvania, VA	KIA	(Dup of W. Nathaniel ?)	HOM,CTA,HOW
Johnson, Neighbor H.	Pvt.	I 25th SCVI	35	CL	08/24/64	Petersburg, VA	DOW	Blandford Church Pbg., VA	ROH,BLC,PP
Johnson, Neil D.	Pvt.	G 8th SCVI	27	MO	05/08/62	Charlottesville	DOW	Univ. Cem. Charlottesville	HOM,ACH,UD1,UD2
Johnson, Nelson	Sgt.	E 21st SCVI		CD	05/16/64	Drury's Bluff VA	DOW		CDC,HAG
Johnson, Noel J.	Pvt.	A 7th SCVIBn	27	CD	04/23/63	Adams Run, SC	DOD		ROH,JR,HIC,PP

SOUTH CAROLINA DEAD IN CSA SERVICE 1861-1865

NAME	RANK	C	REGIMENT	AGE	DS	DIED	WHERE	WHY	BURIED	SOURCES
Johnson, O.P.	Pvt.		(Detached)			10/01/64	Charleston, SC	DOD	Magnolia Cem. Charleston	MAG
Johnson, P.	Pvt.	C	10th SCVI		HY	/ /	Corinth, MS	DOD		RAS
Johnson, P.C.	Pvt.	F	10th SCVI	19	MN	/ /	Tupelo, MS	DOD		RAS,HMC
Johnson, R.S.	Pvt.		4th SCV			/ /	Columbia, SC	DOD	Elmwood Cem. Columbia, SC	ROH,MP,PP
Johnson, R.T.	Pvt.	F	6th SCVI		CR	12/20/61	Blackstock, VA	DOW	(Wdd @ Dranesville, VA)	HHC
Johnson, R.W.	Pvt.	K	1st SCVIR			02/22/65	Columbia, SC	DOD	Elmwood Cem. Columbia, SC	ROH,MP,SA1,PP
Johnson, Randall	Pvt.	D	6th SCVC		CN	02/08/64	Charleston, SC	DOD	Magnolia Cem. Charleston	ROH,MAG
Johnson, S.A.	Cpl.	E	12th SCVI		LR	11/09/63	Richmond, VA	DOW	Hollywood Cem.Rchmd. I108	ROH,JR,HC,LAN
Johnson, S.S. Burdett	Pvt.	D	1st SCVIH		LR	10/06/62		DOW	(Wdd @ 2nd Manassas)	ROH,JR,LAN,JRH
Johnson, Samuel D.	Pvt.	F	2nd SCVI	20	AE	10/13/61	At home	DOD	(JR=Measles 10/13/62)	ROH,JR,KEB,H2
Johnson, Samuel R.	Pvt.	K	2nd SCVIRi	24	AN	02/12/64	At home	DOD	(NI KEB)	ROH
Johnson, Samuel S.	Pvt.	H	23rd SCVI		MN	08/07/64	Petersburg, VA	DOW		ROH,HMC,PP
Johnson, Stanmore	Pvt.	A	19th SCVI	28	ED	07/22/64	Atlanta, GA	KIA	(ROH & JR= Samuel)	ROH,JR,HOE.UD3
Johnson, Stephen M.	Pvt.	B	12th SCVI	18	YK	07/03/63	Gettysburg, PA	DOW		JR,YEB
Johnson, T.H.	Pvt.	C	10th SCVI		HY	04/19/63	Fair Gds Atlanta	DOD	Oakland C. Atlanta R18#6	RAS,BGA
Johnson, Theophilus	Pvt.	F	6th SCVI		CR	12/20/61	Dranesville, VA	KIA	(JR=R.T.)	ROH,JR,R46,HHC
Johnson, Thomas			Torpedo S.			12/27/63	Charleston Hrbr		Magnolia Cem. Charleston	RCD
Johnson, Thomas Albert	Cadet	B	3rd SCVABn	19	NY	03/23/65	Spartanburg, SC	DOD	Rosemont Cem. Newberry, SC	ROH,NCC,ANY
Johnson, Thomas Edward	Pvt.	D	5th SCVI	22	UN	05/31/62	7 Pines, VA	KIA		ROH,JR,SA3
Johnson, V.D.V.	Pvt.	C	2nd SCVA	40	OG	06/15/62	Columbia, SC	DOD		ROH
Johnson, W. Nathaniel	2nd Cpl.	G	15th SCVI	22	WG	09/01/61	Hardeeville, SC	DOD	(KEB= M.M.)	ROH,HOM,KEB
Johnson, W. Newton	Cpl.	C	22nd SCVI	42	SG	04/28/65	Charlotte, NC	DOD	(POW @ Crater, Xchgd)	ROH,P120,HOS,P
Johnson, W.A.	Pvt.	G	15th SCVI			/ /	(Dup of N.M.?)		Spotsylvania C.H., VA	SCH
Johnson, W.B.	Pvt.	L	Orr's Ri.		AN	12/13/62	Fredericksburg	KIA		JR
Johnson, W.P.	Pvt.	G	2nd SCVIRi			06/29/62	Savage Stn., VA	KIA		ROH,JR,CDC
Johnson, W.R.	Pvt.	F	3rd SCVI		LS	12/28/62	Richmond, VA	DOD	Oakwood C.#121,Row N,Div A	ROH,JR,SA2,OWC
Johnson, W.W.	Pvt.	E	P.S.S.		WG	07/15/62	Gaines' Mill, VA	DOW	(Wdd 6/27/62)	ROH,JR
Johnson, W.W.	Cpl.	E	27th SCVI			09/28/64	Richmond, VA	DOD	Oakwood C.#85,Row H,Div G	ROH,OWC
Johnson, Waddy	Pvt.	G	1st SCVA			07/21/63	Bty. Wagner, SC	KIA		ROH
Johnson, Whitfield W.	Pvt.	G	2nd SCVI		KW	07/02/63	Gettysburg, PA	KIA		ROH,JR,GDR,SA2
Johnson, William	Pvt.	H	19th SCVI	25	AE	07/16/62	Enterprise, MS	DOD	C.C. there with unknowns	ROH,PP
Johnson, William	Pvt.	E	1st SCVIG		MN	07/15/63	Richmond, VA	DOD	(Howard Grove Hospital)	SA1,HMC
Johnson, William	Pvt.	B	16th SCVI		GE	06/25/64	At home	DOD		16R,PP
Johnson, William	Pvt.	I	12th SCVI		LR	08/29/62	2nd Manassas, VA	KIA		LAN
Johnson, William	Pvt.	E	12th SCVI		LR	05/12/64	Spotsylvania, VA	KIA		JR,LAN
Johnson, William D.	Pvt.	B	4th SCVC		CR	06/24/64	Nance's Shop VA	KIA		ROH,CDC,HHC,CB
Johnson, William D.	Pvt.	E	26th SCVI			05/14/65	Pt. Lookout, MD	DIP	C.C. Pt. Lookout, MD	FPH,P6,P114
Johnson, William F.	Pvt.	B	18th SCVAB	19	HY	12/24/63	Legareville, SC	KIA		STR,DOC,TOD
Johnson, William F.	Pvt.	I	1st SCVIR			11/12/64	Charleston, SC	DOD	Magnolia Cem. Charleston	ROH,MAG,SA1
Johnson, William G.	Pvt.	G	P.S.S.	23	YK	06/15/63	Richmond, VA		Oakwood C.#65,Row D,Div C	OWC,YEB,SA3
Johnson, William H.	1st Sgt.	K	2nd SCVIRi	28	AN	03/09/64	Bristol, TN	DOD		ROH
Johnson, William H.	Pvt.	E	3rd SCVI		CN	10/28/63	Fair Gds Atlanta	DOW	Oakland C. Atlanta R17#2	ROH,SA2,ANY,BG
Johnson, William H.	Pvt.	A	15th SCMil		RD	04/02/65	New Bern, NC	DOW	Cedar Grove C. Newbern, NC	P1,P6,WAT,PP,P
Johnson, William L.	Pvt.	B	5th SCVI		YK	09/21/61		DOD		SA3
Johnson, William M.	Pvt.	E	13th SCVI	17	SG	05/27/64	Richmond, VA	DOW	Hollywood Cem.Rchmd. E20	ROH,HC,HOS,P12
Johnson, William R.	Pvt.	E	19th SCVI	25	WG	05/18/62	Lauderdale Ss MS	DOD	Con.Cem., with unknowns	CTA,PP
Johnson, William W.	Pvt.	D	27th SCVI	28	CN	09/28/64	Weldon RR, VA	DOW	(Wdd 8/21/64)	ROH,HAG
Johnston, David M.	1st Cpl.	B	5th SCVI			05/15/64	Wilderness, VA	DOW		SA3
Johnston, Hugh Wilson	Pvt.	E	Orr's Ri.	24	PS	10/01/64	Richmond, VA	DOD	(JR=7/21/64 @ Jackson H.)	ROH,JR,CDC
Johnston, James Harvey	Pvt.	E	Orr's Ri.	26	PS	07/07/62	Richmond, VA	DOW	Oakwood C.#91,Row D,Div C	ROH,JR,OWC,PCS
Johnston, Jesse C.	Pvt.	D	24th SCVI	20	BT	10/31/63	Tennessee	DOD		ROH,EJM

J

SOUTH CAROLINA DEAD IN CSA SERVICE 1861-1865

NAME	RANK	C REGIMENT	AGE	DS	DIED	WHERE	WHY	BURIED	SOURCES
Johnston, John M.	Pvt.	H 1st SCVIG		BT	07/15/62	Richmond, VA	DOD	Oakwood C.#78,Row L,Div B	ROH,SA1,OWC,CDC
Johnston, Robert Dixon	Pvt.	E Orr's Ri.	20	PS	09/01/62	2nd Manassas, VA	DOW		ROH,JR
Johnston, William G.	Pvt.	B 5th SCVI			07/03/63	Wilson, NC	DOD		JR,SA3,PP
Joiner, D.E.	Pvt.	A 1st SCVIH		BL	08/30/62	2nd Manassas, VA	KIA	UD3	ROH,JR,SA1,JRH
Joiner, P.	Pvt.	D 6th SCRes		OG	03/05/65	Columbia, SC	DOD		ROH,PP
Joiner, Thomas A.	Pvt.	M 10th SCVI	29	HY	06/15/62	MS	DOD		ROH,RAS
Jolley, D.	Pvt.	4th SCV			/ /	Richmond, VA		Oakwood C.#14,Row N,Div A	ROH,OWC
Jolley, J.L.	Pvt.	2nd SCVIRi			09/20/62	Mt. Jackson, VA	DOW	(Wdd. @ Sharpsburg)	ROH,JR,CDC
Jolley, James J.	Pvt.	E Orr's Ri.	25	PS	05/03/63	Chancellorsville	KIA		ROH
Jolley, Levi D.	Pvt.	G 22nd SCVI		AN	07/30/64	Crater Pbg., VA	KIA		ROH
Jolley, William E.	Sgt.	G 22nd SCVI	22	AN	12/14/62	Kinston, NC	KIA		ROH,CDC,PP,UD2
Jolly, B.A.	Pvt.	A 18th SCVI		UN	07/30/64	Crater, Pbg., VA	KIA		ROH,BLM
Jolly, B.F.	Pvt.	A 18th SCVI		UN	07/30/64	Crater Pbg., VA	KIA		JR
Jolly, J. Knott	Pvt.	H P.S.S.		SG	/ /	Richmond, VA '64	DOW	Hollywood Cem.Rchmd. E22	HC,HOS
Jolly, James	Pvt.	E Orr's Ri.		PS	05/03/63	Chancellorsville	KIA		ROH,JR
Jolly, James	Cpl.	A 18th SCVI		UN	12/18/62	At home	DOD		JR
Jolly, Joseph	Pvt.	A 18th SCVI		UN	07/30/64	Crater, Pbg., VA	KIA		ROH,JR,BLM
Jolly, Joshua	Pvt.	A 18th SCVI		UN	07/30/64	Crater Pbg., VA	KIA		JR
Jolly, S.C.	Pvt.	F 1st SCVIH		MN	11/16/63	Campbell Stn.,TN	KIA		ROH,SA1,JRH
Jolly, W.N.	Pvt.	H P.S.S.			10/25/64	Richmond, VA	DOW		ROH,P12
Jones, A.		CSN			01/16/65	Richmond, VA			ROH
Jones, A.	Pvt.	2nd SCV			05/13/63	Richmond, VA		Hollywood Cem.Rchmd. T25	HC
Jones, Alexander	Pvt.	I 3rd SCVI	35	LS	09/08/62	Richmond, VA	DOD	Shady Grove Ch. Joanna, SC	SA2,KEB,LSC
Jones, Amos	Pvt.	H 10th SCVI	17	WG	01/08/63	Tulahoma, TN	DOD		RAS,HOW,PP
Jones, Benjamin R.	Pvt.	A 26th SCVI	22	HY	08/20/64	Petersburg, VA	DOD		ROH,PP
Jones, Bennett C.	Cpt.	B SC Troops	43	GE	03/15/64	Easley, SC	DOD	Jones Gvyd. Easley, SC	PCS,GEE
Jones, Caswell J.	Pvt.	B 10th SCVI		HY	/ /		DOD	(POW @ Mission Ridge)	RAS,P39
Jones, Clayton	Pvt.	15th SCVI			/ /		DOD	(JR=Co.L)	JR
Jones, Columbus	Pvt.	F 18th SCVI	26	UN	08/15/64	Crater, Pbg., VA	DOW		ROH,BLM,PP
Jones, D.	Pvt.	D 13th SCVI		NY	07/09/62	Richmond, VA		Hollywood Cem.Rchmd. O32	HC
Jones, D.M.	Pvt.	E 23rd SCVI		MN	06/17/64	Petersburg, VA	KIA		JR,HMC
Jones, D.M.	Pvt.	H 7th SCVIBn		RD	10/10/64	Elmira, NY	DIP	Woodlawn N.C.#666 Elmira	FPH,HAG,P6,P65
Jones, Daniel	2nd Lt.	K 9th SCVIBn		LN	01/23/62	Centreville, VA	DOD		JR,R46
Jones, David Rumph	Maj. Gen.		38	OG	01/15/63	Richmond, VA	DOD	Hollywood Cem.Rchmd.	ROH,GIG
Jones, E.	Sgt.	K 19th SCVI	38	ED	/ /		DOD		HOE
Jones, Eban W.	Pvt.	C 10th SCVI		HY	07/22/64	Griffin, GA	DOW	Stonewall Cem. Griffin, GA	RAS,CDC,BGA,UD2
Jones, Eber	Pvt.	G 3rd SCVI		SG	05/01/63		DOD		ROH,SA2,HOS,KEB
Jones, Edwin C.	Pvt.	D 2nd SCVI		SR	12/23/61	Centreville, VA	DOD	(SA2=Measles @ Culpepper)	H2,SA2,KEB
Jones, Edwin Chandler	Pvt.	K 3rd SCVABn	23	SR	09/11/63	Charleston, SC	DOD		ROH
Jones, F.	Pvt.				/ /	Richmond, VA		Oakwood C.#22,Row N,Div A	OWC
Jones, G.F.	Pvt.	H 2nd SCVIRi			11/15/62	Staunton, VA		Thornrose C. Staunton, VA	ROH,TOD
Jones, Gabriel Capers	Pvt.	G 24th SCVI	43	RD	09/22/64	At home	DOD		ROH
Jones, George	Pvt.			WG	/ /		DOD	(1861)	CTA,HOW
Jones, George Irvin	Pvt.	D 19th SCVI	32	ED	12/01/64	Franklin, TN	DOW	(HOE= Irvin G.)	ROH,HOE,PP,UD3
Jones, Gideon B.	Pvt.	I 20th SCVI		LN	07/27/64	Deep Bottom, VA	KIA	(JR=7/30/64)	ROH,JR,CDC,KEB
Jones, H.C.	Pvt.	D 9th SCVIB		CL	02/06/61	Manchester, VA	DOD		ROH,JR
Jones, H.C.	Pvt.	D 3rd SCVIBn		NY	06/15/63	Danville, VA	DOD	(Date aprox)	ANY,KEB
Jones, H.J.M.	Pvt.	G 20th SCVI		SR	07/28/64	New Mkt. Hts. VA	KIA	(JR=7/30/64)	ROH,JR,CDC,KEB
Jones, H.S.	Sgt.	7th SCVI			07/03/63	Gettysburg, PA	KIA	Magnolia Cem. Charleston	MAG
Jones, Hampton Plowden	Pvt.	D 2nd SCVI		SR	08/12/61	Fairfax C.H., VA	DOD	(Typhoid)	JR,KEB,SA2
Jones, Hansford Smith	Pvt.	A 1st SCVIH	27	BL	12/15/63	Bean's Stn., TN	KIA		ROH,SA1,JRH,UD3

SOUTH CAROLINA DEAD IN CSA SERVICE 1861-1865

NAME	RANK	C	REGIMENT	AGE	DS	DIED	WHERE	WHY	BURIED	SOURCES
Jones, Henry	Pvt.	E	15th SCVI			/ /	(Pos 9th SCVIB)			JR
Jones, J.	Pvt.	I	1st SC Mil			02/09/65	Charleston, SC	DOD	Magnolia Cem. Charleston	MAG
Jones, J.	Pvt.		3rd SCVI			10/29/61	Richmond, VA		Hollywood Cem.Rchmd. B246	HC
Jones, J. Pinckney	Pvt.	A	26th SCVI	36	HY	04/21/63	Charleston, SC	DOD		ROH,JR
Jones, J. Walker	Pvt.	A	25th SCVI		BT	10/31/63	Ft. Sumter, SC	KIA	Magnolia Cem. Charleston	ROH,JR,DOC,PP
Jones, J. William	Pvt.	I	16th SCVI		GE	07/22/63	Decatur, GA	KIA		ROH,16R
Jones, J.A.	Sgt.	B	24th SCVI		MO	/ /	Franklin, TN	KIA	Williamson Cty C.C. TN	HOM,WCT
Jones, J.B.	Pvt.	H	Orr's Ri.		MN	/ /	Lynchburg, VA	DOD		JR
Jones, J.B.	Pvt.		Ward's LA			12/25/63	Georgetown, SC	DOD		PP
Jones, J.F.	Pvt.	A	Orr's Ri.		AN	07/05/62	Richmond, VA		Hollywood Cem.Rchmd. M179	ROH,JR,HC,CDC
Jones, J.G.	Pvt.	K	10th SCVI		CN	/ /		DOD		RAS
Jones, J.H.	Pvt.	B	9th SCVIB			10/31/61	Virginia	DOD		JR
Jones, J.M.	Pvt.	H	12th SCVI		YK	05/23/64	Jericho Ford, VA	KIA		CWC
Jones, J.P.	Pvt.	I	1st SCVIR			07/18/63	Bty. Wagner, SC	KIA		ROH,CDC
Jones, J.Q.	Pvt.	A	Ham.Leg.		CN	/ /		DOW		ROH,WLI
Jones, J.R.	Pvt.	G	4th SCVC		CO	02/09/65	Columbia, SC	DOW	Elmwood Cem. Columbia, SC	ROH,JR,MP,PP
Jones, J.S.	Pvt.	F	10th SCVI		MN	06/15/64		KIA		JR
Jones, J.V.	Pvt.	G	2nd SCVIRi			06/16/62	Richmond, VA		Hollywood Cem.Rchmd. M405	ROH,HC
Jones, J.W.	Pvt.	F	22nd SCVI		PS	11/15/64	Petersburg, VA	KIA		ROH
Jones, James	Pvt.	I	19th SCVI	34	AE	09/20/63	Chickamauga, GA	KIA	Con. Cem. Marietta, GA	ROH,JR,CDC,CCM
Jones, James	Pvt.	C	4th SCVI		AN	10/15/61		DOD	(Rchmd effects list)	SA2,UDC
Jones, James	Pvt.	C	1st SCVIH		BL	05/06/64	Wilderness, VA	KIA		SA1,HAG
Jones, James A.	Pvt.	L	21st SCVI	47	MN	02/25/65	Elmira, NY	DIP	Woodlawn N.C.#2122 Elmira	ROH,FPH,P6,P65
Jones, James A.	Pvt.	E	14th SCVI		LS	08/15/64	Petersburg, VA	KIA		JR
Jones, James L.	Pvt.	E	14th SCVI		LS	08/16/64	Fussel's Mill VA	KIA	(CGS=Deep Bottom)	ROH,JR,CGS
Jones, James Moon	Pvt.	G	Orr's Ri.		AE	01/28/63	Lynchburg, VA	DOD	Lynchburg CSA Cem. #10R3	ROH,JR,CDC,BBW
Jones, James Starke	Pvt.	G	19th SCVI		AE	06/24/62	Enterprise, MS	DOD	(Brain fever)	JR,HOL,PP
Jones, James W.	Pvt.	A	14th SCVI	30	DN	07/01/63	Gettysburg, PA	KIA		ROH,GDR,BIG
Jones, Jesse	Pvt.	I	8th SCVI		MN	/ /	Virginia	DOD	(1861)	HMC,KEB
Jones, Jesse S.	Lt. Col.		24th SCVI	32	CO	12/07/64	Franklin, TN	DOW	Cross Swamp Ch. Islandton	ROH,WCT,CUC,PP
Jones, John	Pvt.	E	21st SCVI	43	CD	06/24/64	Petersburg, VA	KIA		ROH,HAG
Jones, John	Pvt.	E	4th SCVC		MO	07/21/64	Hawes Shop, VA	DOW	Hollywood Cem.Rchmd. V685	ROH,HC,HOM
Jones, John	Pvt.	I	2nd SCVA	18	OG	06/16/62	Secessionville	KIA		ROH,CDC
Jones, John	Pvt.	E	Orr's Ri.	19	PS	09/27/62	Dill Springs, VA	DOD	(JR=Richmond 6/27/62)	ROH,JR
Jones, John	Pvt.	F	Orr's Ri.		PS	08/11/62	Manchester, VA	DOD		JR
Jones, John J.	Pvt.	F	6th SCVI	29	YK	09/26/62	Warrenton, VA	DOW	(Wdd 2nd Man, ROH=Co.I))	ROH,WDB,YEB
Jones, John Milton D.	Sgt.	K	3rd SCVABn	25	SR	09/09/63	Charleston, SC	DOD		ROH
Jones, Joseph A.	Color Cpl.	B	24th SCVI	19	MO	11/30/64	Franklin, TN	KIA		ROH,PP
Jones, Joshua W.	Pvt.	A	14th SCVI		DN	07/01/64	Clay's Farm, VA	KIA		JR
Jones, Joshua W.	Pvt.	B	Orr's Ri.		AE	01/11/62	New Market, VA	DOD		JR,CDC
Jones, L.C.	Pvt.	I	20th SCVI		LN	08/17/64	Richmond, VA		Hollywood Cem.Rchmd. V667	ROH,HC,KEB
Jones, Laban	2nd Sgt.	E	5th SCVI		YK	05/06/64	Wilderness, VA	KIA	Fredericksburg C.C. R6S13	ROH,JR,SA3,FBG
Jones, Leven	Pvt.	E	26th SCVI		HY	09/15/64		KIA		ROH
Jones, Louis	Pvt.			20	WG	/ /		DOD	(1862)	CTA,HOW
Jones, Matthew W.	Pvt.	D	2nd SCVIRi		WG	11/15/62	Mt.Jackson, VA	DOD	Mt. Jackson, VA	ROH,HOW,SHS,PP
Jones, N.C.	Cpl.	F	15th SCVI		FD	/ /		DOD		JR,KEB
Jones, Ned	Pvt.		17th SCVI			10/29/63		DIP	(Chronic Diarrhea)	P12
Jones, Richard M.	Sgt.	E	3rd SCVABn			08/16/62	Charlotte, NC		Prob with unknowns in C.C.	PP
Jones, Riley	Pvt.	G	21st SCVI		CD	05/15/62	At home	DOD		JR,HAG
Jones, Robert T.	Pvt.	B	14th SCVI	31	ED	/ /	Petersburg, VA	KIA	(1864)	HOE,UD3
Jones, Robin Ap Catesby	Cpt.	H	1st SCVC	31	YK	06/09/63	Brandy Stn., VA	KIA		ROH,JR,R43,YEB

J

SOUTH CAROLINA DEAD IN CSA SERVICE 1861-1865

NAME	RANK	C REGIMENT	AGE	DS	DIED	WHERE	WHY	BURIED	SOURCES
Jones, S.C.					/ /			(Rchmd effects list 12/62)	CDC
Jones, Samuel A.	Sgt.	E 6th SCVC		LS	08/03/63	Charlottesville	DOD	Univ. Cem. Charlottesville	ROH,ACH,NCC
Jones, Samuel Dickson	Cpl.	G 2nd SCVI		KW	07/21/61	1st Manassas, VA	KIA	Manassas C. Cem.	ROH,JR,KEB,CV
Jones, Stanmore	Pvt.	I 20th SCVI		LN	08/01/63	Bty. Wagner, SC	KIA	Magnolia Cem. Charleston	MAG,KEB,CDC
Jones, Stephen P.	Pvt.	G 1st SCVIG		ED	07/25/62	Richmond, VA	DOD	(JR=Typhoid 6/20/62)	ROH,JR,SA1,HOE
Jones, T.	Pvt.	I 23rd SCVI		CL	01/09/65	Richmond, VA			ROH
Jones, Thadeus	Pvt.	C 2nd SCVI		UN	01/05/63	Farmville, VA	DOD		SA2,H2
Jones, Thomas	Pvt.	G 27th SCVI		CN	08/21/64	City Pt., VA	DOW	City Pt. N.C. Hopewell, VA	ROH,P12
Jones, Thomas	Pvt.	C 14th SCVI			11/16/61	Garners Crnr. SC	DOD	(Typhoid)	JR
Jones, Thomas S.	Pvt.	H 1st SCVIG		CN	08/10/63	Gettysburg, PA	DOW	(Fractured thigh)	ROH,SA1,P1,P5
Jones, Thornton F.	Pvt.	C 22nd SCVI	34	SG	06/15/62	Washington, DC	DOW	Nazareth P.C. GE Cty., SC	ROH,GEC
Jones, V.	Pvt.	A 1st SCVIH		BL	07/14/64	Richmond, VA		Hollywood Cem.Rchmd. U562	ROH,HC,SA1,UD3
Jones, W.P.	Pvt.	I 24th SCVI	43	ED	09/25/63	Chickamauga, GA	DOW		ROH,CDC
Jones, W.S.	Pvt.	H 6th SCVI		FD	05/05/65	Richmond, VA	DOD	Hollywood Cem.Rchmd. W503	ROH,HC,HFC,P6
Jones, W.W.	Pvt.	B 24th SCVI	22	MO	/ /	At home	DOD		HOM
Jones, Wesley	Pvt.	H 23rd SCVI		MN	07/30/64	Crater, Pbg., VA	KIA		JR,BLM,HMC
Jones, Wesley	Pvt.	H Orr's Ri.		MN	/ /	Danville, VA	DOD	(1862)	HMC,CDC
Jones, William	Pvt.	15th SCVI			/ /	Richmond, VA		Oakwood C.#71,Row A,Div A	ROH,OWC
Jones, William	Pvt.	G 9th SCVIBn	40	HY	04/04/62	Georgetown, SC	DOD		ROH,JR,PP
Jones, William	Pvt.	B 23rd SCVI		CN	10/28/64	Pt. Lookout, MD	DIP	C.C. Pt. Lookout, MD	FPH,P6,P114,P120
Jones, William Clayton	Pvt.	C 4th SCVI		AN	12/25/61	Warrenton Sps VA	DOD	(JR=14th SCVI)	JR,SA2,HOF
Jones, William H.	Pvt.	H 7th SCVIBn	34	RD	06/09/64	Fts. Monroe, VA	DOW	Prob. N.C. Hampton, VA	ROH,JR,HAG,P12
Jones, William M.	Pvt.	E 14th SCVI		LS	08/28/62	Richmond, VA	DOD	(JR=Typhoid 8/10/62)	ROH,JR,CGS
Jones, William M.	Pvt.	A 1st SCVIG		BL	10/11/64	Richmond, VA	DOD	Hollywood Cem.Rchmd. V397	HC,SA1
Jones, William S.	Pvt.	F 24th SCVI		AN	04/02/64	Rock Island, IL	DIP	C.C.#862 Rock Island, IL	FPH,HOL
Jones, Willis L.	Pvt.	A 17th SCVI	20	CR	08/23/62	Rapppahanock Stn	ACD	(Rifle discharged)	ROH,JR,HHC,CB
Jones, Y	Pvt.	I 20th SCVI		LN	/ /	Richmond, VA		Oakwood C.#26,Row J,Div G	OWC
Jones, Zachariah	Cpl.	K 11th SCVI	35	CO	06/03/64	Cold Harbor, VA	KIA		ROH,JR,HAG
Jordan, A.	Pvt.	D 8th SCVI		CD	06/16/61	At home	DOD	(Typhoid)	JR,KEB
Jordan, A.M.	Pvt.	E 3rd SCVABn			05/04/63	Columbia, SC	DOD		ROH,PP
Jordan, Andrew D.	Pvt.	E 21st SCVI		CD	05/16/64	Drury's Bluff VA	KIA		ROH,JR,HAG,CDC
Jordan, B.E.	Pvt.	L 1st SCVIG		CN	05/23/64	Lynchburg, VA	DOW	Lynchburg CSA Cem. #10R3	ROH,JR,SA1,BBW
Jordan, Colin	Pvt.	A 7th SCVIBn	38	CD	07/22/64	Richmond, VA	DOD		ROH,JR,HIC,HAG
Jordan, Columbus	Pvt.	I 18th SCVI	23	DN	09/15/62	Richmond, VA	DOD		ROH,JR
Jordan, D.	Pvt.	D 15th SCVI		KW	09/14/62	Maryland Hts.,MD	DOW		JR,HIC,KEB
Jordan, Edwin	Pvt.	PeeDee LA		DN	12/13/62	Fredericksburg	KIA		ROH,PDL
Jordan, Elijah H.	Pvt.	A 17th SCVI	31	CR	08/30/62	2nd Manassas, VA	KIA		ROH,CDC,HHC,CB
Jordan, Green B.	Pvt.	E 16th SCVI		GE	/ /		DIP	(POW @ Ringgold 11/26/63)	16R,P39
Jordan, H.	Sgt.	I 18th SCVI		DN	/ /	Richmond, VA		Oakwood C.#108,Row P,Div B	ROH,OWC
Jordan, I.B.	Pvt.	M 10th SCVI		HY	06/26/64	New Hope Ch., GA	KIA	(On picket)	ROH,JR,RAS
Jordan, J.H.A.	Pvt.	A 7th SCRes			02/06/65	Columbia, SC	DOD	Elmwood Cem. Columbia, SC	ROH,PP
Jordan, J.J.	Sgt.	F 26th SCVI			05/23/64	Pt. Lookout, MD	DOW	C.C. Pt. Lookout, MD	FPH,P6,P12
Jordan, J.R.	Pvt.	E 7th SCVI		ED	08/01/64	Richmond, VA			ROH
Jordan, J.T.	3rd Lt.	G 14th SCVI	33	AE	07/07/63	Gettysburg, PA	DOW	(Severe thigh Wd.)	ROH,CDC,R47
Jordan, J.T.	Pvt.	L 7th SCVI		HY	09/17/62	Sharpsburg, MD	KIA		ROH,JR,KEB
Jordan, Jacob	Pvt.	D 25th SCVI		MN	05/16/64	Drury's Bluff VA	KIA		HMC,HAG
Jordan, Jesse T.	Pvt.	A 17th SCVI	33	CR	05/02/62	Johns Island, SC	DOD		ROH,JR,HHC,CB
Jordan, John	Pvt.	PeeDee LA		DN	/ /				ROH
Jordan, John J.	Pvt.	B 13th SCVI		SG	05/17/62	Richmond, VA	DOD	Oakwood C.#92,Row A,Div B	ROH,JR,HOS,OWC
Jordan, John Walker	Cpl.	F 6th SCVC	22	CN	09/22/64	Elmira, NY	DIP	Woodlawn N.C.#486 Elmira	FPH,CAG,P6,P65
Jordan, N.	Pvt.	A 14th SCVI	45	DN	03/20/62	At home	DOD	(JR=3/10/62)	ROH,JR

SOUTH CAROLINA DEAD IN CSA SERVICE 1861-1865

NAME	RANK	C REGIMENT	AGE	DS	DIED	WHERE	WHY	BURIED	SOURCES
Jordan, S.	Pvt.	B 1st Bn Res		GE	03/13/65	Columbia, SC	DOD		ROH,PP
Jordan, S.G.	Pvt.	B 26th SCVI			06/20/62		DOD		JR
Jordan, T.J.	Pvt.	B Orr's Ri.		AE	07/20/62	Richmond, VA	DOD		JR
Jordan, Thomas	Pvt.	H 10th SCVI		WG	12/31/62	Murfreesboro, TN	KIA		ROH,RAS,HOW,CD
Jordan, W. Julius	Pvt.	PeeDee LA		DN	12/13/62	Fredericksburg	KIA		ROH,PDL
Jordan, W.B. (W.S.?)	Pvt.	D 1st SCVIG		DN	09/21/61	Richmond, VA	DOD	Hollywood Cem.Rchmd. G28	ROH,HC,SA1,PDL
Jordan, W.H.	Pvt.	D 15th SCVI		KW	/ /	Lynchburg, VA	DOD	Lynchburg CSA Cem. #5R5	JR,HIC,KEB,BBW
Jordan, W.J.	Pvt.	B 26th SCVI		HY	12/30/64	Pt. Lookout, MD	DIP	C.C. Pt. Lookout, MD	FPH,P6,P113
Jordan, Wiley	Pvt.	Inglis LA		DN	06/15/64	Florence, SC	DOD		ROH
Jordan, William	Pvt.	A 8th SCVI		DN	07/26/62	Richmond, VA	DOD	(Typhoid)	ROH,JR
Jordan, William F.	Pvt.	Palm. LA		CD	05/03/64	Charlottesville	DOD		SOB
Jordan, William Henry	Pvt.	Chfld LA		CD	07/20/63	Richmond, VA	DOD		ROH
Jordan, William J.	Pvt.	M 10th SCVI		HY	07/28/64	Atlanta, GA	KIA	(On picket)	ROH,RAS
Jordan, William J.	Pvt.	F 1st SCVIG		HY	07/11/62	Richmond, VA	DOD	(JR=DOW 7/10/62)	ROH,JR,SA1,PDL
Jordan, William King	Pvt.	I 21st SCVI		MN	09/16/64	Elmira, NY	DIP	Woodlawn N.C.#168 Elmira	FPH,HMC,HAG,P6
Jordan, William T.	Pvt.	M 26th SCVI	17	HY	07/15/63	Jackson, MS	DOD		ROH,JR,PP
Jordan, Zebedee	Pvt.	K 7th SCVC		KW	/ /	VA	DOD		HIC
Josey, B. Flemming	Pvt.	K 23rd SCVI	20	SR	10/23/63	Winchester, VA	DOD	Stonewall C. Winchester VA	ROH,JR,WIN,UD3
Josey, George W.	Pvt.	K 23rd SCVI	22	SR	08/30/62	2nd Manassas, VA	KIA		ROH,JR,K23,UD3
Josey, J.R.	Pvt.	C 21st SCVI			07/11/64	Richmond, VA		Hollywood Cem.Rchmd. U119	HC
Journegan, John	Pvt.	H 14th SCV			/ /	Hosp.	DOW	(wounded May 1863)	UD2
Jowers, F.M.	Pvt.	C 17th SCMil		CD	04/13/65	Hart's Island NY	DIP	Cypress Hills N.C.#2510 NY	FPH,P6,P79
Jowers, J.P.	Pvt.	K 2nd SCVI		BL	08/31/62	Manchester, VA	DOD		H2,SA2,KEB
Jowers, J.W.	Pvt.	A 23rd SCVI		CD	05/29/65	Hart's Island NY	DIP	Cypress Hills N.C.#2897 NY	ROH,FPH,P6,P42
Jowers, Thomas	Pvt.	H 1st SCV			07/30/64	Ft. Delaware, DE	DIP	Finn's Pt., NJ Nat. Cem.	FPH,P6
Joy, Samuel J.	Pvt.	Hart's Bty			/ /	Petersburg, VA			CNM
Joyner, J.M.	Pvt.	F 2nd SCVC		GE	03/19/65	Salisbury, NC		Prob Old Lutheran C. there	PP
Joyner, P.H.	Pvt.	F P.S.S.		LN	10/15/61	Richmond, VA		Hollywood Cem.Rchmd. F47	HC
Judd, G.M.	Sgt.	Wash. Arty		CN	09/17/62	Sharpsburg, MD	KIA		JR,CDC
Judy, John	Pvt.	C 24th SCVI	18	CO	/ /	Atlanta, GA	KIA	(1864)	ROH,TEB,UD2
Judy, Lewis	Pvt.	C 24th SCVI	26		/ /	Atlanta, GA	DOW		TEB
Jumper, J. Benjamin	2nd Lt.	C 15th SCVI	25	LN	07/07/64	Cold Harbor, VA	DOW		ROH,KEB,TOD,H1
Jumper, J.L.	Pvt.	B 1st SCVIH		LN	05/06/64	Wilderness, VA	KIA		SA1
June, A.H.	Pvt.	G 15th SCVI		WG	10/11/63	Ft. Delaware, DE	DIP	Finn's Pt., NJ Nat. Cem.	ROH,FPH,P5,P40
June, James Stacey	Pvt.	A 10th SCVI		WG	07/22/64	Atlanta, GA	KIA		ROH,GRG,RAS,HO
Junkens, William	Pvt.	K 12th SCVI	22	PS	09/17/62	Sharpsburg, MD	KIA		ROH
Justice, J.F.	Pvt.	D 22nd SCVI		PS	08/27/64	Pt. Lookout, MD	DIP	C.C. Pt. Lookout, MD	ROH,FPH,P5,P11
Justus, Lionel	Pvt.	I 22nd SCVI		OG	06/16/62	Secessionville	KIA		ROH,CDC,PP

SOUTH CAROLINA DEAD IN CSA SERVICE 1861-1865

NAME	RANK	C REGIMENT	AGE	DS	DIED	WHERE	WHY	BURIED	SOURCES
Kadle, James M.	Pvt.	F 7th SCVI	20	ED	11/05/63	Ft. Delaware, DE	DIP	Finn's Pt., NJ Nat. Cem.	ROH,FPH,GDR,P5
Kaessler, Fritz	Pvt.	Bachman's	22	CN	09/17/62	Sharpsburg, MD	KIA		ROH,CDC
Kairick, Artemus	Pvt.	E 1st SCVC		OG	03/15/62	Adams run, SC	DOD		ROH,
Kaler, James E.	Pvt.	C 25th SCVI		WG	05/16/64	Drury's Bluff VA	KIA		CTA,HOW,HAG
Kallstrom, A.	Pvt.	C 2nd SCVI		RD	09/20/63	Chickamauga, GA	KIA		ROH,JR,SA2
Kalsbrour,	Pvt.		30	RD	/ /	NC	KIA	(1865)	ROH
Kane, Nicholas J.	2nd Sgt.	K 1st SCVIG		CN	05/12/64	Spotsylvania, VA	KIA		ROH,JR,SA1,CDC
Kaney, John	Pvt.	F P.S.S.		SR	05/05/62	Williamsburg, VA	KIA		ROH,CDC
Kaslan, Thomas	Pvt.	B 1st SCVA			07/28/64	Bty. Pringle, SC	DOW		R44
Kassey, John L.	Pvt.	C 14th SCVI		LS	06/27/62	Gaines' Mill, VA	KIA		JR
Kay, Charles W.	5th Sgt.	I 19th SCVI	26	AE	08/04/64	Atlanta, GA	DOW	(Wdd 7/28/64)	ROH
Kay, David M.	Pvt.	K Orr's Ri.	24	AN	07/08/62	Richmond, VA	DOD	Hollywood Cem.Rchmd. M118	ROH,JR,HC
Kay, E.J.	Pvt.	L Orr's Ri.		AN	08/12/62	Richmond, VA	DOD	Oakwood C.#37,Row F,Div C	ROH,JR,OWC,CDC
Kay, James Harry	Pvt.	I 19th SCVI	29	AE	12/02/62	Columbia, SC	DOD		ROH
Kay, James W.	Pvt.	G 2nd SCRes	18	AE	01/06/65	Columbia, SC	DOD	Broadmouth B.C. Honeapath	ROH,CAE,PP
Kay, Ludie F.	Pvt.	G 2nd SCRes	18	AE	01/05/65	Columbia, SC	DOD	Broadmouth B.C. Honeapath	ROH,CAE,PP
Kay, Reuben B.	Pvt.	I 19th SCVI	21	AE	01/27/62	Charleston, SC	DOD		ROH
Kay, Robert C.	Pvt.	K Orr's Ri.	22	AN	06/26/62	Gaines' Mill, VA	KIA		ROH,JR,CDC
Kay, Robert M.	Pvt.	K Orr's Ri.		AN	05/20/65	Hart's Island NY	DIP	Cypress Hills N.C.#2836 NY	ROH,FPH,P6,P12
Kay, Robert W.	Pvt.	K Orr's Ri.	28	AN	12/02/63	At home	DOD	(JR=3/5/62)	ROH,CDC
Kay, W.A.	Pvt.	D 7th SCVI			08/08/62			Piedmont Inst., VA	ROH,KEB
Keans, J.J.	Pvt.	C 23rd SCVI		CN	12/10/63	Charleston, SC	DOD	Magnolia Cem. Charleston	ROH,MAG,RCD
Kearney, J.C.	Pvt.	21st SCVI			/ /			City Pt.N.C. Hopewell, VA	ROH
Kearse, Blake W.	Pvt.	D 11th SCVI	17	BT	08/15/62	Hardeesville, SC	DOD	(ROH= W.B.)	ROH,HAG
Keasley, J.B.	Pvt.	L Orr's Ri.		AN	09/27/62	Warrenton, VA	DOW	(Kirsan,J.B./CDC Wdd@Wtn)	ROH
Keathers, Sampson	Pvt.	E 13th SCVI		SG	06/15/62		DOD	(Typhoid)	JR
Keaton, Benjamin F.	Pvt.	K Orr's Ri.	42	AN	06/18/62		DOD		ROH
Keaton, Reuben	Pvt.	K Orr's Ri.	26	AN	06/27/62	Gaines' Mill, VA	KIA	Ebenezer B.C. Belton, SC	ROH,JR,ANC
Keaton, William P.	Pvt.	K Orr's Ri.	37	AE	09/20/64	Petersburg, VA	DOW	(Wdd 8/16/64)	ROH,CDC
Kee, Henry M.	Pvt.	A 6th SCVI		CR	/ /	At home	DOD	(1862, HHC=Huey M.)	JR,HHC,CB
Keels, E.C.	3rd Lt.	I 4th SCVC	39	WG	11/08/65	Richmond, VA	DOD	Hollywood Cem.Rchmd. W726	CTA,HOW,HC
Keels, Elliott M.F.	Cpt.			CL	/ /	Charlestown, VA		(1st Cpt. of H,2nd SCVI).	ROH
Keels, R.F.	Pvt.	E 19th SCVI		SR	06/04/62	Okolona, MS	DOD		PP,TOD
Keels, W. Elliot	Pvt.	I 7th SCVI	31	WG	09/14/62	Maryland Hts. MD	KIA		JR,CTA,HOW
Keen, Abner N.	Pvt.	Tucker's C		GN	03/19/63	Alton, IL	DIP	Confed. Cem. Alton, IL	FPH
Keese, Benjamin F.	Pvt.	D 2nd SCVIRi			11/08/63	Bridgeport, AL	DOW	(In enemy hands)	P6,P12
Keese, John R.	Pvt.	C 2nd SCVI		PS	12/13/62	Fredericksburg	KIA		ROH,JR,SA2
Keese, Livingston W.	Pvt.	E 4th SCVI	24	AN	08/28/61	Culpepper, VA	DOD	Pendleton, SC	JR,CGH,SA2
Keever, Daniel A.	Sgt.	D 25th SCVI		MN	08/28/64	Alexandria, VA	DOW	Christ Ch. Alexandria, VA	HMC,CV,P1,P6
Kegway, B.C.	Pvt.	D 6th SCVC			06/12/64	Trevillian Stn.	KIA		JR
Keiffe, Eli	Pvt.	C 26th SCVI		MN	06/15/63		DOD		JR
Keimer, Michael		CSN			03/29/65	Richmond, VA			ROH
Keise, B.F.	Pvt.	D 2nd SCVIRi		PS	10/28/63	Bridgeport, AL	DOW	(Wdd. @ Lookout Valley)	ROH,JR,P6,CDC
Keisler, G.A.	Pvt.	K 13th SCVI		LN	07/28/63	Davids Island NY	DOW	Cypress Hills N.C.#694 NY	ROH,FPH,P6,P12
Keisler, Mark W.C.	Cpl.	C 15th SCVI	23	LN	05/06/64	Wilderness, VA	KIA		ROH,JR,H15,TOD
Keisler, Wade	2nd Lt.	I 15th SCVI	38	LN	09/14/62	South Mtn., MD	KIA		ROH,JR,KEB,H15
Keist, H.C.	Pvt.	D 5th SCVI			02/15/63	Lynchburg, VA	DOD	Lynchburg CSA Cem. #8R4	SA3,BBW
Keith, Elliott Monroe	Ord. Sgt.	A Orr's Ri.		AN	02/08/62	Sullivans I., SC	DOD	(JR=9/1/62)	ROH,JR
Keith, Evander	Pvt.	E 1st SCVIG		MN	06/08/62	Richmond, VA	DOD	Hollywood Cem.Rchmd. P145	ROH,JR,HC,SA1
Keith, James	Pvt.	E 1st SCVIG		MN	/ /			(On rolls 12/31/64)	HMC,SA1
Keith, John Randolph	Pvt.	A Orr's Ri.		AN	09/01/62	At home	DOD	(JR=Measles 2/8/62)	ROH,JR,CDC

SOUTH CAROLINA DEAD IN CSA SERVICE 1861-1865

NAME	RANK	C	REGIMENT	AGE	DS	DIED	WHERE	WHY	BURIED	SOURCES
Keith, Thomas Jefferson	4th Sgt.	A	Orr's Ri.		PS	08/09/62	Richmond, VA	DOD	Hollywood Cem.Rchmd. Q143	ROH,JR,HC,CDC
Keith, W.A.	Pvt.	D	2nd SCVI		SR	12/13/62	Fredericksburg	KIA	(JR=W.B.)	ROH,JR,SA2
Keitt, Lawrence M.	Col.		20th SCVI	40	OG	06/04/64	Richmond, VA	DOW	(Wdd 6/2 @ Cold Harbor)	ROH,JR,LC,EMC
Keitt, W.H.	Pvt.	K	Orr's Ri.		AN	02/23/62	Greenville, SC	DOD		JR
Kellam, J.W.	Pvt.	I	6th SCVI		CR	03/01/65	Richmond, VA		Hollywood Cem.Rchmd. W333	HC
Keller, J.W. (T.W.?)	Pvt.	B	22nd SCVI		SG	05/12/65	Pt. Lookout, MD	DIP	C.C. Pt. Lookout, MD	P12
Keller, James	Pvt.	I	5th SCVI		SG	08/29/62	2nd Manassas, VA	MIA	(HOS=KIA @ Wilderness)	SA3,HOS
Keller, John	Pvt.	B	22nd SCVI		SG	08/23/62	Rappahanock Stn.	KIA		ROH
Keller, Joseph Wilds	Pvt.	F	4th SCVI		GE	07/21/61	1st Manassas, VA	KIA		ROH,SA2
Keller, William H.	Pvt.	H	Ham.Leg.		OG	11/15/63	Lookout Valley	DOW		ROH,CDC
Keller, Y. Alexander	Cpl.	B	22nd SCVI		SG	04/13/65	Pt. Lookout, MD	DIP	C.C. Pt. Lookout, MD	ROH,FPH,P6,P113
1Kellers, F.W.	Cpl.	F	25th SCVI		OG	05/16/64	Drury's Bluff VA	KIA		JR
Kellers, James F.	4th Cpl.	A	25th SCVI	24	CN	05/20/64	Drury's Bluff VA	KIA		ROH,JR,HAG,WLI
Kellett, J.	Pvt.	K	SCVI			/ /			Charlestown, VA	ROH
Kelley,	Pvt.	G	16th SCVI		GE	/ /	Georgia	DOD		16R
Kelley, C.	Pvt.					/ /	Richmond, VA		Oakwood C.#80,Row A,Div G	ROH,OWC
Kelley, E.	Pvt.	E	2nd SCV			05/16/65	Newport News, VA	DIP	Newport News, VA Cem. #59	P6
Kelley, Hiram	1st Lt.	F	8th SCVI	24	DN	11/22/63	Richmond, VA	DOD	(JR=5/31/62)	ROH,JR,KEB,R46
Kelley, J.C.	Pvt.	D	18th SCVI		AN	/ /	Wilmington, NC			ROH
Kelley, J.J.	Pvt.	C	Orr's Ri.		PS	10/02/62	Winchester, VA		Stonewall C. Winchester VA	ROH,WIN,CDC
Kelley, J.W.	Pvt.	B	2nd SCVIRi		PS	/ /	Winchester, VA			ROH
Kelley, James	Pvt.	E	1st SCVIR			03/16/65	Averysboro, NC	KIA		ROH,SA1,WAT,PP
Kelley, James	Sgt.	B	21st SCVI		DN	02/08/65	Elmira, NY	DIP	Woodlawn N.C.#1912 Elmira	FPH,HAG,P5,P65
Kelley, Joseph	Pvt.	D	13th SCVI	18	NY	05/18/64	Spotsylvania, VA	DOW	Spotsylvania C.H., VA	ROH,SCH
Kelley, M.	Pvt.	C	Orr's Ri.		PS	07/28/62	Danville, VA	DOD		JR
Kelley, Pinckney H.	Cpl.	E	18th SCVI		SG	07/30/64	Petersburg, VA	KIA		ROH,JR,HOS
Kelley, Simon H.	Pvt.	G	21st SCVI		CD	02/16/65	Elmira, NY	DIP	Woodlawn N.C.#2202 Elmira	FPH,CDC,P5,P65
Kelley, T.J.	Pvt.	E	18th SCVI		SG	07/30/64	Crater, Pbg., VA	KIA		BLM,HOS
Kelley, T.K.	Pvt.	G	21st SCVI		CD	05/17/64	Pt. Walthall Jtn	DOW		CDC,HAG
Kelley, Wiley	Pvt.	H	5th SCVI		UN	03/15/63	Lynchburg, VA	DOD	Lynchburg CSA Cem. #6R2	JR,SA3,BBW
Kelley, William J.	Pvt.	D	13th SCVI	23	NY	05/12/64	Spotsylvania, VA	KIA	Spotsylvania C.H., VA	ROH,JR,SCH
Kellingsworth, J.M.	Pvt.	C	Orr's Ri.		PS	04/15/65	Richmond, VA	DOD	(Bronchitus, Jackson Hos.)	P10,CDC
Kelly J.J.	Pvt.	A	20th SCVI		PS	01/12/64	Charleston, SC	DOD	Magnolia Cem. Charleston	ROH,MAG
Kelly, A.O.	Pvt.	F	Orr's Ri.		PS	07/11/63	Richmond, VA	DOD	Hollywood Cem.Rchmd. M184	ROH,HC,CDC
Kelly, B.L.	2nd Cpl.	H	2nd SCVI		LR	09/06/62	Charleston, SC	DOD	(SA2=Home, ACD Wdd,1864)	LAN,SA2,KEB
Kelly, B.P.	Pvt.	D	15th SCVI		KW	/ /	Virginia	KIA	(1864)	HIC,KEB
Kelly, Benjamin E.	Pvt.	E	2nd SCVI	26	KW	01/13/63	Richmond, VA	DOD	(Kelley in HIC)	ROH,SA2,HIC,KEB
Kelly, Brooks B.	Pvt.	H	3rd SCVI		LN	/ /	At home	DOD	(POW 5/23 Exchd 11/01/64)	ROH,KEB,SA2,P113
Kelly, D.	Pvt.	A	1st SCVAR			08/20/62		MUR	(in an affray)	ROH
Kelly, Daniel	Pvt.	I	2nd SCVA	28	OG	06/16/62	Secessionville	KIA	(JR=DOW 6/27/62)	ROH,JR,CDC,PP
Kelly, Daniel E.	1st Lt.Adj		23rd SCVI		CL	07/30/64	Crater, Pbg., VA	KIA		JR,BLM,HCL,R48
Kelly, David	Pvt.	B	21st SCVI	20	DN	03/17/62	Georgetown, SC	DOD		ROH,JR,PP
Kelly, Elbert J.	Pvt.	C	25th SCVI		WG	10/06/64	Philadelphia, PA	DOW	Nat. Cem.#136 Phila., PA	FPH,CDC,P1,P5,P6
Kelly, Elisha	Pvt.	E	2nd SCVIRi		PS	05/16/65	Newport News, VA	DIP	Greenlawn C. Newport News	PP,P12
Kelly, George Jackson	Pvt.	A	2nd SCVI		PS	09/17/62	Sharpsburg, MD	KIA	(JR=MD Hts. 9/13/62)	ROH,JR,SA2,H2
Kelly, H.T.	Pvt.	G	Ham.Leg.			08/12/62		ACD	(Drowned)	JR
Kelly, Harrison	Pvt.	B	21st SCVI		DN	05/16/64	Drury's Bluff VA	DOW		ROH,HAG
Kelly, Harvey	Pvt.	D	Ham.Leg.		AN	05/31/62	7 Pines, VA	KIA		GRS
Kelly, I. Jasper	Pvt.	E	3rd SCVI		NY	10/19/64	Strasburg, VA	KIA	(Also Wdd. 6/1/64)	ROH,SA2,ANY,KEB
Kelly, J. Harrison	Pvt.	C	3rd SCVI		NY	10/15/62		DOD	(JR=Co.B & DOD 8/13/62)	ROH,JR,SA2,ANY
Kelly, J.A.	Pvt.	A	1st SCVIBn		CN	06/03/52	Legare's Place	KIA		JR

SOUTH CAROLINA DEAD IN CSA SERVICE 1861-1865

NAME	RANK	C REGIMENT	AGE	DS	DIED	WHERE	WHY	BURIED	SOURCES
Kelly, J.M.	Pvt.	H 25th SCVI		CN	02/13/65	Elmira, NY	DIP	Woodlawn N.C.#2067 Elmira	FPH,P5,P12,P65
Kelly, James	Pvt.	K 1st SCVIG		CN	12/30/62	Fredericksburg	DOW		SA1
Kelly, James Bainwater	Pvt.	H 13th SCVI		LN	10/18/61	Columbia, SC	DOD	(Measles)	ROH,JR,PP
Kelly, James D.	2nd Lt.	C Ham.Leg.		CL	09/11/62		DOD	(JR=1st Lt. Co.A 2/8/62)	JR,R48
Kelly, James M.	5th Cpl.	C 3rd SCVI	26	NY	06/30/62	Savage Stn., VA	KIA		ROH,JR,SA2,CDC
Kelly, Jasper	Pvt.	D 13th SCVI	21	NY	05/02/63	Chancellorsville	KIA		ANY
Kelly, John	Pvt.		30	RD	/ /	NC	KIA	(1865)	ROH
Kelly, John	Pvt.	C 27th SCVI		CN	08/15/63		DOD		JR,HAG
Kelly, John A.	Pvt.	A 25th SCVI		CN	06/03/62	James Island, SC	KIA	Magnolia Cem. Charleston	ROH,MAG
Kelly, John C.	Pvt.	H 25th SCVI		CN	02/28/65	Elmira, NY	DIP	Woodlawn N.C.#2112 Elmira	FPH,HAG,P5,P65
Kelly, John F.M.	Pvt.	H 2nd SCVI		LR	09/06/62	Charlestown, VA	DOD		ROH,SA2,LAN,H2
Kelly, P.	Pvt.	I 2nd SCVA	50	OG	06/20/62	Secessionville	DOW		ROH
Kelly, P.J.	Pvt.	K Orr's Ri.			08/29/62	2nd Manassas, VA	KIA		JR
Kelly, Samuel L.	Pvt.	F 1st SCVIG		HY	07/06/63	Williamsport, MD	KIA	(JR=Gettysburg 7/2/63)	ROH,JR,SA1,PDL
Kelly, W.D.	Pvt.	I 23rd SCVI		CL	09/21/62	Warrenton, VA	DOW	(Wdd @ 2nd Man)	ROH,CDC
Kelly, Walter J.	Pvt.	D 13th SCVI	21	NY	05/02/63	Chancellorsville	KIA	(Kelley, William J.?)	ANY
Kelly, William	Pvt.	D 1st SCVIR		TN	11/15/64	Ft. Sumter, SC	KIA	(Day estimated)	SA1
Kelly, William B.	Pvt.	F 3rd SCVABn	18	CN	01/22/65	Adams Run, SC	DOD		ROH
Kelly, William H.	1st Lt.	D 5th SCVI		UN	12/26/64	New Market, VA	DOW	(Wdd 12/10/64)	SA3
Kelly, William M.	Pvt.	D 3rd SCVI		SG	/ /	Richmond, VA	DOD	(Around 7/15/61)	SA2,KEB,HOS
Kelly, Z. Simpson	Pvt.	C 3rd SCVI		LN	12/13/62	Fredericksburg	KIA	(Y.in ANY/KEB- p198,KEB)	ROH,JR,SA2,ANY
Kelsey, F.U.	Pvt.	15th SCVIB		CR	09/21/63	Charleston, SC	DOD		ROH
Kelsey, William E.	Pvt.	A 17th SCVI	45	CR	08/28/62	Culpepper, VA	DOD		ROH,JR,HHC,CB
Kemmerlin, T.A.	2nd Sgt.	C 1st SCVIH		OG	01/11/62		DOD		SA1
Kemp, James	Pvt.	A 6th SCVC			05/05/65	Hart's Island NY	DIP	Cypress Hills N.C. 2708	FPH,P6,P12,P79
Kemp, James H.	Pvt.	K 6th SCVI		GE	11/25/61	Culpepper, VA	DOD	Fairview Cem. Culpepper VA	CGH
Kemp, Jesse	2nd Lt.	C 22nd SCVI	36	SG	03/12/65	Ft. Delaware, DE	DIP	Finn's Pt., NJ Nat. Cem.	ROH,FPH,P5,R48
Kemp, John L.	Pvt.	F 5th SCVI		SG	10/01/61		DOD		ROH,SA3
Kemp, John W.	Cpt.	G 7th SCVI	29	ED	05/06/64	Wilderness, VA	KIA		ROH,JR,HOE,UD2
Kemp, Joseph	Pvt.	B 2nd SCVA	16	OG	03/19/65	Bentonville, NC	KIA		ROH,WAT,PP
Kemp, Leonard D.	Pvt.	E 22nd SCVI		GE	06/23/62	Charleston, SC	DOD	Magnolia Cem. Charleston	ROH,MAG
Kemp, Tira.	Pvt.	D 15th SCVI		KW	10/19/61	Columbia, SC	DOD	(JR=P.S.S.) PP	ROH,JR,HIC,CDN
Kemp, W.H.	Pvt.	C 22nd SCVI	18	GE	09/02/64	Elmira, NY	DIP	Woodlawn N.C.#211 Elmira	ROH,FPH,P5,P65
Kempson, Levi Christian	2nd Cpl.	H 3rd SCVI		LN	05/06/64	Wilderness, VA	KIA	Kempson Gvyd. Little Mtn.	ROH,NCC,ANY,SA
Kemsey, A.F.R.	Pvt.	E 26th SCVI			05/20/64	Virginia	KIA		ROH
Kendrick, John	Pvt.	B 22nd SCVI		SG	07/30/64	Crater, Pbg., VA	KIA		HOS
Kendrick, M.B.	Sgt.	F P.S.S.			/ /		DOD		JR
Kendrick, M.S.	Pvt.	F 18th SCVI		UN	06/15/62	Richmond, VA	DOD	Gilead C. Jonesville UN Cy	UD3
Kendrick, Smith	Pvt.	F 15th SCVI	34	UN	12/27/62	Howard Grove Hos	DOD		ROH,UD2
Kendrick, T.F.	5th Sgt.	H 1st SCVIH		UN	01/15/64	Knoxville, TN	DIP		ROH,SA1
Kendrick, T.J. (J.T.?)	Pvt.	F 15th SCVI		UN	/ /	Fredericksburg	DOW	Skull Shoals Ch. UN Cty.	ROH,JR,UNC,KEB
Kendrick, W.R.	2nd Sgt.	B 13th SCVI		SG	08/29/62	2nd Manassas, VA	DOW		JR,HOS
Kenemore, Moses	Pvt.	D 18th SCVI		PS	09/29/64	Elmira, NY	DIP	Woodlawn N.C.#434 Elmira	ROH,FPH,P120
Kennedy, A.V.	Pvt.	H Ham.Leg.		OG	12/15/62	Frederick, MD	DIP	Rose Hill C. Hagerstown MD	ROH,JR,FPH,BOD
Kennedy, Allen D.	Pvt.	H 7th SCVIBn	26	CR	05/16/64	Drury's Bluff VA	KIA		ROH,JR,HAG,HHC
Kennedy, Daul J.	Pvt.	E 1st SCVC		OG	04/15/65	At home	DOD		ROH
Kennedy, Evander	Pvt.	C 18th SCVAB		MN	/ /	Charleston, SC	DOD		HMC
Kennedy, Evander	Pvt.	D 25th SCVI		MN	10/16/62	Elliot Cut, SC	DOD	(On Stono River)	JR,HMC,HAG
Kennedy, H.E.	Pvt.	A Ham.Leg.		CN	/ /				WLI
Kennedy, H.G.	Pvt.	K 17th SCVI	17	BL	09/08/62	Warrenton, VA	DOW	(Wdd @ 2nd Man)	ROH,JR
Kennedy, Hugh Reid	Cpl.	Brooks GA		CN	07/10/63	Gettysburg, PA	DOW	(1st in Co.K, 2nd SCVI)	ROH,JR,KEB,SA2

K

SOUTH CAROLINA DEAD IN CSA SERVICE 1861-1865

NAME	RANK	C REGIMENT	AGE	DS	DIED	WHERE	WHY	BURIED	SOURCES
Kennedy, Isaac C.	Pvt.	G 19th SCVI		AE	03/12/65	Salisbury, NC	DOD	Prob Old Lutheran C. there	HOL,PP
Kennedy, J.R.	Pvt.	G 6th SCVI		FD	09/30/64	Chaffin's Farm	KIA		ROH
Kennedy, James M.	Pvt.	C 7th SCVI	19	AE	09/17/62	Sharpsburg, MD	KIA		ROH,JR,KEB
Kennedy, John	Pvt.	C 24th SCVI	37	CO	04/20/64	James Island, SC	DOD	(? Rgt.not in SC then)	ROH
Kennedy, John	Cpt.	CN Post QM		CN	01/16/64		DOD		ROH
Kennedy, John L.	Cpt.	B 7th SCVIBn	39	FD	08/10/64	Petersburg, VA	DOD	(JR=8/12/64) PP	ROH,JR,HAG,HFC
Kennedy, John M.	Pvt.	SCRes		LS	/ /	Cheraw, SC	DOD		UD3
Kennedy, Joseph	Pvt.	B 19th SCVI		ED	/ /		DOD		HOE
Kennedy, Robert	Pvt.	I 6th SCVI		CR	/ /	Charlottesville	DOD		CB,HHC
Kennedy, Robert	Seaman	CS Navy			04/24/65	Pt. Lookout, MD	DIP	C.C. Pt. Lookout, MD	FPH,P12
Kennedy, Robert W.	2nd Lt.	B 7th SCVIBn	26	FD	08/21/64	Weldon RR, VA	KIA	(JR=6/30/64)	ROH,JR,HFC,R46
Kennedy, Rufus Caloin	Sgt.	D Ham.Leg.	22	AN	09/17/62	Sharpsburg, MD	KIA		ROH,JR,GRS
Kennedy, S.S.	Pvt.	G 4th SCVC			05/24/64	Hawe's Shop, VA	DOW	Mrs. W.N. Newton's house	ROH,JR,CDC,P12
Kennedy, W.	Pvt.				/ /	Charleston, SC		Magnolia Cem. Charleston	MAG
Kennedy, William	Pvt.	G 1st SCVIG		ED	08/21/64	Petersburg, VA	KIA	(Sniper, see Pg154 LSS)	LSS,HOE
Kennedy, William Jay	1st Sgt.	D 1st SC Res	17	PS	02/24/65	Charleston, SC	DOD	Magnolia Cem. Charleston	ROH,MAG
Kennedy, William R.	Pvt.	I 6th SCVI		CR	/ /		DOD		CB,HHC
Kennemore, M.	Pvt.	D 18th SCVI		UN	09/30/64	Elmira, NY	DIP		FPH,P65,P66,P120
Kennerly, Dant	Pvt.	6th SCVC	45	OG	06/15/63	At home	DOD		ROH
Kennerly, J. Robert	Cpl.	G 25th SCVI	25	OG	05/16/64	Drury's Bluff VA	KIA		ROH,JR,EDL,CV
Kennerly, J.S.	Pvt.	K 2nd SCVA		ED	/ /		DOD		HOE,UD3
Kennerly, Samuel N.	1st Lt.	G 25th SCVI	36	OG	08/21/64	Weldon RR, VA	KIA		ROH,HAG,EDR,DOC
Kennerly, Vastino V.	Pvt.	H Ham. Leg.	37	OG	/ /	Virginia	DOW	(1863, in enemy hands)	ROH
Kennes, C.C.	Pvt.	E 25th SCVI		CN	06/04/64	Fts. Monroe, VA	DOW	(In enemy hands)	ROH
Kennett, G.W.	Sgt.	H P.S.S.		sG	06/27/62	Gaines' Mill, VA	KIA	(CDC=Kenneth, G.M.)	ROH,JR,HOS,CDC
Kenney, J.C.	Cpl.	Ficklin's			05/08/64	Spotsylvania, VA	KIA		JR
Kenney, Peter	Pvt.	H 27th SCVI		CN	09/01/64	Greensboro, NC			PP,HAG
Kennimore, George	Pvt.	Fergsons A		PS	06/27/63	Mt. Vernon, MS	DOD	(On drill ground)	ROH
Kennington, G.W.	Sgt.	F 7th SCVIBn		LR	05/16/64	Drury's Bluff VA	KIA	(? LAN & HIC=survived war)	HAG,SA2
Kennington, G.W.	Pvt.	H 2nd SCVI		LR	09/13/62	Maryland Hts. MD	KIA	(JR=Hunnington)	JR,SA2,KEB
Kennington, John	Pvt.	H 2nd SCVI		LR	02/04/62	Danville, VA	DOD	(Typhoid pneumonia)	H2,SA2,KEB
Kennington, Naaman	Pvt.	H 2nd SCVI	28	LR	07/28/64	Deep Bottom, VA	KIA		ROH,SA2,LAN
Kennington, Richard R.	Pvt.	H 2nd SCVI		LR	05/06/64	Wilderness, VA	DOW	(SA2=AWL 6/30/64, at home)	LAN,SA2
Kennington, W.J.	Pvt.	H 2nd SCVI		LR	09/17/62	Sharpsburg, VA	KIA		SA2,LAN,H2,KEB
Kennington, William H.	Pvt.	H 2nd SCVC	19	LR	06/12/63	Newtown, VA	KIA	Stonewall C. Winchester VA	ROH,WIN,LAN,P12
Kennington, William R.	3rd Sgt.	H 2nd SCVI	27	LR	11/12/64	Winchester, VA	DOW	(Wdd @ Cedar Creek)	ROH,SA2,KEB,LAN
Keough, P.H.	1st Sgt.	F 3rd SCVIBn	35	RD	09/14/62	South Mtn., MD	KIA		ROH,JR,KEB
Keown, Carter D.	Pvt.	C P.S.S.		PS	05/16/64	Orange C.H., VA	DOW	(GMJ=Wdd @ Wilderness)	ROH,JR,GMJ
Keown, W.M.	Pvt.	C P.S.S.		AN	08/30/62	2nd Manassas, VA	KIA		ROH,JR,CDC,GMJ
Kernels, L.	Cpl.	A 2nd SCVIRi			10/07/64	Darbytown, VA	KIA		JR
Kerr, C.H.	Pvt.	A 18th SCVAB		CN	02/10/65	Grimball's, SC	KIA		STR,DOC
Kerr, John Thomas	Pvt.	I 19th SCVI		AE	11/12/62	Tazewell, TN	DOD		ROH,PP
Kerr, T.J.	Pvt.	A 18th SCABn		CN	02/10/65	James Island, SC	KIA	Unitarian Ch. Charleston	MAG,RCD
Kerrison, Edwin L.	Pvt.	I 2nd SCVI	23	CN	05/05/64	Spotsylvania, VA	KIA	Magnolia Cem. Charleston	ROH,JR,MAG,SA2
Kersey, H.	Pvt.	E 23rd SCVI		MN	09/28/64	(ROH=Keisler)		Piedmont Inst., VA	ROH,HMC
Kersey, John	Pvt.	Chn Guards		MN	08/03/61	Richmond, VA	DOD	Hollywood Cem.Rchmd. K2	HC
Kersey, William	Pvt.	H 23rd SCVI		MN	12/13/62	Kinston, NC	KIA	(HMC=KIA @ Goldsboro)	ROH,HMC
Kersh, A.J.	Pvt.	G 1st SCVIH		BL	05/30/63		DOD	(Wdd @ Sharpsburg)	ROH,SA1
Kervin, Mercer J. (L.?)	Pvt.	M 8th SCVI		DN	/ /	Greenville, SC			CDC,KEB
Kerwick, William	Pvt.	A 24th SCVI	26	CN	06/01/64	New Hope Ch., GA	KIA	(JR=Marietta, GA 6/19/64)	ROH,JR,CDC
Kesiah, John H.M.	Pvt.	E 21st SCVI	19	CD	02/03/64	Pt. Lookout, MD	DIP	C.C. Pt. Lookout, MD	ROH,FPH,P5,P113

SOUTH CAROLINA DEAD IN CSA SERVICE 1861-1865

NAME	RANK	C REGIMENT	AGE	DS	DIED	WHERE	WHY	BURIED	SOURCES
Ketchum, J.C.	2nd Lt.	G 6th SCVI		FD	10/03/64	Petersburg, VA	DOW	(HFC= Ketchim)	R46,HFC
Ketts, Joseph	Pvt.	SCVA			/ /	High Point, NC		Oakwood Cem. High Point NC	WAT
Key, David	Pvt.	H 14th SCVI		BL	04/01/65	Elmira, NY	DIP	Woodlawn N.C.#2596 Elmira	FPH,P6,P65,P12
Key, Giles	Pvt.	D Hol.Leg.		BL	05/10/64	Weldon, NC			PP
Key, John F.	Pvt.	I 17th SCVI		LR	/ /	Wilmington, NC	DOD	(JR=Warrenton, VA)	JR,LAN
Key, John Oliver	Pvt.	A 1st SCVIG		BL	07/01/63	Gettysburg, PA	KIA		ROH,JR,SA1,CDC
Key, M. Jackson	Pvt.	Chrfld. LA		CD	05/08/63	Petersburg, VA		Blandford Church Pbg., VA	BLC,PP
Key, R.R.	Cpl.	I 17th SCVI		LR	05/28/65	Elmira, NY	DIP	Woodlawn N.C.#2912 Elmira	FPH,LAN,P6,P65
Keys, Jeff	Pvt.	SCVA			04/20/65	High Point, NC		Oakwood Cem. High Point NC	CV
Keyser, Lewis	Pvt.	F 3rd SCVABn	30	CN	03/06/65	Cheraw, SC	DOD		ROH
Kibbin, Joseph W.	Pvt.	D 8th SCVI		CD	02/21/62	Culpepper, VA	DOD	Fairview Cem. Culpepper,VA	JR,CGH,KEB
Kibler, C.R.	Pvt.	C 17th SCVI		YK	08/10/64	Petersburg, VA	KIA		ROH
Kiddell, Theodore	Pvt.	A 27th SCVI		CN	05/07/64	Port Walthal Jct	KIA		ROH,JR,CDC,HAG
Kidwell, S.P.	Pvt.	G 24th SCV			/ /	Griffin Hosp.		Spaulding Cnty GA	UD2
Kilby, J.S.	Pvt.	H 7th SCVI		PS	01/29/65	Pt. Lookout, MD	DIP	C.C. Pt. Lookout, MD	FPH,P5,P12,P11
Kilcrease, A.	Pvt.	B 6th SCVC		ED	06/11/64	Trevillian Stn.	KIA	(HOE=SUR, 1865?)	ROH,JR
Kilgore, James L.	Cpl.	E 6th SCVI	25	DN	05/31/62	7 Pines, VA	KIA		ROH,JR,JLC,WDB
Kilgore, Peter A.	Pvt.	E 6th SCVI	23	DN	05/31/62	7 Pines, VA	KIA		ROH,JR,JLC,WDB
Killiam, J.W.	Pvt.	I 6th SCVI		CR	02/28/65	Richmond, VA		Hollywood Cem.Rchmd. W82	ROH,HC,HHC,CB
Killian, H.V.	Pvt.	H 24th SCVI	27	CR	06/10/64	Pine Mountain GA	DOW	(JR=Marietta, GA 6/19/64)	ROH,JR,HHC,CB
Killian, William M.	Pvt.	C 3rd Bn Res		YK	04/24/65		DOD		DEM
Kilpatrick, Franklin W.	Col.	1st SCVIH	26	PS	10/28/63	Lookout Valley	KIA	(Wauhatchie, TN)	ROH,JR,LC,SA1
Kilpatrick, Robert	Pvt.	D 17th SCVI	25	FD	08/31/64	At home	DOD		ROH
Kilroy, H.T.					/ /	Virginia		(Rchmd effects list 1/63)	CDC
Kimbrel, John	Pvt.	F 13th SCVI		SG	07/29/62	Laurel Hill, VA	DOD	(Typhoid)	HOS,JR
Kimbrel, Lawrence K.	Pvt.	K 6th SCVI	27	YK	10/07/64	Petersburg, VA	KIA	(YEB=Darby Inn)	ROH,YEB
Kimbrell, James	Pvt.	I 24th SCVI	32	ED	05/16/64	Calhoun, GA	KIA	(JR=Marietta, GA 6/19/64)	ROH,JR,CDC,UD2
Kimbrell, John	Pvt.	E 13th SCVI		SG	09/27/62	White Sulpher VA	DOD	(Typhoid)	JR
Kimbrell, Joseph P.	Pvt.	B 6th SCVI		YK	12/27/63	White Sulpher Ss		(YEB=Lost in TN)	ROH,YEB,PP
Kimbrell, Thomas	Pvt.	H 6th SCVI		YK	06/15/61	Germantown, VA	DOD		ROH,YEB
Kimbrell, William	Pvt.	E 13th SCVI		SG	06/10/62	(ROH=F,18th)	DOD	Hollywood Cem.Rchmd. P184	ROH,JR,HC,HOS
Kimmey, Augustus A.	Pvt.	Brooks GA		CN	05/02/64	Lynchburg, VA	DOD	(Typhoid)	H2,SA2,KEB
Kinard, B.	Pvt.	F 20th SCVI		NY	10/19/64	Newtown, VA	KIA	Stonewall C. Winchester VA	ROH,WIN
Kinard, Bennett J.	1st Lt.	H Hol. Leg.	32	NY	08/30/62	2nd Manassas, VA	KIA	Zion U.M.C. Prosperity SC	ROH,JR,NCC,ANY
Kinard, H. Calvin	Pvt.	D 5th SCVI		NY	10/13/64	Darbytown Rd. VA	KIA	Kinard Gvyd #1 Newberry SC	NCC,ANY,SA3
Kinard, Isaac	Pvt.	E 24th SCVI	22	CO	09/20/63	Chickamauga, GA	KIA	Con. Cem. Marietta, GA	ROH,JR,CDC,CCM
Kinard, J.A.	Cpl.	G 17th SCVI		BL	/ /		DOW		JR
Kinard, John	Pvt.	G 13th SCVI		NY	05/15/64		KIA		JR
Kinard, John Martin	Cpt.	F 20th SCVI	31	NY	10/13/64	Strasburg, VA	DOW	Old Newberry Village Cem.	ROH,JR,NCC,ANY
Kinard, Levi C.	Pvt.	C 3rd SCVI		NY	06/29/62	Savage Stn., VA	KIA	KEB	ROH,JR,SA2,ANY
Kinard, M.D.	Cpl.	G 17th SCVI		BL	/ /	John's Island SC	DOD		JR
Kinard, Minor D.	Pvt.	F 20th SCVI		NY	06/22/64	Petersburg, VA	DOW	(Head wound)	ROH,ANY,CDC
Kinard, Walter J.	Pvt.	D 13th SCVI	21	NY	07/01/63	Gettysburg, PA	KIA		ROH,JR,ANY
Kincaid, James H.	Pvt.	B 12th SCVI		YK	08/29/62	2nd Manassas, VA	KIA		ROH,JR,YMD,CDC
Kinchen,	Pvt.	F Orr's Ri.			05/06/64	Wilderness, VA	KIA		ROH,CDC
Kinemore, M.	Pvt.	D 18th SCVI			09/29/64	Elmira, NY	DIP	Woodlawn N.C. #434 Elmira	FPH,P6
King, Allen	Pvt.	K 14th SCVI		ED	07/01/63	Gettysburg, PA	KIA	(JR=DOW 7/25/63)	JR,GDR,HOE
King, Calvin	Pvt.	B 10th SCVI		HY	10/15/62	Vicksburg, MS	DOD	(POW @ Corinth Hospital)	RAS,LOR,P14
King, Charles W.	Refugee				02/25/64	Hilton Head, SC	DOD	Hilton Head N.C. #283	P6
King, D.D.	Pvt.	21st SCVI			/ /	(? E,6th SCVI)		Oakwood C.#5, Row F, Div F	ROH,OWC
King, G. Lucas	Pvt.	K 2nd SCVIRi	25	AN	06/19/64	Petersburg, VA	KIA		ROH,JR

SOUTH CAROLINA DEAD IN CSA SERVICE 1861-1865

NAME	RANK	C REGIMENT	AGE	DS	DIED	WHERE	WHY	BURIED	SOURCES
King, George	Pvt.	I 24th SCVI	20	ED	10/08/63	Atlanta, GA	DOD		EJM
King, George W.	Pvt.	E 2nd SCVI		KW	09/21/62	Lynchburg, VA	DOD	Lynchburg CSA Cem. #8R4	SA2,HIC,KEB,BBW
King, George W.	Pvt.	L 7th SCVI	25	HY	04/20/64	Emory, VA		Con. Cem. Emory, VA	PP
King, Henry C.	Cpt.	D 27th SCVI		CN	06/16/62	Secessionville	DOW	1st P.C.(Scotch)Charleston	ROH,JR,PP,HAG
King, J.	Pvt.	C 20th SCVI		LN	12/29/61	Charleston, SC	DOD	Magnolia Cem. Charleston	ROH,MAG
King, J.E.	Pvt.	F 16th SCVI		GE	11/30/64	Franklin, TN	KIA		ROH,16R,PP
King, J.H.	Pvt.	C 2nd SCVI		RD	01/15/63	Richmond, VA	DOD	Oakwood C.#155,Row M,Div A	ROH,SA2,OWC
King, J.J.	Pvt.	L 7th SCVI			/ /	Savage Stn., VA	DOW		CNM
King, James	Pvt.	F 1st SCVIR		LS	01/03/62		DOD		SA1
King, James M.	Pvt.	H Hol.Leg.	18	NY	02/14/62	Adams Run, SC	DOD		ROH,ANY,PP
King, Joel J.	Pvt.	A 3rd SCVIBn		LS	04/24/65	Pt. Lookout, MD	DIP	C.C. Pt. Lookout, MD	ROH,FPH,P6,P113
King, John	Sgt.	E 25th SCVI		CN	12/11/63	Ft. Sumter, SC	ACD	(Magazine explosion)	ROH,JR,HAG,CDC
King, John	Pvt.	A Tucker's R			02/25/65	Salisbury, NC	DOD	Prob Old Lutheran Ch there	PP
King, John C.	Cpl.	D 9th SCVIBn		HY	03/16/62	Camp Lookout, SC	DOD	(JR=3/10/62)	ROH,JR,PP
King, John J.	Pvt.	I 2nd SCV			06/04/65	Fts. Monroe, VA	DIP	Prob. N.C. Hampton, VA	P6,P12
King, John M.	Pvt.	E 12th SCVI	29	LR	07/16/62	At home	DOD	(LAN=KIA @ Gaines Mill)	ROH,JR,LAN
King, Joseph	Pvt.	I 1st SCVIG		AN	09/12/64	Elmira, NY	DIP	Woodlawn N.C.#174 Elmira	FPH,SA1,P65,P120
King, Joseph H.	Pvt.	A Hol.Leg.	19	SG	08/30/62	2nd Manassas, VA	KIA	(JR=James)	JR,HOS
King, Josiah W.	Pvt.	I 3rd SCVI		LS	11/13/62	Winchester, VA	DOD	(JR=10/30/62)	JR,SA2
King, Lewis Jefferson	Pvt.	E 4th SCVI		PS	01/14/62	Charlottesville	DOD		ROH,SA2
King, Luther	Pvt.	C 15th SCVI	31	LN	01/01/65	At home	DOD	Cedar Grove L.C. Leesville	NCC,TOD,KEB
King, R.R.	Pvt.	C Ham.Leg.		CL	10/11/62			Stonewall Cem. Winchester	WIN
King, Robert C.	Pvt.	E Orr's Ri.	30	PS	12/13/62	Fredericksburg	KIA	(Also Wdd @ Gaines' Mill)	ROH,JR,CDC
King, Robert W.	Pvt.	H 25th SCVI		DN	10/21/64	At home	DOW	1st B.C. Hartsville, SC	CTA,HOW,HAG,PP
King, W.	Pvt.	E 21st SCVI		CN	06/23/65	Elmira, NY	DIP	Woodlawn N.C.#2818 Elmira	FPH,P6,P65,P120
King, W. Capers	Pvt.	K 13th SCVI		LN	07/07/62	Richmond, VA	DOD	(JR=Typhoid @ Winder H.)	ROH,JR
King, W. Harrison	Pvt.	C 2nd SCVI		RD	08/24/61		DOD		SA2,KEB,H2
King, W.R.	Pvt.	I 2nd SCVIRi			08/02/64	Richmond, VA		Hollywood Cem.Rchmd. V40	ROH,HC
King, W.R.	Pvt.	A 3rd SCVIBn		LS	/ /	Manchester, VA		(Same man buried in HC?)	ROH
King, William	Pvt.	K Orr's Ri.	33	AN	09/03/63	Richmond, VA	DOD	(JR=8/23/62)	ROH,JR,CDC
King, William	Pvt.	F 13th SCVI		SG	12/13/62	Fredericksburg	KIA		ROH,JR,HOS
King, William	Pvt.	K 11th SCVI			/ /	(? P.S.S.NI HAG)		Oakwood C.#1, Row 23,Div D	OWC
King, William A.	1st Cpl.	L 1st SCVIG		CN	12/15/64	Fussel's Mill VA	DOW	St.Pauls Ch. Charleston SC	MAG,SA1,CDC
King, William B.	Pvt.	L 2nd SCVIRi	30	AN	01/15/65	Richmond, VA	DOD		ROH
King, William C.	Pvt.	C Ham.Leg.		CL	07/21/61	1st Manassas, VA	KIA		ROH,JR,CDC
King, William H.	Pvt.	B 3rd SCVI		NY	09/02/63	At home	DOD		ROH,SA2,ANY,KEB
Kingman, Robert W.	Cpt. QM	24th SCVI	26	CD	01/02/63	Columbia, SC	DOD	Wentworth St.C. Charleston	ROH,MAG,CDC,PP
Kinloch, Henry Wright	1st Lt.	D 6th SCVC	30	CN	10/24/62	Aiken, SC	DOD	St. Philips Ch. Charleston	ROH,MAG,RCD
Kinman, James B.	Pvt.	F Ham.Leg.		GE	07/21/61	1st Manassas, VA	KIA		ROH
Kinman, James D.	Pvt.	A 2nd SCVI		RD	04/01/62	Richmond, VA	DOD	Oakwood C.#21,Row F,Div A	ROH,JR,SA2,OWC
Kinney, John E.	Pvt.	Palm. LA		SR	06/13/64	Danville, VA	DOD	(Typhoid, 1st D,2nd SCVI)	SOB,H2,SA2,KEB
Kinney, John N.	Pvt.				06/30/64	Petersburg, VA		Blandford Church Pbg., VA	BLC
Kinrass, John	Pvt.	A 16th SCVI		GE	/ /	Lovejoy, GA	KIA		16R
Kinsey,	Pvt.	E SCVI			/ /	High Point, NC		Oakwood Cem. High Point NC	CV,WAT,TOD
Kinsey, Jesse	Pvt.	H 17th SCVI		BL	/ /	Charleston, SC	DOD	(Charlotte?)	JR
Kinsler, A.	Pvt.	K 13th SCVI		LN	07/29/63		DOW	(Wdd @ Gettysburg)	ROH
Kirby, Andrew	Pvt.	I 13th SCVI	30	SG	07/03/63	Gettysburg, PA	KIA		ROH,HOS
Kirby, Calvin (L.C.?)	Pvt.	I 13th SCVI	29	SG	05/14/62	Richmond, VA	DOD		ROH,JR
Kirby, Franklin A.	Pvt.	I 13th SCVI	19	SG	09/03/61	Columbia, SC	DOD	Elmwood Cem. Columbia, SC	ROH,JR,MP,HOS,PP
Kirby, H.	Pvt.	E 8th SCVI		DN	04/15/62	Richmond, VA	DOD	(Pneumonia, Rchmd effects)	JR,KEB,CDC
Kirby, H.M.	Cpt.	C 27th SCVI		CN	05/16/64	Richmond, VA	DOW	Oakwood C.#4, Row J,Div F	ROH,OWC,HAG

SOUTH CAROLINA DEAD IN CSA SERVICE 1861-1865

NAME	RANK	C REGIMENT	AGE	DS	DIED	WHERE	WHY	BURIED	SOURCES
Kirby, Henry	Pvt.	I 13th SCVI	28	SG	12/15/61		DOD	(Typhoid)	ROH,JR,HOS
Kirby, J.	Pvt.	K 1st SCVC			06/08/63	Charleston, SC	DOD	Magnolia Cem. Charleston	ROH,MAG
Kirby, J.	Pvt.	C 7th SCVI			05/25/62	Richmond, VA	DOD	Hollywood Cem.Rchmd. I123	ROH,HC
Kirby, J.F.	Pvt.	C 25th SCVI		WG	09/07/63	Bty. Wagner, SC	KIA		ROH,JR,CTA,HOW
Kirby, J.W.	Pvt.	D 15th SCVI		KW	11/20/63	Ft. Delaware, DE	DIP	Finn's Pt., NJ Nat. Cem.	ROH,FPH,P6,HIC
Kirby, James	Pvt.			SG	/ /	Petersburg, VA		(J.M. K, 27th SCVI?)	ROH
Kirby, Jasper W.	Pvt.	I 13th SCVI		SG	06/01/62		DOD		ROH,JR,HOS
Kirby, John	Pvt.	G 7th SCVIBn	26	KW	05/16/64	Drury's Bluff VA	KIA		ROH,JR,HIC,HAG
Kirby, John	Pvt.	G 2nd SCVI		KW	01/15/63	Richmond, VA	DOW	(Erysipelas, Wdd Fredbg.)	H2,SA2,KEB
Kirby, John Q.	Pvt.	E 16th SCVI	18	GE	02/03/64	Cassville, GA	DOD		ROH,16R
Kirby, Jonas	Pvt.	M P.S.S.	23	SG	07/07/62	Petersburg, VA	DOD		ROH,JR,PP
Kirby, Joseph	Pvt.	B 18th SCVI		UN	08/15/64	Petersburg, VA	KIA		ROH,JR
Kirby, L.C.	Pvt.	K 27th SCVI		SG	04/11/65	Pt. Lookout, MD	DIP	C.C. Pt. Lookout, MD	FPH,HOS,P6,P11
Kirby, M.L.	Pvt.	K 22nd SCVI		PS	04/10/65	Pt. Lookout, MD	DIP	C.C. Pt. Lookout, MD	ROH,P12
Kirby, R.L.	Pvt.	B Hol.Leg.	18	SG	07/09/64	Stony Creek, VA	DOD	(HOS=R.B.M.)	ROH,HOS
Kirby, Reuben W.	Pvt.	H 10th SCVI	18	WG	12/31/62	Murfreesboro, TN	KIA		ROH,RAS,CTA,HO
Kirby, S.	Pvt.	M P.S.S.			07/08/62	Petersburg, VA			ROH
Kirby, Thomas J.	Pvt.	I 13th SCVI	25	SG	06/01/62	Richmond, VA	DOD		ROH,JR,HOS
Kirby, Trust	Pvt.	G 7th SCVIBn	25	KW	05/20/64	Richmond, VA	DOW	(Wdd @ Drury's Bluff, VA)	ROH,JR,HIC,HAG
Kirby, W.J.	Pvt.	Culpeppers			12/24/64	Ship Island, MS	DIP	Ship Island, MS	PP,P3
Kirett, F.	Pvt.	M 22nd SCVI			03/16/65	Elmira, NY	DIP	Woodlawn N.C.#1709 Elmira	FPH,P5
Kirk, James H.	Cpt.	D 1st SCVIH		LR	09/30/64	Ft. Harrison, VA	KIA		ROH,SA1,LAN
Kirk, William J.	Pvt.	I 12th SCVI		LR	08/29/62	2nd Manassas, VA	KIA		JR,LAN
Kirkland, A.M.	Pvt.	F P.S.S.			/ /		DOD		JR
Kirkland, David Clarke	Pvt.	I 1st SCVIG	23	FD	07/01/61	Centreville, VA	DOD	(Typhoid Pneumonia)	ROH,JR
Kirkland, Richard R.	1st Sgt.	G 2nd SCVI	23	KW	09/20/63	Chickamauga, GA	KIA	Quaker Cem. Camden, SC	ROH,SA2,CDN,PP
Kirkland, W. Franklin	Pvt.	E 15th SCVI	21	FD	09/14/62	South Mtn., MD	KIA		ROH,JR,KEB,HFC
Kirkland, William L.	Pvt.	K 4th SCVC	36	CO	06/19/64	Richmond, VA	DOW	Hollywood Cem., Rchmd.	ROH,CLD,HIC
Kirkley, Daniel M.	1st Cpl.	G 2nd SCVI		KW	12/07/62	Frederick, MD	DIP	Mt.Olivet C.#179 Frederick	ROH,FPH,P6,BOD
Kirkpatrick, G.J.	Pvt.	G 18th SCVI		UN	05/11/62	Wilmington, NC	DOD		JR
Kirkpatrick, J. Madison	Pvt.	I 6th SCVI		CR	/ /		KIA		CB
Kirkpatrick, Robert	Pvt.	D 17th SCVI		CR	/ /	At home	DOW		HHC,CB
Kirksey. W.H.	Pvt.	A 22nd SCVI	17	ED	06/26/62	Augusta, GA	DOD	Magnolia Cem. Augusta, GA	ROH,EDN,BGA
Kirkwood, W.D.H.	Cpt.	ADC, staff		CN	01/02/62	Charleston, SC	DOD	Wentworth St.C. Charleston	MAG,RCD
Kirton, Kenneth	Pvt.	E 26th SCVI		HY	04/15/62	Camp Lookout, SC	DOD		ROH
Kirvin, C.A.	Pvt.	A 5th SCVI		DN	09/30/64	Ft. Harrison, VA	KIA		ROH,SA3
Kirvin, G.W.	Pvt.	D 21st SCVI		DN	06/15/64	Petersburg, VA			ROH,HAG
Kirvin, Mercer L.	Pvt.	M 8th SCVI	35	DN	02/10/63	Gordonsville, VA	DOD	(Pneumonia)	ROH,JR
Kiser, F.D.	Pvt.	B 20th SCVI		OG	/ /	At home	DOD		ROH
Kissick, H.G.	Pvt.	D 14th SCVI	22	ED	05/10/63		DOD		D14,HOE
Kissick, P.B.	Pvt.	D 14th SCVI	24	ED	05/23/64	Noel Stn., VA	KIA		D14,HOE
Kissick, W.F.	Pvt.	B 3rd SCVIBn		LS	05/03/63	Richmond, VA	DOD	Hollywood Cem.Rchmd. T520	ROH,HC,KEB
Kitchens, C.T.	1st Sgt.	K 1st SCVC			10/09/63	James City, VA	KIA		ROH
Kitchens, Charles	Pvt.	A 17th SCVI	30	CR	01/15/62	Charleston, SC	DOD	(Brain fever) CB	ROH,JR,HHC,CMO
Kitchens, John I.	Pvt.	A 6th SCVI	22	CR	09/16/62	Petersburg, VA	DOD		ROH,CMO
Kitchens, John S.	Pvt.	A 6th SCVI		CR	06/25/62	Richmond, VA	DOD		ROH,GLS,HHC,CB
Kitchens, John T.	2nd Lt.	B 4th SCVC		CR	06/22/64	Richmond, VA	DOW	(Wdd. @ Old Church, VA)	ROH,JR,R43,CB
Kitchens, John T.	1st Lt.	A P.S.S.		UN	06/30/62	Frayser's Fm. VA	KIA		ROH,JR,CDC,R47
Kitchens, Joshua	Pvt.	A 6th SCVI	30	CR	05/31/62	7 Pines, VA	DOW	CB	ROH,CDC,GLS,HH
Kitchens, Samuel	Pvt.	F 23rd SCVI		CR	/ /	Petersburg, VA	KIA		HHC
Kitchens, William	Pvt.	A 17th SCVI	35	CR	04/05/65	Washington, DC	DIP	(Wdd & POW @ Ft. Steadman)	ROH,CMO,P6,CB

K

SOUTH CAROLINA DEAD IN CSA SERVICE 1861-1865

NAME	RANK	C REGIMENT	AGE	DS	DIED	WHERE	WHY	BURIED	SOURCES
Kitsinger, A.J.	Pvt.	D Ham.Leg.		PS	/ /	Bacon Race, VA	DOD		GRS
Kittere, Daniel	Pvt.	G 12th SCVI		PS	/ /	Lynchburg, VA		Lynchburg CSA Cem. #1R2	BBW
Kitterel, J.D.O.	Pvt.	I 3rd SCVI		LS	11/12/62	Richmond, VA	DOD	Oakwood C.#65,Row L,Div B	ROH,SA2,OWC,CDC
Kittrell, J.C.	Pvt.	D 8th Bn Res			02/01/65	Columbia, SC	DOD		ROH,PP
Kittrell, John	Pvt.	A 6th SCResB		OG	06/15/64	Columbia, SC	DOD		PP
Klance, John	Pvt.	27th SCVI	34		08/03/64	Weldon RR, VA	KIA	(Klink ?)	CDC
Klinck, Theodore	1st Lt.	A Ham.Leg.		CN	06/08/62	7 Pines, VA	DOW	Magnolia Cem. Charleston	ROH,MAG,CDC,WLI
Klinck,Jr., John	Pvt.	A 25th SCVI	34	CN	08/02/64	Ream's Stn., VA	KIA		ROH,WLI,HAG
Klugh, Pascal D.	2nd Lt.	B 7th SCVI	22	AE	06/09/62	Richmond, VA	DOD	(Typhoid, effects list)	ROH,JR,KEB,R46
Knapp, Herman	Pvt.	K 1st SCVIR		LA	03/16/65	Averysboro, NC	KIA		ROH,SA1,WAT,PP
Knecht, J. Martin	Sgt.	K 12th SCVI	30	PS	09/09/64	Fussel's Mill VA	DOW		ROH,JR
Knight, A.M.	Sgt.	K 12th SCVI		PS	09/09/64	Richmond, VA		Hollywood Cem.Rchmd. V459	ROH,HC
Knight, D.A.	Pvt.	C 24th SCVI	25	CO	04/25/62		DOD		EJM
Knight, D.T.	Pvt.	I 16th SCVI		GE	11/30/64	Franklin, TN	KIA	(Color Guard)	PP,16R
Knight, Elijah	Pvt.	B 17th SCVI		FD	09/20/62	Adams Run, SC	DOD	(HFC=Elmore)	JR,PP
Knight, Erwin R.	Cpl.	H 2nd SCVI	21	LR	07/20/61	Richmond, VA	DOW	(SA2=on rolls Pvt.4/30/62)	ROH,LAN,SA2,H2
Knight, F.R.	Pvt.	F 21st SCVI		MO	11/03/63	Charleston, SC	DOD	Magnolia Cem. Charleston	ROH,MAG
Knight, G.R.	Pvt.	C 14th SCVI		LS	07/10/62	Richmond, VA	DOD	(Congestive Fever)	JR
Knight, Hilton	Pvt.	E 12th SCVI	17	LR	06/27/62	Gaines' Mill, VA	KIA	(? Hilton, Knight)	ROH,JR,LAN,CNM
Knight, J. Allen	Pvt.	G 2nd SCVI		KW	08/04/61	Vienna, VA	DOD		SA2,KEB,HIC
Knight, James	Pvt.	C 14th SCVI		LS	07/25/62	Donaldsville, SC	DOD	(Typhoid)	JR
Knight, Joseph M.	Pvt.	B 1st SCVIR		LR	10/31/64	Mt. Pleasant, SC	DOD		ROH,SA1,LAN
Knight, Josiah	Pvt.	G 3rd SCVI		LS	04/14/63	Richmond, VA	DOD	Oakwood C.#16, Row 17,Div D	ROH,JR,SA2,OWC
Knight, M.C.	Pvt.	E 6th SCVC.		LS	08/23/64	Ream's Stn., VA	KIA		ROH,JR
Knight, William	Pvt.	I 16th SCVI		GE	11/30/64	Franklin, TN	KIA	Macgavock C. Frkln Gv#40	ROH,16R,WCT
Knight, William A.	Pvt.	G 2nd SCVI		KW	11/18/63	Knoxville, TN	KIA		SA2,KEB,HIC,H2
Knighton, J.T.	Pvt.	D 8th SCVI		CD	10/28/61	Charlottesville	DOD	Univ. Cem. Charlottesville	JR,ACH,KEB
Knotts, J.V.	Pvt.	G Ham.Leg.			06/27/62		DOD	(Typhoid Dysentery)	JR
Knotts, Joel Elvin	1st Lt.	K 1st SCVIH		OG	08/30/62	2nd Manassas, VA	KIA		ROH,JR,SA1,JRH
Knotts, Thomas D.	Pvt.	K 1st SCVIH		OG	09/14/62	South Mtn., MD	DOW	(Left in enemy hands)	ROH,SA1,JRH
Knowles, M.	Pvt.	K 13th SCVI		LN	12/15/62	Fredericksburg	DOW		JR
Knowlton, J.	Pvt.	I 25th SCVI		CL	03/15/62	Georgetown, SC	DOD		JR
Knowlton, J.K.	Pvt.	A 21st SCVI		CN	03/31/62	Georgetown, SC	DOD		JR,PP
Knowlton, John W.	Pvt.	I 25th SCVI		CL	12/15/62	At home	DOD	(Measles)	JR,HAG
Knox, C.D.	Pvt.	C 7th SCVC		UN	11/03/62	Staunton, VA	DOD		ROH
Knox, George F.	Pvt.	F 5th SCVI	28	YK	02/14/65	Camp Morton, IN	DIP	Green Lawn C. Indianapolis	FPH,SA3,P6,YEB
Knox, James	Pvt.	F 15th SCVI		UN	05/30/64	Richmond, VA	DOW	Hollywood Cem.Rchmd. D135	ROH,JR,HC,KEB
Knox, James M.	Cpl.	B P.S.S.		PS	06/30/62	Frayser's Farm	KIA		ROH
Knox, John C.	Pvt.	E Orr's Ri.	25	PS	06/02/64	Staunton, VA	DOW	Thornrose C.(TOD=C,7th SC)	ROH,CDC,PP,TOD
Knox, John H.	2nd Lt.	H SCVI			05/29/64	Staunton, VA		(PP=11th SC, NI HAG)	PP
Knox, Miles	2nd Sgt.	E Orr's Ri.	32	PS	06/27/62	Gaines' Mill, VA	KIA		ROH,JR,CDC
Knox, Nathaniel	Pvt.	A 2nd SCVIRi	30	AE	06/29/62	Savage Stn., VA	KIA	Long Cane C. Abbeville, SC	ROH,CDC,UD1
Knox, R.C.	Pvt.	2nd SC Res			02/04/65	Charleston, SC	DOD	Magnolia Cem.Charleston	ROH,MAG
Knox, Samuel	Pvt.	C 7th SCVI		AE	07/01/62	Malvern Hill, VA	KIA		ROH,JR,CDC,KEB
Knox, William L.	Pvt.	G 2nd SCVI		KW	09/17/61	Culpepper, VA	DOD	Fairview Cem. Culpepper VA	CGH,SA2,H2,KEB
Kolb, A.L.	Pvt.	I 23rd SCVI	47	CL	11/17/64	Petersburg, VA	DOW	(Also Wdd Deep Bottom7/27)	ROH,PP
Koon, Aaron Hamilton	Pvt.	I 15th SCVI		NY	08/18/64	At home	DOW	Prosperity Cem. SC TOD	JR,NCC,ANY,H15
Koon, George Elias	Cpl.	I 15th SCVI		LN	03/14/65	Camp Chase, OH	DIP	C.C.#1656 Columbus OH	FPH,P6,TOD,H15
Koon, George W.	Pvt.	E 3rd SCVI		NY	09/20/63	Chickamauga, GA	KIA	Con. Cem. Marietta, GA	ROH,JR,SA2,CCM
Koon, J. Barnet	Pvt.	I 15th SCVI	19	LN	10/19/63	Staunton, VA	DOW	Thornhill C. Staunton, VA	H15,TOD,KEB
Koon, J.F.	Pvt.	I P.S.S.			/ /		KIA		JR

SOUTH CAROLINA DEAD IN CSA SERVICE 1861-1865

NAME	RANK	C REGIMENT	AGE	DS	DIED	WHERE	WHY	BURIED	SOURCES
Koon, J.G.	Pvt.	C 4th SCRes		LN	02/16/65	Columbia, SC	DOD		ROH,PP
Koon, John	Pvt.	H 13th SCVI		LN	03/03/62	Whitehall, SC	DOD (Erysipelas)		JR
Koon, John B.	Pvt.	I 15th SCVI	35	LN	10/19/63	Staunton, VA	DOW	Thornrose C. Staunton, VA	ROH,KEB,H15,TO
Koon, Samuel A.	2nd Lt.	F 2nd SCVI	22	RD	05/06/64	Wilderness, VA	KIA		ROH,JR,KEB,CDC
Koon, T.J.	Pvt.	C 20th SCVI	27	LN	04/18/65	At home	DOD		ROH
Koon, Walter W.	Pvt.	I 15th SCVI	26	NY	07/10/63	Gettysburg, PA	DOW	Magnolia Cem. Charleston	ROH,JR,GDR,ANY
Kornekee, H.W.	Pvt.	A 8th SC Res		CN	03/07/65	Columbia, SC	DOD		ROH
Kreps, Cornelius J.W.	2nd Lt.	A 19th SCVI	22	ED	07/22/64	Atlanta, GA	KIA		ROH,HOE,R47,UD
Kurby, A. (Kirby ?)	Pvt.	23rd SCVI		CN	02/24/62			Magnolia Cem. Charleston	MAG
Kyle, Augustine	Cpl.	B Orr's Ri.		AE	09/07/62	Gaines' Mill, VA	DOW		JR,CDC
Kyser, S.J.	Pvt.	C 15th SCVI	33	LN	01/29/63	Richmond, VA	DOD (G.J.?)		ROH,KEB,H15
Kyser, Solomon W.	1st Sgt.	C 15th SCVI	30	LN	09/17/62	Sharpsburg, MD	KIA	TOD	ROH,JR,KEB,H15

SOUTH CAROLINA DEAD IN CSA SERVICE 1861-1865

NAME	RANK	C	REGIMENT	AGE	DS	DIED	WHERE	WHY	BURIED	SOURCES
La Coste, William A.	Pvt.	F	9th SCVIB	20	SR	08/22/61	Manassas, VA	DOD	Manassas CSA Cem.	ROH,JR,CV
LaBorde, Oscar M.	1st Lt.	A	1st SCVA		RD	03/16/65	Averysboro, NC	KIA	Trinity Ch. Columbia, SC	ROH,MP,SCA,PP
LaCoste, William O.	1st Lt.		Chestfd LA	24	CD	01/04/62	Portsmouth, VA	DOD		ROH,R44
LaFoy, Franklin W.	Pvt.	G	16th SCVI		GE	10/06/63	Lauderdale, MS	DOD	Prob in Con. Cem. there	16R,PP
LaMance, Erwin	Pvt.	H	16th SCVI		GE	03/10/64	Rock Island, IL	DIP	C.C.#771 Rock Island, IL	FPH,P5,P12
LaRoche, Edward W.	Pvt.				CO	10/15/61	SC	DOD	(Probably in 9th SCVIH)	ROH
Lacey, John M.	Pvt.	H	10th SCVI		WG	/ /	Okolona, MS	DOD	(1863)	RAS,HOW,PP,TOD
Lack, Jacob F.	Pvt.	A	12th SCVI		AE	07/18/62	Richmond, VA	DOD	Hollywood Cem.Rchmd. Q111	ROH,HC
Ladd, A.W.	Pvt.	G	6th SCVI		FD	05/31/62	7 Pines, VA	DOW		CDC,HFC
Ladd, F.M.	Pvt.	F	Hol.Leg.		AE	03/14/65	Elmira, NY	DIP	Woodlawn N.C.#2189 Elmira	FPH,P6,P10
Ladson, W.H.	Major		QM 2nd Div		CN	05/18/61	Charleston, SC	DOD	Magnolia Cem. Charleston	JR,MAG
Lady, W.	Pvt.	K	12th SCVI		PS	10/03/62	Richmond, VA	DOD		JR
Lagare, Solomon E.	Pvt.	F	6th SCVC		CN	07/22/65	Pt. Lookout, MD	DIP	C.C. Pt. Lookout, MD	CAG,P12
Lake, Edward	Pvt.	B	27th SCVI		CN	11/18/63	Ft. Sumter, SC	KIA	(JR=11/16/63)	ROH,HAG,JR
Lake, Elijah M.	Pvt.	C	Hol.Leg.		NY	02/08/62	Adams Run, SC	DOW		ANY,PP
Lake, G.W.	Pvt.	E				/ /	Richmond, VA		Oakwood C.#20,Row G,Div B	ROH,OWC
Lake, George P.	Pvt.	C	Hol.Leg.		NY	/ /	Adams Run, SC	DOD		ANY
Lake, Isaac K.	Sgt.	C	23rd SCVI		LN	07/30/64	Crater, Pbg., VA	KIA		ROH,JR,ANY,BLM
Lake, John	Pvt.	B	27th SCVI		CN	09/28/63	At home	DOD		JR,HAG
Lake, John B.	Pvt.	D	13th SCVI	22	NY	06/15/65	At home	DOD	(ANY=KIA @ Spotsylvania)	ROH,ANY
Lake, Thomas Hunter	3rd Sgt.	E	3rd SCVI		NY	09/26/61	Flint Hill, VA	DOD	Prosperity C. SC (Typhoid)	ROH,JR,NCC,ANY
Lake, W.F.	Pvt.	E	3rd SCVI		NY	06/01/62	Richmond, VA	DOD	Hollywood Cem.Rchmd. L71	ROH,JR,HC,ANY
Lake, William W.	Pvt.		13th SCVI		NY	/ /	NC	DOD		ROH
Lalane, George M.	2nd Lt.	E	25th SCVI		CN	05/31/64	Drury's Bluff VA	DOW	St.Mary's R.C. Charleston	ROH,MAG,HAG,SA
Lally, James L.	Pvt.	E	1st SCVIR		CN	09/08/63	Ft. Moultrie, SC	KIA	(Explosion at gun)	ROH,SA1,CDC
Lamar, Thomas G.	Colonel		2nd SCVA	35	ED	10/17/62	Charleston, SC	DOD	Lamar Fam.Cem. Hamburg, SC	ROH,R44,EDN,SO
Lamaster, John J.	Pvt.	G	18th SCVI	21	YK	05/20/64	Clay's Farm, VA	KIA		ROH,JR,YMD
Lamaster, Richard S.	Pvt.	A	18th SCVI		UN	07/30/64	Crater, Pbg., VA	KIA		JR,BLM
Lamb, A.K.	Pvt.	D	23rd SCVI		CN	09/24/62	Raleigh, NC		Oakwood C. Raleigh, NC	TOD
Lamb, Barrett	Pvt.	G	1st SCVIG		ED	12/13/62	Fredericksburg	KIA	(JR=Co.B)	JR,SA1,HOE
Lamb, D.C.	Pvt.	B	15th SCVI		UN	/ /		DOD	(May be Lamb, David/KEB)	JR
Lamb, Elijah	Pvt.	B	15th SCVI		UN	/ /		DOD		JR,KEB
Lamb, John	Pvt.	G	27th SCVI		CN	11/15/64	At sea	DIP	(Onway to Savannah for Ex)	CDC,HAG,P65,P1
Lamb, John C.	Pvt.	B	15th SCVI	20	UN	03/01/63	Petersburg, VA		Blandford Church Pbg., VA	BLC,KEB,PP
Lamb, John S.	Pvt.	G	1st SCVIG		ED	12/13/62	Fredericksburg	KIA		JR,SA1,HOE
Lamb, Robert	Cpl.	H	25th SCVI	27	WG	02/15/65	Pt. Lookout, MD	DIP	C.C. Pt. Lookout, MD	ROH,FPH,HOW,P6
Lamb, Robert	Pvt.	C	18th SCVI	25	UN	07/27/62	Richmond, VA	DOD	Hollywood Cem.Rchmd. Q266	ROH,JR,HC
Lamb, S.	Pvt.	E	2nd SCVIRi		PS	/ /	Charlottesville		Univ. Cem. Charlottesville	ACH
Lamb, Samuel D.	Pvt.	K	25th SCVI	27	WG	09/06/63	Bty. Wagner, SC	KIA	(JR=S.B. in 15th SC)	ROH,JR,HAG,HOW
Lambers, E.H.	Pvt.	B	18th SCVAB		CN	11/13/64	Columbia, SC	DOD		ROH,PP
Lambers, J. Francis	Sgt.	A	1st SCVIBn		CN	07/18/63	Bty. Wagner, SC	KIA	Magnolia Cem. Charleston	ROH,JR,MAG,R45
Lambert, Charles A.	Pvt.	A	Ham.Leg.	35	CR	07/01/65	Columbia, SC	DOD		ROH,PP
Lambert, D.H.	Cpl.	D	10th SCVI		MN	01/06/63	Murfreesboro, TN	DOW	(In enemy hands)	P12,P38
Lambert, J.H.	Pvt.	D	10th SCVI		MN	/ /		DOD		RAS
Lambert, P.	Pvt.	D	10th SCVI		MN	/ /		DOD		RAS,HMC
Lambert,Jr., Charles H.	Pvt.	I	6th SCVI		CR	10/07/64	Darbytown, VA	KIA	(HHC=Co.E)	JR,HHC,CB
Lambeth, L.	Pvt.	G	27th SCVI		CN	07/02/64	Petersburg, VA	KIA		ROH
Lambrick, George	Pvt.	C	23rd SCVI		CN	07/30/64	Petersburg, VA	KIA		JR
Lamersey, Joel W.	Pvt.	C	20th SCVI		LN	08/30/63	Atlanta, GA	DOD	Oakland C. Atlanta R19#2	BGA
Laminack, J.J.	Pvt.	C	15th SCVI	21	LN	09/14/62	South Mtn., MD	DOW		ROH,JR,KEB,H15
Laminack, J.S.	3rd Sgt.	C	15th SCVI	24	LN	08/31/64	Richmond, VA	DOD	(Diarrhea)	ROH,KEB,H15

L

SOUTH CAROLINA DEAD IN CSA SERVICE 1861-1865

NAME	RANK	C	REGIMENT	AGE	DS	DIED	WHERE	WHY	BURIED	SOURCES
Laminack, John	Pvt.	G	P.S.S.		YK	02/18/64		DOD		ROH,JR
Laminack, Noah	Pvt.	C	15th SCVI	29	LN	05/07/64	Wilderness, VA	KIA		ROH,JR,KEB,H15
Laminack, Paul	Pvt.	C	15th SCVI	23	LN	04/29/62		DOD		JR,KEB,H15
Laminack, Samuel	Pvt.	C	15th SCVI	16	LN	01/09/62	SC coast	DOD		ROH,JR,KEB,H15
Lamotte, Henry J.	Pvt.	D	27th SCVI	36	CN	02/27/63		DOD (Cancer)		ROH,JR,HAG
Lamson, John	Pvt.	G	27th SCVI			07/08/64	Pt. Lookout, MD	DIP		ROH,HAG,P12,P113
Lan, D.S.	Pvt.		Melchoir's			03/28/64	Georgetown, SC	DOD (Prob Co.B, German Arty)		PP
Lancaster, F.M.	Pvt.	B	15th SCVI		UN	/ /	Charlottesville	DOD	Univ. Cem. Charlottesville	JR,ACH,KEB
Lancaster, L.L.	Pvt.	B	14th SCMil		SG	04/17/65	Hart's Island NY	DIP	Cypress Hills N.C.#2543 NY	FPH,P1,P6,P79
Lancaster, T.D.	Pvt.	H	1st SCVIH		UN	08/24/62		DOD		SA1
Lancaster, William Henry	Pvt.	K	3rd SCVI	21	SG	12/29/62	Fredericksburg	DOW (A 2nd JR entry=1/27/63)		ROH,JR,SA2,KEB
Lance, Archibald St.John	2nd Lt.	D	27th SCVI	38	CN	05/14/64	Drury's Bluff VA	KIA		ROH,JR,HAG,R48
Lance, L.L.	Pvt.	E	Orr's Ri.		PS	/ /	Gordonsville, VA			ROH
Land, J. Edward	Pvt.	F	6th SCVI	25	YK	08/30/62	2nd Manassas, VA	KIA (HHC & CB=Co.I of CR Dst)		WDB,YEB,HHC,CB
Land, Reed R.	Pvt.	K	5th SCVI		SG	04/15/62	Gordonsville, VA	DOD	Gordonsville, VA Cem.	ROH,JR,GOR,SA3
Land, Richard	Pvt.	C	6th SCVI	26	CR	01/22/62	Charlottesville	DOD		ROH,HHC
Land, William	Pvt.		Ham.Leg.			07/30/62	Richmond, VA		Hollywood Cem.Rchmd. Q290	HC
Landas, E.	Pvt.	E	22nd SCVI		LR	10/22/62			Stonewall C. Winchester VA	WIN
Landreth, Lewis	Pvt.	G	16th SCVI		GE	02/20/64	At home	DOD (? on active duty)		16R,PP
Landrum, A.P.	Pvt.	A	2nd SCVI		RD	11/06/62	Richmond, VA	DOD (H2=Culpepper, VA 11/1/62)		ROH,SA2,KEB,H2
Landrum, J.A.	1st Sgt.	K	14th SCVI		ED	05/12/64	Spotsylvania, VA	KIA (JR=J.S.)		JR,HOE
Landrum, James Caldwell	Pvt.	E	2nd SC Mil	16	ED	04/10/65	Greenville, SC	DOD		ROH,PP
Landrum, John Smyly	Lt.	K	14th SCVI	20	ED	05/12/64	Spotsylvania, VA	KIA		ROH,CSL,UD1
Landrum, L.W. (L.M.?)	Pvt.	A	2nd SCVI		RD	11/04/62	Winchester, VA	DOD	Stonewall C. Winchester VA	ROH,WIN,SA2,KEB
Lands, Richard	Pvt.	B	Hol.Leg.	26	SG	09/06/62	Winchester, VA	DOW (Sent to Hospital & lost)		ROH,HOS
Lands, William	Pvt.	C	7th SCVI	28	AE	09/13/62	Maryland Hts. MD	KIA		ROH,CDC,KEB
Lands, William	Pvt.	B	Hol.Leg.	34	SG	07/30/62	Richmond, VA	DOD	Hollywood Cem.Rchmd. Q290	ROH,HC,HOS
Lane, D.F.	Pvt.	H	23rd SCVI		MN	09/14/62	South Mtn., MD	KIA		ROH,JR,CDC
Lane, David	Pvt.	H	Orr's Ri.		MN	/ /		DOD (1864)		HMC
Lane, Elisha	Pvt.		1st SCMil			04/26/65	New Bern, NC	DIP	Cedar Grove C. Newbern, NC	P1,P6,P12,WAT,PP
Lane, Evander	Pvt.	L	8th SCVI		MN	06/01/64	Cold Harbor, VA	KIA		HMC,KEB
Lane, Ferdinand	Pvt.	D	25th SCVI		MN	/ /		DIP		HMC,HAG
Lane, James	Pvt.	B	1st SCVIG	16	NY	05/03/63	Chancellorsville	KIA		ANY
Lane, John	Pvt.	H	17th SCVI		BL	04/26/65	Farmville, VA	DOW	Hospital C. Farmville, VA	ROH,P6,P12
Lane, John	Pvt.	G	1st SCVIG		RD	08/13/64	Richmond, VA	DOD	Hollywood Cem.Rchmd. V584	ROH,SA1,HOE
Lane, Joseph B. (V.?)	2nd Cpl.	L	21st SCVI	21	MN	06/07/64	Cold Harbor, VA	DOW	Hollywood Cem.Rchmd. U579	ROH,HC,HMC,HAG
Lane, Lemuel L.	Pvt.	E	1st SCVIG		MN	01/10/64	Gordonsville, VA	DOD	Gordonsville, VA Cem.	SA1,HMC,GOR
Lane, Leonard L.	Pvt.	E	23rd SCVI		MN	10/19/61	Secessionville	ACD		ROH,HMC
Lane, Olin	4th Sgt.	B	1st SCVIH		OG	08/30/62	2nd Manassas, VA	KIA		ROH,JR,SA1,JRH
Lane, R.F.	Pvt.		7th SCVI			07/15/64	Malvern Hill, VA	KIA		JR
Lane, R.F.	1st Sgt.		18th SCVI			06/15/64		DOW		JR
Lane, Stephen L.	Pvt.	H	23rd SCVI		MN	04/08/65	Appomatox, VA	KIA		HMC
Lane, W.S.	Pvt.	G	1st SCVIH		BL	11/30/62	Warrenton, VA	DOW (Wdd 2nd M.,Rchmd effects)		ROH,SA1,CDC,JRH
Lane, Walter R.	Pvt.	D	13th SCVI	21	NY	05/06/64	Wilderness, VA	KIA (ANY says William)		ROH,ANY
Lanes, J.A.	Pvt.	B	13th SCVI		SG	04/23/62	Richmond, VA	DOD	Hollywood Cem.Rchmd. B8	HC
Laney, George L.	Pvt.	E	22nd SCVI		LR	09/14/62	South Mtn., MD	KIA		LAN
Laney, L.L.	Pvt.	H	5th SCVI	18	YK	/ /	Manassas, VA	DOD (JR=Lancey, Co.B)		JR,SA3,YEB
Laney, Obediah C.	Pvt.	E	22nd SCVI	33	LR	08/18/64	Crater, Pbg., VA	DOW	Blandford Church Pbg., VA	ROH,BLM,BLC,PP
Lanford, B.	Pvt.	G	3rd SCVI		SG	12/25/62	Richmond, VA	DOD		ROH
Lanford, F. Marion	5th Sgt.	K	3rd SCVI		SG	07/02/63	Gettysburg	KIA		ROH,JR,GDR,SA2
Lanford, Greene L.	2nd Lt.	E	Hol.Leg.	38	SG	04/07/65	Petersburg, VA	DOW (Fair Grounds Hos.)		ROH,R48,P5,P12

SOUTH CAROLINA DEAD IN CSA SERVICE 1861-1865

NAME	RANK	C REGIMENT	AGE	DS	DIED	WHERE	WHY	BURIED	SOURCES
Lanford, Hosea	Pvt.	Macbeth LA		SG	03/05/63	Goldsboro, NC	DOD	(Smallpox)	JR
Lanford, J. Merril	Pvt.	E Hol.Leg.	29	SG	12/14/62	South Mtn., MD	KIA	Old Bethel Ch. Spg.	ROH,HOS,RCD
Lanford, John L.	Pvt.	K 5th SCVI		SG	08/25/61	Charlottesville	DOD	Univ. Cem. Charlottesville	JR,SA3,ACH
Lanford, Patillo	Pvt.	G 3rd SCVI		SG	12/20/62	At home	DOW	(Wdd @ Fredericksburg)	ROH,JR,SA2,KEB
Lanford, Seaborn M.	Cpt.	K 3rd SCVI		SG	06/29/62	Savage Stn., VA	DOW	(JR=6/30/62)	JR,SA2,HOS,KEB
Lanford, Thomas P.	Pvt.	D P.S.S.		SG	09/30/64	Ft. Harrison, VA	DOW	Hollywood Cem.Rchmd. W540	ROH,HC,HOS
Lanford, W.L.	Pvt.	H Ham.Leg.		SG	09/18/62	Warrenton, VA	DOW	(Wdd @ 2nd Man.)	ROH
Lanford, William J.	Pvt.	E Hol.Leg.	21	SG	10/09/62	Warrenton, VA	DOW	(Wdd @ 2nd Man)	ROH,HOS
Langdon, Newton	Pvt.	C P.S.S.		AN	10/28/63	Lookout Valley	KIA		ROH,CDC
Lange, N.	Pvt.	I 18th SCVI		DN	10/18/62	Richmond, VA	DOD		JR
Langford,	Pvt.	B 1st SCV			05/09/64	Spotsylvania, VA	KIA		JR
Langford, Daniel A.	Pvt.	E Hol.Leg.		SG	05/29/65	Pt. Lookout, MD	DIP	C.C. Pt. Lookout, MD	FPH,P6,P12,P11
Langford, J.	Pvt.	C 23rd SCVI		CN	07/09/64	Richmond, VA	DOD		P12
Langford, L.A.	Pvt.	B 14th SCVI		ED	08/10/62	Ft. Delaware, DE	DIP	(Typhoid)	JR
Langford, Marion	Pvt.	B 14th SCVI			/ /	Ft. Delaware, DE	DIP		UD3
Langford, Patrick J.	Pvt.	B 14th SCVI	17	ED	08/20/62	Port Royal, SC	DOW	(JR=Ft. Delaware, Typhoid)	JR,UD3,P85,PP
Langford, Pickens B.	3rd Lt.	E 3rd SCVI		NY	07/02/63	Gettysburg, PA	KIA	Magnolia Cem. Charleston	ROH,JR,GDR,KEB
Langford, Stanmore	Pvt.	C 23rd SCVI		NY	07/13/64	Richmond, VA		(In 6mths 2nd SC Res,1863)	ROH,ANY
Langford, T.M.	Pvt.	B 14th SCVI		ED	08/11/62	Petersburg, VA	DOD	Blandford Church Pbg., VA	BLC,PP
Langley, G.W.	Sgt.	Matthews A		BL	04/07/63	Bty. Wagner, SC	KIA	(Explosion of ammo)	ROH
Langley, J.C.	Pvt.	H 4th SCVC		LR	05/28/64	Hawes shop, VA	KIA		LAN
Langley, Robert	3rd Sgt.	D 1st SCVIH		LR	05/06/64	Wilderness, VA	KIA		LAN,SA1
Langley, S.G.	Pvt.	I 12th SCVI		LR	07/21/62	Richmond, VA	DOD		LAN
Langston,	Pvt.	D 19th SCVI	20	SR	/ /		MIA		HOE,UD3
Langston, B.J.	Pvt.	C 9th SCVIB			12/05/61	Virginia	DOD	(Typhoid)	JR
Langston, B.W.	Pvt.	3rd SCV			/ /	Richmond, VA		Oakwood C.#5,Row A,Div A	OWC
Langston, David Mason H.	Cpt.	I 3rd SCVI	30	LS	07/02/63	Gettysburg, PA	KIA		UD3 ROH,JR,GDR,SA2
Langston, Elias G.	Pvt.	G 1st SCVIR		GE	09/08/63	Ft. Moultrie, SC	KIA	(Explosion at gun)	ROH,SA1,CDC
Langston, Ezra E.	Cpl.	E 6th SCVI		SR	09/30/64	Ft. Harrison, VA	KIA	(Also POW @ 7 Pines)	ROH,JLC
Langston, Ira D.	Pvt.	A 8th SCVI		DN	04/16/62	Huguenot Spgs VA	DOD	(JR=Richmond)	ROH,JR,KEB
Langston, J.N.	Pvt.	E 1st SCVIR		GE	09/08/63	Ft. Moultrie, SC	KIA	(Explosion at gun)	ROH,SA1
Langston, M.C.	Pvt.	H 10th SCVI		WG	09/20/63	Chickamauga, GA	KIA		ROH,JR,RAS,HOW
Langston, W. Newton	Pvt.	C P.S.S.		AN	10/28/63	Lookout Valley	KIA	(JR=Racoon Mtn., TN)	ROH,JR,CDC,GMJ
Langston, W.H.	Pvt.	G 26th SCVI		DN	07/03/62		DOD		JR
Lanham, Walter W.	Pvt.	A Ham.Leg.		ED	07/08/62	At home	DCD	(On sick leave)	EDN,HOE,UD2
Lanier, J.M.	Pvt.	L P.S.S.			10/07/64	Atlee's Farm, VA	KIA		JR
Lanier, Jabez J.	Pvt.	I 24th SCVI	25	ED	01/01/62	Charleston, SC	DOD		RJM
Lanier, James	Pvt.	C 17th SCVI	27	YK	/ /	Wilmington, NC	DOD	(1863)	YEB
Lanier, L.W.	4th Sgt.	K 7th SCVI		ED	06/27/62	Gaines' Mill, VA	DOW	(HOE=Wdd.furlough home)	ROH,HOE,KEB
Lanier, Peterson	Pvt.	C 17th SCVI	33	YK	07/30/64	Crater, Pbg., VA	KIA		ROH,BLM,YEB,PP
Lanier, Richard	Pvt.	H 6th SCVI	18	YK	/ /			(Lost sight of)	YEB
Lanier, W.M.	Pvt.	B 12th SCVI		YK	09/12/62		DOW		JR
Lankford, Lewis M.	Pvt.	B 14th SCVI	19	ED	/ /	Ft. Lafayette NY	DOW	(Wdd,POW @ Port Royal, SC	HOE,P85,UD3
Lanneau,Jr., Fleetwood	1st Sgt.	B 25th SCVI	23	CN	06/16/62	Secessionville	KIA	2nd P.C. Charleston WLI	ROH,JR,MAG,LED
Larabee, O.	Pvt.	A Tucker's R			02/15/65	Salisbury, NC	DOD	Prob in Old Lutheran Ch.	PP
Larger, Nicholas	Pvt.	I 18th SCVI	25	DN	10/16/62	Richmond, VA	DOD		ROH
Largins, M.C.					/ /	Virginia		(Rchmd effects list 1863)	CDC
Lariscy, Joel W.	Pvt.	C 24th SCVI	30	CO	08/30/63	Atlanta, GA	ACD	(RR accident)	ROH,TEB
Lariscy, Richard	Pvt.	F 11th SCVI	22	CO	10/13/64	At home	DOD		ROH,HAG
Lark, James Wallace	Pvt.	B 3rd SCVI		NY	01/28/62	At home	DOD	Cross Rds.B.C. Chappels SC	ROH,JR,NCC,SA2
Lark, William F.	Pvt.	C P.S.S.		GE	11/15/63	Lookout Valley	DOW	(In enemy hands)	ROH,JR,CDC,GMJ

L

SOUTH CAROLINA DEAD IN CSA SERVICE 1861-1865

NAME	RANK	C	REGIMENT	AGE	DS	DIED	WHERE	WHY	BURIED	SOURCES
Larkin, A.M.	Pvt.	I	26th SCVI		CN	07/16/64	Richmond, VA			ROH
Larr, Benjamin	Pvt.	I	2nd SCVA	45	OG	06/15/63	SC	DOD		ROH
Larr, Samuel	Pvt.	I	2nd SCVA	39	OG	06/15/63	SC	DOD		ROH
Larr, W.P. (Law ?)	Pvt.	A	1st SCVIH		OG	06/15/61	At home	DOD	(HAG= Law, W.P.)	ROH,EDR,HAG
Larrick, J.	Pvt.	H	6th SCVI		FD	/ /	Richmond, VA		Oakwood C.#71,Row O,Div B	ROH,OWC
Laster, W.H.	Pvt.		6th SCVI			09/14/61	Richmond, VA	DOD	Hollywood Cem.Rchmd. G188	HC
Latham, Andrew C.	Pvt.	I	17th SCVI		LR	05/20/64	Clay's Farm, VA	KIA	(JR=Co.K)	ROH,JR,LAN
Latham, D.A.Y.	Sgt.	I	17th SCVI		LR	11/09/64	Richmond, VA	DOW	Hollywood Cem.Rchmd.W305	ROH,LAN,HC
Latham, J.B.	Pvt.	F	24th SCVI	40	AN	07/04/64	Augusta, GA	DOD	Magnolia Cem. Augusta, GA	HOL,BGA
Latham, J.H.L.	Pvt.	I	17th SCVI		LR	07/18/65	Pt. Lookout, MD	DIP	C.C. Pt. Lookout, MD	P12,P114
Latham, S.M.	Cpl.	I	12th SCVI		LR	07/21/62	Richmond, VA	DOD	Hollywood Cem.Rchmd. H71	ROH,JR,HC,LAN
Latham, W.J.	Pvt.	G	4th SC Res		LR	01/23/65	Columbia, SC	DOD	(ROH=2nd SCRes)	ROH,PP
Latham, William W.	Pvt.	K	6th SCVC	38	PS	08/08/64	Kittrell Spgs.NC		Kittrell Springs, NC Cem.	CV,WAT,PP
Lathan, David A.	Pvt.	H	4th SCVC		LR	07/14/64	Hawes Shop, VA	DOW		ROH,LAN
Lathan, J.T.	Pvt.	H	2nd SCVI		LR	07/21/61	1st Manassas, VA	KIA		LAN,SA2,KEB
Latimer, Benjamin M.	2nd Lt.	G	Orr's Ri.		AE	07/13/62	Gaines' Mill, VA	DOW	(JR=DOD)	ROH,JR,BOS,R45
Latimer, W.T.	Pvt.	G	Orr's Ri.		AE	/ /	Richmond, VA		Oakwood C.#58,Row D,Div C	ROH,OWC
Latta, Robert	Cpl.	A	12th SCVI	20	YK	07/09/62	Petersburg, VA	KIA		YEB
Lavender, Warren	Pvt.	C	9th SCVIB		CL	09/02/61	Germantown, VA	DOD	(JR=Typhoid 9/7/61)	ROH,JR
Law, A.S.	Pvt.	E	7th SCVI		BT	08/04/64	Petersburg, VA	DOW	(Wdd 7/30/64)	ROH
Law, Abner S.	Pvt.	E	11th SCVI		BT	03/22/64	Richmond, VA		Hollywood Cem.Rchmd.V520	HC,HAG
Law, Augustus E.	Cpl.	B	21st SCVI		DN	05/16/64	Plains Stn., VA	DOW		ROH,HAG,DAR
Lawhon, James	2nd Cpl.		PeeDee LA		DN	12/13/62	Fredericksburg	KIA		PDL
Lawless, Edmund	Pvt.	G	22nd SCVI	33	AN	07/30/64	Crater, Pbg., VA	KIA		ROH,BLM
Lawrence,	Pvt.	A	1st SCVA			07/18/63	Bty. Wagner, SC	KIA		ROH
Lawrence, A.L.	Pvt.	G	6th SCVC		DN	02/21/65	Columbia, SC	DOD		ROH
Lawrence, C.C.	Pvt.	I	7th SCVI		ED	/ /			Charlestown, VA	ROH
Lawrence, G.W.	Pvt.	A	23rd SCVI		WG	05/31/64		DOD		ROH
Lawrence, Henry T.	Pvt.	E	Orr's Ri.	19	PS	10/02/63	Anderson Xrds TN	KIA	(Also Wdd @ Sharpsburg)	ROH
Lawrence, Jefferson I.	Pvt.	I	Hol.Leg.		SG	/ /	At home	DOW	(Wdd @ 2nd Manassas)	HOS
Lawrence, Joseph N.	Pvt.		2nd SCVIRi			09/28/63	Columbia, SC	DOD	(Detailed as Hos. Stwd.)	ROH,PP
Lawrence, Moses E.	Pvt.	K	21st SCVI		DN	05/16/64	Drury's Bluff VA	KIA		ROH,JR,HAG,CDC
Lawrence, W.B.	Pvt.	G	Orr's Ri.		AE	03/04/65	Elmira, NY	DIP	Woodlawn N.C. Elmira, NY	P12
Lawrence, W.E.	Pvt.					/ /	Columbia, SC		Elmwood Cem. Columbia, SC	MP,PP
Lawrence, William D.	Pvt.	K	3rd SCVI	21	SG	12/13/62	Fredericksburg	KIA		ROH,JR,SA2,KEB
Lawson, D.	Pvt.	D	4th Bn Res			02/21/65	Columbia, SC	DOD		ROH,PP
Lawson, Elijah	Pvt.	B	15th SCVI		UN	05/29/63	Richmond, VA	DOD	(JR=DOW)	ROH,JR,KEB
Lawson, Fincher	Pvt.	C	18th SCVI		UN	07/22/62	Columbia, SC	DOD		ROH,JR,PP
Lawson, J. Monroe	Pvt.	B	15th SCVI	19	UN	07/18/62	At home	DOD		ROH,JR,KEB
Lawson, J.M.	Pvt.		Ham.Leg.			02/22/64			Hollywood Cem.Rchmd. I9	HC
Lawson, Jefferson G.	Pvt.	K	22nd SCVI		PS	06/15/62	Columbia, SC	DOD	(PP=J.J.)	ROH,PP
Lawson, Joseph	Pvt.	K	1st SCVC	54	PS	04/12/65	Goldsboro, NC	ACD	(Rifle fell from stack)	ROH,GRD
Lawson, Joseph T.	Pvt.	H	21st SCVI		DN	01/15/65	Ft. Fisher, NC	KIA		PP,HAG
Lawson, L.E. (Lemuel?)	Pvt.	B	15th SCVI		UN	/ /	Richmond, VA		Oakwood C.#86,Row G,Div G	ROH,OWC,KEB
Lawson, Levi	Pvt.	C	18th SCVI	28	UN	04/15/62	At home	DOD	(KEB=B, 15th SCVI)	ROH,JR
Lawson, M.H.	Pvt.	H	3rd SCVI		LN	09/13/62	Maryland Hts. MD	KIA		ROH,JR,SA2
Lawson, T.L.	Pvt.	I	P.S.S.		PS	05/31/62	7 Pines, VA	KIA	(JR=T.S.)	ROH,JR,CDC
Lawson, Thomas	Pvt.	C	18th SCVI	22	UN	04/11/64	At home	DOD	(ROH=1862)	ROH,JR
Lawson, W.F.	Pvt.	D	3rd SCVI		SG	09/13/62	Maryland Hts. MD	KIA		ROH,JR,SA2,CDC
Lawson, W.M.	2nd Lt.	C	18th SCVI	22	UN	07/30/64	Crater, Pbg., VA	KIA		ROH,JR,BLM,R47
Lawson, Wiley Mitchell	Cpl.	C	18th SCVI	25	UN	03/18/63	Meridian, MS	DOD	(JR=Madison, MS 5/22/62)	ROH,JR,UNC,PP

SOUTH CAROLINA DEAD IN CSA SERVICE 1861-1865

NAME	RANK	C REGIMENT	AGE	DS	DIED	WHERE	WHY	BURIED	SOURCES
Lawson, William L.	Pvt.	C 10th SCVI		HY	07/22/64	Atlanta, GA	KIA		ROH,JR,RAS,CDC
Lawton, Amos B.	Pvt.	B 27th SCVI		CN	11/10/62	At home	DOD	(JR=Bee's Creek 11/12/62)	ROH,JR,CDC
Lawton, George W.	Pvt.	C 27th SCVI	53	CN	08/01/64	Charlotte, NC	DOD	(Coming home from VA)	ROH,HAG,PP
Lawton, J.W.	Pvt.	K 15th SCVI		AE	10/13/64	Strasburg, VA	KIA		ROH,JR,KEB
Lawton, Jenkins Mikell	Pvt.	B 7th SCVC	21	AE	06/06/64	Virginia	DOD	Methodist Ch. Greenwood SC	ROH,UD3
Lawton, Joseph Charles	Pvt.	B 7th SCVC	23	CN	04/06/65	Farmville, VA	KIA	Mem. Mkr Greenwood, SC	ROH,UD3
Lawton, William Y.	Lt.			CN	01/15/61		DOD		ROH
Lay, E.	Pvt.	Ward's LA	20	HY	07/31/64	Georgetown, SC	DOD	(Lay, E.J. age 37 in CEN?)	PP,CDC
Lay, Joseph H.	Pvt.	D 9th SCVIBn	19	HY	06/16/62	Secessionville	KIA		ROH,JR,PP
Layne, R.F.	Pvt.	B 18th SCVI		UN	06/15/63	Petersburg, VA	DOW	(Wdd 6/4/63)	ROH
Layton, B.W.	Pvt.	D 3rd SCVI		SG	08/16/61	Richmond, VA	DOD		ROH,JR,SA2
Layton, Christopher C.	Pvt.	E 18th SCVI	22	SG	07/11/63	Jackson, MS	ACD		ROH,JR,PP
Layton, D.P.	Pvt.	B 1st SCVC	26	SG	09/13/63	Culpepper, VA	KIA		ROH,HOS,R43
Layton, J. Oliver	Pvt.	B 1st SCVC	30	SG	06/15/61	Adams Run, SC	DOD	(HOS=DOW)	ROH,HOS,PP
Layton, John M.	Pvt.	H 1st SCVIG		SG	04/20/65	Pt. Lookout, MD	DIP	C.C. Pt. Lookout, MD	SA1,FPH,P6,P11
Layton, Maynard C.	Pvt.	K P.S.S.		SG	/ /	Chattanooga, TN	DOD	(Also Wdd @ Fraysers Fm)	ROH,JR,HOS
Layton, Robert	Pvt.	G 1st SCVIR		CR	09/15/62	Kingville, SC	DOD	(DES, Exposure in swamp)	CDC,SA1
Layton, T.J.	Pvt.	B 1st SCVC		SG	09/14/63	Rapidan River VA	KIA		R43
Layton, Thomas C.	Pvt.	E 18th SCVI	24	SG	03/12/64	Belden, FL	DOD		ROH,HOS
LeGrand, Lucius	Pvt.	C 6th SCVI	18	KW	06/07/62	Petersburg, VA	DOD	Blandford Church Pbg., VA	HIC,BLC,PP
LeGrand, Marshall Leard	Pvt.	6th SCVI		KW	06/07/62	Petersburg, VA	DOD	(Typhoid, 1st in E,2nd SC)	H2,SA2
LeRebour, Joseph F.	1st Sgt.	A 10th SCVI		GN	07/22/64	Atlanta, GA	KIA	(NC native)	ROH,GRG,RAS,HO
LeRoach, William T.	Pvt.	A 1st SC		CO	06/07/65	Hart's Island NY	DIP	Cypress Hills N.C.#2903 NY	FPH,P12,P79
LeRoy, Abraham A.	2nd Lt.	E Orr's Ri.	25	PS	03/22/63	Richmond, VA	DOW	(Wdd @ 2nd Man,)	ROH,JR,CDC,R45
LeRoy, Charles T.	Pvt.	H 19th SCVI	40	AE	08/09/64	Forsyth, GA	DOW	Forsyth, GA	ROH,CKB
LeRoy, David T.	Pvt.	E Orr's Ri.	26	PS	07/31/62	Richmond, VA	DOW	(CDC=David S.)	ROH,JR,CDC
LeRoy, J.N.	Pvt.	C 7th SCVI	36	AE	12/05/61	Manchester, VA	DOD	Willington Cem. McC Cty SC	ROH,MCC,KEB
LeRoy, Samuel P.	Pvt.	E Orr's Ri.	22	PS	08/09/62	Richmond, VA	DOD	(Rchmd effects list)	ROH,JR,CDC
LeRoy, William J.H.	Pvt.	E Orr's Ri.	24	PS	06/27/62	Gaines' Mill, VA	KIA		ROH,JR,CDC
Lea, J.C.	Pilot		48	CN	05/10/63	Petersburg, VA	DOD		PP
Leach, C.	Pvt.	C 25th SCVI		LN	08/28/64	Richmond, VA	DOD	(1st in C, 2nd SCVI)	ROH,H2,SA2,KEB
Leach, Duncan N.	Pvt.	E 1st SCVIG		MN	06/07/64	Richmond, VA	DOW	Hollywood Cem.Rchmd. R39	ROH,HC,PDL,SA1
Leach, E. Morgan	Pvt.	D 7th SCVC	29	YK	06/15/64	Malvern Hill, VA	KIA	(1st served in B,5th SCVI)	ROH,JR,SA3,YEB
Leach, John	Pvt.	A 7th SCVIBn	39	KW	09/27/62	At home	DOD	(HIC=Adams Run, JR=8/27/62)	ROH,JR,HIC
Leach, John A.	3rd Sgt.	E 1st SCVIG		MN	05/15/64	Spotsylvania, VA	DOW		ROH,SA1,CDC
Leach, Julius M.	Pvt.	H 8th SCVI		MN	07/02/63	Gettysburg, PA	KIA	(ROH & JR=Leitch)	ROH,JR,HMC,GDR
Leach, P.L.	Pvt.	L Perrin's			/ /	Griffin, GA		(14th SCVI ? no Co. L)	UD2
Leach, William F.	Pvt.	E 7th SCVIBn		KW	07/25/65	Elmira, NY	DIP	Woodlawn N.C.#2868 Elmira	HIC,FPH,P1,P66
Leadbetter, Thomas Deas	Cpt.	C 11th SCVI		CN	05/14/64	Drury's Bluff VA	KIA		ROH,HAG,R47
Leadholt, J.M.	Pvt.	C 1st SCV			12/07/62	Staunton, VA		Thornrose C. Staunton, VA	TOD
League, G.R.	Pvt.	D 2nd SCVIRi		AN	10/28/63	Lookout Valley	KIA		ROH,CDC
League, Henry	Pvt.	I 5th SCVI		SG	05/31/62	7 Pines, VA	KIA		HMC
League, J.M.	Pvt.	B P.S.S.		PS	01/15/63	At home	DOW	(Wdd @ Fraysers Fm.'62)	ROH,JR
League, Joshua	Pvt.	A 16th SCVI	20	GE	09/01/64	Jonesborough, GA	KIA	Clearsprings B.C. GE Cty.	ROH,16R,GEC
League, Willialm	Pvt.	A 16th SCV			/ /		SOW	Marietta GA	UD2
League, William	Pvt.	A 16th SCVI	39	GE	02/20/64	Marietta, GA	DOD	Con. Cem. Marietta, GA	ROH,16R,BGA,CC
Leahey, Michael	Pvt.	B 1st SCVIBn		CN	09/15/62	Charleston, SC	ACD	(Drowned)	ROH,JR,CDC
Leaird, D.H.	Pvt.	G 27th SCVI		OG	06/18/64	Petersburg, VA	KIA	(JR=6/19)	ROH,JR,HAG
Leaird, J. (T.?)	Pvt.	G 27th SCVI			06/18/64	Petersburg, VA	KIA	(Dup of John H.?)	ROH,JR
Leaird, John H.	Pvt.	G 27th SCVI		CN	09/25/64	Petersburg, VA	KIA	(? J.H. or J.J. in HAG)	ROH,HAG,PP
Leak, Thomas J.	Pvt.			LS	05/06/64	Wilderness, VA	KIA		LSS

L

SOUTH CAROLINA DEAD IN CSA SERVICE 1861-1865

NAME	RANK	C REGIMENT	AGE	DS	DIED	WHERE	WHY	BURIED	SOURCES
Leake, William G.	Pvt.	F 22nd SCVI	43	GE	05/24/65	Pt. Lookout, MD	DIP	C.C. Pt. Lookout, MD P6	FPH,GEC,LSC,P114
Leaphart, B.A.M.	Pvt.	F 5th SCVC	30	LN	06/12/64	Trevillian Stn.	DOW		ROH,JR,CDC
Leaphart, Charlton	Pvt.	I 1st SCVC	18	LN	12/15/64	James Island, SC	ACD	(Accidental gunshot)	ROH
Leaphart, Franklin E.	Sgt.	C 15th SCVI	40	LN	09/19/64	Winchester, VA	DOW	(In enemy hands)	DOT,H15,KEB
Leard, Bonner	Pvt.	G 14th SCVI	19	AE	/ /		DOW	(1865, Wdd. @ Pbg)	ROH
Leard, James	Pvt.	G 14th SCVI		AE	05/14/65	Richmond, VA	DIP	106 Hollywood C. Rchmd. VA	ROH,P6,P12
Leathe, John M.	Pvt.	2nd SCVA			03/19/65	Bentonville, NC	KIA		WAT,PP
Leatherman, J.L.	Pvt.	H 1st SC			05/26/64	Richmond, VA			ROH
Leavell, Richard A.	2nd Cpl.	E 3rd SCVI		NY	11/30/63	Knoxville, TN	DOW	Bush River B.C. NY Cty	ROH,NCC,ANY,KEB
Leay, Sinclair	Pvt.	H 15th SCVI		UN	/ /	Manchester, VA	DOD		ROH,JR
Ledbetter, Daniel A.	Colonel	Orr's Ri.	50	AN	09/01/62	2nd Manassas, VA	DOW	Bushy Park Farm, VA	ROH,JR,HOS,LC
Ledbetter, Thomas E.	Cpt.	C 11th SCVI		CN	05/09/64	Swift Creek, VA	KIA		JR,HAG
Lee, A.C.	Pvt.	F 10th SCVI		MN	/ /		DOD		RAS
Lee, A.R.	Pvt.	H 10th SCVI		WG	/ /		DOD	(1863)	RAS,HOW
Lee, Anderson J.	Pvt.	K 1st SCVC			11/01/62		DOD	(Typhoid)	JR
Lee, B.	Pvt.	H 10th SCVI		WG	/ /		DOD	(1863)	RAS,HOW
Lee, B.H.	Pvt.	I 2nd SCVA	40	OG	09/05/63	Charleston, SC	DOD		ROH
Lee, C.W.	Pvt.	H 10th SCVI		WG	12/15/62		DOD	(Day approx)	RAS,HOW
Lee, D.P.	Pvt.	C 15th SCVI		LN	08/11/62	Richmond, VA	DOD		H15
Lee, E.V.B.	Cpl.	C 10th SCVI		MN	/ /	Chattanooga, TN	DOD		RAS
Lee, F.F.	Pvt.	C			09/17/62	Richmond, VA		(Richmond effects list)	ROH,CDC
Lee, G.W.	Pvt.	E 27th SCVI			07/16/64	Richmond, VA			ROH
Lee, H.	Pvt.	B 2nd SCVIRi		PS	11/13/64	Richmond, VA		Hollywood Cem.Rchmd. W197	ROH,HC
Lee, Harry J.	Pvt.	C P.S.S.	18	AN	06/07/62	7 Pines, VA	DOW	Oakwood C.#96,Row K,Div B	ROH,JR,OWC,GMJ
Lee, Henry D.	Sgt.	A 24th SCVI	26	CN	05/16/64	Calhoun, GA	KIA		RJM
Lee, Ira	Pvt.	I 26th SCVI	23	WG	/ /	Petersburg, VA	KIA	(1864)	CTA,HOW
Lee, J.A.	Pvt.	H 10th SCVI		WG	/ /		DIP	(1863)	RAS,HOW
Lee, J.L.	Pvt.	H 10th SCVI		WG	/ /		DIP	(Dup Lee, J.W.?)	RAS,P39
Lee, James	Pvt.	C 7th SCVIBn	26	RD	09/28/63	Charleston, SC	DOD	Magnolia Cem. Charleston	ROH,HAG,RCD
Lee, James	Pvt.	B Hol.Leg.	19	SG	08/04/62	Richmond, VA	DOD	Bethesda B.C. SG Cty.	JR,SSC,HOS
Lee, James	Pvt.	C Orr's Ri.		PS	08/29/62	2nd Manassas, VA	KIA		JR
Lee, James A.	Pvt.	E 15th SCVI	42	FD	01/12/63	Charlottesville	DOD	Univ. Cem. Charlottesville	ROH,JR,ACH
Lee, James S.	Pvt.	B 7th SCVIBn	52	RD	05/16/64	Drury's Bluff VA	KIA		ROH,JR,HAG
Lee, Jeremiah	Pvt.	C Orr's Ri.		PS	07/22/62	Laurel Hill, VA	DOD		JR
Lee, Jesse	Pvt.	C 1st SCVIG		RD	/ /	Richmond, VA		(On roll of 10/31/64)	ROH,SA1
Lee, John	Pvt.	L 7th SCVI		HY	/ /	Richmond, VA		Oakwood C.#10,Row P,Div B	ROH,OWC
Lee, John Dozier	1st Lt.	E P.S.S.	22	SR	06/30/62	Frayser's Farm	KIA	(Rgmtl Adjutant)	ROH,CDC,R48,CNM
Lee, John W.	Pvt.	H 10th SCVI		WG	03/02/64	Rock Island, IL	DIP	C.C.#699 Rock Island, IL	FPH,P5,RAS,HOW
Lee, Joseph	Cpl.	D P.S.S.			/ /		DOD		JR
Lee, Joseph	Pvt.	Palm. LA		CD	06/01/64	Cold Harbor, VA	DOW		SOB
Lee, Joseph E.	Cpt.	F P.S.S.		LN	09/17/62	Sharpsburg, MD	DOW		JR,CDC,R48
Lee, Lawrence D.	Cpl.	G 19th SCVI		AE	12/31/62	Murfreesboro, TN	DOW	Evergreen C. Murfreesboro	HOL,TOD
Lee, Lawrence S.	Pvt.	A 25th SCVI		CN	10/31/64	Ft. Sumter, SC	KIA	St.Phillips C. Charleston	ROH,JR,PP,DOC
Lee, Noah	Pvt.	Ferguson's			/ /	Marietta, GA		Con. Cem. Marietta, GA	CCM
Lee, P.D.	Pvt.	H 10th SCVI		WG	06/15/62	Tupelo, MS	DOD		RAS,CTA,HOW
Lee, Philip	Pvt.	I 1st SCVIR	59	AN	08/08/62	At home		Shady Grove B.C. Belton SC	AMC,SA1
Lee, R.W.	Pvt.	H 23rd SCVI		MN	09/14/62	South Mtn., MD	KIA	(?HMC =Living in 1901)	ROH,JR,CDC
Lee, Ransom	Pvt.	B 22nd SCVI		SG	/ /				HOS
Lee, Robert A.	Pvt.	D Ham.Leg.	19	AN	12/09/61	Manassas, VA	DOD		ROH,GRS
Lee, S.D.	Pvt.	C 9th SCVIB			08/24/61	Germantown, VA	DOD	(Typhoid)	JR
Lee, S.S.	Pvt.	A			10/31/63	Ft. Sumter, SC	KIA	(Falling of a wall)	JR

SOUTH CAROLINA DEAD IN CSA SERVICE 1861-1865

L

NAME	RANK	C	REGIMENT	AGE	DS	DIED	WHERE	WHY	BURIED	SOURCES
Lee, Samuel R.	Pvt.	I	2nd SCVA	35	OG	10/07/64	James Island, SC	DOD		ROH,CDC
Lee, Thomas	1st Cpl.	F	5th SCVI		SG	09/16/61	Charlottesville	DOD	Univ. Cem. Charlottesville	ROH,JR,SA3,ACH
Lee, Timothy	Pvt.	I	26th SCVI	38	WG	/ /	Petersburg, VA	KIA		CTA,HOW
Lee, Uriah H.	4th Cpl.	C	2nd SCVI		RD	09/20/63	Chickamauga, GA	KIA (Also Wdd 5/8/63)		ROH,JR,SA2,KEB
Lee, W.A.	Pvt.	I	10th SCVI		MN	/ /	Mississipppi	DOD		RAS,HMC
Lee, W.C.	Pvt.	H	10th SCVI		WG	/ /		DIP (? DUP Lee, C.W.)		RAS,HOW
Lee, W.H. Harrison	Pvt.	H	16th SCVI		GE	08/15/63	Meridian, MS	DOD		16R,PP
Lee, William C.	Pvt.	H	10th SCVI		WG	/ /		DOD (1863)		RAS,HOW
Lee, William H.	Pvt.	F	6th SCVI		CR	09/09/61		DOD (Measles)		JR,HMC,HHC
Lee, William J.D.	Pvt.	E	Orr's Ri.	19	PS	07/01/62	Richmond, VA	DOD	Hollywood Cem.Rchmd. M287	ROH,JR,HC
Lee, William P.	Qm. Sgt.		3rd SCVI		LS	01/10/64	Camp Chase, OH	DIP	C.C.#90 Columbus, OH	FPH,SA2,ANY,P5
Leech, D.M.	Pvt.	A	1st SC			05/30/64	Richmond, VA		Hollywood Cem.Rchmd. I250	HC
Leek, Richard S.	Pvt.	B	1st SCVIG	21	LS	02/08/63	Danville, VA	DOD		ROH,ANY,SA1
Leek, William Y.	Pvt.	B	1st SCVIG	23	NY	10/30/61	Suffolk, VA	DOD (Body returned home)		ROH,JR,SA1,ANY
Lefton, James	Pvt.	G	4th Bn Res			09/21/64	Charleston, SC	DOD	Magnolia Cem. Charleston	ROH,RCD
Legette, Hannibal	Cpt.	L	21st SCVI	24	MN	07/02/64	At home	DOW (Wdd Walthal Jct. 5/7/64)		ROH,HMC,HAG
Legette, Henry C.	Pvt.	L	21st SCVI	54	MN	02/15/65	Wilmington, NC	DOD (1st served/ H,Orr's Ri.)		ROH,HMC,HAG
Legette, Morgan	Cpl.	H	Orr's Ri.		MN	06/27/62	Gaines' Mill, VA	KIA		ROH,JR,HMC,CDC
Legg, West	Pvt.	A	7th SCV			05/06/64	Wilderness, VA	DOW	Fredericksburg C.C. R6S13	JR,FBG
Leigh, Benjamin Watkins	Major		A.A.G. GS	33		07/03/63	Gettysburg, PA	KIA (Gen. Ed. Johnson's Staff)		ROH,GDR
Leister, Albert	Pvt.	B	1st SCVIG	30	NY	04/15/61	Morris Island SC	DOD (6Mths Org.?)		ANY
Leister, Jefferson	3rd Cpl.	B	22nd SCVI		SG	07/30/64	Crater, Pbg., VA	KIA		BLM
Leitch, Robert Miller	Pvt.	I	1st SCVIG	39	LN	07/05/63	Richmond, VA	DOD (Wdd @ Gaines' Mill)		ROH,SA1
Leitner, Benjamin F.	Pvt.	E	2nd SCVI	19	FD	07/09/62	Savage Stn., VA	DOW		ROH,SA2,HIC,KE
Leitner, John Wesley	Pvt.	G	24th SCVI	31	RD	07/25/64	Atlanta, GA	DOW (Wdd 7/22)		ROH
Leitzey, David M.	2nd Lt.	H	13th SCVI		NY	07/02/63	Gettysburg, PA	DOW (May be from LN)		ROH,GDR,ANY,BO
Leitzey, J.G.	Pvt.		Hol.Leg.			07/27/65	Petersburg, VA	DIP		ROH,P6
Leitzey, Jacob	Pvt.	G	Hol.Leg.		NY	/ /	Point Lookout MD	DIP		ANY
Leitzsey, William L.	Cpt.	H	13th SCVI	20	NY	08/22/64	Fussel's Mills	KIA	Hollywood Cem.Rchmd. V434	JR,HC,ANY,R47
Leman, J.H.	Pvt.	H	8th SCVI		MN	07/02/63	Gettysburg, PA	KIA (Leach, Julius M.?)		JR
Leman, J.T.	Pvt.	E	P.S.S.			/ /		DOD		JR
Leman, L.B.	Pvt.	G	11th SCVI		CN	03/10/65	Pt. Lookout, MD	DIP	C.C. Pt. Lookout, MD	HAG,P12
Leman, Mitchell	Pvt.	L	1st SCVIG	17	CN	07/20/62	Gaines' Mill, VA	DOW (ROH=Leasman)		ROH,JR,SA1,CDC
Leman, William	Pvt.	F	15th SCVI		UN	/ /		DOD (Leonard/KEB?)		JR
Lemans, C.S.	Pvt.	F	3rd SCVC		BT	01/15/65		DIP		P12
Lemmon, J.P.	Pvt.	D	9th SCVIB		SR	10/03/61	Centreville, VA	DOD (JR=Semmon)		JR,CNM
Lemon, George	Pvt.	F	15th SCVI		UN	10/13/64	Strasburg, VA	KIA (Rgmt. consolidated /8th)		ROH
Lemon, James M.	Pvt.	H	24th SCVI	33	CR	11/24/64	Lookout Mtn. GA	KIA		RJM,HHC,CB
Lemon, John M.	Pvt.	H	24th SCVI	21	CR	03/13/65	Milledgeville GA	DOD		ROH,HHC,CB
Lenderman, Andrew J.	Pvt.	B	16th SCVI		GE	09/02/64	Lovejoy, GA	KIA		ROH,16R
Lenderman, John S.	Pvt.	H	7th SCVI		GE	/ /	Mt. Jackson, VA		Mt. Jackson, VA	ROH,PP
Lenderman, Lewis	Pvt.	B	16th SCVI		GE	/ /	Charleston, SC	DOD (1862)		16R
Lenderman, Newton	2nd Lt.	B	16th SCVI		GE	07/11/63	Yazoo City, MS	DOD		16R,R47,PP
Lenerieux, Francis M.	Pvt.	G	15th SCVI	26	WG	07/27/63	Gettysburg, PA	DOW		ROH,JR,GDR,KEB
Lenhardt, Lawrence	Pvt.	K	6th SCVI	22	GE	12/20/61	Dransville, VA	KIA	Lenhardt Fam. C. GE Cty.	GEC,CDC
Lenley, James	Pvt.		2nd SC			09/04/61	Richmond, VA			ROH
Lennou, George	Pvt.	F	15th SCVI			10/13/64	Petersburg, VA	KIA (Leonard?)		JR
Lenton, T.W.	Pvt.	C	P.S.S.		CD	/ /		DOD		ROH
Leonard, D. Clark	Pvt.	C	22nd SCVI		SG	09/17/62	Sharpsburg, MD	KIA (HOS= South Mountain)		ROH,HOS
Leonard, David Anderson	Pvt.	I	5th SCVI	28	GE	/ /	Richmond, VA(62)	DOD	Oakwood C.#4,Row N,Div A	ROH,SA3,GEC,OW
Leonard, G.	Pvt.	F	5th SCV		UN	/ /			Gilead C. Jonesville UN Cy	UD3

L

SOUTH CAROLINA DEAD IN CSA SERVICE 1861-1865

NAME	RANK	C REGIMENT	AGE	DS	DIED	WHERE	WHY	BURIED	SOURCES
Leonard, J.D.	Pvt.	B 13th SCVI		SG	07/20/63	Davids Island NY	DOW	Cypress Hills N.C.#670 NY	ROH,FPH,CDC,P1
Leonard, John	Pvt.	G 18th SCVI		SG	08/30/62	2nd Manassas, VA	KIA		ROH,JR,CDC
Leonard, Joseph	Pvt.	I 6th SCVI		CR	/ /		KIA		CB,HHC
Leonard, Vardry A.	Pvt.	F 2nd SCVI	28	AE	09/25/61	Charlottesville	DOD	Univ. Cem. Charlottesville	ROH,SA2,KEB,ACH
Leonard, W.	Pvt.	H 5th SCV		UN	/ /			Gilead C. Jonesville UN Cy	UD3
Leopard, Elijah	Pvt.	F 7th SCVI	31	ED	/ /	At home	DOD		HOE,KEB
Leopoldt, W.	Pvt.	A German A			/ /			St.Lawrence C. Charleston	MAG
Leppard, W. Caughman	2nd Lt.	K 13th SCVI		LN	09/01/62	Ox Hill, VA	KIA		ROH,HOS,R47
Lequeaux, William B.	Pvt.	I 27th SCVI	20	CN	09/06/64	Elmira, NY	DIP	Woodlawn N.C.#246 Elmira	ROH,FPH,P5,P65
Lesesne, Francis James	1st Lt.	K 25th SCVI		WG	05/16/64	Swift Creek, VA	DOW	Blandford Church Pbg., VA	ROH,HOW,BLC,PP
Lesesne, Francis Kinloch	Pvt.	Marion A.	20	CN	06/24/65	Charleston, SC	DOD	St.Philips C. Charleston	MAG,RCD
Lesesne, Henry Russell	Cpt.	H 1st SCVA	23	CN	03/16/65	Averysboro, NC	KIA	St. Philips Ch. Charleston	ROH,SCA,RCD,PP
Lesesne, Nabor D.	Pvt.	C Ham.Leg.		WG	08/29/61	Culpepper, VA	DOW	Lesesne Community, WG Cty.	JR,HOW,3RC
Lesesne, Patrick H.	Pvt.	K 25th SCVI	26	WG	06/16/64	Swift Creek, VA	DOW	(PP=5/16/64)	ROH,HOW,PP,HAG
Lesesne, William Cantey	Pvt.	K 25th SCVI	19	WG	08/21/64	City Pt. VA	DOW	City Pt. N.C. Hopewell, VA	ROH,HOW,P12,PP
Lesher, William	Pvt.	A 15th SCVI		RD	08/26/64	Charlestown, VA	KIA		ROH,JR,KEB
Lesley, M.H.	Pvt.	E 2nd SCVIRi		PS	05/15/64	Virginia	KIA		ROH,JR
Leslie, A.P.	Pvt.	B 22nd SCVI		SG	10/22/62	Winchester, VA		Stonewall C. Winchester VA	ROH,WIN,P12
Leslie, G.W. (J.W.?)	Pvt.	K 25th SCVI		WG	08/25/64	City Point, VA	DOW	City Pt. N.C. Hopewell, VA	ROH,TOD
Leslie, J.N.	Pvt.	B 6th SCVI		YK	10/01/62	Winchester, VA	DOD		ROH
Leslie, Thomas	Pvt.	B Orr's Ri.		AE	02/24/62	At home	DOD		JR,CDC
Lespair, Malcolm	Pvt.	C 26th SCVI		MN	03/31/64	Petersburg, VA		(Lupo? Not in HMC)	ROH
Lester, Alfred M.	Pvt.	C 3rd SCVI		NY	08/15/63	Richmond, VA	DOD	Oakwood C.#6, Row 25,Div D	ROH,NCC,ANY,OWC
Lester, B.	Pvt.	I 2nd SC			01/03/63	Richmond, VA		Hollywood Cem.Rchmd. D91	HC
Lester, Isaac B.	2nd Sgt.	G 8th SCVI	23	MO	04/12/62	Richmond, VA	DOD	Oakwood C.#54,Row G,Div A	ROH,HOM,OWC,UD2
Lester, L.W.	Pvt.	K 21st SCVI		DN	08/26/64	City Pt., VA	DOW	Prob. N/C/ Hopewell, VA	P12
Lester, W.	Pvt.				/ /	Richmond, VA		Oakwood C.#15, Row 44,Div D	ROH,OWC
Lester, W.J.	Pvt.	11th SCVI			05/20/65	Charleston, SC	DOD	(U.S. Hospital)	P6
Lever, Stephen S.	Sgt.	G 24th SCVI	38		11/10/62	Columbia, SC	DOD	(JR=Congaree Rifles)	JR,EJM,PP
Leverett, D.C.	Pvt.	F 24th SCVI	23	AN	01/09/63	Charleston, SC	DOD	Magnolia Cem. Charleston	ROH,MAG
Leverett, William Harvey	Pvt.	F 24th SCVI	27	AN	01/24/64	Newman, GA	DOD		ROH,HOL
Leverette, C.J.	Pvt.	F 24th SCVI		AN	/ /		DOD		HOL
Leverette, Frederick B.	Surgeon	Fields Bgd	33	BT	07/23/64	Richmond, VA	DOD	(Exhaustion, Wilderness)	ROH
Leverette, Thomas S.	Pvt.	F 24th SCVI	20	AN	02/02/64	Marietta, GA	DOD	Con. Cem. Marietta, GA	EJM,BGA,CCM
Levester, George T.	Pvt.	D 5th SCVI		UN	11/15/61	Centreville, VA	DOD	(To Hosp 12/31/61)	JR,SA3
Levett, J.	Pvt.	L 10th SCVI		MN	05/24/64	Macon, GA		Macon, GA Cem.	CV
Levin, Samuel S.	Pvt.	A 15th SCVI	19	RD	10/04/62	Sharpsburg, MD	DOW	Hebrew Cem. Columbia SC	ROH,JR,MP,PP
Levina, Perry	Pvt.	E 1st SCVIR		CD	09/08/63	Ft. Moultrie, SC	KIA		SA1
Levister, John T.	Pvt.	B 7th SCVIBn	18	CR	03/26/64	James Island, SC	DOD		ROH,HAG,HHC
Levy, David S.	Pvt.	D 2nd SCV			07/21/61		DOD		JR
Levy, J.N.	Pvt.	C 7th SCVI			12/15/61	Richmond, VA	DOD	(Typhoid)	JR
Levy, Jesse	Pvt.	B 3rd SC			09/17/62	Sharpsburg, MD	KIA		ROH
Levy, Julian				KW	/ /		KIA	(7 days battles)	HIC
Levy, Saul				KW	/ /		DOD		HIC
Lewellen, Benjamin F.	Pvt.	I 6th SCVC		MN	09/01/64	Elmira, NY	DIP	Woodlawn N.C.#71 Elmira	FPH,P5,P65,P120
Lewie, Emanuel W.	1st Sgt.	C 15th SCVI	19	LN	07/02/63	Gettysburg, PA	KIA	Magnolia Cem. Charleston	JR,MAG,GDR,H15
Lewie, Samuel Isaiah	1st Lt.	C 15th SCVI	23	LN	09/15/62	South Mtn., MD	KIA	TOD	ROH,JR,KEB,H15
Lewis Robert S.	1st Lt.	D 1st SCVC	27	CR	09/14/63	Raccoon Ford, VA	KIA		ROH,R43
Lewis, A.C.	Pvt.	E 26th SCVI		HY	07/14/63	Jackson, MS	KIA	(Shot on picket, JR=P.C.))	ROH,JR,PP
Lewis, Angus	Pvt.	E 1st SCVIG		MN	07/17/63	Gettysburg, PA	DOW		SA1,GDR,HMC,PDL
Lewis, Augustus	3rd Lt.	K Orr's Ri.	35	AN	05/03/63	Chancellorsville	KIA	(Dup of Jesse A.?)	ROH

SOUTH CAROLINA DEAD IN CSA SERVICE 1861-1865

NAME	RANK	C REGIMENT	AGE	DS	DIED	WHERE	WHY	BURIED	SOURCES
Lewis, Daniel M.	Pvt.	A 21st SCVI		GN	03/18/65	Elmira, NY	DIP	Woodlawn N.C.#1731 Elmira	FLR,HAG,FPH,P6
Lewis, David S.	Pvt.	4th SCVI	19	AN	05/15/61	Charlottesville	DOD	(Lewis, S.D.in SA2 ?)	ROH
Lewis, E.D.S.	Pvt.	B P.S.S.		PS	06/24/62	Manchester, VA	DOD	(JR=DOW)	ROH,JR
Lewis, Earle	Pvt.	C P.S.S.		AN	01/15/63	Fredericksburg			ROH
Lewis, Granby Thomas	Pvt.	F 23rd SCVI	34	CR	10/04/62	Culpepper, VA	DOD	Fairview Cem. Culpepper VA	ROH,CGH
Lewis, Hardee	Pvt.	E 1st SCVIG		MN	05/12/64	Spotsylvania, VA	KIA		ROH,JR,SA1,PDL
Lewis, Isaac	Pvt.	G 10th SCVI	32	HY	06/05/62	Enterprise, MS	DOD	Prob/unknowns, C.C. there	PP,RAS,CEN
Lewis, J.R.	Pvt.	F 10th SCVI		MN	/ /	Knoxville, TN	DOD		RAS,HMC
Lewis, James	Pvt.	K 26th SCVI	19	HY	07/12/63	Jackson, MS	KIA	(Or father James age 38)	ROH,JR,PP,CEN
Lewis, Jesse A.	1st Lt.	K Orr's Ri.	33	AN	09/30/64	Jones Farm, VA	KIA	Honea Path P.C. SC	ROH,JR,ANC,BOS
Lewis, John	Pvt.	D 11th SCVI	26	BT	11/07/61	Bay Point, SC	DOD		ROH,HAG
Lewis, John	Pvt.	Hart's Bty		SR	06/20/64	White House, VA	KIA	(Exploding Caison)	ROH,CNM
Lewis, John	Pvt.	M 16th SCVI			11/30/64	Franklin, TN	KIA	Macgavock C. Fr'kln GV#36	16R,WCT
Lewis, John H.	Pvt.	E 1st SCVIG		MN	08/19/64	Fussell's Mill	DOW	Hollywood Cem.Rchmd. V699	HC,SA1,PDL,CDC
Lewis, John J.	Pvt.	M 10th SCVI		HY	12/15/64	Nashville, TN	KIA		RAS,PP
Lewis, Joseph	Pvt.	C 18th SCVIB		CN	10/19/63	Charleston, SC	DOD	Magnolia Cem. Charleston	ROH,MAG
Lewis, M.J.	Sgt.	D 1st SC			10/12/64	Richmond, VA			ROH
Lewis, Manning	Pvt.	D Orr's Ri.		AN	03/25/65	Petersburg, VA	KIA		LSS,CDC
Lewis, Moses J.	Sgt.	B 10th SCVI		HY	07/22/64	Atlanta, GA	KIA	(JR=died in June)	ROH,JR,RAS
Lewis, Posey	Pvt.	K 27th SCVI		CN	07/14/64	Pt. Lookout, MD	DIP	(POW @ Pbg. 6/24/64)	ROH,HAG,P12,P1
Lewis, Robert G.	Pvt.	K Orr's Ri.	27	AN	08/15/62		DOD		ROH
Lewis, Robert O.	Pvt.	B 4th SCVI		AN	12/21/61	Richmond, VA	DOD	(POW @ 1st Manassas, wdd?)	ROH,JR,SA2,GMJ
Lewis, Robert S.	1st Lt.	D 1st SCVC		CR	09/14/63	Raccoon Ford, VA	KIA	(HHC=DOW @ Georgetown)	R43,HHC
Lewis, Samuel D.	Pvt.	C P.S.S.		AN	08/14/64	Fussel's Mill VA	KIA		ROH,JR,GMJ
Lewis, Theophilus G.	Cpl.	F 10th SCVI	35	MN	09/20/63	Chickamauga, GA	KIA	Con. Cem. Marietta, GA	ROH,RAS,HMC,CC
Lewis, W.	Pvt.	A 1st SCV			/ /	Richmond, VA		Oakwood C.#40,Row 26,Div D	OWC
Lewis, W.H.	Pvt.	D 7th SCVIBn	24	KW	04/30/64	At home	DOD		ROH,HIC,CDN,HA
Lewis, William	Pvt.	G 9th SCVIBn *4	5H		03/02/62	Camp Lookout, SC	DOD	(JR=W.R. 2/13/62)	ROH,JR,PP
Lewis, William E.	Pvt.	A 12th SCVI	22	YK	06/15/64	Ft. Delaware, DE	DIP	Finn's Pt., NJ Nat. Cem.	ROH,FPH,P5,YEB
Lewis, William E.	Sgt.	A 6th SCVI	23	CR	05/31/62	7 Pines, VA	KIA		ROH,WDE,HHC,GL
Liddell, George W.	Pvt.	E Orr's Ri.	35	PS	11/08/61	Sullivans I., SC	DOD		ROH,CDC
Lide, James E.	Pvt.	PeeDee LA	21	DN	11/30/62		DOD		ROH,SA1,PDL
Lieber, Oscar M.	Pvt.	A Ham.Leg.		RD	05/07/62	Elthams Ldg., VA	KIA		ROH,MAG,WLI
Lifrage, Theodore M.	Sgt.	K 25th SCVI	34	WG	04/03/65	Elmira, NY	DIP	Woodlawn N.C.#2567 Elmira	FPH,HOW,HAG,P6
Liggett, Adam	Pvt.	8th SCVI			08/28/61	Richmond, VA	DOD	(Leggette ?)	ROH
Lightler, Jasper	Pvt.	C 7th SCVIBn	19	LN	06/16/64	Petersburg, VA	KIA		ROH
Ligon, George Anderson	Sgt. Maj.	3rd SCVIbn	22	LS	10/18/62	Richmond, VA	DOD		ROH,KEB
Ligon, R.N.	Pvt.	C 7th SCVI		AE	11/28/61	Richmond, VA	DOD	(Typhoid)	JR
Liles, Sherwood H.	Cpl.	B 24th SCVI	16	MO	06/21/64	Kennesaw Mt., GA	KIA	(By sharpshooter)	ROH,JR,HOM,CDC
Liles, W.B.	Pvt.	C 2nd SCVIRi			05/16/64	Drury's Bluff VA	KIA		JR
Limehouse, Thomas R.	3rd Sgt.	C 11th SCVI	26	CN	05/09/64	Swift Creek, VA	KIA		ROH,JR,HAG,CDC
Linam, M.C.L.	Pvt.	I 1st SC		SR	/ /			Spotsylvania C.H., VA	SCH
Linam, Thomas Mack	Pvt.	D 2nd SCVI		SR	07/31/61	Culpepper, VA	DOD	(JR=Sunstroke 7/21/61)	ROH,JR,SA2,KEB
Lindall, J.N.	Cpl.	H 2nd SCVIRi			07/13/63	Gettysburg, PA	DOW		ROH,CDC,P1,P12
Linder,	Pvt.	I 16th SCVI		GE	07/20/63	Peachtree Crk GA	KIA		16R
Linder, Charles	Pvt.	A Hol.Leg.		SG	04/07/64		DOW		P12
Linder, J.	Pvt.	K 18th SCVI			07/13/62	Jackson, MS	KIA	(18th in MS in 62?)	JR
Linder, J.W.	Pvt.	K P.S.S.			/ /		KIA		JR
Linder, R.M.	Pvt.	I 23rd SCVI			08/30/62	2nd Manassas, VA	KIA	(JR=28th SCVI)	JR
Linder, Thomas R.	Sgt.	I 11th SCVI		CO	06/23/64	Drury's Bluff VA	DOW		ROH,HAG
Linder, W.S.	Pvt.	I 16th SCVI		GE	07/20/64	Peachtree Crk GA	KIA		16R

L

SOUTH CAROLINA DEAD IN CSA SERVICE 1861-1865

NAME	RANK	C REGIMENT	AGE	DS	DIED	WHERE	WHY	BURIED	SOURCES
Linder, Willis	Pvt.	I 13th SCVI	35	SG	08/05/62	Laurel Hill, VA	DOD	Hollywood Cem.Rchmd. M218	ROH,JR,HC,HOS
Lindler, Jacob	Pvt.	I 15th SCVI	41	LN	09/29/63	Atlanta, GA	DOW	Oakland Cem. Atlanta R29#1	ROH,KEB,BGA,H15
Lindler, Osman Pinckney	Pvt.	H 13th SCVI	23	LN	05/12/64	Spotsylvania, VA	KIA	(JR=Clay's Fm. 5/20/64)	ROH,JR
Lindley, W.T.	Pvt.	C 3rd SCVIBn		LS	09/14/62	Maryland Hts. MD	KIA		JR
Lindley, Winfield W.	Pvt.	G Orr's Ri.	26	AE	11/20/62	Berryville, VA	DOD	Due West A.R.P. AE Cty. SC	ROH,JR,CAE
Lindsay, A. Poinsett	Cpl.	G Orr's Ri.	28	AE	06/27/62	Gaines' Mill, VA	KIA	Due West A.R.P. AE Cty. SC	ROH,JR,CV,CAE
Lindsay, Albert	Pvt.	F 3rd SCVI		LS	08/29/61	Richmond, VA	DOD	Hollywood Cem.Rchmd. K72	ROH,JR,HC,SA2
Lindsay, Henry A.	Pvt.	D 27th SCVI	33	CN	03/06/63		DOD	(Consumption)	ROH,JR,HAG
Lindsay, James	Pvt.	E 3rd SCVI		NY	01/04/65	Pt. Lookout, MD	DIP	C.C. Pt. Lookout, MD	ROH,FPH,P6,SA2
Lindsay, John	Pvt.	K 22nd SCVI		PS	03/11/62	Columbia, SC	DOD		ROH,PP
Lindsay, John	Pvt.	H 16th SCVI		GE	07/22/64	Atlanta, GA	KIA		16R
Lindsay, John W.	Cpl.	A 12th SCVI	33	YK	07/09/62	Enroute home	DOW	Bethesda Cem. Yk Cty. SC	JR,YMD,RCD,YEB
Lindsay, William K.	Pvt.	E 3rd SCVI		NY	09/20/63	Chickamauga, GA	KIA		SA2,ANY,KEB
Lindsay, William R.	Pvt.	K 3rd SCVI	30	SG	09/26/62	Sharpsburg, MD	DOW	Rose Hill C. Hagerstown MD	ROH,JR,SA2,BOD
Lindsey, A.R.	Pvt.	E 3rd SCVI		NY	09/20/63	Chickamauga, GA	KIA		JR,CDC
Lindsey, Isaac Jasper	Pvt.		18	LS	08/30/62	2nd Manassas, VA	KIA	Cedar Grove B.C. LS Cty.	LSC
Lindsey, J.C.	Pvt.	H 4th SCVC		LR	05/28/64	Hawes Shop, VA	KIA	(JR=Lindsay)	ROH,JR,LAN
Lindsey, J.H.	Cpl.	E Hol.Leg.	20	SG	08/30/62	2nd Manassas, VA	KIA		ROH
Lindsey, J.R.	Pvt.	2nd SCVIRi			10/02/62	Sharpsburg, MD	DOW		ROH,CDC
Lindsey, J.R.	3rd Sgt.	I 12th SCVI		LR	07/01/63	Gettysburg, PA	KIA		LAN
Lindsey, P. Butler	Pvt.	I 12th SCVI		LR	07/01/63	Gettysburg, PA	KIA		JR,LAN
Lindsey, T.H.	Pvt.	A 17th SCVI		CR	06/20/62			Hollywood Cem.Rchmd. L169	HC
Lindsey, W.H.	Pvt.	K 22nd SCVI		PS	07/30/64	Crater, Pbg., VA	KIA		BLM
Lindsey, William B.	2nd Sgt.	H 23rd SCVI		MN	12/15/62	Lynchburg, VA	DOW	Lynchburg CSA Cem.#2 R2	JR,HMC,BBW
Lindsey, William Bailey	Pvt.		30	LS	09/17/62	Sharpsburg, MD	DOW	Cedar Grove B.C. LS Cty.	LSC
Lindsey, William H.	Pvt.	A 12th SCVI	23	YK	06/24/62	Richmond, VA	DOW	Hollywood Cem.Rchmd. O216	ROH,JR,HC,YEB
Lindsy,	Pvt.	D Hol.Leg.		BL	08/30/62	2nd Manassas, VA	KIA		JR
Ling, J.W.	Pvt.	Ham.Leg.			04/29/62	Richmond, VA	DOD		ROH
Lining, Thomas	Pvt.	K 4th SCVC	34	CN	06/11/64	Trevillian Stn.	KIA		ROH,JR,CDC,CLD
Link, Joseph J.	Pvt.	C 7th SCVI	24	AE	08/10/61	Vienna, VA	DOD		ROH,KEB
Link, W. Edward	Pvt.	G 1st SCVC	18	AE	03/05/62	Adams Run, SC	DOD	(PP=3/19/62)	ROH,PP
Link, W.T.	Pvt.	C 7th SCVI	23	AE	10/01/62	At home	DOD	(JR=7/10/62)	ROH,JR,KEB
Linsey, John	Pvt.	E 6th SCVC		LS	10/27/64	Burgess' Mill VA	KIA	(JR=White Oak Rd.)	JR,CDC
Linson, Jesse	Pvt.	E P.S.S.		CO	/ /		KIA		ROH
Linton, Charles	Pvt.	Coit's LA			/ /	Kelly's Fm, VA	KIA	(Suffolk, April '63)	ROH
Linton, J.W.	Pvt.	M P.S.S.			/ /		DOD		JR
Lipford, James Alexander	1st Sgt.	H 24th SCVI		CR	06/27/63	Canton, MS	DOW	Con.Cem. Canton, MS Gv#265	ROH,HHC,CB,TOD
Lipscomb,	Pvt.	F 27th SCVI			05/16/64	Drury's Bluff VA	KIA	(Prob. W.S. in G,27th)	ROH,JR,ODC
Lipscomb, James C.	Pvt.	I 13th SCVI	18	SG	06/15/62	Richmond, VA	DOD	(Typhoid)	ROH,JR,HOS
Lipscomb, Martin	Pvt.	M P.S.S.	22	UN	05/31/62	7 Pines, VA	KIA		ROH,JR,CDC
Lipscomb, Moses	Pvt.	G 5th SCVI	21	SG	06/15/61		DOD		ROH,SA3
Lipscomb, Smith	Sgt.	F 15th SCVI		SG	03/16/65	Averysboro, NC	KIA	(Promoted for bravery)	HOS,KEB
Lipscomb, Thomas H.	Pvt.	I 13th SCVI	28	SG	09/21/62	Lynchburg, VA	DOD	Lynchburg CSA Cem. #5 R4	ROH,JR,HOS,BBW
Lipscomb, Thomas S.	Pvt.	B Hol.Leg.	41	SG	08/30/62	2nd Manassas, VA	KIA		ROH,JR,HOS
Lipscomb, W.E.	4th Sgt.	I 13th SCVI	21	SG	05/03/63	Chancellorsville	KIA		ROH,JR,HOS
Lipsey, James	Pvt.	H 5th SCVI		YK	02/28/62	Manassas, VA	DOD	(SA3=Joseph in one place)	SA3,UD1
Lisenby, Samuel	Pvt.	E 21st SCVI		CD	05/18/64	Petersburg, VA	DOW	Blandford Church Pbg., VA	BLC,HAG,PP
Lisenby, Samuel	Pvt.	B 8th SCVI		CD	09/08/61	Flint Hill, VA	DOD		JR,KEB
Listen, W.J.	Pvt.	G 15th SCVI			/ /		DOD		JR
Lister, A.S.	Pvt.	B 22nd SCVI		SG	10/27/62	Winchester, VA	DOD		ROH,HOS
Lister, Austin H.	Pvt.	H 22nd SCVI	37	SG	07/30/64	Crater, Pbg., VA	KIA	Pleasant Hill B.C. Greer	GEC,BLM,HOS

SOUTH CAROLINA DEAD IN CSA SERVICE 1861-1865

NAME	RANK	C	REGIMENT	AGE	DS	DIED	WHERE	WHY	BURIED	SOURCES
Lister, E.C.	Pvt.	B	22nd SCVI		SG	03/06/62	At home	DOD		ROH
Lister, James A.	Pvt.	B	22nd SCVI		SG	12/01/62	Goldsboro, NC	DOD	Prob Willowdale C. there	ROH,PP
Litchfield, John L.	Cpt.	I	7th SCVI	26	HY	09/13/62	Maryland Hts. MD	KIA		ROH,JR,KEB,R46
Little, George	Pvt.	D	19th SCVI	25	ED	09/20/63	Chickamauga, GA	KIA	Con. Cem. Marietta, GA	HOE,CCM,UD3
Little, H. Camillis	Pvt.	D	Hol.Leg.		BL	05/05/62	Adams Run, SC	DOD		PP
Little, J.R.	Pvt.	B	Orr's Ri.		AE	12/26/62	Richmond, VA	DOD	Oakwood C.#147,Row M,Div A	ROH,JR,OWC,CDC
Little, James C.	Pvt.	B	24th SCVI		MN	05/13/63	At home	DOD		ROH
Little, M.C.	Pvt.	K	14th SCVI		ED	05/03/63	Chancellorsville	KIA	(JR=DOW 5/4/63)	JR,HOE
Little, R.H.	Pvt.	B	9th SCVI			09/10/61		DOD	(Typhoid)	JR
Little, Thomas H.	Pvt.		Boyce's LA		LS	12/07/62	Lynchburg, VA	DOD	Duncan Creek P.C. LS Cty.	ROH,LSC
Little, W.E.	Pvt.	D	P.S.S.			09/17/62	Sharpsburg, MD	KIA	Rose Hill C. Hagerstown MD	ROH,BOD
Little, William	Pvt.	M	P.S.S.			/ /		DOD		JR
Little, William A.	Pvt.	G	5th SCVI	18	SG	07/21/61	1st Manassas, VA	KIA		ROH,SA3
Little, Wright	Pvt.	E	7th SCVI		ED	12/07/62	Richmond, VA	DOD	Oakwood C.#63,Row M,Div A	ROH,UD3,OWC,KE
Littlefields, Albert	Pvt.	E	18th SCVI		SG	02/07/62	Charleston, SC	DOD		JR,HOS
Littlejohn, J.	Pvt.	B	18th SCVI		UN	07/07/62		DOD		JR
Littlejohn, J.A.	Pvt.	E	4th SCMil			02/06/65	Columbia, SC		Elmwood Cem. Columbia, SC	PP
Littlejohn, Lafayette	Pvt.	B	18th SCVI		UN	06/15/62		DOD	Family C. Jonesville UN Cy	UD3
Littlejohn, M.R.	Pvt.	F	15th SCVI		SG	/ /	James Island, SC	KIA		JR,HOS,KEB
Littlejohn, Salathiel	Pvt.	I	6th SCVC		MN	12/15/64	Elmira, NY	DIP	Woodlawn N.C.#1115 Elmira	FPH,P6,P65,P12
Littlejohn, W.F.	Pvt.	C	5th SCVI		UN	05/08/64	Wilderness, VA	DOW	(Wdd 5/6/64)	SA3
Littlejohn, W.G.	Pvt.		24th SCVI			/ /	Richmond, VA		Oakwood C.#22,Row K,Div G	ROH,OWC
Littlejohn, Ward H.						05/15/64	Spotsylvania CH	KIA		UD2
Littleton, E.	Pvt.	G	12th SCVI		PS	09/17/62	Sharpsburg, MD	KIA		JR
Littleton, J.	Pvt.		12th SCVI			11/03/62	Winchester, VA	DOD	Stonewall C. Winchester VA	ROH,WIN,P12
Littleton, John T.	Pvt.	G	12th SCVI		PS	09/15/62		DOD	(J. in Winchester C.?)	JR
Littleton, L.W.	Pvt.	H	7th SCVI			/ /	Richmond, VA		(1862 Rchmd effects list)	ROH,CDC
Littleton, W.C.	Pvt.	G	12th SCVI		PS	09/15/62	Whitehall, SC	DOD		JR
Littleton, William	Pvt.	G	12th SCVI		PS	09/15/62		DOD	(Dup of W.C.?)	JR
Lively, G. Jasper	Pvt.	I	Hol.Leg.		SG	08/30/64	Elmira, NY	DIP	Woodlawn N.C.#97 Elmira	HOS,FPH.P5,P65
Lively, R. Capers	Pvt.	I	14th SCVI		AE	/ /	Richmond, VA	DOD	(Wdd Gaines'M. & Chancvle)	HOL
Liverman, N.W.	Pvt.	E	1st SCVIH		BL	12/07/63	Richmond, VA	DOD	Oakwood C. #26 Row H Div E	ROH,SA1,OWC
Livingston, A.P.	Pvt.	E	Ham.Leg.		CN	/ /	Brentsville, VA	DOD	(08/18/?)	ROH
Livingston, George	Pvt.	G	13th SCVI		NY	/ /		KIA	(MIA, presumed dead)	ROH,ANY
Livingston, Henry	Pvt.	B	3rd SCVI		NY	11/02/62	Staunton, VA	DOD	Thornrose C. Staunton, MS	ROH,JR,SA2,TOD
Livingston, J. Marshall	Pvt.	C	3rd SCVI		NY	11/18/63	Knoxville, TN	KIA		ROH,SA2,ANY,KE
Livingston, J.B.	Sgt.	A	2nd SCVI		RD	07/02/63	Gettysburg, PA	DOW		CDC,KEB
Livingston, James Calvin	Pvt.	F	20th SCVI		NY	11/23/62	Sullivans I., SC	DOD	Livingston Gvyd Newberry	NCC,ANY,KEB
Livingston, John W.P.	Pvt.	D	13th SCVI	19	NY	07/03/62	Richmond, VA	DOD	(JR=Typhoid 7/13/62)	ROH,JR,ANY
Livingston, M.	Pvt.	D	2nd SCVIRi		NY	07/03/64	Petersburg, VA	KIA		ROH,ANY
Livingston, M.	Pvt.	H	3rd SCVI		LN	06/15/63	Richmond, VA	DOD		JR,KEB
Livingston, Robert J.	Pvt.	F	20th SCVI		NY	/ /	Sullivans I., SC	DOD		ANY,KEB
Livingston, Samuel J.	Pvt.	B	1st SCVIG	27	NY	06/15/62		DOD	(Date approximate)	ROH,SA1,ANY
Livingston, W.J. (W.F.?)	Pvt.		SCV			03/16/65	Raleigh, NC		Oakwood C. Raleigh, NC	TOD
Livingston, William	Pvt.	D	13th SCVI	25	NY	08/23/62	Richmond, VA	DOD		ROH
Lloyd, Charles	Pvt.		PeeDee LA		DN	08/29/62	2nd Manassas, VA	DOW	(Perhaps in Warrenton)	ROH,PDL
Lloyd, H.M.	Pvt.	A	1st SCVC			02/05/62	Charleston, SC	DOD	(Measles)	JR
Lloyd, Henry	Pvt.	I	8th SCVI		AL	06/19/61	Centreville, VA	DOD	(Congestive brain fever)	JR,HMC,KEB
Lloyd, Joseph	Pvt.	K	6th SCVI		MO	10/06/62	Ft. McHenry, MD	DOD		3RC,P12
Lloyd, J.E.	Pvt.	D	1st SCVIG	24	DN	07/04/62	Petersburg, VA	DOD		ROH,PP,SA1
Lloyd, James	Pvt.	D	10th SCVI		MN	07/15/62	Meridian, MS	DOD	Prob Rose Hill C, there	RAS,HMC,PP

L

SOUTH CAROLINA DEAD IN CSA SERVICE 1861-1865

NAME	RANK	C REGIMENT	AGE	DS	DIED	WHERE	WHY	BURIED	SOURCES
Lloyd, Samuel James	Pvt.	2nd SCV			11/15/61		DOD	(Diabetes)	JR
Lloyd, William	Pvt.	C 18th SCVIB		MN	/ /	Charleston, SC	DOD		HMC
Loadholt, Charles N.	Pvt.	C 1st SCVIH		BL	04/30/63		DOD	(JR=4/28/63)	ROH,JR,SA1,JRH
Loadholt, J.M.	Pvt.	C 1st SCVIH		BL	12/07/62	Staunton, VA	DOD	(JR=12/27/62)	ROH,JR,SA1,JRH
Lochlier, A.	Pvt.	D 9th SCVIB		SR	02/26/62	Manassas, VA	DOD		JR,CNM
Lochlier, Alexander	Pvt.	F 21st SCVI		MO	07/20/62	Charleston, SC	DOD		ROH,HOM,HAG
Lochlier, John	Pvt.	G 23rd SCVI		MO	08/01/64	Kittrell Spgs NC	DOD	Kittrell Spgs. NC	HOM,CV,PP
Lock, Josiah H.	Pvt.	A 17th SCVI	36	CR	06/17/64	Petersburg, VA	DOW	(SA3=DIS 8/22/61)	JR,SA3,CB
Locke, Andrew H.	Pvt.	D 5th SCVI		UN	05/06/64	Wilderness, VA	KIA	(JR=5/5/64)	ROH,JR,SA3
Locke, F. Otis	Pvt.	A 25th SCVI		CN	05/09/64	Swift Creek, VA	KIA		ROH,HAG,CDC,WLI
Locke, Jesse J.	Pvt.	I 16th SCVI	35	GE	06/04/64	At home	DOD	Standing Spgs. B.C. GE Cty	16R,GEE,PP
Lockey, Benjamin B.	Pvt.	B 1st SCVIG		MN	03/23/65	Ft. Delaware, DE	DIP	Finn's Pt., NJ Nat. Cem.	ROH,SA1,FPH,P6
Lockhart, Edmond M.	Pvt.	I 5th SCVI	24	YK	/ /	Virginia	DOD	(1865)	YEB,SA3
Lockhart, J.A. (J.N.?)	Pvt.	F 15th SCVI		UN	/ /		DOD		JR
Lockhart, J.C.	Pvt.	E 8th SCVI		DN	06/29/62	Savage Stn., VA	KIA	(JR=Malvern Hill 7/2/62)	ROH,JR,KEB
Lockhart, James Yancey	Pvt.	G 19th SCVI		AE	06/26/62	Lauderdale Ss MS	DOD	Prob/unknown in C,C, there	HOL,PP
Lockhart, R.A.	Pvt.	A 12th SCVI		YK	06/21/63	Richmond, VA	DOD		JR
Lockhart, R.M.	Pvt.	F 15th SCVI		UN	/ /	Richmond, VA	DOD	(On Richmond effects list)	ROH,JR,CDC,KEB
Lockler, E.	Pvt.	D 12th SCVI		RD	08/29/62	2nd Manassas, VA	KIA		ROH,JR
Lockridge, W.L.	Pvt.	D 7th SCVI		AE	/ /	Charlottesville		Univ. Cem. Charlottesville	ACH,KEB
Lockwood,	Pvt.	B Orr's Ri.		AE	06/27/62	Gaines' Mill, VA	KIA		ROH
Lockwood, Henry A.	Pvt.	H Ham.Leg.		CN	10/07/62	Winchester, VA	DOW	(Wdd 2nd Man)	ROH,JR,CDC
Lockwood, James P.	2nd Lt.	K P.S.S.		SG	05/28/64	Spotsylvania, VA	DOW	(HOS says only Wdd.)	ROH,JR,R48,HOS
Loden, William	Pvt.	K 12th SCVI	50	PS	10/05/62	Richmond, VA	DOD		ROH
Loftis, Solomon	Pvt.	D 16th SCVI		GE	05/28/64	New Hope Church	KIA	(JR=Petersburg 6/19)	ROH,JR,16R
Lofton, John	2nd Cpl.	I 1st SCVIH		MN	06/19/64	Petersburg, VA	KIA		SA1,HMC
Logan, Andrew Silas	Pvt.	B Orr's Ri.		AE	03/13/62		DOD	(Typhoid	JR,CDC
Logan, Black	Pvt.	M 5th SCVC	18	SG	/ /		DOD	(JR=P.S.S.)	ROH,JR
Logan, Daniel D'Oyley	Pvt.	A Ham.Leg.	28	CN	12/10/62	Culpepper, VA	DOD	(JR=Pneumonia 12/1/62)	ROH,JR
Logan, David J.	1st Lt.	F 17th SCVC	26	YK	06/18/64	Petersburg, VA	KIA	Bethesda Cem. York Cty. CB	ROH,JR,RCD,YEB
Logan, Elijah B.	Pvt.	I 5th SCVI		SG	11/15/61	Richmond, VA	DOD	Oakwood C.#151,Row A,Div A	ROH,OWC,SA3
Logan, Francis	Pvt.	F Hol.Leg.	25	AE	03/03/65	Elmira, NY	DIP	Woodlawn N.C.#1997 Elmira	ROH,FPH,P6,P65
Logan, G.R.	Pvt.	D 2nd SCVIRi			10/28/63	Lookout Valley	KIA	(JR=Racoon Mtn., TN)	JR
Logan, Thomas J.	Pvt.	Palm. LA		SR	02/22/63	At home	DOD		JR,SOB
Logan, W.H.	Pvt.	E P.S.S.		SR	/ /	Manchester, VA	DOD	(1862, JR=H.W.)	ROH,JR
Loggans, Madison E.	Pvt.	C Orr's Ri.		PS	08/17/62		DOD	(Typhoid)	JR,CDC
Logwood,	Pvt.	B Orr's Ri.		AE	06/27/62	Gaines' Mill, VA	KIA		JR
Lollis, E.W.	Pvt.	E 16th SCVI		GE	/ /	At home	DOD	(1865, after the war ?)	16R
Lomas, William	Pvt.	C 7th SCVIBn		RD	03/28/65	Elmira, NY	DIP	Woodlawn N.C.#2523 Elmira	HAG,FPH,P1,P6
Lomax, George	Pvt.	A 1st SCVC	38	AE	06/15/63	At home	DOD		ROH
Lomax, William G.	Pvt.	F 2nd SCVI	22	AE	07/02/63	Gettysburg, PA	KIA	RCD	ROH,JR,GDR,SA2
Lominack, Daniel	Pvt.	K 20th SCVI		LN	03/15/65		DOD		ROH,KEB
Lominack, David W.	Pvt.	D 5th SCVC		CN	10/12/62	Winchester, VA	DOD	Stonewall C. Winchester VA	JR,WIN
Lominack, James J.	Pvt.	C 15th SCVI	21	LN	09/29/62	South Mtn., MD	DOW		TOD,H15,KEB
Lominack, James S.	Sgt.	C 15th SCVI	24	LN	08/31/64	Richmond, VA	DOD	(Acute Diarrhea)	TOD,H15,KEB
Lominack, John	Pvt.	G P.S.S.	22	YK	/ /	Morristown, TN	DOD		YEB
Lominack, Noah	Pvt.	C 15th SCVI	29	LN	05/07/64	Wilderness, VA	DOW		TOD,H15,KEB
Lominack, Paul	Pvt.	C 15th SCVI	23	LN	04/29/62	Charleston, SC	DOD		TOD,H15,KEB
Lominack, Samuel	Pvt.	C 15th SCVI	19	LN	01/09/62	Charleston, SC	DOD		TOD,H15,KEB
Lominack, William Frank	1st Sgt.	G Hol.Leg.		LS	08/29/62	2nd Manassas VA	KIA		ROH,ANY
Loner, William Lloyd	Pvt.	I 19th SCVI	19	AE	02/06/63	Shelbyville, TN	DOD	Willowmount C.Shelbyville	ROH,PP,TOD

SOUTH CAROLINA DEAD IN CSA SERVICE 1861-1865

L

NAME	RANK	C REGIMENT	AGE	DS	DIED	WHERE	WHY	BURIED	SOURCES
Long,	Cpl.	1st SCVIR			03/16/65	Averysboro, NC	KIA	(Thomas H.in B or Wm.in H)	ROH
Long,			60	SR	02/15/65	Dingle's Mill	KIA		UD3
Long, A.F.	Pvt.	I 1st SCVIR		AN	07/18/63	Bty. Wagner, SC	KIA		ROH,SA1
Long, D.S.	Pvt.	H 3rd SCVI		LN	01/21/65	Ft. Delaware, DE	DIP	Finn's Pt., NJ Nat. Cem.	ROH,SA2,FPH,P6
Long, David Patrick	2nd Sgt.	I 15th SCVI	20	LN	09/05/62	Leesburg, VA	DOD	TOD	ROH,JR,KEB,H15
Long, E.C.	Pvt.	K 10th SCVI		CN	/ /		DOD		RAS
Long, G.W.M.	Pvt.	B 7th SCVI		AE	05/15/64		KIA	Spotsylvania C.H., VA	JR,SCH,KEB
Long, Gabriel W.	Sgt.	G Orr's Ri.		AE	08/13/64	Dutch Gap, VA	KIA		ROH,CDC
Long, George J.	Pvt.	I 15th SCVI	27	LN	08/07/62	Chafins Farm, VA	DOD	(James River Rd. Whs.) TOD	ROH,JR,LNC,H15
Long, George W.	Pvt.	K 2nd SCVA		ED	/ /		KIA		HOE,UD3
Long, Henry	Pvt.	E 10th SCVI		WG	/ /	South Island, SC	DOD		RAS,HOW
Long, Henry A.	3rd Lt.	E 4th SCVC	23	MO	08/14/64	At home	DOD		ROH,HOM,R43
Long, Henry A.	Pvt.	G 8th SCVI		MO	06/21/61	1st Manassas, VA	KIA		KEB,UD1
Long, Henry M.	Pvt.	H 3rd SCVI		LN	08/12/61	Richmond, VA	DOD		ROH,JR,SA2,ANY
Long, J. Michael	Pvt.	C 3rd SCVI		NY	08/24/61	Richmond, VA	DOD	Hollywood Cem.Rchmd. K112	ROH,JR,HC,ANY
Long, J.B.	Pvt.	F Orr's Ri.		PS	/ /	Richmond, VA	DOD	(JR=P.S.S.)	ROH,JR
Long, J.H.	Pvt.	E P.S.S.		SR	07/22/64		DOW		ROH
Long, J.L.	Cpl.	D 12th SCVI		RD	05/06/64	Wilderness, VA	KIA		JR
Long, J.L.	Pvt.	C 14th SCVI		LS	11/11/62	Staunton, VA		Thornrose C. Staunton, VA	TOD
Long, J.M.	Pvt.	20th SCVI			04/10/65	Dingle's Mill SC	KIA	(Probably Co.K from LN)	ROH
Long, J.M.	Pvt.	C 20th SCVI			07/10/62	Richmond, VA	DOD	(Typhoid)	JR
Long, John	Pvt.	C 7th SCVC	38	UN	06/13/64	Riddle's Shop VA	KIA	Gilead B.C. UN Cty., SC	ROH,JR,UNC,UD3
Long, John	Pvt.	H 3rd SCVI		LN	06/15/63	Richmond, VA	DOD		JR,SA2,KEB
Long, John C.	Pvt.	K 20th SCVI		LN	10/13/64	Strasburg, VA	KIA		ROH,JR,CDC,KEB
Long, John J.	Pvt.	I 15th SCVI		LN	07/21/64	Richmond, VA	DOW	Hollywood Cem.Rchmd. U247	HC,KEB,TOD,P12
Long, John Oliver	Pvt.	F 24th SCVI		AN	06/17/63	Jackson, MS	DOW		HOL,PP
Long, Joseph	Pvt.	E P.S.S.		SR	09/29/64	Ft. Harrison, VA	KIA		ROH
Long, Joseph Henry	Pvt.	E	20	CN	07/21/64	Petersburg, VA	KIA		ROH
Long, Matthew Thompson	Pvt.	D Orr's Ri.	22	AN	08/01/63	At home	DOD		ROH,JR
Long, N.G.	Sgt.	A 15th SCVI		RD	05/24/64	Hanover C.H., VA	KIA		ROH
Long, P.W.	Pvt.	F 24th SCVI		AN	/ /		DOD	(1862)	HOL
Long, Samuel Gentry	Pvt.	D Orr's Ri.	18	AN	06/27/62	Dill Spring, VA	DOD		ROH
Long, Simeon	Pvt.	H 13th SCVI	30	LN	/ /		DIP	(POW in Wilderness 5/6/64)	ROH
Long, Thomas	Pvt.	E 5th SCVI		UN	02/02/62	Centreville, VA	DOD	Gilead C, Jonesville UN Cy	UD1,UD3
Long, W.R.	Sgt.	H 7th SCVI		PS	09/25/63	Chickamauga, GA	DOW		ROH,JR
Long, William	Pvt.	C 7th SCVC		UN	06/15/65			Gilead C. Jonesville UN Cy	UD3
Long, William B.	Pvt.	E Orr's Ri.	20	PS	07/04/62	Dill Springs, VA	DOD		ROH,JR,CDC
Long, William W.	Pvt.	E 15th SCVI	24	FD	01/28/63	Charlottesville	DOD	Univ. Cem. Charlottesville	ROH,JR,ACH,KEB
Longshore, Andrew J.	Pvt.	B 3rd SCVI		NY	12/14/62	Fredericksburg	DOW		ROH,JR,SA2,ANY
Longshore, Milton W.	Pvt.	G Hol. Leg.	22	NY	11/10/64	Petersburg, VA	DOW		ROH,ANY
Loomis, Hayne H.	Pvt.	A 2nd SCVI		RD	08/26/64	Deep Bottom, VA	KIA	(JR=6/28/64)	ROH,JR,SA2,KEB
Loomis, John H.	Pvt.	C 2nd SCVC	23	RD	09/13/63	Culpepper, VA	KIA		ROH
Looney, Dennis	Pvt.	K 1st SCVIG		PS	07/26/62	Richmond, VA	DOD	Oakwood C.#115,Row N,Div C	ROH,JR,OWC,SA1
Looney, J.T.	Pvt.	B P.S.S.		PS	05/23/62	Washington, DC	DOW	(Wdd & POW, Wmsbg. 5/6/62)	ROH,JR,CDC
Looper, James	Pvt.	C 26th SCVI		MN	10/30/63		DOD		JR
Looper, William F.				PS	10/30/64	Lynchburg, VA		Crossroads B.C. Table Rock	PCS
Loper, D.	Pvt.	B 23rd SCVI	28	BT	05/27/62	Charleston, SC	DOD	Magnolia Cem. Charleston	ROH,MAG
Loper, J.	Pvt.	G 2nd SC			05/27/62	Charleston, SC		Magnolia Cem. Charleston	RCD
Loper, S.D.	Pvt.	G 1st SCVIH		BL	02/02/63	Richmond, VA	DOD	Oakwood C.#9,Row F,Div E	ROH,SA1,OWC
Lorance, Lawson	Pvt.	H Orr's Ri.		MN	07/15/61	At home	DOD		JR,HMC,CDC
Loring, A.H.	Pvt.	I 6th SCVI		CR	/ /		DOD	(CB=Lansing)	CB,HHC

L

SOUTH CAROLINA DEAD IN CSA SERVICE 1861-1865

NAME	RANK	C REGIMENT	AGE	DS	DIED	WHERE	WHY	BURIED	SOURCES
Loring, Thomas F.	Pvt.	D Ham. Leg.		UN	10/28/63	Lookout Valley	KIA		ROH
Lott, Jesse A.	Pvt.	A 19th SCVI	32	ED	06/20/62	Enterprise, MS	DOD	(Left wife & 3 children)	HOE,EDN,PP,UD3
Lott, John	Pvt.	A 19th SCVI	40	ED	/ /	Chattahoochee R.	DOW		HOE,UD3
Lott, John Bolivar	Pvt.	H 7th SCVI	19	ED	07/02/63	Gettysburg, PA	KIA		ROH,GDR,CV
Lott, Luther	Pvt.	E 7th SCVI	25	ED	03/15/62	Richmond, VA	DOD	Dry Creek B.C. ED Cty.	ROH,JR,EDN,UD3
Loustro, J.R. (Sp.?)	Pvt.	G 7th SCVI			10/26/62	Staunton, VA	DOD		ROH
Love, A.M.	Pvt.				05/06/64	Wilderness, VA	KIA		ROH
Love, Daniel Moore	Pvt.	A 12th SCVI	24	YK	05/12/64	Spotsylvania, VA	KIA		ROH,JR,YEB
Love, James W.	Pvt.	E 5th SCVI	19	YK	06/27/62	Gaines' Mill, VA	KIA	(ROH says DOD in Pbg)	ROH,JR,SA3,YEB
Love, John A.	Pvt.	E 5th SCVI		YK	06/27/62	Gaines` Mill, VA	KIA		JR,SA3
Love, John E.	Pvt.	G 5th SCVI	22	YK	02/16/62	Centreville, VA	DOD	(ROH=M, P.S.S.)	ROH,SA3,YMD,YEB
Love, John H.	Pvt.	B 16th SCVI		GE	11/30/64	Franklin, TN	KIA		16R
Love, John W.	Pvt.	G 5th SCVI	22	YK	01/15/63	Virginia	DOD	Beersheba P.C. YK Cty.	SA3,YEB
Love, Jones S.	Pvt.	B 1st SCVIG	16	NY	05/02/63	Chancellorsville	KIA	(JR=5/3/63)	ROH,JR,SA1
Love, Lawrence W.	Pvt.	E 2nd SCVI		KW	03/25/64	Bristol, TN	DOW	(Wdd Beans Stn 12/14/63)	SA2,KEB,HIC
Love, McDuffie Rutledge	Pvt.	G 2nd SCVI		KW	07/02/63	Gettysburg, PA	KIA	Magnolia Cem., Charleston	JR,SA2,GDR,HIC
Love, P.P.	Lt.	H 27th SCVI			/ /	Petersburg, VA			ROH
Love, Richard A.	1st Sgt.	E 12th SCVI	30	LR	02/28/62	White Hall, SC	DOD		ROH,JR,LAN
Love, Robert	Pvt.		19	YK	05/05/62	Williamsburg, VA	KIA	(5th SCVI?)	YMD,YEB
Love, Robert John W.	Pvt.	G 5th SCVI	22	YK	03/02/63	Petersburg, VA	DOD	Canaan M.C. Cherokee Cty.	JR,SA3,TCC,BLC
Love, V.B.H.	Pvt.	H 2nd SCVI		LR	06/01/64	Cold Harbor, VA	KIA		SA2,LAN,KEB
Love, William	Pvt.	E 2nd SCVI		KW	/ /	Virginia	KIA	(SA2=Discharged underage)	HIC,KEB,SA2
Lovelace, J.	Pvt.	I 2nd SCV			10/17/62	Mt. Jackson, VA	DOW	(Prob Wdd @ Sharpsburg)	JR
Lovelace, John	Pvt.	H 1st SCVA		ED	09/10/63	Charleston, SC	DOD	Magnolia Cem. Charleston	ROH,MAG
Lovelace, John C.	1st Lt.	H 7th SCVI		ED	09/20/63	Chickamauga, GA	KIA	(HOE=Loveless)	ROH,JR,R46,HOE
Lovelace, N.L.	Pvt.	H P.S.S.		SG	05/06/64	Wilderness, VA	KIA	(2nd JR entry=Loveland)	ROH,JR,HOS
Lovelace, Ransom	Pvt.	B 7th SCVI			08/24/62	Richmond, VA	DOD		ROH,CDC
Lovelace, W.P.	Pvt.	I 5th SCV			04/20/62	Yorktown, VA	DOD	(Pneumonia)	JR
Loveless, Benjamin F.	Pvt.	C 24th SCVI		CO	05/31/63	Canton, MS	DOW	Con.Cem. Canton, MS Gv#303	EJM,PP,TOD
Loveless, C.H.	Pvt.	F Orr's Ri.		PS	09/18/62	Sharpsburg, MD	DOW		JR,CDC
Loveless, J.	Pvt.	F 2nd SCVIRi		AE	10/17/62	Sharpsburg, MD	DOW		ROH,CDC
Loveless, James L.	Pvt.	F 2nd SCVIRi		AE	/ /		DOD	(1863)	ROL,JR
Lovett, John	Pvt.	L 10th SCVI		MN	05/24/64	Macon, GA		Rose Hill Cem. Macon, GA	PP,BGA
Lovin, Pressley	Pvt.	E Hol.Leg.	42	LS	12/23/62	Goldsboro, NC	DOD	(? SG)	ROH,HOS,PP
Loving, Thomas F.	Pvt.	D Ham.Leg.		VA	10/28/63	Will's Valley TN	KIA		GRS,CDC
Low, J.H.	Pvt.	I 13th SCVI		SG	10/12/61	Columbia, SC	DOD		PP
Low, James H.	Pvt.	B Hol.Leg.		SG	06/07/65	Pt. Lookout, MD	DIP	C.C. Pt. Lookout, MD	HOS,FPH.P6,P114
Lowder, H.J.	Pvt.	I 23rd SCVI		CL	/ /			(ROH=Lowden, no Co.)	ROH,HCL
Lowe, A.R.	Pvt.	I 5th SCVI		SG	04/18/64	Ft. Delaware, DE	DIP	Finn's Pt., NJ Nat. Cem.	ROH,SA3,FPH,P5
Lowe, Pleasant W.	Pvt.	F 3rd SCVI		LS	12/25/61	At home	DOD		ROH,JR,SA2,KEB
Lowe, Thomas G.	Pvt.	G Orr's Ri.		AE	06/05/62	Richmond, VA	DOD		ROH,CDC
Lowery, Calvin	Cpl.	K 6th SCVC			08/30/64	Elmira, NY	DIP	Woodlawn N.C.#96 Elmira	FPH,P5,P65,P120
Lowery, James F.	Pvt.	E Orr's Ri.	22	PS	07/27/62	Richmond, VA	DOD	Hollywood Cem.Rchmd. C120	ROH,JR,HC,CDC
Lowery, Joseph	Pvt.	C 23rd SCVI		CN	07/30/64	Crater, Pbg., VA	KIA		ROH,JR,BLM
Lowery, R.J.	Pvt.	H 2nd SCVI		LR	/ /		KIA	(After 6/30/64)	SA2,LAN,KEB
Lowman, John Preston	Pvt.	C 20th SCVI	20	LN	07/03/64	Petersburg, VA	KIA	(JR=6/23/64)	ROH,JR,KEB
Lowman, Solomon F.	Pvt.	F 19th SCVI	35	LN	/ /		DOD	(March)	ROH
Lowrimore, David R.W.	Pvt.	13th SCVI		GN	05/12/64	Spotsylvania, VA	kIA		FLR
Lowrimore, Hanson L.	Pvt.	I 21st SCVI		MN	10/23/64	Pt. Lookout, MD	DIP	C.C. Pt. Lookout, MD	HMC,HAG,FPH,P5
Lowrimore, John R.	Pvt.	A 26th SCVI	20	HY	12/15/64	Petersburg, VA	KIA		ROH
Lowrimore, John R.	Pvt.	F 1st SCVIG		HY	09/17/62	Sharpsburg, MD	KIA		JR,SA1

SOUTH CAROLINA DEAD IN CSA SERVICE 1861-1865

L

NAME	RANK	C	REGIMENT	AGE	DS	DIED	WHERE	WHY	BURIED	SOURCES
Lowrimore, John W.	Pvt.	I	21st SCVI		MN	06/15/62	Ft. Reliance, SC	DOD	(On the PeeDee River)	JR,HMC,HAG
Lowrimore, R.	Pvt.	E	11th SCVI		MN	05/28/64	Richmond, VA	DOD	Hollywood Cem.Rchmd. E17	ROH,HC
Lowrimore, Richard A.	4th Sgt.	F	1st SCVIG		HY	08/29/62	2nd Manassas, VA	KIA		ROH,JR,SA1,PDL
Lowrimore, Robert	Pvt.	F	1st SCVIG		HY	06/01/64	Wilderness, VA	DOW	(Wdd 5/6/64)	ROH,SA1,PDL,CD
Lowry, J.H.	Lt.	D	8th SCVI		CD	/ /	Manchester, VA		(ROH=Loring, J.M.)	ROH,KEB,R46
Lowry, James	Pvt.	E	5th SCVI	29	YK	08/30/62	2nd Manassas, VA	KIA		YEB,SA3
Lowry, Samuel Catawba	2nd Lt.	F	17th SCVI	22	YK	07/30/64	Crater, Pbg., VA	KIA		ROH,JR,YMD,YEB
Lowry, T.	Pvt.	B	4th SCVC		CR	06/13/64	Riddle's Shop VA	KIA	(JR=Co.I, 7th SCVC 6/15)	ROH,JR
Lowry, W.H.C.	Pvt.	A	12th SCVI	18	UN	10/23/62	Richmond, VA	DOW	Oakwood C.#48,Row P,Div B	ROH,JR,OWC,YEB
Lowry, William	Pvt.	B	1st SCVIG	40	NY	09/15/62	Warrenton, VA	DOW	(Wdd @ 2nd Man.)	ROH,SA1,ANY,CD
Luarls, G.W. (Sp?)	2nd Lt.	D	22nd SCVI		PS	07/24/64	Petersburg, VA	KIA		R48
Lubanks, C.	Pvt.					/ /	(Lubkin?)		Fredericksburg C.C. R6S13	FBG
Lucas, C.D.	Pvt.	C	1st SCVIH		BL	11/16/63	Campbell's Stn.	KIA	(Terrible Wd. p232 JRH)	ROH,SA1,JRH
Lucas, C.D.	Pvt.	F	2nd SCVIRi	50	SG	11/29/63	Knoxville, TN	KIA		ROH
Lucas, David Harrison	Pvt.	I	17th SCVI		LR	06/11/64	Petersburg, VA	KIA		ROH,LAN,BLC
Lucas, J.H.	Pvt.	H	13th SCVI		LN	07/16/62	Laurel Hill, VA	KIA		JR
Lucas, Jacob Harrison	Pvt.	H	13th SCVI	18	LN	06/27/62	Gaines' Mill, VA	KIA	(PP=DOW @ Pbg 6/11/62)	ROH,JR,CDC,PP
Lucas, Jacob Lee	Pvt.	H	13th SCVI	28	LN	08/29/62	2nd Manassas, VA	DOW		ROH
Lucas, James Field M.	Pvt.	K	13th SCVI		LN	08/29/62	2nd Manassas, VA	KIA		ROH,JR,CDC
Lucas, John	Pvt.	C	12th SCVI		FD	01/13/64	Pt. Lookout, MD	DIP	C.C. Pt. Lookout, MD P5	ROH,HFC,FPH,P1
Lucas, K.D.	Pvt.		PeeDee LA		DN	/ /	Richmond, VA		Oakwood C.#93,Row O,Div B	ROH,OWC,SA1,PD
Lucas, Samuel F.	Pvt.	K	1st SCVIH		OG	05/18/63		DOD		ROH,SA1,JRH
Lucas, Thomas Hendrix	Pvt.	H	13th SCVI		LN	07/01/63	Gettysburg, PA	KIA		ROH
Lucius, D.F.	Pvt.	D	2nd SCVIRi		RD	12/31/62	Richmond, VA	DOD		ROH
Luckey, Samuel J.	Cpl.	C	6th SCVI		SR	06/03/62	Fts. Monroe, VA	DOW	(Wdd. & POW @ 7 Pines)	ROH,JLC,CDC,WD
Luke, J.W.	Pvt.	K	17th SCVI		DN	10/17/62	Richmond, VA	DOD		ROH
Luke, J.W.	Pvt.	L	1st SCVIG		LS	07/14/62	Richmond, VA	DOD	Hollywood Cem.Rchmd. G221	HC,SA1
Luke, John H.	Pvt.	F	3rd SCVI		LS	11/25/61	Charlottesville	DOD	(KEB & JR= Lake)	ROH,JR,SA2,KEB
Luke, R.S.	Pvt.	B	3rd SCVIBn		LS	08/29/62	Manchester, VA	DOD	Little River P.C. SC	NCC,KEB
Luke, Richard S.	Pvt.		Orr's Ri.			02/17/63	Richmond, VA	DOD		ROH
Lumpkin, A.J.	Pvt.	B	Ham.Leg.			05/31/62	Richmond, VA	DOW	(Wd.West Point, VA 5/7/62)	ROH,JR,CDC
Lumpkin, E.T.	Pvt.	G	1st SCVIR		AN	11/30/61		DOD		SA1
Lumpkin, J.	Pvt.		5th SCVC			/ /	Richmond, VA		Oakwood C.#42,Row B,Div A	ROH,OWC
Lumpkins, T.T.	Pvt.	B	4th SCVC		CR	05/30/64	Old Church, VA	KIA	(ROH=P.P.)	ROH,JR,HHC,CB
Lundy, James	Pvt.	C	1st SCVA			06/15/65	Hart's Island NY	DIP	Cypress Hills N.C.#3006 NY	FPH,P6,P79
Lundy, John	Pvt.	I	18th SCVI	30	DN	02/15/62	Charleston, SC	DOD	(JR=Dd. in Chester 3/15)	ROH,JR
Lunn, Lazarus M.	Pvt.	G	9th SCVIB		DN	10/15/61	Richmond, VA	DOD		ROH,JLC,JR
Lunn, S.J. Timmons	Pvt.	G	9th SCVIB		DN	09/19/61	Germantown, VA	DOD		ROH,JLC,JR
Lupo, Evan	Pvt.	C	26th SCVI		MN	/ /	Petersburg, VA			HMC
Lupo, James	Pvt.	C	26th SCVI		MN	/ /	Mt. Pleasant, SC	DOD		HMC
Lupo, Malcom	Pvt.	C	26th SCVI		MN	05/01/64	Bermuda Hundred	DOW	Blandford Church Pbg., VA	HMC,BLC,PP
Lupo, Thomas A.	Pvt.	C	18th SCVIB		MN	/ /	Charleston, SC	DOD		HMC
Lusby, J.S.	Pvt.	F	1st SCVIR		CN	04/07/63	Ft. Moultrie, SC	KIA		SA1
Lusk, D.B.	Pvt.	A	Orr's Ri.		AN	07/14/62	Richmond, VA		Hollywood Cem.Rchmd. H2	ROH,JR,HC,CDC
Lusk, Henry C.	Pvt.	A	Orr's Ri.		AN	07/08/62	Richmond, VA	DOD	(Winder Hos.)	JR,CDC
Lusk, R.H.	Pvt.	G	12th SCVI		PS	12/18/61	Whitehall, SC	DOD		JR
Lustin, A.S.	Pvt.	B	22nd SCVI		SG	10/16/62			Stonewall C. Winchester VA	WIN
Lybrand, H. Elsey	Sgt.	A	19th SCVI	22	ED	/ /	Chickamauga, GA	DOW		HOE,UD3
Lybrand, John N.	2nd Lt.	I	15th SCVI	25	LN	06/01/62	Hardeeville, SC	DOD	(Typhoid) TOD	JR,R47,KEB,H15
Lybrand, Joshua E.	Pvt.	I	15th SCVI		LN	02/23/62	Hardeeville, SC	DOD	(Camp Elliott)	H15,KEB
Lybrand, Martin	Pvt.	A	19th SCVI	17	ED	09/20/63	Chickamauga, GA	KIA	(10th Co. 10/19th Consol)	ROH,JR,HOE,UD3

L

SOUTH CAROLINA DEAD IN CSA SERVICE 1861-1865

NAME	RANK	C	REGIMENT	AGE	DS	DIED	WHERE	WHY	BURIED	SOURCES
Lyles, Erskine	Pvt.	B	1st SCVIG	24	NY	09/15/62	Warrenton, VA	DOW	(Wdd @ 2nd Man. 8/29/62)	ROH,JR,SA1,CDC
Lyles, George W.	Pvt.	E	12th SCVI	18	LR	05/12/64	Spotsylvania, VA	KIA	(Bloody Angle)	ROH,JR,LAN
Lyles, H.J.	Pvt.	H	6th SCVI	46	FD	09/23/62	Germantown, VA			ROH
Lyles, J.T.	Sgt.	K	12th SCVI		PS	09/30/64	Richmond, VA	KIA		JR
Lyles, J.W.	Pvt.	F	Orr's Ri.		PS	03/25/62	Liberty, VA	DOD		JR
Lyles, James B.	Cpl.	E	15th SCVI	24	FD	07/28/64	Deep Bottom, VA	KIA		ROH,KEB
Lyles, James M.	Pvt.	F	Orr's Ri.		PS	06/27/62	Gaines' Mill, VA	KIA		ROH,JR,CDC
Lyles, James W.	Pvt.	F	12th SCVI		FD	/ /	Petersburg, VA	KIA		HFC
Lyles, Jesse E.	Pvt.	B	3rd SCVI		NY	04/22/62	Richmond, VA	DOD		ROH,JR,SA2,ANY
Lyles, Obadiah	Pvt.	F	Orr's Ri.		PS	07/12/62		DOD		JR
Lyles, R.M.	Pvt.	F	Orr's Ri.		PS	09/01/62	Ox Hill, VA	KIA		JR,CDC
Lyles, Richard W.	Pvt.	I	12th SCVI		LR	04/05/64	Gordonsville, VA	DOD	Gordonsville, VA Cem.	ROH,JR,LAN,GOR
Lyles, Thomas Henry	1st Lt.	B	1st SCVIG	22	NY	12/13/62	Fredericksburg	KIA	Lyles/Hughey Cem. Newberry	ROH,JR,SA1,NCC
Lyles, W.T.	Pvt.	F	14th SCVI		LS	09/16/62	Danville, VA	DOD		JR
Lyles, Wallace W.	Pvt.	E	15th SCVI	19	FD	09/15/62	South Mtn., MD	KIA		ROH,JR,KEB
Lyles, William	Pvt.	B	15th SCVAB			04/04/65	Pt. Lookout, MD	DIP	C.C. Pt. Lookout, MD	FPH,P6
Lyles, William Boykin	Cpt.	H	6th SCVI	26	FD	05/31/62	7 Pines, VA	KIA	R46	ROH,JR,HFC,WDB
Lyles, William Woodward	Pvt.	H	6th SCVI	19	FD	10/18/64	Ft. Harrison, VA	DOW		ROH
Lyman, H.J.	Pvt.	I	23rd SCVI		CL	09/17/62	Sharpsburg, MD	KIA	(JR=Lynch, H.J.)	ROH,JR,HCL
Lyman, W.T.	Cpl.	G	23rd SCVI		MO	07/30/64	Petersburg, VA	KIA		JR
Lynch, A.	Pvt.	H	10th SCVI		WG	/ /		DOD	(1863)	RAS,HOW
Lynch, Francis R.	1st Lt.	I	27th SCVI		CN	10/20/63	Spartanburg, SC	DOD	(Consumption)	ROH,JR,R48
Lynch, George W.	Pvt.	I	26th SCVI		WG	09/16/64	Elmira, NY	DIP	Woodlawn N.C.#296 Elmira	FPH,P5,P10,P65
Lynch, Hugh P.	1st Lt.	D	21st SCVI		CD	/ /	Cheraw, SC	ACD	(RR accident in 1863)	ROH,HAG
Lynch, J. Elian	Pvt.	H	25th SCVI	30	WG	09/06/63	Bty Wagner, SC	KIA		ROH,JR,CTA,HOW
Lynch, J.L.	Pvt.	H	10th SCVI		WG	/ /		DOD		RAS
Lynch, J.M.	Pvt.				WG	/ /		DOD	(1863)	CTA,HOW
Lynch, James	Pvt.	K	1st SCVA			04/30/65	New Bern, NC	DIP	Cedar Grove C. Newbern, NC	P1,WAT,PP
Lynch, John F.	Pvt.	D	3rd SCVI		SG	11/18/63	Knoxville, TN	KIA		SA2,R45,HOS,KEB
Lynch, T.	Pvt.	C	Ham.Leg.		CL	07/21/61	1st Manassas, VA	KIA		ROH,JR,CDC
Lynch, William H.	Pvt.		Walters By	22	CN	07/11/64	Johns Island, SC	DOW		ROH
Lynch, William H.	Pvt.	H	Orr's Ri.		MN	04/05/63	Camp Chase. OH	DIP	C.C.#2109 Columbus, OH	FPH,P5,P22
Lynes, G.A.	Pvt.	B	23rd SCVI	26	BT	01/28/63	Goldsboro, NC	DOD	Prob Willowdale C. there	ROH,PP
Lynes, George W.	Pvt.	C	1st SCVIH		BL	09/25/62	Warrenton, VA	DOW	(Wdd 2nd Man. 8/30/62)	ROH,SA1,JRH
Lynn, P.G.	Pvt.		Columbia P			12/22/63	Columbia, SC	DOD	(Provost Guard, Columbia)	ROH
Lynn, Samuel Mc.	Pvt.	I	12th SCVI		LR	08/06/62	Richmond, VA	DOD	Hollywood Cem.Rchmd. H253	JR,HC,LAN,ROH
Lynn, W.W.	Pvt.	G	18th SCVI		UN	09/15/64	Petersburg, VA	DOW	(Wdd 9/7/64)	ROH
Lynn, William Mc.	Pvt.	A	17th SCVI	20	CR	01/24/62	At home	DOD	(Measles)	ROH,JR,HHC,CB
Lynn, William Peter	Pvt.	H	2nd SCVI	20	LR	08/16/61	Culpepper, VA	DOD	Fairview Cem. Culpepper VA	ROH,JR,SA2,CGH
Lynor, W.M.	Pvt.	G	18th SCVI		UN	07/30/64	Crater, Pbg., VA	KIA		BLM
Lynson, J.	Pvt.	E	P.S.S.		SR	12/07/65	Richmond, VA		Hollywood Cem.Rchmd. W383	HC
Lyon, P.G.	Pvt.		Post Guard			12/22/63	Columbia, SC	DOD		PP
Lyon, Robert Newton	Pvt.	C	7th SCVI		AE	11/21/61		DOD		ROH,KEB
Lyons,	Sgt.	G	11th SCVI		CO	05/09/64	Swift Creek, VA	KIA	(Lyons,Ben or Lynes,Jacob)	ROH
Lyons, G.W.	Pvt.	C	Orr's Ri.		PS	09/24/62	Warrenton, VA	DOW	(Wdd 2nd Man.)	ROH
Lyons, George W.	Cpl.	I	16th SCVI		GE	03/27/64	Dalton, GA	DOD		16R,PP
Lythgoe, Augustus J.	Colonel		19th SCVI	32	ED	12/31/62	Murfreesboro, TN	KIA	Upper Long Cane P.C. AE	ROH,JR,R47,HOL

SOUTH CAROLINA DEAD IN CSA SERVICE 1861-1865

NAME	RANK	C	REGIMENT	AGE	DS	DIED	WHERE	WHY	BURIED	SOURCES
Mabrey,	Pvt.	K	18th SCVI			02/27/62	Camp Guerin, SC	ACD	(struck by lightening)	UD2
Mabrey, Francis	Pvt.		18th SCVI		UN	/ /	Camp Guerin, SC	DOD	Measles (Jan or Feb 1862)	UD2
Mabry, J.	Pvt.	H	19th SCVI		AE	/ /	Okolona, MS			TOD
Macauley,	Pvt.	B	Ham.Leg.			07/21/61	1st Manassas, VA	KIA		ROH,CDC
Mace, James C.	Pvt.	I	8th SCVI		MN	/ /	Virginia	DOD		HMC,KEB
Mace, Joseph C.	Pvt.	A	21st SCVI		MN	01/15/65	Ft. Fisher, NC	KIA		ROH,HAG,PP
Mace, William Gregg	1st Lt.	H	Orr's Ri.		MN	12/13/62	Fredericksburg	KIA		ROH,JR,HMC,CDC
Machem, James M.	Sgt.	E	16th SCVI	23	GE	08/04/64	Atlanta, GA	KIA		ROH,16R
Mack, H.L.	Pvt.	H	20th SCVI		LN	06/01/64	Beulah Church VA	KIA		ROH,KEB
Mack, J. Montgomery	Cpl.	A	2nd SCVI		RD	07/16/62	Manchester, VA	DOW	Hollywood Cem.Rchmd. N16	ROH,JR,HC,SA2,
Mack, J.F.	Pvt.	H	20th SCVI		LN	/ /	Richmond, VA	KIA		ROH,KEB
Mack, J.G.	Pvt.	K	1st SCVIH		OG	12/22/64	Petersburg, VA	EXC		SA1
Mack, Jacob A.	Pvt.	I	27th SCVI	34	OG	09/10/64	Pt. Lookout, MD	DIP	C.C. Pt. Lookout, MD	ROH,FPH,P6,P11
Mackay, George Chisolm	1st Sgt.	H	1st SCVIG		BT	05/12/64	Spotsylvania, VA	KIA	(JR=Co.L)	ROH,JR,SA1,BBC
Mackerson, J.M.	Pvt.	A	12th SCVI		UN	/ /	Richmond, VA		Oakwood C.#92,Row H,Div B	OWC
Mackey, Daniel N.	Pvt.	H	4th SCVC			05/28/64	Hawe's Shop, VA	KIA		ROH,JR,LAN
Mackey, William	Pvt.	I	12th SCVI		LR	10/01/62	Columbia, SC	DOD		JR,LAN
Macoursin, David	Pvt.	K	18th SCVI	36	SG	/ /	Germantown, VA	DOD	(Maconison?)	ROH
Madden, C.S.	Pvt.	F	3rd SCVI		GE	01/23/63	Manchester, VA	DOD	(KEB=S.C.)	ROH,JR,SA2,KEB
Madden, Charles D.	Pvt.	G	12th SCVI		PS	10/28/62	Frederick, MD	DOW	Mt.Olivet C.#156 Frederick	ROH,FPH,P1,BOD
Madden, E.M.	Pvt.	I	P.S.S.		PS	05/10/64	Orange C.H., VA	DOD	(JR=DOW)	ROH,JR
Madden, James H.	Pvt.	F	3rd SCVI	29	LS	09/03/61	Richmond, VA	DOD		ROH,JR,SA2,KEB
Madden, L.C. (S.C.?)	Pvt.	E	27th SCVI	23	AE	08/09/64	Petersburg, VA	KIA		ROH,HAG,PP
Madden, Messer	Pvt.	I	P.S.S.		PS	05/06/64	Wilderness, VA	KIA	(JR=Spotsylvania 5/12/64)	ROH,JR
Madden, Moses	Pvt.	D	27th SCVI	41	LS	06/23/64				ROH,HAG
Madden, Obediah	Pvt.	F	Hol.Leg.	17	LS	06/28/64	Sappony Creek VA	KIA	(Sappony Church ?)	ROH
Maddigan, Lawrence	4th Sgt.	C	1st SCVIBn		CN	12/05/62	Charleston, SC	MUR	St.Lawrence C. Charleston	ROH,JR,MAG,HAG
Maddon, Thomas	Pvt.	E	2nd SCVI		KW	/ /	Richmond, VA	DOD	(KEB & HIC=Maddox)	SA2,HIC,KEB
Maddox, J.T.	Pvt.	D	Orr's Ri.		AN	12/15/62	At home	DOD		JR
Maddox, Jacob W.	Pvt.	G	3rd SCVI		LS	12/09/62	Farmville, VA	DOD		JR,SA2,KEB
Maddox, N.L.	Pvt.	D	Orr's Ri.		AN	07/17/62	Laurel Hill, VA	DOD		JR
Maddox, P.	Pvt.	A	3rd SCVI			09/13/62	South Mtn., MD	KIA		JR
Maddox, Thomas Pinckney	Pvt.	G	22nd SCVI	25	AN	05/13/65	Savannah, GA	DIP	Laurel Grove C. Savannah	ROH,AR,P1,P6,B
Madison, J.N.	Pvt.	A	20th SCVI		PS	07/01/64	Richmond, VA		Hollywood Cem.Rchmd. U32	HC
Madison, L.	Pvt.	E	Ham.Leg.		GE	05/07/62	Ashland, VA	DOD		ROH
Madray, J.M.	Pvt.	F	1st SCVA		CN	10/07/62	Charleston, SC	DOD	Magnolia Cem. Charleston	ROH,MAG
Maffett, Adolphus	Sgt.	A	4th SC Res		NY	10/10/64	Charleston, SC	DOD		ROH,ANY,CDC
Maffett, Daniel Smiley	1st Lt.	C	3rd SCVI	25	NY	11/20/63	Knoxville, TN	DOW	Cannon Crk. ARP Cem. NY Cy	ROH,NCC,ANY,SA
Maffett, Jacob Lawson	Pvt.	H	Hol.Leg.	19	NY	04/30/65	Pt. Lookout, MD	DIP	(ANY=Lamar not Lawson)	ROH,ANY
Maffett, James M.	Cpt.	H	Hol.Leg.	41	NY	08/06/63	Lockhart, MS	DOD		ROH,ANY,R48
Maffett, Robert Clayton	Lt. Col.		3rd SCVI	29	NY	02/15/65	Ft. Delaware, DE	DIP	Finn's Pt., NJ Nat. Cem.	ROH,FPH,ANY,KE
Maffett, Robert Drayton	Pvt.	C	3rd SCVI	36	NY	09/20/63	Chickamauga, GA	KIA	Con. Cem. Marietta, GA	ROH,JR,SA2,CCM
Magee, J.J.	Cpt.	G	7th SCVC		CN	05/30/64	Old Church, VA	KIA		ROH,CDC,R43
Magill, Thomas	Cpl.	C	P.S.S.		AN	06/30/62	Frayser's Farm	KIA	(JR=Co.B)	ROH,JR,CDC
Magills, J.T.	Pvt.	B	11th SCVI		CO	07/18/64	Richmond, VA		(HAG=Meagles, J.)	ROH,HAG
Magors, D.K.	Pvt.	F	1st SC			08/17/64			Hollywood Cem.Rchmd. V414	HC
Maguire, John J.	Cpt.	H	6th SCVC		CN	08/23/64	Ream's Stn., VA	KIA	Magnolia Cem. Charleston	ROH,JR,MAG,R43
Mahaffey, Green L.	Pvt.	B	13th SCVI		SG	07/20/64	Richmond, VA	DOD	Hollywood Cem.Rchmd. U199	JR,HC,HOS
Mahaffey, J. Rufus	Pvt.	F	16th SCVI		GE	11/30/64	Franklin, TN	KIA		16R
Mahaffey, Q.D. (L.D.?)	Pvt.	C	14th SCVI		LS	05/24/62	Richmond, VA	DOD	Hollywood Cem.Rchmd. J104	ROH,JR,HC
Mahaffy, D.	Pvt.	B	13th SCVI		SG	07/24/64	Richmond, VA			ROH

M

SOUTH CAROLINA DEAD IN CSA SERVICE 1861-1865

NAME	RANK	C	REGIMENT	AGE	DS	DIED	WHERE	WHY	BURIED	SOURCES
Mahaffy, E.	Pvt.	C	14th SCVI		LS	07/28/64	Petersburg, VA	KIA		ROH,JR
Maher, John	Pvt.	C	1st SCVIBn		CN	12/02/62		DOW	(JR=H, 27th SCVI)	JR,HAG
Mahon, S.H. (KEB=Mann)	Pvt.	E	20th SCVI		OG	02/21/65	Pt. Lookout, MD	DIP	C.C. Pt. Lookout, MD	FPH,KEB,P6,P115
Mahoney, D.	Pvt.	F	14th SCVI			07/02/62	Fraysers Farm VA	DOW		JR
Mahoney, David A.	Pvt.	A	25th SCVI		CN	05/07/64	Pt. Walthal Jctn	KIA		ROH,JR,WLI,HAG
Main, J.A.	Pvt.	G	1st SCVIH		BL	04/01/63		DOD		ROH,SA1
Main, J.W.	Pvt.	G	1st SCVIG		BL	06/12/63		DOD		ROH,SA1
Main, M.M.	Pvt.	E	1st SCVIH		BL	01/02/63		DOD	(Wdd @ Shpsbg/Pneumonia)	ROH,SA1,JRH
Mainar, W.T.	Pvt.	B	6th SCVI			08/30/62	2nd Manassas, VA	KIA		ROH
Mallard, W.C.H.	Pvt.	H	11th SCVI		CO	06/09/64	Cold Harbor, VA	DOW	Hollywood Cem.Rchmd U631	ROH,HAG,HC
Mallett, John	Pvt.	I	24th SCVI	21	ED	01/03/63	Wilmington, NC	DOD		EJM,HOE
Mallett, Preston B.	Pvt.	I	24th SCVI	18	ED	08/17/64	Atlanta, GA	KIA	(Shot on picket line)	EJM
Mallon, S.A.	Pvt.	A	7th SCVI			12/11/64	Pt. Lookout, MD	DIP		ROH
Mallony,	Pvt.	C	2nd SCVIRi			07/18/61		KIA		JR
Malloy, George	Pvt.	A	16th SCVI		GE	/ /	Charleston, SC	DOD		16R
Malloy, William P.	Pvt.	B	27th SCVI		CN	11/02/64	Fts. Monroe, VA	DOW		ROH
Malone, C.H.	Pvt.	C	BennettsBn			02/15/65	Charleston, SC	DOD	Magnolia Cem. Charleston	MAG
Malone, David	Pvt.	G	14th SCVI	40	AE	05/03/63	Chancellorsville	KIA		ROH,JR
Malone, James D.	Cpl.	B	Orr's Ri.	21	AE	05/03/63	Chancellorsville	KIA		ROH,JR,CDC
Malone, Medlock	Pvt.	E	26th SCVI		AE	09/04/64		KIA		ROH
Malone, Patrick	Pvt.	C	27th SCVI		CN	11/20/64	Elmira, NY	DIP	Woodlawn N.C.#941 Elmira	FPH,HAG,P65,P120
Manchett, Jonas	Pvt.		4th SCVI			07/29/61		DOW		JR
Maner, M.	Pvt.	G	13th SCVI		BT	02/28/65	Richmond, VA			ROH
Mangrum, Andrew J.	Pvt.	I	Hol.Leg.		SG	/ /	Mississippi		(1863)	HOS
Mangum, Joseph W.	Sgt.		Chfld. LA	23	CD	08/31/62	Petersburg, VA	DOD		PP
Mangum, W.P.	Pvt.	D	8th SCVI		CD	/ /	Petersburg, VA		(Also Wdd @ Chickamauga)	ROH,KEB
Manigault, Alfred	Cpl.	K	4th SCVC	24	CN	02/20/65	Winnsboro, SC	DOD	St.Philips C. Charleston	ROH,MAG,CDC
Manigault, Peter	Pvt.	H	3rd SCVC	59	CN	11/23/64	Bell's Ferry, GA	KIA	Huguenot Ch. Charleston SC	MAG,STR,DOC,UD1
Manion, Francis	Pvt.	K	1st SCVIG		CN	01/11/63	Richmond, VA	DOW	Hollywood Cem.Rchmd. D89	HC,SA1
Manley, J.P. (BLM=P.F.)	Pvt.	F	22nd SCVI	22	PS	08/07/64	Crater, Pbg., VA	DOW	Blandford Ch. Pbg., VA PP	ROH,JR,BLM,BLC
Manley, James M.	Pvt.	D	Ham.Leg.		PS	07/28/64	Riddle's Shop VA	KIA		ROH,GRS
Manly, Tyre	Cpl.	D	22nd SCVI		PS	06/05/64	Petersburg, VA			PP
Mann, A.	Pvt.		Orr's Ri.			07/20/64			Hollywood Cem.Rchmd. U21	HC
Mann, Aaron	Pvt.	I	P.S.S.		PS	07/01/64	Richmond, VA	DOD	(JR=Jackson Hos. 7/19/64)	ROH
Mann, James A.	Pvt.	I	14th SCVI	24	AE	05/20/64	Wilderness, VA	DOW		ROH,HOL
Mann, John M.	Pvt.	I	14th SCVI	20	AE	08/10/62	Richmond, VA	DOD	(JR=Typhoid 8/12/62)	ROH,JR,HOL,CDC
Mann, Robert R.	Pvt.	G	19th SCVI		AE	12/31/62		DOD		HOL
Mann, Thomas	Pvt.	F	5th SCVI			/ /	Staunton, VA	DOD	(1862)	CB,SA3
Manning, George P.	Pvt.	F	2nd SCVIRi	28	AN	03/17/63	Petersburg, VA	DOD		ROH,PP
Manning, H.W.	Pvt.	F	Orr's Ri.			/ /	Richmond, VA			ROH
Manning, John Mauldin	Pvt.	C	P.S.S.		AN	07/15/62	Richmond, VA	DOD		JR,SA2,GMJ
Manning, John	Pvt.	C	4th SCVI		AN	/ /	Richmond, VA	DOW	(1862, Prob in 4th SCVIBn)	HOF,SA2
Manning, Robert L.	Pvt.	B	12th SCVI	25	YK	08/07/62	Lynchburg, VA	DOD	Lynchburg CSA Cem. #6 R4	ROH,JR,YEB,BBW
Manning, William C.	Pvt.	B	12th SCVI	23	YK	09/17/62	Sharpsburg, MD	KIA		JR,YEB
Manning, William L.	2nd Lt.	I	1st SCVIH		MN	08/29/62	Groveton, VA	KIA		ROH,JR,SA1,HMC
Mansel, Joseph H.	Pvt.	E	2nd SCVIRi	16	PS	08/20/62	Richmond, VA	DOD		ROH
Mansel, Richard Harrison	Pvt.	F	2nd SCVC	36	PS	12/11/63	Richmond, VA	DOD		ROH
Mansell, J.E.	Pvt.		1st SCV			08/29/62	2nd Manassas, VA	KIA	(Manoell?)	JR
Mansell, J.H.	Pvt.		Brooks GA			/ /		DOD		JR
Manship, Aaron	Pvt.	F	21st SCVI		MO	08/21/64	Petersburg, VA	KIA		ROH,HOM,HAG
Manship, John H.	Pvt.	K	8th SCVI		MO	02/05/65	Columbia, SC	DOD		ROH,HOM,KEB

SOUTH CAROLINA DEAD IN CSA SERVICE 1861-1865

NAME	RANK	C REGIMENT	AGE	DS	DIED	WHERE	WHY	BURIED	SOURCES
Manship, Travis	Pvt.	F 1st SCVIG		MO	09/15/64		DOD		SA1
Manude, John A.	Cpl.	H 27th SCVI		CN	10/26/64	Pt. Lookout, MD	DIP	C.C. Pt. Lookout, MD	FPH,HAG,P5,P11
Manuel, John	Pvt.	D 19th SCVI	30	CR	07/22/64	Atlanta, GA	KIA	(? Mannel)	HOE,UD3
Manus, J.H.	Pvt.	K 5th SCVI		SG	05/31/62	7 Pines, VA	KIA		SA3
Manus, W.J.	Pvt.	B 6th SCVI		SG	08/30/62	2nd Manassas, VA	KIA		WDB
Mapus, Jacob	Pvt.	F 19th SCVI		ED	08/12/62	Okolona, MS	DOD	(HOE=DIS 2/26/62)	PP,HOE
Marce, Daniel	Pvt.	C 26th SCVI		MN	06/25/64	Petersburg, VA	DOW	(Wdd 6/23/64)(NI HMC)	ROH
March, H.	Pvt.	E 2nd SCVI		KW	12/10/62	Richmond, VA	DOD	(Marsh, H. in Oakwood C.?)	ROH,SA2,H2
March, J.M.	Pvt.	L Orr's Ri.		AN	/ /	Richmond, VA		Oakwood C.#105,Row M,Div A	ROH,OWC
Marchant, John	Sgt.	I 2nd SCVA	43	OG	10/03/64	Charleston, SC	DOD		ROH,JR
Marchbanks, Elkanah	Pvt.		23	GE	09/18/62	Shepherdstown VA	DOD	Shepherdstown, VA	GEC,ROH
Mardis, W.J.	Pvt.	B 18th SCVI		UN	08/30/62	2nd Manassas, VA	KIA	(JR=W.T.)	ROH,JR,CDC
Mardner, J.O.	Pvt.	H 1st SCVC		YK	02/01/65	Richmond, VA			ROH
Maret, M.A.	Pvt.	K 22nd SCVI		PS	07/22/64	Richmond, VA	DOD	(JR=Jackson Hospital)	ROH,JR
Maret, R.M.	Sgt.	E 17th SCVI		YK	07/30/64	Crater, Pbg., VA	KIA	(BKM=Maret, P.W.)	ROH,BLM
Marett, G.B.	Pvt.	F P.S.S.		LN	07/08/64		DOW		ROH
Marett, W.H.	Pvt.	B P.S.S.		AN	10/28/63	Lookout Valley	KIA		ROH,JR
Marfield, J.B.	Pvt.	H 6th SCVI		FD	05/31/62	7 Pines, VA	KIA	(Mayfield ? NI HFC)	WDB
Marins, W.D.	Pvt.	B 6th SCVI			08/30/62	2nd Manassas, VA	KIA		ROH,JR,CDC
Marion, F.	Pvt.	C 1st SCVC		ED	01/11/63	Richmond, VA	DOD		ROH
Marion, John Francis	2nd Sgt.	B 25th SCVI	21	CN	06/26/64	Richmond, VA	DOD	St.Mary's R.C. Charleston	ROH,JR,MAG,HAG
Marion, T.S.	Pvt.	K 4th SCVC			/ /				CLD
Marion, W.T.	Pvt.	5th SCVI			10/28/63	Lookout Valley	KIA		CDC
Mark, Isaac	Pvt.	C 15th SCVAB		CN	08/23/63	Bty. Wagner, SC	DOW		CDC
Markley, Charles A.	Pvt.	B 2nd SCVI	25	GE	07/02/63	Gettysburg, PA	KIA		JR,GDR,SA2,KEB
Markley, John	Pvt.	B 2nd SCVI		GE	/ /	Georgia	DOD	(1862 on sick leave)	ROH,KEB,SA2
Marks, T.	Pvt.	A Tucker's R			02/26/65	Salisbury, NC	DOD	Prob Old Lutheran Ch.there	PP
Marler, V.A.	Pvt.	F 10th SCVI		MN	/ /	Corinth, MS	DOD		HMC,RAS
Marler, William S.	Pvt.	I 1st SCVIG		CN	09/05/65	Richmond, VA	DOD	(POW 3/25/65 Rlsd 6/29/65)	ROH,P115
Marlow, J.A.	Pvt.	A 7th SCVC		GN	12/12/64	Pt. Lookout, MD	DIP	C.C. Pt. Lookout, MD	P113
Marlow, O.S.	Pvt.	A 10th SCVI		GN	/ /		DOD		GRG,RAS
Marlow, R. William	Pvt.	I 21st SCVI		MN	06/25/64	Petersburg, VA	DOW	(Wdd 6/23/64)	ROH,HMC,HAG
Marlow, Thomas M.	Pvt.	D 10th SCVI		MN	01/23/63	Brandon, MS	DOD	(RAS=Marlor)	RAS,HMC,PP
Maroney, James	Pvt.	K 2nd SCVIRi	35	AN	06/30/62	Frayser's Farm	KIA	(JR=Co.I 6/29/62)	ROH,JR,CDC
Maroney, S.S.	Cpl.	A 18th SCVI		UN	07/30/64	Crater, Pbg., VA	KIA		ROH,BLM
Marsh, Gates	Pvt.	D 15th SCVI		KW	/ /	Richmond, VA	KIA		JR,HIC,KEB
Marsh, H.	Pvt.	E 2nd SCVI		KW	/ /	Richmond, VA		Oakwood C.#42,Row A,Div B	OWC,CDC
Marsh, Isaac	Pvt.	C 15th SCVAB		CN	04/05/65	Pt. Lookout, MD	DIP	C.C. Pt. Lookout, MD	FPH
Marsh, R.H.	Pvt.	F P.S.S.		LN	07/24/62	Richmond, VA	DOW	(JR=March, R.H.)	ROH,JR,CDC
Marsh, Samuel P.	Pvt.	A Alexdrs A.			05/03/63	Chancellorsville	KIA		JR
Marsh, William	Pvt.	E 24th SCVI	18	CO	12/10/62	Secessionville	KIA	Bethel U.M.C. CO Cty. SC	ROH,CUC
Marshall, George W.	Pvt.	PeeDee LA		DN	/ /				ROH,PDL
Marshall, J.J.	Pvt.	I 4th SCVC		WG	05/29/64	Hawes Shop, VA	KIA		JR,CTA,HMC
Marshall, J.R.	Pvt.	G 21st SCVI		CD	03/15/62		DOD		JR,HAG
Marshall, J.S.	Pvt.	L P.S.S.			05/20/64		DOD		ROH,JR
Marshall, James L.	Pvt.	M 8th SCVI		DN	05/26/63	Columbia, SC	DOD	(Consumption, PP=Co.F)	JR,PP
Marshall, James S.	Pvt.	E 14th SCVI	18	LS	07/30/62	Richmond, VA	DOD	Liberty Spgs. P.C. LS Cty.	ROH,JR,CGS,LSC
Marshall, Jehu Foster	Colonel	Orr's Ri	45	AE	08/29/62	2nd Manassas, VA	KIA	Abbeville, SC	ROH,JR,LC,BOS
Marshall, John		CS Hunley		ACD	10/16/63	Charleston H'bor	ACD		RCD
Marshall, John T.	Pvt.	E 10th SCVI		WG	06/07/62	West Point, MS	DOD	(JR=Corinth, MS)	JR,RAS,HOW
Marshall, Thomas P.	Pvt.	E 3rd SCVI		NY	09/15/63	Chattanooga, TN	DOD	(NI KEB)	ROH,SA2,ANY

SOUTH CAROLINA DEAD IN CSA SERVICE 1861-1865

NAME	RANK	C	REGIMENT	AGE	DS	DIED	WHERE	WHY	BURIED	SOURCES
Marshall, W.D.	Pvt.	G	2nd SCVI		KW	12/05/62	Lynchburg, VA	DOD	Lynchburg CSA Cem. #2 R2	JR,SA2,H2,BBW
Marshburn, William W.	Pvt.	B	5th SCVC	23	CN	09/05/64	Raleigh, NC	DOD	Magnolia Cem. Charleston	ROH,MAG,MDM
Martin, A.J.	Pvt.	A	Orr's Ri.		AN	08/11/62	Rabun Cty., GA	DOD		JR
Martin, Albert	Pvt.				LN	/ /				ROH
Martin, Andrew	Cpl.		Brooks GA		CN	07/03/63	Gettysburg, PA	KIA	Gettysburg, PA	ROH,JR,GDR,WV,H2
Martin, B.	Pvt.		Ferguson's			06/27/65	Camp Chase, OH	DIP	C.C.#2056 Columbus, OH	FPH,P27
Martin, B.B.	Pvt.	D	4th SC Res			/ /	Charleston, SC			ROH
Martin, B.W.	Pvt.	L	7th SCVI		HY	05/08/64	Spotsylvania, VA		Spotsylvania C.H., VA	JR,SCH,KEB
Martin, C. Bookter	Pvt.	C	2nd SCVI		RD	03/28/62	Richmond, VA	DOD	Oakwood C.#36,Row F,Div A	ROH,SA2,KEB,OWC
Martin, C.M.	Pvt.	D	18th SCVI		AN	02/03/62	Charleston, SC	DOD		ROH,JR
Martin, D.J.V.	1st Lt.	H	P.S.S.	21	SG	09/02/62	2nd Manassas, VA	DOW	(HOS=J.D.V. JR=8/30/62)	ROH,R48,HOS,CDC
Martin, D.S.	Pvt.	B	4th SCVC		CR	04/06/65	Raleigh, NC	DOW	(Wdd Fayetteville)	CB
Martin, Ebenezer Reed	Pvt.	C	25th SCVI	40	WG	07/28/64	Richmond, VA	DOD	Hollywood Cem.Rchmd. U116	HC,ROH,HOW,HAG
Martin, F.M.	Pvt.	F	Orr's Ri.		PS	05/26/64	Washington, DC	DOW		ROH,CDC
Martin, Francis M.	Pvt.	L	1st SCVIG		CN	05/14/64	Washington, DC	DOW	(Wdd & POW @ Spotsylvania)	ROH,JR,SA1,P6
Martin, G.H.	Pvt.	M	P.S.S.	29	SG	06/15/65	Danville, VA	DOD		ROH
Martin, G.P. (C.R.?)	Pvt.	C	25th SCVI		WG	07/19/64	Richmond, VA	DOD		ROH
Martin, G.W.	Pvt.		Matthews A		CN	/ /	High Point, NC		Oakwood Cem. High Point NC	CV,WAT,TOD
Martin, George	Pvt.	C	P.S.S.	25	AN	09/30/64	Ft. Harrison, VA	KIA		ROH,SA2,GMJ
Martin, George W.	Pvt.	M	7th SCVI		ED	09/14/64	Pt. Lookout, MD	DIP	C.C. Pt. Lookout, MD	ROH,FPH,HOE,P113
Martin, George W.	Pvt.	C	7th SCVI	18	AE	05/13/62	Charlottesville	DOD	(JR=Co.B)	ROH,JR,KEB
Martin, H.P.	Cpl.	B	11th SCVI		CO	06/24/64	Petersburg, VA	KIA		ROH,JR,HAG
Martin, Henry H.	Pvt.	D	27th SCVI	39	LS	08/07/63		DOD		ROH,HAG
Martin, Irwin James	Pvt.	C	25th SCVI		WG	05/09/65	Pt. Lookout, MD	DIP	C.C. Pt. Lookout, MD P6	ROH,FPH,HAG,P115
Martin, J. Alfred	Pvt.	G	22nd SCVI	20	AN	07/30/64	Crater, Pbg., VA	KIA		ROH,BLM
Martin, J. Allen	Pvt.	C	3rd SCVI		NY	05/06/64	Wilderness, VA	KIA		ROH,JR,SA2,ANY
Martin, J. Douglas	Pvt.	A	6th SCVI		CR	09/16/61	Fairfax C.H., VA	DOD	(Typhoid)	JR,HHC
Martin, J.A.	Pvt.	D	3rd SCVIBn		LS	09/20/63	Chickamauga, GA	KIA	Con. Cem. Marietta, GA	ROH,JR,KEB,CCM
Martin, J.K.	Pvt.	D	18th SCVI		AN	08/10/62		DOW		JR
Martin, J.O.	Pvt.	K	Hol.Leg.			08/20/64	Pt. Lookout, MD	DIP	C.C. Pt. Lookout, MD	FPH,P5,P113
Martin, J.O.	Pvt.	E	13th SCVI		SG	/ /		DOD		HOS
Martin, J.P.A.	Pvt.	C	10th SCVI		HY	/ /	At home	DOD		RAS
Martin, J.R.	Pvt.	D	18th SCVI		AN	/ /	At home			ROH
Martin, J.S.	Pvt.	D	2nd SCV			/ /	LaGrange, GA		Con. Cem. LaGrange, GA	TOD
Martin, J.W.	2nd Lt.	I	22nd SCVI		OG	07/30/64	Crater, Pbg., VA	KIA		JR,BLM,R48
Martin, James C.P.	Pvt.	E	10th SCVI	27	WG	05/13/62	Corinth, MS	DOD	(JR=Canton, MS 5/27/62)	ROH,JR,RAS,HOW
Martin, James E.	Pvt.	C	Orr's Ri.		PS	10/17/62	Winchester, VA	DOD	Stonewall C. Winchester VA	ROH,JR,WIN,CDC
Martin, James F.	Pvt.	K	2nd SCVI		BL	08/05/63	Gettysburg, VA	DOW	(JR=Joseph) P5	ROH,JR,SA2,GDR
Martin, James G.	Pvt.	G	Orr's Ri.		AE	07/01/62	Gaines' Mill, VA	DOW	(JR=7/3/62)	ROH,JR
Martin, James Warren	2nd Sgt.	D	4th SCVI		AN	07/02/61		DOD	(Delirium Tremens)	SA2,HOF
Martin, Joel	Pvt.	C	7th SCVIBn	30	RD	12/20/63	At home	DOD	(HAG lists a Joseph)	ROH
Martin, Joel L.	Pvt.	C	2nd SCVI			06/11/62	Richmond, VA	DOD		H2,SA2,KEB
Martin, John	Pvt.	F	3rd SCVIBn	35	RD	07/02/63	Gettysburg, PA	KIA		ROH,JR,GDR,CDC
Martin, John Alvin	Cpl.	E	1st SCVC		OG	08/19/63	Brandy Stn., VA	KIA	Hollywood Cem.Rchmd. T78	ROH,HC
Martin, John C.	Sgt.	C	7th SCVI	25	AE	09/17/63	Petersburg, VA	DOD	(Also Wdd @ Gettysburg)	ROH,KEB
Martin, John F.	Pvt.	B	Orr's Ri.		AE	05/03/63	Chancellorsville	KIA	(JR=5th SCVI)	ROH,JR,CDC
Martin, John M.	Cpt.	H	P.S.S.	34	SG	07/12/62	Gaines' Mill, VA	DOW	(HOS=Frayser's Farm)	ROH,JR,R48,SCS
Martin, John V.	Sgt.	C	Hol.Leg.	22	SG	08/30/62	2nd Manassas, VA	KIA		ROH,HOS
Martin, Joseph B.	2nd Lt.	E	15th SCVI		FD	07/02/63	Gettysburg, PA	KIA		ROH,GDR,KEB,R047
Martin, Joseph L.	Pvt.	G	2nd SCV			08/06/63	Gettysburg, PA	DOW		P6
Martin, Joseph R.	Pvt.	F	12th SCVI		FD	09/14/62	Gordonsville, VA	DOD	(JR=Typhoid Dysentery)	JR,HFC

SOUTH CAROLINA DEAD IN CSA SERVICE 1861-1865

NAME	RANK	C REGIMENT	AGE	DS	DIED	WHERE	WHY	BURIED	SOURCES
Martin, Joshua	Pvt.	G 3rd SCVI	23	LS	08/15/62	North Carolina	DOW	(Wdd Savage Stn 6/29/62)	ROH,JR,SA2,KEB
Martin, Lafayette	Pvt.	K 24th SCVI		ED	12/12/63		DOD		HOE
Martin, M.	Pvt.	G 11th SCVI		CN	04/13/65	Pt. Lookout, MD	DIP	C.C. Pt. Lookout, MD	FPH,HAG,P6,P11
Martin, M.A.	Pvt.	A Orr's Ri.		AN	08/10/64	Richmond, VA	DOW	Oakwood C.#94,Row B,Div B	ROH,JR,OWC
Martin, M.G.	Pvt.	G 3rd SCVI		LS	02/24/65	Pt. Lookout, MD	DIP	C.C. Pt. Lookout, MD	ROH,FPH,KEB,P6
Martin, M.M.	Pvt.	G 10th SCVI		HY	/ /	Saltillo, MS	DOD	(RAS=DIS, Manassah M.?)	PP,RAS
Martin, Marshall Monroe	Pvt.	D Orr's Ri.	20	AN	01/16/62	Sullivans I., SC	DOD	Hardshell Baptist site AN	ACC,CDC
Martin, Noah J.	2nd Lt.	D 1st SCVC	30	CR	10/17/63	Charlottesville	DOD	Univ. Cem. Charlottesville	ROH,ACH,R43,HH
Martin, Pinckney B.	Pvt.	D 4th SCResB			03/26/65	Charlotte, NC			PP
Martin, R.B.	Pvt.	H 6th SCVI		FD	/ /	Farmville, VA			ROH
Martin, Robert H.	Sgt.	H 18th SCVI	33	YK	07/30/64	Crater, Pbg., VA	KIA		ROH,JR,BLM,YEB
Martin, Robert Marshall	Pvt.	I 19th SCVI	27	AE	09/30/63	At home	DOD	Due West A.R.P. AE Cty. SC	ROH,JR,CAE
Martin, S.	Pvt.	K 2nd SCVC		GE	10/25/62			Stonewall C. Winchester VA	ROH,WIN
Martin, S.	Pvt.	L 7th SCVI		HY	09/13/62	Maryland Hts. MD	KIA		ROH,JR
Martin, S.V.	Pvt.	D 27th SCVI		CN	06/25/64	Drury's Bluff VA	DOW	Hollywood Cem.Rchmd. U12	ROH,HC,HAG
Martin, Samuel	Pvt.	A 17th SCVI	21	CR	04/07/65	Staunton, VA	DOW	(Wdd @ Ft. Steadman)	ROH,HHC,CB
Martin, T. Ogier	Pvt.	E 1st SCVIBn	17	CN	08/17/63	Bty. Wagner, SC	KIA	Old Scotch P.C. Charleston	ROH,JR,HAG,RCD
Martin, Thomas Cooper	Pvt.	D 4th SCVI		AN	07/25/61	Culpepper, VA	DOD	Fairview Cem. Culpepper VA	CGH,SA2
Martin, Thomas Nelson	3rd Cpl.	E 10th SCVI	25	WG	05/15/62	Corinth, MS	DOD	(JR & PP=Macon, MS)	ROH,JR,RAS,PP
Martin, W.	Pvt.	C 10th SCVI		HY	/ /		DOD		RAS
Martin, W. Walker	Pvt.	C 17th SCVI	22	YK	09/15/63	At home	DOD		YEB
Martin, W.A.	Pvt.	D 18th SCVI		AN	08/27/62	Rappahanock R.	KIA	(JR=8/30/62)	ROH,JR,CDC
Martin, W.D.	Pvt.	D 4th SCV			/ /	At sea	DIP	(To Savannah for exchange)	CDC
Martin, W.T.	Pvt.	F Orr's Ri.		PS	08/05/62	Richmond, VA	DOW	(Wdd @ Gaines' Mill)	ROH,JR,CDC
Martin, Washington	Pvt.	F 5th SCVI		YK	07/15/62	Gaines' Mill, VA	DOW	(JR=7/5/62)	JR,SA3,CB
Martin, Whitfield	Pvt.	K 24th SCVI		ED	07/20/64	Peachtree Crk.GA	KIA		ROH,JR,HOE,CDC
Martin, William				RD	/ /	Columbia, SC	DOD		ROH
Martin, William	Pvt.	F 17th SCVI		YK	05/20/64	Clay's Farm, VA	KIA	(JR=Drury's Bluff 5/16/64)	ROH,JR,CB
Martin, William	Pvt.	A 16th SCVI		GE	/ /	At home	DOD	(? on active duty)	16R
Martin, William A.	3rd Sgt.	G 22nd SCVI	25	AN	07/30/64	Crater, Pbg., VA	KIA		ROH,BLM
Martin, William Hayland	Pvt.	H 1st SCVIG	22	BT	07/15/62	Richmond, VA	DOD		ROH,SA1,CDC
Martin, William Henry	Pvt.	Santee LA	18	CN	04/01/63		DOD		ROH
Martin, William J.	Pvt.	A 26th SCVI	27	HY	03/15/65	At home	DOD		ROH
Martin, William Maxwell	Pvt.	Green's Co			02/21/61	Ft. Moultrie, SC	DOD	Washington St.M.C.Columbia	MP,PP
Martin, William Ogier	Pvt.	A 25th SCVI		CN	06/16/62	Secessionville	KIA	1st P.C.(Scotch)Charleston	MAG,RCD
Martin, William R.	Pvt.	F 12th SCVI		FD	08/06/62	Richmond, VA	DOW	(Wdd @ Gaines' Mill)	ROH,HFC
Martin, William R.	Cpl.	H 23rd SCVI		MN	07/27/64	Pt. Lookout, MD	DIP	(POW 6/17/64 @ Pbg.)	HMC,P113,P120
Marting, J.H.	Pvt.				/ /			Rose Hill C. Hagerstown MD	BOD
Marton, J.A.	Pvt.	A 7th SCVC		GN	12/12/64	Pt. Lookout, MD	DIP	C.C. Pt. Lookout, MD	FPH,P5
Marvin, William D.	Cpt.	C 5th SCVC		CO	08/23/64	Gravelly Run, VA	KIA		ROH,JR,CDC
Masengill, Joseph	Pvt.	B 37th VAVCB		PS	03/17/65	Camp Chase, OH	DIP	C.C.#1695 Columbus, OH	37V,FPH,P6,P27
Mash, J.T.F.	Pvt.	C 8th SCVI		CD	11/16/64	Camp Chase, OH	DIP	C.C.#479 Columbus, OH	FPH,KEB
Mason, A.F.	Pvt.	K 22nd SCVI		PS	09/19/62	Lynchburg, VA	DOD	Lynchburg CSA Cem. #3 R3	JR,CDC,BBW
Mason, A.J.	Pvt.	K 22nd SCVI		PS	07/30/64	Crater, Pbg., VA	KIA		BLM
Mason, A.P.	Pvt.	K 15th SCVI			10/13/63	Chickamauga, GA	DOW	(KEB=Mayson, P.A.)	ROH,JR,KEB
Mason, A.T.	Pvt.	K 22nd SCVI		PS	09/18/62	Virginia	DOD		ROH
Mason, Benjamin F.	Pvt.	B 22nd SCVI		SG	07/03/62	Columbia, SC	DOD		ROH,PP
Mason, G.W.	Pvt.	B 22nd SCVI		SG	07/30/64	Crater, Pbg., VA	KIA		BLM,HOS
Mason, George W.	Pvt.	H 5th SCVI	35	YK	06/10/61	Columbia, SC	DOD	(YMD=KIA Bethel Ch., VA)	JR,YMD,YEB
Mason, Henry F.	Pvt.	A Hol.Leg.	32	SG	08/30/62	2nd Manassas, VA	KIA		ROH,JR,HOS
Mason, J. (Mann, J.A.?)	Pvt.	I 14th SCVI		AE	06/09/64	Richmond, VA		Hollywood Cem.Rchmd. U130	HC

SOUTH CAROLINA DEAD IN CSA SERVICE 1861-1865

NAME	RANK	C REGIMENT	AGE	DS	DIED	WHERE	WHY	BURIED	SOURCES
Mason, J. Ross	4th Sgt.	B 22nd SCVI		SG	07/30/64	Crater, Pbg., VA	KIA		BLM,HOS
Mason, J.B.	Pvt.	K 22nd SCVI		PS	07/30/64	Crater, Pbg., VA	KIA		BLM
Mason, J.P.	Pvt.	B 22nd SCVI		SG	07/30/64	Crater, Pbg., VA	KIA		HOS
Mason, James P.	Pvt.	D 11th SCVI	30	BT	07/20/64	Petersburg, PA	DOD		ROH
Mason, John	Pvt.	G P.S.S.	31	YK	/ /	Richmond, VA	DOD	(1864)	YEB
Mason, John K.	Pvt.	K 22nd SCVI		PS	10/11/62	Frederick, MD	DOW	Rose Hill c. Hagerstown MD	ROH,FPH,BOD
Mason, Josiah	Pvt.	K 22nd SCVI		PS	/ /	At home		(7/20/?)	ROH
Mason, Rufus	Pvt.	D 23rd SCVI		CR	08/30/62	2nd Manassas, VA	KIA		HHC
Mason, T.M.	Pvt.	B 22nd SCVI		SG	07/30/64	Crater, Pbg., VA	KIA		BLM
Mason, T.R.	Pvt.	G 2nd SCVI		KW	11/12/62	Winchester, VA	DOD	Stonewall C. Winchester VA	ROH,WIN,SA2,H2
Massengill, James G.	Pvt.	I P.S.S.		PS	05/31/62	7 pines, VA	KIA		ROH,JR,CDC
Massey, B.F.	Pvt.	B 8th SCVI		CD	07/21/61	1st Manassas, VA	KIA		JR,KEB,R46
Massey, J.B.	Pvt.	E 2nd SCVA			02/02/64	Charleston, SC	DOD	Magnolia Cem. Charleston	ROH,MAG
Massey, J.C.	Pvt.	K 6th SCVC		CD	06/11/64	Trevillian Stn.	KIA		ROH,JR
Massey, John W.	Pvt.	H 4th SCVC		LR	06/09/63	McPhersonville	DOD		ROH,LAN
Massey, Leon	5th Sgt.	F 17th SCVI		YK	04/01/65	Five Forks, VA	KIA		DEM,YEB
Massey, Oliver	Pvt.	C 15th SCVAB		CN	04/16/63	Columbia, SC	DOD		ROH,PP
Masterman, Alfred H.	2nd Lt.	B 27th SCVI		CN	05/07/64	Pt. Walthal Jctn	KIA	Blandford Church Pbg., VA	ROH,JR,PP,BLC
Mastrip, A. (Manship?)	Pvt.				02/06/65	Richmond, VA		Elmwood Cem. Columbia, SC	MP,PP
Masville, J.	Pvt.	B 7th SCVI		AE	05/18/64	Richmond, VA			ROH
Matherson, Hugh	Pvt.	K 8th SCVI		MO	11/15/61		DOD	(Pneumonia)	JR,HOM,KEB
Mathews, G.	Pvt.	H 12th SCVI		YK	06/15/62		DOD	(YEB=DIS 6/62)	CWC,YEB
Mathews, George W.	Pvt.	K 6th SCVI		SR	08/30/62	2nd Manassas, VA	KIA		ROH,CDC
Mathews, J.A.	Pvt.	H 18th SCVI		YK	05/02/65	Elmira, NY	DIP	Woodlawn N.C.#2743 Elmira	FPH,P6,P65,P120
Mathews, J.P.	Pvt.	H 10th SCVI		WG	09/20/63	Chickamauga, GA	KIA	(JR=Co.C)	ROH,JR,CDC
Mathews, J.R.	Pvt.	H 20th SCVI		LN	/ /	Gordonsville, VA		(Mathias, J.B.?)	ROH
Mathews, James K.	Pvt.	G 6th SCVI	21	FD	07/01/62	Fraysers Fm., VA	DOW		ROH,WDB
Mathews, John A.	Pvt.	F 12th SCVI		FD	05/12/64	Spotsylvania, VA	KIA	(JR=DOD 5/3/63)	ROH,JR,HFC
Mathews, Marion M.	3rd Cpl.	B 6th SCVI		YK	11/16/63	Campbell's Stn.	KIA		ROH,YEB
Mathews, Robert N.	Pvt.	D 11th SCVI	41	BT	/ /	Fts. Monroe, VA	DOW	(Wdd Pbg. 6/16/64)	ROH,HAG
Mathews, T. Alexander	Cpl.	A 10th SCVI		GN	07/22/64	Atlanta, GA	DOW	(Left shoulder)	ROH,GRG,RAS,CDC
Mathews, W.M.	Pvt.	K 18th SCVI		SG	09/15/64	Elmira, NY	DIP	Woodlawn N.C.#282 Elmira	FPH,P5,P65,P120
Mathis, Benjamin H.	Pvt.	G 13th SCVI		NY	07/13/62	Laurel Hill, VA	DOD	St.Lukes L.C. Prosperity	ROH,JR,NCC,ANY
Mathis, D.L.	Pvt.	H 19th SCVI	18	AE	09/20/63	Chickamauga, GA	KIA		ROH,CDC
Mathis, J.	Pvt.	E 7th SCVI			07/02/63	Gettysburg, PA	KIA		JR
Mathis, J. Nelson	Pvt.	K 23rd SCVI	31	SR	03/29/65	Petersburg, VA	DOW	(Wdd 3/25/65)	ROH,PP
Mathis, Jeff	Pvt.	I 12th SCVI		LR	02/17/65	Pt. lookout, MD	DIP	C.C. Pt. Lookout, MD	ROH,FPH,LAN,P6
Mathis, Joab	Pvt.	G 13th SCVI		NY	07/01/63	Gettysburg, PA	KIA		ROH,ANY,CDC
Mathis, John	Sgt.	B 7th SCVI			10/17/63	Chickamauga, GA	DOW	Con. Cem. Marietta, GA	ROH,KEB,CDC,CCM
Mathis, John	Pvt.	F 2nd SC Res		NY	02/03/64	Charleston, SC	DOD	(6 mths service in '63)	ROH,ANY
Mathis, Simpson	Pvt.	I 2nd SCVA		ED	05/15/63		DOD		ROH
Mathis, Thomas M.	Pvt.	G 14th SCVI	31	AE	05/16/65	Hart's Island NY	DIP	Cypress Hills N.C.#2803 NY	ROH,P6,FPH
Mathis, William H.	Cpl.	I 7th SCVI		ED	07/02/63	Gettysburg, PA	KIA		ROH,JR,GDR,KEB
Mathis, William J.	Pvt.	K 23rd SCVI		SR	08/30/62	2nd Manassas, VA	DOW	(ROH= Wdd 7/4/64 @ Pbg)	ROH,K23,UD3
Matt, Edwin G.	Pvt.				08/04/64	Petersburg, VA		Blandford Church Pbg., VA	BLC
Matthewes,	Pvt.				/ /			Magnolia Cem. Charleston	MAG
Matthewes, T.M.	Pvt.			WG	07/22/64	Atlanta, GA	KIA		HOW
Matthews,	Overseer				10/31/63	Ft. Sumter, SC	KIA		PP
Matthews, A.	Pvt.	H 10th SCVI		WG	/ /		DOD	(1863)	RAS,HOW
Matthews, A.M.	Pvt.	D 2nd SC Res	22	WG	/ /		DOD	(1863)	CTA
Matthews, B.C.	Pvt.	A 1st SCVIG	20	BL	07/01/63	Gettysburg, PA	KIA	(JR=7/2/63)	ROH,JR,SA1,GDR

SOUTH CAROLINA DEAD IN CSA SERVICE 1861-1865

NAME	RANK	C REGIMENT	AGE	DS	DIED	WHERE	WHY	BURIED	SOURCES
Matthews, Benjamin	Pvt.	I 26th SCVI	28	WG	05/20/64	Clay's Farm, VA	KIA		ROH,HOW,CTA
Matthews, E.A.	Pvt.	I 26th SCVI		WG	08/20/64			Hollywood Cem.Rchmd. V586	HC
Matthews, Elijah	Pvt.	A 1st SCVIG	22	BL	07/27/63	Davids Island NY	DOW	Cypress Hills N.C.#691 NY	ROH,FPH,GDR,P6
Matthews, Francis	Pvt.	H 10th SCVI		WG	06/15/63	Chattanooga, TN	DOD	City C, Chattanooga, TN	RAS,HOW,TOD
Matthews, G.C.	Sgt.	H 2nd SCVA		BL	09/07/63	Bty. Wagner, SC	KIA		ROH
Matthews, G.W.	Pvt.	H 10th SCVI		WG	12/31/62	Murfreesboro, TN	KIA		RAS,HOW
Matthews, George	Pvt.	B 6th SCVI	35	YK	06/15/63	Lynchburg, VA	DOD	Lynchburg CSA Cem.#27R4	ROH,BBW,YEB
Matthews, Gideon	Sgt.	1st SCVA	38	BL	08/22/63	Bty. Wagner, SC	KIA		ROH
Matthews, H.H.	Pvt.			WG	/ /		DOD	(1863)	CTA,HOW
Matthews, H.M.	Pvt.	H 10th SCVI		WG	/ /		DOD		RAS
Matthews, H.W.	Pvt.	H 25th SCVI		WG	05/16/64	Drury's Bluff VA	KIA		ROH,JR,HOW,HAG
Matthews, Jacob L.	Pvt.	H Hol. Leg.		NY	05/01/65	Pt. Lookout, MD	DIP	C.C. Pt. Lookout, MD	FPH,P6,P115
Matthews, James	Pvt.	E 13th SCVI		SG	08/06/63	Davids Island NY	DOW	(Prob. in Cypress Hills C)	ROH,P1,CDC
Matthews, James N.	Pvt.	H 10th SCVI		WG	01/07/63	Murfreesboro, TN	DOW	(In enemy hands)	RAS,HOW,P38
Matthews, John J.	Pvt.	G 15th SCVI	28	WG	/ /		DOD		JR,CTA,HOW,KEB
Matthews, John T.	Pvt.	A 3rd SCResB			/ /	Raleigh, NC		Oakwood C. Raleigh, NC	TOD
Matthews, M.	Pvt.	H 10th SCVI		WG	/ /		DOD	(1863)	RAS,HOW
Matthews, Mark	Pvt.	C 19th SCVI		ED	07/18/62	Enterprise, MS	DOD	(EDN= Mathis)	ROH,HOE,EDN,UD
Matthews, Pleasant	Pvt.	H 10th SCVI		WG	/ /		DOD	(1863, J.P.?)	RAS,HOW
Matthews, Pleasant	Pvt.	I 26th SCVI	24	WG	09/20/63	Chickamauga, GA	KIA		CTA,HOW
Matthews, R.M.	Pvt.	H 10th SCVI		WG	/ /		DOD	(1863)	RAS,HOW
Matthews, Robert	Pvt.	H 10th SCVI		WG	/ /		DOD		RAS,HOW
Matthews, Robert W.	Pvt.		36	BL	03/20/63	SC coast	DOD		ROH
Matthews, Simeon	Pvt.	C 19th SCVI	23	ED	03/10/62	Charleston, SC	DOD	(EDN= Mathis)	ROH,HOE,EDN,UD
Matthews, W.A.	Pvt.	E 8th SCVI		DN	09/13/62	Maryland Hts. MD	KIA		JR,KEB
Matthews, W.J.	Pvt.	H 25th SCVI		CN	04/07/65	Elmira, NY	DIP	Woodlawn N.C.#2649 Elmira	FPH,HAG,P6,P65
Matthews, William J.	Pvt.	K 6th SCVI	30	WG	08/30/62	2nd Manassas, VA	KIA	(WDB= J.W.)	ROH,HOW,WDB,3R
Matthias, John T.	Pvt.	C 1st SCVIG		RD	04/14/65	Petersburg, VA	DOW	(Near Fair Gds. Hos. Pbg.)	ROH,SA1,P6
Mattison, G.F.	Pvt.	F 1st SCVIG		AN	08/13/64	Pt. Lookout, MD	DIP	(P5=Madison)	SA1,FPH,P5,P11
Mattison, J. Marion	Pvt.	G Orr's Ri.		AE	05/07/63	Chancellorsville	DOW	(Wdd 5/6, JR=Co.C)	ROH,JR,CDC
Mattison, James F.	3rd Lt.	E 20th SCVI		AN	06/30/64	Richmond, VA		Shady Grove B.C. Belton SC	ROH,ANC,KEB,R4
Mattison, L.W.	Pvt.	E Ham.Leg.	41	AN	05/08/62	Ashland, VA	DOD		ROH
Mattison, N. Colbert	Pvt.	D Ham.Leg.	37	AN	11/20/63	Campbell's Stn.	DOW	(CDC= V.C.)	ROH,GRS,CDC
Mattison, Uriah J.	Pvt.	G Orr's Ri.		AE	08/13/64	Chaffin's Farm	DOD		ROH
Mattison, William Newton	2nd Lt.	I 19th SCVI	33	AE	07/28/64	Atlanta, GA	DOW	(R47=dropped 5/8/62)	ROH,R47
Mattox, Henry	Pvt.	I 19th SCVI	19	AE	04/01/63	Chattanooga, TN	DOD	City C. Chattanooga, TN	ROH,TOD
Mattox, Jacob	Pvt.	E 18th SCVI	21	SG	10/26/64	Petersburg, VA	KIA	(HOS= Maddox)	ROH,HOS,PP
Mattox, Perry	Pvt.	K 3rd SCVI	19	SG	09/13/62	Maryland Hts. MD	KIA		ROH,SA2,HOS,KE
Mattox, Samuel	Pvt.	D 15th SCVI		KW	06/02/65	Pt. Lookout, MD	DIP	C.C. Pt. Lookout, MD	FPH,KEB,P6,P11
Mattox, W.M.	Pvt.	D Ham.Leg.		AN	05/31/62	7 Pines, VA	KIA		GRS
Mauldin, A.M.	Pvt.	E 1st SCVIR			01/27/64	At home	DOD		SA1
Mauldin, Edmund	Pvt.	B 16th SCVI		GE	/ /	At home	DOD	(1862)	16R
Mauldin, Elbert	Pvt.	E 2nd SCVIRi	22	PS	08/27/62	Manchester, VA	DOD	Kenmore Fam. C. Pickens SC	UD2
Mauldin, James D.	Pvt.	I 14th SCVI	18	AE	11/01/63	Ft. Delaware, DE	DIP	(ROH=Hart's Island, NY)	ROH,JR,FPH,P5
Mauldin, James G.	Pvt.	A Orr's Ri.		AN	06/20/62	Richmond, VA	DOD		JR,CDC
Mauldin, Joab L.	Cpl.	B 2nd SCVI	26	GE	08/15/61	Fairfax C.H., VA	DOD		ROH,SA2,KEB,H2
Mauldin, John E.	Pvt.	D Ham.Leg.		PS	10/28/63	Lookout Valley	KIA		ROH,GRS
Mauly, B.	Pvt.			PS	06/07/64	Petersburg, VA		Blandford Church Pbg., VA	BLC
Maw, John F.	Pvt.	K Orr's Ri.	28	PS	12/19/62	Staunton, VA	DOD	Thornrose C. Staunton, VA	ROH,JR,CDC,TOD
Mawley, Tyre	Pvt.	D 22nd SCVI		PS	06/05/64	Petersburg, VA		Blandford Church Pbg., VA	BLC
Maxwell, George H.	Pvt.	G 1st SCVIG		ED	12/24/61	Suffolk, VA	DOD	(Pneumonia)	JR,SA1,HOE

SOUTH CAROLINA DEAD IN CSA SERVICE 1861-1865

NAME	RANK	C REGIMENT	AGE	DS	DIED	WHERE	WHY	BURIED	SOURCES
Maxwell, John D.	Pvt.	I	20	AN	07/15/64	Richmond, VA	DOD		ROH
Maxwell, L.L.	Pvt.	B Orr's Ri.		AE	08/29/62	2nd Manassas, VA	KIA		JR
Maxwell, Samuel	Cpl.	G 14th SCVI	28	AE	09/16/62		DOD	Rose Hill C. Hagerstown MD	ROH,BOD
Maxwell, T. Edward	Pvt.	B Orr's Ri.	24	AN	08/29/62	2nd Manassas, VA	KIA		ROH,JR,CDC
May, James	Pvt.	D 21st SCVI		CD	01/15/65	Ft. Fisher, NC	KIA		PP
May, James A.	Pvt.	G 7th SCVI	19	ED	08/09/61	Charlottesville	DOD	Univ. Cem. Charlottesville	HOE,UD2,ACH,EDN
May, Jesse M.	Pvt.	K 14th SCVI	20	ED	07/18/62	Richmond, VA	DOW	(JR=8/15/62)	ROH,JR,HOE,EDN
May, John A.	2nd Lt.	A 12th SCVI	26	YK	08/29/62	2nd Manassas, VA	KIA		ROH,JR,YEB,CWC
May, John A.	Pvt.	D 6th SCVI		CR	/ /	Richmond, VA		Oakwood C.#27,Row J,Div B.	ROH,OWC,WDB
May, Michael	Pvt.	K 1st SCVIG		CN	03/15/63	Richmond, VA	DOW	(Wdd @ Ox Hill 9/1/62)	SA1
May, Robert Franklin	Pvt.	A 8th SCVI	19	DN	09/22/61	Culpepper, VA	DOD	Fairview Cem. Culpepper VA	ROH,JR,CGH,KEB
May, Thomas	Pvt.	B Ham.Leg.			07/21/61	1st Manassas, VA	KIA		ROH,JR,CDC
May, W. Frank	3rd Sgt.	C 19th SCVI		ED	09/30/63	Chickamauga, GA	DOW	Con. Cem. Marietta, GA	HOE,CCM,UD3
May, W.J.	Pvt.	C 5th SCVI			12/28/62	Lynchburg, VA	DOD	(To Hosp. 12/17/62)	JR,SA3
Mayberry, Francis	Pvt.	B 18th SCVI		UN	02/15/62	At home	DOD		JR
Maybry, Foster	Pvt.	B 18th SCVI		UN	10/26/64	Pt. Lookout, MD	DIP	C.C. Pt. Lookout, MD	FPH,P5,P115,P120
Mayer, Daniel	Sgt.	B 19th SCVI	30	ED	12/30/64	Camp Douglas, IL	DIP	Oak Woods C. Chicago, IL	ROH,FPH,HOE
Mayer, Jesse	Cpl.	B 19th SCVI		ED	09/20/63	Chickamauga, GA	DOW	Con. Cem. Marietta, GA	ROH,HOE,CDC,CCM
Mayer, John A.	Cpl.	H 3rd SCVI		LN	10/10/63	Chickamauga, GA	DOW		ROH,JR,SA2,KEB
Mayers, Dove	Pvt.				/ /	Camp Douglas, IL	DIP		ROH,CDC
Mayers, J. Wiley	Pvt.	B 6th SCVC		ED	06/12/64	Trevillian Stn.	KIA	(ROH= Moyers)	ROH,HOE,UD3
Mayers, John	Pvt.	K SCVA			06/28/62	Ft. Sumter, SC	KIA	Magnolia Cem. Charleston	RCD
Mayes, John	Pvt.	H 5th SCVI		UN	05/31/62	7 Pines, VA	KIA		JR,SA3,NHU,UD1
Mayes, John B.	Pvt.	E 3rd SCVI		NY	09/20/63	Chickamauga, GA	KIA	Con. Cem. Marietta, GA	ROH,JR,SA2,CCM
Mayes, Robert	Pvt.	E 18th SCVI		SG	/ /	Virginia			HOS
Mayes, Samuel Scott	Pvt.	K 3rd SCVI	20	SG	07/30/62	Richmond, VA	DOD	(HOS=DOW, JR=7/28/62)	ROH,JR,SA2,UNC
Mayes, T.	Pvt.	SCVI			07/24/62			Hollywood Cem.Rchmd. H136	HC
Mayes, William D.S.	1st Sgt.	E P.S.S.		SR	08/01/62	Richmond, VA	DOW	(Wdd 6/27/62, JR=8/2/62)	ROH,JR
Mayes, William J.	Pvt.	K 3rd SCVI	27	SG	06/27/63	Richmond, VA	DOW	(Wdd @ Fbg. 12/13/62)	ROH,JR,SA2,HOS
Mayfield, Abraham	Pvt.	F 23rd SCVI	30	CR	/ /	Richmond, VA	DOW	(1862, Wdd @ 2nd Man.)	ROH,JR,CDC,HHC
Mayfield, B.L.	Pvt.	D 18th SCVI		AN	11/27/64	Charleston, SC	DOD		ROH
Mayfield, D. Massey	Pvt.	B 13th SCVI		SG	08/19/64	Fussel's Mill VA	DOW	Oakwood C.#74,Row J,Div G	ROH,OWC,HOS
Mayfield, David T.	Pvt.	F 16th SCVI		GE	09/18/62	Charleston, SC	DOD	(PP=At home 9/9/62)	JR,16R,PP
Mayfield, I.J.	Cpl.	B 22nd SCVI		SG	/ /				HOS
Mayfield, J.L.	Pvt.	Ham.Leg.		GE	08/09/64	Richmond, VA	DOD	Hollywood Cem.Rchmd. V51	ROH,HC
Mayfield, John	Pvt.	D Ham.Leg.		AN	06/15/62		DOD		GRS
Mayfield, John M.	Pvt.	C 22nd SCVI		SG	01/18/63	Charleston, SC	DOD		ROH
Mayfield, Sanford V.	Pvt.	D 4th SCVI		AN	08/26/61	Orange C.H., VA	DOD		SA2
Mayharue, A.	Pvt.	B 1st SCVC	30	LS	/ /	Johns Island, SC	KIA	(1862)	ROH
Maynard, James E.	Pvt.	Orr's Ri.		AE	06/16/62	Richmond, VA	DOD		ROH
Maynard, S.	Pvt.	K 13th SCVI		LN	06/01/62			Hollywood Cem.Rchmd. M391	HC
Mayo, W.P.	Pvt.	D 6th SCVI		CR	06/01/62	7 Pines, VA	KIA		ROH,WDB,CDC
Mayrant, John G.	3rd Sgt.	G 7th SCVIBn	21	RD	05/23/64	Drury's Bluff VA	DOW	(JR=KIA 5/16/64)	ROH,JR,HIC,HAG
Mayrant, William K.	Sgt.	C 7th SCVIBn	24	RD	07/10/63	Morris Island SC	KIA		ROH,JR
Mays, Dannett	Pvt.	K 4th SCVI		AN	04/07/62	Lynchburg, VA	DOD	Lynchburg CSA Cem.#6 R5	ROH,JR,SA2,BBW
Mays, Francis Whitfield	Pvt.	D 6th SCVI	20	ED	05/31/62	7 Pines, VA	KIA		JR,EDN
Mays, John C.	2nd Sgt.	G 1st SCVIG		BL	07/03/63	Gettysburg, PA	KIA	Magnolia Cem. Charleston	ROH,JR,GDR,SA1
Mays, John W.	Pvt.	I 2nd SCVC		ED	07/07/64	Gervais Fld.JnsI	KIA		ROH,CDC,HOE
Mays, L.W.	Pvt.	B 6th SCVC		ED	04/15/64	At home	DOD		ROH,HOE,UD3
Mays, William S.	Pvt.	G 5th SCVI		YK	01/06/63	Fredericksburg	DOD	(JR=6/6/63)	JR,SA3
Mazyck, J.M.	Pvt.	H 17th SCVI		BL	/ /		DOW		JR

SOUTH CAROLINA DEAD IN CSA SERVICE 1861-1865

NAME	RANK	C	REGIMENT	AGE	DS	DIED	WHERE	WHY	BURIED	SOURCES
Meacham, W.A.	Pvt.	G	18th SCVI		YK	07/30/64	Crater, Pbg., VA	KIA		ROH,JR
Meadors, Robert	Pvt.	F	16th SCVI		GE	07/22/64	Decatur, GA	KIA		16R
Meadows, J.A.	Pvt.	E	17th SCVI	22	YK	07/30/64	Crater, Pbg., VA	KIA		ROH,BLM
Meadows, N.	Pvt.		Ham.Leg.			08/26/62	Richmond, VA	DOD	Hollywood Cem.Rchmd. H55	ROH,HC,CDC
Meadows, T.S.	Pvt.	K	3rd SCVI		SG	01/05/62	Lynchburg, VA	DOW	Lynchburg CSA Cem. #8 R1	ROH,JR,BBW,KEB
Meadows, Warren D.	Pvt.	D	2nd SCVIRi	22		07/10/62	Petersburg, VA	DOD	Blandford Church Pbg., VA	BLC,PP
Mealey, Charles	Pvt.	C	Orr's Ri.		PS	12/14/62	Fredericksburg	DOW		JR,CDC
Mealing, Drury J.	Pvt.	B	19th SCVI	19	ED	06/02/62	Enterprise, MS	DOD	Republican B.C. ED Cty. SC	ROH,HOE,EDN,PP
Means, Beverly W.	Sgt. Major		6th SCVI	28	FD	06/01/62	7 Pines, VA	DOW	(In enemy hands)	ROH,JR,HCD,CDC
Means, John Harvey	Cpl.	G	19th SCVI		AE	06/25/62	Lauderdale Ss MS	DOD		HOL,PP
Means, John Hugh	Colonel		17th SCVI	50	FD	09/01/62	2nd Manassas, VA	DOW		ROH,JR,LC,HHC
Means, T.J.	Pvt.	E	14th SCVI		LS	05/02/63	Chancellorsville	KIA		ROH,CDC
Meares, J.A.	1st Sgt.	E	14th SCVI		LS	07/02/63	Gettysburg, PA	KIA	(JR=Means)	JR,CGS
Meares, P.L.	Pvt.	L	10th SCVI		MN	/ /		DOD		RAS,HMC
Meares, T.J.	2nd Sgt.	E	14th SCVI		LS	05/12/64	Spotsylvania, VA	KIA		CGS
Mearies, W.T.	Pvt.	E	14th SCVI		LS	05/03/63	Chancellorsville	KIA	(JR=Means)	ROH,JR,CGS
Measles, J.	Pvt.	B	11th SCVI		CO	07/19/64	Petersburg, VA	DOW	(Wdd 7/12/64)	ROH,HAG
Meders,	Sgt.	E	Hol.Leg.	34	SG	08/25/62	Richmond, VA	DOD		ROH
Medlin, Brit	Pvt.	B	P.S.S.			02/01/64	Chafin's Farm VA	KIA	(JR=DOD 2/1/64)	JR,LSS
Medlin, Calvin	Pvt.	C	7th SCVIBn	48	RD	01/04/64	Charleston, SC	DOD	Magnolia Cem. Charleston	ROH,JR,RCD,HIC
Medlin, Chesley D.	Pvt.	B	P.S.S.		PS	06/02/64	At home			ROH,JR
Medlin, Daniel	Cpl.	C	7th SCVIBn		RD	02/03/65	Elmira, NY	DIP	Woodlawn N.C.#1747 Elmira	FPH,HAG,P6,P65
Medlin, H.	Pvt.	H	6th SCVI		FD	/ /	Richmond, VA		Oakwood C.#1,Row A,Div A	ROH,OWC
Medlin, Irvin	Pvt.	C	7th SCVIBn	19	RD	06/30/64	Petersburg, VA	DOD		ROH
Medlin, J.V.	Pvt.	A	Orr's Ri.			/ /	Richmond, VA		Oakwood C.#42,Row G,Div C	ROH,OWC
Medlin, John	Pvt.	C	7th SCVIBn	23	RD	09/20/63	Charleston, SC	DOD	(JR=10/17/63)	ROH,JR,HAG
Medlin, Joseph B.	Pvt.	I	P.S.S.		PS	09/17/62	Sharpsburg, VA	KIA		ROH,JR,CDC
Medlin, W.	Pvt.	F	2nd SC Res		RD	02/09/65	Columbia, SC	DOD	Elmwood Cem. Columbia, SC	ROH,MP,PP
Medlin, Wesley	Cpl.	C	7th SCVIBn	35	RD	10/10/63	Charleston, SC	DOD	(JR=12/31/63)	ROH,JR,HAG
Medling, A.	Pvt.	H	6th SCVI		FD	/ /	Richmond, VA		(1862)	ROH
Medlock, Ander	Pvt.	C	3rd SCVIBn	41	LS	09/05/64			Medlock Fam.C. Princeton	LSC,KEB
Medlock, John	Pvt.	F	7th SCVI	24	ED	/ /	Richmond, VA	DOD		ROH,HOE
Medlock, Martin	Pvt.	B	24th SCVI	17	MO	/ /		DOD		EJM
Meek, E.F.	Pvt.			23	YK	06/27/62	Gaines' Mill, VA	KIA	(I,5th SCVI before Reorg)	YEB
Meek, Emmet R.	2nd Lt.	E	5th SCVI	24	YK	06/15/62	Frayser's Farm	DOW		ROH,R46
Meekins, Oscar F.	Pvt.	B	24th SCVI		MO	09/01/64	Jonesboro, GA	DOW	Rose Hill C. Macon, GA	ROH,HOM,BGA,PP
Meekins, William E.	Cpl.	B	24th SCVI		MN	07/22/64	Decatur, GA	KIA		ROH,JR,HOM
Meeks, Thomas B.	Pvt.	I	3rd SCVI		LS	09/18/61	Richmond, VA	DOD	(JR=9/13/61)	ROH,JR,SA2,KEB
Meener, D.D. (Munn?)	Pvt.	G	7th SCVIBn	36	KW	/ /	Richmond, VA	DOW	(Wdd Pbg. 6/17/64)	ROH,HIC
Meger, Thomas	Pvt.					02/11/65	Richmond, VA			ROH
Meggs, Stephen	Pvt.	D	7th SCVIBn	49	KW	07/11/63	Bty. Wagner, SC	KIA	(ROH & JR=Co.G.)	ROH,JR,HAG,HIC
Meggs, William	Pvt.	H	Orr's Ri.		MN	06/14/62	Farmville, VA	DOD	(Typhoid Pneumonia)	ROH,JR,HMC
Mehrton, George	Pvt.	I	3rd SCVI		LS	01/06/63	Richmond, VA	DOD		ROH,SA2,KEB
Meitzler, William	Pvt.		Ham.Leg.		CN	12/07/61	Bacon Race, VA	DOD		ROH
Mellett, M.M.	Pvt.	H	26th SCVI		SR	09/16/63	Charleston, SC	DOD	Magnolia Cem. Charleston	ROH,RCD
Mellichamp, Edward Henry	Pvt.		Eng. Corps.	45	CN	05/25/65	Pt. Lookout, MD	DIP	(Savannah, GA post)	ROH,FPH
Mellichamp, James Manly	Pvt.	A	25th SCVI	28	CN	02/12/65	Elmira, NY	DIP	Woodlawn N.C.#2052 Elmira	ROH,FPH,HAG,P6
Mellichamp, William S.	Pvt.	A	27th SCVI	26	CN	03/02/64	Charleston, SC	DOD	Circular Church Charleston	ROH,MAG,CDC,HA
Melton, B.A.	Pvt.		Inglis LA		DN	12/30/63	At home	DOD		ROH
Melton, C.W.	Pvt.	B	8th SCVI		CD	10/15/61	Orange C.H., VA	DOD	(Typhoid)	JR
Melton, J.A.	Pvt.	H	7th SCVI			09/03/63	Richmond, VA	DOD	Hollywood Cem. Rchmd. T412	ROH,HC

M

SOUTH CAROLINA DEAD IN CSA SERVICE 1861-1865

NAME	RANK	C	REGIMENT	AGE	DS	DIED	WHERE	WHY	BURIED	SOURCES
Melton, J.B.	Pvt.	A	5th SCVI		DN	06/09/64	Petersburg, VA	KIA		JR,SA3,LAN,WAT
Melton, Jesse	Pvt.	H	24th SCVI	40	CR	09/24/63	Atlanta, GA	KIA		ROH,HHC,CB
Melton, Samuel	Pvt.	I	1st SCVC		CO	01/06/64	Charleston, SC	DOD		ROH
Melton, W.D.M.	Pvt.	G	21st SCVI		CD	10/10/64	Elmira, NY	DIP	Woodlawn N.C.#690 Elmira	FPH,P5,P65,P120
Mendelsohn, Mendel	1st Sgt.		10th SCVI			09/20/63	Chickamauga, GA	KIA		ROH
Menig, William	Pvt.	H	12th SCVI		YK	/ /	Richmond, VA			ROH
Menniken, J.A.	Pvt.	F	20th SCVI	19	OG	05/14/62	At home	DOD	(age 19Y6M24D)	CNM
Mentley, James (Mobley?)	Pvt.	H	6th SCVI			/ /	Richmond, VA		Oakwood C.#15,Row R,Div C	ROH,OWC
Menude, John A.	Cpl.	I	27th SCVI	18	CN	10/21/64	Pt. Lookout, MD	DIP		ROH,HAG,CDC,P113
Merce, Thomas Daniel	Cpl.	B	23rd SCVI	24	CN	03/25/63	Richmond, VA	DOD		ROH
Mercer, J.B.	Pvt.	C	21st SCVI			02/01/64	Pt. Lookout, MD	DIP		ROH
Merchant, Edgar D.	Pvt.	B	14th SCVI	18	ED	01/01/62	Port Royal, SC	KIA	(JR=Marchant, DOW 6/10/62)	JR,HOE,UD3
Meree, G.W.	Pvt.	D	6th SCVI	27		02/18/63	Adams Run, SC	DOD	(Meares?)	PP
Meret, Lewis R.	Pvt.	C	2nd SCVI		RD	07/09/63	Gettysburg, PA	DOW	P1	ROH,JR,GDR,SA2
Merit, Henry	Pvt.	B	6th SCVI	50	YK	10/07/64	Petersburg, VA	KIA	(YEB=Darbytown Rd.)	ROH,JR,YEB
Merit, R.	Pvt.		SCVA			08/11/62	Ft. Sumter, SC		Magnolia Cem. Charleston	RCD
Meritt, George B.	Pvt.	F	P.S.S.	18	LN	05/08/64	Wilderness, VA	DOW	Hollywood Cem.Rchmd. U343	ROH,JR,HC
Meriweather, Thos. N.	Cpl.	F				11/04/63	Kelly's Ford VA	DOD		UD2
Meross, J.M.	Pvt.					06/16/64	Richmond, VA			ROH
Merrett, T.M.	Pvt.	L	Orr's Ri.		AN	12/16/62	Fredericksburg	DOW		JR,CDC
Merriman, Burrell	Pvt.	E	21st SCVI		CD	08/02/62	Richmond, VA			ROH,HAG
Merrit, Robert N.	Cpl.	E	17th SCVI	22	YK	07/30/64	Crater, Pbg., VA	KIA		JR,BLM,YEB
Merrit, William Harvey	Pvt.	H	18th SCVI		YK	05/20/64	Clay's Farm, VA	KIA	(YEB=E, 17th SCVI)	ROH,JR,YEB
Merritt, M.A.	Pvt.	K	22nd SCVI		PS	07/22/64	Richmond, VA		Hollywood Cem.Rchmd. V297	ROH,HC
Merritt, Wiley	Pvt.	B	P.S.S.		PS	10/28/63	Lookout Valley	KIA	(JR=Racoon Mtn., TN)	ROH,JR,CDC
Merritt, William B.	Sgt.		Marion LA		CN	05/11/62	Charleston, SC		1st Baptist Ch, Charleston	JR,MAG
Merritt, William Henry	5th Sgt.	B	6th SCVI	23	YK	12/10/64	New Market Hts.	KIA		ROH,YEB
Merriwether, William N.	Pvt.	F	2nd SCVI	21	AE	04/18/62	Charlottesville	DOD	(Typhoid)	ROH,JR,SA2,H2
Messer, L.H.	Color Sgt.	B	P.S.S.		PS	08/30/62	2nd Manassas, VA	KIA		ROH,JR,CDC
Metts, Edward	Pvt.	C	20th SCVI		LN	09/21/64	Mt. Pleasant, SC	DOD		ROH,KEB
Metts, John	Pvt.	H	11th SCVI		CO	12/11/61	Hardeeville, SC	DOD	(JR=25th SCVI)	ROH,JR,HAG
Metts, John T.	Pvt.	C	20th SCVI	40	LN	09/21/64	Mt. Pleasant, SC	DOD		ROH,KEB
Metts, L.	Pvt.		1st SC			09/17/62	Sharpsburg, MD	KIA		ROH,CDC
Metts, Thomas M.	Pvt.	H	11th SCVI		CO	12/30/61	Hardeeville, SC	DOD	(JR=12/30/62)	ROH,JR,HAG
Metts, William	Pvt.	C	24th SCVI		CO	05/01/63	Columbia, SC	DOD		EJM,PP
Metzells, Joseph S.	Pvt.	B	11th SCVI		CN	06/17/64	Richmond, VA		Hollywood Cem.Rchmd. U669	HC,HAG
Mew, Alexander C.	3rd Sgt.	E	11th SCVI		BT	08/21/64	Welden RR, VA	KIA		ROH,HAG
Meyer, Claus	Pvt.	B	1st SCVA		CN	11/07/61	Port Royal, SC	KIA	(German Artillery)	ROH,JR,CDC
Meyer, H.	Pvt.	B	1st SCVA		CN	06/29/62		DOD		JR
Meyer, J.H.	Pvt.	F	1st SCVA			05/03/65	Hart's Island NY	DIP	Cypress Hills N.C.#2682 NY	FPH,P6,P79
Meyer, Peter O.	Pvt.	C	1st SCVIH		BL	05/24/63	Carrsville, VA	DOW	(wdd 5/12/64)	ROH,SA1
Meyerhoff, B.	Lt.	B	1st SCVA			11/07/61	Port Royal, SC	KIA	(German Artillery)	ROH,JR,CDC
Meyers, George W.	Sgt.	B	15th SCVI	21	UN	06/17/64	At home	DOD		ROH,KEB
Meyers, Joseph	Pvt.	D	8th SCVI	24	CD	03/07/65	Camp Chase, OH	DIP	C.C.#1589 Columbus, OH	ROH,FPH,KEB
Meyers, Washington	Pvt.	K	7th SCVC	40	KW	12/18/62		DOD		HIC,CDN,HIC
Michel, D.E.	Cpl.	B	18th SCVI		UN	08/30/62	2nd Manassas, VA	KIA		ROH,CDC
Michel, G.A.	Pvt.	I	1st SCVA			03/28/64	Charleston, SC	DOD	Magnolia Cem. Charleston	ROH,MAG,RCD
Michel, Lloyd	Pvt.	C	1st SCVC		BL	06/15/64	Staunton, VA	DOD		ROH
Michell,	Pvt.	A	18th SCVI		UN	07/30/64	Crater, Pbg., VA	KIA		ROH
Mickell, Ephraim S.	Pvt.	I	3rd SCVC	37	CN	01/07/65	Charleston, SC	DOD	(Farrier)	ROH
Mickle, Joseph	Pvt.	G	7th SCVIBn	18	KW	06/10/64	Richmond, VA	DOW	(Wdd Cold Harbor 6/3/64)	ROH,HAG,HIC

SOUTH CAROLINA DEAD IN CSA SERVICE 1861-1865

NAME	RANK	C	REGIMENT	AGE	DS	DIED	WHERE	WHY	BURIED	SOURCES
Mickle, Samuel T.	Pvt.	A	17th SCVI	28	CR	07/20/65	At home	DOD	(DOD contracted in prison)	ROH,P120,HHC,C
Mickle, William T.	Pvt.	C	12th SCVI		FD	06/27/62	Gaines' Mill, VA	DOW	(JR=Mitchell, W.S.)	JR,HFC
Mickler, Huger	Cpl.	B	2nd SCVC		BL	/ /	Greenwood Ch. VA	KIA	Greenwood Ch. Cem. VA	AOA
Middleton, D.M.	Pvt.					07/21/63			Magnolia Cem. Charleston	RCD
Middleton, David J.	Pvt.	E	2nd SCVI		KW	/ /	Virginia	DOD	(1862)	SA2,HIC,KEB
Middleton, Edward B.	1st Lt.	H	1st SCVA	21	CN	03/16/65	Averysboro, NC	KIA		ROH,R44
Middleton, Francis K.	Pvt.	K	4th SCVC	28	CN	05/30/64	Hawes Shop, VA	KIA	Magnolia Cem. Charleston	ROH,MAG,CLD
Middleton, Henry A.	Pvt.	A	Ham.Leg.	31	GN	07/27/61	1st Manassas, VA	DOW	St. Philips Ch. Charleston	ROH,MAG,CDC
Middleton, J.	Pvt.	H	1st SCVIH		SG	01/01/63		DOD	(Sent from Fredericksburg)	ROH,SA1,JRH
Middleton, J. Henry	Pvt.	B	3rd SCVI		NY	09/21/63	Chickamauga, GA	DOW		ROH,JR,SA2,KEB
Middleton, Oliver Hering	Pvt.	K	4th SCVC		CN	05/31/64	Hawes Shop, VA	DOW	Magnolia Cem. Charleston	MAG,ROH,CLD
Middleton, W.E.	Pvt.	I	7th SCVI		ED	01/08/62	At home	DOD		EDN
Middleton,Sr., Thomas	1st Lt.	A	15th SCVAB	31	CN	01/30/64	Charleston, SC	DOD	Magnolia Cem. Charleston	ROH,MAG,R44
Milam, A.R.	Cpl.	B	3rd SCVIBn		LS	05/08/64	Spotsylvania, VA	KIA	Spotsylvania C.H., VA	ROH,JR,SCH,KEB
Milam, M.F.	Pvt.	A	3rd SCVI		LS	09/20/63	Chickamauga, GA	KIA	Con. Cem. Marietta, GA	ROH,SA2,KEB,CC
Milam, Madison B.	Pvt.	A	13th SCVI		LS	08/30/62	2nd Manassas, VA	KIA	(JR=8/29/62)	ROH,JR,CDC
Milam, R. Griffin		B	Orr's Ri.		AE	06/22/62		DOD	(Typhoid Pneumonia)	JR
Milam, W.H.	Pvt.	F	22nd SCVI		LS	02/23/65	Pt. Lookout, MD	DIP	C.C. Pt. Lookout, MD	ROH,FPH,P6,P11
Milam, William L.	Pvt.	F	14th SCVI	24	LS	07/01/62	Petersburg, VA	DOD	Blandford Church Pbg., VA	ROH,JR,BLC,PP
Milam, William M.	Pvt.	E	7th SCVC	35	LS	02/13/65	Pt. Lookout, MD	DIP	C.C. Pt. Lookout, MD P6	ROH,FPH,ANY,P1
Milan, John	Pvt.	B	3rd SCV			09/19/62	Richmond, VA		(Prob Milam, J.A. 3rd Bn.)	ROH
Milan, R.G.	Pvt.	B	Orr's Ri.		AE	08/29/62	2nd Manassas, VA	KIA		JR,CDC
Milbank, W.J.	Pvt.	K	12th SCVI		PS	04/19/65	Unknown	DIP	Cypress Hills N.C.#2560 NY	FPH
Miles, Albert	Pvt.	A	7th SCVI			06/30/62	Frayser's Farm	KIA	(JR=6/28/62)	ROH,JR,CDC,KEB
Miles, Allen	Pvt.	H	26th SCVI		SR	07/10/63		DOD		JR
Miles, Benjamin	Pvt.	I	26th SCVI		WG	11/06/63		DOD		JR
Miles, Francis	Pvt.	I	26th SCVI		WG	10/20/63	Columbia, SC	DOD		JR,PP
Miles, Francis Alexander	Pvt.	G	24th SCVI			02/09/65	Camp Chase, OH	DIP	(PP=Miles, A. Dd 4/24/93)	P23,P27
Miles, Henry B.	Pvt.	C	7th SCVIBn	18	RD	06/26/64	Richmond, VA	DOD	Hollywood Cem.Rchmd. U167	ROH,HC,HAG
Miles, Hezekiah	Pvt.	E	9th SCVIBn	22		03/03/62	Georgetown, SC	DOD	(PP=3/5/62)	JR,PP
Miles, J. Allen	Sgt.	K	4th SCVC	30	CN	05/28/64	Hawes Shop, VA	KIA		ROH,JR,CDC,CLD
Miles, J.A.	Pvt.		1st SCVA			02/01/65	Charleston, SC	DOD	Magnolia Cem. Charleston	ROH,MAG,RCD
Miles, J.J.	Pvt.	I	26th SCVI		WG	09/20/63		DOD		JR
Miles, J.R.	Pvt.	H	10th SCVI		WG	09/20/63	Chickamauga, GA	KIA		ROH,RAS,HOW,CD
Miles, Jesse	Cpl.	G	24th SCVI	25		07/22/64	Atlanta, GA	KIA		ROH,JR,CDC
Miles, N.J.	Pvt.	I	26th SCVI		WG	/ /	Petersburg, VA	DOW	(Between 6/17 & &/27,1864)	CDC
Miles, Newton T.	1st Sgt.	A	7th SCVI		ED	07/01/62	Malvern Hill, VA	KIA	(KEB=Smiles, N.G.)	ROH,JR,EDN,KEB
Miles, R.W.	Pvt.	I	26th SCVI		WG	10/10/63		DOD		JR
Miles, Septimus Charles	Pvt.	I	2nd SCVI		CN	07/02/63	Gettysburg, PA	KIA	Magnolia Cem. Charleston	ROH,JR,GDR,WV
Miles, Spias	Pvt.	H	10th SCVI		WG	06/15/64	Macon, GA	DOD	Rose Hill C. Macon, GA	RAS,HOW,PP,BGA
Miles, Stephen	Pvt.	H	7th SCVIBn	30	RD	05/19/64	Drury's Bluff VA	DOW		ROH,JR,HAG
Miles, Stephen	Pvt.	B	1st SCVIR		LR	07/10/63	Morris Island SC	KIA		SA1,CDC
Miles, T. Monroe	Pvt.	E	18th SCVI	23	SG	08/30/62	2nd Manassas, VA	KIA	(JR=T. Morris)	ROH,JR,HOS,CDC
Miles, Thomas	Cpl.	I	26th SCVI	34	WG	10/28/63	Columbia, SC	DOD	(PP=11/17/63)	ROH,HOW,PP
Miley, G.W.	Pvt.	E	24th SCVI	27	CO	07/20/63	Alabama	DOD		ROH
Miley, J.K.	Pvt.	E	24th SCVI	22	CO	09/01/64	Jonesboro, GA	KIA		ROH
Miley, Martin B.	Sgt.	F	11th SCVI		BT	06/27/64	Richmond, VA	DOD		ROH,HAG
Milford, A.J.	Pvt.	F	Orr's Ri.		PS	01/31/63	Richmond, VA	DOD	(JR=7/31/64)	ROH,JR,CDC
Milford, G.V.	Pvt.	F	12th SCVI			/ /	Lynchburg, VA		Lynchburg CSA Cem.#4 R3	BBW
Milford, H.F.	Pvt.	L	Orr's Ri.		AN	09/30/64	Weldon RR, VA	DOW		HR,CDC
Milford, J.W.	Pvt.	D	27th SCVI	38	AE	07/08/64	Petersburg, VA	DOW	Blandford Church Pbg., VA	ROH,HAG,BLC,PP

SOUTH CAROLINA DEAD IN CSA SERVICE 1861-1865

NAME	RANK	C REGIMENT	AGE	DS	DIED	WHERE	WHY	BURIED	SOURCES
Milford, James T.	Pvt.	F 2nd SCVI		AE	01/15/63	Lynchburg, VA	DOD		SA2,KEB,H2
Milford, L.C.	Pvt.	F 24th SCVI		AN	08/18/64	Forsyth, GA	DOW	Forsyth, GA	HOL,CKB
Milhous, Casper P.	Pvt.	K 1st SCVIH	19	BL	11/10/61	At home	DOD	(Fever from coast)	ROH,SA1
Milhous, J.C.	Pvt.	A 1st SCVIH	25	BL	01/10/63	Richmond, VA	DOD		ROH,SA1,JRH,UD3
Mill,	Pvt.	F 2nd SC Res			01/28/65	Columbia, SC	DOD	Elmwood Cem. Columbia, SC	MP,PP
Millen, John A.	2nd Lt.	H 24th SCVI		CR	12/30/64	Nashville, TN	DOW	(Wdd & POW @ Franklin)	ROH,P3,P6,HHC,PP
Millen, Samuel	Pvt.	A 6th SCVI	26	CR	05/30/62	7 Pines, VA	KIA	Fishing Creek P.C. CR Cty.	ROH,WDB,HHC,GLS
Miller,	Pvt.				01/01/62			Stonewall C. Winchester VA	ROH,WIN
Miller, A.J.	Pvt.	C 15th SCVAB		CN	05/19/65	Pt. Lookout, MD	DIP	C.C. Pt. Lookout, MD	FPH,P6,P115
Miller, Alexander Fraser	1st Lt.	H 1st SCVIG		CO	10/03/64	Jones Farm, VA	DOW	(Wdd 9/30/64 Pbg.)	ROH,SA1,BOS,R45
Miller, Andrew H.	Pvt.	K P.S.S.		SG	02/01/63	Richmond, VA	DOD		ROH,JR,HOS
Miller, B.	Pvt.	Macbeth LA			09/17/62	Sharpsburg, MD	DOW	(Boyce's Bty.)	ROH,JR,CDC
Miller, Barr Napoleon	Pvt.	Macbeth LA			09/19/62	Sharpsburg, MD	DOW		JR
Miller, Benjamin	Pvt.	A 18th SCVI		UN	08/25/63	Savannah, GA	DOD		JR
Miller, Benjamin F.	3rd Lt.	B Orr's Ri.	24	AE	05/12/64	Spotsylvania, VA	DOW	Old Rocky River P.C. AE	ROH,JR,CDC,CAE
Miller, C.L.	Pvt.	H 1st SC			10/02/64	Richmond, VA		Hollywood Cem.Rchmd. V22	HC
Miller, C.W.	Pvt.	I Ham.Leg.			12/07/63	Camp Morton, IN	DIP	Green Lawn C. Indianapolis	FPH,P5,CV
Miller, Calis C.	Pvt.	A 18th SCVI		UN	08/10/62	Richmond, VA	DOD	Hollywood Cem.Rchmd. Q93	ROH,JR,HC
Miller, E.	Pvt.	F 10th SCVI		MN	/ /		MIA	(? missing from camp)	HMC,RAS
Miller, E.P.	Lt.				12/11/63	Fredericksburg	KIA		UD2
Miller, F.	Pvt.	H 25th SCVI		CN	09/15/63	Bty. Wagner, SC	KIA	(Mullins, F.?)	ROH,JR,CDC
Miller, F.P.	Pvt.	B 3rd SCVIBn		LS	07/02/63	Gettysburg, PA	KIA	(Miller, W.P. in KEB?)	CDC
Miller, G.W.	Cpl.	C 2nd SCVA			04/07/65	Charlotte, NC			PP
Miller, George T.	Pvt.	E 12th SCVI	21	LR	05/05/64	Wilderness, VA	KIA		ROH,LAN
Miller, Harry C.	Pvt.	A 3rd SCVI	19	AN	10/19/64	Cedar Creek, VA	KIA	St. Paul's E.C. Pendleton	ROH,JR,SA2,ACC
Miller, Henry	Pvt.	PeeDee LA		DN	12/13/62	Fredericksburg	KIA	(Wdd twice before)	PDL
Miller, Henry	Pvt.		46	LS	03/03/64			Liberty Springs P.C. LS	LSC
Miller, I.J.	Pvt.	I 18th SCVI	32	DN	11/15/64	Florence, SC	DOD		ROH
Miller, Isaac		SCV			/ /	(1862)		Nat. Cem. Hampton, VA	PP,TOD
Miller, J.A.	Pvt.	E 2nd SCVI		NY	05/11/63	Richmond, VA	DOD	(Detached to pioneers)	ROH,SA2,HIC,KEB
Miller, J.A.	Pvt.	G 5th SCVI		YK	12/19/62	Richmond, VA	DOD	Oakwood C.#121,Row M,Div A	ROH,SA3,OWC
Miller, J.C.					07/20/62	Richmond, VA			ROH
Miller, J.F.	Pvt.	H 12th SCVI	21	YK	06/27/62	Gaines' Mill, VA	DOW		JR,YEB,CNM
Miller, J.R.	Pvt.	K 13th SCVI		LN	07/01/63	Gettysburg, PA	KIA		ROH,LGS
Miller, J.T.	Pvt.	C 4th SCVC		PS	/ /	Richmond, VA		Oakwood C.#125,Row D,Div G	ROH,OWC
Miller, James B.	Pvt.	A 20th SCVI		PS	03/07/65	Charlotte, NC		(ROH=Co.B)	ROH,PP
Miller, James Boyce	Pvt.	F 12th SCVI	23	FD	08/30/62	2nd Manassas, VA	KIA	(JR=8/28/62)	ROH,JR,HFC
Miller, James P.	2nd Sgt.	B 6th SCVI		YK	05/06/64	Wilderness, VA	KIA	(Also wdd @ 7 Pines)	ROH,JR,CDC
Miller, Jesse	Cpl.	I P.S.S.		PS	06/30/62	Frayser's Fm. VA	KIA		JR,CDC
Miller, Joel	Pvt.	M 7th SCVI		ED	07/08/63	Gettysburg, PA	DOW	Magnolia Cem. Charleston	ROH,GDR,HOE
Miller, John	Pvt.	G 26th SCVI	30	AN	01/27/65	Elmira, NY	DIP	Woodlawn N.C.#1648 Elmira	ROH,FPH,P5,P120
Miller, John	Pvt.	C 26th SCVI		MN	10/01/62		DOD		JR
Miller, John	Pvt.	G 5th SCVC		YK	07/10/63	At home	DOD	(Dropsy of brain)	JR
Miller, John Alexander	2nd Lt.	F 26th SCVI	21	CD	08/23/63	Lauderdale Ss MS	DOD		ROH,JR,R48,PP
Miller, John Lucas	Colonel	12th SCVI		YK	05/06/64	Wilderness, VA	DOW	Hollywood Cem.Rchmd. X106	ROH,JR,HC,YEB
Miller, John R.	Cpl.	D 22nd SCVI		PS	10/18/64	Petersburg, VA	KIA		ROH,PP
Miller, Joseph H.	Pvt.	F 23rd SCVI		CR	07/30/64	Crater, Pbg., VA	KIA		JR,BLM,HHC
Miller, Joseph T.	Pvt.	F 20th SCVI		NY	06/12/64	Gaines' Mill, VA	DOW		ANY,KEB
Miller, L.W.	Cpl.	L 10th SCVI		MN	/ /	SC	DOD	(On March GN-CN Spring'62)	RAS,HMC
Miller, P.B.	Pvt.	B 1st SCVC		SG	/ /	At home	DOD		HOS
Miller, Paul Gervais	Pvt.	I 2nd SCVI	16	CN	12/19/61	Warrenton, VA	DOD	(Palmetto Guards)	SA2,KEB,CNM

SOUTH CAROLINA DEAD IN CSA SERVICE 1861-1865

NAME	RANK	C REGIMENT	AGE	DS	DIED	WHERE	WHY	BURIED	SOURCES
Miller, Pink	Pvt.	B Orr's Ri.	31	SG	/ /	At home	DOD	(1862)	ROH
Miller, Robert M.	Pvt.	B 24th SCVI	27	CN	10/08/63	Atlanta, GA	DOW	Oakland C. Atlanta R32#7	BGA
Miller, Robert P.	2nd Lt.	K P.S.S.		SG	11/16/63	Campbell Stn. TN	KIA		ROH,JR,HOS,R48
Miller, S.D.	Pvt.	G 1st SCVIH		BL	09/26/63	Chattanooga, TN	DOW		ROH,SA1,JRH
Miller, Samuel	Pvt.	A 6th SCVI		CR	05/31/62	7 Pines, VA	KIA		JR,CDC,HHC
Miller, Samuel W.	Pvt.	K P.S.S.	23	SG	06/30/62	Frayser's Farm	KIA	Nazareth P.C. SG Cty.	ROH,JR,HOS,GEC
Miller, T.M.	Pvt.			WG	/ /		DOD	(1862)	CTA
Miller, Tado	Pvt.	I Hol.Leg.	32	SG	11/27/63	Mt. Pleasant, SC	DOD	(HOS= Dado)	ROH,HOS
Miller, Thomas A.	Pvt.	F Orr's Ri.		PS	02/14/62	At home	DOD		JR,CDC
Miller, Thomas H.	Pvt.	B 14th SCVI	18	ED	07/02/63	Gettysburg, PA	KIA		HOE,UD3
Miller, Thomas McConnell	Cpt.	E 10th SCVI	23	WG	07/07/62	Tupelo, MS	DOD	(JR=Pneumonia 7/10/62)	ROH,JR,RAS
Miller, W.J.	Pvt.	H 12th SCVI		YK	06/27/62	Gaines' Mill, VA	KIA		CDC
Miller, W.L.	Pvt.	A 2nd SCVI		RD	06/15/61	Charlottesville	DOD	Univ. Cem. Charlottesville	ACH,SA2,KEB
Miller, W.W.	Pvt.	I 17th SCVI		LR	/ /	Petersburg, VA	KIA		LAN
Miller, Wiley	Pvt.	C 19th SCVI		ED	02/04/63	Charleston, SC	DOD	(7th SCVI also given)	HOE,UD3
Miller, William	Cpl.	I 6th SCVI	28	FD	10/22/61	Culpepper, VA	DOD	Fairview Cem. Culpepper VA	CGH
Miller, William D.L.	2nd Cpl.	B 14th SCVI	21	ED	07/28/64	Deep Bottom, VA	KIA		HOE,UD3
Miller, William Hamilton	Pvt.	A Hol.Leg.	46	SG	09/17/62	Sharpsburg, MD	DOW	Nazareth P.C. SG Cty.	GEC,GEE,HOS
Miller, William P.	Pvt.	B 3rd SCVIBn		LS	07/02/63	Gettysburg, PA	KIA	(JR=W.B.)	JR,GDR,KEB
Miller, William R.	Pvt.	C Hol.Leg.		SG	09/14/62	South Mtn., MD	DOW	(Wdd & POW)	HOS
Millford, Cador Gantt	Pvt.	C 4th SCVIBn		AN	05/05/62	Eltham's Ldg. VA	KIA		ROH,SA2,CNM
Milligan, Joseph	Pvt.	F 1st SCVIG		HY	08/29/62	2nd Manassas, VA	KIA		ROH,JR,PDL,SA1
Milligan, Joseph B.	Pvt.	F 1st SCVIG		HY	07/03/63	Gettysburg, PA	KIA		ROH,JR,GDR,PDL
Milligan, R.J.	Pvt.	D Orr's Ri.		AN	08/29/62	2nd Manassas, VA	KIA		JR
Millikin, S.W.	2nd Cpl.	G 22nd SCVI		AN	07/30/64	Crater, Pbg., VA	KIA		BLM
Millikin, William	Pvt.	I 4th SCV			10/15/62	Georgetown, SC	DOD	(Prob B, 12th SCVCBn WG)	JR
Milling, J.R.	Pvt.	A 2nd SCVC		FD	10/19/64	Columbia, SC	DOD		ROH,PP
Milling, John McK.	Pvt.	F 6th SCVC	39	FD	06/11/64	Trevillian Stn.	KIA		ROH,JR,CAG
Milling, John R.	1st Lt.	G 6th SCVI		FD	10/02/64		DOW		R46
Milling, W.A.	Sgt.	G 6th SCVI		FD	05/31/62	7 Pines, VA	DOW		CDC,HFC,WDB
Milling, W.D.	Pvt.	PeeDee LA		DN	/ /				ROH,PDL
Mills, Benjamin	Pvt.	F 11th SCVI	27	CO	06/06/64	Cold Harbor, VA	KIA	(JR=8/ /64)	ROH,JR,HAG
Mills, Benjamin	Pvt.	F 7th SCVIBn		KW	06/15/64		DOW		JR
Mills, Edmund James	Pvt.	I 2nd SCVI	21	CN	07/02/63	Gettysburg, PA	KIA	Magnolia Cem. Charleston	ROH,JR,GDR,WV
Mills, H. Edmund	Pvt.	G 1st SCVIG		ED	05/15/64	Wilderness, VA	DOW	(Wdd 5/5/64 exact DoD UK)	ROH,SA1,HOE
Mills, J.A.	Pvt.	F P.S.S.			/ /		DOW	(Miles?)	JR
Mills, J.S. (J.C.?)	Pvt.	G 14th SCVI	25	AE	08/01/62	Richmond, VA	DOD	Oakwood C.#40, Row S,Div C	ROH,JR,OWC
Mills, James S.	Pvt.	K 19th SCVI	46	ED	/ /		DOD	(1864)	ROH,HOE
Mills, John B.	Pvt.	D 4th SCVC		CN	05/03/63		DOD		ROH,JR
Mills, John I.	Pvt.		19		05/03/63	McClellanville	DOD		ROH
Mills, Luther	Pvt.	K 19th SCVI	21	ED	/ /		DOD		HOE
Mills, Simeon M.	Pvt.	H 7th SCVI		ED	09/21/61	Culpepper, VA	DOD	Fairview Cem. Culpepper VA	ROH,CGH
Mills, Thomas	Pvt.	E 13th SCVI		SG	/ /	Virginia	KIA		HOS
Mills, Wade	Pvt.	K 2nd SCVA		ED	09/18/63	Bty Haskell, SC	KIA	(Burst gun)	STR,MOE,DOC,UD
Mills, William	Pvt.	A 1st SCVIG		BL	05/05/64	Lynchburg, VA	DOW	Lynchburg CSA C.#4 R4	ROH,SA1,CDC,BB
Mills, William	Pvt.	K 2nd SCVA		ED	/ /		DOD		HOE,UD3
Mills, William J.	Pvt.	I 26th SCVI	43	WG	06/15/64	Petersburg, VA	KIA	(Also listed as Miles)	CTA,HOW
Millson, John	Pvt.	L P.S.S.			/ /		DOD		JR
Millwee, John	Pvt.	J 4th SCVI		AN	11/29/61	Centreville, VA	DOD		ROH,SA2
Millwood, Edward B.	Pvt.	H 15th SCVI		UN	07/02/63	Gettysburg, PA	KIA		ROH,JR,GDR,KEB
Millwood, James E.	Pvt.	H 5th SCVI		UN	07/15/62	Gaines' Mill, VA	DOW	(Died in Manchester, VA)	JR,SA3

SOUTH CAROLINA DEAD IN CSA SERVICE 1861-1865

NAME	RANK	C	REGIMENT	AGE	DS	DIED	WHERE	WHY	BURIED	SOURCES
Millwood, Tilman	Pvt.	D	Ham.Leg.		UN	/ /	Richmond, VA			ROH
Milps, A.S.	Pvt.		1st SC			/ /	Richmond, VA		Oakwood C.#43,Row D,Div E	ROH,OWC
Milton, J.	Pvt.	G	2nd SCVIRi			06/03/62	Richmond, VA		Hollywood Cem.Rchmd. M364	ROH,HC,
Milton, W.M.	Pvt.	G	6th SCVI			06/05/62	Richmond, VA		Hollywood Cem.Rchmd. M404	ROH,HC
Mims,	Sgt.	A	7th SCVI			07/02/63	Gettysburg, PA	KIA		JR,CDC
Mims, A. Pinckney	Pvt.	G	11th SCVI		CO	05/09/64	Swift Creek, VA	KIA		ROH,JR,HAG
Mims, C.P.	Pvt.	A	18th SCVI		UN	09/10/64	Pt. Lookout, MD	DIP	C.C. Pt. Lookout, MD	ROH,FPH,P6
Mims, David	Pvt.	G	11th SCVI		CN	12/15/61	At home	DOD		ROH,HAG
Mims, J.A.	Pvt.	K	21st SCVI		DN	07/08/62	At home	DOD		JR
Mims, J.W.	Pvt.	A	14th SCVI	25	DN	03/02/64	Orange C.H., VA	DOD	(Also Wdd @ Gaines' Mill)	ROH,CNM
Mims, Josiah S.	Pvt.	G	11th SCVI		CN	07/30/64	Kittrell Spgs NC	DOD	Kittrell Springs, NC Cem.	ROH,CV,HAG,WAT
Mims, M.D.	Pvt.	A	7th SCV			/ /	Richmond, VA		(W.P. in KEB?)	ROH
Mims, R.A.	Pvt.	I	23rd SCVI		CL	07/30/64	Crater, Pbg., VA	KIA		BLM,ROH,HCL
Mims, R.M.	Pvt.	A	1st SCVIG		BL	08/12/62	At home	DOD	(Typhoid)	JR,SA1
Mims, Robert E.	Pvt.	K	10th SCVI		CN	02/02/61	Georgetown, SC	DOD		JR,RAS
Mims, Robert L.	Pvt.	A	7th SCVI	22	ED	07/02/63	Gettysburg, PA	KIA		ROH,GDR,KEB
Mims, S.J.	Pvt.	K	21st SCVI		DN	05/07/63	Columbia, SC	DOD		JR,PP
Mims, Samuel P.	2nd Lt.	A	16th SCVI		GE	05/16/64	Calhoun, GA	KIA	(R47= 5/20/64)	ROH,16R,R47
Mims, Thomas E.	Pvt.	K	10th SCVI		CN	01/15/63	Georgia	DOD		JR,RAS
Mims, W.	Pvt.	E	7th SCVIBn		SR	03/08/63	At home	DOD		JR
Mims, W.D.	Pvt.	A	7th SCVI			07/01/62	Malvern Hill, VA	DOW		CNM
Mims, Washington	Pvt.	H	1st SCVIG		CN	12/15/64	At home	DOD		ROH,SA1
Mims, William E.	Pvt.	K	10th SCVI		CN	01/15/63	Dalton, GA	DOD		JR,RAS
Mince, Drayton	Pvt.	C	17th SCVI		YK	09/14/62	South Mtn., MD	KIA		JR,CB
Mincey, M.						/ /			(Richmd.effects list 1/63)	CDC
Mincy, Alva	Pvt.	G	9th SCVIBn	21	HY	03/08/62	Camp Lookout, SC	DOD		ROH,PP
Mincy, B.	Pvt.	C	10th SCVI		HY	/ /		DOD		RAS
Mincy, Eli A.	Pvt.	K	26th SCVI		HY	02/11/65	Petersburg, VA	KIA		ROH,PP
Mincy, Frederick	Pvt.	F	1st SCVIG		HY	06/11/63	At home	DOD	(Wdd @ Sharpsburg)	PDL
Mincy, Hugh J.	Pvt.	F	1st SCVIG	25	HY	10/09/61	Suffolk, VA	DOD		JR,SA1
Mincy, Isaac	Pvt.	C	10th SCVI		HY	11/06/62	Knoxville, TN	DOD	Bethel C. Knoxville, TN	RAS,TOD
Mincy, N.B.	Pvt.	K	26th SCVI	37	HY	08/17/64	Petersburg, VA	DOD	Blandford Church Pbg., VA	ROH,BLC
Mincy, William	Pvt.	F	1st SCVIG	18	HY	08/26/62	Richmond, VA	DOD	Hollywood Cem.Rchmd. H118	ROH,JR,HC,PDL
Miner, Robert S.	Pvt.	H	7th SCVIBn	37	ED	05/27/64	Richmond, VA	DOW	(Wdd Drury's Bluff 5/16)	ROH,HAG
Miniard, Thomas	Pvt.	A	3rd SCVI		LS	11/18/63	Knoxville, TN	KIA		ROH,SA2
Minor, Ransom	Pvt.	K	7th SCVI		ED	08/26/64	Charlestown, VA	KIA		ROH
Minsall, R.H.	Pvt.	F	2nd SC			12/12/63	(?Mancil, R.J.)		Hollywood Cem.Rchmd. I178	HC
Minter, John	Pvt.	K	17th SCVI		YK	08/21/64	Crater, Pbg., VA	DOW		ROH,JR,BLM
Minter, W. Jesse	Pvt.	E	5th SCVI	22	YK	10/28/63	Lookout Valley	KIA	(JR=Racoon Mtn., TN) UD3	ROH,JR,SA3,YEB
Minton, Columbus	Pvt.	D	15th SCVI		KW	07/02/63	Gettysburg, PA	KIA		ROH,JR,HIC,GDR
Minton, F.M.	Pvt.	K	22nd SCVI		PS	07/30/64	Crater, Pbg., VA	KIA		BLM
Minton, John B.	Pvt.	D	15th SCVI		KW	07/03/63	Gettysburg, PA	KIA		HIC,KEB
Mishoe, S.C.	Pvt.	C	10th SCVI		HY	/ /		DOD		RAS
Miskelly, DeKalb	Pvt.	K	17th SCVI	29	YK	08/30/62	2nd Manassas, VA	KIA		YEB
Miskelly, J.W.	Pvt.	C	27th SCVI		CN	05/20/64	Petersburg, VA	DOW		ROH,HAG
Miskelly, James D.	Pvt.	D	6th SCVI		YK	03/04/64	Nashville, TN	DOW	(Wdd & POW @ L.O. Mtn.)	P2
Missola, J.	Pvt.	B	11th SCVI		CO	07/17/64	Petersburg, VA	DOW	(HAG=Mizzles)	JR,HAG
Missola, John	Pvt.	K	10th SCVI		WG	12/31/62	Murfreesboro, TN	KIA		ROH,JR,RAS,HOW
Mitcham, Andrew J.	Pvt.	G	18th SCVI	31	YK	07/30/64	Crater Pbg., VA	KIA		YEB
Mitcham, H.	Pvt.	K	25th SCVI		WG	07/09/63	James Island, SC	DOD		JR
Mitchel, John C.	Cpt.	I	1st SCVA		CN	07/20/64	Ft. Sumter, SC	KIA		SCA

SOUTH CAROLINA DEAD IN CSA SERVICE 1861-1865

NAME	RANK	C REGIMENT	AGE	DS	DIED	WHERE	WHY	BURIED	SOURCES
Mitchell, Aaron A.	Pvt.	L Orr's Ri.		AN	06/27/62	Gaines' Mill, VA	KIA	(JR=DOD 10/ /62)	ROH,JR
Mitchell, B.B.	Pvt.	A 7th SCVI			/ /	Lynchburg, VA		Lynchburg CSA Cem.#10 R2	BBW
Mitchell, B.L.O.	Pvt.	D Orr's Ri.		AN	08/23/62	Richmond, VA			ROH,CDC
Mitchell, D.E.	Cpl.	B 18th SCVI		UN	08/30/62	2nd Manassas, VA	KIA		JR,CDC
Mitchell, David H.	Pvt.	Brooks GA			07/03/63	Gettysburg, PA	KIA		ROH,JR,GDR,H2
Mitchell, E. Marshall	Pvt.	F 24th SCVI	30	AN	04/04/63	Ballouville, SC	DOD	Ballouville, SC	HOL
Mitchell, Edward	Sgt.	E 7th SCVI		ED	/ /		KIA		HOE,KEB,UD3
Mitchell, Elias T.	2nd Cpl.	I 5th SCVI		SG	11/16/63	Campbell's Stn.	KIA		HOS,SA3
Mitchell, G.F.	Pvt.	I 1st SCVIR		AN	11/07/64	Charleston, SC	DOD	Magnolia Cem. Charleston	ROH,MAG,SA1
Mitchell, George W.	Pvt.	K Orr's Ri.	20	AN	09/07/64	Elmira, NY	DIP	Woodlawn N.C.#213 Elmira	ROH,FPH,P5,P12
Mitchell, H.H.	Sgt.	K P.S.S.		SG	08/30/62	2nd Manassas, VA	DOW		CDC
Mitchell, Hezekiah W.	Pvt.	G 22nd SCVI	32	AN	07/30/64	Crater, Pbg., VA	KIA		ROH,BLM
Mitchell, J. Thomas	Pvt.	E 17th SCVI	18	YK	03/15/62	Johns Island, SC	DOD		ROH,JR,YEB
Mitchell, J.H.	Pvt.	I 5th SCVI		SG	06/30/62	Frayser's Farm	KIA		JR,SA3
Mitchell, J.J.	Pvt.	I 9th SCVIB		SG	09/18/61	Manassas, VA	DOD	(JR=Warrenton Springs, VA)	ROH,JR,HOS
Mitchell, J.M.	Pvt.	A 18th SCVI		UN	07/30/64	Crater, Pbg., VA	KIA		BLM
Mitchell, J.R.	Pvt.	E 17th SCVI	21	YK	03/15/62	At home	DOD		ROH
Mitchell, James M.	Pvt.	D Orr's Ri.		AN	01/25/65	Ft. Delaware, DE	DIP	Finn's Pt., NJ Nat. Cem.	ROH,FPH,P5,CDC
Mitchell, James T.	Pvt.	K Orr's Ri.	22	AN	06/27/62	Gaines' Mill, VA	KIA		ROH,JR
Mitchell, John C.	Cpt.	I 1st SCVA	25	CN	07/20/64	Ft. Sumter, SC	KIA	Magnolia Cem. Charleston	ROH,DOC,RCD,R4
Mitchell, John W.T.	Pvt.	K Orr's Ri.	20	AN	06/27/62	Gaines' Mill, VA	KIA	(JR=DOD 10/ /62)	ROH,JR,CDC
Mitchell, L.L.	Pvt.	C 1st SCVC		ED	03/26/63	Staunton, VA		Thornrose C. Staunton, VA	ROH,TOD
Mitchell, Leonidas W.	Pvt.	H 18th SCVI		YK	05/20/64	Clay's Farm, VA	KIA		ROH,JR
Mitchell, Michael	Pvt.	K 1st SCVIG		CN	01/15/64		MUR	(Killed by Pvt Pat Morris)	SA1
Mitchell, Paul M.	Pvt.	E 7th SCVI		ED	07/02/63	Gettysburg, PA	KIA		ROH,GDR,HOE,UD
Mitchell, R.S.	Pvt.	A 19th SCVI			07/02/64	Med. C. Atlanta		Oakland C. Atlanta R16#5	BGA
Mitchell, Reuben	1st Cpl.	K 2nd SCVIRi	26	PS	06/27/63	Suffolk, VA	MUR	(Hung by the enemy)	ROH
Mitchell, W.P. (W.B.?)	Pvt.	A 1st SCVIG		BL	10/16/62	Lynchburg, VA	DOD	Lynchburg CSA Cem.#2 R4	ROH,JR,SA1,BBW
Mitchell, William A.	Pvt.	A 19th SCVI	16	ED	12/31/62	Murfreesboro, TN	KIA		HOE,UD3
Mitchell, William R.	Pvt.	E 17th SCVI	22	YK	/ /	John's Island SC	DOD	(1862)	JR,DEM,YEB
Mitchum, C.H.	Pvt.	K 25th SCVI		WG	04/25/63	Clarendon, SC	DOD		JR,CTA,HOW
Mitchum, Sylvester S.	Sgt.	C 25th SCVI	38	WG	03/06/65	Richmond, VA	DOD	Oakwood C.#28, Row L, Div G	HOW,HAG,OWC,P6
Mix, E.M.	Pvt.	F 22nd SCVI		PS	12/13/63	Charleston, SC		Magnolia Cem. Charleston	ROH,MAG,RCD
Mixon, Anthony W.	Pvt.	I 25th SCVI		CL	02/14/65	Elmira, NY	DIP	Woodlawn N.C.#2185 Elmira	FPH,HAG,P6,P65
Mixon, D.V.	Pvt.	K 10th SCVI		CN	/ /		DOD		RAS
Mixon, John S. (James?)	Pvt.	A 7th SCVIBn	27	KW	05/20/64	Drury's Bluff VA	DOW	Hollywood Cem.Rchmd. I160	ROH,HIC,HAG,HC
Mixon, L. Simeon	Pvt.	A 7th SCVIBn	19	KW	02/10/62	Adams Run, SC	DOD	(JR=T.S.)	ROH,JR,HIC,HAG
Mixon, M.	Pvt.	K 10th SCVI		CN	/ /		DOD		RAS
Mixson, John A.	Pvt.	F 11th SCVI	46	BT	06/15/64	Petersburg, VA	DOD	Blandford Church Pbg., VA	ROH,BLC,HAG,PP
Mize, James	Pvt.	C 2nd SCVI		RD	01/01/62	Winchester, VA	DOD	Stonewall C. Winchester VA	WIN,SA2,H2
Mizell, Randolph	Pvt.	D 17th SCVI	18	CR	08/21/64	Petersburg, VA			PP
Moates, Jefferson L.	Pvt.	B 3rd SCVI		NY	12/01/63	Richmond, VA	DOD	(ANY= Winchester)	ROH,JR,SA2,ANY
Mobley, A.	Pvt.	6th SC Res			02/10/65	Charleston, SC	DOD	Magnolia Cem. Charleston	ROH,MAG,RCD
Mobley, Edward Isaiah	Sgt.	B 4th SCVC	17	CR	02/02/63	Hardeeville, SC	DOD	(Measles)	ROH,JR,HHC
Mobley, Edwin R.	5th Sgt.	K 14th SCVI		ED	07/02/63	Gettysburg, PA	KIA	(JR=K, 13th SCVI) UD2	ROH,JR,HOE,GDR
Mobley, G.W.	Pvt.	H 4th SCVC		LR	06/15/62	Camden, SC	DOD	(Wayside Hospital)	LAN
Mobley, Langdon Cheves	Pvt.	H 7th SCVI	61	ED	11/22/61	Charlottesville	DOD	(Typhoid Pneumonia)	ROH,JR,EDN
Mobley, Oliver R.	Pvt.	H 6th SCVI		FD	01/05/64	Morristown, TN	DOD	(JR=M, P.S.S.)	ROH,JR
Mobley, P.T.	Pvt.	G 3rd SCVABn		LR	02/15/65	Columbia, SC	DOD		ROH,LAN,PP
Mobley, Warren	Pvt.	B 9th SCVIB			08/25/61	Germantown, VA	DOD		JR
Mobly, Eldridge V.	Pvt.	I 2nd SCVC		ED	12/29/64	Wilmington, NC	KIA		ROH,HOE

M

SOUTH CAROLINA DEAD IN CSA SERVICE 1861-1865

NAME	RANK	C REGIMENT	AGE	DS	DIED	WHERE	WHY	BURIED	SOURCES
Mochatt, Joseph	Pvt.	L P.S.S.			/ /		DOD		JR
Mock, J.S. (J.F.?)	Pvt.	E 14th SCVI		LS	07/29/63	Chester, PA	DOW	Magnolia Cem. Charleston	FPH,JR,CGS,P1,P6
Mock, Thomas	Pvt.	D 24th SCVI		BT	11/30/64	Franklin, TN	KIA		CDC
Mock, W.F.	Pvt.	E 14th SCVI		LS	06/11/62	Cranshaws Fm. VA	DOD	(JR=W.C., Pneumonia)	JR,CGS
Moffitt, A.	Pvt.	A 4th Bn Res			10/08/64	Charleston, SC	DOD	Magnolia Cem. Charleston	ROH,MAG,RCD
Moffitt, J.L.	Pvt.	H Ham.Leg.		RD	04/30/65	Pt. Lookout, MD	DIP		ROH
Moffitt, William W.	Pvt.	E 4th SCVI		PS	01/20/62	Charlottesville	DOD	Univ. Cem. Charlottesville	ROH,JR,SA2,ACH
Moise, George	Pvt.	E 6th SCVI	25	DN	/ /		DOD		ROH
Mole, John A.	1st Sgt.	D 11th SCVI	22	BT	05/16/64	Drury's Bluff VA	KIA		ROH,HAG
Molloy, W.P.	Pvt.	A 27th SCVI		CN	/ /	At sea	DIP	(To Savannah for exchange)	CDC,P113,P120
Molony, P.K.	Cpt.	F&S Hagood	30	BL	08/21/64	Ream's Stn., VA	KIA	(AAG Hagood's Brigade)	ROH,SA1,HAG,CSO
Moncier, J.	Pvt.	H 1st SCVA			11/05/62	Charleston, SC	DOD	Magnolia Cem. Charleston	ROH,MAG,RCD
Monday, James C.	Pvt.	F Ham. Leg.	40	AE	/ /		DOD	(1865, on way home)	ROH
Moneyham, William W.	Pvt.	E 23rd SCVI		KW	/ /	Petersburg, VA	KIA		ROH,HMC
Monjoy, William	Pvt.	C 15th SCVAB		CN	11/02/64	James Island, SC	DOD		ROH
Monk, John A.	Sgt.	C 22nd SCVI	43	SG	06/15/62	Richmond, VA		Oakwood C.#104,Row L,Div A	ROH,OWC,HOS
Monoghan, Thomas	Pvt.	E 1st SCVIR		TN	01/17/63	Sullivans Isl SC	MUR	(Knifed in an affray)	ROH,SA1,CDC
Monro, Wesley E.	Pvt.	F 3rd SCVI		LS	05/05/63	Chancellorsville	KIA	(RHL & UD3= Sharpsburg)	SA2,RHL,UD3
Monroe, George W.	Pvt.	E 2nd SCVI		KW	01/26/63	Richmond, VA	DOW	(Wdd at Fredericksburg)	ROH,SA2,HIC,KEB
Monroe, James B.	Pvt.	E 2nd SCVI		KW	04/26/62	Richmond, VA	DOD	Oakwood C.#146,Row J,Div A	ROH,SA2,HIC,OWC
Monroe, John P.	3rd Cpl.	E 2nd SCVI		KW	02/20/65	Camp Chase, OH	DIP	C.C.#1350 Columbus, OH	FPH,SA2,KEB,P6
Montgomery, Charles K.	Pvt.	F 12th SCVI	22	FD	05/12/64	Spotsylvania, VA	KIA		ROH,JR,HFC
Montgomery, Daniel B.	Pvt.	B 1st SCVIG	30	NY	07/15/62	Richmond, VA	DOD	(Typhoid)	ROH,JR,ANY,SA1
Montgomery, G.W.	Pvt.	B SCVI			/ /	Richmond, VA		Oakwood C.#42,Row L,Div B	OWC
Montgomery, Green B.W.	2nd Lt.	F 3rd SCVIBn	27	RD	07/02/63	Gettysburg, VA	KIA	(JR=DOW 7/3/63)	ROH,JR,GDR,KEB
Montgomery, Hugh N.	Pvt.	F 9th SCVIB	27	SR	08/27/61	Germantown, VA	DOD		ROH,JR
Montgomery, J. Franklin	Pvt.	C 25th SCVI	30	WG	06/15/64	Drury's Bluff VA	DOW	(Wdd & POW 5/14)	ROH,HOW,HAG,CDC
Montgomery, J. Quigley	Pvt.	E 12th SCVI	32	LR	06/27/62	Gaines' Mill, VA	DOW		ROH,JR,LAN,CNM
Montgomery, J.B.	Pvt.	B 1st SC			/ /	Richmond, VA		(?in E,1st SCVIH,reorgd.)	ROH,SA1,CDC
Montgomery, J.O.	Cpl.	A 12th SCVI	19	UN	08/29/62	2nd Manassas, VA	KIA		ROH,JR,YMD,YEB
Montgomery, Josiah A.	Pvt.	D 1st SCVIH		LR	04/04/63	Charlottesville	DOD	Univ. Cem. Charlottesville	ROH,SA1,LAN,ACH
Montgomery, Prater S.G.	2nd Sgt.	K 27th SCVI	38	SG	02/09/65	Elmira, NY	DIP	(POW @ Pbg.6/24/64)	ROH,HOS,HAG,P120
Montgomery, Richard F.	Cpl.	K 17th SCVI	36	YK	/ /	At home	DOD	(1862)	YEB
Montgomery, Robert	Pvt.	I 17th SCVI		LR	07/15/63	Jackson, MS	KIA		ROH,JR,LAN,PP
Montgomery, S. Edgar	Pvt.	C 25th SCVI	32	WG	06/15/65	Fts. Monroe, VA	DIP	(POW @ Ft.Fisher, Elmira)	CTA,HOW,HAG,PO65
Montgomery, S. Isaac	2nd Lt.	C 25th SCVI		WG	09/03/64	Alexandria, VA	DOW	(In enemy hands)	ROH
Montgomery, S. Leroy	Pvt.	F 12th SCVI	28	FD	01/18/63	At home	DOD		ROH,JR,HFC
Montgomery, Samuel	Sgt.	C 25th SCVI	26	WG	05/14/64	Drury's bluff VA	KIA		ROH,JR,HOW,HAG
Montgomery, Thomas W.	Pvt.	C 25th SCVI	18	WG	09/03/64	Alexandria, VA	DOW	Christ Ch. Alexandria	ROH,HOW,HAG,P6
Montgomery, W.H.	Pvt.	A 25th SCVI			10/10/64	Greensboro, NC			PP
Montgomery, William A.	Pvt.	B Orr's Ri.	30	AE	05/03/63	Chancellorsville	KIA	(ROH=R.M.)	ROH,JR,CDC
Montgomery, William John	Pvt.	C 25th SCVI	40	WG	10/05/64	Petersburg, VA	DOD		ROH,HOW,CTA,HAG
Montgomery,Jr., Henry	2nd Lt.	C 25th SCVI	31	WG	09/05/63	Bty. Wagner, SC	KIA		ROH,HAG,HOW,R45
Monts, Nelson C.	Pvt.	H 3rd SCVI		LN	01/15/63	Richmond, VA	DOD	(ROH=Morets,KIA @ Shpsbg)	ROH,JR,SA2,KEB
Monts, Thomas H.	Pvt.	H 3rd SCVI		LN	09/13/62	Maryland Hts. MD	KIA	(ROH= Morets)	ROH,JR,SA2,KEB
Monts, Walter F.	3rd Lt.	I 15th SCVI	24	NY	07/10/63	Gettysburg, PA	DOW	(Leg amp, Pvt.on NY Mon.)	JR,ANY,H15,KEB
Mood, Samuel	Pvt.	B P.S.S.		PS	08/30/62	2nd Manassas, VA	KIA		ROH
Moody, Calvin C.	Pvt.	F 1st SCVIG		HY	08/02/64	Ft. Delaware, DE	DIP	Finn's Pt., NJ Nat. Cem.	ROH,JR,FPH,P5
Moody, Curtis	Pvt.	E 1st SCVIG		MN	07/09/62		DOD		ROH,JR,SA1
Moody, Edward Rutledge	Pvt.	G Ham.Leg.	23	SR	04/17/62	Ashland, VA	DOD		ROH
Moody, Ezra Allen	Pvt.	G Ham. Leg.	20	SR	12/15/62	Richmond, VA	DOD		ROH

SOUTH CAROLINA DEAD IN CSA SERVICE 1861-1865

M

NAME	RANK	C REGIMENT	AGE	DS	DIED	WHERE	WHY	BURIED	SOURCES
Moody, Jeremiah	Pvt.	E Orr's Ri.	30	PS	06/29/62	Dill Springs, VA	DOD		ROH,JR,CDC
Moody, Joel	Pvt.	E Orr's Ri.	35	PS	09/01/62	Lynchburg, VA	DOD	Lynchburg CSA Cem.#5 R5	ROH,CDC,BBW
Moody, John M.	Pvt.	E Orr's Ri.	18	PS	07/26/62	Richmond, VA	DOW		ROH,JR
Moody, Miles Eugene	Pvt.	G Ham. Leg.	28	SR	01/28/63	At home	DOD		ROH
Moody, Oliver A.	Pvt.	E 1st SCVIG		MN	10/15/62		DOW	(Wdd @ Sharpsburg)	JR,SA1,HMC
Moody, Peter	Pvt.	K 7th SCVI		ED	05/08/64	Spotsylvania, VA	KIA	Spotsylvania C.H., VA	ROH,JR,SCH
Moody, Robert M.	Pvt.	H Orr's Ri.		MN	10/27/62	Liberty Hospital	DOD	Piedmont Institute, VA	ROH,JR,HMC,CDC
Moody, Thomas	Pvt.	H 14th SCVI		BL	08/02/62	Richmond, VA	DOD	Oakwood C.#50,Row J,Div G	ROH,JR,OWC
Moody, W. Dudley	Pvt.	D P.S.S.		SG	07/12/64	Petersburg, VA	KIA	(Also Wdd @ Sharpsburg)	ROH,HOS
Moody, William Wheeler	Sgt.	E 7th SCVIBn	33	SR	10/23/63	Sullivans I., SC	DOD	(HAG= W.M.)	ROH,HAG
Moon, P.	Pvt.	A Ham.Leg.			01/13/65	Petersburg, VA	DOD		ROH
Moon, Robert P.	Sgt.	C 16th SCVI		GE	/ /	Georgia	DOD		16R
Moone, O.P.	Lt.	E 3rd SCVIBn		LS	09/20/63	Chickamauga, GA	KIA	(KEB= Moore)	ROH,JR,CDC,KEB
Moore, A.A.	Pvt.	K 7th SCVI		ED	10/15/64	Williamsburg, VA		Oakwood C.#18,Row A,Div G	ROH,OWC
Moore, A.C.	Pvt.	E 18th SCVI		SG	08/30/62	2nd Manassas, VA	KIA	Manassas, VA CSA Cem.	JR,CDC
Moore, A.J.	Pvt.	A 17th SCVI		CR	12/15/62	Kinston, NC	DOW		ROH
Moore, Albertus W.	Pvt.	F 5th SCVI		YK	10/07/64	Darbytown Rd. VA	KIA	(SA3=Co. E)	CB,SA,YEB
Moore, Alexander			33		/ /	(1862)		Choctaw County, MS	MCG
Moore, Alexander A.	Pvt.	F 5th SCVI	21	YK	10/07/64	Darbytown Rd. VA	KIA		ROH,JR,SA3
Moore, Allen	Pvt.	F 3rd SCVIBn	17	RD	06/02/64	Cold Harbor, VA	KIA		ROH,KEB
Moore, Andrew Charles	Sgt.	E 18th SCVI	24	SG	08/30/62	2nd Manassas, VA	KIA	Nazareth P.C. SG Cty.	ROH,HOS,GEC,GE
Moore, Augustus	Pvt.	SC Arty	21	YK	08/30/62	2nd Manassas, VA	KIA		YEB
Moore, B.	Pvt.	A Ham.Leg.			01/13/65	Petersburg, VA			ROH
Moore, B.F.	Pvt.	B 21st SCVI		DN	04/10/65	Elmira, NY	DIP	Woodlawn N.C.#2607 Elmira	ROH,FPH,P6,P65
Moore, Benjamin	3rd Cpl.	A 24th SCVI	30	CN	04/22/62	Folly Island, SC	ACD		ROH,CDC
Moore, Benjamin J.	Pvt.	E 21st SCVI		MO	02/07/64	Pt. Lookout, MD	DIP	C.C. Pt. Lookout, MD	ROH,FPH,P5,P23
Moore, Berry	Pvt.	F 16th SCVI		GE	/ /	Charleston, SC	DOD		16R
Moore, Blaney J.	1st Sgt.	H 8th SCVI		MN	01/29/65	Camp Chase. OH	DIP	C.C.#956 Columbus, OH	FPH,HMC,P6,P23
Moore, Blanton	Pvt.	F 17th SCVI		YK	/ /	Richmond, VA	DOD		JR,CB
Moore, Charles	Pvt.	A 12th SCVI	26	YK	06/27/62	Gaines' Mill, VA	KIA	(YEB=Mechanicsville)	YEB
Moore, Charles R.	Pvt.	G P.S.S.	28	YK	07/07/62	Fraser's Farm VA	DOW	Hollywood Cem.Rchmd. O20	ROH,JR,UD2,HC
Moore, D.	Pvt.	E 9th SCVIB			03/23/61	Virginia	DOD		JR
Moore, D.S.	Pvt.	C 17th SCVI		YK	/ /	Adams Run, VA	DOD		JR
Moore, Daniel Williams	Cpl.	A 12th SCVI	21	YK	10/01/62	Warrenton, VA	DOW	(Wdd 2nd Man)	ROH,JR,YMD,YEB
Moore, David W.	Pvt.	D P.S.S.		SG	08/30/62	2nd Manassas, VA	KIA		ROH,JR,HOS,CDC
Moore, E.B.	Pvt.	D 18th SCVI		AN	12/05/62	Goldsboro, NC	DOD		JR
Moore, E.R.	Pvt.	D 18th SCVI		AN	06/12/64	Richmond, VA	DOW		ROH
Moore, Edward	2nd Lt.	K 5th SCVC	29	YK	06/12/64	Cold Harbor, VA	DOW	Hollywood Cem.Rchmd. U355	ROH,HC,RCD,YEB
Moore, Edward	Pvt.	B 2nd SCVI		GE	04/15/64	Rock Island, IL	DIP	C.C.#1047 Rock Island, IL	FPH,SA2,KEB
Moore, Edward W.	Pvt.	E 14th SCVI	22	LS	10/10/61	Camp Butler, SC	DOD	(Measles)	ROH,JR
Moore, Eli	Cpl.	C 4th SCVC			07/19/64	Armory Sq. H. DC	DOW	(POW @ Hawes Shop, VA)	P6
Moore, Frederick E.	1st Lt.	H 6th SCVI	26	YK	12/20/61	Dranesville, VA	KIA		ROH,YMD,CDC,YE
Moore, Frederick R.	Pvt.	H Hol.Leg.	35	NY	08/30/62	2nd Manassas, VA	KIA		ROH,JR,ANY
Moore, G. Watts	Sgt.	F 17th SCVI	24	YK	07/31/64	Crater, Pbg., VA	DOW	Blandford Church Pbg., VA	ROH,BLM,BLC,TC
Moore, G.B.	Pvt.	F 3rd SCVI		LS	12/19/61	Richmond, VA	DOD		ROH,JR,SA2,KEB
Moore, G.M.	Pvt.	E 3rd SCVIBn		LS	05/08/64	Spotsylvania, VA	KIA	Spotsylvania C.H., VA	ROH,JR,SCH,KEB
Moore, G.W.	Pvt.	Inglis LA		DN	02/28/64	Summerville, SC	DOD		ROH
Moore, G.W.	Pvt.	D 25th SCVI		MN	/ /	Little Rock, SC	MUR	(Wdd 5/16, FUR & MUR in MN)	HMC,HAG
Moore, George E.	Pvt.	H 1st SCVIH		SG	09/23/63	Columbia, SC	DOD		ROH,SA1,HOS,PP
Moore, George W.	Pvt.	G 27th SCVI	18	SG	08/05/64	Petersburg, VA	DOD	Blandford Church Pbg., VA	ROH,HOS,BLC,HA
Moore, H.	Pvt.	D 23rd SCVI		CN	08/30/62	2nd Manassas, VA	KIA		ROH,JR,CDC

SOUTH CAROLINA DEAD IN CSA SERVICE 1861-1865

NAME	RANK	C REGIMENT	AGE	DS	DIED	WHERE	WHY	BURIED	SOURCES
Moore, H.J.	Pvt.	B 8th SCVI		CD	11/18/61	Richmond, VA	DOD	(Typhoid)	ROH,JR,KEP
Moore, H.P.	Pvt.	B 5th SCVC	19	BT	/ /		DOD		MDM
Moore, Henry	Pvt.	F 2nd SCVI	40	AE	08/08/62	Manchester, VA	DOD		ROH,SA2,KEB
Moore, Henry F.	Pvt.	F 24th SCVI		AN	05/16/63	Jackson, MS	DOW		HOL,PP
Moore, Hugh H.	Pvt.	G P.S.S.		YK	05/30/62	7 Pines, VA	KIA		CNM,YEB
Moore, J.	Pvt.	B 1st SC Res		GE	02/04/65	Columbia, SC	DOD	Elmwood Cem. Columbia SC	ROH,MP,PP
Moore, J.	Pvt.	D 1st SCVA		CN	08/11/63	Chester, PA	DOW	(Wdd @ Gettysburg)	ROH,CDC,P1
Moore, J. Mickell	1st Lt.	F 6th SCVI	28	CR	06/27/62	Gaines' Mill, VA	KIA	(Also Ltly. Wdd.@ 7 Pines)	ROH,WDB,CDC,HHC
Moore, J.A.	Pvt.	F 3rd SCVI		LS	11/04/62	Richmond, VA		Hollywood Cem.Rchmd. C41	ROH,HC
Moore, J.D.	Pvt.	B 17th SCVI		FD	02/12/65	Petersburg, VA			ROH,HFC,PP
Moore, J.G.	Sgt.	E 8th SCVI		DN	05/13/62	Richmond, VA	DOD		JR,KEB
Moore, J.J.	Pvt.	A 23rd SCVI		CN	04/01/65	Five Forks, VA	KIA		ROH
Moore, J.M.	Sgt.	C 17th SCVI		YK	09/14/62	South Mtn., MD	KIA		JR
Moore, J.R.	Pvt.	G 22nd SCVI		AN	/ /	Charleston, SC	DOD	(7/21/?)	ROH
Moore, James	Pvt.	D Hol.Leg.	28	BL	12/06/64	Petersburg, VA	KIA		ROH
Moore, James A.	Cpl.	K P.S.S.		SG	05/31/62	7 Pines, VA	KIA	(JR=Co.A)	JR,HOS,CDC
Moore, James A.	Pvt.	C 2nd SCV			/ /	Lynchburg, VA		Lynchburg CSA Cem.#10 R1	BBW
Moore, James D.	Pvt.	E 8th SCVI		DN	01/15/62	Manchester, VA	DOD	Hollywood Cem.Rchmd. L67	ROH,JR,HC,KEB
Moore, Jesse N.	2nd Lt.	G P.S.S.	26	YK	05/06/64	Wilderness, VA	KIA	Bethesda C. York, SC UD2	ROH,JR,RCD,YEB
Moore, John	Pvt.	H 1st SC		SG	09/14/63	Columbia, SC	DOD		ROH
Moore, John	Sgt.	A 26th SCVI	28	HY	10/15/64	Petersburg, VA	KIA		ROH
Moore, John	Pvt.	F 18th SCVI		YK	07/30/64	Crater, Pbg., VA	KIA		BLM
Moore, John J.	Pvt.	A 21st SCVI		CN	02/17/65	Elmira, NY	DIP	Woodlawn N.C.#2213 Elmira	FPH,HAG,P6,P65
Moore, John Kennedy	Sgt.	D 12th SCVI		RD	08/22/62	Richmond, VA	DOD	(JR=Typhoid 4/22/62)	ROH,JR,PP
Moore, John R.	1st Sgt.	F 21st SCVI		MO	07/13/65	Elmira, NY	DIP	(POW @ Ft Fisher 1/15/65)	ROH,HOM,HAG,P65
Moore, John V.	Colonel	2nd SCVIRi		AN	09/03/62	Haymarket, VA	DOW	Haymarket, VA Cem.	ROH,JR,LC,CV,R45
Moore, Levi	Pvt.	A 9th SCVIBn	32	HY	07/25/62	Waccamaw Neck SC	DOD		ROH,JR
Moore, Levi	Pvt.	E 2nd SCVI		KW	/ /	Richmond, VA	DOD		SA2,KEB,HIC
Moore, N.	Pvt.	K 10th SCVI		CN	/ /		DOD		RAS
Moore, N.C.	Pvt.	G 3rd SCVABn			07/25/64	Columbia, SC	DOD		ROH
Moore, Newton Whitner	Pvt.	C 2nd SCVIRi			06/29/62	Richmond, VA	KIA		JR
Moore, O. Perry	3rd Lt.	E 3rd SCVIBn		LS	09/20/63	Chickamauga, GA	KIA		ROH,KEB,R45
Moore, P.	Pvt.			SG	01/14/64	Petersburg, VA		Blandford Church Pbg., VA	BLC
Moore, Peter H.	Pvt.	B 13th SCVI		SG	/ /	Coosawatchie, SC			HOS
Moore, Planter	Pvt.	F 17th SCVI		YK	07/30/64	Crater, Pbg., VA	KIA		BLM
Moore, Prescott T.E.	Sgt.	I 24th SCVI		ED	07/22/64	Atlanta, GA	KIA		JR
Moore, R. Brown	Pvt.	G 13th SCVI		NY	07/01/63	Gettysburg, PA	KIA	(CDC=Brown, Moore)	ROH,JR,ANY
Moore, Robert	Pvt.	A 21st SCVI		GN	02/18/63	Morris Island SC	DOD		ROH,JR,HAG
Moore, Robert	Pvt.	D 16th SCVI		GE	/ /		DOD		16R
Moore, Robert Morgan	Pvt.	D 4th SCVI		AN	08/20/61	Culpepper, VA	DOD	Fairview Cem. Culpepper VA	JR,CGH,SA2,CDC
Moore, S.	Pvt.	E 2nd SCVIRi			07/01/62	Malvern Hill, VA	KIA	(JR=6/29/62)	ROH,JR,CDC
Moore, S.B.	Pvt.	E 14th SCVI		LS	08/05/62	Richmond, VA	DOD	(Typhoid)	JR,CGS
Moore, Samuel	Pvt.	B P.S.S.		PS	08/30/62	2nd Manassas, VA	KIA		ROH,JR,CDC
Moore, Stephen	Pvt.	D 10th SCVI		MN	07/22/64	Atlanta, GA	KIA		ROH,JR,RAS,HMC
Moore, T. Ezra	Pvt.	I 24th SCVI	22	ED	07/20/64	Peachtree Ck. GA	KIA		CDC
Moore, T.A.	Pvt.	E P.S.S.		SR	09/29/64	Ft. Harrison, VA	KIA		ROH
Moore, T.B.	Pvt.	K 10th SCVI		CN	/ /		DOD		RAS
Moore, T.H.	Pvt.	SCVI	39		/ /	LaGrange, GA		Con. Cem. LaGrange, GA	TOD
Moore, T.J.	Pvt.	C 17th SCVI		YK	09/14/62	South Mtn., MD	KIA		JR,CB
Moore, Thomas	Pvt.	C 3rd SCV			07/26/64	Spotsylvania, VA	DOW	(Wdd Wilderness)	ROH,JR
Moore, Thomas	Pvt.	E 4th SCV			/ /	Manchester, VA		(Co.K, 4th SCVI?)	ROH

SOUTH CAROLINA DEAD IN CSA SERVICE 1861-1865

NAME	RANK	C REGIMENT	AGE	DS	DIED	WHERE	WHY	BURIED	SOURCES
Moore, Thomas O.	Pvt.	D 18th SCVI		AN	06/28/63	Jackson, MS	DOD		ROH,JR,PP
Moore, Thomas W.	Pvt.	F 6th SCVI	20	CR	02/10/63	Petersburg, VA	DOD		ROH,HHC
Moore, Trapp E.	Pvt.	K 17th SCVI	44	YK	/ /	Petersburg, VA	KIA		YEB
Moore, W.	Pvt.	B 10th SCVI		HY	/ /		DOD		RAS
Moore, W.	Pvt.	H 12th SCVI	41	YK	/ /	Richmond, VA	DOD	(Left behind in camp 1862)	CWC,YEB
Moore, W.A.	Pvt.	D 12th SCVI		RD	06/27/62	Gaines' Mill, VA	KIA		ROH,JR,CNM
Moore, W.C.	Sgt.	I 1st SCVIR			07/18/63	Bty. Wagner, SC	KIA		ROH,CDC
Moore, W.C.	Pvt.	G 3rd SCVABn			07/25/64	Columbia, SC	DOD		PP
Moore, W.D.	Color Sgt.	I 17th SCVI		LR	08/30/62	2nd Manassas, VA	KIA		ROH,JR,LAN
Moore, W.D.	Pvt.	B 1st SCVIH		BL	07/24/63		DOD	(To hosp 12/17/62)	ROH,SA1,JRH
Moore, W.H.	Pvt.	F 3rd SCVI		LS	01/11/62	Manassas, VA	DOD		ROH,JR,SA2,KEB
Moore, W.J.	Pvt.	1st SC	20	CD	07/15/64	At home	DOD		ROH
Moore, W.J.	Pvt.	I 26th SCVI		WG	10/10/63		DOD		JR
Moore, W.J.	Pvt.	F 17th SCVI		YK	09/14/62	South Mtn., MD	DOW		CB
Moore, W.P.C.	Pvt.	B 13th SCVI		SG	12/25/61		DOD	(Measles)	JR
Moore, W.W.	Pvt.	7th SCVI			/ /			Stonewall C. Winchester VA	ROH,WIN
Moore, W.W.	Pvt.	I 1st SCVIG			07/28/64	Deep Bottom, VA	KIA		ROH,CDC
Moore, William	Pvt.	A 6th SCVI	24	CR	05/30/62	7 Pines, VA	KIA	(ROH= Moon) HHC,CB	ROH,JR,WDB,GLS
Moore, William	Pvt.	A 21st SCVI		GN	03/20/62	At home	DOD		ROH,JR
Moore, William	Pvt.	A 21st SCVI		GN	08/09/63	Morris Island SC	DOW	Magnolia Cem. Charleston	ROH,JR,MAG,RCD
Moore, William	Pvt.	A 6th SCVI			06/01/62	7 Pines, VA	DOW		ROH,CDC
Moore, William	Pvt.	E 1st SCVIR		CD	09/08/63	Ft. Moultrie, SC	KIA		ROH,SA1,CDC
Moore, William	Pvt.	F 16th SCVI		GE	/ /	Adams Run, SC	DOD		16R
Moore, William	Pvt.	H Orr's Ri.		MN	07/28/64	Deep Bottom, VA	KIA		JR
Moore, William A.	Pvt.	F 5th SCVI		YK	05/31/62	7 Pines, VA	KIA		SA3,CB
Moore, William E.K.	Pvt.	A Hol.Leg.	18	SG	01/14/65	Petersburg, VA	DOD		ROH,HOS,PP
Moore, William H.	2nd Lt.	C 17th SCVI		YK	10/01/62		DOW		JR,R47,CB
Moore, William J.	Pvt.	7th SCVIBn			/ /		DOD	(JR=Co,C,HAG=D)	JR
Moore, William R.	Pvt.	A 21st SCVI		CN	04/12/62	Georgetown, SC	DOD		PP
Moore, Zimri	Pvt.	C 3rd SCVIBn		LS	06/12/62	Adams Run, SC	DOD		JR
Moore,Jr., J.T.	Pvt.	H 12th SCVI	19	YK	08/29/62	2nd Manassas, VA	KIA		JR,CWC,YEB
Moorer, Francis Marion	Pvt.	A 5th SCVC	30	OG	06/12/64	Trevillian Stn.	DOW	Family Gvyd. Orangeburg SC	ROH,JR,CDC,ETW
Moorer, Henry L.	Cpl.	F 3rd SCVABn	27	CN	10/04/64	At home	DOD		ROH
Moorer, Jacob F.	Cpt.	K 2nd SCVI		CN	07/05/63	Gettysburg, PA	DOW	(Wdd 7/2/63)	ROH,GDR,SA2,R4
Moorhead, W.G.	Sgt.	F 18th SCVI	30	UN	08/07/63	Montgomery, AL	ACD	(RR accident)	ROH,JR
Moorhead, William L.	Pvt.	F 15th SCVI		UN	07/15/64	Petersburg, VA	DOD		ROH,KEB
Moorman, Lemuel	2nd Sgt.	C 13th SCVI		SG	08/16/64	Fussells Mill VA	KIA		ROH,JR,HOS
Moose, Joseph A.	Pvt.	A 17th SCVI	28	CR	12/26/62	Kinston, NC	DOW	(PP=12/31/62)	ROH,JR,HHC,PP,
Moragne, William C.	Colonel	19th SCVI		ED	10/05/62	At home	DOD		ROH,JR,HOE,PP
Mordecai,Jr., Thomas W.	Pvt.	K 4th SCVC		CN	05/11/61	Ft. Moultrie, SC	DOD	Beth Elohim, Charleston SC	JR,MAG,RCD,CLD
Moreton, J.T.	Sgt.	E 10th SCVI		WG	03/19/65	Bentonville, NC	DOW		RAS,CTA,HOW
Moreton, R.G.	Sgt.	E 10th SCVI		WG	07/22/64	Atlanta, GA	DOW	(From slight leg wound)	ROH,RAS,CDC
Morgan, B.E.	Pvt.	E 14th SCVI		LS	06/30/62	Frayser's Farm	KIA		ROH,JR,CGS
Morgan, B.F.	Pvt.	E Orr's Ri.		PS	12/09/62	Richmond, VA	DOD		JR
Morgan, Bailey B.	Pvt.	I 2nd SCVIRi		PS	08/27/63	Petersburg, VA	DOW	Blandford Church Pbg., VA	ROH,BLC,PP
Morgan, Barnes	Pvt.	H 24th SCVI		CR	09/20/63	Chickamauga, GA	KIA		HHC
Morgan, D.	Pvt.	E Orr's Ri.		PS	06/27/62	Gaines' Mill, VA	KIA		CDC
Morgan, Daniel	Pvt.	Hart's LA			10/27/64	Boydton Plank Rd	KIA		ROH,CNM,CDC
Morgan, David	Pvt.	K 24th SCVI	38	ED	01/09/64	Dalton, GA	DOD		ROH,HOE,PP
Morgan, E.C.	Pvt.	I 7th SCVI			/ /	LaGrange, GA		Con. Cem. LaGrange, GA	TOD
Morgan, F.M.	Pvt.	K 18th SCVI			11/04/64	Charlotte, NC			PP

SOUTH CAROLINA DEAD IN CSA SERVICE 1861-1865

NAME	RANK	C REGIMENT	AGE	DS	DIED	WHERE	WHY	BURIED	SOURCES
Morgan, G.E.	Pvt.	K 24th SCVI			/ /	Marietta, GA		Con. Cem. Marietta, GA	CCM
Morgan, George	Pvt.	C 1st SCVC	21	BL	04/15/65	Goldsboro, NC	KIA		ROH
Morgan, Isaac	Pvt.	A 21st SCVI	34	GN	07/16/64	Petersburg, VA	DOW	(PP=8/1/64)	ROH,CDC,HAG,PP
Morgan, Isaac Charles	Pvt.	A 15th SCVI	19	RD	09/20/63	Chickamauga, GA	KIA		ROH,JR,KEB
Morgan, J.A.	Pvt.	E 1st SCVIH		BL	04/06/63	Richmond, VA	DOD	Oakwood C.#90,Row N,Div A	ROH,SA1,OWC
Morgan, J.C.	Pvt.	F 3rd SCVI		LS	10/06/62	Sharpsburg, MD	DOW	Rose Hill C. Hagerstown MD	ROH,CDC,KEB,BOD
Morgan, J.C.	Pvt.	2nd SCV			10/05/62		DOW		JR
Morgan, Jesse M.	Pvt.	D P.S.S.		SG	02/23/62	At home	DOD		ROH,HOS
Morgan, Jesse S.	1st Sgt.	B 22nd SCVI	23	SG	06/17/64	Petersburg, VA	KIA	(HOS=Crater)	ROH,HOS
Morgan, John W.	Pvt.	E Orr's Ri.	23	PS	06/27/62	Gaines' Mill, VA	KIA	(JR=John J.)	ROH,JR,CDC
Morgan, Joseph Evan	3rd Lt.	K 24th SCVI		ED	09/20/63	Chickamauga, GA	KIA		ROH,JR,HOE,BIG
Morgan, Lewis	Pvt.	K 19th SCVI			01/23/64	Med. C. Atlanta		Oakland C. Atlanta R11#13	BGA
Morgan, O. Peter	Pvt.	I 5th SCVI		SG	/ /	Virginia		(On rolls 2/28/65)	HOS,SA3
Morgan, T.M.	Pvt.	K 18th SCVI			/ /	Charlottesville			ROH
Morgan, Thomas J.	Pvt.	E Orr's Ri.	25	PS	08/13/62	Richmond, VA	DOD		ROH,JR,CDC
Morgan, W. Collin	Pvt.	L 8th SCVI		MN	06/29/64	Richmond, VA	KIA	(Malvern Hill ?)	ROH,HMC,KEB
Morgan, W.D.	Pvt.	B 5th SCV			05/03/63	Chancellorsville	KIA		JR
Morgan, W.E.	Pvt.	F Ham.Leg.	26		08/29/62	Columbia, SC	DOW	(Wdd @ 7 Pines, JR=8/20)	ROH,JR
Morgan, W.H.	Pvt.	G 12th SCVI		PS	05/06/64	Lynchburg, VA	DOW	Lynchburg CSA Cem.#3 R5	JR,BBW
Morgan, Warren D.	Pvt.	D Orr's Ri.	19	AN	05/27/62	Gaines' Mill, VA	KIA	(JR=Co.E)	ROH,JR
Morgan, William	Pvt.	A 6th SCVI	35	CR	05/15/63	Virginia	DOD		ROH,GLS,HHC,CB
Morgan, William D.	Pvt.	G 3rd SCVIBn		FD	09/20/63	Chickamauga, GA	KIA	Con. Cem. Marietta, GA	ROH,CDC,KEB,CCM
Morgan, William F.	Pvt.	E Orr's Ri.	21	PS	12/10/62	Gaines' Mill, VA	DOW	Oakwood C.#70,Row L,Div A	ROH,JR,OWC,CDC
Morgan, William T.	Pvt.	F 24th SCVI		AN	05/14/63	Jackson, MS	KIA		ROH,HOL,CDC,PP
Morie, William P.	Pvt.	E 1st SCVIR		LR	09/09/62	Ft. Moultrie, SC	KIA	(Morris in ROH)	ROH,SA1,CDC
Mornett, Willey	Pvt.	P.S.S.			10/28/63	Lookout Valley	KIA		CDC
Morre, H.H.	Pvt.	G P.S.S.			05/31/62	7 Pines, VA	KIA		JR
Morrell, John	Pvt.	G 24th SCVI	37		06/16/62	Secessionville	KIA	(JR=DOW 9/19/64)	JR,EJM,PP
Morrell, Peter	Pvt.	M 8th SCVI	25	DN	09/15/62	Maryland Hts. MD	KIA	(JR=1st Sgt.)	ROH,KEB
Morrell, William E.	Pvt.	A 8th SCVI		DN	11/23/62	Fredericksburg	DOD	(Pneumonia)	ROH,JR,KEB
Morris,	Pvt.	K 3rd SCVC		BL	04/27/62	Beaufort area SC	DOD		ROH
Morris, Aaron	Pvt.	G 2nd SCVIRi			06/03/62	Adams Run, SC	DOD		PP
Morris, Alexander	Pvt.	C 17th SCVI	37	YK	/ /		DOD	(1863)	YEB
Morris, Amos	Pvt.	D 2nd SCVIRi			07/02/62	Richmond, VA	DOD	(Typhoid, on effects list)	ROH,JR,CDC
Morris, B.C.	Pvt.	C 18th SCVI	40	UN	07/30/64	Crater, Pbg., VA	KIA		ROH,JR
Morris, Chauncey H.	Pvt.	H Hol.Leg.		NY	04/08/65	Pt. Lookout, MD	DIP	C.C. Pt. Lookout, MD P6	ROH,FPH,ANY,P115
Morris, D.B.					/ /			(Rchmnd effects list 1/63)	CDC
Morris, D.S.	Pvt.	C (?3rd Inf)			/ /	Richmond, VA		Oakwood C.#130,Row L,Div C	ROH,OWC,CDC
Morris, E.	Pvt.	G 2nd SCVA			07/20/63	Ft. Johnson, SC	KIA	(Shell Point Battery)	ROH,CDC
Morris, Howard	Pvt.	F 6th SCVI	22	CR	06/23/62	7 Pines, VA	DOW	Hollywood Cem.Rchmd. 089	ROH,CRM,HHC,HC
Morris, J. Abner	Pvt.	F P.S.S.			/ /		DOW		JR
Morris, J.H.	Pvt.	B 4th SCVC	33	AE	07/21/64	Trevillian Stn.	DOW	(Severe thigh wound)	ROH,CDC
Morris, J.J.	Pvt.	G 22nd SCVI		AN	07/09/63	Petersburg, VA		Blandford Church Pbg., VA	BLC
Morris, J.M.	2nd Lt.	G 26th SCVI		DN	07/28/64	Richmond, VA	DOD	Hollywood Cem.Rchmd. V363	ROH,HC,R48
Morris, J.S.	Pvt.	D 8th SCVI			07/14/62	Richmond, VA	DOW	(J.L. in Co.E?)	JR
Morris, J.W.	Pvt.	G 18th SCVI		UN	06/28/62	Augusta, GA	DOD		JR
Morris, Jacob	Pvt.	H 17th SCVI		BL	09/21/63	Charleston, SC	ACD	(RR accident near CN)	ROH,JR
Morris, James H.	Pvt.	B 5th SCVC			06/29/64		DOW		JR
Morris, James J.M.	Pvt.	G 2nd SCVIRi	24	AN	07/09/63	Petersburg, VA			PP
Morris, James M.	Pvt.	C 23rd SCVI	41	CD	08/08/64	Petersburg, VA		Blandford Church Pbg., VA	BLC,PP
Morris, John	Pvt.	G 1st SCVIH		BL	10/13/61	Cole's Isl., SC	DOD		SA1

SOUTH CAROLINA DEAD IN CSA SERVICE 1861-1865

NAME	RANK	C REGIMENT	AGE	DS	DIED	WHERE	WHY	BURIED	SOURCES
Morris, John D.	Pvt.	G 13th SCVI		NY	05/28/62	Ashland, VA	DOD	(Typhoid)	ROH,JR,ANY
Morris, John S.	Pvt.	A 14th SCMil			04/20/65	Hart's Island NY	DIP	Cypress Hills N.C.#2588 NY	FPH,P1,P6,P79
Morris, Joseph	Pvt.	K 24th SCVI		ED	/ /	Meridan, MS	DOD	(To Hospital 1/28/65)	EJM
Morris, Marion	Pvt.	H 16th SCVI		GE	09/03/64	Lovejoy's Stn.GA	KIA		ROH,16R
Morris, Miles	Pvt.	I 13th SCVI	18	SG	/ /	Petersburg, VA	MIA		ROH
Morris, P.F.	Pvt.	D Orr's Ri.		AN	07/16/63		DOW		JR,CDC
Morris, R.	Pvt.	G 1st SCVIH		BL	08/30/62	2nd Manassas, VA	KIA		ROH,SA1,CDC
Morris, Ralph	Pvt.	K 2nd SCVA		ED	/ /		KIA		HOE,UD3
Morris, Robb	Pvt.	I 13th SCVI	20	SG	09/30/64	Jones Farm, VA	KIA		ROH
Morris, Robert	Pvt.	H 17th SCVI			/ /				JR
Morris, Robert Harrison	5th Sgt.	H 6th SCVI	25	FD	12/20/61	Dranesville, VA	KIA	(JR=Co.C)	ROH,JR,R46,HFC
Morris, S.P.	Lt.	A 16th SCVI		GE	06/19/64	Louisa C.H., VA	KIA		ROH,JR
Morris, Stephen H.	Pvt.	I 18th SCVI	32	DN	03/14/65	Petersburg, VA	DOD	(1865)	ROH
Morris, T.E.	Color Sgt.	E 8th SCVI		DN	09/17/62	Sharpsburg, MD	KIA		JR,KEB
Morris, T.R.	Pvt.	G 2nd SCV			/ /	Lynchburg, VA		Lynchburg CSA Cem.#2 R3	BBW
Morris, Thomas S.	Pvt.	E 15th SCVI			/ /		DOD		JR
Morris, W.A.	Pvt.	C 17th SCVI		YK	/ /	Mt. Vernon, MS	DOD		JR
Morris, W.C.	Pvt.	K Orr's Ri.		AN	07/10/62		DOW		JR
Morris, W.T.	Pvt.	K P.S.S.			/ /		DOD		JR
Morris, William	Pvt.	E 7th SCVIBn	36		03/08/63	Adams Run, SC	ACD	(ROH=Co.F, PP=Co.A)	ROH,HAG,PP
Morris, William	Pvt.	A 24th SCVI	44	CN	11/23/62	Charleston, SC	DOD	Magnolia Cem. Charleston	ROH,MAG,RCD
Morris, William T.	Pvt.	B 5th SCVI		CR	05/06/64	Wilderness, VA	KIA	(JR=W.P. & Co.A)	ROH,JR,SA3,HHC
Morrisey, Abner	Pvt.	K 26th SCVI			03/08/62		DOD		JR
Morrisey, J.S.	Cpl.	A 18th SCVI		UN	07/30/64	Crater, Pbg., VA	KIA		JR
Morrisey, Patrick	Pvt.	B 27th SCVI		SG	10/05/63	Columbia, SC	DOD	(ROH= Morrison)	ROH,JR,HAG
Morrison, Angus	Pvt.	A 1st SCVIR			05/13/65	Hart's Island NY	DIP	Cypress Hills N.C.#2774 NY	FPH,SA1,P6,P11
Morrison, Charles A.	Pvt.	A 16th SCVI		GE	/ /	Camp Douglas, IL	DIP		16R,P23
Morrison, Daniel	Pvt.	A 1st SCVIR			06/12/62	Ft. Moultrie, SC	DOD		SA1
Morrison, T.L.	Pvt.	K Orr's Ri.		AN	10/15/62	Richmond, VA	DOD		JR
Morrison, Thomas M.	Pvt.	K Orr's Ri.	24	AN	06/27/62	Gaines' Mill, VA	KIA		ROH,JR,CDC
Morrison, William L.	Pvt.	K Orr's Ri.		AN	06/27/62	Gaiines' Mill VA	KIA		JR
Morrison, William P.	Pvt.	G Orr's Ri.		AE	06/27/62	Gaines' Mill, VA	KIA		ROH,JR,CDC
Morriss, J.	Pvt.	I 13th SCVI		SG	02/27/65			Hollywood Cem.Rchmd. W41	HC
Morriss, James	Pvt.	G 2nd SCVIRi			07/09/63	Petersburg, VA	DOD		ROH
Morriss, James M.	Pvt.	C 23rd SCVI		CN	08/08/64	Petersburg, VA			ROH
Morriss, P.L.H.	Pvt.	I 18th SCVI		DN	03/12/65	Richmond, VA		Hollywood Cem.Rchmd. W183	HC
Morrow, C.C.	Pvt.	A Hol. Leg.		SG	08/30/62	2nd Manassas, VA	DOW		HOS
Morrow, Daniel	Pvt.	G 7th SCV			/ /		DOD		JR
Morse, D.	Pvt.	C 25th SCVI		WG	08/20/64	Petersburg, VA	DOW	(Wdd 8/17/64)	ROH
Morse, George W.	Sgt.	B 21st SCVI		DN	09/10/63	Morris Island SC	DOW	(JR=7/12/63)	JR,R48,HAG
Morse, J.P.	Pvt.	H 22nd SCVI		GE	09/02/64	Elmira, NY	DIP	Woodlawn N.C.#85 Elmira	FPH,P5,P65,P12
Mortimer, LaBruce	4th Sgt.	I 2nd SCVI	21	CN	07/04/63	Gettysburg, PA	DOW	(JR=DOW 8/8/63)	ROH,JR,GDR,SA2
Morton, J.F.	Pvt.	E 10th SCVI		WG	/ /	Kentucky	DOD	(HOW=Moreton)	RAS,HOW,LOR
Morton, Robert E.	Sgt.	E 10th SCVI		GN	07/21/64	Atlanta, GA	KIA	(RAS=Robert G.)	FLR,RAS
Morton, W.S.	Pvt.	I Orr's Ri.			09/03/64			Hollywood Cem.Rchmd. W51	HC
Mosby, John T.	Pvt.	Rhett's LA			05/03/63	Chancellorsville	KIA		JR
Moseley, Craddock L.	Pvt.	G 2nd SCVI		KW	12/14/63	Bean's Stn., TN	KIA		ROH,SA2,HIC,KE
Moseley, Frank	Pvt.	G 2nd SCVI		KW	11/18/63	Knoxville, TN	KIA		SA2,KEB,HIC,H2
Moseley, Levi	Pvt.	C 6th SCVI		KW	/ /	Virginia	DOD	(1st in E, 2nd SCVI)	JLC,H2,SA2
Moseley, Thomas	Cpl.	H 14th SCVI		BL	08/03/62	Richmond, VA	DOD	(Typhoid, Chimbarazo Hos.)	ROH,JR,CDC,UD2
Moseley, W.B.	Pvt.	C 14th SCVI		LS	/ /	Richmond, VA			ROH

M

SOUTH CAROLINA DEAD IN CSA SERVICE 1861-1865

NAME	RANK	C	REGIMENT	AGE	DS	DIED	WHERE	WHY	BURIED	SOURCES
Moseley, W.D.	Pvt.	F	P.S.S.			/ /		DOD		JR
Mosely, B.	Pvt.	A	1st SCV			05/15/64		KIA		JR
Mosely, William	Pvt.	H	P.S.S.		SG	/ /				HOS
Moses, Edwin L.	Pvt.	D	27th SCVI	32	CN	06/11/65	Camp Chase, OH	DIP	Beth Elohim, Charleston SC	ROH,FPH,P6,RCD
Moses, Joshua L.	Lt.		Culpeppers		CN	04/09/65	Ft. Blakely, AL	KIA	(1st in I, 2nd SCVI)	H2,SA2,KEB
Moses, Perry	Pvt.	D	2nd SCVI	18	RD	09/12/62	Malvern Hill, VA	DOW	Hebrew Cem. Columbia, SC	MP,ROH,HIC,PP,H2
Mosley, H.T.	Pvt.	H	4th SCVI		PS	01/27/62	Manassas, VA	DOD		SA2
Mosley, J.A.	Pvt.	C	2nd SCV			10/13/63	Atlanta, GA		Oakland C. Atlanta R4#3	BGA
Moss, George W.	2nd Sgt.	K	5th SCVI		SG	09/17/62	Sharpsburg, MD	KIA	(HOS=1st Sgt.)	ROH,JR,SA3,HOS
Moss, J.L.	Pvt.					/ /	Richmond, VA		Oakwood C.#57, Row K,Div G	OWC
Moss, J.W.	Pvt.	D	22nd SCVI		PS	08/12/64	Petersburg, VA			ROH,PP
Moss, James P.	Pvt.	I	2nd SCVC		ED	/ /	Malvern Hill, VA	DOW	(J.L. in OWC ?)	HOE
Moss, John F.	Pvt.	K	5th SCVI		SG	09/17/62	Sharpsburg, MD	KIA		ROH,JR,SA3,HOS
Moss, John H.	Pvt.	B	6th SCVC		ED	06/12/64	Trevillian Stn.	KIA	UD3	ROH,JR,HOE,ETW
Moss, Joseph	Pvt.	A	17th SCVI		YK	12/14/62	Kinston, NC	KIA		YEB
Moss, Matthew	Pvt.	B	6th SCVC		ED	06/12/64	Trevillian Stn.	KIA	UD3	ROH,JR,HOE,ETW
Moss, Roland	Pvt.	C	12th SCVI		FD	07/02/63	Gettysburg, PA	KIA	(JR=DOW 7/4/63)	JR,GDR,HFC
Moss, Singleton A.	Pvt.	I	14th SCVI	30	AE	05/15/63	Richmond, VA	DOW	(Wdd @ Chancellorsville)	ROH,JR,HOL
Motes, Joseph B.	Pvt.	K	1st SCVIG	31	LS	05/25/64	Richmond, VA	DOW	Hollywood Cem.Rchmd. I235	ROH,HC,SA1
Motes, S.T.	Pvt.	G	3rd SCVI		LS	12/25/62	Richmond, VA	DOD	Oakwood C.#45, Row L,Div B	OWC
Motes, S.T.	Pvt.	G	3rd SCVI		LS	12/23/62	Lynchburg, VA	DOD	Lynchburg CSA Cem.#1 R2	JR,BBW,SA2
Motes, Thomas F.	Pvt.	B	1st SCVIG	25	NY	11/22/62	Charlottesville	DOD	Univ. Cem. Charlottesville	ROH,JR,SA1,ACH
Motley, James	Pvt.	C	6th SCVI		KW	07/05/62	7 Pines, VA	DOW	Oakwood C.#4, Row M, Div C	ROH,JR,OWC,CDC
Motley, Ransom L.	Sgt.	H	7th SCVIBn	34	RD	05/16/64	Drury's Bluff VA	KIA		ROH,JR,HAG
Motley, Warren G.	Pvt.	E	9th SCVI			08/25/61		DOD	(Measles)	JR
Motte, Jeff	Pvt.	H	15th SCVI		UN	/ /		DOD		JR,KEB
Motte, John	Pvt.	H	15th SCVI		UN	/ /		DOD		JR,KEB
Motte, Joshua W.	1st Sgt.	E	14th SCVI	21	LS	08/03/64	Richmond, VA	DOW	(Wdd 7/28/64)	ROH,JR,CGS
Moulton, R.F.	Pvt.	A	5th SCVI		DN	06/30/62	Frayser's Fm. VA	DOW	(JR=Mouton)	ROH,JR,SA3,LAN
Moushet, Jonas	Pvt.	C	4th SCVI		AN	07/28/61	Culpepper, VA	DOD	Fairview Cem. Culpepper VA	ROH,SA2,CGH,CDC
Mouton, C.B.	Pvt.	C	2nd SCVIRi			/ /	Richmond, VA			ROH
Mox, G.	Pvt.	A	14th SCVI	22	DN	08/16/64	Richmond, VA	KIA		ROH
Moyer, W.F.	Pvt.					/ /	Marietta, GA		Con.Cem. Marietta, GA	CCM
Moyers, Daniel	Sgt.	B	19th SCVI			12/30/64	Camp Douglas, IL	DIP	Oakwoods Cem. Chicago, IL	FPH,P5
Moylan, Peter	Cpl.	I	3rd SCVI		LS	07/05/63	Gettysburg, PA	DOW	(KEB= Maylan)	ROH,GDR,KEB
Mozingo, Henry	Pvt.		PeeDee LA		DN	/ /			(PDL= A.M.)	ROH,PDL
Mozingo, N.E.	Cpl.	M	8th SCVI		DN	02/15/63	Richmond, VA	DOD	Oakwood C.#48, Row L, Div C	ROH,JR,OWC,KEB
Muckenfuss, Henry T.	Pvt.	G	11th SCVI		CO	10/15/63	SC	DOD		ROH,CDC
Muckenfuss, William C.	Pvt.	A	25th SCVI	18	CN	07/29/62	James Island, SC	DOD	Bethel M.C. Charleston, SC	ROH,MAG,HAG
Muden, Charles D.	Pvt.	G	12th SCVI		PS	10/31/62	Frederick, MD			ROH
Muff, J.N.	Pvt.	C	14th SCVI		LS	06/06/64			Hollywood Cem.Rchmd. U588	HC
Muldrow, John H.	Cpt.	A	8th SCVI		DN	07/01/62	Malvern Hill, VA	KIA		ROH,JR,TRR,R46
Muldrow, W.W.	Pvt.	B	12th SCVI		YK	08/29/62	2nd Manassas, VA	KIA		JR
Mulkey, William E.	Pvt.	I	2nd SCVI		PS	12/03/62	Richmond, VA	DOD	(Mackey ?)	ROH,SA2,H2
Muller, L.	Sgt.		P.S.S.			08/30/62	2nd Manassas, VA	KIA	CSA Cem. Manassas, VA	CDC
Mulligan, W.H.	Pvt.	E	11th SCVI		BT	01/26/65	Elmira, NY	DIP	Woodlawn N.C.#1634 Elmira	FPH,HAG,P5,P120
Mullikin, B.M.	Pvt.	D	18th SCVI		AN	08/27/62	Rappahannock Stn	DOW	(JR=KIA 3/30/62)	ROH,JR,CDC
Mullikin, Francis Marion	Pvt.	G	22nd SCVI	21	AN	07/30/64	Crater, Pbg., VA	KIA		ROH,BLM
Mullikin, James H.	Pvt.	C	P.S.S.	34	AN	09/17/62	Richmond, VA	DOW	(Wdd @ Frayser's Farm)	ROH,JR,SA2,GMJ
Mullikin, James M.	1st Lt.	G	19th SCVI		AN	07/22/64	Atlanta, GA	KIA	(HOL= Cpt. Mulligan)	ROH,JR,HOL,R47
Mullikin, John Ferdinand	Pvt.	D	Orr's Ri.	38	AN	10/04/62	Hillsboro, NC	DOD	Charlestown, VA	ROH,JR

M

SOUTH CAROLINA DEAD IN CSA SERVICE 1861-1865

NAME	RANK	C REGIMENT	AGE	DS	DIED	WHERE	WHY	BURIED	SOURCES
Mullikin, John William	Pvt.	G 22nd SCVI	17	AN	09/14/62	Maryland Hts. MD	KIA		ROH
Mullikin, Richard Jasper	Pvt.	D Orr's Ri.	32	AN	08/29/62	2nd Manassas, VA	KIA		ROH
Mullikin, Samuel Warren	Cpl.	G 22nd SCVI	30	AN	07/30/64	Crater, Pbg., VA	KIA		ROH
Mullinax, A. Richard	Pvt.	A 17th SCVI	35	YK	12/14/62	Kinston, NC	KIA	UD2	ROH,JR,PP,YEB,
Mullinax, Alexander	Pvt.	C 17th SCVI	22	YK	07/30/64	Crater, Pbg., VA	KIA		ROH,BLM,YEB
Mullinax, Andrew Jackson	Pvt.	F 18th SCVI		UN	07/30/64	Crater, Pbg., VA	KIA		ROH,JR,BLM
Mullinax, Emanuel K.	2nd Lt.	I P.S.S.		PS	05/28/64	Old Church, VA	KIA	(JR=5/31/64)	ROH,JR,R48
Mullinax, Huston	Pvt.	F 18th SCVI		UN	01/21/63	Kinston, NC	DOD		JR
Mullinax, J.S.	Pvt.	I P.S.S.		PS	02/12/64	Camp Morton, IN	DIP	Green Lawn C. Indianapolis	FPH,JR,CV
Mullinax, James	Pvt.	F 18th SCVI		UN	02/05/62	Charleston, SC	DOD		JR
Mullinax, John	Pvt.	H 16th SCVI		GE	01/12/65	Nashville, TN	DOW	(Wdd @ Nashville 12/15/64)	P4,16R
Mullinax, John G.	Pvt.	F 17th SCVI	34	YK	01/12/62	Charleston, SC	DOD	(YMD=Co.C)	JR,YMD,TCC,CB
Mullinax, Joseph	Pvt.	F 18th SCVI	24	YK	06/01/64	Petersburg, VA	DOW	(HOS=SG & Co.G)	ROH,HOS
Mullinax, W.	Pvt.	B 12th SCVI			08/29/62	2nd Manassas, VA	KIA		JR
Mullinax, William	Pvt.	H 22nd SCVI		GE	04/01/63	At home	DOD		PP
Mullins, R.A.	Pvt.	B 12th SCVI		YK	07/03/63	Gettysburg, PA	KIA		JR
Mullins, Richard	Pvt.	B 1st SCVA			07/10/64	Bty. Pringle, SC	DOW		R44
Mullins, Thomas	Pvt.	H 1st SCVIR		CN	06/15/62	Columbia, SC	DOD	(Exact date unknown)	SA1
Mullins, W.W.	Pvt.	B 12th SCVI		YK	08/29/62	2nd Manassas, VA	KIA		ROH,JR,CDC
Multon, J.J.	Pvt.				07/23/64	Richmond, VA			ROH
Mulvin, D.	Cpl.	F 4th SCVC		MN	11/03/64	Richmond, VA			ROH
Mumford, James	Pvt.	D 26th SCVI		MO	/ /	Petersburg, VA	KIA		HOM
Mundle, William W.	Pvt.	F 12th SCVI		FD	07/02/63	Gettysburg, PA	KIA		JR,GDR,HFC,CDC
Mundy, Milledge B.	Pvt.	I 7th SCVI		BL	03/26/62	Richmond, VA	DOD	Antioch B.C. ED Cty.	ROH,EDN
Mungo, E. Mack	Pvt.	K 6th SCVI			10/23/64	Baltimore, MD	DIP	Loudon Pk. C. B-102 Balto	FPH,CV,PP,P3
Mungo, William	Pvt.	E 12th SCVI	18	LR	07/26/62	Richmond, VA	DOD	(JR=Mender)	ROH,JR,LAN
Munion, J.C.	Pvt.	H SCVABn			03/28/62	Ft. Sumter, SC	KIA	Magnolia Cem. Charleston	MAG,RCD
Munn, J.	Pvt.	G P.S.S.		YK	08/21/62			Hollywood Cem.Rchmd. V413	HC
Munn, W.J.	Pvt.	I 10th SCVI		MN	07/28/64	Atlanta, GA	KIA	(HOW & RAS= Murfreesboro)	ROH,RAS,HOW,HM
Munnerlyn, William H.	1st Lt.	D 10th SCVI		WG	07/22/64	Atlanta, GA	KIA		ROH,RAS,HOW,CD
Munro, John	2nd Lt.	L 1st SCVIG		CN	08/29/62	2nd Manassas, VA	KIA		ROH,JR,SA1,R45
Murchison, Allan A.	Pvt.	E 2nd SCVI	20	KW	07/23/61	Culpepper, VA	DOD	Fairview Cem. Culpepper VA	ROH,CGH,SA2,CD
Murchison, Julius J.	1st Sgt.	G 2nd SCVI		KW	05/08/64	Wilderness, VA	DOW	Fredericksburg C.C. R6S1?	ROH,JR,SA2,FBG
Murdaugh, L.B.	1st Lt.	K 11th SCVI	23	CO	04/15/65	Goldsboro, NC	DOD		ROH,HAG
Murden, E.O.	Cpt.	D 23rd SCVI		CN	08/30/62	2nd Manassas, VA	DOW		CDC
Murdock, John F.	Sgt. Major	G 8th SCVI	18	MO	/ /	At home	DOD	Dischged, died April 1865	UD2
Murphy, Charles T.	Pvt.	C 18th SCVI	20	UN	07/24/62	Charleston, SC	DOD		ROH,JR
Murphy, David F.	Pvt.	G 25th SCVI		OG	02/23/65	Elmira, NY	DIP		EDR,HAG,P65
Murphy, Duncan	2nd Lt.	I 1st SCVIH		MN	05/12/64	Spotsylvania, VA	KIA	Spotsylvania C.H., VA	ROH,SCH,SA1,HM
Murphy, E.A.	Pvt.	D 18th SCVI		AN	0?/29/62	Charleston, SC	DOD		ROH,JR
Murphy, Edward M.	Pvt.	A 12th SCVI	23	YK	06/15/62	At home	DOD		JR,YMD,YEB
Murphy, Enoch E.	Pvt.	E 15th SCVI	19	FD	09/02/63	David's Isl. NY	DOW	Cypress Hills N.C.#863 NY	ROH,JR,FPH,P1,
Murphy, Erastus J.	Pvt.	G 9th SCVIB			09/27/61	Warrenton Ss. VA	DOD		JR
Murphy, George D.	Pvt.	A 2nd SCVI		RD	02/08/63	Fredericksburg	DOD	Fredericksburg C.C. R1S11	ROH,JR,FBG,SA2
Murphy, J.M.	Pvt.	F 15th SCVI		UN	12/08/64	Pt. Lookout, MD	DIP	C.C. Pt. Lookout, MD	ROH,FPH,P5,P11
Murphy, James B.	Pvt.	H 6th SCVI	41	FD	07/17/62	Frayser's Fm. VA	DOW		ROH,WDB,HFC
Murphy, John J.	Pvt.	E 1st SCVC	21	OG	05/15/62	Adams Run, SC	DOD		ROH,PP
Murphy, John R.	Pvt.	E 15th SCVI	23	FD	12/15/62	Fredericksburg	DOW		ROH,JR,KEB,HFC
Murphy, Joseph E.	Pvt.	G 9th SCVIB		DN	10/07/61	Richmond, VA	DOD	Hollywood Cem.Rchmd. F44	JR,HC,JLC
Murphy, L.D.	Pvt.	H 25th SCVI		CN	02/28/65	Elmira, NY	DIP	Woodlawn N.C.#2134 Elmira	FPH,HAG,P6,P65
Murphy, Robert Elijah	Pvt.	D 3rd SCVI	25	SG	10/19/64	Cedar Creek, VA	KIA		ROH,SA2,HOS,KE

SOUTH CAROLINA DEAD IN CSA SERVICE 1861-1865

NAME	RANK	C REGIMENT	AGE	DS	DIED	WHERE	WHY	BURIED	SOURCES
Murphy, Samuel A.	Pvt.	E 15th SCVI		FD	12/15/62	Fredericksburg	DOW		CDC,KEB
Murray, A.	Pvt.				/ /			Elmwood Cem. Columbia, SC	MP,PP
Murray, Francis Marion	Pvt.	C 4th SCVI	21	AN	08/23/61	Culpepper, VA	DOD	At home	CGH,SA2,HOF
Murray, George		CS Navy			11/10/64	Richmond, VA			ROH
Murray, Henry	Pvt.	H 11th SCVI		CO	02/02/65	Elmira, NY	DIP	Woodlawn N.C.#1771 Elmira	FPH,HAG,P6,P65
Murray, J.E.	Pvt.	7th SCVC			05/30/64	Cross Roads, VA	KIA		ROH
Murray, J.J. (J.E.?)	Lt.	H 11th SCVI		CO	05/14/64	Drury's Bluff VA	KIA	(HAG= Sgt. & J.E.)	ROH,HAG
Murray, J.R.	Pvt.				/ /	Columbia, SC		Elmwood Cem. Columbia, SC	MP
Murray, John D.	Pvt.	B 13th SCVI		SG	01/22/64	At home	DOW	(Crawfordsville, SC)	JR,HOS
Murray, P.P.	Cpl.	SCVA			04/14/65	Charlotte, NC			PP
Murray, T.J.	1st Lt.	C 24th SCVI	33	CO	08/06/62	At home	DOD		ROH,CDC,R48
Murray, William B.	Pvt.	D 5th SCVC	34	CO	07/23/64	Samaria Ch., VA	DOW	Hollywood Cem.Rchmd. V579	ROH,HC,CDC
Murrell, W.S.	Pvt.	C 5th SCVI			06/02/64	Cold Harbor, VA	KIA		SA3
Murry,	Pvt.				/ /			Fredericksburg C.C. R6S13	FBG
Music, J.M.	Pvt.	A 7th SCVC		GN	09/08/64	Pt. Lookout, MD	DIP	C.C. Pt. Lookout, MD	FPH,P113
Mybern, A.F.	Pvt.	F 22nd SCVI		PS	07/15/64	Petersburg, VA	DOW	(Wdd 7/7/64)	ROH
Myers, Alexander	Pvt.	C 24th SCVI	30	CO	09/20/63	Chickamauga, GA	KIA		ROH,JR,CDC
Myers, Alexander	Pvt.	C 3rd SC Res	17	CD	01/28/65	Charleston, sC	DOD	Magnolia Cem. Charleston	ROH,MAG,RCD
Myers, D.J.	Pvt.	F 7th SCVI		ED	06/07/64	Richmond, VA		Hollywood Cem.Rchmd. U453	ROH,HC
Myers, F.A.	Pvt.	I 24th SCVI		ED	02/09/65	Camp Chase, OH	DIP	C.C.#1145 Columbus, OH	FPH,P6
Myers, Frederick	Pvt.	F 25th SCVI	47	OG	07/15/64	Petersburg, VA	KIA	(HAG= Meyers)	ROH,HAG,EDR
Myers, G.J.	Pvt.	K 7th SCVC			/ /		DIP		HIC
Myers, George Matthews	1st Lt.	H 8th SCVI		MN	07/02/63	Gettysburg, PA	KIA	UD1	ROH,JR,GDR,HMC
Myers, H.	Pvt.	G 1st SCVIR		TN	09/15/61	Charleston, SC	MUR	(Axed by Pvt. D. Simpson)	SA1
Myers, Jacob S.	Pvt.	A Ham.Leg.		CN	10/28/63	Lookout Valley	DOW		ROH,WLI,CDC
Myers, John	Pvt.	G 3rd SCVABn	40	KW	01/05/64	Hardeeville, SC	DOD	Antioch Ch. KW Cty.	ROH,CDN
Myers, John	Pvt.	E 1st SCVIR		CN	09/08/63	Ft. Moultrie, SC	KIA	(Ammo chest explosion)	ROH,SA1,CDC
Myers, John Eaton	Pvt.	I 8th SCVI	23	MN	06/16/63	Gordonsville, VA	DOD	(JR=Moyers, Rchmd 6/14)	ROH,JR,KEB,GOR
Myers, John W.	Pvt.	F 25th SCVI	26	OG	05/07/64	Pt. Walthal Jctn	KIA		ROH,CDC,PP,HAG
Myers, Joseph	Pvt.	D 8th SCVI		CD	03/07/65	Camp Chase, OH	DIP		P6,P23,KEB
Myers, Ransom G.	Pvt.	F 2nd SC Res	17	OG	03/15/65	Kingstree, SC	DOD		ROH
Myers, T.G.	Pvt.	K 25th SCVI		WG	/ /	Petersburg, VA			ROH
Myers, W.H.	Pvt.	F Orr's Ri.		PS	06/05/62	Richmond, VA		Hollywood Cem.Rchmd. P73	ROH,HC

Mc

SOUTH CAROLINA DEAD IN CSA SERVICE 1861-1865

NAME	RANK	C REGIMENT	AGE	DS	DIED	WHERE	WHY	BURIED	SOURCES
McAbee, Abner	Pvt.	I 5th SCVI		SG	07/01/64	Petersburg, VA	KIA	Petersburg Heights	HOS,SA3,WAT
McAbee, J. Joyce	Pvt.	D P.S.S.		SG	08/07/62	Frayser's Farm	DOW	Hollywood Cem.Rchmd. S55	ROH,JR,HC,HOS
McAbee, James	Pvt.	I 5th SCVI		SG	06/28/64	Petersburg, VA	KIA	(NI SA3)	ROH,HOS
McAbee, James H.	Pvt.	I 13th SCVI	24	SG	03/30/65	Hatcher's Run VA	KIA		ROH,HOS
McAbee, Leslie	Pvt.	A 3rd SCVI		SG	01/15/63	Richmond, VA	DOW	(Wdd @ Fredericksburg)	ROH,JR,SA2,KEB
McAbee, T.	Pvt.	17th SCVI		SG	08/08/62			Hollywood Cem.Rchmd. H75	HC
McAbee, William A.	Pvt.	I 13th SCVI	25	SG	09/17/62	Richmond, VA	DOD	Hollywood Cem.Rchmd. H75	ROH,JR,HC
McAbee, William B.	Pvt.	A 3rd SCVI		SG	05/06/64	Wilderness, VA	KIA	Oakwood C.#66,Row M,Div A	ROH,JR,SA2,OWC
McAdams, James R.	Pvt.	G Orr's Ri.		AE	07/15/62	Dill's Farm, VA	DOD	(Dill's Farm, SC ?)	ROH,JR,CDC
McAfee, William P.	Pvt.	G 18th sCVI		YK	05/22/62		DOD	Beersheba P.C. YK Cty.	YMD
McAliley, Samuel L.	Sgt.	I 6th SCVI		CR	06/30/62	Frayser's Fm. VA	KIA		WDB,CB,HHC
McAlister, C.	Pvt.	C 2nd SCV			08/22/63	Mobile, AL		Magnolia Cem. Mobile, AL	TOD
McAlister, C.R.	Pvt.	G 22nd SCVI	19	AN	08/15/63	Morton, MS	DOD		ROH
McAlister, David B.	Pvt.	E Orr's Ri.	28	PS	05/25/62	Guinea's Stn. VA	DOD	(JR=Spotsylvania C.H.)	ROH,JR,*CDC
McAlister, E.	Pvt.	H 25th SCVI		CN	02/28/65	Elmira, NY	DIP	Woodlawn N.C.#1378 Elmira	HAG,FPH,P6,P65
McAlister, J.A.	Pvt.	F 24th SCVI	39	AN	06/24/64	Milledgeville GA	DOD		HOL
McAlister, M.	Pvt.	B 22nd SCVI		SG	03/03/65	Richmond, VA	DOD		ROH
McAlister, O.B.	Pvt.	F 24th SCVI		AE	05/14/63	Jackson, MS	KIA		ROH,JR,PP,HOL
McAllister, George W.	Pvt.	F 24th SCVI		AN	02/01/64	Rock Island, IL	DIP	C.C.#337 Rock Island, IL	FPH,HOL,P5
McAnerna, James	Pvt.	H 1st SCVIG		GA	11/25/61	Suffolk, VA	DOD	(JR=John 12/11/61)	SA1,JR
McAnge, William	Sgt.	M 10th SCVI	33	HY	/ /	Holly Springs MS	DOD		ROH,RAS,PP
McArthur, D.J.	3rd Lt.	I 5th SCVI		SG	06/21/62		DOD	(JR=DOW @ 7 Pines)	JR,SA3,R46
McArthur, James A.	Pvt.	I 1st SCVIH		MN	12/01/62	Culpepper, VA	DOD	(To hos 11/15 dd:approx))	ROH,SA1,HMC
McArthur, William Walker	Pvt.	G 18th SCVI	45	YK	07/30/64	Crater, Pbg., VA	KIA		ROH
McAteer, Francis Marion	Pvt.	D 1st SCVIH	23	LR	08/30/62	2nd Manassas, VA	KIA		ROH,LAN,HAG,CD
McAteer, Marion	Pvt.	B 1st SCV			08/30/62	2nd Manassas, VA	KIA		JR
McBowers,	Pvt.	D 24th SCVI		BT	05/14/63	Jackson, MS	KIA		ROH,JR,CDC
McBride, Edward L.	Pvt.	G 24th SCVI	20		09/30/63	Atlanta, GA	DOW	Oakland C. Atlanta	EJM,CVGH
McBride, Edward L.	Pvt.	F 24th SCVI		AN	/ /		DOD	(1864,? Dup of Co.G man)	HOL
McBride, H.C.	Pvt.	Ham.Leg.			10/08/64	Richmond, VA		Oakwood C.#7,Row H,Div G	ROH,OWC
McBride, J.B.	Sgt.	K 15th SCVI			/ /		DOD	(JR=G.B.)	JR,KEB
McBride, J.C.	Pvt.	G 14th SCVI	24	AE	09/24/61	Camp Butler, SC	DOD	(Measles)	ROH,JR
McBride, T.A.	Pvt.	G 7th SCVC		CN	10/28/64	Petersburg, VA			ROH
McCabe, John Wesley	Pvt.	A 25th SCVI		CN	12/19/64	Pt. Lookout, MD	DIP	C.C. Pt. Lookout, MD	ROH,FPH,HAG,P5
McCafferty, George A.	Pvt.	F 15th SCVI		UN	06/15/62		DOD	Gilead B.C. Union Cty. SC	JR,KEB,UD3
McCaha, Thomas	Pvt.	G 22nd SCVI		AN	07/30/64	Crater, Pbg., VA	KIA		BLM
McCahon, J.V.	Pvt.	D 12th SCVI		RD	07/10/62	Richmond, VA			ROH
McCain, James W.	Pvt.	E 9th SCVIB		LR	01/15/62	Culpepper, VA	DOD	Fairview Cem. Culpepper VA	CGH
McCain, John Allen	Pvt.	B 3rd SCV			09/19/62	Richmond, VA	DOD	(Winder Hos., Dysentery)	JR
McCalister, William J.	Pvt.	G 15th SCVI	30	WG	09/17/62	Sharpsburg, MD	KIA	(MD Hts.?)	ROH,JR,HOW,KEB
McCall, C.W.	Pvt.	F 1st SCVIH		GE	10/07/64	Virginia	KIA		SA1
McCall, Cameron	Pvt.	K 8th SCVI		MO	09/15/61	Richmond, VA	DOD	Oakwood C.#31,Row A,Div A	ROH,JR,OWC,KEB
McCall, Daniel	Pvt.	G 23rd SCVI		MO	08/25/63	Lauderdale Sc MS	DOD	(HOM=Jackson, MS)	HOM,PP
McCall, Hugh	Pvt.	H 22nd SCVI		GE	06/02/64	Virginia	KIA		ROH
McCall, Hugh B.	1st Sgt.	K 8th SCVI		MO	10/20/62	Maryland Hts. MD	DOW		JR,HOM,KEB
McCall, Hugh S.	Pvt.	E 4th SCVC		MO	10/10/64	Elmira, NY	DIP	Woodlawn N.C.#680 Elmira	FPH,HOM,P5,P65
McCall, J.	Pvt.	L 10th SCVI		MN	03/19/65	Bentonville, NC	KIA		RAS,HMC
McCall, Martin Crawford	Sgt.	K 8th SCVI	20	MO	07/02/63	Gettysburg, PA	KIA		ROH,JR,GDR,KEB
McCall, Nathan	2nd Sgt.	I 1st SCVIH		MN	11/15/62	At home	DOD	(To Hosp @ Wchstr.,10/17)	SA1,HMC
McCall, William	Pvt.	A 21st SCVI		CN	10/19/62	Morris Island SC	DOD	(PP=Georgetown, SC 11/13)	ROH,JR,PP
McCalla,	Pvt.	1st SCVC		AE	09/17/64	Ebenezer Church	KIA	(On the beefsteak raid)	BHC,CV

Mc

SOUTH CAROLINA DEAD IN CSA SERVICE 1861-1865

NAME	RANK	C REGIMENT	AGE	DS	DIED	WHERE	WHY	BURIED	SOURCES
McCalla, J.D.	Sgt.	H Orr's Ri.		YK	05/15/65		KIA		ROH
McCallister, F.	Pvt.			WG	/ /	Weldon RR, VA	KIA		CTA,HOW
McCallister, G.W.	Pvt.	F 24th SCVI		AN	/ /		DOD (1864)		HOL
McCallister, James E.	Pvt.	I 26th SCVI		WG	/ /	Petersburg, VA	KIA (1864)		HOW,CTA
McCallister, Pleasant	Pvt.	K 6th SCVI	35	MO	/ /	Frederick, MD	DOD		ROH,3RC
McCammon, Albert T.	Pvt.	A 15th SCVI	21	RD	09/17/62	Sharpsburg, MD	KIA		ROH,JR,KEB,CDC
McCammon, Gerald L.	Pvt.	A 15th SCVI	23	RD	09/14/62	South Mtn., MD	KIA (JR=Sharpsburg)		ROH,JR,KEB,CDC
McCann, Seaborn S.	Pvt.	G 19th SCVI		AE	05/20/62	Meridian, MS	DOD		PP
McCannon, M.C.	Pvt.	H 12th SCVI	27	YK	05/12/64	Spotsylvania, VA	KIA (YEB=McCammon)		CWC,YEB
McCants, David B.	Pvt.	D 5th SCVI	24	YK	07/23/63	Petersburg, VA	DOD	Blandford Church Pbg., VA	ROH,JR,SA3,BLC
McCants, Frank S.	Pvt.	A 10th SCVI		GN	12/15/64	Nashville, TN	KIA		GRG,HOW,FLR,RAS
McCants, John E.	Pvt.	C 25th SCVI	19	WG	08/21/64	Welden RR, VA	KIA		ROH,HOW,CTA,HAG
McCants, P.J.	Pvt.	A 5th SCVI		OG	04/11/63	Pocotaligo, SC	DOD (NI SA3, Prob 5th Cav)		ROH,JR
McCants, S.E.	Pvt.	A 7th SCVC		WG	/ /		DOD		CTA,HOW,FLR
McCants, Thomas M.	1st Lt.	H 7th SCVIBn	36	FD	06/03/64	Cold Harbor, VA	DOW (Wdd 6/3/64)		ROH,JR,R46,HAG
McCaran, J.T.	Pvt.	A 26th SCVI		HY	01/10/65			Hollywood Cem.Rchmd. W237	HC
McCarlan, James	Pvt.	E			03/13/64	White Sulpher VA	(McCaslan ?)		ROH
McCarlan, Thomas	Sgt.	2nd SCVIRi		AE	08/30/62	2nd Manassas, VA	KIA		ROH
McCarley, John	Pvt.	F 2nd SCVIRi			03/12/64	White Sulpher Ss			PP
McCarley, William	Pvt.	G 2nd SCVIRi			03/03/64			Piedmont Institute, VA	ROH
McCarroll,	3rd Lt.	C 11th SCVI			08/23/64	Petersburg, VA	KIA		ROH
McCarter, B.F.D.	Pvt.	3rd SCVABn			07/03/62		DOD (Pneumonia)		JR
McCarter, David A.G.	Pvt.	H 5th SCVI		YK	06/15/61	Charlottesville	DOD	Univ. Cem. Charlottesville	JR,SA3,ACH,YEB
McCarter, Harvey S.	2nd Sgt.	B 5th SCVI	30	YK	11/14/61	Centreville, VA	DOD (YEB=Harvey G.)		SA3,YEB,CB
McCarter, Irvin E.	Pvt.	G 18th SCVI		YK	07/30/64	Crater, Pbg., VA	KIA		ROH,JR,YEB,BLM
McCarter, J.W.	Pvt.	D 18th SCVI		AN	08/30/62	2nd Manassas, VA	KIA		ROH,CDC
McCarter, Joseph	Pvt.	H 5th SCVI		SG	06/28/62	Richmond, VA	DOD		ROH,SA3
McCarter, Owen N.	Pvt.	G 18th SCVI	37	YK	09/07/64	Petersburg, VA	KIA	Blandford Church Pbg., VA	ROH,BLC,PP
McCarter, W. Elias	Pvt.	H 18th SCVI	27	YK	05/20/64	Clay's Farm, VA	KIA		ROH,JR,YEB
McCartha, Joshua	Pvt.	C 20th SCVI	40	LN	09/25/63	Mt. Pleasant, SC	DOD		ROH,KEB
McCartha, Michael	Pvt.			LN	/ /				ROH
McCartha, Randolph	Pvt.	C 20th SCVI	35	LN	05/14/64	At home	DOD		ROH,KEB
McCartha, Silas	Pvt.			LN	/ /				ROH
McCarthy, George W.	Pvt.	B 14th SCVI	26	ED	08/20/62	Gaines' Mill, VA	DOW (Rptd Wdd a Chanc'Ville)		JR,HOE,UD3
McCarty, Alexander P.	3rd Cpl.	B 1st SCVIG	25	ED	06/04/63	Richmond, VA	DOW	Hollywood Cem.Rchmd. T151	ROH,HC,UD3,SA1
McCarty, D.D.W.	Pvt.	E 7th SCVI		ED	05/02/65	High Point, NC	DOD	Oakwood C. High Point, NC	HOE,UD3,KEB,TOD
McCarty, L. W.	Pvt.	H 17th SCVI		BL	/ /	Richmond, VA			ROH
McCaskill, Finley	1st Lt.	A 7th SCVIBn	44	KW	08/21/64	Weldon RR, VA	KIA		ROH,JR,HAG,HIC
McCaskill, J.A.	Cpl.	A 5th SCVI		KW	07/15/62	Mechanicsville	DOW (Wdd 5/31/62,JR=M.A.)		JR,LAN,SA3
McCaskill, Neal C.	2nd Sgt.	F 21st SCVI		MO	08/21/64	Petersburg, VA	KIA		ROH,HAG
McCaslan, James M.	Pvt.	B Orr's Ri.	24	AE	08/29/62	2nd Manassas, VA	KIA		ROH,JR,CDC
McCaslan, Thomas O.	Sgt. Maj.	2nd SCVIRi		AE	06/30/62	Frayser's Farm	KIA (JR=6/29/62)		ROH,JR,CDC
McCaslin, John F.	Pvt.	G 1st SCVC			05/06/64	Columbia, SC	DOD		ROH,PP
McCauley,	Pvt.	B Ham.Leg.		ED	07/21/61	1st Manassas, VA	KIA		JR
McCauley,Jr., H.H.	Pvt.	F 1st SCVIH		GE	08/31/62	2nd Manassas, VA	DOW (JRH= H.M.)(JR=8/29/62)		ROH,JR,SA1,JRH
McCaw, C.C.	Pvt.	8th SCVI			/ /	Richmond, VA		Oakwood C.#3,Row A, Div A	ROH,OWC
McCaw, F.M.	Sgt.	1st SCVC			09/17/63	Richmond, VA	DOD		ROH
McCaw, John T.	Pvt.	B Orr.s Ri.		AE	08/29/62	2nd Manassas, VA	KIA		ROH,JR,CDC
McCaw, Robert G.	Pvt.	G P.S.S.		AE	06/06/62	7 Pines, VA	DOW (On Rchmd effects list)		ROH,JR,CDC,UD2
McCay, George Washington	Pvt.	K 4th SCVI	22	AN	05/31/62	7 Pines, VA	KIA		ROH,SA2
McCelvy, J.C.	1st Lt.	M 7th SCVI		AE	09/17/62	Sharpsburg, MD	KIA		JR,KEB,R46

Mc

SOUTH CAROLINA DEAD IN CSA SERVICE 1861-1865

NAME	RANK	C	REGIMENT	AGE	DS	DIED	WHERE	WHY	BURIED	SOURCES
McCelvy, J.W.	Pvt.	G	14th SCVI	25	AE	09/20/62	Boteler's Ford	KIA		ROH
McCelvy, William H.	Pvt.	C	7th SCVI	22	AE	03/10/62	Charlottesville	DOD	(JR=Typhoid 5/10/62)	ROH,JR,KEB
McChesley, J.M.	Pvt.	G	3rd SC			11/18/62	Staunton, VA			ROH
McClain, James M.	Pvt.	I	19th SCVI	22	AE	02/12/63	Newman, GA	DOD	Oak Hill C. Newman, GA	ROH,BGA
McClain, Jonathan E.	Pvt.	F	17th SCVI	22	YK	08/30/62	2nd Manassas, VA	KIA	(JR=8/29/62)	JR,YMD,CDC
McClain, Robert	Pvt.	C	7th SCVI	21	AE	09/24/63	Chattanooga, TN	KIA		ROH,KEB
McClain, Samuel Carlisle	Cpl.	I	19th SCVI	24	AE	03/19/65	Bentonville, NC	KIA		ROH,WAT,PP
McClain, Samuel M.	Pvt.	I	19th SCVI	26	AE	08/15/64	Newman, GA	DOW	(Dup of James M.?)	ROH
McClain, William	Pvt.	B	7th SCVIBn	29	FD	08/29/63	Church Flats, SC	DOD		ROH,HAG
McClam, William S.	Sgt.	H	10th SCVI		WG	07/28/64	Savannah, GA	DOW	Laurel Grove C. Savannah	ROH,RAS,HOW,BG
McClane, J.W.	Pvt.	B	8th SCVI		CD	08/02/64	Petersburg, VA	DOD	Blandford Church Pbg., VA	ROH,JR,BLC,KEB
McClary, James Henry	Pvt.	I	4th SCVC		WG	/ /		DOD	(1864)	CTA,HOW
McClaughlin, E.A.	Pvt.	A	1st SCVAR		CN	09/15/62	Charleston, SC	DOD	Magnolia Cem. Charleston	ROH,MAG
McClawrin, T.B.	Pvt.		Citadel		MO	05/14/61	Sullivans I., SC	DOD		ROH
McCleary, J.L.	Sgt.	C	25th SCVI		WG	09/04/64	Petersburg, VA	DOW	(Wdd 8/21, leg amputated)	ROH,CDC
McCleland, L.	Pvt.	B	P.S.S.		PS	12/01/64	Knoxville, TN	KIA	(JR=M. 11/28/63)	ROH,JR
McCleland, Samuel L.	Pvt.	G	1st SCVC	35	AE	01/08/63	Petersburg, VA	DOD	Blandford Church Pbg., VA	ROH,BLC,PP
McClellan, P.C.	Pvt.	I	21st SCVI		MN	03/02/65	Elmira, NY	DIP	Woodlawn N.C.#2020 Elmira	FPH,P6,P65
McClellan, William P.	Sgt.	F	Hol.Leg.	24	AE	10/11/64	Elmira, NY	DIP	Woodlawn N.C.#579 Elmira	ROH,FPH,P5,P65
McClelland, Samuel	Pvt.	L	Orr's Ri.		AN	07/27/63	Mt. Jackson, VA			PP
McClenaghan, John C.	Cpt. AQM		21st SCVI	28	MN	03/06/63	Charleston, SC	DOD	(Consumption)	ROH,JR,UD3,HAG
McClendon, F.P.	Pvt.	A	22nd SCVI			04/07/65	Elmira, NY	DIP	Woodlawn N.C.#2654 Elmira	FPH,P6,P65,P12
McClendon, G.K.	Pvt.	G	8th SCVI		MO	05/12/63	Richmond, VA		Oakwood C.#17,Row 23,Div D	ROH,OWC
McClendon, George	Pvt.	G	6th SCVI		DN	05/31/62	7 Pines, VA	KIA		ROH
McClendon, J.M.	Pvt.	G	21st SCVI		CD	01/25/64	Pt. Lookout, MD	DIP		ROH,HAG,P113
McCleod, Alexander A.	Pvt.	C	1st SCVA	22	NC	07/25/63	Bty. Gregg, SC			ROH
McCleton, W.	Pvt.		P.S.S.			11/23/63	Knoxville, TN	DOW	Knoxville City Cem.	P5
McClimons, John P.	Pvt.	F	1st SCVA	43	GE	05/09/65	Pt. Lookout, MD	DIP	C.C. Pt. Lookout, MD	ROH,FPH,GEC,P5
McClintock, J.L.	3rd Lt.	F	14th SCVI		LS	07/28/64	Deep Bottom, VA	KIA		ROH,JR,BOS
McClintock, John H.	Cpl.	H	24th SCVI	19	CR	03/07/65	Louisville, KY	DIP	Cave Hill N.C.31R62 , KY	ROH,FPH,P4,HHC
McClintock, Robert Y.	Cpl.	H	24th SCVI	21	CR	09/20/63	Chickamauga, GA	KIA	(HHC=R.N., CB=R.M.)	ROH,JR,HHC,CB
McClinton, Robert A.	Cpl.	G	2nd SCVIRi	30	AN	07/24/62	Frayser's Farm	DOW	(Wdd 6/30/62, Winder Hos.)	ROH,JR,HOF
McClinton, Robert S.	Pvt.	B	Orr's Ri.		AE	11/29/62	Sullivans I., SC	DOD		ROH,JR,CDC
McClinton, William H.	5th Sgt.	G	2nd SCVIRi	21	AN	04/19/65	NC	ACD	(Shelter fall, going home)	ROH,AR
McCluney, James	Cpl.	D	3rd SCVIBn	20	LS	05/06/64	Wilderness, VA	KIA	(KEB= McCawley)	ROH,KEB,UD3
McClung, A.S.	Pvt.	I	14th SCVI		AE	06/27/62	Gaines' Mill, VA	KIA		CNM
McClung, David P.	Pvt.	G	Hol.Leg.	18	NY	08/28/63	Lauderdale Ss MS	DOD	(NI ANY roster, on Monum)	ROH,PP
McClung, Robert	Pvt.	G	Hol.Leg.		NY	/ /		DOD		ANY
McClung, William P.	Pvt.	G	Hol.Leg.	23	NY	03/16/62	Adams Run, SC	DOD		ROH,ANY,PP
McClure, C.R.	Pvt.	F	13th SCVI		SG	09/30/64	Weldon RR, VA	KIA		JR,HOS
McClure, David	Pvt.	G	3rd SCVABn			06/05/62			Magnolia Cem. Charleston	RCD
McClure, W.D.	Sgt.	D	2nd SCVIRi			08/30/62	2nd Manassas, VA	KIA		ROH,JR,CDC
McCluskey, William	Pvt.	K	4th SCVI		PS	/ /	Charlottesville	DOD	Univ. Cem. Charlottesville	ACH,SA2
McCollum, Andrew J.	1st Sgt.	D	13th SCVI	25	NY	05/04/63	Chancellorsville	KIA		ROH,JR,ANY
McCollum, T.E.	Pvt.	L	1st SCVIG		CN	06/27/62	Gaines' Mill, VA	KIA		JR,SA1
McCombs, Morgan C.	Pvt.	K	18th SCVI		SG	09/04/64	Elmira, NY	DOW	Woodlawn N.C.#73 Elmira	ROH,FPH,P5,P65
McComson, David	Pvt.		6th SCVI		SG	/ /		DOD		HOS
McConnell, A.C.	Sgt.	G	3rd SCVIBn		FD	03/25/64	Knoxville, TN	DOW	Knoxville City Cem.	KEB,P1,P5
McConnell, A.J.	1st Lt.	B	17th SCVI		FD	07/30/64	Crater, Pbg., VA	KIA	UD3	ROH,JR,BLM,HFC
McConnell, D.	Pvt.	D	11th SCVI		BT	07/21/62	Richmond, VA			ROH
McConnell, G. Butler	Pvt.	G	3rd SCVIBn		FD	06/28/64	Richmond, VA	DOD	Hollywood Cem.Rchmd. U614	ROH,HC,KEB,HFC

Mc

SOUTH CAROLINA DEAD IN CSA SERVICE 1861-1865

NAME	RANK	C REGIMENT	AGE	DS	DIED	WHERE	WHY	BURIED	SOURCES
McConnell, James D.	Pvt.	D Orr's Ri.		AN	07/23/62	Gaines' Mill, VA	DOW		JR,CDC
McConnell, Robert A.	Pvt.	K 17th SCVI	23	YK	08/30/62	2nd Manassas, VA	KIA		ROH,JR,YEB
McConnell, Thomas A.	Pvt.	C 25th SCVI		WG	05/16/64	Drury's Bluff VA	KIA		CTA,HOW,HAG
McConnell, William Scott	Pvt.	E 10th SCVI	18	WG	06/08/62	Columbus, MS	DOD	Friendship C. Columbus, MS	ROH,RAS,HOW,PP
McCook, J.J.	Pvt.	K 18th SCVI		CD	08/01/62	Petersburg, VA	DOD	Blandford Church Pbg., VA	ROH,BLC
McCool, W.	Pvt.	A 2nd SCVIRi		AE	/ /	Lynchburg, VA		Lynchburg CSA Cem.#8 R2	BBW
McCord, David W.	Pvt.	F 2nd SCVI		AE	07/01/62	Malvern Hill, VA	KIA		ROH,SA2,KEB,H2
McCord, Frank	Cpl.	G Orr's Ri.	26	AE	08/01/63	Richmond, VA	DOW		ROH
McCord, John	Pvt.	G Orr's Ri.	19	AE	02/15/63	Stevensburg, VA	DOD		ROH
McCord, Langdon Cheves	Cpt.	H Ham.Leg.	21	LN	01/23/63	Richmond, VA	DOW	Elmwood Cem. Columbia, SC	ROH,MP,PP,R48
McCormac, James A.	Cpl.	H Orr's Ri.		MN	06/27/62	Gaines' Mill, VA	KIA	(JR=DOW 10/ /62)	ROH,JR,HMC,CDC
McCormac, Thomas J.	Pvt.	H Orr's Ri.		MN	08/29/62	2nd Manassas, VA	KIA	(JR=J.F.)	JR,HMC,CDC
McCormack, Simeon P.	Pvt.	E 1st SCVIG		MN	06/05/64	Richmond, VA	DOD	Hollywood Cem.Rchmd. U583	ROH,HC,PDL,HMC
McCormick, B.F.	Cpl.	I 1st SCVIH		MN	08/29/62	2nd Manassas, VA	KIA	(Not in SA1)	ROH,JR,CDC,JRH
McCormick, F.B.	Sgt.	E 26th SCVI		HY	02/15/64	Virginia	DOW		ROH
McCormick, G.W.	Pvt.	P.S.S.			/ /	Richmond, VA		Oakwood C.#15, Row G,Div G	OWC
McCormick, George	Pvt.	A 1st SCVIH		BL	10/07/64	Darbytown Rd. VA	KIA	(SA2 hints DES to Enemy)	ROH,JR,SA1,UD3
McCormick, John	Cpt.	A 18th SCVI		UN	07/30/64	Crater, Pbg., VA	KIA		ROH,JR,R47
McCormick, John	Pvt.	C 1st SCVIR		TN	07/25/61	South Carolina	DOD		SA1
McCormick, Joseph	Pvt.	A 1st SCVIH		BL	11/01/62	Richmond, VA	DOD	Oakwood C.#67,Row L,Div A	ROH,SA1,OWC,JRH
McCormick, Samuel	Sgt.	A 18th SCVI		UN	07/30/64	Crater, Pbg., VA	KIA		BLM
McCormick, Thomas	Pvt.	D 9th SCVIBn	15	HY	04/15/62	Camp Lookout, SC	DOD	(JR=5/12/62,PP=3/15/62)	ROH,JR,PP
McCown, J.T.	Pvt.	A 26th SCVI	42	AN	11/15/64	Richmond, VA	DOW	(Wdd @ Pbg)	ROH
McCoy, Charles D.	Pvt.	E 8th SCVI		DN	02/25/65	Camp Chase, OH	DIP	C.C.#1424 Columbus, OH	FPH,KEB,P6,P23
McCoy, E.C.S.	Pvt.	3rd SCVABn	37	SR	08/25/62	Charleston, SC	DOD		ROH
McCoy, E.V.	Pvt.	B 1st SC Res		AN	02/19/65	Columbia, SC	DOD		ROH,PP
McCoy, G.F.	Pvt.	E 3rd SCV			09/17/62	Sharpsburg, MD	KIA	(JR=Fredericksburg)	JR
McCoy, J. Wesley	Pvt.	E P.S.S.		SR	06/30/63	Frayser's Farm	KIA		ROH,JR,CDC
McCoy, J.B.	Pvt.	D P.S.S.			/ /		DOD		JR
McCoy, J.J.	Pvt.	E 8th SCVI		DN	08/05/62	Richmond, VA	DOD	(Typhoid)	JR,KEB
McCoy, James F.	Pvt.	K 6th SCVI			05/15/65	Newport News, VA	DIP	Greenlawn C. Newport News	PP,P6
McCoy, Robert	Pvt.	A 14th SCVI		DN	10/31/61	Camp Butler, SC	DOD	(Measles)	JR
McCoy, Robert M.	Pvt.	E 6th SCVI		SR	05/12/64	Spotsylvania, VA	DOW		ROH,JLC
McCoy, Samuel T.	Pvt.	E 3rd SCVI		NY	09/17/62	Sharpsburg, MD	KIA	Rose Hill C. Hagerstown MD	ROH,ANY,SA2,BOD
McCoy, Thomas	Pvt.	B 2nd SCVIRi		PS	/ /				ROH
McCoy, Warren S.	Pvt.	L 1st Eng'rs			09/25/62	Petersburg, VA	DOD		ROH
McCracken, Arthur	Pvt.	K 12th SCVI	22	PS	05/05/63	Guinea Stn., VA	DOD	(JR=5/8/63)	ROH,JR
McCracken, R. Hayne	Pvt.	D 13th SCVI	25	NY	08/04/63	Chester, PA	DOW	Magnolia Cem. Charleston	ROH,GDR,ANY,P1
McCracken, W. Wilson	Pvt.	B 10th SCVI		HY	02/21/65	Camp Chase, OH	DIP	C.C.#1371 Columbus, OH	FPH,RAS,P6,P23
McCracken, W.A.	Sgt.	B Orr's Ri.		AE	02/02/63	Richmond, VA	DOW	(Wdd @ Fredericksburg)	ROH,JR,CDC
McCracken, W.T.	Pvt.	B 10th SCVI		HY	/ /	Mississippi	DOD		RAS
McCrackin, John R.	Pvt.	C 3rd SCVI		NY	06/06/64	Cold Harbor, VA	KIA		ROH,SA2,ANY,KEB
McCrady, James Berry	Pvt.	F Hol.Leg.	18	AE	04/06/65	Pt. Lookout, MD	DIP	C.C. Pt. Lookout, MD	ROH,FPH,P6,P115
McCrady, Robert S.	Pvt.	A 13th SCVI		LS	01/06/61	Camp Pemberton	DOD	(Consumption)	JR
McCrae, A.D.	Pvt.	K 8th SCVI		MO	06/15/62		DOD		HOM,KEB
McCrae, John C.	Pvt.	K 8th SCVI		MO	/ /	Virginia	DOW	(Wdd @ Maryland Hts.8/14)	HOM,KEB
McCrany, Daniel A.	Pvt.	B 8th SCVI	18	CD	12/15/61	Richmond, VA	DOD	Oakwood C.#114, Row C,DivA	ROH,KEB,OWC
McCrany, John	Sgt.	D 26th SCVI	40	CD	07/15/62	Charleston, SC	DOD		ROH
McCrarey,	Pvt.	H 6th SCVI		FD	08/30/62	2nd Manassas, VA	DOW		WDB
McCrary, John	Pvt.	K Ham.Leg.		SG	05/31/62	7 Pines, VA	KIA		HOS
McCrary, Samuel	Cpl.	G 2nd SC Res	17	AN	01/31/65	Columbia, SC	DOD		ROH,PP

SOUTH CAROLINA DEAD IN CSA SERVICE 1861-1865

NAME	RANK	C REGIMENT	AGE	DS	DIED	WHERE	WHY	BURIED	SOURCES
McCrary, Spencer R.	Pvt.	A 13th SCVI		LS	01/06/62	Ashland, VA	DOD		JR
McCravy, Hartwell A.	Pvt.	K 5th SCVI		SG	07/21/61	1st Manassas, VA	KIA	(JR=K, P.S.S.)	JR, SA3
McCravy, Samuel	Pvt.	D 3rd SCVI	24	SG	06/29/62	Savage Stn., VA	KIA	Friendship Ch. SG Cty. SC	ROH, JR, KEB, UNC
McCray, James H. (A.?)	Sgt.	H 7th SCVC		KW	08/23/64	White Oak Swamp	KIA	Oakwood C.#55, Row G, Div G	ROH, OWC, HIC
McCreary, C. Wycliffe	Col.	1st SCVIG	29	BL	03/31/65	Hatchers Run, VA	KIA	Family Cem. Williston, SC	ROH, LC, BOS
McCreary, James	Pvt.	I 16th SCVI		GE	/ /	Adams Run, SC	DOD		16R
McCreary, Judson	Surgeon	1st SC Res			02/09/64	At home	DOD		ROH
McCreight, J.G. (J.T.?)	Pvt.	G 6th SCVI		FD	09/30/64	Chaffins Farm VA	KIA		ROH, HFC
McCreight, J.H.	Pvt.	C 3rd SCResB			04/08/65	Raleigh, NC		Oakwood C. Raleigh, NC	TOD
McCreless, James	Pvt.	H 19th SCVI	40	ED	01/15/62	At home	DOD		ROH, EDN
McCrelus, James M.	Pvt.	C 19th SCVI		ED	02/09/62	Charleston, SC	DOD		HOE, UD3
McCright, J.W.	Pvt.	H 12th SCVI	22	YK	07/15/62	Richmond, VA	DOD		CWC, YEB
McCright, John E.D.	Pvt.	C 5th SCVI		UN	/ /	At home	DOD	(Furlough 7/10/62)	JR, SA3
McCright, W.T.	Pvt.	H 12th SCVI	20	YK	07/15/62	Richmond, VA	DOD		CWC, YEB
McCron, G.	Pvt.	H 6th SCVI		FD	08/30/62	2nd Manassas, VA	DOW		CDC
McCrorey, J.L.	2nd Lt.	B 4th SCVC		CR	08/21/64	Ft. Delaware, DE	DIP	Finn's Pt., NJ Nat. Cem.	ROH, JR, FPH, P5,
McCrown, P.F.	Pvt.	F 14th SCVI		LS	12/29/62	Richmond, VA		Oakwood C.#102, Row N, Div A	ROH, OWC
McCue, H.W.	Pvt.	B 22nd SCVI		SG	/ /				ROH
McCue, J.M.	Sgt.	B 22nd SCVI		SG	/ /				HOS
McCue, James	Pvt.	B 22nd SCVI		SG	/ /				ROH
McCue, M.A.	Pvt.	B 22nd SCVI		SG	07/30/64	Crater, Pbg., VA	KIA		HOS
McCue, William M.	Pvt.	A 1st SCVIH		BL	08/30/62	2nd Manassas, VA	KIA	UD3	ROH, JR, SA1, JRH
McCuir, J.T.	Pvt.	B Orr's Ri.	35	AE	05/05/64	Wilderness, VA	KIA	(Prob Dup of McCaw, J.T.)	ROH, JR
McCulley, John Emory	Pvt.	D 17th SCVI	19	CR	11/22/62	Richmond, VA	DOD	(HHC=DOW, JR=11/27)	ROH, JR, HHC, CB
McCullom, W.	Pvt.	A 6th SCVI		CR	01/03/65	Richmond, VA		Hollywood Cem. Rchmd. W240	HC
McCullough, C.T.	Pvt.	D Orr's Ri.		AN	/ /	Petersburg, VA			ROH
McCullough, H.B.	Cpl.	A 22nd SCVI	32	ED	05/09/64	Petersburg, VA		Blandford Church Pbg., VA	BLC, PP
McCullough, Hiram	Pvt.	A 17th SCVI		CR	/ /	Charlotte, NC	DOD	(Charlottesville ?)	HHC
McCullough, J.H.	Pvt.	G 13th SCVI		NY	05/12/64	Spotsylvania, VA	KIA	Spotsylvania C.H., VA	ROH, JR, SCH, ANY
McCullough, J.H.	1st Sgt.	E 16th SCVI	26	GE	08/07/62	Adams Run, SC	DOD	(Typhoid)	ROH, JR, 16R
McCullough, J.H.	Pvt.	H 18th SCVI		YK	08/06/62	Petersburg, VA	DOD	(JR=McCully, S.H.)	ROH, JR
McCullough, John	Pvt.	B 4th SCVC		CR	08/15/64	Elmira, NY	DIP	Woodlawn N.C.#25 Elmira	FPH, P5, P65, HHC
McCullough, John A.	Pvt.	A 22nd SCVI	18	ED	04/18/62	Charleston, SC	DOD		ROH, EDN
McCullough, John D.	Pvt.	C Hol.Leg.		SG	/ /		DOW	(In Enemy Hands)	HOS
McCullough, L.M.	Pvt.	H 18th SCVI		YK	/ /	Petersburg, VA			ROH
McCullough, T.R.	Pvt.	A 6th SCVI	24	CR	09/15/64	At home	DOD		ROH, GLS, HHC
McCullough, Thomas	Pvt.	A 17th SCVI	36	CR	09/10/62	Danville, VA	DOD	(JR=Memphis 9/17, Typhoid)	ROH, JR, HHC, CB
McCullough, Thomas	Cpl.	B 4th SCVC		CR	08/18/64	Elmira, NY	DIP	Woodlawn N.C.#121 Elmira	FPH, P5, HHC, CB
McCullough, Thomas	Pvt.	B 6th SCVI	29	YK	/ /	At home	DOD	(1862)	YEB
McCullough, William F.	Pvt.	A 12th SCVI	35	UN	07/05/63	Williamsport, MD	KIA		ROH, JR, YEB
McCullough, William L.	Pvt.	A 5th SCVI		CR	08/15/63	Morristown, TN	DOD		LAN, SA3, HHC
McCullough, William M.	Pvt.	K 6th SCVI	32	WG	11/03/64	Wilderness, VA	DOW	McCullough/Grayson C. WG	ROH, HOW, CTA, 3R
McCully, Samuel	Pvt.	H 18th SCVI	24	YK	/ /	Raleigh, NC	DOD		YEB
McCurry, Augustus	Pvt.	I 14th SCVI	21	AE	06/27/62	Gaines' Mill, VA	KIA	(HOL= Frayser's Farm)	ROH, HOL
McCurry, D.S.	Pvt.	I 14th SCVI		AE	06/27/62	Gaines' Mill, VA	KIA		JR
McCurry, John S.	Pvt.	I 14th SCVI	23	AE	09/12/63	Davids Island NY	DOW	Cypress Hills N.C.#855 NY	ROH, JR, FPH, GDR
McCurry, Seaborn S.	Pvt.	G 19th SCVI		AE	06/24/62	Enterprise, MS	DOD	(PP=5/29/62)	HOL, PP
McCurry, William L.	Sgt.	D 7th SCVI		AE	07/02/63	Gettysburg, PA	KIA	(KEB=McCurne)	ROH, GDR, KEB, CD
McCutchen, George H.	Pvt.	E 6th SCVI		SR	/ /	At home	DOW	(Wdd 7P, 2nd M.& Ft Harsn)	JLC, CDC
McDaniel, A.	Pvt.	L 10th SCVI		MN	/ /		DOD		RAS, HMC
McDaniel, Amos	Pvt.	I 1st SCVIH		MN	05/19/64	Spotsylvania, VA	DOW		SA1, HMC

Mc

SOUTH CAROLINA DEAD IN CSA SERVICE 1861-1865

NAME	RANK	C REGIMENT	AGE	DS	DIED	WHERE	WHY	BURIED	SOURCES
McDaniel, B.F.	Pvt.	B P.S.S.			04/20/64		DOD		ROH, JR
McDaniel, Benjamin W.	Cpl.	B 16th SCVI		GE	09/23/63	Newton, MS	DOD	(16R=Griffin, GA)	16R, PP
McDaniel, E. Jackson	Pvt.	F 6th SCVI	30	CR	02/01/65	At home	DOW	(Also Wdd @ 7 Pines)	ROH, HHC
McDaniel, E.H.	Pvt.	C Orr's Ri.		PS	06/15/62	Lynchburg, VA	DOD	Lynchburg CSA Cem.#8 R2	ROH, JR, CDC, BBW
McDaniel, George	Pvt.	E 16th SCVI	28	GE	03/26/64	At home	DOD		ROH, 16R, PP
McDaniel, Isaac	Pvt.	C 6th SCVI		KW	/ /	Virginia	DOD	(May be Co.C, 9th SCVI)	HIC
McDaniel, James	Pvt.	H Orr's Ri.		MN	08/15/62	Sullivans I., SC	DOD	(Feb. in HMC)	ROH, HMC
McDaniel, James	Pvt.	K 2nd SCVC			07/26/64	Adams Run, SC	DOD		PP
McDaniel, James A.	Pvt.	G 15th SCVI	23	WG	09/29/62	Richmond, VA	DOD	Hollywood Cem.Rchmd. S185	ROH, JR, HC, KEB
McDaniel, James A.	Pvt.	F Ham.Leg.		GE	06/15/61	Brentsville, VA	DOD		ROH
McDaniel, James B.	Pvt.	E 2nd SCVI		KW	08/07/64	Richmond, VA	DOD	(Not on rolls 11/1/62)	JR, HIC, SA2, KEB
McDaniel, James R.	Pvt.	K 8th SCVI		MO	12/03/63	Chattanooga, TN	DIP		HOM, KEB, P1, P39
McDaniel, John Francis	Pvt.	B 18th SCVI	33	UN	07/30/64	Crater, Pbg., VA	KIA		ROH, JR, BLM
McDaniel, John R.	3rd Sgt.	I 21st SCVI		MN	/ /	Elmira, NY	DIP	(! see McDonald, J.R.)	HMC, HAG
McDaniel, Joseph	Pvt.	I 1st SCVIH		MN	08/15/62	Charleston, SC	DOD		HMC, JRH
McDaniel, Joseph P.	Pvt.	F 6th SCVI	23	CR	10/19/64	Richmond, VA	DOW	(Wdd on Darbytown Road)	ROH, CDC, HHC
McDaniel, P.B.	Pvt.	B 1st SCSSBn	37	ED	10/22/62	Pocotaligo, SC	KIA		JR, HOE, HAGUD3, PP
McDaniel, Randall	Pvt.	I 1st SCVIH		MN	10/28/63	Lookout Valley	KIA	(HMC= died in 1868)	ROH, JRH, HMC
McDaniel, Robert S.	Pvt.	A P.S.S.		UN	03/19/62	Rapidan River VA	ACD	(Falling tree)	JR, SA3, UD1
McDaniel, Simeon	Pvt.	H 7th SCVI		PS	09/04/61	Charlottesville	DOD	Univ. Cem. Charlottesville	ROH, JR, ACH
McDaniel, W. Preston	Pvt.	H Orr's Ri.		MN	02/15/62	Sullivans I., SC	DOD	(JR=12/14/61)	ROH, HMC, CDC, CNM
McDaniel, William L.	Pvt.	F 6th SCVI	22	CR	06/05/62	7 Pines, VA	DOW		ROH, CRM, WDB, HHC
McDaniel, William Tate	Pvt.	E 5th SCVI			08/16/64	Whites Tavern VA	KIA	In the field	ROH, JR, SA3, UD3
McDaniels, J.E.	Pvt.	K 26th SCVI	33	HY	12/28/63	At home	DOD		ROH
McDaniels, J.H.	Pvt.	M 10th SCVI		HY	/ /		DOD		RAS
McDaniels, M.T.	Pvt.	H 1st SCVC		YK	03/15/62		DOD		ROH
McDavid, William L.	Sgt.	K Orr's Ri.	23	AN	05/12/64	Spotsylvania, VA	KIA		ROH
McDermott, Michael	2nd Sgt.	K 1st SCVIG		CN	06/10/62	Virginia	ACD	(Accid'tly shot on picket)	JR, SA1
McDill, David T.	Pvt.	G Orr's Ri.		AE	12/25/61	At home	DOD	Due West A.R.P. AE Cty.	ROH, JR, CAE, CDC
McDill, J. Hervey	2nd Lt.	F 23rd SCVI		CR	07/31/64	Petersburg, VA	DOW	(Wdd 7/28/64)	ROH, R48, HHC
McDill, William Simonton	Pvt.	G 6th SCVI	21	CR	12/20/61	Dranesville, VA	KIA		ROH, JR, HHC, R46
McDill, William W.	Pvt.	F 2ns SCVIRi	23	AE	12/31/64	Strawberry Pl'ns	DIP	Due West A.R.P.	CAE, P1, P5
McDonald, A.	Pvt.	K 1st SCV			10/15/63	Gordonsville, VA		Gordonsville, VA	GOR
McDonald, A.A.	Pvt.	C 27th SCVI		CN	04/22/65	Pt. Lookout, MD	DIP		HAG, P113
McDonald, Alexander G.	Pvt.	A Ham.Leg.	18	RD	05/31/62	7 Pines, VA	KIA		ROH, JR, CDC, WLI
McDonald, Frank	Pvt.	B P.S.S.		PS	12/15/64	At home	DOD		ROH
McDonald, G.	Pvt.	E 9th SCVIB			01/15/62	Charlottesville	DOD	Univ. Cem. Charlottesville	JR, ACH
McDonald, Ishmael C.	Pvt.	C 2nd SCVC		RD	07/26/64	Adams Run, SC	DOD	Magnolia Cem. Charleston	ROH, MAG, PP
McDonald, J.	Pvt.	G 15th SCVI		WG	09/14/62	South Mtn., MD	KIA		CTA, HOW, KEB
McDonald, J.R.	Pvt.	I 21st SCVI		MN	06/11/65	Elmira, NY	DIP	Woodlawn N.C.#2885 Elmira	FPH, P6, P66
McDonald, James E.	Pvt.	K 3rd SCVI		SG	06/05/64	Lynchburg, VA	DOW	Lynchburg CSA Cem.#7 R4	ROH, SA2, HOS, BBW
McDonald, Jerome B.	Pvt.				/ /	Petersburg, VA		Blandford Church Pbg., VA	BLC
McDonald, John M.	Cpt.	G 19th SCVI		AE	12/15/64	Nashville, TN	KIA	(HOL=Lt.Col.)	ROH, HOL
McDonald, M.	Pvt.	H 3rd SCVIBn			09/20/62	(!no such unit)		Stonewall C. Winchester VA	ROH, WIN
McDonald, Samuel Newell	1st Lt.	K 25th SCVI	27	WG	09/15/63	Bty. Wagner, SC	DOW		ROH, JR, HOW, HAG
McDonald, T.S.	Pvt.	B 5th SCVI			06/27/62	Gaines' Mill, VA	KIA		ROH, SA3
McDonald, William	Pvt.	B 21st SCVI		DN	/ /				ROH
McDonaldson, William	Cpl.	A 3rd SCV			10/13/64	Strasburg, VA	KIA		ROH, JR
McDougal,	Pvt.	1st SCVA		CN	11/15/64	Ft. Sumter, SC	DOW		ROH
McDougal, J.C.	Pvt.	A 10th SCVI		GN	05/08/62	Macon, MS	DOD	(Typhoid)	JR, GRG, RAS, PP
McDougal, Matthew	Pvt.	K 7th SCV			06/30/64	Charlotte, NC			PP

Mc

SOUTH CAROLINA DEAD IN CSA SERVICE 1861-1865

NAME	RANK	C	REGIMENT	AGE	DS	DIED	WHERE	WHY	BURIED	SOURCES
McDougal, R.	Pvt.	K	7th SCVI		ED	09/21/63	Chickamauga, GA	DOW		ROH,JR
McDow, J.T.	1st Sgt.	H	4th SCVC		CR	02/15/65	Kittrell Spgs.NC	DOD	Kittrell Springs, NC N.C.	LAN,CV,WAT,PP
McDow, James P.	Pvt.	I	12th SCVI		LR	06/27/62	Gaines' Mill, VA	KIA		ROH,JR,LAN,CNM
McDow, Johnston	Pvt.	I	17th SCVI		LR	09/14/62	South Mtn., MD	KIA	(R.J. or H.J.)	JR,LAN
McDow, W.A.	Pvt.	I	12th SCVI		LR	11/10/62	Staunton, VA	DOD	(JR=I,P.S.S.)	ROH,JR,LAN
McDow, William	Pvt.	I	P.S.S.		PS	05/31/62	7 Pines, VA	DOW		ROH
McDowall, George M.	Cpt.	F	2nd SCVI	24	AE	07/03/63	Gettysburg, PA	KIA	Magnolia Cem. Charleston	ROH,JR,GDR,SA2
McDowall, Patrick H.	Pvt.	E	Orr's Ri.		PS	04/14/65	Old Capitol P.DC	DOW		P6,CDC
McDowell, Alexander T.M.	Pvt.	A	5th SCVI		LR	03/19/63	Richmond, VA	DOD	(Also Wdd @ Frayser's Fm.)	ROH,JR,SA3,LAN
McDowell, Benjamin F.	Pvt.	K	24th SCVI		ED	02/16/65	Rock Island, IL	DIP	C.C.#567 Rock Island, IL	FPH,P5
McDowell, G.W.	2nd Cpl.	F	3rd SCVI	23	LS	08/15/62	Lynchburg, VA	DOW	Huntsville Ch. Clinton, SC	ROH,JR,SA2,LSC
McDowell, George A.	Cpl.	F	6th SCVC	22	CN	02/09/64	John's Island SC	KIA		ROH,CDC,CAG
McDowell, George W.	Lt.	L	2nd SCVIRi	41	AN	07/15/62	Manchester, VA	DOW		ROH
McDowell, J. Daniel	Pvt.	C	19th SCVI		ED	06/15/64	Covington, GA	DOD	Covington, GA Con. Cem.	HOE,CV,BGA,UD3
McDowell, J.B.	Pvt.	H	3rd SCVABn		GE	/ /				ROH
McDowell, James H.	Pvt.	F	13th SCVI		SG	08/25/64	Richmond, VA	KIA		ROH,HOS
McDowell, James J.	2nd Sgt.	F	5th SCVI		SG	08/15/61			DOD (HOS=Co. D,P.S.S.)	HOS,SA3
McDowell, Jerome B.	Pvt.	F	13th SCVI		SG	06/12/64	Petersburg, VA		(Dup of McDonald, Jerome?)	ROH,HOS,PP
McDowell, Jonas	Pvt.	K	5th SCVI		SG	07/16/62	Richmond, VA	DOW	Hollywood Cem.Rchmd. M237	ROH,JR,HC
McDowell, M.V.	2nd Lt.	K	5th SCVI		SG	05/31/62	7 Pines, VA	KIA	(HOS=Pvt.)	JR,SA3,HOS,R46
McDowell, Marcus	Pvt.	K	5th SCVI		SG	07/27/63			DOD (HOS=2nd Lt.)	SA3,HOS
McDowell, Newman J.	Sgt.	A	3rd SCVI		LS	09/20/63	Chickamauga, GA	KIA		ROH,JR,SA2,KEB
McDowell, R.R.	Pvt.	F	5th SCVI		SG	08/24/61	At home	DOD	(JR=D,P.S.S.)	ROH,JR,SA3,HOS
McDowell, S.L.	Pvt.	F	12th SCVI		FD	08/15/62	Richmond, VA	DOD	Oakwood C.#40,Row K,Div B	ROH,JR,HFC,OWC
McDowell, W.A.	Pvt.	I	13th SCVI		SG	11/09/62	Staunton, VA		Thornrose C. Staunton, VA	TOD
McDowell, W.J.	Pvt.	K	5th SCVI		SG	09/17/62	Sharpsburg, MD	DOW	(SA3=DIS 8/3/64 lost arm)	ROH,JR,CDC
McDowell, Wm. Alexander	Pvt.	E	15th SCVI	23	FD	09/03/61	Camp Johnson, SC	DOD	(JR=Lightwood Knot Spgs.)	ROH,JR,KEB
McDowell, Wm. Grafton	Pvt.	A	12th SCVI	22	YK	07/27/62	Richmond, VA	DOD	Hollywood Cem.Rchmd. C119	JR,HC,YEB
McDrew, John	Pvt.	D	1st SCVIR		TN	05/29/65	Pt. Lookout, MD	DIP	C.C. Pt. Lookout, MD	FPH,SA1,P6,P11
McDuffie, B.	Pvt.	F	Orr's Ri.		PS	08/29/62	2nd Manassas, VA	KIA		JR
McDuffie, Daniel Q.	Sgt.	I	8th SCVI		MN	07/01/63	Gettysburg, PA	KIA	Magnolia Cem. Charleston	JR,GDR,MAG,HMC
McDuffie, Duncan	Lt.		SCVA		RD	06/09/62	Charleston, SC	DOD	Magnolia Cem. Charleston	ROH,MAG
McDuffie, J.F. (F.J.?)	Pvt.	C	8th SCVI		CD	/ /	Richmond, VA		Oakwood C.#87,Row B,Div A	ROH,OWC,KEB
McDunn, N.A.	Pvt.		SCVI			07/25/62			Hollywood Cem.Rchmd. S234	HC
McEachern, John	Pvt.	G	23rd SCVI		MO	11/04/64	Richmond, VA		Hollywood Cem.Rchmd. W204	HC,HOM
McElduff, Henry	Pvt.	F	6th SCVI	28	CR	07/01/62	Richmond, VA	DOD	(Slight Wd. @ 7 Pines)	ROH,CDC,HHC
McElduff, James	Pvt.	G	6th SCVI	27	CR	10/07/61	Germantown, VA	DOD		ROH,HHC
McElduff, John	Pvt.	D	17th SCVI		CR	09/14/62	South Mtn., MD	KIA		HHC
McElduff, John B.	Pvt.	D	17th SCVI		CR	09/14/62	South Mtn., MD	KIA	(JR=J.A.)	ROH,JR,CB
McElduff, Thomas L.	Pvt.	D	17th SCVI		CR	11/09/64	Jerusalem Plk Rd	KIA		ROH,R4,HHC
McElhany, William	Pvt.	H	11th SCVI		CO	/ /	Petersburg, VA	KIA		ROH,HAG
McElheney, J.S.	Pvt.	F	6th SCVI		CR	/ /	At home	DOD	(1864)	HHC
McElmary, J.A.	Pvt.	D	Hol. Leg.	28	BL	12/06/64	Petersburg, VA	KIA		ROH
McElmurry, M.C.	Pvt.	G	2nd SCV			/ /			Con. Cem. Marietta, GA	CCM
McElrath, David T.	Pvt.	B	27th SCVI	33	SG	08/23/64	Petersburg, VA	DOW	Blandford Church Pbg., VA	ROH,BLC,PP
McElrath, Manly	Pvt.	B	13th SCVI		SG	11/28/61	Coosawatchie, SC	DOD	(JR=15th SCVI, Apoplexy)	JR,HOS
McElroy, Thomas	Pvt.	E	25th SCVI		CN	12/11/63	Ft. Sumter, SC	ACD	(Magazine explosion)	ROH,JR,CDC
McElveen, H.D.	Pvt.	B	9th SCVIB		WG	12/14/61	Centreville, VA	DOD	(JR=Co.D)	ROH,JR
McElveen, J.L.	Cpl.	G	P.S.S.		YK	09/17/62	Sharpsburg, MD	KIA	(Color guard)	ROH,JR,CDC
McElveen, Nelson	Pvt.	C	9th SCVIB	23	CL	03/15/62	At home	DOD		ROH
McElvey, W.F.	Pvt.	F	14th SCVI		SG	09/09/62	Richmond, VA	DOD	(Typhoid, McKelvey?)	JR

Mc

SOUTH CAROLINA DEAD IN CSA SERVICE 1861-1865

NAME	RANK	C	REGIMENT	AGE	DS	DIED	WHERE	WHY	BURIED	SOURCES
McElwaine, Charles	Pvt.	E	17th SCVI	29	YK	/ /		DIP	(1865)	ROH,YEB
McElwee, J.N.	Pvt.	A	12th SCVI	36	YK	/ /	At home	DOD	(1862)	YEB
McElwee, James Leslie	Pvt.	H	5th SCVI	20	YK	10/17/62	Virginia	DOD	(YEB=KIA)	YMD,SA3,YEB
McEureen, John	Pvt.	B	1st CSEng.		CR	05/27/65	Newport News, VA		Greenlawn C. Newport News	PP
McFadden, Edward D.	4th Cpl.	A	6th SCVI	24	CR	05/13/64	At home	DOD		ROH,GLS,HHC,CB
McFadden, F.	Pvt.	D	1st SC			04/04/64	Ft. Delaware, DE	DIP		ROH
McFadden, Samuel N.	Pvt.	B	5th SCVI		CR	06/27/62	Gaines` Mill, VA	KIA	(GLS & HHC=A,6th SCVI)	JR,SA3,GLS,HHC
McFadden, Thomas S.	Pvt.	D	1st SCVC	40	CR	04/04/64	Ft. Delaware, DE	DIP	Finn's Pt., NJ Nat. Cem.	ROH,FPH,P5,HHC
McFadden, W.D.	Pvt.	K	6th SCVI		WG	/ /	7 days battles	KIA	Burgess Cem. Wmbg, SC	CTA
McFadden, W.S.	Pvt.	B	6th SCVI			05/31/62	7 Pines, VA	KIA		WDB
McFadden, William	Pvt.	A	6th SCVI		CR	12/20/61	Dranesville, VA	DOW	(CB=Cpt.)	ROH,HHC,CB
McFadden, William L.	Pvt.	A	6th SCVI	22	CR	06/01/62	7 Pines, VA	DOW		ROH,CDC,HHC,CB
McFadden, William S.F.	Pvt.	B	6th SCVI		YK	05/31/62	7 Pines, VA	KIA		ROH,JR,,CDC,YEB
McFall, S.N.W.	Pvt.	E	Orr's Ri.	19	PS	07/08/62	Gaines' Mill, VA	DOW	Bethel P.C. West Union, SC	ROH,JR,OCS,CDC
McFall, Samuel R.	2nd Lt.	E	Orr's Ri.	50	PS	06/27/62	Gaines' Mill, VA	KIA		ROH,JR,CDC,R45
McFarland, Archibald	Cpl.	E	21st SCVI		CD	08/24/64	Pt. Lookout, MD	DIP	C.C. Pt. Lookout, MD	ROH,FPH,HAG,P5
McFarland, C.P.	Pvt.	K	1st SCVIR		CD	04/28/62		DOD		SA1
McFarland, W.L.	Sgt.	B	9th SCVIBn			06/16/62	Secessionville	DOW		PP
McFarland, William	Pvt.	K	P.S.S.		SG	/ /		DOD		HOS
McGaha, Thomas	Pvt.	G	22nd SCVI		AN	07/30/64	Crater, Pbg., VA	KIA		ROH
McGarity, David	Pvt.	A	17th SCVI		CR	07/15/65	At home	DOW		ROH,HHC,CB
McGarity, Henderson	Sgt.	H	24th SCVI	23	CR	03/11/65	Camp Chase, OH	DIP	C.C.#1636 Columbus, OH	ROH,FPH,P6,HHC
McGarity, John	Pvt.	A	6th SCVI		CR	05/31/62	7 Pines, VA	DOW	(CDC= Missing in action)	ROH,HHC,WDB,GLS
McGarity, Joseph	Pvt.	A	6th SCVI	23	CR	06/15/62	7 Pines, VA	DOW		ROH,GLS,HHC,CB
McGarity, Lemuel L.	Pvt.	A	6th SCVI	25	CR	11/16/63	Campbell Stn. TN	KIA	(HHC=7 Pines)	ROH,HHC,CB
McGarity, Lewis J.	Pvt.	A	6th SCVI		CR	05/31/62	7 Pines, VA	KIA	(Prob in another unit)	HHC
McGaugh, M.	Pvt.	C	1st SCV			/ /	Lynchburg, VA		Lynchburg CSA Cem.#4 R1	BBW
McGee, Abner H.	Sgt. Major		Orr's Ri.		AE	08/09/63	Gaines' Mill, VA	DOW	(Former 1st Sgt. Co.G)	ROH,JR,CDC
McGee, Andrew G.	Pvt.	B	14th SCVI	21	ED	05/04/62	Port Royal, SC	DOD	(Typhoid)	JR,HOE,UD3
McGee, Chesley	Pvt.		7th SCVI		ED	/ /	Richmond, VA		Oakwood C.#25,Row A,Div A	ROH,OWC
McGee, G.	Pvt.	G	Ham.Leg.			/ /	Charlottesville		Univ. Cem. Charlottesville	ACH
McGee, G.W.	Pvt.	F	7th SCVI		ED	09/13/62	Maryland Hts. MD	KIA	(KEB=J.W.)	JR,KEB
McGee, J.M.	Pvt.	F	3rd SCVI		LS	06/29/62	Savage Stn., VA	KIA		ROH,JR,SA2,KEB
McGee, J.M.	Pvt.	B	7th SCVI		AE	09/13/62	Maryland Hts. MD	KIA		JR,KEB
McGee, James A.	Pvt.	B	4th SCVI	25	AN	08/08/61	Culpepper, VA	DOD	Fairview Cem. Culpepper VA	ROH,JR,CGH,SA2
McGee, James W.	Sgt.	A	Ham.Leg.	18	CN	09/08/62	Warrenton, VA	DOW	(Wdd 8/29 @ 2nd Man)	ROH,JR,CDC,WLI
McGee, John C.	Sgt.	H	10th SCVI	28	WG	09/15/62		DOD	(On the march)	JR,RAS,CTA,HOW
McGee, John J.	Pvt.	I	26th SCVI	28	WG	/ /	Petersburg, VA	KIA		CTA,HOW
McGee, John Lewis	Sgt.	F	24th SCVI	20	AN	07/22/64	Decatur, GA	KIA		HOL
McGee, Joseph	Pvt.	B	14th SCVI	18	ED	07/28/64	Deep Bottom, VA	KIA		HOE,UD3
McGee, Julius W.	Pvt.	F	7th SCVI	19	AN	09/14/62	Maryland Hts.,MD	KIA	(G.W. in ROH)	ROH,HOE,KEB
McGee, Sylvester W.	Pvt.	F	24th SCVI		MN	01/30/65	Camp Douglas, IL	DIP	Oak Woods Cem. Chicago, IL	ROH,FPH,HOL,P5
McGee, T.	Pvt.	A	4th SCVIBn			09/30/62			Hollywood Cem.Rchmd. S73	HC
McGee, T.	Pvt.		P.S.S.			02/11/65			Hollywood Cem.Rchmd. W29	HC
McGee, T.M.	Pvt.	F	4th SC			08/31/62	Richmond, VA		(Probably McGee, T in HC)	ROH
McGee, U.G.	Cpl.	E	7th SCVI		ED	07/02/63	Gettysburg, PA	KIA	(KEB=U.R.,UD3=U.B.)	UD3 ROH,JR,GDR,KEB
McGee, W.H.	Sgt.	B	7th SCVI		AE	09/17/62	Sharpsburg, MD	KIA		JR
McGee, W.R.D.	Pvt.	B	4th SCVI		AN	08/15/61	Culpepper, VA	DOD		SA2,GMJ
McGee, William W.	Pvt.	A	26th SCVI		HY	07/15/64	Petersburg, VA	KIA		ROH
McGee,Jr., Abner H.	Pvt.	G	Orr's Ri.		AE	08/15/62	Gaines' Mill, VA	DOW		ROH,CDC
McGeehe, George	Pvt.	A	19th SCVI	30	ED	07/22/64	Atlanta, GA	KIA		HOE,UD3

SOUTH CAROLINA DEAD IN CSA SERVICE 1861-1865

Mc

NAME	RANK	C REGIMENT	AGE	DS	DIED	WHERE	WHY	BURIED	SOURCES
McGill, Colin	Pvt.	L 8th SCVI		MN	03/27/63	Richmond, VA	DOD	(JR=Savage St.DOW 7/11/62)	ROH,JR,HMC,KEB
McGill, D.	Pvt.	K 4th SCVI		AN	/ /	Charlottesville	DOD	Univ. Cem. Charlottesville	ACH
McGill, J.F.	Pvt.	G 26th SCVI		DN	05/05/65	Charlotte, NC			PP
McGill, J.H.	Pvt.	2nd SCV			/ /			Mt. Jackson, VA	ROH,CDC
McGill, James	Pvt.	K 1st SCVIG		CN	01/15/63	Richmond, VA	DOD	(Approx,to Hos 6/10/62)	SA1
McGill, James M.	Pvt.	K 17th SCVI	18	YK	06/17/64	Petersburg, VA	DOD	Blandford Church Pbg., VA	ROH,YMD,BLC,PP
McGill, Robert	Pvt.	B 17th SCVI		FD	11/12/62	Staunton, VA	DOD	Thornrose C. Staunton, VA	ROH,JR,TOD
McGill, Thomas	Cpl.	C P.S.S.		AN	06/30/62	Frayser's Farm	KIA		SA2,GMJ
McGill, Thomas C.	Pvt.	G 18th SCVI	18		07/30/64	Crater, Pbg., VA	KIA		ROH,BLM,PP
McGill, William Thompson	Pvt.	D 3rd SC Res	17	YK	11/18/64	Florence, SC	DOD	(Gill's Bn.prison Gds ?)	ROH,PP
McGilvray, B.F.	Pvt.	G 23rd SCVI		MO	04/01/65	5 Forks, VA	KIA		HOM
McGinness, P.B.	Pvt.	Ham.Leg.			06/02/64			Hollywood Cem.Rchmd. U106	HC
McGinness, P.B.	Pvt.	Ham.L.Arty			06/30/64			Hollywood Cem.Rchmd. X83	HC
McGinness, William M.	Pvt.	H 2nd SCVC		PS	03/29/64	Ft. Delaware, DE	DIP	Finn's Pt., NJ Nat. Cem.	ROH,CDC,FPH,P5
McGinnis, Michael	Pvt.	I 1st SCVIG		CN	07/02/63	Gettysburg, PA	KIA		SA1,GDR,CDC
McGinnis, W.A.	Pvt.	F 13th SCVI		SG	07/29/62	Laurel Hill, VA	DOD	(Typhoid)	JR
McGivens, James		CS Navy			/ /	Richmond, VA			ROH
McGlenn, G.	Pvt.	I 6th SCVI		CR	07/15/64			Hollywood Cem.Rchmd. U250	HC
McGou, J.G.	Pvt.	G 1st SCVC		AE	09/12/64	Charleston, SC		Magnolia Cem. Charleston	ROH,MAG
McGougan, Archibald	Pvt.	F 7th SCVIBn		KW	01/01/65	Pt. Lookout, MD	DIP	C.C. Pt. Lookout, MD	FPH,P5,HIC,HAG
McGougan, John	Pvt.	F 7th SCVIBn	23	KW	10/24/62	Pocotaligo, SC	DOW		ROH,HIC,HAG,PP
McGouin, Thomas	Pvt.	18th SCVI	UN		/ /	Camp Guerin, SC	DOD	Measles (Jan or Feb 62)	UD2
McGovern, John	Pvt.	K 16th SCVI		GE	11/30/64	Franklin, TN	KIA	(16R= Morgan)	ROH,16R
McGovern, Peter	Pvt.	E 1st SCVIR		GE	09/08/63	Ft. Moultrie, SC	DOW	(CDC & ROH= McGowan)	ROH,SA1,CDC
McGowan, Alexander H.	Cpt.(AQM)			LS	01/04/63	At home	DOD	(Lung Hemourage)	ROH,JR
McGowan, J.M.	Pvt.	F 15th SCVI		UN	09/21/62	Frederick, MD	DOW	Mt.Olivet C.#25 Frederick	FPH,P6,BOD
McGowan, M.B.	Lt.	K 3rd SCVI		SG	07/03/63	Gettysburg, PA	KIA	Magnolia Cem. Charleston	MAG
McGowan, S.	Pvt.	F 3rd SCVI		LS	04/18/62	Orange C.H., VA	DOD		ROH,JR,KEB
McGowan, Thomas	Pvt.	B 18th SCVI		UN	02/15/62	Charleston, SC	DOD		ROH,JR
McGowin, Thomas	Pvt.	B 2nd SCVIRi		PS	/ /				ROH
McGraw, Nathan C.	Pvt.	B 7th SCVIBn	22	FD	06/30/64	Petersburg, VA		(HAG= McGrath)	ROH,HAG,HFC,PP
McGreen, J		CS Navy			03/23/65	Richmond, VA			ROH
McGuffin, W.S.	Pvt.	F Orr's Ri.		PS	07/01/62	Richmond, VA		Hollywood Cem.Rchmd. M384	ROH,JR,CDC
McGuire, George	Pvt.	H 18th SCVI		YK	09/10/62	Warrenton, VA	DOW	(YEB=E,17th SCVI)	ROH,JR,YEB
McGuire, Henry	Pvt.	D 15th SCVI		KW	/ /		DOD		JR,KEB
McHugh, Charles		CS Hunley			10/16/63	Charleston area	ACD	Magnolia Cem. Charleston	RCD
McIher, Francis	Pvt.	D Orr's Ri.		LR	08/30/62	2nd Manassas, VA	KIA		ROH
McIlvaine, Thomas	Pvt.	F 8th SCVI	27	DN	/ /	Richmond, VA	DOD	(1862)	ROH
McIlveen, George M.	Pvt.	I 6th SCVC	18	DN	07/15/64	Richmond, VA	DOD	(Jackson Hos.)	ROH,JR
McIlwain, Andrew	Cpl.	K 2nd SCVIRi	29	AE	03/17/63	Jerusalem, VA	DOD		ROH,JR
McIlwain, J.M.	Pvt.	F Hol.Leg.		AE	04/09/65	Charlotte, NC			PP
McIlwain, Jonathan	Pvt.	H 4th SCVC		LR	06/09/63	McPhersonville	DOD		LAN
McIlwain, William M.	Pvt.	F Hol.Leg.			01/02/65	Elmira, NY	DIP	Woodlawn N.C.#1345 Elmira	FPH,P5,P66
McIlwaine, James	Pvt.	B Orr's Ri.		AE	07/10/62	Richmond, VA	DOW		ROH,JR,CDC
McInery, James	Pvt.		23	CN	12/26/61	Otter Island, SC	ACD	(Exploding gun, S.Santee)	ROH
McInnes, N.H. (N.M.?)	Pvt.	D 15th SCVI		KW	/ /		KIA	(1863)	HIC,KEB
McInnes, Nicholas H.	Pvt.	C 6th SCVI		KW	/ /		KIA		HIC
McInnis, Murdaugh	3rd Cpl.	I 1st SCVIH		MN	01/13/63	Fredericksburg	DOW	(JR=Gettysburg)	ROH,JR,SA1,HMC
McInnis, Norman H.	Pvt.	H Orr's Ri.		MN	07/15/64	Petersburg, VA	DOW	(Wdd 7/11 @ Riddles Shop)	ROH,HMC
McIntosh, Alexander	Cpl.	G 8th SCVI		MO	07/02/63	Gettysburg, PA	KIA	(Pvt. in HOM) UD1,UD2	ROH,JR,GDR,HOM
McIntosh, G.E.	Pvt.	D 2nd SCVA			12/29/63	Charleston, SC		Magnolia Cem. Charleston	ROH,MAG

Mc

SOUTH CAROLINA DEAD IN CSA SERVICE 1861-1865

NAME	RANK	C	REGIMENT	AGE	DS	DIED	WHERE	WHY	BURIED	SOURCES
McIntosh, George	Pvt.		Inglis LA	18	DN	12/26/64	Charleston, SC	DOD		ROH
McIntosh, J.E.	Pvt.		Inglis LA		DN	/ /				ROH
McIntosh, John F.	Pvt.	I	25th SCVI		CL	10/30/64	Richmond, VA	DOD	(POW from Pt.L.O. 10/11)	ROH,P113
McIntosh, Robert W.J.	Pvt.	C	9th SCVIB	20	WG	11/23/61	Charlottesville	DOD	Univ. Cem. Charlottesville	JR,CTA,HOW,ACH
McIntosh, Thomas R.	Pvt.		Palm. LA		SR	07/04/63	Gettysburg, PA	DOW	Hollywood Cem.Rchmd.	ROH,JR,CDR,SOB
McIntosh, W.	Pvt.	I	25th SCVI		CL	10/09/64	Richmond, VA		Hollywood Cem.Rchmd. W243	HC
McIntyre, Duncan	Pvt.	H	Orr's Ri.		MN	/ /	Richmond, VA	DOD	(1862)	HMC
McIntyre, F.	Pvt.	D	1st SCV			08/30/62	2nd Manassas, VA	KIA		JR
McIntyre, I. Archibald	2nd Lt.	E	1st SCVIG		MN	09/17/62	Sharpsburg, MD	DOW	In the field UD3	ROH,JR,SA1,BOS
McIntyre, John T.	Sgt. Maj.		21st SCVI		MO	03/05/65	Elmira, NY	DIP	Woodlawn N.C.#2413 Elmira	ROH,FPH,P6,P65
McIntyre, T. Curtis	Pvt.	E	13th SCVI		SG	08/25/62		DOD	(Typhoid, On effects list)	JR,CDC
McInville, J.C.	Pvt.	B	1st SCVIH		OG	11/03/63	Lookout Valley	DOW	(Wdd 10/28/63)	ROH,SA1,CDC
McInville, Rufus K.	Pvt.	E	6th SCVI		DN	06/30/62	Frayser's Farm	KIA		ROH,JLC,WDB
McIver, Bruner A.	Pvt.	F	25th SCVI		OG	05/16/64	Drury's Bluff VA	DOW		ROH,HAG,CDC,CV
McIver, J.J.	Pvt.	K	1st SCVIH		OG	05/06/64	Wilderness, VA	KIA		SA1
McIver, John Kalb	Cpt.	F	8th SCVI	29	DN	10/15/63	Pt. Lookout, MD	DOW	C.C. Pt. Lookout, MD	ROH,FPH,GDR,P5
McJunkin, Pinkney						07/15/62	Virginia?	KIA		UD2
McJunkin, R.L.	Pvt.	C	18th SCVI		UN	02/09/62		DOD	(Measles)	JR
McJunkin, Robert C.	Pvt.	C	4th SCVIBn		AN	09/07/62		DOD	(Typhoid)	JR,SA2
McJunkin, S.P.	Cpl.	B	P.S.S.		PS	06/30/62	Frayser's Farm	KIA		ROH,JR,CDC
McJunkins, James D.	Pvt.	D	5th SCVI		UN	06/25/62	Richmond, VA	DOW	(Wdd @ 7 Pines)	JR,SA3
McJunkins, Thomas W.	Pvt.	D	5th SCVI		OG	07/10/61		DOD	(Measles)	JR,SA3
McKagen, Henry Green	3rd Sgt.	E	2nd SCVI	24	KW	01/06/63	Fredericksburg	DOW	(Wdd 12/13/62) KEB	ROH,SA2,HIC,CDN
McKain, John J.	3rd Lt.	E	2nd SCVI	25	KW	04/15/62	Warwick River VA	DOW	Quaker Cem. Camden, SC	ROH,SA2,HIC,CDN
McKaskill, Neal C.	2nd Sgt.	F	21st SCVI		MO	/ /	Petersburg, VA	KIA		HOM,HAG
McKay,	Pvt.	L	P.S.S.			/ /		DOD		JR
McKay, A.R.	Pvt.	B	12th SCVI		YK	/ /		DOD		YEB
McKay, G.W.	Sgt.	L	P.S.S.			/ /		DOW		JR
McKay, Isaiah Jefferson	Pvt.	E	8th SCVI	26	DN	08/05/62	Richmond, VA	DOD	(Typhoid)	ROH,JR
McKay, J.	Pvt.		PeeDee Leg			12/15/62	Georgetown, SC	DOD	(Measles)	JR
McKay, James	Pvt.	C	1st SCResB			04/09/65	Raleigh, NC		Oakwood C. Raleigh, NC	TOD
McKay, Robert	Pvt.	A	14th SCVI	20	DN	11/08/61	At home	DOD		ROH
McKee, Cornelius	Pvt.	A	2nd SCVIRi		AE	04/04/62		DOD		ROH
McKee, Francis M.	Pvt.	G	2nd SCVIRi		AE	06/02/62	Richmond, VA	DOD	(Typhoid Pneumonia)	ROH,JR
McKee, Henry	Pvt.	F	6th SCVI	25	CR	10/30/63	At home			ROH
McKee, John A.	Pvt.	A	2nd SCVIRi		AE	09/17/62	Sharpsburg, MD	DOW	Shepherdstown, VA	JR,CDC,CV
McKee, Joseph G.	Pvt.	A	2nd SCVI		RD	06/20/64	Petersburg, VA	KIA	(On picket)	ROH,SA2,KEB,H2
McKee, Robert	Pvt.	E	1st SCVA			11/30/64	Camp Douglas, IL	DIP	Oak Woods Cem. Chicago, IL	ROH,FPH,P5,P53
McKee, S.L.	Pvt.	B	17th SCVI		FD	/ /	(ROH=J.L.,11th)		Oakwood C.#92,Row J,Div C	ROH,OWC
McKee, S.W.	Pvt.	G	24th SCVI			/ /	Camp Douglas, IL	DIP		CDC
McKee, T.J.	Pvt.	G	Orr's Ri.		AE	06/02/62	Richmond, VA		(McGee, J.L.?)	ROH
McKellar, Leonard W.	Pvt.	F	2nd SCVI	19	AE	07/01/62	Malvern Hill, VA	KIA		ROH,SA2,KEB,H2
McKellar, Peter	Pvt.	H	Orr's Ri.		MN	/ /	PA	KIA	(1864)	HMC
McKeller, John D.	1st Sgt.	I	1st SCVIH		MN	03/16/64	East TN	DOD		ROH,SA1,HMC,JRH
McKelvey, J.H.	Pvt.	E	13th SCVI		SG	/ /	Richmond, VA	DOD		HOS
McKelvey, J.W.	Pvt.	G	14th SCVI		AE	09/17/62	Sharpsburg, MD	KIA		JR
McKelvey, Philip K.	Pvt.	A	18th SCVAB	26	CN	09/27/62	Pineville, SC	DOD	(Typhoid)	ROH,JR,CDC
McKelvey, W.F.	Pvt.	H	P.S.S.		SG	05/08/64	Bermuda Hundred	KIA		ROH,JR,HOS
McKelvey, W.H.	Pvt.	C	7th SCVI			/ /	Charlottesville		Univ. Cem. Charlottesville	ACH,KEB
McKelvy, James T.	Pvt.	I	3rd SCVI		LS	09/20/63	Chickamauga, GA	KIA		SA2,KEB
McKenney, J.	Pvt.	H	11th SCVI		CO	05/23/62	Richmond, VA		Oakwood C.#61,Row D,Div B	ROH,OWC

Mc

SOUTH CAROLINA DEAD IN CSA SERVICE 1861-1865

NAME	RANK	C REGIMENT	AGE	DS	DIED	WHERE	WHY	BURIED	SOURCES
McKenny, J.W.	Pvt.	G 21st SCVI		CD	/ /	Petersburg, VA		(NI HAG McClendon?)	ROH
McKensie, J.D.	Pvt.	E 9th SCVIB		KW	10/06/61	Charlottesville	DOD	Univ. Cem. Charlottesville	JR,ACH,HIC
McKensie, John Potser	Pvt.	C 18th SCVI	27	YK	07/30/64	Crater, Pbg., VA	KIA		ROH,JR,BLM,YEB
McKensie, Lowry	Pvt.	H 26th SCVI		SR	09/19/63	Charleston, SC		Magnolia Cem. Charleston	ROH,JR,MAG
McKensie, Noah R.	Pvt.	E P.S.S.		CL	05/15/64	Cold Harbor, VA	DOW	(#2 JR entry=Spotsylvania)	ROH,JR
McKenzie, George W.	Pvt.	F 2nd SCVI	22	RD	11/04/64	Mt. Jackson, VA	DOD	Elmwood Cem. Columbia, SC	MP,SA2,KEB,PP,
McKenzie, J.B.	Pvt.	E 9th SCVIB		SR	02/15/62	At home	DOD		JR
McKenzie, J.R.	Pvt.			WG	/ /	Petersburg, VA	KIA	(Perhaps Co.I, 26th SCVI)	CTA,HOW
McKenzie, John	Pvt.	B 19th SCVI		ED	05/31/62	Atlanta, GA		Oakland C. Atlanta R7#21	CVGH,BGA
McKenzie, Ladson	Sgt.	E 1st SCVC		OG	01/15/65	James Island, SC	DOD		ROH
McKenzie, R.	Pvt.				/ /			Elmwood Cem. Columbia, SC	MP
McKenzie, R.H.	Pvt.	G 23rd SCVI		MO	09/17/62	Sharpsburg, MD	KIA	(HOM= South Mtn., MD)	ROH,JR,CDC,HOM
McKenzie, S.	Pvt.	I 7th SCVI		ED	09/13/62	Maryland Hts. MD	KIA		JR
McKeon, C.M.	Pvt.	E 23rd SCVI		MN	07/06/61	Columbia, SC	DOD	(Typhoid)	JR
McKeon, Peter	3rd Sgt.	K 1st SCVIG		CN	12/15/62		DOW	(Wdd@ Sharpsburg JR=10/18)	JR,SA1
McKeon, W.F.	Sgt. Major	P.S.S.			/ /		KIA		JR
McKeown, F.M.	Pvt.	F 15th SCVI		UN	09/21/62	Frederick, MD	DOW	(In enemy hands)	ROH,JR,P1
McKeown, George W.	Pvt.	A 12th SCVI		UN	/ /	Spotsylvania CH	KIA	(YEB=8/30/62?)	YEB
McKeown, James	Pvt.	F 6th SCVI		CR	12/20/61	Dranesville, VA	KIA		ROH,JR,HHC,R46
McKeown, John	Pvt.	D 17th SCVI		CR	/ /	John's Island SC	DOW		CB,HHC
McKeown, John Bingham	Pvt.	D 17th SCVI	31	CR	08/10/64	Crater, Pbg., VA	DOW		ROH,BLM,HHC,PP
McKeown, John James	Pvt.	B 5th SCVI	24	CR	05/05/62	Williamsburg, VA	KIA		ROH,JR,SA3,HHC
McKeown, John M.	Pvt.	A 12th SCVI	27	UN	05/31/62	Richmond, VA	DOD	(Richmond effects list)	YEB,CDC
McKeown, Samuel Scott	Pvt.	D 17th SCVI	21	CR	12/09/64	Elmira, NY	DIP	Woodlawn N.C.#1157 Elmira	ROH,FPH,P5,HHC
McKeown, William O.	Pvt.	C 17th SCVI	23	YK	07/30/64	Crater Pbg., VA	KIA		ROH,YEB
McKeown, William S.	Pvt.	C P.S.S.		AN	08/30/62	2nd Manassas, VA	KIA	Manassas CSA Cem.	ROH,CDC
McKerrill, J.J.	Pvt.				/ /	Petersburg, VA	DOW	(Wdd 9/5/64)	ROH
McKethan, J.A.	Pvt.	L 1st SCVIG		NC	08/03/63	Davids Island NY	DOW	Cypress Hills N.C.#734 NY	ROH,FPH,GDR,SA
McKewn, W. Fordham	Sgt. Maj.	P.S.S.	22	OG	12/13/62	Fredericksburg	KIA		ROH,JR
McKilby, H.A.	Pvty.	K Hol.Leg.			12/28/64	Savannah, GA	DIP		P1,P5
McKillups, M.W.	Pvt.	A 15th SCVI			11/02/62			Hollywood Cem.Rchmd. S9	HC
McKinney, B.J.	Pvt.	F 7th SCVI		ED	11/02/62	Staunton, VA		Thornrose C. Staunton, VA	ROH,TOD
McKinney, Clayborne C.	1st Sgt.	E Orr's Ri.	28	PS	07/20/62	At home	DOW		ROH,CDC
McKinney, George	Pvt.	I 5th SCVI		SG	02/24/65	Richmond, VA	DOD	(POW from Pt.L.O. 2/10)	ROH,SA3,P113
McKinney, J. Hampton	Pvt,	G P.S.S.	31	YK	06/10/64	Cold Harbor, VA	DOW	(JR=1/5/64)	ROH,JR,YEB
McKinney, J.B.	Pvt.	Columbia G		LS	12/12/63	Columbia, SC	DOD	(Prob. Cpt. Senn's Co.)	ROH,PP
McKinney, Jeff	Sgt.	I 16th SCVI		GE	/ /	Griffin, GA		Stonewall C. Griffin, GA	BGA,UD2
McKinney, John W.	Pvt.	G 22nd SCVI	37	PS	06/30/64	Bermuda Hundred	DOW		ROH,PP
McKinney, Norton A.	Pvt.	I 16th SCVI		GE	02/23/64	Dalton, GA	DOD		16R,PP
McKinney, W.T.	Pvt.	LafayetteA			03/07/65	Raleigh, NC		Oakwood C. Raleigh, NC	TOD
McKinnie, P. Franklin	Pvt.	G 22nd SCVI	33	AN	07/07/64	Richmond, VA	DOD		ROH
McKinnon, John C.	Pvt.	E 1st SCVIR		LR	09/24/63	Charleston, SC	DOW	Magnolia Cem. Charleston	ROH,MAG,SA1
McKinsey, W.J.	Pvt.	E 4th Bn Res			10/08/64	Charleston, SC	DOD	Magnolia Cem. Charleston	ROH,MAG,CDC,RC
McKinsey, Walter	Pvt.	F 7th SCVI	28	ED	11/29/63	Knoxville, TN	DOW	(KEB=McKenzie)	HOE,KEB
McKintree, T.C.	Pvt.	E 13th SCVI		SG	08/26/62	(HC=McIntyre)		Hollywood Cem.Rchmd. H46	ROH,HC,HOS
McKinzie, R.	Pvt.	F			/ /			Spotsylvania C.H., VA	SCH
McKissick, Edward D.J.	1st Lt.	H 5th SCVI		UN	05/31/62	7 Pines, VA	KIA	McKissick Fam. Cem. UN Cty	ROH,JR,SA3,UNC
McKittrick, J.	Pvt.	B 27th SCVI		CN	07/18/64	Richmond, VA		Hollywood Cem.Rchmd. U552	ROH,HC
McKittrick, Samuel	Cpt.	I 16th SCVI		GE	07/23/64	Decatur, GA	DOW	Fairview P.C. GE Cty.	ROH,16R,GEC,GE
McKnight, Hiram W.	Pvt.	A 3rd SCVI		LS	12/13/62	Fredericksburg	KIA		ROH,JR,KEB,SA2
McKnight, James E.	Pvt.	E 5th SCVI	27	YK	02/10/63	At home	DOD	(Wdd 5/31/62, Brain Dropsy)	JR,SA3,YEB

Mc

SOUTH CAROLINA DEAD IN CSA SERVICE 1861-1865

NAME	RANK	C	REGIMENT	AGE	DS	DIED	WHERE	WHY	BURIED	SOURCES
McKnight, James R.	2nd Lt.	B	12th SCVI	28	YK	05/05/64	Wilderness, VA	KIA	Beersheba P.C. YK Cty.	ROH,JR,HCD,YEB
McKnight, John T.	1st Sgt.	E	5th SCVI	25	YK	06/27/62	Gaines` Mill, VA	KIA		JR,SA3,YEB
McKnight, Robert	Pvt.				WG	06/15/62		DOD	(Prob Co. H, 10th SCVI)	CTA,HOW
McLain, James	Pvt.	F	17th SCVI		YK	/ /	At home	DOD		JR
McLane, J.B.	Pvt.	E	11th SCVI		BT	05/10/65	Elmira, NY	DIP	Woodlawn N.C.#2792 Elmira	FPH,P6,P65,P120
McLane, M.	Pvt.		6th SCVI			/ /	Richmond, VA		Oakwood C.#92,Row J,Div A	OWC
McLard, M.P.	Pvt.	A	3rd SCVI			09/20/63	Chickamauga, GA	KIA		ROH,JR
McLary, James Lane	Pvt.	C	25th SCVI		WG	08/15/64	Weldon RR, VA	DOW		ROH,HOM
McLaughlin, Alexander	Pvt.	D	21st SCVI		CD	08/27/63	Charleston, SC	DOD	Magnolia Cem. Charleston	ROH,JR,RCD,HAG
McLaughlin, H.	Pvt.	G	26th SCVI		DN	04/14/64	Charleston, SC	DOD		ROH,CDC
McLaughlin, R.H.	Pvt.	G	9th SCVIB		DN	09/23/61	Germantown, VA	DOD		ROH,JR
McLaughlin, Samuel	Pvt.	F	6th SCVI	25	CR	12/28/64	Richmond, VA	DOW	Hollywood Cem.Rchmd. W165	ROH,HC,HHC
McLaurin, Angus	Pvt.	A	7th SCVIBn	18	KW	06/03/64	Cold Harbor, VA	KIA		ROH,JR,HIC,HAG
McLaurin, D.McQ.	Pvt.	G	23rd SCVI		MO	08/25/62	Lynchburg, VA	DOD	Lynchburg CSA Cem.#9 R3	ROH,JR,HOM,CDC
McLaurin, Hugh	Pvt.	G	23rd SCVI		MO	/ /	Jackson, MS			HOM
McLean, Daniel A.	Pvt.	B	8th SCVI		CD	03/06/62	Charlottesville	DOD	Univ. Cem. Charlottesville	ROH,JR,CDC,ACH
McLean, G.M.	Pvt.	D	Orr's Ri.		AN	07/07/62	Richmond, VA	DOD	Oakwood C.#53,Row J,Div C	ROH,JR,OWC,CDC
McLean, John W.	Pvt.	B	8th SCVI	23	CD	08/01/62	Petersburg, VA	DOD		PP,KEB
McLean, Jonathan	Pvt.	F	17th SCVI		YK	08/30/62	2nd Manassas, VA	KIA		ROH
McLees, Judd A.	Pvt.	E	4th SCVIBn		AN	05/31/62	Philadelphia, PA	DOW	(Wdd & POW @ 7 Pines)	ROH,HOF
McLees, William Rufus	Pvt.	E	4th SCVIBn		AN	06/04/62	Richmond, VA	DOD	(1st in Co,C, 4th SCVI)	HOF,SA2
McLelland, M.	Pvt.	B	P.S.S.		AN	11/24/63	Knoxville, TN	KIA		ROH
McLemore, Francis Marion	4th Cpl.	B	5th SCVI		CR	09/25/63	Chattanooga, TN	KIA		ROH,JR,SA3
McLemore, J.O.	Pvt.	A	1st SCVIG		BL	08/09/64	Richmond, VA	DOD	Hollywood Cem.Rchmd. V304	ROH,HC,SA1
McLemore, John Caldwell	Cpt.	B	1st SCVIG	26	NY	09/19/62	Richmond, VA	DOW	(Wdd 2nd Man 8/29) ANY	ROH,JR,SA1,BOS
McLemore, Thomas	Pvt.	D	5th SCVI		CR	09/25/63	Chattanooga, TN	DOW	(In enemy hands)	ROH,JR,SA3,HHC
McLendon, G.K.	Pvt.	M	8th SCVI		DN	05/15/63		DOD	(Pneumonia)	JR
McLendon, George R.	Pvt.	E	6th SCVI		DN	05/31/62	7 Pines, VA	KIA		ROH,JR,JLC,WDB
McLendon, James	Pvt.		PeeDee LA		DN	06/26/62	Mechanicsville	DOW		PDL
McLendon, James Miller	Pvt.	G	21st SCVI	22	DN	01/25/64	Pt. Lookout, MD	DIP	C.C. Pt. Lookout, MD	ROH,FPH,P5,HAG
McLendon, Jesse	Pvt.		PeeDee LA		DN	12/13/62	Fredericksburg	KIA		ROH,PDL
McLendon, John	Pvt.	E	7th SCVI		ED	/ /		KIA		HOE,KEB,UD3
McLendon, William	Pvt.	F	7th SCVIBn		KW	/ /	Virginia	DOW	(Possibly DOD)	HIC,HAG
McLeod, Angus	Pvt.	E	6th SCVI	25	DN	11/15/61	Richmond, VA	DOD	(JR=Warrenton Springs)	ROH,JR,JLC
McLeod, Donald McDairmed	Major		8th SCVI	41	MO	07/05/63	Cashtown, VA	DOW	(Wdd 7/2/63,Gettysburg)	ROH,JR,GDR,LC
McLeod, N.A.	Cpl.	D	15th SCVI		KW	/ /		DOD		JR
McLeskey, J.W.	Pvt.	H	7th SCVI		PS	05/08/64	Spotsylvania, VA	KIA	Spotsylvania C.H., VA	JR,SCH
McLester, Thomas	Pvt.	F	26th SCVI		KW	/ /	Columbia, SC	DOD	Elmwood Cem. Columbia, SC	ROH,MP,PP
McLewain, J.M.	Pvt.	F	Hol. Leg.		AE	/ /	Charlottesville			ROH
McLin, Elijah	Pvt.	K	3rd SCVC	40	BL	04/21/62	At home	DOD		ROH
McLucas, Archibald C.	Pvt.	K	8th SCVI	18	MO	09/15/63	At home	DOD		ROH,JR,HOM,KEB
McLucas, Hugh	Sgt.	K	8th SCVI	22	MO	07/02/63	Gettysburg, PA	KIA		ROH,JR,GDR,KEB
McLure, William	Pvt.	F	3rd SCVI		GE	12/27/62	Richmond, VA	DOD	Oakwood C.#88,Row N,Div A	ROH,JR,SA2,OWC
McMahan, A.H.	Pvt.	F	24th SCVI		AN	12/10/63	Rock Island, IL	DIP	(POW @ Mission Ridge)	HOL,P5
McMahan, F. Alexander	Pvt.	G	19th SCVI		AE	12/20/62	Tullahoma, TN	DOD	(PP=11/20/62)	HOL,PP
McMahan, Obediah M.	Pvt.	G	19th SCVI		AE	06/24/62	Meridan, MS	DOD	(PP=Macon, MS)	HOL,PP
McMahan, W.S.	Pvt.		14th SCVI	38		/ /	(1863)		Grenada County, MS	MCG
McMahon,	Pvt.		5th SCVI			03/19/62	Madison Mills VA	ACD	(Falling tree)	HOF
McMahon, John T.	Pvt.	I	14th SCVI	20	AE	06/27/62	Gaines' Mill, VA	KIA	(HOL= Frayser's Farm)	ROH,JR,HOL
McMakin, George	Pvt.	I	3rd SCVI		LS	01/29/62	Richmond, VA	DOD		JR,KEB
McMakin, J.P.	Pvt.	F	4th SCVI		GE	06/15/62	Richmond, VA	DOD	Oakwood C.#143,Row A,Div A	ROH,SA2,OWC

Mc

SOUTH CAROLINA DEAD IN CSA SERVICE 1861-1865

NAME	RANK	C REGIMENT	AGE	DS	DIED	WHERE	WHY	BURIED	SOURCES
McManus, Albert	Pvt.	I 17th SCVI		LR	/ /	2nd Manassas, VA	DOW		JR,LAN
McManus, John L.	Pvt.	B 26th SCVI	23	CD	01/03/65	Petersburg, VA	DOD		ROH,PP
McManus, Samuel F.	Pvt.	H 2nd SCVI	25	LR	11/17/61	Manassas, VA	DOD	(LAN=S.T.)	ROH,LAN,H2
McManus, Thomas	Pvt.	C 19th SCVI		ED	04/07/64	Rock Island, IL	DIP	C.C.#1001 Rock Island, IL	FPH,P5,HOE,UD3
McManus, W.H.	Pvt.	H 2nd SCV		LR	09/20/63	Chickamauga, GA	DOW	(?SA2=Furloughed 6/30/64)	LAN,KEB,SA2,P4
McMatters, C.L.	Pvt.	D 17th SCVI		CR	/ /		DOD		JR
McMatters, R.L.	Pvt.	D 17th SCVI		CR	/ /	Johns Island, SC	DOD		JR
McMayfield, John	Pvt.	C 22nd SCVI		SG	01/18/63	Charleston, SC	DOD		ROH
McMeekin, Andrew	Pvt.	F 12th SCVI		FD	08/29/62	2nd Manassas, VA	KIA		JR,HFC
McMeekin, Robert	Pvt.	F 12th SCVI		FD	09/04/62	Laurel Hill, VA	DOD		JR,HFC
McMeekin, Thomas	Sgt.	F 12th SCVI		FD	05/20/64	Spotsylvania, VA	DOW	Arlington N.C. Section 16	HFC,PP
McMeekin, William B.	Cpl.	F 12th SCVI		FD	01/16/65	Pt. Lookout, MD	DIP	C.C. Pt. Lookout, MD	ROH,FPH,HFC,P5
McMichael, John B.	Pvt.	Hart's Bty	37	OG	06/12/64	Trevillian Stn.	DOW	(Severe leg wound)	ROH,CDC,CNM
McMillan, David M.	Pvt.	F 13th SCVI		SG	07/05/62	Richmond, VA	DOD	Hollywood Cem.Rchmd. M95	ROH,JR,HC,HOS
McMillan, Elijah	Pvt.	A Hol.Leg.	30	SG	10/09/64	Wilson, NC	DOD		ROH,HOS,PP
McMillan, F.M.	Pvt.	C 1st SCVIH		BL	09/14/62	South Mtn., MD	KIA		SA1
McMillan, J.E.	Pvt.				/ /	Lynchburg, VA	DOW	Meth. Ch. Lynchburg, VA	BIG
McMillan, James D.	Cpl.	A 4th SCVC		CD	03/10/65	Monroe's XRd. NC	KIA		ROH
McMillan, Joel A.	Pvt.	E 2nd SCVI		KW	/ /	Richmond, VA		(EXC?, deserted 5/3/63)	H2,SA2
McMillan, John	Cpl.	B 11th SCVI		CO	12/16/62	Blufton, SC	DOD		ROH,JR,HAG
McMillan, L. Pinckney	2nd Lt.	A 1st SCVIH		BL	06/21/64	Petersburg, VA	KIA	(Sniper)	ROH,SA1,UD3
McMillan, L.N.P.	Pvt.	D			/ /	Petersburg, VA	DOW	(ROH=Wdd 1/8/62)	ROH
McMillan, R.H.	Pvt.	C 1st SCVIH		BL	08/08/62	James Island, SC	DOD		ROH,SA1,JRH
McMillan, Thomas E.	Pvt.	L 1st SCVIG	23	CN	11/20/62	Winchester, VA	DOD	(Pneumonia)	ROH,JR,SA1
McMillan, William J.	Pvt.	E 3rd SCVI		NY	12/14/62	Fredericksburg	DOW	(JR=McWilliams, J.) KEB	ROH,JR,ANY,SA2
McMillen, Thomas B.	Sgt.	A Hol.Leg.		SG	08/30/64	2nd Manassas, VA	KIA		JR,HOS
McMillon, Peter	Pvt.	D 5th SCVI			09/07/61	Orange C.H., VA	DOD	(Measles)	JR,SA3
McMore, M.	Pvt.				/ /	Richmond, VA		Oakwood C.#57,Row G,Div A	OWC
McMorries, John	Pvt.	D 13th SCVI	22	NY	06/01/62	Ashland, VA	DOD	(Typhoid)	JR,ANY
McMorrow, Barney	Pvt.	I 1st SCVIG		GE	12/26/64	Petersburg, VA	DOW		SA1
McMulken, James	Pvt.	A 10th SCVI		GN	12/31/62	Murfreesboro, TN	KIA	HOW	ROH,JR,RAS,GRG
McMurray, J.S.	Sgt.	I 17th SCVI		LR	07/30/64	Crater, Pbg., VA	KIA		ROH,JR,BLM,LAN
McMurray, R.	Pvt.	E 1st CSEng			06/07/65	Newport News, VA	DIP	Greenlawn C. Newport News	PP
McMurray, William	Pvt.	K Orr's Ri.	27	AN	06/27/62	Gaines' Mill, VA	KIA		ROH,JR,CDC
McMurton, M.	Pvt.	B 22nd SCVI		SG	03/01/65	Richmond, VA		Hollywood Cem.Rchmd. W547	ROH,HC
McMurtrey, Bender	Pvt.	G 22nd SCVI	26	AN	05/15/63	Columbia, SC	DOD		ROH
McMurtrey, J. Foster	Pvt.	G 22nd SCVI	24	AN	07/30/64	Crater, Pbg., VA	KIA		ROH
McNab, William R.	Pvt.	L 7th SCVI		HY	/ /	Charlottesville		Univ. Cem. Charlottesville	KEB,ACH
McNabb, Joseph	Pvt,	K 1st SCVIG		CN	05/03/63	Chancellorsville	KIA		ROH,SA1,CDC
McNabb, W.R.	Pvt.	L 7th SCVI		HY	/ /	Charlottesville	DOD	Univ. Cem. Charlottesville	ROH,CDC,ACH
McNair, D.D.	Pvt.	D 8th SCVI		CD	12/17/61	Charlottesville	DOD	(Typhoid)	JR,KEB
McNair, Duncan N.	Pvt.	E 8th SCVI		DN	12/17/61	Mt. Jackson, VA	DOD		PP
McNair, John W.	Pvt.	B 8th SCVI		CD	10/04/61	Culpepper, VA	DOD	Fairview Cem. Culpepper VA	JR,CGH,KEB
McNamee, William	Pvt.	D 10th SCVI		MN	05/14/64	Resaca, GA	KIA	(CDC= McNance)	ROH,JR,RAS,HMC
McNaughton, W.D.N.	Pvt.	D 7th SCVIBn	37	KW	06/19/64	Petersburg, VA	KIA	(JR=McMouton)	ROH,JR,HIC,HAG
McNeal, G.	Pvt.	7th SCVI			08/12/61	Culpepper, VA	DOW	(JR=4th SCVI)	ROH,JR
McNealy, Robert	Pvt.	E 1st SCVIR		GE	06/20/64	At home	DOD		SA1
McNeel, Ludwig Gustavus	Pvt.	A 12th SCVI	21	YK	08/30/62	2nd Manassas, VA	DOW		ROH,JR,YEB
McNeely, A.Y.	5th Sgt.	G 3rd SCVI		LS	09/17/62	Sharpsburg, MD	KIA	Rose Hill C. Hagerstown MD	ROH,JR,SA2,BOD
McNeely, Josiah K.	Cpt.	D Ham.Leg.	32	GE	06/19/64	Riddle's Shop VA	DOW	Hollywood Cem.Rchmd. U53	ROH,HC,GRS,R48
McNeely, Robert A.	Cpl.	B 16th SCVI		GE	11/30/64	Franklin, TN	KIA		ROH,16R,PP

Mc

SOUTH CAROLINA DEAD IN CSA SERVICE 1861-1865

NAME	RANK	C REGIMENT	AGE	DS	DIED	WHERE	WHY	BURIED	SOURCES
McNeil, Henry	Pvt.	G 7th SCVIBn	40	RD	05/16/64	Drury's Bluff VA	KIA		ROH,JR,HIC,HAG
McNeil, James Y.	Pvt.	G 7th SCVIBn	22	RD	10/12/64	At home	DOD		ROH
McNeil, Jerry	Pvt.	F 10th SCVI	37	MN	/ /	South Island. SC	DOD	(PP=Enterprise, MS)	ROH,RAS,HMC,PP
McNeil, K.	Sgt.	G 14th SCVI		AE	07/02/63	Gettysburg, PA	KIA		JR
McNeil, W.R.	Pvt.	B 4th SCVC		CR	06/11/64	Trevillian Stn.	KIA	(JR=M.C., CB=W.H.)	ROH,JR,CB
McNeil, William R.	Pvt.	5th SCVC	28	YK	05/28/64	Hawe's Shop, VA	KIA		YEB
McNeille, Robert	2nd Lt.	G 14th SCVI	21	AE	07/03/63	Gettysburg, PA	KIA		ROH
McNinch, George	Pvt.	23rd SCVI		CR	07/30/64	Crater Pbg., VA	KIA		HHC
McNinch, J.	Pvt.	C 14th SCVI		LS	02/05/62	McPhersonville	DOD	(Erysipelas)	JR
McNinch, J.I.	Pvt.	F 6th SCVI		CR	/ /	Lynchburg, VA		Lynchburg CSA Cem.#6 R2	BBW
McNinch, J.M.	Pvt.	F 23rd SCVI		CR	08/20/62	Richmond, VA	DOD	Hollywood Cem.Rchmd. C131	ROH,HC
McNinch, James	Pvt.	23rd SCVI		CR	07/30/64	Crater Pbg., VA	KIA		HHC
McNinch, John	Pvt.	F 23rd SCVI		CR	08/30/62	2nd Manassas, VA	KIA		HHC
McNinch, John	Pvt.	A 6th SCVC	30		05/15/64	Adams Run, SC	DOD		PP
McNinch, S.S.	Pvt.	I 6th SCVI		CR	08/30/62	Richmond, VA	DOD	Hollywood Cem.Rchmd. S66	ROH,HC
McNinch, Samuel	Pvt.	F 23rd SCVI		CR	08/30/62	2nd Manassas, VA	KIA		HHC
McNinch, William C.	2nd Lt.	G 13th SCVI		NY	07/01/63	Gettysburg, PA	KIA		ROH,GDR,ANY,BOS
McNutt, W.R.	Pvt.	B 4th SCVC		CR	06/11/64	Trevillian, Stn.	KIA	(JR=7/12/64)	ROH,JR,CDC
McPhail, John	Pvt.	F 24th SCVI		AN	01/15/64		DOD		HOL
McPhaul, Daniel	Pvt.	L 8th SCVI		MN	/ /	Richmond, VA		(KEB=McPhane)	HMC,KEB
McPherson, Angus M.	Pvt.	K 8th SCVI	25	MO	07/02/63	Gettysburg, PA	KIA		ROH,JR,GDR,KEB
McPherson, J.E.	1st Lt.ADC	G. Garnett	24	CN	08/25/61	Monterey, VA	DOD	St. Philips Ch. Charleston	RCD
McPherson, Jacob	Pvt.	3rd SCVABn			07/21/62		DOD		JR
McPherson, James M.	Pvt.	3rd SCVABn			07/28/62	Charleston, SC	DOD	Magnolia Cem. Charleston	ROH,JR,MAG,RCD
McPherson, John	Pvt.	C 2nd SCVI		RD	09/10/61	1st Manassas, VA	DOW	(JR=Co.A DOD 9/10/62)	ROH,JR,SA2,KEB
McPherson, Malcom	Pvt.	K 8th SCVI	27	MO	07/02/63	Gettysburg, PA	KIA		ROH,JR,GDR,KEB
McPherson, Robert E.	Pvt.	M 8th SCVI		DN	07/15/62	Malvern Hill, VA	DOW		JR,KEB
McPherson, Samuel	Pvt.	C 2nd SCVI		RD	08/17/61	Charlottesville	DOW	Univ. Cem. Charlottesville	JR,SA2,KEB,ACH
McQuage, Colin	Pvt.	A 4th SCVC		CD	06/11/64	Trevillian Stn.	KIA	(JR=7/12/64)	ROH,JR,CDC
McQueen, William A.	1st Lt.	Palm. LA		RD	04/09/65	Dingle's Mill SC	KIA	(1st in D, 2nd SCVI)	ROH,HSU,CV,H2
McQuerns, John A.	Pvt.	C 7th SCVI	31	AE	10/01/62	Maryland Hts. MD	DOW		ROH,JR,KEB
McQuinn,	Pvt.	A 18th SCVI		UN	07/30/64	Crater, Pbg., VA	KIA		ROH,JR
McQuown, M.M.	Pvt.	I 3rd SCVI		LS	06/22/64	Petersburg, VA	KIA	(KEB= McInown)	SA2,KEB
McRae, A.D.	Pvt.	K 8th SCVI		MO	/ /			(1862)	HOM,KEB
McRae, A.L.	Cpt.	G 23rd SCVI		MO	08/30/62	2nd Manassas, VA	KIA		ROH,JR,HOM,R48
McRae, Angus	Pvt.	E 4th SCVC		MO	/ /	Pocotaligo, SC	DOD		HOM
McRae, Colin	Pvt.	L 8th SCVI		MN	07/30/62	Savage Stn., VA	DOW	(JR=7/11/62)	JR,HMC,KEB
McRae, Frank	Sgt.	K 8th SCVI		MO	12/05/64	Mt. Jackson, VA			HOM,KEB,PP
McRae, James A.	Sgt.	H 7th SCVC		KW	08/25/64	White Oak Swamp	KIA		HIC,CDC
McRae, James C.H.	Pvt.	K 8th SCVI		MO	09/11/61	Germantown, VA	DOD	(JR=B,7th SCVI 9/28/61)	ROH,JR,HOM,KEB
McRae, John T.	Pvt.	K 8th SCVI		MO	10/15/62	Maryland Hts. MD	DOW	(TFD frm G,23rd SCVI)	JR,HOM
McRae, Norman	Pvt.	L 8th SCVI		MN	01/27/63	Virginia	DOD	(Typhoid)	JR,HMC,KEB
McRae, Virgil A.	Pvt.	H 7th SCVC		CD	03/28/65	Elmira, NY	DIP	Woodlawn N.C.#1856 Elmira	FPH,HIC,P6,P65
McRae, William P. (B.?)	Pvt.	A 23rd SCVI		CD	07/30/64	Crater, Pbg., VA	KIA		ROH,JR,BLM
McRainey, J.	Pvt.	H 12th SCVI		YK	/ /		DOD	(1864)	CWC
McRea, Daniel	Pvt.	7th SCVC			05/14/64	Washington, DC	DOW		P5
McSwain, Hicks H.	Pvt.	E 5th SCVI		YK	04/10/63	LaGrange, GA	DOD	Con. Cem. LaGrange, GA	SA3,TOD,YEB
McSwain, Horace A.	1st Sgt.	K P.S.S.	19	SG	08/30/62	2nd Manassas, VA	KIA	UD1	ROH,JR,SA3,HOS
McSwain, John	Pvt.	G 17th SCVI	19	YK	/ /	Crater Pbg., VA	DOW	(YEB=Discharged but DOW)	YEB
McSween, William	1st Lt.	F 7th SCVIBn	35	CD	06/02/64	Weldon RR, VA	DOW	(Wdd 5/16/64)	ROH,HIC,HAG,PP
McSweeney, Miles	1st Sgt.	K 27th SCVI		CN	06/18/64	Petersburg, VA	KIA		ROH,JR,HAG

SOUTH CAROLINA DEAD IN CSA SERVICE 1861-1865

NAME	RANK	C REGIMENT	AGE	DS	DIED	WHERE	WHY	BURIED	SOURCES
McTureous, Joseph Cowen	Pvt.	G 5th SCVC	20	CN	07/18/63	Charleston, SC	DOD	1st Baptist C. Charleston	ROH,MAG,RCD
McTurner, A.	Pvt.	McBeth LA			06/08/62	Charleston, SC		Magnolia Cem. Charleston	MAG,RCD
McVay, John D.	Pvt.	B 13th SCVI		SG	06/27/62	Gaines' Mill, VA	KIA		ROH,HOS
McVay, Joseph B.	Pvt.	F 5th SCVI		SG	07/30/61	Charlottesville	DOD	Univ. Cem. Charlottesville	ROH,SA3,HOS,AC
McWalters, Samuel H.	Pvt.	F 6th SCVI	23	CR	06/22/62	7 Pines, VA	DOW	(HHC=McWatters)	ROH,CDC,WDB,HH
McWaters, Ansil	Pvt.	D 17th SCVI		CR	02/20/65	Elmira, NY	DIP		ROH,P65,HHC,CB
McWaters, Benjamin L.	Pvt.	D 17th SCVI		CR	04/19/62	Johns Island, SC	DOD		ROH,HHC,CB
McWaters, Charles L.	Pvt.	D 17th SCVI		CR	03/20/62	Johns Island, SC	DOD		ROH,HHC
McWaters, J.B.	Pvt.	B 14th SCVI		ED	10/08/64	Richmond, VA			ROH
McWaters, J.P.	Pvt.	D 17th SCVI		CR	/ /	John's Island SC	DOD		HHC
McWaters, James D.	Pvt.	F 24th SCVI	17	CR	07/20/62	Charleston, SC	DOD	Magnolia Cem. Charleston	ROH,MAG,RCD,HH
McWaters, Jesse	Pvt.	D 17th SCVI		CR	11/09/65	Elmira, NY	DIP	Woodlawn N.C.Elmira #834W	ROH,P65,HHC,CB
McWaters, John	Pvt.	D 17th SCVI		CR	04/11/65	Elmira, NY	DIP	Woodlawn N.C.#2676 Elmira	ROH,FPH,P65,HH
McWaters, William L.	1st Sgt.	D 17th SCVI		CR	/ /	(1865)	DOD	(Enroute from Elmira P.C.)	ROH,P113,HHC,C
McWhirter, W.F.	Pvt.	D Ham.Leg.		PS	06/15/62	7 Pines, VA	DOW		GRS
McWhite, A.A.	Pvt.	H 8th SCVI		MN	09/14/62	Maryland Hts. MD	KIA		HMC,KEB
McWhite, Evander	Cpl.	H 8th SCVI		MN	09/13/62	Maryland Hts. MD	KIA		UD1,KEB
McWhite, George W.	Pvt.	I 10th SCVI	37	MN	06/02/62	Enterprise, MS	DOD		ROH,RAS,HMC
McWhorter, G.W.	Pvt.	I P.S.S.		PS	06/30/62	Frayser's Farm	KIA		ROH,CDC
McWhorter, John S.	Pvt.	A 16th SCVI		GE	11/30/64	Franklin, TN	KIA		ROH,16R
McWhorter, John T.	Pvt.	G Orr's Ri.		AE	07/15/62	Dill Farm, VA	DOD		ROH,CDC
McWhorter, M.	Pvt.	A 20th SCVI		PS	03/16/63	Richmond, VA	DOD	Magnolia Cem. Charleston	ROH,RCD
McWilliams, A.	Pvt.	L 2nd SCVIRi		AE	07/07/62	Petersburg, VA	DOD		ROH
McWilliams, Samuel	Pvt.	F 3rd SCVI	28	LS	08/28/61	Culpepper, VA	DOD	Fairview Cem. Culpepper VA	JR,CGH,SA2,KEB
McWithers, J.B.	Pvt.	E 2nd SCV			10/07/64			Hollywood Cem.Rchmd. V389	HC
Mclendon, James F.	Pvt.	PeeDee LA		DN	/ /				ROH
Mcleod, Norman A.	Pvt.	D 15th SCVI	23	KW	01/21/63	Richmond, VA	DOW	Antioch Ch. KW Cty.	ROH,KEB,HIC,CD
Mcleod, William W.	Pvt.	K 4th SCVC		CN	02/17/65	At home	DOD		ROH,CLD

SOUTH CAROLINA DEAD IN CSA SERVICE 1861-1865

NAME	RANK	C	REGIMENT	AGE	DS	DIED	WHERE	WHY	BURIED	SOURCES
Nabers, Austin	Lt.	G	2nd SCVC		AE	09/05/63	Gettysburg, PA	DOW	Magnolia Cem. Charleston	ROH,P5,GDR,RCD
Nabers, Zachariah Linden	Sgt.	F	14th SCVI	20	LS	05/21/63	Richmond, VA	DOW	(Wdd @ Fredericksburg)	ROH,JR
Nagle, William P.	Cpl.	A	1st SCVABn		CN	02/10/65	Grimball's, SC	KIA	Magnolia Cem. Charleston	MAG,STR,DOC,CD
Nail, J. Polk	Pvt.	A	6th SCVI	20	CR	06/02/62	7 Pines, VA	DOW	(Wdd 5/30/62 in leg) CB	ROH,HHC,WDB,GL
Nailer, J.C.	Pvt.		SCVI			06/20/62	Richmond, VA		Hollywood Cem.Rchmd. N37	HC
Nalley, John	Pvt.	B	16th SCVI		GE	/ /	At home	DOD	(1862)	16R
Nance, James Drayton	Colonel		3rd SCVI	27	NY	05/06/64	Wilderness, VA	KIA	Rosemont Cem. Newberry, SC	ROH,NCC,ANY
Nance, Thomas Davis	Pvt.	A	P.S.S.		UN	05/06/64	Wilderness, VA	KIA		ROH,CDC
Napper,	Pvt.	G	6th SCVC		RD	10/27/64	Burgess' Mill VA	KIA		CDC
Napper, Allen	Pvt.	D	5th SCRes		RD	12/19/62	Adams Run, SC	DOD		PP
Napper, James W.	Pvt.	B	6th SCVC		ED	10/01/64	Hatcher's Run VA	KIA		ROH,HOE,UD3
Napper, William	Pvt.	B	19th SCVI	18	ED	01/21/62	At home	DOD	(JR=Typhoid,Graniteville)	ROH,JR,HOE
Nations, M.	Pvt.	A	20th SCVI		PS	10/23/63	Charleston, SC		Magnolia Cem. Charleston	ROH,MAG
Neal, D.M.						/ /			(Rchmd effects list 1/63)	CDC
Neal, G.D.	Pvt.	C	16th SCVI		GE	/ /	At home	DOD		16R
Neal, George W.	Pvt.	G	7th SCVI	19	ED	08/12/61	Flint Hill, VA	DOD	Fairview Cem. Culpepper VA	ROH,CGH,HOE,UD
Neal, J.J.	Pvt.	A	11th SCVI		DN	06/02/64	Cold Harbor, VA	KIA	(No Co. A in HAG)	ROH
Neal, J.O.	Pvt.		2nd SCV			/ /	Richmond, VA		Oakwood C.#124,Row N,Div C	ROH,OWC
Neal, James R.	Pvt.	A	Orr's Ri.	32	PS	07/19/62	Petersburg, VA	DOD	Pickens Court House	ALC,PP,CDC
Neal, John B.	Pvt.	I	P.S.S.		PS	03/15/63	Jerusalem, VA	DOD		ROH,JR
Neal, John B.	Pvt.	G	16th SCVI		GE	12/13/63				P6,16R
Neal, R.L.	Pvt.	E	27th SCVI		NY	/ /	Petersburg, VA			ROH,ANY,HAG
Neal, S.H.	Pvt.	I	3rd SCVI		LS	/ /		DOD		SA2,KEB
Neal, W.H.	Pvt.	K	14th SCVI		ED	/ /		DOW		HOE
Neal, W.M.	Pvt.	A	Orr's Ri.		AN	02/16/64	Ft. Delaware, DE	DIP	Finn's Pt., NJ Nat. Cem.	ROH,FPH,CDC,P5
Neal, William A.	Pvt.	G	P.S.S.	26	YK	10/28/63	Lookout Valley	KIA		ROH,SA3,YEB,UD
Neal, William C.	Pvt.	D	17th SCVI		CR	02/23/65	Elmira, NY	DIP	Woodlawn N.C.#1397 Elmira	ROH,FPH,P6,HHC
Neal, William M.	3rd Sgt.	H	7th SCVIBn	25	RD	10/19/62	Adams Run, SC	DOD	(JR=McNeal)	ROH,HAG,JR,PP
Neal, William M.	Pvt.	H	2nd SCVI		LR	09/21/63	Chickamauga, GA	DOW		ROH,SA2,LAN,H2
Neal, Willis	Pvt.	K	14th SCVI		ED	06/17/64	Richmond, VA	DOW		ROH,HOE
Nealey, Robert	Pvt.	A	21st SCVI		GN	09/15/64	Petersburg, VA	KIA		ROH,HAG
Nealy, Jackson	Pvt.	F	16th SCVI		GE	07/10/63	Jackson, MS	KIA		16R
Neel, John	Pvt.	G	14th SCVI	19	AE	/ /	Petersburg, VA	DOW	(1865)	ROH
Neelands, Abraham	Pvt.	F	17th SCVI	35	YK	/ /	Columbia, SC	DOD	(YEB=Co,K, DOD 1862)	JR,YEB
Neely, Alexander P.W.	Pvt.	A	6th SCVI	23	CR	07/15/62	At home	DOW	(Wdd hand @ 7 Pines 5/30)	ROH,HHC,WDB,GL
Neely, George Washington	Pvt.	F	3rd SCVI		LS	08/02/61	Charlottesville	DOD	Univ. Cem. Charlottesville	JR,SA2,KEB,ACH
Neely, H.	Pvt.	D	7th SCVI			11/16/62	Winchester, VA		Stonewall C. Winchester VA	ROH,WIN
Neely, Henry	Pvt.	E	14th SCVI		LS	01/18/62		DOD	(Pneumonia)	JR,CGS
Neely, Hiram S.	Pvt.	C	16th SCVI		GE	/ /		DIP		16R,P39
Neely, James H.	Pvt.	B	26th SCVI	23	CR	04/23/62	Kinston, NC	DOD		HHC
Neely, Miles	Pvt.		Kanapaux's	26	YK	/ /	Gillisonville SC	DOD		YEB
Neely, Richard	Pvt.	C	12th SCVI		FD	06/15/63	Richmond, VA	DOD	(On Rchmd effects list)	ROH,HFC,CDC
Neely, Thomas A.	Pvt.	L	5th SC Res		CR	01/28/64		DOD		ROH,HHC
Neighbor, F.G.	Pvt.		6th SCVI			/ /	Richmond, VA		Oakwood C.#102,Row A,Div A	OWC
Neighbors, George	Pvt.	E	16th SCVI	43	GE	/ /	Griffin, GA	DOD	Stonewall C. Griffin, GA	ROH,16R,BGA,UD
Neighbors, Green F.	Pvt.	C	5th SCVI		OG	10/24/61	Richmond, VA	DOD	(Perhaps F.G. in Oakwood)	ROH,SA3
Neighbors, H.N.	Pvt.	G	20th SCVI		SG	01/28/65	Charleston, SC		Magnolia Cem. Charleston	ROH,MAG,KEB
Neighbors, H.S.	Pvt.	D	Ham.Leg.		UN	09/17/62	Sharpsburg, MD	KIA	(JR=H.L.)	ROH,JR
Neighbors, H.T.	Pvt.	D	Ham.Leg.		PS	09/17/62	Sharpsburg, MD	KIA	(Probably Dup of H.S.)	ROH,GRS
Neighbors, J.	Pvt.	G	27th SCVI		CN	/ /	Fts. Monroe, VA	DIP		ROH,HAG
Neighbors, J.E.	Pvt.	D	Ham.Leg.		PS	/ /	Double Gates, ?	KIA		GRS

N

SOUTH CAROLINA DEAD IN CSA SERVICE 1861-1865

NAME	RANK	C REGIMENT	AGE	DS	DIED	WHERE	WHY	BURIED	SOURCES
Neighbors, J.R.M. (MJM?)	Pvt.	E 18th SCVI		SG	07/30/64	Crater, Pbg., VA	KIA		BLM,HOS
Neighbors, W.R.	Pvt.	A 13th SCVI		LS	05/24/62	Ashland, VA	DOD	(Measles)	JR
Neighbors, William	Pvt.	I Hol.Leg.	18	SG	07/10/62	Adams Run, SC	DOD		ROH,HOS,PP
Neighbors, William S.	Pvt.	G 27th SCVI		CN	10/03/64	Elmira, NY	DIP	Woodlawn N.C.#631 Elmira	FPH,HAG,CDC,P65
Neil, James H.	Pvt.	E 15th SCVI	18	FD	01/09/62	Camp DeSaussure	DOD	(JR=E,P.S.S.)	ROH,KEB
Neil, John Calhoun.	Pvt.	G P.S.S.	19	YK	08/30/62	2nd Manassas, VA	KIA	(Citadel cadet on leave)	ROH,JR,YEB,CAG
Neil, S.H.	Sgt.	F 22nd SCVI		PS	/ /	Petersburg, VA		(1864)	ROH
Neil, William M.	Pvt.	G 7th SCVI	24	ED	11/13/63	At home	DOD	(ROH=Neal)	ROH,HOE,KEB,UD2
Neill, Daniel	Pvt.	B 27th SCVI		CN	05/07/64	Pt. Walthal Jctn	KIA		ROH,CDC,HAG
Neill, J. Spencer	Pvt.	C 3rd SCVI		NY	09/20/63	Chickamauga, GA	KIA	Con. Cem. Marietta, GA	ROH,ANY,SA2,CCM
Neilson, Frank	Pvt.	1st SC	19	BL	10/15/63	Marietta, GA	DOD		ROH
Nelligan, Michael	Pvt.	H Tucker's R			11/14/64	Columbia, SCMS			PP
Nelson, Andrew	Pvt.	B 3rd SCVIBn		LS	02/05/62	Adams Run, SC	DOD		PP,KEB
Nelson, Calvin	Pvt.			FD	/ /	Virginia	DOD	(1861)	ROH
Nelson, Elihu D.	Pvt.	A 3rd SCVIBn		LS	02/07/62	Adams Run, SC	DOD	(Measles)	JR,KEB,PP
Nelson, Ervine (Erwin?)	Pvt.	F 21st SCVI		MO	/ /	Pt. Lookout, MD	DIP	(POW 7/10/63 Took Oath)	ROH,HOM,HAG,P1
Nelson, George	Pvt.	E 2nd SCVI	26	KW	06/30/61	Culpepper, VA	DOD	Fairview Cem. Culpepper VA	CGH,SA2,HIC,CDC
Nelson, Harvey L.	3rd Cpl.	E 5th SCVI		YK	12/21/62	Charlottesville	DOD	Univ. Cem. Charlottesville	JR,SA3,ACH,YEB
Nelson, J.D.	Pvt.	L Orr's Ri.		AN	/ /	Richmond, VA		Oakwood C.#18,Row 38,Div C	ROH,OWC,CDC
Nelson, J.G.	Pvt.	C SC Res			12/16/64	Columbia, SC	DOD		ROH,PP
Nelson, J.J.	1st Cpl.	E 17th SCVI	22	YK	10/10/62	Winchester, VA	DOW	Stonewall C. Winchester VA	ROH,JR,WIN
Nelson, J.N.	Pvt.	C Ham.Leg.		CL	08/30/62	2nd Manassas, VA	KIA	(JR=L.M.)	ROH,JR
Nelson, James F.	Pvt.	B 3rd SCVIBn		LS	04/22/64	Emory, VA		Con. Cem. Emory, VA	PP,KEB
Nelson, John	Pvt.	B 8th SCVI		CD	06/15/62	Richmond, VA	DOD	Oakwood C.#96,Row D,Div A	ROH,JR,OWC
Nelson, John	Pvt.	G 24th SCVI			09/20/63	Chickamauga, GA	KIA		ROH,JR,CDC
Nelson, John T.	Pvt.	G 3rd SCVIBn		FD	07/10/62	Columbia, SC	DOD		PP,KEB
Nelson, Josiah	Pvt.	D 27th SCVI	39	LS	11/30/64	Richmond, VA			ROH,HAG
Nelson, Leander	Pvt.	G 18th SCVI	23	YK	/ /	Charleston, SC	DOD	(In service ?)	YEB
Nelson, Meek	Pvt.	G 18th SCVI	25	YK	/ /	Charleston, SC	DOD	(In service ?)	YEB
Nelson, Patrick Henry	Lt. Col.	7th SCVIBn	40	SR	06/24/64	Petersburg, VA	KIA	(see p278,HAG)	ROH,HAG,LC,DOC
Nelson, Thomas J.	Pvt.	K 7th SCVC		KW	05/20/65	Pt. Lookout, MD	DIP	C.C. Pt. Lookout, MD	ROH,FPH,H2,P6
Nelson, Thomas Singleton	1st Lt.	I 4th SCVC		WG	06/04/64	Richmond, VA	DOW	Hollywood Cem.Rchmd. U132	ROH,HC,HOW,CTA
Nelson, W.A.	Pvt.	D 27th SCVI	32	LS	02/10/64	James Island, SC	DOD	Magnolia Cem. Charleston	ROH,SCL,RCD,HAG
Nelson, William A.	Pvt.	A 3rd SCVIBn	30	LS	07/15/64	Petersburg, VA	DOW	Blandford Church Pbg., VA	BLC,KEB,PP
Nesbit, James Franklin	Pvt.	F 5th SCVI	25	YK	07/15/62	Weldon, NC	DOW	(Wdd @ Gaines Mill)	JR,SA3,YMD,YEB
Nesbit, S.J.	Pvt.	B 1st SCVIBn		CN	07/18/63	Bty. Wagner, SC	KIA		ROH,CDC,R45
Nesbit, W.A.	1st Lt.	H 1st SCVIH		BL	08/30/62	2nd Manassas, VA	KIA		ROH,JR,SA1,R45
Nesbit, William A.	Pvt.	A 3rd SCVIBn		SG	07/15/64	Petersburg, VA		(Began as Cpl. K,3rd SCVI)	ROH,HOS,SA2
Nesbit, William C.	Pvt.	I 17th SCVI		LR	06/02/64	Petersburg, VA		Blandford Church Pbg., VA	BLC,PP
Nesbitt, Alexander J.	Pvt.	D P.S.S.		SG	10/15/64	Ft. Harrison, VA	DOW	(Wdd 9/30/64 & 2nd Man)	ROH,HOS
Nesbitt, John Preston	Pvt.	A 6th SCVC	23	GE	09/17/63			Fairview P.C. GE Cty.	GEE
Nesbitt, P.L.	Pvt.	D P.S.S.		SG	10/22/64	Richmond, VA		Hollywood Cem.Rchmd. E6	HC
Nesbitt, Wilson	Pvt.	D P.S.S.		SG	06/30/62	Fraysers Farm VA	KIA		ROH,JR,HOS,CDC
Nesmith, Daniel Conyers	Pvt.	K 2nd SCVI		WG	09/17/62	Sharpsburg, VA	KIA	(KEB=E.C.)	ROH,JR,SA2,HOW
Nesmith, Nathaniel	Pvt.	E 10th SCVI		WG	09/20/63	Chickamauga, GA	KIA		ROH,JR,RAS,HOW
Nesmith, Samuel	Pvt.	A 7th SCVC		GN	05/16/65	Pt. Lookout, MD	DIP	C.C. Pt. Lookout, MD	ROH,FPH,P6,P115
Nesmith, William B.	Pvt.	A Tucker's C		WG	08/04/63	Georgetown, SC	DOD		JR,CTA,HOW,R43
Netherford, James	Pvt.	H 14th SCVI		BL	01/01/62	Port Royal Ferry	KIA		CNM
Nettles, Benjamin F.	Pvt.	F 8th SCVI	20	DN	11/30/61	Centreville, VA	DOD	(NI KEB but Nettles, R.F.)	ROH,JR
Nettles, D.W.	Pvt.	F 2nd SCVA	29	OG	10/15/64	James Island, SC	DOD		ROH,CDC
Nettles, F.L.	Sgt.	E 8th SCVI		DN	08/18/63	Gettysburg, PA	DOW	Magnolia Cem. Charleston	ROH,GDR,P1,KEB

SOUTH CAROLINA DEAD IN CSA SERVICE 1861-1865

N

NAME	RANK	C REGIMENT	AGE	DS	DIED	WHERE	WHY	BURIED	SOURCES
Nettles, J.S.	Pvt.	23rd SCVI			02/21/61	Culpepper, VA	DOD	(May be Jesse S.)	JR
Nettles, Jesse S.	Pvt.	E 2nd SCVI	18	KW	07/23/61	Fairfax C.H., VA	DOW	Fairview Cem. Culpepper VA	ROH,CGH,HIC,KE
Nettles, John R.	Cpt.	H 10th SCVI		WG	01/14/63	Murfreesboro, TN	DOW	(In enemy hands)	ROH,RAS,CGW,P3
Nettles, Joseph H.	3rd Lt.	D 2nd SCVI		SR	12/20/61	Richmond, VA	DOD		SA2,H2,R45,KEB
Nettles, S.J.	Pvt.	H 10th SCVI	26	WG	/ /	Lookout Valley	DOD	(1863)	RAS,CTA,HOW,P1
Nettles, W.	Pvt.	C 11th SCVI		CN	/ /	Petersburg, VA	DOW	(Wdd 9/14/64)	ROH
Nettles, W.D.	Pvt.	K 11th SCVI		CO	02/15/63	Hardeesville, SC	DOD		ROH,HAG
Nettles, William	Pvt.	K 11th SCVI	40	CO	09/14/64	Weldon RR, VA	DOW		ROH,HAG,PP
Nettles, William Joseph	2nd Lt.	F 6th SCVC		ED	10/27/64	Burgess Mill, VA	KIA		CAG,EDN,CDC,R4
Neuffer, Abram	Pvt.	K 7th SCVC		RD	05/30/64	Old Church, VA	KIA		ROH,HIC
Neuffer, Charles E.	Pvt.	A 2nd SCVI		RD	07/03/63	Gettysburg, VA	KIA	(1st reported MIA)	ROH,GDR,SA2,H2
Neuffer, Harmon F.	Pvt.	C 2nd SCVI	25	RD	08/11/61	Vienna, VA	DOD	Elmwood Cem. Columbia, SC	ROH,MP,SA2,PP
Neufville, W.L.	Pvt.	B 5th SCVC	41	CN	01/19/65	Columbia, SC	DOD	(W.J.?)	ROH,PP
Nevels, R.F.	Pvt.	K 2nd SCVI		BL	/ /	(POW '64)	DIP	Charlestown, VA	ROH,SA2,KEB
Neville, L.F.	Pvt.	H 17th SCVI		BL	/ /	At home	DOD		JR
Nevils, George	Pvt.	2nd SCVA			/ /	NC	KIA		UD1
Nevitt, John W.	Pvt.	H 6th SCVI		FD	01/17/64	Danbridge, TN	KIA	(HFC= Joseph K.,WDB=J.K.)	ROH,CDC,WDB
Nevitt, Robert C.	Sgt.	C P.S.S.		AN	05/31/62	7 Pines, VA	KIA		ROH,SA2,GMJ
New, Edward	Pvt.	K 24th SCVI	28	ED	/ /		DOD	(1862)	HOE
New, John	Pvt.	C 7th SCVI		AE	12/13/62	Fredericksburg	KIA	(KEB=New, F.)	ROH,JR,KEB
Newby, George W.	Pvt.	K 15th SCVI	24	ED	03/07/63	Petersburg, VA	DOD	Blandford Church Pbg., VA	JR,BLC,KEB,PP
Newby, William	Pvt.	F 1st SCVIH		GE	01/10/64		DOD		ROH,SA1,JRH
Newcomen, John G.	Cpl.	A 25th SCVI	21	CN	09/04/63	Bty. Wagner, SC	KIA	Magnolia Cem. Charleston	ROH,JR,MAG,WLI
Newel, Thomas A.	Pvt.	F 24th SCVI		AN	/ /		DOD	(1862)	HOL
Newell, J.T.	Pvt.	F 2nd SCVIRi			/ /	Richmond, VA		Oakwood C.#107,Row E,Div G	ROH,OWC
Newham, B.F.	Pvt.	I 18th SCVI	22	DN	01/23/65	Petersburg, VA	KIA		ROH,PP
Newham, John	Pvt.	I 18th SCVI	35	DN	11/15/65	Petersburg, VA	DOD		ROH
Newman, J.A.	Pvt.	A 1st SCV			/ /	Richmond, VA		Oakwood C.#89,Div L,Div C	OWC
Newman, John F.	Pvt.	E 6th SCVI		SR	05/15/63	Franklin, VA	DOD	(Blackwater,Suffolk)	ROH,JLC
Newman, Johnson J.	Pvt.	F 13th SCVI		SG	/ /			(POW Xchd 2/27/65)	HOS,P41
Newman, M.H.	Sgt.	A 11th SCVI		BT	02/16/64	Camp Morton, IN	DIP	Green Lawn C.C. Chicago IN	FPH
Newman, Milberry, W.	Pvt.	F 7th SCVIBn	24	KW	08/24/62	Adams Run, SC	DOD		ROH,HIC,HAG,R4
Newman, Richard Burke	4th Cpl.	A 2nd SCVI		RD	12/14/63	Bean's Stn., TN	KIA		ROH,SA2,KEB,PP
Newman, S.E.	Pvt.	A 1st SCVIG		BL	07/19/62	Richmond, VA	DOD	(JR=Typhoid 8/19)	ROH,JR,SA1
Newman, Thomas S.	Pvt.	F 9th SCVIB	18	SR	08/21/61	Germantown, VA	DOD		ROH,JR
Newsom, Bennett	Pvt.	H 21st SCVI		DN	08/17/63	Charleston, SC	DOD	Magnolia Cem. Charleston	ROH,MAG,RCD,HA
Newton, E. Carew	Pvt.	Brooks LA	24		01/07/64	Ft. Delaware, DE	DIP	Finn's Pt., NJ Nat. Cem.	ROH,FPH.P40
Newton, George	Pvt.	B 11th SCVI		CO	08/21/64	Weldon RR, VA	KIA		ROH,HAG
Newton, J.	Pvt.	7th SC Res			02/19/65	Charleston, SC	DOD	Magnolia Cem. Charleston	ROH,MAG,RCD
Newton, John	Sgt.	Hart's Bty			07/02/63	Gettysburg, PA	DOW		ROH,GDR
Newton, John C.	Pvt.	F 21st SCVI		MO	05/16/64	Drury's Bluff VA	KIA		ROH,HAG,CDC,HO
Newton, John W.	2nd Lt.	A 26th SCVI	28	HY	12/30/63	At home	DOD		ROH,R48
Newton, N.H.	Pvt.	A 1st SCV			07/31/64	High Point, NC	KIA	(PP=Orr's Ri. ?)	PP
Newton, Richard D.	Sgt.	E 4th SCVC		MO	01/10/65	Wilson, NC		(PP=Weldon, NC)	HOM,PP
Newton, William S.	2nd Lt.	A 26th SCVI	27	HY	06/17/64	Petersburg, VA	KIA		ROH,CDC,R48
Nexas, Thomas	Pvt.	I 3rd SCV		LS	10/28/61	Richmond, VA		Hollywood Cem.Rchmd. B245	HC
Nich, S.G.	Pvt.	E 6th SCVI		DN	08/30/62	Richmond, VA		Hollywood Cem.Rchmd. C109	HC
Nicholes, Benjamin B.	Pvt.	H Ham.Leg.		GE	08/06/61	Virginia	DOD	(Benjamin F.?)	ROH,JR,SOB
Nicholls, E.P.M.	Pvt.	D P.S.S.		SG	06/30/62	Frayser's Farm	KIA	(JR=E.M.P.)	ROH,JR,CDC
Nichols, Benjamin	Pvt.	H 23rd SCVI		MN	08/30/62	2nd Manassas, VA	KIA		JR
Nichols, E.A.	Pvt.	B 12th SCVI	41	YK	06/27/62	Gaines' Mill, VA	KIA		CNM,YEB

N

SOUTH CAROLINA DEAD IN CSA SERVICE 1861-1865

NAME	RANK	C	REGIMENT	AGE	DS	DIED	WHERE	WHY	BURIED	SOURCES
Nichols, Henry B.	Pvt.	F	Hol.Leg.		AE	12/13/64	Pt. Lookout, MD	DIP	C.C. Pt. Lookout, MD	FPH,P115
Nichols, Irvin	Pvt.	B	12th SCVI	19	YK	06/27/62	Gaines' Mill, VA	KIA		YEB
Nichols, Isaac	Pvt.	A	7th SCVIBn		KW	10/21/65	Elmira, NY	DIP	Woodlawn N.C.#1587 Elmira	FPH,HIC,P5,P65
Nichols, James A.	Pvt.	B	12th SCVI	35	YK	08/25/64	Richmond, VA	DOD	Hollywood Cem.Rchmd. V435	ROH,HC,YEB
Nichols, James M.	Pvt.	C	17th SCVI	25	YK	03/11/62	At home	DOD	(Pneumonia, Hickory Grove)	JR,YEB
Nichols, John			CS Navy			04/29/65	Richmond, VA			ROH
Nichols, John	Pvt.	H	19th SCVI		AE	11/06/62	Knoxville, TN		Bethel C. Knoxville, TN	TOD
Nichols, Kendre	1st Lt.	H	23rd SCVI		MN	08/30/62	2nd Manassas, VA	KIA	(HMC=Kendre, Nichols)	JR,CDC,R48,HMC
Nichols, R.F.	Sgt.	A	SC CadetBn	21		02/14/65	James Island, SC	DOD		ROH,CAG
Nichols, R.G.	Pvt.	B	10th SCVI		HY	/ /	Kentucky	DOD		RAS
Nichols, R.M.	4th Cpl.	F	3rd SCVI		LS	09/20/63	Chickamauga, GA	KIA	Con. Cem. Marietta, GA	ROH,JR,SA2,CCM
Nichols, Thomas A.	Pvt.	B	6th SCVI		CR	08/15/61	Germantown, VA	DOD		GLS,HHC,CNM
Nichols, W.T.	Pvt.	B	19th SCVI		ED	02/22/62	At home	DOT	(Typhoid @ Graniteville)	JR
Nicholson, C.W.	Pvt.					/ /	Richmond, VA		Oakwood C.#1,Row C,Div G	OWC
Nicholson, James	Pvt.	H	21st SCVI		DN	04/04/62	Georgetown, SC	DOD		PP,HAG
Nickels, John	Pvt.	F	Hol.Leg.	30	AE	10/04/62	Warrenton, VA	DOW	(Wdd 2nd Man)	ROH
Nickolds, W. Thomas	Pvt.	A	5th SCVI		LR	09/17/62	Sharpsburg, MD	KIA	(NI SA3)	JR,LAN,CDC
Nielson, B.F.	Pvt.	E	1st SCVIH		BL	10/19/63	Newnan, GA	DOD		SA1
Niles, Edward C.	1st Lt. QM		2nd SCVI	26	KW	11/18/62	At home	DOD		ROH,SA2,HIC,CDN
Nimmons, William A.J.	Pvt.	A	1st SCVIG		RD	05/01/65	Farmville, VA	DOW	(Wdd Hatcher's Run 2/5)	SA1,P6
Nipson, James J.	Pvt.	B	5th SCVC	25	CN	10/27/64	Boydton Plank Rd	KIA	(PP=11/3/64	ROH,MDM,PP
Nisbet, Gilmore G.	Pvt.	A	5th SCVI		LR	10/07/64	Darlington Rd.	DOW	(Near Gaines' Mill, POW)	LAN,SA3
Nisbet, J.A.	Pvt.	I	12th SCVI		LR	07/01/63	Gettysburg, PA	KIA		LAN
Nisbet, James Blackstock	Pvt.	I	17th SCVI		LR	08/30/62	2nd Manassas, VA	KIA	(JR=Nesbit)	ROH,JR,LAN
Nisbet, John Calhoun	Cpl.	I	17th SCVI		LR	08/30/62	2nd Manassas, VA	DOW		JR,LAN
Nisbet, W.E.	Pvt.	I	17th SCVI		LR	07/30/64	Crater, Pbg., VA	KIA		LAN
Nisbet, W.M.	Pvt.	I	17th SCVI		LR	06/20/63	Petersburg, VA	DOD	(Nesbit in E,1st SCVIH)	ROH,LAN,SA1,JRH
Nisbett, W.E.	Pvt.	D	1st SCVIH		LR	05/10/64	Spotsylvania, VA	KIA	(SA1= Nesbit)	LAN,SA1
Nix, B.W.J.	2nd Lt.	H	17th SCVI		BL	10/25/62	At home	DOD		JR,R47
Nix, G.M.	Pvt.	B	11th SCVI		BT	11/16/63	Charleston, SC		Magnolia Cem. Charleston	ROH,MAG,RCD
Nix, Henry E.	Pvt.	E	11th SCVI	25	BT	06/09/64	Cold Harbor, VA	KIA		ROH,HAG
Nix, J.B.	Pvt.	K	2nd SCVI		BL	10/12/62	Farmville, VA	DOD	(Brain inflamation)	H2,SA2,KEB
Nix, Stephen	Pvt.	D	3rd SCVI		SG	06/29/62	Savage Stn., VA	KIA		KEB ROH,JR,HOS,SA2
Nix, W.H.	Sgt.	E	11th SCVI	25	BT	08/23/62	Hardeesville. SC	DOW	(Pinckney Island)	ROH,CDC
Nix, Wiley J.	Pvt.	B	1st SCVA		BL	06/16/62	Secessionville	KIA	(PP=2nd SCVA)	ROH,JR,CDC,PP
Nixon, W.J.	Pvt.	F	3rd SCVI		LS	09/05/61	Richmond, VA	DOD	(JR=9/15/61)	ROH,JR,SA2,KEB
Noah, Jacob	Pvt.	D	8th SCVI			06/19/62	Richmond, VA			ROH
Nobels, Joshua	Pvt.	E	24th SCVI	33	CO	02/23/64	Dalton, GA	DOD	(PP=2/22/64)	ROH,PP
Noble, Edward	1st Lt.	G	19th SCVI		AE	05/26/62				R47
Noble, J.W.	Pvt.	B	6th SCVC			06/11/64	Elmira, NY	DIP	(POW @ Trevillian)	ROH,P120
Noble, Joseph	Pvt.	B	19th SCVI		ED	12/19/62	Lauderdale Spgs.	DOD		PP
Noble, Russel	Pvt.	B	SC CadetBn	18	AE	03/15/65	Chester, SC	DOD		ROH,CAG
Noble, William	Pvt.	B	19th SCVI		ED	/ /		DOD		HOE
Nobles, A.B.	Pvt.	E	14th SCVI		LS	08/01/64	Richmond, VA	DOW	Hollywood Cem.Rchmd. V38	ROH,HC,CGS
Nobles, B.B.	Pvt.	G	10th SCVI		HY	/ /		DOD		RAS
Nobles, H.	Pvt.	D	10th SCVI		MN	/ /		DOD		RAS,HMC
Nobles, J. Pinckney	Pvt.	F	10th SCVI	21	MN	/ /	Tupelo, MS	DOD		ROH,RAS,HMC
Nobles, J.W.	Pvt.	D	10th SCVI		MN	09/20/63	Chickamauga, GA	MIA		RAS,HMC
Nobles, N.	Pvt.	D	10th SCVI		MN	07/22/64	Atlanta, GA	MIA		RAS,HMC
Nobles, William F.	Pvt.	G	13th SCVI		NY	06/24/65	Pt. Lookout, MD	DIP	C.C. Pt. Lookout, MD	ROH,FPH,ANY,P6
Nohrden, C.	Cpt.	A	German Art		CN	07/15/61	Charleston, SC	DOD		ROH

SOUTH CAROLINA DEAD IN CSA SERVICE 1861-1865

NAME	RANK	C	REGIMENT	AGE	DS	DIED	WHERE	WHY	BURIED	SOURCES
Nolan, J.	Pvt.	G	Orr's Ri.		AE	06/05/64	Richmond, VA		Hollywood CEm.Rchmd. S266	HC
Nolan, J.N.						/ /			Magnolia Cem. Charleston	MAG
Nolan, James P.	Pvt.	A	1st SCVIG		BL	08/29/62	2nd Manassas, VA	DOW		JR,SA1,CDC
Noland, L.	Pvt.	K	P.S.S.			/ /		DOD		JR
Noland, Leander S.	Pvt.	K	5th SCVI		SG	08/07/61	Richmond, VA	DOW	Hollywood Cem.Rchmd. K10	HC,SA3
Nolans, N.J.	Pvt.		5th SCVI			08/07/61	Richmond, VA			ROH
Norman, John P.	Pvt.	C	18th SCVI	22	UN	05/20/64	Clay's Farm, VA	KIA		ROH
Norman, Robert M.	Pvt.	D	13th SCVI	28	NY	11/28/63	At home	DOD	(ANY=Robert K. DIS)	ROH,ANY
Norman, Robert M.	Cpt. ADC		Gen.Gregg	27	SG	11/23/64	At home	DOD		ROH
Norman, Thomas Franklin	Cpl.	A	P.S.S.	24	UN	06/30/62	Frayser's Farm	KIA	Padgett Crk. B.C. UN Cty.	ROH,JR,CDC,UNC
Norman, Thomas W.	Cpl.	C	18th SCVI	20	UN	07/28/64	Columbia, SC	DOD	Padgett Crk. B.C. UN Cty.	ROH,UNC
Norman, W. Thomas	Sgt.	C	18th SCVI	27	UN	08/30/62	2nd Manassas, VA	KIA	Padgett Crk. B.C. UN Cty.	ROH,JR,UNC,CDC
Norris, A. Christopher	Pvt.	A	7th SCVIBn	21	KW	02/11/62	Adams Run, SC	DOD		ROH,HIC,HAG,PP
Norris, Franklin	Pvt.	F	3rd SCVABn	17		02/05/63		ACD	(Acd disch of own pistol)	ROH
Norris, George	Pvt.	A	7th SCVIBn	48	KW	09/11/64	At home	DOD		ROH,HIC,HAG
Norris, Isaac	Pvt.	K	26th SCVI		HY	01/23/65	Richmond, VA	DOD		ROH
Norris, J.A.J.	Pvt.	B	P.S.S.			/ /		DOD		JR
Norris, J.R.	Pvt.	A	14th SCVI	23	DN	01/02/63	Lynchburg, VA	DOD	Lynchburg CSA Cem.#6 R5	ROH,DEB,BBW
Norris, J.R.	Pvt.	K	26th SCVI		HY	12/24/64	Richmond, VA			ROH
Norris, James	1st Lt.	F	15th SCVI	22	UN	11/09/61	Savannah, GA	DOW	Fernandez Fam. Cem. UN Cty	ROH,JR,UNC,KEB
Norris, Jesse Wetherall	1st Sgt.	C	4th SCVI		AN	07/21/61	1st Manassas, VA	KIA	(JR=L,P.S.S.)	JR,SA2
Norris, John Thomas	2nd Lt.	A	19th SCVI		ED	01/09/63	Chattanooga, TN	DOW	(Wdd @ Murfreesboro)	JR,HOE,R47,UD3
Norris, Jordan	Pvt.	K	16th SCVI		GE	06/27/62	Adams Run, SC	DOD	(Congestive Chill)	JR,16R,PP
Norris, Thomas Patrick	Sgt.	F	2nd SCVA	22	OG	03/22/65	Bentonville, NC	DOW		ROH,WAT,PP,UD1
Norris, W.B.M.	Pvt.	H	6th SCVI		FD	10/15/64	Tennessee	DOW	Con. Cem. Emory, VA	ROH,WDB,HFC,PP
Norris, William C.	1st Lt.	K	Orr's Ri.		AN	07/10/62	Gaines' Mill, VA	DOW		ROH,BOS,CDC,R4
Norris, William H.	Cpt.	F	19th SCVI		LN	05/28/62	Atlanta, GA	KIA		HOE,R47
Norris, William T.	1st Lt.	C	5th SCVI	34	UN	11/11/64	Point O Rocks MD	DOW	Norris Fam. Cem. UN Cty.	SA3,UNC,R45
Norris,Jr., J. Ewing	Pvt.	B	4th SCVI		AN	09/16/61	Germantown, VA	DOD		SA2,BIG,GMJ
Northworth, B.J.						11/01/62	Staunton, VA		(Northsworthy?)	ROH
Norton, Alexander	Pvt.	C	25th SCVI		CN	06/26/62	Charleston, SC	DOD	Magnolia Cem. Charleston	ROH,MAG,RCD
Norton, J.M.	Pvt.	I	7th SCVI		ED	09/13/62	Maryland Hts. MD	KIA		JR
Norton, James P.	Pvt.	B	24th SCVI	22	MO	06/15/62	Augusta, GA	DOD		ROH,HOM
Norton, Miles M.	Cpt.	E	Orr's Ri.	45	PS	08/30/62	2nd Manassas, VA	DOW		ROH,JR,CDC,R45
Norton, Samuel S.	Pvt.	B	24th SCVI		MO	12/16/64	Nashville, TN	KIA	(Franklin per HOM)	ROH,HOM
Norton, Sandy	Pvt.	D	25th SCVI		MN	/ /	Virginia	KIA	(? Alexander in Co. C)	HMC,HAG
Norton, W.C.	Pvt.	H	2nd SCV			07/04/63	Gettysburg, PA	DOW		JR
Norwood, J.	Pvt.	A	Orr's Ri.		AN	06/09/62	Richmond, VA		Hollywood Cem.Rchmd. P46	ROH,HC
Norwood, James	Pvt.	M	8th SCVI		DN	12/19/62	Racoon Ford, VA	DOD		JR,KEB
Norwood, Samuel G.	Pvt.	K	Orr's Ri.	23	AN	07/28/62		DOD		ROH,CDC
Norwood, Wesley	Pvt.	A	1st SCVC		AE	05/24/63	Staunton, VA	DOD		ROH
Norwood, William Tully	2nd Lt.	E	6th SCVI		AE	01/17/64	Johnson's I., OH	DIP		ROH,CV,R46
Norwood, Wyatt L.	Pvt.	K	Orr's Ri.	32	AN	04/20/62		DOD		ROH,CDC
Nowell, Edward W.	Pvt.	K	4th SCVC		CN	/ /				CLD
Nowles, Michael	Pvt.	K	1st SCVIG		CN	12/13/62	Fredericksburg	DOW		ROH,JR,SA1,CDC
Noyer, J.W.	Pvt.	B	6th SCVC			06/11/64	Trevillian Stn.	KIA		ROH
Nueller, A.	Pvt.		7th SCVC			05/30/64	Old Church, VA	KIA		CDC
Nugent, George H.	Pvt.	A	7th SCVI			10/19/64		KIA	Stonewall C. Winchester VA	ROH,WIN
Nunn, L.D.	Pvt.	B	15th SCVAB			03/23/65	Savannah G.H.	DOW	(Wdd @ Bentonville, NC)	P1,P6
Nunnamaker, Sidney	1st Lt.	H	3rd SCVI		LN	10/09/62	Union Church, VA	DOW	(Wdd @ Sharpsburg)	ROH,SA2,KEB
Nunnamaker, Tillman C.	2nd Sgt.	H	3rd SCVI		LN	09/20/63	Chickamauga, GA	KIA	(See p279,KEB)	ROH,JR,SA2,KEB

N

SOUTH CAROLINA DEAD IN CSA SERVICE 1861-1865

NAME	RANK	C	REGIMENT	AGE	DS	DIED	WHERE	WHY	BURIED	SOURCES
Nunnery, Peter	Pvt.	E	7th SCVIBn	32	SR	05/16/64	Drury's Bluff VA	KIA		ROH,HAG

O

SOUTH CAROLINA DEAD IN CSA SERVICE 1861-1865

NAME	RANK	C	REGIMENT	AGE	DS	DIED	WHERE	WHY	BURIED	SOURCES
O'Brannon, Sampson	Pvt.	H	14th SCV		BL	/ /		DOD	(To hospital April, 1864)	UD2
O'Brian, W.H.	Pvt.					/ /	Richmond, VA			ROH
O'Briant, Asbury	Pvt.	F	24th SCVI		AN	/ /		DOD	(1863)	HOL
O'Brien, Daniel	Pvt.	A	1st SCVIR		CN	02/28/62	Ft. Moultrie, SC	ACD	(drowned)	SA1
O'Cain, John M.	Pvt.	G	25th SCVI	45	OG	11/23/64	At home	DOD		ROH,HAG,EDR
O'Connell, Edward	Pvt.	C	15th SCVAB		CN	12/05/64	Camp Morton, IN	DIP	Green Lawn C. Indianapolis	FPH
O'Connell, Stephen	Pvt	K	1st SCVIG		CN	12/13/62	Fredericksburg	DOW	(Prob O..., S.W. in FBG)	ROH,JR,SA1,CDC
O'Conner, Patrick	Pvt.	C	1st SCVA			04/27/65	Unknown	DIP	Cypress Hills N.C.#2613 NY	FPH
O'Daniel, Francis M.	Pvt.	H	1st SCVIH	23	YK	05/06/64	Wilderness, VA	KIA		ROH,SA1,HOS,YE
O'Donnell, Alexander V.	1st Sgt.	K	1st SCVIG		CN	10/06/63	Gordonsville, VA	DOD		SA1
O'Donnell, Charles	Pvt.	C	1st SCVIG		RD	12/15/62	Fredericksburg	DOW		JR,SA1
O'Farrell, George H.	Sgt.	G	P.S.S.	25	YK	05/12/64	Orange C.H., VA	DOW	(Wdd. 5/6 in Wilderness)	ROH,SA2,YEB,UD
O'Hara, William P.	Pvt.	B	25th SCVI		CN	04/15/64	Ft. Sumter, SC	KIA		ROH,HHS,WLI,HA
O'Hear, James W.	2nd Lt.	K	4th SCVC		CN	05/28/64	Hawes Shop, VA	KIA		ROH,CLD,HAG,R4
O'Neal, John B.	Cpt.	F	3rd SCVI		LS	07/15/63	Williamsport, MD	DOW	Rose Hill C. Hagerstown MD	ROH,KEB,SA2,BO
O'Neal, W.R.	Pvt.	E	1st SC			04/28/64	Richmond, VA		Hollywood Cem.Rchmd. I242	ROH,HC
O'Neil, Charles C.	Major		16th SCVI		GE	06/22/64	Kennesaw Mtn. GA	KIA		ROH,16R,CDC
O'Neil, John	Pvt.	K	2nd SCVI		CN	03/09/62	At home	DOD	(H2=TFD to Ficklin's LA)	ROH,SA2,H2
O'Neill, J.J.A.	Pvt.	K	4th SCVC			/ /				CLD
O'Rourke, John	Pvt.	K	1st SCVIG		CN	06/27/62	Gaines' Mill, VA	KIA		JR,SA1
O'Sullivan, James	Cpl.	E	1st SCVIR		NC	03/17/63	At home	DOD		SA1
O____, L.W.			SCV			/ /	Marietta, GA		Con. Cem. Marietta, GA	CCM
O____, S.W.	Pvt.					/ /			Fredericksburg C.C. R6S13	FBG
Oakley, Fielden F.	Pvt.	C	Orr's Ri.	22	PS	08/10/62	Petersburg, VA	DOD	Blandford Church Pbg., VA	ROH,CDC,BLC,PP
Oates, S.L. McElwee	Pvt.	A	12th SCVI	22	YK	08/29/62	2nd Manassas, VA	KIA		ROH,JR,CDC,YEB
Oates, Thomas	Pvt.	B	14th SCVI		ED	07/21/62	Laurel Hill, VA	DOD	(Typhoid)	JR
Odam, Andrew P.	Pvt.	D	16th SCVI		GE	06/27/62	Adams Run, SC	DOD		16R,PP
Odanion, G.B.(O'Banion?)	Pvt.	E	2nd SCVA			/ /	High Point, NC		Oakwood C. High Point, NC	TOD
Odell, James A.	Pvt.	H	2nd SCVIRi		PS	04/27/63	Petersburg, VA		Blandford Church Pbg., VA	BLC,PP
Odom, Alfred	Pvt.	C	1st SCVIG		RD	06/18/63	Chancellorsville	DOW		SA1
Odom, B.J. (S.J.?)	Pvt.	A	8th SCVI		DN	06/13/62	Richmond, VA		Hollywood Cem.Rchmd. P193	ROH,HC,KEB
Odom, Henry	Pvt.	F	21st SCVI		MO	06/18/64	Petersburg, VA	KIA		ROH,HOM,HAG
Odom, Henry E.	Pvt.	B	24th SCVI	20	MO	05/14/63	Jackson, MS	KIA		ROH,JR,HOM,PP
Odom, J.A.	Pvt.	H	25th SCVI		WG	08/21/64	Weldon RR, VA	KIA	(HOW= 21st SCVI)	CTA,HOW,HAG
Odom, J.J.	Pvt.	D	12th SCVI		RD	07/13/64	Ft. Delaware, DE	DIP	Finn's Pt., NJ Nat. Cem.	ROH,FPH,CDC,P5
Odom, James E.	Pvt.	F	21st SCVI	50	MO	01/20/62	Georgetown, SC	DOD		ROH,HOM,HAG,PP
Odom, James G.	Pvt.	B	24th SCVI		MO	07/20/64	Peachtree Creek	DOW		ROH,HOM
Odom, James T.	Pvt.	E	4th SCVC		MO	06/11/64	Trevillian Stn.	KIA		ROH,HOM,CDC
Odom, Jesse	Pvt.	I	18th SCVI	33	DN	09/15/62		DOD		ROH
Odom, Joel	1st Sgt.	H	21st SCVI		DN	09/13/64	Philadelphia, PA	DOW	Philadelphia N.C.#101 OFS	FPH,HAG,P6
Odom, John	Pvt.	E	3rd SCVABn			07/22/62	Charleston, SC	DOD	Magnolia Cem. Charleston	MAG,RCD,CDC
Odom, John	Pvt.	E	4th SCVC		MO	05/28/64	Hawes Shop, VA	KIA		HOM
Odom, Josiah	Pvt.		6th SCV	21	MO	/ /			Trfd from G, 8th SCVI)	UD2,KEB
Odom, Leggett	4th Sgt.	G	8th SCVI	20	MO	08/29/61	Richmond, VA	DOD	(Typhoid)	JR,HOM,KEB,UD2
Odom, Marion	Cpl.	F	7th SCVI	27	ED	05/04/62	Richmond, VA	DOD	(Erysipelas,on effects L.)	JR,HOE,KEB,CDC
Odom, Philip W.	Pvt.	B	24th SCV		MO	/ /			(Trfd from G, 8th SCVI)	UD2,KEB
Odom, Richard W.	Pvt.	H	17th SCVI		BL	11/11/62	At home	DOD		ROH,JR
Odom, Runnels	Pvt.	F	1st SCVIH		GE	06/25/62	Charleston, SC	DOD		ROH,SA1
Odom, S.J.	Cpl.	A	8th SCVI		DN	08/28/61	Richmond, VA	DOD	Hollywood Cem.Rchmd. K69	ROH,JR,HC
Odom, Sion W.	Pvt.	B	24th SCVI	25	MO	09/20/63	Chickamauga, GA	KIA	(Tfd from G, 8th SCVI)	ROH,JR,UD2,KEB
Odom, Thomas	Pvt.				WG	08/21/64	Weldon RR, VA	KIA		CTA,HOW

O

SOUTH CAROLINA DEAD IN CSA SERVICE 1861-1865

NAME	RANK	C REGIMENT	AGE	DS	DIED	WHERE	WHY	BURIED	SOURCES
Odom, W.	Pvt.	6th SC Res	18	OG	/ /	North Carolina	DOD	(1865)	ROH
Odom, W.A.	Pvt.	H 17th SCVI		BL	08/30/62	2nd Manassas, VA	KIA		ROH,JR
Ogden, Darius S.	Pvt.	E 1st SCVIH		BL	05/28/65	Pt. Lookout, MD	DIP	C.C. Pt. Lookout, MD	ROH,FPH,SA1,P6
Ogden, Isaac	Cpl.	G 1st SCVIH	24	BL	08/30/62	2nd Manassas, VA	KIA	(ROH=Sgt. Co.E,)	ROH,JR,SA1
Ogier, Thomas L.	Asst. Surg	24th SCVI		CN	07/31/63	Merton, MS	DOD		ROH,SRG
Oglesby, David	Pvt.	H 4th SC	17	SG	/ /	Salisbury, NC	DOD		ROH
Oldham, M.R.	Pvt.	F 7th SCVI			05/06/62	Richmond, VA		Oakwood C.#95,Row J,Div A	ROH,OWC
Oldham, Thomas	Pvt.	D 18th SCVI		AN	02/25/64	Florida	ACD	(RR accident in Florida)	ROH
Olfert, Bernard	Pvt.	Bachman's		CN	06/28/62	Mechanicsville	ACD		ROH,CDC
Oliver, C. Winter	Pvt.	G 19th SCVI		AE	/ /		DOD		HOL
Oliver, H.C.	Pvt.	F 15th SCMil			05/07/65	Pt. Lookout, MD	DIP	C.C. Pt. Lookout, MD	ROH,FPH,P6,P115
Oliver, J. Walter	Pvt.	Ferguson's			05/25/63	Jackson, MS			PP
Oliver, John	Pvt.	6th SCVI			07/09/62	Richmond, VA			ROH
Oliver, John J.	Pvt.	I 14th SCVI	22	AE	06/25/62	Richmond, VA	DOD	(Typhoid)	ROH,JR,HOL
Oliver, M.M.	Pvt.	H 11th SCVI			05/25/63	Petersburg, VA	DOW	(Wdd 5/22/63, ? NI VA '63)	ROH
Oliver, P.E.	Pvt.	D 7th SCVI			09/04/64			Stonewall C. Winchester VA	ROH,WIN,KEB
Oliver, Sidney	Pvt.	K 21st SCVI		DN	01/15/65	Ft. Fisher, NC	KIA		PP,HAG
Oliver, Thomas P.	Pvt.	B 25th SCVI		OG	03/15/65		DIP		ROH,HAG,WLI
Oliver, William W.	Pvt.	H 26th SCVI		SR	05/21/64	Petersburg, VA			PP
Olmstead,	Pvt.	H 1st SCVA		CR	06/11/63	Charleston, SC		Magnolia Cem. Charleston	ROH,MAG,RCD
Olney, Alfred L.	Sgt.	A 25th SCVI	24	CN	06/06/64	Richmond, VA	DOD	Magnolia Cem. Charleston	ROH,HAG,CDC,CV
Omelveny, James	Pvt.	F 23rd SCVI	19	CR	08/04/64	Crater Pbg., VA	DOW	(Wdd 7/30/64) PP	ROH,BLM,BLC,HHC
Onyness, J.J.	Pvt.	E 14th SCVI			/ /	Richmond, VA		Oakwood C.#91,Row M,Div B	ROH,OWC
Opry, E.G.	Pvt.	C 3rd SCVABn			12/02/64	Ship Island, MS	DIP	Ship Island Cem., MS	PP,P3
Opry, Sidney	Pvt.	C 3rd SCVABn			12/02/64	Ship Island, MS	DIP	#57 Ship Island, MS Cem.	P6
Orander, Lewis R.	Pvt.	I 2nd SCVI		ED	07/28/63	Gettysburg, PA	DOW	(JR=7/27/62)	ROH,JR,GDR,SA2
Ord,Jr., Robert H.R.	Pvt.	L 21st SCVI	16	MN	01/15/65	Ft. Fisher, NC	KIA		PP
Orr, Alexander	4th Sgt.	B 2nd SCVIRi		PS	/ /			(Rchmd effects list 1/63)	ROH,CDC
Orr, Francis	Pvt.	I 6th SCVI		CR	06/30/62	Frayser's Fm. VA	KIA		WDB,HHC,CB
Orr, Harvey D.	Pvt.	G 22nd SCVI	20	AN	06/16/62	Secessionville	KIA	(PP=Henry D.)	ROH,CDC,PP
Orr, Joseph Andrew	Pvt.	F 6th SCVC	36	UN	10/27/64	Burgess' Mill VA	KIA		ROH,CDC,CAG
Ortray, John T.	Pvt.	F 3rd SCVIBn		RD	11/07/62	Mt. Jackson, VA		(Altee, Autry ?	PP
Orvin, Henry J.	Pvt.	K 10th SCVI		CN	12/31/62	Murfreesboro, TN	KIA		RAS
Osborne, E.B.	Pvt.	A 1st SCVIR		LR	07/24/64	Mt. Pleasant, SC	DOD		SA1,LAN
Osborne, J.D.	Pvt.	14th SCVI		LS	11/20/62	Richmond, VA	DOD	Hollywood Cem.Rchmd. S240	ROH,HC
Osborne, John Francis	Pvt.	E 6th SC Res	18	ED	/ /	NC	DOD	(1865, Chaplain in Rgt.?)	ROH
Osborne, John Rutledge	Pvt.	H 6th SCVI	19	FD	06/30/62	Frayser's Farm	KIA		ROH,WDB,HFC
Osborne, Thomas J.	Cpl.	H 16th SCVI		GE	/ /	Marietta, GA	DOD	Con. Cem. Marietta, GA	16R,BGA,CCM
Osborne, Thomas J.	Pvt.	D 1st SCV			/ /	Lynchburg, VA		Lynchburg CSA Cem.#5 R4	BBW
Osborne, W.F.	Pvt.	D 2nd SC			10/21/62			Stonewall C. Winchester VA	ROH,WIN
Osgood, Henry	Pvt.	D P.S.S.			/ /		DOD		JR
Osmer, D.	Pvt.	I Orr's Ri.			05/04/64	Richmond, VA		Hollywood Cem.Rchmd. I12	ROH,HC
Osteen, Alfred M.	Pvt.	K 23rd SCVI		CL	04/15/62	Christ Church SC	DOD		K23,UD3
Osteen, Caleb C.	Pvt.	A 1st SCVC		AE	03/01/62		DOD	(Measles)	JR
Oswald, P.H.	Pvt.	C 11th SCVI			/ /	Richmond, VA			ROH
Oswald, S.	Pvt.	K 14th SCVI		AE	07/31/63	Davids Island NY	DOW	(Prob Oswalt, Simeon 15th)	ROH
Oswalt, Daniel	Pvt.	K 20th SCVI		LN	07/29/64	Chaffin's Bluff	KIA		ROH,KEB
Oswalt, David Wilson	Pvt.	C 15th SCVI	33	LN	07/04/63	Gettysburg, PA	DOW	(Exchd South Mtn. POW)	ROH,H15,KEB,TOD
Oswalt, James T.	Pvt.	C 15th SCVI	23	LN	06/05/63	Rapidan, VA	DOD	(On march)	ROH,KEB,H15
Oswalt, Simeon O.	Pvt.	C 15th SCVI		LN	07/31/63	Gettysburg, PA	DOW	Cypress Hills N.C. #706	ROH,FPH,P4,P6
Oswalt, W.D.	Pvt.	G 3rd SCVI		LN	10/02/62	Strasburg, VA	DOW	(Wdd 9/13/62)	ROH,SA2,KEB

SOUTH CAROLINA DEAD IN CSA SERVICE 1861-1865

NAME	RANK	C REGIMENT	AGE	DS	DIED	WHERE	WHY	BURIED	SOURCES
Otey, Henry (Outz ?)	Pvt.	D 14th SCVI		ED	/ /	Richmond, VA		Oakwood C.#72,Row N,Div A	ROH,OWC
Otis,	Pvt.	23rd SCVI			/ /				ROH,CDC
Otis, James	Pvt.	F 23rd SCVI		CR	/ /	Lynchburg, VA		Lynchburg CSA Cem.#9 R4	BBW,HHC
Ott, Elias	Pvt.	G 25th SCVI	45	OG	07/10/64	Petersburg, VA	DOW	(Wdd 1/2/64)	ROH,HAG,EDR,PP
Ott, John David	Pvt.	G 25th SCVI		OG	03/15/65	Charleston, SC	DIP	(Died on way home/Elmira)	EDR,P1,P65
Ott, William Elmore	Pvt.	G 25th SCVI		OG	03/05/65	Elmira, NY	DIP	Woodlawn N.C.#1981 Elmira	ROH,FPH,EDR,P6
Otts, James M.	Pvt.	G 20th SCVI		SR	07/12/64	Richmond, VA		Hollywood Cem.Rchmd. V227	ROH,HC,KEB,CDC
Otts, John M.	Pvt.	I 5th SCVI	26	SG	06/30/62	Frayser's Farm	KIA	Nazareth P.C. SG Cty.	JR,SA3,GEC,GEE
Otts, John W.	Pvt.	C 13th SCVI		SG	07/03/62	Frayser's Farm	DOW	Hollywood Cem.Rchmd. M65	ROH,JR,HC
Otts, Martin (Outz ?)	Pvt.	1st SC Res		GE	05/09/65	Hart's Island NY	DIP	Cypress Hills N.C.#2978 NY	FPH,P6,P79
Outen, J.J.	Pvt.	E 12th SCVI	17	LR	03/12/64	Spotsylvania, VA	KIA	Spotsylvania C.H., VA	ROH,SCH,LAN
Outlaw, B.R.	Pvt.	B 9th SCVIBn	24		03/29/62	Georgetown, SC	DOD		PP
Outlaw, Bentley	Pvt.	G 7th SCVIBn	23	KW	05/16/64	Drury's Bluff VA	KIA		ROH,HIC,KEB
Outz, C.N.	Pvt.	K 14th SCVI		ED	12/16/62	Richmond, VA			ROH
Outz, John H.	Pvt.	B 14th SCVI	20	ED	/ /	Petersburg, VA	KIA		HOE,LSS,UD3
Outz, Thomas	Pvt.	B 14th SCVI	23	ED	/ /	Richmond, VA	DOW	(Wdd @ Chancellorsville)	HOE,UD3
Ouzts, Abdell	Pvt.	K 24th SCVI		ED	/ /		DOD	(1862)	HOE
Ouzts, Andrew Jackson	Pvt.	K 14th SCVI	24	ED	06/27/62	Gaines' Mill, VA	KIA		ROH,JR,HOE,EDN
Ouzts, E.M.	3rd Cpl.	K 14th SCVI		ED	12/13/62	Fredericksburg	KIA	(JR=DOW 12/16)	JR,HOE
Ouzts, Franklin	Pvt.	K 24th SCVI		ED	09/20/63	Chickamauga, GA	KIA		JR,CDC
Ouzts, George Martin	Pvt.	K 14th SCVI	21	ED	07/15/63	Gettysburg, PA	DOW	(Left to enemy)	ROH,GDR,HOE,P1
Ouzts, Henry	Pvt.	K 14th SCVI		ED	12/30/62	Richmond, VA	DOD	(Typhoid)	JR
Ouzts, J. Brantly	3rd Sgt.	C 19th SCVI		ED	12/31/62	Murfreesboro, TN	KIA		ROH,HOE,UD3
Ouzts, J.D.	Pvt.	C 14th SCVI		LS	/ /	Richmond, VA	DOD		JR
Ouzts, James	Pvt.	K 14th SCVI	19	ED	07/02/63	Gettysburg, PA	KIA		ROH,GDR,HOE,UD
Ouzts, James L.	Pvt.	K 14th SCVI	22	ED	05/05/64	Wilderness, VA	KIA		ROH,HOE
Ouzts, John H.	1st Sgt.	H 7th SCVIBn	24	ED	05/16/64	Drury's Bluff VA	KIA	(ROH= Co.G)	ROH,HAG
Ouzts, Marion	Pvt.	K 14th SCVI	21	ED	06/27/62	Gaines' Mill, VA	KIA	(Not listed dead in HOE)	ROH,JR,HOE,CNM
Ouzts, Shemvel W,	Pvt.	K 24th SCVI		ED	05/30/64	Calhoun, GA	DOW	Sleepy Creek Ch. ED Cty.	ROH,HOE
Overstreet, George	Pvt.	K 19th SCVI	35	ED	02/03/63	Shelbyville, TN	DOD	Willowmount C. Shelbyville	PP,HOE,TOD
Overstreet, L.	Pvt.	D 24th SCVI		BT	03/05/65	Camp Chase, OH	DIP	C.C.#1563 Columbus, OH	FPH,P1,P6
Owen, D.	Pvt.	H P.S.S.			01/17/64	Danbridge, TN	KIA		ROH,CDC
Owen, David T.	Pvt.	K 10th SCVI		CN	12/31/62	Murfreesboro, TN	DOW	(JR=7/11/63 & in Co.G)	JR,RAS
Owen, Leslie D.	Sgt.	Wshgtn LA		CN	04/22/62	Adams Run, SC	ACD	(drowned)	ROH
Owen, Leslie Dunlap	Pvt.	C 13th SCVI		SG	07/16/62	Laurel Hill, VA	KIA		JR
Owen, Moses Taggart	Cpt.	A 1st SCVC		AE	08/04/63	At home	DOW	(Wdd @ Williamsport)	ROH,JR,LC,R43
Owens, A.Y.	Pvt.	E 3rd SCVIBn		LS	05/08/64	Spotsylvania, VA	KIA	Spotsylvania C.H., VA	ROH,SCH,KEB
Owens, Albert P.	3rd Cpl.	E 1st SCVIG		MN	08/05/63	Davids Island NY	DIP	Cypress Hills N.C.#717 NY	FPH,GDR,SA1,P6
Owens, Alexander W.	Pvt.	F 6th SCVC	20	CN	/ /	Richmond, VA	DOD	(To hospital 12/20/64)	CAG
Owens, Alfred	Pvt.	A 25th SCVI	44	MN	08/26/64	Petersburg, VA	KIA	Blandford Church Pbg., VA	ROH,BLC,PP
Owens, Benjamin	Pvt.	E 22nd SCVI		LR	/ /	Richmond, VA '62		Oakwood C.#154,Row B,Div B	ROH,OWC,CDC
Owens, D.	Pvt.	A 5th SCVC		OG	09/12/64	Elmira, NY	DIP	Woodlawn N.C.#178 Elmira	FPH,P5,P65,P12
Owens, D.B.	Pvt.	B 7th SCVI		AE	01/15/62		DOW		JR,KEB
Owens, David R.	Pvt.	I 8th SCVI		MN	01/21/63	Richmond, VA	KIA	Oakwood C.#8,Row A,Div C	ROH,HMC,OWC,KE
Owens, E.	Pvt.	D 10th SCVI		MN	/ /		DOD		RAS,HMC
Owens, E.A.	Pvt.				/ /			Fredericksburg C.C. R6S13	FBG
Owens, Elijah (Elisha?)	Pvt.	A 21st SCVI		GN	06/24/64		DIP	(POW Pbg 6/24/64)	ROH,CDC,HAG
Owens, Ellis	Pvt.	D Hol.Leg.	21	BL	10/01/62	At home	DOW	(Wdd @ Rappahannock, VA)	ROH
Owens, George W.	Pvt.	F 16th SCVI		GE	01/23/62	Adams Run, SC	DOD		PP
Owens, H. Newton	Pvt.	A 6th SCVI	25	CR	05/06/64	Wilderness, VA	KIA	CB	ROH,GLS,HHC,YM
Owens, Harris	Pvt.	B 22nd SCVI		SG	07/30/64	Crater, Pbg., VA	KIA		HOS

SOUTH CAROLINA DEAD IN CSA SERVICE 1861-1865

NAME	RANK	C	REGIMENT	AGE	DS	DIED	WHERE	WHY	BURIED	SOURCES
Owens, Henry	Pvt.	C	22nd SCVI		SG	01/07/65	Elmira, NY	DIP	Woodlawn N.C.#1500 Elmira	ROH,FPH,P6,P65
Owens, Henry A.	Pvt.	H	1st SCVIG	21	BT	08/16/64	Fussel's Mills	MIA		ROH,SA1
Owens, J.C. *	Pvt.	A	44th SCVI			07/20/65	Richmond, VA		Hollywood Cem.Rchmd. U649	HC
Owens, James	Pvt.	E	13th SCVI		SG	06/25/62	At home	DOD	(Typhoid)	JR,HOS
Owens, James D.	Cpl.	B	Hol.Leg.		SG	/ /	Virginia 1864	DOD	1st P.C. Columbia, SC	ROH,HOS,PP
Owens, James W.	Cpt.	K	21st SCVI	44	LS	05/18/64	Richmond, VA	DOW	(Wdd Swift Ck. 5/9)	ROH,STR,HAG,R48
Owens, Jesse	Pvt.	B	16th SCVI		GE	11/30/64	Franklin, TN	KIA		16R
Owens, Jesse D.	Pvt.	A	1st SCVIG		BL	08/20/64	Fussel's Mill VA	DOW	Hollywood Cem.Rchmd. V353	ROH,SA1,CDC
Owens, John	Pvt.	G	3rd SCVI		SG	09/20/63	Chickamauga, GA	KIA	Con. Cem. Marietta, GA	ROH,JR,SA2,CCM
Owens, John	Pvt.	B	23rd SCVI	20	CN	06/30/64	Petersburg, VA	KIA		ROH
Owens, John	Pvt.	F	21st SCVI		MO	/ /	Point Lookout MD	DIP	(? P125= Jnd.USA 2/25/64)	HOM,P1,P124,P125
Owens, John	Pvt.	I	16th SCVI		GE	08/01/62	Adams Run, SC	DOD		PP
Owens, John A.	Pvt.	G	15th SCVI	23	WG	07/28/64	Deep Bottom, VA	KIA		ROH,KEB
Owens, John I.	Pvt.	E	1st SCVIH		BL	01/21/65	Camp Morton, IN	DIP	Green Lawn C. Indianapolis	ROH,FPH,SA1,P6
Owens, John Perry	Pvt.	F	4th SC Res	17	LS	04/24/65	At home	DOD		ROH
Owens, Lott	Pvt.	D	25th SCVI		MN	/ /	Virginia	KIA		HMC,HAG
Owens, M.	Pvt.	D	10th SCVI		MN	06/22/64	Kennesaw Mtn. GA	KIA		RAS,HMC
Owens, Mattison	Pvt.	F	16th SCVI		GE	/ /	Charleston, SC	DOD	(1862)	16R
Owens, Miller	Pvt.	I	Hol.Leg.	20	SG	08/10/62	Richmond, VA	DOD		ROH,HOS
Owens, Newt	Pvt.	I	1st SCVIH		MN	07/14/62	Columbia, SC	DOD	(Measles, NI SA1)	ROH,JRH,PP
Owens, R.H.	Pvt.	D	10th SCVI		MN	/ /		DOD		HMC,RAS
Owens, R.S.	Pvt.	C	13th SCVI		SG	07/16/62	Richmond, VA	DOW		JR
Owens, R.W.	Pvt.	E	25th SCVI		CN	05/07/64	Pt. Walthal Jctn	KIA		ROH,CDC
Owens, Richard	Pvt.	B	22nd SCVI		SG	07/30/64	Crater, Pbg., VA	KIA		ROH,BLM
Owens, Robert D.	Pvt.	K	P.S.S.		SG	/ /	Tennessee	DOD	(In enemy hands)	HOS
Owens, Robert J.	Pvt.	C	13th SCVI		SG	06/30/62	Frayser's Farm	KIA		ROH,JR,HOS,CDC
Owens, Robert S.	Cpt.	F	14th SCVI		LS	07/14/62	Frayser's Farm	DOW	(JR=7/11/62)	JR,CGS,R47
Owens, S.	Pvt.	B	7th SCVI		AE	05/13/61		DOD		JR,KEB
Owens, S.E.	Pvt.	D	10th SCVI		MN	12/29/62	Lauderdale Ss MS	DOD		RAS,HMC,PP
Owens, Samuel	Pvt.	A	21st SCVI		GN	02/21/65	Elmira, NY	DIP	Woodlawn N.C.#2301 Elmira	FPH,HAG,P6,P65
Owens, Shadrack S.	Pvt.	I	8th SCVI		MN	08/24/63	Richmond, VA	DOW	Hollywood Cem.Rchmd. U311	ROH,HC,HMC,KEB
Owens, T.	Pvt.	E	Orr's Ri.		PS	/ /	Richmond, VA		Hollywood Cem.Rchmd. W484	HC
Owens, T.A.	Pvt.	E	16th SCVI	20	GE	08/01/63	Jackson, MS	DOD		ROH,16R,PP
Owens, T.R.	Sgt.	F	14th SCVI		LS	07/02/63	Gettysburg, PA	KIA		ROH,JR,GDR
Owens, Thomas	Pvt.	D	Hol.Leg.	47	BL	12/07/64	Petersburg, VA	KIA		ROH
Owens, Thomas	Cpl.	D	11th SCVI	22	BT	05/16/64	Drury's Bluff VA	KIA		ROH,HAG
Owens, Thomas A.	Pvt.	C	22nd SCVI		SG	10/10/64	Elmira, NY	DIP	Woodlawn N.C.#669 Elmira	ROH,FPH,HOS,P6
Owens, W. Riley	Pvt.	A	20th SCVI		PS	10/13/64	Strasburg, VA	KIA		ROH,KEB
Owens, W.A.	Pvt.		7th SCVA			03/12/64	Charleston, SC		Magnolia Cem. Charleston	ROH,MAG,RCD
Owens, W.H.	Pvt.	K	25th SCVI		WG	03/21/65	Elmira, NY	DIP	Woodlawn N.C.#1537 Elmira	FPH,P6,P65
Owens, William	Pvt.	A	21st SCVI		GN	04/26/65	Elmira, NY	DIP	Woodlawn N.C. #1424 Elmira	ROH,FPH,P6,P65
Owens, William	Pvt.	C	22nd SCVI		SG	11/29/64	Elmira, NY	DIP	Woodlawn N.C.#987 Elmira	ROH,FPH,P6,P65
Owens, William	Pvt.	E	23rd SCVI		MN	08/24/63	Richmond, VA		Hollywood Cem.Rchmd. C195	ROH,HC
Owens, William	Pvt.	H	P.S.S.		SG	12/13/63	Dandridge, TN	KIA		HOS
Owens, William Capers	1st Sgt.	A	25th SCVI	20	CN	10/31/63	Ft. Sumter, SC	KIA	Magnolia Cem. Charleston	ROH,JR,DOC,PP
Owensby, David A.	Pvt.	F	4th SCVI		GE	11/08/61	Mt. Jackson, VA	DOD	(Place & day unknown)	SA2,PP
Owings, Eugene	Pvt.	E	14th SCVI		LS	06/16/62	At home	DOD	(Typhoid)	JR
Owings, J.T.	Pvt.	C	15th SCVI		LN	/ /		DOD		JR
Owings, J.W.	Pvt.	E	14th SCVI		LS	07/02/63	Gettysburg, PA	KIA		CGS
Owings, James A.L.	Pvt.	I	1st SCVIG		LS	05/02/63	Chancellorsville	KIA		ROH,SA1
Owings, John H.	Pvt.	E	14th SCVI		LS	01/05/63	At home	DOD	(Consumption)	JR,CGS

SOUTH CAROLINA DEAD IN CSA SERVICE 1861-1865

NAME	RANK	C	REGIMENT	AGE	DS	DIED	WHERE	WHY	BURIED	SOURCES
Owings, Osteen	Pvt.		16th SCVCb			07/16/62	At home	DOD (Typhoid)		JR
Owings, S.J.	Pvt.	E	14th SCVI		LS	06/06/62	Richmond, VA	DOD (Measles)		JR
Owings, W.H.	Pvt.	E	14th SCVI		LS	08/09/64	Richmond, VA		Hollywood Cem.Rchd. V90	ROH,HC
Ownes, William	Pvt.	C	22nd SCVI		SG	04/26/65	Elmira, NY	DIP	Woodlawn N.C.#1424 Elmira	FPH
Oxendine, Richard	Pvt.	C	6th SCVI		SR	/ /		KIA		HIC
Oxendine, Warren	Pvt.	A	14th SCVI	30	DN	05/12/64	Spotsylvania, VA	KIA		ROH,DEB,LSS
Oxener, Alfred Jackson	Cpl.	C	23rd SCVI		LN	07/24/64			Darby/Jones/Oxner Gvyd. NY	NCC
Oxner, D.	Pvt.	I	1st SCVIG		ED	06/15/64	Richmond, VA		Hollywood Cem.Rchmd. I13	HC,SA1

SOUTH CAROLINA DEAD IN CSA SERVICE 1861-1865

NAME	RANK	C REGIMENT	AGE	DS	DIED	WHERE	WHY	BURIED	SOURCES
P...., E.C.	Pvt.				/ /			Fredericksburg C.C. R6S13	FBG
P____, C.P.					/ /			Con. Cem. Marietta, GA	CCM
Pace, J.F.	Pvt.	D Ham.Leg.		AN	/ /	At home	DOD		GRS
Pace, J.L.	Pvt.	F 7th SCVIBn		KW	09/13/63	Charleston, SC	DOD	Magnolia Cem. Charleston	MAG,HIC,HAG,RC
Pace, James A.	Pvt.	I 21st SCVI	31	MN	12/15/63	Pt. Lookout, MD	DIP	C.C. Pt. Lookout, MD	ROH,FPH,HMC,P5
Pace, Reuben	Pvt.	G 2nd SC Res	16	NY	01/19/65	Columbia, SC	DOD		ROH,PP
Pace, Richard W.	Pvt.	F 10th SCVI		MN	11/13/62	Tennessee	DOD	(Erysipelas)	JR,RAS,HMC
Pace, W.H.	Pvt.	Palm. LA		SR	06/15/62	Lynchburg, VA	DOD	Lynchburg CSA Cem.#6 R3	BBW,SOB
Pack, B.J.	Pvt.	C Ham.Leg.		CL	09/18/62	Warrenton, VA	DOW	(Wdd 2nd Man)	ROH,JR
Pack, Elijah (J.H.?)	Pvt.	G 2nd SCVIRi	23	AN	06/15/62	Charlottesville	DOW	Univ. Cem. Charlottesville	ROH,ACH
Padget, A.R.	Pvt.	A 19th SCVI	26	ED	/ /	Lynchburg, VA	DOD	Lynchburg CSA Cem.#1 R2	HOE,BBW,UD3
Padget, Albert M.	Pvt.	M 7th SCVI	19	ED	01/03/63	Frederick, MD	DOW	Rose Hill C. Hagerstown MD	ROH,JR,FPH,BOD
Padget, Edwin Ernest	Pvt.	B 6th SCVC	19	ED	06/12/64	Trevillian Stn.	KIA	(See p249,BHC)	ROH,BC,HOE,UD3
Padget, Emanuel	Cpl.	E 7th SCVI		ED	/ /	Petersburg, VA			ROH,HOE,KEB,UD
Padget, Joel	Pvt.	B 11th SCVI		CO	01/15/62	At home	DOD	(?POW 2/20/65 in Co.K)	ROH
Padget, Wilbert	Pvt.	A 19th SCVI	25	ED	/ /	Chattanooga, TN	DOD	City C. Chattanooga, TN	HOE,UD3,TOD
Padgett, A.M.	Pvt.	M 7th SCVI			09/13/62	Maryland Hts. MD	dow	Rose Hill C. Hagerstown MD	BOD
Padgett, D.	Pvt.	K 11th SCVI	25	CO	09/22/62	At home	DOD	(Two men/name in HAG)	ROH,HAG
Padgett, Daniel A.	Pvt.	K 11th SCVI	22	CO	03/15/65	Pt. Lookout, MD	DIP	C.C. Pt. Lookout, MD	ROH,FPH,HAG,P6
Padgett, David	Pvt.	E 24th SCVI	30	CO	06/11/64	Georgia	DOD		ROH
Padgett, Enrie		F 19th SCV			07/05/64	?	?		UD2
Padgett, Francis M.	Pvt.	K 11th SCVI	22	CO	12/28/64	Pt. Lookout, MD	DIP	C.C. Pt. Lookout, MD	ROH,FPH,HAG,P5
Padgett, H.	Pvt.	K 11th SCVI	19	CO	04/30/65	North Carolina	DOD		ROH
Padgett, H.	Pvt.	B 3rd SCVI			04/06/62	Richmond, VA			ROH
Padgett, Isaac	Pvt.	F 3rd SCVABn	30	CN	08/15/63	At home	DOD		ROH
Padgett, Isom	Pvt.	G 4th SCVC		CO	03/21/64	Green Pond, SC	DOD		PP
Padgett, J.M.	Pvt.	K 22nd SCVI		PS	07/30/64	Crater, Pbg., VA	KIA		BLM
Padgett, James	Pvt.	E 24th SCVI	22	CO	12/07/63	Col. H. Atlanta	DOW	Oakland C. Atlanta R6#5	ROH,BGA.EJM
Padgett, James D.	2nd Lt.	I 24th SCVI	30	RD	11/30/64	Franklin, TN	KIA	Williamson Cty., TN C.C.	ROH,WCT,CDC,PP
Padgett, Lawson	Pvt.	B 14th SCVI	17	ED	/ /	Petersburg, VA	KIA	(1864)	HOE,UD3
Padgett, Mahlon	Pvt.	B 14th SCVI	17	ED	/ /	Orange C.H., VA	DOD	(1863)	HOE,UD3
Padgett, Samuel	Pvt.	D 19th SCVI	31	ED	/ /	Atlanta, GA	DOD	Oakland Cem. Atlanta, GA	HOE,CVGH,UD3
Padgett, Thomas	Pvt.	E 24th SCVI	22	CO	11/01/64	Camp Douglas, IL	DIP	Oakwood Con.Mound, Chicago	ROH,FPH,P5,P38
Padgett, Wesley P.	Pvt.	B 14th SCVI	18	ED	07/03/63	Gettysburg, PA	KIA		HOE,UD3
Padgett,Jr., Isham	Pvt.	E 24th SCVI	21	CO	02/19/64	Chickamauga, GA	DOW		ROH
Padgett,Sr., Isham	Pvt.	E 24th SCVI	41	CO	04/13/64	Atlanta, GA	DOW		ROH
Pagbell, Calock (? SP)	Pvt.	B 15th SCVI		UN	/ /	(Bagwell ?)		Oakwood C.#150,Row A,Div A	OWC
Page, A.	Pvt.	L 10th SCVI		MN	05/14/64	Resacca, GA	DOW		ROH,CDC
Page, Alfred M.	Pvt.	E Hol.Leg.	39	SG	08/13/62	Richmond, VA	DOD	(On Rchmd effects list)	ROH,HOS,CDC
Page, D.N.	Pvt.	L 8th SCVI		MN	04/26/63	Richmond, VA	DOD	Hollywood Cem.Rchmd. T315	HC,ROH,HMC,KEB
Page, Harrison	Pvt.	H 23rd SCVI		MN	08/30/62	2nd Manassas, VA	KIA		ROH,HMC,CDC
Page, J.B.	Cpl.	F 13th SCVI		SG	08/15/62			(Day approx, ?dup J.P./HC)	HOS
Page, J.J.	Pvt.	D 16th SCVI		GE	11/30/64	Franklin, TN	KIA	Macgavock C. Frkln Gv# 39	ROH,16R,WCT,PP
Page, J.L.	Pvt.	F 15th SCVI		UN	06/24/62	Richmond, VA	DOD	Hollywood Cem.Rchmd. O265	ROH,JR,HC
Page, James Singleton	Pvt.	F 15th SCVI	21	UN	06/10/62	Hardeeville, SC	DOD	(J.L. in KEB?)	ROH
Page, John J.	Pvt.	K 2nd SCVI		BL	01/13/63	Richmond, VA	DOD		ROH,SA2,KEB,H2
Page, M.R.	Pvt.	B 1st SC Res		GE	02/27/65	Columbia, SC	DOD	(1st SC Militia?)	ROH,PP
Page, P.C.	2nd Lt.	C 26th SCVI		MN	07/27/63	Jackson, MS	DOD		HMC,R48
Page, Pleasant G.	1st Lt.	F 13th SCVI		SG	04/15/62		DOD	(JR=Peay)	JR,HOS,R47
Page, Willis D.	Pvt.	E Hol.Leg.	37	SG	07/11/62	Adams Run, SC	DOD		ROH,HOS,PP
Paget, J.	Pvt.	German Art		CN	03/05/65	Columbia, SC	DOD		ROH

P

SOUTH CAROLINA DEAD IN CSA SERVICE 1861-1865

NAME	RANK	C REGIMENT	AGE	DS	DIED	WHERE	WHY	BURIED	SOURCES
Pagett, E.M.	Pvt.	H 26th SCVI		SR	11/08/64	Richmond, VA		Hollywood Cem.Rchmd. W375	ROH,HC
Pagett, J.	Pvt.	C 24th SCVI		CO	04/14/64	Med. C. Atlanta		Oakland C. Atlanta R5#12	BGA
Pagett, J. Andrew	1st Lt.	L Orr's Ri.		AN	12/13/62	Fredericksburg	KIA		ROH,CDC
Paine,	Pvt.				07/05/62	Richmond, VA		Hollywood Cem.Rchmd. M123	HC
Paine, G.W.					07/03/62	Richmond, VA		Hollywood Cem.Rchmd. M250	HC
Paine, P.F.	Pvt.	I 2nd SCV			10/24/62	Raleigh, NC		Oakwood C. Raleigh, NC	TOD
Paine, Robert	Pvt.	A 4th SCVC		CD	05/28/64	Hawes Shop, VA	KIA		ROH
Painter, Bailus	Pvt.	I Hol.Leg.		SG	/ /	Elmira, NY	DIP	(POW @ Stoney Creek)	HOS
Pair, N.	Pvt.	E Orr's Ri.		PS	/ /	Richmond, VA			ROH
Paison, George	Pvt.	F 1st SC			/ /	Manchester, VA			ROH
Palmer, Barnwell W.	Cpt.	A 27th SCVI	38	CN	06/16/64	Hare's Hill, Pbg	KIA	Magnolia Cem. Charleston	ROH,CDC,HAG,R48
Palmer, E.	Pvt.	H 15th SCVI		UN	04/15/64	Gordonsville, VA		Gordonsville, VA	ROH,GOR,KEB
Palmer, Edwin C.	Pvt.	C 10th SCVI		HY	01/02/65	Alton, IL	DIP	Con. Cem. Alton, IL	FPH,RAS,P6,P14
Palmer, Francis Gendron	Lt. Col.	Hol.Leg.	29	CN	12/05/62	Warrenton, VA	DOW	(Wdd 2nd Man)	ROH,LC,CDC
Palmer, Francis Marion	Pvt.	B Orr's Ri.	19	AE	05/12/64	Spotsylvania, VA	KIA		ROH,CDC
Palmer, G.P.	Pvt.	B Ham.Leg.			11/21/64	Pt. Lookout, MD	DIP	C.C. Pt. Lookout, MD	FPH,P5,P115
Palmer, J. Clarence	1st Lt.	24th SCVI	22	CN	09/20/63	Chickamauga, GA	KIA	Con. Cem. Marietta, GA	ROH,JR,R48,BGA
Palmer, J.T.	Pvt.	2nd SCVIRi			06/29/62	Savage Stn., VA	KIA	(One report = Gaines'Mill)	ROH,JR,CDC
Palmer, J.W.	Pvt.	D 6th SCVC		CN	06/07/65	Pt. Lookout, MD	DIP	C.C. Pt. Lookout, MD	FPH,P6,P115
Palmer, James Jerman	Cpl.	K P.S.S.		CR	08/30/62	2nd Manassas, VA	KIA	(1st in I, 2nd SCVI)	ROH,JR,HOS,UD1
Palmer, John C.	Pvt.	K 2nd SCVIRi	24	AN	10/01/62	Winchester, VA	DOD	Stonewall C. Winchester VA	ROH,WIN
Palmer, John D.	Pvt.				06/24/64	Petersburg, VA		Blandford Church Pbg., VA	BLC
Palmer, John S.	Cpt.	K 10th SCVI		CN	07/28/64	Atlanta, GA	KIA	Magnolia Cem. Charleston	ROH,MAG,RAS
Palmer, S.D.	Pvt.	D 4th SCVC		CN	06/17/64	Trevillian Stn.	DOW		ROH
Palmer, W. O'Neal	Pvt.	C 7th SCVI	20	AE	01/17/63	Richmond, VA	DOD	(Pneumonia)	ROH,JR,KEB
Palmer, W.J.	Sgt.	D 5th SCVC	38	CN	06/15/62	Charleston, SC	DOD		ROH
Palmer, William McDonald	Pvt.	A 12th SCVI	25	YK	06/29/62	Gaines' Mill, VA	DOW		JR,YMD,YEB,CNM
Palmore, John A.	Pvt.	C 6th SCVI		PS	04/04/65	Pt. Lookout, MD	DIP	(?,Co.C was from Kershaw)	ROH
Palson, William	Pvt.	8th SCVI			/ /	(Poston,W. Co C?		Oakwood C.#49,Row D,Div A	ROH,OWC
Pannel, Israel	Pvt.	F 23rd SCVI		CR	09/17/62	Sharpsburg	KIA	(HHC=South Mtn.)	CRM,HFC,HHC
Pannell, Robert Elijah	Pvt.	H 6th SCVI	30	CR	09/20/61	Manassas, VA	DOD	(Died @ Morkely's house)	ROH,HHC
Parater, Madison	Pvt.	L P.S.S.			08/19/64	Richmond, VA		Hollywood Cem.Rchmd. V106	ROH,HC
Pardue, Alfred A.	Sgt.	A 19th SCVI	35	ED	10/29/62	Knoxville, TN	DOD	Bethel C. Knoxville, TN	ROH,HOE,UD3,TOD
Pardue, D.	Pvt.	K 24th SCVI		ED	/ /		DOD		HOE
Pardue, John	Pvt.	A 16th SCVI		GE	/ /	Atlanta, GA	DOD		16R
Pardue, John H.	Pvt.	A 22nd SCVI			08/23/62	Rappahannock Stn	KIA		ROH
Parham, Frank	Pvt.	B 1st SCVC	25	SG	06/15/62	Adams Run, SC	DOD	(PP=age 22)	ROH,HOS,PP
Parham, Frederick L.	Pvt.	C 13th SCVI		SG	07/03/63	Gettysburg, PA	KIA	(ROH=Frederick J.)	ROH,GRD,HOS
Parham, Samuel	Pvt.	B 24th SCVI		MO	07/22/64	Peachtree Ck. GA	KIA		ROH,HOM,CDC
Parham, William	Pvt.	D 26th SCVI		MO	12/01/64	Stony Creek Stn.	KIA	Hollywood CEm.Rchmd. W584	ROH,HC
Paris, P.P.	Pvt.	H P.S.S.			06/30/62	Frayser's Farm	KIA		ROH
Parish, Armstead	Pvt.	D 19th SCVI	28	ED	/ /	Mississippi	DOD		HOE,UD3
Parish, C.W.	Pvt.	B 12th SCVI	30	YK	/ /				YEB
Parish, Doc	Pvt.	G P.S.S.	25	YK	11/24/63	Lookout Mtn., TN	KIA		YEB
Parish, J.	Pvt.	SCVA			06/01/62	Richmond, VA		Hollywood Cem.Rchmd. L66	HC
Parish, James A.	Pvt.	G P.S.S.	18	YK	05/16/64	Abbeville, SC	DOD		YMD
Park, Thomas W.		CS Hunley			10/16/63	Charleston, SC	ACD	Magnolia Cem. Charleston	RCD
Parker, A.	Pvt,	C 6th SCVI		KW	06/08/62	Richmond, VA	DOD	Hollywood CEm.Rchmd. P59	ROH,HC,HIC
Parker, Armis	Pvt.	E 2nd SCVI		KW	05/13/62	Richmond, VA	DOD	(Typhoid)	H2,SA2
Parker, Arthur	Pvt.	F 7th SCVI	18	ED	07/01/62	Malvern Hill, VA	KIA	(JR=2nd Manassas 8/29)	ROH,JR,HOE,KEB
Parker, Badgegood B.	Sgt.	E 21st SCVI		CD	07/12/65	Elmira, NY	DIP	Woodlawn N.C.#2847 Elmira	FPH,P6,HAG

SOUTH CAROLINA DEAD IN CSA SERVICE 1861-1865

NAME	RANK	C	REGIMENT	AGE	DS	DIED	WHERE	WHY	BURIED	SOURCES
Parker, Bartimens	Pvt.	A	23rd SCVI		HY	04/01/65	Five Forks, VA	KIA		ROH
Parker, Benjamin B.	Pvt.	D	15th SCVI		KW	/ /		DOD		JR,HIC,KEB
Parker, Calvin	Pvt.	D	21st SCVI		CD	04/21/65	Pt. Lookout, MD	DIP	C.C. Pt. Lookout, MD	ROH,FPH,HAG,P6
Parker, E.L.	Pvt.		7th SCVI			/ /	Richmond, VA		Oakwood C.#17,Row U,Div F	ROH,OWC
Parker, G.A. (G.W.?)						/ /			(Rchmd effects list 12/62)	CDC
Parker, G.W.	Pvt.	D	Hol.Leg.	27	BL	08/23/62	Rappahannock Stn	KIA	(JR=2nd Manassas 8/30)	ROH,JR
Parker, George W.	Pvt.	F	1st SCVIG		HY	07/10/63	Gettysburg, PA	DOW	(Wdd 7/3/63)	SA1,GDR,CDC
Parker, H.H.	Pvt.	L	7th SCVI		HY	01/30/64	Columbia, SC	DOD	(Tetanus, PP=1/15/64)	ROH,KEB,PP
Parker, H.J.	Pvt.	G	P.S.S.		YK	06/30/62	Frayser's Farm	KIA		ROH,JR,CDC
Parker, Hardy	Cpl.	G	10th SCVI		HY	09/20/63	Chickamauga, GA	KIA	(RAS=Mission Ridge)	ROH,JR,RAS,CDC
Parker, Irwin	Pvt.	F	4th SCVC		MN	02/21/65	Elmira, NY	DIP	Woodlawn N.C.#2310 Elmira	FPH,HMC,P6,P65
Parker, Isaac L.	Cpl.	A	12th SCVI	23	UN	08/16/64	Fussel's Mill VA	KIA		ROH,YEB
Parker, J.	Pvt.		PSS			06/15/62	Near /Richmond	DOW		UD2
Parker, J.A.	Pvt.	L	2nd SCVIRi			08/26/62	Richmond, VA			ROH,CDC
Parker, J.G.	Pvt.	A	3rd SCVC		CO	/ /	Richmond, VA		Oakwood C.#8,Row B,Div B	ROH,OWC
Parker, J.J.	Pvt.	D	14th SCVI		ED	06/19/62	Richmond, VA		Hollywood Cem.Rchmd. O214	HC
Parker, J.S. (J.J.?)	Pvt.					/ /	Columbia, SC		Elmwood Cem. Columbia, SC	MP,PP
Parker, J.S. (J.L.?)	Pvt.	I	11th SCVI		CO	05/19/64	Drury's Bluff VA	DOW	Oakwood C.#3,Row H,Div F	ROH,OWC
Parker, James W.	Pvt.	C	P.S.S.		AN	05/09/65	Richmond, VA	DOD	Hollywood Cem.Rchmd. W612	HC,P6,SA2,GMJ
Parker, Jaby	Pvt.	K	6th SCVI	28	WG	/ /	Lynchburg, VA		Lynchburg CSA Cem.#4 R4	ROH,BBW
Parker, James	Pvt.	D	Hol.Leg.	25	ED	08/23/62	Rappahannock Stn	KIA	(JR=2nd Manassas 8/30)	ROH,JR
Parker, James	Pvt.	F	1st SCVIR			05/15/65	Hart's Island NY	DIP	Cypress Hills N.C.#2797 NY	FPH,P6,P79,SA1
Parker, James	2nd Sgt.	B	19th SCVI		ED	12/27/64	Camp Chase, OH	DIP	C.C.#674 Columbus, OH	FPH,HOE,P6,P22
Parker, James K.	Pvt.	E	21st SCVI		CD	04/14/62	Georgetown, SC	DOD		PP,HAG
Parker, John	Pvt.	F	7th SCVI	18	ED	07/21/64	Richmond, VA	DOD	Hollywood Cem.Rchmd. V624	ROH,HC,HOE,KEB
Parker, John	Pvt.	A	10th SCVI		GN	/ /		KIA	(1861, NI RAS)	FLR
Parker, John E.	Sgt.	F	Hol.Leg.		KW	12/26/61	Culpepper, VA	DOD	Fairview Cem. Culpepper VA	CGH
Parker, John Emelius	Sgt.	H	7th SCVC	24	KW	12/24/61	Dumfries, VA	DOW	St.Paul's C. Charleston SC	ROH,JR,MAG,HIC
Parker, John F.	Pvt.	A	12th SCVI	31	UN	04/15/65	Staunton River	ACD	(Drowned)	YEB
Parker, Joseph	Pvt.	L	1st SCVIG		CN	03/10/65	Richmond, VA	DIP	(POW 8/31/64)	ROH,SA1
Parker, M.	Pvt.		SCVA			08/21/64	City Point, VA	DOW	City Pt. N.C. Hopewell, VA	ROH,PP,TOD
Parker, M. Turner	Pvt.	B	14th SCVI	22	ED	/ /	Lynchburg, VA	DOD	Lynchburg CSA Cem.#2 R5	HOE,BBW,UD3
Parker, Marion D.	Pvt.	E	1st SCVIH	19	BL	03/01/63	Petersburg, VA	DOD	Blandford Church Pbg., VA	ROH,JR,SA1,BLC
Parker, N.G.	Pvt.	H	10th SCVI		WG	/ /		DOD	(1863)	RAS,HOW
Parker, Peter	1st Cpl.	D	26th SCVI		MO	/ /	At home	DOD		HOM
Parker, Redding	Pvt.	D	15th SCVI		KW	07/29/63	Gordonsville, VA	DOD	Gordonsville, VA	ROH,JR,GOR,CDN
Parker, Samuel A.	Pvt.	B	6th SCVI		YK	09/30/64	Ft. Harrison, VA	KIA		ROH
Parker, Solomon	Pvt.	B	26th SCVI	23	CD	03/05/64	New Bern, NC	KIA		ROH,PP
Parker, Thomas	Pvt.	A	1st SCVIBn	30	AE	06/16/62	Secessionville	KIA	Trinity E.C. Abbeville, SC	ROH,CDC,CAE
Parker, Thomas H.	Pvt.	D	9th SCVIBn	30	HY	04/15/62	Camp Lookout, SC	DOD		ROH,PP
Parker, W.	Pvt.					/ /	Columbia, SC		Elmwood Cem. Columbia, SC	MP,PP
Parker, W.A.	Pvt.	F	17th SCVI		YK	08/29/62	2nd Manassas, VA	KIA		ROH,JR,CDC,CB
Parker, W.N.	Pvt.	G	5th SCVI		YK	03/15/63	Jerusalem, VA	DOD	(Prob Pbg. area)	JR,SA3
Parker, William McK.	Cadet		SC Mil Aca	18		05/09/65	Anderson, SC	MUR	Huguenot Ch. Charleston	MAG,CAG
Parker, William W.	Pvt.	B	24th SCVI	23	MO	06/15/63	Griffin, GA	DOD	Stonewall C. Griffin, GA	ROH,HOM,BGA,UD
Parkes, James F.	Pvt.	L	2nd SCVIRi	26	AN	09/15/62	Richmond, VA	DOD		ROH
Parkins, Daniel	Pvt.	D	Ham.Leg.		PS	/ /	Winchester, VA	DOD		GRS
Parkman, Jesse	Pvt.	K	14th SCVI		ED	07/01/63	Gettysburg, PA	KIA		GDR,HOE,UD2
Parkman, Saunders	Pvt.	A	22nd SCVI		ED	12/14/62	Kinston, NC	KIA		ROH,CDC,PP
Parkman, Saunders	Pvt.	A	22nd SCV			/ /	Kinston 12/62	KIA		UD2
Parkman, Simeon	Pvt.	C	19th SCVI		ED	12/31/62	Murfreesboro, TN	DOW	Willowmount C. Shelbyville	ROH,JR,TOD,PP

P

SOUTH CAROLINA DEAD IN CSA SERVICE 1861-1865

NAME	RANK	C REGIMENT	AGE	DS	DIED	WHERE	WHY	BURIED	SOURCES
Parks, A.R.	Pvt.	D 3rd SCVIBn		LS	11/29/63	Knoxville, TN	KIA		RHL,KEB,UD3
Parks, Alexander	Pvt.	D 26th SCVI		MO	/ /	Charleston, SC	DOD	(1863)	HOM
Parks, E.	Pvt.	C 1st SCVC		ED	01/02/64	Ft. Delaware, DE	DIP	Finn's Pt., NJ Nat. Cem.	ROH,FPH,P5,CDC
Parks, John M.	Pvt.	A 3rd SCVI		LS	09/15/62	Richmond, VA	DOD		ROH,JR,SA2,KEB
Parks, Monroe	Pvt.	K 17th SCVI	20	YK	/ /	Virginia	DOD		YEB
Parks, R.E.	Pvt.	G 18th SCVI		UN	03/05/64	Charleston, SC	KIA	Magnolia Cem. Charleston	ROH,MAG,CDC
Parks, Thomas J.	Pvt.	H 6th SCVI	35	YK	12/20/61	Dranesville, VA	KIA		ROH,JR,CDC,YEB
Parks, William G.	Pvt.	F 2nd SCVI	20	AE	04/09/64	Knoxville, TN	DOW	(Wdd 11/23/63,Chattanooga)	ROH,SA2,KEB,H2
Parler, Aldrich J.M.	Pvt.	F 25th SCVI	21	OG	08/24/64	Weldon RR, VA	KIA		ROH
Parler, Edward N.	Pvt.	A 8th SC Res	17	OG	12/02/64	Columbia, SC	DOD	(ROH=Charleston)	ROH,PP
Parler, John	Pvt.	A 6th SCRes	18	OG	06/15/64	Columbia, SC	DOD		ROH,PP
Parlitz, F.M.		24th SCV			/ /	Griffin, GA		Spaulding County, GA	UD2
Parlor, Edwin	Pvt.	D 4th SCVC		CN	10/04/64	Elmira, NY	DIP	Woodlawn N.C.#606 Elmira	ROH,FPH,P5,P65
Parnel,	Pvt.	23rd SCVI		CN	/ /				ROH,CDC
Parnell, H.W.	Pvt,	F 3rd SCVC		DN	03/28/65	Ft. Delaware, DE	DIP	Finn's Pt., NJ Nat. Cem.	ROH,FPH,P6,P41
Parnell, Henry E.	Pvt.	H 21st SCVI		DN	07/10/63	Morris Island SC	KIA		ROH,JR,CDC,HAG
Parnell, J.H.	Pvt.	A 14th SCVI	27	DN	09/20/62	Oxford, VA	KIA	(JR=Sharpsburg 9/17/62)	ROH,JR
Parnell, John H.	Pvt.	G 3rd SCVIBn		FD	07/02/63	Gettysburg, PA	MIA	(J.H. in P115? Xchd)	JR,HFC,CDC
Parnell, John H.	Pvt.	A 1st SC			07/02/63	Gettysburg, PA	KIA	(? Jere H.in H,1st SCVIG)	ROH
Parnell, W.J.	Pvt.	G 26th SCVI		DN	09/15/64	Petersburg, VA	DOW	(Wdd 9/8/64)	ROH
Paroll, Mathew	Pvt.	F Orr's Ri.		PS	06/13/62	Richmond, VA			ROH
Parr, James	Pvt.	E 5th SCVI		UN	08/14/61	Camp Pettus, VA	DOD	(Typhoid)	SA3,UD1
Parr, N.	Pvt.	E 1st SCV			/ /	Richmond, VA		Oakwood C.#24,Row L,Div B	OWC
Parr, William P.	2nd Lt.	H 15th SCVI		UN	07/02/63	Gettysburg, PA	KIA		ROH,JR,GDR,KEB
Parris, David	Pvt.	A 13th SCVI		LS	08/14/62	Richmond, VA	DOD	Hollywood Cem.Rchmd. Q129	ROH,JR,HC,CDC
Parris, Green B.	Pvt.	K Hol.Leg.		SG	06/07/62	Richmond, VA	DOD	(JR=H,P.S.S.)	ROH,JR
Parris, J.W.	Pvt.	A 5th SCVI	21	OG	05/31/62	7 Pines, VA	KIA	(JR=A,P.S.S.)	ROH,JR,SA3
Parris, James	Pvt.	H P.S.S.		SG	06/30/62	Frayser's Farm	KIA	(CDC=P.P.)	JR,HOS,CDC
Parrish, C.W.	Pvt.				08/21/64	Petersburg, VA	KIA	(Sniper, see pg154 LSS)	LSS
Parrish, Doctor F.	Pvt.	F 5th SCVI		YK	08/06/64	Camp Morton, IN	DIP	Green Lawn C. Indianapolis	FPH,P5,SA3
Parrish, G.B.	Pvt.	G			06/07/62	Richmond, VA			ROH
Parrish, W.P.	Pvt.	G 5th SCVI		YK	01/15/63	Richmond, VA	DOD		ROH,SA3
Parrison, John Thomas					/ /		DOW		JMB
Parrott, Benjamin	Pvt.	M 8th SCVI	22	DN	05/12/62	Richmond, VA	DOD		ROH,KEB
Parrott, Franklin	Pvt.	B 21st SCVI	20	DN	08/02/64	Petersburg, VA	DOW	Blandford Church Pbg., VA	ROH,BLC,HAG,PP
Parrott, George W.	Pvt.	B 21st SCVI		DN	01/15/65	Ft. Fisher, NC	KIA		PP,HAG
Parrott, James M.	Pvt.	B 21st SCVI		DN	07/16/65	Elmira, NY	DIP	Woodlawn N.C.#2873 Elmira	ROH,FPH,HAG,P65
Parrott, John	Pvt.	B 21st SCVI		DN	07/24/64	Petersburg, VA	DOW	Blandford Church Pbg., VA	ROH,BLC,HAG,PP
Parrott, Joseph	Pvt.	D 2nd SCVI			12/22/62		DOD		H2,SA2
Parrott, Nicholas	Pvt.	B 21st SCVI	20	DN	07/10/63	Morris Island SC	KIA	(CDC=S.J., NI HAG)	ROH,CDC,R48,UD2
Parrott, S.	Pvt.	B 21st SCVI		DN	07/10/63	Bty. Wagner, SC	KIA		ROH,JR,CDC,HAG
Parrott, William J.	4th Cpl.	E 17th SCVI	21	YK	07/28/64	Petersburg, VA	KIA	Blandford Church Pbg., VA	ROH,BLC,PP,YEB
Parsons, Frank R.	Pvt.	C 25th SCVI		WG	05/21/64	Bermuda Hundred	DOW	Blandford Church Pbg., VA	CTA,SA1,BLC
Parsons, J. Benjamin	Pvt.	B 2nd SCVIRi		PS	09/17/62	Sharpsburg, MD	DOW	(Color bearer)	ROH,R45
Parsons, J.T.L.	Pvt.	I P.S.S.		PS	08/12/62		DOD		ROH
Parsons, R.E. (R.A.?)	Pvt.	E 14th SCVI		LS	08/22/62	Charlottesville	DOD	Univ. Cem. Charlottesville	JR,CGS,ACH
Parsons, T.J.	Pvt.	E P.S.S.		SR	06/15/62	Manchester, VA	DOD		ROH,JR
Pase, William	Pvt.	H 16th SCVI		GE	07/29/64	Lovejoy, GA	KIA		16R
Pasley, M.E.	Pvt.	E 2nd SC		LS	/ /	Richmond, VA			ROH
Pasley, William H.	Pvt.	F 6th SCVC	17	LS	10/15/63	Johns Island, SC	DOD		ROH,CAG
Pate, Alfred D.	Pvt.	F 21st SCVI		MO	01/15/65	Ft. Fisher, NC	DOW		ROH,HOM,HAG,PP

SOUTH CAROLINA DEAD IN CSA SERVICE 1861-1865

NAME	RANK	C	REGIMENT	AGE	DS	DIED	WHERE	WHY	BURIED	SOURCES
Pate, James P.	Pvt.	G	1st SCVIG		ED	07/02/62	Gaines' Mill, VA	DOW		JR,SA1,HOE
Pate, Jr., Levi	Pvt.	F	7th SCVIBn	42	KW	07/13/64	Virginia	DOD		ROH,HIC,HAG
Patjens,	Pvt.		SC Lt. Art		CN	03/05/65	Columbia, SC			PP
Patrice, L.M. (Petree?)	Pvt.	K	3rd SCVI		SG	/ /	Richmond, VA		Oakwood C.#85,Row L,Div B	ROH,OWC
Patrick, J.F.	Pvt.	B	20th SCVI		UN	07/28/64	New Market Hts.	KIA		ROH,CDC,KEB
Patrick, Jasper	Pvt.	F	18th SCVI	19	UN	07/18/62	Charleston, SC	DOD		ROH
Patrick, Robert C.	Pvt.	F	18th SCVI		YK	02/05/65	Elmira, NY	DIP	Woodlawn N.C.#1918 Elmira	FPH,P6,P65,P66
Patrick, Robert V. (L.?)	Pvt.	F	5th SCVI	22	YK	12/13/61	Culpepper, VA	DOD	Fairview Cem. Culpepper VA	JR,CGH,SA3,YEB
Patrick, W.S.	Pvt.	H	11th SCVI		CO	09/15/62	Hardeeville, SC	DOD		ROH,HAG
Patrick, William	Pvt.	A	1st SCVIH		BL	02/01/63	Richmond, VA	DOD	(Also severe Wd.@ 2nd M.)	ROH,SA1,JRH,UD
Patterson, J.J.	Pvt.	G	18th SCVI		UN	07/11/63	Jackson, MS	KIA	(YEB=POW @ Crater)	ROH,JR,PP
Patterson, J.R.	Pvt.	C	Orr's Ri.		PS	06/30/62	Frayser's Farm	KIA	Hollywood Cem.Rchmd. M11	ROH,HC
Patterson, J.W.	Pvt.		ColumbiaGd		HY	02/03/65	Columbia, SC	DOD		ROH,PP
Patterson, James	Pvt.	K	Orr's Ri.	18	AN	07/23/62		DOD		ROH
Patterson, James Burt	Cpl.	I	14th SCVI	25	AE	05/22/64	Staunton, VA	DOW	(Wdd Wilderness)	ROH,HOL,PP
Patterson, Joseph			CS Hunley			10/16/63	Charleston, SC	ACD	Magnolia Cem. Charleston	RCD
Patterson, T.D.	Sgt.	K	22nd SCVI		PS	07/30/64	Crater, Pbg., VA	KIA		BLM
Patterson, W. Smith	Pvt.	K	P.S.S.		SG	/ /	Ft. Harrison, VA	KIA		HOS
Patterson, William	Pvt.	C	Hol.Leg.	30	SG	10/01/62	Richmond, VA	DOD	(HOS= John)	ROH,HOS
Patterson, William	Pvt.	C	19th SCVI		LS	07/22/64	Atlanta, GA	KIA		HOE,UD3
Patterson, William B.	Sgt.	F	24th SCVI		AN	01/01/64		DOD		HOL
Patterson, William L.B.	Pvt.	A	SC CadetBn	18	CN	12/17/64	Tulifinny, SC	DOW	Magnolia Cem. Charleston	ROH,MAG,CDC,CA
Patterson, William N.	Pvt.	A	25th SCVI		CN	10/31/63	Ft. Sumter, SC	KIA	Magnolia Cem. Charleston	ROH,JR,DOC,PP
Patton, R.	Pvt.	H	12th SCVI	41	YK	03/15/62		DOD		CWC,YEB
Patton, R. Franklin	Pvt.	E	17th SCVI	18	YK	09/14/62	South Mtn., MD	KIA		ROH,JR
Patton, W.H.	Pvt.	H	14th SCVI		BL	12/07/63	Richmond, VA		Hollywood Cem.Rchmd. I63	ROH,HC
Patton, W.M. (W.B.?)	Pvt.	E	3rd SCVIBn		LS	/ /			Stonewall C. Winchester VA	WIN,KEB
Paul, James W.	Pvt.	F	12th SCVI		FD	/ /	Richmond, VA	DOD		ROH,HFC
Paul, Thomas	Pvt.	C	12th SCVI		FD	06/15/63	Hamilton Xng, VA	DOD	(Date approx)	HFC
Paul, William	Pvt.	I	1st SCVIH		MN	10/15/62	Winchester, VA	DOD		ROH,HMC,JRH
Paxton, J.R.	Pvt.		Pee Dee LA		DN	06/14/64	Ft. Delaware, DE	DIP	Finn's Pt., NJ Nat. Cem.	FPH,P5
Payne, B.F.	Pvt.	E	7th SCVC		ED	/ /		DOD		HOE
Payne, I.P.	Pvt.	F	2nd SCVC		GE	08/16/64	At home	DOD		PP
Payne, J.F.	Pvt.	K	2nd SCVI		GE	10/20/62	Raleigh, NC	DOD		SA2,KEB,H2
Payne, James R.	5th Sgt.	C	Hol.Leg.		ED	05/26/62	Adams Run, SC	DOD	(Left wife & 3 children)	ANY,EDN,CV
Payne, John	Pvt.	B	2nd SCVI	23	GE	07/21/61	1st Manassas, VA	KIA		ROH,SA2,KEB
Payne, John	Pvt.	B	16th SCVI		GE	/ /	At home	DOD	(1862)	16R
Payne, Richard	Pvt.	B	16th SCVI		GE	/ /	At home	DOD	(1862)	16R
Payne, Robert	Pvt.	A	4th SCVC		LR	05/28/64	Hawes Shop, VA	KIA		ROH,LAN
Paysinger, Benjamin F.	Pvt.	F	22nd SCVI	42	NY	01/28/65	Richmond, VA	DOD	Hollywood Cem.Rchmd. M49	ROH,HC,CDC,ANY
Paysinger, David S.	Pvt.	D	13th SCVI	23	NY	08/09/62	Richmond, VA	DOD	Colony L.C. Prosperity, SC	ROH,JR,NCC,ANY
Paysinger, Henry M.	5th Sgt.	C	3rd SCVI	23	NY	09/06/63	Gettysburg, PA	DOW	Magnolia Cem. Charleston	ROH,P5,GDR,ANY
Peabody, Charles W.	Pvt.	H	Orr's Ri.		MO	/ /		DOD	(1864)	HMC,CDC
Peace, George	Pvt.	I	22nd SCVI		OG	/ /	Lynchburg, VA		Lynchburg CSA Cem.#7 R2	BBW
Peach, William	Pvt.	G	2nd SCVI		KW	07/02/63	Gettysburg, PA	KIA		P2,SA2,KEB
Peacock, E.L.	Pvt.	A	1st SCVIG		BL	07/01/63	Gettysburg, VA	KIA		ROH,JR,GDR,SA1
Peacock, George W.	Pvt.	G	7th SCVC		CN	01/08/65	Elmira, NY	DIP	Woodlawn N.C.#1229 Elmira	FPH
Peacock, Isaac	Pvt.	I	5th SCVI		YK	10/23/62			Stonewall C. Winchester VA	ROH,WIN
Peagler, James R.	Pvt.	K	10th SCVI		CN	07/21/62	Okolona, MS	DOD		RAS,PP
Peagler, Thomas H.	Pvt.	H	1st SCVIG			09/28/64	Ft. Delaware, DE	DIP		SA1,P41,P42
Peahuff, J.L.	Pvt.	C	Hol.Leg.	22	GE	05/12/62	Adams Run, SC	DOD	(PP=3/24/62)	ROH,PP

P

SOUTH CAROLINA DEAD IN CSA SERVICE 1861-1865

NAME	RANK	C REGIMENT	AGE	DS	DIED	WHERE	WHY	BURIED	SOURCES
Peahuff, William	Pvt.	G 16th SCVI		GE	/ /	At home	DOD	(On active duty ?)	16R
Peak, George	Pvt.	F 12th SCVI		FD	06/01/64	Cold Harbor, VA	KIA		HFC
Peake, Samuel L.	Pvt.	G 24th SCVI			02/14/65	Camp Chase, OH	DIP	C.C.#1240 Columbus, OH	FPH,P6,P23
Peal, A.D. (Deserted)	Pvt.	D 5th SCVI		UN	09/20/64	Elmira, NY	DIP	Woodlawn N.C.#344 Elmira	FPH,SA3,P5,P65
Peal, T.J.	Pvt.	I 14th SCVI		AE	07/07/62	Richmond, VA		Hollywood Cem.Rchmd. M470	HC
Pearce, G.	Pvt.	C 18th SCVI		UN	11/06/62	Richmond, VA		Hollywood Cem. Rchmd. C35	HC
Pearson, A. Fitchue	Pvt.	G 16th SCVI		GE	01/01/64	At home	DOD	(16R=Georgia)	16R,PP
Pearson, A. John	Pvt.	G 16th SCVI		GE	06/16/64	Macon, GA	DOD	Rose Hill C. Macon, GA	16R,CV,BGA,PP
Pearson, Anthony Jackson	Pvt.	C 22nd SCVI		SG	10/16/64	Elmira, NY	DIP	Woodlawn N.C.#552 Elmira	ROH,FPH,P5,P120
Pearson, B. (R.?)	Pvt.	B 2nd SCVIRi		PS	09/17/62	Sharpsburg, MD	KIA		ROH,JR
Pearson, J. Alexander	Pvt.	F 13th SCVI		SG	09/01/62	Ox Hill, VA	KIA		ROH,JR,HOS
Pearson, J.E.	Pvt.	C 1st SCVIH		BL	01/02/63	Richmond, VA	DOD	Hollywood Cem.Rchmd. D2	ROH,HC,SA1
Pearson, J.H.	Pvt.	K 2nd SCVI		BL	07/13/63	Emory, VA	DOD	(SA2=Pierson)	SA2,KEB,H2
Pearson, J.P.	Pvt.	I Hol.Leg.		SG	04/23/65	Petersburg, VA	DOW	Near Fair Grounds Hospital	CDC,P6
Pearson, James H.	Pvt.	K 2nd SCVIRi			07/13/63	Emory, VA		Con. Cem. Emory, VA	PP
Pearson, John	Pvt.	E 14th SCVI		SG	05/12/64	Spotsylvania, VA	KIA	Spotsylvania C.H., VA	ROH,SCH,CGS,UD1
Pearson, John C.	Pvt.	E Hol. Leg.	18	SG	09/05/62	Warrenton, VA	DOW	(Wdd 2nd Man)	ROH,HOS
Pearson, L.G. (S.Y.?)	Pvt.	E 14th SCVI		RD	06/15/62	Richmond, VA		Oakwood C.#49,Row P,Div C	ROH,CGS,OWC
Pearson, P.A.	Pvt.	E Hol.Leg.		SG	08/30/62	2nd Manassas, VA	DOW		HOS
Pearson, Robert C.	Pvt.	G 8th SCVI	18	MO	09/27/62	Virginia	DOD	(Pneumonia)	JR,HOM,UD2
Pearson, Robert Raiford	Pvt.	C 2nd SCVI		RD	07/13/63	Gettysburg, PA	DOW		ROH,JR,GDR,SA2
Pearson, Samuel J.	Pvt.	C 22nd SCVI	37	SG	09/24/64	Elmira, NY	DIP	Woodlawn N.C.#461 Elmira	ROH,FPH,GEC,P5
Pearson, Simeon B.		Orr's Ri.		SG	12/20/62	Fredericksburg	DOW		HOS
Pearson, Thomas	Pvt.	B 27th SCVI		CN	09/23/64	Petersburg, VA			PP
Pearson, William	Sgt.	M P.S.S.	21	UN	06/22/64	Petersburg, VA	KIA		ROH
Pearson, William	Pvt.	I 5th SCVI		SG	/ /	Virginia	KIA		HOS
Pease, John	Pvt.	D 3rd SCVIBn		NY	07/25/63	Gettysburg, PA	DOW	Cypress Hills 689 N.C. NY	FPH,ANY,KEB,P1
Peaster, F.J.	Pvt.	C 6th SCVC			06/11/64	Trevillian Stn.	KIA		ROH
Peavy, J.	Pvt.	F 1st SCVIR		CD	03/14/62		DOD		SA1
Peavy, Jeremiah	Pvt.	I 1st SCVIR		MO	12/19/63	Mt. Pleasant, SC	DOD		SA1
Peay,	Pvt.				08/02/61	Charlottesville	DOW	(Wdd,1st M. ROH=23rd SCVI)	ROH,CDC
Peay, George	Pvt.	F 23rd SCVI		CR	08/30/62	2nd Manassas, VA	KIA		JR,HHC
Peay, James R.	Pvt.	F 6th SCVI		CR	06/30/62	Frayser's Farm	KIA	(Also slight Wd @ 7 Pines)	ROH,WDB,HHC,JR
Peck, E.D.	Pvt.	5th SC			/ /	Mt. Jackson Hos.	DOD	Mt. Jackson, VA	ROH,CDC
Peck, James F.	Pvt.	L 1st SCVIG		CN	08/29/62	2nd Manassas, VA	KIA		ROH,JR,SA1,CDC
Peden, A.M.	Pvt.	A 6th SCVC		GE	08/25/64	Ream's Stn., VA	KIA		ROH
Peden, James B.	Pvt.	B 1st SCVC	26	LS	09/15/63	Gordonsville, VA		Gordonsville Cem., VA	ROH,GOR
Peden, James S.	Pvt.	I 16th SCVI	43	GE	07/26/64	Decatur, GA	DOW	Fairview P.C. (wdd 7/22)	16R,GEC,GEE
Peden, Joseph C.	Pvt.	F 6th SCVI	23	CR	12/15/63	At home	DOD	(Also slight Wd @ 7 Pines)	ROH,HHC
Peebles, Addison S.	Pvt.	E 6th SCVI		DN	11/15/63	Racoon Mtn., TN	DOW	(AKA Wauhatchie)	ROH,JLC
Peebles, Edward S.	Pvt.	H 21st SCVI	22	DN	05/14/63	Pt. Walthall Jct	DOW	Blandford Church Pbg., VA	ROH,BLC,PP,HAG
Peebles, R.F.	Pvt.	A 7th SCVI			07/29/64	Richmond, VA		Hollywood Cem.Rchmd. V47	ROH,HC
Peebles, R.S.	Pvt.	E 6th SCVI			01/24/63	Inst.H. Atlanta		Oakland C. Atlanta R30#4	BGA
Peele, Lamartine	Pvt.	D Hol.Leg.		BL	/ /	Richmond, VA			ROH
Peeler, A.W.	Pvt.	F 5th SCVI		YK	01/10/62	Charlottesville	DOD		ROH,CB
Peeples, Abraham	Pvt.	F 11th SCVI		BT	01/15/65	Ft. Fisher, NC	KIA		ROH,CNM,HAG,PP
Peeples, J.R.	Pvt.	B 5th SCVC		BT	11/06/64	Boydton Plank Rd	DOW	(Wdd 11/5/64)	ROH,MDM,PP
Peeples, John A.	Pvt.	F 11th SCVI	24	BT	06/24/64	Petersburg, VA	KIA		ROH,HAG
Peeples, Joseph E.	Pvt.	K 1st SCVIH		OG	12/12/62	Richmond, VA	DOD		ROH,SA1,JRH
Pegler, Isaac	Pvt.	D 5th SCVC		CN	06/20/64	White House, VA	KIA	(JR=Begeler)	ROH,JR,CDC
Pehuff, S.S.	Pvt.	K 5th SCVI		SG	07/18/64	Petersburg, VA	DOD		SA3,HOS

SOUTH CAROLINA DEAD IN CSA SERVICE 1861-1865

NAME	RANK	C	REGIMENT	AGE	DS	DIED	WHERE	WHY	BURIED	SOURCES
Pelfrey, Joseph	Pvt.	K	12th SCVI	25	PS	01/22/63	Lynchburg, VA	DOD		ROH
Pelgrin, P.P.	Pvt.		Bachmans A		CN	07/18/64	Charleston, SC		Magnolia Cem. Charleston	ROH,MAG,RCD
Pelham, E.L.	Pvt.	G	1st SCVIH		BL	10/24/64	Ft. Harrison, VA	DOW	Hollywood Cem.Rchmd. W722	ROH,HC,SA1
Pelot, William L.	2nd Lt.	D	2nd SCVI		SR	06/03/64	Cold Harbor, VA	KIA		ROH,SA2,KEB,R4
Pence, Harrison	Pvt.	F	2nd SCV			08/12/64	Elmira, NY	DIP	Woodlawn N.C.#18 Elmira	FPH,P5
Pendarvis, Enoch	Pvt.	H	11th SCVI		CO	12/27/64		DOD		ROH,HAG
Pendarvis, H.L.	Pvt.	H	11th SCVI	23	CO	07/02/64	Petersburg, VA	DOW	(Wdd 6/27/64,PP=Dd 7/26)	ROH,HAG,PP
Pendarvis, J.A.	Pvt.	C	24th SCVI	23	CO	08/26/62	James Island, SC	DOD		ROH
Pendarvis, John B.	Pvt.	G	11th SCVI		CO	08/15/62	SC	DOD		ROH,HAG
Pendarvis, Rufus	Pvt.	F	3rd SCVABn	18	CN	03/14/65	Rockingham, NC	DOD		ROH
Pendarvis, W.J.	Pvt.	C	24th SCVI		CO	08/26/62	Charleston, SC		Magnolia Cem. Charleston	ROH,MAG,RCD
Pender, Perry H.	Pvt.					07/26/64	Petersburg, VA		Blandford Church Pbg., VA	BLC
Pendergrass, James H.	Pvt.	H	1st SCVIG		CR	05/12/64	Spotsylvania, VA	KIA		ROH,SA1,CDC,HH
Pendergrass, Joseph	Pvt.	G	7th SCVI			/ /		ACD	(HIC=Burned boat)	HIC,H2
Penn, E.M.	3rd Lt.	A	22nd SCVI	28	ED	09/29/62	Frederick, MD	DOW	Willow Brook B.C. ED Cty.	ROH,FPH,EDN,BO
Penn, S.	Pvt.	E	Orr's Ri.		PS	/ /	Richmond, VA		(1862)	ROH
Pennal, James A.	Pvt.	C	7th SCVI	21	AE	01/17/63	At home	DOD		ROH,KEB
Penny, J.T.	Pvt.	B	Orr's Ri.		AE	06/05/62	Richmond, VA		Hollywood Cem.Rchmd. P108	HC
Penny, N.C.	Cpl.	F	2nd SC Res	17	PS	01/20/65	Columbia, SC	DOD	Elmwood Cem. Columbia, SC	ROH,MP,PP
Penson, James	Pvt.	C	14th SCVI		GE	07/25/62	Richmond, VA			ROH
Pentick, A.	Pvt.	K	13th SCVI		LN	07/10/62	Richmond, VA			ROH
Pepper, John H.	Pvt.	K	Orr's Ri	28	AN	08/19/62	Richmond, VA	DOD	Hollywood Cem.Rchmd. H119	ROH,HC,CDC
Percy, J.						/ /				ROH
Perdieux, Colleton	Pvt.	E	21st SCVI		CD	06/21/65	Elmira, NY	DIP	Woodlawn N.C.#2812 Elmira	FPH,HAG,P6,P65
Perdon, O.P.	Pvt.	H	1st SC			06/15/65	Richmond, VA		Hollywood Cem.Rchmd. W416	HC
Perish, P.W.	Pvt.	B	12th SCVI	28	YK	/ /				YEB
Perkins, B.P.	Pvt.	L	7th SCVI		HY	/ /	Charlottesville		Univ. Cem. Charlottesville	ACH,KEB
Perkins, Elihu	Pvt.	H	Hol.Leg.	43	NY	02/01/65	Petersburg, VA	DOD		ROH,ANY,PP
Perkins, J.P.	Cpl.	H	26th SCVI		CN	06/17/64	Petersburg, VA		Blandford Church Pbg., VA	BLC,PP
Perkins, Miles	Pvt.	D	26th SCVI		MO	03/11/64	Charleston, SC	DOD	Magnolia Cem. Charleston	ROH,MAG,HOM,CD
Perkins, Roger Griswold	Pvt.	E	Hol.Leg. C	28	KW	08/15/61	Charleston, SC	DOD	Quaker Cem. Camden, SC	CNM,HIC,PP
Perkins, Samuel	Pvt.	E	1st SCVIR		PS	08/26/63	At home	DOD		SA1
Perkins, William	Pvt.	F	Orr's Ri.		PS	06/04/62	Richmond, VA	DOD	Hollywood Cem.Rchmd. P122	ROH,HC
Perkinson, Samuel	Pvt.	F	15th SCVI		SG	10/07/62	Winchester, VA	DOD	Stonewall C. Winchester VA	JR,WIN,HOS,KEB
Perkson, J.	Pvt.	B	1st SCVIBn		CN	/ /				ROH
Perrin, Abner M.	Brig. Gen.			37	ED	05/12/64	Spotsylvania, VA	KIA	Fredericksburg C.C. Sec.3	ROH,FBG
Perrin, James Monroe	Colonel		Orr's Ri.	41	AE	05/05/63	Chancellorsville	DOW	(Wdd 5/2/63)	ROH,JR,LC,CDC
Perrin, Samuel	Pvt.		LafayetteA			01/03/65	Charleston, SC		Magnolia Cem. Charleston	ROH,MAG,RCD
Perrin, Thomas S.	Pvt.	B	Orr's Ri.		AE	05/03/63	Chancellorsville	KIA	Upper Long Cane P.C. AE	ROH,JR,CAE
Perrin, William Henry	Pvt.	B	Orr's Ri.	25	AE	06/27/62	Gaines' Mill, VA	KIA	Upper Long Cane P.C. AE	ROH,JR,CDC,CAE
Perritt, M.	Pvt.	E	3rd SCVABn			/ /	Bty. Wagner, SC	DOW	(Between 8/30/63 & Evac)	CDC
Perry, Andrew M.	1st Lt.	H	2nd SCVI		LR	10/10/63	Walker Co., GA	DOW	(Wdd @ Chickamauga)	ROH,JR,SA2,H2
Perry, Benjamin C.	Pvt.	H	2nd SCVI		LR	08/03/61	Charlottesville	DOD		LAN,SA2,KEB,H2
Perry, J. Franklin	2nd Lt.	H	2nd SCVI		LR	07/21/62	Richmond, VA	DOW	(H2=Wdd @ Savage Stn.)	JR,LAN,KEB,H2
Perry, James	Pvt.	C	2nd SCVI		RD	07/11/62	Manchester, VA	DOW	(H2=Savage Stn.)	ROH,SA2,KEB,H2
Perry, John J.	Pvt.	G	7th SCVIBn	21	FD	05/16/64	Drury's Bluff VA	KIA		ROH,HIC,HAG
Perry, Lawrence Thomas	Pvt.	B	14th SCVI	19	ED	06/11/64	Spotsylvania, VA	DOW		ROH,HOE,UD3
Perry, Presley	Pvt.	E	22nd SCVI		LR	08/09/64	Elmira, NY	DIP	Woodlawn N.C.#138 Elmira	FPH,LAN,P5,P65
Perry, Samuel G.	Pvt.	G	7th SCVIBn	26	FD	06/20/64	Drury's Bluff, VA	DOW		ROH,HFC
Perry, Simon N.	Pvt.	G	7th SCVIBn	18	FD	07/18/62	Adams Run, SC	DOD		ROH,HFC,PP
Perry, T.W.	Pvt.	I	18th SCVI		DN	08/08/64	Crater, Pbg., VA	DOW	Blandford Church Pbg., VA	BLM,BLC

P

SOUTH CAROLINA DEAD IN CSA SERVICE 1861-1865

NAME	RANK	C	REGIMENT	AGE	DS	DIED	WHERE	WHY	BURIED	SOURCES
Perry, Thomas J.	Pvt.	G	2nd SCVI		KW	04/15/62	Gordonsville, VA	DOD	Gordonsville Cem., VA	JR,SA2,HIC,GOR
Perry, W.H.	Pvt.		6th SCVI			01/29/62	Richmond, VA		Hollywood Cem.Rchmd.066	HC
Persley,	Pvt.	G	5th SCVC		AE	08/16/64	Gravelly Run, VA	KIA		ROH
Pert, John	Pvt.	K	2nd SCVIRI	31	AE	11/11/63	LaGrange, GA	DOD	Con. Cem. LaGrange, GA	ROH,TOD
Pervis, S.G.	Pvt.	E	14th SCVI	33	CD	/ /	Richmond, VA		Oakwood C.#9, Row M, Div F	ROH,OWC
Peterkin, John A.	3rd Lt.	K	8th SCVI		MO	12/25/61	Richmond, VA	DOD	(Typhoid)	JR,HOM,R46,KEB
Peters, David	Pvt.	A	12th SCVI	35	YK	/ /	Richmond, VA	DOD		YEB
Peterson, George	Pvt.	F	1st SCVIG		HY	03/04/63	Manchester, VA	DOD		SA1
Peterson, William Spence	Cpt.	D	19th SCVI		ED	07/28/64	Atlanta, GA	DOW		ROH,ANY,HOE,UD3
Petit, Henry	Pvt.	H	P.S.S.		SG	06/30/62	Frayser's Farm	KIA		ROH,HOS,CDC
Petit, J.J.	Pvt.	A	25th SCVI	30	CN	/ /	Alexandria, VA	DOW	(POW Reams Stn 8/21)	ROH,HAG
Petree, James	Pvt.	K	3rd SCVI	18	SG	08/15/63	Winchester, VA	DOD	(1 Rpt=Patrice 11/12/62)	ROH,JR,SA2
Petsch, Emanuel	Pvt.	B	1st SCVIBn		CN	/ /				ROH
Pettigrew, Daniel H.	Pvt.	E	15th SCVI	25	FD	04/20/63	Richmond, VA	DOD		ROH,JR,KEB
Pettigrew, Joseph H.	Sgt.	E	15th SCVI	23	FD	05/04/63	Richmond, VA	DOD		ROH,JR,KEB
Pettit, G.W.	Pvt.	I	5th SCVI		SG	08/28/63	Lookout Valley	KIA	(JR=Racoon Mtn. 10/28)	ROH,JR,SA3,CDC
Pettitt, Nathan H.	Cpl.	K	3rd SCVI	21	SG	09/20/63	Chickamauga, GA	KIA	Con. Cem. Marietta, GA	ROH,JR,SA2,CCM
Pettus, Henry	Pvt.	A	12th SCVI	23	YK	08/29/62	2nd Manassas, VA	KIA		YEB
Petty, Asbury	Cpl.	B	Hol.Leg.	23	SG	02/15/62	Adams Run, SC	DOD		ROH,HOS,PP
Petty, Ira G.	Cpl.	C	Hol.Leg.	19	SG	09/15/62	Warrenton, VA	DOW	(Wdd 2M, HOS=Rappahanock)	ROH,HOS
Petty, James	Pvt.	I	9th SCVIB		SG	09/13/61	Germantown, VA	DOD		ROH,HOS
Petty, Joseph	Pvt.	K	P.S.S.		SG	/ /		DOD		JR,HOS
Petty, Newton	Pvt.	M	P.S.S.	17	UN	08/17/62	Sharpsburg, MD	KIA	Rose Hill C. Hagerstown MD	ROH,JR,CDC,BOD
Phelps, George L.	Pvt.	K	Ham. Leg.		CN	07/21/61	1st Manassas, VA	KIA		ROH,CDC,WLI
Philips, A.	Pvt.	H	13th SCVI		LN	09/04/64	Richmond, VA		Hollywood Cem.Rchmd. V214	HC
Phillip, William E.	1st Lt.	F	16th SCVI		GE	/ /	Adams Run, SC	DOD		16R
Phillips, A.B.	Pvt.	K	4th SCVC		CN	/ /				CLD
Phillips, Charles	Pvt.	E	14th SCVI		SG	11/12/64	Deep Bottom, VA	KIA	Hollywood Cem.Rchmd. W665	ROH,HC,CGS,HOS
Phillips, Clayburn	Pvt.	I	16th SCVI		GE	/ /	At home	DOD	(On active duty ?)	16R
Phillips, Eli	Pvt.	A	21st SCVI		GN	02/20/65	Elmira, NY	DIP	Woodlawn N.C.#2328 Elmira	ROH,FPH,P6,P65
Phillips, Franklin	Pvt.	K	12th SCVI	20	PS	12/05/62	Lynchburg, VA	DOD	Oakwood C.#145, Row L, Div A	ROH,OWC,CDC
Phillips, H.G.	Sgt.	C	26th SCVI	26	MN	07/11/63	Jackson, MS	KIA		ROH,HMC,CDC,PP
Phillips, H.L.	Pvt.	H	2nd SCVI		LR	09/17/62	Sharpsburg, VA	KIA	(JR=Maryland Hts. 9/13)	ROH,JR,SA2,LAN
Phillips, Hampton	Pvt.	I	P.S.S.		PS	06/15/62	Petersburg, VA	DOD	(JR=W.H.)	ROH,JR
Phillips, J.P.	Pvt.	I	6th SCVI		CR	/ /		DOD		CB
Phillips, J.T.	Pvt.	M	P.S.S.			11/14/62	Charlottesville	DOD	Univ. Cem. Charlottesville	ROH,JR,ACH
Phillips, James H.	1st Lt.	K	1st SCVIH		OG	09/11/62	Warrenton, VA	DOW	(Wdd 8/30/62 @ 2nd Man)	ROH,SA1,R45
Phillips, John	Pvt.	A	21st SCVI		GN	02/06/65	Elmira, NY	DIP	Woodlawn N.C.#1916 Elmira	ROH,FPH,P6,P65
Phillips, John	Sgt.	H	9th SCVIBn	34	CD	07/15/62	Columbia, SC	DOD		ROH,PP
Phillips, John	Pvt.	F	11th SCVI	21	BT	/ /	Weldon RR, VA	DOW	(In enemy hands)	ROH,HAG
Phillips, Joseph D.	Pvt.	F	27th SCVI	26	UN	08/10/62	Charleston, SC	DOD	(NI HAG)	ROH
Phillips, L.D.	Pvt.	E	16th SCVI	41	AN	07/22/64	Decatur, GA	KIA		ROH,16R
Phillips, L.S.	Pvt.	G	3rd SC			/ /	Maryland			ROH
Phillips, Lemuel Milner	Pvt.	E	25th SCVI	29	CN	09/15/64	Ream's Stn., VA	DOW	(Wdd & POW 8/24/64)	ROH,HAG
Phillips, Manning	Pvt.	E	Orr's Ri.	34	PS	03/30/65	White Oak Rd. VA	KIA		ROH
Phillips, Marion	Pvt.	B	22nd SCVI		SG	06/30/62				ROH
Phillips, Nelson	Pvt.	A	21st SCVI		GN	01/15/65	Ft. Fisher, NC	KIA		ROH,HAG,PP
Phillips, Peter	Pvt.	F	15th SCVI		PS	01/01/64	Pt. Lookout, MD	DIP	C.C. Pt. Lookout, MD	ROH,FPH,P5,P113
Phillips, Reuben	Pvt.	I	P.S.S.		PS	06/24/62	Petersburg, VA	DOD	Blandford Church Pbg., VA	ROH,JR,BLC,PP
Phillips, S.P.	Cpl.	M	8th SCVI	30	DN	09/20/63	Chickamauga, GA	KIA	Con. Cem. Marietta, GA	ROH,JR,CDC,CCM
Phillips, S.W.	Pvt.	G	7th SCVC			06/10/65	Pt. Lookout, MD	DIP	C.C. Pt. Lookout, MD	FPH,P6

SOUTH CAROLINA DEAD IN CSA SERVICE 1861-1865

NAME	RANK	C	REGIMENT	AGE	DS	DIED	WHERE	WHY	BURIED	SOURCES
Phillips, Seaborn F.	Pvt.	F	15th SCVI	23	UN	06/10/62		DOD	(KEB=S.G.)	ROH,JR,KEB
Phillips, Stephen F.	Sgt.	F	7th SCVIBn		KW	/ /	Petersburg, VA	KIA		HIC,HAG
Phillips, Thomas	Pvt.	E	5th SCVC		GN	/ /	Drury's Bluff VA	KIA		FLR
Phillips, William	Pvt.	K	10th SCVI		CN	/ /		DOD		RAS
Phillips, William E.	1st Lt.	F	16th SCVI		GE	07/11/62	Adams Run, SC	DOD		JR,16R,R47,PP
Philpot, Amon	Pvt.		19th SCVCB	29	PS	06/15/64	Richmond, VA	DOD	(? Trenholm's Cav. in VA?)	ROH
Philpot, James	Pvt.		7th SCVC		PS	02/17/65	At home	DOD	Mt.Zion U.M.C. Central, SC	PCS,UD3
Philpot, John W.	1st Lt.	A	Orr's Ri.	30	PS	09/10/62	Frayser's Farm	DOW	Mt.Zion U.M.C. Central, SC	ROH,PCS,CDC,UD
Philpot, Richard W.	Pvt.	A	Orr's Ri.		PS	12/07/61	Sullivans I., SC	DOD	Mt.Zion U.M.C. Central, SC	PCS,CDC,UD3
Philson, W.F.	Pvt.		Orr's Ri			04/29/62	Richmond, VA	DOD	Hollywood Cem.Rchmd. B296	ROH,JR,HC
Phinney, James Monroe	Cpt.	G	6th SCVI	29	FD	05/31/62	7 Pines, VA	KIA	Oakwood C.#4,Row B,Div A	ROH,JR,OWC,WDB
Phipps, J.W.	Pvt.	K	26th SCVI	35	HY	09/01/63	Mobile, AL	DOD		ROH
Phipps, L.G.	Cpl.	K	26th SCVI		HY	05/20/64	Drury's Bluff VA	KIA		ROH
Phylen, F.M.	Pvt.	H	22nd SCVI		GE	10/09/62			Stonewall C. Winchester VA	WIN
Pickens, Andrew Monroe	Pvt.	D	Ham.Leg.	23	AN	05/17/62	Richmond, VA	DOD	Pickens Chapel Pickens, SC	ROH,PCS,GRS
Pickens, T. Jeff	3rd Sgt.	G	22nd SCVI		AN	07/30/62	Columbia, SC	DOD	Elmwood Cem. Columbia, SC	ROH,MP,PP
Pickens, Thomas J.	3rd Lt.		16th SCVI		PS	07/30/62	Columbia, SC	DOD	Pickens Chapel Pickens, SC	PCS
Pickett, Elijah	Pvt.		SCVI			11/08/62	Richmond, VA	DOD	Hollywood Cem.Rchmd. S45	ROH,HC
Pie, G.R.	Pvt.	B	18th SCVI		UN	09/01/62	Richmond, VA	DOD	Hollywood Cem.Rchmd. S128	ROH,HC,CDC
Pierce, Andrew M.	Pvt.	M	10th SCVI	18	HY	/ /	Corinth, MS	DOD	(ROH=NC,PP=Okolona, MS)	ROH,RAS,PP
Pierce, James	Pvt.	K	2nd SCVIRi	20	PS	10/15/63	Richmond, VA	DOD		ROH
Pierson, Charles H.	Pvt.	H	1st SCVIG		SG	07/13/64	Richmond, VA	DOD		ROH,SA1
Pierson, D.W.	Pvt.	C	27th SCVI		CN	/ /	Fts. Monroe, VA	DIP	(MIA 6/24/64)	ROH,HAG
Pierson, J.B.	Pvt.	I	Ham.Leg.			/ /	Petersburg, VA	DOW	(Wdd 4/28/65)?	ROH
Pierson, J.P.	Pvt.	D	Ham.Leg.		UN	04/22/62	Petersburg, VA		(NI GRS)	ROH
Pierson, Thomas J.	Pvt.	B	27th SCVI			09/28/64	Petersburg, VA			ROH
Piester, James Spencer	3rd Lt.	C	3rd SCVI		NY	12/13/62	Fredericksburg	KIA	DeWalt/Gallman Gvyd Nby,SC	ROH,JR,NCC,SA2
Pigg, D.M.	Pvt.	C	3rd SC Res		CD	02/03/65	Charleston, SC	DOD	Magnolia Cem. Charleston	ROH,MAG,RCD
Pigg, Dallas	Pvt.	B	26th SCVI	18	CD	06/03/64	New Bern, NC	DOW		ROH
Pigg, Hollis	Pvt.	B	9th SCVIBn	22	CD	04/01/62	Georgetown, SC	DOD		PP
Pigg, O.K.	Pvt.	B	26th SCVI		CD	07/30/64	Petersburg, VA	KIA		ROH
Pigg, Pleasant P.	Pvt.	A	23rd SCVI		CD	07/30/64	Crater, Pbg., VA	KIA		ROH,BLM,PP
Pigg, William P.	Pvt.	B	26th SCVI		CD	06/19/65	Pt. Lookout, MD	DIP	C.C. Pt. Lookout, MD	ROH,FPH,P6,P11
Pigg, Young John	Pvt.	A	23rd SCVI		CD	08/11/64	Crater, Pbg., VA	DOW	Blandford Church Pbg., VA	ROH,BLC
Pigler, Benjamin F.	Sgt.	A	18th SCVI		UN	07/11/63	Jackson, MS	KIA		ROH,JR,PP
Pike, L.M.	Pvt.	F	16th SCVI		GE	/ /	Adams Run, SC	DOD	(On active duty ?)	16R
Pilgrim, R.R.	Pvt.		14th SCVI		AN	07/08/62	Richmond, VA		Hollywood Cem.Rchmd. O19	HC,CDC
Pilgrim, Sidney	Pvt.	D	4th SCVI		AN	07/05/61	Leesburg, VA	DOD		SA2,HOF
Pilgrim, Thomas F.	Pvt.	K	Ham.Leg.		AN	/ /	Lynchburg, VA		Lynchburg CSA Cem.#3 R1	BBW,SA2
Pilgrim, W.	Pvt.		Bachmans A		PS	07/16/64	McPhersonville	DOD		ROH
Pilgrim, W.H.	Pvt.	G	Hol.Leg.		PS	08/12/64	Stony Creek, VA			ROH
Pinckney, Alfred G.	Pvt.	L	1st SCVIG	19	CN	06/28/62	Gaines' Mill, VA	DOW	St.Philip's Ch. Charleston	ROH,JR,MAG,SA1
Pinckney, George C.	Pvt.	L	1st SCVIG		CN	12/13/62	Fredericksburg	KIA		ROH,JR,SA1,CDC
Pinckston, William	Pvt.	B	12th SCVI	40	YK	/ /				YEB
Pinner, John F.	Pvt.	L	1st SCVIG		CN	06/15/62	Richmond, VA	DOD	Hollywood Cem.Rchmd. R2	ROH,HC,SA1
Pinner, Thomas A.	Pvt.	A	26th SCVI	35	HY	09/28/65	At home	DOD		ROH
Pinson, Cornelius F.	Pvt.	A	3rd SCVIBn		AE	05/14/65	Pt. Lookout, MD	DIP	C.C. Pt. Lookout, MD	ROH,FPH,KEB,P6
Pinson, Elijah M.	Cpl.	A	3rd SCVIBn		AE	09/20/63	Chickamauga, GA	KIA	Con. Cem. Marietta, GA	ROH,JR,KEB,CCM
Pinson, H.H.	Pvt.	C	14th SCVI		LS	07/12/63	Hagerstown, MD	KIA		ROH
Pinson, J.	Pvt.	E	2nd SCV			/ /	Lynchburg, VA		Lynchburg CSA Cem.#5 R2	BBW
Pinson, J.H. (J.W.?)	Pvt.	F	3rd SCVI		LS	/ /	Richmond, VA		Oakwood C.#107,Row C,Div B	ROH,OWC,SA2,KE

P

SOUTH CAROLINA DEAD IN CSA SERVICE 1861-1865

NAME	RANK	C REGIMENT	AGE	DS	DIED	WHERE	WHY	BURIED	SOURCES
Pinson, James Milton	Pvt.	C 14th SCVI	18	LS	07/24/64	Richmond, VA	DOD		ROH
Pinson, Jesse	2nd Lt.	A Hol.Leg.	31	SG	11/07/64	Petersburg, VA	KIA	Blandford Church Pbg., VA	ROH,HOS,BLC,PP
Pinson, John V.	Pvt.	F 2nd SCVI		AE	05/06/64	Wilderness, VA	KIA	(Pinson, J. Bd.Lynchburg?)	ROH,SA2,CDC,KEB
Piper, F.D.	Pvt.	I 1st SC		CN	09/02/62	Richmond, VA		Hollywood Cem.Rchmd. A2	HC
Pipken,	Pvt.				05/18/62	Richmond, VA		Hollywood Cem.Rchmd. F99	HC
Pipkin, Elisha C.	1st Lt.	G 23rd SCVI		MO	/ /			(Dropped @ reOrg)	HOM,R48
Pipkin, W.J.	Pvt.	E 10th SCVI		GN	/ /	MS	DOD		RAS,HOW
Pitman, Bennett	Pvt.	D 1st SCVIH		LR	07/07/64	Petersburg, VA	DOD	(Also Wdd @ 2nd Man.)	SA1,LAN
Pitman, Laban	Pvt.	I 17th SCVI		LR	08/18/64	Petersburg, VA	DOD		ROH,LAN,PP
Pitman, S.D.	1st Lt.	L 7th SCVI		HY	09/17/62	Sharpsburg, MD	KIA	(ROH & KEB=Petman)	ROH,JR,R46,KEB
Pitman, Wylie	Pvt.	H 12th SCVI		YK	05/20/63		DOW		YEB,JR
Pitt, J.	Pvt.	C 5th SCV			10/23/62			Stonewall C. Winchester VA	ROH,WIN
Pittman, H.M.	1st Sgt.	F 4th SCVC		MN	05/28/64	Hawes Shop, VA	KIA		ROH,HMC
Pittman, J. David	Pvt.	F 4th SCVC		MN	01/29/65	Richmond, VA	DOD	Hollywood Cem.Rchmd. W581	HC,HMC
Pitts, A.	Pvt.	G 1st SCVIR		AN	11/17/61	Charleston, SC	DOD	Magnolia Cem. Charleston	MAG,SA1
Pitts, Drayton	3rd Sgt.	G Hol.Leg.	31	NY	/ /	Petersburg, VA	KIA		ANY
Pitts, J.F.	Pvt.	B 3rd SCVIBn		LS	09/03/64	Berrysville, VA	KIA	Stonewall C. Winchester VA	ROH,JR,WIN,KEB
Pitts, J.J.	Pvt.	A 2nd SCV			06/26/64	Richmond, VA		Hollywood Cem.Rchmd. U304	ROH,HC
Pitts, J.W.	Pvt.	F 3rd SCVI		LS	05/21/62	Richmond, VA	DOD		ROH,JR,SA2,KEB
Pitts, James M.	Pvt.	B 3rd SCVI		NY	12/13/62	Lynchburg, VA	DOW	Lynchburg CSA Cem.#7 R5	ROH,JR,SA2,BBW
Pitts, Milledge	Pvt.	K 2nd SCVA		ED	/ /		KIA		HOE,UD3
Pitts, P.A.	Pvt.	I 1st SCVC		CO	01/27/65	Columbia, SC	DOD	Elmwood Cem. Columbia, SC	ROH,MP,PP
Pitts, Robert	Pvt.	I 1st SCVC	45	LN	02/15/64	Columbia, SC			ROH
Pitts, W.A.	Pvt.	G 1st SC			11/09/61	Charleston, SC	DOD		ROH
Pitts, William	Pvt.	B 3rd SCVI		NY	07/15/62	Manchester, VA	DOW	(Wdd @ Savage Stn. 6/29)	ROH,JR,SA2,ANY
Pitts, William	Pvt.	B P.S.S.		PS	/ /		DIP	(POW Williamsburg,1862)	ROH
Pitts, William H.	Pvt.	D 13th SCVI	23	NY	06/29/62	Gaines' Mill, VA	DOW		ROH,JR,ANY,CDC
Pladith, S. (Plunkett?)	Pvt.	D 13th SCVI		NY	09/22/64	Richmond, VA		Hollywood Cem.Rchmd. V209	HC
Platt, William M.	Pvt.	C 5th SCVC		CO	08/26/64	City Point, VA	DOW	City Pt. N.C. Hopewell, VA	ROH,PP,TOD
Platte, W.W.	Sgt.	I 1st SCVC		CO	03/15/63	Lynchburg, VA	DOD	Lynchburg CSA Cem.#8 R1	ROH,BBW
Platts, William F.	Pvt.	C 1st SCVIH	18	BL	03/17/63	Petersburg, VA	DOD		ROH,SA1,JRH,PP
Plaxico, William S.	Pvt.	F 18th SCVI	18	YK	08/24/64	Petersburg, VA	DOW	Blandford Church Pbg., VA	ROH,BLC
Playdes, W.	Pvt.	F 18th SCVI		YK	/ /	Petersburg, VA			ROH
Player, J.G.	Pvt.			WG	05/07/64	Walthall Jctn VA	KIA		HOW
Player, Robert	Pvt.	G 21st SCVI		CD	01/15/65	Ft. Fisher, NC	KIA		PP
Plexico, John S.	Pvt.	A 12th SCVI	40	YK	07/08/62	At home	DOD		YEB
Plindell, Noah	Pvt.	K 19th SCVI	25	ED	/ /		DOD		HOE
Plowden, H. Isaac B.	Pvt.	C Ham.Leg.		CL	09/18/62	Warrenton, VA	DOW	(Wdd 2nd Man)	ROH,JR,CDC
Plowden, James	Pvt.	B 14th SCVCB	45	WG	09/20/62	Georgetown, SC	DOD		ROH,CDC,PP
Plowden, John C.	Pvt.	I 25th SCVI		CL	05/03/65	Elmira, NY	DIP	Woodlawn N.C.#2754 Elmira	FPH,HAG,P6,P65
Plumer, James M.	5th Sgt.	B 1st SCVIG	25	NY	09/04/63	Chester, PA	DOW	Magnolia Cem. Charleston	ROH,GDR,SA1,P6
Plumley, J. Davis	Pvt.	H 22nd SCVI	22	GE	07/25/62	Columbia, SC	DOD	Glassy Mt. B.C. GE Cty	GEE,PP
Plumly, Benjamin	Pvt.	H 22nd SCVI	18	GE	08/10/64	Crater, Pbg., VA	DOW	Blandford Church Pbg., VA	ROH,BLM,BLC,PP
Plummer, Charles H.	Pvt.	E 8th SCVI		DN	10/05/63	Ft. Delaware, DE	DIP	Finn's Pt., NJ Nat. Cem.	ROH,FPH,KEB,P5
Plummer, H.B.	Pvt.	I 6th SCVC	21	DN	02/02/65	Columbia, SC	DOD	Elmwood Cem. Columbia, SC	ROH,MP,PP
Plunckett, C.P.	Pvt.				/ /			Fredericksburg Cem. R8S12	FBG
Plunkett, Daniel Stewart	Pvt.	D 13th SCVI	22	NY	06/25/62	Richmond, VA	DOD	(ANY=Drayton S.)	ROH,JR,ANY
Plunkett, David	Pvt.	B 6th SCVI		ED	06/12/64	Trevillian Stn.	KIA		HOE
Plunkett, O.C.	2nd Lt.	H 14th SCVI		BL	06/27/62	Gaines' Mill, VA	KIA	(JR=Co.A)	ROH,JR,BOS,UD3
Plunkett, Patrick C.	Pvt.	H 14th SCV		BL	01/15/63	Camp Gregg, VA	DOD		UD2
Plyler, D.H.	Pvt.	D 22nd SCVI		LR	07/24/62	Charleston, SC	DOD	Magnolia Cem. Charleston	ROH,MAG,RCD,LAN

SOUTH CAROLINA DEAD IN CSA SERVICE 1861-1865

NAME	RANK	C REGIMENT	AGE	DS	DIED	WHERE	WHY	BURIED	SOURCES
Plyler, F.N.	Pvt.	D 1st SC		LR	12/15/62		DOD	(Prob Co. H, 4th SCVC)	ROH
Plyler, F.P.	Pvt.	A 4th SCVC		LR	09/18/64	Pt. Lookout, MD	DIP	C.C. Pt. Lookout, MD	ROH,FPH,P6,P11
Plyler, General W.	Pvt.	D 1st SCVIH		LR	02/15/63	Richmond, VA	DOD	Oakwood C.#184,Row L,Div A	ROH,SA1,OWC,LA
Plyler, John Wesley	2nd Sgt.	A 5th SCVI		LR	08/16/64	New Market, VA	KIA	(On picket duty)	ROH,SA3,LAN
Plyler, N.B.	Pvt.	I 17th SCVI		LR	/ /	Adams Run, SC	DOD		JR,LAN
Plyler, N.L.	Pvt.	I 17th SCVI		LR	/ /	At home	DOD		JR,LAN
Plyler, T.M.	Pvt.	H 22nd SCVI		LR	10/09/62			Winchester, VA	ROH
Plymale, Michael	Pvt.	B 14th SCVI	23	ED	01/02/62	McPhersonville	DOW	(Wdd @ Port Royal Ferry)	ROH,JR,HOE,UD3
Plymale, W.W.	Pvt.	C 15th SCVI	17	LN	06/05/62	Hardeeville, SC	DOD		H15,KEB,TOD
Poag, Alonzo Walker	1st Lt.	H 12th SCVI	24	YK	07/03/63	Gettysburg, PA	KIA	YEB	ROH,GDR,BOS,BB
Poag, B.Z.	Pvt.	E 17th SCVI		BT	10/06/61	Culpepper, VA	DOD	Fairview Cem. Culpepper VA	CGH
Poag, Benjamin	Pvt.	E 17th SCVI	25	YK	08/27/62	2nd Manassas, VA	MIA	(May be B.Z CGH '61)	ROH,JR
Poag, David Randolph	Pvt.	F 6th SCVI	22	CR	09/10/62	Warrenton, VA	DOW	Fishing Creek P.C.	ROH,FCP,HHC
Poag, J.R.	Pvt.	18th SCVI			07/10/62	Charleston, SC	DOD	Magnolia Cem. Charleston	ROH,MAG,RCD
Poag, James M.	Pvt.	E 3rd SC Res	46	CR	04/07/65	At home	DOD		ROH,HHC
Poag, John	Pvt.	E 5th SCVI	34	YK	10/28/63	Lookout Valley	KIA	(YEB=Will's Valley)	SA3,CDC,YEB,UD
Poag, John Minor	4th Cpl.	E 17th SCVI		YK	05/20/64	Clay's Farm, VA	KIA		ROH
Poag, P. William	Pvt.	F 6th SCVI	40	CR	10/18/64	Ft. Harrison, VA	DOW	Hollywood Cem.Rchmd. V128	ROH,HC,HHC
Poag, Robert M.	1st Sgt.	F 6th SCVI	32	CR	03/04/64	Greenville, TN	DOD	Fishing Creek P.C.	ROH,FCP,HHC
Poag, Samuel G.	Cpl.	K 17th SCVI	34	YK	04/09/65	City Point, VA	DOW	(Wdd & POW 3/65)	ROH,RCD,P6,YEB
Poag, Thomas	Pvt.	A 6th SCVI	29	YK	09/17/62	Sharpsburg, MD	KIA	(Same man as Thomas J.?)	YEB
Poag, Thomas J.	Pvt.	A 6th SCVI	29	CR	08/22/61	Centreville, VA	DOD	Fishing Creek P.C.	ROH,FCP,HHC,CB
Poag, William H.	Pvt.	5th SC Res		YK	12/04/64	(RR in SC)	ACD	Bethesda Cem. YK Cty.	ROH,RCD
Poat, Charles John	Pvt.	C 1st SCVIG		RD	09/15/62	Warrenton, VA	DOW	(Wdd 2nd M., Dth date apr)	SA1
Poe, William	1st Lt.	C P.S.S.		AN	12/22/63	Lookout Valley	DOW	(GMJ=Chattanooga 11/28)	ROH,CDC,R48,GM
Polatty, James M.	Pvt.	C 19th SCVI		ED	12/06/64	Camp Chase, OH	DIP	C.C.#559 Columbus, OH	FPH,HOE,P6,UD3
Polk, H.M.	Pvt.	H 7th SCVI		PS	10/15/62	Winchester, VA		Stonewall C. Winchester VA	ROH,WIN
Polk, Isaac	Pvt.	K 11th SCVI		CO	06/07/64	Richmond, VA		Oakwood C.#10.Row T,Div F	ROH,OWC,HAG
Polk, J.W.	Pvt.	E 2nd SCVI		KW	07/02/63	Gettysburg, PA	KIA	Magnolia Cem. Charleston	ROH,JR,GDR,SA2
Polk, James M.	Pvt.	K 11th SCVI	23	CO	01/10/62	Hardeesville, SC	DOD		ROH
Polk, John	Pvt.	D 21st SCVI	30	CD	05/16/64	Drury's Bluff VA	KIA	(?POW 8/16/64)	ROH,P113
Pollard, James B.	Asst. Surg	Ham.Leg.	34	ED	02/20/62	Richmond, VA	DOD	(A Virginia native)	CNM
Pollard, John R.	Cpl.	D P.S.S.		SG	11/15/63	Campbell Stn. TN	DOW		ROH,HOS
Pollard, William C.	Pvt.	F 17th SCVI	18	YK	07/30/64	Crater, Pbg., VA	KIA		ROH,YMD,BLM
Pollard, William W.	Pvt.	F 3rd SCVABn	25	LS	11/05/62	Adams Run, SC	DOD		ROH
Pollock, Clarence J.	Pvt.	C 1st SCVIG	22	RD	05/12/64	Spotsylvania, VA	KIA	Hebrew Cem. Columbia, SC	ROH,MP,CDC,PP
Polly, John A.	Pvt.	D 17th SCVI		FD	04/02/62	Johns Island, SC	DOD		ROH,JR
Polson, Alexander	Pvt.	G 23rd SCVI		MO	/ /		DOW		HOM
Polson, Elihu	Pvt.	21st SCVI		CD	/ /				ROH
Polson, James H.	Pvt.	D 21st SCVI		CD	01/09/64	Pt. Lookout, MD	DIP	C.C. Pt. Lookout, MD	ROH,FPH,HAG,P5
Polson, John	Pvt.	B 8th SCVI	16	CD	11/15/61	Manassas, VA			ROH,KEB
Polson, John M.	Pvt.	E 6th SCVI		CD	06/30/62	7 Pines, VA	DOW	Hollywood Cem.Rchmd. M92	ROH,JLC,CDC,HC
Polson, John M.	Pvt.	E 21st SCVI		CD	/ /				ROH,HAG
Polson, Robert H.	Pvt.	G 21st SCVI		CD	06/04/62	Columbia, SC	DOW		ROH,HAG,PP
Polson, W.H.	Cpl.	G 21st SCVI	23	CD	07/10/63	Morris Island SC	KIA		ROH,JR,HAG
Polston, William	Pvt.	F 21st SCVI		MO	01/12/62	Georgetown, SC	DOD	(HAG=Polson)	ROH,HOM,HAG
Pond, Josiah W.	Pvt.	K 11th SCVI		CO	08/24/64	Petersburg, VA			ROH
Ponder, Thomas Milton	Pvt.	H 5th SCVC	19	GE	12/18/64	Beaufort, SC	KIA	(Heyward's Place, Argyle)	ROH,CDC
Ponds, Joseph	Pvt.	K 11th SCVI		CO	09/15/64	Petersburg, VA	DOD		ROH
Pool, Albert	Pvt.	I 5th SCVI		YK	/ /	Lookout Mtn., TN	KIA		YEB
Pool, Alfred P.	Pvt.	H 16th SCVI		GE	12/08/63	Atlanta, GA	DOD	Oakland C. Atlanta R38#6	ROH,BGA

P

SOUTH CAROLINA DEAD IN CSA SERVICE 1861-1865

NAME	RANK	C	REGIMENT	AGE	DS	DIED	WHERE	WHY	BURIED	SOURCES
Pool, C. F.	Pvt.	B	2nd SCVIRi		PS	/ /				ROH
Pool, Ephraim Manning	Pvt.	G	22nd SCVI	34	AN	07/30/64	Crater, Pbg., VA	KIA		ROH,BLM
Pool, G.R. (J.R.?)	Pvt.	B	2nd SCV			12/24/64	Knoxville, TN	DOW	(In enemy hands)	P1,P5
Pool, Green P.	Cpt.	F	4th SCVI		GE	07/31/61	Culpepper, VA	DOW	Springwood Cem. GE Cty.	ROH,JR,GEC,PP
Pool, J.C.	2nd Lt.	C	14th SCVI		LS	07/16/63				R47
Pool, J.P.	pvt.	B	2nd SCVIRi			12/24/64	Knoxville, TN	DIP		P5
Pool, Jeremiah P.	Pvt.	D	3rd SCVI		SG	03/19/65	Bentonville, NC	KIA		HOS
Pool, Jesse	Pvt.	G	16th SCVI		GE	/ /	At home	DOD	(On active duty ?)	16R
Pool, John D.	Pvt.	E	18th SCVI	19	SG	09/15/62	Warrenton, VA	DOW	New Hope Church SG Cty.	ROH,HOS,UNC
Pool, L.	Pvt.	H	14th SCVI		BL	06/28/62	Richmond, VA		Hollywood Cem.Rchmd. M15	HC
Pool, Martin Shuford	Pvt.	E	5th SCVI		YK	10/28/63	Lookout Valley	DOW	(POW @ Chattanooga?)	SA3,CDC,YEB,UD3
Pool, Robert W.	2nd Sgt.	B	2nd SCVI	22	GE	07/03/63	Gettysburg, PA	DOW		ROH,JR,GDR,SA2
Poole, Baylus E.	2nd Sgt.	E	Orr's Ri.	34	PS	01/18/62	Sullivans I., SC	DOD		ROH,CDC
Poole, D.	Pvt.	F	9th SCVIH		CN	11/07/61	Port Royal, SC	KIA		ROH
Poole, G.G.	Pvt.	F	14th SCVI		LS	08/18/62	Richmond, VA	DOD	(Typhoid)	ROH,JR
Poole, G.W.S.	Cpl.	B	Hol.Leg.	28	SG	02/09/62	Adams Run, SC	DOD	(PP=age 21)	ROH,HOS,PP
Poole, John H.F.	Pvt.	C	Hol.Leg.	23	SG	02/26/62	Adams Run, SC	DOD	Nazereth P.C. GE Cty.	HOS,GEC,GEE,PP
Poole, Robert C.	Pvt.	D	3rd SCVI		SG	08/08/61	Richmond, VA	DOD		JR,SA2,KEB,HOS
Poole, Robert L.	Cpt.	H	P.S.S.		SG	05/31/62	7 Pines, VA	KIA	(? Martin was Cpt @ 7P)	HOS
Poole, W.D.D.	4th Sgt.	I	5th SCVI		SG	02/25/65	Camp Douglas, IL	DIP	Oak Woods C.C. Md. Chicago	FPH,SA3,P3,P6
Poor, John W.	Pvt.	B	2nd SCVI	22	GE	08/12/61	Fairfax C.H., VA	DOD	(Typhoid)	ROH,SA2,KEB,H2
Poor, John W.	Pvt.	G	1st SCVA			06/18/65	Hart's Island NY	DIP	Cypress Hills N.C.#3024 NY	FPH,P6,P79
Pooser, Emanuel L.	Pvt.	B	20th SCVI		OG	04/30/65	New Bern, NC	DOW	Cedar Grove C. Newbern, NC	ROH,P1,KEB,P6,PP
Pooser, W.L.	Pvt.	A	1st SCVIH		BL	03/15/64	At home	DOD		SA1,UD3
Pope, Burrell	Pvt.	D	Ham.Leg.		RD	02/17/62	Virginia	DOD	Elmwood Cem. Columbia, SC	MP,PP
Pope, Burton H.	Pvt.	B	1st SCVIG	17	NY	07/17/62	Petersburg, VA	DOD	Blandford Church Pbg., VA	ROH,JR,SA2,BLC
Pope, David E.	Cpl.	I	Hol.Leg.		SG	10/14/64	Baltimore, MD	DOW	Loudon Pk.C. B-74 Balto.MD	FPH,P1,P5,P10,PP
Pope, J.B.	Pvt.					/ /	Virginia		(Rchmd. effects list 1/63)	CDC
Pope, J.R.E.	Pvt.	A	2nd SCVC			08/25/63	Richmond, VA			ROH
Pope, M.J.	Pvt.			42	SG	08/31/62	Warrenton, VA	DOW		TCC
Pope, M.T.	Pvt.	D	27th SCVI	39	LS	08/19/63		DOD		ROH,HAG
Pope, William Henry	Pvt.	E	3rd SCVI		NY	03/17/65	Averysboro, NC	KIA	PP	ROH,ANY,SA2,KEB
Popwell, Robert James	Pvt.	K	23rd SCVI		SR	08/19/64	Salisury, NC	DOD	(PP=Charlotte, NC 5/18/65)	ROH,K23,PP,UD3
Porcher, Isaac	Pvt.	L	1st SCVIG		CN	/ /		DOD	(Carolina Light Inf. 1861)	ROH
Porcher, Julius Theodore	Lt. Col.		10th SCVI	34	CN	11/25/63	Missionary Ridge	KIA		ROH,RAS
Porcher, Percival R.	Pvt.	K	4th SCVC		CN	06/02/64	Richmond, VA	DOW	(Wdd Hawes Shop)	ROH,CDC,CLD
Porcher, Philip	Lt.		CSS Juno		CN	/ /	Charleston, SC	KIA	(Running blockade)	DOC
Porcher, Thomas F.	Pvt.		Rutldge MR	33	CN	08/17/61	Sullivans I., SC	ACD	(Drwnd trying save sister)	ROH
Porcher, William C.	Pvt.	B	2nd SCVC		CN	07/07/64	Johns Island, SC	KIA		CDC,AOA
Port, Jehu	Pvt.	D	10th SCVI		MN	/ /		DOD		HMC
Port, L.	Pvt.	D	10th SCVI		MN	/ /		DOD		RAS,HMC
Porte, Thomas	Pvt.	E	10th SCVI		MN	/ /	South Island, SC	DOD	(WG ?)	RAS,HOW
Porter, A.G.	Pvt.	F	1st SC			10/07/62	(? E,15th SCVI)		Stonewall C. Winchester VA	WIN
Porter, C.C.	Pvt.	H	12th SCVI		YK	06/15/64	Lynchburg, VA	DOD	Lynchburg CSA Cem.#9 R3	CWC,BBW
Porter, Francis M.	Pvt.	F	18th SCVI	17	YK	07/28/62	Richmond, VA	DOD		ROH,PP
Porter, J.M.	Pvt.	F	18th SCVI		YK	07/28/62	Petersburg, VA			ROH
Porter, James W.	Pvt.	H	19th SCVI	40	AE	04/09/65	Camp Chase, OH	DIP	C.C.#1847 Columbus, OH	ROH,FPH,P6,P23
Porter, John G.	Pvt.	G	5th SCVI		SG	02/16/62	Manassas, VA	DOD	(JR=M,P.S.S.)	ROH,JR,SA3
Porter, John L.C.	Pvt.	I	12th SCVI		LR	05/12/64	Spotsylvania, VA	KIA		LAN
Porter, John R.	Pvt.	G	1st SCVIG		ED	05/12/64	Spotsylvania, VA	KIA		ROH,SA1,HOE,CDC
Porter, Joseph M.	1st Lt.	H	15th SCVI		WG	07/03/63	Gettysburg, VA	KIA	Magnolia Cem Charleston	ROH,JR,GDR,KEB

SOUTH CAROLINA DEAD IN CSA SERVICE 1861-1865

NAME	RANK	C REGIMENT	AGE	DS	DIED	WHERE	WHY	BURIED	SOURCES
Porter, Phillip H.	Pvt.	B 2nd SCVIRi			05/10/62	Adams Run, SC	DOD		PP
Porter, R.H.	1st Lt.	H 4th SCVC		LR	08/22/64	Virginia	DOD		LAN,R43
Porter, Samuel	Pvt.	G 1st SCVIG		ED	05/12/64	Spotsylvania, VA	KIA		ROH,SA1,HOE,CD
Porter, Theodore	Pvt.	C 17th SCVI		YK	/ /				YEB
Porterfield, J.H.	Pvt.	G 14th SCVI	24	AE	05/12/64	Spotsylvania, VA	KIA		ROH
Portress, John H.	Pvt.	H 1st SCVIG	24	BT	08/15/62	Laurel Hill, VA	DOD		ROH,SA1
Posey, E.	Pvt.	H 14th SCVI		BL	06/27/62	Gaines' Mill, VA	KIA		CNM
Posey, J. William	Pvt.	L Orr's Ri.		AN	11/04/62	Winchester, VA		Stonewall C. Winchester VA	ROH,WIN,CDC
Posey, Newton	Pvt.	D Ham.Leg.		PS	10/28/63	Will's Valley TN	KIA		GRS
Posey, W.H.	Pvt.	D 14th SCVI	21	ED	06/09/63	Richmond, VA	DOD	Oakwood C.#41,Row 33,Div C	ROH,D14,OWC,HO
Posey, W.H.	Pvt.	E Ham.Leg.		GE	11/28/63	Lookout Valley	DOW		CDC
Posey, W.W.	Pvt.	E 1st SCVA		SG	03/10/65	Columbia, SC	DOD		ROH,PP
Posey, William	Pvt.	E 2nd SCVIRi		AE	11/11/63	Bridgeport, AL	DOW	(Wdd & POW, Shell Mnd. AL)	ROH,CDC,P2,P6
Posey, William	Pvt.				/ /	(Posey, W.W.?)		Magnolia Cem. Charleston	MAG
Poster, J.H.	Pvt.	B 2nd SCVIRi		PS	/ /				ROH
Postern, Samuel	Pvt.	H 1st SCVIR		CD	02/02/64	At home	DOD		SA1
Poston, Bryant	Pvt.	C 26th SCVI		MN	10/27/64	Burgess' Mill VA	KIA		HMC
Poston, Canton	Pvt.	D 2nd SCVA		DN	03/30/64	Adams Run, SC	DOD	(Inglis L.A.)	ROH,PP
Poston, Christopher	Pvt.	I 10th SCVI	22	MN	/ /	Tennessee	DOD		ROH,RAS,HMC
Poston, Hampton	Pvt.	I 10th SCVI		MN	/ /	South Carolina	DOD		RAS
Poston, Henry A.	Pvt.	G 15th SCVI	25	WG	05/12/64	Spotsylvania. VA	KIA	Spotsylvania C.H., VA	ROH,HOW,KEB,SC
Poston, Josiah H.	Pvt.	I 10th SCVI	40	MN	06/04/62	Macon, GA	DOD	(RAS=died in TN)	ROH,RAS,HMC,PP
Poston, W.H.	Pvt.	I 10th SCVI		MN	11/25/63	Missionary Ridge	KIA	(WG ?)	RAS,WOW,HMC
Poston, William	Pvt.	I 10th SCVI		MN	05/18/62	Canton, MS	DOD		PP,RAS
Poston, William L.	Pvt.	D 21st SCVI		CD	06/15/63	At home	DOD		ROH
Poteet, Jacob A.	Pvt.	B 7th SCVIBn	38	FD	05/16/64	Drury's Bluff VA	KIA	(HAG=Poteat)	ROH,HAG,HFC
Potter, Peyton A.	Pvt.	E 13th SCVI		SG	08/29/62	2nd Manassas, VA	DOW	(JR=DOW 9/5/62)	HOS,JR,CDC
Potterfield, A.		3rd SCV		AN	/ /	Griffin, GA		Griffin, Spaulding Cty, GA	UD2
Potterfield, Patrick H.	Pvt.	D 18th SCVI	33	AN	07/23/64	Petersburg, VA	KIA	Blandford Church Pbg., VA	ROH,BLC,PP
Pou, John	Cpl.	E 7th SCVI		ED	/ /		KIA	(KEB=Powe)	HOE,KEB,UD3
Pou, W.G.	Pvt.	D 20th SCVI		OG	/ /	Charlottesville		Univ. Cem. Charlottesville	ACH,KEB
Powe, James F.	Pvt.	D 21st SCVI	38	CD	05/15/65	Elmira, NY	DIP	Woodlawn N.C.#2764 Elmira	ROH,FPH,HAG,P6
Powe, Joseph E.	Pvt.	D 21st SCVI		CD	03/08/65	Elmira, NY	DIP	Woodlawn N.C.#2364 Elmira	ROH,FPH,HAG,P6
Powe, Thomas Erasmus	Cpt.	C 8th SCVI	25	CD	07/10/63	Gettysburg, PA	DOW		ROH,JR,GDR,KEB
Powell, A. Louis	Pvt.	C 22nd SCVI		PS	08/14/64	Elmira, NY	DIP	Woodlawn N.C.#127 Elmira	ROH,FPH,CDC,P5
Powell, A.D.	Pt.	A 4th SCResB			03/12/65	Raleigh, NC		Oakwood C. Raleigh, NC	TOD
Powell, Benjamin	Pvt.	I 12th SCVI		LR	05/06/64	Wilderness, VA	KIA	(Wdd 8/16/64 @ Newmarket)	LSS,LAN
Powell, Charles	Pvt.	H 25th SCVI	21	WG	08/21/64	Weldon RR, VA	KIA		CTA,HOW,HAG
Powell, David	Pvt.	H 25th SCVI	31	WG	01/15/65	Ft. Fisher, NC	KIA		CTA,HOW,HAG
Powell, E.	Pvt.	H 25th SCVI		WG	06/23/65	Elmira, NY	DIP	Woodlawn N.C.#2815 Elmira	FPH,HOW,HAG,P6
Powell, H.A.	Pvt.	G 14th SCVI	20	AE	05/06/64	Wilderness, VA	KIA	(Also wdd @ 2nd Man.)	ROH
Powell, J.A.	Pvt.	I 3rd SCVI		LS	08/13/64	Pt. Lookout, MD	DIP	C.C. Pt. Lookout, MD	ROH,FPH,SA2,P5
Powell, J.B.	Pvt.	C Orr's Ri.		PS	06/27/62	Gaines' Mill, VA	KIA		ROH,JR,CDC
Powell, James	Pvt.	G 6th SCVI		FD	05/31/62	7 Pines, VA	KIA	(Boyce Guards)	ROH,JR,CDC,HFC
Powell, James V.	Pvt.	H 23rd SCVI		MN	12/20/64	Elmira, NY	DIP		P5
Powell, Jesse C.	2nd Cpl.	E 1st SCVIG		MN	05/12/64	Spotsylvania, VA	KIA		ROH,SA1,PDL,HM
Powell, John	Pvt.	C 18th SCVI	18	UN	/ /	MD	DOD	(1862)	ROH
Powell, John H.	Pvt.	G 1st SCVIG		ED	07/03/62	Richmond, VA	DOD	(JR=7/21/62)	JR,SA1,HOE
Powell, L.	Pvt.	I 7th SCVI		ED	/ /	Charlottesville	DOD	Univ. Cem. Charlottesville	ROH,CDC,ACH
Powell, Madison	Pvt.	A 5th SCVI		LR	08/02/61	Charlottesville	DOW	(Wdd @ 1st Man)	ROH
Powell, Noah P.	Pvt.	I 21st SCVI		MN	06/18/64	Petersburg, VA	KIA		HMC,HAG

P

SOUTH CAROLINA DEAD IN CSA SERVICE 1861-1865

NAME	RANK	C REGIMENT	AGE	DS	DIED	WHERE	WHY	BURIED	SOURCES
Powell, P.N.	Pvt.	G 6th SCVI		ED	05/31/62	7 Pines, VA	KIA	(Boyce Guards)	ROH,JR,WDB,CDC
Powell, Thomas W.	2nd Lt.	F 1st SCVIH	42	GE	06/30/62	Columbia, SC	DOD	Ebenezer B.C. GE Cty.	ROH,SA1,GEC,GEE
Powell, W.H.	Pvt.	I 3rd SCVI		LS	05/02/63	Frederick, MD	DOW	Mt.Olivet C. Frederick, MD	ROH,JR,FPH,P1,P6
Powell, Wiley	Pvt.	I 22nd SCVI		OG	04/27/64	Kinston, NC			PP
Powell, Willis A.	Sgt.	D 21st SCVI		CD	06/15/63	At home	DOD		ROH,HAG
Power, J. Alexander	3rd Lt.	E 14th SCVI	26	LS	01/01/62	Port Royal Ferry	KIA	New Harmony B.C. GE Cty.	ROH,JR,GEC,LSC
Power, James M.	Pvt.	E 14th SCVI		LS	/ /		DOD	(1863)	CGS
Powers, Alvin	Pvt.	B 13th SCVI		SG	07/01/64	Richmond, VA	DOD	Hollywood Cem.Rchmd. U14	HC,HOS
Powers, George	Pvt.	G 27th SCVI		CN	04/12/65	Elmira, NY	DIP	Woodlawn N.C.#2677 Elmira	FPH,HAG,P65,P120
Powers, George G.	Pvt.	B 1st SCVA			05/24/65	Pt. Lookout, MD	DIP	C.C. Pt. Lookout, MD	FPH,P6,P115
Powers, J.A.	Pvt.	I 15th SCVI		LN	10/10/62	Frederick, MD	DOW	(Wdd @ Sharpsburg, NI KEB)	P1,P6
Powers, James H.	Pvt.	A 21st SCVI		GN	01/22/65	Charleston, SC	DOD	Magnolia Cem. Charleston	ROH,MAG,RCD,P115
Powers, John H.	Pvt.	A 21st SCVI		GN	01/24/63		DOD		FLR,HAG
Powers, John W.	Pvt.	F 2nd SCVI	31	AE	11/27/63	Knoxville, TN	DOW	(Wdd 11/24/63)	ROH,SA2,KEB
Powers, Percy H.	Pvt.	E 3rd SCVIBn		LS	07/26/64	Petersburg, VA			ROH,KEB
Powers, S.	Pvt.	E 16th SCVI			/ /	Gainesville, AL		Gainesville, AL	TOD
Powers, Thomas	Pvt.	B 1st SCVA		CN	08/23/63	Bty. Wagner, SC	DOW	Magnolia Cem. Charleston	ROH,MAG,CDC,RCD
Powers, Tilman B.	Pvt.	A Orr's Ri.		AN	05/17/65	Hart's Island NY	DIP	Unknown, Prob Cypress Hiil	FPH,P6,P113,P124
Powers, W.T.	Pvt.	G 2nd SCVI	21	ED	09/20/63	Chickamauga, GA	KIA	(JR=W.D.)	ROH,JR,SA2,HIC
Powers, W.T.	Pvt.	D Ham.Leg.		UN	05/31/62	7 Pines, VA	KIA		GRS
Poznanski, Gustavus	Pvt.	D 1st SCVIBn		CN	06/16/62	Secessionville	KIA	Beth Elohim Charleston, SC	MAG,PP,RCD,HAG
Prant, W.J.	Pvt.	G 17th SCVI		BL	07/30/64	Crater, Pbg., VA	KIA		BLM
Prater, Drewry A.	Pvt.	19th SCVI	25	LN	/ /				ROH
Prater, James	Pvt.	E 5th SCVI	20	YK	06/01/63	Jerusalem, VA	DOD	(Typhoid)	JR,SA3,YEB
Prater, Larkin C.	Pvt.	A 19th SCVI	28	ED	07/22/64	Atlanta, GA	KIA		HOE,UD3
Prater, M.	Pvt.	L P.S.S.			08/18/64		DOD		ROH
Prater, Pressley M.	Pvt.	D 14th SCVI	21	ED	12/18/64	Elmira, NY	DIP	Woodlawn N.C.#1067 Elmira	ROH,FPH,D14,P120
Prather, Hamilton H.	Pvt.	A 2nd SCVIRi	27	AE	07/15/62	Richmond, VA	DOD	Oakwood C.#64,Row R,Div C	ROH,JR,OWC
Prather, Henry	Pvt.	G P.S.S.		LN	05/28/64	Old Church, VA	KIA		ROH
Prather, W.G.	4th Cpl.	H 1st SCVIH		LS	05/06/64	Wilderness, VA	KIA		ROH,SA1
Prather, William	Pvt.	B P.S.S.		AE	10/07/64	Darbytown Rd. VA	KIA		ROH
Pratt, Henry	1st Lt.	C 17th SCVI	28	YK	07/30/64	Crater, Pbg VA	KIA		ROH,YEB,BLM,KEB
Pratt, John S.	Pvt.	A 12th SCVI	26	YK	/ /	Richmond, VA	DOW		YEB
Pratt, Jonathan	Pvt.	D 1st SC		CR	/ /	Manassas, VA	DOD	(Died @ Morkely's Fm 1861)	HHC
Pratt, S. Langdon	3rd Sgt.	G Orr's Ri.		AE	06/05/62	Richmond, VA	DOD		ROH,CDC
Pratt, Samuel R.	Pvt.	A 12th SCVI	24	YK	09/19/62	Sharpsburg, MD	DOW		ROH,YEB
Pratt, Thomas A.	Pvt.	D 7th SCVC		RD	01/15/65	Elmira, NY	DIP	(FPH=26th VAVI)	FPH,P65,P66
Pratt, W.A.	Pvt.	B 7th SCVI		AE	09/20/63	Chickamauga, GA	KIA		ROH,JR,CDC,KEB
Preacher, J. Minney	Pvt.	E 24th SCVI	27	CO	02/07/65				ROH
Preacher, William E.	Cpl.	E 24th SCVI	19	CO	02/17/65	Camp Chase, OH	DIP	C.C.#1314 Columbus, OH	ROH,FPH,P6,P23
Prendergast, Joseph	Pvt.	G 7th SCVI			01/15/65	Smithville, NC	KIA	(NI KEB, Co.D,7th SCVIBn?)	ROH
Prentiss, C.B.	Pvt.	Hart's LA			/ /				CNM
Prentiss, F.J.	Sgt.	A Orr's Ri.		AN	07/28/63	Davids Island NY	DOW		ROH,P1
Prescott, J.H.	Pvt.	H 7th SCVI	27	BL	11/18/61	Culpepper, VA	DOD	Fairview Cem. Culpepper VA	CGH,HOE
Prescott, Memphis W.	Sgt.	I 24th SCVI		ED	07/20/64	Peachtree Creek	KIA		ROH,CDC
Prescott, Thomas D.	Pvt.	E 7th SCVIBn	20	SR	07/13/64	Petersburg, VA	DOD		ROH,HAG
Prescott, William M.	Pvt.	C 23rd SCVI	38	SR	08/11/64	Crater, Pbg., VA	DOW	Blandford Church Pbg., VA	ROH,BLM,BLC,PP
Prescott,Jr., William D.	Pvt.		33	ED	07/30/63	TN	DOW	(b:12/16/29)	FLR
Presher, Henry	Pvt.	D 22nd SCVI		PS	06/16/62	Secessionville	KIA		ROH,CDC,PP
Presley, David A.	Pvt.	D 5th SCVI		UN	10/14/62	Richmond, VA	DOW	(Wdd @ 7 Pines)	SA3
Presley, E.W.	Pvt.			CR	/ /	Charlottesville		Univ. Cem. Charlottesville	ACH

SOUTH CAROLINA DEAD IN CSA SERVICE 1861-1865

NAME	RANK	C	REGIMENT	AGE	DS	DIED	WHERE	WHY	BURIED	SOURCES
Presley, James B.	Pvt.	E	6th SCVI		CR	/ /	Charlottesville		Univ. Cem. Charlottesville	ACH,HHC
Presley, William	Pvt.	D	21st SCVI		CD	06/15/64	At home	DOD		ROH,HAG
Pressley, Thomas N.	Pvt.	I	7th SCVI		CR	07/03/63	Gettysburg, PA	KIA		ROH,JR,GDR,KEB
Preston, William C.	Major		CSA Arty.		RD	07/21/64	Peachtree Ck GA	KIA	Trinity C. Columbia, SC	MP,ROH,SCA,PP
Prewett, Philip H.	Pvt.	F	24th SCVI	17	AN	11/30/64	Franklin, TN	KIA		ROH,HOL,PP
Prewitt, Benjamin C.	Pvt.	B	22nd SCVI		SG	/ /				HOS
Prewitt, Elijah	Pvt.	D	16th SCVI		GE	/ /	Charleston, SC	DOD	(1862)	16R
Prewitt, J.	Pvt.	B	22nd SCVI		SG	/ /				HOS
Prewitt, Marcus W.	Pvt.	B	22nd SCVI		SG	09/08/62		DOD	(Pneumonia)	JR,HOS
Price,	Cpl.	G	4th SCVC		CD	05/28/64	Hawe's Shop, VA	DOW	(In enemy hands)	SSO
Price, A.E.	Pvt.	I	5th SCVI		SG	05/31/62	7 Pines, VA	KIA	(JR=Henry)	JR,SA3
Price, B.F.	Pvt.	B	Ham.Leg.	29	ED	08/11/63	Petersburg, VA	DOD	Blandford Church Pbg., VA	ROH,BLC,PP
Price, C. Frederick	Pvt.	C	7th SCVIBn	25	RD	05/25/63	Adams Run, SC	DOD	(PP=6/9/62)	ROH,JR,HAG,PP
Price, C.A.	Sgt.	F	22nd SCVI		PS	07/30/64	Crater, Pbg., VA	KIA		BLM
Price, Daniel	Pvt.	C	15th SCVI	44	LN	10/07/64	Camp Chase, OH	DIP	C.C.#286 Columbus, OH	ROH,FPH,H15,P2
Price, E.M.	Pvt.	K	Hol.Leg.	25	SG	08/25/62	Richmond, VA	DOD	New Pleasant B.C. Cherokee	ROH,TCC
Price, F.M.	Sgt.	B	26th SCVI	21	CD	08/22/63	Savannah, GA	DOD	Laurel Grove C. Savannah	ROH,BGA
Price, G. Wesley	Pvt.	K	13th SCVI		LN	07/07/62	Richmond, VA	DOD	(Typhoid)	ROH,JR
Price, George S.	Pvt.	C	15th SCVI	22	LN	11/22/62	Richmond, VA	DOD	(TOD=James Island)	ROH,JR,H15,TOD
Price, George W.	Pvt.	C	15th SCVI	22	LN	06/05/62	Hardeeville, SC	DOD	Rehobeth U.M.C. Saluda, SC	ROH,JR,KEB,TOD
Price, H.P.	Pvt.	H	6th SCVI		YK	12/20/61	Dranesville, VA	KIA		ROH,JR,CDC,R46
Price, Isaiah	Pvt.	K	20th SCVI		LN	12/26/64	At home	DOD	St. Paul's L.C. Lexington	ROH,KEB,NCC
Price, J. Whitfield	Pvt.	E	15th SCVI	27	FD	12/25/63	At home			ROH,KEB
Price, J.P.	Pvt.		4th SCVC	22	CO	05/29/64	Hawes Shop, VA	KIA		ROH
Price, J.S.	Pvt.	K	7th SCVI		ED	/ /	Charlottesville		Univ. Cem. Charlottesville	ACH
Price, James	Pvt.	D	3rd SCVIBn		LS	12/01/62	Staunton, VA	DOD	Thornrose C. Staunton, VA	ROH,KEB,TOD
Price, James Green	Pvt.	D	12th SCVI		RD	07/01/63	Gettysburg, PA	DOW	(ROH=died in Richmond)	ROH,GDR,CDC
Price, John	Pvt.	K	18th SCVI	28		09/18/64	Elmira, NY	DIP	Woodlawn N.C.#314 Elmira	ROH,FPH,P65,P1
Price, Joseph S.	Pvt.	C	23rd SCVI		CN	/ /	Charlottesville		Univ. Cem. Charlottesville	ROH,ACH
Price, Paul	Pvt.		15th SCMil			05/12/65	Newbern, NC	DIP	Cedar Grove C. Newbern, NC	WAT,P6,PP
Price, R.E.	Pvt.	C	15th SCVI	30	LN	01/30/65	Camp Chase, OH	DIP	C.C.#968 Columbus, OH	ROH,FPH,H15,P6
Price, R.S.	Sgt.	I	1st SCVC	35	CO	03/23/63	Columbia, SC	DOD		ROH,PP
Price, Robert	Cpl.	E	13th SCVI		SG	05/06/62	Charleston, SC	DOD	(Typhoid)	JR,HOS
Price, S.S.	Pvt.	H	23rd SCVI		MN	09/14/62	South Mtn., MD	KIA		ROH,JR,HMC,CDC
Price, Simeon R.	Pvt.	E	3rd SCVI		NY	12/15/64	Staunton, VA	DOD		ROH,ANY,SA2,KE
Price, Skirving (M.D.)			15th SCVI			08/15/64	Strasburg, VA	KIA		ROH
Price, Thomas J.	Pvt.	C	7th SCVIBn	28	RD	08/10/64	Petersburg, VA	DOD	Blandford Church Pbg., VA	ROH,HAG,BLC,PP
Price, Thomas J.	Pvt.	C	17th SCVI	21	YK	09/17/62	Sharpsburg, MD	KIA		YEB
Price, Thomas K.	Pvt.	F	Orr's Ri.		PS	02/24/65	Pt. Lookout, MD	DIP	C.C. Pt. Lookout, MD	FPH,P6,CDC
Price, W.C.	Pvt.	K	15th SCVI		LN	/ /	Lynchburg, VA		Lynchburg CSA Cem.#8 R5	JR,BBW,KEB
Price, William H.	Pvt.	E	1st SCVIG		MN	08/06/62	Richmond, VA	DOD	(On Rchmd effects list)	JR,HMC,SA1,CDC
Price, William J.	Pvt.	C	12th SCVI		FD	/ /	Charlottesville	DOD	Univ. Cem. Charlottesville	HFC,ACH
Prichard, A.C.	Pvt.	B	1st SCVIR		AN	04/07/65	Averysboro, NC	DOW		ROH,SA1,WAT,PP
Prichard, William L.	Cpl.	G	22nd SCVI	28	AN	07/30/64	Crater, Pbg., VA	KIA		ROH
Prichett, Elias M.	Pvt.	G	16th SCVI		GE	/ /	At home	DOD	(On active duty ?)	16R
Prickett, James H.	Sgt.	H	25th SCVI	31	OG	06/15/65	Elmira, NY	DIP	Woodlawn N.C.#2880 Elmira	ROH,FPH,HAG,P6
Prickett, John W.	Cpl.	F	25th SCVI	25	OG	05/08/64	Pt. Walthall Jtn	DOW	Blandford Church Pbg., VA	ROH,HAG,BLC,PP
Prickett, William A.	Pvt.	E	16th SCVI		GE	/ /	TN	DOD		16R
Pridgeon, John	Pvt.	D	9th SCVIBn	22	HY	03/06/62	Camp Lookout, SC	DOD		ROH,PP
Pridgeon, W.	Pvt.	C	10th SCVI		HY	/ /		DOD		RAS
Priem, S.W.	Pvt.	F	24th SCV			/ /	Griffin, GA	DOW	Griffin, Spaulding Cty, GA	UD2

P

SOUTH CAROLINA DEAD IN CSA SERVICE 1861-1865

NAME	RANK	C REGIMENT	AGE	DS	DIED	WHERE	WHY	BURIED	SOURCES
Priester, J.R.	Pvt.	E 24th SCVI	23	CO	05/16/64	Marietta, GA	DOW	(Wdd.5/16 @ Calhoun Stn.)	ROH,CDC,SA1
Priester, U.	Pvt.	G 1st SCVIH		CO	06/19/64	Petersburg, VA	KIA		SA1
Prince, Berryman	Pvt.	B 2nd SCVIRi		PS	04/25/65	Elmira, NY	DIP	Woodlawn N.C.#1413 Elmira	ROH,FPH,CDC,P65
Prince, C.	Pvt.	H 1st SC			07/12/64	Richmond, VA		Hollywood Cem.Rchmd. U563	HC
Prince, D.	Pvt.	I 7th SCVI		ED	07/01/62	Malvern Hill, VA	KIA		ROH,JR,CDC,CNM
Prince, Edward C.	Pvt.	F 24th SCVI		AN	/ /		DOD	(1864)	HOL
Prince, G.W.	Pvt.	D 12th SCVI		RD	/ /	Richmond, VA		Oakwood C.#11,Row 33,Div D	OWC
Prince, Gist	Pvt.	C 18th SCVI	30	UN	11/15/62	Richmond, VA	DOD		ROH
Prince, H.M.	Pvt.	H 24th SCVI	17	UN	01/12/65	Columbia, SC			PP
Prince, J. Frank	Pvt.	I 4th SCVI		AN	08/26/61	Culpepper, VA	DOD	Fairview Cem. Culpepper VA	ROH,JR,CGH,SA2
Prince, J.L.	Sgt.				/ /			Fredericksburg C.R6S13	FBG
Prince, J.L.	Sgt.				/ /			Fredericksburg C. R14S14	FBG
Prince, James	Pvt.	M 10th SCVI		HY	/ /	Corinth, MS	DOD	(1862)	RAS
Prince, Jefferson C.	Pvt.	C 18th SCVI	35	UN	07/30/64	Crater, Pbg., VA	KIA	Blandford Church Pbg., VA	ROH,BLM,BLC
Prince, John F.	Pvt.	Ferguson's			01/09/64	Rock Island, IL	DIP	C.m.#169 Rock Island, IL	FPH,P5
Prince, Jonathan	Pvt.	C 18th SCVI	36	UN	06/17/64	Petersburg, VA			PP
Prince, Joseph A.	Pvt.	H 1st SCVA			/ /	Hilton Head, SC		NC Beaufort, SC #53-6370	PP,BNC
Prince, Lott	Sgt.	C 10th SCVI		HY	11/04/62	Knoxville, TN	DOD	Bethel C. Knoxville, TN	RAS,TOD
Prince, Marion	Pvt.	E 4th SC Res	17	UN	01/25/65	Columbia, SC	DOD	Elmwood Cem. Columbia, SC	ROH,MP,PP
Prince, Noah	Pvt.	H 4th SCVI		PS	09/15/61		DOD		SA2
Prince, Spencer	Pvt.	B 15th SCVI		UN	09/14/62	South Mtn., MD	KIA	(Prob MD Hts. 9/13)	ROH,JR,KEB
Prince, W.H.	Pvt.	Orr's Ri.			/ /	Richmond, VA		Oakwood C.#70,Row R,Div B	ROH,OWC
Prince, William F.	2nd Lt.	B Ham.Leg.		BT	03/08/62		DOD	Springwood Cem. GE Cty.	R43,GEE
Pringle, Charles Alston	2nd Lt.	H 1st SCVIR		CN	06/29/62	Charleston, SC	DOD	St.Michaels C. Charleston	ROH,JR,SA1
Pringle, J.R.P.	Pvt.	K 4th SCVC		CN	08/23/64	Old Church, VA	DOW	Mrs. Wm. Newton's House	ROH,CDC,CLD
Pringle, James	Cpl.	C 27th SCVI	27	CN	06/24/64	Petersburg, VA	KIA	Old Scotch P.C. Charleston	ROH,RCD,HAG
Pringle, Robert	Cpt.	B 15th SCVAB		CN	08/21/63	Bty. Wagner, SC	KIA	St.Michaels C. Charleston	ROH,MAG,HAG,CDC
Pringle, Samuel McBride	1st Lt.	Palm. LA	23	SR	09/24/62	Winchester, VA	DOW	(Wdd @ Sharpsburg)	ROH,JR,R44,SOB
Prioleau, Charles E.	Cpl.	K 4th SCVC	24	CN	05/28/64	Hawes Shop, VA	KIA	St.Philip's Ch. Charleston	ROH,RCD
Prior, Alexander	Pvt.				05/12/63	Richmond, VA	DOD		ROH
Prior, S.J.	Pvt.				11/10/64	Richmond, VA		Hollywood Cem.Rchmd. V391	HC
Prisson, John	Pvt.	F 2nd SCVIRi	21	AE	05/06/64	Wilderness, VA	KIA		ROH
Pritchard, Benjamin J.	Pvt.	B 6th SCV			/ /	High Point, NC		Oakwood Cem. High Point NC	CV,WAT,TOD
Pritchard, William	Pvt.	A 25th SCVI		CN	08/16/62	Charleston, SC	DOD	St. Philips Ch. Charleston	MAG,HAG
Pritchard, William	Pvt.	A 25th SCVI	30	CN	09/12/62		DOD		CDC,HAG,WLI
Pritchett, Elias M.	Pvt.	G 16th SCVI		GE	02/18/64	At home	DOD		16R,PP
Privatt, Evander	Pvt.	G 8th SCVI	22	DN	09/20/63	Chickamauga, GA	KIA	Con. Cem. Marietta, GA	ROH,JR,CCM,UD2
Privel, J.	Pvt.	18th SCVI			09/05/62	Richmond, VA		Hollywood Cem.Rchmd. S24	HC
Procter, Daniel	Pvt.	E 7th SCVC	21	ED	06/02/64	Old Church, VAA	KIA		ANY,HOE,CDC,UD2
Proctor, Aaron	Pvt.	G 23rd SCVI		MO	07/30/64	Crater, Pbg., VA	KIA		ROH,HOM,BLM
Proctor, Balam	Pvt.	C 24th SCVI	25	CO	12/14/62	James Island, SC	DOD		ROH,DRE
Proctor, Henry G.	Pvt.	A 25th SCVI		CN	09/18/64	Alexandria, VA	DOW	Christ Ch. Alexandria, VA	ROH,HAG,WLI,P1
Proctor, Joseph	Pvt.	C 24th SCVI	22	CO	08/04/64	Macon, GA	DOD		ROH
Proctor, M.L.B.	Pvt.	A 17th SCVI	24	CR	04/01/65	Five Forks, VA	KIA	(CB=MIA)	ROH,HHC,CB
Proctor, Micajah	Pvt.	H 24th SCVI	18	CR	06/15/63	Macon, GA	DOW	(Wdd @ Jackson, MS)	ROH
Proctor, Michael C.	Pvt.	H 24th SCVI		CR	12/06/63	Macon, GA	DOD		EJM,HHC,PP
Proctor, William M.	Pvt.	H 24th SCVI	30	CR	07/20/62	Columbia, SC	DOD		ROH,HHC,PP,CB
Propes, M.M.	Pvt.	F 3rd SCVI		LS	08/05/62	Richmond, VA	DOD	(JR=Winchester)	ROH,JR,KEB,SA2
Propst, Henry E.	Pvt.	B 7th SCVIBn	22	FD	11/03/62	Church Flats, SC	DOD		ROH,HAG
Prosser, Ira L.	Sgt.	F 10th SCVI	22	MN	09/20/62	Tompkinsville KY	DOW	(Wdd @ Murfreesboro)	ROH,RAS,HMC
Prosser, M.					/ /			(Rchmd. effects list 1/63)	CDC

P

SOUTH CAROLINA DEAD IN CSA SERVICE 1861-1865

NAME	RANK	C REGIMENT	AGE	DS	DIED	WHERE	WHY	BURIED	SOURCES
Prosser, Nathan	Pvt.	I 10th SCVI	30	MN	/ /	South Carolina	DOD		ROH,RAS,HMC
Pruit, Enoch Washington	Pvt.	G Orr's Ri.	22	AE	06/27/62	Gaines' Mill, VA	KIA	Due West, SC A.R.P.	ROH,JR,CV,CAE
Pruitt, John	Pvt.	D 3rd SCVI		SG	02/13/63	New Market, TN	DOD		SA2,HOS
Puckett, Allen	Pvt.	I 5th SC Res	37	AE	01/09/63	At home	DOD		ROH
Puckett, George W.	2nd Cpl.	H 5th SCVI		UN	07/30/62	Richmond, VA	DOD	Hollywood Cem.Rchmd. Q222	ROH,JR,HC,SA3
Puckett, H.R.	Pvt.	B 15th SCVI		UN	/ /	Richmond, VA	DOW	Oakwood C.#19,Row 37,Div D	ROH,JR,OWC,KEB
Puckett, J.T.	Pvt.	G 14th SCVI	18	AE	07/06/62	Richmond, VA	DOD		ROH
Puckett, Richard M.	Pvt.	F 3rd SCVI		LS	11/08/61	Front Royal, VA	DOD	(Typhoid)	ROH,JR,KEB,SA2
Puckett, William A.	Pvt.	E 16th SCVI	42	LS	/ /	Kentucky	DOD	(1865, ? LS man in 16th)	ROH
Puckett, William C.	Cpl.	I 5th SC Res	43	AE	01/01/63	Adams Run, SC	DOD		ROH,PP
Pulaski, T.W.	Pvt.	C 24th SCVI	38	CO	/ /	Atlanta, GA	DOW	Stonewall C. Griffin, GA	EJM,TEB,BGA
Pulley, E.P.	Pvt.	B 3rd SCVI			07/02/63	Gettysburg, PA	KIA	Magnolia Cem. Charleston	MAG,RCD
Pulley, James H.	Pvt.	C 14th SCVI		LS	05/12/64	Spotsylvania, VA	KIA		ROH
Pulliam, Benjamin S.	Pvt.	F Hol.Leg.	38	AE	11/06/64	Petersburg, VA	KIA		ROH
Pulliam, George W.	Pvt.	A 2nd SCVIRi	21	AE	12/18/61	At home	DOD		ROH
Pulliam, Robert C.	Cpt.	B 2nd SCVI	34	GE	07/03/63	Gettysburg, PA	DOW	Magnolia Cem. Charleston	ROH,JR,GDR,SA2
Pulliam, Zachary C.	Cpt.	H 2nd SCVIRi		GE	10/12/62	Warrenton, VA	DOW	Liberty Springs S.P.C.	ROH,JR,LSC,R45
Pullig, Samuel W.	3rd Lt.	B 3rd SCVI		NY	10/19/64	Cedar Creek, VA	DOW	(? POW released per P45)	SA2,KEB
Pulling, N.P.	Pvt.	K 12th SCVI		PS	07/28/64	Chester, PA	DOW	(Also Wd @ Champions Hill)	P1
Pullman, P.	Pvt.	B 6th SCV			/ /	High Point, NC		Oakwood C. High Point, NC	WAT,TOD
Pulman, W.	Pvt.	H 14th SCVI		BL	/ /	Lynchburg, VA		Lynchburg CSA Cem.#5 R4	BBW
Purcell, J.H.	Pvt.	G 1st SC			/ /	Richmond, VA		Oakwood C.#127,Row L,Div B	ROH,OWC
Purdvis, H.L. (SP?)	Pvt.				07/26/64	Petersburg, VA	DOW	Blandford Church Pbg., VA	BLC
Purdy, James	Pvt.	H 19th SCVI	22	AE	10/15/62		DOD		ROH
Purseley, David E.	Pvt.	B Orr's Ri.		AE	/ /	South Carolina	DOD	(1861)	ROH,CDC
Purseley, W. Calvin	Pvt.	A 12th SCVI	19	YK	10/07/61	At home	DOD		YMD,YEB
Pursley, Franklin	2nd Cpl.	G 18th SCVI	25	YK	07/30/64	Crater, Pbg., VA	KIA		BLM,YEB
Pursley, James W.	Pvt.	G 16th SCVI		GE	/ /	Charleston, SC	DOD		16R
Pursley, John C.	Pvt.	B Orr's Ri.	23	AE	05/12/64	Spotsylvania, VA	KIA		ROH
Pursley, Jonathan	Pvt.	G 16th SCVI		GE	06/14/64	Pine Mtn., GA	KIA		16R
Purtell, J.	Pvt.	B 10th SCVI		HY	/ /	Tennessee	DOD		RAS
Purvis, J. Henry	Pvt.	K 21st SCVI		DN	02/12/65	Elmira, NY	DIP	Woodlawn N.C.#2057 Elmira	FPH,HAG,P6,P65
Purvis, James	Pvt.	E 21st SCVI		CD	05/16/64	Drury's Bluff VA	KIA		ROH,HAG
Pusser, Drayton	Pvt.	C 18th SCVI	25	UN	06/15/62				ROH
Putman, J. Perry	Pvt.	B 1st SCVIR		LS	04/15/65	Averysboro, NC	DOW	Oakwood C. High Point, NC	ROH,SA1,PP,WAT
Putman, John	Pvt.	B 1st SCVIR		LS	/ /		DOW	(1865, in enemy hands)	ROH,SA1
Putnam, J.R.	Pvt.	E 6th SCVC		LS	08/23/64	Ream's Stn., VA	KIA		ROH
Pye, Henry	Pvt.	H 13th SCVI		KW	08/25/64	Ream's Stn., VA	KIA		ROH
Pye, J. Strother	Pvt.	K 10th SCVI		CN	07/17/62	Macon, MS	DOD		RAS,PP
Pye, Peter	Pvt.	K 10th SCVI		CN	/ /		DOD		RAS
Pylant, Joseph	Cpl.	F 19th SCVI		ED	08/12/62	Enterprise, MS	DOD		PP,HOE
Pyles, Newton M.	Pvt.	G 27th SCVI	19	LS	07/30/64	Pt. Lookout, MD	DIP	C.C. Pt. Lookout, MD	ROH,FPH,HAG,P6
Pyles, R.W.	Sgt.	F 2nd SCVIRi		LS	08/30/62	2nd Manassas, VA	KIA		ROH,JR,CDC

SOUTH CAROLINA DEAD IN CSA SERVICE 1861-1865

NAME	RANK	C REGIMENT	AGE	DS	DIED	WHERE	WHY	BURIED	SOURCES
Quailes, James R.	Pvt.	K 7th SCVI		ED	04/06/62	Richmond, VA	DOD		ROH
Quails, J.	Pvt.	D SCVA		AN	02/11/62	Charleston, SC		Magnolia Cem. Charleston	ROH,MAG
Quarles, David R.	Pvt.	B 6th SCVC		ED	03/10/65	Fayetteville, NC	KIA	(Raid, Kilpatrick's Camp)	ROH,HOE,PP,UD3
Quarles, Hugh M.	Pvt.	K 7th SCVI		ED	09/13/62	Maryland Hts. MD	KIA		ROH,JR,KEB,HOE
Quarles, Jackson	Pvt.	I 2nd SCVC		ED	07/23/62	Richmond, VA		(James W. in HOE?)	ROH
Quattlebaum, H.D.	Pvt.	K 14th SCVI		ED	/ /	Lynchburg, VA	DOD	Lynchburg CSA Cem.#2 R4	HOE,BBW
Quattlebaum, Harman D.	2nd Sgt.	C 19th SCVI		ED	/ /	At home	DOD	(1862)	HOE,UD3
Quattlebaum, J.	Pvt.	G 19th SCVI		NY	07/22/64	Atlanta, GA	KIA	(On Newberry Monument)	ROH,NCC
Quattlebaum, J.D.	3rd Lt.	C 22nd SCVI	22	ED	07/30/64	Crater, Pbg., VA	KIA		ROH,R48,BLM
Quattlebaum, Jacob	Cpt.	F P.S.S.		LN	10/07/64	Atlee's Farm, VA	KIA	(ROH=Quintle)	ROH,R48
Quattlebaum, James	Pvt.	G 19th SCVI		AE	/ /	Atlanta, GA	KIA	(1864)	HOL
Quattlebaum, James A.	Pvt.	G 7th SCVI	24	ED	05/06/64	Wilderness, VA	KIA	UD2	ROH,HOE,KEB,UD
Quattlebaum, James B.	Pvt.	H Hol.Leg.	26	NY	03/05/62	At home	DOD	Quattlebaum Gvyd. Newberry	ROH,NCC,ANY
Quattlebaum, John D.	Pvt.	C 19th SCVI		ED	12/31/62	Murfreesboro, TN	KIA		HOE,UD3
Quattlebaum, S.P.	Pvt.	G 13th SCVI		NY	08/29/62	2nd Manassas,VA	KIA	(CDC=S.F.)	ROH,JR,ANY,CDC
Quattlebaum, T.A.	2nd Lt.	K 1st SCVIR		LN	03/17/65	Averysboro, NC	DOW	Quattlebaum C.Batesburg SC	ROH,SA1,TOD,PP
Queen, D.	Pvt.	F 18th SCVI		YK	11/06/62			Stonewall C. Winchester VA	WIN
Queen, J.W.	pvt.	c 17th SCVI		YK	/ /		DOW	(Wdd. @ Sharpsburg)	JR
Quick, Angus	Pvt.	F 21st SCVI		MO	/ /		DIP	(POW @ Ft. Fisher)	HOM,HAG,P65
Quick, B.	Pvt.	C 8th SCVI		CD	06/09/61	Richmond, VA	DOD	Hollywood Cem.Rchmd. U109	ROH,HC,KEB
Quick, D.	Pvt.	K 8th SCVI		MO	08/15/62	Richmond, VA	DOD	(Pneumonia)	JR
Quick, Daniel	Pvt.	G 23rd SCVI		MO	/ /	At home	DOD		HOM
Quick, Henry	Pvt.	F 21st SCVI		MO	/ /		KIA		HOM,HAG
Quick, Henry D.	Pvt.	G 23rd SCVI		MO	08/30/62	2nd Manassas, VA	KIA	(JR=Co.C)	JR,HOM,CDC
Quick, Herbert T.	4th SGT.	F 21st SCVI		MO	/ /	Cold Harbor, VA	DOD		ROH,HOM,HAG
Quick, James	Pvt.	B 24th SCVI	34	MO	/ /	At home	DOD		HOM
Quick, Jesse E.	Pvt.	H 21st SCVI	20	DN	07/17/64	Petersburg, VA	DOW	Blandford Church Pbg., VA	ROH,BLC,HAG,PP
Quick, John B.	Pvt.	F 21st SCVI		MO	06/15/65	Pt. Lookout, MD	DOW	(Wdd & POW Ft. Fisher 1/15	ROH,HOM,HAG,P1
Quick, Philip	Pvt.	G 23rd SCVI		MO	/ /	Savannah, GA	DOD		HOM
Quick, Pleasant	Pvt.	G 23rd SCVI		MO	/ /	Petersburg, VA	KIA		HOM
Quick, Richmond	Pvt.	C 5th SCVI			12/09/62	Lynchburg, VA	DOD	Lynchburg CSA Cem.#5 R3	JR,SA3,BBW
Quick, Robert	1st Sgt.	D 26th SCVI		MO	/ /	Petersburg, VA	KIA		HOM
Quick, Robert W.	Pvt.	D 26th SCVI		MO	/ /	At home	DOD		HOM
Quick, Thomas P.	5th Sgt.	D 26th SCVI		MO	09/01/64	Petersburg, VA	DOW	(Wdd 8/18 date d: approx)	ROH,HOM
Quick, Wyatt	Pvt.	D 26th SCVI		MO	/ /	At home	DOD	(1863)	HOM
Quigley, Charles T.	Sgt.	B 15th SCVAB			03/19/65	Bentonville, VA	KIA		WAT,PP
Quinn, Daniel	Pvt.				05/05/63	Fredericksburg	KIA	(1st a Cpl. I, 1st SCVIG)	ROH,SA1
Quinn, David R.	Pvt.	A Hol.Leg.	24	SG	07/05/63	Jackson, MS	DOW		ROH,HOS
Quinn, F.J.E.	1st Sgt.	B 7th SC Res		YK	01/20/63	Mt. Pleasant, SC	DOD		R46,YEB
Quinn, J. Warren	Lt.	B 12th SCVI	30	YK	/ /	At home	DOD	(1861)(NI R47)	YEB
Quinn, James H.	4th Sgt.	F 5th SCVI	27	YK	10/28/63	Lookout Valley	KIA		ROH,JR,SA3,YEB
Quinn, Josephus	Pvt.	B Hol.Leg.	25	SG	12/17/62	Kinston, NC	KIA		ROH,PP
Quinn, L.C.	Pvt.	K 27th SCVI		CN	06/24/64	Petersburg, VA	KIA		ROH,HAG,CDC
Quinn, Leroy D.	Pvt.	H 5th SCVI	21	YK	11/21/61	Culpepper, VA	DOD	Fairview Cem. Culpepper VA	JR,CGH,SA3,YEB
Quinn, McDuffie	Pvt.	A 18th SCVI		UN	07/30/64	Crater, Pbg., VA	KIA		ROH,BLM
Quinn, Wesley	Pvt.	A 18th SCVI		UN	07/30/64	Crater, Pbg., VA	KIA		BLM
Quinn, William B.	Pvt.	I 13th SCVI	40	SG	09/17/62	Sharpsburg, MD	KIA		ROH,JR,HOS
Quinton, Arden	Pvt.	G 18th SCVI		UN	07/30/64	Crater, Pbg., VA	KIA		BLM
Quinton, John B.	Pvt.	B 12th SCVI	20	YK	07/03/63	Gettysburg, PA	KIA		YEB
Quinton, William	Pvt.	K 1st SCVIG		CN	09/30/64	Jones' Farm, VA	KIA		SA1

SOUTH CAROLINA DEAD IN CSA SERVICE 1861-1865

NAME	RANK	C REGIMENT	AGE	DS	DIED	WHERE	WHY	BURIED	SOURCES
R....., J.C.	Pvt.	D 14th SCVI		ED	/ /	Richmond, VA		Oakwood C.#36,Row 32,Div D	OWC
R....., J.E.	Pvt.				/ /			Fredericksburg C.C. R1S11	FBG
Rabb, C.W.	Pvt.	G 6th SCVI		FD	08/09/64	Richmond, VA			ROH
Rabb, E.A.	Cpt.	CN Comms'y	42	FD	10/13/64	At home	DOD		ROH,CDC
Rabb, John W.	Sgt.	G 6th SCVI	21	FD	06/30/62	Frayser's Farm	KIA	(Color Sgt. also Wd @ 7P)	ROH,WDB,HFC
Rabon, John	Pvt.	G 24th SCVI	40	HY	01/24/65	Camp Chase, OH	DIP	C.C.#861 Columbus, OH	FPH,P6,P23
Raborn, William M.	Pvt.	D 19th SCVI	35	ED	01/15/63	Murfreesboro, TN	DOW	(Wdd 12/31/62)	ROH,HOE,UD3
Rabun, W.	Sgt.	7th SCVC			06/22/64	Virginia	KIA		ROH
Raburn, J.W.	Pvt.	A 22nd SCVI		ED	06/18/64	Petersburg, VA	KIA		ROH
Racklen, L.	Pvt.	G 12th SCVI		PS	/ /	Richmond, VA		Oakwood C.#27,Row J,Div B	ROH,OWC
Rackley, James Hamilton	Pvt.	B P.S.S.	23	PS	06/01/64	Virginia	DOD		ROH,JR
Rackley, W.B.	Pvt.	B P.S.S.		PS	/ /		DIP		ROH
Radcliffe, H.J.	Pvt.	B 5th SCVC	19	CN	01/22/65	Charleston, SC	DOD	Magnolia Cem. Charleston	ROH,MAG,RCD,MD
Radcliffe, W.J.	Sgt.	F Hol.Leg.	29	AE	07/20/62	At home	DOD	Due West, SC	ROH
Radcliffe,Jr., Thomas W.	Pvt.	2nd SCVC		RD	09/22/63	Madison C.H., VA	KIA		ROH,JR
Rader, Eli C.	Sgt.	F 6th SCVI	23	CR	05/24/64	Verdiersville VA	DOW	Fishing Creek P.C.	ROH,FCP,HHC
Radford, J.A.	Pvt.	A 7th SCVI		ED	04/19/63	Richmond, VA	DOD	Oakwood C.#28,Row 23,Div D	ROH,OWC,KEB
Radford, Thomas	Pvt.	I 1st SCVC	28	CO	06/15/63	Richmond, VA			ROH
Radish, Isham	Pvt.	E 24th SCVI	25	CO	06/30/63	Georgia	DOD		ROH
Radish, Peter	Pvt.	E 24th SCVI	28	CO	09/30/63	Mississippi	DOD		ROH
Radrick, J.H.	Pvt.	F 7th SCVI		ED	06/14/64	Pt. Lookout, MD	DIP		ROH
Ragin, C.H.	Lt.	A 21st SCVI			/ /				WLI
Ragin, H.T.	Pvt.	D 9th SCVIB			11/22/61	Richmond, VA	DOD		ROH,JR
Ragin, Henry J.	Pvt.	C 25th SCVI		WG	/ /	Bty Wagner, SC	KIA		CTA,HOW
Ragin, T.E.	Pvt.			WG	/ /		KIA	(PeeDee Lgn. Cpt.Maurice)	HOW
Ragsdale, A.K.	Pvt.	G 3rd SCVIBn		FD	11/19/62	Richmond, VA		Hollywood Cem.Rchmd. S256	HC
Raines, Anthony	Pvt.	C 12th SCVI		FD	07/02/63	Gettysburg, PA	KIA	(Color bearer)	HFC,GDR
Raines, Damisey	Pvt.	8th SCVI		FD	/ /			Oakwood C.#149,Row A,Div A	ROH,OWC,
Rainey, J.M.C.	Pvt.	C 12th SCVI		FD	04/12/65	Richmond, VA	DOD	SW corner Jackson Hos Gds.	P6
Rainey, O.H.P.	Pvt.	H 12th SCVI	21	YK	05/05/64	Wilderness, VA	KIA	Fredericksburg C.C. R6S12	FBG,CWC,YEB
Rainey, S.J.	Pvt.	C 16th SCVI		GE	/ /	At home	DOD	(On active duty ?)	16R,PP
Rainey, T.	Pvt.	C Orr's Ri.		PS	07/24/63	Richmond, VA	DOD	Hollywood Cem.Rchmd. U24	ROH,HC
Rainey, Thomas W.	Pvt.	B 12th SCVI	25	YK	/ /	Guinea Stn., VA	DOD		YEB
Rains, John Newton	Pvt.	Pal Bn LA	20	GE	02/14/62	At home	DOD	(Typhoid)	ROH,JR
Rains, William	Pvt.	B 15th SCVI		UN	/ /		DOD		JR,KEB
Rainwater, J.P.	Pvt.	G 27th SCVI		SG	07/19/64	Pt. Lookout, MD	DIP	C.C. Pt. Lookout, MD	ROH,FPH,HAG,P6
Rainwaters, Joshua W.	Pvt.	E 4th SCVC		MO	10/21/64	Elmira, NY	DIP	Woodlawn N.C.#526 Elmira	ROH,HOM,FPH,P6
Raley, Dove	Pvt.	F 7th SCVIBn	18	CR	08/23/64	Petersburg, VA	KIA	(PP=8/30/64)	ROH,HIC,HAG,PP
Ralls, J.W.	Pvt.	G 6th SCVI			/ /	Richmond, VA			ROH
Ramage, Drayton W.	6th Cpl.	E 3rd SCVI		NY	05/04/62	Charlottesville	DOD		ROH,JR,ANY,SA2
Ramage, Isaac W.T.	Pvt.	A 13th SCVI		LS	11/07/62	Lynchburg, VA	DOD	Duncan Creek B.C. LS Cty.	LSC
Ramage, James C.	Pvt.	E 7th SCVI		ED	12/21/62	Richmond, VA			ROH,HOE,UD3
Ramage, Peter B.	Pvt.	B 1st SCVIG	21	ED	01/04/63	Fredericksburg	DOD	(JR=Typhoid 6/16/62)	ROH,JR,UD2,UD3
Rambo, John	Pvt.	A 7th SCVI		ED	09/20/63	Chickamauga, GA	KIA		ROH,HOE
Ramick, John Peter G.	Pvt.	H 20th SCVI		LN	06/15/63	Charleston, SC	DOD		ROH,KEB
Ramper, John P.	Pvt.	I 14th SCVI	25	AE	01/13/65	Pt. Lookout, MD	DIP	C.C. Pt. Lookout, MD	ROH,FPH,P6,P11
Rampey, George P.	Pvt.	F 2nd SCVI		AE	07/24/64	(HC=Ramsey, J.)	DOW	Hollywood Cem.Rchmd. V45	HC,SA2,KEB
Rampey, J.R.	Pvt.	F Hol.Leg.		AE	07/29/64	Pt. Lookout, MD	DIP	C.C. Pt. Lookout, MD	ROH,FPH,P6,P11
Rampey, W.F.	Pvt.	L Orr's Ri.		AN	07/28/64	Deep Bottom, VA	KIA		ROH
Ramsay, A.P.	Pvt.	C 5th SCVI			06/15/64		DOD	(To Hosp 5/15/64)	SA3
Ramsey, Abraham	Sgt.	G 5th SCVI		YK	06/30/62	Columbia, SC	DOD		JR,YEB

SOUTH CAROLINA DEAD IN CSA SERVICE 1861-1865

NAME	RANK	C REGIMENT	AGE	DS	DIED	WHERE	WHY	BURIED	SOURCES
Ramsey, Alexander	Pvt.	G 5th SCVI	25	YK	04/12/63	Columbia, SC	DOD	(JR=Cleveland Cty, NC)	JR,SA3,YEB
Ramsey, Arthur Crozier	Pvt.			YK	06/05/64	Piedmont, VA	DOW		YMD
Ramsey, Calvin	Cpl.	M P.S.S.	21	UN	07/30/62	Frayser's Farm	DOW	(Dup of Ramsey, C.?)	ROH
Ramsey, David	Major	1st SCVIBn	33	CN	08/06/63	Bty. Wagner, SC	DOW	Cirular Ch. Charleston	ROH,MAG,DOC,R48
Ramsey, Hugh	Pvt.	SC Lt.Arty			/ /	Lynchburg, VA		Lynchburg CSA Cem.#3 R1	BBW
Ramsey, James A.	Pvt.	F 7th SCVI	24	ED	05/24/64	North Anna River	DOW	(JR=Sharpsburg)	JR,HOE,KEB
Ramsey, James A.	Pvt.	B 4th SCResB	16	YK	/ /	At home	DOD	(1864)(Florence Prsn Gds)	YEB
Ramsey, John	Pvt.	M P.S.S.	22	UN	08/30/62	2nd Manassas, VA	KIA	(JR=Co.F.)	ROH,JR,CDC
Ramsey, Picking	Pvt.	F 5th SCVI	24	YK	/ /	Richmond, VA	DOD		YEB
Ramsey, Richard	Pvt.	H Orr's Ri.		MN	09/01/62	Ox Hill, VA	KIA		HMC,CDC
Ramsey, S.	Pvt.	F 7th SCVI		ED	07/24/64	Richmond, VA		(NI KEB,Ramsey, J.A.?)	ROH
Ramsey, Thomas S.	Pvt.	E Orr's Ri.		PS	07/20/64	Richmond, VA		(ROH=Ramsey, T.)	ROH,CDC
Ramsey, W. Harvey	Pvt.	G P.S.S.	25	YK	08/30/62	2nd Manassas, VA	KIA		JR,YEB
Ramsey, W.J.	Pvt.	H 1st SCV			08/29/62	2nd Manassas, VA	KIA		JR
Randall, George W.	Pvt.	A 19th SCVI	30	ED	/ /	Charleston, SC	DOD		HOE,UD3
Randall, James	Pvt.	F 16th SCVI		GE	/ /	Dalton, GA	DOD	(S.M. in Newman, GA ?)	16R
Randall, Jefferson	Pvt.	A 19th SCVI	23	ED	07/22/64	Atlanta, GA	KIA		HOE,UD3
Randall, Lafayette	Pvt.	A 19th SCVI	17	ED	07/22/64	Atlanta, GA	KIA		ROH,HOE,UD3
Randall, P.	Pvt.			ED	/ /	Virginia	DOD	(TFD from B,6th SCVC)	HOE,UD3
Randall, Robert H.	Pvt.	C 17th SCVI	24	YK	03/28/64	Ft. Steadman, VA	DOW		ROH,PP,CB
Randall, S.M.	Pvt.	F 16th SCVI		GE	/ /	Newman, GA		Oak Hill Cem. Newman, GA	BGA
Randall, Seaborn	Pvt.	A 19th SCVI	23	ED	09/20/63	Chickamauga, GA	DOW	(10th Co. 10/19 Consol)	ROH,HOE
Randall, William	Pvt.	K 19th SCVI	30	ED	01/30/65	Camp Douglas, IL	DIP	Oak Woods Cem. Chicago, IL	FPH,HOE,P3,P6
Randall, William	Pvt.	K 23rd SCVI		SR	04/01/65	5 Forks, VA	KIA		K23,UD3
Randolph, A.	Pvt.	A 14th SCVI	32	DN	12/27/62	Mt. Jackson, VA	DOD	(PP=Dd 1/12/63)	ROH,PP,CDC,SHS
Randolph, Hugh J.	Pvt.	D 7th SCVIBn	28	KW	12/15/63	At home	DOD		ROH,HAG,HIC
Randolph, R.	Pvt.	A 7th SCVIBn		KW	06/05/63	Richmond, VA		Hollywood Cem.Rchmd. U177	HC
Randolph, Thomas	Pvt.	A 7th SCVIBn	26	KW	06/04/64	Cold Harbor, VA	DOW	(Wdd 6/3/64)	ROH,HIC,HAG
Randolph, William	Pvt.	K 23rd SCVI		RD	04/01/65		KIA		ROH
Rankin, David C.	Pvt.	E Orr's Ri.	21	PS	07/21/62	Richmond, VA	DOW	Hollywood Cem.Rchmd. H166	ROH,HC,CDC
Rankin, George W.	Pvt.	H Hol.Leg.		AN	04/23/65	Pt. Lookout, MD	DIP	C.C. Pt. Lookout, MD	ROH,FPH,P6,P115
Rankin, J.W.	Pvt.	E 11th SCVI		BT	/ /	Richmond, VA		Oakwood C.#78, Row G,Div C	ROH,OWC,CDC
Rankin, John M.	Pvt.	E Orr's Ri.	25	PS	11/12/62	Winchester, VA	DOW	(Wdd Gaines' Mill, VA)	ROH,CDC
Rankin, Joshua	Pvt.	E Orr's Ri.	23	PS	08/31/62	Richmond, VA	DOD		ROH,CDC
Rankin, William	Pvt.	E Orr's Ri.		PS	01/30/65	Elmira, NY	DIP	Woodlawn N.C.#1785 Elmira	FPH,P6,P65,P120
Rannerty, J.M.	Pvt.	E 3rd SCV			/ /	Richmond, VA		Oakwood C.#10, Row 39,Div D	OWC
Ransom, Pleiades Orion	4th Sgt.	G 1st SCVIG	19	ED	07/31/63	Staunton, VA	DOW	Thornrose C. Staunton, VA	ROH,SA1,GDR,TOD
Ransom, Reuben	Pvt.	Ham.Leg.			08/02/61	Charlottesville	DOW	(Wdd 1st Man)	ROH
Ransom, Robert Henry	1st Cpl.	C 4th SCVI		AN	08/02/61	1st Manassas, VA	DOW	(JR=L,P.S.S.)	JR,SA2
Ransom, William N.	Pvt.	C Orr's Ri.		PS	/ /			Con. Cem. Marietta, GA	CDC,CCM
Rascoe, Daniel	Pvt.	K 8th SCVI		MO	08/09/61	Vienna, VA	DOD		JR,HOM,KEB
Rascoe, Harris	Pvt.	B 24th SCVI	24	MO	01/06/62	Charleston, SC	DOD	Magnolia Cem. Charleston	ROH,MAG,HOM,RCD
Rascoe, William M.	Pvt.	F 21st SCVI		MO	07/31/64	Florence, SC	DOD	(HAG= Roscoe)	ROH,HOM,HAG,PP
Rast, Fred M.	Pvt.	G 25th SCVI		OG	06/15/66	At home	DOD	(From effects of prison)	ROH,P115,HAG
Rast, Jacob E.	Sgt.	G 25th SCVI	24	OG	03/07/64	Pt.Walthal Jctn.	KIA	(1st in A, 1st SCVIH)	ROH,JR,HAG,CV
Rast, John	Pvt.	I 1st SC	25	CO	10/15/62	Richmond, VA			ROH
Rast, Thomas F.	Pvt.	B 20th SCVI		OG	02/23/65	Pt. Lookout, MD	DIP	C.C. Pt. Lookout, MD	ROH,FPH,P6,KEB
Rast, William R.	Pvt.	C 14th SCMil		OG	05/13/65	Hart's Island NY	DIP	Cypress Hills N.C.#2781 NY	FPH,P6,P79
Rateree, Alexander	Pvt.	D 17th SCVI		CR	10/21/62	Shepherdstown VA	DOW	(Wdd 9/14 @ South Mtn.,MD)	ROH,JR,HHC,CB
Rateree, Henry	Pvt.	B 5th SCVI		CR	08/22/64	Richmond, VA	DOW	Hollywood Cem.Rchmd. V55	ROH,HC,SA3
Rathrock, Jacob J.	Pvt.	K 1st SCVC	32	CR	09/27/64	Charleston, SC	DOD	(HHC=Rothrock)	ROH,HHC

SOUTH CAROLINA DEAD IN CSA SERVICE 1861-1865

NAME	RANK	C REGIMENT	AGE	DS	DIED	WHERE	WHY	BURIED	SOURCES
Ratteree, James	Pvt.	H 12th SCVI	19	YK	07/01/63	Gettysburg, PA	KIA		CWC,YEB,GDR
Ratteree, T.D.	Pvt.	B 5th SCVI		YK	08/30/62	2nd Manassas, VA	KIA		ROH,JR,SA3,CDC
Rauch, Wallace W.	Pvt.	K 20th SCVI		LN	11/05/64	Baltimore, MD	DOW	Loudon Pk.C. B-70 Balto MD	ROH,FPH,P1,PP
Rauch,Jr., Henry A.	2nd Lt.	B 14th SCVI	19	ED	07/16/63	Gettysburg, PA	DOW	Gettysburg, PA	HOE,R47,WV,UD3
Ravan, J.	Pvt.	I 7th SCVI		GE	06/16/65	Ft. Delaware, DE	DIP	Finn's Pt., NJ Nat. Cem.	FPH,P6
Ravenel, Elias Prioleau	1st Lt.	I 1st SCVA	27	CN	07/24/63	Aiken, SC	DOD	Magnolia Cem. Charleston	ROH,MAG,SCA,R4
Ravenel, Francis Gualdo	Cpt.	ADC Ripley		CN	07/01/62	Malvern Hill, VA	KIA	Huegenot Ch.,Charleston	ROH,MAG,CDC,RC
Ravenel, William	Cadet	Citadel A.	17	CN	08/23/63	Charleston, SC	DOD	St.Michaels C. Charleston	MAG,RCD,CAG
Ravin, J.J.	Pvt.	B 12th SCVI		YK	07/10/62	Richmond, VA		Hollywood Cem.Rchmd. H261	HC
Rawl, Emanuel	Pvt.	C 15th SCVI	23	LN	09/13/62	Richmond, VA	DOD	Hollywood Cem.Rchmd. H16	ROH,JR,HC
Rawl, Emanuel	Pvt.	C 15th SCVI	22	LN	09/13/62		DOD	(Acute Diarrhea)	TOD,H15
Rawl, J. Saunders	Pvt.	C 3rd SCVI		LN	06/15/64	Charlottesville	DOW	Univ. Cem. Charlottesville	ROH,SA2,ANY,AC
Rawlings, Charles A.	Pvt.	C 1st SCVIG		RD	01/28/63		DOD		SA1
Rawlinson, Abraham S.	Pvt.	G 25th SCVI		OG	03/15/65		DOD		ROH,HAG,EDR
Rawlinson, George	Pvt.	B 1st SCVIG	28	RD	07/27/62	Richmond, VA	DOD	(JR=Robinson)	ROH,JR,SA1
Rawlinson, Moses A.	Pvt.	G 25th SCVI		OG	09/05/63	Bty. Wagner, SC	KIA		ROH,JR,HAG,EDR
Rawls, Ezra	Pvt.	K 9th SCVIB			12/21/61	Centreville, MD	DOD		JR
Rawls, H.A.	Pvt.	F P.S.S.		LN	07/15/64	Petersburg, VA	KIA		ROH
Rawls, James L.	Pvt.	A 21st SCVI		CN	04/05/65	Elmira, NY	DIP	Woodlawn N.C.#2548 Elmira	FPH,HAG,P6,P65
Ray,					/ /			Magnolia Cem. Charleston	MAG
Ray, A.	Pvt.	H 8th SCVI		MN	/ /	Richmond, VA		Oakwood C.#97,Row D,Div A	ROH,OWC,KEB,HM
Ray, A.	Pvt.	H 1st SCV			02/23/62	Richmond, VA	DOD	(Typhoid)	JR
Ray, A.J.	Pvt.	A 13th SCVI		LS	08/17/64	Richmond, VA			ROH
Ray, Abraham	Pvt.	C 22nd SCVI	24	SG	11/29/64	Petersburg, VA	KIA		ROH,PP
Ray, Edward S.	Pvt.	E 10th SCVI		WG	10/04/62	Bardstown, KY	DOD		RAS,PP
Ray, Elijah	Cpl.	B P.S.S.	30	UN	07/18/62	Philadelphia, PA	DOW	Philadelphia N.C. PA	ROH,JR,FPH,CV
Ray, H.H.	Pvt.				/ /			(Rchmd. effects list 1/63)	CDC
Ray, J.	Pvt.	C 10th SCVI		HY	07/22/64	Atlanta, GA	KIA	(MIA & lost)	RAS,CDC
Ray, J.C.	Pvt.	A 13th SCVI		LS	09/28/63	Pt. Lookout, MD	DIP	C.C. Pt. Lookout, MD	ROH,FPH,CDC,P6
Ray, James	Pvt.	D 15th SCVI		KW	06/24/62	Charleston, SC	DOD	Magnolia Cem. Charleston	JR,HIC,RCD,KEB
Ray, Jeremiah	Pvt.	B 15th SCVI		UN	/ /		DOD	(Ray, J.H. in P115?)	JR
Ray, Jesse	Pvt.	B 15th SCVI	43		/ /			Tippah County, MS 1864	MCG
Ray, John A.	Pvt.	E 1st SCVIG		MN	08/16/64	Fussel's Mill VA	KIA		ROH,SA1,PDL,HM
Ray, John Thompson	2nd Lt.	D 3rd SCVI	22	SG	06/30/62	Savage Stn., VA	DOW	Padgett Creek B.C.	ROH,JR,SA2,UNC
Ray, M.J.	Pvt.	H 25th SCVI		CN	07/19/62	Richmond, VA		Hollywood Cem.Rchmd. C122	HC
Ray, R.S.	Pvt.	K Orr's Ri.		AN	06/27/62	Gaines' Mill, VA	KIA		ROH,JR,CDC
Ray, Robert Landrum	1st Sgt.	D 3rd SCVI	31	SG	09/24/63	Chickamauga, GA	DOW	Con. Cem. Marietta, GA	ROH,JR,SA2,CCM
Ray, S.G.	1st Lt.	H 17th SCVI	24	BL	09/01/62	2nd Manassas, VA	DOW		ROH,JR,R47
Ray, S.J.	1st Lt.	C 18th SCVI		UN	07/30/64	Crater, Pbg., VA	KIA		ROH,BLM
Ray, Thomas J.	Pvt.	D 3rd SCVI	23	SG	09/20/63	Chickamauga, GA	KIA	Padgett Creek B.C.	ROH,JR,SA2,UNC
Ray, William	Pvt.	I 3rd SCVI	25	UN	07/10/62	Savage Stn., VA	DOW	(Wdd 6/29/62)	ROH,JR,SA2,KEB
Ray, William H.H.	Pvt.	A 13th SCVI		LS	05/25/62		DOD	(Typhoid Pneumonia)	JR
Ray, William J.	Pvt.	E 1st SCVIH		BL	12/14/62	At home	DOW	(Wdd 2nd Man)	ROH,SA1,JRH
Rayan, Charles	Pvt.	F 13th SCVI		SG	05/12/64	Spotsylvania, VA	KIA	(ROH= Ravin)	ROH,HOS
Raysor, James M.	Pvt.	G 7th SCVC		BT	12/25/64	Pt. Lookout, MD	DIP	C.C. Pt. Lookout, MD	ROH,FPH,P5,P11
Read, Jefferson	Pvt.	D Hol.Leg.	39	BL	11/11/62	Richmond, VA	DOD	Oakwood C.#43,Row P,Div B	ROH,OWC
Ready, George (Reddy?)	Pvt.	D Hol.Leg.	33	BL	01/04/65	Petersburg, VA	DOW	Blandford Church Pbg., VA	ROH,BLC,PP
Ready, J.P.	Pvt.	E 27th SCVI		BL	03/09/65	Columbia, SC	DOD	Elmwood Cem. Columbia, SC	ROH,MP,HAG,PP
Ready,Jr., John C.	Pvt.	K 22nd SCVI		ED	08/30/62	Petersburg, VA	DOD	(One of 3 brothers in CSA)	ROH,FDN
Reagan, H.J.	Pvt.	D 9th SCVIB		SR	11/22/62	Richmond, VA	DOD	Hollywood Cem.Rchmd. B131	ROH,HC
Reagan, N.T.	Pvt.	D P.S.S.			/ /		DOD	(Ragin, H.T. 9th SC ?)	JR

R

SOUTH CAROLINA DEAD IN CSA SERVICE 1861-1865

NAME	RANK	C REGIMENT	AGE	DS	DIED	WHERE	WHY	BURIED	SOURCES
Reagin, Henry W.	Pvt.	C 3rd SCVI		NY	03/21/65	Bentonville, NC	KIA	Reagin Gyd Newberry, SC	ROH,NCC,PP,SA2
Reams, W.	Cpl.	L P.S.S.			/ /		DOD		JR
Reardon, J.	Pvt.	Ham.Leg.			/ /	Richmond, VA		Oakwood C.#85,Row J,Div A	ROH,OWC
Reardon, James E.	Cpt.	F 7th SCVI	23	ED	09/26/63	Chickamauga, GA	DOW	(Also Wdd @ Sharpsburg)	HOE,R46,UD3
Reardon, John	Pvt.	A 16th SCVI		GE	07/22/64	Atlanta, GA	KIA		ROH,16R
Reardon, Samuel M.	Pvt.	C 9th SCVIB	25	CL	02/15/62	Charlottesville	DOD		ROH
Reardon, William E.	Cpl.	F 7th SCVI	21	ED	09/17/62	Sharpsburg, MD	KIA	(Left wife & 1 child)	ROH,JR,HOE,EDN
Reaves, Charles W.	1st Cpl.	E 1st SCVIG		MN	07/01/63	Gettysburg, PA	KIA		ROH,JR,GDR,HMC
Reaves, David	Pvt.	D 7th SCVIBn	30	KW	06/21/64	Petersburg, VA	DOW	(Wdd 6/20/64)	ROH,HIC,HAG
Reaves, G.B.	Pvt.	I 13th SCVI	27	SG	06/15/63	Richmond, VA			ROH,HOS
Reaves, Henry R.	Pvt.	H 1st SCVIG		BT	07/15/62	Danville, VA	DOD		ROH,SA1
Reaves, John A.	Pvt.	I 13th SCVI	25	SG	/ /	Fredericksburg	DOD		ROH
Reaves, Joseph Lide	2nd Lt.	F 4th SCVC		MN	06/23/64	Washington, DC	DOW	(Wdd & POW @ Hawes Shop)	HMC,UD3,P5,P6
Reaves, Lewis	Pvt.	5th SCVC		CO	09/29/64	Wyatt's Farm, VA	KIA		ROH,CDC
Reaves, Thomas J.	Pvt.	I 13th SCVI	21	SG	08/29/62	2nd Manassas, VA	KIA		ROH,HOS
Reaves, W.L.	Pvt.	F 22nd SCVI		LR	12/13/64	Elmira, NY	DIP	Woodlawn N.C.#1124 Elmira	FPH,P6,P65,P120
Reaves,Jr., Robert H.	Pvt.	L 21st SCVI	16	MN	01/15/65	Ft. Fisher, NC	KIA	(HAG=1st Sgt. father?)	ROH,HMC
Reay, G.C. (Reary ?)	Pvt.	E 4th SCV			/ /	Richmond, VA		Oakwood C.#45,Row B,Div G	ROH,OWC
Rector, David L.	Pvt.	D 16th SCVI		GE	01/29/64	Rock Island, IL	DIP	C.C.#302 Rock Island, IL	FPH,P6,16R
Rector, J.P.	Pvt.	A 3rd SCVABn	19	GE	/ /	Hardeeville, SC	DOD	(1864,Mem'l in Rector F.C)	GEC
Reddick, William H.	Pvt.	A 8th SCVI		DN	06/18/64	Petersburg, VA	KIA		ROH,KEB
Redford, James B.	Pvt.	D 2nd SCVI	27	SR	10/13/64	Strasburg, VA	KIA	(Hupp's Hill)	ROH,SA2,KEB,P2
Redman, A.L.	Pvt.	B 10th SCVI		HY	12/31/62	Murfreesboro, TN	DOW		RAS
Redman, E.	Pvt.	B 20th SCVI		OG	09/09/64	Richmond, VA		Hollywood Cem.Rchmd. V440	ROH,HC,KEB
Redman, Jacob W.	Pvt.	D 25th SCVI		MN	09/03/64	Alexandria G.H.	DOW	Christ Ch. Alexandria, VA	HMC,HAG,P1,P6,CV
Redman, Thomas	Pvt.	11th SCVI		CO	/ /	At home	DOD		ROH
Redmond, John W.C.	Pvt.	B 1st SCVA		BL	06/16/62	Secessionville	KIA	(JR=3rd SCVA, PP=2nd SCVA)	ROH,JR,CDC,PP
Reece, G.C.	Pvt.	F 13th SCVI		SG	/ /			(1862)	HOS
Reed, A.	Pvt.	A 5th SCVI			10/04/62	Staunton, VA		Thornrose C. Staunton, VA	TOD
Reed, Benjamin F.	Pvt.	B 3rd SCVIBn		LS	02/16/62	Adams Run, SC	DOD		PP,KEB
Reed, J.J.	Pvt.	C 4th SCVC		PS	08/30/64	Elmira, NY	DIP	Woodlawn N.C.#95 Elmira	FPH,P5,P65,P120
Reed, James R.	Pvt.	H 25th SCVI		CN	03/13/65	Elmira, NY	DIP	Woodlawn N.C.#2436 Elmira	FPH,P6,P65,HAG
Reed, L.S.	Pvt.	A 1st Bn SCT		SG	/ /		DOD		HOS
Reed, Oscar J.	Pvt.	D 5th SCVC	24	CN	03/20/65	Bentonville, NC	KIA		ROH,WAT,PP
Reed, Samuel	Pvt.	D 25th SCVI		MN	10/11/64	Greensboro, NC			PP
Reed, Samuel J.	Cpt.	B 2nd SCVA	35	BL	06/16/62	Secessionville	KIA	(JR=Richmond 6/30/62)	ROH,JR,CDC,PP
Reed, T.Y. (J.Y.?)	Pvt.	B 3rd SCVIBn		LS	/ /	Richmond, VA		Oakwood C.#55,Row P,Div B	ROH,OWC,KEB
Reed, W. Massey	Pvt.	A 20th SCVI		PS	10/13/64	Strasburg, VA	KIA		ROH,KEB
Reed, W.W.	Pvt.	F 2nd Bn.Res			05/15/65	Thomasville, NC		Con. Cem. Thomasville, NC	CV,PP
Reeder, Abner M. (N.?)	Pvt.	G Hol.Leg.	28	NY	07/12/64	Weldon, NC	DOW		ROH,PP
Reeder, James J.	2nd Lt.	G Hol.Leg.	33	NY	05/16/65	Petersburg, VA	DOW	(Wdd Hatcher's Run 3/29)	ROH,ANY,R48
Reeder, James R.C.	1st Sgt.	B 3rd SCVI	29	NY	09/24/63	Chickamauga, GA	DOW	(Wdd 9/20)	ROH,JR,SA2,KEB
Reeder, Thomas Henry	Pvt.	A 18th SCVAB	23	CN	07/28/64	Charleston, SC	DOD	Bethel M.C. Charleston, SC	ROH,MAG,CDC,H2
Reeder, William	Pvt.	A 3rd SCVABn	22	CN	04/11/65	Dingle's Mills	KIA		ROH,HSR,UD#
Reeder,Jr., Alfred M.	Pvt.	B 3rd SCVI	18	NY	06/10/63	At home	DOD		ROH,JR,SA2,ANY
Rees, B.F.	Pvt.	C 27th SCVI		CN	07/17/64	Richmond, VA	DOW	(Wdd 5/7/64)	ROH,HAG,P6
Reese, Alexander	Pvt.	D 1st SC Res	16		01/27/65	Columbia, SC	DOD	Elmwood Cem. Columbia, SC	ROH,MP,PP
Reese, B.F.	Pvt.	D 2nd SCVIRi			11/18/63	Bridgeport, AL	DIP	(In US Gnl. Hospital)	P6
Reese, B.R.	Pvt.	C 22nd SCVI		SG	07/17/63	Richmond, VA		Hollywood Cem.Rchmd. U154	HC
Reese, E.S.	Pvt.	B 22nd SCVI		SG	07/30/64	Crater, Pbg., VA	KIA		BLM
Reese, G.	Pvt.	G 27th SCVI		CN	03/14/65	Pt. Lookout, MD	DIP	C.C. Pt. Lookout, MD	FPH,P6,P113

SOUTH CAROLINA DEAD IN CSA SERVICE 1861-1865

NAME	RANK	C REGIMENT	AGE	DS	DIED	WHERE	WHY	BURIED	SOURCES
Reese, J.D.	1st Sgt.	B 24th SCVI	30	MO	06/15/62	At home	DOD		ROH,HOM
Reese, Jeptha	Pvt.	B 2nd SCVIRi		PS	/ /				ROH
Reese, Robert M.	1st Sgt.	B 22nd SCVI		SG	11/14/64	Beaufort, SC	DIP	NC Beaufort, SC #53-6400	ROH,BLM,PP,P12
Reese, T.J.	Pvt.	I 7th SCVI	23	ED	06/29/62	Savage Stn., VA	KIA		ROH,JR,CDC,EDN
Reeves,	Pvt.	2nd SCVA			10/28/63	Ft. Johnson, SC	KIA		ROH
Reeves,	Pvt.	A 27th SCVI		CN	06/15/62	Charleston, SC		Trinity Ch. Charleston, SC	MAG
Reeves, A.D.	Pvt.	F 22nd SCVI		PS	/ /			Stonewall C. Winchester VA	ROH,WIN
Reeves, Charles D.	Pvt.	H 11th SCVI		CO	/ /	Hardeeville, SC	DOD	(Dorchester Enroll Book)	ROH,HAG,TEB
Reeves, Charles J.W.	Pvt.	F 4th SCVC		MN	06/11/64	Trevillian Stn.	KIA		HMC,CDC
Reeves, Daniel E.	Sgt.	B 25th SCVI		CN	08/28/64	Alexandria G.H.	DOW	(Wdd @ Weldon RR 8/21)	P1,P6
Reeves, Henry	Pvt.	E 1st SCVC		OG	03/20/62	Adams Run, SC	DOD		ROH,PP
Reeves, James R.	Pvt.	L 2nd SCVIRi	30	AN	07/15/62	Richmond, VA	DOD		ROH
Reeves, John	Pvt.	H 5th SCVI		DN	05/31/62	7 Pines, VA	KIA	(JR=1st SCVI)	JR,SA3,NHU,UD1
Reeves, M.G. (W.D.?)	Pvt.	A Orr's Ri.		AN	06/27/62	Gaines' Mill, VA	KIA		ROH,JR,CDC
Reeves, T.J.	Pvt.	I 13th SCVI		SG	08/30/62	2nd Manassas, VA	KIA		ROH,JR,CDC,HOS
Reeves, Thomas J.	Pvt.	H 5th SCVI			03/15/64	Emory, VA		Con. Cem. Emory, VA	PP,SA3
Register, Ira	Pvt.	B 21st SCVI		DN	01/15/65	Ft. Fisher, NC	KIA		ROH,HAG,PP
Reid, D.F. (D.L.?)	Pvt.	G 13th SCVI		NY	12/25/61	Coosawatchie, SC	DOD	(JR=Measles 11/12/62)	ROH,JR,ANY
Reid, David P.	Pvt.	A 17th SCVI	20	CR	08/31/62	2nd Manassas, VA	DOW		ROH,JR,HHC,CB
Reid, G.W.	Pvt.	H 10th SCVI	33	WG	06/15/63		DOD	(Date approx)	RAS,HOW
Reid, H. Bachman	Cpl.	E 3rd SCVI		NY	08/15/62	Richmond, VA	DOW	(Wdd Savage Stn.6/29/62)	ROH,JR,SA2,ANY
Reid, H.T.	Pvt.	D 22nd SCVI		PS	07/30/64	Crater, Pbg., VA	KIA		BLM
Reid, Hiram N.	Pvt.	B 1st SCVIG	24	NY	07/27/62	Gaines' Mill, VA	KIA		ROH,JR,SA1,ANY
Reid, J.W.	Pvt.	B 6th SCVI	19	YK	05/31/62	7 Pines, VA	KIA		YEB
Reid, James L.	Pvt.	B 4th SCVI	21	AN	08/14/61	Culpepper, VA	DOD	Fairview Cem. Culpepper VA	ROH,JR,CGH,SA2
Reid, John B.	Pvt.	A 6th SCVI	26	CR	05/31/61	Charleston, SC	DOD	Fishing Creek Ch. Chester	ROH,YEB,HHC,UD
Reid, John M.	Pvt.	E 3rd SCVI		NY	04/08/62	Richmond, VA	DOD	Cannon Creek ARP Newberry	ROH,JR,NCC,SA2
Reid, John W.	Sgt.	B Orr's Ri.	21	AE	06/28/64	Riddle's Shop VA	DOW	City Pt.N.C. Hopewell, VA	ROH,CDC,PP,TOD
Reid, Joseph	Pvt.	H 16th SCVI		GE	07/22/64	Atlanta, GA	KIA		ROH,16R
Reid, L.S.	Pvt.	A 1st SCResB		UN	/ /	In camp	DOD		UD3
Reid, M.	Pvt.	K 1st SCVC		CN	08/24/64	Charleston, SC	DOD	Magnolia Cem. Charleston	ROH,MAG,RCD
Reid, Samuel O.	Pvt.	G Orr's Ri.		AE	07/15/62	Gaines' Mill, VA	DOW	Oakwood C.#26,Row H,Div C	ROH,JR,OWC,CDC
Reid, Samuel Pressley	Pvt.	C 3rd SCVI		NY	03/01/62	Manchester, VA	DOD	Cannon Creek ARP Newberry	JR,NCC,SA2,KEB
Reid, T.G.	Pvt.	C P.S.S.		AN	08/15/62		DOD		JR,GMJ
Reid, T.W.	Pvt.	G 13th SCVI		NY	/ /		DOD	(Not on NY monument)	ANY
Reid, Thomas J.	Pvt.	C 4th SCVC		PS	08/30/64	Elmira, NY	DIP	(POW 6/11/64 Trev Stn)	ROH
Reid, Thomas Simpson	Pvt.	A 6th SCVI	25	YK	05/31/62	7 Pines, VA	KIA	UD1	ROH,WDB,GLS,YE
Reid, W.W.	Pvt.	H 12th SCVI	16	YK	06/15/64		DOD	(YEB=discharged)	CWC,YEB
Reid, William	Pvt.	F 3rd SCVI		LS	05/03/63	Chancellorsville	KIA	(Reed, M. in SA2?)	JR
Reid, William W.	Pvt.	E 3rd SCVI		NY	05/05/63	Chancellorsville	KIA	(Wdd 5/2/63)	ROH,JR,SA2,KEB
Reide, J.M.					/ /			(Rchmd effects list 12/62)	CDC
Reilly, D.	Pvt.	B 1st SCVA		BL	06/16/62	Secessionville	KIA		ROH,CDC
Reilly, James	Pvt.	K 1st SCVIG		CN	03/15/63	Rchmd, Wdd @ Sbg	DOW	Oakwood C.#83,Row P,Div B	ROH,JR,SA1,OWC
Reilly, John C.	2nd Lt.	I 11th SCVI		CO	06/24/64	Petersburg, VA	KIA		ROH,R47,HAG
Remley, A.H.K.	Pvt.	E 26th SCVI	17	CO	05/20/64	Petersburg, VA	KIA		ROH,CDC
Remly, K.F.L.	Pvt.	E 26th SCVI	18	AE	05/20/64	Petersburg, VA	KIA		ROH
Rennel, W.	Pvt.	B Orr's Ri.		AE	06/27/62	Gaines' Mill, VA	KIA		ROH,JR,CDC
Rentz, Charles	Pvt.	D 11th SCVI	36	BL	04/15/64	Lake City, FL	DOD		ROH,HAG,PP
Rentz, George W.	Sgt.	K 11th SCVI	32	CO	12/29/64	Elmira, NY	DIP	Woodlawn N.C.#1305 Elmira	ROH,FPH,HAG,P6
Rentz, Isaac	Pvt.	G 17th SCVI		BL	09/27/61		DOW		JR
Rentz, J.D.	Pvt.	G 1st SCVIG		BL	05/07/64	Orange C.H., VA	DOW	(Wdd Wilderness)	ROH,SA1

SOUTH CAROLINA DEAD IN CSA SERVICE 1861-1865

NAME	RANK	C REGIMENT	AGE	DS	DIED	WHERE	WHY	BURIED	SOURCES
Rentz, W.C.	Pvt.	H 17th SCVI		BL	09/17/62		DOW		JR
Renwick, Hugh Toland	Pvt.	E 3rd SCVI	29	NY	04/27/62	Richmond, VA	DOD	Kings Crk. ARP Newberry SC	ROH,NCC,ANY,SA2
Reseman, G.W.	Pvt.	D 1st SCResB			11/29/65	Raleigh, NC		Oakwood C. Raleigh, NC	TOD
Resons, T.R.	Pvt.	K 10th SSCVI		CN	/ /		DOD		RAS
Revel, J.A.	Pvt.	B 1st SCVIH		DN	10/28/63	Lookout Valley	MIA		ROH,SA1,CDC
Revel, John		PeeDee LA		DN	/ /				ROH
Revel, John W.	Pvt.	C 20th SCVI	19	LN	03/16/62	James Island, SC	DOD		ROH,KEB
Revels, George Madison	Pvt.	I 6th SCVI		CR	/ /		DOD		CB,HHC
Revels, John J.	Pvt.	G 18th SCVI	34	YK	05/26/65	Pt. Lookout, MD	DIP	C.C. Pt. Lookout, MD	FPH,P6,P115,YEB
Reyburn, William	Pvt.	9th SCVIB			10/19/61	Richmond, VA	DOD		ROH
Reynolds, B.F.	Pvt.	C 22nd SCVI		SG	11/14/64	Elmira, NY	DIP	Woodlawn N.C.#797 Elmira	FPH,P6,P65,P120
Reynolds, David	Pvt.			ED	/ /	Virginia	DOD	(TFD frm B,6th SCVC)	HOE,UD3
Reynolds, Drury J.	Pvt.	A Hol. Leg.	20	SG	08/30/62	2nd Manassas, VA	KIA		ROH,JR,HOS
Reynolds, George N.	Major		24	CN	03/24/63	Winnsboro, SC	DOD		ROH
Reynolds, Hastings	Pvt.	C 12th SCVI		FD	06/15/61	St. Helena, SC	ACD	(Drowned in Sound)	HFC
Reynolds, J.B.	Pvt.	A 1st SCV			08/15/62		KIA		JR
Reynolds, J.C.	Pvt.	K 7th SCVI		ED	09/17/62	Sharpsburg, MD	KIA		JR,KEB
Reynolds, J.H.	Pvt.	C 22nd SCVI		SG	07/19/63	Richmond, VA		Hollywood Cem.Rchmd. U704	ROH,HC
Reynolds, J.W.	Pvt.	Ham.Leg.			08/20/62	Richmond, VA		Hollywood Cem.Rchmd. H248	HC
Reynolds, James	Pvt.	C 22nd SCVI	19	SG	/ /	Petersburg, VA	DOW		ROH
Reynolds, John H.	Pvt.	C 15th SCVAB			08/23/63	Bty. Wagner, SC	DOW		CDC
Reynolds, John M.	Asst Surg.		23	BT	06/22/62	Richmond, VA	DOD	Hollywood Cem.Rchmd. O168	ROH,HC,CDC
Reynolds, John McKellar	Pvt.	F 2nd SCVI	19	AE	07/02/63	Gettysburg, PA	KIA	Magnolia Cem. Charleston	ROH,JR,GDR,SA2
Reynolds, P.J.	Pvt.	D 5th SCVC		CO	03/27/65	Columbia, SC	DOD		ROH,PP
Reynolds, R.	Pvt.	E 23rd SCVI		MN	07/08/64	Richmond, VA		Hollywood Cem.Rchmd. U554	ROH,HC
Reynolds, Riley D.	Pvt.	B 13th SCVI		SG	/ /	Columbia, SC			HOS
Reynolds, T.	Pvt.	C 18th SCVI		UN	10/17/62	Richmond, VA			ROH
Reynolds, T. Zion	Pvt.	G 22nd SCVI	37	AN	11/08/64	Petersburg, VA	DOW		ROH
Reynolds, T.G.	Pvt.	G 22nd SCVI	35	AN	11/08/64	Petersburg, VA			ROH,PP
Reynolds, W.M.	Sgt.	K 7th SCVI		ED	09/13/62	Maryland Hts. MD	KIA		JR,KEB
Reynolds, W.P.	Pvt.	I 3rd SCVI		LS	12/03/62	Richmond, VA	DOD		ROH,JR,SA2
Reynolds, W.R.	Pvt.	H 2nd SC			/ /	Richmond, VA		Oakwood C.#10,Row G,Div B	ROH,OWC
Reynolds, William C.	Pvt.	A 14th SCVI	23	DN	07/01/63	Gettysburg, PA	KIA		ROH
Reynolds,Jr., William F.	Pvt.	F 18th SCVI	34	UN	08/10/64	Petersburg, VA	DOD	Goudelock F. Cem. UN Cty.	ROH,BLC,UNC,PP
Rhaime, John E.	Pvt.	A 2nd SCVC	22	KW	07/16/64	Green Pond, SC	ACD	(Drowned in Ashepoo R.)	ROH,AHB
Rhame, John B.	Pvt.	C Ham.Leg.		RD	08/17/61	Culpepper, VA	DOW	Fairview Cem. Culpepper VA	JR,CGH,CDC
Rhames, Nathaniel	Pvt.	A 21st SCVI		CN	06/10/65	Elmira, NY	DIP	Woodlawn N.C.#2887 Elmira	FPH,HAG,P6,P65
Rhea, William	Cpl.	B 6th SCVI		YK	08/30/62	2nd Manassas, VA	DOW	(Color bearer)	ROH,CDC
Rhett, J. Grimke	2nd Lt.	H 1st SCVIG		CN	06/27/62	Gaines' Mill, SC	KIA		ROH,JR,SA1,BBC
Rhett, Robert Woodward	2nd Lt.	I 1st SCVIG	23	CN	06/30/62	Gaines' Mill, VA	DOW	St. Philips Ch. Charleston	ROH,MAG,CDC,R45
Rhinehart, A. Pickens	Pvt.	H Hol.Leg.	16	ED	09/01/62	2nd Manassas, VA	DOW		ROH,JR
Rhode, D.	Pvt.	C 27th SCVI		CN	05/16/64	Drury's Bluff VA	KIA		ROH,CDC,HAG
Rhoden, H.W.	Pvt.	H 17th SCVI		BL	06/27/64	Petersburg, VA	KIA		ROH
Rhoden, Wiley	Pvt.	A 19th SCVI	35	ED	07/22/64	Atlanta, GA	KIA		ROH,HOE,UD3
Rhodes, Everett E.	Pvt.	I 18th SCVI	32	DN	11/15/64	Florence, SC	DOD		ROH,PP
Rhodes, F. Everett	Pvt.	F 8th SCVI	40	DN	/ /	Florence, SC	DOD		ROH,KEB
Rhodes, J.B.	Pvt.	G 7th SCVI		ED	08/09/61	Culpepper, VA	DOD	Fairview Cem. Culpepper VA	CGH,KEB,HOE
Rhodes, J.F.	Pvt.	PeeDee LA		DN	/ /				ROH,PDL,SA1
Rhodes, J.P.	Pvt.	I 1st SC	24	CO	04/15/62	Adams Run, SC	DOD		ROH
Rhodes, J.T.	Pvt.	D 1st SC			/ /	Richmond, VA			ROH
Rhodes, James	Pvt.	I 1st SCVC	28	CO	04/15/62	Adams Run, SC	DOD		ROH,PP

SOUTH CAROLINA DEAD IN CSA SERVICE 1861-1865

NAME	RANK	C	REGIMENT	AGE	DS	DIED	WHERE	WHY	BURIED	SOURCES
Rhodes, James	Pvt.	A	26th SCVI	25	HY	09/15/63	Charleston, SC	DOD		ROH
Rhodes, James Burt	Pvt.	B	21st SCVI		DN	05/16/64	Drury's Bluff VA	KIA		ROH,CDC,HAG
Rhodes, James Joseph	Pvt.	G	9th SCVIB		DN	08/08/61	Culpepper, VA	DOD	(CDC=7th SCVI 8/9/61)	ROH,JR,JLC,CDC
Rhodes, James M.	Pvt.	E	18th SCVI	35	SG	06/15/62	Spartanburg, SC	ACD		ROH,HOS
Rhodes, John	Pvt.	A	8th SCVI		DN	/ /				ROH
Rhodes, John B.	1st Cpl.	G	1st SCVIG		ED	05/03/63	Chancellorsville	KIA		SA1,HOE
Rhodes, John Dawsey	Pvt.	F	8th SCVI	20	DN	07/02/63	Gettysburg, PA	KIA	(JR=2nd Sgt.)	ROH,JR,GDR,KEB
Rhodes, Joseph	Pvt.	B	21st SCVI		DN	/ /				ROH,HAG
Rhodes, L. Miles	Pvt.	K	19th SCVI	17	ED	02/15/62	Charleston, SC	DOD	(Typhoid)	JR,HOE
Rhodes, R.J.	Pvt.	C	8th SCV		CD	10/15/62	Staunton, VA	DOD		JR
Rhodes, R.L.	Pvt.	G	1st SCVIH		BL	08/30/62	2nd Manassas, VA	DOW	(JR=R.S.)	ROHJR,,CDC,JRH
Rhodes, T. Augustus	3rd Sgt.	H	1st SCVIG	32	BT	07/03/63	Gettysburg, PA	KIA	Magnolia Cem. Charleston	ROH,Jr,GDR,BBC
Rhodes, Wiley S.	3rd Cpl.	H	1st SCVIH		SG	01/27/63	White Sulpher Ss	DOD	PP	ROH,SA1,HOS,JR
Rhodes, William B.	2nd Lt.	M	8th SCVI		DN	07/28/64	Deep Bottom, VA	KIA		TRR,KEB,R46
Rhodus, Joel G.	5th Cpl.	C	25th SCVI	40	WG	/ /			(1864)	HOW,CTA
Rials, T.A.	Pvt.	G	10th SCVI		HY	/ /		DOD		RAS
Ricard, J.F.	Pvt.	B	Orr's Ri.		AE	08/29/62	2nd Manassas, VA	KIA	(JR=Rykird)	ROH,JR
Rice,	Pvt.	A	17th SCVI		CR	12/13/62	Kinston, NC	KIA		ROH
Rice,						09/17/62	Sharpsburg, MD	DOW	Rose Hill C. Hagerstown MD	WAT
Rice, D.H.	Pvt.	C	8th SCVI		CD	09/09/62	(NI KEB)		Piedmont Institute, VA	ROH
Rice, Henry	Pvt.	I	5th SCVI		SG	05/31/62	7 Pines, VA	KIA		HOS
Rice, Ibzan L.	Pvt.	C	P.S.S.		AN	06/30/62	Frayser's Farm	KIA		SA2,ROH,JR,CDC,GMJ
Rice, James H. (E.?)	Pvt.	E	16th SCVI	28	GE	/ /	Camp Chase, OH	DIP	(P 11/26/63 Graysville GA)	ROH,16R,P2
Rice, James P. (T.?)	Pvt.	I	7th SCVI		ED	10/05/62		DOW		JR
Rice, M.	Pvt.		Ham.Leg.			11/02/64	Richmond, VA		Hollywood Cem.Rchmd. W376	ROH,HC
Rice, Wilkinson	Pvt.	K	14th SCVI		ED	07/01/63	Gettysburg, PA	KIA	(HOE=Williamson)	HOE,GDR,UD2
Rice, William R.	Pvt.	F	24th SCVI		AN	12/10/64	Camp Douglas, IL	DIP	Oak Woods Cem. Chicago, IL	ROH,FPH,P5,HOL
Rich, William Henry	Pvt.	B	23rd SCVI	25	CN	06/27/64	Petersburg, VA	KIA		ROH,RCD
Richard, G.G.	Pvt.	G	Orr's Ri.		AE	06/27/62	Gaines' Mill, VA	KIA		ROH,JR,CDC
Richard, Hiram H.	1st Lt.	D	5th SCVI	24	UN	08/16/64	Deep Bottom, VA	DOW	Tucker F. Cem. UN Cty.	ROH,SA3,UNC,UD
Richards, D.M.	Pvt.	F	14th SCVI		LS	07/02/63	Gettysburg, PA	KIA	(JR=Co.D)	ROH,JR
Richards, J.M.	Pvt.	H	15th SCVI		UN	07/05/64	Richmond, VA			ROH
Richards, James A.	Pvt.		16th SCVI		GE	12/05/62	Adams Run, SC	DOD		GEC
Richards, James H.	Pvt.		3rd SCVABn	24	GE	05/19/64	McPhersonville	DOD		ROH
Richards, John M.	Pvt.	B	22nd SCVI		SG	07/30/64	Crater, Pbg., VA	KIA		ROH,HOS,BLM
Richards, Levi	Pvt.	B	22nd SCVI		SG	07/30/64	Crater, Pbg., VA	KIA		ROH,BLM,HOS
Richards, Louis	Pvt.	F	1st SCVIR			06/10/63	Columbia, SC	DOD		SA1,PP
Richards, M.G. Berry	2nd Lt.	K	5th SCVC		LS	03/27/65	Smithfield, NC	DOW	Richards Gvyd Newberry, SC	ROH,JR,NCC,ANY
Richards, N.L.	4th Cpl.	G	22nd SCVI		AN	07/30/64	Crater, Pbg., VA	KIA		BLM
Richardson, A.J.	Pvt.	F	10th SCVI		MN	/ /		DOD		RAS
Richardson, A.R.	Sgt.	B	5th SCVC	23	BT	02/25/65	Lynch's Creek SC	KIA		ROH,MDM
Richardson, Benjamin F.	Pvt.	D	P.S.S.		SG	03/29/63	Franklin, VA	DOD	(JR=DOW)	ROH,JR,HOS
Richardson, C.P.	Pvt.	D	Ham.Leg.		AN	05/31/62	7 Pines, VA	KIA		GRS
Richardson, Charles	Pvt.	I	P.S.S.		PS	07/15/62	Frayser's Farm	DOW	(Wdd 6/30/62)	ROH
Richardson, D.H.	Pvt.	E	1st SCV			09/07/62	Richmond, VA	DOD	(Typhoid)	JR
Richardson, David W.	Pvt.	I	21st SCVI		MN	05/09/64	Swift Creek, VA	KIA		HMC,HAG
Richardson, F.M.	Pvt.	L	10th SCVI		MN	/ /		DOD		RAS,HMC
Richardson, Gaillard	Pvt.	F	12th SCVI		FD	/ /	At home	DOD		HFC
Richardson, Gonan	Pvt.	B	14th SCVI	22	ED	05/16/62	Petersburg, VA	ACD	(RR wreck near Pbg) UD3,PP	ROH,JR,HOE,BLC
Richardson, I.J.	Pvt.	D	1st SC			04/07/62	Richmond, VA			ROH
Richardson, I.N.	Pvt.	H	12th SCVI	28	YK	05/12/64	Spotsylvania, VA	KIA	(YEB=J.N.)	CWC,YEB

SOUTH CAROLINA DEAD IN CSA SERVICE 1861-1865

NAME	RANK	C REGIMENT	AGE	DS	DIED	WHERE	WHY	BURIED	SOURCES
Richardson, J.R.	Pvt.	C 26th SCVI		MN	02/19/64	Charleston, SC	DOD	Magnolia Cem. Charleston	ROH,MAG,RCD
Richardson, J.W.	Pvt.	H 15th SCVI		UN	07/06/64	Richmond, VA	KIA	Hollywood Cem.Rchmd. X87	HC
Richardson, Jesse James	Pvt.	D 14th SCVCB	19	BL	10/22/62	Pocotaligo, SC			ROH,PP
Richardson, John	Pvt.	C 12th SCVI		FD	06/30/64	Ft. Delaware, DE	DIP	Finn's Pt., NJ Con. Cem.	ROH,FPH,P5,HFC
Richardson, John L.D.	Pvt.	H 13th SCVI	22	LN	07/06/64	Virginia	DOD		ROH
Richardson, John S.	Pvt.	C 12th SCVI		FD	06/27/62	Gaines' Mill, VA	KIA		HFC
Richardson, Oliver P.	1st Lt.	A 10th SCVI		GN	06/27/64	Forsyth, GA	DOW	(Leg & shoulder)	ROH,RAS,GRG,CKB
Richardson, Reuben J.	Pvt.	C 12th SCVI		FD	09/17/62	Sharpsburg, MD	KIA		HFC
Richardson, S.	Pvt.	26th SCVI			05/30/62	Charleston, SC	DOD	Magnolia Cem. Charleston	ROH,MAG
Richardson, S.T.	Pvt.	D 7th SCVI			10/28/62			Stonewall C. Winchester VA	ROH,WIN
Richardson, Samuel F.	Cpl.	A 3rd SCVI		LS	07/20/64	Pt. Lookout, MD	DIP	C.C. Pt. Lookout, MD UD3	ROH,FPH,KEB,P6
Richardson, T.	Pvt.	21st SCVI		PS	01/27/62			Magnolia Cem. Charleston	RCD
Richardson, Thomas	Pvt.	L 21st SCVI		MN	/ /	Columbia, SC	DOD	(1862)	HMC,HAG
Richardson, Thomas	Pvt.	I 21st SCVI		MN	/ /	Charleston, SC			HMC,HAG
Richardson, W.E. Murphy	Sgt.	I P.S.S.	20	PS	07/02/62	Malvern Hill, VA	DOW		ROH,JR
Richardson, W.W.	Pvt.	H 12th SCVI	31	YK	08/15/62		DOD	(CWC=DOW)	YEB,CWC
Richardson, William	Pvt.	C 12th SCVI		FD	03/31/64	Petersburg, VA			ROH,HFC
Richardson, William	Pvt.	Gregg's By			04/21/65	Pt. Lookout, MD	DIP	C.C. Pt. Lookout, MD	FPH
Richardson, William S.	Pvt.	K P.S.S.		SG	06/30/62	Frayser's Farm	DOW		HOS,JR
Richardson, Wylie A.	Pvt.	D 1st SCVIH		LR	10/20/64	Ft. Harrison, VA	DOW	Hollywood Cem.Rchmd. E12	ROH,SA1,LAN
Richbourg, A.D.	Pvt.	C Ham.Leg.		SR	05/31/62	7 Pines, VA	KIA		ROH,JR,CDC
Richbourg, Edwin	Pvt.	C Ham.Leg.		SR	05/31/62	7 Pines, VA	KIA		ROH,JR,CDC
Richbourg, F.D.	Pvt.	E 19th SCVI		SR	01/19/63		DOW		JR
Richbourg, James A.H.	Cpl.	K 23rd SCVI	25	SR	09/15/64	Petersburg, VA	DOW	(Wdd 9/4/64, 3rd wd)	ROH,K23,BLM
Richbourg, John J.	Pvt.	D 15th SCVI		KW	/ /		DOD		HIC,KEB
Richbourg, R.D. (B.D.?)	Pvt.	I 25th SCVI		CL	04/24/65	Elmira, NY	DIP	Woodlawn N.C.#1409 Elmira	FPH,HAG,P6,P65
Richburg, B.R.	Cpt.	E 19th SCVI			10/13/64		DOW		R47
Richburg, James H. (W.?)	Pvt.	I 25th SCVI		CL	05/23/64	Richmond, VA		Hollywood Cem.Rchmd. I168	ROH,HC,HAG
Richburg, Pinkey S.	Pvt.	I 23rd SCVI		CL	09/27/62	Culpepper, VA	DOW	Fairview Cem. Culpepper VA	CGH,CDC
Richburg, R.	Pvt.	E 10th SCVI			08/07/64	Macon, GA		Rose Hill Cem. Macon, GA	CV,BGA
Richburg, Reuben L.G.	Pvt.	E 19th SCVI		SR	08/07/64	Macon, GA		Prob Rosehill C. Macon, GA	PP
Richer, W.E.	Pvt.				09/09/62	Richmond, VA		Hollywood Cem.Rchmd. H48	HC
Richey, George B. (R.?)	Pvt.	G Orr's Ri.		AE	06/27/62	Gaines' Mill, VA	KIA		ROH,CV,CDC
Richey, George W.	Pvt.	G 1st SCVIG		RD	08/01/64	Richmond, VA	DOD		SA1
Richey, John	Pvt.	C P.S.S.		AN	05/08/64	Spotsylvania, VA	KIA		ROH,CDC,SA2,GMJ
Richey, John Robert	Pvt.	D 4th SCVI	18	AN	08/04/62	(? in B,37thVa)	DOD	Fairview U.M.C. Easley, SC	ACC
Richie, William M.	Pvt.	D 17th SCVI		CR	07/16/64	Petersburg, VA	KIA		ROH,HHC,CB
Rick, G.W.	Pvt.	F 1st SC			08/01/62	Richmond, VA		Hollywood Cem.Rchmd. C107	HC
Rickenbaker, Fred. M.	Pvt.	B 1st SCVIH	25	OG	09/22/62	Warrenton, VA	DOW	(Wdd 2nd Man)(JR=4/22)	ROH,JR,SA1,JRH
Rickenbaker, Harmon	Pvt.	H Ham.Leg.		OG	/ /	Virginia	DOW		ROH
Rickenbaker, William	Pvt.	H Ham. Leg.	20	OG	09/15/62	Frederick, MD	DOW		ROH
Rickets, Peter	Pvt.	I 19th SCVI	39	AE	07/10/63	Rome, GA	DOD	(Teamster)	ROH
Riddle, Benjamin	Pvt.	B 22nd SCVI		SG	07/30/64	Crater, Pbg., VA	KIA		BLM
Riddle, D.B. (D.V.?)	Pvt.	E 3rd SCVIBn		LS	04/24/63	Staunton, VA		Thornrose C. Staunton, VA	ROH,KEB,TOD
Riddle, D.L.	Pvt.	E 3rd SCVIBn		LS	09/25/63	Weldon, NC		(Maybe Dup of D.B.)	PP
Riddle, George M.A.C.	Pvt.	D 6th SCVI	30	YK	/ /	Lynchburg, VA	DOD		YEB
Riddle, Melmoth	Pvt.	E 3rd SCVIBn		LS	05/08/64	Spotsylvania, VA	KIA	Spotsylvania C.H., VA	ROH,SCH,KEB
Riddlehuber, William F.	4th Cpl.	H 13th SCVI	21	NY	07/01/63	Gettysburg, PA	KIA		ANY
Rider, G.E.	Pvt.	G SCVA			01/27/62	Charleston, SC	DOD	Magnolia Cem. Charleston	MAG,RCD
Ridge, Daniel	Pvt.	G 14th SCVI	45	AE	07/10/63	Richmond, VA	DOD	Hollywood Cem.Rchmd. T387	ROH,HC
Ridge, William L.	Pvt.	G 14th SCVI	25	AE	03/20/63	Gordonsville, VA	DOD	Gordonsville, VA Cem.	ROH,GOR

SOUTH CAROLINA DEAD IN CSA SERVICE 1861-1865

NAME	RANK	C REGIMENT	AGE	DS	DIED	WHERE	WHY	BURIED	SOURCES
Ridgedell, Felix	Pvt.	D 14th SCVI	17	ED	07/01/63	Gettysburg, PA	KIA		HOE,GDR,D14
Ridgell, Norris	Pvt.	F 19th SCVI	30	ED	06/20/62	Okolona, MS	DOD		ROH,PP
Ridgell, T.T.	Pvt.	D 14th SCVI	20	ED	/ /	Petersburg, VA	KIA		HOE,D14
Ridgell, William	Pvt.	E 7th SCVI		ED	/ /		DOD		HOE,KEB,UD3
Ridgeway, David Carter	Pvt.		29	GE	06/11/64	Trevillian Stn.	KIA	(Memorial on battlefield)	GEC,GEE
Ridgeway, J.M.	Pvt.	I 25th SCVI		CL	04/06/65	Elmira, NY	DIP	Woodlawn N.C.#2549 Elmira	FPH,HAG,P6,P65
Ridgeway, S.C.	Pvt.	I 7th SCVI		WG	07/02/63	Gettysburg, PA	KIA		ROH,JR,GDR,CDC
Ridgway, Hopewell W.	Pvt.	K 23rd SCVI		CL	09/15/64	Petersburg, VA	KIA		ROH,K23,UD3
Ridgway, John W.	Pvt.	K 23rd SCVI		CL	06/17/64	Petersburg, VA	KIA		ROH,K23,UD3
Ridlehuber, Henry Walter	1st Sgt.	B 1st SCVIG	21	NY	05/05/64	Wilderness, VA	KIA		ROH,SA1,ANY,CD
Ridlehuber, William L.	Pvt.	F 20th SCVI	33	NY	06/17/63	At home	DOD	Ridlehuber Gyd. Newberry	ROH,NCC,ANY
Rigdon, J.M.	Pvt.	B 2nd SCVIRi		PS	/ /				ROH
Rigdon, Thomas B.	Pvt.	H 2nd SCVIRi	19	GE	01/24/63	Petersburg, VA		Blandford Church Pbg., VA	BLC,PP
Riggins, A.R.	Pvt.	F 22nd SCVI		PS	07/30/64	Crater, Pbg., VA	KIA		BLM
Riggins, Allen	Pvt.	B 2nd SCVIRi		PS	02/04/64	Louisville, KY	DIP	Cave Hill C. Louisville KY	ROH,FPH,P5,CV
Riggins, Allen R.	Pvt.	B 2nd SCVIRi		PS	07/30/64	Petersburg, VA	KIA		PCS
Riggins, William P.	Pvt.	A Orr's Ri.		AN	05/06/64	Wilderness, VA	KIA		ROH
Riggles, D.W.	Pvt.	B 1st SCV		CN	04/08/63	Richmond, VA			ROH
Riggs, John S.	1st Sgt.	G 11th SCVI		CO	06/24/64	Petersburg, VA	KIA		ROH,HAG
Rikard, A.J.	Pvt.	D 13th SCVI	24	NY	06/30/62	Frayser's Farm	KIA		ROH,ANY
Rikard, Andrew C.	Pvt.	D 13th SCVI	23	NY	08/29/62	2nd Manassas	KIA	(CNM=Mort Wdd @ 7 Days)	ROH,JR,ANY,CNM
Rikard, J.M.	Pvt.	G 13th SCVI		NY	05/12/64	Spotsylvania, VA	KIA		ROH,ANY
Rikard, John A.	Pvt.	G 13th SCVI		NY	07/01/63	Gettysburg, PA	KIA		ROH,GDR,ANY,CD
Rikard, L.C.	Pvt.	H 3rd SCVI		LN	09/17/62	Sharpsburg, MD	KIA		SA2,KEB
Rikard, Levi	Pvt.	G 13th SCVI			/ /		DOD	(Not on NY monument)	ANY
Rikard, Walter M.	Pvt.	D 13th SCVI	21	NY	12/13/62	Fredericksburg	KIA		ROH,ANY
Rikard, Wiley	Pvt.	H Hol.Leg.	20	NY	08/19/62	Richmond, VA	DOD		ROH,ANY
Riley	Pvt.	G 1st SCVAR			01/27/62	Ft. Sumter, SC	ACD	(Fell from wall)	CDC
Riley, C.W.	Pvt.	A 5th SCVI		LR	02/27/63	Richmond, VA	DOD	Hollywood Cem.Rchmd. D156	ROH,HC,SA3,LAN
Riley, David A.	Pvt.	A 1st SCVIH		CN	02/15/62		DOD	(Date approx)	SA1
Riley, Edward C.	Pvt.	B Orr's Ri.	22	AE	05/03/63	Chancellorsville	KIA	(1st in F, 2nd SCVI)	ROH,JR,H2,SA2
Riley, George S.	Pvt.	K 1st SCVIG		BL	01/29/65	Columbia, SC			PP,SA1
Riley, J.P.	Cpl.	A 1st SCVIG		BL	08/29/62	2nd Manassas, VA	KIA		JR,SA1
Riley, J.S.	Pvt.	H 7th SCVI		PS	01/28/65	Pt. Lookout, MD	DIP		ROH
Riley, J.W.	Pvt.	A 1st SCVIG		BL	12/13/62	Fredericksburg	KIA	(JR=DOW 9/18/62)	ROH,JR,SA1
Riley, James W.	Pvt.	B 1st SCVIH		OG	07/12/62		DOD	(Typhoid Fever)	JR,SA1,JRH
Riley, John	Pvt.	D 15th SCVI		KW	/ /		DOD		JR
Riley, John B.	Pvt.	K 2nd SCVA		ED	/ /		DOD		HOE,UD3
Riley, Nathan	Pvt.	5th SCV	43		/ /			Itawamba County, MS	MCG
Riley, Pinckney	Pvt.	B Orr's Ri.	22	AE	06/15/64	(Andrew P.?/CDC)	DOW	(Wdd, died in enemy Hands)	ROH
Riley, W.B.	Pvt.	B Orr's Ri.		AE	05/03/63	Chancellorsville	KIA	(ROH=Burt)	ROH,JR,CDC
Riley, W.B.	Pvt.	B 5th SCV			05/03/63	Chancellorsville	KIA		JR
Riley, William Newton	Pvt.	F 2nd SCVI	22	AE	07/02/63	Gettysburg, PA	KIA	Magnolia Cem. Charleston	ROH,JR,GDR,SA2
Ringe, J.W. (Ramage ?)	Pvt.	I 3rd SCVI		LS	10/30/62	(KEB=Ramage)		Stonewall C. Winchester VA	WIN
Ripley, Edward	Pvt.	B 19th SCVI	30	ED	10/23/62	Enterprise, MS	DOD		ROH,HOE,PP
Riser, Francis Marion	Pvt.	B 14th SCVI	18	ED	01/01/62	Port Royal Ferry	KIA	St.Marks LC Saluda Cty. SC	JR,NCC,PP,EDN
Riser, George A.	Pvt.	F 1st SCVA		NY	03/19/65	Bentonville, NC	KIA		ANY
Rish, John Adams	Pvt.	I 15th SCVI		LN	06/23/62	Hardeeville, SC	DOD	(TOD=At home)	H15,TOD,KEB
Rish, William Ivey	Pvt.	I 15th SCVI	24	LN	06/06/62	Hardeeville, SC	DOD		H15,TOD,KEB
Risher, H.B.	2nd Sgt.	G 1st SCVIH		CO	07/20/64	Petersburg, VA	KIA	(Also wdd @ Boonsboro)	SA1,JRH
Risher, Jack	Pvt.	I 1st SCVC		CO	06/15/63	Lynchburg, VA	DOW	Lynchburg CSA Cem.#1 R5	ROH,BBW

SOUTH CAROLINA DEAD IN CSA SERVICE 1861-1865

NAME	RANK	C REGIMENT	AGE	DS	DIED	WHERE	WHY	BURIED	SOURCES
Risher, Junius	Sgt.	G 4th SCVC		CO	10/20/64	Wilson, NC	DOW	(Wdd @ Burgess Mills, VA)	SSO,PP
Risher, R.B.	Pvt.	11th SCVI		CO	06/15/62	At home	DOD		ROH
Risher, Silas	Cpl.	I 1st SCVC	24	CO	11/15/63	Staunton, VA	DOD		ROH
Risinger, David	Pvt.	C 15th SCVI	29	LN	04/24/63	Richmond, VA	DOD	Hollywood Cem.Rchmd. T307	JR,HC,KEB,H15
Risinger, Noah	Pvt.	C 15th SCVI		LN	05/06/64	Wilderness, VA	KIA		ROH,KEB,H15
Risk, J.A.	Pvt.	I 15th SCVI		LN	/ /		DOD		JR,KEB
Risk, W.I.	Pvt.	I 15th SCVI		LN	/ /		DOD		JR,KEB
Ritchens, W.E.	Pvt.	7th SCVI			09/09/62	(Richey, Co.D?)		Hollywood Cem.Rchmd. A83	HC
Ritter, John A.	Pvt.	K 2nd SCVI		BL	11/06/62	Richmond, VA	DOD	Oakwood C.#22,Row L,Div B	ROH,SA2,OWC,H2
Ritters, William					/ /			(Rchmnd effects list 1/63)	CDC
Ritz, John	Cpl.	B 11th SCVI		CO	06/21/64	Petersburg, VA	DOW	(Wdd 6/18/64)	ROH,HAG
Rivers, C.H.	Pvt.	H 25th SCVI		CN	10/25/64	Charleston, SC	DOD	Magnolia Cem. Charleston	ROH,MAG,HAG,RCD
Rivers, Dempsey	Pvt.	B 8th SCVI		CD	11/09/61	Richmond, VA	DOD	(Typhoid)	ROH,JR
Rivers, Drew	Citizen			CD	05/08/65	Pt. Lookout, MD	DIP	C.C. Pt. Lookout, MD	FPH,P6,P115
Rivers, F. Tyler	Pvt.	E 11th SCVI		BT	07/02/64	Petersburg, VA	DOW	(Wdd 6/24/64)	ROH,HAG
Rivers, George M.	Pvt.	D 11th SCVI	21	BT	08/15/62	Hardeeville, SC	DOD		ROH,HAG
Rivers, J.M.	Sgt.	B 8th SCVI		CD	02/15/61		DOD	(Typhoid)	JR
Rivers, Joseph T.	Cpl.	D 11th SCVI	26	BT	05/08/64	Swift Creek, VA	KIA		ROH,HAG
Rivers, L.B.	Pvt.	D 6th SCVC	24		07/13/63	Adams Run, SC	DOD		PP
Rivers, L.I.	Pvt.	B 26th SCVI			03/02/65	Charleston, SC	DOD	Magnolia Cem. Charleston	ROH,MAG,P65,P120
Rivers, Robert H.	Pvt.	D 11th SCVI	27	BT	06/18/64	Petersburg, VA	KIA		ROH,HAG
Rivers, Rollins H.	2nd Cpl.	I 2nd SCVI	20	CN	10/01/63	Chickamauga, GA	DOW	(Wdd 9/20/63, JR=Sgt.)	ROH,JR,SA2,KEB
Rivers, Sterling Worth	Pvt.	G 22nd SCVI	54	RD	07/30/64	Crater, Pbg., VA	KIA	(BLM= Rives)	ROH,BLM
Rivers, W.A.	Pvt.	P.S.S.			08/17/63	Petersburg, VA			ROH
Rivers, William	Pvt.	8th SCVI	25	CD	07/15/64	Petersburg, VA	KIA	(Dup of William B.?)	ROH
Rivers, William B.	Cpl.	B 8th SCVI		CD	07/19/61	Richmond, VA	DOW	(JR=Wdd 1st Man., NI KEB)	ROH,JR
Roach, B.F.	Pvt.	E 5th SCVI		YK	06/27/62	Gaines' Mill, VA	KIA		JR,SA3
Roach, Berry	Pvt.	E Orr's Ri.	19	PS	08/02/62	Camp Jackson(?)	DOD		ROH
Roach, James Leroy	Pvt.	H 12th SCVI	22	YK	09/17/62	Sharpsburg, MD	KIA	(ROH=2nd Manassas)	ROH,JR,YEB,DEM
Roach, William	Pvt.	D 22nd SCVI		PS	06/16/62	Secessionville	KIA		ROH,CDC
Roach, William J.	Pvt.	A 2nd SCVI		RD	07/02/63	Gettysburg, PA	KIA	Magnolia Cem. Charleston	ROH,JR,GDR,SA2
Roane, W.B.	Pvt.	K 8th SCVI			/ /	Richmond, VA		Oakwood C.#118,Row C,Div A	ROH,OWC
Robb, A.S.	Pvt.			CL	11/17/64	Petersburg, VA		Blandford Church Pbg., VA	BLC
Robb, C.W. (Rabb ?)	Pvt.	E 3rd SCV			08/09/64	Richmond, VA		Hollywood Cem.Rchmd. V431	HC
Robb, J.C.	Pvt.	I 9th SCVIB			08/27/61	Germantown, VA	DOD		JR
Robbel, John	Pvt.	E 20th SCVI	20	LN	03/20/62	James Island, SC	DOD		ROH
Robbins, Jackson	Pvt.	E 13th SCVI		SG	11/27/62	Mt. Jackson Hos.	DOD	Mt. Jackson, VA	ROH,HOS,CDC,PP
Robbins, James S.	Pvt.	H P.S.S.			06/07/65	Pt. Lookout, MD	DIP	C.C. Pt. Lookout, MD	FPH,P6,P115
Robbins, John B.	4th Cpl.	I 8th SCVI		MN	07/02/63	Gettysburg, PA	KIA	Rose Farm, Gettysburg, PA	ROH,JR,GDR,WV
Robbins, S.A.	Pvt.	C 11th SCVI			08/31/62	Lynchburg, VA	DOD	Lynchburg CSA Cem.#2 R4	ROH,CDC
Robbins, S.F.	Pvt.	E 13th SCVI		SG	07/08/62	Richmond, VA	DOD	(JR=DOW)	ROH,JR,HOS
Robbins, Thomas G.	Cpl.	I Hol. Leg.		SG	/ /	Elmira, NY	DIP		HOS
Robbins, William P.	Pvt.	K 5th SCVI		SG	08/24/62	Richmond, VA	DOD	(JR=9/1/62)	ROH,JR,SA3,HOS
Robbs, J.C.	Pvt.	H 9th SCVIB	28	SG	08/15/61	Germantown, VA	DOD		ROH
Roberson, H.A.	Pvt.	C 19th SCVI		ED	07/15/62	Enterprise, MS	DOD		HOE
Roberson, Higdon	Pvt.	C 19th SCVI		ED	07/15/62	Enterprise, MS	DOD		HOE,UD3
Roberson, James M.	Pvt.	C 19th SCVI		ED	/ /	Mississippi	DOD	(1863)	HOE
Roberson, T.J.	Pvt.	P.S.S.			08/19/64	Richmond, VA		Hollywood Cem.Rchmd. V34	HC
Roberson, W.	Pvt.	Hart's Bty			01/29/65	Kittrell Spgs NC		Kittrell Springs, NC Cem.	CV
Roberson, W.E.	Pvt.	E 9th SCVIB			04/20/62	Richmond, VA	DOD	(Typhoid)	JR
Robert, James H.	3rd Cpl.	L 8th SCVI		MN	06/29/62	Savage Stn., VA	KIA		ROH,HMC,KEB

SOUTH CAROLINA DEAD IN CSA SERVICE 1861-1865

NAME	RANK	C	REGIMENT	AGE	DS	DIED	WHERE	WHY	BURIED	SOURCES
Roberts, A.J.	Pvt.	A	1st SCVIR			03/19/65	Bentonville, NC	KIA		ROH,WAT,SA1,PP
Roberts, Andrew J.	Pvt.	K	17th SCVI		YK	07/15/64	Petersburg, VA	DOW		ROH,YEB
Roberts, Benjamin F.	Pvt.	E	1st SCVIG		MN	05/12/64	Spotsylvania, VA	KIA		ROH,SA1,PDL,HM
Roberts, David A.	Pvt.	H	2nd SCVI		LR	/ /	Richmond, VA	DOD	Oakwood C.#11,Row B,Div E	ROH,OWC,H2,SA2
Roberts, E.C.	Pvt.	A	2nd SCVIRi			06/29/62	Savage Stn., VA	KIA	(Gaines M.? CDC= 7/8/62)	ROH,JR,CDC
Roberts, J.C.	1st Lt.	B	3rd SCVIBn		LS	10/19/64	Cedar Creek, VA	KIA		ROH,KEB,R45
Roberts, J.H.	Pvt.	B	10th SCVI		HY	/ /	Kentucky	DOD		RAS
Roberts, J.L.						/ /			(Rchmd effects list 1/63)	CDC
Roberts, J.W.	Pvt.	G	14th SCVI	38	AE	05/03/63	Chancellorsville	KIA		ROH
Roberts, James F.	Pvt.	F	23rd SCVI		CR	08/22/62	Richmond, VA			ROH,HHC
Roberts, James F.	Pvt.	A	2nd SCVI		RD	07/02/63	Gettysburg, PA	KIA	Magnolia Cem. Charleston	ROH,JR,GDR,SA2
Roberts, James M.	1st Lt.	C	16th SCVI		GE	01/29/65	Nashville, TN	DOW	(Wdd & POW at Franklin)	16R,P3,P5
Roberts, James W.	Pvt.	B	10th SCVI		HY	06/10/62	Columbus, MS	DOD	Friendship C. Columbus, MS	RAS,PP
Roberts, John	Lt. Col.		23rd SCVI		MN	11/04/62	At home	DOW	(Wdd @ 2nd Manassas)	HMC,LC,CDC
Roberts, John Newton	Pvt.	E	1st SCVIR		AN	09/08/63	Ft. Moultrie, SC	KIA		ROH,SA1,CDC
Roberts, Leroy R.	Pvt.	E	12th SCVI	18	LR	06/27/62	Gaines' Mill, VA	KIA		ROH,JR,LAN
Roberts, O.M.	Hosp. Stwd		1st LA Hos			10/11/64	Charleston, SC	DOD	Magnolia Cem. Charleston	ROH,MAG,CDC
Roberts, P.C.	Pvt.	E	Ham.Leg.		GE	07/21/61	1st Manassas, VA	KIA	(Bozeman Guards)	ROH,JR,CDC
Roberts, R.T.W.	Pvt.	K	11th SCVI	45	CO	/ /		DOD		ROH
Roberts, W.	Pvt.	A	21st SCVI			04/11/64	Petersburg, VA		Blandford Church Pbg., VA	BLC
Roberts, W.H.	Pvt.	A	15th SCVI		RD	09/14/62	South Mtn., MD	KIA	(Prob MD Hts. 9/13)	ROH,JR,KEB
Roberts, Wiley W.	1st Sgt.	F	1st SCVIG		HY	09/25/62	Manchester, VA	DOD		ROH,SA1
Roberts, William	Pvt.	D	5th SCVI		UN	09/15/63	Chattanooga, TN	KIA	(NI SA3,JR=Co.B))	ROH,JR
Roberts, William	Pvt.	B	16th SCVI		GE	07/25/62	Adams Run, SC	DOD		16R,PP
Roberts, William E.	Pvt.	C	16th SCVI		GE	11/30/64	Franklin, TN	DOW	Macgavock C. Fr'kln GV#32	16R,WCT,PP
Roberts, Wilson A.	Pvt.	F	11th SCVI		BT	06/04/65	Pt. Lookout, MD	DIP	C.C. Pt. Lookout, MD	FPH,P6,P115,HA
Robertson, C.E.	Pvt.	E	14th SCVI		LS	/ /	Richmond, VA	KIA		CGS
Robertson, Christopher	Pvt.	B	18th SCVI	45	UN	08/19/64	Petersburg, VA		Blandford Church Pbg., VA	ROH,BLC,PP
Robertson, D.J.B.	Pvt.	E	Orr's Ri.		PS	06/30/62	Gaines' Mill, VA	DOW	Craig Gvyd, Pickens, SC	PCS
Robertson, E.H.	Pvt.	G	2nd SCVI		KW	05/26/64	Spotsylvania, VA	DOW	Spotsylvania C.H., VA	SCH,SA2,HIC,KE
Robertson, E.R.	Pvt.	K	4th SCVC		FD	10/01/64	Peebles' Farm VA	KIA		ROH,CLD
Robertson, Henry	Pvt.	E	14th SCVI		LS	/ /		DOD		CGS
Robertson, Isam	Pvt.	C	22nd SCVI		SG	10/15/64	Elmira, NY	DIP	(? Dup of Robinson, J.E.)	ROH
Robertson, J.	Pvt.	H	22nd SCVI		GE	11/20/64	Richmond, VA		Hollywood Cem.Rchmd. W497	HC
Robertson, J.H.	Pvt.	G	18th SCVI		UN	11/27/64	Richmond, VA		Hollywood Cem.Rchmd. W727	ROH,HC
Robertson, John M.	Pvt.	F	2nd SCVI	28	ED	05/08/64	Wilderness, VA	DOW	Fredericksburg C.C. R6S13	ROH,SA2,FBG
Robertson, Jonathan	Pvt.	F	2nd SCV			11/09/62	Staunton, VA	DOD	Thornrose C. Staunton, VA	H2,TOD
Robertson, L.B.	Pvt.	D	1st SCVA			02/13/63	Charleston, SC	DOD	Magnolia Cem. Charleston	ROH,MAG,RCD
Robertson, Lee	Pvt.	E	14th SCVI		LS	05/12/64	Spotsylvania, VA	KIA		CGS
Robertson, Nathan B.	Pvt.	E	Orr's Ri.	19	PS	06/30/62	Gaines' Mill, VA	DOW	Oakwood C.#21,Row A,Div C	ROH,OWC,CDC
Robertson, Richard	5th Sgt.	G	3rd SCVI	29	LS	11/30/63	Knoxville, TN	DOW		ROH,SA2,KEB,CD
Robertson, S.F.	Pvt.		19th SCVI			/ /	Richmond, VA		(Exchgd POW?)	ROH
Robertson, Thomas L.	Pvt.	I	14th SCVI	21	AE	02/03/63	Fredericksburg	DOD		ROH
Robertson, Vaughan	Pvt.	F	23rd SCVI		CR	08/30/62	2nd Manassas, VA	KIA		ROH,CDC,HHC
Robertson, W.	Pvt.	C	1st SC			/ /	Charlottesville		Univ. Cem. Charlottesville	ACH
Robertson, William	Pvt.	F	5th SCRes	42		12/24/62	Adams Run, SC	DOD		PP
Robertson, William G.	Pvt.	F	12th SCVI		FD	12/03/63			Stonewall C. Winchester VA	ROH,WIN
Robertson,Jr., Alexander	Pvt.	K	4th SCVC		CN	05/28/64	Hawes Shop, VA	KIA		ROH,CDC,CLD
Robeson, Jacob	Pvt.	K	Orr's Ri.	23	AN	04/06/65		DOD		ROH
Robeson, Jacob B.	Pvt.	K	1st SC Res			04/14/65	Charleston, SC	DOD	Magnolia Cem Charleston	MAG,RCD
Robin, Jackson	Pvt.	E	13th SCVI		SG	/ /	Mt. Jackson, VA	DOD	Mt. Jackson, VA	CV,SHS

SOUTH CAROLINA DEAD IN CSA SERVICE 1861-1865

NAME	RANK	C	REGIMENT	AGE	DS	DIED	WHERE	WHY	BURIED	SOURCES
Robins, F.G.	Pvt.	H	Ham.Leg.		RD	11/05/62			Stonewall C. Winchester VA	WIN
Robins, S.A.	Pvt.	C	11th SCVI		CN	08/31/62	Lynchburg, VA		Lynchburg CSA Cem.#2 R4	BBW
Robinson, A.W.	Pvt.	C	12th SCVI		FD	/ /	Lynchburg, VA	DOD	Lynchburg CSA Cem.#5 R3	HFC,BBW
Robinson, Abe	Pvt.	A	3rd SCVI		LS	01/25/63	Richmond, VA	DOW	(Wdd Fbg 12/13/62) UD3	ROH,JR,SA2,RHL
Robinson, Albert B.	Pvt.	D	Ham. Leg.	18	AN	07/21/61	1st Manassas, VA	KIA		ROH,JR,GRS,CDC
Robinson, Allen J.	Pvt.	I	17th SCVI		LR	11/08/64	Elmira, NY	DIP	Woodlawn N.C.#781 Elmira	FPH,P6,P120,LAN
Robinson, Arthur	Cpl.	K	4th SCVC	22	CN	05/28/64	Hawes Shop, VA	KIA	2nd P.C. Charleston, SC	ROH,MAG,CDC,CLD
Robinson, B.E.	Pvt.	C	6th SCVI		KW	/ /		DOD		HIC
Robinson, C.S.	Pvt.	L	P.S.S.			06/30/62	Frayser's Farm	KIA		ROH,JR,CDC
Robinson, Charles L.D.	Pvt.	B	1st SCVIH		OG	11/15/62	At home	DOW	(Wdd 8/30 2nd Man)	ROH,JR,SA1,JRH
Robinson, Clarence	Pvt.			15	ED	07/01/62	Malvern Hill, VA	KIA		ROH
Robinson, Franklin	Cpl.	B	18th SCVAB			11/05/62	Charleston, SC	DOD	Magnolia Cem. Charleston	ROH,MAG
Robinson, G.W.M.	Pvt.	A	2nd SCVIRi		AE	/ /	Richmond, VA		(Rchmd effects list 1/63)	ROH,CDC
Robinson, George	Pvt.	C	2nd SCVI		RD	11/21/62	Richmond, VA	DOD	(H2=Co, D)	SA2,H2
Robinson, H.W.	Pvt.	C	19th SCVI		ED	11/27/62	Atlanta, GA	DOD	Oakland C. Atlanta R8#1	BGA
Robinson, Henry	Pvt.	C	6th SCVC	33		05/23/63	Adams Run, SC	DOD		PP
Robinson, Hilton	Pvt.	F	26th SCVI			03/04/64	Charleston, SC	DOD		CDC
Robinson, Hugh Y.	Sgt.	E	15th SCVI	24	FD	07/06/63	Gettysburg, PA	DOW	(Wdd 7/2/63)	ROH,JR,GDR,KEB
Robinson, J.A.	Pvt.	K	17th SCVI		YK	/ /	Petersburg, VA		(ROH=Robertson)	ROH,YEB
Robinson, J.E.	Pvt.	C	22nd SCVI		SG	10/01/64	Elmira, NY	DIP	Woodlawn N.C.#412 Elmira	FPH,CDC,P65,P120
Robinson, J.O.	Pvt.	E	1st SCVIR		CN	06/12/63	Ft. Moultrie, SC	DOD		SA1
Robinson, J.P.	Pvt.	I	12th SCVI		LR	08/29/62	2nd Manassas, VA	KIA		JR,LAN
Robinson, J.T.	Pvt.	E	5th SCV			/ /	Richmond, VA		Oakwood C.#32,Row G,Div E	OWC
Robinson, Jabez P.R.	Sgt.	C	7th SCVI	22	AE	06/29/62	Savage Stn., VA	KIA		ROH,JR,CDC,KEB
Robinson, James B.	Pvt.	G	6th SCVI		FD	/ /	Virginia		(1861)	ROH,HFC
Robinson, James F.	1st Sgt.	H	7th SCVI		ED	09/13/62	Maryland Hts. MD	KIA		ROH,JR,EDN,RME
Robinson, James T.	Pvt.	H	4th SCVI	32	PS	01/25/62	Charlottesville	DOD	Peter's Creek B.C. PS Cty.	SA2,UD2
Robinson, John	Pvt.	C	2nd SCVA	30	OG	06/15/64	At home	DOD		ROH
Robinson, John Barnes	Sgt.	H	7th SCVIBn	22	FD	05/16/64	Drury's Bluff VA	KIA	(Color Sgt.)	ROH,HAG
Robinson, John S.	Cpl.	H	7th SCVIBn	35	FD	05/10/64	Drury's Bluff VA	DOW		ROH,HAG
Robinson, John Simmons	Pvt.	D	5th SCVC	23	CN	10/19/62	Green Pond, SC	DOD	Magnolia Cem. Charleston	ROH,MAG
Robinson, John T. (C.?)	Pvt.	A	5th SCVI		LR	08/01/62	Richmond, VA	DOD	Hollywood Cem.Rchmd. Q197	JR,HC,LAN,SA3
Robinson, L.B.	Pvt.	D	6th SCVI		CR	11/03/62	Staunton, VA		Thornrose C. Staunton, VA	ROH,TOD
Robinson, Larkin	Pvt.	D	6th SCVI	31	YK	/ /	At home	DOD	(Dup of L.B.?)	YEB
Robinson, M.	Pvt.	F	26th SCVI			02/22/65	Richmond, VA	DOD		ROH
Robinson, M.C.	Cpl.	D	1st SCVC	30	CR	01/15/63	Stevensburg, VA	DOD		ROH,HHC
Robinson, Nathaniel	Pvt.	F	23rd SCVI		CR	08/30/62	2nd Manassas, VA	KIA		JR,HHC
Robinson, Robert R.	Cpl.	G	P.S.S.	24	YK	06/19/64	Petersburg, VA	KIA		ROH,YEB
Robinson, S.	Pvt.	D	7th SCVI			09/13/62	Maryland Hts. MD	KIA		ROH,JR
Robinson, S.A.	Pvt.	A	25th SCVI		CN	/ /		DOD		ROH,HAG,WLI
Robinson, S.J.	Pvt.		Brook's LA			/ /	Shepherdstown VA	DOW	Shepherdstown, VA C.C. AP6	ROH,CV,BOD
Robinson, Samuel J.	2nd Lt.	I	2nd SCVI		CN	09/17/62	Sharpsburg, VA	KIA	2nd P.C. Charleston, SC	ROH,JR,MAG,SA2
Robinson, Samuel J.	Pvt.	B	3rd SCVI		SG	12/13/62	Fredericksburg	KIA	(KEB=Robertson)	ROH,JR,SA2,HOS
Robinson, Smith	Pvt.				AE	01/12/64	Petersburg, VA	DOW	Blandford Church Pbg., VA	BLC
Robinson, T.J.	Pvt.	E	P.S.S.		SR	08/23/64		DOW		ROH
Robinson, Thomas A.	Pvt.	G	14th SCVI	20	AE	08/06/64	Petersburg, VA	KIA	Blandford Church Pbg., VA	ROH,BLC,PP
Robinson, W.H.	Pvt.	E	14th SCVI		LS	05/03/64	Richmond, VA		(CGS=Robertson)	ROH
Robinson, W.S.B.	Pvt.	A	18th SCVI		UN	10/28/64	Pt. Lookout, MD	DIP	C.C. Pt. Lookout, MD	FPH,P5,P125,BLM
Robinson, W.T.	3rd Cpl.	H	6th SCVI		YK	12/20/61	Dranesville, VA	KIA		ROH,JR,CDC,R46
Robinson, William	Pvt.	H	Ham.Leg.		RD	01/16/64	Camp Morton, IN	DIP	Green Lawn C. Indianapolis	FPH,CV
Robinson, William D.	Pvt.		Hart's Bty	27	BL	01/23/65	Kitrell Ss, NC	DOW	C.C. Kitrell Springs, NC	ROH,CNM,CDC

SOUTH CAROLINA DEAD IN CSA SERVICE 1861-1865

NAME	RANK	C REGIMENT	AGE	DS	DIED	WHERE	WHY	BURIED	SOURCES
Robinson, William F.T.	Pvt.	I 12th SCVI		LR	/ /	Virginia	DOD		LAN
Robinson, William J.	Pvt.	I 17th SCVI		LR	08/06/64	Clay's Farm, VA	DOW	Hollywood Cem.Rchmd. V532	ROH,HC,LAN
Roche, William	Pvt.	D 22nd SCVI		PS	06/16/62	Secessionville	KIA		PP
Rochelle, J.A.	Pvt.	I 24th SCVI	17	ED	11/30/64	Franklin, TN	KIA	Williamson Cty, TN C.C.	ROH,WCT,CDC,PP
Rochester, J.S.	Pvt.	L 7th SCVI		HY	09/13/62	Maryland Hts. MD	KIA		ROH,JR
Rochester, James	Pvt.	K 12th SCVI	28	PS	11/15/62	At home	DOD		ROH
Rochester, M.A.	Pvt.	A 1?th SCVI		CN	/ /	Richmond, VA		Oakwood C.#89,Row A,Div C	ROH,OWC
Rochester, William	Pvt.	K 16th SCVI		GE	09/12/64	Rock Island, IL	DIP	C.C.#1498 Rock Island, IL	FPH,P5,16R
Rochester, William	Pvt.	A 16th SCVI		GE	/ /	At home	DOD	(On active duty ?)	16R
Rockley, W.	Pvt.	A 20th SCVI		PS	06/18/64	Richmond, VA		Hollywood Cem.Rchmd. U330	HC
Rockwell, J.H.	Pvt.	F Hol.Leg.			06/15/64	Pt. Lookout, MD	DIP		P6,P113
Roddy, Nathaniel	Pvt.	F 13th SCVI		SG	12/13/62	Fredericksburg	KIA	(HOS= Matthew)	ROH,JR,HOS
Roddy, T.E.	1st Sgt.	H 12th SCVI	22	YK	09/18/61		DOD		CWC,YEB
Roden, John D.	Pvt.	B 5th SCVI		CR	09/30/64	Chattanooga, TN	DOW	(In enemy hands 9/25/64)	ROH,JR,SA3
Rodgen, Josiah	Pvt.	D 19th SCVI		ED	/ /	Chattanooga, TN	DOD	(1863)	HOE
Rodgers, Arthur	Pvt.	Ham.Leg.		SG	05/31/62	7 Pines, VA	KIA		HOS
Rodgers, C.E.J.	Pvt.	18th SCVI			08/30/62	2nd Manassas, VA	KIA	Manassas CSA Cem.	CDC
Rodgers, Daniel M.	1st Lt.	G 3rd SCVABn	27		02/15/64		DOD	(R44=RES 11/21/63)	ROH,R44
Rodgers, Duff	Pvt.	D Ham.Leg.		UN	01/17/64	Danbridge, TN	KIA	(Dandridge ?)	ROH,GRS
Rodgers, E.J. (C.R.?)				SG	/ /	Shepherdstown VA	DOW	Shepherdstown, VA C.C.AP3	ROH
Rodgers, G.W.	Cpl.	F Ham.Leg.		GE	10/28/63	Lookout Valley	KIA	(JR=Racoon Mtn., TN)	ROH,JR,CDC
Rodgers, J.H.	Pvt.	A 25th SCVI		SR	08/30/64	Petersburg, VA	DOW	(Wdd 8/21/64)	ROH
Rodgers, J.R.	Pvt.	H 12th SCVI	46	YK	03/15/62	At home	DOD	(YEB=Discharged)	CWC,YEB
Rodgers, James Dickinson	Pvt.	A 7th SCVIBn	21	KW	05/20/64	Drury's Bluff VA	DOW	(Wdd 5/16)	ROH,HIC,HAG
Rodgers, Jesse	5th Sgt.	K 26th SCVI	28	HY	05/20/64	Clay's Farm, VA	KIA		ROH,TOD
Rodgers, Josiah	Pvt.	K 1st SCVIH		OG	06/21/65	Pt. Lookout, MD	DIP	C.C. Pt. Lookout, MD	FPH,P6,P115,SA
Rodgers, L.P.	Pvt.	G 27th SCVI	42	GE	03/26/65	Chester, SC	DOD	New Harmony B.C. GE Cty.	GEC,HAG,P65,P1
Rodgers, Micajah	Pvt.	B 6th SCVI		CR	08/06/61	Culpepper, VA	DOD	Fairview Cem. Culpepper VA	JR,CGH,HHC,GLS
Rodgers, P.	Pvt.	A 1st SCSSBn			07/31/63	Georgetown, SC	DOD		PP
Rodgers, Shadrack C.	Pvt.	A 7th SCVIBn	19	KW	07/03/64	Drury's Bluff VA	DOW	(Wdd 5/16/64)	ROH,HIC,HAG
Rodgers, W.D.	Pvt.	C Orr's Ri.		PS	07/04/62	Richmond, VA		Hollywood Cem.Rchmd. M454	ROH,HC
Rodgers, William	Pvt.	K Hol.Leg.	19		09/20/62	Staunton, VA	DOW	(Wdd 2nd Man)	ROH
Rodgers, William	Pvt.	I 25th SCVI		CL	05/16/64	Drury's Bluff VA	KIA		ROH,HAG,CDC
Rodgers, William Andrew	Pvt.	F 15th SCVI		UN	09/24/62	Winchester, VA	DOD	Stonewall C. Winchester VA	ROH,JR,WIN,KEB
Rodman, Alexander K.	Pvt.	H 24th SCVI	37	CR	01/01/64	Nashville, TN	DIP	Nashville Cem. 9V547	EJM,P6,HHC,CB
Rodman, Charles E.	Pvt.	C 15th SCVAB			08/23/63	Bty. Wagner, SC	DOW		CDC
Roe, Absolom	Pvt.	D 7th SCVIBn	18	KW	02/15/62	Charleston, SC	DOD		ROH,HIC,HAG
Roe, Erwin	Pvt.	E 13th SCVI		SG	/ /	Richmond, VA		(1863)	HOS
Roe, William F.	Pvt.	B 7th SCVIBn	22	FD	10/17/63	Charleston, SC	DOD	Magnolia Cem. Charleston	ROH,MAG,HAG,RC
Roebuck, Isaac	Pvt.	G Hol.Leg.		NY	/ /	At home	DOD		ANY
Roebuck, James V.	Cpl.	B 1st SCVIG	27	NY	09/03/62	Warrenton, VA	DOW	(Wdd 2nd Man)	ROH,JR,SA1,ANY
Roebuck, Jerry H.	Pvt.	E Hol.Leg.	23	SG	09/27/62	Warrenton, VA	DOW	(Wdd 2nd Man)	ROH,HOS
Roebuck, Jesse J.	Pvt.	K 3rd SCVI	21	SG	09/27/61	Lynchburg, VA	DOD	(JR=Richmond)	ROH,JR,HOS,SA2
Roebuck, Thomas	Pvt.			NY	/ /				ANY
Roebuck, William P.	Pvt.	K 3rd SCVI	29	SG	05/17/64	Spotsylvania, VA	DOW	Spotsylvania C.H., VA	ROH,SCH,SA2,KE
Rogers, Cade	Pvt.	McQueens A			10/30/64	Richmond, VA	DOD		ROH,CDC
Rogers, Carey	Pvt.	L 21st SCVI		MN	08/25/64	Petersburg, VA		Blandford Church Pbg., VA	ROH,HMC,BLC,PP
Rogers, D.S.	Pvt.	E 6th SCVC		LS	06/22/64	Nance's Shop, VA	KIA		ROH
Rogers, David	Pvt.	B 16th SCVI		GE	/ /	Adams Run, SC	DOD	(1862)	16R
Rogers, David	Pvt.	1st SC			/ /	Alexandria, VA	DOW	Christ Ch. Alexandria, VA	CV
Rogers, Dennis B.	Pvt.	E 1st SCVIG		MN	07/28/64	Deep Bottom, VA	KIA	(Escaped from Pt.L.O.)	HMC,SA1,P125

SOUTH CAROLINA DEAD IN CSA SERVICE 1861-1865

NAME	RANK	C REGIMENT	AGE	DS	DIED	WHERE	WHY	BURIED	SOURCES
Rogers, E. Dawkins	Sgt. Major	18th SCVI	22	UN	08/30/62	2nd Manassas, VA	KIA		ROH,CDC,UD3
Rogers, Ebenezer	Sgt.	L 8th SCVI		MN	07/08/63	Gettysburg, PA	DOW		ROH,JR,GDR,HMC
Rogers, Edward Eben	Pvt.	H Orr's Ri.		MN	/ /	Virginia	DOD (1862)		HMC,CDC
Rogers, Frank M.	Pvt.	E 7th SCVI		ED	09/13/62	Maryland Hts. MD	KIA (JR= Rodgers)		ROH,JR,HOE,UD3
Rogers, Hinyard	Pvt.	C 26th SCVI		MN	03/24/64	Charleston, SC	DOD		ROH,HMC,CDC
Rogers, Hobby	Pvt.	A 1st Bn SCT		SG	/ /	Combahee River	DOD		HOS
Rogers, Hugh G. (Huger?)	2nd Lt.	H Orr's Ri.		MN	09/30/64	Jones' Farm, VA	KIA		ROH,BOS,HMC,R45
Rogers, I.S.	Sgt.	F 14th SCVI		LS	08/14/64	Richmond, VA		Hollywood Cem.Rchmd. V587	ROH,HC
Rogers, J.	Sgt.	K 26th SCVI			05/20/64	Virginia	KIA		ROH
Rogers, J. Newton	Pvt.	G 7th SCVI	23	AE	11/29/61	Culpepper, VA	DOD	Fairview Cem. Culpepper VA	JR,CGH,ROH
Rogers, J.A. (A.J.?)	Pvt.	F Orr's Ri.		PS	08/10/62	Richmond, VA		Hollywood Cem.Rchmd. Q102	ROH,HC,CDC
Rogers, J.B.	Pvt.	F 21st SCVI		MO	/ /	Virginia	KIA (1864)		ROH
Rogers, J.L.	Pvt.	D 10th SCVI		MN	/ /	Gainesville, AL	DOD	Gainesville, AL	RAS,HMC,TOD
Rogers, J.M.	Pvt.	E 14th SCVI		LS	10/07/61	Camp Butler, SC	DOD (Measles)		JR,CGS
Rogers, James	Pvt.	C 22nd SCVI		SG	/ /	At home			ROH,HOS
Rogers, James	Pvt.	Boyce's By			09/17/62	Sharpsburg, MD	DOW		ROH,JR,CDC
Rogers, James	Pvt.	E 1st SCVIG		MN	07/28/64	Deep Bottom, VA	KIA (SA1= POW 7/28/64)		HMC,SA1
Rogers, James H.	Pvt.	A 21st SCVI		CN	09/14/64	Petersburg, VA			ROH,HAG
Rogers, Jasper G.	Pvt.	H 7th SCVIBn			05/16/64	Drury's Bluff VA	KIA		ROH,HAG
Rogers, John	Pvt.	G 18th SCVI	28	YK	07/30/64	Crater, Pbg., VA	KIA		ROH,BLM,YEB
Rogers, John	Pvt.	H 23rd SCVI		MN	/ /	Virginia			HMC
Rogers, John J.	Pvt.	L 8th SCVI		MN	06/29/62	Savage Stn., VA	KIA (JR=Malvern Hill 7/1)		ROH,JR,HMC,KEB
Rogers, Joseph	Pvt.	H Orr's Ri.		MN	/ /	Sullivans I., SC	DOD (1862)		HMC,CDC
Rogers, Joseph B.	Pvt.	H Orr's Ri.		MN	/ /	Virginia	DOD (1862)		HMC,CDC
Rogers, Joseph S.	Pvt.	K 3rd SCVI		SG	09/20/63	Chickamauga, GA	DOW	Con. Cem. Marietta, GA	ROH,SA2,HOS,CCM
Rogers, Matthew	Pvt.	K 3rd SCVI	29	SG	09/13/62	Maryland Hts. MD	KIA	KEB	ROH,JR,SA2,HOS
Rogers, Owen M.	Pvt.	L 21st SCVI	30	MN	06/16/64	Petersburg, VA	KIA (HMC= Darbytown Rd.)		ROH,HMC,HAG
Rogers, Robin	Pvt.	C 18th SCVAB		MN	/ /	Charleston, SC	DOD		HMC
Rogers, Sanford V.	Pvt.	C 22nd SCVI	27	SG	10/31/64	Elmira, NY	DIP	Woodlawn N.C.#749 Elmira	ROH,FPH,HOS,P65
Rogers, Thomas	Sgt.	F 23rd SCVI		CR	11/19/62	Staunton, VA		(HHC=A, 17th SCVI)	ROH
Rogers, Thomas G.	Pvt.	I 21st SCVI		MN	02/16/65	Elmira, NY	DIP	Woodlawn N.C.#2188 Elmira	FPH,HMC,HAG,P65
Rogers, Timothy	Pvt.	H 23rd SCVI		MN	12/13/62	Kinston, NC	KIA		ROH,HMC,CDC,PP
Rogers, W.D. (Rodgers?)					/ /		(Rchmd effects list 12/62)		CDC
Rogers, W.F.	Pvt.	Gregg's By			07/30/64	Petersburg, VA	KIA		CDC
Rogers, W.S.	Pvt.	H 23rd SCVI		MN	08/05/62	Petersburg, VA	DOD	Blandford Church Pbg., VA	ROH,HMC,BLC,PP
Rogers, William	Pvt.	C 26th SCVI		MN	/ /	Jackson, MS	KIA		HMC
Rogers, William C.	Pvt.	H Orr's Ri.		MN	12/13/62	Fredericksburg	KIA		HMC,CDC
Rogers, William M.	1st Lt.	K 15th SCVI	36	AE	10/18/63	Rome, GA	DOW	Willington Cem. AE	ROH,R47,KEB
Rogers, William W.	Pvt.	H Orr's Ri.		MN	12/13/62	Fredericksburg	KIA (HMC=TFD in 1862)		JR,CDC,HMC
Rogers, Zadock	Pvt.	C 22nd SCVI	40	SG	08/04/62	Charleston, SC	DOD (ROH=Fedric)		ROH,JR,HOS
Roland, Henry	Pvt.	D 15th SCRes		LN	/ /		(1865)		ROH
Roland, John N.	Pvt.	I 1st SC			11/10/64	Baltimore, MD	DIP	Loudon Park Cem. Balto MD	CV,P1
Roland, Jonas B.	Pvt.	G 13th SCVI			08/29/62	Laurel Hill, VA	(2nd M?)		JR
Role, James	Pvt.	K 23rd SCVI		SR	/ /	Petersburg, VA	KIA		K23
Roller, John	4th Cpl.	D 26th SCVI		MO	06/16/62	Secessionville	KIA		HOM
Rollins, C.W. (G.W.?)	Pvt.	D 8th SCVI		CD	12/13/61	Charlottesville	DOD	Univ. Cem. Charlottesville	JR,ACH,KEB
Rollins, J.C.	Pvt.	D 8th SCVI		CD	10/25/62	Staunton, VA	DOD	Thornrose C. Staunton, VA	ROH,JR,KEB,TOD
Rollins, James	Pvt.	E 9th SCVIBn	26		03/04/62	Georgetown, SC	DOD		PP
Rollins, L.P.	Pvt.	G 24th SCVI			12/24/63	Rock Island, IL	DIP	C.C.#53 Rock Island, IL	FPH,P5
Rollins, R. Baxter	Pvt.	PeeDee LA		DN	09/20/62	Sharpsburg, MD	DOW (In enemy hands)		ROH,PDL,SA1,CV
Rollins, T.J.	Pvt.	K 5th SCVI		SG	05/30/62	Williamsburg, VA	KIA		JR,SA3,HOS

SOUTH CAROLINA DEAD IN CSA SERVICE 1861-1865

NAME	RANK	C	REGIMENT	AGE	DS	DIED	WHERE	WHY	BURIED	SOURCES
Rollins, Theophilus	Pvt.	I	18th SCVI	35	DN	09/02/64	Elmira, NY	DIP	Woodlawn N.C.#75 Elmira	ROH,FPH,P5,P65
Rollins, Thomas	Pvt.	C	1st SCVIR		CN	06/23/65	Unknown	DIP	Cypress Hills N.C.#3048 NY	FPH,SA1
Rollins, W. Lewis P.	Sgt. Major	B	1st SCVCBn	17	DN	04/06/62	Camp Lookout, SC	DOD	(CNM=Col. Nesbitt's)	PP,CNM
Rollins, W.R.A.	Pvt.	H	2nd SCVI	20	LR	06/28/62	Richmond, VA	DOD	(NI SA2,ROH=Rallings)	ROH,LAN
Rollison, Benjamin G.	2nd Lt.	K	Orr's Ri.	32	AN	09/30/64	Jones' Farm, VA	KIA		ROH,BOS,R45
Roman, Morris	Pvt.		Wagner's A		CN	09/29/64	Charleston, SC		Magnolia Cem. Charleston	MAG,RCD
Roney, Newton	Pvt.	A	1st SCVIG		BL	12/06/61	Suffolk, VA	DOD	(Dropsy)	JR,SA1
Roney, Patrick	Pvt.	A	17th SCVI	21	CR	07/30/64	Crater, Pbg., VA	KIA		ROH,BLM,HHC,CB
Roof, David	Pvt.	D	15th SCVI		LN	/ /			(1865)	ROH
Roof, Thomas E. (Ruff?)	Pvt.	H	20th SCVI		LN	08/13/62		DOD		ROH,KEB
Rook, Franklin	Pvt.	B	15th SCVI		SG	09/14/62	South Mtn., MD	KIA	(Prob MD Hts. 9/13)	ROH,JR,HOS,KEB
Rook, James	Pvt.	B	15th SCVI		SG	/ /		KIA		HOS,KEB
Rook, Permain	Pvt.	K	21st SCVI		DN	04/03/65	Elmira, NY	DIP	Woodlawn N.C.#2564 Elmira	FPH
Rook, Samuel L.	Pvt.	A	27th SCVI			01/16/65	Elmira, NY	DIP	Woodlawn N.C.#1446 Elmira	FPH,P1,P6,P65
Roon, S.A.	Pvt.					/ /			Fredericksburg C.C. R6S13	FBG
Rooper, T.L.	Pvt.	B	37th VAVCB		PS	03/01/65	Pt. Lookout, MD	DIP	C.C. Pt. Lookout, MD	P6
Roper, Charles B.	Pvt.	B	6th SCVC		ED	10/15/64	At home	DOD		ROH,HOE,UD3
Roper, D.	Cpl.		Orr's Ri.		PS	10/16/64	Richmond, VA		Hollywood Cem.Rchmd. V196	HC
Roper, David	2nd Cpl.	K	2nd SCVIRi	26	PS	09/30/64	Ft. Harrison, VA	KIA	(Roper,D.Orr's in HC?)	ROH
Roper, David F.	Pvt.	F	7th SCVI	32	PS	10/27/62	Staunton, VA	DOD		ROH,PCS
Roper, John W.	Pvt.	B	19th SCVI	18	ED	09/20/63	Chickamauga, GA	KIA	(10th Co. 10/19th Consol)	ROH,JR,HOE,CDC
Ropp, Arthur S.	Pvt.				NY	/ /	Ft. Sumter, SC	KIA	(At one time in F,20th)	ANY,KEB
Ropp, Ivy	Pvt.	G	Hol.Leg.		NY	/ /		DOD		ANY
Rosamond, James F.	2nd Lt.		4th SCVIBn		GE	07/18/62	Manchester, VA	DOW	(Wdd. @ Gaines' Mill)	JR,SA2,CNM
Rosborough, John	3rd Sgt.	E	5th SCVI	28	YK	06/30/62	Frayser`s Farm	KIA	(JR=3rd SCVI)	JR,SA3,YMD,YEB
Rose, Alexander	Lt. (ADC)		G. Gadsden	24	CN	03/24/63	Jackson, MS	DOD	Unitarian C. Charleston	MAG,PP
Rose, J. Alexander	Pvt.	B	7th SCVIBn	28	FD	05/16/64	Drury's Bluff VA	KIA		ROH,HFC,HAG
Rose, Joseph	Sgt.	C	12th SCVI		FD	07/02/63	Gettysburg, PA	KIA	(Commissary Sgt. per HFC)	ROH,JR,GDR,HFC
Rose, Joseph H. (Rowe?)	Pvt.	B	24th SCVI		MO	/ /		DIP	(P@ Egypt Stn. MS 2/19/64)	ROH
Rose, Samuel C.	5th Cpl.	C	12th SCVI		FD	06/10/62	Richmond, VA	DOD	Hollywood Cem.Rchmd. P205	ROH,HC,HFC
Rose, William N.	1st Lt.	K	16th SCVI		GE	11/30/64	Franklin, TN	KIA	Macgavock C. Frkln Gv# 18	ROH,16R,WCT,PP
Rose, Willoughby C.	Pvt.	B	7th SCVIBn	26	FD	07/29/64	Petersburg, VA	KIA	(HFC=W.B.)	ROH,HFC,HAG
Rosier, J.	Pvt.	B	1st Eng Cp			/ /	Richmond, VA		Oakwood C.#51,Row G,Div G	ROH,OWC
Ross, David A.	Pvt.	E	Orr's Ri.	26	PS	06/27/62	Gaines' Mill, VA	KIA		ROH,JR,CDC
Ross, Donald J.	Pvt.	D	2nd SCVI		SR	11/28/62	At home	DOD		SA2,KEB,H2
Ross, J. Newton	1st Lt.	I	8th SCVI		MN	07/28/64	Deep Bottom, VA	DOW	Hopewell Cem. Florence, SC	HMC,KEB,R46,UD
Ross, James A.	2nd Lt.	A	25th SCVI		CN	08/21/64	Ream's Stn., VA	KIA	Old Scotch P.C. Charleston	ROH,HAG,R47
Ross, James S.	Pvt.	B	5th SCVI	26	YK	05/31/62	7 Pines, VA	DOW	Oakwood C.#47,Row N,Div B	JR,SA3,OWC,YEB
Ross, John	Pvt.	B	1st SCVIR		LR	10/03/64	Charleston, SC	DOD		ROH,SA1,LAN
Ross, John Henry	Pvt.	K	20th SCVI		PS	02/02/62	Pickens, SC	DOD	Old Pickens P.C.	OCS
Ross, Julius A.	Lt.			25	AN	/ /	VA	KIA	(1864)	ROH
Ross, M. Calvin	Pvt.	A	12th SCVI	27	YK	08/30/62	2nd Manassas, VA	KIA	(JR=8/29/62)	ROH,JR,CDC,YEB
Ross, Thomas Mallory	Pvt.	F	2nd SCVI	31	AE	05/15/62	Manchester, VA	DOD		ROH,SA2,KEB,H2
Ross, Wiley N.	Pvt.	F	2nd SCVI	17	AE	07/15/62	Richmond, VA	DOD		ROH,SA1,KEB
Ross, Wiley W.	3rd Lt.	F	16th SCVI		GE	/ /	Selma, AL	DOD		16R
Ross, William M.	Pvt.	D	5th SCVI		SG	05/26/64	Orange C.H., VA	DOW	(Wdd Wilderness 5/6/64)	ROH,SA3,HOS
Rosser,	Lt.					/ /			Fredericksburg C.C. R8S12	FBG
Rosser, D.F.	Pvt.	F	7th SCVI			10/26/62	Staunton, VA		Thornhill C. Staunton, VA	TOD
Rotherick, J.I.	Pvt.	K	1st SCVC			09/27/64	Charleston, SC		Magnolia Cem. Charleston	MAG,RCD
Rothrock, J.H.	Pvt.	F	Hol.Leg.	18	AE	06/15/64	Pt. Lookout, MD	DIP	C.C. Pt. Lookout, MD	ROH,FPH
Rothschild, Benjamin	Pvt.	B	Orr's Ri.	30	AE	08/29/62	2nd Manassas, VA	KIA		ROH,JR,CDC,ALH

R

SOUTH CAROLINA DEAD IN CSA SERVICE 1861-1865

NAME	RANK	C REGIMENT	AGE	DS	DIED	WHERE	WHY	BURIED	SOURCES
Roton, David	Pvt.	D 6th ResBn		ED	03/19/65	Bentonville, NC	KIA		UD1
Roundtree, G.F.	Pvt.	D Hol.Leg.	27	BL	12/06/64	Petersburg, VA	KIA		ROH
Rounsey, E.	Pvt.	M Orr's Ri.		AE	/ /	Richmond, VA		Oakwood C.#22,Row L,Div C	ROH,OWC
Rountree, Joseph R.	2nd Cpl.	K 3rd SCVI	25	SG	09/25/63	Chickamauga, GA	DOW		ROH,JR,SA2,HOS
Rountree, Thomas J.	Pvt.	K 7th SCVI		ED	12/08/62	Frederick, MD	DOW	Mt.Olivet C.#180 Frederick	ROH,JR,FPH,BOD
Rourk, John E.	Pvt.	H 1st SCVIG		CN	/ /	Richmond, VA	KIA	(1862, SA1= AWOL)	ROH,SA1
Rouse, D.J.	1st Lt.	C 3rd St.Tps			/ /	Georgetown, SC	DOD	(1863)	R45
Roux, Henry P.	Pvt.	A Ham.Leg.		CN	08/30/62	2nd Manassas, VA	KIA	St. Philips Ch. Charleston	ROH,JR,RCD,WLI
Row, Louis J.	Pvt.	A 15th SCVI		RD	10/15/63	TN		(ROH=25th SCVI)	ROH,KEB
Rowan, Morris	Pvt.	Wagner's A			09/29/64	Charleston, SC	DOD	Magnolia Cem. Charleston	ROH,MAG
Rowand, Elliot	Pvt.				/ /			Magnolia Cem. Charleston	MAG
Rowe, A. Govan	Pvt.	A 1st SCVIH		OG	02/15/62	At home	DOD	(SA1=DIS before 2/28/62)	EDR,SA1
Rowe, Cornelius E.	Pvt.	D 19th SCVI	34	ED	07/24/64	Atlanta, GA	KIA		ROH,HOE
Rowe, J.	Pvt.	A 21st SCVI		GN	/ /		DIP	(POW 6/24/64,ROH=25th SC)	ROH,HAG
Rowe, Joseph H.	Pvt.	24th SCV	18		/ /	Egypt	KIA	Trnsfd from Co.G 8th SCV	UD2
Rowe, Joseph H. (Rose?)	Pvt.	B 24th SCVI		MO	/ /		DOD	(1861, TFD frm G,8th SCVI)	HOM
Rowe, William D.	Pvt.	B 24th SCVI	25	MO	/ /			(HOM=died in 1896)	
Rowell, Alfred	Pvt.	4th Mtd.Mi		BT	02/05/62	St.Luke's Par.SC	KIA	(Boyd's Ldg., Fripp's Pln)	ROH,CDC,R43,CNM
Rowell, David Albert	Pvt.	I 21st SCVI	23	MN	06/21/63	Morris Island SC	DOD		ROH,HMC,HAG
Rowell, Elihu	Pvt.	E 22nd SCVI		LR	07/16/62	Columbia, SC	DOD		PP,LAN
Rowell, James V.	5th Sgt.	H 23rd SCVI		MN	12/20/64	Elmira, NY	DIP	Woodlawn N.C.#1073 Elmira	FPH,HMC,P1,P120
Rowell, Thomas	Cpl.	D Hol.Leg.	27	BL	08/30/62	2nd Manassas, VA	KIA	(JR=Rowell, S.L.)	ROH,JR,SAS
Rowell, W.T.	Pvt.			WG	/ /		KIA		HOW
Rowell, William	Pvt.	E 22nd SCVI		LR	04/18/65	Lincoln G.H., DC	DOD	(Malaria)	P6
Rowell, William P.	Pvt.	I 21st SCVI	18	MN	05/10/64	Pt. Walthal Jctn	DOW	(Wdd 5/7/64)	ROH,HMC,HAG
Rowland, James A.	1st Sgt.	F 15th SCVI		SG	09/14/62	South Mtn., MD	KIA	(Prob MD Hts. 9/13)	ROH,JR,HOS,KEB
Rowland, Samuel C.	4th Cpl.	E Orr's Ri.	20	PS	07/10/62	Dill Springs, VA	DOD	(ROH=Roland, Daniel C.)	ROH,CDC
Rowland, William R.	5th Sgt.	C 5th SCVI		SG	05/27/64	Orange C.H., VA	DOW	(Wdd Wilderness 5/6/64)	ROH,SA3
Rowley, William	Pvt.	A Tucker's R			02/03/65	Salisbury, NC	DOD		PP
Rowley, Willis E.	Pvt.	A 3rd SCVI		SG	03/19/65	Bentonville, NC	KIA		HOS
Royal, James Peronneau	Pvt.	I 2nd SCVI	22	CN	07/01/62	Malvern Hill, VA	DOW		ROH,SA2,KEB,CDC
Royals, George L.	Pvt.	F 1st SCVIG		HY	08/03/62	Richmond, VA	DOD		ROH,JR,SA1,PDL
Royalston, L.R.	Pvt.	I 5th SCVC			06/18/64	Richmond, VA		Hollywood Cem.Rchmd. U306	HC
Royston, Joel E.	Pvt.	K 5th SCVI		SG	/ /	Petersburg, VA	KIA	(SA3=MIA since 5/6/64)	HOS,SA3
Rozier, Robert A.	Pvt.	F 11th SCVI	23	BT	05/05/64	Fts. Monroe, VA	DOW	(Wdd & POW @ Swift Creek)	ROH,HAG
Rucker, Addison					/ /			(Rchmd effects list 1/63)	CDC
Rucker, Gerhard	Pvt.	B 1st SCVIH		OG	08/16/62		DOD		ROH,SA1
Rucker, H.L.	Pvt.	B 1st SCVIH		LN	03/17/64	Rock Island, IL	DIP	C.C.#837 Rock Island, IL	FPH,P5,SA1
Rucker, Henry L.	Pvt.	F 25th SCVI		LN	10/18/64	Columbia, SC	DOW		ROH,PP,HAG
Rucker, U.S.L.	2nd Lt.	B 1st SCVIH		OG	05/06/64	Wilderness, VA	KIA	(Wdd Shpsbg & L.O. Valley)	ROH,SA1,JRH,R45
Rucker, William A.	Pvt.	H 3rd SCVI		LN	12/08/62	Richmond, VA	DOW	(SA2= lost in MD)	ROH,SA2,KEB
Rudicil, A.A.	Pvt.	D 5th SCVI		UN	09/25/62	Staunton, VA	DOW	(JR=10/25/62)	ROH,JR,SA3
Rudicil, David	1st Sgt.	F 13th SCVI		SG	12/13/62	Fredericksburg	KIA		HOS
Rudisil, M.	Pvt.	H 6th SCVC			06/11/64	Trevillian Stn.	KIA		ROH
Rudisill, G. Alexander	Cpl.	H 6th SCVCI		SG	08/19/64	Elmira, NY	DIP	Woodlawn N.C.#119 Elmira	FPH,HOS,P65,P120
Rudisill, W.V.	Cpl.	D 17th SCVI		CR	05/28/65	Elmira, NY	DIP	Woodlawn N.C.#2911 Elmira	ROH,FPH,P65,HHC
Ruff, Benjamin Franklin	Pvt.	G 24th SCVI	20		05/14/63	Jackson, MS	KIA		EJM,PP
Ruff, C.F. (C.T.?)	Pvt.	G 24th SCVI	20		05/14/63	Jackson, MS	KIA	(JR=Co.F)	ROH,JR,CDC
Ruff, D.W.	2nd Lt.	C 2nd SCVC		RD	11/01/62	Winchester, VA	DOD	Stonewall C. Winchester	ROH,WIN,R43
Ruff, J.C.	Pvt.	K 13th SCVI		LN	09/07/62	Richmond, VA			ROH
Ruff, J.J.	Pvt.	E 7th SCVI		LN	06/01/64	Richmond, VA			ROH

SOUTH CAROLINA DEAD IN CSA SERVICE 1861-1865

NAME	RANK	C REGIMENT	AGE	DS	DIED	WHERE	WHY	BURIED	SOURCES
Ruff, John J.	3rd Cpl.	B 1st SCVIG	18	NY	06/02/64	Spotsylvania, VA	DOW	Old Newberry Village Cem.	ROH,NCC,ANY,CD
Ruff, John J.	Pvt.	D 13th SCVI	22	NY	/ /	Gaines' Mill, VA	KIA		ANY
Ruff, Martin	Pvt.	H 20th SCVI		LN	/ /	Charlottesville		Univ. Cem. Charlottesville	ACH,KEB
Ruff, Reuben F.	Pvt.	E 3rd SCVI	23	NY	08/27/61	Culpepper, VA	DOD	Ruff Cem. Newberry, SC	ROH,JR,NCC,ANY
Ruff, T.E.	Pvt.	K 13th SCVI		LN	09/07/62	Richmond, VA	DOD	Oakwood C.#61,Row B,Div A	ROH,JR,OWC
Ruff, William W.	Pvt.	E 3rd SCVI		NY	07/22/64	Petersburg, VA	DOW	(Wdd 6/20/64)	ROH,SA2,ANY,KE
Rugg, Andrew Jackson	Pvt.	PeeDee LA		DN	05/15/63	Richmond, VA	DOW	(Wdd Chancellorsville 5/1)	ROH,PDL,UD4
Ruppe, Henry	Pvt.	K Hol.Leg.	27		07/04/62	Adams Run, SC	DOD		ROH
Ruppe, John W.	Pvt.	K Hol.Leg.	20		11/26/64	Richmond, VA	DOW	Hollywood Cem.Rchmd. W307	ROH,HC
Ruppe, Ward M.	Cpl.	K Hol.Leg.	22		09/09/64	Elmira, NY	DIP	Woodlawn N.C.#204 Elmira	ROH,FPH,P5,P11
Ruppe, William	Pvt.	K Hol.Leg.	28		08/03/62	Richmond, VA	DOD		ROH
Rupy, J.L.	Pvt.	G 14th SCVI		AE	06/27/62	Gaines' Mill, VA	KIA		JR
Ruse, George C.	Pvt.	C 13th SCVI		SG	08/07/62		DOD	(Typhoid)	JR
Rush, A.W.	Pvt.	I 3rd SCVI		LS	09/20/63	Chickamauga, GA	KIA	Con. Cem. Marietta, GA	ROH,JR,SA2,CCM
Rush, Andrew J.	Pvt.	A 1st SCVIR		LR	01/13/64	Pt. Lookout, MD	DIP	C.C. Pt. Lookout, MD	FPH,SA1,P5,LAN
Rush, Calvin	Pvt.	F 3rd SCVABn	25	CN	12/26/63	Adams Run, SC	DOD	(PP=age 37)	ROH,PP
Rush, Capers	Pvt.	B 11th SCVI		CO	10/22/62	Pocotaligo, SC	ACD		ROH,HAG,PP
Rush, Henry	Pvt.	H 7th SCVIBn	27	ED	08/24/64	Petersburg, VA	DOD		ROH,DOD
Rush, J.A.	Pvt.	K 10th SCVI		CN	/ /		DOD		RAS
Rush, J.G.	Pvt.	K 1st SCVC			10/03/64	Charleston, SC	DOD		ROH
Rush, J.M.	Pvt.	E P.S.S.		CL	11/15/63	Knoxville, TN	KIA		ROH
Rush, Lewis F.	Pvt.	G 25th SCVI	22	OG	06/07/64	Cold Harbor, VA	KIA		ROH,HAG,EDR
Rush, Paul D.	1st Lt.	A 5th SCVC		OG	05/24/63	At home	DOD		ROH,R43
Rush, R.H.	Pvt.	G 17th SCVI		LR	05/27/65	Lincoln G.H., DC	DOW		P6
Rush, Samuel	Pvt.	B 11th SCVI		CO	06/20/64	Cold Harbor, VA	KIA	Oakwood C.#42,Row A,Div G	ROH,OWC,HAG
Rush, Simeon	Pvt.		30	BL	/ /	New York	DOW	(POW died in NY)	ROH
Rush, Thomas	Pvt.	26th SCVI			09/14/63	Charleston, SC			ROH
Rush, Warren R.	Pvt.	G 22nd SCVI	23	AN	07/23/62	Charleston, SC	DOD		ROH
Rush, William A.	Pvt.	H 7th SCVIBn	20	ED	05/16/64	Drury's Bluff VA	KIA		ROH,HAG
Rush, William H.	Pvt.	C 7th SCVIBn		RD	04/17/65	New Bern, NC	DOW	Cedar Grove C. Newbern, NC	HAG,WAT,P1,P6,
Rushen, J.J.	Pvt.	F 26th SCVI			11/13/64	Richmond, VA		Hollywood Cem.Rchmd. W498	HC
Rushing, C.	Pvt.	E 11th SCVI		BT	/ /	Richmond, VA		Oakwood C.#96,Row H,Div G	ROH,OWC
Rushing, J.H.	Pvt.	E 11th SCVI		BT	11/20/64		DOD	(Contracted in prison)	ROH,P113,HAG
Rushing, James	Pvt.	D 25th SCVI		MN	/ /	Ft. Delaware, DE	DIP		HMC,HAG
Rushing, Samuel R.	Pvt.	E 3rd SCVC	20	BT	/ /	At home	DOD		ROH
Rushing, William	Pvt.	F 26th SCVI		BL	09/22/64	Richmond, VA		Hollywood Cem.Rchmd. V316	ROH,HC
Rushing, William H.	Pvt.	E 1st SCVIG		MN	12/13/62	Fredericksburg	KIA		ROH,JR,SA1,PDL
Rushton, Henry D.	Cpl.	M 7th SCVI		ED	09/20/63	Chickamauga, GA	KIA	(Co. M roster not in KEB)	ROH,JR,CDC,HOE
Ruskin, J.J.	Pvt.	F 26th SCVI			11/14/64	Richmond, VA			ROH
Russ, E.	Pvt.	B 10th SCVI		HY	11/25/63	Missionary Rdge	KIA		ROH,RAS
Russ, Joseph B.	Pvt.	E 10th SCVI	40	MN	01/03/63	Murfreesboro, TN	DOW	(In enemy hands)	ROH,RAS,HOW,P3
Russ, Thomas	Pvt.	A 26th SCVI	25	HY	09/15/63	Charleston, SC	DOD		ROH
Russ, Thomas B.	2nd Lt.	L 10th SCVI		MN	07/22/64	Atlanta, GA	DOW	(Slight neck wound 11/12)	ROH,RAS,CDC,CK
Russ, W.H.	Sgt.	Ham.Leg.			11/16/63	Campbell's Stn.	KIA		ROH,CDC
Russel, J.N.	Pvt.	K 8th SCVI		MO	08/30/62	Richmond, VA		Hollywood Cem.Rchmd. S70	HC
Russell, A.A.	Pvt.	E 5th SCVC	25	CN	10/17/64	Petersburg, VA	KIA		ROH
Russell, Charles S.	Sgt.	K 17th SCVI		YK	03/27/64	City Point, VA	DOW	City Pt. N.C. Hopewell, VA	PP,YEB,TOD
Russell, Eli Giles	Pvt.	I 5th SCVI		YK	04/02/63		DOD	(Consumption)	JR,YEB
Russell, H.R.	Pvt.	G 14th SCVI	20	AE	07/10/63	Richmond, VA	DOD	Oakwood C.#2, Row 31,Div D	ROH,OWC
Russell, Henry	Pvt.	D 1st SCVIR		CN	09/11/63	Charleston, SC	DOD	Magnolia Cem. Charleston	ROH,MAG,SA1,RC
Russell, J.B.	Pvt.	A Orr's Ri.		AN	09/13/64	Elmira, NNY	DIP	Woodlawn N.C.#267 Elmira	FPH,P5,P65,P11

SOUTH CAROLINA DEAD IN CSA SERVICE 1861-1865

NAME	RANK	C	REGIMENT	AGE	DS	DIED	WHERE	WHY	BURIED	SOURCES
Russell, James	Cook	C	24th SCVI		CO	11/25/63	Mission Ridge GA	KIA	(Free black)	EJM
Russell, John B.	Pvt.	G	3rd SCVIBn		LN	09/28/62			Stonewall C. Winchester VA	ROH,WIN,KEB
Russell, Josiah T.	Pvt.	I	19th SCVI	20	AE	02/21/63	Shelbyville, TN	DOD		ROH,PP
Russell, L. Fletcher	Pvt.	H	3rd SCVI	18	LN	06/29/62	Savage Stn., VA	KIA		ROH,SA2,ANY,KEB
Russell, M.B.	Pvt.	F	12th SCVI	25	FD	07/31/63	Baltimore, MD	DOW	Loudon Pk. C.A-86 Balto MD	ROH,FPH,GDR,PP
Russell, S.F.	Pvt.	H	5th SCVI			06/29/62	Savage Stn., VA	DOW	(NI SA3)	JR
Russell, Samuel O.	Pvt.	A	1st SCVC.		AE	08/05/63	Culpepper, VA	DOW	(Wdd Brandy Stn 8/1/63)	ROH,JR,R43
Russell, Sterling	Pvt.				YK	/ /	7 Pines, VA	DOW		ROH
Russell, Timothy	Pvt.	G	14th SCVI	20	AE	09/05/63	Ft. Delaware, DE	DIP	Finn's Pt., NJ Nat. Cem.	ROH,FPH,P5,P40
Russell, W.	Pvt.	F	1st SCVIH		PS	11/16/63	Campbell Stn. TN	KIA		ROH,SA1,JRH
Russell, William	Pvt.	E	11th SCVI		BT	12/15/62	South Carolina	DOD		ROH
Russell, William	Pvt.	K	17th SCVI		YK	07/30/64	Petersburg, VA	KIA		ROH
Rust, John	Pvt.	I	1st SCV			11/15/62	Gordonsville, VA		Gordonsville, VA Cem.	GOR
Rutherford, W. Drayton	Colonel		3rd SCVI	27	NY	10/13/64	Cedar Creek, VA	KIA	Rosemont Cem. Newberry, SC	ROH,NCC
Ruthven, H.G.	Pvt.		Inglis LA		DN	12/25/63	Johns Island, SC	KIA		ROH
Rutland, Ezekiel Watson	1st Lt.	B	14th SCVI	35	ED	10/18/61	At home	DOD	(Measles @ Camp Butler)	JR,HOE,R47,UD3
Rutland, George	Pvt.	L	1st SCVIG		OG	05/12/64	Spotsylvania, VA	KIA		ROH,SA1,CDC
Rutland, Michael	Pvt.	A	19th SCVI	16	ED	03/08/65	Kinston, NC	KIA		HOE,UD3
Rutland, William A.	1st Lt.	E	7th SCVI		ED	07/08/63	Gettysburg, PA	DOW	UD3	GDR,HOE,R46,KEB
Rutledge, John B.	Sgt.	B	P.S.S.		AN	06/30/62	Frayser's Farm	KIA		ROH,JR,CDC
Ryan, Benjamin G.	Sgt.	A	7th SCVI		ED	09/11/62	Sharpsburg, MD	KIA	(Left wife & 2 children)	ROH,JR,EDN,HOE
Ryan, David Rogers	2nd Sgt.	E	2nd SCVI	25	CN	07/02/63	Gettysburg, PA	KIA	Magnolia Cem. Charleston	ROH,JR,GDR,WV
Ryan, Henry J.	Pvt.	A	24th SCVI	37	CN	05/14/63	Jackson, MS	KIA		ROH,CDC,PP
Ryan, Jabez B.	Cpl.	A	Ham.Leg.		ED	01/03/62	Manassas, VA	DOD	(Cavalry Bn.)	HOE,EDN
Ryan, Thomas	Pvt.	E	25th SCVI		CN	05/07/64	Pt. Walthal Jctn	KIA	(Ryan J. in HAG ?)	ROH,CDC
Ryan, Thomas	Pvt.	H	27th SCVI		CN	/ /	Richmond, VA		Oakwood C.#41,Row C,Div G	ROH,OWC,HAG
Ryan, William H.	Cpt.	I	1st SCVIBn	32	CN	07/18/63	Bty. Wagner, SC	KIA	St.Lawrence C. Charleston	ROH,MAG,DOC,HAG
Ryan, William P.	Pvt.	A	24th SCVI	19	CN	09/20/64	Chickamauga, GA	KIA	Con. Cem. Marietta, GA	ROH,JR,CDC,CCM
Rye, William	Pvt.	D	26th SCVI		MO	03/10/64	Charleston, SC	DOD	Magnolia Cem. Charleston	ROH,MAG,CDC,RCD
Ryfield, Marion	Pvt.	G	5th SCVI		YK	12/30/62	Fredericksburg	DOD	(To Hosp 12/22/62)	JR,SA3,YEB

S

SOUTH CAROLINA DEAD IN CSA SERVICE 1861-1865

NAME	RANK	C REGIMENT	AGE	DS	DIED	WHERE	WHY	BURIED	SOURCES
S......, J.W.	Pvt.	H 6th SCVI		FD	/ /	Richmond, VA		Oakwood C.#6,Row B,Div A	OWC
S......, Y.S.	Pvt.	H 6th SCVI		FD	/ /	Richland, VA		Oakwood C.#6,Row C,Div A	OWC
Saddler, J.K.	Sgt.	F 24th SCVI	23	AN	05/14/63	Jackson, MS	KIA	(J.H.?)	ROH,JR,PP,HOL
Saddler, Willis	Pvt.	F 2nd SCVI	51	AE	01/04/64	Knoxville, TN	DOD		ROH,SA2,KEB,H2
Sadler, Isaac Newton	Pvt.	A 12th SCVI		YK	05/23/64	Bethesda Ch., VA	KIA		YMD,CDC
Sadler, John A.	Pvt.	D 7th SCVI		AN	11/05/62	Richmond, VA		Hollywood Cem.Rchmd. S14	ROH,HC
Sadler, Joseph R.	2nd Lt.	D Orr's Ri.		AN	10/07/64	Staunton, VA			R45,CDC,PP
Sadler, Kiah H.	Pvt.	K 5th SCVC	23	YK	06/11/64	Trevillian Stn.	KIA		ROH,MDM,YEB
Sadler, William	Pvt.	E 20th SCVI		OG	01/19/65	Elmira, NY	DIP	Woodlawn N.C.#1205W Elmira	FPH,KEB,P5,P65
Sale, William Augustus	Pvt.	G 1st SCVIG		ED	10/23/63	Davids Island NY	DOW	Cypress Hills N.C.#902 NY	FPH,P6,GDR,SA1
Salisbury, John	Pvt.	D 5th SCVC	29	CN	08/13/64		DOD		ROH
Salley,	Pvt.	E 1st SCVIR			09/08/63	Ft. Moultrie, SC	KIA	(Ammo chest explosion)	ROH
Salmon, Samuel J.	1st Sgt.	H Orr's Ri.		MN	08/29/62	2nd Manassas, VA	KIA		JR,HMC,CDC
Salmons, Ellis W.	5th Sgt.	G 4th SCVI	23	GE	09/18/61	Culpepper, VA	DOD	Fairview Cem. Culpepper VA	CGH,SA2
Salter, J.L.	Cpl.	A P.S.S.		AN	08/14/64	Richmond, VA	KIA	(Skirmish below Richmond)	ROH
Salter, John C.	Pvt.	D 19th SCVI	31	ED	11/30/64	Franklin, TN	KIA		HOE,UD3
Salter, Lemuel	Pvt.	D 19th SCVI	41	ED	11/30/64	Franklin, TN	KIA		PP,HOE
Salter, Thomas	Pvt.	F 18th SCVI		UN	08/30/62	2nd Manassas, VA	KIA		ROH
Salter, William R.	Pvt.	D 19th SCVI	29	ED	11/30/64	Franklin, TN	KIA		ROH,HOE
Salters, John	Pvt.	I 4th SCVC		WG	/ /		DOD		HOW
Salters, Samuel	Pvt.	B 25th SCVI	22	CN	06/16/62	Secessionville	KIA	1st Baptist Ch. Charleston	ROH,MAG,PP,WLI
Sammons, William D.	Pvt.	F 23rd SCVI	22	CR	11/15/62	At home	DOD	(HHC=Sammonds, Wm.M.)	ROH,HHC
Sample, William E.	Pvt.	E 7th SCVI	24	ED	06/26/62	At home	DOD	(Bn: 6/15/38)(Pneumonia)	JR,UD3,EDN,KEB
Samuel, Joseph G.	Pvt.	H 7th SCVI	23	ED	11/01/61	Charlottesville	DOD	(Typhoid)	JR,EDN
Samuels, George W.	1st Sgt.	C 1st SCVA	24	ED	10/06/64	James Island, SC	DOD		ROH,CDC
Sanderfer, Phillip R.	Pvt.	K 17th SCVI	36	YK	09/23/64	Petersburg, VA	DOW	Blandford Church Pbg., VA	ROH,BLC,YEB
Sanderfer, S.T. (L.F.?)	Pvt.	5th SCV			11/14/62	Richmond, VA		Hollywood Cem.Rchmd. S277	ROH,HC
Sanderford, J.M.	Pvt.	E Ham.Leg.			12/15/62	Fredericksburg	DOW		JR
Sanders, Andrew P.	2nd Lt.	E 6th SCVI		CR	04/01/62		DOD		R46,HHC
Sanders, Benjamin F.G.	Pvt.	F 18th SCVI		UN	08/30/62	2nd Manassas, VA	KIA	(JR=Saunders)	ROH,JR,CDC
Sanders, C.W.	Pvt.	B 4th SCVC		CR	06/11/64	Washington, DC	DOW	(Wdd & POW 5/30/64)	P5
Sanders, E.B.	Pvt.	I 1st SC Res		PS	02/18/65	Columbia, SC	DOD		ROH,PP
Sanders, Edward	Pvt.	H 6th SCVI	20	YK	/ /	Centreville, VA	DOD		YEB
Sanders, Ephraim	Pvt.	A 21st SCVI		GN	/ /		DIP	(POW 6/24/64)	ROH,HAG
Sanders, Ezekiel W.	Pvt.	E 5th SCVI		YK	04/07/65	Sutherland Stn.	KIA		SA3,UD3
Sanders, F.T.	Pvt.	K 10th SCVI		CN	/ /		DOD		RAS
Sanders, George E.	Pvt.	A 21st SCVI		GN	07/13/63	Bty. Wagner, SC	KIA		ROH,CDC,HAG
Sanders, Isaac	Pvt.	B 24th SCVI	34	MO	01/15/64	Dalton, GA	DOD	(Dropped dead of apoplexy)	ROH,PP
Sanders, J.A.	Pvt.	G 2nd SC Res	17	AN	01/06/65	Columbia, SC	DOD	Elmwood Cem. Columbia, SC	ROH,MP,PP
Sanders, J.B.	Pvt.	Ward's LA			02/05/63	Georgetown, SC	DOD		PP,CDC
Sanders, J.P.	Pvt.	13th SCVI			04/07/64	Richmond, VA			ROH
Sanders, J.S.	Cpl.	H Ham.Leg.		CN	09/14/62		DOW		ROH
Sanders, J.W.	Pvt.	F 3rd SCVIBn	30	RD	/ /	Deep Bottom, VA	KIA	(KEB=Saunders)	ROH,KEB
Sanders, James	Pvt.	E 5th SCVI			05/31/62	7 Pines, VA	KIA	(JR=Saunders)	JR,SA3
Sanders, James	Pvt.	H 6th SCVI	19	YK	08/30/62	2nd Manassas, VA	KIA		YEB
Sanders, James W.	Pvt.	A 1st SCVIR		HY	06/16/63	Ft. Moultrie, SC	DOD	Corinth L.C. Saluda, SC	NCC,SA1
Sanders, John	Pvt.	E 7th SCVIBn	29	SR	02/10/62	Kingsville, SC	ACD		ROH,HAG
Sanders, John	Pvt.	A 20th SCVI	19	ED	05/15/64	Petersburg, VA	KIA	(NI KEB, Co.A was from PS)	ROH
Sanders, John	Pvt.	5th SCV		YK	09/15/64	Richmond, VA	DOW		ROH
Sanders, John	Pvt.	I 13th SCVI	20	SG	05/12/64	Spotsylvania, VA	KIA	(NI HOS)	ROH
Sanders, M.V.	Pvt.	F 3rd SCVC		BT	04/11/65	Ft. Delaware, DE	DIP	Finn's Pt., NJ Nat. Cem.	FPH,P6,P41

S

SOUTH CAROLINA DEAD IN CSA SERVICE 1861-1865

NAME	RANK	C REGIMENT	AGE	DS	DIED	WHERE	WHY	BURIED	SOURCES
Sanders, Patrick	Pvt.	D 7th SCVIBn	42	KW	11/12/62	Adams Run, SC	DOD	(ROH=Saunders)	ROH,HIC,HAG,PP
Sanders, Reid	Major	CN Commisy			09/03/64	Ft. Warren, MS	DIP	(POW @ CN 1/5/63)	FPH,P2
Sanders, Richard Thomas	1st Lt.	G 2nd SCVA	27		10/13/62	Secessionville	DOD		ROH,R44
Sanders, S. Daniel	Pvt.	I 5th SCVI		SG	06/22/62	7 Pines, VA	DOW	Hollywood Cem.Rchmd. O201	ROH,JR,HC,SA3
Sanders, Thomas	Pvt.	D 5th SCVC	36	CN	12/13/62	Charleston, SC	DOD		ROH
Sanders, W.F.	Sgt.	C 15th SCVI	28	LN	12/18/64	Camp Chase, OH	DIP	C.C.#627 Columbus, OH	FPH,KEB,P23,H15
Sanders, William	Pvt.	G 7th SCVIBn	25	KW	01/10/65	Wilmington, NC	DOD		ROH
Sanders, William	Pvt.	A 14th SCVI	45	DN	06/07/63	At home	DOD		ROH
Sanders, William	Pvt.	B 4th SCVC		CR	06/11/64	Trevilian C.H.	KIA	(Dup of C.W.?)	HHC,CB
Sanders, William	Lt.	E 6th SCV		CR	/ /	Washington, DC	DOW		HHC
Sanders, William Thomas	Cpt.	H 17th SCVI		BL	03/15/62	At home	DOD	(?R47=dropped 4/28/62)	JR,DEM,R47
Sandifer, D.W.	Pvt.	H 17th SCVI		BL	01/24/62	Charleston, SC	DOD		CNM
Sandifer, Jacob	Pvt.	H 17th SCVI		BL	/ /	Charleston, SC	DOD		JR
Sandifer, Phillip R	Pvt.	K 17th SCVI	37	YK	09/23/64	Petersburg, VA	KIA		PP,YEB
Sandlin, Andrew Didd	Pvt.	C 17th SCVI	36	YK	/ /	Charleston, SC	DOD	(1862)	JR,YEB
Sandlin, Dempsey M.	Pvt.	F 16th SCVI		YK	02/02/64	Rock Island, IL	DIP	C.C.#347 Rock Island, IL	FPH,P5,16R
Sandlin, Jonothan A.	Pvt.	K 17th SCVI	29	YK	/ /	At home	DOD	(1862)	JR,YEB
Sandlin, W.E.	Pvt.	F 16th SCVI		GE	08/09/62	At home	DOD		PP,16R
Sands, W.W.	Pvt.	C 7th SCVI		AE	09/13/62	Maryland Hts. MD	KIA	(NI KEB)	ROH,JR
Sanford, Jesse	Pvt.	G 25th SCVI	37	OG	03/20/65	Elmira, NY	DIP	Woodlawn N.C.#1549 Elmira	ROH,FPH,EDR,P65
Sanford, Lewis	Pvt.	H Ham.Leg.	26	OG	/ /		DOW		ROH
Sanford, Wade B.	Pvt.	C 15th SCVI	23	LN	05/09/64	Spotsylvania, VA	KIA	Spotsylvania C.H., VA	ROH,SCH,KEB,H15
Sanford, William	Pvt.	A 1st SCVIH		LN	05/06/64	Wilderness, VA	KIA	(Oldest man in his Co.)	SA1,UD3
Sansbury, Cowen L.	1st Lt.	K 21st SCVI		DN	05/09/64	Swift Creek, VA	KIA		ROH,HAG,CDC,R48
Sansbury, E. Burdell	Pvt.	K 21st SCVI		DN	07/10/63	Bty. Wagner, SC	KIA	(JR=Gettysburg 7/3/63)	ROH,HAG,CDC,JR
Santhem, Berry	Pvt.	H 16th SCVI		GE	/ /	Chattanooga, TN	DOD	(Prob. Southern, Berry)	16R
Sargeant, L.F.	Pvt.	B 2nd SCVIRi		PS	/ /				ROH
Sargeant, Tyler	Pvt.	B 2nd SCVIRi		PS	/ /				ROH
Sargent, A.B.	Pvt.	D 4th SCVI		AN	08/28/61	Richmond, VA	DOD	(Measles)	JR,SA2
Sargent, S.L.	Pvt.	K 2nd SCVIRi			/ /	Richmond, VA			ROH
Sargins, M.E.	Pvt.	C 11th SCVI			08/15/62	Richmond, VA		(NI HAG,11th NI VA in 62)	ROH
Sarratt, A.	Pvt.	F 18th SCVI	19	YK	/ /	At home	DOD		ROH
Sarratt, Cortez	Pvt.	M P.S.S.	18	SG	08/17/62	Gaines' Mill, VA	DOW	(JR=DOD)	ROH,JR
Sarratt, Edwin C.	Pvt.	E 4th SC Res	17	SG	01/06/65	Charleston, SC	DOD	Sarratt Fam. Cem Cherokee	ROH,TCC,UD3
Sarratt, William A.	Pvt.	F 6th SCVC	24	SG	06/16/64	Trevillian Stn.	DOW	Providence B.C. Cherokee	ROH,TCC,CAG
Sarter, R.W.	2nd Lt.	B 18th SCVI		UN	02/22/64	Charleston, SC	DOD		ROH,CDC,R47
Sarter, William	1st Lt.	B 18th SCVI	34	UN	09/25/62	Warrenton, VA	DOW	Fishdam Ch. Union Cty.	ROH,UNC,R47
Sartor, D.T.	Pvt.	D 5th SCVI		UN	11/16/62	Richmond, VA	DOD	Oakwood C.#110,Row L,Div A	ROH,SA3,OWC
Sartor, Thomas	Pvt.	F 18th SCVI		UN	08/30/62	2nd Manassas, VA	KIA	(ROH=8/29/62)	ROH,JR,CDC
Sarvance, Elias	Pvt.	A 14th SCVI		DN	11/27/62	Staunton, VA			ROH
Sarvis, A.R.	Pvt.	K 8th SCVI		MO	/ /	Gordonville, VA	DOD	(KEB=S.L.,HOM=S.L.)	ROH,HOM,KEB
Sarvis, Joseph A.	2nd Lt.	B 10th SCVI		HY	07/28/64	Atlanta, GA	KIA		ROH,RAS
Sarvis, William F.	Pvt.	G 9th SCVIBn	17	HY	03/05/62	Georgetown, SC	DOD	(ROH=W.J. age 18)	ROH,PP
Sarvis,Jr., John F.	Pvt.	A 4th SCVC		HY	05/30/64	Cold Harbor, VA	KIA		ROH
Sassard, James A.	Pvt.	I 27th SCVI	23	CN	06/05/64	Cold Harbor, VA	KIA	(Sniper)	ROH,CDC,HAG
Sasser, Benjamin	Pvt.	H Orr's Ri.		MN	05/12/64	Spotsylvania, VA	KIA		HMC
Satcher, Henry	Pvt.	A 19th SCVI	17	ED	/ /	At home	DOD		HOE,UD3
Satcher, Henry A.	Pvt.	C 15th SCVI	19	LN	09/14/62	South Mtn., MD	KIA	(KEB=Salther) TOD	ROH,JR,H15,KEB
Satcher, Isaiah	Pvt.	B 6th SCVC		ED	07/15/64	Raleigh, NC	DOD		ROH
Satcher, Robert	Pvt.	A 19th SCVI	28	ED	/ /	Chattanooga, TN	DOD	City C. Chattanooga, TN	HOE,TOD
Satchwell, T.M.	Pvt.	I 3rd SC			09/26/62	Richmond, VA		Hollywood Cem.Rchmd. H177	HC

SOUTH CAROLINA DEAD IN CSA SERVICE 1861-1865

NAME	RANK	C REGIMENT	AGE	DS	DIED	WHERE	WHY	BURIED	SOURCES
Satterfield, E.A.	Pvt.	D 18th SCVI		GE	07/30/64	Crater, Pbg., VA	KIA		ROH
Satterfield, J. Wade	Pvt.	A Hol.Leg.	26	SG	04/01/62	Adams Run, SC	ACD	(Accidentaly shot,PP=2/14)	ROH,HOS,PP
Satterfield, J.N.	Pvt.	A 7th SCVI			11/06/62	Staunton, VA		Thornrose C. Staunton, VA	ROH,TOD
Satterfield, James	Pvt.	B 16th SCVI		GE	11/30/64	Franklin, TN	KIA		16R,WCT
Satterfield, William O.	Pvt.	K 16th SCVI		GE	11/30/64	Franklin, TN	KIA		ROH,16R,PP
Satterwhite, Pascal	Pvt.	D 5th SCVI		UN	06/27/62	Gaines' Mill, VA	KIA		SA3
Satterwhite, W.F.	Pvt.	B 1st SCVIG	40	NY	05/16/62	Richmond, VA	DOD	(ANY= John F.)	JR,SA1,ANY
Sauls,	Pvt.	23rd SCVI		CO	/ /				ROH,CDC
Sauls, Benjamin	Pvt.	K 11th SCVI	20	CO	06/24/64	Petersburg, VA	KIA		ROH,HAG
Sauls, Charles	Pvt.	I 11th SCVI		CO	05/16/64	Drury's Bluff VA	KIA		ROH,HAG
Sauls, James	Pvt.	E 10th SCVI		WG	/ /		DOD	(1863)	RAS,HOW
Sauls, James	Pvt.	D 24th SCVI		BT	09/20/63	Chickamauga, GA	DOW	(Hip wound)	CDC
Sauls, John B. (Soles?)	Pvt.	G 10th SCVI		HY	01/24/65	Rock Island, IL	DIP	C.C.#1814 Rock Island, IL	FPH,P3
Sauls, John E.	Pvt.	D 11th SCVI	23	BT	12/25/61	Hardeeville, SC	DOD	(Co. I?)	ROH
Saunders, James	Pvt.	1st SC			07/20/63	Charleston, SC		Magnolia Cem. Charleston	ROH,MAG
Saunders, Jeremiah S.	Pvt.	H 1st SCVA			07/18/63	Bty. Wagner, SC	KIA		ROH,CDC
Saunders, John	Pvt.	G 5th SC			06/26/62	Columbia, SC	DOD		JR
Saunders, L.A.	Pvt.	D 22nd SCVI		PS	/ /	Richmond, VA		Oakwood C.#5,Row P,Div B	ROH,OWC
Saunders, S.L.	Pvt.	K 2nd SCVIRi	37	PS	11/20/63	Newman, GA	DOD		ROH
Saunders, W.C.	Pvt.	H 18th SCVI		YK	08/15/64	Petersburg, VA	DOW	(Wdd 8/1/64)	ROH
Saunders, W.F.	Pvt.	A 2nd SCVC			/ /	Lynchburg, VA	DOD	Lynchburg CSA Cem. YS	BBW
Saunders, W.W.	Pvt.	G 2nd SCVA			03/01/65	High Point, NC		Oakwood C. High Point, NC	CV,WAT,TOD
Saunders, William	Pvt.	A 18th SCVI	41	UN	07/30/64	Crater, Pbg., VA	KIA	(BLM=Sanders)	ROH,BLM
Savage, James	Sgt.	H 15th SCVI		UN	/ /		KIA		JR,KEB,UD3
Saville, Harris M.	Pvt.	C 3rd SCResB	48	YK	/ /	Raleigh, NC	DOD	(On active duty ?)	YEB
Sawyer, James L.	Cpl.	E 3rd SCVI		NY	11/19/63	Knoxville, TN	DOW		ROH,SA2,ANY,CD
Sawyer, Levi	Pvt.	G 23rd SCVI		MO	08/30/62	2nd Manassas, VA	KIA		ROH,JR,HOM,CDC
Sawyer, Thomas M.	Pvt.	D 14th SCVI	35	ED	08/23/64	Jericho Ford, VA	KIA	(JR=DOW 8/2/62)	ROH,JR,D14,HOE
Sawyer, William	Pvt.	B 14th SCVI	23	ED	/ /	Richmond, VA		(On Rchmd effects list)	HOE,CDC,UD3
Saxon, A.	Pvt.	C 14th SCVI		LS	/ /	Lynchburg, VA		Lynchburg CSA Cem.#6 R2	BBW
Saxon, James S.	Pvt.	14th SCVI			04/16/62	Pocotaligo, SC	DOD	(Congestive fever)	JR
Saxon, William P.	Pvt.	G 19th SCVI		AE	04/08/64	Rock Island, IL	DIP	C.C.#996 Rock Island, IL	FPH,P5,HOL
Saye, Abraham Richard	Pvt.	F 9th SCVIB	21	UN	08/29/61	Germantown, VA	DOD		ROH,JR
Saylor, Henry E.	Sgt.	D 27th SCVI	30	CN	08/23/65	Columbia, SC	DOW	St.John's L.C. Charleston	ROH,MAG,CDC,PP
Saylors, W.G.	Pvt.	I 4th SCVI	23	AN	06/06/61		DOD	(NI SA2,JR=L,P.S.S.)	ROH,JR
Scaff, Matthew	Pvt.	K 21st SCVI		DN	08/25/64	City Point, VA	DOW	City Pt. N.C. Hopewell, VA	PP,HAG,TOD
Scaff, R.	Pvt.	A 14th SCVI	45	DN	08/18/64	Richmond, VA			ROH
Scaife, Benjamin F.	Pvt.	F 6th SCVI		CR	/ /	Centreville, VA	DOD	(1861)	HHC
Scales, G.G.	Pvt.			UN	/ /	Petersburg, VA			ROH
Scales, Joseph	Pvt.	F 17th SCVI		UN	/ /	Winchester, VA	DOD	Stonewall C. Winchester VA	JR,WIN
Scales, L.	Pvt.	F 15th SCVI		UN	/ /		KIA	(KEB=Scates)	JR,KEB
Scales, Stewart	Pvt.	M P.S.S.	17	UN	08/30/62	2nd Manassas, VA	DOW		ROH,JR,CDC
Scales, William	Pvt.	M P.S.S.		UN	01/10/63		DOD		ROH
Scalf, Joseph	Pvt.	E 1st SCVIR		GE	09/08/63	Ft. Moultrie, SC	KIA	(Ammo chest explosion)	ROH,SA1,CDC
Scarborough, A.M.	2nd Lt.	A 14th SCVI	23	DN	05/12/64	Spotsylvania, VA	KIA		ROH,DEB,BOS,R4
Scarborough, Bryant S.	Pvt.	A 7th SCVIBn		KW	12/12/63	Sullivans I., SC	DOD	(HAG=B.A.)	ROH,HIC,HAG
Scarborough, James H.	Pvt.	C Ham.Leg.		CL	07/21/61	1st Manassas, VA	KIA		ROH,JR,CDC
Scarborough, John R.	Pvt.	K 23rd SCVI	34	SR	08/30/62	2nd Manassas, VA	KIA	(JR=DOW 8/31)	ROH,JR,K23,UD3
Scates, A.J.	Pvt.	D 2nd SCVI		SR	09/20/63	Chickamauga, GA	KIA		ROH,JR,SA2,H2
Scheffelin, J.	Pvt.	C 27th SCVI		CN	05/16/64	Drury's Bluff VA	KIA	(HAG=Shoeflin)	ROH,HAG,CDC
Scheider, J. McPherson	Pvt.	H 11th SCVI		CO	07/27/64	Petersburg, VA	DOW	(Wdd 6/24/64)	ROH,CDC,HAG,PP

S

SOUTH CAROLINA DEAD IN CSA SERVICE 1861-1865

NAME	RANK	C REGIMENT	AGE	DS	DIED	WHERE	WHY	BURIED	SOURCES
Schenk, John M.	Pvt.	C 19th SCVI		ED	08/10/64	Rock Island, IL	DIP	C.C.#1400 Rock Island, IL	FPH,HOE,UD3
Schmidt, James Merritt	Sgt.	C 11th SCVI	32	CO	05/16/64	Drury's Bluff VA	KIA		ROH,CDC,WLI
Schmidt, M.	Pvt.	I 11th SCVI		CO	08/21/64	Weldon RR, VA	KIA		ROH
Schmitz, J. David	Pvt.	C 20th SCVI	24	LN	06/29/63	At home	DOD	Schmitz/Koon Gvyd Peak, SC	ROH,NCC,KEB
Schnekenberger, Adam	Pvt.	G 1st SCVIR		CN	11/12/64	Mt. Pleasant, SC	DOD		SA1
Schnierle, Vincent	Pvt.	A 27th SCVI		CN	06/16/64	Hare's Hill, VA	DOW	(Wdd 6/17/64)	ROH,HAG,CDC
Schroder, H.	Pvt.	B German Art			/ /			St. Lawrence C. Charleston	MAG
Schroder, J.C.	Cpl.	B German Art			/ /			St. Lawrence C. Charleston	MAG,PP
Schroeder, Charles	Pvt.	Hart's LA		CN	/ /	Richmond, VA	KIA	(Seven days battles)	CNM,STC
Schroeder, Henry	Pvt.	C 27th SCVI		CN	03/04/65	Elmira, NY	DIP	Woodlawn N.C.#1978	FPH,P6,P65,HAG
Schroeder, J.C.L.	Pvt.	A German art		CN	08/15/63	Columbia, SC	DOD	Elmwood Cem. Columbia, SC	ROH,MP
Schumpert, A.	Pvt.	F 20th SCVI		NY	08/11/62	Columbia, SC	DOD		ROH
Schumpert, Benjamin H.G.	Pvt.	E 3rd SCVI		NY	09/20/63	Chickamauga, GA	KIA	(See p394,ANY)	ROH,JR,SA2,ANY
Schumpert, George A.	Pvt.	D 19th SCVI	18	ED	09/20/63	Chickamauga, GA	KIA		ROH,JR,HOE,UD3
Schumpert, I.P.	Pvt.	C 23rd SCVI		CN	03/01/65	Richmond, VA		Hollywood Cem.Rchmd. W528	HC
Schumpert, J.L.	Pvt.	F 20th SCVI	18	NY	08/10/63	Morris Island SC	DOW		ROH,ANY
Schumpert, J.L.	Pvt.	E 7th SCVC	18	NY	/ /	Coffin's Farm	DOD	(1864)	ANY
Schumpert, M.L.	Pvt.	F 20th SCVI		NY	08/12/63	Columbia, SC	DOD		PP
Schumpert, Peter	Pvt.	K 2nd SCVA		ED	/ /		DOD		HOE,UD3
Schwartz, Barney	Pvt.	B 1st SCVIR		CN	12/22/61	Ft. Sumter, SC	DOD		ROH,RCD,SA1
Schwartz, G.W.	Pvt.	H 13th SCVI		LN	08/07/64	Ft. Delaware, DE	DIP	Finn's Pt., NJ Nat. Cem.	ROH,FPH,P5,P40
Schwartz, Henry C.	Pvt.	H 13th SCVI	33	LN	08/29/62	2nd Manassas, VA	KIA	(ROH=8/30)	ROH,JR,CDC
Schwartz, J.M.	Pvt.	C 20th SCVI	15	LN	02/27/65	Raleigh, NC	DOD		ROH
Schwartz, Jasper				LN	/ /				ROH
Schwartz, John Benedict	Pvt.	C 12th SCVI	19	FD	07/02/63	Gettysburg, PA	KIA	(ROH=7/3)	ROH,JR,GDR,HFC
Schwartz, William	Pvt.	M P.S.S.			/ /		DOD		JR
Schwecke, H.	Pvt.	A German Art		CN	/ /			St.Lawrence C. Charleston	MAG
Scott, Alexander	Pvt.	F 3rd SCVABn	35	CN	11/08/62	At home	DOD		ROH
Scott, Allen	Pvt.	C 26th SCVI		MN	/ /	Iron Bridge, ?	DOW		HMC
Scott, Barry B.	Pvt.	M P.S.S.		SG	02/14/64	Rock Island, IL	DIP	C.C.#489 Rock Island, IL	FPH,P5
Scott, Benjamin F.	4th Sgt.	K 6th SCVI	20	WG	05/05/62	Williamsburg, VA	KIA	(Died in enemy hands)	ROH,JR,CTA,HOW
Scott, Daniel	Pvt.	L 2nd SCVIRi	38	GE	12/15/63	Augusta, GA	DOW	Magnolia Cem. Augusta, GA	ROH,BGA
Scott, E. Brainard	3rd Lt.	K 6th SCVI	20	WG	06/03/62	Manchester, VA	DOD	Williamsburg P.C. WG Cty.	ROH,HOW,3RC,R46
Scott, G.C.	Pvt.	G 15th SCVI		WG	/ /		DOD		JR,KEB
Scott, G.W.	Pvt.	I Hol.Leg.	18	SG	06/25/64	Pt. Lookout, MD	DIP	C.C. Pt. Lookout, MD	ROH,FPH,P6,P113
Scott, George W.	Pvt.	E 7th SCVIBn		SR	04/14/65	Pt. Lookout, MD	DIP	C.C. Pt. Lookout, MD	ROH,FPH,P6,HAG
Scott, H.W.	Pvt.	F 15th SCVI		UN	09/14/62	South Mtn., MD	KIA		ROH,JR,KEB
Scott, Henry	Pvt.	E 7th SCVIBn	49	SR	02/28/62	At home	DOD		ROH,HAG
Scott, J.L.	Pvt.	C 23rd SCVI		CN	06/21/64	Petersburg, VA	KIA		ROH
Scott, J.M.	Pvt.	B 27th SCVI		CN	08/01/64	Fts. Monroe, VA	DOW	Nat. Cem. Hampton, VA	ROH,PP,TOD
Scott, James	Pvt.	E Ham.Leg.		GE	03/12/64	White Sulpher Ss			ROH,PP
Scott, James R.	Pvt.	C 2nd SCVI		RD	/ /	(SA2=1862)	DOD	(H2=TFD Earle's LA & KIA)	SA2,KEB,H2
Scott, James Thornwell	1st Lt.	C 2nd SCVI		RD	07/02/63	Gettysburg, PA	KIA		ROH,JR,GDR,SA2
Scott, Jesse W.	Pvt.	I 14th SCVI	24	AE	05/10/63	Fredericksburg	DOD		ROH,HOL
Scott, John	Pvt.	G 22nd SCVI	34	PS	07/30/64	Crater, Pbg., VA	KIA		ROH,BLM
Scott, John James	Pvt.	E 7th SCVIBn	23	SR	08/21/64	Weldon RR, VA	KIA	(HAG=James J.)	ROH,HAG
Scott, John L.	Pvt.	I 26th SCVI	32	WG	/ /		DOD	(1863)	CTA,HOW
Scott, Junius Lawton	Pvt.	G 25th SCVI		OG	/ /	Elmira, NY	DIP	(P65=Released 7/11/65)	EDR,HAG,P65
Scott, Lewis	Pvt.	G 11th SCVI		CO	10/24/62	Hardeeville, SC	DOD		ROH,CDC
Scott, Lewis	Pvt.	A 24th SCVI		CN	06/23/62	Charleston, SC		Magnolia Cem. Charleston	ROH,MAG,RCD
Scott, M.M.	Pvt.	K 25th SCVI		WG	07/09/64	Petersburg, VA	KIA		ROH,HOW,CTA,CDC

SOUTH CAROLINA DEAD IN CSA SERVICE 1861-1865

NAME	RANK	C	REGIMENT	AGE	DS	DIED	WHERE	WHY	BURIED	SOURCES
Scott, Maxwell O.	Pvt.		J.Davis L.		CN	05/12/64	Middlesex, VA	KIA	(TFD frm I, 2nd SCVI)	H2,SA2,KEB
Scott, Pinckney	Pvt.	E	1st SCVIH		BL	08/30/62	2nd Manassas, VA	DOW		ROH,JR,CDC
Scott, T.	Pvt.	I	1st SC		MN	07/16/62	South Carolina	DOD		ROH
Scott, Thomas E.	Pvt.	F	15th SCVI		UN	06/28/62	Columbia, SC	DOD	Elmwood Cem. Columbia, SC	ROH,JR,MP,KEB,
Scott, Wainwright	Pvt.	A	8th SC Res		CN	02/10/65	Columbia, SC	DOD	Elmwood Cem. Columbia, SC	ROH,MP,PP
Scruggs, A.M.	2nd Lt.	H	P.S.S.		SG	06/30/62	Frayser's Farm	KIA		ROH,JR,R48,HOS
Scruggs, Alfred	Pvt.	K	Hol.Leg.		SG	/ /	At home	DOD		ROH
Scruggs, Charles S.W.	Sgt.	K	Hol.Leg.	36	SG	08/25/62	Brandy Stn., VA	DOD	Scruggs Fam. Cem. Ck'kee	ROH,TCC
Scruggs, W.L.M.A.	Pvt.	B	2nd SCVI	33	GE	09/25/61	Lewensville, VA	DOW		ROH,SA2,KEB,H2
Scruggs, W.W.	Pvt.	K	Hol.Leg.	20	SG	02/28/65	Baltimore, MD	DIP	Loudon Park C. Balto. MD	PP,P65,P120,P1
Scruggs, Wilson N.	Pvt.	K	Hol.Leg.	35	SG	10/23/63	At home	DOD	State Line B.C. Cherokee	ROH,TCC
Scurry, E.M.	Sgt.	H	10th SCVI		WG	11/23/62	Atlanta, GA	DOD	Oakland C. Atlanta R7#6	RAS,HOW,CVGA,B
Seaborn, Wm. Robinson	Pvt.	B	P.S.S.	22	AN	05/30/62	7 Pines, VA	KIA	On the field	ROH,JR,CDC,ACC
Seabrook, Cato A.	Cpt.(AAG)		P.S.S.		YK	08/30/62	2nd Manassas, VA	KIA	Haymarket, VA	ROH,JR,YEB,CV
Seabrook, Cotesworth P.	2nd Lt.	H	1st SCVIG	23	BT	05/03/63	Chancellorsville	KIA	St. Johns C. Flat Rock, NC	ROH,JR,SA1,BOS
Seabrook, E. Smyley	Cpl.	B	27th SCVI		CO	08/05/64	Richmond, VA		Hollywood Cem.Rchmd. V49	ROH,HC,HAG
Seabrook, George W.	Cpt.				CO	04/15/61		DOD	(Palmetto Volunteers)	ROH
Seabrook, Julius C.	1st Cpl.	I	2nd SCVI	21	CN	12/20/62	Fredericksburg	DOW		ROH,JR,SA2,KEB
Seabrook, Paul H.	Cpt.	B	23rd SCVI	39	BT	09/09/62	2nd Manassas, VA	DOW	(Prob in Warrenton, VA)	ROH,JR,CDC,R48
Seabrook, Samuel	Pvt.	E	1st SCVIG			12/13/62	Fredericksburg	KIA		CDC
Seabrook, Whitemarsh H.	1st Lt.	H	25th SCVI		CO	05/21/64	Fts. Monroe, VA	DIP	Nat. Cem. Hampton, VA	ROH,HAG,R48,PP
Seaford, M.H.	Pvt.	A	Ham.Leg.		FD	01/17/64	Dandridge, TN	KIA		ROH,CDC,WLI
Seals, John R.	Pvt.	F	2nd SCVI		AE	09/02/61	Richmond, VA	DOD	Hollywood Cem.Rchmd. G58	HC,SA2,KEB,H2
Searight, Isaac Cowan	1st Cpl.	I	19th SCVI	28	AE	06/28/62	West Point, MS	DOD		ROH,PP
Searight, Jacob	Pvt.	F	20th SCVI		OG	02/10/62	Charleston, SC	DOD	(CNM=Sawright)	CNM
Sears, J.P.	Pvt.	L	P.S.S.			/ /		DOD		JR
Sears, T.N.	Pvt.	L	P.S.S.			06/30/62	Frayser's Farm	KIA	(ROH=J.N.)	ROH,JR,CDC
Sease, Daniel Isaiah	Cpl.	C	15th SCVI	31	LN	03/18/65	Camp Chase, OH	DIP	C.C.#1801 Columbus, OH	ROH,FPH,P23,KE
Sease, F. Marion	Pvt.	C	15th SCVI	18	LN	11/05/61	Columbia, SC	DOD		H15,TOD,PP
Sease, S.M.	Pvt.	C	15th SCVI		LN	/ /		DOD		JR
Seay, Daniel E.	Pvt.	F	5th SCVC	40	LN	01/30/65	Elmira, NY	DIP	Woodlawn N.C.#1786 Elmira	ROH,FPH,P6,P12
Seay, Daniel P.	Pvt.	C	15th SCVI	32	LN	/ /	Richmond, VA	DOD		TOD,H15
Seay, Franklin	Pvt.	F	13th SCVI		SG	07/01/63	Gettysburg, PA	KIA	(HOS=Chancellorsville)	ROH,HOS
Seay, George W.	Pvt.	F	27th SCVI	25	ED	07/30/64	Richmond, VA	DOW	Hollwood Cem.Rchmd. U335	ROH,HC,HOE,UD3
Seay, H. Harley	1st Lt.	B	15th SCMil	55	LN	04/29/65	Newbern, NC	DIP	Cedar Grove C. Newbern, NC	LNC,KEB,PP,P6
Seay, Irvin	Pvt.	I	6th SCVI		CR	/ /		KIA		CB,HHC
Seay, J.N.	Pvt.	K	5th SCVI		SG	/ /	Virginia	DOD	(To Hospital 2/10/63)	JR,HOS,SA3
Seay, L.H.	Pvt.	H	6th SC		SG	01/27/63	Richmond, VA			ROH
Seay, Mountain	Pvt.	K	13th SCVI		LN	04/04/62	Camp Gregg, SC	DOD	(Brain Congestion)	ROH,JR
Seay, R.B.	2nd Lt.	K	27th SCVI		SG	05/14/64	Drury's Bluff VA	DOD	(Exhaustion)	HAG,CDC,R47
Seay, R.B.	Cpt.	K	5th SCVI		SG	/ /	Virginia	DOD	(Biography in HOS)	HOS,SA3
Seay, Wilson	Cpl.	F	13th SCVI		SG	05/15/64	Spotsylvania, VA	KIA		ROH,HOS
Seedorff, H.C.	Pvt.	B	German Art		CN	11/07/61	Port Royal, SC	KIA	(JR=C.H.)	ROH,JR,CDC
Segagne, William			SC			/ /			Cedar Grove C. Newbern, NC	PP
Segars, W.G.	Pvt.	A	23rd SCVI		CD	01/10/64	Petersburg, VA	DOD		ROH
Segemore, Starling	Pvt.	I	1st SCVA		CN	09/09/62	Charleston, SC	DOD	Magnolia Cem. Charleston	ROH,MAG,RCD
Sego, Thomas A.	Pvt.	B	6th SCVC		ED	03/16/65	Fayetteville, NC	DOW	(Chg on Kilpatrick's Camp)	ROH,HOE,BHC,UD
Segrist, W.D.	Pvt.	I	5th SCVC	36	OG	06/17/64	Washington, DC	DOW	Soldier's Burial Ground	ROH,P6
Seigler, H.G.	Cpl.	K	24th SCVI		ED	09/01/64	Jonesborough, GA	KIA		HOE
Seigler, William Young	Pvt.	H	6th SCVI		FD	11/17/61	Richmond, VA		Oakwood C.#5,Row B,Div A	ROH,OWC
Seilaff, C.W.	1st Cpl.	A	2nd SCVI		RD	07/16/63	Gettysburg, PA	DOW		P1,SA2,KEB

S

SOUTH CAROLINA DEAD IN CSA SERVICE 1861-1865

NAME	RANK	C REGIMENT	AGE	DS	DIED	WHERE	WHY	BURIED	SOURCES
Seiley, G.W.	Pvt.	G 1st SCVIG		ED	06/27/62	Gaines' Mill, VA	KIA		JR,SA1,HOE
Seitzes, John	Pvt.	F 7th SCVI	35	ED	10/01/62	Frederick, MD	DOW	Mt.Olivet C.#61 Frederick	ROH,FPH,HOE,BOD
Selby, Edmund C.	Pvt.	F 2nd SCVI	23	AE	03/02/62	Manassas, VA	DOD	(Typhoid)	ROH,SA2,KEB,H2
Selby, John	Pvt.	F Hol.Leg.	24	AE	03/09/62	Adams Run, SC	DOD		ROH,PP
Self, A.S.	Pvt.	K 18th SCVI			08/30/62	2nd Manassas, VA	KIA		CDC
Sell, Andrew	Pvt.	K 21st SCVI			02/16/65	Elmira, NY	DIP	Woodlawn N.C.#2187 Elmira	FPH,P6
Sellars, S.A.	Pvt.	A 10th SCVI		GN	07/15/62		DOD	(Typhoid)	JR,RAS
Sellers, Bryant J.	Pvt.	E 4th SCVC		MO	08/13/63	McPhersonville	DOD		HOM
Sellers, Elijah	Pvt.	A 4th SCVC		CD	05/28/64	Hawes Shop, VA	KIA		ROH
Sellers, Hardy	Pvt.	Ch'fld LA	40	CD	08/15/63	Petersburg, VA		Blandford Church Pbg., VA	ROH,BLC,PP
Sellers, Henry	Pvt.	M P.S.S.	26	UN	05/16/64	Charlottesville	DOW	Univ. Cem. Charlottesville	ROH,ACH
Sellers, J.D.	Pvt.	B 8th SCVI		CD	10/15/61	Richmond, VA	DOD	(Typhoid)	JR,KEB
Sellers, John E.	1st Sgt.	A 4th SCVC		CD	05/28/64	Hawes Shop, VA	KIA		ROH
Sellers, Martin Henry	Cpt.	F 25th SCVI	25	OG	08/21/64	Globe Tavern, VA	KIA	(See p300,HAG)	ROH,HAG,DOC,R48
Sellers, R.A.	Pvt.	C 27th SCVI		CN	07/27/64	Richmond, VA	DOW	Hollywood Cem.Rchmd. V624	ROH,HAG,HC
Sellers, Thomas	Pvt.	K 6th SCVI	45	CD	03/10/64		DOD		ROH
Sellers, W. Riley	Pvt.	A 4th SCVC		CD	03/23/65	Elmira, NY	DIP	Woodlawn N.C.#2438 Elmira	ROH,FPH,P6,P65
Sellers, W.R.	Pvt.	B 8th SCVI		CD	05/11/62	Richmond, VA			ROH,KEB
Sellers, William	Pvt.	F 15th SCVI		UN	03/03/63	Richmond, VA			ROH
Semmes, J.H.	Pvt.	C 23rd SCVI		CN	/ /	Petersburg, VA	KIA	(1864)	ROH
Semmes, J.K.	Pvt.	G P.S.S.		YK	03/12/63	Petersburg, VA			ROH
Senn, A.C.	Pvt.	F 5th SCVC	22	LN	05/30/64	Cold Harbor, VA	KIA		ROH
Senn, A.D.	Sgt.	H 20th SCVI		LN	08/30/64	Petersburg, VA	DOW		ROH,KEB
Senn, A.D.	Pvt.	C 20th SCVI		LN	07/31/64	Richmond, VA		Hollywood Cem.Rchmd. V658	ROH,HC
Senn, Daniel	Pvt.	C 15th SCVI		LN	07/18/62	Richmond, VA			ROH
Senn, Dederick	Pvt.	F 3rd SCVIBn	45	RD	09/14/62	South Mtn., MD	KIA		ROH,KEB
Senn, Drayton	Pvt.	D 13th SCVI	19	NY	02/17/63	Richmond, VA	DOD		ROH
Senn, Ivel	Sgt.	H 20th SCVI		LN	10/25/62	Summerville, SC	DOD		ROH
Senn, James P.	Pvt.	D 13th SCVI	19	NY	12/12/64	Ft. Delaware, DE	DIP	Finn's Pt., NJ Nat. Cem.	ROH,ANY,FPH,P40
Senn, John D.	Pvt.	D 13th SCVI	24	NY	05/15/64	Lynchburg, VA	DOW	Lynchburg CSA Cem.#9 R3	BBW,ANY
Senn, Ketchem M.	Pvt.	D 13th SCVI	21	NY	07/01/63	Gettysburg, PA	KIA	(ANY=Petersburg)	ROH,JR,ANY
Senn, Oland	Sgt.	B 7th SCVI			08/30/62	2nd Manassas, VA	KIA		JR
Senn, S.	Pvt.	F 5th SCVC		LN	05/29/64	Atlee's Stn., VA	KIA		ROH,CDC
Sepoch, Jacob	Pvt.	F 17th SCVI		YK	09/14/62	South Mtn., MD	KIA		JR,CB
Sepoch, Noah	Pvt.	F 17th SCVI		YK	07/30/64	Crater Pbg., VA	KIA	(Sepaugh?)	CB
Serat, J.	Pvt.	I Prestons A			06/19/64	Charleston, SC		Magnolia Cem. Charleston	MAG,RCD
Service, Thomas O.	Pvt.	F 5th SCVC		LN	12/27/63	Baltimore, MD		Loudon Pk. C. Baltimore MD	PP
Settle, William E.	Pvt.	D P.S.S.		SG	09/17/62	Sharpsburg, MD	KIA		ROH,JR,HOS,CDC
Severance, E.J.	Pvt.	A 14th SCVI	30	DN	02/09/63	Lynchburg, VA	DOD		ROH
Severance, George W.	Pvt.	A 14th SCVI	19	DN	02/06/63	Fredericksburg	DOD	(From vacination)	ROH,DEB
Severance, J.J.W.	Pvt.	A 14th SCVI	22	DN	08/16/64	Fussel's Mill VA	KIA		ROH,DEB
Severance, Joseph	Pvt.	A 14th SCVI	35	DN	04/03/65		DOD		ROH
Severance, R.E.	Pvt.	A 8th SCVI		DN	06/03/63	Richmond, VA	DOD	(Pneumonia)	ROH,JR,KEB
Severence, E.	Pvt.	A 14th SCVI		DN	11/27/62	Staunton, VA		Thornrose C. Staunton, VA	TOD
Severence, Thomas G.	Pvt.	C 3rd SCVABn			12/27/64	Ship Island, MS	DIP	N.C. Ship Island, MS	PP,P3
Sexton, B.W.	Sgt.	C 18th SCVI	33	UN	10/08/62	Richmond, VA	DOD	Hollywood Cem.Rchmd. C54	ROH,JR,HC
Sexton, C.	Pvt.	H 12th SCVI	21	YK	12/15/62	Richmond, VA	DOD	Oakwood C.#59,Row L,Div A	ROH,OWC,YEB
Sexton, Curran P.	Pvt.	K 5th SCVC		UN	06/21/64	Richmond, VA	DOW	Hollywood Cem.Rchmd. U436	ROH,HC
Sexton, Daniel	Pvt.	H 24th SCVI		CR	/ /		DOD		CB,HHC
Sexton, David	Pvt.	C 13th SCVI		OG	09/30/64	Jones Farm, VA	KIA	(Near Petersburg)	ROH
Sexton, E.T.	Pvt.	C 18th SCVI	35	UN	10/17/62	Richmond, VA	DOD		ROH,JR

SOUTH CAROLINA DEAD IN CSA SERVICE 1861-1865

NAME	RANK	C REGIMENT	AGE	DS	DIED	WHERE	WHY	BURIED	SOURCES
Sexton, J.A.	Pvt.	F 1st SCVIBn		CN	03/27/63		DOD		JR
Sexton, James	Pvt.	E 3rd SCResB			03/25/65	Raleigh, NC		Oakwood C. Raleigh, NC	TOD
Sexton, Newton W.	Pvt.	C 18th SCVI	18	UN	02/07/62	At home	DOD		ROH,JR
Sexton, Samuel	Pvt.	F 1st SCVIBn		CN	08/11/63	Columbia, SC	DOD	(HOS= E,18th SCVI)	ROH,JR,HOS,PP
Sexton, William Allen	Pvt.	A 17th SCVI	30	CR	08/30/62	2nd Manassas, VA	KIA		ROH,JR,CDC,HHC
Sexton, William C.	Pvt.	C 13th SCVI		SG	08/29/62	2nd Manassas, VA	KIA	(JR=8/30/62)	ROH,JR,HOS,CDC
Seybet, George W.B.	1st Sgt.	I 27th SCVI	23	CN	06/18/64	Petersburg, VA	KIA	(HAG=Seybt, Robert F.)	ROH
Seymore, James	Pvt.	B 17th SCVI		FD	/ /	Goldsboro, NC	DOD		JR
Seymore, Jerome	Pvt.	D 6th SCVI		CR	06/30/62	Frayser's Farm	KIA		WDB
Shackleford, B.F.	Pvt.	M 10th SCVI		GN	02/04/63	At home		Mt.Olive B.C. Georgetown	GNG,RAS
Shackleford, J.L.	2nd Lt.	E 18th SCVI		SG	12/10/62	Richmond, VA	DOD	Oakwood C.#166,Row L,Div A	ROH,OWC,HOS,R4
Shackleford, John G.	Pvt.	E 18th SCVI	21	SG	07/27/62	Richmond	KIA	(? Rgt NI VA, NI HOS)	ROH
Shackleford, T.C.	Pvt.	B 10th SCVI		HY	/ /	Nashville, TN	DIP		RAS,P38
Shafer, John	Pvt.	K 24th SCVI		ED	08/21/63	Funderdale Spgs	DOD	(Lauderdale Spgs,MS?)	HOE,PP
Shafer, John	Pvt.	G 7th SCV			/ /				UD2
Shafer, John C.	Pvt.	G 1st SCVIG		ED	07/03/62	Gettysburg, PA	KIA		ROH,JR,GDR,SA1
Shaler, F.E.	Lt.	F 27th SCVI		CN	/ /	Richmond, VA		Oakwood C.#3, Row E, Div F	ROH,OWC
Shaler, H.A.	Pvt.	D 25th SCVI		CN	11/12/62	(2nd Cav in ROH)		Stonewall C. Winchester VA	ROH,WIN
Shalock, H.T.	Pvt.	B Ham.Leg.		ED	05/31/62	7 Pines, VA	KIA		ROH,JR,CDC
Shands, Adolphus Duroe	Pvt.	A 1st SC Res	17	SG	03/14/65	Camden, SC	DOD	New Hope Ch. Spartanburg	ROH,UNC
Shands, L.S.	Pvt.	A 1st Bn SCT		SG	03/16/65	Averysboro, NC	KIA		HOS
Shands, P.W.	Pvt.	D 6th SCVI		SG	/ /	Richmond, VA		Oakwood C.#77,Row B,Div B	ROH,OWC
Shands, Samuel	Pvt.	D 3rd SCVI		SG	03/19/65	Bentonville, NC	KIA		HOS,KEB
Shands, Samuel	Pvt.	A 1st SC Res		SG	03/16/65	Averysboro, NC	KIA		HOS,KEB,UD3
Shands, Silas W.	2nd Cpl.	H 1st SCVIH		SG	08/30/62	2nd Manassas, VA	KIA		ROH,JR,SA1,JRH
Shannon, Allison E.	Pvt.	A 2nd SCVC	21	KW	03/15/65	Neuse River, NC	KIA		ROH,HIC
Shannon, Hiram	Pvt.	F 6th SCVI	23	CR	05/14/64	Spotsylvania, VA	KIA	Spotsylvania C.H., VA	ROH,SCH,HHC
Shannon, James	Pvt.			UN	07/07/65	At home		Mt.Tabor M.C. Newberry SC	NCC
Shannon, R.A.	Pvt.	G 10th SCVI		HY	/ /	At home	MUR	(RAS=killed at home)	RAS
Sharp, Amos L.	Pvt.	A 3rd SCVI		LS	12/14/61	Centreville, VA	ACD	(Dropped pistol, fired)	ROH,SA2,KEB
Sharp, Franklin	Pvt.	H 20th SCVI		LN	01/03/62		DOD		ROH
Sharp, H.N.	Pvt.	M P.S.S.			05/23/63	Franklin, VA	KIA	(JR=DOD)	ROH,JR
Sharp, J.A.	Pvt.	B 18th SCVI	19	NY	08/12/62	Petersburg, VA	DOD		ROH,PP
Sharp, J.J.	Pvt.	B 5th SCVC	35	BT	05/28/64	Price's Farm, VA	KIA		ROH,CDC,MDM
Sharp, R.	Pvt.	F Hol.Leg.	25	AE	02/07/62	At home	DOD		ROH
Sharpe, C.C.	Pvt.	H 15th SCVI		UN	12/04/63	Ft. Delaware, DE	DIP	Finn's Pt., NJ Nat. Cem.	ROH,FPH,P5,KEB
Sharpe, C.M.	Pvt.	B Orr's Ri.		AE	05/28/64	Staunton, VA			PP
Sharpe, E. Hooker	Pvt.	E 5th SCVI		UN	08/01/61	Charlottesville	DOD	(Typhoid)	SA3,UD1
Sharper, H.	Pvt.	I Orr's Ri.			07/15/62	Richmond, VA		(Sharpe?, no Co.I)	ROH
Sharpton, Benjamin	Pvt.	F 7th SCVI	19	ED	06/27/62	Gaines' Mill, VA	DOW		HOE,CV,KEB,UD3
Sharpton, E. Moody	Pvt.	G 24th SCVI	16	ED	05/17/62	Charleston, SC	DOD		CDC
Sharpton, J.F.	Pvt.	G 14th SCVI	18	AE	05/26/64	Staunton, VA	DOW	(Wdd Wilderness)	ROH,PP
Sharpton, J.S.	Pvt.	I 7th SCVI		ED	06/29/62	Savage Stn., VA	DOW	(KEB=Shafton)	ROH,CDC,HOE,KE
Sharpton, William	Pvt.	B 19th SCVI	23	ED	08/15/62	Lauderdale Ss MS	DOD		ROH,HOE,PP
Shaver, William	Pvt.	K 15th SCVI			05/15/65	Hart's Island NY	DIP	Cypress Hills N.C.#2782 NY	FPH,P6,P79,KEB
Shaw, Abraham B.	Pvt.	D 10th SCVI		MN	11/30/64	Franklin, TN	KIA		PP
Shaw, Andrew	Pvt.	H 12th SCVI	31	YK	/ /		DOD	(1862)	YEB
Shaw, Benjamin A.	Pvt.	L 23rd SCVI	25	MN	11/02/63	Pt. Lookout, MD	DIP	C.C. Pt. Lookout, MD	ROH,FPH,HMC,P1
Shaw, E.	Pvt.	D 10th SCVI		MN	/ /		DOD		ROH,RAS,HMC
Shaw, H.B.	Pvt.	21st SCVI			06/09/64	Richmond, VA			ROH
Shaw, H.J.	Pvt.	K Orr's Ri.		AN	07/08/62	Richmond, VA			ROH

S

SOUTH CAROLINA DEAD IN CSA SERVICE 1861-1865

NAME	RANK	C REGIMENT	AGE	DS	DIED	WHERE	WHY	BURIED	SOURCES
Shaw, Isaac T.	Pvt.	K Orr's Ri.	21	AN	12/13/62	Fredericksburg	KIA		ROH,CDC
Shaw, J.H.	Pvt.	D 2nd SCVI		SR	06/14/63	Richmond, VA	DOD	Hollywood Cem.Rchmd. T40	HC,SA2,KEB
Shaw, J.H.	Pvt.	F 10th SCVI		MN	11/30/64	Franklin, TN	KIA	(HMC= wdd @ Resaca,GA)	RAS,HMC
Shaw, J.M. (Jr. or Sr.?)	Pvt.	K 11th SCVI		CO	11/20/63	Charleston, SC	DOD	Magnolia Cem. Charleston	ROH,MAG,RCD,HAG
Shaw, John C.A.	1st Lt.	B 19th SCVI	30	ED	07/24/64	Atlanta, GA	KIA		ROH,HOE,R47
Shaw, John F.	Pvt.	B 13th SCVI		SG	09/07/62	Lynchburg, VA	DOD	Lynchburg CSA Cem.#7 R1	ROH,JR,HOS,BBW
Shaw, R. Dwight	Cpl.	K 23rd SCVI	27	SR	07/30/64	Crater, Pbg., VA	KIA		ROH,K23,BLM,UD3
Shaw, Samuel L.	Pvt.	I 14th SCVI	23	AE	09/01/62	Ox Hill, VA	KIA	(JR=2nd M. 8/30)	ROH,JR,HOL
Shaw, Thomas J.	2nd Lt.	B P.S.S.			/ /		DOD		JR
Shaw, William	Pvt.	B 11th SCVI		CO	09/15/63	SC	DOD	Magnolia Cem. Charleston	ROH,RCD,HAG
Shaw, William	Pvt.	A 7th SCVIBn		KW	/ /	At home	DOD	(1862)	ROH,HAG,HIC
Shaw, William A.	Pvt.	I 14th SCVI	55	AE	10/13/62	Winchester, VA	DOD		ROH,JR,HOL
Shaw, William F.	Pvt.	K Orr's Ri.	20	AN	07/16/62		DOD		ROH,CDC
Shaylor, J.D.	Pvt.	D Ham.Leg.		KW	10/17/62		DOD	(In enemy hands)	JR
Shaylor, Thomas S.	Pvt.	D 15th SCVI		KW	11/18/62	Staunton, VA	DOD	Thornrose C. Staunton, VA	ROH,JR,KEB,TOD
Shealey,	Pvt.	F 15th SCVI			/ /	Richmond, VA		Oakwood C.#50,Row A,Div B	OWC
Shealey, A.O.	Pvt.	K 13th SCVI		LN	06/16/62	Richmond, VA	DOD	(Typhoid)	ROH,JR
Shealey, Abram	Pvt.	E 7th SCVI		ED	07/08/64	Richmond, VA		Hollywood Cem.Rchmd. U598	ROH,HC,HOE,UD3
Shealey, Adam	Pvt.	E 7th SCVI		ED	/ /		DOD		HOE,KEB
Shealey, George W.	Pvt.	I 15th SCVI		LN	06/22/62	Hardeeville, SC	DOD	TOD	ROH,JR,H15,KEB
Shealey, John	Pvt.	E 7th SCVI		ED	06/15/61		DOD	(Typhoid)	JR,HOE,KEB,UD3
Shealey, Samuel S.	Pvt.	K 13th SCVI		LN	06/15/62	Richmond, VA	DOD	(Typhoid)	ROH,JR
Shealey, W. Riley	Pvt.	K 20th SCVI		ED	11/17/64	Pt. Lookout, MD	DIP	(Shurley, W.B. in FPH)	ROH,FPH,KEB
Shealey, Wm. Walter	Pvt.	K 13th SCVI		LN	07/08/62	Richmond, VA	DOD	(Typhoid)	ROH,JR
Shealy, Amos	Pvt.	M 7th SCVI	33	LN	02/07/63	At home	DOD	Union L.C. Lexington, SC	TOD
Shealy, Azariah	Pvt.	C 15th SCVI	17	LN	10/05/63	Atlanta, GA	DOW	Oakland Cem. Atlanta, GA	ROH,KEB,CVGH,H15
Shealy, Ephraim	Pvt.	H Hol.Leg.	32	ED	09/26/62	Richmond, VA	DOD		ROH,JR
Shealy, F.P.	Pvt.	G 13th SCVI		NY	/ /		MIA	(Assumed dead)	ROH,ANY
Shealy, Franklin	Pvt.	13th SCVI		NY	04/02/65	Appomattox R. VA	ACD	(LSS=Drowned)	LSS,ANY
Shealy, Henry	Pvt.	C 15th SCVI	28	LN	12/10/64	LaGrange, GA	DOD	Con. Cem. LaGrange, GA	ROH,KEB,H15,TOD
Shealy, Henry	Pvt.		29	LN	12/10/63			Union L.C. Lexington, SC	TOD
Shealy, J.M.	Pvt.	I 15th SCVI		LN	09/14/62	South Mtn., MD	KIA		JR
Shealy, James D.	Cpl.	G 13th SCVI		NY	08/16/64	Fussel's Mills	KIA	(ANY says Deep Bottom)	ROH,ANY
Shealy, John H.	Pvt.	G 13th SCVI	20	AE	05/31/64	Richmond, VA	DOW	(Wdd @ Spotsylvania)	ROH
Shealy, L. Melvin	Pvt.	I 15th SCVI	22	NY	08/13/62	At home	DOD		JR,ANY,KEB,H15
Shealy, Levi	Cpl.	H Hol.Leg.	34	ED	08/30/62	2nd Manassas, VA	KIA		ROH,JR
Shealy, Littleton	Pvt.	C 15th SCVI		LN	12/23/64	Camp Chase, OH	DIP	C.C.#658 Columbus, OH	ROH,FPH,KEB,P23
Shealy, Noah F.	Pvt.	I 15th SCVI	21	LN	06/29/62	Summerville, SC	DOD		ROH,JR,KEB,H15
Shealy, Peter W.	Pvt.	C 15th SCVI		LN	10/15/63	Chickamauga, GA	DOW	Con. Cem. Marietta, GA	ROH,JR,KEB,H15
Shealy, Simeon	Pvt.	M 7th SCVI	35	LN	03/10/63	At home	DOD	Union L.C. Lexington, SC	TOD
Shealy, Solomon	Pvt.	I 15th SCVI	38	LN	06/22/62	At home	DOD	Salem L.C. Leesville, SC	JR,H15,KEB
Shealy, Thomas	Pvt.	I 15th SCVI	26	LN	/ /	(Before 12/5/63)	DOD		TOD
Shealy, Tyra	Pvt.	F P.S.S.			/ /		DOD		JR
Shealy, Westly Walter	Pvt.	I 15th SCVI	22	LN	05/08/64	Spotsylvania, VA	KIA	Spotsylvania C.H., VA	ROH,SCH,KEB,H15
Shealy, Wiley	Pvt.	C 15th SCVI	23	LN	08/19/63	Chester, PA	DOW	Finn's Point N.C., NJ	ROH,FPH,P40,KEB
Shealy, William H.	Pvt.	G 13th SCVI		NY	09/30/64	Jones Farm, VA	KIA		ROH,ANY
Shearer, B.H.	Pvt.	G 7th SCVC		CN	08/11/64	Elmira, NY	DIP	Woodlawn N.C.#14 Elmira	FPH,P5,P65,P120
Shearer, Samuel David	Pvt.	E 4th SCVI		PS	12/30/61	Charlottesville	DOD		ROH,SA2
Sheares, Perry O.	Pvt.	G 22nd SCVI		AN	07/30/64	Crater, Pbg., VA	KIA		ROH,BLM
Sheath, D.D.	Pvt.				/ /	Columbia, SC		Elmwood Cem. Columbia, SC	MP
Shedd, James P.	2nd Lt.	G 3rd SCVIBn		BL	09/14/62	South Mtn., MD	KIA		KEB,R45

SOUTH CAROLINA DEAD IN CSA SERVICE 1861-1865

NAME	RANK	C REGIMENT	AGE	DS	DIED	WHERE	WHY	BURIED	SOURCES
Shedd, Jesse P.	Pvt.	D 15th SCVI		KW	05/12/64	Spotsylvania, VA	KIA		HIC,KEB
Shedd, William H.	Pvt.	G 3rd SCVIBn		FD	07/28/62	Columbia, SC	DOD	(PP=7/26/62)	ROH,KEB,PP
Sheehan, Patrick	Pvt.	H 27th SCVI		CN	06/24/64	Petersburg, VA	KIA		ROH,CDC
Sheeley, James	Pvt.	SC Res	17	LN	03/29/65	At home	DOD		ROH
Sheeley, Julius	Pvt.	C 20th SCVI	18	LN	05/26/64	Richmond, VA	DOD		ROH,KEB
Sheeley, Paul P.	Pvt.	C 20th SCVI	20	LN	10/13/64	Strasburg, VA	KIA		ROH,KEB,CDC,UD
Sheeley, Thomas	Pvt.	I 15th SCVI	25	LN	/ /		DOD	(Before 12/6/63,JR=DOW)	ROH,JR,H15
Sheeley, Yerby	Pvt.	C 2nd SCVI		RD	01/26/65	Pt. Lookout, MD	DIP	C.C. Pt. Lookout, MD	FPH,P6,P113,SA
Sheely, Daniel	Pvt.	F 3rd SCVABn	38	CN	08/19/64	Willtown Bluff SC	DOD		ROH
Sheely, Irvin	Pvt.	G 3rd SCVI		LN	09/13/62	Maryland Hts. MD	KIA	(KEB=Shesly, E.)	ROH,JR,SA2,KEB
Shehan, John	Pvt.	D 5th SCRes		KW	06/10/65	Pt. Lookout, MD	DIP	C.C. Pt. Lookout, MD	FPH,P6,P115,HI
Shehane, A.T.	Pvt.	A 5th SCVI		GE	07/05/62	Frayser's Farm	DOW	Hollywood Cem.Rchmd. M340	ROH,HC,SA3
Shehorne, James	Pvt.	G 2nd SCVI		KW	06/29/62	Savage Stn., VA	KIA	(KEB=Sheorn)	SA2,KEB,H2
Shehorne, Morris D.	Pvt.	G 2nd SCVI		KW	12/21/61	Warren Spgs., VA	DOD	(KEB=Sheorn, H2=12/31/61)	SA2,KEB,H2
Shelden, J. (I.?)	Pvt.	1st SCVA			07/16/63	Charleston, SC		Magnolia Cem. Charleston	ROH,MAG,RCD
Shelden, S.H.	Cpt.	B 15th SCVI	24	UN	10/04/64	Charleston, SC	DOD	Belmont Cem. UN Cty.	ROH,KEB,CDC,UN
Shell, T. Franklin	Pvt.	A 3rd SCVI	18	LS	10/13/64	Fisher's Hill VA	KIA	Hurricane B.C. Laurens SC	ROH,NCC,LSC
Shelley, David	2nd Lt.	I 21st SCVI		MN	10/04/64	Pt. Lookout, MD	DIP	C.C. Pt. Lookout, MD	ROH,FPH,P6,P11
Shelly, John W.	Pvt.	F 1st SCVIG		HY	06/27/62	Gaines' Mill, VA	KIA		SA1
Shelton, J.L.	Pvt.	C 4th SCVC		AN	07/05/64	Richmond, VA		Hollywood Cem.Rchmd. U62	HC
Shelton, Perry M.	Pvt.	G 4th SCVI		GE	10/25/61	Richmond, VA	DOD		SA2
Shely, George	Pvt.	C 25th SCVI		WG	01/22/65	Pt. Lookout, MD	DIP		ROH
Shepard, Charles	Pvt.	I 22nd SCVI		OG	09/14/62	South Mtn., MD	KIA		ROH
Shepherd, S. (L.?)	Pvt.	H 7th SCVI		ED	/ /	Charlottesville		Univ. Cem. Charlottesville	ACH
Sheppard, Benjamin T.	Pvt.	A 25th SCVI	24	ED	11/13/62	Charleston, SC	DOD	Magnolia Cem. Charleston	ROH,JR,MAG,HAG
Sheppard, J.H.	Pvt.	Ham.Leg.			07/30/64	Richmond, VA		Hollywood Cem.Rchmd. V293	ROH,HC
Sheppard, J.W.	Pvt.	E 1st SCVIH		BL	07/07/64	Richmond, VA	DOD	Hollywood Cem.Rchmd. U610	ROH,HC,SA1
Sheppard, James Oscar	Sgt. Major	6th SCVC	22	ED	06/12/64	Trevillian Stn.	DOW		ROH,CAG,SMC
Sheppard, John H. Heise	4th Cpl.	C 1st SCVIG	19	RD	05/05/64	Wilderness, VA	KIA		ROH,SA1,CDC
Sheppard, Thomas George	Pvt.	L 1st SCVIG	18	CN	09/17/62	Warrenton, VA	DOW	Magnolia Cem. Charleston	ROH,JR,MAG,SA1
Shepperd, Thomas	Seaman	CS Gunboat			12/04/63	Charleston, SC		Magnolia Cem. Charleston	RCD
Sheppy, Muckolls					09/30/63	Chickahominy, VA	KIA		ROH
Sherard, W.G.	1st Lt.	F 2nd SCVIRi	26	AN	10/21/64	Ft. Harrison, VA	DOW	Hollywood Cem.Rchmd. E59	ROH,HC,R45
Sherbert, Carlisle W.	Pvt.	E 18th SCVI	32	SG	06/15/64	Petersburg, VA	DOD		ROH,HOS
Sheriff, John	Pvt.	G 22nd SCVI	36	AN	07/30/64	Crater, Pbg., VA	KIA		ROH,BLM
Sherley, Elijah	Pvt.	McBeth LA			/ /			Stonewall C. Winchester VA	WIN
Sherley, L.P.	Pvt.	C 15th SCVI			10/31/62	(KEB=Shirey,I.P.)		Stonewall C. Winchester VA	ROH,WIN,KEB
Sherrer, J. George	Pvt.	12th SCVI		YK	/ /			(YEB=Killed @ railroad)	YEB
Sherrer, S.	Pvt.	F 6th SCVI		YK	12/01/62		DOD		ROH
Sherry, W. (Shealy?)	Pvt.	I 15th SCVI		LN	02/02/63	Richmond, VA		Oakwood C.#6,Row F,Div E	ROH,OWC
Sherry, William L.	Pvt.	C 4th SCVC			02/16/65	Elmira, NY	DIP	Woodlawn N.C.#2198 Elmira	FPH,P6,P65,P12
Sherwood, Richard	Pvt.	I 1st SCVIH		MN	05/25/63	Columbia, SC	DOD	(HMC=6/2/62)	ROH,SA1,HMC,PP
Shibley, Luke D.	2nd Sgt.	K 7th SCVI		ED	07/15/63		DOD	(HOE=Shipley)	ROH,KEB,HOE
Shields, E.P.	Pvt.	K 5th SCVI		SG	/ /	Chattanooga, TN			HOS,SA3
Shields, S.	Pvt.	G Orr's Ri.		AE	06/27/62	Gaines' Mill, VA	KIA		ROH,JR,CDC
Shilbefield, William	Sgt.	G 1st SCVA			07/04/64	Ft. Johnson, SC	KIA	Magnolia Cem. Charleston	ROH,MAG,RCD
Shiletto, George W.	1st Cpl.	B Orr's Ri.	21	AE	05/12/64	Spotsylvania VA	KIA		ROH,CDC
Shiletto, William	Pvt.	B Orr's Ri.	23	AE	07/15/62	Richmond, VA	DOD		ROH,CDC
Shillinglaw, S. William	Pvt.	D 5th SCVI		YK	10/03/62	Winchester, VA	DOW	Stonewall C. Winchester VA	ROH,JR,WIN,YEB
Shillingworth, Marcus	Pvt.	I Orr's Ri.		AE	04/15/65	Richmond, VA	DOD		ROH
Shipes, Jacob J.	Pvt.	D 11th SCVI		BT	12/08/64	Elmira,NY	DIP	Woodlawn N.C.#1174 Elmira	FPH,P5,P65,P12

S

SOUTH CAROLINA DEAD IN CSA SERVICE 1861-1865

NAME	RANK	C REGIMENT	AGE	DS	DIED	WHERE	WHY	BURIED	SOURCES
Shipper, J.J.	Pvt.	K 5th SCVC		UN	06/03/64	Richmond, VA		Hollywood Cem.Rchmd. U224	HC
Shippey, M.	Pvt.	F 15th SCVI		SG	09/20/63	Chickamauga, GA	KIA	(Also Wdd @ Chanc'lsville)	HOS,KEB
Shippy, Wallace	Pvt.	M P.S.S.	19	UN	12/24/61	Richmond, VA	DOD		ROH,JR
Shirar, Henry W.	Pvt.	F 25th SCVI	27	OG	06/30/65	Elmira, NY	DIP	Woodlawn N.C.#2830 Elmira	ROH,FPH,HAG,P65
Shirer, William David	Pvt.	E 1st SCVC	21	OG	08/14/63	Gettysburg, PA	DOW		ROH,GDR,P1,CDC
Shirers, John	Pvt.	A 15th SCVAB		OG	07/04/64	James Island, SC	KIA	(Exploding gun)	ROH,CDC
Shirey, Joseph P.	Pvt.	C 15th SCVI		LN	/ /	At home	DOD	(1864)	TOD,H15
Shirley, Allen Andrew	Pvt.	D 4th SCVI		AN	07/21/61	1st Manassas, VA	KIA		SA2
Shirley, E.	Pvt.	Boyce's By			08/30/62	2nd Manassas, VA	DOW	(JR=Sharpsburg 9/17)	JR,CDC
Shirley, E.P.	Pvt.	B 1st SCVIR		AN	08/24/64	Sullivans I., SC	ACD	(Falling roof in storm)	ROH,SA1
Shirley, Ephraim	Pvt.	B 17th SCVI		FD	06/25/63	Charleston, SC	DOD	Magnolia Cem. Charleston	ROH,MAG,RCD
Shirley, Hampton	Pvt.	G 24th SCVI			02/12/65	Camp Chase, OH	DIP	C.C.#1449 Columbus, OH	FPH,P6,P23
Shirley, J. Enoch	Pvt.	B 1st SCVIR		AN	12/18/64	Mt. Pleasant, SC	DOD		ROH
Shirley, J.J.	Pvt.	Matthews A		AN	09/06/63	Charleston, SC	DOD	Magnolia Cem. Charleston	ROH,MAG,RCD
Shirley, James	Pvt.	I 19th SCVI	37	AE	02/14/64	Rock Island, IL	DIP	C.C.#462 Rock Island, IL	ROH,FPH,P5
Shirley, James	Pvt.	H 19th SCVI		AE	11/23/63	Chattanooga, TN	KIA	(8th Co. 10/19th Consol)	ROH,CDC
Shirley, John P.	Pvt.	F 3rd SCVI		LS	07/03/63	Gettysburg, PA	KIA		ROH,JR,GDR,KEB
Shirley, R.	Pvt.	C 11th SCVI		CN	/ /	Richmond, VA		Oakwood C.#103,Row K,Div A	ROH,OWC,CDC
Shirley, Richard	Pvt.	L Orr's Ri.	32	AN	08/16/62	Richmond, VA	DOD		ROH
Shirley, Stephenson	Pvt.	K 22nd SCVI		PS	07/30/64	Crater, Pbg., VA	KIA		BLM
Shirley, Thomas	Pvt.	F 23rd SCVI		CR	/ /	Long Island, SC	ACD		HHC
Shirley, W. Newton	Pvt.	G Orr's Ri.		AE	07/15/62	Dill Farm, VA	DOD	(L, P.S.S.'s ?)	ROH,CDC
Shirley, W.B.	Pvt.	K 20th SCVI		LN	11/18/64	Pt. Lookout, MD	DIP	C.C. Pt. Lookout, MD	FPH,P6
Shirley, William	Sgt.	G 24th SCVI		AN	11/30/64	Franklin, TN	KIA	Williamson Cty, TN C.C.	ROH,WCT,PP
Shiver, Joseph	Pvt.	D 15th SCVI		KW	/ /	VA	DOD	(1863, KEB=Shivey))	HIC,KEB
Shiver, S.D.	Pvt.	B P.S.S.			/ /		DOD		JR
Shoolbred, Rives G.	2nd Sgt.	I 2nd SCVI		CN	09/22/63	Chickamauga, GA	DOW	(H2=Reeve G.)	JR,SA2,KEB,H2
Shooter, Charles F.	5th Sgt.	E 1st SCVIG		MN	05/06/64	Wilderness, VA	KIA		ROH,SA1,PDL,HMC
Shooter, Evander C.	2nd Lt.	E 1st SCVIG		MN	05/12/64	Spotsylvania, VA	KIA		ROH,SA1,BOS,HMC
Shooter, Washington P.	Lt. Col.	1st SCVIG	27	MN	05/12/64	Spotsylvania, VA	KIA	Spotsylvania C.H., VA	ROH,SCH,SA1,BOS
Short, Clark D.	Pvt.	I 12th SCVI		LR	/ /	Petersburg, VA	KIA	(1864)	LSS,LAN
Shott, Richard M.	Pvt.	K Orr's Ri.		AN	06/27/62	Gaines' Mill, VA	KIA		JR,CDC
Shrift, Thomas J.	Sgt.	K 12th SCVI	30	PS	09/05/62	Warrenton, VA	DOW	(Wdd 2nd Man)	ROH
Shuler, A.T.	Pvt.	F 2nd SCVA	24	OG	08/07/63		DOD	(EDR=H.T., ROH=1st SCVA)	ROH,EDR
Shuler, Bennett	Pvt.	SC Res			06/03/65	Pt. Lookout, MD	DIP	C.C. Pt. Lookout, MD	FPH,P6,P115
Shuler, Daniel M.	Pvt.	C 14th SCRes	51	OG	05/05/65	Hart's Island NY	DIP	Cypress Hills N.C.#2707 NY	ROH,FPH,P79
Shuler, F. Pinckney H.	Pvt.	F 25th SCVI	32	OG	04/07/65	Richmond, VA	DIP	Hollywood Cem., Rchmd, VA	ROH,P6,P65,HAG
Shuler, Franklin Elmore	2nd Lt.	F 25th SCVI	24	OG	05/19/64	Drury's Bluff VA	DOW		ROH,HAG,CV,R48
Shuler, H.	Pvt.	D 8th SCVI		OG	01/20/65	Columbia, SC	DOD		ROH
Shuler, Hamilton H.	Pvt.	1st SC	35	OG	06/24/61	At home	DOD		ROH
Shuler, Harrison A.	Pvt.	2nd SCVC		CN	11/12/63	Winchester, VA	DOD		ROH
Shuler, Henry	Pvt.	A 6th SCResB	48	OG	04/29/65	Columbia, SC	DOD	(PP=age 41)	ROH,PP
Shuler, Julius A.R.	Pvt.	I 2nd SCVA	17	OG	06/16/62	Secessionville	KIA		ROH,JR,CDC,PP
Shuler, M.J.	Pvt.	I 3rd SCVI		LS	09/17/62	Sharpsburg, MD	KIA	Rose Hill C. Hagerstown MD	JR,CDC,BOD
Shuler, Peter L.	Pvt.	C 20th SCVI	25	LN	02/12/65	Pt. Lookout, MD	DIP	C.C. Pt. Lookout, MD	ROH,FPH,KEB,P115
Shuler, S.M.	Pvt.	B 5th SCVI			05/15/62	Williamsburg, VA	DOW		JR,SA3
Shuler, Samuel	Pvt.	K 13th SCVI		LN	06/15/62	Richmond, VA		Hollywood Cem.Rchmd. O108	HC
Shuler, Wade A.	Pvt.	B 1st SCVIH		OG	08/15/63	Richmond, VA	DOD	Hollywood Cem.Rchmd. T29	ROH,HC,SA1
Shull, H.M.	Pvt.	H 20th SCVI		LN	09/09/64	Richmond, VA	DOW	Hollywood Cem.Rchmd. V91	ROH,HC,KEB,CDC
Shull, Henry W.	Pvt.	H 20th SCVI		LN	08/30/64	Deep Bottom, VA	KIA		ROH,KEB
Shull, J.E.	Pvt.	H 20th SCVI		LN	10/19/63	Chattanooga, TN	KIA		ROH

SOUTH CAROLINA DEAD IN CSA SERVICE 1861-1865

NAME	RANK	C REGIMENT	AGE	DS DIED	WHERE	WHY	BURIED	SOURCES
Shull, W.M.	Pvt.	L P.S.S.		05/31/62	7 Pines, VA	KIA	(CNM=Sherley, W.M.)	JR,CNM
Shull,Jr., John	Pvt.	C 15th SCVI	21	LN 12/27/62	Columbia, SC	DOW	Shiloh M.C. Gilbert, SC	ROH,JR,LNC,H15
Shumake, George Nelson	Pvt.	F 7th SCVIBn	34	KW 08/26/64		DOD		ROH,HIC,HAG
Shumake, Samson	Pvt.	F 8th SCVI	35	DN 12/15/61	Charlottesville	DOD	(KEB=Shumaker, JR=4/62)	ROH,JR,KEB
Shumaker, M.T.	Pvt.	F 2nd SCVA	18	OG 08/20/64		DOD		ROH
Shumate, James S.	Pvt.	B 2nd SCVI	29	GE 06/01/64	Cold Harbor, VA	KIA	Lebanon M.C. GE Cty.	ROH,SA2,GEC,KE
Shumpert, J.P.	Pvt.	C 23rd SCVI		ED 03/03/65	Richmond, VA			ROH
Shumpert, Meredith	Pvt.	F 20th SCVI		NY / /	Charleston, SC	DOW	(1864)	ROH
Shumpert, S.A.	Pvt.	K 1st SCVA		OG 09/12/63		DOD		ROH
Shumpert, William J.	Pvt.	K Orr's Ri.	22	AN 08/17/62		DOD		ROH,CDC
Shurbert, John	Pvt.	I Hol.Leg.	21	SG 06/19/62	At home	DOD		ROH
Shurbut, A. Thomas	Pvt.	K 3rd SCVI	24	SG 11/26/61	Centreville, VA	DOD	(Typhoid pneumonia)	ROH,JR,SA2,HOS
Shurley, T.S.	Pvt.	H 12th SCVI	29	YK / /		DOD	(1862)	CWC,YEB
Shurlnight, Lewis	Pvt.	F 25th SCVI	24	OG 05/16/64	Drury's Bluff VA	KIA		ROH,CV,CDC,HAG
Sian, George S.T.	Pvt.	A Ham.Leg.	25	GN 12/12/61	Charlottesville	DOD	Univ. Cem. Charlottesville	ROH,ACH
Siblet, Joshua	Pvt.	A 17th SCVI		CR 07/30/64	Crater, Pbg., VA	KIA		BLM
Siddall, John	3rd Lt.	A 20th SCVI		PS 10/13/64	Strasburg, VA	KIA	(R48=Sindall)	ROH,CDC,R48
Sidly, John				/ /			Rose Hill C. Hagerstown MD	WAT
Sief, A.S.	Pvt.	K 18th SCVI		SG 08/30/62	2nd Manassas, VA	KIA		ROH
Sighler, A.	Pvt.	K 7th SCVI		ED 10/15/62			Stonewall C. Winchester VA	ROH,WIN
Sightler, A.M.	2nd Sgt.	K 1st SCVIH		OG 10/15/62	VA	DOD	(To Hospital 10/10/62)	ROH,SA1
Sightler, Rufus Harmon	Pvt.	B 9th SCVIB		BT 09/10/61	Germantown, VA	DOD		ROH,JR
Sightler, S.B.	Pvt.	K 1st SCVIH		OG 06/16/62		DOD		ROH,SA1
Sightler, Thomas A.	Pvt.	A 5th SCVC	30	OG 09/10/64	At home	DOD		ROH
Sightler, W.S. (W.H.?)	Pvt.	K 1st SCVIH		OG 05/04/64	Lynchburg, VA	DOD	Lynchburg CSA Cem.#8 R1	SA1,BBW
Sigman, Jesse Eugene	Pvt.	C 3rd SCVI	25	NY 02/14/65	Orangeburg, SC	KIA		ROH,SA2,ANY,KE
Sigman, S.	Pvt.	B 13th SCVI		SG 08/28/62	Richmond, VA		Hollywood Cem.Rchmd. S83	HC
Signs, J.W.	Pvt.	C 26th SCVI		MN 04/27/62	Richmond, VA		Hollywood Cem.Rchmd. F116	HC
Silcox, James	Pvt.	B 25th SCVI	20	CN 08/22/64	Petersburg, VA	DOD	Magnolia Cem. Charleston	ROH,MAG,PP,HAG
Sill, B.	Pvt.	K 1st SCVA		12/12/63	Ft. Sumter, SC	ACD	(Magazine explosion)	ROH,CDC
Sill, John H.	Pvt.	A 23rd SCVI		KW 07/30/64	Crater, Pbg., VA	KIA		ROH,HIC,BLM
Sills, A.N.	Pvt.	I 14th SCVI		AE 05/27/64	Richmond, VA		Hollywood Cem.Rchmd. I95	HC
Sills, O.M.	Pvt.	E 14th SCVI		LS 05/03/64	Richmond, VA			ROH
Simkins, John	Pvt.			/ /	Columbia, SC		Elmwood Cem. Columbia, SC	MP
Simkins, P.P.	Pvt.	B 4th SCVC		BT 05/30/64	Old Church, VA	KIA		ROH
Simmons,	Pvt.	SCVI		/ /			Stonewall C. Winchester VA	WIN
Simmons, Charles	Pvt.	K P.S.S.		SG / /		DOW		JR
Simmons, D.J.	Pvt.	G Orr's Ri.		AE / /	Richmond, VA			ROH
Simmons, D.L.	Pvt.	B P.S.S.		PS 06/30/62	Frayser's Farm	KIA	(JR=6/27)	ROH,JR,CDC
Simmons, Edwin Bryant	2nd Lt.	E 14th SCVI	19	LS 10/01/64	Jones Farm, Va	DOW		ROH,BOS,RHL,UD
Simmons, G.	Pvt.	H 1st SCVIH		SG 10/30/63	Lookout Valley	DOW		SA1,CDC
Simmons, George	Pvt.	K 3rd SCVI	27	SG 06/01/64	Cold Harbor, VA	KIA	(HOS=Deep Bottom, VA)	ROH,SA2,HOS,KE
Simmons, J.	Pvt.	A 1st SCVIG		BL 07/28/62	Gaines' Mill, VA	DOW		ROH,JR,SA1
Simmons, John	Pvt.	C 17th SCVCB		CN 10/19/62		DOD		JR
Simmons, R.	Pvt.	D Orr's Ri.		AN 09/01/62	Ox hill, VA	KIA		JR
Simmons, Tully Sullivan	Pvt.	I 19th SCVI	34	AN 08/07/64	Griffin, GA	DOW	Stonewall C. Griffin, GA	ROH,BGA,UD2
Simmons, Warren	Pvt.	A 16th SCVI	18	GE 07/30/62	Adams Run, SC	DOD	Taylor/Gibson Fam. Cem.	16R,GEC,GEE,PP
Simmons, William	Sgt.	H Ham.Leg.		OG 06/16/64		DOW		ROH
Simmons, William	Pvt.	K 26th SCVI	18	HY 05/31/63	Jackson, MS	DOD		ROH,PP
Simmons, William	Pvt.	D 24th SCVI		BT 12/01/64	Camp Douglas, IL	DIP	Oak Woods Cem. Chicago, IL	FPH,P5,P58
Simmons, William	Pvt.	B 16th SCVI		GE 06/16/62	At home	DOD		PP

S

SOUTH CAROLINA DEAD IN CSA SERVICE 1861-1865

NAME	RANK	C REGIMENT	AGE	DS	DIED	WHERE	WHY	BURIED	SOURCES
Simmons, William A.	1st Sgt.	K 1st SCVIR		GE	03/16/65	Averysboro, NC	KIA		ROH,SA1,WAT,PP
Simms, W.N.	Pvt.	A 13th SCVI		LS	05/15/62	Ashland, VA	DOD		ROH
Simnson, James A.	Pvt.	F 24th SCVI		AN	07/20/64	Peachtree Creek	KIA		HOL
Simon, James	Pvt.	C 3rd SCVABn			11/27/64	Ship Island, MS	DIP	N,C, Ship Island, MS	PP
Simons, D.	Pvt.	D 1st SCVC		CR	/ /	Lynchburg, VA		Lynchburg CSA Cem.#9 R4	BBW
Simons, Harris	Pvt.	H 1st SCVIG		CN	07/17/62	Richmond, VA	DOD	Hollywood Cem.Rchmd. N8	ROH,JR,HC,SA1
Simons, J.	Pvt.	A 2nd SCVIRi		AE	07/29/62	Richmond, VA		Hollywood Cem.Rchmd. H259	HC
Simons, James	Pvt.		23	CN	06/14/63		DOD		ROH,RCD
Simons, James R.	5th Sgt.	K 2nd SCVI		CN	05/12/64	Spotsylvania, VA	KIA	Spotsylvania C.H., VA	ROH,SCH,SA2,KEB
Simons, Thomas Young	Pvt.	3rd SCVC	33	CN	08/27/64	Savannah, GA	DOD		ROH
Simonton, Charles P.	Pvt.	H 6th SCVI	30	FD	09/30/64	Ft. Harrison, VA	KIA		ROH
Simonton,, W. Boyce	Pvt.	H 6th SCVI		FD	06/15/62	Fts. Monroe, VA	DOW	(Wdd @ POW 7 Pines)	ROH,JR,CDC,HFC
Simpkins, John C.	Lt. Col.	1st SCVIR	36	NY	07/18/63	Bty. Wagner, SC	KIA	Trinity E.C. Abbeville, SC	ROH,SA1,DOC,ANY
Simpson, A.	Pvt.	G Orr's Ri.		AE	06/27/62	Gaines' Mill, VA	KIA		ROH,JR,CDC
Simpson, Alexander	Pvt.	E 6th SCVC	24		03/12/63	Adams Run, SC	DOD		ROH,PP
Simpson, Anderson	Pvt.	E Hol.Leg.	41	AN	05/20/63	Montgomery, AL	DOD		ROH,HOS
Simpson, Colin M.	Pvt.	C 24th SCVI	18	CO	/ /	James Island, SC	DOD	(Dorchester Enroll Book)	ROH,TEB
Simpson, Elisha R.	Pvt.	K Orr's Ri.	21	AN	12/09/61		DOD		ROH
Simpson, G.S.	Pvt.	A 13th SCVI	07	LS	07/01/63	Gettysburg, PA	KIA	(JR=E.S.)	ROH,JR,CDC
Simpson, J.C. (J.H.?)	Pvt.	7th SCVI			/ /	Richmond, VA			ROH
Simpson, J.L.	Pvt.	F Hol.Leg.	18	AE	06/29/64	Sappony Ch., VA	DOW		ROH
Simpson, James A.	Pvt.	D Ham.Leg.		AN	/ /	Brentsville, VA	DOD	(1861)	ROH,GRS
Simpson, Jesse M.	Pvt.	F 24th SCVI		AN	03/10/62		DOD		HOL
Simpson, John	Pvt.	E 14th SCVI		LS	06/27/62	Gaines' Mill, VA	KIA		ROH,JR,CGS,CDC
Simpson, John	Pvt.	J 4th SCVI		AN	07/21/61	1st Manassas, VA	KIA	(JR=L,P.S.S.)	JR,SA2
Simpson, John D.	Pvt.	B 7th SCVIBn	18	CR	03/22/62	James Island, SC	DOD		ROH,HAG,HHC
Simpson, John F.	Pvt.	F Hol.Leg.			01/19/65	Elmira, NY	DIP	Woodlawn N.C.#1429 Elmira	FPH,P65,P120
Simpson, Luke	Pvt.	I 2nd SCVI		CN	05/28/63	Richmond, VA	DOD	Oakwood C.#13,Row 30,Div D	ROH,SA2,OWC,H2
Simpson, Mathew	Pvt.	F 24th SCVI		AN	03/18/64	Marietta, GA	DOD	Con. Cem. Marietta, GA	HOL,BGA,UD2
Simpson, R. Caspar	3rd Cpl.	A 3rd SCVI	24	LS	09/17/62	Sharpsburg, MD	KIA	(KEB=Simpson, B.C.) UD3	ROH,JR,SA2,KEB
Simpson, Taliaferro N.	1st Cpl.	A 3rd SCVI	24	AN	09/20/63	Chickamauga, GA	KIA	Simpson Cem. Pendleton SC	ROH,SA2,CDC,KEB
Simpson, W.J.	Pvt.	B P.S.S.		AN	01/25/64		DOD		ROH
Simpson, W.L.	Pvt,	G 14th SCVI		AE	/ /	Richmond, VA		Oakwood C.#10,Row L,Div A	ROH,OWC
Simpson, W.S.	Pvt.	D Orr's Ri.		AN	/ /	Richmond, VA		Oakwood C.#18,Row F,Div C	ROH,OWC
Simpson, Wiley Wade	Pvt.	G 3rd SCVI	25	LS	06/15/64	Petersburg, VA	KIA	(By Sharpshooter) UD3	ROH,SA2,KEB,RHL
Simpson, William H.	Pvt.	G Orr's Ri.		AE	06/27/62	Gaines' Mill, VA	KIA		ROH,CV,CDC
Simpson, William L.	Pvt.	I 14th SCVI	17	AE	01/15/63	Farmville, VA	DOW	(Wdd 6/30/62)	ROH,HOL
Simril, Franklin M.	Pvt.	H 18th SCVI	21	YK	05/20/64	Clay's Farm, VA	KIA		ROH,YEB
Simril, John J.	Pvt.	5th SCVI	22	YK	05/15/62	Richmond, VA	DOD		YMD,YEB
Sims, Clough L.	1st Lt Adj	18th SCVI		UN	11/21/64	Petersburg, VA	DOW	(UD3=Crater, DOW 8/15/64)	R47,UD3
Sims, David	Pvt.	D 13th SCVI	23	NY	08/01/62	Richmond, VA	DOD	(Typhoid)	JR,
Sims, Edward T.	Pvt.	D 5th SCVI		UN	07/29/63	Charleston, SC	DOD	(ROH=Simons, NI SA3)	ROH,SA3
Sims, Garrett T.	Pvt.	I 12th SCVI		LR	09/07/62	Cold Harbor, VA	KIA	Hollywood Cem.Rchmd. V491	ROH,HC,LAN
Sims, J. Frank	Pvt.	I 12th SCVI		LR	06/27/62	Gaines' Mill, VA	KIA		ROH,LAN,CNM
Sims, J. Terry	Pvt.	E 16th SCVI	37	GE	07/25/62	Adams Run, SC	DOD	(PP=7/22/62)	ROH,16R,PP
Sims, J.H.	Pvt.	C 23rd SCVI		CN	07/30/64	Crater, Pbg., VA	KIA		BLM
Sims, J.K.S.	Pvt.	G P.S.S.	20	UN	04/15/63	Petersburg, VA	DOD		JR,PP
Sims, J.O. (J.D.?)	Pvt.	A 13th SCVI		LS	06/21/62	Richmond, VA	DOD		JR
Sims, James R.	Pvt.	I 19th SCVI		AE	09/20/63	Chickamauga, GA	KIA		ROH,CDC
Sims, James S.	4th Cpl.	B 1st SCVIG	23	LS	09/01/64	Richmond, VA	DOD		ROH,SA1,ANY
Sims, John	Pvt.	D 16th SCVI		GE	/ /	At home	DOD	(1864)	16R

SOUTH CAROLINA DEAD IN CSA SERVICE 1861-1865

NAME	RANK	C REGIMENT	AGE	DS	DIED	WHERE	WHY	BURIED	SOURCES
Sims, John P.	Pvt.	D 13th SCVI	25	NY	/ /	Richmond, VA	DOD		ANY
Sims, M.G.	Pvt.	F Hol.Leg.		LS	11/12/64	Richmond, VA	DOW (Wdd @ Pbg)		ROH
Sims, Martin S.	Pvt.	E 16th SCVI	40	GE	02/01/64	Oxford, GA	DOD		ROH,16R
Sims, Michael J.	5th Sgt.	D 1st SCVIH		LR	10/12/64	Ft. Harrison, VA	DOW	Hollywood Cem.Rchmd. V392	HC,SA1,LAN
Sims, T.	Pvt.	A 13th SCVI		LS	/ /	Richmond, VA		Oakwood C.#1,Row 26,Div D	ROH,OWC
Sims, Thomas R.	Sgt. Major	18th SCVI		DN	05/20/64	Clay's Farm, VA	KIA		ROH,UD3
Sims, W.	Pvt.	C 12th SCVI		FD	/ /	Richmond, VA		Oakwood C.#134,Row L,Div A	ROH,OWC
Sims, W.N.	Pvt.	A 13th SCVI		LS	05/31/62	Richmond, VA	DOD (Measles & Pneumonia)		JR
Sims, W.P.	Pvt.	A 13th SCVI		LS	05/21/62	Ashland, VA	DOD (Measles)		JR
Sims, William	Pvt.	E 12th SCVI	26	LR	08/10/62	Richmond, VA	DOD		ROH,LAN
Sims, William	2nd Lt.	D 22nd SCVI		PS	07/10/64	Petersburg, VA	KIA		R48
Sinam, T.M.	Pvt.	2nd SCV			07/31/61	Culpepper, VA	DOD	Fairview Cem. Culpepper VA	CGH
Sinclair, D.R.	2nd Cpl.	F 21st SCVI		MO	06/24/64	Petersburg, VA	KIA (D.M. ?)		ROH,HOM
Sinclair, Malcom G.	Pvt.	H Orr's Ri.		MN	08/15/62	Charlottesville	DOD		HMC
Sindal, (Tindal?)	Pvt.				/ /	Columbia, SC		Elmwood Cem. Columbia, SC	MP
Sineath, Joseph P.	Pvt.	I 21st SCVI		MN	/ /	Morris Island SC	DOD		HMC,HAG
Sing, Solomon	Pvt.	A 26th SCVI		HY	02/15/65	At home	DOD		ROH
Sing, W.J.	Pvt.	E 26th SCVI		HY	08/28/63	Savannah, GA	DOD	Laurel Grove C. Savannah	ROH,BGA
Singletary, C.W.	Pvt.	E 8th SCVI		DN	12/15/61	Richmond, VA	DOD	Oakwood C.#42,Row D,Div A	ROH,JR,OWC,KEB
Singletary, J.C.	Pvt.	K 10th SCVI		CN	09/20/63	Chickamauga, GA	KIA		ROH,RAS,HOW,CD
Singletary, W.D.	Pvt.	I 4th SCVC		WG	/ /		DOD (1864)		CTA,HOW
Singleton, Armisted R.	Pvt.	G Orr's Ri.		AE	08/15/62	Richmond, VA		(On Rchmd effects list)	ROH,CDC
Singleton, J.P.	Pvt.	F 14th SCVI		LS	/ /	Lynchburg, VA		Lynchburg CSA CEm.#2 R2	BBW
Singleton, Solomon R.	Cpl.	A 26th SCVI	18	HY	12/15/62	At home	DOD		ROH
Singley, D.C.	Pvt.	G 13th SCVI		NY	09/18/62	Sharpsburg, MD	DOW		ROH,ANY
Singley, G.M.	Pvt.	F 20th SCVI		NY	05/06/64	Charleston, SC	DOD (Soldiers Relief Hospital)		ROH,CDC,KEB
Singley, George M.	Sgt.	H Hol.Leg.		NY	02/05/65	Hatcher's Run VA	KIA (May be an earlier Engmt)		ANY
Singley, James E.	Pvt.	G Hol.Leg.	18	NY	11/04/64	Petersburg, VA	KIA		ROH,ANY
Singley, Miles S.	Pvt.	H 13th SCVI	22	NY	03/03/64	Ft. Delaware, DE	DIP	Finn's Pt., NJ Nat. Cem.	ROH,FPH,P40,AN
Sippel, Henry	Pvt.	A 18th SCVI		UN	07/30/64	Crater, Pbg., VA	KIA		ROH,BLM
Sisson, J.C.	Pvt.	L 7th SCVI		HY	/ /	Richmond, VA		(Sessions?)	ROH
Sistare, A.J.	Pvt.	D 1st SCVIH		LR	08/30/62	2nd Manassas, VA	DOW		LAN,CDC
Sistare, J.H.	Pvt.	A 5th SCVI		LR	10/28/62	Winchester, VA	DOW	Stonewall C. Winchester VA	ROH,JR,WIN,LAN
Sistare, Will T.	Pvt.	I 12th SCVI		LR	/ /	Wilderness, VA	KIA		LAN
Size, R.M.					03/29/64	Emory, NC		Con. Cem. Emory, VA	PP
Sizemore,	Pvt.	A 22nd SCVI			01/12/65	Richmond, VA		Hollywood Cem.Rchmd. 948	HC
Sizemore, Berry	Pvt.	G 22nd SCVI	30	AN	07/30/64	Crater, Pbg., VA	KIA		ROH,BLM
Sizemore, David	Pvt.	F 13th SCVI		SG	/ /		DOD (1861)		HOS
Sizemore, Edward D.	Pvt.	C 22nd SCVI	27	GE	11/19/64	Elmira, NY	DIP	Woodlawn N.C.#948 Elmira	ROH,FPH,P65,P1
Sizemore, J.	Pvt.	K 22nd SCVI		PS	12/20/64	Richmond, VA			ROH
Sizemore, J. Thomas	5th Sgt.	C 22nd SCVI	23	GE	03/01/64	Charlotte, NC	DOD (PP=3/22/64)		ROH,PP
Sizemore, Powell	Pvt.	H 14th SCVI		BL	07/28/64	Ft. Delaware, DE	DIP	Finn's Pt., NJ Nat. Cem.	ROH,FPH,P5,P40
Sizemore, Stephen	Pvt.	B 13th SCVI		SG	08/29/62	Richmond, VA			ROH,HOS
Skates, William	Pvt.	G P.S.S.		YK	/ /	Lynchburg, VA		Lynchburg, CSA Cem.#7 R5	BBW
Skelton, Andrew J.	Pvt.	B 15th SCVAB			05/07/65	Pt. Lookout, MD	DIP	C.C. Pt. Lookout, MD	FPH,P6,P115
Skelton, James	Pvt.				/ /		DOW (7 days)		HOF
Skinner, B. Witherspoon	Pvt.	C Ham.Leg.		CL	02/01/62	At home	DOD		JR
Skinner, Franklin	Pvt.	H 21st SCVI		DN	04/09/65	Elmira, NY	DIP	Woodlawn N.C.#2612 Elmira	FPH,P6,P65,HAG
Skinner, J.R.	Pvt.	A 14th SCVI	19	DN	07/22/63	Richmond, VA	DOD		ROH
Skinner, Richard M.	Cpt.	H 5th SCVC		CL	06/24/64	Ladd's Store, VA	KIA		ROH,CDC,R43
Skinner, Simpson	Pvt.	H 21st SCVI	38	DN	03/24/62	Georgetown, SC	DOD		PP

S

SOUTH CAROLINA DEAD IN CSA SERVICE 1861-1865

NAME	RANK	C REGIMENT	AGE	DS	DIED	WHERE	WHY	BURIED	SOURCES
Skipper, Arthur B.	Pvt.	A 10th SCVI		GN	09/20/63	Chickamauga, GA	DOW		GRG,LOR,HOW,CDC
Skipper, James M.	Pvt.	G 8th SCVI		MO	03/04/62		DOD (Pneumonia)		JR
Skipper, John	Pvt.	F 1st SCVIG		HY	08/29/62	2nd Manassas, VA	KIA (JR=Co.E)		ROH,JR,SA1,PDL
Skipper, Samuel T.	Pvt.	A 21st SCVI		GN	07/27/64	Pt. Lookout, MD	DIP	C.C. Pt. Lookout, MD	ROH,FPH,HAG,P113
Skipper, Thomas	Pvt.	G 21st SCVI			01/15/65	Ft. Fisher, NC	KIA		PP
Skipper, Timothy	Pvt.	A 21st SCVI		GN	07/10/63	Morris Island SC	KIA		ROH,CDC,HAG
Skippers, James	Pvt.	M P.S.S.		MO	/ /		DOD (1862)		ROH
Slagle, John W.	Pvt.	F 25th SCVI		LN	/ /		KIA		ROH
Slagle, William F.	Pvt.	B 1st SCVIH		LN	08/30/62	2nd Manassas, VA	KIA		ROH,JR,SA1,CDC
Slater, Edward D.	Pvt.	C Orr's Ri.		PS	06/27/62	Gaines' Mill, VA	KIA (ROH= Slatter)		ROH,CDC
Slater, J.C.	Pvt.	D 18th SCVI		AN	09/10/64	Columbus, GA	DOD		ROH
Slatten, Jeff	Pvt.	D Ham.Leg.		AN	10/28/63	Will's Valley TN	KIA		GRS
Slice, James Frederick	Pvt.	H 13th SCVI	22	LN	08/28/62	Warrenton, VA			ROH
Slice, John Jefferson	Pvt.	C 20th SCVI	25	LN	10/13/64	Cedar Creek, VA	KIA		ROH,KEB
Slice, Richard Godfrey	Pvt.	H 3rd SCVI	23	LN	12/13/62	Fredericksburg	KIA		ROH,JR,SA2,KEB
Sligh, David B.	Pvt.	D 13th SCVI	30	NY	12/27/61	Coosawatchie, SC	DOD (Typhoid)(JR=1/6/62)		JR,ANY
Sligh, David P.	Pvt.	C 3rd SCVI		NY	07/16/62	Malvern Hill, VA	DOW	Ebenezer U.M.C Newberry SC	ROH,JR,NCC,ANY
Sligh, John N.	Pvt.	H Hol.Leg.		NY	03/25/65	Ft. Steadman, VA	KIA		ANY
Sligh, Monroe	Pvt.	F 20th SCVI		NY	/ /	Charleston, SC	DOD		ANY,KEB
Sligh, Thomas W.	Pvt.	E 3rd SCVI	20	NY	07/02/63	Gettysburg, PA	KIA	Magnolia C. Charleston, SC	ROH,JR,GDR,WV
Sloan, Calvin Washington	Pvt.	F 12th SCVI		FD	09/26/62		DOW (Wdd @ Sharpsburg)		JR,HFC
Sloan, Enoch Berry	Pvt.	D Orr's Ri.	30	AN	06/15/62	At home	DOD		ROH,CDC
Sloan, J. Wiley	1st Sgt.	G 6th SCVI		AN	05/31/62	7 Pines, VA	KIA (ROH=J.B., WDB=I.W.)		ROH,WDB,CDC
Sloan, John B.	2nd Lt.	D Orr's Ri.	38	AN	09/23/62	Charlottesville	DOD		ROH,CDC,R45
Sloan, John Ebenezer P.	Pvt.	E 3rd SCVI	19	NY	11/18/63	Knoxville, TN	KIA	Cannon Creek ARP Newberry	ROH,NCC,ANY,KEB
Sloan, John Matheson	Sgt.	F 12th SCVI		FD	08/29/62	2nd Manassas, VA	KIA		ROH,JR,HFC
Sloan, Joseph Berry	1st Lt.	D Orr's Ri.	30	AN	12/13/62	Fredericksburg	KIA (JR=DOD)		ROH,JR,R45
Sloan, Robert	Pvt.	Ham. Leg.		FD	/ /	Richmond, VA			ROH
Sloan, Seth M.	Pvt.	B Hol.Leg.	21	SG	08/30/62	2nd Manassas, VA	KIA (Wdd once before)		ROH,HOS
Sloan, Thomas G.	2nd Cpl.	E 3rd SCVI		LS	/ /	At home	DOW (ANY=Wdd.@ Chickamauga)		SA2,ANY,KEB
Sloan, Thomas Jefferson	2nd Lt.	E 4th SCVI		PS	02/15/62	Charlottesville	DOD		ROH,SA2
Small, Alexander T.	Pvt.	E 12th SCVI	17	LR	04/25/62	McPhersonville	DOD (Bled to death. cause?)		ROH,LAN
Small, Amos C.	Pvt.	K 26th SCVI	23	HY	12/07/64	Elmira, NY	DIP	Woodlawn N.C.#1185 Elmira	ROH,FPH,P65,P120
Small, Frederick W.	Pvt.	E 12th SCVI	17	LR	11/05/61	Bay Point, SC	DOD		ROH,LAN
Small, Henry	Pvt.	A 21st SCVI		GN	06/15/62	At home	DOD		ROH
Small, J.C.	Pvt.	A 10th SCVI			09/20/63	Chickamauga, GA	KIA (Not listed as KIA in RAS)		CTA
Small, James M.	2nd Cpl.	H 2nd SCVI		LR	07/13/63	Gettysburg, PA	DOW		ROH,JR,GDR,SA2
Small, John C.	Pvt.	E 12th SCVI	19	LR	06/27/62	Gaines' Mill, VA	KIA	Oakwood C.#39,Row L,Div C	ROH,OWC,LAN,CNM
Small, John Canda	Pvt.	E 12th SCVI	22	LR	06/27/62	Gaines' Mill, VA	KIA		ROH,LAN
Small, Joseph J.	Pvt.	A 25th SCVI	22	CN	05/27/64	Pt. Walthal Jctn	DOW (Body sent home)		ROH,PP,WLI,HAG
Small, P.	Pvt.	I 3rd SC Res			02/19/65	Charleston, SC	DOD	Magnolia Cem. Charleston	ROH,MAG,RCD
Small, Robert F.	Cpl.	Palm. LA	20	SR	07/07/63	Hagerstown, MD	DOW (AWOL from E,2nd SCVI)		ROH,JR,GDR,SA2
Small, Thomas	Pvt.	E 12th SCVI	22	LR	02/19/62	McPhersonville	DOD		ROH,LAN
Small, W. Seaborn	Pvt.	H 2nd SCVI		LR	08/26/61	Richmond, VA	DOD (Typhoid)		H2,SA2
Small, W.T.	Pvt.	H 12th SCVI		LR	08/26/61		DOR (Typhoid, KEB=W.F.)		JR,LAN,KEB
Smalley, Isaiah	Pvt.	I 8th SCVI		MN	09/21/61	Culpepper, VA	DOD	Fairview Cem. Culpepper VA	JR,CGH,HMC,KEB
Smart, Thomas H.	2nd Lt.	E 15th SCVI	24	FD	12/07/61	Savannah, GA	DOW (Wdd 11/7/61 Port Royal)		ROH,JR,KEB,PP
Smiley, D.S.	Pvt.	G 4th SCVC		CO	06/04/64	Richmond, VA	DOW (Wdd @ Hawe's Shop, VA)		ROH,SSO
Smith, A.C.	Pvt.	I 21st SCVI		MN	01/10/65	Fayetteville, SC			PP
Smith, A.J.	Pvt.	F Hol.Leg.	28	AE	09/05/64	Elmira, NY	DIP	Woodlawn N.C.#239 Elmira	ROH,FPH,P5,P66
Smith, A.M.	Cpl.	SCVA	23	CD	12/15/61	Portsmouth, VA	DOD		ROH

SOUTH CAROLINA DEAD IN CSA SERVICE 1861-1865

NAME	RANK	C	REGIMENT	AGE	DS	DIED	WHERE	WHY	BURIED	SOURCES
Smith, A.T.	Pvt.	C	17th SCVI	35	YK	07/30/64	Crater, Pbg., VA	KIA		ROH,BLM,YEB
Smith, A.W.	Pvt.	E	24th SCVI		CO	06/15/64	Pine Mtn., GA	DOW		CDC
Smith, Aaron John	1st Sgt.	G	22nd SCVI	34	AN	07/30/64	Crater, Pbg., VA	KIA		ROH,BLM
Smith, Abraham T.	Cpt.	D	16th SCVI		GE	09/07/63		DOD		16R,R47
Smith, Adam L.	Pvt.	E	1st SCVC		OG	12/15/61	Fripp's Bluff SC	ACD		ROH
Smith, Albert	Pvt.	A	13th SCVI		NY	07/01/63	Gettysburg, PA	KIA	Fairview B.C. Newberry, SC	ROH,JR,NCC,GDR
Smith, Alexander D.	Col.		26th SCVI		MO	/ /	At home	DOW	(Wdd @ Pbg. after 6/1/64)	HOM,LC
Smith, Ambrose	Pvt.	I	P.S.S.		PS	06/27/62	Gaines' Mill, SC	KIA		ROH
Smith, Anderson A.	Pvt.	G	22nd SCVI		AN	04/29/65	Pt. Lookout, MD	DIP	C.C. Pt. Lookout, MD	ROH,FPH,P6,P11
Smith, Andrew A.	Pvt.	K	12th SCVI	30	PS	07/15/63	Richmond, VA	DOD		ROH
Smith, Andrew Kindrey	Cpt.	I	13th SCVI	39	SG	08/29/62	2nd Manassas, VA	KIA		ROH,JR,HOS,R47
Smith, Andrew N.	Pvt.		Kanapaux's	22	YK	02/10/65	Columbia, SC	DOD	Elmwood Cem. Columbia, SC	ROH,MP,PP,YEB
Smith, Augustus Marshall	Lt. Col.		1st SCVIG	35	AE	06/30/62	Gaines' Mill, VA	DOW	Hollywood Cem.Rchmd. M3	ROH,JR,HC,SA1,
Smith, B.	Pvt.	F	Ham.Leg.		GE	06/01/62	7 Pines, VA	DOW	(JR=5/31)	ROH,JR,CDC
Smith, B.A.	Pvt.	C	25th SCVI		WG	05/21/64	Petersburg, VA		Blandford Church Pbg., VA	BLC
Smith, B.M.	Pvt.	K	3rd SCVI	20	SG	05/09/62	Richmond, VA	DOD	Oakwood C.#69,Row K,Div A	ROH,JR,SA2,OWC
Smith, B.S.	Cpl.	C	P.S.S.		AN	07/15/62	Richmond, VA	DOW	(Wdd @ Frayser's Farm)	SA2,BMJ
Smith, B.T.	Pvt.	D	4th SCVI		AN	/ /	Lynchburg, VA	DOD	Lynchburg CSA Cem.#7 R1	JR,BBW,SA2
Smith, Ben	Sgt.	A	4th SCVI	22		06/15/61	Richmond, VA	KIA		ROH
Smith, Benjamin F.	Pvt.	E	11th SCVI		BT	05/03/65	Elmira, NY	DIP	Woodlawn N.C.#2753 Elmira	FPH,HAG,P65,P1
Smith, Benjamin G.	Pvt.	F	16th SCVI		GE	06/19/64	Marietta, GA	KIA	(16R= DOD in MS,1863)	ROH,16R
Smith, Benjamin R.	Pvt.	G	22nd SCVI	20	AN	07/30/64	Crater, Pbg., VA	KIA		ROH,BLM
Smith, Benjamin R.	Pvt.	M	7th SCVI		ED	07/02/63	Gettysburg, PA	KIA		ROH,JR,GDR,CDC
Smith, Benjamin W.	Pvt.	H	7th SCVI		ED	07/02/63	Gettysburg, PA	KIA		ROH,GDR
Smith, Berry	Pvt.	D	22nd SCVI		PS	03/02/62	Columbia, SC	DOD		PP
Smith, C.	Pvt.		Orr's Ri.			07/05/62	Richmond, VA			ROH
Smith, C. Perry	Pvt.	A	1st SCResB			/ /	In prison	DIP		UD3
Smith, C.C.	Cpl.		5th SCVC			06/15/64	Petersburg, VA	KIA		ROH
Smith, Calvin	Pvt.	H	24th SCVI	20	CR	07/11/63	Brownsville, MS	DOD		ROH,HHC,CB
Smith, Cannon	Pvt.	G	1st SCVIBn		CN	/ /	Morris Island SC	DOW	(1863)	ROH
Smith, Capers M.	Cpl.	A	20th SCVI	19	PS	09/02/63	Mt. Pleasant, SC	DOD		ROH,JR,KEB
Smith, Charles	Pvt.	F	2nd SCVIRi			06/27/62	Columbia, SC	DOD		PP
Smith, Charles C.	Cpl.	F	11th SCVI	20	BT	05/09/64	Swift Creek, VA	KIA		ROH,HAG
Smith, Charles S.	Pvt.	I	11th SCVI		CO	06/16/64	Drury's Bluff VA	DOW		ROH,HAG
Smith, D.N.	Pvt.	A	3rd SCVI		LS	09/20/63	Chickamauga, GA	KIA		CDC
Smith, D.P.	Cpl.	K	13th SCVI		LN	07/01/63	Gettysburg, PA	KIA		ROH,JR
Smith, D.P.	Pvt.	I	13th SCVI		SG	06/05/62	Richmond, VA		Hollywood Cem.Rchmd. P42	HC
Smith, D.R.	Pvt.	D	7th SCVIBn	22	KW	12/21/63	At home	DOD	(ROH=Co.G)	ROH,HAG,HIC
Smith, Daniel	1st Sgt.	G	22nd SCVI	31	AN	03/25/62	Charleston, SC	DOD		ROH
Smith, Daniel	Pvt.	B	13th SCVI		SG	08/29/62	2nd Manassas, VA	KIA		HOS
Smith, David M.	Pvt.	C	25th SCVI	20	WG	05/16/64	Drury's Bluff VA	KIA		CTA,HOW,CDC,HA
Smith, David N.	Pvt.	F	1st SCVIG		HY	05/18/63	Richmond, VA	DOW	Hollywood Cem.Rchmd. T482	HC,SA1,PDL
Smith, Davis W.S.	Pvt.	A	20th SCVI	20	PS	07/23/63	Petersburg, VA	DOD	Blandford Church Pbg., VA	ROH,BLC,KEB,PP
Smith, E.	Pvt.	G	26th SCVI		DN	07/18/64	Richmond, VA			ROH
Smith, E.A.	Pvt.	I	11th SCVI		CO	06/15/64	Richmond, VA		Hollywood Cem.Rchmd. U173	HC
Smith, E.B.	Pvt.	D	21st SCVI			03/02/65	Elmira, NY	DIP	(POW @ Ft. Fisher)	P65,P66
Smith, E.C.	Pvt.	A	23rd SCVI	39	RD	08/05/64	Crater, Pbg., VA	DOW		ROH,BLM,PP
Smith, Edmond	Pvt.	A	Hol.Leg.	30	SG	07/01/62	Adams Run, SC	DOD	(PP=age 43 & 7/3/62)	ROH,HOS,PP
Smith, Elihu P.	Pvt.	E	6th SCVC	19	SG	02/20/65	Elmira, NY	DIP	Woodlawn N.C.#2322 Elmira	FPH,UNC,P65,P1
Smith, Elijah	Pvt.	F	18th SCVI		YK	08/30/62	2nd Manassas, VA	KIA		YEB
Smith, Elijah H.	Pvt.	A	16th SCVI	24	GE	01/25/62			DOD Standing Springs B.C.	GEC,GEE

S

SOUTH CAROLINA DEAD IN CSA SERVICE 1861-1865

NAME	RANK	C	REGIMENT	AGE	DS	DIED	WHERE	WHY	BURIED	SOURCES
Smith, F.	Pvt.	F	Hol.Leg.	20	AE	01/24/62	Adams Run, SC	DOD		ROH
Smith, Fias	Pvt.	E	26th SCVI		HY	04/15/62	Camp Lookout, SC	DOD		ROH
Smith, George	Pvt.	E	8th SCVI		DN	/ /	Petersburg, VA			ROH
Smith, George W.	Pvt.	G	1st SCVIG		ED	05/05/63	Chancellorsville	DOW	Fredericksburg C.C. R6S13	JR,FBG,SA1,HOE
Smith, H.	Pvt.	K	1st SCVA			05/11/63	Charleston, SC	DOD	Magnolia Cem. Charleston	ROH,MAG,RCD
Smith, H.	Pvt.	H	10th SCVI			/ /	Chattanooga, TN		City C. Chattanooga, TN	TOD
Smith, H.A.	Pvt.	B	6th SCVI		CR	05/05/62	Williamsburg, VA	KIA		WDB,CNM
Smith, H.H.	Pvt.	C	Hol.Leg.	25	SG	04/10/62	Adams Run, SC	DOD	(PP=6/22/62)	ROH,HOS,PP
Smith, H.H.	Pvt.					02/08/64	Richmond, VA			ROH
Smith, H.H.	Pvt.		Macbeth LA			01/24/63	Goldsboro, NC		Prob Willowdale C. there	PP
Smith, H.S.	Pvt.		Marion Art			02/15/64	Charleston, SC	DOD		ROH
Smith, H.S.	Pvt.	F	P.S.S.		LN	/ /		DOW		JR
Smith, Henry	Pvt.	A	22nd SCVI		ED	11/28/64	Petersburg, VA	KIA		ROH,PP
Smith, Henry	Pvt.	A	6th SCVI	26	CR	11/15/61	Centreville, VA	DOD		ROH,GLS,HHC,CB
Smith, Henry Abbott	1st Sgt.	D	27th SCVI	34	CN	08/24/64	Weldon RR, VA	DOW	(Wdd & POW 8/21/64)	ROH,HAG,CDC,R48
Smith, Henry Julius	Cpt.	D	Ham.Leg.	30	GE	09/20/62	Sharpsburg, MD	DOW	Elmwood C. Shepherdstown	ROH,JR,GRS,BOD
Smith, Herbert M.	Pvt.	E	4th SCVC		MO	09/16/64	Elmira, NY	DIP	Woodlawn N.C.#304 Elmira	FPH,HOM,P65,P120
Smith, Hinson L.	Pvt.	B	16th SCVI		GE	01/19/65	Camp Douglas, IL	DIP	Oak Woods Cem. Chicago, IL	ROH,FPH,P5,16R
Smith, Horace Waring	Pvt.	A	27th SCVI		CN	02/15/64	Charleston, SC	DOD	Circular Church Charleston	MAG,RCD,HAG
Smith, Hugh	Pvt.	B	6th SCVI		FD	05/05/64	Williamsburg, VA	KIA		ROH,WDB
Smith, I.H.	Pvt.	A	Ham.Leg.	27	GN	05/04/62	Richmond, VA	DOD	Hollywood Cem.Rchmd. G174	ROH,HC
Smith, I.K.	Pvt.	C	10th SCVI		HY	/ /		DOD		RAS
Smith, J.	Cpl.	C	4th SC Res		NY	02/02/65	Columbia, SC	DOD	Elmwood Cem. Columbia, SC)	ROH,MP,PP
Smith, J.	Pvt.					/ /			Fredericksburg C.C. R6S13	FBG
Smith, J. Enoch	Pvt.	L	21st SCVI	31	MN	04/23/63	Morris Island SC	DOD		ROH,HMC,HAG
Smith, J. Frank	Pvt.	C	5th SCVI			/ /		DOD	(AWOL 7/16/62)	SA3
Smith, J. Jesse	Pvt.	E	P.S.S.		CL	06/30/62	Frayser's Farm	KIA		ROH,JR
Smith, John Laurens N.	Pvt.	C	P.S.S.	19	AN	05/31/62	7 Pines, VA	KIA	St. Paul's E.C. Pendleton	ROH,JR,ACC,SA2
Smith, J. Walker	Pvt.	F	6th SCVI		CR	12/20/61	Dranesville, VA	KIA		ROH,JR,HHC,R46
Smith, J.B.	Pvt.	F	10th SCVI		MN	11/30/64	Franklin, TN	KIA	(Not KIA in RAS)	HMC,RAS
Smith, J.B.	Pvt.	D	2nd SCV			/ /	Charlottesville		Univ. Cem. Charlottesville	ACH
Smith, J.B.	Pvt.	I	19th SCVI		AN	09/20/63	Chickamauga, GA	KIA		JR
Smith, J.B.E.	Pvt.	D	4th SCVI		AN	07/17/62	Richmond, VA	DOD	Hollywood Cem. Rchmd. H224	ROH,HC,SA2
Smith, J.B.H.	Pvt.	G	1st SCVI			06/30/62	Fraysers Farm VA	DOW		JR
Smith, J.C.	Pvt.					/ /	Richmond, VA		Oakwood C.#3,Row M,Div A	ROH,OWC
Smith, J.D.	Pvt.	B	13th SCVI		SG	08/30/62	2nd Manassas, VA	KIA	(JR=8/29)	ROH,JR,CDC
Smith, J.D.	Pvt.	B	27th SCVI		SG	/ /	Fts. Monroe, VA	DIP		ROH
Smith, J.D.	Pvt.	D	19th SCVI		NY	05/04/64	At home		Rosemont Cem. Newberry, SC	NCC
Smith, J.E.	Pvt.	G	13th SCVI		NY	/ /		DOD	Stonewall C. Winchester VA	ROH,WIN,ANY
Smith, J.E.	Pvt.	H	12th SCVI	22	YK	/ /		DOD	(1863)	YEB
Smith, J.F.	Pvt.	F	Hol.Leg.	20	AE	01/24/62	Adams Run, SC	DOD		PP
Smith, J.H.	Pvt.	D	12th SCVI		YK	08/02/63	Davids Island NY	DOW	Cypress Hills N.C.#733 NY	ROH,FPH,P1,CDC
Smith, J.H.	Pvt.	H	12th SCVI	25	YK	05/15/64	Charlottesville	DOW	Univ. Cem. Charlottesville	ACH,CWC,YEB
Smith, J.J.	Pvt.	A	25th SCVI		CN	05/07/64	Pt. Walthall Jn.	KIA	(Smythe, J. Adgers ?)	CDC
Smith, J.M.	Pvt.	D	P.S.S.		SG	05/31/62	7 Pines, VA	KIA		ROH,JR
Smith, J.N.	Pvt.	E	16th SCVI	18	GE	10/30/63	Newman, GA	DOD		ROH,16R
Smith, J.N. (R.N.?)	Pvt.	B	7th SCVI		AE	06/24/64	Richmond, VA		Hollywood Cem.Rchmd. U350	ROH,HC,KEB
Smith, J.R.	Pvt.	F	19th SCVI		ED	10/03/62	Danville, KY	DIP	Con. lot Danville Cem., KY	FPH
Smith, J.T.	Pvt.	E	24th SCVI	30	CO	02/18/63	Charleston, SC	DOD		ROH
Smith, J.W.	Pvt.	B	22nd SCVI		SG	10/16/62	Winchester, VA			ROH
Smith, J.W.	Pvt.	I	P.S.S.		PS	/ /		DOD		JR

SOUTH CAROLINA DEAD IN CSA SERVICE 1861-1865

NAME	RANK	C	REGIMENT	AGE	DS	DIED	WHERE	WHY	BURIED	SOURCES
Smith, Jacob J.	Pvt.	G	1st SCVIH		BL	01/15/63	Lynchburg, VA	DOD	Lynchburg CSA Cem.#6 R1	ROH,SA1,JRH,BB
Smith, James	Pvt.	I	19th SCVI	34	AE	04/06/65	High Point, NC	DOD		ROH,PP
Smith, James	Pvt.	H	1st SCVA			09/27/62	Charleston, SC	DOD	Magnolia Cem. Charleston	ROH,MAG,RCD
Smith, James	Pvt.	A	Ham. Leg.	18	OG	04/25/64	James Island, SC	DOD		ROH
Smith, James	Pvt.	E	Orr's Ri.	22	PS	02/21/62	Sullivans I., SC	DOD		ROH
Smith, James	Pvt.	A	Hol.Leg.		SG	06/16/65	Pt. Lookout, MD	DIP	C.C. Pt. Lookout, MD	FPH,P6,P115,HO
Smith, James	Pvt.	F	4th SCVC		MN	/ /	At home	MUR	(1865, after the war ?)	HMC
Smith, James	Pvt.	G	P.S.S.	22	YK	08/31/63	Wills Valley, TN	KIA		YEB
Smith, James Madison	Cpl.	E	16th SCVI	25	GE	11/30/64	Franklin, TN	KIA	Macgavock C. Frkln Gv# 48	ROH,16R,WCT,PP
Smith, James B.	Pvt.	F	3rd SCVABn	35	CN	05/03/64	Adams Run, SC	DOD		ROH
Smith, James B.	Pvt.	A	Ham.Leg.		CN	06/29/62	Savage Stn., VA	KIA		CNM
Smith, James F.	Pvt.	I	25th SCVI		CL	03/16/65	Elmira, NY	DIP	Woodlawn N.C.#1554 Elmira	FPH,P6
Smith, James H.	Pvt.	I	13th SCVI	35	SG	12/07/62	At home	DOD		ROH,HOS
Smith, James H.	Pvt.	E	7th SCVI		ED	/ /		KIA		HOE,KEB,UD3
Smith, James H.	Pvt.	E	10th SCVI	24	WG	11/23/63	Chattanooga, TN	KIA	(Not listed as KIA in RAS)	CTA,HOW,RAS
Smith, James H.	Pvt.	B	12th SCVI	19	YK	06/27/62	Gaines' Mill, VA	KIA		YEB
Smith, James L.	4th Sgt.	K	12th SCVI	32	PS	05/12/64	Spotsylvania, VA	KIA		ROH
Smith, James Lewis	Pvt.	A	4th SCVIBn			08/02/62	Richmond, VA	DOD	(Dropsy of the chest)	JR
Smith, James M.	Pvt.	G	Orr's Ri.		AE	06/27/62	Gaines' Mill, VA	KIA		ROH,JR,CDC
Smith, James Sparkman	Pvt.	A	Ham. Leg.	22	GN	06/21/62	Savage Stn., VA	KIA		ROH,JR,WLI,LOR
Smith, James W.	Pvt.	E	11th SCVI		BT	07/28/64	Richmond, VA		Hollywood Cem.Rchmd. V574	ROH,HC,HAG
Smith, James W.	Pvt.	B	1st SCVIH		OG	08/20/62	Richmond, VA	DOD	Hollywood Cem.Rchmd. C194	ROH,HC,SA1,JRH
Smith, Jesse	Pvt.	A	1st SCVIG		RD	05/29/64	Lynchburg, VA	DOW	Lynchburg CSA Cem.#6 R2	SA1,BBW
Smith, Jesse A.	Pvt.	B	4th SCVI		AN	08/11/61	Culpepper, VA	DOD	Fairview Cem. Culpepper VA	ROH,JR,CGH,SA2
Smith, Jesse W.	1st Sgt.	E	11th SCVI	30	BT	/ /	Petersburg, VA	KIA		ROH,HAG
Smith, John	Pvt.	B	11th SCVI		CO	01/15/62	At home	DOD		ROH
Smith, John	Pvt.	G	1st SCVIH		BL	04/09/63		DOD		ROH,SA1
Smith, John	Seaman		CS Ch'ston			10/12/63	Charleston, SC	ACD	(Drowned)	CDC
Smith, John	Pvt.	G	P.S.S.	20	YK	/ /	Chattanooga, TN	KIA		YEB
Smith, John	Pvt.		PSS			06/15/62	Near Richmond	DOW	(Rchmd effects list)	UD2,CDC
Smith, John B.	Pvt.	I	11th SCVI		CO	07/20/64	Petersburg, VA	KIA		ROH,HAG
Smith, John B.	Pvt.	G	P.S.S.		YK	06/30/62	Frayser's Farm	KIA		ROH,JR,CDC,YEB
Smith, John E.	Pvt.		19th SCVI			08/28/62	Savannah, GA		Laurel Grove C. Savannah	BGA
Smith, John L.	Pvt.	F	2nd SCVIRi			02/15/64	Rock Island, IL	DIP	C.C.#503 Rock Island, IL	FPH,P5
Smith, John N.	Pvt.	G	1st SCVIG		BL	07/05/62	Gaines' Mill, VA	DOW	(HOE=J.H.)	ROH,JR,SA1,HOE
Smith, John O.	Pvt.	D	24th SCVI	25	BT	02/16/65	Camp Chase, OH	DIP	C.C.#1285 Columbus, OH	ROH,FPH,P6,P23
Smith, John W.	Pvt.	G	13th SCVI		NY	01/15/61		DOD		ROH,ANY
Smith, John W.	Pvt.	E	11th SCVI		BT	07/24/64	Petersburg, VA	DOW	(Wdd 6/24/64)	ROH
Smith, John W.	Pvt.	K	Orr's Ri.	33	AN	07/19/62		DOD		ROH
Smith, John W.	Pvt.	F	1st SCVIG		GE	11/09/64	Fussell's Mill	DOW	(Wdd 8/16/64)	SA1
Smith, John W.	Pvt.	B	13th SCVI		SG	/ /	Richmond, VA			HOS
Smith, Joseph	Pvt.	I	P.S.S.		PS	06/15/62		DOD		ROH
Smith, Joseph C.	Sgt.	A	1st SCVIR			09/26/61	Ft. Moultrie, SC	ACD	(Drowned)	SA1
Smith, Joseph W.	Pvt.	C	17th SCVI	35	YK	01/09/65	Elmira, NY	DIP	Woodlawn N.C.#1216 Elmira	FPH,P5,P65,YEB
Smith, Joseph W.	Pvt.	F	Hol.Leg.		AE	02/08/65	Elmira, NY	DIP	Woodlawn N.C.#1932 Elmira	FPH,P6,P65,P11
Smith, Josiah	Pvt.	D	9th SCVIBn	40		03/05/62	Georgetown, SC	DOD		PP
Smith, Josiah H.	Pvt.	H	1st SCVIG		CN	09/15/62	Warrenton, VA	DOW	(Wdd 2nd Man)	ROH,SA1
Smith, K.	Pvt.	B	15th SCVAB			07/27/63	Bty. Wagner, SC	KIA		ROH,CDC
Smith, L.	Pvt.	B	1st SCVC	28	LS	06/15/62	Staunton, VA	DOD		ROH
Smith, L.A.	Cpl.	E	7th SCVI		ED	/ /		KIA	(KEB=Smith, L.L.)	HOE,KEB,UD3
Smith, L.H.	Sgt.	K	17th SCVI		YK	/ /	Goldsboro, NC	DOD		JR

S

SOUTH CAROLINA DEAD IN CSA SERVICE 1861-1865

NAME	RANK	C REGIMENT	AGE	DS	DIED	WHERE	WHY	BURIED	SOURCES
Smith, L.K.	Pvt.	G 24th SCVI			10/31/63		DOW		EJM
Smith, L.T.	Pvt.	1st SCVC			11/18/62	Staunton, VA		Thornrose C. Staunton, VA	TOD
Smith, Lawrence A.	1st Sgt.	C 1st SCVIG		RD	08/29/62	2nd Manassas, VA	KIA		ROH,JR,SA1,CDC
Smith, Lawrence T.	Pvt.	P.S.S.	30		05/31/62	7 Pines, VA	KIA		ROH,CDC
Smith, Lewis R.	Pvt.	B 2nd SCVI	27	GE	08/01/63	Gettysburg, PA	DOW		ROH,GDR,SA2,KEB
Smith, Linsey	Pvt.	Matthews A			07/18/62	Charleston, SC	DOD	Magnolia Cem. Charleston	ROH,MAG,RCD
Smith, M.	Pvt.	D 2nd SCVI		SR	11/15/62	Richmond, VA	DOD	Oakwood C.#76,Row L,Div A	ROH,SA2,OWC,H2
Smith, M.M.	Pvt.	D 18th SCVI		AN	03/24/64	FL	DOD		ROH
Smith, Malachi F.	Pvt.	A 4th SCVC		MO	05/30/64		DOD		ROH
Smith, Martin W.	Pvt.	D P.S.S.		SG	05/31/62	7 Pines, VA	KIA		HOS
Smith, Moses J.	Pvt.	G Orr's Ri.		AE	07/15/62	Laurel Hill, VA	DOD		ROH
Smith, N.	Pvt.	H 6th SCV			/ /	Richmond, VA			ROH
Smith, Nathaniel J.	Pvt.	B 13th SCVI		SG	07/12/62	Richmond, VA			ROH,HOS
Smith, Neil	1st Sgt.	H Orr's Ri.		MN	06/27/62	Gaine's Mill, VA	KIA		JR,HMC,CDC
Smith, Nevin D.	Pvt.	A 4th SCVC		CD	05/28/64	Hawes Shop, VA	KIA		ROH
Smith, P.J.	Pvt.	I 1st SCVIH		BL	10/11/61	At home	DOD		SA1
Smith, Patrick	Pvt.	A 3rd SCVI		LS	09/20/63	Chickamauga, GA	KIA		SA2,KEB
Smith, Perry L.	Pvt.	I 13th SCVI	26	SG	07/01/63	Gettysburg, PA	KIA		ROH,JR,GDR,HOS
Smith, Peter	Pvt.	B 37th VAVCB		GE	08/01/64	Virginia	DOD		37V
Smith, Peter	Pvt.	B 16th SCVI		GE	/ /	Yazoo City, MS			PP
Smith, Pinckney A.	Pvt.	C 1st SCVIR		CN	11/23/61	Charleston, SC	DOD		SA1
Smith, R.	Pvt.	A 14th SCVI	35	DN	/ /	At home	DOD		ROH
Smith, R. Yeadon	Cpl.	A Ham.Leg.		CN	/ /	Richmond, VA			ROH,WLI
Smith, R.C.	Pvt.	F 2nd SCVIRi			06/25/64	Richmond, VA		Hollywood Cem.Rchmd. U416	ROH,HC
Smith, R.C.	Pvt.			RD	08/05/64	Petersburg, VA		Blandford Church Pbg., VA	BLC
Smith, R.E.	Pvt.	F 16th SCVI		GE	11/30/64	Franklin, TN	KIA		ROH,CDC,PP
Smith, R.M.	Pvt.	B 4th SCVC		CR	11/16/64	Elmira, NY	DIP	Woodlawn N.C.#954 Elmira	FPH,P5,P65,HHC
Smith, R.T.	Pvt.	K 21st SCVI		DN	07/26/62	Petersburg, VA	DOD	(HAG=1 Smith, Thomas)	ROH
Smith, Ralph H.	Pvt.	C 5th SCVI	24	SG	06/25/62	7 Pines, VA	DOW	Smith Fam. C. SG Cty.	ROH,JR,SA3,UNC
Smith, Richard	Pvt.	E 14th SCVI		LS	09/05/62	Frederick, MD	DOW	Mt.Olivet C.#6 Frederick	ROH,FPH,CGS,BOD
Smith, Richard W.	Pvt.	B 14th SCVI	19	ED	11/18/63	Ft. Delaware, DE	DIP	Finn's Pt., NJ Nat. Cem.	ROH,FPH,P5,UD3
Smith, Riley	Sgt.	A 17th SCVI		CR	08/30/62	2nd Manassas, VA	KIA		HHC
Smith, Robert	Pvt.	C 13th SCVI		SG	08/29/62	2nd Manassas, VA	KIA	(JR=Co.E)	ROH,JR,CDC,HOS
Smith, Robert	Pvt.	D 4th SCVI		AN	10/21/61	Richmond, VA	DOD	Hollywood Cem.Rchmd. B143	ROH,HC,SA2
Smith, Robert	Pvt.	K 2nd SCVI		BL	12/28/62	Lynchburg, VA	DOD	Lynchburg CSA Cem.#4 R3	SA2,BBW,KEB,H2
Smith, Robert A.	Pvt.	G 22nd SCVI	29	AN	07/30/64	Crater, Pbg., VA	KIA		ROH,BLM
Smith, Robert B.	Sgt.	G P.S.S.	23	YK	/ /		DOW		JR,YEB
Smith, Robert J.	Pvt.	F 25th SCVI	18	OG	02/27/65	Elmira, NY	DIP	Woodlawn N.C.#2159 Elmira	ROH,FPH,P65,HAG
Smith, S.	Pvt.	H 11th SCVI		CO	/ /	(NI HAG)		Stonewall C. Winchester VA	ROH,WIN
Smith, Samuel W.	Pvt.	A 6th SCVI	23	CR	09/29/64	Ft. Harrison, VA	KIA		ROH,GLS,HHC,CB
Smith, Savid A.	Pvt.	H 6th SCVI	28	FD	09/01/61	Germantown, VA	DOD	(Died @ Morkely's house)	ROH
Smith, Scott Nimrod	Pvt.	G 2nd SC Res		AN	01/18/65	Columbia, SC	DOD	Elmwood Cem. Columbia, SC	ROH,MP,PP
Smith, Signes N.	1st Cpl.	F 18th SCVI		YK	08/30/62	2nd Manassas, VA	KIA		ROH
Smith, Simson	Pvt.	F 19th SCVI	19	LN	03/15/62	At home	DOD		ROH
Smith, Solomon	Pvt.	F 3rd SCVIBn	20	LN	04/19/62	Adams Run, SC	DOD		ROH,KEB,PP
Smith, Solomon J.	Pvt.	M 10th SCVI		HY	/ /		DOD		RAS
Smith, Stephen E.	Pvt.	F 16th SCVI		GE	06/23/64	Kenesaw Mtn. GA	DOW	Con. Cem. Marietta, GA	ROH,16R,BGA,CCM
Smith, T.H.	Pvt.	A Ham.Leg.		GN	05/04/62	Richmond, VA		Hollywood Cem.Rchmd. F70	HC,LOR,WLI
Smith, T.R.	Pvt.	F 2nd SCVIRi			06/29/63	Petersburg, VA	DOD		ROH
Smith, Thomas	Sgt.	A 1st SCV	40	AE	/ /				ROH
Smith, Thomas	Pvt.	C 8th SCVI		CD	07/12/64	Petersburg, VA			ROH,KEB

SOUTH CAROLINA DEAD IN CSA SERVICE 1861-1865

NAME	RANK	C	REGIMENT	AGE	DS	DIED	WHERE	WHY	BURIED	SOURCES
Smith, Thomas	Pvt.	F	16th SCVI		GE	11/30/64	Franklin, TN	KIA		16R
Smith, Thomas	Pvt.	F	23rd SCVI		CR	08/30/62	2nd Manassas, VA	KIA		HHC
Smith, Thomas G.	Pvt.	K	P.S.S.		SG	07/18/62	7 Pines, VA	DOW	Hollywood Cem.Rchmd. S173	JR,HC,HOS
Smith, Thomas J.	Pvt.	H	7th SCVI		ED	07/02/63	Gettysburg, PA	KIA		ROH,JR,GDR,CDC
Smith, Thomas J.	Pvt.	G	1st SCVIG		ED	05/21/62		DOD	(Typhoid pneumonia)	JR,SA1,HOE
Smith, Thomas M.C.	Pvt.	F	3rd SCVIBn	16	LN	09/14/62	South Mtn., MD	KIA		ROH,KEB
Smith, Thomas W.	Pvt.	A	1st SCVC	35	AE	09/19/63		DOD		ROH
Smith, W. (W.R.T.?)	Pvt.	H	6th SCVI		FD	/ /	Richmond, VA		Oakwood C.#3,Row A,Div A	ROH,OWC
Smith, W. Bryant	Pvt.	M	8th SCVI		DN	11/05/64	Baltimore, MD	DIP	Loudon Pk.C. B-68 Balto.MD	FPH,P4,P5,KEB,
Smith, W.A.	Pvt.	I	P.S.S.		PS	07/15/62	Richmond, VA	DOW	Hollywood Cem.Rchmd. X21	ROH,JR,HC
Smith, W.F.	Pvt.	C	10th SCVI		MN	09/20/63	Chickamauga, GA	KIA	(RAS=W.J.)	ROH,CDC,RAS
Smith, W.G.	Pvt.	C	4th SCVC		PS	09/29/64	Pt. Lookout, MD	DIP	C.C. Pt. Lookout, MD	ROH,FPH,P5,P11
Smith, W.H.	Pvt.		1st SC Mil			02/10/65	Charleston	DOD	Magnolia Cem. Charleston	ROH,MAG
Smith, W.H.	6th Cpl.	C	12th SCVI		FD	/ /		KIA		HFC
Smith, W.H.	Pvt.		1st SCV			02/10/65			Magnolia Cem. Charleston	RCD
Smith, W.M.	Cpl.	D	16th SCVI		GE	07/20/64	Peachtree Ck. GA	KIA		16R
Smith, W.R.	Pvt.	B	2nd SCVIRi		PS	/ /				ROH
Smith, W.R.	Pvt.	A	1st SCVIG		BL	12/13/62	Fredericksburg	KIA		SA1
Smith, W.T.	Pvt.	C	4th SCV			07/05/64	Richmond, VA			ROH
Smith, W.T.	Pvt.	G	14th SCVI	40	AE	02/22/63	Lynchburg, VA	DOD	Lynchburg CSA Cem.#7 R1	ROH,BBW
Smith, W.W.	Pvt.	E	7th SCVI		ED	/ /		DOD		HOE,KEB,UD3
Smith, Wahington Irving	Pvt.	E	18th Bn A	19	CN	08/12/63	Bty. Wagner, SC	DOW	Magnolia Cem. Charleston	ROH,MAG,RCD
Smith, Walter D.	Pvt.	C	Ham.Leg. C		BT	05/07/62		DOD	(Consumption)	JR
Smith, Warren	Pvt.	D	1st SCVA			07/17/63	Charleston, SC	DOD	Magnolia Cem. Charleston	ROH,MAG,RCD
Smith, Warren	Pvt.	I	P.S.S.		PS	07/15/62	Frayser's Farm	DOW	Hollywood Cem.Rchmd. Q247	ROH,HC
Smith, Whiteford Andrew	Pvt.	K	P.S.S.	18	SG	08/31/62	2nd Manassas, VA	DOW	Manassas CSA Cem.	ROH,JR,HOS,UD1
Smith, William	Pvt.	H	15th SCVI		UN	04/10/64	Columbia, SC	DOD	(PP=4/15/64)	ROH,KEB,PP
Smith, William	Pvt.	D	P.S.S.		SG	06/27/62	Gaines' Mill, VA	KIA		ROH,JR,HOS,CDC
Smith, William	Pvt.	B	22nd SCVI		SG	10/20/62	Winchester, VA	DOD		ROH
Smith, William	Pvt.	B	11th SCVI		CO	06/05/62	At home	DOD		ROH
Smith, William	Pvt.	B	16th SCVI		GE	11/30/64	Franklin, TN	KIA		16R
Smith, William	Pvt.	F	16th SCVI		GE	06/22/64	Kennesaw Mtn. GA	KIA		16R
Smith, William	Pvt.	H	Ham.Leg.		RD	11/16/63	Campbell Stn. TN	DOW		CDC
Smith, William A.	6th Cpl.	K	3rd SCVI	22	SG	06/29/62	Savage Stn., VA	KIA		ROH,JR,SA2,HOS
Smith, William G.	Cpl.	G	24th SCVI	38	FD	05/28/64	Macon, GA		Rose Hill C. Macon, GA	CV,BGA,PP
Smith, William James	Pvt.	E	5th SCVI		YK	10/28/63	Lookout Valley	KIA	(See p. 89, STC)	SA3,STC,CDC,UD
Smith, William Kirkwood	1st Sgt.	D	27th SCVI	26	CN	07/18/63	Bty. Wagner, SC	KIA		ROH,CDC,HAG
Smith, William L.	Pvt.	B	37th VAVCB		AN	09/19/64	Winchester, VA	KIA	Stonewall C. Winchester VA	37V
Smith, William M.	2nd Lt.	B	15th SCVI		UN	09/17/62	Sharpsburg, MD	KIA	(ROH=KIA @ Sharpsburg)	ROH,JR,R47,KEB
Smith, William Mason	1st Lt.Adj		27th SCVI	21	CN	08/16/64	Richmond, VA	DOW	St.Philip's Ch. Charleston	ROH,MAG,R48,MS
Smith, William Robert	Pvt.	E	1st SCVIR			05/09/65	Newbern, NC		Cedar Grove C. Newbern, NC	PP,SA1
Smith, William S.	Pvt.	D	3rd SCVI	20	SG	07/07/61	Charlottesville	DOD		ROH,JR,SA2,KEB
Smith, William S.	Pvt.	F	16th SCVI		GE	11/30/64	Franklin, TN	KIA	Macgavock C. Frkln Gv# 49	ROH,16R,WCT,PP
Smith, William T.	Sgt.	A	26th SCVI	22	HY	04/15/65	Charlotte, NC	DOD		ROH,PP
Smith, Wilson	1st Lt.	E	11th SCVI	25	BT	07/20/64	Petersburg, VA	DOW	(R47=DOW 6/14/64)	ROH,R47,HAG
Smith, Z.D.	Pvt.	D	1st SCV	33	CR	10/15/62	Summerville, SC	DOD		ROH,HHC,YEB
Smith, Zacharia Brown	2nd Lt.	E	1st SCVIG	21	MN	09/01/63	At home	DOW	(Wdd Falling Water 7/?/63)	ROH,SA1,PDL,HM
Smith,Jr., George W.	Pvt.	E	11th SCVI	19	BT	/ /	At home	DOD		ROH,HAG
Smitherman, J.D.	Pvt.	D	14th SCVI	28	ED	06/30/62	Fraser's Farm VA	KIA	(ROH= T.L.)	ROH,JR,D14,HOE
Smithgan, A.	Pvt.		1st SC			06/16/62	Richmond, VA		Hollywood Cem.Rchmd. O186	HC
Smithson, Silas N.	Pvt.	C	2nd SCVIRi	28	PS	03/06/63	Petersburg, VA		Blandford Church Pbg., VA	BLC,PP

S

SOUTH CAROLINA DEAD IN CSA SERVICE 1861-1865

NAME	RANK	C	REGIMENT	AGE	DS	DIED	WHERE	WHY	BURIED	SOURCES
Smoak, Adam E.	Pvt.	F	25th SCVI	18	OG	02/20/65	Elmira, NY	DIP	(Dup of man in Co.H?)	ROH,HAG
Smoak, Andrew A.	Pvt.	F	25th SCVI		OG	08/21/64	McClellan H.Phil	DOW	Odd Fellows Plot Phila C.	ROH,HAG,EDR,P6
Smoak, Andrew J.	Pvt.	G	25th SCVI		OG	09/19/64	Philadelphia, PA	DOW	N.C.OFS #279 Philadelphia	FPH,P6,HAG
Smoak, D.S.	Pvt.	A	1st SCVIH		OG	08/24/64	Ream's Stn., VA	KIA	(Also Wdd @ 2nd Manassas)	SA1,UD3
Smoak, H.E.	Pvt.	H	25th SCVI		CN	02/11/65	Elmira, NY	DIP	Woodlawn N.C.#2264 Elmira	FPH,HAG
Smoke, A.E.	Pvt.	K	11th SCVI	25	CO	06/16/64	Petersburg, VA	KIA		ROH,HAG
Smoke, Daniel	Pvt.	B	3rd SCVC	17	CO	07/18/63	Hardeeville, SC	DOD	(? SSO=MIA @ Hawe's Shop)	ROH
Smoke, George	Pvt.	D	1st SCVA			10/12/62	Charleston, SC	DOD	Magnolia Cem. Charleston	ROH,MAG,RCD
Smoke, J. Wesley	Pvt.	B	20th SCVI	35	OG	08/23/63	Bty. Wagner, SC	KIA	(KEB=Smoak, G.W.)	ROH,CDC
Smoke, John	Pvt.	B	20th SCVI		OG	/ /	Mt. Pleasant, SC	DOD		ROH
Smoke, Joshua	Pvt.	K	11th SCVI	23	CO	06/05/64	Cold Harbor, VA	DOW	Hollywood Cem.Rchmd. U317	ROH,HC,HAG
Smoke, Jr., George W.	Sgt.	H		19	BL	10/11/62	Boonsville, MD	DOD		ROH
Smoke, W.F.	2nd Lt.	A	5th SCVC	37	OG	06/23/64	Charlottesville	DOW	Univ. Cem. Charlottesville	ROH,ACH,CDC
Smoke, W.M.	Pvt.	I	3rd SCVI		LS	09/25/63	Chickamauga, GA	DOW	(KEB=Snook, W.M.)	ROH,JR,SA2,KEB
Smoke, W.P.	Pvt.	E	24th SCVI	19	CO	09/01/64	Montgomery, AL	DOD		ROH
Smoke, William	Pvt.			25	OG	/ /	Tennessee		(1864)	ROH
Smoot, Joshua	2nd Lt.	M	8th SCVI		DN	07/02/63	Gettysburg, PA	KIA		GDR,KEB,R46
Smothers, J.K.	Pvt.	F	26th SCVI			09/30/63	Charleston, SC	DOD	Magnolia Cem. Charleston	ROH,MAG,RCD
Smothers, L.	Pvt.	G	21st SCVI		CD	03/14/65	Richmond, VA		Hollywood Cem.Rchmd. W212	ROH,HC
Smothers, Wiley	Pvt.	G	21st SCVI		CD	01/15/65	Ft. Fisher, NC	KIA		PP
Smyer, Miles A.	Pvt.	B	2nd SCVI	28	GE	05/06/64	Wilderness, VA	KIA		ROH,SA2,CDC,KEB
Smyley, Duncan	Pvt.	G	4th SCVC	22	CO	05/30/64	Hawes Shop, VA	DOW		ROH
Smyley, John	Pvt.	G	4th SCVC	24	CO	06/25/65	Pt. Lookout, MD	DIP	C.C. Pt. Lookout, MD	ROH,FPH,P6,P115
Smyley, Joseph	Pvt.	G	4th SCVC	23	CO	05/30/64	Hawes Shop, VA	DOW		ROH
Smyrle, James K.	Pvt.	E	2nd SCVI		KW	11/18/62	Richmond, VA	DOD	Hollywood Cem.Rchmd. S303	HC,SA2,HIC,KEB
Smythe, John	Pvt.	B	7th SCVC	20	CN	06/13/64	Riddle's Shop VA	KIA	(CDC=6/19/64)	ROH,CDC
Snaars, F.	Pvt.	A	German Art		CN	/ /			St.Lawrence C. Charleston	MAG
Snead, C.P.	5th Sgt.	I	3rd SCVI		LS	05/15/64	Spotsylvania, VA	DOW	(Wdd 5/8/64)	SA2,KEB
Sneed, R.	Pvt.	I	Orr's Ri.		PS	/ /			Stonewall C. Winchester VA	ROH
Snelgrove, Chesney	Pvt.	H	Hol.Leg.	40	ED	04/25/62	Adams Run, SC	DOD	(Dysentery)	ROH,JR,ANY,PP
Snelgrove, Francis M.	Pvt.	B	14th SCVI	20	ED	07/02/63	Gettysburg, PA	KIA		HOE,UD3
Snelgrove, Joshua A.	Pvt.	C	1st SCVIG		LN	04/17/64	Richmond, VA	DOD	Hollywood Cem.Rchmd. I261	ROH,HC,SA1
Snider, George	Pvt.		11th SCVI		BT	/ /	Richmond, VA			ROH
Snimes, W.A.	Pvt.	C	6th SC Bn			05/10/65	Pt. Lookout, MD	DIP	(? name, unit NI FPH)	ROH
Snipes, Allen	Pvt.	E	1st SCVIG		MN	11/15/62		DOD		HMC,SA1
Snipes, Asa	Pvt.	H	2nd SCVI	31	LR	12/22/62	Lynchburg, VA	DOD	Lynchburg CSA Cem.#9 R4	ROH,JR,SA2,BBW
Snipes, Burrell M.	Pvt.	A	1st SCVIR	18	LR	07/08/63	Ft. Moultrie, SC	DOD		ROH,SA1,LAN
Snipes, Chesley	Pvt.	B	21st SCVI		DN	03/18/62	Georgetown, SC	DOD		ROH,PP
Snipes, J.L.	Pvt.	H	12th SCVI		YK	/ /	Richmond, VA		Oakwood C.#84,Row G,Div C	ROH,OWC
Snipes, Jackson	Pvt.	B	14th SCVI	23	ED	06/07/62	Richmond, VA	DOD	(Typhoid)	JR,HOE,UD3
Snipes, James	Pvt.	L	10th SCVI		MN	11/30/64	Franklin, TN	KIA		ROH,RAS
Snipes, Michael	Pvt.	I	8th SCVI		MN	10/13/64	Cedar Creek, VA	KIA		HMC,KEB
Snipes, P.L.	Pvt.	K	1st SCVIR		LR	07/29/62	Adams Run, SC	DOD		SA1
Snipes, Perry	Pvt.	C	18th SCVAB		MN	/ /	Charleston, SC	DOD		HMC
Snipes, R.P. (R.S. ?)	Pvt.	E	23rd SCVI		MN	08/28/64	Richmond, VA	DOD	Hollywood Cem.Rchmd. V648	ROH,HC,HMC
Snipes, Ruffin H.	Pvt.	L	Orr's Ri.		AN	05/03/63	Chancellorsville	KIA		ROH,JR,CDC
Snipes, William C.	1st Sgt.	A	1st SCVIR	31	LR	09/07/63	Morris Island SC	DOW	(Wdd Bty Gregg 9/5)	ROH,SA1
Snoddy, John Crawford	Pvt.	C	22nd SCVI	19	SG	10/28/64	(25th in FPH)	DIP	Woodlawn N.C.#727 Elmira	ROH,FPH,P6,P120
Snoddy, Robert A.	1st Lt.	D	P.S.S.		SG	11/30/63	Campbells Stn TN	DOW	(Wdd 11/16)	ROH,HOS,R48
Snow, Frost	Pvt.	K	Orr's Ri.	25	AN	07/23/62	Richmond, VA	DOW	Hollywood Cem.Rchmd. D1	ROH,HC,CDC
Snow, Jesse L.	Pvt.	L	1st SCVIG	17	GN	05/10/65	Hart's Island NY	DIP	Cypress Hills N.C.#2770 NY	ROH,FPH,P6,SA1

SOUTH CAROLINA DEAD IN CSA SERVICE 1861-1865

NAME	RANK	C	REGIMENT	AGE	DS	DIED	WHERE	WHY	BURIED	SOURCES
Snowden, DuBose	Sgt.	A	7th SCVC			10/07/64	Darbytown Rd. VA	KIA		CV,ALH
Snyder, Joseph	Pvt.	B	2nd SCVI	38	GE	07/11/64	Petersburg, VA	DOD		ROH,SA2,KEB,H2
Snyder, W.	Pvt.		18th SCVI			08/05/62	Richmond, VA		Hollywood Cem.Rchmd. Q47	HC
Someril, W.W.	Pvt.	E	3rd SCVIBn		LS	09/19/62	Frederick, MD	DOW	Mt. Olivet C.#28 Frederick	FPH,P1,KEB,BOD
Somers, Adolphus	1st Sgt.	D	15th SCVI		KW	04/23/61	Charleston, SC	ACD	(Drowned in harbor)	HIC,CDN,KEB
Son, A. Solomon	Pvt.	C	15th SCVI		LN	05/11/63	Lynchburg, VA	DOD	Lynchburg CSA Cem.#6 R1	ROH,BBW,H15,TO
Sorrill, H.M.	Pvt.	A	4th SCResB			03/16/65	Raleigh, NC		Oakwood C. Raleigh, NC	TOD
Souls, B.	Pvt.	C	5th SCVC		CO	03/15/65		DOW	(Wdd 3/11)	ROH
Souls, J.W.	Pvt.	H	23rd SCVI		HY	/ /	Charlottesville		Univ. Cem. Charlottesville	ACH,HMC
Southerlin, S.E.	Pvt.	B	2nd SCVIRi		PS	/ /				ROH
Southerlin, William	Pvt.	E	24th SCVI	38	CO	09/07/63	MS	DOD		ROH
Southern, B.J.	Pvt.	H	16th SCVI		GE	05/07/64	Marietta, GA		Con. Cem. Marietta, GA	BGA
Southern, William R.	Pvt.	F	1st SCVIH		GE	01/14/63		DOD		ROH,SA1
Sowell, Abram	Pvt.	H	2nd SCVI		LR	06/09/62	Petersburg, VA	DOD	(Rheumatism)	H2,SA2,KEB
Sowles, John	Pvt.	F	1st SCVIG		HY	06/27/62	Mechanicsville	DOW	Oakwood C.#135,Row L, Div B	ROH,JR,SA1,OWC
Sox, Samuel	Pvt.	D	15th Mil	57	LN	04/29/65	Pt. Lookout, MD	DIP	C.C. Pt. Lookout, MD	ROH,P115
Spady, Southey G.	Sgt.	A	27th SCVI		CN	12/08/64	Pt. Lookout, MD	DIP	C.C. Pt. Lookout, MD	ROH,FPH,P5,HAG
Spakes, Samuel S.	Pvt.	F	3rd SCVI		LS	12/13/62	Fredericksburg	KIA	(KEB=Sparks, S.) RHL	ROH,JR,SA2,UD3
Spann, Edward C.	Pvt.		Inst. Camp	32	SR	08/28/64	Columbia, SC	DOD	(B:05/15/32)	ROH,CDC
Spann, J.F.	1st Lt.	F	P.S.S.		SR	06/20/64	Petersburg, VA	KIA		ROH,R48
Spann, P.P.	Pvt.	M	7th SCVI		ED	09/13/62	MD	KIA		ROH,JR,KEB,HOE
Spann, Walter D.	Pvt.	K	2nd SCVA		ED	/ /		DOD		HOE,UD3
Sparkman, A.J.	3rd Cpl.	K	2nd SCVI		CN	02/21/62	Charlottesville	DOD	Univ. Cem. Charlottesville	ROH,SA2,KEB,AC
Sparkman, George R.	Pvt.	I	8th SCVI		MN	/ /	Virginia			HMC,KEB
Sparkman, Levi	3rd Cpl.	I	8th SCVI		MN	/ /	Virginia	DOD		HMC,KEB
Sparks Bolton O'N.	Pvt.	H	1st SCVIR		GE	07/18/63	Bty. Wagner, SC	KIA		ROH,CDC,SA1
Sparks, A.	Pvt.	E	1st SCV			10/16/62		DOD		JR
Sparks, J.C.	Pvt.	H	12th SCVI	21	YK	06/15/64		DOD	(Wdd 8/29/62,YEB=DIS '64)	CWC,YEB
Sparks, Jesse	Pvt.	D	13th SCVI	29	NY	02/23/63	Richmond, VA	DOD		ROH,ANY
Sparks, John Calhoun	Sgt.	K	2nd SCVC		GE	01/06/64	Catlett Stn., VA	KIA	(Wdd twice)	ROH,TRR,AOA
Sparks, John T.	Pvt.	A	18th SCVI	28	UN	11/23/62	Richmond, VA		Hollywood Cem.Rchmd. S323	ROH,HC
Sparks, Thomas	Pvt.	K	5th SC Res			11/24/63	Columbia, SC	DOD		ROH,PP
Sparks, Thomas	Pvt.	I	1st SCVIR		SG	03/16/65	Averysboro, NC	KIA		ROH,SA1,WAT,PP
Sparks, W.A.	Pvt.	H	12th SCVI	22	YK	02/15/63	Lynchbrg, VA	DOD	Lynchburg CSA Cem.#6 R2	CDC,BBW,YEB
Sparks, William M.	Pvt.	B	15th SCVI		UN	/ /		DOD		JR
Sparks, William T.	Pvt.	I	13th SCVI	25	SG	10/20/61		DOD	Padgett Creek B.C. UN Cty.	ROH,JR,UNC
Speaks, W.T.	2nd Lt.		Kirk's P.R	45	BT	10/22/62	Pocotaligo, SC	KIA	(Speights?)	ROH,R43,MDM,PP
Spear, J.						/ /			(Rchmd effects list 12/62)	CDC
Spearman, Benjamin J.	Pvt.	D	18th SCVI	20	AN	03/18/65	Petersburg, VA		(PP=3/8/65)	ROH,PP
Spearman, David D.	Pvt.	D	18th SCVI		AN	06/09/64	Columbia, SC	ACD	(Gunshot+RR Accident)	ROH,PP
Spearman, J.W.	Cpl.	D	18th SCVI		AN	05/20/64	Clay's Farm, VA	KIA		ROH
Spearman, James K.P.	Pvt.	C	Hol.Leg.		NY	/ /	Adams Run, SC	DOD		ANY
Spearman, John F.	Pvt.	C	Hol.Leg.		NY	02/10/62	At home	DOD	(Not on NY Mon list)	ANY
Spearman, William H.	Pvt.	F	24th SCVI		AN	09/23/63	Lauderdale Sp.MS	DOD		HOL
Spears, George S.	Cpl.	F	15th SCVI	39	UN	02/04/65	Pt. Lookout, MD	DIP	C.C. Pt. Lookout, MD	ROH,FPH,KEB,P1
Spears, J.C.	Pvt.	H	12th SCVI	23	YK	08/08/62	Richmond, VA	DOD	Oakwood C.#13,Row B,Div B	ROH,JR,OWC,YEB
Spears, J.E.	Pvt.	H	Ham.Leg.		MO	/ /			(1865)	HOM
Spears, J.T.	Sgt.	H	15th SCVI		NY	07/02/63	Gettysburg, PA	KIA	Magnolia Cem., Charleston	JR,MAG,RCD,NCC
Spears, James A.	Pvt.	F	21st SCVI		MO	06/20/64	Petersburg, VA	KIA		ROH,HOM,HAG
Spears, Jesse	Pvt.	D	13th SCVI	19	NY	07/01/63	Gettysburg, PA	KIA	(ANY says Gaines' Mill)	ROH,JR,ANY
Spears, Joseph	Pvt.	F	15th SCVI	20	UN	07/03/63	Gettysburg, PA	KIA		ROH

S

SOUTH CAROLINA DEAD IN CSA SERVICE 1861-1865

NAME	RANK	C REGIMENT	AGE	DS	DIED	WHERE	WHY	BURIED	SOURCES
Spears, Joseph C.	Pvt.	H 12th SCVI		YK	07/15/62	Richmond, VA	DOD	(ROH=Speavy)	ROH,CWC,YEB
Spears, R.S.	Pvt.	D 3rd SCVIBn		NY	11/13/62	Richmond, VA			ROH,ANY,KEB
Spears, S.C.	Pvt.	I 8th SCVI		MN	05/19/64	Richmond, VA		Hollywood Cem.Rchmd. I264	ROH,HC
Spears, T.	Pvt.	B 13th SCVI		SG	10/29/62	Richmond, VA		Hollywood Cem.Rchmd. C24	HC
Spell, D.Y.	Sgt.	E 24th SCVI	22	CO	05/16/64	Calhoun, GA	KIA		ROH,CDC
Spell, Joseph E.F.	Pvt.	A 24th SCVI	32	CN	10/07/64	Camp Douglas, IL	DIP	Oak Woods Cem. Chicago, IL	ROH,FPH,P5,P43
Spell, Paul	Pvt.	G 4th SCVC		CO	10/27/64	Southside RR, VA	KIA		SSO
Spell, W. Allen	Pvt.	A 24th SCVI		CN	10/26/63	Atlanta, GA	DOW	Oakland C. Atlanta R15#8	BGA
Spelts, Robert J.	Pvt.	E 3rd SCVIBn		LS	07/08/64	Columbia, SC			PP,KEB
Spence, David C.	Pvt.	F 3rd SCVABn	17	CN	09/10/65	At home	DOD	(D, Ham.Leg. ?)	ROH
Spence, Milton	Pvt.	C 5th SC Res			11/15/63		DOD		ROH
Spence, Moses E.	Pvt.	G 21st SCVI	20	CD	03/21/62	Georgetown, SC	DOD		PP,HAG
Spence, Samuel H.	Pvt.	C 3rd SCVI		NY	05/02/63	Chancellorsville	KIA	(JR=Sprouse)	ROH,JR,SA2,ANY
Spencer, Jasper M.	Pvt.	G 18th SCVI		UN	11/28/64	Elmira, NNY	DIP	Woodlawn N.C.#991 Elmira	FPH,CDC,P65,P120
Spencer, Robert	Pvt.	C Orr's Ri.		/	/	Petersburg, VA	KIA		UD4
Spencer, T.J.	Pvt.	G Orr's Ri.		AE	06/05/62	Richmond, VA			ROH
Spencer, W. Henry	Pvt.	H P.S.S.		SG	05/05/62	Williamsburg, VA	KIA		ROH,HOS,CDC
Sperrell, H.E.	Pvt.			/	/	Richmond, VA		Oakwood C.#11,Row C,Div E	OWC
Sperry, E.C.	Pvt.	K 15th SCVI		CN	01/15/63	Richmond, VA	DOD	(ROH=Sperrin)	ROH,JR,KEB
Spetts, R.G.	Pvt.	G 3rd SC			07/08/64	Columbia, SC	DOD		ROH
Spigener, George Paul	Pvt.	B 20th SCVI	16	OG	01/20/62	At home	DOD		ROH
Spigner, W.F.	Pvt.	D 12th SCVI		YK	06/27/62	Gaines' Mill, VA	KIA		ROH,CNM
Spillers, Herbert M.	Cpl.	H 1st SCVIH		UN	05/15/64	Lynchburg, VA	DOW	Lynchburg CSA Cem.#10 R4	ROH,SA1,HOS,BBW
Spillers, Louis	Pvt.	H 3rd SCVI		LN	09/21/63	Chickamauga, GA	DOW	(See p279,KEB)	ROH,JR,SA2,ANY
Spillers, William F.	Pvt.	K 2nd SCVI		GE	04/30/64	Ft. Delaware, DE	DIP	Finn's Pt., NJ Nat. Cem.	ROH,FPH,P5,KEB
Spires, D.	Pvt.	H 20th SCVI		LN	10/20/63		DOW	(Wdd 10/19/63)	ROH,KEB
Spires, Michael	Cpl.	E 1st SCVIR		LN	09/08/63	Ft. Moultrie, SC	KIA	(Ammo chest explosion)	ROH,SA1,CDC
Spivey, Ephraim	Pvt.	E 26th SCVI		HY	/ /	Virginia	KIA		ROH
Spivey, R.W.	Pvt.	B 10th SCVI	34	HY	12/22/64	Goldsboro, NC	DOD		PP
Spivey, W.L.	Pvt.	D Ham.Leg.		CL	08/31/63	Will's Valley TN	KIA		GRS
Spoonauger,	Pvt.	A Orr's Ri.		AN	05/03/63	Chancellorsville	KIA		ROH,JR
Spooner, J.F.	Pvt.	I 4th SCVC		GN	06/11/64	Trevillian Stn.	KIA	(HOW= WG & T.J.,CDC=J.T.)	ROH,HOW,CDC
Sports, W.B.	Pvt.	G 23rd SCVI		MO	/ /				HOM
Spradley, Benjamin F.	Pvt.	F P.S.S.		LN	03/14/64	Rock Island, IL	DIP	C.C.#816 Rock Island, IL	FPH,P5
Spradley, John	Pvt.	D 15th SCVI		KW	05/06/64	Wilderness, VA	KIA	(Also Rptd MIA @ Gettysbg)	HIC,KEB
Spradley, W. James	Pvt.	D 15th SCVI		KW	09/17/62	Sharpsburg, MD	DOW	(Wdd & missing)	HIC,CDC,KEB
Sprague, Charles L.		CS Hunley			10/16/63	Charleston, SC	ACD	Magnolia Cem. Charleston	RCD
Sprawls, John F.	4th Sgt.	A 1st SCVIG	27	BL	07/25/63	Davids Island NY	DOW	Cypress Hills N.C.#685 NY	ROH,FPH,GDR,P1
Spray, Jefferson J.	Pvt.	E 22nd SCVI		LR	06/16/62	Secessionville	KIA		ROH,JR,CDC,LAN
Spray, John J.	Pvt.	E 22nd SCVI		LR	07/30/64	Crater, Pbg., VA	KIA		BLM,LAN
Spring, George W.	Pvt.	G 15th SCVI	35	WG	09/14/62	Charlottesville	DOW	Univ. Cem. Charlottesville	ROH,JR,HOW,ACH
Spring, R.	Pvt.	H 10th SCVI		WG	06/15/62		DOD	(Date approx)	RAS,HOW
Springfield, T.W.	Pvt.	B 1st SC Res		GE	02/12/65		DOD	Elmwood Cem. Columbia, SC	ROH,MP,PP
Springs, William	Pvt.	A 21st SCVI		CN	02/19/65	Elmira, NY	DIP	Woodlawn N.C.#2340 Elmira	FPH,P6,P65,HAG
Sprinkle, Hiram T.	Pvt.	E 15th SCVI	47	FD	09/28/62	Winchester, VA	DOD	Stonewall C. Winchester VA	ROH,JR,WIN,KEB
Sprouse, Alfred	Pvt.	C 5th SCVI		SG	10/15/62	Staunton, VA	DOW	(Anson Sprouse I, 9th ?)	JR,SA3,HOS
Sprouse, Calvin	Pvt.	B Hol.Leg.	25	SG	11/07/64	Petersburg, VA	DOD	(PP=age 31)	ROH,HOS,PP
Sprouse, George W.	Pvt.	I 9th SCVIB		SG	/ /	Richmond, VA		Oakwood C.#60,Row E,Div A	ROH,OWC,HOS
Sprouse, H.H. (W.H.?)	Pvt.	A 6th SCVC		UN	04/15/65	Pt. Lookout, MD	DIP	C.C. Pt. Lookout, MD	ROH,P6,P115,CDC
Sprouse, John	Pvt.	I 5th SCVI		SG	/ /	Mitchell's St.TN	KIA	(1st in Co.I, 9th SCVIB?)	HOS,SA3
Sprouse, R.L.	Pvt.	C Hol.Leg.		SG	06/29/64	Sappony Ch., VA	KIA		HOS

SOUTH CAROLINA DEAD IN CSA SERVICE 1861-1865

NAME	RANK	C REGIMENT	AGE	DS	DIED	WHERE	WHY	BURIED	SOURCES
Sprouse, R.M.	Pvt.	E Hol.Leg.	18	SG	06/29/64	Sappony Ch., VA	KIA		ROH
Sprouse, Walter	Pvt.	F 15th SCVI		UN	/ /		DOD		JR
Spruel, John S.	Pvt.	B 3rd SCVI		NY	06/29/62	Manchester, VA	DOW	(Wdd @ Savage Stn.)	ROH,JR,SA2,ANY
Spruel, William F.	Pvt.	B 3rd SCVI		NY	06/29/62	Mancheste, VA	DOW	(Wdd @ Savage Stn.)	ROH,JR,SA2,ANY
Spruell, James W.	Pvt.	G 19th SCVI		AE	10/29/62	Knoxville, TN	DOD	Bethel C. Knoxville, TN	HOL,TOD
Spruell, S.	2nd Lt.	C 15th SCVI	55	LN	01/10/62	At home	DOD	(KEB=Spence)	R47,TOD,H15
Spurgess, A.	Pvt.	A 26th SCVI		HY	04/27/62	Richmond, VA		Hollywood Cem.Rchmd. B66	HC
Squires, Robert N.	Pvt.	F 1st SCVIG		HY	07/17/62	Richmond, VA	DOD		JR,SA1
St..., G.N. (Stokes?)	Pvt.	F 3rd SCVIBn	27		10/03/62	(age 27Ys 3Mths)		Stonewall C. Winchester VA	WIN
Stabler, D.V.	Pvt.	D 20th SCVI		OG	01/20/65	Pt. Lookout, MD	DIP	C.C. Pt. Lookout, MD	ROH,FPH,P6,P11
Stabler, George W.	Pvt.	B 1st SCVIH		OG	07/15/62	At home	DOD	(Typhoid)	ROH,JR,SA1
Stacey, S.	Pvt.	B 10th SCVI		HY	12/15/64	Nashville, TN	DOW	(Wdd & POW)	RAS
Stacey, Thomas	Pvt.	B 4th SCResB		AE	03/19/65	Charlotte, NC	DOD		ROH,PP
Stacey, W.R.	Pvt.	K 18th SCVI	25	UN	03/07/65	Elmira, NY	DIP	Woodlawn N.C.#2386 Elmira	ROH,FPH,P65,P1
Stackhouse, John W.	Pvt.	E 4th SCVC	27	MN	09/19/64	Elmira, NY	DIP	Woodlawn N.C.#520 Elmira	ROH,FPH,HOM,P1
Stacy, R.M.	Pvt.	K 18th SCVI	20	SG	11/10/64	Pt. Lookout, MD	DIP	C.C. Pt. Lookout, MD	ROH,FPH,P5,P11
Stafford, Duncan C.	1st Lt.	I 8th SCVI		MN	/ /	Richmond, VA	KIA	Oakwood C.#91,Row E,Div G	ROH,HMC,OWC,KE
Stager, J.W.	Pvt.	Mwthr's Bn			/ /	Raleigh, NC		Oakwood C.(Merriweather's)	TOD
Staggs, Thomas M.	Pvt.	B 13th SCVI		SG	05/22/64	Jericho Ford, VA	KIA		ROH,HOS
Stain, S.M.	Pvt.	A 12th SCVI		YK	/ /	Richmond, VA			ROH
Staley, Henry J. (I.?)	Pvt.	F 25th SCVI	24	OG	01/13/65	Richmond, VA	DOD	Hollywood Cem.Rchmd. W647	ROH,HC,HAG,EDR
Stallings, Paul	Pvt.	2nd SCVA	19	BL	/ /	James Island, SC	DOD		ROH
Stallings, S.H.	Pvt.	SC Res	52	BL	/ /	Charleston, SC	DOD		ROH
Stalmaker, D.F.	Pvt.	H 7th SCVIBn		ED	10/07/64	Elmira, NY	DIP	Woodlawn N.C.#585W Elmira	FPH,HAG,P65,P1
Stalnaker, R.	Pvt.	H 7th SCVIBn		ED	06/04/64	Pt. Lookout, MD	DIP	C.C. Pt. Lookout, MD	ROH,FPH,HAG,P1
Stalnaker, Samuel	Pvt.	G 14th SCVI	25	ED	07/10/63	Gettysburg, PA	DOW	(Died in enemy hands)	ROH,GDR,HOE
Stalvey, A.	Pvt.	A 10th SCVI		GN	/ /		DOD		GRG
Stalvey, A.	Pvt.	F 7th SCVC		HY	04/03/65	Newport News, VA	DIP	Newport News Cem.	P6
Stalvey, Henry	Pvt.	E 26th SCVI	18	HY	08/15/63	Charleston, SC	DOD		ROH
Stalvey, J.P.	Pvt.	A 10th SCVI		GN	10/15/62		DOD	(Typhoid)	JR,GRG,RAS
Stalvey, John P.	Pvt.	D 9th SCVIBn	25	HY	04/15/62	Camp Lookout, SC	DOD		ROH,PP,CEN
Stalvey, Mabry	Pvt.	E 26th SCVI	31	HY	06/16/62	Secessionville	KIA		ROH
Stancel, Joseph A.	Pvt.	Ferguson's			12/14/63	Rock Island, IL	DIP	C.C.#26 Rock Island, IL	FPH,P5
Stancell, John S.	Pvt.	1st SC Mil			04/30/65	New Bern, NC	DIP	Cedar Grove C. Newbern, NC	P1,P6,WAT,PP
Stancill, John	1st Sgt.	C 8th SCVI		CD	07/25/63	Gettysburg, PA	DOW		ROH,GDR,P1,KEB
Standard,	Pvt.	A 23rd SCVI		CN	07/15/62	Richmond, VA		Hollywood Cem.Rchmd. 097	HC
Stanfield, John M.	Pvt.	G 1st SCVIR		CN	07/20/62		DOD	(Dropsy)	JR,SA1
Stanfill, James R.	Pvt.	B 3rd SCVC		CO	07/18/63	Hardeeville, SC	DOD		ROH
Stanhouse, J.D.	Pvt.	E 9th SCVI		KW	01/15/62		DOD		JR
Stanley, Edward A.	3rd Cpl.	PeeDee LA		DN	/ /				ROH,SA1,PDL
Stanley, Jefferson T.	Pvt.	I 21st SCVI		MN	06/30/64	Petersburg, VA		Blandford Church Pbg., VA	BLC,PP
Stanley, John F.	Pvt.	I 21st SCVI		MN	05/09/64	Pt. Walthall Jn.	DOW	(Wdd 5/7/64,PP=Dd 6/30)	ROH,HMC,HAG,PP
Stansell, M	Pvt.	F 22nd SCVI		AN	02/06/65	Pt. Lookout, MD	DIP	(Stancer, M. Co. A in FPH)	ROH,FPH,P113
Stanton, E.G.	Pvt.	B 24th SCVI	18	MO	11/30/64	Franklin, TN	KIA		EJM
Stanton, Harvey	Pvt.	F 12th SCVI		FD	/ /	Richmond, VA	DOD		HFC
Stanton, J.H.	Pvt.	G 23rd SCVI		MO	04/01/65	5 Forks, VA	KIA		HOM
Stanton, John	Cpl.	D 26th SCVI		MO	07/15/64	Petersburg, VA	KIA	(Day approx, 6/17-7/27)	ROH,HOM,CDC
Stanton, John A.	Pvt.	G 8th SCVI		MO	/ /	Petersburg, VA	KIA	(1864)	HOM,KEB
Stanton, Milton B.	Pvt.	B 24th SCVI	18	MO	06/13/65	Camp Chase, OH	DIP	C.C.#2041 Columbus, OH	ROH,FPH,HOM,P2
Stanton, Noah	Pvt.	B 24th SCVI		MO	11/30/64	Franklin, TN	KIA	(TRFD frm G, 8th SCVI)	ROH,HOM,UD2,PP
Stanton, R.E.	2nd Lt.	B 17th SCVI		FD	10/28/62	Warrenton, VA	DOW	(Wdd @ 2nd M.)	JR,R47,UD3

S

SOUTH CAROLINA DEAD IN CSA SERVICE 1861-1865

NAME	RANK	C	REGIMENT	AGE	DS	DIED	WHERE	WHY	BURIED	SOURCES
Stark, Adolphus	Pvt.	A	15th SCVI		RD	09/14/62	South Mtn., MD	KIA	(JR=M,13th SCVI)	ROH,JR,KEB
Stark, John	Pvt.	F	3rd SCResB			/ /	Raleigh, NC		Oakwood C. Raleigh, NC	TOD
Starling, John	Pvt.	A	2nd SCVI		RD	10/25/63	Newman, GA	DOW	Oak Hill Cem. Newman, GA	ROH,SA2,KEB,BGA
Starling, Robert	Pvt.	A	2nd SCVI		RD	05/07/62	Richmond, VA	DOD	Hollywood Cem.Rchmd. G14	ROH,HC,SA2,KEB
Starnes, John T.	Pvt.	B	6th SCVI	19	YK	/ /	Virginia	DOD		YEB
Starnes, T.A.	Pvt.	G	3rd SCVI	20	LS	12/13/62	Fredericksburg	KIA	(KEB= Starms)	ROH,JR,SA2,KEB
Starns, A.H.	Pvt.	D	3rd SCVI		SG	07/02/63	Gettysburg, PA	KIA	(KEB=Stearns, A.B.)	ROH,JR,GDR,SA2
Starns, R. Thomas	Pvt.	E	17th SCVI	22	YK	/ /	Mississippi	DOD	(1864)	ROH,DEM,YEB
Starns, Robert C.	Cpl.	D	27th SCVI		LS	08/24/64	Weldon RR, VA	KIA	(Rptd MIA 8/21/64)	ROH,HAG
Starr, H.A.						/ /			Rose Hill C. Hagerstown MD	BOD
Starr, W.	Pvt.	K	17th SCVI		YK	07/30/64	Crater, Pbg., VA	KIA		BLM
Statter, W.D.					PS	/ /	Petersburg, VA			ROH
Staubs, Jacob	3rd Sgt.	F	27th SCVI	31	ED	06/06/64	Cold Harbor, VA	KIA	(HOE=11/7@ Attlee's Fm.)	HOE,HAG,UD3
Staunton, George	Pvt.	K	6th SCVI	30	MO	09/02/62	Warrenton, VA	DOW	(Wdd 2nd Man)	ROH,3RC
Stavart, J.D.	Pvt.	B	7th SCVC		CN	12/25/64	Pt. Lookout, MD	DIP	(Prob Stewart, J.D. 7thBn0	ROH
Steadham, G.D.	Pvt.	H	25th SCVI		CL	06/17/64	Petersburg, VA			ROH,HAG
Steading, George F.	Sgt.	D	P.S.S.		SG	10/15/64	Darbytown Rd. VA	DOW	City Pt. N.C. Hopewell, VA	ROH,HOS,PP,TOD
Steadman, Henry C.	Pvt.	G	7th SCVI		ED	06/29/62	Savage Stn., VA	KIA	(? Rgtl.Sgt. Major)	JR,HOE,UD2,KEB
Steadman, James C.	Pvt.	G	7th SCVI		ED	06/29/62	Savage Stn., VA	KIA		JR,HOE,KEB,UD2
Steame, J.	Pvt.	H	15th SCVI		UN	07/03/64	Richmond, VA		Hollywood Cem.Rchmd. U301	HC
Stedham, S.D.	Pvt.	A	14th SCVI		DN	08/11/62	Lynchburg, VA	DOD		JR
Stedham, Thomas L.	Pvt.	K	14th SCVI		ED	08/11/62		DOD		JR,HOE
Stedwell, D.	Pvt.	E	24th SCVI		CO	/ /	Atlanta, GA		Oakland C. Atlanta, GA	CVGA
Steedly, A.T.	Pvt.	G	1st SCVIH		BL	05/12/62		DOD		ROH,SA1
Steedman, James B.	3rd Sgt.	L	1st SCVIG	39	CN	12/18/63	Ft. Delaware, DE	DIP	Finn's Pt., NJ Nat. Cem.	ROH,FPH,P40,SA1
Steedman, James B.	Cpt.	H	5th SCVI		UN	/ /	At home	DOW	(Wdd 2M,RES 7/63?)	JR,SA3
Steel, J.T.	QM Sgt.		22nd SCVI			07/30/64	Crater, Pbg., VA	KIA		BLM
Steel, S.	Pvt.	H	3rd SCVI		LN	12/23/62	Richmond, VA	DOD	Hollywood Cem.Rchmd. S353	HC,SA2
Steele, J.B.	Pvt.	H	12th SCVI	47	YK	01/15/64		DOD	(Also wdd 6/27/62, 9/1/62)	CWC,YEB
Steele, John J.	Pvt.	H	10th SCVI		WG	06/25/62	Canton, MS	DOD	Con. Cem. Canton, MS Gv#89	PP,RAS,TOD
Steele, S.H.	Pvt.	H	12th SCVIi	22	YK	04/02/65	Sutherland Stn.	KIA		CWC,YEB
Steele, W.	Pvt.	H	1st SCVC	19	YK	01/15/64		DOD		ROH,YEB
Steele, W.A.	Pvt.	H	12th SCVI	31	YK	/ /	At home	DOD		YEB
Steele,Jr., W.A.	Pvt.	H	12th SCVI	22	YK	/ /		DOD	(1861)	YEB
Steen, Allen	Pvt.	F	21st SCVI		MO	02/17/65	(POW Ft.Fsh1/16)	DIP	Woodlawn N.C.#2221 Elmira	ROH,FPH,HOM,P65
Steen, George	1st Lt.	F	15th SCVI	32	UN	05/24/64	Richmond, VA	DOW	(Wdd 5/8/64)	ROH,R47,KEB
Steen, Maccany	Pvt.	B	26th SCVI	38	CD	10/15/63	At home	DOD		ROH
Steine, Alexander	Pvt.	F	1st SCVIR		CD	11/08/63	Charleston, SC	DOD		ROH,SA1
Steinmeyer,Jr., J.H.	Cpt.	A	24th SCVI		CN	05/16/64	Calhoun, GA	KIA		CDC,R48
Stell, R.M.	Pvt.	K	Orr's Ri.		AN	06/27/62	Gaines' Mill, VA	KIA		ROH,CDC
Stellings, S.B.	Major		SC Res		BL	09/12/64	Charleston, SC	DOD		ROH
Stenhouse, John Taylor	2nd Lt.	E	Ham.Leg.	34	RD	08/27/61	Culpepper, VA	DOW	Fairview P.C. GE Cty.	JR,CGH,GEC,R48
Stentson, Andrew	Pvt.	F	24th SCVI		AN	01/10/64	Rock Island, IL	DIP	C.C.#159 Rock Island, IL	FPH,P5
Stephens, A.	Pvt.	G	7th SCVIBn	35	KW	07/11/64	Richmond, VA	DOD	Hollywood Cem.Rchmd. U468	ROH,HC
Stephens, Allen	Pvt.	C	26th SCVI		MN	05/28/64	Petersburg, VA	KIA	(HMC=KIA @ 5 Forks, VA)	ROH,HMC
Stephens, B.	Pvt.	C	10th SCVI		HY	/ /	Corinth, MS	DOD		RAS
Stephens, Edward T.	Pvt.	B	1st SCVIG		NY	06/29/62	Gaines Mill	DOW	(SA1=DIS,not on NY Mon.)	ANY,SA1
Stephens, Elisha	Pvt.	C	Hol.Leg.	37	SG	05/22/62	Adams Run, SC	DOD	(ROH=Co.E,PP=2/20/62)	ROH,HOS,PP
Stephens, F.H.	Pvt.	B	2nd SCVIRi		PS	/ /				ROH
Stephens, F.J.	Pvt.	A	Orr's Ri.		AN	06/27/62	Gaines' Mill, VA	KIA		JR,ROH
Stephens, Green B.	Pvt.	A	Orr's Ri.	22	PS	06/27/62	Gaines' Mill, VA	KIA		ROH,CDC

SOUTH CAROLINA DEAD IN CSA SERVICE 1861-1865

NAME	RANK	C REGIMENT	AGE	DS	DIED	WHERE	WHY	BURIED	SOURCES
Stephens, J.B.	Pvt.	A 7th SCVI			06/02/63	Richmond, VA		Hollywood Cem.Rchmd. T534	ROH,HC
Stephens, James E.	Pvt.	F 21st SCVI		MO	02/23/65	Elmira, NY	DIP	Woodlawn N.C.#2254 Elmira	ROH,FPH,HAG,P6
Stephens, Jack D.	Pvt.	E Hol.Leg.		SG	/ /	At home	DOD		HOS
Stephens, James Adger	Pvt.	Hart's Bty			07/18/64	Richmond, VA			ROH,CNM
Stephens, James H.	Pvt.	A Orr's Ri.	34	PS	05/05/64	Wilderness, VA	KIA		ROH
Stephens, James J.	Sgt.	C 10th SCVI		HY	08/26/63	Forsyth, GA	DOW	Forsyth, GA	RAS,CDC,CKB
Stephens, Joel W.	Pvt.	D 10th SCVI		MN	06/15/62	Holly Springs MS	DOD		RAS,HMC,PP
Stephens, John R.	Pvt.	E 9th SCVIBn	20		03/26/62	Georgetown, SC	DOD		PP
Stephens, John W.	Pvt.	E 1st SCVIG		MN	07/10/64	Wilderness, VA	DOW	(Wdd 5/6/64)	SA1,HMC
Stephens, M.	Pvt.	C 10th SCVI		HY	/ /		DOD		RAS
Stephens, R.R.	Pvt.	K 11th SCVI	18	CO	01/15/64	At home	DOD		ROH,HAG
Stephens, Reuben	Pvt.	F 21st SCVI		MO	02/23/64	Pt. Lookout, MD	DIP	C.C. Pt. Lookout, MD	ROH,FPH,HOM,P1
Stephens, S. Perry	Pvt.	G 27th SCVI		CN	02/19/65	Elmira, NY	DIP	Woodlawn N.C.#2341 Elmira	FPH,P6,P65,P12
Stephens, Wesley Chapple	Pvt.	SC Militia	17	CD	04/01/65	New Bern, NC	DOW	Cedar Grove C, Newbern, NC	P1,P6,WAT,PP
Stephenson, J.L.	Pvt.	D 17th SCVI		CR	/ /	Petersburg, VA			ROH
Stepp, John	Pvt.	G 16th SCVI		GE	02/04/64	Rock Island, IL	DIP	C.C.#363 Rock Island, IL	FPH,16R,P5,P8
Stepp, Thomas	Pvt.	I 16th SCVI		GE	/ /	Pt. Lookout, MD	DIP	C.C. Pt. Lookout, MD	16R
Sterling, C.M.	Pvt.	A Ham.Leg.		CN	/ /	Richmond, VA	KIA		ROH,WLI
Sterling, Charles Thomas	Pvt.	B 1st SCVIG	18	NY	01/15/65	At home	DOD		ROH,SA1,ANY
Sterling, D.	Pvt.	Ward's LA			03/08/64	Georgetown, SC	DOD		PP
Sterling, G. Pinckney	Pvt.	B 3rd SCVI		NY	03/11/65	Elmira, NY	DIP	Woodlawn N.C.#1836 Elmira	FPH,SA2,KEB,P6
Sterling, John Calvin	Pvt.	B 4th SCVC		CR	07/01/64	Nance's Shop, VA	KIA	Hollywood Cem.Rchmd. U302	ROH,HC,HHC,CB
Sterling, Samuel A.	Pvt.	B 7th SCVIBn	34	CR	01/22/64	Sullivans I., SC	DOD		ROH,HHC
Stevens, Benjamin	Pvt.	F 1st SCVIG		HY	11/14/61	Suffolk, VA	DOD		JR,SA1
Stevens, Clement Huffman	Brig.Gen.			PS	07/25/64	Atlanta, GA	DOW	St. Pauls E.C. Pendleton	ACC,GIG
Stevens, Frederick W.	Pvt.	L 1st SCVIG	22	CN	09/09/62	Richmond, VA	DOD	Hollywood Cem.Rchmd. A90	ROH,JR,HC,SA1
Stevens, Hugh	Pvt.	M 10th SCVI		HY	/ /		DOD		RAS
Stevens, J.D.	Pvt.	SCVA			07/17/64	Richmond, VA		Hollywood Cem.Rchmd. U66	HC
Stevens, J.F.	Pvt.	D 3rd SCVI		SG	12/21/61	Centreville, VA	DOD	(KEB & HOS=Stephens)	JR,SA2,KEB,HOS
Stevens, James	Pvt.	F 1st SCVIG		HY	02/07/64	Orange C.H., VA	DOD		SA1
Stevens, James Adger	5th Sgt.	A 25th SCVI		CN	10/31/63	Ft. Sumter, SC	KIA	Old Scotch P.C. Char'ston)	ROH,JR,DOC,PP
Stevens, James W.	Pvt.	M 10th SCVI		HY	/ /	Booneville, MS	DOD		ROH,RAS
Stevens, M.W.	Pvt.	K 14th SCVI		ED	07/01/63	Gettysburg, PA	KIA		HOE,GDR,UD2
Stevens, Richard	Pvt.	G 7th SCVI		ED	/ /		DOD		HOE,KEB,UD2
Stevens, Simeon	Pvt.	I Hol. Leg.		SG	12/04/64	Pt. Lookout, MD	DIP	C.C. Pt. Lookout, MD	FPH,P5,P115
Stevens, T.W.					/ /			(Rchmd. effects list 1/63)	CDC
Stevens, W.H.	Pvt.	F 1st SCVIBn		CN	/ /		DOD	Magnolia Cem. Charleston	RCD
Stevenson, A T.	Pvt.	F 24th SCVI		AN	01/07/64	Rock Island, IL	DIP	C.C.#159 Rock Island, IL	ROH,JR,FPH,P5
Stevenson, Albert D.	1st Cpl.	C 4th SCVI		AN	05/31/62	7 Pines, VA	KIA		ROH,SA2
Stevenson, Amaziah F.	Pvt.	F 24th SCVI		AN	05/24/63	Jackson, MS	KIA		PP,HOL
Stevenson, D.S.	Pvt.	I 22nd SCVI		OG	07/30/64	Crater, Pbg., VA	KIA		BLM
Stevenson, David	Pvt.	H 6th SCVI		FD	09/13/61	Germantown, VA	DOD		ROH,HFC
Stevenson, David	Pvt.	C 3rd SCVCBn		BL	/ /		DOD	(Mem to CNM 2/3/62)	CNM
Stevenson, E.J.	Pvt.	F 2nd SC Res			04/02/65	Thomasville, NC		Con. Cem. Thomasville, NC	CV,PP
Stevenson, Elbert	Pvt.	L P.S.S.			/ /		ACD		JR
Stevenson, J.C.	Pvt.	2nd SCVIRi			10/03/62	Mt. Jackson, VA	DOW	Mt. Jackson, VA	ROH,JR,CDC
Stevenson, J.E.	Pvt.	F Hol.Leg.		AE	02/28/65	Elmira, NY	DIP	Woodlawn N.C.#2138 Elmira	FPH,P6,P120,P6
Stevenson, Joel P.	Pvt.	K 1st SCVIH		OG	09/07/62	2nd Manassas, VA	DOW	(Wdd 8/30/62)	ROH,SA1,JRH
Stevenson, John Young	Pvt.	H 6th SCVI	26	FD	07/01/62	Frayser's Farm	DOW		ROH,WDB,HFC
Stevenson, R.A.	Pvt.	F 6th SCVI	28	CR	06/15/62	Richmond, VA	DOD		ROH,HHC
Stevenson, Samuel W.	Pvt.	H 6th SCVI	21	FD	06/01/62	7 Pines, VA	KIA		ROH,JR,CDC,WDB

S

SOUTH CAROLINA DEAD IN CSA SERVICE 1861-1865

NAME	RANK	C REGIMENT	AGE	DS	DIED	WHERE	WHY	BURIED	SOURCES
Stevenson, T.W.	Pvt.	G P.S.S.		YK	/ /		DOD	(Stephenson, Thompson ?)	JR
Stevenson, Thomas J.	Pvt.	B 5th SCVI		UN	09/30/64	Chaffin's Farm	KIA		ROH,SA3
Stevenson, W. Foster	Pvt.	F 24th SCVI	20	AN	01/15/64		DOD		HOL
Stevenson, William	Pvt.	F Hol.Leg.	41	AE	03/06/62	At home	DOD		ROH
Steward, Frank A.	Pvt.	K 17th SCVI	25	YK	/ /	Manassas, VA	ACD		JR,YEB
Steward, P.M.	Pvt.	A 17th SCVI		CR	05/17/64	Petersburg, VA		Blandford Church Pbg., VA	BLC
Steward, William	Pvt.	A Tucker's R			05/07/65	Salisbury, NC	DOD	Prob old Lutheran C. there	PP
Stewart, A. Jackson	2nd Lt.	H 4th SCVC		LR	06/28/64	Hawes Shop, VA	KIA		ROH,LAN,R43
Stewart, A.B.	Pvt.	F 22nd SCVI		PS	07/30/64	Crater, Pbg., VA	KIA		BLM
Stewart, D.T.	Pvt.	E 14th SCVI		LS	05/03/63	Chancellorsville	KIA		ROH,CGS
Stewart, Daniel	Pvt.	B 2nd SCVIRi		PS	08/30/62	2nd Manassas, VA	KIA	(MIA, assumed dead)	ROH,CDC
Stewart, G.L.	Pvt.	K 1st SCVIH		OG	06/01/64	At home	EXC	(killed near home as DES)	SA1
Stewart, George W.	Pvt.	G 1st SCVIG		ED	05/23/64	Jericho Ford, VA	KIA		ROH,SA1,HOE,CDC
Stewart, George W.	Pvt.	F 23rd SCVI		CR	09/06/62	2nd Manassas, VA	DOW		JR
Stewart, Isaac	Pvt.	16th SCVI			10/15/62	(16th not in VA)		Stonewall C. Winchester VA	ROH,WIN
Stewart, J.	Pvt.	A 20th SCVI		PS	07/27/64	Richmond, VA		Hollywood Cem.Rchmd. V2	ROH,HC
Stewart, J.B.				DN	07/15/62	Petersburg, VA			ROH
Stewart, J.C. Alvin	Pvt.	G 3rd SCVI	23	LS	01/10/63	At home	DOD	New Harmony B.C.	ROH,JR,SA2,CEC
Stewart, J.F.	Pvt.	A 13th SCVI		LS	06/17/62	Richmond, VA		Hollywood Cem.Rchmd. O240	ROH,HC
Stewart, J.K.	Pvt.	G 5th SCVC		AE	08/16/64		KIA		ROH
Stewart, J.W.	Pvt.	B 25th SCVI		CN	04/24/65	Elmira, NY	DIP	Woodlawn N.C.#1410 Elmira	FPH,P6
Stewart, Jackson J.	Pvt.	H 24th SCVI	37	CR	06/10/62	Charleston, SC	DOW	Magnolia Cem. Charleston	ROH,MAG,RCD,HHC
Stewart, James Dallas	Pvt.	B 7th SCVIBn	18	FD	05/21/64	Weldon RR, VA	KIA		ROH,HAG,HFC
Stewart, James H.	Surgeon	3rd SCVCBn		YK	/ /		DOD		YEB
Stewart, James S.	Pvt.	G 1st SCVIG		ED	09/16/64	Ream's Stn., VA	DOW	Hollywood Cem.Rchmd. V557	ROH,HC,SA1,HOE
Stewart, James W.	Pvt.	F 24th SCVI		AN	/ /		DOD	(1864)	HOL
Stewart, John H.	2nd Lt.	B 6th SCVI	31	YK	09/30/64	Ft. Harrison, VA	KIA	Hollywood Cem.Rchmd. I119	ROH,HC,R46,YEB
Stewart, John P.	Pvt.	B 3rd SCVI		NY	03/02/64	Rock Island, IL	DIP	C.C.#700 Rock Island, IL	ROH,FPH,P5,ANY
Stewart, Joseph	Pvt.	E 3rd SCVIBn		LS	10/04/62	Frederick, MD	DOW	Mt.Olivet C.#81 Frederick	FPH,KEB,BOD
Stewart, Joseph W.	Pvt.	E 3rd SCVIBn		RD	07/02/63	Gettysburg, PA	KIA	Magnolia Cem. Charleston	ROH,JR,MAG,CDC
Stewart, Littleton G.	Pvt.	F 24th SCVI		AN	05/14/63	Jackson, MS	DOW		EJM,PP
Stewart, M.J.H.	Pvt.	A Wash. LA			02/25/65	Charleston, SC	DOD	St.Johns Chapel Charleston	MAG,RCD
Stewart, R. Hardy	Pvt.	A 8th SCVI	17	DN	07/19/62	Petersburg, VA	DOD	(Typhoid)	ROH,JR,KEB,PP
Stewart, R.J.	Pvt.	E 14th SCVI		LS	06/25/62	Richmond, VA	DOD	(Typhoid, JR=P.J.)	JR,CGS
Stewart, Robert	Pvt.	E Orr's Ri.		PS	06/20/62	Richmond, VA			ROH
Stewart, Robert G.	1st Sgt.	G 3rd SCVIBn	35	LS	02/24/62	Adams Run, SC	DOD	New Harmony B.C. GE Cty.	JR,GEC,LSC
Stewart, Samuel C.	Pvt.	B 21st SCVI		DN	04/04/65	Elmira, NY	DIP	Woodlawn N.C.#2555 Elmira	FPH,HAG,P6,P65
Stewart, Spencer F.	Pvt.	F 20th SCVI		NY	/ /	Strasburg, VA	KIA		ANY,KEB
Stewart, Thomas M.	Pvt.	A 17th SCVI	21	CR	05/21/64	Petersburg, VA			PP
Stewart, Thomas S.	Pvt.	A 17th SCVI	23	CR	05/23/64	Clay's Farm, VA	DOW		ROH,HHC,CB
Stewart, W.	Pvt.	C 6th SCVI		FD	/ /	Lynchburg, VA		Lynchburg CSA Cem.#6 R5	BBW,HFC
Stewart, W.B.	Pvt.	Macbeth LA		LS	02/13/63	Petersburg, VA	DOD	Blandford Church Pbg., VA	ROH,BLC,PP
Stewart, W.C.	Pvt.	D Ham.Leg.		LS	/ /	At home	DOD		GRS
Stewart, W.F.	Pvt.	C 20th SCVI		LN	05/05/65	Richmond, VA			ROH
Stewart, W.M.	Pvt.	E 22nd SCVI		PS	10/24/62			Stonewall C. Winchester VA	ROH,WIN
Stewart, W.S.	Pvt.	F 20th SCVI			05/05/65	Richmond, VA	DOD	Hollywood Cem.Rchmd. W481	HC,P6
Stewart, William	Pvt.	I 16th SCVI		GE	/ /	Mississippi	DOD		16R
Stewart, Wilson H.	Pvt.	D 16th SCVI		GE	11/23/63	At home	DOD	(16R=H.W.)	16R,PP
Stewman, John A.	Sgt. Major	9th SCVIB			02/09/62	Richmond, VA	DOD		JR,LAN
Stewman, Philip A.H.	Sgt.	D 15th SCVI		LR	/ /	Charleston, '62	DOD	Lancaster P.C. LR Cty.	JR,HIC,LAN
Stidham, L.D.	Pvt.	A 14th SCVI		DN	08/11/62	Lynchburg, VA	DOD	Lynchburg CSA Cem.#9 R1	ROH,CDC,BBW

SOUTH CAROLINA DEAD IN CSA SERVICE 1861-1865

NAME	RANK	C REGIMENT	AGE	DS	DIED	WHERE	WHY	BURIED	SOURCES
Stigall, Hensley	Pvt.	E 12th SCVI	25	LR	09/17/62	Sharpsburg, MD	KIA		ROH,LAN
Still, D.C.	Pvt.	1st SC			07/26/62	Richmond, VA		Hollywood Cem.Rchmd. Q121	HC
Still, Isaac	Pvt.	A 14th SCMil			05/16/65	Hart's Island NY	DIP	Cypress Hills N.C.#2805 NY	FPH,P6,P79
Still, James T.	Pvt.	H 17th SCVI		BL	01/06/65	Elmira, NY	DIP	Woodlawn N.C.#1234 Elmira	FPH,P5,P65,P12
Still, Thomas E.	Pvt.	B 14th SCMil			04/28/64	Hart's Island NY	DIP	Cypress Hills N.C.#2637 NY	FPH,P6,P79
Stillinger, Frank	Pvt.	B 20th SCVI	20	OG	06/02/64	Cold Harbor, VA	KIA		ROH,KEB
Stillman, W.T.	Pvt.	K 24th SCVI		ED	05/20/63	Calhoun, GA	DOW		HOE
Stine, W.D.	Sgt.	I 19th SCVI		AN	11/30/64	Franklin, TN	KIA		ROH
Stinson, Lewis P.	Pvt.	Ward's Bty		GN	05/15/64	Wilderness, VA	DOW		ROH
Stinson, William G.	1st Cpl.	B 5th SCVI			10/07/64	Darbytown Rd.	KIA		SA3
Stinton, J.	Pvt.	D 26th SCVI		CN	/ /	Petersburg, VA	KIA		ROH
Stirling, Thomas P.	Pvt.	A Ham.Leg.	35	CR	08/25/64	Deep Bottom, VA	DOW	(Wdd in left lung)	ROH,CDC,HHC
Stivender, William F.	Pvt.	E 1st SCVIH		BL	01/17/63		DOD		ROH,SA1
Stockhart, R.M.	Pvt.	F 15th SCVI		UN	/ /	Richmond, VA		Oakwood C.#54,Row M,Div A	ROH,OWC
Stockman, J. Belton C.	Pvt.	H Hol.Leg.	37	NY	05/07/63	Wilmington, NC	DOD		ROH,ANY
Stockman, J.H.	Pvt.	G 13th SCVI		NY	03/30/65	At home	DOD	(ANY says KIA)	ROH,ANY
Stockman, John C.	Pvt.	C 3rd SCVI	26	NY	07/15/62	Malvern Hill, VA	DOW	(Wdd 7/1/62)	ROH,JR,SA2,ANY
Stockman, Wiley M.	Pvt.	G 13th SCVI		NY	07/05/62	Richmond, VA	DOD	(Typhoid)	ROH,JR,ANY
Stocks, John	Pvt.	L 8th SCVI		MN	08/22/62	Richmond, VA	DOD	Oakwood C.#58,Row H,Div A	ROH,JR,OWC
Stoddard, D.C.	Pvt.	G 3rd SCVI		LS	10/09/62	Mt. Jackson, VA	DOD	Mt. Jackson, VA	ROH,JR,SA2,PP
Stoddard, D.F.	Pvt.	E 14th SCVI	20	LS	02/26/62	McPhersonville	DOD	New Harmony B.C. GE Cty.	JR,GEC,LSC
Stoddard, David F.	Pvt.	G 3rd SCVI	24	LS	06/29/62	Savage Stn., VA	KIA	New Harmony B.C. LSC	ROH,JR,SA2,GEC
Stoddard, W.C.	Pvt.	E 14th SCVI	23	LS	04/11/63	Staunton, VA	DOD	New Harmony B.C.	ROH,JR,CGS,GEC
Stogner, Thomas	Pvt.	F 21st SCVI		MO	03/26/64	Pt. Lookout, MD	DIP	C.C. Pt. Lookout, MD	ROH,FPH,HOM,P1
Stogner, William	Pvt.	F 21st SCVI		MO	/ /	At home	DOD		HOM,HAG
Stokes, Alexander D.	Pvt.	I 18th SCVI	23	DN	07/10/63	Jackson, MS	KIA		ROH,PP
Stokes, B.F.	Pvt.	7th SCVI			02/11/63	Richmond, VA			ROH
Stokes, Charles Spencer	Pvt.	F 7th SCVIBn	17	KW	06/11/64	Bermuda Hundred	DOW	Blandford Church Pbg., VA	ROH,HIC,BLC,PP
Stokes, Coleman M.	Pvt.	B 16th SCVI		GE	09/24/62	Adams Run, SC	DOD	(Brain fever,PP=Calvin)	JR,16R,PP
Stokes, F. Marion	Pvt.	C 6th SCVI		KW	/ /		KIA	(ROH=Co. D	HIC
Stokes, H.	Pvt.	K 6th SCVI		WG	07/20/62		DOD		3RC
Stokes, Henry Y.	Pvt.	B 16th SCVI		GE	07/25/62	Adams Run, SC	DOD		PP
Stokes, J.F.	2nd Sgt.	E 13th SCVI		SG	08/29/62	2nd Manassas, VA	KIA		HOS
Stokes, James Frieson	Pvt.	B 15th SCVAB	22	DN	03/16/65	Averysboro, NC	KIA		ROH,WAT,PP
Stokes, Josiah W.	Pvt.	K 2nd SCVIRi	43	AE	01/05/64	Morristown, TN	DOD		ROH
Stokes, M.	Pvt.	D 6th SCVI		CR	10/31/62	Staunton, VA		Thornrose C. Staunton, VA	ROH,TOD
Stokes, R.	Pvt.	F 8th SCVI	22	DN	12/15/62	Orange C.H., VA	DOD	(Typhoid)	ROH,JR,KEB
Stokes, Reddier	Pvt.	M 8th SCVI	30	DN	/ /		DOD	(1862)	ROH
Stokes, Thomas	Pvt.	G 19th SCVI		AE	09/22/64	Atlanta, GA	KIA		HOL
Stokes, William Elias	Pvt.	H 21st SCVI	27	DN	10/18/64	Augusta, GA	DOD		ROH,HAG
Stokes, William Jarvis	Pvt.	A 7th SCVIBn	24	KW	05/30/64	Drury's Bluff VA	DOW		ROH,HIC,HAG
Stokes,Jr., Elwood R.	Sgt.	F 3rd SCVIBn	23	RD	07/02/63	Gettysburg, PA	KIA	(1st in A, 2nd SCVI)	ROH,JR,GDR,SA2
Stoll, John T.	Cpl.	K 10th SCVI		CN	06/24/62	Canton, MS	DOD	Con.Cem. Canton, MS Gv#289	JR,RAS,PP,TOD
Stoll, Richard M.	Pvt.	K Orr's Ri.	47	AN	06/27/62	Gaines' Mill, VA	KIA		ROH
Stom, Robert (Strom?)					/ /			(Rchmd effects list 12/62)	CDC
Stone, C.	Pvt.	C 4th SCRes			02/01/65	Charleston, SC	DOD	Magnolia Cem. Charleston	ROH,RCD
Stone, C.W.	Pvt.	21st SCVI			/ /	Charlestown, VA			ROH
Stone, F.H.	Pvt.	H 7th SCVI		ED	06/15/61	Charlottesville	DOD	Univ. Cem. Charlottesville	ROH,ACH
Stone, Francis F.	Pvt.	H 8th SCVI		MN	07/21/61	1st Manassas, VA	KIA	(JR=Typhoid 9/3/61)	JR,HMC,KEB
Stone, Francis Marion	Pvt.	B Ham.Leg.		ED	06/13/65	Newport News, VA		Greenlawn C. Newport News	PP
Stone, Frank	Pvt.	19th SCVI	18	LN	07/15/64	Lagrange, GA	DOD		ROH

S

SOUTH CAROLINA DEAD IN CSA SERVICE 1861-1865

NAME	RANK	C	REGIMENT	AGE	DS	DIED	WHERE	WHY	BURIED	SOURCES
Stone, Henry E.	Pvt.	A	17th SCVI		CR	06/15/65	At home	DOD	(Died after discharge)	ROH,HHC,CB
Stone, J.B.	Pvt.	K	12th SCVI	21	PS	03/07/62	Green Pond, SC	DOD		ROH,PP
Stone, J.H.	Pvt.	E	16th SCVI	20	GE	07/13/64	Columbia, SC	DOD		ROH,16R,PP
Stone, J.H.	Pvt.	H	8th SCVI		MN	09/03/61	Charlottesville	DOD	(Measles)	JR
Stone, J.P.	Pvt.	E	6th SCVC		LS	08/13/64	Wilson, NC			PP
Stone, James	1st Cpl.	E	Orr's Ri.	22	PS	07/29/62	Gaines' Mill, VA	DOW	City Pt. N.C. Hopewell, VA	ROH,CDC,PP,TOD
Stone, James	Pvt.	I	1st SCVA			03/08/64	Pt. Lookout, MD	DIP	C.C. Pt. Lookout, MD	ROH,FPH,P5,P113
Stone, James	Pvt.	F	13th SCVI		SG	06/01/62	Richmond, VA	DOD	(Apoplexy in camp)	JR,HOS
Stone, John	Pvt.	F	19th SCVI	29	LN	07/15/63	Rome, GA	DOD	Myrtle Hill C. Rome, GA	ROH,HOE,BGA
Stone, John	Pvt.	B	14th SCVI	20	ED	06/27/62	Gaine's Mill, VA	KIA		JR,HOE,UD3
Stone, Leonard B.	Pvt.	E	7th Bn Res	17	WG	01/31/65	Green Pond, SC	DOD		ROH
Stone, M.	Pvt.	D	27th SCVI	37	LS	07/20/63	Bty. Wagner, SC	KIA		ROH,HAG
Stone, Micajah	Pvt.	E	16th SCVI	26	GE	07/25/62	Adams Run, SC	DOD		ROH,16R
Stone, Oliver	Pvt.	D	24th SCVI	16	BT	06/18/64	Kenesaw Mtn., GA	KIA		EJM
Stone, Palvey T.	Pvt.	G	15th SCVI	26	WG	05/24/63	Richmond, VA	DOW	Hollywood Cem.Rchmd. T493	ROH,JR,HC,HOW
Stone, Patilla A.	Pvt.	D	P.S.S.		SG	07/10/62	Petersburg, VA	DOD		ROH,JR,HOS,PP
Stone, R.J.	Pvt.	G	2nd SCVIRi			09/19/62	Warrenton, VA	DOW	(Wdd and Man.)	ROH
Stone, R.W.	Pvt.	F	10th SCVI		MN	/ /	Glasgow, KY	DOD	(not a casualty in RAS)	HMC,RAS
Stone, Reuben C.	Pvt.	K	12th SCVI		PS	09/14/63	Ft. Delaware, DE	DIP	Finn's Pt.,NJ Nat. Cem.	ROH,FPH,P5,P40
Stone, Robert	Pvt.	K	1st SCVC	35	PS	12/30/64	Hilton Head, SC	DOW	(Wdd & POW 12/13/64)	ROH,P2,P6
Stone, Thomas	Pvt.	E	1st SCVIR			11/02/63	Charleston, SC	DOD		SA1
Stone, Thomas	Pvt.	L	P.S.S.			/ /		KIA		JR
Stone, W.A.	Pvt.	G	27th SCVI		SG	08/06/64	Pt. Lookout, MD	DIP	C.C. Pt. Lookout, MD	ROH,FPH,HAG,P113
Stone, W.C.P.	3rd Sgt.	H	8th SCVI		MN	05/12/64	Spotsylvania, VA	KIA		HMC,KEB,UD1
Stone, W.L.	1st Cpl.	F	27th SCVI	40	ED	07/04/63	At home	DOD		HOE,HAG
Stone, W.T.	Pvt.	D	18th SCVI		AN	08/27/62	Rappahanock, VA	KIA		ROH
Stone, William	Pvt.	K	1st SCVC	32	CR	06/18/63	Washington, DC	DOW	Soldier's Home Nat. Cem.	ROH,HHC,CV,P6,CB
Stone, William Diamond	Sgt.	I	19th SCVI	29	AE	11/30/64	Franklin, TN	KIA	Williamson Cty., TN C.C.	ROH,WCT,PP
Stonecypher, Benjamin						10/16/63	AthensGA Armory	DOD		UD2
Stoney, George M.	2nd Lt.	C	1st SCVIR		RD	03/19/65	Bentonville, NC	KIA		ROH,SA1,WAT,PP
Stoney, William R.	Cpt. ADC		Hagood'sBd			05/07/64	Pt. Walthal Jctn	KIA	(Also wdd @ Bty. Wagner)	ROH,CDC
Storey, George H.	Pvt.	K	3rd SCVI		SG	09/21/61	Richmond, VA	DOD		JR,SA2,HOS,KEB
Story, D.G.	Pvt.	A	1st SCResB			/ /			DOD After the surrender	UD3
Story, Jesse	Pvt.	C	22nd SCVI	19	SG	07/30/64	Petersburg, VA	KIA	(Killed after capture)	ROH
Story, Thomas E.	Pvt.	E	7th SCVI		ED	/ /	Charlottesville	DOD	Univ. Cem. Charlottesville	HOE,ACH,KEB
Story, Thomas G.	Pvt.		2nd SCVIRi			09/17/62	Sharpsburg, VA	DOW	(JR=Stoney, T.J.)	ROH,JR,CDC
Story, W.L.	Pvt.	F	Ham.Leg.	21	GE	07/21/61	1st Manassas, VA	KIA	(Davis Guards)	ROH,JR,CV,CDC
Stott, D.C.	Pvt.	L	Orr's Ri.		AN	07/25/62	Richmond, VA			ROH,CDC
Stott, W.D.	Pvt.		Ham. Leg.		AN	/ /	Richmond, VA			ROH
Stoudemire, A.J.	Pvt.	H	13th SCVI		LN	09/17/62	Culpepper, VA	DOW	(Wdd 2nd Man) Culpepper VA	JR,CGH
Stoudenmire, David C.	Pvt.	E	1st SCVC		OG	11/26/62	Orange C.H., VA	DOD	(general debility)	ROH
Stoudenmire, John B.	Pvt.	H	13th SCVI	25	LN	07/01/63	Gettysburg, PA	KIA	(JR=A.B.)	ROH,JR
Stoudenmire, John David	Pvt.	E	5th SCVC	18	OG	11/03/64	Summerville, SC	DOW	(Wdd @ Price's Farm, VA)	ROH,CDC
Stoutamire, E.W.	Cpl.	C	11th SCVI		CN	07/20/62	At home	DOD		ROH,HAG,CDC
Stoutmire, J.T.	Pvt.	G	5th SCVC		AE	05/31/64	Old Church, VA	DOW	Mrs. Wm. Newton's Place	ROH
Stover, David G.	Pvt.	G	2nd SCVI		KW	06/29/62	Savage Stn., VA	KIA		JR,HIC,KEB,SA2
Stover, Thomas B.	Pvt.	H	4th SCVC		LR	05/31/64	Old Church, VA	DOW	Mrs. Wm. Newton's Place	ROH,CDC,LAN
Stover, W.G.	Cpt.	I	12th SCVI		LR	09/17/62	Sharpsburg, MD	DOW		LAN,R47
Stowe, Robert S.	Pvt.	K	1st SCVC			12/30/64	Hilton Head, SC		NC Beaufort, SC #53-6336	PP,BNC
Stowe, S.D.	Pvt.		Kanapaux's	35	YK	/ /	At home	DOD	(YEB= Stone ?)	YEB
Strain, Archibald W.	Pvt.	A	12th SCVI	19	UN	06/03/62	Richmond, VA	DOD	(Measles)	JR,YMD,YEB

SOUTH CAROLINA DEAD IN CSA SERVICE 1861-1865

NAME	RANK	C	REGIMENT	AGE	DS	DIED	WHERE	WHY	BURIED	SOURCES
Strain, Joseph E.	Pvt.	E	5th SCVI	27	YK	05/22/63	Gastonia, NC	DOD		JR,SA3,YMD,YEB
Strain, Joseph J.	Pvt.	E	5th SCV		YK	/ /	Petersburg, VA	DOD (Dup of J.E.?)		YEB
Strain, Samuel M.	Pvt.	A	12th SCVI	29	UN	08/08/62	Richmond, VA	DOD (Typhoid)		JR,YEB
Strain, William H.	Pvt.	I	27th SCVI		CN	06/15/64		DOD	Magnolia Cem. Charleston	MAG,HAG
Strait, G.L.	Cpt.	A	6th SCVI	30	CR	10/15/63	At home	DOD (Severe Wnd. @ 2nd Man.)		ROH,CDC,HHC
Strait, George W.	Pvt.	A	17th SCVI	22	CR	03/25/65	Ft. Steadman, VA	KIA		ROH,HHC,CB
Strait, Hugh D.	Pvt.	A	17th SCVI			/ /	Savannah, GA	DOW (When? CR or YK?)		HHC,YEB
Strait, Lafayette	Post Surg.		17th SCVI	29	CR	10/10/63		DOD		ROH,HHC
Strait, William L.	Pvt.	A	17th SCVI	30	CR	05/15/65	Petersburg, VA	DOW (Wdd 4/4/62)		ROH,YEB,HHC,P6
Strange, Henry J.	Pvt.	C	7th SCVIBn	25	RD	05/14/64	Drury's Bluff VA	KIA		ROH,CDC,HAG
Strange, John	Pvt.	E	18th SCVI		SG	/ /	Charleston, SC	DOD		HOS
Strange, N.W.	Pvt.		12th SCVI			06/05/62	Richmond, VA			ROH
Strange, T.A.	Pvt.	I	Hol.Leg.	40	SG	04/06/64	Savannah, GA	DOD		ROH
Strange, W.P.	Cpt.	G	2nd SCVIRi		PS	07/10/64	Richmond, VA	DOD	Hollywood Cem.Rchmd. U17	ROH,HC,R45
Strange, William	Pvt.	A	Hol.Leg.	34	SG	08/30/62	2nd Manassas, VA	KIA		ROH,HOS
Strawhorn, Robert T.	Pvt.	F	Hol.Leg.	23	AE	08/31/62	2nd Manassas, VA	DOW		ROH
Strawinski, Thaddeus S.	Pvt.				RD	06/15/61	Castle Pinckney	ACD	1st P.C.(Scots) Charleston	ROH,MAG
Street, Edward	Pvt.		Brooks GA		CN	07/02/63	Gettysburg, PA	KIA (1st in K, 2nd SCVI)		ROH,JR,GDR,SA2
Street, George	Pvt.	F	23rd SCVI		CR	08/30/62	2nd Manassas, VA	KIA		HHC
Street, Jeff	Pvt.	F	23rd SCVI		CR	08/30/62	2nd Manassas, VA	KIA		HHC
Street, Robert J.	Pvt.	H	7th SCVIBn	22	FD	06/18/64	Petersburg, VA	KIA		ROH,HAG
Stribling, James M.	Cpl.	E	Orr's Ri.	19	PS	12/13/62	Fredericksburg	KIA		ROH
Stribling, James M.	Lt. CSNavy		CS Florida		PS	09/13/62	At sea	DOD	At sea off Montrose	CDC
Stribling, Jones H.	4th Sgt.	E	Orr's Ri.	28	PS	07/07/62	Dill Springs, VA	DOD		ROH,CDC
Stribling, Thomas Asbury	Pvt.	G	22nd SCVI	29	AN	06/24/62	Secessionville	KIA		ROH,CDC,PP
Stribling, Thomas J.	Pvt.	E	Orr's Ri.	21	PS	05/01/65		DOW		ROH
Stribling, William B.	Pvt.	E	Orr's Ri.	23	PS	08/06/62	Richmond, VA	DOD		ROH,CDC
Strickland, D.J.	Pvt.	F	1st SCVIG		HY	01/03/62	Suffolk, VA	DOD		JR,SA1
Strickland, D.O.	Pvt.	G	6th SCVC		AE	05/31/65	Pt. Lookout, MD	DIP	C.C. Pt. Lookout, MD	FPH,P6,P115,CD
Strickland, H.S.	Pvt.	K	1st SCVIH		OG	12/15/63		DOD		ROH,SA1,JRH
Strickland, Henry	Pvt.	D	26th SCVI		MO	06/14/65	Hart's Island NY	DIP	Cypress Hills N.C.#3005 NY	FPH,HOM,P79
Strickland, J.	Pvt.	D	7th SCVI			10/29/62			Stonewall C. Winchester VA	ROH,WIN
Strickland, J.J.	Pvt.	K	1st SCVIH		OG	09/20/64	Petersburg, VA	EXC (Deserter)		SA1
Strickland, John B.	Pvt.	G	Orr's Ri.		AE	06/15/64	At home	DOD		ROH
Strickland, Laban	Pvt.	G	9th SCVIBn	31	HY	07/17/62	Secessionville	DOW	Magnolia Cem. Charleston	ROH,MAG,RCD,PP
Strickland, M.R.	Pvt.	D	8th SCVI		CD	10/25/62	Richmond, VA		Hollywood Cem.Rchmd. B139	HC,KEB
Strickland, R.	Pvt.	H	23rd SCVI		HY	08/30/62	2nd Manassas, VA	KIA		ROH,HMC,CDC
Strickland, Starling	Pvt.	H	7th SCVIBn			07/06/63	Petersburg, VA			ROH,HAG
Strickland, W.L.	Pvt.	G	6th SCVC	28	RD	06/30/63	Adams Run, SC	DOD		PP
Strickland, W.R.	Pvt.	K	26th SCVI	38	HY	12/16/63	Charleston, SC	DOD		ROH
Strickland, Yancey L.	Pvt.	I	1st SCVIR	20	AN	04/30/65	New Bern, NC	DOW	Cedar Grove C. Newbern, NC	P1,P6,SA1,WAT,
Stricklen, Westley	Pvt.	D	8th SCVI	18	CD	/ /	Georgia	DOD (1863)		ROH
Stricklin, N.	Pvt.	B	8th SCVI		CD	10/27/61	Richmond, VA	DOD	Oakwood C.#5,Row C,Div A	ROH,JR,OWC
Stricklin, Nathan	Pvt.	D	8th SCVI		CD	10/12/61	Charlottesville	DOD (Typhoid)		JR,KEB
Strickling, Elmore	Pvt.	D	11th SCVI	16	BT	05/16/64	Drury's Bluff VA	KIA (NI HAG)		ROH
Strickling, John	Pvt.	D	24th SCVI		BT	07/25/64	Peachtree Creek	KIA		ROH,CDC
Strickln, W.W.	Pvt.	B	8th SCVI			12/18/61	Front Royal, VA	DOD	Prospect Hill C. Frt.Royal	TOD
Stringfellow, Lemuel	Pvt.	A	1st SCVIG		BL	03/01/65	Richmond, VA	DOW	Hollywood Cem.Rchmd. W526	ROH,HC,SA1
Stringfield, Edwin	Pvt.	F	7th SCVI	23	ED	/ /	Charlottesville		Univ. Cem. Charlottesville	ACH,KEB,HOE
Strobhart, James A.	Sgt.	I	2nd SCVI	20	BT	06/23/62	Manchester, VA	DOD		ROH,JR,SA2,KEB
Strobhart, James M.	Pvt.		Boyce's LA			09/17/62	Sharpsburg, MD	KIA		JR

S

SOUTH CAROLINA DEAD IN CSA SERVICE 1861-1865

NAME	RANK	C REGIMENT	AGE	DS	DIED	WHERE	WHY	BURIED	SOURCES
Strock, Bozeman	Pvt.	A Ham.Leg.	18	OG	/ /	At home	DOD		ROH
Strock, E.B.	Pvt.	F 25th SCVI	19	OG	03/17/65	Richmond, VA	DOW	Hollywood Cem.Rchmd. W213	ROH,HC,CDC,P65
Strock, H.D.	Pvt.	K 9th SCVIB		LN	09/19/61	Germantown, VA	DOD	(JR=F,P.S.S.)	ROH,JR
Strock, Samuel B.	Pvt.	E Ham.Leg.		GE	02/13/63		DOD	(Consumption)	JR
Strohecker, Oswald E.	Cpl.	A Ham. Leg.	26	CN	10/27/64	Richmond, VA	KIA		ROH,CDC,WLI
Strom, G.B.	Pvt.	D 14th SCVI		ED	05/17/65	Hart's Island NY	DIP	Cypress Hills N.C.#2809 NY	FPH,P6,P79
Strom, H.A.	Pvt.	D 14th SCVI	17	ED	05/30/64	Alexandria, VA	DOW	(Wdd & POW @ Noel Stn.)	D14,HOE,P1,P5
Strom, Harrison	Cpl.	K 24th SCVI		ED	09/01/64	Jonesboro, GA	KIA	(HOE=SUR @ Greensboro)	EJM
Strom, Robert					/ /			(Rchmd effects list 1/63)	CDC
Strom, S.B.	Pvt.	K 24th SCVI		ED	06/15/65	At home	DOD	Rehobeth B.C. McCormick	HOE,EDN
Strom, Thomas J.	Pvt.	D 14th SCVI	20	ED	08/18/64	Petersburg, VA	KIA		ROH,HOE,D14
Strom, W. Silas	Pvt.	K 24th SCVI		ED	11/30/64	Franklin, TN	KIA		ROH,HOE,CDC,PP
Stroman, Absolom	Pvt.	A 14th SCMil	57	OG	04/29/65	Hart's Island NY	DIP	Cypress Hills N.C.#2665 NY	ROH,FPH,P6,P79
Stroman, Charles	Pvt.	F 25th SCVI		OG	05/10/65	Elmira, NY	DIP	Woodlawn N.C.#2788 Elmira	ROH,FPH,HAG,P65
Stroman, D.P.	Pvt.	I 2nd SCVA	25	OG	08/03/63		DOD	(Stroman, P.B. in EDR?)	ROH
Strong, Andrew	Pvt.	D 17th SCVI	37	CR	10/30/64	Elmira, NY	DIP	Woodlawn N.C.#732 Elmira	ROH,FPH,P65,HHC
Strong, George	2nd Lt.	1st SCV		BT	03/10/65	Bentonville, NC	KIA		ROH
Strother, George J.	2nd Lt.	G 7th SCVI		ED	/ /		DOD		HOE,KEB,R46,UD2
Strother, James C.	Pvt.	8th SCVI	26	CD	09/15/62	Warrenton, VA	DOW	(Wdd 2nd Man)	ROH
Strother, Joseph C.	Sgt.	C 8th SCVI		CD	09/14/62	Maryland Hts. MD	KIA		JR,KEB
Stroud, Pinckney	Pvt.	B 1st SCVC		SG	07/21/62	Adams Run, SC	DOD		PP
Stroup, M.A.	Pvt.	K 18th SCVI		SG	12/09/64	Elmira, NY	DIP	Woodlawn N.C.#1167 Elmira	ROH,FPH,P65,P120
Stuart, Allan	Lt. ADC	Gen.Cantey		BT	01/04/64	Aiken, SC	DOD	St. Thadeus E.C. Aiken, SC	ROH,TOD
Stuart, Edmund Rhett	Pvt.	H 1st SCVIG	19	BT	08/29/62	2nd Manassas, VA	KIA		ROH,SA1
Stuart, George F.	Pvt.	B 7th SCVC		CN	12/26/64	Pt. Lookout, MD	DIP	C.C. Pt. Lookout, MD	FPH,P5,P115
Stuart, Henry Middleton	1st Lt.	B 1st SCVA	22	BT	03/16/65	Averysboro, NC	KIA	St. Thadeus E.C. Aiken, SC	ROH,SCA,DOC,PP
Stuart, R.	Pvt.	A 1st SC			06/20/62	Richmond, VA		Hollywood Cem.Rchmd. 091	HC
Stuart, R.M.	Pvt.	Boyce's By			/ /	Lynchburg, VA		Lynchburg CSA Cem.#9 R2	BBW
Stuart, Samuel	Pvt.	C Ham.Leg.		CL	05/31/62	7 Pines, VA	KIA		ROH,JR,CDC
Stuart, T.W.	Pvt.	D 2nd Bn.Res			03/31/65	Thomasville, NC		Thomasville, NC C.C.	CV,PP
Stubblefield, R.	Sgt.	G 1st SCVA		PS	07/03/64	Ft. Johnson, SC	DOW		CDC
Stubbs, Joel	Pvt.	G 23rd SCVI	17	MO	07/03/64	Petersburg, VA	DOD		ROH,HOM,PP
Stubbs, John	Pvt.	G 23rd SCVI		MO	09/17/62	Sharpsburg, MD	KIA	Rose Hill C. Hagerstown MD	JR,HOM,CDC,BOD
Stubbs, Lucius C.	Pvt.	K 8th SCVI		MO	02/15/62	Richmond, VA	DOD	Bennettsville B.C., SC	ROH,JR,HOM,KEB
Stubbs, Maston W.	Pvt.	F 21st SCVI		MO	06/09/64	Swift Creek, VA	DOW	(Wdd 5/9/64)	ROH,HOM,HAG
Stubbs, Paul	Pvt.			MO	08/01/64	Petersburg, VA		Blandford Church Pbg., VA	BLC
Stubbs, Samuel F.	Pvt.	F 21st SCVI		MO	02/11/65	Elmira, NY	DIP	Woodlawn N.C.#2059 HAG	ROH,FPH,HOM,P65
Stuck, Jacob Barnett	Pvt.	H 13th SCVI	37	LN	07/02/63	Gettysburg, VA	KIA		ROH
Stuckey, Anderson	Pvt.	G 7th SCVIBn	32	KW	08/13/63	Charleston, SC	DOW	Magnolia Cem. Charleston	ROH,MAG,HIC,HAG
Stuckey, Andrew Newton	Pvt.	I 14th SCVI	19	AE	06/30/62	Frayser's Farm	KIA		ROH,JR,HOL
Stuckey, Christopher C.	Pvt.	C 6th SCVIB		KW	09/14/62	South Mtn., MD	KIA	(JR=Sharpsburg 9/17)	JR,HIC,WDB,CDC
Stuckey, H.G.	Pvt.	H 7th SCVI		PS	07/13/64	Fts. Monroe, VA	DIP		ROH
Stuckey, Hardy C.	Pvt.	B 21st SCVI		DN	/ /				HAG
Stuckey, Jasper E.	Sgt.	E 19th SCVI		SR	03/04/65	Camp Chase, OH	DIP	C.C.#1545 Columbus, OH	FPH,P6,P23
Stuckey, R. Foley	Pvt.	F 9th SCVIB	22	SR	12/09/61	Manchester, VA	DOD		ROH,JR
Stuckey, Wiley D.	Pvt.	H 21st SCVI		DN	01/22/65	Pt. Lookout, MD	DIP	C.C. Pt. Lookout, MD	ROH,FPH,HAG,P6
Stucky, J.	Pvt.	H 21st SCVI			/ /	Fts. Monroe, VA	DIP		ROH
Stukes, Alfred M.	Pvt.	D 4th SCVC		CL	09/02/64	Elmira, NY	DIP	Woodlawn N.C.#87 Elmira	ROH,FPH,P65,P120
Stukes, H.H.	Pvt.	K 25th SCVI		WG	05/09/64	Swift Creek, VA	KIA		HOW,CTA
Stukes, Henry	Pvt.	K 6th SCVI	35	CL	07/26/62	Richmond, VA	DOD		ROH
Stukes, Samuel James	Pvt.	C Ham.Leg.	21	CL	05/31/62	7 Pines, VA	DOW	(In enemy hands)	ROH,JR,CDC

SOUTH CAROLINA DEAD IN CSA SERVICE 1861-1865

NAME	RANK	C	REGIMENT	AGE	DS	DIED	WHERE	WHY	BURIED	SOURCES
Sturgeon, J. Thomas	Pvt.	H	7th SCVIBn	18	RD	/ /	Richmond, VA	DOW	(Wdd Drury's Bluff)	ROH,HAG
Sturgeon, Richard D.	Pvt.	H	7th SCVIBn		RD	12/10/64	Elmira, NY	DIP	Woodlawn N.C.#1055 Elmira	FPH,HAG,P65,P1
Sturgis, J.T.	Pvt.	H	12th SCVI	23	YK	05/12/64	Spotsylvania, VA	KIA		CDC,YEB
Sturgis, W.			SC			03/02/65			Loudon P. C. Baltimore	PP
Sturkey, D.P.	Sgt.	B	Ham.Leg.	22	AE	01/17/64	Dandridge, KY	KIA	Sturkey Fam.C. Plum Branch	ROH,CDC,MCC
Sturkey, Gabriel	Pvt.	I	2nd SCVA	52	LN	/ /		DOD	(1865)	ROH
Sturkey, Green N.	Pvt.	I	2nd SCVA		LN	/ /		DOD		ROH
Sturkey, John Wesley	Pvt.	K	20th SCVI		LN	08/15/64	At home	DOD	(KEB=Storey, Wesly, Co.I)	ROH
Stutts, J.H.	Cpl.	G	11th SCVI		CO	01/02/65	SC	DOD	(HAG=Stutts, G.H.)	ROH,HAG
Stutts, Thomas M.	Cpl.	G	11th SCVI		CO	09/15/62	SC	DOD		ROH,HAG
Styles, Daniel W.	Pvt.	C	13th SCVI		OG	/ /	Winchester, VA	DOD	(Sent to Hos 9/?/62)	ROH
Styres, John	Pvt.	C	14th SCVI		LS	12/07/62			Stonewall C. Winchester VA	ROH
Styron, Charles T.	Cpl.	K	19th SCVI	23	ED	07/28/64	Atlanta, GA	KIA		ROH,HOE
Styron, Thomas J.	Pvt.	G	1st SCVIG		ED	05/28/62		DOD	(Dropsy)	JR,SA1,HOE
Suares, Basil Manly	Pvt.	A	27th SCVI	22	CN	02/03/63	Charleston, SC	DOD	1st Baptist Ch. Charleston	ROH,MAG
Suber, Andrew	Pvt.	B	3rd SCVI		NY	09/15/61	Culpepper, VA	DOD	Fairview Cem. Culpepper VA	ROH,JR,SA2,UD1
Suber, Andrew Pinckney	Pvt.	H	3rd SCVI		LN	05/01/62	Richmond, VA	DOD		ROH,JR,SA2,ANY
Suber, Enoch	Pvt.	B	1st SCVIG	45	NY	02/28/63	Lynchburg, VA	DOD	Lynchburg CSA Cem.#6 R1	ROH,SA1,ANY,BB
Suber, George A.	Pvt.	B	3rd SCVI		NY	12/13/62	Fredericksburg	DOW	(ANY says Richmond)	ROH,JR,SA2,ANY
Suber, J.J.	Pvt.	C	4th SCResB		NY	01/26/65	Columbia, SC	DOD	Elmwood Cem. Columbia, SC	ROH,MP,PP
Suber, James Madison	2nd Sgt.	G	Hol.Leg.	36	NY	08/30/62	2nd Manassas, VA	KIA		ROH,ANY
Suber, M. Drayton	3rd Sgt.	G	Hol.Leg.	27	NY	10/15/62	Staunton, VA	DOD		ROH,ANY
Suber, Marion S.	Pvt.	I	3rd SCVI		LS	09/17/62	Sharpsburg, MD	KIA		ROH,SA2,KEB
Suber, Middleton	6th Cpl.	B	3rd SCVI		NY	10/31/61	Culpepper, VA	DOD	(JR=Richmond)	ROH,JR,SA2,ANY
Suber, Robert David	Pvt.	D	13th SCVI	21	NY	06/29/62	Savage Stn., VA	KIA		ROH,JR,ANY,CDC
Sudam, John M.	Pvt.	G	10th SCVI		HY	/ /	Forsyth, GA	DOW	Forsyth, GA	CKB,RAS
Sudduth, Lewis W.	Pvt.	F	16th SCVI	49	GE	05/20/65	Augusta, GA	DOD	Ebenezer M.C. GE Cty.	16R,GEE
Suggs, Arthur	Pvt.	A	Ham.Leg.		HY	/ /		DOD		ROH,WLI
Suggs, J.W.	Pvt.	C	10th SCVI		HY	/ /		DOD		RAS
Suggs, W.L.	Pvt.	A	7th SCVI			/ /	Richmond, VA		Oakwood C.#110,Row J,Div G	ROH,OWC
Suggs, William	Pvt.	G	2nd SCVI		KW	/ /	Manchester, VA	DOD	(1862)	HIC,KEB,H2,SA2
Sulledge, J.	Pvt.	D	SCVI			/ /	Richmond, VA		Oakwood C.#42,Row E,Div G	ROH,OWC
Sullivan, Andrew J.	Pvt.	I	12th SCVI		LR	06/19/64	Jericho Ford, VA	DOW	Hollywood Cem.Rchmd. U279	ROH,HC,LAN
Sullivan, D.	Pvt.	I	11th SCVI		CO	09/23/64		DOD		ROH,HAG
Sullivan, John	Pvt.	A	5th SCVI		LR	06/15/62	7 Pines, VA	DOW	(LAN=Mechanicville)	JR,SA3,LAN
Sullivan, John C.	Pvt.	E	16th SCVI	18	GE	/ /	Atlanta, GA	DOD	(1864)	ROH,16R
Sullivan, M.R.	Pvt.	D	4th SCVC		CN	11/20/64	Baltimore, MD	DIP	Loudon Pk.C. B-17 Balto MD	FPH,P4,P5,CV,P
Sullivan, Milton Arnold	Cpt.	A	6th SCVC	35	YK	02/19/65	Columbia, SC	DOD	Lebanon M.C. GE Cty.	ROH,GEC,GEE,PP
Sullivan, Nimrod	Pvt.	C	Orr's Ri.		PS	06/27/62	Gaines' Mill, VA	DOW	(Rchmd effects list 1/63)	CDC
Sullivan, Pressley O.	Pvt.	I	24th SCVI	30	ED	05/16/64	Calhoun Stn., GA	KIA		ROH,CDC
Sullivan, Sampson W.	Pvt.	I	24th SCVI	33	ED	09/20/63	Chickamauga, GA	KIA	Con. Cem. Marietta, GA	ROH,JR,CDC,CCM
Sullivan, Steven	Pvt.	D	8th SCVI	36	CD	12/15/63	Fredericksburg	DOD		ROH
Sullivan, T.	Pvt.	B	2nd SCV			06/13/64	Richmond, VA		Hollywood Cem.Rchmd. U578	HC
Sullivan, Thomas	Pvt.	D	8th SCVI	21	CD	07/15/64	Maryland	DOW		ROH
Sullivan, W.H.	Sgt.	C	Hol.Leg.		SG	/ /	Mt. Pleasant, SC	DOD	Magnolia Cem. Charleston	HOS,RCD
Sullivan, W.J.	Pvt.	B	27th SCVI		SG	03/04/65	Elmira, NY	DIP	Woodlawn N.C.#1979 Elmira	FPH,P6,P65,P12
Sullivan, W.P.	1st Sgt.	I	5th SC Res	42	AE	07/17/63	At home	DOD		ROH
Sullivan, W.S.	Pvt.	C	2nd SCVIRi			03/18/62		DOD	(Typhoid pneumonia)	JR
Sullivan, Warren P.	1st Cpl.	A	3rd SCVI		LS	10/30/61	Charlottesville	DOD		ROH,SA2,RHL,KE
Sulman, W.T.	Pvt.	K	24th SCVI		ED	05/20/64	Med.C. Atlanta		Oakland C. Atlanta R10#5	BGA
Sultan, Joseph R.	Pvt.	I	15th SCVI	47	LN	05/15/64	Lynchburg, VA	DOW	(Wdd Wilderness, died ?)	TOD

S

SOUTH CAROLINA DEAD IN CSA SERVICE 1861-1865

NAME	RANK	C REGIMENT	AGE	DS	DIED	WHERE	WHY	BURIED	SOURCES
Sultan, Robert J.	Pvt.	C 3rd SCVI		NY	05/15/63		DOD	(Date approx)	ROH,ANY,KEB,SA2
Summary, William	Pvt.	D 24th SCVI		BT	/ /	Camp Douglas, IL	DIP		ROH,CDC
Summer, Bluford M.	Pvt.	D 13th SCVI	23	NY	09/13/63	Ft. Delaware, DE	DIP	(May be Summer, Martin B.)	NCC,ANY
Summer, Francis M.	Pvt.	E 3rd SCVI	22	NY	07/12/62	Savage Stn., VA	DOW		ROH,JR,SA2,KEB
Summer, Franklin	Pvt.	H 13th SCVI		LN	/ /		DOD		ROH
Summer, George W.	Sgt.	H 13th SCVI		LN	07/14/62	Martinsburg, VA	DOD	Greenhill C. Martinsburg	ROH,JR,PP,UD1
Summer, J.B.	Pvt.	H 3rd SCVI		LN	03/06/62	Charlottesville	DOD		ROH,JR,SA2,KEB
Summer, J.D.	Pvt.	A 13th SCVI		LS	06/20/62	Richmond, VA		Hollywood Cem.Rchmd. Q305	ROH,HC
Summer, J.G.	Pvt.	B 15th SCVI		UN	/ /		DOD		JR
Summer, J.J.	Pvt.	G 13th SCVI		NY	08/02/62	Richmond, VA			ROH,ANY
Summer, John	Pvt.	B 15th SCVI		UN	/ /		DOD		JR,KEB
Summer, John Calhoun	Cpt.	H 3rd SCVI		LN	12/13/62	Fredericksburg	KIA	Summer Gvyd #2 Little Mtn.	JR,NCC,KEB,ANY
Summer, John Garrett	Pvt.	H 13th SCVI		LN	03/23/63	Guinea Stn., VA	DOD	(Smallpox)	ROH,JR
Summer, Martin B.	Hos. Stwd.	13th SCVI		NY	09/13/63	Ft. Delaware, DE	DIP	Finn's Pt., NJ Nat. Cem.	ROH,FPH,P5,ANY
Summer, Mattison M.	Pvt.	B 15th SCVI		LN	06/12/64	Richmond, VA	DOD	Hollywood Cem.Rchmd. U276	ROH,JR,HC,KEB
Summer, P.B.	Pvt.				/ /	Richmond, VA		Oakwood C.#8,Div N,Div F	OWC
Summer, Pinckney				LN	/ /			(May be Summer, P.B.)	ROH
Summer, R.H.	Pvt.	A Ham.Leg.		CN	07/16/61	Richmond, VA		Hollywood Cem.Rchmd. K51	ROH,HC,CDC
Summer, R.P.	Pvt.	H 3rd SCVI		LN	12/13/62	Richmond, VA	DOD	Oakwood C.#41,Row O,Div E	ROH,JR,SA2,OWC
Summer, William L.	Pvt.	H 13th SCVI		LN	01/28/63	Guinea Stn., VA	DOD	(Smallpox)	ROH,JR
Summerall, E.	Cpl.	E 3rd SCVIBn		LS	10/19/64	Strasburg, VA	KIA		ROH
Summerall, John	Pvt.	C 14th SCVI		LS	10/16/61	SC Coast	DOD		JR
Summerall, M.	Cpl.	C 3rd SCVIBn		LS	05/06/64	Wilderness, VA	KIA	(KEB= Co.E)	ROH
Summerall, W.W.	Pvt.	E 3rd SCVABn			09/19/62	Frederick, MD	DOW	Frederick G.H. Cem.	P6
Summers, Adam Samuel	Pvt.	C 13th SCVI		SG	12/10/64	Coosawatchie, SC	ACD	(ACD, by pistol shot)	ROH,JR,HOS
Summers, B. Frank	Pvt.	E 3rd SCVI		NY	/ /	Richmond, VA	DOW	(? Francis M.?)	ANY
Summers, David A.F.	Pvt.	I 2nd SCVA	37	OG	02/03/64	James Island, SC	DOD		ROH
Summers, George	Pvt.	D 5th SCVC		CN	/ /	Petersburg, VA	KIA	(Dorchester Enroll Book)	TEB
Summers, George T.	Pvt.	F 6th SCVC	25	CN	10/27/64	Burgess' Mill VA	KIA		CAG,CDC
Summers, John Franklin	Pvt.	H 13th SCVI		LN	05/22/62	Ashland, VA	DOD	(Typhoid)	ROH,JR
Summers, P.H.	Pvt.	SCVI			07/26/61	Richmond, VA		Hollywood Cem.Rchmd. K90	HC
Summers, Richard H.	Pvt.			CN	/ /	Virginia	DOD	(Dorhester Enroll Book)	TEB
Summers, William A.	Pvt.	C 6th Bn.Res			05/11/65	Pt. Lookout, MD	DIP	C.C. Pt. Lookout, MD	FPH,P6,P115
Summerville, J. Bluford	Pvt.	F 14th SCVI		LS	08/29/62	2nd Manassas, VA	KIA	(JR=Summerall)	ROH,JR,CDC
Super, A.P. (Suber?)					/ /			(Rchmd effects list 12/62)	CDC
Surrat, F.C.	Pvt.	M P.S.S.		SG	/ /		DOW	(In enemy hands)	HOS
Surrat, J.	Pvt.	I 3rd SCVABn		GE	06/19/64	Charleston, SC	DOD	(1st. Louisiana Hospital)	ROH,CDC
Surrat, W.A.	Pvt.	SCVC		SG	/ /		KIA		HOS
Surten, A.	Pvt.	K 1st SCVA			12/11/63	Ft. Sumter, SC	ACD	(Magazine explosion)	ROH,CDC
Sutherland, Elisha J.	Pvt.	I 14th SCVI	22	AE	12/24/62	Fredericksburg	DOW	(Wdd 6/27 & 12/15)	ROH,HOL
Sutherland, Francis M.	Pvt.	I 14th SCVI	24	AE	10/13/62	Winchester, VA	DOD	(Also Wdd @ Frayser's Fm.)	ROH,HOL
Sutherland, J.F.	Pvt.	F 2nd SCVC			03/26/64	Raleigh, NC		Oakland C. Raleigh, NC	TOD
Sutherland, L.N.	Pvt.	K 5th SCVI		SG	11/24/63	Lookout Valley	DOW		HOS,SA3,CDC
Sutherling, Wilson	Pvt.	E 24th SCVI	24	CO	/ /	At home	DOD		ROH
Sutner, J.W.	Pvt.	G 24th SCVI			07/25/64	Atlanta, GA	DOW		ROH
Sutton, B.F.	Pvt.	H 2nd SCVI		LR	09/20/63	Chickamauga, GA	DOW	(SA2=died @ Cedar Creek)	LAN,SA2
Sutton, E.	Pvt.	G 2nd SCVI	36	KW	09/19/63	At home	DOD		ROH,SA2,KEB,HIC
Sutton, Euriah	Sgt.	K 17th SCVI	19	YK	10/04/62	Winchester, VA	DOD	(YEB=I, 12th SCVI)	JR,YEB
Sutton, James Irwin	Pvt.	I 5th SCVI		YK	09/20/61	Germantown, VA	DOD	(YEB=SUR)	JR,SA3,YEB
Sutton, T.J.	Pvt.	G 7th SCVIBn	26	KW	05/16/64	Drury's Bluff VA	KIA	(HAG=Sutton, T.G.)	ROH,HIC,HAG
Swain, E.	Pvt.	K 17th SCVI		YK	07/30/64	Petersburg, VA	KIA		ROH

SOUTH CAROLINA DEAD IN CSA SERVICE 1861-1865

NAME	RANK	C REGIMENT	AGE	DS	DIED	WHERE	WHY	BURIED	SOURCES
Swancy, Richard D.	Cpl.	G Orr's Ri.		AE	05/30/62	Richmond, VA	DOD		ROH
Swaney, James	Pvt.	G 1st SCVA			06/27/63	Charleston, SC		Magnolia Cem. Charleston	ROH,MAG,RCD
Swann, Eaton	Pvt.	K 17th SCVI	38	YK	07/30/64	Crater, Pbg., VA	KIA		BLM,YEB
Swann, H. Lorraine.	Pvt.	E 5th SCVI	36	YK	11/16/63	Campbell's Stn	KIA		ROH,SA3,YEB,UD
Swansey, J.R.	Pvt.	G Orr's Ri.		AE	05/31/62	Richmond, VA			ROH,CDC
Swanston, Robert	Sgt.	K 1st SCVA			12/11/63	Ft. Sumter, SC	ACD	(Magazine explosion	ROH,CDC
Swatsel, Richard L.	Pvt.	C 13th SCVI		SG	08/29/62	2nd Manassas, VA	KIA	(HOS= William)	ROH,JR,HOS,CDC
Swearengen, Benjamin T.	3rd Cpl.	D 14th SCVI	21	ED	01/20/62	Coosawatchie, SC	DOD	(Typhoid)	JR,D14,HOE,EDN
Swearingen, Richard V.	Pvt.	H 7th SCVI		ED	06/29/62	Savage Stn., VA	KIA		ROH,JR,CDC,HOE
Sweat, Benjamin	Pvt.	D 26th SCVI		MO	/ /		KIA	(1862)	HOM
Sweat, G.	Pvt.	K 10th SCVI		CN	/ /		DOD		RAS
Sweat, George	Pvt.	G 1st SCVIH		BL	02/27/63		DOD		ROH,SA1
Sweat, James W.	Pvt.	B 24th SCVI		MO	/ /	At home	DOD		HOM
Sweat, John	Pvt.	D 26th SCVI		MO	/ /	Secessionville	DOD	(1862)	HOM
Sweat, Joseph	Pvt.	A 17th SCVI		CR	07/30/64	Crater Pbg., VA	KIA		HHC
Sweat, Joshua	Pvt.	D 17th SCVI	18	CR	03/01/62	John's Island SC	DOD		ROH,JR,HHC,CB
Sweat, Lawrence J.	Cpt.	G 1st SCVIH	25	BL	10/15/63	Chattanooga, TN	DOW		ROH,SA1
Sweat, Leonard	Pvt.	D 26th SCVI		MO	07/15/64	Petersburg, VA	DOW	(Wdd 7/1/64)	ROH,HOM,CDC
Sweat, Robert	Pvt.	I 6th SCVI		CR	/ /		DOD		CB,HHC
Sweat, Robert S.	Pvt.	A Ham.Leg.	24	BT	08/19/61	Culpepper, VA	DOW	Fairview Cem. Culpepper VA	ROH,CGH,WLI,CN
Sweat, S.	Pvt.	K 10th SCVI		CN	/ /		DOD		RAS
Sweat, Samuel	Pvt.	B 24th SCVI		MO	/ /		DOW	(1863)	HOM
Sweat, Samuel C.	4th Cpl.	E 5th SCVI		YK	09/30/64	Ft. Harrison, VA	KIA		SA3,UD3
Sweat, Simeon	Pvt.	B 24th SCVI		MO	12/06/64	Nashville, TN	KIA	(1863)	HOM
Sweat, Warren W.	Pvt.	G 9th SCVIB		DN	11/15/61	Virginia	DOD		ROH,JLC
Sweat, William	Pvt.	B 4th SCVC	36	CR	09/02/64	Lincoln G.H., DC	DIP	Soldier's Burial Ground	ROH,P6,HHC,CB
Sweat, William W.	Pvt.	G 9th SCVIB	29	CD	12/15/61	Richmond, VA	DOD	Oakwood C.#75,Row B,Div A	ROH,OWC
Sweatt, Josiah L.	Pvt.	A 17th SCVI	23	CR	07/30/64	Crater Pbg., VA	KIA		ROH,HHC,CB
Sweeney, Calvin	Pvt.	G 1st SCVA			06/30/65	Greensboro, NC			PP
Sweester, Theodore	Pvt.	1st SC			11/23/63	Unknown	DIP	Cypress Hills N.C.#937 NY	FPH
Sweet, David	Cpl.	D 25th SCVI		MN	/ /	VA		(1864)	HMC,HAG
Sweet, William Phillip	Pvt.	L 10th SCVI		MN	05/14/62	Macon, GA	DOD		RAS,HMC,PP
Swift, G.	Pvt.	E 1st SCV		CN	07/19/62	Columbia, SC	DOD	(Swift, John 1st SCVIR?)	ROH
Swigart, John J.	Pvt.	F 5th SCVC	31	LN	08/12/64	At home	DOD		ROH
Swigart, M.S.	Pvt.	F 5th SCVC	22	LN	08/28/63	Charleston, SC	DOD		ROH
Swittenburg, D.R.	Pvt.	H 3rd SCVI		LN	05/06/64	Wilderness, VA	KIA	Fredericksburg C.C. R6S13	SA2,FBG
Switzer, John D.	Pvt.	A Hol.Leg.		SG	03/29/65	Hatcher's Run VA	DOW		HOS
Swords, Jasper	Pvt.	C 20th SCVI			02/28/64	Raleigh, NC		Oakwood C. Raleigh, NC	TOD
Swygart, Emanuel Z.	1st Lt.	C 15th SCVI	38	LN	11/07/62	Ft. Walker, SC	KIA		TOD ROH,JR,KEB,PP
Sykes,	Sgt.	F 7th SCVI		ED	09/17/62	Sharpsburg, MD	KIA		JR
Sykes,Sr., A.	Pvt.	H 6th SCVI		FD	08/30/62	2nd Manassas, VA	DOW		JR,CDC
Syphech, Richard	Pvt.	E 1st SCVC		OG	05/15/64	Charleston, SC	DOD		ROH
Syphret, Obadiah J.	Pvt.	G 25th SCVI	18	OG	06/23/65	Elmira, NY	DIP	(POW @ Fort Fisher 1/15)	ROH,HAG,P65
Syphrett, J.W.W.	Pvt.	C 18th SCVIB			/ /	Charleston, SC			HMC

SOUTH CAROLINA DEAD IN CSA SERVICE 1861-1865

NAME	RANK	C REGIMENT	AGE	DS	DIED	WHERE	WHY	BURIED	SOURCES
Tachnas, D.	Pvt.	C 5th SCVC		CO	06/27/64	Samaria Church	DOW		ROH
Taft, Robert Martin	2nd Lt.	B 25th SCVI	28	CN	05/16/64	Drury's Bluff VA	KIA	Magnolia Cem. Charleston	ROH,WLI,HAG,R4
Tager, Anderson	Pvt.	E 1st SCVIR		RD	08/20/63	Charleston, SC	DOD		SA1
Tagett, James A.	1st Lt.	L Orr's Ri.		AN	01/06/63				R45
Tait, William J.	Pvt.	F 21st SCVI		MO	03/06/62	Georgetown, SC	DOD	(ROH & HOM= Tart)	ROH,HOM,HAG,PP
Talbert, Ansel Wayne	Pvt.		16	AE	03/14/65	At home	DOD	Talbert Cem. Plum Branch	ROH,MCC
Talbert, John	Pvt.	I 3rd SC Res			02/17/65	Columbia, SC	DOD		ROH,PP
Talbert, Joseph L.	1st Lt.	K 7th SCVI		ED	09/19/62	Maryland Hts. MD	DOW	Charlestown, WV	ROH,JR,EDN,R46
Talbert, O.W.	Pvt.	D 8th SCVI		CD	06/16/61	At home	DOD	(Typhoid)	JR
Talbert, T.	Pvt.	E 26th SCVI			09/16/64	Pt. Lookout, MD	DIP		ROH
Talbot, Andrew G.	Pvt.	D 21st SCVI		CD	01/01/65	Richmond, VA		Hollywood Cem.Rchmd. W597	ROH,HC,HAG
Talbot, James Franklin	Pvt.	G 19th SCVI		AE	01/27/65	Camp Chase, OH	DIP	C.C.#902 Columbus, OH	FPH,P6,P22,HOL
Tallant, Patrick A.	Pvt.	C 1st SCVIG		RD	09/02/62	Warrenton, VA	DOW	(Wdd 2nd Man 8/29)	ROH,JR,SA1,CDC
Tallarast, J.A.	Pvt.	K 6th SCVI	20	MO	02/18/63	Charlottesville	DOD	(3RC=Talwast, DOW	ROH,3RC
Tallent, T.J.	Pvt.	H 22nd SCVI		GE	/ /	Columbia, SC			PP
Tallevast, Alexander	Pvt.	B 21st SCVI		DN	04/04/65	Elmira, NY	DIP	Woodlawn N.C.#2556 Elmira	ROH,FPH,P5,P65
Tallicum, A.					/ /			Rose Hill C. Hagerstown MD	WAT,BOD
Tann, Oliver J.	Pvt.	A 5th SCVC	30	OG	06/11/64	Trevillian Stn.	KIA	(CDC=Taut)	ROH,CDC
Tanner, Edward D. (V.?)	Pvt.	F 27th SCVI	19	MN	08/06/64	Petersburg, VA	DOD	Blandford Church Pbg., VA	ROH,BLC,HAG,PP
Tanner, T.H.	Pvt.	H 18th SCVI		YK	10/23/63	Pt. Lookout, MD	DIP		ROH
Tant, N.J.N.	Pvt.	K 1st SCVIH		BL	10/14/61	At home	DOD		SA1
Tapp, A.J.	Pvt.	A 3rd SCVI		LS	06/25/65	Richmond, VA	DOD	Oakwood C.#149,Row N,Div A	ROH,JR,SA2,OWC
Tapp, Joshua	Sgt.	I Hol.Leg.	25	SG	05/27/62	Adams Run, SC	DOD	(Joshua R. in HOS?)	ROH,PP
Tarborough, C.	Pvt.	F 14th SCVI		SG	02/22/62	Columbia, SC	DOD		JR
Tarrant, Sumter W.	Pvt.	K P.S.S.	18	AE	11/17/62	Warrenton, VA	DOD		ROH,JR
Tarrant, Wesley F.	Pvt.	A 13th SCVI		LS	07/08/62	Richmond, VA	DOD	(Typhoid)	JR
Tart, Godi	Pvt.	D 25th SCVI		MN	07/26/64	Petersburg, VA	DOD	Blandford Church Pbg., VA	ROH,HMC,BLC,PP
Tart, L.C.	Pvt.	D 10th SCVI		MN	12/15/65	Harrodsburg, KY	DIP	Spring Hill Cem. KY	FPH,RAS,HMC
Tate, R.L.	Pvt.	G 11th SCVI			03/16/63	Richmond, VA	DOD	Oakwood C.#11, Row 6,Div D	ROH,OWC
Tate, Thomas R.	Pvt.	G 1st SCVIG		ED	02/01/63		DOW	(Wdd @ Fredericksburg)	SA1,HOE,CDC
Tate, Willis G.	Pvt.	C 16th SCVI		GE	/ /	Dalton, GA	DOD	Con. Cem. Marietta, GA	16R,BGA,CCM,UD
Tatum, William T.	Cpt.	I 1st SCVIR		AE	07/18/63	Bty. Wagner, SC	KIA		ROH,SA1,DOC,CD
Taverner, John Howard	Pvt.	B 25th SCVI	26	CN	06/16/62	Secessionville	KIA	2nd P.C.(Flynn's) Chlstn	ROH,JR,MAG,LED
Tayler, Caleb	Pvt.	C 20th SCVI	21	ED	06/01/64	Cold Harbor, VA	KIA		ROH,KEB
Taylor,		H 2nd SCVIRi			09/11/63	Petersburg, VA	EXC	(For desertion)	UD2
Taylor, A.J.	Pvt.	G 3rd SCVABn			10/28/63	Charleston, SC		Magnolia Cem. Charleston	ROH,MAG,RCD
Taylor, Alexander	Pvt.	D 1st SCVIH		LR	08/31/62	2nd Manassas, VA	DOW		ROH,JR,LAN,JRH
Taylor, Amos	Pvt.	K 13th SCVI	22	BT	12/13/61	At home	DOD	(JR=12/13/62)	ROH,JR,TOD
Taylor, Benjamin B.	Pvt.	H 23rd SCVI		MN	06/28/65	Pt. Lookout, MD	DIP	C.C. Pt. Lookout, MD	FPH,P6,P115,HM
Taylor, Benjamin F.	Pvt.	F 7th SCVI	20	ED	06/29/62	Savage Stn., VA	KIA	(JR=9 Mile Rd.)	ROH,JR,HOE,CV
Taylor, Calvin Smith	1st Sgt.	B 1st SCVIG	23	NY	12/26/62	At home	DOD	Beth Eden L.C. Newberry SC	NCC,ROH,ANY
Taylor, D.T.	Pvt.	B 13th SCVI		SG	07/22/62	Richmond, VA		Hollywood Cem.Rchmd. Q280	ROH,HC
Taylor, David	4th Cpl.	E 1st SCVIG		MN	05/06/64	Wilderness, VA	KIA		ROH,SA1,PDL,HM
Taylor, David A.	Pvt.	I 12th SCVI		LR	09/02/62	2nd Manassas, VA	DOW	(JR=D.E. KIA 8/29/62)	JR,LAN
Taylor, Drayton	Pvt.	G 13th SCVI		NY	07/25/62	Richmond, VA	DOD	(Typhoid)	ROH,JR,ANY
Taylor, F. Harmon	Pvt.	B 1st SCVIG	25	NY	05/05/64	Wilderness, VA	DOW	(MIA, wounded)	ROH,SA1,ANY,CD
Taylor, G.A.	Cpt. AQM	22nd SCVI			05/30/63	West Point, GA	DOD		JR,R48
Taylor, G.B.	Pvt.	A 3rd SCVIBn		LS	/ /	Charlottesville		Univ. Cem. Charlottesville	ACH,KEB
Taylor, George	Pvt.	H 14th SCVI		BL	06/10/62	Richmond, VA	DOD	Hollywood Cem.Rchmd. P173	ROH,JR,HC,UD3
Taylor, H. Clarence	Pvt.	A Ham.Leg.		CN	05/31/62	7 Pines, VA	KIA		ROH,JR,CDC,WLI
Taylor, H.J.	Pvt.	K 10th SCVI		CN	/ /		DOD		RAS

T

SOUTH CAROLINA DEAD IN CSA SERVICE 1861-1865

NAME	RANK	C REGIMENT	AGE DS	DIED	WHERE	WHY	BURIED	SOURCES
Taylor, H.P.	Pvt.	E 3rd SCV		10/11/63	Inst H. Atlanta		Oakland C. Atlanta R38#10	BGA
Taylor, Henry		CS Navy		11/18/64	Richmond, VA			ROH
Taylor, J.	Pvt.	D 16th SCVI	GE	/ /		DOD		16R
Taylor, J.	Pvt.	K 10th SCVI	CN	/ /		DOD		RAS
Taylor, J. Jacob	Pvt.	K 13th SCVI	LN	06/17/62	Richmond, VA	DOD		ROH
Taylor, J.A.	Pvt.	G 2nd SCRes	AN	01/29/65	Columbia, SC	DOD	Elmwood Cem. Columbia, SC	ROH
Taylor, J.C.	Pvt.	E 1st SCVIG	MN	05/05/64	Wilderness, VA	KIA		ROH,SA1,PDL,CDC
Taylor, J.C.	Pvt.	I 2nd SCVC	ED	07/16/64	Charleston, SC	DOW	Magnolia Cem. Charleston	ROH,MAG,RCD
Taylor, J.H.	Pvt.	H 12th SCVI	19 YK	07/01/63	Gettysburg, PA	KIA		GDR,CWC,YEB
Taylor, J.H.	Pvt.	H 1st SCVIH		11/13/63	Dalton, GA	DOD		PP,SA1
Taylor, J.W.	Pvt.	F 27th SCVI		06/06/64	Bermuda Hundred	KIA		ROH,CDC,HAG
Taylor, Jacob Riley	Pvt.	K 13th SCVI	LN	06/09/62	Richmond, VA	DOD (Typhoid)		ROH,JR
Taylor, James	Pvt.	H 1st SCVIH	SG	01/15/64	South Carolina	DOD (On recruiting detail)		ROH,SA1,HOS
Taylor, James	Pvt.	G 24th SCVI	30	11/30/64	Franklin, TN	KIA	Williamson Cty., TN C.C.	ROH,WCT,PP
Taylor, James	Pvt.	I 12th SCVI	LR	05/06/64	Wilderness, VA	KIA		LAN
Taylor, James	Pvt.	H 2nd SCVIRi	25 PS	09/11/63	Petersburg, VA		(Taylor EXC in UD2 DES?)	PP
Taylor, James H.	Pvt.	I 2nd SCVC	ED	07/07/64	Johns Island, SC	KIA		ROH,HOE,CDC
Taylor, James Hunt	4th Sgt.	C 1st SCVIG	RD	06/27/62	Gaines' Mill, VA	KIA (Color Bearer)	UD4	ROH,JR,UD2,SA1
Taylor, James Jacob	Pvt.	K 13th SCVI	LN	06/15/62	Richmond, VA	DOD	Hollywood Cem.Rchmd. O138	JR,HC
Taylor, James Julius	Pvt.	K 13th SCVI	LN	11/29/62	Orange C.H., VA	DOD		ROH,JR
Taylor, James S.	4th Cpl.	G 23rd SCVI	MO	09/28/62	Warrenton, VA	DOW (Wdd 2nd Man)		ROH,HOM,CDC
Taylor, James W.	Pvt.	K 20th SCVI	LN	07/25/63		DOD		ROH,KEB
Taylor, John	Pvt.	E 22nd SCVI	LR	12/11/62	Kinston, NC	KIA		ROH,CDC
Taylor, John	Pvt.	A 3rd SCVIBn	LS	/ /	Richmond, VA		Oakwood C.#148,Row L,Div A	ROH,OWC,KEB
Taylor, John	Pvt.	G 1st SCVIR	AE	11/29/61	Charleston, SC	DOD	Magnolia Cem. Charleston	ROH,MAG
Taylor, John D.S.	Pvt.	A 3rd SCVIBn	LS	02/26/62	Adams Run, SC	DOD		PP,KEB
Taylor, John M.	Pvt.	H 23rd SCVI	MN	11/27/64	Petersburg, VA	DOW	Blandford Church Pbg., VA	ROH,HMC,BLC
Taylor, Jolley	Pvt.	K 13th SCVI	LN	07/10/62	Richmond, VA		Hollywood Cem.Rchmd. M183	ROH,JR,HC
Taylor, Joseph	Pvt.	E 1st SCVIG	MN	08/29/62	2nd Manassas, VA	KIA		HMC
Taylor, M.	Pvt.	M 20th SCVI	LN	03/16/65	Richmond, VA			ROH
Taylor, M.C.	Pvt.	E 2nd SCVA		11/25/64	James Island, SC	DOD		ROH
Taylor, M.S.				/ /		(Rchmnd effects list 1/63)		CDC
Taylor, Marion	Pvt.	H 14th SCVI	BL	09/15/62	Harpers Ferry VA	KIA (CDC=Shpsbg,JR=Ox Hill)		ROH,JR,CDC,UD2
Taylor, Michael	Pvt.	I 14th SCVI	25 AE	01/13/63	Fredericksburg	DOD		ROH,HOL
Taylor, Middleton E.	Pvt.	F 25th SCVI	22 OG	03/15/65	Richmond, VA	DOD (Returning from prison)		ROH,HAG,P65
Taylor, Noah Aquilla	Pvt.	E 1st SCVIG	MN	08/29/62	2nd Manassas, VA	DOW (JR=8/30)		ROH,JR,SA1,CDC
Taylor, P.	Pvt.	E 1st SCVIH	BL	01/17/63		DOW (Wdd @ Sharpsburg)		ROH,JR,SA1,JRH
Taylor, P.C.	Pvt.	Rhett's LA		/ /	Lynchburg, VA		Lynchburg CSA Cem.#6 R5	BBW
Taylor, Reuben	Pvt.	C 15th SCVI	19 LN	11/10/62	Front Royal, VA	DOW	TOD	ROH,JR,KEB,H15
Taylor, Riley	Pvt.	F 13th SCVI	SG	06/10/62	Richmond, VA		Hollywood Cem.Rchmd. P172	ROH,HC
Taylor, Robert	Pvt.	M P.S.S.		/ /		DOW		JR
Taylor, Robert B.	Pvt.	PeeDee LA	DN	/ /				ROH,PDL
Taylor, Robert W.	Pvt.	F 10th SCVI	MN	06/26/62	Macon, GA	DOD (Typhoid)		JR,RAS,HMC,PP
Taylor, Samuel	Pvt.	2nd SCVIRi	AN	/ /	At home	DOD (1864)		ROH
Taylor, Samuel J.	Pvt.	L P.S.S.		05/08/64		DOD		ROH
Taylor, Solomon H.	Pvt.	A 5th SCVI	LR	12/18/62	Fredericksburg	DOW (JR=DOD 10/18/62)		JR,SA3,LAN
Taylor, Thomas	Pvt.	K 13th SCVI	LN	07/08/62	Richmond, VA	DOD	Hollywood Cem.Rchmd. O37	ROH,JR,HC
Taylor, Toliver L.	Pvt.	F 24th SCVI	AN	11/30/64	Franklin, TN	KIA	Williamson Cty., TN C.C.	ROH,WCT,CDC
Taylor, W.	Pvt.	H 1st SCVIH	SG	07/08/64	Petersburg, VA	ACD (discharge of his own gun)		ROH,SA1,HOS
Taylor, W.E.	Pvt.	G 2nd SCRes		01/03/65	Columbia, SC			PP
Taylor, W.J.	1st Lt.	K 26th SCVI	30 GN	07/29/64	Petersburg, VA	KIA		ROH,R48

SOUTH CAROLINA DEAD IN CSA SERVICE 1861-1865

NAME	RANK	C REGIMENT	AGE	DS	DIED	WHERE	WHY	BURIED	SOURCES
Taylor, W.J.	Pvt.	I 3rd SCVI		LS	09/28/64	At home	DOD		SA2,KEB
Taylor, W.M.	Pvt.	I 12th SCVI		LR	09/17/62	Sharpsburg, MD	KIA		LAN
Taylor, W.P.	Pvt.	I Ham.Leg.			04/07/65	USGH Farmville	DOW	Farmville Hospital Cem.	P6
Taylor, William	Pvt.	H 7th SCVIBn	32	RD	05/16/64	Drury's Bluff VA	KIA		ROH,HAG
Taylor, William	Pvt.	K 13th SCVI		LN	05/22/64	Charlottesville	DOW	Univ. Cem. Charlottesville	ROH,ACH
Taylor, William C.	Pvt.	K 20th SCVI		LN	06/03/64	Virginia	KIA		ROH,KEB
Taylor, William H.	2nd Lt.	C 7th SCVIBn		AE	/ /	Columbia, SC		Elmwood Cem. Columbia, SC	MP,PP
Taylor, William Hayne	1st Lt.Adj	Ham.Leg.		RD	04/18/62	Petersburg, VA	DOD	Taylor Family Cem.Columbia	ROH,MP,PP
Taylor, William J.	Cpt.	K 26th SCVI		WG	07/29/64	Petersburg, VA	KIA		HOW,R48
Taylor, William L.	Pvt.	G 2nd SCVI		KW	09/22/62	Richmond, VA	DOD	(Bilious fever)	ROH,SA2,HIC,H2
Taylor, William M.	Pvt.	E 18th SCVI		SG	/ /	Charleston, SC	DOD		HOS
Taylor, William W.	Pvt.	G 25th SCVI		OG	09/11/64	Alexandria G.H.	DOW	Christ Church Alexandria	ROH,P1,CV,HAG
Teague, Henry	Pvt.	I 5th SCVI		SG	06/09/62	Fts. Monroe, vA	DOW	Williamsburg N.C.	ROH,JR,SA3,HOS
Teague, J.W. (Isaac?)	Pvt.	A 20th SCVI		PS	07/31/62	Charleston, SC		Magnolia Cem. Charleston	ROH,MAG,RCD,KE
Teague, R. Ewell	2nd Sgt.	H 1st SCVIH		SG	08/30/62	2nd Manassas, VA	KIA		ROH,JR,SA1,HOS
Teague, Washington	Pvt.	I 17th SCVI		LR	09/12/62	Richmond, VA			ROH
Teague, William C.	Pvt.	E 6th SCVC		LS	02/01/65	Elmira, NY	DIP	Woodlawn N.C.#1769 Elmira	FPH,P5,P65,P12
Teal, George Washington	Pvt.	D 21st SCVI		DN	04/07/65	Elmira, NY	DIP	Woodlawn N.C.#2646 Elmira	ROH,FPH,HAG,P6
Teal, J.T. (T.J.?)	Pvt.	B 8th SCVI		CD	08/15/61	Charlottesville		Univ. Cem. Charlottesville	JR,ACH
Teal, John	Pvt.	D 21st SCVI		DN	05/07/64	Pt.Walthal Jctn.	KIA		ROH,CDC
Teal, William	Pvt.	A 23rd SCVI		CD	08/10/64	Petersburg, VA	DOW	(Wdd 6/18/64)	ROH
Teal, William	Pvt.	23rd SCVI	38	CD	07/19/64	Petersburg, VA	KIA		ROH
Teal, William	Pvt.	23rd SCVI			09/15/63		DOW	(Wdd 8/22/63)	ROH
Teal, William J.	Pvt.	E 21st SCVI	18	CD	07/10/64	At home	DOW		ROH,HAG
Team, John W.	Pvt.	E 2nd SCVI	18	KW	09/01/61	Lynchburg, VA	DOD	(Body sent home)	ROH,JR,CDN,KEB
Teat, Aaron H.	Pvt.	L 2nd SCVIRi	25	AN	07/06/62	Richmond, VA	DOW	(JR=7/15)	ROH,JR
Teat, John C.	Pvt.	L 2nd SCVIRi	34	AN	06/15/62	Manchester, VA	DOD	(Measles)	ROH,JR
Teate, J.R.	Pvt.	F 2nd SCVIRi			08/23/62	Richmond, VA			ROH
Teate, Jasper R.	Pvt.	K 2nd SCVIRi		AN	/ /			(DUP of J.R.?)	ROH
Teddards, David F.	Pvt.	F 2nd SCVI		AE	/ /	Manchester, VA	DOD	(1862)	SA2,KEB,H2
Tedder, Benjamin H.	Pvt.	G 9th SCVIB		DN	10/20/61	Charlottesville	DOD	Univ. Cem. Charlottesville	ROH,JR,JLC,ACH
Tedder, James J.	Pvt.	I 18th SCVI	25	DN	12/15/64	At home	DOD		ROH
Tedder, Stephen	Pvt.	G 3rd SCVC		CN	05/18/65	Hart's Island NY	DIP	Cypress Hills N.C. #2760	FPH,P6,P79
Teetz, Martin	Pvt.	I 25th SCVI		CL	05/17/64	Richmond, VA	DOW	(Wdd @ Drury's Bluff 5/16)	ROH,HAG,CDC
Televast, J.	Pvt.	K 6th SCVI		SR	/ /	Charlottesville		Univ. Cem. Charlottesville	ACH
Telford, James	Pvt.	G 2nd SCVIRi	19	AN	06/30/62	Frayser's Farm	KIA	(? Savage Stn.)	ROH,JR,CDC
Telford, John Calvin	Pvt.	K Orr's Ri.	17	AN	06/27/62	Gaines' Mill, VA	KIA	(JR=6/29)	ROH,JR,CDC
Telford, William J.	Sgt.	C 7th SCVIBn	35	RD	06/22/64	Petersburg, VA	DOW	Blandford Church Pbg., VA	ROH,BLC,PP
Tellers, W.L.	Pvt.	13th SCVI		LN	/ /	Richmond, VA		Oakwood C.#134,Row H,Div C	ROH,OWC
Templeton, G.M.	Pvt.	F 14th SCVI		LS	/ /	Lynchburg, VA		Lynchburg CSA Cem.#7 R1	BBW
Templeton, H.B.	Pvt.	B 14th SCMil			06/01/65	Hart's Island NY	DIP	Cypress Hills N.C.#2929 NY	FPH,P6,P79
Templeton, Ira Griffin	Pvt.	A 15th SCVI	18	RD	09/14/62	South Mtn., MD	DOW	(In enemy hands)	ROH,JR,KEB,CDC
Templeton, J.D.	Pvt.	I 3rd SCVI		LS	05/07/64	Wilderness, VA	DOW	(Wdd 5/6/64)	ROH,SA2,KEB
Templeton, James L.	Pvt.	A 3rd SCVI	26	LS	05/30/63	Charlottesville	DOW	(Wdd @ Fbg)	ROH,JR,SA2,KEB
Templeton, R.M.	Pvt.	C 3rd SCVI		LS	04/05/62	Williamsburg, VA	DOD		JR,SA2
Templeton, Waddy	Pvt.	G 3rd SCVI		LS	06/29/62	Savage Stn., VA	KIA		JR
Templeton, William A.	Pvt.	C 3rd SCVI	21	NY	07/06/62	Petersburg, VA	DOD	Blandford Church Pbg., VA	ROH,JR,SA2,BLC
Tenant, W.F.	Pvt.	A 13th SCVI		LS	07/09/62	Richmond, VA			ROH
Tending, J.W.	Pvt.	H 7th SCVI		PS	09/29/62	Richmond, VA		Hollywood Cem.Rchmd. S182	ROH,HC
Tennant, J.S.	Pvt.	Ham.Leg.		GE	06/17/64	Richmond, VA		Hollywood Cem.Rchmd. U141	ROH,HC
Tennel, G.A.	Pvt.	Ham.Leg.			/ /	Richmond, VA		Oakwood C.#93,Row A,Div B	ROH,OWC

SOUTH CAROLINA DEAD IN CSA SERVICE 1861-1865

NAME	RANK	C	REGIMENT	AGE	DS	DIED	WHERE	WHY	BURIED	SOURCES
Tennent, Edward S.	Pvt.	D	27th SCVI		CN	08/15/62	Secessionville	DOW		ROH
Tennent, Gilbert V.	Pvt.	A	27th SCVI	18	CN	/ /	Charleston, SC	DOD	Circular Church Charleston	ROH,MAG,HAG
Tennent, William M.	Pvt.	G	22nd SCVI	32	PS	/ /	Pt. Lookout, MD	DIP		ROH
Terrell, James B.	Pvt.	B	5th SCVI		LR	11/26/63	Bridgeport, AL	DOW	(POW @ Shell Mound, TN)	P2,P6,SA3
Terrell, Solomon	Pvt.				PS	/ /		KIA	(perhaps in Orr's Ri.)	UD3
Terrell, William T.	Pvt.	F	21st SCVI		MO	05/07/64	Pt.Walthal Jctn.	KIA	Blandford Church Pbg., VA	ROH,HOM,BLC,PP
Terrett, A.H.	Pvt.		SCVA			04/12/62	Richmond, VA		Hollywood Cem.Rchmd. B24	ROH,HC
Terry, Champ P.	Pvt.	D	21st SCVI	48	CD	04/23/62	At home	DOD		ROH,HAG,PP
Terry, Charles W.	Pvt.	E	Ham.Leg.	22	GE	07/13/64	Riddle's Shop VA	KIA	Pisgah U.M.C. Fork Shoals	ROH,GEC,GEE
Terry, Cyrus C.	4th Sgt.	K	2nd SCVIRi	33	PS	09/30/64	Ft. Harrison, VA	KIA		ROH
Terry, H.	Pvt.	E	Orr's Ri.		PS	06/27/64	Richmond, VA		Hollywood Cem.Rchmd. W268	HC
Terry, J.P.	Pvt.	A	22nd SCVI			11/10/64	Richmond, VA		Hollywood Cem.Rchmd. W248	ROH,HC
Terry, James A.	Pvt.	E	Ham.Leg.		GE	05/30/62	7 Pines, VA	KIA	Pisgah U.M.C. Fork Shoals	GEC,GEE
Terry, James E.	Pvt.	D	1st SCVIR		CD	06/14/62	SC	DOD		SA1
Terry, James W.	Pvt.		7th SCVIBn			07/13/62	Charleston, SC		Magnolia Cem. Charleston	RCD
Terry, John M.	Pvt.	E	18th SCVI	18	SG	04/03/65			Mosteller Fam. C. Greer SC	HOS,GEE
Terry, W. James	Pvt.	F	9th SCVIB	24	SR	01/11/62	Charlottesville	DOD	Univ. Cem. Charlottesville	ROH,JR,ACH
Terry, W.J.	Pvt.	B	8th SCVI		CD	11/15/61	Charlottesville	DOD	(Typhoid)	JR
Terry, W.S.	Pvt.		16th SCVI		GE	/ /	GA	KIA	(7/?/64)	ROH
Terry, William M. (H.?)	Sgt.	F	11th SCVI	25	BT	10/04/64	Gillisonville SC	DOW	(Wdd @ Swift Creek 5/9)	ROH,HAG
Terry, William S.	Pvt.	C	19th SCVI	35	ED	10/07/63	At home	DOW	(Wdd @ Chickamauga)	ROH,HOE,UD3
Terry, William T.	Pvt.	B	24th SCVI		MO	01/09/65	Camp Chase, OH	DIP	C.C.#730 Columbus, OH	FPH,P5,P22
Tew, Thomas Russell	Pvt.		Hart's Bty		CN	/ /		KIA	(1865)	ROH
Thackston, W.P.	Cpl.	F	Ham.Leg.		GE	07/27/64	Virginia	KIA		ROH
Thackston, Z.A.	Pvt.	I	3rd SCVI		LS	07/21/64	Charlottesville	DOW	Univ. Cem. Charlottesville	SA2,ACH,KEB
Thamell, C.	Pvt.	I	8th SCVI		MN	/ /	Richmond, VA		Oakwood C.#32,Row D,Div G	ROH,OWC
Thames, J.P.	Pvt.	E	P.S.S.		CL	06/03/64	Cold Harbor, VA	KIA		ROH
Thames, R.J.	Pvt.	D	4th SCVC		SR	07/15/64	Charlottesville	DOD		ROH
Thames, W.S.	Pvt.	E	P.S.S.		CL	07/15/62	Frayser's Farm	DOW		ROH
Thanell, Henry	Pvt.	B	8th SCVI	18	CD	08/30/64	Petersburg, VA	KIA	(Threatt?)	ROH
Thanell, Lewis	Pvt.	D	8th SCVI	16	CD	05/12/64	Spotsylvania, VA	KIA	Spotsylvania C.H., VA	ROH,SCH
Tharen, Edward B.	Pvt.	B	25th SCVI	20	CN	05/07/64	Pt.Walthal Jctn.	KIA	Blandford Church Pbg., VA	ROH,BLC,HAG,PP
Tharp, Wingate	Pvt.	M	10th SCVI	20	HY	06/15/62	Georgetown, SC	DOD		ROH,RAS,PP
Thiele, Henry	Pvt.	D	5th SCVI		UN	06/27/62	Gaines' Mill, VA	KIA		JR,SA3
Thigpen, J.	Pvt.	H	26th SCVI		CN	08/15/64	Richmond, VA		Hollywood Cem.Rchmd. V372	ROH,HC
Thigpin, H.J.	Pvt.	I	26th SCVI	18	CL	08/13/64	Richmond, VA	DOW	Hollywood Cem.Rchmd. V288	ROH,HC
Thode, Henning Peter	1st Lt.	K	12th SCVI	48	PS	06/19/63	At home	DOD	St.Johns L.C. Walhalla, SC	ROH,OCS,R47
Thomas, A.	Pvt.	L	10th SCVI		MN	07/22/64	Atlanta, GA	KIA		ROH,CDC
Thomas, Albert	Pvt.	A	6th SCVI	31	CR	05/06/64	Wilderness, VA	KIA		ROH,GLS,HHC,CB
Thomas, B.	Pvt.	F	22nd SCVI		PS	02/04/65	Pt. Lookout, MD	DIP		ROH
Thomas, Charles M.	Pvt.	I	24th SCVI		ED	05/15/64	Calhoun, GA	DOW		EJM
Thomas, D.	Pvt.	H	1st SCVIH		SG	10/28/63	Lookout Valley	DOW	(Left in enemy hands)	ROH,SA1,CDC,JRH
Thomas, David L.	Pvt.		Gregg's A			06/10/65	Pt. Lookout, MD	DIP	C.C. Pt. Lookout, MD	FPH,P6,P115
Thomas, E.	Pvt.	D	10th SCVI		MN	/ /		DOD		RAS,HMC
Thomas, Ediphus	Pvt.	A	1st SCSSBn			08/11/63	Georgetown, SC	DOD		PP
Thomas, Elliot O.	Pvt.	B	13th SCVI		SG	/ /	Columbia, SC			HOS
Thomas, Enoch	Pvt.	H	1st SCVIH		SG	08/04/62	At home	DOD		ROH,SA1,HOS,JRH
Thomas, George W.	Pvt.	A	Hol.Leg.	22	SG	10/27/64	Petersburg, VA	KIA	(Killed leading a charge)	ROH,HOS
Thomas, Griffin	Pvt.	B	1st SCVIG	23	NY	07/27/64	Petersburg, VA	KIA	(Also wdd @ 2nd Man.)	ROH,SA1,ANY
Thomas, H.	Pvt.	H	20th SCVI			06/21/64	Richmond, VA		Hollywood Cem.Rchmd. U459	HC
Thomas, Henry B.	Pvt.	E	5th SCVI		YK	05/06/64	Wilderness, VA	KIA		ROH,SA3,UD3

SOUTH CAROLINA DEAD IN CSA SERVICE 1861-1865

NAME	RANK	C	REGIMENT	AGE	DS	DIED	WHERE	WHY	BURIED	SOURCES
Thomas, Isaiah T.	Pvt.	A	6th SCVI	30	CR	01/15/64	At home	DOD		ROH,GLS,HHC,CB
Thomas, J.	Pvt.	C	7th SCVI			/ /	Richmond, VA		Oakwood C.#11,Row T,Div F	ROH,OWC
Thomas, J.G.	Pvt.	B	Orr's Ri.		AE	07/02/63		DOD		ROH
Thomas, J.L.	Lt.	D	3rd SCVIBn			05/08/64	Spotsylvania, VA	KIA		ROH
Thomas, J.M.	Pvt.	M	8th SCVI		DN	01/29/65	Camp Chase, OH	DIP	C.C.#960 Columbus, OH	FPH,KEB,P6,P22
Thomas, James	Pvt.					/ /			Fredericksburg C.C. R6S13	FBG
Thomas, James	Pvt.	E	4th SCVC		MO	/ /	Camp Marion, SC	DOD		HOM
Thomas, John	Pvt.	A	7th SCVI			07/19/64	Charleston, SC		Magnolia Cem. Charleston	MAG,RCD
Thomas, John D.	Pvt.	H	Hol.Leg.	30	ED	10/10/62	At home	DOD		ROH
Thomas, John M.	Pvt.	G	15th SCVI	35	WG	09/17/62	Sharpsburg, MD	KIA		ROH,JR,KEB
Thomas, John T.	Pvt.	D	21st SCVI		CD	05/16/64	Drury's Bluff VA	KIA		ROH,HAG
Thomas, John Wesley	Pvt.	C	17th SCVI	35	CR	07/31/64	Crater Pbg., VA	DOW		CB
Thomas, Joseph	Pvt.	F	21st SCVI		MO	07/21/64	Richmond, VA	DOD	Hollywood Cem.Rchmd. U155	ROH,HC,HOM,HAG
Thomas, Joseph	Pvt.	H	Orr's Ri.		MN	06/14/64	Richmond, VA	DOW	Hollywood Cem.Rchmd. U97	ROH,HC,HMC,CDC
Thomas, L.P.	Pvt.	K	3rd SCVI	20	SG	07/02/63	Gettysburg, PA	KIA		ROH,JR,SA2,GDR
Thomas, M.F.	Pvt.	F	20th SCVI		NY	06/22/64	Richmond, VA			ROH
Thomas, Mabry C.G.	Pvt.	D	5th SCVI		UN	11/15/61	Charlottesville	DOD		JR,SA3
Thomas, Marion L.	Pvt.	C	13th SCVI		SG	08/29/62	2nd Manassas, VA	KIA		ROH,JR,HOS,CDC
Thomas, Newton H.	Sgt.		McBeth LA	22	UN	01/29/64	Charleston, SC	DOD	Gilliam Chapel UN Cty.	ROH,UNC
Thomas, Oliver	Pvt.	F	27th SCVI		ED	02/05/65	Pt. Lookout, MD	DIP	C.C. Pt. Lookout, MD	FPH,P5,P113,HA
Thomas, Philip	Pvt.	E	5th SCVC		CN	10/01/64	Elmira, NY	DIP	Woodlawn N.C.#421 Elmira	FPH,P5,P65,P11
Thomas, R.	Pvt.	H	26th SCVI		SR	03/09/65	Richmond, VA		Hollywood Cem.Rchmd. W694	ROH,HC
Thomas, Ransom	Pvt.	K	11th SCVI	34	CO	08/07/64		DIP	(Alive,Elmira 3/2/65)	ROH,HAG,P65,P1
Thomas, Renatus	Cpl.	C	2nd SCVC		RD	08/16/63	At home	DOD		PP
Thomas, Richard W.	Pvt.					/ /			Magnolia Cem. Charleston	MAG,RCD
Thomas, Robert	Pvt.	H	15th SCVI			/ /		DOD	(Thomas, R. in 26th?)	JR
Thomas, Robert E.	Pvt.	M	8th SCVI		DN	07/02/63	Gettysburg, PA	KIA		ROH,JR,GDR,CDC
Thomas, S.	Pvt.	D	10th SCVI		MN	09/20/63	Chickamauga, GA	KIA		RAS,HMC
Thomas, Samuel W.	Pvt.	E	1st SCVIG		MN	07/03/63	Gettysburg, PA	KIA		SA1,GDR,HMC
Thomas, Simpson	Cpl.	A	Hol.Leg.		SG	03/29/65	Hatcher's Run VA	KIA		HOS
Thomas, W.	Pvt.	A	1st SCVC		AE	/ /	John's Island SC	KIA	(1862)	ROH
Thomas, W.	Pvt.	F	13th SCVI		SG	03/17/65	Elmira, NY	DIP	Woodlawn N.C.#1717 Elmira	FPH
Thomas, W. Henry	Pvt.	D	10th SCVI		MN	09/06/62	Lauderdale Ss MS	DOD		JR,RAS,HMC,PP
Thomas, W.N.	Pvt.	K	3rd SCVABn			11/07/63	Charleston, SC		Magnolia Cem. Charleston	ROH,MAG,RCD
Thomas, W.S.	Pvt.	E	P.S.S.			/ /		KIA		JR
Thomas, W.T.	Pvt.	E	5th SCVC		CN	05/20/64	Charlottesville	DOW	Univ. Cem. Charlottesville	ROH,ACH
Thomas, Wesley J.	Pvt.	C	17th SCVI		CR	08/15/64	Crater Pbg., VA	DOW		ROH,BLM,HHC,CB
Thomas, William	Cpl.	D	24th SCVI		BT	07/22/64	Atlanta, GA	KIA		ROH,CDC
Thomas, William	Pvt.	F	6th SCVI		CR	12/20/61	Dranesville, VA	KIA	(NI Chester Blues CNM)	HHC
Thomas, William L.	Pvt.	C	22nd SCVI	22	SG	08/10/64	Petersburg, VA	DOW	Blandford Church Pbg., VA	ROH,BLC,PP
Thomas, William L.	Pvt.	B	7th SCVIBn	26	CR	03/10/64	James Island, SC	DOD		ROH,HAG
Thomas, William R.	3rd Lt.	K	3rd SCVI	27	SG	07/04/62	Gettysburg, PA	DOW	Magnolia Cem. Charleston	ROH,JR,GDR,SA2
Thomas, William R.	Pvt.	A	Orr's Ri.		AN	05/06/64	Wilderness, VA	KIA		ROH
Thomason, J.F.	Pvt.	F	Ham.Leg.		GE	12/31/61	Richmond, VA	DOD		R48
Thomason, James B.	Pvt.	F	Ham.Leg.		GE	05/30/65	Pt. Lookout, MD	DIP	C.C. Pt. Lookout, MD	FPH,P6,P115
Thomason, R.E.	2nd Lt.	F	Ham.Leg.	21	GE	07/22/64	Richmond, VA	KIA		ROH,R48
Thomason, W.F.	Pvt.	G	3rd SCVI		GE	06/15/63	At home	DOD	(KEB=Thompson)	ROH,SA2,KEB
Thomasson, Arnold D.	Pvt.	G	Hol.Leg.		NY	/ /	Lynchburg, VA		Lynchburg CSA Cem.#1 R4	ANY,BBW
Thomasson, J.B.	Pvt.	H	12th SCVI		YK	10/15/62		DOD		CWC
Thomasson, James F.	Pvt.	H	18th SCVI		YK	09/14/62	South Mtn., MD	KIA		ROH
Thomasson, William	Pvt.	G	18th SCVI	37	YK	05/20/64	Clay's Farm, VA	KIA		YEB

T

SOUTH CAROLINA DEAD IN CSA SERVICE 1861-1865

NAME	RANK	C REGIMENT	AGE	DS	DIED	WHERE	WHY	BURIED	SOURCES
Thompson, Andrew	Pvt.	E 15th SCVAB			09/02/62	Charleston, SC		Magnolia Cem. Charleston	ROH,MAG,RCD
Thompson, B.L.	Pvt.	H 2nd SCVC		RD	04/05/65	Charlotte, NC			ROH,PP
Thompson, C.	Pvt.	I 12th SCVI		LR	/ /	Richmond, VA	DOD	(1862)	LAN
Thompson, C.D.	Pvt.	B 26th SCVI	18	CD	08/15/64	Richmond, VA	DOD		ROH
Thompson, Charles	Pvt.	D 12th SCVI		RD	07/16/62	Petersburg, VA	DOD	Blandford Church Pbg., VA	ROH,JR,BLC
Thompson, Charles L.	Pvt.	I 13th SCVI	26	SG	07/16/62	Petersburg, VA	DOD		PP
Thompson, Charles S.	Pvt.	B 20th SCVI	18	CD	08/23/64	Petersburg, VA	DOD	Blandford Church Pbg., VA	ROH,BLC,PP
Thompson, E.P.	Pvt.	G 15th SCVI		WG	07/08/62	Richmond, VA		Hollywood Cem.Rchmd. M296	ROH,HC
Thompson, F.S.	Pvt.	G 1st SCVIH		BL	11/08/62	Warrenton, VA	DOW	(Wdd 8/30/62 2nd Man)	ROH,JR,SA1,JRH
Thompson, H.W.	Pvt.	K 11th SCVI	22	CO	07/01/64	Petersburg, VA	KIA		ROH,HAG
Thompson, Henry	Pvt.	G 23rd SCVI		MO	10/21/64	Elmira, NY	DIP	Woodlawn N.C.#870 Elmira	FPH,P5,P65,P120
Thompson, Henry A.	Pvt.	E 14th SCVI		LS	05/21/64	Spotsylvania, VA	DOW	Hollywood Cem.Rchmd. I71	ROH,HC,CGS
Thompson, Isaac M.	Pvt.	B 5th SCVI	19	YK	06/30/62	Frayser's Farm	KIA	(JR & HHC=Gaines'Mill)	ROH,JR,SA3,HHC
Thompson, J.C.	Pvt.	I 17th SCVI		LR	09/13/64	Elmira, NY	DIP	Woodlawn N.C.#270 Elmira	FPH,P65,P120,LAN
Thompson, J.C.C.	Pvt.	F 1st SCVC		PS	06/29/64	Columbia, SC			PP
Thompson, J.T.	Pvt.	B 21st SCVI		DN	/ /				ROH
Thompson, J.T. (J.J.?)	Pvt.	K 23rd SCVI		SR	09/04/64	Crater, Pbg., VA	DOW	Blandford Church Pbg., VA	ROH,BLM,BLC,PP
Thompson, J.W.	1st Cpl.	G 1st SCVIH		BL	10/08/64	Ft. Harrison, VA	DOW	Hollywood Cem.Rchmd. V450	ROH,HC,SA1
Thompson, J.W.	Pvt.	E Ham.Leg.		GE	12/22/62	Richmond, VA			ROH
Thompson, J.W. (D.W.?)	Pvt.	D 14th SCVI		ED	06/28/62	Richmond, VA		Hollywood Cem.Rchmd. M379	HC
Thompson, James	Pvt.	E 16th SCVI	30	GE	11/30/64	Franklin, TN	KIA		ROH,16R,PP
Thompson, James	Pvt.	D 21st SCVI		CD	11/15/63	Pt. Lookout, MD	DIP		ROH
Thompson, James	Pvt.	H 6th SCVI		FD	09/30/64	Chaffin's Farm	KIA		ROH
Thompson, James	Pvt.	H 16th SCVI		GE	08/15/62	At home	DOD		PP,16R
Thompson, James A.	Pvt.	I 18th SCVI	20	DN	03/15/64	At home	DOD	(Florence, SC)	ROH,PP
Thompson, James A.	Cpl.	C P.S.S.			12/22/63	Lookout Valley	DOW	(Wdd 10/29/63)	ROH
Thompson, James J.	Pvt.	B Hol.Leg.	20	SG	07/01/62	Adams Run, SC	DOD		ROH,HOS,PP
Thompson, John	Pvt.	K 14th SCVI		AE	07/13/62	Richmond, VA			ROH
Thompson, John	Pvt.			SR	04/09/65	Dingle's Mill SC	KIA		HSR
Thompson, John A.	Pvt.	E 7th SCVIBn		KW	10/14/62	Staunton, VA	DOD	Thornrose C. Staunton, VA	HIC,HAG,TOD
Thompson, John H.	3rd Sgt.	G 1st SCVIH		BL	09/25/63	Chattanooga, TN	KIA	(JRH=Thomson)	ROH,JR,SA1,JRH
Thompson, John J.	Pvt.	D 16th SCVI		GE	05/02/64	Rock Island, IL	DIP	C.C.#1109 Rock Island, IL	FPH,P5,P39,16R
Thompson, Joseph A.	Pvt.	E 7th SCVI		ED	10/14/62	Staunton, VA	KIA		ROH,HOE,KEB,UD3
Thompson, Pressley	Pvt.	G Hol.Leg.	30	NY	10/01/62	Richmond, VA	DOD		ROH,SA1
Thompson, S.	2nd Sgt.	E 5th SCVC		GN	10/27/64	Burgess' Mill VA	KIA		ROH,LOR,CDC
Thompson, Samuel D.	Pvt.	D 21st SCVI		CD	11/05/63	Pt. Lookout, MD	DIP	C.C. Pt. Lookout, MD	FPH,P6,P113,HAG
Thompson, Samuel R.	Sgt.	D 1st SCVC	23	CR	09/15/63	Lynchburg, VA	DOD	Lynchburg CSA Cem.#7 R2	ROH,BBW,HHC
Thompson, Thomas J.	Pvt.	C 3rd SCVI	27	NY	05/12/64	Wilderness, VA	DOW		ROH,SA2,ANY,KEB
Thompson, W.H.	Pvt.	G Ham.Leg.		SR	06/01/62	7 Pines, VA	DOW		ROH,CDC
Thompson, W.M.	Pvt.	B 7th SCVC		CN	06/13/64	Riddle's Shop VA	KIA		ROH
Thompson, Waddy	Pvt.	G 3rd SCVI	27	LS	06/29/62	Savage Stn., VA	KIA		ROH,SA2,KEB
Thompson, William	Pvt.	E 16th SCVI	32	GE	09/06/63	Lauderdale, MS	DOD	(16R & PP=Macon, MS)	ROH,16R,PP
Thompson, William A.	Sgt.	C 13th SCVI		SG	10/18/64	Jones' Farm, VA	DOW	Hollywood Cem.Rchmd. V266	ROH,HC,HOS
Thompson, William F.	Pvt.	B 21st SCVI		DN	02/17/65	Elmira, NY	DIP	Woodlawn N.C.#2230 Elmira	FPH,P5,P65,P66
Thompson, William H.	Pvt.	E 3rd SCVI		NY	06/18/62	9 Mile Rd. Rchmd	DOW	(Skirmish near Richmond)	ROH,JR,SA2,ANY
Thompson, William M.	Pvt.	L 10th SCVI		MN	12/31/62	Murfreesboro, TN	KIA		ROH,JR,RAS,HMC
Thompson, William T.	2nd Sgt.	A 7th SCVC		WG	/ /	Ream's Stn., VA	KIA	(May be in E,15th SCVI)	HOW
Thompson, Wm. Lawson	2nd Lt.	B 5th SCVI	26	YK	06/30/62	Frayser's Farm	KIA		ROH,JR,SA3,YEB
Thomson, J.A.	Pvt.	F 1st SCVC		PS	06/29/64	Columbia, SC	DOD		ROH
Thomson, John	Pvt.	20th SCRes		SR	04/10/65	Dingle's Mill SC	KIA		ROH
Thomson, John H.	Cpt.	E 1st SCVIH		BL	08/30/62	2nd Manassas, VA	KIA		ROH,JR,SA1,R45

SOUTH CAROLINA DEAD IN CSA SERVICE 1861-1865

NAME	RANK	C	REGIMENT	AGE	DS	DIED	WHERE	WHY	BURIED	SOURCES
Thorn, J. Christon	Pvt.	I	5th SCVI		SG	05/06/64	Wilderness, VA	KIA		ROH,SA3,HOS
Thorn, J.F.	Pvt.	H	18th SCVI		YK	07/30/64	Crater, Pbg., VA	KIA		ROH,BLM
Thornhill, B.B.	Pvt.	F	27th SCVI		DN	08/21/64	Weldon RR, VA	KIA		ROH,CDC,HAG
Thornton, James McComb	Pvt.	H	19th SCVI	20	AE	11/25/63	Missionary Ridge	KIA		ROH
Thornton, John	Pvt.	C	7th SCVIBn	30	RD	03/24/62	Adams Run, SC	DOD	(PP=3/22/62)	ROH,HAG
Thornton, Thurgood	Pvt.	B	1st SCVIG	30	RD	06/27/62	Gaines' Mill, VA	DOW	(JR=Thompson, T.)	ROH,JR,SA1,ANY
Thornwell, Charles A.	Pvt.	G	8th SCVI	18	MO	07/27/64	Deep Bottom, VA	KIA		ROH,HOM,KEB,UD
Thornwell, Gillespie R.	Pvt.	H	1st SCVC	19	RD	05/04/63	Alexandria, VA	DOW	Elmwood Cem. Columbia, SC	ROH,MP,AOA,PP
Thrailkill, Clifton	Pvt.	A	17th SCVI	20	CR	09/14/62	South Mtn., MD	KIA		ROH,JR,HHC,CB
Threat, John R.	Pvt.	B	9th SCVIBn		CD	07/03/62	Secessionville	DOW	Magnolia Cem. Charleston	ROH,MAG,RCD
Threatt, H.A.	Pvt.	B	26th SCVI	36	CD	/ /	Petersburg, VA	DOD	(6/1/?)	ROH
Threatt, J.W.	Pvt.	D	8th SCVI		CD	12/13/62	Fredericksburg	KIA		JR,KEB
Threatt, Thomas	Pvt.	B	26th SCVI	28	CD	07/14/64	Petersburg, VA	KIA		ROH,CDC
Thrift, Calvin B.	Pvt.	B	3rd SCVI	23	NY	09/20/61	Culpepper, VA	DOD	Fairview Cem. Culpepper VA	ROH,JR,CGH,SA2
Thrift, Jesse	Pvt.	I	5th SCVI		SG	/ /	Virginia	DOD		HOS
Thurman, Joseph C.	Pvt.	A	4th SCVC	23	CD	05/28/64	Hawes Shop, VA	KIA		ROH
Thurmond, Phillip M.	Pvt.	I	24th SCVI		ED	11/30/64	Franklin, TN	KIA	Williamson Cty., TN C.C.	ROH,WCT,CDC,PP
Thurston, J.W.	Pvt.	D	4th SCVC		CN	02/17/65	Elmira, NY	DIP	Woodlawn N.C.#2229 Elmira	FPH,P5,P65,P12
Thurston, James M.	Pvt.	H	1st SCVA		CN	09/16/62	Charleston, SC		Magnolia Cem. Charleston	ROH,MAG,RCD
Tidwell, Clark	Pvt.	E	18th Bn A		LR	05/11/65	Davids Island NY	DIP	Cypress Hills N.C.#2748 NY	FPH,P6,LAN,P79
Tidwell, S.P.	Pvt.	G	24th SCVI	30	FD	09/17/64	Atlanta, GA	DOW	Stonewall Cem. Griffin, GA	EJM,HFC,BGA
Tidwell, Thomas	Pvt.	C	6th SCVI		KW	/ /	Virginia	DOD	(Perhaps in E,9th SCVIB)	HIC
Tidwell, W.L.	Lt.		Marion LA			08/30/62	2nd Manassas, VA	KIA		JR
Tigue, W. (Teague?)	Pvt.	I	14th SCVI		AE	09/14/62	Richmond, VA		Hollywood Cem.Rchmd. A134	HC
Tiler, Benjamin	Pvt.	C	1st SCV	20	BL	04/15/65	Goldsboro, NC	KIA		ROH
Tilgham, J.J.	Cpl.	A	10th SCVI			09/20/63	Chickamauga, GA	KIA		CDC
Till, Henry	Pvt.	E	24th SCVI	20	CO	01/14/64	At home	DOD		ROH
Tilley, G.D.	Pvt.	A	5th SCVC		OG	06/15/65	At home	DOD		ROH
Tilley, William	Pvt.	F	2nd SC Res			01/28/65	Columbia, SC	DOD		ROH,PP
Tillison, John J.	Pvt.	C	Hol.Leg.		SG	06/06/65	Pt. Lookout, MD	DIP	C.C. Pt. Lookout, MD	FPH,P6,P115,HO
Tillman, James	Cpt.	I	24th SCVI		ED	/ /		KIA		UD3
Tillotson, Greenberry W.	Cpl.	I	5th SCVI		SG	10/10/62	Manchester, VA	DOD	(JR=Tillison)	JR,SA3
Tilly, William	Pvt.	D	14th SCMil			04/23/65	Davids Island NY	DOW	Cypress Hills N.C.#2593 NY	FPH,P1,P5,P79
Tillywill, Solomon						/ /			Rose Hill C. Hagerstown MD	WAT,BOD
Tilton, W.J.	Pvt.	C	15th SCVI			/ /	Lynchburg, VA		Lynchburg CSA Cem.#5 R3	BBW
Timberlake, Richard	Pvt.	A	12th SCVI	42	YK	09/20/62	Richmond, VA	DOD	Oakwood C.#58,Row F,Div B	ROH,OWC,YEB
Timmerman, B.M.	Pvt.	K	14th SCVI		ED	01/25/64	Ft. Delaware, DE	DIP	(FPH=Tumbland)	ROH,FPH,HOE
Timmerman, Felix	Pvt.	K	14th SCVI		ED	08/26/62	Richmond, VA	DOD	(ROH= Zimmerman)	ROH,JR,HOE
Timmerman, Felix L.	Pvt.	K	7th SCVI	20	ED	07/14/62	Malvern Hill, VA	DOW	(ROH= Zimmerman)	ROH,JR,EDN,CNM
Timmerman, Francis H.	Pvt.	K	15th SCVI		ED	07/23/64	Petersburg, VA	KIA	(ROH= Zimmerman)	ROH,KEB,HOE
Timmerman, Frank A.	Pvt.	K	24th SCVI		ED	01/30/64	Camp Douglas, IL	DIP	Oak Woods Cem. Chicago, IL	ROH,FPH,P5,HOE
Timmerman, George H.	Pvt.	K	7th SCVI		ED	07/14/62	Malvern Hill, VA	KIA	(HOE=11/08/63)	ROH,HOE,KEB
Timmerman, George H.	Pvt.	K	24th SCVI		ED	09/01/64	Jonesborough, GA	KIA		HOE
Timmerman, Henry	Pvt.	K	24th SCVI		ED	09/20/63	Chickamauga, GA	KIA		HOE,BIG
Timmerman, J. Talbert	Pvt.	C	19th SCVI		ED	06/15/63	Enterprise, MS	DOD	(UD3=W. Talbert)	HOE,EDN,PP,UD3
Timmerman, J.L.	Pvt.	K	14th SCVI		ED	07/15/62	Richmond, VA	DOW	Oakwood C. #42 Row R Div C	ROH,HOE,OWC
Timmerman, J.T.	Pvt.	K	14th SCVI		ED	09/19/63	Ft. Delaware, DE	DIP	Finn's Pt., NJ Nat. Cem.	ROH,FPH,P40,CV
Timmerman, Jacob B.	Pvt.	G	1st SCVIG		ED	/ /		DIP	(1865 per HOE)	HOE
Timmerman, John B.	1st Sgt.	K	19th SCVI	32	ED	04/24/62	Enterprise, MS	ACD	(M & O RR wreck) PP	ROH,JR,HOE,EDN
Timmerman, N.D.	Pvt.	I	2nd SCVC		ED	12/29/64	Wilmington, NC	KIA		ROH,HOE
Timmerman, R.W.	Pvt.	K	14th SCVI		ED	12/08/62	Winchester, VA	DOD	Stonewall C. Winchester VA	ROH,HOE,WIN

T

SOUTH CAROLINA DEAD IN CSA SERVICE 1861-1865

NAME	RANK	C REGIMENT	AGE	DS	DIED	WHERE	WHY	BURIED	SOURCES
Timmons, John	Pvt.	I 18th SCVI	44	DN	07/30/64	Crater, Pbg., VA	KIA		ROH
Timmons, John M.	Pvt.	I 18th SCVI		DN	12/16/64	Elmira, NY	DIP	Woodlawn N.C.#1270 Elmira	FPH,P65,P66
Timmons, Luther R.	Pvt.	C 26th SCVI		MN	01/29/63	McClellanville	DOD		ROH,HMC
Timmons, Robert E.	Pvt.	C 3rd SCVABn		MN	05/30/63	Meridian, MS	DOD	(Wilson Lt. Artillery)	ROH,PP
Timmons, William H.	Pvt.	E 8th SCVI	32	DN	09/07/62	Petersburg, VA	DOD		ROH,JR,KEB,PP
Timmons, William J.	Pvt.	I 25th SCVI		CL	11/19/63	Pt. Lookout, MD	DIP	C.C. Pt. Lookout, MD	ROH,FPH,P5,HAG
Timms, David	Pvt.	G 6th SCVI		CR	06/30/62	Frayser's Farm	KIA		ROH,WDB
Timms, J.M.	Pvt.	D 27th SCVI	37	CR	08/15/63	Bty. Wagner, SC	KIA		ROH
Timms, J.T.	Pvt.	B 7th SCVI		AE	08/30/62	2nd Manassas, VA	KIA	(JR=J.J.)	JR,KEB
Timons, Abraham	Pvt.	G 4th SCVI		GE	06/17/62	Richmond, VA	DOD		ROH,SA2
Tims, H.M.	Pvt.	D 18th SCVI		AN	02/28/64	Richmond, VA			ROH
Tims, Jesse Simpson	Cpl.	F 23rd SCVI	19	CR	07/12/63	Jackson, MS	KIA	(UD3=Trim)	ROH,HHC,PP,UD3
Tindal, James	Pvt.	A 26th SCVI	19	HY	08/19/64	Richmond, VA	DOW	(Wdd @ Pbg)	ROH
Tindal, Solomon	Pvt.	I 21st SCVI		MN	02/13/63	At home	DOD	(JR=2/17/62)	JR,HMC,HAG
Tindall, Henry F.	Pvt.	I 5th SCVC	27	BL	05/02/65	Hart's Island NY	DIP	Cypress Hills N.C.#2679 NY	ROH,FPH,P5,P79
Tindall, James	Pvt.	D 24th SCVI	16	BT	08/30/63	Mississippi	DOD		ROH
Tindall, James S.	1st Lt.	A 14th SCVCB			02/23/62		DOD		R43
Tindall, John W.	Pvt.	C 20th SCVI	42	OG	07/11/64	Petersburg, VA	DOW		ROW
Tindall, Nathaniel T.	Pvt.	F 1st SCVIG		HY	07/07/62	Gaines' Mill, VA	DOW	Oakwood C.#11,Row L,Div L	ROH,JR,SA1,OWC
Tindall, Zachariah A.	Pvt.	Hart's Bty	39	BL	05/19/62	Richmond, VA			ROH
Tines,	1st Sgt.	A 15th SCVAB			/ /	Bty Wagner, SC	DOW	(See page 187 HAG)	HAG
Tinkler, George S.	Pvt.	G 3rd SCVIBn		FD	04/27/63	At home	DOD	(Consumption)	JR,KEB
Tinkler, R.H.	Pvt.	G 6th SCVI		FD	06/26/64	Richmond, VA		Hollywood Cem.Rchmd. U538	ROH,HC,WDB
Tinsley, A.R.	Pvt.	D 3rd SCVI		SG	07/11/62	Savage Stn., VA	DOW		JR,SA2,KEB,HOS
Tinsley, Brackin A.	2nd Cpl.	G 16th SCVI		GE	02/06/65	Nashville, TN	DOW		16R,P3,P5
Tinsley, J.P.	5th Sgt.	D 3rd SCVI		SG	08/03/63	At home	DOD	(Sent home 4/6/63)	JR,,KEB,HOS
Tinsley, J.T.	Pvt.	F 1st SCV			02/02/63	Richmond, VA			ROH
Tinsley, James	Pvt.	I 1st SCVIR		SG	08/02/62	Adams Run, SC	SUI		SA1
Tinsley, Jesse G.	Pvt.	D P.S.S.		SG	06/15/62	7 Pines, VA	DOW	(Wdd 5/31/62)	ROH,JR,HOS,SA1
Tinsley, John	Pvt.	G 16th SCVI		GE	01/15/64	Covington, GA	DOD	Con. Cem. Newton, GA	16R,BGA
Tinsley, Ransom	Pvt.	E 1st SCVIR		SG	09/08/63	Ft. Moultrie, SC	KIA	(Ammo chest explosion)	ROH,SA1,CDC
Tinsley, Thomas	Pvt.	F 13th SCVI		SG	07/24/62	Laurel Hill, VA	DOD	(Typhoid)	JR,HOS
Tinsley, Thomas J.	Pvt.	D P.S.S.		SG	06/30/62	Frayser's Farm	KIA		ROH,JR,HOS
Tinsley, William W.	Pvt.	C 13th SCVI		SG	07/29/62	Laurel Hill, VA	DOD	(Typhoid)	JR,HOS
Tinson, C.F.	Pvt.	A 3rd SCVIBn			05/13/65	Pt. Lookout, MD	DIP		ROH
Tippins, Simpson	Pvt.	K 17th SCVI	29	YK	/ /	Petersburg, VA	KIA		YEB
Tippins, T.S.	Pvt.	F 17th SCVI		YK	05/09/65	Elmira, NY	DIP	Woodlawn N.C.#2779 Elmira	FPH,P65,P113
Titson, J.D.	Pvt.	I 15th SCVI		LN	10/11/62			Stonewall C. Winchester VA	WIN
Tobias, John B.	Pvt.	K 6th SCVI	28	CL	05/05/62	Williamsburg, VA	KIA		ROH,3RC,WDB
Tobias, John S. (H.?)	Pvt.	I 25th SCVI		CL	02/23/65	Elmira, NY	DIP	Woodlawn N.C.#2244 Elmira	FPH,P5,P65,HAG
Tobias, Thomas N.	Pvt.	I 25th SCVI	27	CL	05/16/64	Petersburg, VA			PP,HAG
Tobin, C.F.	Pvt.	C 8th Bn Res			10/08/64	Charleston, SC	DOD	Magnolia Cem. Charleston	ROH,MAG,RCD
Tobin, William	Pvt.	K 1st SCVIG		CN	07/15/62	Gaines' Mill, VA	DOW	(Date approx)	JR,SA1
Todd, Addison C.	Pvt.	Ward's LA	28	HY	03/05/65	Georgetown, SC	DOD	(Spinal Menengitis)	PP,TOD
Todd, Andrew W.	Pvt.	F 14th SCVI		LS	08/15/62	Richmond, VA	DOD	Oakwood C.#24,Row K,Div C	ROH,JR,OWC,TOD
Todd, D.W.	Pvt.	G 10th SCVI	35	HY	07/10/62	Columbus, MS	DOD	Friendship C, Columbus, MS	RAS,TOD
Todd, David H.	Pvt.	E Orr's Ri.	21	PS	06/27/62	At home	DOW	(Wdd 6/22/62)	ROH,CDC,TOD
Todd, Dennis	Pvt.	G 10th SCVI		HY	/ /	At home	MUR	Cherry Hill C. Horry Cty.	RAS,TOD
Todd, G.W.	Pvt.	B 4th SCVI			08/08/61	Culpepper, VA	DOD	(JR=DOW)	CDC
Todd, H.J.	Pvt.	G 10th SCVI	32	HY	/ /		DOD	(Age 30 in 1860 Census)	RAS,CEN
Todd, Heyward P.	Pvt.	E 12th SCVI	29	LR	01/08/64	Richmond, VA	DOD	(age 35 ?)	ROH,LAN

SOUTH CAROLINA DEAD IN CSA SERVICE 1861-1865

NAME	RANK	C REGIMENT	AGE	DS	DIED	WHERE	WHY	BURIED	SOURCES
Todd, Isaac Harrison	Pvt.	F 1st SCVIG		HY	07/04/62	Richmond, VA	DOD	(JR=7/7/62)	JR,SA1,TOD
Todd, J.	Pvt.	H 1st SC Res		AN	03/15/65	Columbia, SC	DOD		ROH,PP
Todd, Jackson J.	Pvt.	A 26th SCVI		HY	03/08/65	Richmond, VA	DOD	Hollywood Cem.Rchmd. W292	HC,TOD
Todd, James	Pvt.	H 27th SCVI		CN	06/17/64	Petersburg, VA	DOW	Blandford Church Pbg., VA	ROH,BLC,TOD,PP
Todd, James E.	Pvt.	C Orr's Ri.	35	PS	08/27/62	Lynchburg, VA	DOD	Lynchburg CSA Cem.#5 R4	ROH,JR,BBW,TOD
Todd, James F. (C.?)	Pvt.	C Orr's Ri.		PS	06/15/62	Richmond, VA		Oakwood C.#68,Row M,Div C	ROH,OWC
Todd, James Melvin	Pvt.	G 10th SCVI		HY	05/21/63	Chattanooga, TN	DOD	City C. Chattanooga, TN	RAS,TOD
Todd, James T.	Pvt.	C P.S.S.	25	AN	06/07/62	7 Pines, VA	DOW	(Wdd 5/31/62)	SA2,ROH,JR,GMJ,TOD
Todd, John H.	Pvt.	G 10th SCVI	33	HY	08/24/63	Shelbyville, TN	DOD	Willowmount C. Shelbyville	RAS,PP,TOD
Todd, John N.	Sgt.	E Orr's Ri.	29	PS	05/06/64	Wilderness, VA	DOW		CDC,TOD
Todd, John T.	Pvt.	F 1st SCVIG	19	HY	05/16/63	Richmond, VA	DOW	Oakwood C.#28,Row 32,Div D	ROH,SA1,PDL,TO
Todd, Joseph D.	Pvt.	C 10th SCVI		HY	08/18/62	Brandon, MS	DOD		RAS,PP
Todd, Joseph Thomas	Pvt.	F 14th SCVI	19	LS	02/01/65	Pt. Lookout, MD	DIP	C.C. Pt. Lookout, MD	FPH,P5,P115,TO
Todd, Lemuel M.	Pvt.	G 10th SCVI	27	HY	06/10/63	Chattanooga, TN	DOD	City C. Chattanooga, TN	RAS,TOD
Todd, Nathan C.	Pvt.	F 20th SCVI		LS	06/02/63	Charleston, SC	DOW	Magnolia Cem. Charleston	ROH,MAG,RCD,TO
Todd, Robert F.	Cpl.	I P.S.S.		PS	08/07/62	At home	DOW	(Wdd @ Frayser's Farm)	ROH,JR,TOD
Todd, S.D.	Pvt.	M P.S.S.	18	PS	01/28/64	Lynchburg, VA	DOD	Lynchburg CSA Cem.#6 R2	ROH,BBW,TOD
Todd, S.D.	Pvt.	G 10th SCVI		HY	/ /		DOD		RAS
Todd, S.J.	Pvt.	G 10th SCVI	18	HY	09/15/62	Kentucky	DOD	(Fell out on march)	RAS,TOD
Todd, T.H.					/ /			(Rchmnd effects list 1/63)	CDC
Todd, Thaddeus Sabiski	Pvt.	F 1st SCVIG	22	HY	07/11/62	Gaines' Mill, VA	DOW	(TOD=Oakwood C.) TOD	ROH,JR,SA1,PDL
Todd, Thomas L.	Pvt.	F 14th SCVI	25	AE	10/18/62	Lynchburg, VA	DOD	Lynchburg CSA Cem.#3 R4	ROH,JR,TOD,BBW
Todd, W.P.	Pvt.	B 2nd SC Res			02/13/65	Columbia, SC	DOD		ROH,PP
Todd, William A.	Cpl.	K 12th SCVI	33	PS	08/06/62	Richmond, VA	DOD	(TOD=Oakwood C.)	ROH,TOD
Todd, William C.	Pvt.	E Orr's Ri.	25	PS	08/01/62	Richmond, VA	DOD	(TOD=Oakwood C.)	ROH,CDC,TOD
Todd, William H.	Pvt.	A Ham.Leg.		CN	08/30/62	2nd Manassas, VA	KIA		ROH,JR,WLI,RDC
Toland, William H.	Cpl.	I Ham.Leg.			11/05/64	Richmond, VA		Hollywood Cem.Rchmd. W724	ROH,HC
Tolar, (Taylor?)	Pvt.	L Orr's Ri.		AN	10/23/62	Richmond, VA		Hollywood Cem.Rchmd. C76	ROH,HC
Tolar, John H.	1st Lt.	H Orr's Ri.	30	MN	05/05/64	Wilderness, VA	KIA	(HMC=Plank Rd. April)	ROH,BOS,HMC,R4
Tolar, Thomas B.	Pvt.	B 10th SCVI		HY	08/25/63	Union Point, GA	DOW	(Wdd @ Murfreesboro)	RAS,CV
Tolbert, Tillman	Pvt.	E 12th SCVI	18	LR	01/27/62	McPhersonville	DOD		ROH,LAN
Tolleson, Daniel	Pvt.	E 16th SCVI	28	GE	03/01/64	(POW11/26/63GA)	DIP	C.C.#748 Rock Island, IL	ROH,FPH,P6,16R
Tolleson, John	Pvt.	I 3rd SCVI		LS	10/09/64	Greensboro, NC	DOW	(Wdd near Strasburg, VA)	PP,KEB,SA2
Tollison, Alfred James	1st Lt.	C Hol.Leg.	22	SG	06/27/65	Richmond, VA	DOW	(Trfd frm P.S.S.)	ROH,HOS
Tollison, Edward	Pvt.	E 16th SCVI	26	GE	07/22/62	Adams Run, SC	DOD		ROH,16R,ETT,PP
Tollison, Francis Marion				GE	09/17/62	Sharpsburg, MD	MIA		BOD
Tollison, J. Belton	Sgt.	C Hol.Leg.	29	SG	09/13/62	Warrenton, VA	DOW	(Wdd 2nd Man)	ROH,HOS
Tollison, J.W.	Ord. Sgt.	Hol.Leg.		SG	05/03/65	Richmond, VA	DOD		P6,HOS
Tollison, Thomas	Pvt.	E 16th SCVI	28	GE	09/15/63	Rome, GA	DOD	Myrtle Hill Cem. Rome, GA	ROH,16R,BGA
Tollison, William B.	Pvt.	I 13th SCVI	26	SG	07/02/62	Richmond, VA	DOD	Hollywood Cem.Rchmd. L111	ROH,JR,HC
Tolloph, T.	Pvt.	E 22nd SCVI		LR	11/10/64	Richmond, VA			ROH
Tolly, Samuel	Pvt.	E 22nd SCVI		LR	09/17/64	Pt. Lookout, MD	DIP	C.C. Pt. Lookout, MD	FPH,P6,P113
Toman, Benjamin		K 26th SCVI			/ /	(NO, 26th NI GA)		Con. Cem. Marietta, GA	CCM
Tomb, S. Julius	Cpt.	B 18th SCVI	24	UN	07/03/64	Petersburg, VA	DOW		ROH,R47,PP
Tomb, Samuel Jukins	Cpt.	B 18th SCVI		UN	07/03/64	Petersburg, VA	DOW	(Wdd 6/18 ?)	ROH,R47
Tomison, W.J. (SP?)	Pvt.	G 18th SCVI		UN	05/05/64	Petersburg, VA		Blandford Church Pbg., VA	BLC
Tomlin, H.H.	Cpl.	E 14th SCVI		LS	/ /	Richmond, VA		Oakwood C.#21,Row A,Div C	ROH,OWC
Tomlin, S.J.	Pvt.	A 10th SCVI			09/20/63	Chickamauga, GA	DOW		CDC
Tomlinson, R. Leander	Pvt.	H 18th SCVI		YK	01/19/62	Charleston, SC	DOD		YMD,YEB
Tomlinson, Robert	Pvt.	D 9th SCVIB		SR	11/07/61	Richmond, VA	DOD	(JR=E,P.S.S.)	ROH,JR
Tompkins, James M.	Pvt.			20	ED	06/27/62	Gaines' Mill, VA	KIA	Tompkins F.C. Plum Branch	MCC

T

SOUTH CAROLINA DEAD IN CSA SERVICE 1861-1865

NAME	RANK	C REGIMENT	AGE	DS	DIED	WHERE	WHY	BURIED	SOURCES
Tompkins, Jan	Pvt.	K 16th SCVI		GE	09/02/64	Jonesboro, GA	KIA		16R,UD2
Tompkins, John	Pvt.	K 14th SCVI		ED	07/13/62	Richmond, VA	DOW	(On Rchmd effects list)	JR,HOE,CDC
Tompkins, John B.	Pvt.	C 10th SCVI		HY	07/22/64	Atlanta, GA	KIA		ROH,RAS,CDC
Tompkins, Jones	Pvt.	K 16th SCVI		GE	/ /	Georgia	KIA		16R
Tompkins, R.W.	Cpt.	B Ham.Leg.	27	ED	09/17/62	Sharpsburg, MD	KIA	Thompkins F.C. McCormick	ROH,JR,HOE,R48
Tompkins, S.G.	Cpl.	G 10th SCVI		HY	09/20/63	Chickamauga, GA	KIA		ROH,JR,RAS,CDC
Tompkins, Stephen A.	Pvt.	G 1st SCVIG		ED	12/13/62	Fredericksburg	KIA	(Hos. Stwd.)	JR,SA1,HOE
Tompkins, W.J.	Pvt.	K 10th SCVI			/ /	Griffin, GA		Stonewall Cem. Griffin, GA	BGA
Toney, Edward	Pvt.	H 2nd SCVIRi	20	ED	10/16/62	Charlestown, VA	DOW	Charlestown, VA	ROH,EDN
Tonyers, Lewis	Pvt.	Hart's Bty		CN	09/14/63	Jack's Shop, VA	DOW		CDC
Toole, C.	Pvt.	B 1st SCVIH		BL	11/28/63	Campbell's Stn.	DOW	(Wdd 11/16 POW, Recaptured)	ROH,SA1,JRH
Toole, Harrison	Pvt.	H 14th SCVI		BL	06/09/62	Richmond, VA	DOW		JR,UD2
Toole, M.	Pvt.	C 1st SCVIBn		CN	07/18/63	Bty. Wagner, SC	KIA		ROH,CDC
Toole, Frank	Pvt.	H 2nd SCVA			/ /	Asheboro, NC	DOW		DI1
Touchberry, H.	Pvt.	B 3rd SCVC		CL	01/28/65	Charleston, SC		Magnolia Cem. Charleston	MAG,RCD
Touchberry, J.J.	Pvt.	C Ham.Leg.		CL	07/21/61	1st Manassas, VA	KIA	(Manning Guards)	ROH,JR,CDC
Towles, E.R.	Pvt.	K 15th SCVI		AE	/ /		DOD		JR,KEB
Town, R.A.	Pvt.	H 2nd SCVA			05/25/64	Charleston, SC		Magnolia Cem.Rchmd.	ROH,MAG,RCD
Townsend, A.E.	Sgt.	G 8th SCVI		MO	07/03/63	Richmond, VA	DOD	(Pneumonia)	JR
Townsend, G.B.	Pvt.			WG	/ /		KIA		HOW
Townsend, Henry E.	2nd Cpl.	G 8th SCVI	17	MO	12/04/62	Richmond, VA	DOD	Hollywood Cem.Rchmd. N10	ROH,JR,HC,UD2
Townsend, J.V.	Pvt.	G 3rd SCVI		RD	06/28/64	Richmond, VA	KIA	(NI KEB)	ROH,SA2
Townsend, Joshua M.	Cpt.	A 3rd SCVIBn		LS	09/20/63	Chickamauga, GA	KIA		ROH,JR,R45,KEB
Townsend, L.J.	Pvt.	G 7th SCVC		CN	01/16/65	Greensboro, NC			PP
Townsend, William	Pvt.	K 6th SCVI	30	MO	06/15/64	Petersburg, VA	DOW		ROH,3RC
Townsend, William	Pvt.	F 13th SCVI		SG	05/12/64	Spotsylvania, VA	KIA		HOS
Tracy, Frederick S.	Pvt.	7th SCVC		GE	04/03/65	Richmond, VA	KIA	(Co.B or G, Rutledge M.R.)	H2,SA2,KEB
Trail, George P.	Pvt.	A Hol.Leg.		SG	/ /	Pt. Lookout, MD	DIP		HOS
Trammell, Bayfield P.	Pvt.	H 22nd SCVI		FD	08/06/64	Richmond, VA	DOD	Hollywood Cem.Rchmd. V569	ROH,HC,HIC,P120
Trammell, Fleming	Pvt.	H 16th SCVI		GE	12/15/63	At home	DOD		PP
Trammell, P.L.	Pvt.	F 1st SCVIH			11/24/63	Med C. Atlanta	DOD	Oakland C. Atlanta R29#3	BGA,SA1
Trammell, Thomas D.	Pvt.	H 2nd SCVIRi			/ /	Lynchburg, VA		Lynchburg CSA Cem.#10 R1	BBW
Trammell, Jr., Jerry	Pvt.	H 22nd SCVI		GE	07/30/62	Columbia, SC	DOD		PP
Transell, A.	Pvt.	A 22nd SCVI		GE	08/20/64	Petersburg, VA	DOW		ROH
Trapp, Allen	Pvt.	B 7th SCVIBn	18	FD	05/16/64	Drury's Bluff VA	KIA		ROH,HFC,HAG
Trapp, Bayfield W.	Pvt.	F 12th SCVI		FD	05/04/64	Richmond, VA		Hollywood Cem.Rchmd. I45	HC,ROH,HFC
Travis, Joshua	Pvt.	SC			12/18/62	Kinston, NC	DOW		PP
Trawick, Peter	Pvt.	B 24th SCVI	25	MO	11/30/64	Franklin, TN	KIA		ROH,HOM,CDC,PP
Traxler, James J.	Pvt.	C 24th SCVI	18	CO	07/25/63	Jackson, MS	DOD	(PP=Lauderdale Springs)	ROH,PP
Traylor, Albert Thomas	1st Lt.	C 7th SCVI	25	AE	07/03/63	Cashtown, PA	DOW	Rife's Farm Cashtown, PA	ROH,GDR,R46,WV
Traylor, William T.	Pvt.	A 12th SCVI	19	YK	09/17/62	Sharpsburg, MD	KIA		YEB
Traynaham, Waddy T.	Pvt.	E 16th SCVI	30	GE	07/07/62	At home	DOD		ROH,16R,PP
Treadaway, G.T.	Pvt.	K 22nd SCVI		PS	07/30/64	Crater, Pbg., VA	KIA		BLM
Treadaway, George T.	Pvt.	B P.S.S.		PS	06/15/63	At home			ROH
Treadaway, James E.	Pvt.	K 22nd SCVI		PS	09/05/64	Richmond, VA	DOW	Hollywood Cem.Rchmd. V608	ROH,HC
Treadaway, John M.	Pvt.	K 22nd SCVI		PS	03/09/62	Columbia, SC			PP
Treat, Frederick W.	Pvt.	I 7th SCVI	20	ED	09/04/61	Charlottesville	DOD	Magnolia Cem. Augusta, GA	EDN,HOE,BGA
Trexler, J.J.	Pvt.	A 18th SCRes			05/02/65	Hart's Island NY	DIP	Cypress Hills N.C.#2680 NY	FPH,P6,P79
Trezevant, Jesse Howell	Lt. ADC	B.G.Archer	19	RD	06/27/62	Gaines' Mill, VA	KIA	Trinity Church Columbia SC	ROH,JR,MP,PP
Trezevant, Willoughby F.	ADC/Evans	1st SCVC	16	RD	09/24/62	Sharpsburg, MD	DOW	Trinity Church Columbia SC	ROH,JR,MP,PP
Tribble, C. John	Pvt.	E 7th SCVC	20	LS	/ /	Tylersville, VA	KIA	(On picket)	ANY

SOUTH CAROLINA DEAD IN CSA SERVICE 1861-1865

NAME	RANK	C	REGIMENT	AGE	DS	DIED	WHERE	WHY	BURIED	SOURCES
Tribble, C.W.	Pvt.	D	Hol.Leg.		NY	01/15/63	Manchester, VA	DOD		ROH,ANY
Tribble, J.C.	Pvt.	C	Hol.Leg.		NY	08/15/63	New Kent C.H. VA	KIA		ANY
Tribble, J.K.	Pvt.	K	1st SC Res		LS	02/10/65	Charleston, SC	DOD	Magnolia Cem. Charleston	ROH,MAG,RCD
Tribble, James R.	Pvt.	E	3rd SCVI		LS	05/15/61	Camp Johnson, SC	DOD		ROH,JR,ANY,KEB
Tribble, L.R.	Pvt.	D	2nd SCV			/ /	Charlottesville		Univ. Cem. Charlottesville	ACH
Tribble, R.W.	Pvt.	B	7th SCVI		AE	12/26/62	Lynchburg, VA		Lynchburg CSA Cem.#5 R4	JR,BBW
Tridel, J.M.	Pvt.				LN	10/15/62	Columbia, SC	DOD		ROH
Tripp, Elias	Pvt.	G	4th SCVI		GE	/ /	Richmond, VA	DOD	Oakwood C.#52,Row C,Div A	ROH,SA2,OWC
Tripp, William	Pvt.	C	4th SCVI		AN	12/25/61		DOD		HOF
Trotter, A.B.	Pvt.	A	7th SCVI			11/07/62	Winchester, VA		Stonewall C. Winchester VA	WIN
Trotter, Butler	Pvt.	B	2nd SCVIRi		PS	/ /				ROH
Trotter, Henry	Pvt.	F	1st SCVC		PS	06/02/62	Adams Run, SC	DOD		PP
Trotter, J.B.	Pvt.	B	2nd SCVIRi		PS	/ /			Spotsylvania C.H., VA	SCH
Trotter, R.	Pvt.	E	1st SCVA			04/04/64	Charleston, SC		Magnolia Cem. Charleston	ROH,MAG,RCD
Trotter, William	Pvt.	K	2nd SCVIRi		PS	/ /	Lynchburg, VA		Lynchburg CSA Cem.#6 R2	BBW
Trouche, Augustus J.	Sgt.	D	27th SCVI	26	CN	02/15/64	Charleston, SC	DOD	St.Mary's R.C. Charleston	ROH,MAG,CDC
Truesdell, Burwell	Pvt.	G	2nd SCVI		KW	06/29/62	Savage Stn., VA	KIA	(JR=Daniel)	JR,HIC,KEB,H2
Truesdell, G.D.	Pvt.	C	2nd SCVI			09/13/62	Maryland Hts. MD	KIA		JR
Truesdell, James T.	Pvt.	G	2nd SCVI	22	KW	09/17/62	Sharpsburg, MD	KIA		ROH,SA2,HIC,KE
Truesdell, John C.	Pvt.	I	12th SCVI		LR	06/19/64	Richmond, VA	DOW	Hollywood Cem.Rchmd. U262	LAN,HC
Truesdell, Wm. Jasper	3rd Cpl.	G	2nd SCVI		KW	06/29/62	Savage Stn., VA	KIA	(JR=1st Sgt.)	JR,HIC,SA2,KEB
Truett, J.D.	Pvt.	A	14th SCVI	21	DN	07/01/63	Gettysburg, PA	KIA		ROH
Truett, Pinckney	Pvt.	K	21st SCVI		DN	05/16/64	Drury's Bluff VA	KIA		ROH,CDC,HAG
Truluck, Ebenezer B.	Pvt.	F	26th SCVI		CL	07/26/63	Lauderdale Ss MS			PP
Tuck, J. Armstrong	Pvt.	K	P.S.S.		SG	/ /	Richmond, VA	DOW	Oakwood C.#49,Row O,Div B	ROH,JR,OWC
Tuck, Richard H.	Sgt.	C	Hol.Leg.	26	SG	11/05/64	Petersburg, VA	KIA		ROH,HOS
Tuck, Thomas M.	Cpl.	C	Hol.Leg.	23	SG	09/30/62	Frederick, MD	DOW	Mt.Olivet C.#63 Frederick	FPH,HOS,P6,BOD
Tucker, B.A.	Pvt.	G	6th SCVI			/ /	Charlottesville		Univ. Cem. Charlottesville	ACH
Tucker, B.F.	Pvt.	F	1st SCVIG		SG	06/27/64	Richmond, VA	DOD	Hollywood Cem.Rchmd. U639	ROH,HC,SA1,PDL
Tucker, Charles W.	Pvt.	C	15th SCVAB			09/03/63	Bty. Wagner, SC	DOW	Magnolia Cem. Charleston	ROH,MAG,CDC,RC
Tucker, Francis Marion	Cpt.	E	18th SCVI	33	SG	08/30/62	2nd Manassas, VA	KIA	Family C. Woodruff, SC	ROH,JR,HOS,UD3
Tucker, G. Pickett	Pvt.	B	Ham.Leg.			09/15/62		DOW		JR
Tucker, John	Pvt.	G	19th SCVI		AE	/ /	Charleston, SC	DOD		HOL
Tucker, John J.	Pvt.	I	14th SCVI	24	AE	06/08/63	At home	DOD	(Typhoid)	ROH,JR,HOL
Tucker, Lewis	Pvt.	C	11th SCVI		CN	05/16/64	Drury's Bluff VA	KIA		ROH
Tucker, P.L.	Lt.	I	24th SCVI	17		/ /	Kennesaw, GA	DOW	(1864)	ROH,CDC
Tucker, Silas	Cpl.		Tucker's R			03/29/65	Salisbury, NC			PP
Tucker, William B.	Pvt.	K	P.S.S.		SG	/ /	Richmond, VA		Oakwood C.#22,Row O,Div B	ROH,OWC
Tumbland, B.M.	Pvt.	K	14th SCVI		ED	01/25/64	Ft. Delaware, DE	DIP	Finn's Point N.C. NJ	FPH,P5
Tumblestone, Henry C.	Pvt.	C	11th SCVI		CO	05/16/64	Drury's Bluff VA	KIA	(HAG=Tumblestow)	ROH,HAG
Tumblin, H.H.	Pvt.	E	14th SCVI		LS	07/01/62	Gaines' Mill, VA	DOW		JR,CGS
Tunsul, J.T.	Pvt.	L	7th SCVI		HY	/ /	Richmond, VA			ROH
Tupper, James A.	Pvt.	I	Hol.Leg.		SG	/ /	Elmira, NY	DIP	(POW @ Stoney Crk., VA)	HOS
Turbeville, Calvin	Pvt.	L	8th SCVI		MN	08/22/62	Richmond, VA	DOD	(Typhoid)	JR,KEB
Turbeville, F.	Pvt.	D	10th SCVI		MN	/ /		DOD		RAS,HMC
Turbeville, P.	Pvt.	D	10th SCVI		MN	/ /		DOD		RAS,HMC
Turbeville, S.	Pvt.	F	10th SCVI		MN	07/24/64	At home	DOW	(Wdd @ Atlanta, 7/22)	RAS,HMC,CDC
Turbeville, S.H.	Pvt.		Ham.Leg.		MN	07/29/64	Richmond, VA			ROH
Turbeville, Solomon	Pvt.	E	1st SCVIG		MN	10/01/62	Frederick, MD	DOW	Mt.Olivet C.#67 Frederick	FPH,SA1,P6,BOD
Turnage, B.F.	Pvt.	C	8th SCVI	22	CD	08/24/61	Orange C.H., VA	DOD	(JR=Measles @ Culpepper)	ROH,JR
Turner, A. (S.?)	Pvt.	G	4th SCVI		GE	06/19/62	Richmond, VA		Hollywood Cem.Rchmd. O79	HC

T

SOUTH CAROLINA DEAD IN CSA SERVICE 1861-1865

NAME	RANK	C REGIMENT	AGE	DS	DIED	WHERE	WHY	BURIED	SOURCES
Turner, B.F.	Pvt.	H 22nd SCVI			/ /	Charlottesville		Univ. Cem. Charlottesville	ACH
Turner, Benjamin James	Cpl.	F 7th SCVIBn	36	KW	06/16/64	Drury's Bluff VA	DOW		ROH,HAG
Turner, C.	Pvt.	1st SCVC			10/15/64	Richmond, VA		Hollywood Cem.Rchmd. V333	HC
Turner, C.L.	Cpl.	K Hol.Leg.	22	SG	08/23/62	Rappahannock Br.	KIA		ROH
Turner, Darling	Pvt.	K 19th SCVI	17	ED	10/03/62	Danville, KY	DIP	Danville Cem. C.L. KY	ROH,FPH,HOE
Turner, David	Pvt.	C 11th SCVI		CO	06/24/64	Petersburg, VA	KIA		ROH,HAG
Turner, Elisha W.	Pvt.	C Hol.Leg.	32	SG	08/30/62	2nd Manassas, VA	KIA		ROH,JR,HOS
Turner, Elliot	Pvt.	E SCVI			09/13/64			Stonewall C. Winchester VA	WIN
Turner, F.P.	Pvt.	E 18th SCVAB	20	SG	/ /	Charleston, SC	DOD		ROH
Turner, Henry A.	5th Sgt.	K 5th SCVI		SG	09/12/62		DOW		JR,SA3
Turner, Henry J.	Cpl.	A Hol.Leg.		SG	08/30/62	2nd Manassas, VA	KIA		HOS
Turner, J.B.	Pvt.	K 6th SCVI	33	CL	09/27/62	Warrenton, VA	DOW (Wdd 2nd Man.)		ROH,3RC
Turner, J.D.	Pvt.	F 19th SCVI		ED	01/14/65	Camp Chase, OH	DIP	C.C.#764 Columbus, OH	FPH,P5,P22
Turner, J.L.	Pvt.	F 10th SCVI		MN	09/20/63	Chickamauga, GA	KIA (JR=Co.A)		ROH,JR,CDC
Turner, J.M.	Cpl.	I 5th SCVI		SG	08/16/64	New Market Hts.	KIA		ROH,SA3,HOS
Turner, J.N.W.	Pvt.	SCVC			06/12/64	Trevillian Stn.	KIA		ROH
Turner, J.P.	Sgt.	E 13th SCVI		SG	10/20/62	Warrenton, VA	DOW (Wdd 2nd Man)		ROH,HOS
Turner, J.S.	Pvt.	B 10th SCVI		HY	09/19/63	Chickamauga, GA	KIA (Color bearer,leading Rgt)		ROH,RAS
Turner, J.S.	Pvt.	A P.S.S.		UN	05/31/62	7 Pines, VA	KIA		JR,CDC
Turner, J.T.	Pvt.	G 22nd SCVI		AN	08/09/63	Gettysburg, PA	DOW (May be T.J.)		ROH,P1,P5,CDC
Turner, J.W.	4th Cpl.	K 18th SCVI			07/30/64	Crater, Pbg., VA	KIA		ROH,BLM
Turner, James	Pvt.	D 10th SCVI		MN	/ /	Meridian, MS	DOD		RAS,HMC,PP
Turner, James	Pvt.	C 17th SCVI	36	YK	02/26/62	Johns Island, SC	DOD		JR,DEM,YEB
Turner, James C.	Sgt.	K 18th SCVI	33	UN	02/17/63	At home	DOD	Padgett Creek B.C. UN Cty.	ROH,UNC
Turner, James C.	Pvt.	G Hol.Leg.	25	UN	02/17/62	Adams Run, SC	DOD		ROH,ANY
Turner, James D.W.	Pvt.	I 12th SCVI		LR	05/06/64	Wilderness, VA	KIA		LAN
Turner, James P.	Pvt.	F 17th SCVI		YK	06/17/65	Pt. Lookout, MD	DIP	C.C. Pt. Lookout, MD	FPH,P6,P115
Turner, James R.	Pvt.	SC Res Trp	17	YK	11/26/64	Florence, SC	DOD		YMD
Turner, Jefferson	Pvt.	F 13th SCVI		SG	/ /		KIA (JR=Co.E)		JR,HOS
Turner, Jeptha	Pvt.	22nd SCVI			/ /	Petersburg, VA	KIA		ROH
Turner, John	Pvt.	B 6th SCVI		YK	10/10/64	Richmond, VA	KIA		ROH
Turner, John	Pvt.	H Orr's Ri.		MN	/ /	Virginia	DOD (1862)		HMC
Turner, John A.	Pvt.	M 7th SCVC			02/13/65	Pt. Lookout, MD	DIP	C.C. Pt. Lookout, MD	FPH
Turner, John C.	Pvt.	I 8th SCVI		MN	10/13/64	Cedar Creek, VA	KIA (8th/15th SCVI Consol)		ROH,HMC,KEB
Turner, John C.	Pvt.	I 8th SCVI		UN	/ /		DOD	Padgetts Creek C. Union SC	UD2
Turner, John L.	4th Sgt.	B 2nd SCVI	32	GE	08/15/61	Vienna, VA	DOD (Typhoid)		ROH,SA2,KEB,H2
Turner, John T.B.	Pvt.	C 13th SCVI		SG	05/12/64	Spotsylvania, VA	KIA		ROH,HOS
Turner, Joseph B.	Pvt.	I Hol.Leg.		SG	03/14/65	Richmond, VA	DOD		ROH,HOS
Turner, L.	Pvt.	B 24th SCVI		MO	/ /	At home	DOD		HOM
Turner, L.	Pvt.	C 1st SCSSBn			06/22/63	Columbia, SC			PP
Turner, Lee L.	Pvt.	E 13th SCVI	22	SG	09/30/64	Jones' Farm, VA	KIA		ROH,HOS
Turner, Lewis	Pvt.	B 2nd SCVIRi		PS	08/30/62	2nd Manassas, VA	KIA (MIA presumed dead)		ROH,CDC
Turner, Lewis H.	Pvt.	I 10th SCVI		MN	05/03/63	Atlanta, GA	DOD	Oakland C. Atlanta R21#8	RAS,HMC,BGA
Turner, R.H.	Pvt.	F 10th SCVI		MN	/ /		DOD		RAS,HMC
Turner, Silas Holloway	Pvt.		38	GE	05/29/62	At home	DOD	Garrison Fam. C. GE Cty.	GEE
Turner, T.J.	Sgt.	G 22nd SCVI		AN	07/02/63	Gettysburg, PA	KIA	Magnolia Cem. Charleston	MAG,RCD
Turner, T.J.	Pvt.	A 18th SCVI		UN	07/30/64	Crater, Pbg., VA	KIA		BLM
Turner, T.J.	Pvt.	K 5th SCVI		SG	/ /	Virginia	DOD		HOS,SA3
Turner, Thomas	Pvt.	H Hol.Leg.	18	ED	04/30/63	Wilmington, SC	DOD		ROH
Turner, Thomas D.	Pvt.	F 10th SCVI		MN	04/05/65	Camp Douglas, IL	DIP	Oak Woods Cem. Chicago, IL	ROH,FPH,P6,RAS
Turner, Thompson	Pvt.	A 18th SCVI		UN	05/20/64	Clay's Farm, VA	KIA		ROH

SOUTH CAROLINA DEAD IN CSA SERVICE 1861-1865

NAME	RANK	C REGIMENT	AGE	DS	DIED	WHERE	WHY	BURIED	SOURCES
Turner, Wiley	Pvt.	3rd SC Res		PS	12/19/62	SC	DOD		ROH
Turner, William	Pvt.	B 24th SCVI		MO	05/07/63	Charleston, SC	DOD	Magnolia Cem. Charleston	ROH,MAG,RCD
Turner, William	Cpl.	K 19th SCVI	24	ED	12/31/62	Murfreesboro, TN	KIA		HOE
Turner, William Elliott	Cpl.	A Hol.Leg.	30	SG	09/13/62	Winchester, VA	DOD		ROH,HOS
Turner, William W.	Pvt.	C 8th SCVI	33	CD	09/30/63	Chattanooga, TN	DOW	(Wdd 9/22/64)	ROH,JR,CDC
Turner, William W.	Pvt.	E 2nd SCVI	18	KW	09/03/61	Lynchburg, VA	DOD	(Body sent home)	ROH,JR,SA2,CDN
Turney, John	Pvt.	F 5th SCVI	41	YK	05/31/62	7 Pines, VA	KIA		JR,SA3,YEB,CB
Turnipseed, Edward A.	Pvt.	C 7th SCVIBn	20	RD	10/22/62	Pocotaligo, SC	KIA		ROH,HAG,R46,PP
Turnipseed, John	Pvt.	G 7th SCVI		ED	/ /		KIA		HOE,UD2
Turpin, William Peter	Pvt.	B 2nd SCVI	20	GE	05/06/64	Wilderness, VA	KIA		ROH,SA2,CDC,KE
Tuten, J.C.C.	Pvt.	B 5th SCVC	19	BT	10/27/64	Boydton Plank Rd	KIA		ROH,MDM
Tuten, J.W.	Sgt.	B 5th SCVC	30	BT	05/06/65		DOD		ROH
Tuten, Jefferson N.	Pvt.	H 1st SCVIG	35	BT	07/15/62	Richmond, VA	DOD	Oakwood C.#13, Row O, Div B	ROH,SA1,OWC
Tuten, Jesse J.	Pvt.	H 1st SCVIG	23	BT	07/15/62	Richmond, VA	DOD		ROH,SA1
Tuten, John	Pvt.	B 5th SCVC		BT	12/25/64	Petersburg, VA	DOW	(Wdd 12/20/64)	ROH,PP
Tuterow, T.P.	Pvt.	M 7th SCVC			01/23/65	Elmira, NY	DIP	Woodlawn N.C.#1603 Elmira	FPH
Twiggs, John D.	Lt. Col.	1st SCVC		ED	09/15/64	Hamburg, SC	MUR	(Killed by Butler, on Lve.)	CRD,LC,R43
Twiner, C.	Pvt.	1st SCVC			10/15/64	Richmond, VA			ROH
Twiner, S.	Pvt.	B 4th SCVIBn			05/31/62	Philadelphia, PA	DIP		ROH
Twiner, W.M.	Pvt.	16th SCVI			01/20/62	Charleston, SC	DOD		ROH
Twitty, Charles Russell	Sgt.	A 16th SCVI	19	GE	05/10/64	Columbia, SC	DOD	(PP=3/13/64)	ROH,PP
Twitty, George W.	Pvt.	E 12th SCVI	23	LR	01/06/62	Pocotaligo, SC	DOW	(JR=Killed by a prisoner)	ROH,JR,LAN
Twitty, Lewis M.	Cpl.	D 7th SCVIBn	21	KW	03/21/63	Adams Run, SC	DOD		ROH,HAG,PP
Twitty, Peter W.	Pvt.	E 12th SCVI		LR	01/06/62	Pocotaligo, SC	DOW	Fort Hill B.C. Cem.	LAN
Tyler,	Pvt.	C 1st SCVC			04/10/65	Moccasin Ck., NC	KIA		CRD
Tyler, D.S.	Pvt.	1st SCVA	38		09/15/64		DOD		ROH
Tyler, Elias	Pvt.	K 26th SCVI	40	HY	08/01/64	Petersburg, VA	DOW		ROH,PP,CEN
Tyler, Hugh	Pvt.	F 1st SCVIG		HY	11/04/63	Ft. Delaware, DE	DIP	Finn's Pt., NJ Nat. Cem.	ROH,FPH,P5,SA1
Tyler, James	Pvt.	D 17th SCVI		CR	12/09/64	Elmira, NY	DIP		ROH
Tyler, Swift	Pvt.	6th SCVC	40	OG	/ /		DOD	(1864)	ROH
Tyler, Wesley	Pvt.	6th SC Res	47	OG	/ /		DOD	(1864)	ROH
Tyner, Caleb	Pvt.	E 6th SCVI		DN	05/31/62	7 Pines, VA	KIA		ROH,JR,WDB,CDC
Tyner, John G.	Pvt.	G 21st SCVI		CD	01/09/64	Pt. Lookout, MD	DIP	C.C. Pt. Lookout, MD	ROH,FPH,P5,HAG
Tynes, Samuel Alexander	1st Sgt.	A 15th SCVAB		RD	07/24/63	Bty. Wagner, SC	DOW	Elmwood Cem. Columbia, SC	ROH,MP,PP,R44
Tyre, Christopher	Pvt.	B 9th SCVIB		RD	01/31/62	Richmond, VA	DOD		JR,CNM

SOUTH CAROLINA DEAD IN CSA SERVICE 1861-1865

NAME	RANK	C	REGIMENT	AGE	DS	DIED	WHERE	WHY	BURIED	SOURCES
Ulm, R.M.	Pvt.	E	27th SCVI		CN	12/11/64	Richmond, VA		Hollywood Cem.Rchmd. W297	ROH,HC,HAG
Ulmer, Adam A.	pvt.	B	1st SCVIH	24	OG	11/11/62	Lynchburg, VA	DOD		ROH,SA1,EDR,JR
Unger, David W.	Pvt.		Bachmans A		LN	12/15/64	Summerville, SC	DOD		ROH
Unger, John J.	Pvt.	F	5th SCVC	19	LN	06/12/64	Trevillian Stn.	DOW (Leg amputated)		ROH,CDC
Unger, P.D.	Pvt.	F	5th SCVC	27	LN	03/23/62	At home	DOD		ROH
Usher, Charles	Pvt.	B	24th SCVI	18	MO	03/21/64	Forsythe, GA	DOD		ROH,HOM
Usher, McMucan	Pvt.	F	21st SCVI		MO	05/07/64	Pt.Walthal Jctn.	DOW	Blandford Church Pbg., VA	ROH,HOM,PP,BLC
Ussery, J.C.	Pvt.	G	Ham.Leg.		LR	/ /		DOD		LAN
Ussery, J.T.	Pvt.		1st SCV		LR	07/10/62	Richmond, VA			ROH
Ussery, S.W.	Pvt.	A	1st SCVIG		BL	07/01/63	Gettysburg, PA	KIA		ROH,JR,GDR,SA1
Ussery, Samuel M.	Pvt.	D	1st SCVIH		LR	07/01/62	Summerville, SC	DOD (NI SA1)		ROH,LAN,JRH
Ussury, Richard Samuel	pvt.	L	2nd SCVIRi	24	LR	07/07/62	Petersburg, VA	DOD	Blandford Church Pbg., VA	ROH,BLC,PP
Utsey, Charles	Pvt.	H	11th SCVI	22	CO	/ /		DOW		DRE
Utsey, D.	Pvt.	C	24th SCVI	39	CO	09/24/63	Georges Stn., SC	DOD		ROH
Utsey, D.W.	Sgt.	H	11th SCVI	28	CO	/ /		DOD		DRE
Utsey, John R.S.	Pvt.	C	24th SCVI	22	CO	06/14/64	Pine Mtn., GA	KIA (Smyrna Church Line)		ROH,CDC,TEB

SOUTH CAROLINA DEAD IN CSA SERVICE 1861-1865

NAME	RANK	C	REGIMENT	AGE	DS	DIED	WHERE	WHY	BURIED	SOURCES
Valentine, Isaac D.	Cpl.	D	1st SCVIBn	29	CN	06/16/62	Secessionville	KIA	Beth Elohim Charleston	ROH,MAG,HAG,PP
Valentine, Joseph	Pvt.	I	11th SCVI		CO	06/29/64		DOW		ROH,HAG
Valentine, T.D.	Pvt.	H	13th SCVI		LN	06/22/62	Richmond, VA		Hollywood Cem.Rchmd. O247	ROH,HC
Valentine, Thomas	Pvt.	A	21st SCVI			10/18/62	(21st not here)		Stonewall C. Winchester VA	ROH,WIN
Vance, H.T.	Pvt.	F	14th SCVI		LS	07/13/62	Richmond, VA	DOD		JR
Vance, William A.	2nd Sgt.	F	3rd SCVI	21	LS	09/20/63	Chickamauga, GA	KIA	Vance Burying Gds. Kinards	ROH,SA2,KEB,LS
Vance, William D.	1st Lt.	E	16th SCVI	23	GE	03/02/62	At home	DOD	(Typhoid @ Belton, SC)	ROH,JR,16R,R47
Vanderford, Alonzo A.	3rd Lt.	D	21st SSCVI		CD	07/30/64	Petersburg, VA	DOW		ROH,R48,HAG
Vanderford, Dudley	Pvt.	D	5th SCVI		UN	02/15/62	Centreville, VA	DOD	(Pneumonia)	JR,SA3
Vanderford, Hampton	Pvt.	H	15th SCVI		UN	07/12/63	Gettysburg, PA	DOW	Magnolia Cem. Charleston	ROH,JR,,GDR,P1
Vanderhorst, Louis M.	Pvt.	K	4th SCVC		CN	05/28/64	Hawes Shop, VA	KIA		MSF,CLD
Vandiver, Augustus W.	1st Lt.	F	2nd SCVIRi			10/28/63	Lookout Valley	KIA	(R45=10/19/63)	ROH,JR,CDC,R45
Vandiver, Edwin C.	Pvt.	G	22nd SCVI	21	AN	03/01/62	Columbia, SC	DOD		ROH,PP
Vandiver, Edwin W.	Pvt.	B	7th SCVI		AE	09/13/62	Maryland Hts. MD	KIA		JR,KEB
Vandiver, Elam. M.	2nd Lt.	L	Orr's Ri.		AN	/ /		DOW	(R45= RES 9/30/63)	ROH,JR,R45
Vandiver, J.R.	Pvt.		5th SCVI			08/21/61	Culpepper, VA	DOD	(JR =DOW from 1st Man.)	JR,CDC
Vandiver, Jephtha M.	3rd Lt.	K	2nd SCVIRi	31	AN	09/30/64	Ft. Harrison, VA	KIA		ROH,R45
Vandiver, John Lambkin	Pvt.	D	4th SCVI	26	AN	08/26/61	Culpepper, VA	DOD	Fairview Cem. Culpepper VA	CGH,SA2
Vandiver, Oliver K.	Pvt.	B	Hol.Leg.	39	SG	11/16/64	Petersburg, VA	DOD		ROH,HOS,PP
Vandyke, M.B.	Pvt.	B	13th SCVI		SG	/ /	Richmond, VA		Oakwood C.#40,Row M,Div A	ROH,OWC
Vanhorn, Arnold A.	Pvt.	I	14th SCVI	19	AE	09/15/63	At sea	DIP	(On ship rtg frm prison)	ROH,P115
Vanhorn, D.	Pvt.	I	14th SCVI		AE	11/05/64	Fts. Monroe, VA	DOW		ROH
Vanhorn, Joseph	Pvt.	1	14th SCVI		AE	/ /	Richmond, VA	DOD		HOL
Vanlandingham, J.C.T.	Pvt.	I	12th SCVI	28	LR	07/01/62	Port Royal Ferry	KIA		LAN,CDC,PP,CNM
Vann, R.G.	Pvt.	H	2nd SCVA			05/31/64	Charleston, SC	DOD	(Soldiers Relief Hospital)	CDC
Vann, R.J.	Pvt.	I	2nd SCVA	18	OG	06/01/64	James Island, SC	DOW	Magnolia Cem. Charleston	ROH,MAG,RCD,R4
Vann, T.J.	Cpl.	K	3rd SCVI			06/14/62	Richmond, VA		(Vaughan?)	ROH
Vanness, William	Pvt.	H	23rd SCVI		MN	08/30/62	2nd Manassas, VA	KIA		ROH,JR,HMC,CDC
Vansant, J.T.	Pvt.	E	7th SCVI	22	ED	06/10/61	At home	DOD		HOE,EDN,KEB,UD
Vansant, Jesse W.	Pvt.	B	14th SCVI	23	ED	08/18/62	Richmond, VA	DOD	(HOE=Vincent)	ROH,JR,HOE,UD3
Vansant, S.W.	Pvt.	B	14th SCVI		ED	08/18/62	Richmond, VA	DOD	(Typhoid)	JR
Varn, Aaron E.	Pvt.	K	11th SCVI	19	CO	06/18/64	Farmville, VA	DOD		ROH,HAG
Varn, G.W.	Pvt.	H	17th SCVI		BL	07/30/64	Petersburg, VA	KIA		ROH
Varn, Hangford D.	Pvt.	K	14th SCMil			05/11/65	Hart's Island NY	DIP	Cypress Hills N.C.#2753 NY	FPH,P6,P79
Varn, P.M.E.	Pvt.	E	24th SCVI	20	CO	09/20/63	Chickamauga, GA	KIA		ROH,CDC
Varn, Thomas J.	Cpl.	K	1st SCVIH	22	OG	06/14/64	Spotsylvania, VA	DOW		ROH,SA1
Varnadoe, Henry	Pvt.	E	15th SCVI	26	FD	07/01/62	Charleston, SC	DOD		ROH,JR,KEB
Varnadore, G. Washington	Pvt.	F	23rd SCVI		CR	08/30/62	2nd Manassas, VA	KIA		HHC
Varner, Isaac N.	Pvt.	A	Hol.Leg.	20	SG	08/30/62	2nd Manassas, VA	KIA	(JR=Co.H)	ROH,JR,HOS
Varner, J. Frank	Pvt.	E	18th SCVI		SG	05/16/64	Clay's Farm, VA	KIA		HOS
Varner, J.B.	2nd Lt.	D	2nd SCVC		CN	12/08/62		DOD		R43
Varner, J.W.	Pvt.	D	3rd SCVI		SG	04/17/62	Richmond, VA	DOD	Oakwood C.#32,Row G,Div A	JR,SA2,OWC,KEB
Varner, Thomas	Pvt.	E	18th SCVI	27	SG	02/17/65	Petersburg, VA	KIA		ROH,HOS,PP
Varnes, W.M.	Pvt.	E	27th SCVI			07/22/62	Richmond, VA		Hollywood Cem.Rchmd. U68	ROH,HC,HAG
Vasser, T.Z.B.	Cpl.	H	26th SCVI		SR	08/15/63	Jackson, MS			PP
Vassey, George	Pvt.	G	5th SCVI	23	SG	10/04/61	Fairfax C.H., VA	DOD	(JR=M,P.S.S.)	ROH,JR,SA3
Vassey, Levy	Pvt.	G	5th SCVC	45	AE	/ /				ROH
Vaughan, Barrington A.	Pvt.	C	3rd SCVIBn	19	LS	11/04/62	Staunton, VA	DOD	Vaughan Fam. C. Laurens	ROH,LSC,KEB,TO
Vaughan, David Y.	Pvt.	B	16th SCVI		GE	06/13/63	At home	DOD		PP
Vaughan, E.C.	Pvt.	H	5th SCVI			01/15/63	Fredericksburg	DOD	Fredericksburg C.C. R6S13	FBG,SA3
Vaughan, Joseph L.	Pvt.	K	3rd SCVI	22	SG	01/03/63	Richmond, VA	DOD	(JR=Fredericksburg)	ROH,JR,SA2,HOS

SOUTH CAROLINA DEAD IN CSA SERVICE 1861-1865

NAME	RANK	C REGIMENT	AGE	DS	DIED	WHERE	WHY	BURIED	SOURCES
Vaughan, Robert	Pvt.	B 16th SCVI		GE	/ /	Adams Run, SC	DOD	(1862)	16R
Vaughan, Stephen	Pvt.	E 24th SCVI	21	CO	05/06/64	At home	DOD	(May have survived war)	ROH
Vaughan, W.B.	Pvt.	A P.S.S.			/ /	Lee's Farm, VA	KIA	(1864)	JR
Vaughan, William	Pvt.	B 13th SCVI		SG	/ /	Richmond, VA	DOW		HOS
Vaughn, A.	Pvt.	A Orr's Ri.		AN	07/08/62	Richmond, VA			ROH,CDC
Vaughn, David	Pvt.	I 1st SCVIR			03/12/64	Charleston, SC	DOD	Magnolia Cem. Charleston	ROH,MAG,CDC,SA1
Vaughn, David	Pvt.	I Ham.Leg.			06/30/65	Pt. Lookout, MD	DIP	C.C. Pt. Lookout, MD	FPH,P6,P115
Vaughn, Francis Oliver	Pvt.	D 2nd SCVI	27	SR	06/11/61	Culpepper, VA	DOD	Fairview Cem. Culpepper VA	ROH,JR,CGH,SA2
Vaughn, G.P.	Pvt.	A 27th SCVI		CN	08/10/64	Richmond, VA		Hollywood Cem.Rchmd. V37	ROH,HC
Vaughn, Henry G.	Sgt.	I 16th SCVI		GE	11/30/64	Franklin, TN	KIA		ROH,16R,PP
Vaughn, J.B.	Pvt.	A 3rd SCVI		LS	07/02/63	Gettysburg, PA	DOW		CDC
Vaughn, Jesse A.	Cpl.	E 16th SCVI		GE	03/03/65	Camp Chase, OH	DIP	C.C.#1523 Columbus, OH	FPH,16R,P2,P6,PP
Vaughn, Joel	Pvt.	B 27th SCVI		SG	06/03/64	Bermuda Hundred	KIA		ROH,CDC
Vaughn, John	Pvt.	A 3rd SCVI		LS	06/12/61	Columbia, SC	ACD	(Killed by train)	ROH,JR,SA2,KEB
Vaughn, Leroy	Cpl.	B 2nd SCVIRi		PS	/ /	Charlottesville	DOD	Univ. Cem. Charlottesville	ROH,ACH
Vaughn, Lewis M.	Pvt.	E 2nd SCVI		KW	09/02/61	Lynchburg, VA	DOD	(Body sent home)	ROH,JR,SA2,HIC
Vaughn, Pascal D.	Sgt.	I 16th SCVI		GE	11/30/64	Franklin, TN	KIA	(CDC=John)	ROH,16R,PP
Vaughn, R. Pickens	Pvt.	A 22nd SCVI	18	ED	07/05/64	Petersburg, VA	KIA		ROH
Vaughn, R.B.	Pvt.	B 27th SCVI		CN	07/21/64	Richmond, VA		Hollywood Cem.Rchmd. V659	ROH,HC
Vaughn, Solomon	Pvt.	C Orr's Ri.		PS	12/09/61	Charleston, SC	DOD		ROH,CDC
Vaughn, T.R.	Pvt.	I 16th SCVI	21	GE	07/01/64	Kennesaw Mtn. GA	DOW		ROH,16R
Vaughn, Thomas	Pvt.	F 16th SCVI		GE	12/15/64	Nashville, TN	KIA		16R
Vaughn, Thomas W.	Pvt.	I 2nd SCVC	26	ED	06/22/64	At home	DOD		ROH,HOE
Vaughn, W.J.P.	Pvt.	A 5th SCVI		UN	/ /	Charlottesville	DOD	Univ. Cem. Charlottesville	CDC,ACH,SA3
Vaughn, William A.	Pvt.	B 13th SCVI		SG	06/26/64	Richmond, VA	DOD	Hollywood Cem.Rchmd. U393	ROH,HC,HOS
Vaughn, William H.	Pvt.	E Ham.Leg.	24	GE	07/21/61	1st Manassas, VA	KIA		ROH,JR,CDC
Vaughn, William H.	Pvt.	L 2nd SCVIRi	44	AN	11/15/62	At home	DOD		ROH
Vehann, J.L.	Pvt.	D 16th SCVI		GE	/ /	Chickamauga, GA	DOD	(1863)	16R
Vehorn, Elias	Pvt.	F 13th SCVI		SG	10/13/63	Philadelphia, PA	DOW	Nat.Cem. Philadelphia PA	ROH,FPH,P6,GDR
Vehorn, Thomas	Pvt.	F 13th SCVI		SG	/ /			(1862)	HOS
Veitch, John C.	Pvt.	H 1st SCVIG	25	BT	07/06/62	Gaines' Mill, VA	DOW		ROH,SA1,CDC,BBC
Venable, Hugh	Pvt.	K 5th SCVI	25	YK	/ /	Lynchburg, VA	DOD		YEB
Venable, Robert P.	Pvt.	B 5th SCVI	21	YK	12/09/61	Richmond, VA	DOD	Oakwood C.#94,Row C,Div A	ROH,JR,SA3,YEB
Venning, Elias	1st Lt.	E 5th SCVC		CN	10/07/63		KIA		R43
Venters, W.H.	Pvt.	E 7th SCVI	24	WG	07/15/64	Lynchburg, VA	DOD	Lynchburg CSA Cem.#6 R2	ROH,BBW,KEB
Ventis, Daniel	Pvt.	10th SCVI			09/20/63	Chickamauga, GA	KIA		JR
Verdier, W.E.	Pvt.	A Ham.Leg.		CN	/ /	Riddle's Shop VA	KIA		ROH,WLI
Vereen, James Allison	1st Sgt.	L 7th SCVI	19	HY	09/02/61	Culpepper, VA	DOD	Hollywood Cem. Rchmd./CNM	JR,CGH,KEB,CNM
Veronee, T. William	1st Lt.	A 18th SCVAB	31	CN	11/09/62	Orange C.H., VA	ACD	(RR)Bethel M.C. Charleston	ROH,JR,MAG,R44
Vick, A.B.	Pvt.	D 5th SCVI		UN	12/01/62	Liberty, VA	DOD	(JR=11/29)	JR,SA3
Vicory, George B.	Pvt.	I 12th SCVI		LR	/ /		DOD	(1862)	LAN
Vierd, Peter	Pvt.	G 11th SCVI		CO	04/03/64	Lake City, FL	DOD	(HAG=Viawd)	ROH,HAG,PP
Villepigue, C.L.	Pvt.	A 7th SCVC		KW	02/04/65	Elmira, NY	DIP	Woodlawn N.C.#1741 Elmira	FPH,P6,P65,P120
Villepigue, John B.	Brig. Gen.			KW	11/09/62	Port Hudson, LA	DOD	Quaker Cem. Camden, SC	HIC,GIG,PP
Villepontaux, Peter	Pvt.	Wash. LA	24	CN	12/01/61	Richmond, VA	DOD		ROH
Vincent, Jesse W.	Pvt.	B 14th SCVI	23	ED	/ /	Richmond, VA	DOD	(1862)	HOE,UD3
Vincent, T.J.	Cpl.	K Orr's Ri.		AN	06/14/64	Richmond, VA		Hollywood Cem.Rchmd. U392	HC
Vincent, William A.	Pvt.	E 22nd SCVI	19	LR	03/15/62	Columbia, SC	DOD		LAN
Vinson, J.C.	Pvt.	H 5th SCVI		UN	10/18/64		DOW		SA3
Vinson, James Walker	3rd Cpl.	C 2nd SCVI	21	RD	09/20/63	Chickamauga, GA	KIA		ROH,JR,SA2,H2
Vinson, Jesse	Pvt.	C Hol.Leg.		SG	/ /	Fisher's Run	MIA	(POW, never heard from)	HOS

SOUTH CAROLINA DEAD IN CSA SERVICE 1861-1865

NAME	RANK	C	REGIMENT	AGE	DS	DIED	WHERE	WHY	BURIED	SOURCES
Vocelle, A. Leonidas	Pvt.	E	25th SCVI	30	CN	06/02/64	Drury's Bluff VA	DOW	Hollywood Cem.Rchmd. U133	ROH,HC,CDC,HAG
Vocelle, Augustus	Pvt.	E	25th SCVI			03/21/65	Elmira, NY	DIP	Woodlawn N.C.#1527 Elmira	FPH,HAG,P6,P65
Voght, M.A.	Cpl.	B	1st SCVIG	20	OG	06/15/63	Richmond, VA	DOW	(Wdd @ Chancellorsville)	ROH,SA1,ANY
Von Dohlen, Nicolas	Pvt.		Bachman'sA		CN	04/13/62	Virginia	DOD	(Dd. Diascore's Building)	ROH
Von Heille, T. (F.W.?)	Pvt.	C	Orr's Ri.		PS	12/27/62	Richmond, VA		Hollywood Cem.Rchmd. S342	ROH,HC

SOUTH CAROLINA DEAD IN CSA SERVICE 1861-1865

NAME	RANK	C REGIMENT	AGE	DS	DIED	WHERE	WHY	BURIED	SOURCES
W..., A.J.	Pvt.				/ /			Spotsylvania C.H., VA	SCH
W...., C.	Pvt,	D 14th SCVI			/ /	Richmond, VA		Oakwood C.#38,Row 32,Div D	OWC
W...., H.S.	Pvt.	A 7th SCVI			11/01/62	(or S...., W.H.)		Stonewall C. Winchester VA	WIN
W.S.	Pvt.	H 7th SCVI			10/30/62			Stonewall C. Winchester VA	WIN
W_____,		A 19th SCVI		ED	/ /			Con. Cem. Marietta, GA	CCM
Waddell, George W.	Pvt.	PeeDee LA		DN	07/02/65	Gettysburg, PA	KIA		ROH,PDL
Waddell, James R.	Pvt.	E 14th SCVI		SG	/ /		KIA		HOS
Waddell, N.T.	Pvt.	D 15th SCVI		KW	/ /		DOD	Stonewall C. Winchester VA	ROH,JR,WIN,HIC
Waddle, George W.	Pvt.	E 14th SCVi		SG	/ /	Pt. Lookout, MD	DIP	(Alive in Pt.L.O. 1/27/65)	CGS,P113,HOS
Waddle, Jeff J.	Pvt.	E Hol.Leg.	23	SG	10/09/62	Warrenton, VA	DOW	(Wdd @ 2nd Man)	ROH,HOS
Waddle, Richard	Pvt.	C 5th SCVI		SG	09/22/61	Culpepper, VA	DOD	Fairview Cem. Culpepper VA	CGH,SA3
Waddle, W.B.	Cpl.	E 14th SCVI		SG	08/16/64		KIA		ROH,CGS,HOS
Wade, George H.	Pvt.	A 15th SCVI		RD	10/13/64	Strasburg, VA	KIA	(KEB=Wade, George McD.)	ROH,KEB
Wade, Hampton	Pvt.	F 7th SCVI		ED	/ /		DOD		HOE,KEB
Wade, James	Pvt.	H 2nd SCVIRi			06/29/62	Savage Stn., VA	KIA	(Rptd 7/8 issue of CDC)	ROH,JR,CDC
Wade, M.C.	Pvt.	G 16th SCVI		GE	/ /	Charleston, SC	DOD		16R
Wade, Thomas H.	Pvt.	A 15th SCVI		RD	10/12/63	At home	DOW	(Wdd @ Chickamauga)	ROH,KEB
Wade,Sr., John	Pvt.	G 16th SCVI		GE	05/29/64	Dallas, GA	KIA		ROH,16R
Wadkins, James	Pvt.	18th SCVI		UN	/ /	Camp Guerin, SC	DOD	Measles (Jan or Feb 1862)	UD2
Wadsworth, D.S.	Cpt.	F 26th SCVI	19	CD	07/11/64	Richmond, VA	DOD	Oakwood C.#3,Row T,Div F	ROH,OWC,R48
Wadsworth, James B.	Pvt.	I 18th SCVI	23	DN	07/30/64	Crater, Pbg., VA	KIA		ROH,BLM
Wadsworth, William W.	Pvt.	F 26th SCVI	18	CD	06/25/62	Petersburg, VA	DOE	Blandford Church Pbg., VA	ROH,BLC,PP
Wages, Aaron	Pvt.	I 6th SCVI		CR	08/30/62	2nd Manassas, VA	DOW		WDB,HHC,CB
Wages, Patrick	Pvt.	D 19th SCVI	20	ED	01/15/62	Charleston, SC	DOD		HOE,UD3
Waggines, Robert	Pvt.	C 18th SCVI	19	UN	/ /		DOD	(1862)	ROH
Wagner, Thomas M.	Lt. Col.	1st SCVA	38	CN	07/17/62	Ft. Moultrie, SC	ACD	(Bursting of rifled gun)	ROH,CDC
Wagner, William H.	Cpt. ADC	B.G.Ripley	34	CN	10/13/63	Charleston, SC	DOD	St.Pauls C. Charleston	ROH,MAG
Waites, Buford	Pvt.	H Hol.Leg.		NY	04/24/65	Pt. Lookout, MD	DIP	C.C. Pt. Lookout, MD	FPH,P6,ANY
Waits, Drayton	Pvt.	H Hol.Leg.		NY	04/24/65	Pt. Lookout, MD	DIP	C.C. Pt. Lookout, MD	ROH,ANY,P115
Waits, John	Pvt.	B 14th SCVI	16	ED	04/19/65	Lincoln G.H., DC	DOW	(P6=Wagers, John)	HOE,P6,UD3
Wakefield, Hezekiah S.	Pvt.	I 14th SCVI	18	AE	07/12/62	(OWC=Co.G)	DOD	Oakwood C.#76,Row N,Div B	ROH,JR,OWC,HOL
Wakefield, James M.	Pvt.	B 13th SCVI		SG	/ /	Laurel Hill, VA		(1862)	HOS
Wakefield, John Williams	Pvt.	I 14th SCVI	18	AN	07/05/63	Gettysburg, PA	DOW	(Wdd 7/3/63)	ROH,GDR,HOL,CD
Wakefield, Miles C.	Pvt.	H 1st SC Res	17	AN	/ /	Mt. Pleasant, SC	DOD		ROH
Walding, R.W.	Pvt.	F 1st SCVA			06/26/62	Charleston, SC		Magnolia Cem. Charleston	MAG,ROH,RCD
Waldrip, Andrew	Pvt.	Palmetto A			09/20/62	Charleston, SC	DOD		JR
Waldrip, John L.	Pvt.	I 13th SCVI	45	SG	05/15/62	Ashland Stn., VA	DOD	(JR=J.W.)	ROH,JR
Waldrip, Thomas	Pvt.	C 18th SCVI		SG	08/02/64	Crater, Pbg., VA	KIA		ROH,BLM,HOS,PP
Waldrop, A.B.	Pvt.	D P.S.S.		SG	01/24/63	Richmond, VA	DOD	(JR=W.B.)	ROH,JR,HOS
Waldrop, B.W.	Pvt.	E 27th SCVI			/ /	Petersburg, VA			ROH
Waldrop, C.P.	Pvt.	F 20th SCVI		NY	01/26/65	Richmond, VA		Hollywood Cem.Rchmd. W167	ROH,HC
Waldrop, J.A.	Pvt.	I Hol.Leg.	17	SG	01/30/63	Goldsboro, NC	DOD		ROH
Waldrop, R.G.	Sgt.	B 3rd SCVIBn		LS	09/08/62			Stonewall C. Winchester VA	ROH,WIN,KEB
Walker,					09/17/62	Sharpsburg, MD	DOW	Rose Hill C. Hagerstown MD	WAT,BOD
Walker,	Sgt.	2nd SCVA			/ /	NC	KIA		UD1
Walker, A.	Pvt.	F 4th SCVC		GN	/ /	At home	DOD	(1862)	HMC
Walker, A.F.	Pvt.	A 17th SCVI	40	CR	/ /	At home	DOD	(1864)	ROH,CB
Walker, A.H.	Pvt.	G 14th SCVI		AE	07/02/63	Gettysburg, PA	KIA		JR
Walker, Absolom Calhoun	Sgt.	A 4th SC Res	16	SG	02/14/65	Blackstocks, SC	DOD	New Hope Church SG Cty.	ROH,UNC
Walker, Allen S.	Pvt.	F 6th SCVI		CR	06/24/64	Richmond, VA	DOD	Hollywood Cem.Rchmd. U103	ROH,HC,HHC
Walker, Berryman W.	Pvt.	A Hol.Leg.	23	SG	07/14/63	Jackson, MS	DOW	(HOS=Benjamin)	ROH,HOS,PP

SOUTH CAROLINA DEAD IN CSA SERVICE 1861-1865

NAME	RANK	C REGIMENT	AGE	DS	DIED	WHERE	WHY	BURIED	SOURCES
Walker, Daniel W.	Pvt.	I 24th SCVI	36	ED	11/30/64	Franklin, TN	KIA	Williamson Cty., TN C.C.	ROH,WCT,CDC,PP
Walker, F.M.	Cpl.	B 3rd SCVIBn		LS	10/29/64	Pt. Lookout, MD	DIP	C.C. Pt. Lookout, MD	FPH,P5,P113,KEB
Walker, F.M.	Pvt.	A 14th SCVI		DN	09/20/62		DOW		JR
Walker, Felix	Pvt.	K P.S.S.		SG	07/11/62	Manchester, VA	DOW	Hollywood Cem. Rchmd. X78	ROH,JR,HC,HOS
Walker, Franklin	Pvt.	A 17th SCVI		CR	/ /		DOD	(1864)	CB,HHC
Walker, George E.	Cpt.	Eng. Corps	36	RD	09/16/63	Columbus, GA	DOD		ROH,CDC
Walker, George M.	Pvt.	G 1st SCVIG		ED	02/25/65	Richmond, VA	DOD		HOE,SA1
Walker, George W.	Pvt.	F 5th SCVI	21	YK	06/27/62	Gaines' Mill, VA	KIA		JR,YEB,SA3,CB
Walker, H.M.	Pvt.	K 18th SCVI			08/06/62	Charleston, SC		Magnolia Cem. Charleston	ROH,MAG
Walker, Harrison	Pvt.	F 23rd SCVI		CR	01/01/63	Kinston, NC	DOD	(HHC=KIA @ 2nd Man)	CRM,HHC
Walker, Henry P.	2nd Lt.	F 1st SCVIBn	21	CN	08/09/62	Ft. Pulaski, GA	DOW	NC Beaufort, SC #53-6432	ROH,CDC,R47,PP
Walker, Holbert Acker	Pvt.	G 22nd SCVI	24	AN	07/30/64	Crater, Pbg., VA	KIA	(BLM=R.A.)	ROH,BLM
Walker, J. Felix	Cpt.	F 18th SCVI	38	SG	09/10/62	2nd Manassas, VA	DOW	Skull Shoals Church	ROH,R47,UNC
Walker, J.C.	Pvt.	K 11th SCVI	18	CO	08/21/64	Ream's Stn., VA	KIA	(NI HAG)	ROH
Walker, J.L.	Pvt.	A 6th SCVI		CR	/ /	Centreville, VA	DOD		CRM
Walker, J.N.	Pvt.	F Ham.Leg.		GE	/ /	Brentsville, VA	DOD		ROH
Walker, J.T.	Pvt.	A 14th SCVI		DN	02/25/65	Richmond, VA		Hollywood Cem.Rchmd. W4	HC
Walker, James	Pvt.	I 6th SCVI		CR	09/01/62	Fts. Monroe, VA	DOW	Nat. Cem. Hampton, VA	ROH,PP,HHC,CB
Walker, James	Pvt.	A 20th SCVI		SR	06/18/64	Petersburg, VA	KIA		ROH,CDC
Walker, James	Pvt.	K 19th SCVI	29	ED	09/20/63	Chickamauga, GA	KIA		ROH,CDC,HOE
Walker, James C.	Pvt.	F 6th SCVI	20	CR	12/15/63	At home	DOD	(CDC=also Wdd @ 7 Pines)	ROH,CDC,HHC
Walker, James D.	Pvt.	E 24th SCVI	29	CO	12/11/64	Camp Douglas, IL	DIP	Oak Woods Cem. Chicago, IL	ROH,FPH,P5,P53
Walker, Jerome W.	Cpt.	D 6th SCVI		ED	05/31/62	7 Pines, VA	KIA		ROH,JR,HCD,WDB
Walker, John	Pvt.	3rd SC Res		PS	12/24/62	SC	DOD		ROH
Walker, John	Pvt.	H 14th SCVI		BL	/ /		DOD	(1862)	UD2
Walker, John Columbus	Pvt.	E Orr's Ri.	30	PS	05/05/64	Wilderness, VA	KIA		ROH,CDC,UD3
Walker, John E.	Pvt.	K P.S.S.		SG	06/21/64	Petersburg, VA	KIA	(Also Wdd @ 2nd M.)	ROH,HOS
Walker, John H.	Pvt.	G 14th SCVI	26	AE	07/01/63	Gettysburg, PA	KIA		ROH,GDR,CDC
Walker, John Henry	3rd Lt.	D 3rd SCVI		SG	07/02/63	Gettysburg, PA	KIA		ROH,SA2,GDR,CDC
Walker, John M.	Pvt.	C 3rd SCV			/ /	White Sulpher Ss		(Prob 3rd SCVIBn)	PP
Walker, John T.	Pvt.	K P.S.S.		SG	06/30/62	Frayser's Farm	DOW		CDC
Walker, John T.	Cpt.	A 6th SCVI		CR	01/15/61	Centreville, VA	DOD	(Pneumonia)	HHC,CB
Walker, John Thomas	Pvt.	1st SC Res		PS	06/15/62			New Mtn. Grove B.C.Pickens	PCS
Walker, L.B.	Pvt.	E 24th SCVI	19	CO	09/20/63	Chickamauga, GA	KIA		ROH,CDC
Walker, Lafayette	Pvt.	F 5th SCVI	22	YK	/ /		DOD	(1861)(NI SA3)	YEB
Walker, M.	Pvt.	A 14th SCVI	30	DN	09/20/62	Oxford, VA	KIA	(AKA Shepherdstown, VA)	ROH
Walker, Manus	Pvt.	K 5th SCVI			05/31/62	7 Pines, VA	KIA		JR
Walker, Marshall E.	Pvt.	G 1st SCVIG		ED	05/09/64	Wilderness, VA	DOW	Fredericksburg C.C. R7S12	ROH,SA1,HOE,FBG
Walker, Micajah T.	Pvt.	G 22nd SCVI	33	AN	05/15/63	Columbia, SC	DOD		ROH,PP
Walker, Milton	Pvt.	C 19th SCVI		ED	04/24/62	Enterprise, MS	ACQ	(M & O RR accident)	ROH,HOE,UD3,PP
Walker, Oliphant P.	Pvt.	D 14th SCVI	19	ED	05/03/63	Chancellorsville	KIA		ROH,JR,D14,HOE
Walker, P.E.	2nd Lt.	A 7th SCVI			07/20/63	Gettysburg, PA	DOW		CDC,KEB,GDR,R46
Walker, Richardson	Pvt.	H P.S.S.			08/30/62	2nd Manassas, VA	KIA		JR
Walker, Robert	Pvt.	H 19th SCVI		AE	12/31/62	Murfreesboro, TN	KIA		ROH,JR
Walker, Robert	Pvt.	Boyce's By	30		10/15/62	Winchester, VA	DOD		ROH
Walker, Robert J.	Pvt.	B 19th SCVI	18	ED	08/05/62	Chesterville, MS	DOD	Sweetwater B.C. Aiken, SC	ROH,HOE,EDN
Walker, Robert L.	Pvt.	B 5th SCVI		OG	06/06/62	Columbia, SC	DOD	(JR=Co.G)	JR,SA3,PP
Walker, S.L.	Pvt.	H 14th SCVI		BL	11/04/61		DOD	(Typhoid)	JR
Walker, Samuel N.	Pvt.	F 5th SCV			/ /	Columbia, SC		Elmwood Cem. Columbia, SC	MP,ROH,PP
Walker, Tillman A.	Pvt.	G 1st SCVIG		ED	05/15/64	Charlottesville	DOW	Univ. Cem. Charlottesville	ROH,SA1,HOE,ACH
Walker, W.E.	Pvt.	SCVI			/ /	Richmond, VA '62		Hollywood Cem.Rchmd. M276	HC

SOUTH CAROLINA DEAD IN CSA SERVICE 1861-1865

NAME	RANK	C REGIMENT	AGE	DS	DIED	WHERE	WHY	BURIED	SOURCES
Walker, W.G.	Pvt.	C 15th SCMil		LN	04/18/65	Pt. Lookout, MD	DIP	C.C. Pt. Lookout, MD	ROH,FPH,P6
Walker, W.H.	Pvt.	H 19th SCVI	25	AE	12/31/62		KIA		ROH
Walker, W.W.	Pvt.	A 13th SCVI		LS	07/03/62	Richmond, VA		Hollywood Cem.Rchmd. M173	ROH,HC,CDC
Walker, Washington W.	Pvt.	A 13th SCVI		LS	10/13/61	Lightwood Knot	DOD	(Measles)	JR
Walker, William	Cpl.	C 7th SCVI	33	AE	05/09/62	Richmond, VA	DOD	Oakwood C.#95,Row K,Div A	ROH,OWC,KEB
Walker, William	Pvt.	I 6th SCVI		CR	08/30/62	2nd Manassas, VA	KIA	CB	ROH,JR,WDB,HHC
Walker, William F.	Pvt.	K Hol.Leg.			04/19/65	Elmira, NY	DIP	Woodlawn N.C.#1373 Elmira	FPH,P6,P65,P12
Walker, William L.	Pvt.	F 2nd SCVI		AE	04/15/62	Williamsburg, VA	DOD		ROH,SA2,KEB,H2
Walker, William M.	Pvt.	C 17th SCVI		YK	08/31/62	Staunton, VA	DOD	Thornrose C. Staunton, VA	ROH,TOD,YEB
Wall, B.H.	Pvt.	C 5th SCVI		SG	09/14/61	Germantown, VA	DOD	(JR=Co.K)	JR,SA3
Wall, C.M.	Pvt.	F 10th SCVI		MN	/ /	Tupelo, MS	DOD		HMC
Wall, Henry W. (A.?)	Pvt.	C 26th SCVI	18	MN	02/15/65	Petersburg, VA	DOD	Blandford Church Pbg., VA	ROH,HMC,BLC,PP
Wall, J.E.	Pvt.	D 24th SCVI		BT	04/29/63	Columbia, SC	DOD		ROH,PP
Wall, James Crawford	Pvt.	F 10th SCVI	21	MN	07/28/64	Atlanta, GA	KIA	Wiggins Cem. Georgetown SC	ROH,RAS,HMC,CD
Wall, James W.	Pvt.	I 1st SC			12/07/63	Richmond, VA		Hollywood Cem.Rchmd. I111	ROH,HC
Wall, Richard J.	Pvt.	B Orr's Ri.		AE	/ /	Lynchburg, VA		Lynchburg CSA Cem.#7 R4	BBW
Wall, Robert F.	Pvt.	C 5th SCVI		SG	09/20/61	Germantown, VA	DOD	(JR=Co.K)	JR,SA3
Wall, Samuel J.	Pvt.	F 11th SCVI	27	BT	05/28/64	Fts. Monroe, VA	DOW	(Wdd&POW Swift Ck 5/9/64)	ROH,HAG,P6
Wall, W.D.	1st Cpl.	F 4th SCVC		MN	09/06/64	Pt. Lookout, MD	DOW	C.C. Pt. Lookout, MD	FPH,P6,P113,HM
Wall, W.J.B.	Pvt.		32	WG	/ /		DOD	(1864)	CTA,HOW
Wallace, Alonzo	Pvt.	F 13th SCVI		SG	04/26/62	Charleston, SC	DOD	(Pneumonia)	JR,HOS
Wallace, Andrew	Pvt.	B 12th SCVI	28	YK	/ /		DIP	(? Sgt. A.S. Rlsd 1865)	YEB
Wallace, Barney	Pvt.	H 25th SCVI	49	WG	08/21/64	Weldon RR, VA	KIA		CTA,HOW,HAG
Wallace, C.	Pvt.	G 1st SCV			09/15/63				ROH
Wallace, D.H.	Pvt.				12/06/62	Richmond, VA			ROH
Wallace, Edward	2nd Lt.	C 2nd SCVI	25	RD	04/09/63	Richmond, VA	DOD	Elmwood Cem. Columbia, SC	ROH,MP,SA2,PP,
Wallace, Frederick J.	Pvt.	D 1st SCVIH		LR	12/15/62	Lynchburg, VA	DOD		ROH,SA1,LAN
Wallace, Henry C.	Pvt.			GE	10/20/63	SC	DOD		ROH
Wallace, Hugh B.	Pvt.	A 5th SCVI		CR	12/14/62	Richmond, VA '62	DOD	Oakwood C.#130,Row L,Div A	ROH,JR,SA3,OWC
Wallace, Hugh K.	Pvt.	H 24th SCVI		CR	01/22/65	Camp Douglas, IL	DIP	Oak Woods C. Chicago, IL	FPH,P6,HHC,CB
Wallace, J.	Pvt.	H P.S.S.			/ /	Richmond, VA			ROH
Wallace, J. Beaufort	Sgt.	D 14th SCVI		ED	07/02/63	Gettysburg, PA	KIA		ROH,GDR,CSL
Wallace, J.A.	Pvt.	H 18th SCVI		YK	07/13/62	Columbia, SC	DOD	(John R. in YEB?)	JR
Wallace, J.B.S.	Sgt.	E 7th SCV			07/03/64	Richmond, VA		Hollywood Cem.Rchmd. U31	ROH,HC
Wallace, J.C.	Pvt.	F 5th SCVI		YK	06/28/62	Gaines' Mill, VA	DOW	Oakwood C.#89 Row 3 Div G	ROH,JR,SA3,OWC
Wallace, J.T.	Pvt.	D 1st SCVIH		LR	12/15/62		DOD		JRH
Wallace, James F.	Pvt.	B 5th SCVI	20	YK	11/24/62	Richmond, VA	DOD	(Pneumonia)	JR,SA3,YEB
Wallace, John J.	Pvt.	G 18th SCVI		YK	10/13/62	Frederick, MD	DOW	Rose Hill C. Hagerstown MD	ROH,FPH,BOD,YE
Wallace, John J.	Pvt.	I 21st SCVI		MN	/ /	At home	DOD	(1862)	HMC,HAG
Wallace, John R.	Pvt.	H 18th SCVI	20	YK	/ /	Charleston, SC	DOD		YEB
Wallace, John R.H.	Pvt.	B 5th SCVI	24	YK	06/27/62	Gaines` Mill, VA	KIA	(YEB=Co.H,JR=Cpl.)	JR,SA3,YEB,CB
Wallace, John T.	Pvt.	K Orr's Ri.	37	AN	12/13/62	Fredericksburg	KIA		ROH
Wallace, Joseph L.	Sgt.	A 16th SCVI		GE	11/30/64	Franklin, TN	KIA	Macgavock C. Frkln Gv# 26	ROH,16R,WCT,PP
Wallace, M.	Pvt.	H 24th SCVI		CR	/ /	Camp Duglas, IL	DIP		CDC
Wallace, Mannes	Pvt.	D 1st SCVIH		LR	09/27/63	Chattanooga, TN	KIA	(LAN= Magnus)	ROH,SA1,LAN,JR
Wallace, Oscar L.	Pvt.	F 17th SCVI	21	YK	08/30/62	2nd Manassas, VA	KIA		ROH,JR,YMD,CDC
Wallace, R.W.	Pvt.	E 1st SCVA			07/08/64	Charleston, SC		Magnolia Cem. Charleston	ROH,MAG,RCD
Wallace, R.W.	Pvt.	K 1st SCV		OG	06/20/62		DOD		ROH
Wallace, S.J.	Pvt.	I 17th SCVI		LR	09/14/62	South Mtn., MD	KIA	(LAN=E,22nd SCVI)	JR,LAN
Wallace, Samuel	Pvt.	I 12th SCVI		LR	09/17/62	Sharpsburg, MD	KIA		LAN
Wallace, William L.	Pvt.	B 16th SCVI		GE	01/12/64	Med C. Atlanta	DOD	Oakwood C. Atlanta R10#12	ROH,BGA

SOUTH CAROLINA DEAD IN CSA SERVICE 1861-1865

NAME	RANK	C REGIMENT	AGE	DS	DIED	WHERE	WHY	BURIED	SOURCES
Wallace, William Logan	Pvt.	E 3rd SCVC	42	BT	/ /	At home	DOD		ROH
Wallace, William S.	Pvt.	E 10th SCVI	19	WG	07/18/62	Corinth, MS	DOD	(W.O. in ROH)	ROH,RAS,HOW,CTA
Wallace,Jr., Joseph F.	Pvt.	B 5th SCVI		YK	11/23/62	Richmond, VA	DOD	Hollywood Cem.Rchmd. S327	ROH,HC,SA3,YEB
Waller, Henry	Pvt.	I 21st SCVI		MN	/ /	Farmville, VA			ROH
Waller, J.	Pvt.	I 17th SCVI		LR	/ /	Richmond, VA			ROH
Waller, J.G.	Pvt.	E 26th SCVI		HY	/ /	Virginia	KIA		ROH
Waller, James L.	Pvt.	Palm. LA	19	AE	10/12/62	Winchester, VA	DOD	(JR=James M. @ Richmond)	ROH,JR,SOB
Waller, R.B.	Pvt.	C 25th SCVI		WG	/ /	Fts. Monroe, VA	DOW		P6
Waller, William W.	Pvt.	F 2nd SCVI	34	AE	07/02/63	Gettysburg, PA	KIA	Magnolia Cem. Charleston	ROH,JR,GDR,SA2
Walling, Robert	Pvt.	K 1st SCVIH		OG	07/12/62	Charleston, SC	DOD	(JRH=Waller, R.W. ?)	ROH,SA1
Wallis,	Sgt.	D 14th SCVI		ED	07/02/63	Gettysburg, PA	KIA		ROH,CDC
Walsh, Henry B.	Pvt.	E 1st SCVIG		MN	07/13/62	Richmond, VA	DOD	(ROH=Welch)	ROH,JR,SA1,HMC
Walsh, James B.	Pvt.	H 23rd SCVI		MN	/ /	MS	DOD	(? 23rd in MS)	HMC
Walter, J.W.					/ /			Charlestown, VA	ROH
Walters, Benjamin L.	Pvt.	H			09/01/63	Lauderdale Ss MS			PP
Walters, J.W. (Waters?)	Pvt.	C 22nd SCVI		SG	07/20/64	Petersburg, VA	DOW	(Wdd 7/15/64)	ROH
Walters, R.G.	Pvt.	C 25th SCVI		WG	06/02/64	Fts. Monroe, VA	DOW		ROH,CDC
Walters, Reuben	Pvt.	F 21st SCVI		MO	06/28/64	Petersburg, VA	KIA	(HOM=Waters)	ROH,HAG,HOM
Walton, Caleb	Pvt.	G 7th SCVI	34	ED	09/13/62	Maryland Hts. MD	KIA		ROH,KEB,HOE,UD2
Walton, Thomas					/ /	Columbia, SC		Elmwood Cem. Columbia, SC	MP,PP
Waltz, Shadrack S.	Pvt.	A 5th SCVC	25	OG	05/28/64	Atlee's Stn., VA	KIA		ROH,CDC
Wannamaker, W.S.	Citizen	Orangeburg		OG	05/11/65	Hart's Island NY	DIP	Prob Cypress Hills N.C.	P6,P79
Wannamaker, Irvin W.	Pvt.	F 25th SCVI		OG	05/16/64	Lincoln G.H., DC	DOW		ROH,HAG,EDR,P6
Wansill, J.C.	Pvt.	8th SCVI			07/02/63	Gettysburg, PA	KIA	Magnolia Cem. Charleston	MAG,RCD
Ward, Alfred L.	Pvt.	F Orr's Ri.	22	PS	08/17/64	Petersburg, VA	DOW	Blandford Church Pbg., VA	ROH,BLC,CDC,PP
Ward, Andrew J.	Pvt.	G 27th SCVI		CN	10/02/64	Elmira, NY	DIP	Woodlawn N.C.#416 Elmira	FPH,P5,P65,HAG
Ward, Benjamin	Pvt.			WG	/ /		DOD	(1863)	CTA,HOW
Ward, C.E.	Cpl.	E 8th SCVI		DN	06/29/62	Savage Stn., VA	KIA	(JR=Malvern Hill 7/1)	ROH,JR,KEB
Ward, D.M.	Pvt.	G 13th SCVI		NY	01/16/65	Richmond,VA		Hollywood Cem.Rchmd. W630	HC,ANY
Ward, James	Pvt.	D 11th SCVI	40	BT	08/01/61	Bay Point, SC	DOD		ROH
Ward, James	Pvt.	F Orr's Ri.		PS	11/02/64	Charleston, SC		Magnolia Cem. Charleston	MAG,CDC
Ward, John N.	Pvt.	I 9th SCVIB	22	UN	09/08/61	Germantown, VA	DOD		ROH
Ward, M. Nathaniel	Pvt.	A 20th SCVI		SR	06/20/63	Charleston, SC		Magnolia Cem. Charleston	ROH,MAG,KEB,RCD
Ward, Nedom	Pvt.	E 26th SCVI		HY	/ /	Christ Church,SC		(1863)	ROH
Ward, R.H.	Sgt.	E 8th SCVI		DN	12/19/65	Camp Chase, OH	DIP		P23
Ward, Richard	Pvt.	C 2nd SCVI			03/27/63		DOD	(Typhoid)	H2,SA2
Ward, S.J. (Wood?)	Pvt.	D 25th SCVI		MN	/ /	Richmond, VA		Oakwood C.#44,Row M,Div C	ROH,OWC
Ward, W.H.	Pvt.	E 17th SCVI	38	YK	03/25/65	Petersburg, VA	KIA	(Ft. Steadman)	ROH
Ward, W.J.	Pvt.	D 9th SCVIB		WG	03/15/62	VA	DOD	(On march from Manassas)	ROH,JR
Ward, William	Pvt.	D 10th SCVI		MN	04/15/62	Mobile, AL	DOD	(Day approximate)	ROH,RAS,HMC,CDC
Ward, William B.	Pvt.	C 9th SCVIB	23	CL	08/15/61	Centreville, VA	DOD	(JR=11/16/61)	ROH,JR
Ward, William S.	Pvt.	C 16th SCVI		GE	08/18/63	At home	DOD	(16R=Charleston)	16R,PP
Warden, George	Pvt.	C Ham.Leg.		SR	/ /	Richmond, VA		Oakwoo C.#17,Row G,Div A	ROH,OWC
Wardlaw, Arthur	Pvt.	B Orr's Ri.	19	AE	05/05/64	Wilderness, VA	KIA		ROH,CDC
Wardlaw, Francis H.	2nd Sgt.	B Orr's Ri.		AE	06/30/62	Manchester, VA	DOD	Hollywood Cem.Rchmd. O63	ROH,HC,CDC
Wardlaw, James Nichols	3rd Sgt.	D 4th SCVI	27	AN	11/13/61	Culpepper, VA	DOD	Fairview Cem. Culpepper VA	ROH,CGH,SA2
Wardlaw, Lewis Alfred	Sgt.	B Orr's Ri.	20	AE	06/06/63	At home	DOW	Upper Long Cane P.C. AE	ROH,CAE,CDC
Wardlaw, Robert Henry	Pvt.	B Orr's Ri.	22	AE	04/15/65	At home	DOW	Upper Long Cane P.C. AE	ROH,CAE,CDC,UD1
Wardlaw, T. Lamar	2nd Lt.	1st SCVA		ED	07/17/62	Ft. Moultrie, SC	ACD	(Wdd 7/15, bursting gun)	ROH,CDC
Wardlaw, W.L.	Pvt.	I 6th SCVI		CR	02/08/65	Richmond, VA			ROH
Ware, B.J.	Pvt.	B 7th SCVC		HY	06/14/64	Richmond, VA	DOW	(Weir?)	JES

SOUTH CAROLINA DEAD IN CSA SERVICE 1861-1865

NAME	RANK	C	REGIMENT	AGE	DS	DIED	WHERE	WHY	BURIED	SOURCES
Ware, D.S.	Pvt.	K	6th SCVI			07/04/62	Petersburg, VA	DOD		ROH
Ware, James R. (Weir?)	Pvt.	H	12th SCVI	42	YK	/ /	Richmond, VA		Oakwood C.#109,Row H,Div B	ROH,OWC,YEB
Ware, W.A.J.	Pvt.	D	27th SCVI	36	AE	07/20/63	Bty. Wagner, SC	DOW	(Wdd 7/18/63)	ROH,HAG
Warfield, J.B.	Pvt.	H	6th SCVI		FD	06/01/62	7 Pines, VA	DOW		ROH,CDC
Waring, Paul Hamilton	Cpt.	B	9th SCVIBn		CN	07/15/63	Bty. Wagner, SC	KIA	Magnolia Cem. Charleston	ROH,MAG,CDC
Waring, Richard G.	Pvt.	A	18th SCVAB			09/11/62	Camp Holmes, SC	DOD		CDC
Warner, Jacob	Cpt.	H	Hol.Leg.	39	NY	11/06/64	Petersburg, VA	DOW	(Wdd 11/5/64)	ROH,ANY,R48
Warney, W.	Pvt.	I	1st SCVA			07/14/63	Columbia, SC	DOD		ROH
Warr, J.R.	Pvt.	B	21st SCVI		DN	/ /				ROH,HAG
Warren, Christopher	Pvt.	H	27th SCVI		CN	08/02/64	Petersburg, VA			ROH,HAG
Warren, Danniel	Pvt.	I	11th SCVI		CO	06/10/64	Drury's Bluff VA	DOW	Oakwood C.#3,Row B,Div G	ROH,OWC,HAG
Warren, Darby M.	Pvt.	E	24th SCVI	20	CO	10/09/62	James Island, SC	DOD		ROH
Warren, G.S.	Pvt.	I	11th SCVI		CO	12/11/64	Baltimore, MD	DIP	Loudon Pk.C. B-10 Balto MD	FPH,P3,P5,PP,C
Warren, J.F.						01/30/65	Columbia, SC		Elmwood Cem. Columbia, SC	MP,PP
Warren, John	Pvt.	H	27th SCVI	32	CN	06/26/64	Petersburg, VA			ROH,HAG,PP
Warren, John	Cpt.	E	24th SCVI	29	CO	07/06/64	Atlanta, GA	DOW	(Wdd 6/16/64)	ROH,R48
Warren, John D. (H.?)	Pvt.	D	Ham.Leg.		AN	11/16/63	Campbells Stn TN	KIA		ROH,GRS,CDC
Warren, Joseph O.	Pvt.	E	2nd SCVI		KW	06/28/63	Front Royal, VA	DOD		SA2,KEB,HIC,H2
Warren, S.J.	Pvt.	F	P.S.S.		LN	08/30/62	2nd Manassas, VA	KIA	(JR=Sharpsburg)	ROH,JR,CDC
Warren, T.G.	pvt.	I	11th SCVI		CO	12/06/64	Baltimore, MD	DIP		P3
Warren, T.J.	Pvt.	I	2nd SCVA			12/15/63			Bethel M.C. Charleston	MAG,RCD
Warren, Thomas	Pvt.	G	17th SCVI		BL	/ /		DOD		JR
Warren, Thomas J.	Cpt.	D	15th SCVI	39	KW	07/02/63	Gettysburg, PA	KIA	(See CWT 9-10/92)	ROH,JR,GDR,PP
Warren, Thomas J.	Asst Surg.				CN	12/12/63	Columbia, SC	DOD		ROH,PP
Warren, Wiley Lanosley	Pvt.	F	7th SCVIBn	18	DN	06/29/64	Petersburg, VA	DOD		ROH,HIC,HAG
Warren, William D.	Pvt.	D	15th SCVI		KW	09/25/62	Warrenton, VA	DOW	(Wdd @ 2nd Man)	ROH,JR,HIC,KEB
Warton, John	Pvt.	D	27th SCVI	38	LS	10/03/63		DOD		ROH
Wash, M.E.	Pvt.					/ /			(Rchmd effects list 1/63)	CDC
Washburn, A.C.	Pvt.	H	P.S.S.		SG	06/27/62	Gaines' Mill, VA	KIA		ROH,JR,CDC
Washburn, N.C.	Pvt.	I	5th SCVI		SG	05/06/64	Wilderness, VA	KIA		HOS
Wasson, J.W.	Pvt.	G	2nd SCVIRi			/ /	Richmond, VA		Oakwood C.#104,Row C,Div G	ROH,OWC
Wate, Charles H.	Pvt.	G	1st SCVIG	16	ED	07/01/63	Gettysburg, PA	KIA	(Veteran of 11 battles)	ROH,JR,GDR,SA1
Waters, Chiddleton	Pvt.	C	24th SCVI		CO	/ /		ACD	(RR accident)	ROH
Waters, Elias	Pvt.	L	9th SCVIB			/ /	Virginia	DOD	(No such unit,JR=F,P.S.S.)	ROH
Waters, H.M.	Pvt.	H	P.S.S.			05/08/64	Spotsylvania, VA	KIA		ROH
Waters, J.H. (A.or M.?)	2nd Sgt.	C	22nd SCVI		SG	06/18/64	Petersburg, VA	KIA		ROH
Waters, John	2nd Lt.	A	17th SCVI	33	CR	08/31/62	Warrenton, VA	DOW	(Wdd @ 2nd Man.)	ROH,JR,HHC,CB
Waters, Perry	Pvt.	H	13th SCVI		SG	/ /	Laurel Hill, VA			HOS
Waters, T.H.	2nd Lt.	I	13th SCVI	31	SG	06/15/62	Richmond, VA	DOD	(Typhoid)	ROH,JR,R47,HOS
Waters, Willis	Pvt.	G	22nd SCVI	21	AN	08/24/62	Rappahanock, VA	KIA		ROH
Watford, J.R.	Pvt.	A	14th SCVI	35	DN	08/02/62	Richmond, VA	DOD		ROH
Waties, T. Davis (P.?)	1st Lt.	G	1st SCVA		CN	04/15/65	Charleston, SC	DOD	(Detached duty)	SCA,R44
Watkins, Alexander F.	Pvt.	E	6th SCVI		DN	06/30/62	Frayser's Farm	KIA	(WDB= A.L.)	ROH,JLC,WDB
Watkins, B.J.	2nd Lt.	D	Orr's Ri.	30	AN	05/05/64	Wilderness, VA	KIA		ROH,R45,CDC,BO
Watkins, E.H.	1st Lt.	G	22nd SCVI	30	AN	08/29/64	Petersburg, VA		(Prob as Pvt. RES 12/63)	PP
Watkins, Edward McD.	Pvt.	A	7th SCVIBn	29	KW	07/24/64	Petersburg, VA	DOD	Blandford Church Pbg., VA	ROH,HIC,HAG,BL
Watkins, J.						/ /	Columbia, SC		Elmwood Cem. Columbia, SC	MP,PP
Watkins, J.F.	1st Cpl.	K	12th SCVI		PS	05/12/64		KIA		ROH
Watkins, J.T.	Pvt.	B	2nd SCVIRi		PS	/ /				ROH
Watkins, Judson	2nd Lt.	F	P.S.S.		LN	08/18/64		DOD		ROH,R48
Watkins, R.	Pvt.					03/16/65	Averysboro, NC	KIA		WAT

SOUTH CAROLINA DEAD IN CSA SERVICE 1861-1865

NAME	RANK	C	REGIMENT	AGE	DS	DIED	WHERE	WHY	BURIED	SOURCES
Watkins, Thomas C.	Lt. Col.		22nd SCVI		AN	09/26/62	Frederick, MD	DOW	Mt.Olivet C.#45 Frederick	ROH,FPH,R48,BOD
Watkins, W.C.	Pvt.	B	37th SCVCB	23	AN	08/07/64	Moorefield, VA	KIA		37V
Watkins, W.D.	Pvt.					02/13/65	Charleston, SC		Magnolia Cem. Charleston	MAG,RCD
Watkins, W.H.	Pvt.	B	Orr's Ri.			/ /	Manchester, VA			ROH
Watkins, William E.	Pvt.	D	19th SCVI		ED	11/11/64	Rock Island, IL	DIP	C.C.#1604 Rock Island, IL	FPH,P5
Watkins, William L.	Pvt.	F	2nd SCVIRi			04/27/62	Richmond, VA		Oakwood C.#161,Row J,Div A	ROH,OWC
Watly, S.S.	Pvt.	A	5th SCVC		OG	05/30/64		KIA		ROH
Watson, (W.W.?)	Pvt.		15th SCVI			10/28/62	Richmond, VA		Hollywood Cem.Rchmd. S117	ROH,HC
Watson, A.J. (A.S.?)	Pvt.	B	SCVI			11/08/64	Richmond, VA		Hollywood Cem.Rchmd. W535	HC
Watson, A.S.	Pvt.	K	6th SCVC		CD	12/15/64	Heyward's Place	DOW	(Near Doyle, SC)	ROH,CDC
Watson, Albert Cephus	Pvt.	F	3rd SCVI	22	LS	06/29/62	Savage Stn., VA	KIA	Smyrna Ch. Waterloo, SC	ROH,JR,SA2,LSC
Watson, Allen N.	Pvt.	K	19th SCVI		ED	09/18/64	Camp Chase, OH	DIP	C.C.#254 Columbus, OH	ROH,FPH,P5,P22
Watson, Ambrose M.	Pvt.	E	18th SCVI	24	SG	/ /	VA	DOD	(1863)	ROH,HOS
Watson, Andrew Jackson	Pvt.	F	16th SCVI		GE	09/13/63	Lauderdale, MS	DOD		16R,PP
Watson, Coleman	Pvt.	D	26th SCVI		MO	/ /	At home	DOD		HOM
Watson, Cornelius	Pvt.	C	27th SCVI		YK	03/23/65	Kittrell Spgs NC	DOD	Kittrell Springs, NC Cem.	PP,WAT,HAG,YEB
Watson, Delavere A.	Cpl.	A	13th SCVI	30	LS	05/30/62	Richmond, VA	DOD	Oakwood C.#51,Row C,Div B	ROH,JR,OWC,RHL
Watson, Fanning M.	Pvt.	D	16th SCVI		GE	04/12/64	Rock Island, IL	DIP	C.C.#841 Rock Island, IL	FPH,P5,16R
Watson, George M.	Pvt.	B	1st SCVA	22	BL	06/16/62	Secessionville	KIA	(PP=2nd SCVA)	CDC,JR,PP
Watson, Henry	Pvt.	E	26th SCVI		HY	07/30/64		KIA		ROH
Watson, J.B.	Pvt.	H	6th SCVI		FD	09/30/64	Chaffin's Farm	KIA		ROH
Watson, J.J.	Pvt.	E	17th SCVI		YK	06/23/64	Richmond, VA		Hollywood Cem.Rchmd. U440	HC
Watson, J.M.	Pvt.	H	4th SCVC		LR	03/16/64	Raleigh, NC		Oakwood C. Raleigh, NC	TOD
Watson, John Drayton	Pvt.	D	27th SCVI	17	LS	07/11/64	Richmond, VA	DOD	Hollywood Cem.Rchmnd. U73	ROH,HC,HAG
Watson, John J.	2nd Lt.	D	16th SCVI		GE	/ /	Columbia, SC	DOD	(1864)	16R
Watson, John R.	Pvt.	L	8th SCVI		MN	06/29/62	Savage Stn., VA	KIA		ROH,HMC,KEB
Watson, John R.	Pvt.	I	8th SCVI		MN	07/01/62	Malvern Hill, VA	KIA		JR,HMC,KEB
Watson, Lindsay	Pvt.	L	8th SCVI		MN	07/18/61	Culpepper, VA	DOD	(JR=DOW)	ROH,JR,HMC,KEB
Watson, M.	Pvt.	H	22nd SCVI		GE	08/06/64	Richmond, VA		Hollywood Cem.Rchmd. V39	ROH,HC
Watson, N.H.	Pvt.	I	8th SCVI		CN	07/18/61	Culpepper, VA	DOD	Fairview Cem. Culpepper VA	JR,CGH
Watson, Orasmus Allen	Cpt.	B	3rd SCVIBn	35	LS	09/20/63	Chickamauga, GA	KIA	Hopewell M.C.	ROH,JR,KEB,R45
Watson, Pierce B.	Pvt.	F	16th SCVI		GE	/ /	Dalton, GA	DOD	Stonewall Cem. Griffin, GA	16R,BGA
Watson, Quinn	Pvt.	L	8th SCVI		MN	06/29/62	Savage Stn., VA	KIA		JR,HMC,KEB
Watson, Richard	Pvt.					08/25/64	Richmond, VA			ROH
Watson, Richard Walker	Pvt.	K	P.S.S.		SG	08/29/62	2nd Manassas, VA	KIA	Con. Cem. Manassas, VA	ROH,HOS,CDC,UD3
Watson, Richardson A.	Pvt.	K	P.S.S.		SG	08/30/62	2nd Manassas, VA	KIA	(HOS= R.W.,JR=8/29)	ROH,JR,HOS,UD1
Watson, S.	Pvt.	L	8th SCVI		MN	08/22/62	Richmond, VA	DOD	(Typhoid)	JR
Watson, W.W.	Pvt.	D	15th SCVI		KW	08/14/62	South Mtn., MD	MIA		JR,HIC,CDC,KEB
Watson, William	Pvt.	F	5th SCVI	26	YK	01/11/64	Bridgeport, AL	DOW		CB ROH,SA3,YEB,P6
Watson, William A.	Pvt.	D	19th SCVI	23	ED	12/31/62	Murfreesboro, TN	KIA		ROH,HOE,UD3
Watson, William Chandler	Pvt.	B	2nd SCVI	22	GE	07/02/62	Malvern Hill, VA	DOW	Springwood Cem. GE Cty.	ROH,SA2,GEC,H2
Watson, William D.	Pvt.	H	5th SCVI	20	YK	06/04/62	Richmond, VA	DOW	Hollywood Cem.Rchmd. L153	HC,SA3,YEB
Watson, William S.	Pvt.	B	5th SCVI			06/27/62	Gaines` Mill, VA	KIA		JR,SA3
Watt, John W.	Cpl.	F	12th SCVI		FD	06/15/62		DOD	(Date approx)	HFC
Watts, B.F.	Pvt.		3rd SCVIBn		LS	/ /	Gordonsville, VA			ROH
Watts, Columbus	Pvt.	D	15th SCVI		KW	09/14/62	South Mtn., MD	MIA		JR,HIC,KEB
Watts, Francis M.	Pvt.	D	15th SCVI		KW	07/02/63	Gettysburg, PA	KIA		ROH,JR,GDR,HIC
Watts, Henry	Pvt.	G	24th SCVI		RD	04/22/64	Columbia, SC	DOD	Elmwood Cem. Columbia, SC	ROH,MP,PP
Watts, I.J.	Pvt.	C	10th SCVI		HY	12/15/64	Nashville, TN	KIA		ROH,RAS
Watts, J. Allen	Pvt.	B	7th SCVIBn	26	FD	11/20/64	Darbytown Rd. VA	DOW		ROH,HFC,HAG
Watts, J.B.	Pvt.	C	Ham.Leg.			07/07/64	Raleigh, NC		Oakwood C. Raleigh, NC	TOD

SOUTH CAROLINA DEAD IN CSA SERVICE 1861-1865

NAME	RANK	C REGIMENT	AGE	DS	DIED	WHERE	WHY	BURIED	SOURCES
Watts, John	Pvt.	F 1st SCVIG		HY	12/04/62	Virginia	DOD		SA1
Watts, Levi	Pvt.	G 10th SCVI		HY	/ /		DOD		RAS
Watts, Pickens Butler	1st Sgt.	F 27th SCVI		LS	06/24/64	Petersburg, VA	KIA	Edgefield Village Cem.	ROH,ANY,HAG,ED
Watts, R.S.	Pvt.	D 27th SCVI	37	LS	09/15/63		DOD		ROH,HAG
Watts, W. Dickens	Pvt.	F 20th SCVI		NY	/ /	Strasburg, VA	KIA		ANY
Watts, W.N.	Pvt.	C 6th SCVI		KW	11/20/63	Charlottesville		Univ. Cem. Charlottesville	ACH,HIC
Watts, Warren	Pvt.	Columbia G		CR	10/06/63		DOD		ROH,HHC
Watts, Warren D.	Pvt.	K 2nd SCVI		SR	/ /		DOD	(Tfd from Co.D)	H2,SA2,KEB
Watts, William	Pvt.	Preston's			12/17/63	Columbia, SC	DOD	Elmwood Cem. Columbia, SC	ROH,MP,PP
Watts, William	Pvt.	C 7th SCVIBn	19	RD	08/20/63	At home	DOD	(PP=9/ /63)	ROH,PP
Watts, William B.	Pvt.	C Orr's Ri.		PS	08/08/63	Frederick, MD	DOW	Rose Hill C. Hagerstown MD	ROH,FPH,P6,BOD
Wattus, Hosey	Pvt.	H P.S.S.			/ /			Spotsylvania C.H., VA	SCH
Way, A.H.	Sgt.	B 20th SCVI		OG	07/27/64	Deep Bottom, VA	KIA		ROH,CDC,KEB
Wayne, David L.	Pvt.	H Orr's Ri.		MN	05/26/62	Ashland, VA	DOD		ROH,HMC
Wayne,Jr., Francis A.	Pvt.	L 1st SCVIG			05/11/65	Hart's Island NY	DIP	Cypress Hills N.C.#2747 NY	FPH,SA1,P6,P79
Weaner, M.J.	Pvt.	A 5th SCVI		LR	06/27/62	Gaines' Mill, VA	KIA	(LAN & JR=J.W.)	JR,SA3,LAN
Weatherall, George	Sgt.	C 14th SCVI	21	LS	01/25/62	Port Royal, SC	DOW	Harmony B.C. LS Cty.	JR,LSC
Weatherford, J E.(J.P.?)	Pvt.	PeeDee LA		DN	/ /	Richmond, VA		Oakwood C.#138,Row L,Div B	ROH,OWC,PDL
Weatherford, James	Pvt.	I Hol.Leg.	32	SG	12/17/62	Kinston, NC	DOW	(Died @ Moseley's Hall)	ROH,HOS,PP
Weatherford, James	Pvt.	F 21st SCVI		MO	/ /	At home	DOD		HOM,HAG
Weatherford, James	Pvt.	H 14th SCVI	18	BL	01/01/62	Port Royal Ferry	DOW		JR,PP,UD2
Weatherford, Lemuel J.	Pvt.	C 11th SCVI		CN	06/17/65	Pt. Lookout, MD	DIP	C.C. Pt. Lookout, MD	FPH,P6,P115,HA
Weatherly, Robert T.	4th Cpl.	E 4th SCVC		MO	/ /	Pocotaligo, SC	DOD	(1863)	HOM
Weathers, J.D.E.	Sgt.	C 24th SCVI	21	CO	09/20/63	Chickamauga, GA	KIA		ROH
Weathers, Jacob W.	2nd Lt.	C 24th SCVI	21	CO	11/20/63	At home	DOW	(Wdd @ Chickamauga)	ROH,R48
Weathers, Morgan	Pvt.	B 20th SCVI		OG	/ /	Mt. Pleasant, SC	DOD		ROH,KEB
Weathers, Simpson D.	Pvt.	I 13th SCVI	20	SG	07/04/62	Richmond, VA	DOD	(Pneumonia)	ROH,JR,HOS
Weathersbee, Charles	Pvt.	A 1st SCVIG		BL	03/15/63	Richmond, VA	DOW	(Wdd @ Fredericksburg)	SA1
Weathersbee, J.B.	Pvt.	A 1st SCVIG		BL	08/11/63	Davids Island NY	DOW	Cypress Hills N.C.#774 NY	ROH,FPH,P6,GDR
Weathersbee, T.V.	Pvt.	A 1st SCVIG		BL	09/20/62	Sharpsburg, MD	DOW	(Date approximate)	JR,SA1
Weathersbee, Thomas C.	Pvt.	E 2nd SCVI		KW	12/21/62	Richmond, VA	DOD		SA2,KEB
Weaver, J.P.	Pvt.	F 27th SCVI	16	ED	05/16/64	Drury's Bluff VA	KIA		HOE,CDC,HAG,UD
Weaver, Lindsey G.	Pvt.	K 6th SCVI		GE	10/01/61	Fairfax, VA	DOD		ROH
Webb, Benjamin	Pvt.	A 1st SCVIG		BL	06/02/64	Lynchburg, VA	DOW	(Wdd W'ness 5/5/64)	ROH,SA1,CDC
Webb, Daniel C.	1st Sgt.	A 27th SCVI	30	CN	06/12/64	Petersburg, VA	DOW	(Wdd 5/6/64)	ROH,PP
Webb, Francis Marion	Pvt.	K 9th SCVIB	25	SR	08/19/61	Germantown, VA	DOD		ROH,JR
Webb, Fred Fraser	Cpl.	B 3rd SCVC	17	CO	08/24/62	At home	DOD		ROH,JR
Webb, J.S.	Pvt.	A 1st SCVIG		BL	08/15/61	Suffolk, VA	DOD		JR,SA1
Webb, James	Pvt.	D 19th SCVI		ED	07/22/64	Atlanta, GA	KIA	(E.J. Wills?)	ROH
Webb, John	Pvt.			CN	08/15/61	Columbia, SC	DOD	Elmwood Cem. Columbia, SC	ROH,MP,PP
Webb, John	Pvt.	L 21st SCVI	29	MN	07/11/63	Morris Island SC	DOW	(Wdd & POW 7/10/63)	ROH,HMC,CDC,HA
Webb, John	Pvt.	E 13th SCVI		SG	07/01/63	Gettysburg, PA	KIA		HOS
Webb, John	Pvt.	B 7th SCVI		AE	06/29/62	Savage Stn., VA	DOW		CDC,KEB,CNM
Webb, John T.	Pvt.	C P.S.S.		AN	07/08/62	Richmond, VA	DOW	(Wdd @ 7 Pines)	JR,SA2,GMJ
Webb, Lockwood States H.	Pvt.	B Orr's Ri.	22	BT	06/27/62	Gaines' Mill, VA	KIA	(1st in I, 2nd SCVI)	ROH,JR,CDC,SA2
Webb, Robert C.	Cpt.	I 7th SCVC	27	SR	05/31/64	Old Church, VA	KIA		ROH,CDC,R43,R4
Webb, Samuel	Pvt.	A 7th SCVIBn	39	KW	05/20/64	Drury's Bluff VA	DOW	(Wdd 5/16)	ROH,HIC,HAG
Webb, Samuel H.	Pvt.	L 2nd SCVIRi	32	AN	07/15/62	Richmond, VA	DOD	Oakwood C.#44,Row L,Div C	ROH,OWC
Webb, William	Pvt.	I 19th SCVI	20	AE	07/28/64	Atlanta, GA	KIA		ROH
Webb,Jr., John	Cpt.	K 2nd SCVI		CN	05/12/64	Spotsylvania, VA	KIA		ROH,SA2,KEB,R4
Webber, Benjamin	Pvt.	C 17th SCVI		YK	07/30/64	Crater Pbg., VA	KIA		CB

SOUTH CAROLINA DEAD IN CSA SERVICE 1861-1865

NAME	RANK	C	REGIMENT	AGE	DS	DIED	WHERE	WHY	BURIED	SOURCES
Webber, Casper K.	Pvt.	C	17th SCVI	21	SG	08/10/64	Petersburg, VA	KIA	Webber Fam. Cem.	TCC
Webster, J. Hartwell	Pvt.	G	8th SCVI		MO	/ /	Richmond, VA	DOW	Oakwood C.#76,Row E,Div A	ROH,UD2,OWC,KEB
Wedaman, John David	1st Sgt.	H	13th SCVI	26	NY	07/08/62	At home	DOD	Wedaman Gyvd Pomaria, SC	JR,NCC,ANY
Wederman, E. Harrison	Pvt.	H	13th SCVI	21	LS	12/15/61	Coosawatchie, SC	DOD	(ANY=Richmond)	JR,ANY
Weed, Caleb A.	Pvt.	C	20th SCVI	24	LN	07/15/62	Sullivans I., SC	DOD		ROH,KEB
Weed, J.A. (J.B.?)	Pvt.	G	14th SCVI	25	AE	07/11/63	Staunton, VA	DOD	Thornrose C. Staunton, VA	ROH,TOD
Weed, William W.	Pvt.	H	3rd SCVI	41	LN	11/20/61	Warrenton, VA	DOD	(ROH=Weed, William Allen)	ROH,JR,SA2,KEB
Weeks, Foster	Pvt.	A	5th SCVI		UN	08/10/61	Richmond, VA	DOD	Hollywood Cem.Rchmd. K60	HC,SA3
Weeks, J.D.	Cpl.	D	4th SCVC	22	CN	07/24/64	Pt. Lookout, MD	DIP	C.C. Pt. Lookout, MD	ROH,FPH,P6,P113
Weeks, John	Pvt.		6th SCVI		UN	08/10/61		DOD	(Weeks, Joel T.-5th SCVI?)	ROH
Weeks, John H.	Pvt.	A	1st SCVIH		SR	12/15/63	Bean's Stn., TN	KIA		ROH,SA1,JRH,UD3
Weeks, John J.	Pvt.	C	24th SCVI	28	CO	06/15/65	Augusta, GA	DOD	(Dorchester Enroll Book)	EJM,TEB
Weeks, S.E. (L.E.?)	Pvt.	H	11th SCVI		CO	06/22/64	Richmond, VA	DOD	Hollywood Cem.Rchmd. U189	ROH,HC,HAG
Weeks, Sampson	Pvt.	K	15th SCVI			07/02/63	Gettysburg, PA	KIA		ROH,GDR,CDC,KEB
Weeks, Sydney	Pvt.					01/09/61	Charleston, SC	ACD		BBC
Weeks, W.D.	Pvt.	D	4th SCVC		CN	04/15/65	Charlotte, NC			ROH,PP
Weeks, Zachariah P.	Sgt.	C	24th SCVI	20	CO	09/20/63	Chickamauga, GA	KIA	(Dorchester Enroll Book)	ROH,JR,CDC,TEB
Weems, J.	Pvt.	A	Orr's Ri.		PS	01/29/64	Pt. Lookout, MD	DIP	C.C. Pt. Lookout, MD	ROH,FPH,P5,P125
Weems, J.H.	Pvt.	K	1st SCVC		AE	/ /	Lynchburg, VA		Lynchburg CSA Cem.#3 R3	BBW
Weems, Thomas	Pvt.	K	1st SCVC	28	PS	/ /	Stevensburg, VA	DOD		ROH
Weicking, Frederick	Pvt.	L	1st SCVIG		CN	10/01/64	Elmira, NY	DIP	Woodlawn N.C.#415 Elmira	FPH,P5,P65,SA1
Weir, David S.	Pvt.	G	6th SCVI	27	FD	08/11/62	Petersburg, VA	DOD	Blandford Church Pbg., VA	BLC,PP
Weir, Harrison Kern	Cpt.	E	3rd SCVIBn	24	LS	07/28/64	Deep Bottom, VA	KIA	Duncan Creek P.C. LS Cty.	ROH,LSC,KEB
Weir, J.G.	Pvt.	G	6th SCVI		FD	05/31/62	7 Pines, VA	KIA		ROH,WDB,CDC
Weir, James T.	2nd Lt.	F	23rd SCVI		CR	12/13/62	Kinston, NC	KIA		ROH,CDC,R48,HHC
Weir, Joseph J.	Pvt.	G	6th SCVI		FD	05/31/64	7 Pines, VA	KIA		ROH,JR,CDC
Weir, Robert Long	2nd Lt.	E	3rd SCVI	32	LS	11/05/61	Centreville, VA	DOD	Duncan Creek P.C. LS Cty.	JR,SA2,LSC,KEB
Weir, Samuel Laurens	2nd Lt.	A	13th SCVI	21	LS	05/06/64	Wilderness, VA	KIA	On field (Mem. @ D.C.M.C.)	ROH,LSC,R47
Weir, W.A.	Pvt.	B	7th SCVI		AE	/ /	Richmond, VA		Oakwood C.#85,Row K,Div A	ROH,OWC,CDC,KEB
Weissinger, James W.	Pvt.	K	13th SCVI		LN	08/30/62	2nd Manassas, VA	KIA		ROH
Welbourn, Monroe W.	Pvt.	K	5th SCVC		UN	07/15/64	Charlottesville	DOW	(Wdd Trevillian Stn 6/11)	ROH
Welch, A.L.	Sgt.	K	10th SCVI		CN	12/20/63	Empire H.Atlanta	DOW	Oakland C. Atlanta R4#8	RAS,BGA
Welch, J.C.	Pvt.	D	1st SCVIG		DN	06/30/62	Frayser's Farm	KIA	Hollywood Cem.Rchmd. M78	HC,SA1,CDC
Welch, J.F.	Pvt.	E	9th SCVIB		KW	11/15/61	Richmond, VA	DOD	Oakwood C.#7,Row B,Div A	ROH,JR,OWC
Welch, James	Pvt.	I	24th SCVI	34	ED	02/24/65	Macon, GA	DOD	Rose Hill Cem. Macon, GA	EJM,BGA
Welch, James P.	Pvt.	C	9th SCVIB	21	CL	08/15/61	Germantown, SC	DOD		ROH,JR
Welch, John	Pvt.	L	2nd SCVIRi	49	AN	08/15/64	At home	DOD		ROH
Welch, Samuel N.	Pvt.	F	27th SCVI		ED	08/21/64	Weldon RR, VA	KIA		ROH,CDC,HAG
Welch, W.H.	Pvt.	K	23rd SCVI		SR	07/24/64	Columbia, SC	DOD	Elmwood Cem. Columbia, SC	ROH,MP,PP
Welfong, Charles F.	Pvt.	E	3rd SC Res			05/26/65	Camp Chase, OH	DIP	(POW 4/15/65 @ Lenoir, NC)	P23
Well, B.	Pvt.	I	1st SCV			/ /	Lynchburg, VA		Lynchburg CSA Cem.#1 R2	BBW
Wells, B.W.	Pvt.	C	13th SCVI		SG	10/29/62	Richmond, VA			ROH
Wells, B.W.	3rd Cpl.	F	3rd SCVI		LS	12/21/62	Charlottesville	DOW	(Wdd @ Fbg,JR=Sharpsbg)	JR,SA2
Wells, David	5th Sgt.	E	P.S.S.		SR	06/30/62	Frayser's Farm	KIA		ROH,JR,CDC
Wells, David Edward	4th Cpl.	E	2nd SCVI		KW	06/30/62	Frayser's Farm	KIA		JR,SA2,KEB,HIC
Wells, Francis A.	Pvt.	C	Ham.Leg.		CL	12/04/61	Charlottesville	DOD		JR
Wells, H.D.	1st Lt.	I	23rd SCVI	35	SR	04/01/65	Five Forks, VA	KIA		ROH,HCL
Wells, James	Pvt.	D	4th SCVC		CN	05/15/63		DOD		ROH
Wells, James	Pvt.	D	7th SCVC		RD	01/30/65	Pt. Lookout, MD	DIP	C.C. Pt. Lookout, MD	FPH,P6
Wells, James Edward	1st Sgt.	I	23rd SCVI	23	SR	09/21/62	Warrenton, VA	DOW	(Wdd @ 2nd Man)	ROH,JR,HCL,CDC
Wells, James G.	Pvt.	E	P.S.S.		SR	06/30/62	Frayser's Farm	KIA	(Co.C?)	ROH,JR,CDC

SOUTH CAROLINA DEAD IN CSA SERVICE 1861-1865

NAME	RANK	C	REGIMENT	AGE	DS	DIED	WHERE	WHY	BURIED	SOURCES
Wells, James Marion	Pvt.	F	24th SCVI	18	AN	03/04/64	Cassville, GA	DOD		ROH,HOL
Wells, Jasper W.	2nd Lt.	I	24th SCVI	35	ED	09/20/63	Chickamauga, GA	KIA	(JR=W.J.)	ROH,JR,CDC,R48
Wells, John A.	Pvt.	G	5th SCVI		YK	11/16/63	Columbia, SC	DOD		ROH,SA3,PP
Wells, John F.	Pvt.	B	1st SCVC	24	SG	/ /	Boonsboro, MD	KIA	(1863,Getttysbg Campaign?)	ROH,HOS
Wells, W.A.	Cpt.	B	3rd SCVIBn		LS	10/19/64	Cedar Creek, VA	KIA	Stonewall C. Winchester VA	WIN,KEB,R45
Welsey, F.W.	Pvt.		15th SCVAB			09/21/63	Charleston, SC		Magnolia Cem. Charleston	MAG,RCD
Welsh, A.	Lt.	F	7th SCVI			11/16/64	Richmond, VA		(7th SCVC?)	ROH
Welsh, S.	Sgt.	D	8th SCVI		CD	05/19/65	Camp Chase, OH	DIP		KEB,P23
Welsh, T.J.	Pvt.	H	2nd SCVI		LR	01/17/63		DOW		SA2,KEB,LAN
Wenley, W.C. (Winn?)	Pvt.	I	3rd SCVI			/ /	Richmond, VA		Oakwood C.#37,Row F,Div B	ROH,OWC
Wertheim, Hyman	1st Lt.	E	8th SCVI		DN	07/02/63	Gettysburg, PA	KIA		ROH,JR,GDR,KEB
Werts, A.A.	Pvt.	A	22nd SCVI		ED	/ /	Charleston, SC	DOD	(8/10/?)	ROH
Werts, Andrew S.	Sgt.	C	3rd SCVI	26	NY	05/06/64	Wilderness, VA	KIA	(SA2=on rolls 7/64)	ROH,ANY,SA2,KE
Werts, Henry Middleton	Pvt.	H	Hol.Leg.		NY	05/16/65	Pt. Lookout, MD	DIP	C.C. Pt. Lookout, MD	ROH,FPH,P6,ANY
Werts, W.H.	Cpl.	H	3rd SCVI		NY	11/08/61	Richmond, VA	DOD		ROH,JR
Werts, Wesley A.	Pvt.	H	3rd SCVI		NY	/ /	Charlottesville	DOD	(SA2=on roll 6/30/64)	ANY,KEB,SA2
Werts, William Henry B.	Pvt.	D	13th SCVI	19	NY	01/07/62	Coosawatchie, SC	DOD	Beth Eden L.C. Newberry SC	ROH,JR,NCC,ANY
Wescoat, Wm. Preston	3rd Sgt.	I	2nd SCVI		CO	05/06/64	Wilderness, VA	KIA	Fredericksburg C.C. R6S13	ROH,FBG,SA2,KE
Wessinger, Henry Mathias	3rd Lt.	I	15th SCVI	35	LN	06/26/62	Savannah, GA	DOW	(PP=11/26/61) PP	ROH,JR,TOD,H15
Wessinger, James	Pvt.	K	13th SCVI		LN	08/29/62	2nd Manassas, VA	KIA	(JR=8/30)	ROH,JR,CDC
Wessinger, John W.	Pvt.	I	15th SCVI		LN	11/14/63	Richmond, VA	DOD	Hollywood Cem.Rchmd. I184	ROH,HC,KEB,TOD
Wessinger, Martin L.	4th Sgt.	B	4th SCVIBn	18	LN	04/08/62	Summerville, SC	DOD		ROH
Wessinger, Noah	Sgt.	K	13th SCVI		LN	/ /	Virginia	KIA	(5/?/64)	ROH
Wessinger, Noah J.	2nd Cpl.	I	15th SCVI	22	LN	03/01/64	At home	DOD	(Wdd @ Gettysburg & Prld.)	ROH,H15,KEB,P1
Wessinger, Washington	Pvt.	A	13th SCVI		LS	10/19/61	Lightwood Knot S	DOD		ROH,JR
Wessinger, Wesley F.	4th Sgt.	I	15th SCVI	24	LN	07/04/63	Gettysburg, PA	DOW	(H15=POW & Rlsd)	ROH,JR,H15,KEB
West, Archibald	Pvt.	E	1st SCVIR		PS	04/01/65	New Bern, NC	DIP	Cedar Grove C. Newbern, NC	P1,P6,WAT,PP,S
West, Edward A.	Lt.		Sec/CdrCSN	37	CN	04/16/64	Charleston, SC	MUR	Magnolia Cem. Charleston	ROH,CDC
West, Elijah	Pvt.	H	1st SCVIH		SG	01/10/64	Tennessee	DOD	(DES in VA in 1863)	ROH,SA1,HOS,JR
West, Frank	Pvt.	A	1st SCResB			/ /		DOD		UD3
West, George W.	Pvt.	K	3rd SCVI	19	SG	10/13/64	Cedar Creek, VA	KIA		ROH,SA2,HOS,KE
West, Henry	Pvt.	K	3rd SCVI	19	SG	06/15/61	Manassas, VA	DOD	(JR=Centreville 12/19/62)	ROH,JR,SA2,KEB
West, Isaac T.	Pvt.	B	15th SCVI		UN	/ /	Richmond, VA	DOD	Oakwood C.#2,Row 20,Div D	ROH,JR,OWC,KEB
West, James	Pvt.	A	3rd SCVI		LS	07/02/63	Gettysburg, PA	KIA		RHL,UD3
West, James F.	Pvt.	A	17th SCVI	22	CR	02/18/64	Green Pond, SC	DOD		ROH,HHC,CB,PP
West, John Arthur	Pvt.			17	CN	09/28/64	Greenville, SC	DOD		ROH,PP
West, John D.	Cpl.	H	11th SCVI		CO	/ /	Petersburg, VA	KIA		ROH,HAG
West, Joseph	Pvt.	A	3rd SCVI	18	LS	07/05/63	Gettysburg, PA	DOD		ROH,SA2,KEB
West, Joseph (James?)	Pvt.	I	Hol.Leg.		SG	02/03/65	Elmira, NY	DIP	Woodlawn N.C.#1954 Elmira	FPH,P65,P120,H
West, Joseph A.	Pvt.	G	7th SCVIBn	32	KW	05/16/64	Drury's Bluff VA	KIA	(1st in G, 2nd SCVI)	ROH,HIC,HAG,SA
West, Lewis Marion	Pvt.	E	Ham.Leg.	39	GE	07/24/61	Culpepper, VA	DOW	Standing Springs B.C. GE	ROH,CGH,GEC,CD
West, Oliver P.	Pvt.				UN	01/15/63		DOD		ROH
West, Philoman Harley	Pvt.	A	16th SCVI	36	GE	01/27/62	Adams Run, SC	DOD	Standing Springs B.C. GE	16R,GEC,GEE
West, Richard	Pvt.	I	Hol.Leg.		SG	/ /	Elmira, NY	DIP	(?prob error POW Stoney C)	HOS
West, Richard Edward	Pvt.	F	7th SCVIBn	29	KW	05/16/64	Drury's Bluff VA	KIA		ROH,HIC,HAG
West, Robert	Pvt.	E	Orr's Ri.	30	PS	11/20/62	Winchester, VA	DOD	(On Rchmd effects list)	ROH,CDC
West, Solomon	Pvt.	E	Orr's Ri.	34	PS	07/01/62	Richmond, VA	DOD	Oakwood C.#34,Row G,Div B	ROH,OWC
West, Solomon W.	Pvt.	A	3rd SCVI	45	LS	06/24/64	Pt. Lookout, MD	DIP	C.C. Pt. Lookout, MD	ROH,FPH,P6,UD3
West, Theodore J.	Pvt.	H	1st SCVIH		SG	08/29/62	2nd Manassas, VA	KIA		ROH,SA1,HOS,R4
West, Thomas D.	Pvt.	H	11th SCVI		CO	/ /	Hardeeville, SC	DOD		ROH,HAG
West, W.D.	Pvt.	F	7th SCVI		ED	/ /	At home	DOD	(KEB=W.A.)	HOE,KEB

SOUTH CAROLINA DEAD IN CSA SERVICE 1861-1865

NAME	RANK	C REGIMENT	AGE	DS	DIED	WHERE	WHY	BURIED	SOURCES
West, W.H.	Sgt.	A 2nd SCVI		RD	06/30/62	Savage Stn., VA	KIA		ROH,SA2,CDC,KEB
West, W.J.	Pvt.	E 1st SCVA			11/20/64	James Island, SC	DOD		ROH
West, William Edwin	Pvt.	B 1st SCResB	17	GE	02/06/65	Columbia, SC	DOD		ROH,PP
West, William M.	Pvt.	G 2nd SCVI		KW	07/28/63	Gettysburg, PA	DOW		ROH,JR,GDR,SA2
West, William Mackey	Pvt.	B 15th SCVI	23	UN	09/08/63	Howard Grove, VA	DOW	Oakwood C.#3,Row 20,Div D	ROH,OWC,KEB
West, William S.	5th Sgt.	G 2nd SCVI		KW	12/28/61	Fairfax, VA	DOD	(H2=Co.D)	SA2,KEB,HIC,H2
Westberry, James P.	Pvt.	C 6th SCVI		KW	/ /	Nashville, TN	DOW		P2,HIC
Westbrook, W.H.H.	Pvt.	G 2nd SCVRi.			/ /			Spotsylvania C.H., VA	SCH
Westbrook, William Y.	Pvt.	B 6th SCVI		CR	08/11/61	Centreville, VA	DOD	(JR=Typhoid 8/13)	JR,CRM,GLS,HHC
Westbrooks, C.C.	Pvt.	H 12th SCVI	19	YK	08/29/62	2nd Manassas, VA	KIA		JR,CWC,YEB
Westbrooks, J.H. (J.A.?)	Pvt.	H 12th SCVI	21	YK	08/29/62	2nd Manassas, VA	KIA	(YEB=J.A.)	JR,YEB
Westbury, D.H.	Pvt.	H 11th SCVI		CO	02/05/63	James Island, SC	DOW	(Wdd 1/27/63)	ROH,HAG
Westbury, Joseph A.	Pvt.	B 23rd SCVI	19	CN	10/03/61	Culpepper, VA	DOD	Fairview Cem. Culpepper VA	ROH,CGH
Westenberger, J.R.	Pvt.	A 1st SCVA		CN	02/22/62	Charleston, SC		Magnolia Cem. Charleston	MAG,RCD
Westendorf, Charles	Pvt.	A 27th SCVI		CN	04/04/65	Pt. Lookout, MD	DIP	C.C. Pt. Lookout, MD	FPH,P6,P115,HAG
Westendorff, M.A.	Pvt.	D 5th SCVC	24	CN	06/01/65	Charleston, SC	DOD	Magnolia Cem. Charleston	ROH,MAG
Westerland,	Cpt.				/ /			Magnolia Cem. Charleston	MAG
Westmoreland, Bluford	Pvt.	E 14th SCVI		SG	05/06/64	Wilderness, VA	DOW		HOS
Westmoreland, E.M.	Pvt.	E 14th SCVI		SG	07/02/63	Gettysburg, PA	KIA		CGS,HOS
Westmoreland, J.A.	Pvt.	I Hol.Leg.	27	SG	04/20/63	Charleston, SC	DOD		ROH
Westmoreland, James G.	Pvt.	I Hol.Leg.		SG	12/10/64	Elmira, NY	DIP	Woodlawn N.C.#1040 Elmira	FPH,P5,P65,HOS
Westmoreland, John A.	Pvt.	E 14th SCVI		SG	05/12/64	Spotsylvania, VA	KIA		CGS,HOS
Westmoreland, Joseph W.	Cpl.	I Hol.Leg.	38	SG	03/18/63	Wilmington, NC	DOD		ROH,HOS
Westmoreland, Lewis S.	Pvt.	I Hol.Leg.		SG	/ /	Columbia, SC	DOD	Elmwood Cem. Columbia, SC	MP,HOS
Westmoreland, Lorenzo D.	Sgt.	I Hol.Leg.	33	SG	07/19/64	Camp Morton, IN	DIP	Green Lawn C. Indianapolis	FPH,P6,HOS,CV
Westmoreland, W. Thomas	Pvt.	E 14th SCVI		SG	/ /	Petersburg, VA	KIA		HOS,CGS
Weston, Francis H.	Cpt.	H 6th SCVI		FD	10/30/63	Lookout Valley	DOW	(Also Wdd @ @nd M.)	ROH,CDC,R46
Weston, Plowden C.J.	Cpt.	A 10th SCVI	44	GN	01/25/64	At home	DOD	All Saints C. Pawleys Isl.	ROH,GNG,RAS
Wetherby, S.S.	Pvt.	F 25th SCVI			10/31/62	(25th NI VA ?)		Stonewall C. Winchester VA	ROH,WIN
Wetherford, James P.	Pvt.	PeeDee LA		DN	/ /				ROH,PDL
Wetherford, Peter E.	Pvt.	PeeDee LA		DN	/ /				ROH,PDL
Wetzel, D.D.	Pvt.				03/19/62	Richmond, VA		Oakwood C.#78,Row E,Div A	ROH,OWC
Wetzel, John M.	Pvt.	Appier's C			/ /			Spotsylvania C.H., VA	SCH
Whale, Charles Dearing	Sgt.	Wash. L.A.	23	CN	02/09/65	Kings Creek, SC	KIA	Magnolia Cem. Charleston	MAG,CDC
Whaley, George W.	Pvt.	H Orr's Ri.		MN	05/12/64	Spotsylvania, VA	KIA		HMC,CDC
Whaley, John H.	Pvt.	I 21st SCVI		MN	11/17/62	At home	DOD		JR,HMC,HAG
Whaley, William M.	Pvt.	I 21st SCVI		MN	02/10/62	At home	DOD		HMC,HAG
Wharton, John	Pvt.	A Ham.Leg.			/ /				WLI
Whatley, John P.	Pvt.	G 7th SCVI		ED	09/23/62		DOD	(Typhoid)	HOE,KEB,UD2
Whatley, Shirly B.	Pvt.	B 6th SCVC		ED	12/10/64	At home	DOD		ROH,HOE,UD3
Whatley, William	Pvt.	G 1st SCVIG		ED	05/23/64	Jericho Ford, VA	KIA	(AKA Noel Stn.)	ROH,SA1,HOE,CDC
Whatley, Wilson Milledge	Pvt.	G 1st SCVIG	22	ED	09/09/62	Richmond, VA	DOW	(Wdd @ 2nd Man)	JR,SA1,HOE,EDN
Wheeler, B. Luther	Pvt.	H 3rd SCVI		LN	09/13/62	Maryland Hts. MD	KIA		ROH,JR,SA2,ANY
Wheeler, George C.	Pvt.	D 2nd SCVA	38	WG	09/18/63	Ft. Johnson, SC	DOD	(ROH= Inglis L.A.)	CTA,HOW,ROH
Wheeler, Henry	Pvt.	I 18th SCVI		DN	/ /	Chattanooga, TN	DIP		P6
Wheeler, J. Smiley	1st Lt.	B 22nd SCVI	25	SG	07/10/63	Jackson, MS	KIA		ROH,R48,HOS,PP
Wheeler, Jacob W.	Pvt.	I 15th SCVI	26	LN	06/15/65	Pt. Lookout, MD	DIP	(POW @ Fisher's Hill, VA)	ROH,P115,KEB,TOD
Wheeler, James A.	3rd Sgt.	B 22nd SCVI		SG	07/30/64	Crater, Pbg., VA	KIA		ROH,BLM
Wheeler, John C.	3rd Lt.	D 19th SCVI	25	ED	07/28/64	Atlanta, GA	KIA		ROH,HOE,ANY,UD3
Wheeler, Joseph W.	Pvt.	C 2nd SCVI		RD	03/17/63		DOD	(H2=Co.I, Dysentery)	ROH,SA2,H2
Wheeler, Peter C.	Pvt.	C 13th SCVI		OG	07/01/63	Gettysburg, PA	KIA		ROH,GDR,HOS

SOUTH CAROLINA DEAD IN CSA SERVICE 1861-1865

NAME	RANK	C REGIMENT	AGE	DS	DIED	WHERE	WHY	BURIED	SOURCES
Wheeler, Robert E.	Cpt.	H 26th SCVI		SR	07/30/64		KIA		R48
Wheeler, W.P.	Pvt.	D 2nd SCV			11/11/62			Stonewall C. Winchester VA	ROH,WIN
Whelan, Edward	Pvt.	H 27th SCVI		CN	05/15/64	Drury's Bluff VA	KIA		ROH,HAG
Whelan, Rhody	Pvt.	H 27th SCVI		CN	10/04/64	Elmira, NY	DIP	Woodlawn N.C.#598 Elmira	FPH,P5,P65,HAG
Wherry, J.F.	Pvt.	H 12th SCVI	19	YK	07/03/62		ACD		CWC,YEB
Wherry, James A.	Pvt.	H 12th SCVI	22	YK	07/22/63	Davids Island NY	DOW	Cypress Hills N.C.#669 NY	ROH,GDR,FPH,P6
Wherry, William C.	Pvt.	K 1st SCVC	20	YK	/ /	Charleston, SC	DOD		ROH,YEB
Whetsell, J.M.	Pvt.	D 5th SCVC		CO	07/15/64	VA	DOD		ROH
Whetstone, Nathan W.	Pvt.	B 1st SCVIH	53	OG	10/02/63	At home	DOD		ROH,SA1,JRH
Whetstone, William	1st Sgt.	Hart's Bty	24	BL	11/25/63	Pt. Lookout, MD	DIP	C.C. Pt. Lookout, MD	ROH,FPH,P6,P11
Whetten, C.P.	Pvt.	C Orr's Ri.		PS	06/27/62	Gaines' Mill, VA	KIA		ROH,JR,CDC
Whever, William W.	Pvt.	A 26th SCVI		HY	05/23/64	Petersburg, VA		Blandford Church Pbg., VA	BLC
Whilden, John M.	Major	23rd SCVI	23	CN	09/06/62	2nd Manassas, VA	DOW	(Prob @ Warrenton)	ROH,JR,LC,R48
Whilden, Louis A.	Cpt.	E 5th SCVC		CN	08/04/64	Virginia	KIA		ROH,R43
Whilton, W.R.	Pvt.	E Orr's Ri.		PS	06/27/62	Gaines' Mill, VA	KIA		ROH,JR
Whisenant, Barton C.	Pvt.	A Orr's Ri.	30	PS	07/03/62	Richmond, VA	DOD	Hollywood Cem.Rchmd. M81	ROH,HC,CDC
Whisenant, David	Pvt.	K 17th SCVI	18	YK	/ /				YEB
Whisenant, John Daniel	Pvt.	D 4th SCResB	18	YK	01/23/65	Florence, SC	DOD	Hopewell P.C. Cherokee Cty	TCC,YEB
Whisenant, Robert D.	4th Cpl.	F 5th SCVI		YK	06/30/62	Frayser's Farm	KIA		JR,SA3,CB
Whisnant, Rufus H.	4th Sgt.	G 5th SCVI		YK	08/01/64	Petersburg, VA	DOD		ROH,SA3
Whisonant, P.H.	Pvt.	F 17th SCVI	39	YK	08/01/64	Crater, Pbg., VA	DOW	Blandford Church Pbg., VA	BLM,BLC,PP,CB
Whitaker, B.F.	Pvt.	I 17th SCVI		LR	09/11/64	Elmira, NY	DIP	Woodlawn N.C.#251 Elmira	FPH,P5,P120,LA
Whitaker, Duncan M.	1st Lt.	F 7th SCVC	36	KW	07/04/64	Richmond, VA	DOD	Hollywood Cem.Rchmd.	ROH,HC,CDN,R43
Whitaker, John W.	Pvt.	B 8th SCVI	22	CD	07/12/62	Richmond, VA	DOD	(Typhoid)	ROH,JR,CDC,KEB
Whitaker, Napoleon	Pvt.	H 7th SCVIBn	17	ED	05/01/64	At home	DOD		ROH,HAG
Whitaker, Thomas	Sgt.	C 6th SCVI		KW	08/30/64	Ft. Harrison, VA	KIA		ROH,HIC
Whitaker, William M.	Sgt.	B 25th SCVI	27	CN	07/15/64	Petersburg, PA	KIA	2nd P.C.(Flynn's) Chlstn.	ROH,MAG,WLI,HA
White,	Pvt.	A 13th SCVI		LS	08/10/64		KIA		ROH
White, A.V.	Pvt.	K 12th SCVI	25	PS	08/26/62	Richmond, VA	DOD		ROH
White, Andrew A.	1st Sgt.	E P.S.S.		SR	06/03/64		KIA		ROH
White, Anthony	2nd Lt.	I 16th SCVI		GE	08/06/64	Atlanta, GA	KIA	Clear Springs B.C. GE Cty.	ROH,16R,GEC,R4
White, Augustus K.	2nd Cpl.	L 21st SCVI	18	MN	08/06/63	Charleston, SC	DOW	(Wdd Morris Isl. 07/10/63)	ROH,HMC,HAG
White, B.T.	Pvt.	B 9th SCVIB		SR	09/06/61	Germantown, VA	DOD	(JR=Co.D)	ROH,JR
White, C.H.	Pvt.	K 5th SCVI		SG	/ /	Virginia	DOD		HOS
White, C.J.	Pvt.	K 18th SCVI			09/01/64	Elmira, NY	DIP	Woodlawn N.C.#89 Elmira	FPH,PO65,P120
White, Calvin L.	Pvt.	SC Res		AE	08/15/64		DOD		ROH
White, David	Pvt.	C 8th SCVI		CD	07/21/61	1st Manassas, VA	KIA		JR,KEB
White, David F.	Pvt.	D 21st SCVI		CD	06/15/62	At home	DOD	(NI HAG)	ROH
White, Edward Bishop	2nd Lt.	H 18th SCVI	23	YK	08/30/62	2nd Manassas, VA	KIA	Manassas Con. Cem.	ROH,JR,YEB,R47
White, Elihu	Pvt.	E 13th SCVI		SG	07/20/63	Davids Island NY	DOW	Cypress Hills N.C.#654 NY	FPH,P1,P6,HOS
White, Evander F.	1st Sgt.	D 21st SCVI		DN	05/07/64	Pt.Walthal Jctn.	KIA		ROH,CDC,HAG
White, G.	Pvt.				/ /			Fresdericksburg C.C. R6S13	FBG
White, G. Moses	Pvt.	I 16th SCVI		GE	11/30/64	Franklin, TN	KIA	Macgavock Cem. Grave #41	16R
White, H.	Pvt.	K 5th SCVI		SG	09/17/72	Sharpsburg, VA	KIA		JR,SA3
White, H.R.	Pvt,	B P.S.S.		AN	09/17/62	Sharpsburg, MD	KIA		JR
White, H.Y.	Pvt.	I 25th SCVI		CL	08/24/64	Petersburg, VA			ROH,HAG
White, Hiram	Pvt.	A 1st SC Res	27	SG	02/17/65	Columbia, SC	DOD	Elmwood Cem. Columbia, SC	ROH,MP,PP,UD3
White, Hugh	Sgt.	D 17th SCVI		CR	/ /	Corinth, MS	KIA	(17th at Corinth?)	HHC
White, J.A.	Pvt.	G 1st SC			06/29/64	Richmond, VA			ROH
White, J.B.H.	Pvt.	G 3rd SCVI		LS	10/07/61	Richmond, VA	DOD		ROH,JR,SA2,KEB
White, J.G.	Pvt.	B 9th SCVIB		SR	09/10/61	Germantown, VA	DOD	(JR=Co.D)	ROH,JR

SOUTH CAROLINA DEAD IN CSA SERVICE 1861-1865

NAME	RANK	C REGIMENT	AGE	DS	DIED	WHERE	WHY	BURIED	SOURCES
White, J.M.	Cpl.	C 22nd SCVI		SG	/ /	Petersburg, VA	DOW	(Wdd 7/18/64)	ROH
White, J.N.	Sgt.	E 24th SCVI	19	CO	04/01/64	Georgia	DOD		ROH
White, J.S.	Pvt.	C 5th SCVI		SG	10/28/61	Culpepper, VA	DOD	Fairview Cem. Culpepper VA	JR,CGH,SA3
White, J.W.	Pvt.	G 22nd SCVI		AN	/ /	Richmond, VA		Oakwood C.#47,Row M,Div A	OWC
White, J.W.C.	Pvt.	K Ham.Leg.		AN	10/28/63	Lookout Valley	KIA	(TFD from K,4th SCVI?)	ROH,JR
White, James	Pvt.	G 14th SCVI	40	AE	05/03/63	Chancellorsville	KIA		ROH
White, James H.	Pvt.	I 21st SCVI		MN	07/14/64	Petersburg, VA	DOW		ROH,HMC,HAG
White, James H.	Pvt.	A 17th SCVI	21	CR	02/06/62	Charleston, SC	DOD	(Measles)	ROH,JR,HHC,CB
White, James H.	1st Sgt.	B 14th SCVI	25	ED	/ /	Petersburg, VA	KIA	(1864)	HOE,UD3
White, John	Pvt.	C 3rd SCV		NY	04/15/61	Richmond, VA	DOD	Oakwood C.#31,Row B,Div A	ROH,OWC
White, John	Pvt.	G 5th SCVI		YK	01/21/63	Richmond, VA			ROH,SA3
White, John	1st Sgt.	F 13th SCVI		SG	08/15/62	Virginia		(Day approx)	HOS
White, John	Pvt.	K 7th SCVI		ED	11/17/61	Richmond, VA	DOD		JR
White, John C.	Pvt.	K 6th SCVI	26	CL	10/15/62	Winchester, VA	DOD		ROH
White, John M.	Pvt.	F 5th SCRes	42		12/14/62	Adams Run, SC	DOD		PP
White, John S.	Lt.		42	CN	11/17/61	At home	DOD	(Etiwan Rangers)	ROH,CNM
White, John W.	Pvt.	G 20th SCVI		SG	07/20/63	Bty. Wagner, SC	KIA	(Trfd frm I, 13th SCVI)	ROH,HOS,CDC,KEB
White, John W.	1st Lt.	K P.S.S.		SG	/ /	Charlottesville	DOW		HOS
White, L.W.	Pvt.	E 7th SCVI		ED	07/24/61	Charlottesville	DOW		ROH,KEB
White, Lafayette	Pvt.	A 17th SCVI		CR	/ /	Charleston, SC	DOD		HHC
White, Leonard Anthony	Sgt.	E P.S.S.	23	SR	06/06/64	Richmond, VA	DOW	(Wdd Chickahominy River)	ROH
White, M.	Pvt.	E			/ /	Richmond, VA		Oakwood C.#40,Row M,Div C	ROH,OWC
White, Moses P.	Pvt.	H 4th SCVC		LR	05/28/64	Hawes Shop, VA	KIA		LAN
White, N.R.	Pvt.	H 2nd SCVIRi			/ /	Virginia		(5/?/64)	ROH
White, O.P.	Pvt.	K 5th SCVI		SG	12/29/63	Chattanooga, TN	DOW	(Wdd @ Knoxville 12/1/63)	ROH,P5,SA3,HOS
White, Oliver H.	Sgt.	I 23rd SCVI		CL	10/01/62	Warrenton, VA	DOW	(Wdd 2nd M.)(JR=Typhoid)	ROH,JR
White, Osborne	Pvt.	L Orr's Ri.		AN	07/10/62	Richmond, VA			ROH
White, P.J.	Pvt.	K 5th SCVI		SG	10/16/62	Richmond, VA	DOD	Hollywood Cem.Rchmd. F169	ROH,JR,HC,SA3
White, R.J.	Pvt.	D 7th SCV			08/29/64	Richmond, VA		Hollywood Cem.Rchmd. V25	ROH,HC
White, R.J.	Pvt.	D 7th SCVIBn		KW	08/01/64	Richmond, VA	DOW	Hollywood Cem.Rchmd. V233	ROH,HC,HAG,HIC
White, R.M.	Pvt.	A 27th SCVI			06/18/64	Petersburg, VA	DOD		ROH
White, R.M.	Pvt.	H 5th SCVI	22	UN	04/03/63	Richmond, VA	DOD	New Hope M.C. UN Cty.	ROH,JR,SA3,UNC
White, R.Q.	Pvt.	D 2nd SCV			07/28/64	Richmond, VA		Hollywood Cem.Rchmd. U482	ROH,HC
White, Robert	Pvt.	I 18th SCVI	20	DN	02/15/62	Charleston, SC	DOD		ROH
White, Robert G.	Sgt.	F 23rd SCVI		CR	08/30/62	2nd Manassas, VA	KIA		JR,HHC
White, Robert P.	Pvt.	G 18th SCVI	25	YK	11/12/64	Petersburg, VA	KIA	(By a sharpshooter)	ROH,YEB
White, Rufus B.	Pvt.	K P.S.S.	23	SG	07/25/62	Frayser's Farm	DOW	(JR=DOD)	ROH,JR,HOS
White, S.C.	2nd Lt.	E 24th SCVI	25	CO	09/20/63	Chickamauga, GA	KIA	Con. Cem. Marietta, GA	ROH,JR,R48,CCM
White, Solomon A.	Pvt.	I 16th SCVI		LS	07/26/64	Augusta, GA	DOD	Magnolia Cem. Augusta, GA	ROH,16R,BGA
White, Steele	Pvt.	D 14th SCVI	45	ED	06/27/62	Gaines' Mill, VA	KIA	(D14=Jericho Fd. 5/23/64)	JR,HOE,D14,EDN
White, T.C.	Pvt.	K 6th SCVI		CL	10/15/62		DOD		3RC
White, T.O.	Pvt.	G 7th SCVI			06/28/64	Richmond, VA		Hollywood Cem.Rchmd. U437	HC
White, Thomas A.	Pvt.	G 1st SCVIG		ED	06/29/64		DOD		SA1,HOE
White, Thomas C.	Pvt.	B Orr's Ri.	23	AE	01/06/63	Richmond, VA	DOW	(Wdd @ Fredericksburg)	ROH,JR,CDC
White, W.A.	Pvt.	B 26th SCVI	22	CD	08/02/64	Petersburg, VA	KIA		ROH
White, W.M.	Pvt.	H			10/04/64	Richmond, VA		Hollywood Cem.Rchmd. V182	ROH,HC
White, W.R.	Pvt.	D P.S.S.		SG	09/17/62	Sharpsburg, MD	DOW		ROH,CDC
White, William	Pvt.	K 24th SCVI	45	ED	09/20/63	Chickamauga, GA	KIA		ROH,JR,HOE,CDC
White, William	Cpl.	E P.S.S.		SR	07/15/62	Frayser's Farm	DOW		ROH,JR
White, William	Pvt.	K P.S.S.	27	SG	06/24/62	Winchester, VA	DOD		ROH,JR
White, William	Pvt.	E 1st SCVIG		MN	06/24/62	Richmond, VA	DOD	Hollywood Cem.Rchmd. O269	ROH,HC,SA1,HMC

SOUTH CAROLINA DEAD IN CSA SERVICE 1861-1865

NAME	RANK	C REGIMENT	AGE	DS	DIED	WHERE	WHY	BURIED	SOURCES
White, William	Cpl.	E 15th SCVI		FD	07/14/62	Frayser's Farm	DOW		JR
White, William					/ /		EXC	(Hanged for ? causes)	PP
White, William C.	Pvt.	F Hol.Leg.	49	AE	11/06/64	Petersburg, VA	KIA		ROH
White, William Capers	Major	7th SCVI	41	GN	09/17/62	Sharpsburg, MD	KIA		ROH,JR,LC,KEB
White, William F.	Pvt.	D 3rd SCV			04/10/64	Rock Island, IL	DIP	C.C.#1016 Rock Island, IL	FPH
White, William H.	Pvt.	I 16th SCVI		GE	04/03/65	Raleigh, NC	DOW	Oakwood C. Raleigh, NC	16R,TOD
White, William Henry	Cpt.	K 2nd SCVIRi	25	AE	08/30/62	2nd Manassas, VA	KIA	Upper Long Cane P.C.	ROH,JR,R45,CAE
White, William J.	Pvt.	B 18th SCVI		UN	10/05/64	Elmira, NY	DIP	Woodlawn N.C.#608 Elmira	FPH,P5,P65,P12
White, Young Moses	Pvt.	I 16th SCVI		GE	11/30/64	Franklin, TN	KIA	Macgavock C. Frkln Gv# 41	ROH,16R,WCT,PP
White,Jr., John	Pvt.	K 7th SCV	28		11/17/61	Richmond, VA	DOD		ROH
Whitehead, A.	Pvt.	E 5th SCVI		YK	01/01/63	Lynchburg, VA	DOD		SA3
Whitehead, B.T.	Pvt.	C 27th SCVI		CN	08/31/64	Richmond, VA	DOW	Hollywood Cem.Rchmd. V176	ROH,HC,HAG
Whitehead, Jacob J.	Pvt.	G 15th SCVI	17	WG	/ /		DOD	(1861)	JR,CTA,HOW,KEB
Whitehead, James W.	Pvt.	B 15th SCVI		UN	07/16/64	Richmond, VA		Hollywood Cem.Rchmd.U532	ROH,HC,KEB
Whitehead, Ransom	Pvt.	C 18th SCVI	30	UN	/ /		DOD	(1862)	ROH
Whitehead, Stephen M.	Pvt.	B 15th SCVI		UN	07/16/64	Richmond, VA		Hollywood Cem.Rchmd. W449	ROH,HC,KEB
Whitehead, William	Pvt.	C 18th SCVI	25	UN	/ /		DOD	(1862)	ROH
Whitemire, J.B.	Pvt.	G 27th SCVI		CN	09/26/64	Richmond, VA		Hollywood Cem.Rchmd. V276	ROH,HC,HAG
Whitemire, Jordan W.	Pvt.	K 12th SCVI	30	PS	07/15/64	Richmond, VA	DOD	Hollywood Cem.Rchmd. U127	ROH,HC
Whites, Abel E.	Pvt.	C 20th SCVI	24	LN	07/05/64	Richmond, VA	DOW	Oakwood C.#27,Row D,Div G	ROH,OWC,KEB
Whites, Godfrey J.	Pvt.	C 3rd SCVI		NY	04/15/62	Richmond, VA	DOD	Oakwood C.#37,Div H,Div A	ROH,SA2,OWC,KE
Whites, Joseph D.	Pvt.	C 3rd SCVI		LN	05/06/64	Wilderness, VA	KIA		ROH,SA2,ANY,KE
Whites, Solomon H.	Pvt.	C 20th SCVI	40	LN	11/14/62	Columbia, SC	DOD		ROH,KEB,PP
Whiteside, R.C. (J.C.?)	Pvt.	G 12th SCVI		YK	05/06/64	Wilderness, VA	KIA	Fredricksburg C.C. R5S12	LSS,FBG,YMD,UD
Whitesides, Austin S.	Pvt.	B 6th SCVI		YK	01/03/63	At home	DOD		YMD,GLS
Whitesides, Calvin C.	Pvt.	B 12th SCVI	21	YK	05/05/64	Wilderness, VA	KIA		YEB
Whitesides, J. Milton	1st Sgt.	G 5th SCVI	34	YK	/ /	TN	DOD	(1863)(SA3=C.M.)	SA3,YEB
Whitesides, James H.	Pvt.	H 1st SCVC		YK	02/15/63	Lynchburg, VA	DOD	Lynchburg Cem.#10 R2	ROH,YMD,BBW
Whitesides, M. Major	Pvt.	F 5th SCVI		YK	06/27/62	Gaines` Mill, VA	KIA		JR,SA3,CB
Whitesides, Newton	1st Sgt.	A 12th SCVI	43	YK	/ /	Tennessee	KIA		YEB
Whitesides, R. Newton	Pvt.	A 12th SCVI	28	YK	11/17/62	Richmond, VA	DOW	(Wdd @ Sharpsburg)	YEB
Whitesides, Samuel R.	Pvt.	B 7th SCVC	21	YK	08/16/64	Richmond, VA	DOW	(ROH=Co.D)	ROH,CDC,YEB
Whitesides, William M.	Pvt.	E 5th SCVI	23	YK	05/06/64	Wilderness, VA	KIA	(YEB=Co.H, 6th SCVI)	ROH,SA3,YEB,UD
Whitfield, Sylvester	Pvt.	K 10th SCVI		CN	12/20/63	Louisville, KY	DIP	Cave Hill C. Louisville KY	ROH,FPH,P5,RAS
Whitford, Isaac B.	Pvt.	K 1st Engrs	21	MO	08/22/64	Petersburg, VA	DOW	Blandford Church Pbg., VA	ROH,BLC,PP
Whitley, Thomas	Pvt.	B Orr's Ri.		AE	/ /		DIP	(1864)	ROH
Whitlock, C.	Pvt.	D 7th SCVC		RD	07/30/64	Richmond, VA			ROH
Whitlock, John	Pvt.	B 27th SCVI	39	UN	03/12/65	Pt. Lookout, MD	DOW	(Died on way to prison)	ROH
Whitlock, Oliver P.	Pvt.	D 7th SCVC	17	UN	07/31/64	Richmond, VA	DOD		ROH
Whitlock, Thomas	Pvt.	B 7th SCVI		AE	12/25/61		DOD		JR
Whitman, Andrew M.	Pvt.	B 14th SCVI	18	ED	/ /	Chester, PA G.H.	DIP	(1863)	HOE,UD3
Whitman, Davis	Pvt.	M P.S.S.		SG	05/31/62	7 Pines, VA	KIA		HOS
Whitman, Elijah Pierce	Pvt.	F 24th SCVI	24	AN	08/03/62	Columbia, SC	DOD	(Same name CSA Dd1912 NBY)	ROH,HOL,PP
Whitman, John B.	Pvt.	C 13th SCVI		SG	07/02/64	Pt. Lookout, MD	DIP	(POW @ Spotsylvania)	ROH,P113
Whitman, Thomas J.	Pvt.	D 13th SCVI	21	NY	07/28/64	Deep Bottom, VA	KIA	(ANY says Chancellorsville	ROH,ANY
Whitman, William J.	Pvt.	F 24th SCVI		AN	05/14/63	Jackson, MS	KIA	(JR=5/4/63)	ROH,JR,HOL,PP
Whitmire, J.F.	Pvt.	B 2nd SCVIRi		PS	/ /				ROH
Whitmire, Michael	Cpl.	K 16th SCVI		GE	/ /	Adams Run, SC	DOD		16R
Whitmire, William Bobo	Pvt.	K 5th SCVC	20	UN	06/25/64	Charlottesville	DOW	(Wdd Trevillian Stn.6/11)	ROH
Whitmore, Elijah H.	Pvt.	B 15th SCVI		SG	08/30/62	2nd Manassas, VA	KIA	(2nd JR entry=Sharpsburg)	ROH,JR,HOS,KEB
Whitmore, M.S. (M.L.?)	Pvt.	A Orr's Ri.		AN	06/02/62	Richmond, VA		Hollywood Cem.Rchmd. L61	CDC,HC

SOUTH CAROLINA DEAD IN CSA SERVICE 1861-1865

NAME	RANK	C	REGIMENT	AGE	DS	DIED	WHERE	WHY	BURIED	SOURCES
Whitmore, R.	Pvt.	F	2nd SCVA	38	OG	09/14/64		DOD		ROH
Whitmore, William M.(H.?	Pvt.	B	15th SCVI		/	/	Richmond, VA	DOD	Oakwood C.#42,Row F,Div E	ROH,JR,OWC,CDC
Whitner, B.M.	Cpt.	G	3rd SCVIBn		FD	10/19/64	Cedar Creek, VA	KIA	(Acting Bn. CO)	ROH,KEB,R45
Whitney, Henry Frost	Pvt.	B	7th SCVC	21	CN	06/13/64	Riddle's Shop VA	KIA	2nd P.C.(Flynn's) Chlstn.	ROH,MAG,CDC
Whitsell, J.M.	Pvt.	D	1st SCVC		CO	07/15/64	Richmond, VA		Hollywood Cem.Rchmd. U296	HC
Whitt, J.W.	Pvt.	G	22nd SCVI		AN	12/17/62	Richmond, VA		(On Rchmd effects list)	ROH,CDC
Whittemore, William	Pvt.	A	Ham.Leg.	25	CN	12/15/61	Manassas, VA	DOD		ROH,WLI
Whitten, Henry	Cpl.	C	18th SCVI		UN	07/30/64	Crater, Pbg., VA	KIA	(BLM= Witten)	ROH,BLM
Whitten, L.P.	Pvt.	A	Ham.Leg.		CN	01/29/64	Rock Island, IL	DIP	C.C.#300 Rock Island, IL	FPH,P5
Whitten, W.R.	Pvt.	E	Orr's Ri.	18	PS	06/27/62	Gaines' Mill, VA	KIA		ROH,CDC
Whittington, John M.	Pvt.	G	9th SCVIB		DN	09/22/61	Germantown, VA	DOD	(JR=Richmond)	ROH,JR,JLC
Whittle, E.	Pvt.	A	22nd SCVI		ED	06/15/64	Petersburg, VA	KIA		ROH
Whittle, Ira	Pvt.	B	14th SCVI	35	ED	/ /	Baltimore, MD	DOW	Magnolia Cem. Charleston	HOE,RCD,UD3
Whittle, Isalm	Pvt.	D	14th SCVI		ED	/ /	Lynchburg, VA		Lynchburg CSA Cem.#8 R1	BBW
Whittle, Joel M.	Pvt.	B	14th SCVI	18	ED	08/19/63	Chester, PA	DOW	Magnolia Cem. Charleston	ROH,FPH,P6,UD3
Whittle, John W.	Pvt.	D	19th SCVI	31	ED	/ /	Chattanooga, TN	DOD	(1863)	HOE,UD3
Whittle, M.L.	Pvt.	B	14th SCVI		ED	11/14/61	Richmond, VA	DOD		JR
Whittle, Tillman	Pvt.	F	19th SCVI		ED	06/25/62	Enterprise, MS	DOD		PP,HOE
Whittle, W.	Pvt.	E	7th SCVI		ED	05/07/62	Richmond, VA			ROH,KEB
Whittle, Wesley	Pvt.	B	14th SCVI	39	ED	06/10/62	Richmond, VA	DOD	(Typhoid)	ROH,JR,HOE,UD3
Whitton, Austin	Pvt.	G	14th SCVI	22	AE	07/07/63	Gettysburg, PA	DOW		ROH
Whitwell, J.M.	Pvt.	C	5th SCVC		CO	07/16/64	Richmond, VA			ROH
Whitworth, John R.	Pvt.	K	2nd SCVIRi	33	AN	11/16/63	At home	DOD		ROH
Whitworth, John S.	Pvt.	C	Ham.Leg.		CL	08/30/62	2nd Manassas, VA	KIA		ROH,JR,CDC
Whitworth, Ransom Hunt	Pvt.	E	4th SCVI		AN	01/09/61	Richmond, VA	DOW	Hollywood Cem.Rchmd. B171	HC,ROH,SA2
Whitworth, W.B.	Pvt.	G	7th SCVC		CN	05/30/64	Old Church, VA	DOW		ROH,CDC
Whoney, William	Pvt.	K	1st SCVC			10/20/64	Charleston, SC		Magnolia Cem. Charleston	ROH,MAG,RCD,CDC
Wicker, Daniel M.E.	Pvt.	D	13th SCVI	26	NY	08/29/62	2nd Manassas, VA	KIA	(JR=DOW 10/28)	ROH,JR,ANY
Wienholtz, L.	Pvt.	B	1st SCVA		CN	11/07/61	Port Royal, SC	KIA		ROH,CDC
Wier, Harrison K.	Cpt.	E	3rd SCVIBn	23	LS	07/28/64	Deep Bottom, VA	KIA		ROH,KEB,R45
Wigg, Samuel Patterson	3rd Cpl.	H	1st SCVIG		BT	09/17/62	Sharpsburg, MD	KIA	(Also Wdd @ 2nd M.)	ROH,JR,SA1
Wiggers, G. Aaron	Pvt.	I	15th SCVI	19	LN	06/18/62	Hardeeville, SC	DOD		H15,KEB,TOD
Wiggers, Henry J.	1st Sgt.	I	15th SCVI	31	LN	06/13/62	Hardeeville, SC	DOD		H15,KEB
Wiggers, James D.	Pvt.	I	15th SCVI		LN	08/20/63	Staunton, VA	DOD	Thornrose C. Staunton, VA	H15,KEB,TOD
Wiggins, A.F.	Pvt.	I	1st SCVIG		SG	05/05/64	Wilderness, VA	KIA	(CDC=A.W.)	ROH,SA1,CDC
Wiggins, Baker	Pvt.	H	Orr's Ri.		MN	05/11/65	Ft. McHenry, MD	DIP	Loudon Pk. C. Balto, MD	FPH,P3,P6,HMC,PP
Wiggins, C.H.	Pvt.	H	23rd SCVI		MN	06/30/62	Richmond, VA		Hollywood Cem.Rchmd. H441	HC
Wiggins, Calvin	Pvt.	H	Orr's Ri.		MN	06/27/62	Gaine's Mill, VA	KIA		HMC,CDC
Wiggins, H. (A.?)	Pvt.	F	4th SCVC		GN	05/29/64	Hawes Shop, VA	KIA		ROH,LOR,HMC
Wiggins, H.H.	Pvt.	E	23rd SCVI		MN	02/02/64	Charleston, SC	DOD		ROH
Wiggins, Ham	Pvt.	G	23rd SCVI		MO	/ /				HOM
Wiggins, J.H.	1st Sgt.	I	15th SCVI		LN	/ /		DOD	(Wiggers, H.J. in KEB?)	JR
Wiggins, J.W.	Pvt.	D	10th SCVI		MN	/ /		DOD		RAS,HMC
Wiggins, John	Pvt.	K	23rd SCVI		SR	08/14/62	Richmond, VA		Hollywood Cem.Rchmd. S89	ROH,HC
Wiggins, John B.	Pvt.	L	10th SCVI		MN	05/21/62	Macon, MS	DOD		RAS,HMC,PP
Wiggins, R.M.	Cpl.	A	21st SCVI		CN	/ /	Charleston, SC			ROH
Wiggins, Simeon	Pvt.	I	11th SCVI		CO	02/23/65	Greensboro, NC			PP,HAG
Wiggins, William S.	Pvt.	I	11th SCVI		CO	05/15/64		DIP		ROH,HAG,P65,P120
Wigginton, G.A.	Pvt.		2nd SCVIRi		AN	04/23/64	Richmond, VA			ROH
Wigginton, J.E.	Sgt.	D	18th SCVI		AN	10/15/62	Winchester, VA		Stonewall C. Winchester VA	ROH,WIN
Wigginton, Robert A.	Pvt.	A	Orr's Ri.		AN	12/24/64	Elmira, NY	DIP	Woodlawn N.C.#1095 Elmira	FPH,P5,P65,CDC

SOUTH CAROLINA DEAD IN CSA SERVICE 1861-1865

NAME	RANK	C	REGIMENT	AGE	DS	DIED	WHERE	WHY	BURIED	SOURCES
Wilbank, W.J.	Pvt.	K	12th SCVI		PS	04/19/65	Hart's Island NY	DIP	(P79 = Wilbank, S.W.)	P6,P79
Wilbern, W.W.	Pvt.	F	Orr's Ri.		PS	05/07/64	Orange C.H., VA			ROH
Wilborn, Hiram J.	Pvt.	C	18th SCVI	18	UN	09/05/62	Culpepper, VA	DOW	Fairview Cem. Culpepper VA	ROH,CGH,CDC
Wilbourn, Robert C.	3rd Sgt.	D	3rd SCVI		SG	07/26/64	Deep Bottom, VA	KIA		SA2,HOS,KEB
Wilbur, Hardy	Pvt.	F	24th SCVI		AN	/ /	Atlanta, GA	KIA		EJM,HOL
Wilburn, Isaac S.	Pvt.	C	Ham.Leg.		CL	12/03/63	Camp Morton, IN	DIP	Green Lawn C. Indianapolis	FPH
Wilburn, W.C.	Pvt.	H	1st SCVA			03/21/65	Camden, SC	DOD	(1st SC Hospital)	CDN
Wilburn, W.F.	Pvt.	H	24th SCVI		CR	/ /	Georgia	DOW		EJM,HHC
Wilburn, Ward	Pvt.	E	17th SCVI	33	YK	/ /	Petersburg, VA	KIA		YEB
Wilburn, William	4th Sgt.	C	5th SCVI			05/31/62	7 Pines, VA	KIA		JR,SA3
Wilcox, W.P.	Pvt.	F	20th SCVI		NY	/ /	Richmond, VA	DOD		ANY,KEB
Wilder, Benjamin K.	Pvt.	K	25th SCVI		WG	03/16/65	Elmira, NY	DIP	Woodlawn N.C.#1693 Elmira	FPH,P6,P65,HAG
Wilder, C.B.	Pvt.	F	6th SCVI		CR	03/20/63	Richmond, VA		Hollywood Cem.Rchmd. T14	ROH,HC
Wilder, J.B. (Wylie?)	Pvt.	H	6th SCVI		FD	/ /	Lynchburg, VA		Lynchburg CSA Cem.#5 R1	BBW
Wilder, John	Pvt.	I	27th SCVI		CN	07/15/64	Petersburg, VA	KIA		ROH,CDC
Wilder, John	Pvt.	K	25th SCVI		WG	/ /	Swift Creek, VA	KIA		CTA,HOW,HAG
Wilder, L.	Pvt.	K	25th SCVI		WG	02/02/65	Elmira, NY	DIP	Woodlawn N.C.#2575 Elmira	FPH,P6,P65,HAG
Wilder, P.E.	Pvt.	G	27th SCVI		SG	/ /	Fts. Monroe, VA	DOW		ROH
Wilder, Samuel	Pvt.	D	2nd SCVI		SR	07/01/62	Malvern Hill, VA	KIA		H2,KEB
Wilder, T.M.	Pvt.	E	18th SCVI		SG	08/30/62	2nd Manassas, VA	KIA	Con. Cem. Manassas, VA	ROH,JR,HOS,CDC
Wilder, A.J.	Pvt.	F	4th SCVC		MN	07/13/64	Richmond, VA		Hollywood Cem.Rchmd. U600	ROH,HC,HMC
Wiles, G.A.	Pvt.	F	25th SCVI	22	OG	09/01/64	Philadelphia, PA	DOW	Philadelphia Nat.Cem.C#266	ROH,FPH,P6,HAG
Wiles, Henry	Pvt.	F	25th SCVI		OG	/ /	At home	DOD	(ROH=Whiles)	ROH,HAG,EDR
Wiles, J. Martin	Pvt.	E	1st SCVC		OG	06/15/64	At home	DOD		ROH
Wiles, James	Pvt.	D	7th SCVI		ED	01/30/65	Pt. Lookout, MD	DIP		ROH
Wiles, William	Pvt.	F	25th SCVI	23	OG	05/11/65	Elmira, NY	DIP	Woodlawn N.C.#2795 Elmira	FPH,P6,P65,HAG
Wiley, J.R.	Pvt.	D	14th SCVI		ED	10/22/62	Lynchburg, VA	DOD	Lynchburg CSA Cem.#8 R3	ROH,JR,CDC
Wiley, P.C.	Pvt.	H	24th SCV			/ /	Griffin, GA		Griffin, Spaulding Cnty GA	UD2
Wiley, Robert D.	Pvt.	E	Orr's Ri.	26	PS	01/18/62	Richmond, VA	DOD		ROH,CDC
Wiley, T.A.	Pvt.	C	Orr's Ri.		PS	/ /	Winchester, VA		Stonewall C. Winchester VA	ROH,WIN
Wiley, Thomas	Pvt.	G	5th SCVC		AE	10/03/64	Charleston, SC			ROH
Wiley, Thomas A.	Pvt.	E	Orr's Ri.	28	PS	01/18/63		DOD	(Duplicate of T.A.?)	ROH
Wiley, Thomas S.	Cpl.	D	17th SCVI		CR	11/30/64	Elmira, NY	DIP	Woodlawn N.C.#994 Elmira	FPH,P5,P65,P12
Wilhelm, Henry	Sgt.	K	12th SCVI	27	PS	05/12/64	Spotsylvania, VA	KIA		ROH
Wilkerny, E.	Pvt.	D	21st SCV		CD	/ /	Richmond, VA		Oakwood C.#44,Row D,Div G	OWC
Wilkerson, Henry W.	Pvt.	H	2nd SCVI		LR	07/02/63	Gettysburg, PA	KIA	Magnolia Cem. Charleston	ROH,JR,GDR,SA2
Wilkerson, J.	Pvt.	E	1st SCVC		OG	/ /	Petersburg, VA	DOW	(Wdd 8/24/64)	ROH
Wilkerson, John S.	Pvt.	F	17th SCVI		YK	/ /	Virginia	DOD		YEB
Wilkes, Daniel M.	Pvt.	E	21st SCVI		CD	05/16/64	Drury's Bluff VA	KIA		ROH,HAG,CDC,UD
Wilkes, David	Pvt.	A	6th SCVI		CR	/ /	Germantown, VA	DOD	(1861)	HHC,CNM
Wilkes, E.M.	Pvt.	E	3rd SCVABn			08/12/62	Columbia, SC	DOD		ROH,PP
Wilkes, Eli Cornwell	Pvt.	D	1st SCVC	27	CR	09/04/63	Luray, VA	KIA	Calvary Ch. Chester, SC	ROH,UNC,HHC
Wilkes, F.	Pvt.	H	1st SCV			/ /	High Point, NC		Oakwood C. High Point, NC	WAT,TOD
Wilkes, G.W.	Pvt.	D	1st SCVC	30	CR	07/23/63	Winchester, VA	DOD	(HHC=Manchester)	ROH,HHC
Wilkes, Garland	Pvt.	E	6th SCVI		CR	/ /	Charlottesville		Univ. Cem. Charlottesville	ACH,HHC
Wilkes, J.C.	Cpl.		SCVC			06/09/63	Brandy Stn., VA	KIA	(Prob D, 1st SCVC)	ROH
Wilkes, James	Pvt.	D	25th SCVI		MN	/ /		DIP		HMC,HAG,P113
Wilkes, John	Pvt.					03/09/64	Richmond, VA		Hollywood Cem.Rchmd. D211	ROH,HC
Wilkes, John W.M.	1st Sgt.	F	8th SCVI	32	DN	12/19/64	Camp Chase, OH	DIP	C.C.#633 Columbus, OH	ROH,FPH,P23,KE
Wilkes, Samuel Marion	1st Lt.		4th SCVI	40	AN	07/21/61	1st Manassas, VA	KIA	(Rgtl Adjutant)	ROH,JR,SA2
Wilkes, Thomas W.	2nd Lt.	E	21st SCVI		CD	09/11/64	Drury's Bluff VA	DOW	(Wdd 6/16/64)	HAG,R48

375

SOUTH CAROLINA DEAD IN CSA SERVICE 1861-1865

NAME	RANK	C REGIMENT	AGE	DS	DIED	WHERE	WHY	BURIED	SOURCES
Wilkes, W. David C.	Pvt.	B 5th SCVI		CR	05/06/64	Wilderness, VA	KIA		ROH,SA3,HHC
Wilkes, Washington	Pvt.	E 1st SCV		CR	/ /	Manchester, VA	DOD		HHC
Wilkins, J.R.	Pvt.	K 2nd SCVI		CN	06/06/61	Manassas, VA	ACD	(H2=Thomas K.)	SA2,KEB,H2
Wilkins, James	Pvt.	H P.S.S.			/ /		DOD	(Prob in prior unit)	JR
Wilkins, John	Pvt.	A 14th SCVI		DN	09/20/62		DOW		JR
Wilkins, John A.	Pvt.	A 6th SCVI	23	DN	10/22/64	Ft. Harrison, VA	DOW	Hollywood Cem.Rchmd. I87	ROH,HC
Wilkins, John E.	Pvt.	B 6th SCVI		DN	08/30/64	Ft. Harrison, VA	DOW	Hollywood Cem.Rchmd. V728	HC,JLC
Wilkins, R.P.	Pvt.	F 5th SCVI		SG	01/03/62	Culpepper, VA	DOD	Fairview Cem. Culpepper VA	ROH,JR,CGH
Wilkins, Robert Y.	Pvt.	A Hol.Leg.		SG	05/21/65	Pt. Lookout, MD	DIP	C.C. Pt. Lookout, MD	FPH,P6,P115,HOS
Wilkins, T.T.	Pvt.	F 15th SCVI	29	SG	08/01/62	At home	DOD		ROH,JR,HOS,KEB
Wilkinson, Edgar F.	Pvt.	Winder's A			05/27/65	Pt. Lookout, MD	DIP	C.C. Pt. Lookout, MD	FPH,P6
Wilkinson, Gorman	Pvt.	D 26th SCVI		MO	/ /	Charleston, SC	DOD		HOM
Wilkinson, Robert S.	Pvt.	H 5th SCVI	22	YK	/ /	Manchester, VA	DOD	(JR=G,P.S.S.)	ROH,JR,SA3,YEB
Wilkinson, S.	Pvt.	B 7th SCVC		CN	/ /	Virginia	KIA	(8/?/64)	ROH,CDC
Wilkinson, William T.	Pvt.	A 5th SCVI		LR	07/15/62	Frayser's Farm	DOW	Oakwood C.#89,Row D,Div C	ROH,SA3,OWC,LAN
Wilks, F.	Pvt.	H 1st SCVA			05/09/65	High Point, NC		Oakwood C. High Point, NC	CV
Wilks, Obadiah	Pvt.	Sc Res	17	CR	01/20/64	At home	DOD		ROH
Wilks, Richard	Pvt.	H 1st SCVIG	26	CR	06/06/64	Richmond, VA	DOD	Hollywood Cem.Rchmd. U629	ROH,HC,SA1,HHC
Wilks, T.H.	Pvt.	H 10th SCVI		WG	/ /		DOD	(1863)	RAS,HOW
Wilks, William Monroe	Pvt.	E 6th SCVI	18	CR	09/01/61	Germantown, VA	DOD		ROH,HHC
Wilks, William Thomas	Cpl.	D 1st SCVC	28	CR	06/09/63	Brandy Stn., VA	KIA		ROH,JR,HHC
Will,	Pvt.	C 13th SCVI		SG	10/30/62	Richmond, VA		Hollywood Cem.Rchmd. C66	HC
Willard,	Sgt.	A 18th SCVI		UN	07/30/64	Petersburg, VA	KIA		ROH
Willard, Benjamin	Pvt.	B 15th SCVI		UN	05/03/63	Chancellorsville	KIA		ROH,JR,KEB
Willard, D.L.	Pvt.	K 1st SCV			05/26/62		DOD	(Pneumonia)	JR
Willard, J.B.	Pvt.	B 10th SCVI		HY	/ /	At home	DOD		RAS
Willard, Jesse W.	Pvt.	I 3rd SCVI		LS	05/12/62	Richmond, VA	DOD	Hollywood Cem.Rchmd. G66	ROH,JR,HC,SA2
Willard, Mabrey	Pvt.	A P.S.S.		UN	/ /		DOD		JR
Willard, O.	Pvt.	H 19th SCVI	30	AE	05/15/62	At home			ROH
Willard, President	Pvt.	A 5th SCVI		UN	08/06/61		DOD	(JR=A,P.S.S.)	JR,SA3
Willbanks, James	Pvt.	K 12th SCVI		PS	05/05/65		DOD		ROH
Willen, Henry	Pvt.	C Hol.Leg.		NY	/ /	VA	DOD	(Not on NY Mon List)	ANY
Williams,	Pvt.	B 23rd SCVI	27	BT	09/15/62	Warrenton, VA	DOW	(Wdd @ 2nd Man.)	ROH
Williams, A.C.	Pvt.	B 7th SCVI		AE	09/17/62	Sharpsburg, MD	KIA		ROH,JR
Williams, A.J.	Sgt.	I 22nd SCVI		OG	09/14/62	South Mtn., MD	KIA		ROH
Williams, Adolphus M.	Pvt.	E 18th SCVI	20	SG	/ /		KIA	(1865, DIP? see P113)	ROH,HOS
Williams, Albert			23		09/25/63	Chickamauga, GA	KIA	Laurens Cemetery, SC	PP
Williams, Alexander W.	4th Sgt.	K 6th SCVI	28	WG	02/07/64	Wilson, NC	DOD		ROH,3RC
Williams, Alexander W.	Pvt.	D 21st SCVI		CD	04/20/65	Elmira, NY	DIP	Woodlawn N.C.#1379 Elmira	ROH,FPH,P6,HAG
Williams, Barnett F.	Pvt.	G Hol.Leg.		GE	09/02/62	Richmond, VA	DOW	Oakwood C.# ,Row F,Div C	ROH,OWC,ANY
Williams, Burton	Cpl.	A 19th SCVI	24	ED	02/04/63	Shelbyville,	DOD	Willowmount C. Shelbyville	HOE,PP,UD3,TOD
Williams, Butler	Pvt.	A 22nd SCVI		ED	/ /	Columbia, SC	DOD	(01/30/?)	ROH,PP
Williams, C.D.	Pvt.	G 2nd SCVI		KW	/ /	Columbia or home	DOW	(Wdd @ Fredericksburg)	HIC,SA2,KEB
Williams, C.T.	Sgt.	G 7th SCVI		CN	01/02/62	Culpepper, VA	DOD	Fairview Cem. Culpepper VA	CGH,HOE,KEB
Williams, D.	Pvt.	H 20th SCVI		LN	/ /		DOW	(KEB=T.D.)	ROH,KEB
Williams, D. Taylor	Pvt.	Brook's A			07/02/63	Gettysburg, PA	KIA		ROH,JR,GDR,CDC
Williams, D.N.	Pvt.	F 10th SCVI		MN	/ /	Kentucky	DOD	(Not a casualty in RAS)	HMC,RAS
Williams, David A.	2nd Sgt.	H 2nd SCVI		LR	07/15/64	Richmond, VA	DOD	Oakwood C.#170,Row A,Div A	LAN,SA2,OWC,P1
Williams, E.D.	Pvt.	K 12th SCVI	27	PS	09/15/63	Charlottesville	DOD	Univ. Cem. Charlottesville	ROH,ACH
Williams, Edwin G.	Ordn. Sgt.	1st SCVIR		KW	07/18/64	Ft. Moultrie, SC	DOW	Quaker Cem. Camden, SC	SA1,PP
Williams, Edwin S.	Pvt.	K 27th SCVI	40	CN	/ /		DOW	Quaker Cem. Camden, SC	PP,HAG

SOUTH CAROLINA DEAD IN CSA SERVICE 1861-1865

NAME	RANK	C	REGIMENT	AGE	DS	DIED	WHERE	WHY	BURIED	SOURCES
Williams, Elijah	Pvt.	I	6th SCVI		CR	12/15/63	Cassville, GA	DOD		ROH,HHC,CB
Williams, Ephraim	1st Cpl.	I	3rd SCVI		LS	06/29/62	Savage Stn., VA	KIA		ROH,JR,SA2,KEB
Williams, F. Lee	Pvt.	E	12th SCVI	22	LR	09/17/62	Sharpsburg, MD	KIA	(LAN=6/27 Mechanicsville)	ROH,LAN
Williams, Fountain	Pvt.	B	1st SCVIH		OG	08/29/62	2nd Manassas, VA	KIA		ROH,SA1,CDC,JR
Williams, G.	Pvt.	B	7th SCVI		AE	/ /	MD		(10/02/?)	ROH,KEB
Williams, G.B.	Lt.		3rd SCV			/ /	Richmond, VA		Oakwood C.#74,Row F,Div B	ROH,OWC
Williams, G.M.	2nd Lt.	K	Ham.Leg.		PS	10/28/63	Lookout Valley	KIA		ROH,SA2,CDC,R4
Williams, G.W.	Pvt.	C	Ham.Leg.		CL	06/12/62	Richmond, VA	DOW		ROH,JR
Williams, G.W.	Pvt.	I	6th SCVI		CR	/ /	Richmond, VA			ROH
Williams, G.W.	Pvt.	A	10th SCVI		GN	/ /		DOD		GRG
Williams, George F.	Cpt.				DN	06/15/61	At home	DOD		ROH
Williams, George W.	Pvt.	B	2nd SCVI	19	GE	05/08/64	Spotsylvania, VA	DOW	Spotsylvania C.H., VA	ROH,SCH,SA2,H2
Williams, Graham	Pvt.	I	P.S.S.		PS	01/15/64	At home	DOD		ROH
Williams, H.	Pvt.	G	17th SCVI		BL	09/27/64	Richmond, VA		Hollywood Cem.Rchmd. V65	ROH,HC
Williams, H.	Pvt.	D	20th SCVI		OG	10/19/64	Winchester, VA		Stonewall C. Winchester VA	ROH,WIN
Williams, H.	Pvt.	A	2nd SCV			03/07/65	Richmond, VA		Hollywood Cem.Rchmd. W548	HC
Williams, H.	Pvt.		18th SCVI			/ /	Culpepper, VA		Fairview Cem. Culpepper VA	CGH
Williams, H. Pickens	Pvt.	A	19th SCVI	18	ED	/ /	Enterprise, MS	DOD		HOE
Williams, H.S.	Pvt.	G	10th SCVI		HY	12/31/62	Murfreesboro, TN	KIA	(RAS= H.T.)	ROH,JR,RAS,CDC
Williams, H.W.	Pvt.	G	P.S.S.		YK	/ /		DOD		JR
Williams, Henry	Pvt.	A	1st SCVIH		BL	03/02/63	Petersburg, VA	DOD	Blandford Church Pbg., VA	ROH,SA1,BLC,JR
Williams, Henry B.	Pvt.	H	8th SCVI		MN	07/21/61	1st Manassas, VA	KIA		JR,HMC,KEB
Williams, Henry J.	Pvt.	G	1st SCVIG	26	ED	06/27/62	Gaines' Mill, VA	KIA		JR,SA1,HOE,EDN
Williams, Henry S.B.	Pvt.	I	21st SCVI		MN	05/09/64	Pt. Walthal Jn.	DOW	Blandford Church Pbg., VA	ROH,HMC,PP,BLC
Williams, Isaac B.	Pvt.	A	19th SCVI	16	ED	/ /	At home	DOD		HOE,UD3
Williams, J.	Pvt.	A	3rd SCVI			/ /	Richmond, VA		Oakwood C.#79,Row C,Div B	ROH,OWC,KEB
Williams, J. Franklin	Pvt.	H	4th SCVI		PS	09/08/61		DOD		SA2
Williams, J.B.	Sgt.	D	Ham.Leg.		AN	11/16/63	Campbell's Stn.	KIA		GRS,CDC
Williams, J.B.	Pvt.	B	37th VAVCB		PS	03/01/64	Virginia	DOD		37V
Williams, J.B.	Pvt.		Boykins R.		KW	10/23/61	Richmond, VA	DOD	(Probably 1862)	JR
Williams, J.D.	Pvt.	D	3rd SCVI		SG	06/16/62	Sumter, SC	ACD	(RR accident)	JR,KEB
Williams, J.E.	Sgt. Major		2nd SCVCBn	20	CO	05/18/62	Grahamville, SC	DOD		CUC,SSO
Williams, J.J.	Cpl.	F	10th SCVI		MN	/ /	At home	DOD	(Not a casualty in RAS)	HMC,RAS
Williams, J.L.	Pvt.	F	17th SCVI		YK	/ /	Kinston, NC	DOD		JR,YEB
Williams, J.M.	Pvt.	G	4th SCV			/ /	Richmond, VA		Oakwood C.#1,Row K,Div F	ROH,OWC
Williams, J.T.	Pvt.	I	1st SCVA			01/14/62	Charleston, SC	DOD	Magnolia Cem. Charleston	ROH,MAG,RCD
Williams, J.W. (J.A.?)	Pvt.	B	7th SCVI			/ /	Richmond, VA		Oakwood C.#79,Row P,Div B	ROH,OWC
Williams, Jackson	Pvt.	I	22nd SCVI	30	OG	09/17/62	Sharpsburg, MD	KIA		ROH
Williams, James	Pvt.	A	1st SCVIH		BL	12/01/62	Culpepper, VA	DOD		ROH,SA1,JRH,UD
Williams, James	Pvt.	F	1st SCVIG		HY	07/28/64	Riddle's Shop VA	KIA		ROH,SA1,PDL,CD
Williams, James A.	Pvt.	B	13th SCVI		SG	02/09/64	Ft. Delaware, DE	DIP	Finn's Pt., NJ Nat. Cem.	ROH,FPH,P5,HOS
Williams, James B.	1st Sgt.	D	Ham.Leg.	23	AN	11/16/63	Knoxville, TN	KIA		ROH
Williams, James C. (O.?)	Pvt.	E	22nd SCVI		LR	08/10/64	Pt. Lookout, MD	DIP	C.C. Pt. Lookout, MD	ROH,FPH,LAN,P1
Williams, James H.	Cpl.	E	22nd SCVI		LR	12/13/62	Kinston, NC	KIA		ROH,UD2,LAN,PP
Williams, James M.	Pvt.	I	19th SCVI	20	AE	07/28/64	Atlanta, GA	KIA		ROH
Williams, James M.	Pvt.	A	Orr's Ri.		AN	05/03/63	Chancellorsville	KIA		ROH,JR,CDC
Williams, James McL.	Sgt.	K	17th SCVI	41	YK	07/30/64	Crater, Pbg., VA	KIA		ROH,BLM,RCD,YE
Williams, John	4th Sgt.	A	5th SCVI		LR	05/26/62	Yorktown, VA	ACD	(Acd shot on picket 5/14)	JR,SA3,LAN
Williams, John B.	Pvt.	L	2nd SCVIRi	18	AN	05/03/63	Blackwater, VA	DOD		ROH
Williams, John Butler	Pvt.	D	14th SCVI	26	ED	06/02/62	Richmond, VA	DOW	Hollywood Cem.Rchmd. L98	ROH,JR,HC,D14
Williams, John C.	Pvt.	I	21st SCVI	16	MN	03/25/62	Georgetown, SC	DOD		HMC,HAG,PP

SOUTH CAROLINA DEAD IN CSA SERVICE 1861-1865

NAME	RANK	C REGIMENT	AGE	DS	DIED	WHERE	WHY	BURIED	SOURCES
Williams, John Dunn	Pvt.	L 1st SCVIG	21	LS	03/09/63	At home	DOD		ROH,SA1
Williams, John Franklin	Pvt.	H 2nd SCVI		LR	10/29/61	Orange C.H., VA	DOD (Typhoid)		H2,SA2,KEB
Williams, John H.	Pvt.	H 4th SCVI		PS	07/24/61	1st Manassas, VA	DOW		SA2
Williams, John J.	Pvt.	F 11th SCVI	19	BT	12/22/64	Virginia	ACD (RR Rchmd-Danville RR)		ROH
Williams, John L.	Pvt.	A 2nd SCVI	19	RD	07/22/61	Culpepper, VA	DOD	Fairview Cem. Culpepper VA	ROH,CGH,KEB,H2
Williams, John N.	Pvt.	G 2nd SCVI		KW	07/19/64	Cold Harbor, VA	DOW (Wdd 6/1/64)		SA2,KEB,HIC,H2
Williams, John Randolph	Sgt.	F 23rd SCVI	31	CR	05/01/65	Petersburg, VA	DOW (Wdd 3/25/ @ Ft. Steadman)		ROH,HHC,P6
Williams, John S.	Pvt.	K 24th SCVI		ED	09/09/64	Atlanta, GA	DOW	Con. Cem. Milner, GA	HOE,CKB,BGA
Williams, Joseph	Pvt.	B 24th SCVI		MO	01/04/64	Atlanta, GA	DOD (PP= Macon, GA 6/1/64)		ROH,HOM,PP
Williams, Joseph	Pvt.	A 19th SCVI	30	ED	09/20/63	Chickamauga, GA	KIA	Con. Cem. Marietta, GA	ROH,JR,UD3,CCM
Williams, Joseph B.	Pvt.	C 1st SCVIH		BL	08/18/62		DOD		ROH,SA1,JRH
Williams, Joseph M.	Pvt.	B 1st SCVIH		OG	11/16/63	Campbell Stn. TN	KIA (JRH=Wdd & POW, Escpd DOW)		ROH,SA1,JRH
Williams, Joseph N.	Pvt.	G 7th SCVIBn	40	KW	05/31/64	Drury's Bluff VA	DOW (Wdd 5/16)		ROH,HIC,HAG
Williams, Joshua	Pvt.	E 12th SCVI	24	LR	10/23/62	Liberty, VA	DOD		ROH,LAN
Williams, Kendrick	Pvt.	Palm. LA		SR	06/06/64	Lynchburg, VA	DOW	Lynchburg CSA Cem.#10 R1	BBW,SOB
Williams, Lewis C.	Pvt.	G 1st SCVIG		ED	07/27/62	Frayser's Farm	DOW	Oakwood C.#30, Row S, Div C	ROH,SA1,HOE,OWC
Williams, M.J.	2nd Sgt.	E 12th SCVI	30	LR	07/18/62	Richmond, VA	DOD	Hollywood Cem.Rchmd. H228	ROH,HC,LAN
Williams, Major	Pvt.	F 1st SCVIG		HY	06/27/62	Gaines' Mill, VA	KIA		JR,SA1
Williams, Martial W.	Pvt.	I 19th SCVI	20	AE	01/28/62	Charleston, SC	DOD		ROH
Williams, N.	Pvt.	K 6th SCVI	37	MO	/ /		MIA		ROH
Williams, Newton J.D.	Pvt.	D 3rd SCVI		SG	06/15/61	Sumter, SC	ACD (Kd on top/RR Car @ Brdg)		JR,SA2,KEB
Williams, Ora	Pvt.	G 7th SCVI		ED	/ /				UD2
Williams, Pierce Butler	2nd Lt.	K 2nd SCVC	25	GE	08/01/63	Brandy Stn., VA	DOW		ROH,CDC,R43
Williams, R.A.	Pvt.	H 8th SCVI		MN	02/23/62	Richmond, VA	DOD (Typhoid)		JR
Williams, R.H.	Pvt.	F 3rd SCVC		BT	04/06/65	Ft. Delaware, DE	DIP	Finn's Pt., NJ Nat. Cem.	ROH,FPH,P6,P45
Williams, R.L.	Pvt.	H 8th SCVI		MN	07/21/61	Charlottesville	DOW	Univ. Cem. Charlottesville	HMC,KEB,ACH
Williams, Reuben R.	Pvt.	H 1st SCVIG		BT	11/26/64	Screven Cty., GA	KIA (Wdd & disabled 12/13/62)		ROH,SA1
Williams, S.	Pvt.	I 22nd SCVI		OG	01/25/65	Richmond, VA		Hollywood Cem.Rchmd. W236	HC
Williams, S.B.	Pvt.	McBeth LA			/ /			Stonewall C. Winchester VA	WIN
Williams, Samuel	Pvt.	C 1st SC Res		ED	03/05/65	Columbia, SC	DOD		ROH,PP
Williams, Samuel	Pvt.	A 26th SCVI	18	HY	04/15/63	Charleston, SC	DOD		ROH
Williams, Samuel	Pvt.	I 10th SCVI		MN	/ /	GA	DOD		RAS,HMC
Williams, T.A.	Pvt.	B 7th SCVI		AE	03/22/63	Richmond, VA		Oakwood C.#198, Row N, Div A	ROH,OWC
Williams, T.C.	Pvt.	I Hol.Leg.	18	SG	01/15/63	Goldsboro, NC	DOD (NI HOS)		ROH
Williams, T.J.	Pvt.	H 20th SCVI		LN	07/28/64	New Market Hts.	KIA (Left leg broken & MIA)		ROH,CDC,KEB
Williams, T.J.	Pvt.	B 2nd SCV			/ /	Richmond, VA		Oakwood C.#62, Row R, Div B	ROH,OWC
Williams, Theodore F.	3rd Sgt.	G 1st SCVIG	30	ED	09/29/62	Warrenton, VA	DOW (Wdd 8/29 @ 2nd Man.)		ROH,JR,SA1,UD3
Williams, Thomas	Pvt.	H 8th SCVI		MN	07/21/61	1st Manassas, VA	KIA		HMC,KEB
Williams, Thomas Elmore	Cpl.	H 2nd SCVI	21	LR	03/21/62	Orange C.H., VA	DOD (Musician)		ROH,SA2,LAN,KEB
Williams, Thomas H.	Pvt.	G 1st SCVIG		ED	08/29/62	2nd Manassas, VA	DOW		ROH,SA1,CDC
Williams, Thomas H.	Pvt.	A 19th SCVI	45	ED	/ /	Enterprise, MS	DOD		HOE,UD3
Williams, Thomas H.	Pvt.	G 7th SCVI	20	ED	08/30/62	2nd Manassas, VA	DOW (Wd 8/29, 1 of 5 Bros.CSA)		EDN,KEB,HOE,UD2
Williams, Thomas R.	Pvt.	B 6th SCVC		ED	11/20/63	Petersburg, VA	DOW (Wdd 11/17/63)		ROH,HOE,UD3
Williams, Uriah Asa M.	Pvt.	H 2nd SCVI	19	LR	05/10/64	Spotsylvania, VA	KIA	Spotsylvania C.H., VA	ROH,SCH,SA2,LAN
Williams, V.B.	2nd Lt.	F 2nd SCVC		GE	09/18/62		DOD (On Rchmd effects list)		R43,CDC
Williams, W.	Pvt.	M 7th SCVI		ED	10/01/64	Elmira, NY	DIP	Woodlawn N.C.#409 Elmira	FPH
Williams, W. Aaron	Cpl.	E 12th SCVI	24	LR	05/12/64	Spotsylvania, VA	KIA		ROH,LAN
Williams, W.C.	Pvt.	D 1st SCVIH		OG	02/06/62	At home	DOD		SA1
Williams, W.H.	Pvt.	C 18th SCVI	36	UN	11/02/62	Winchester, VA	DOD	Stonewall C. Winchester VA	ROH,WIN,UNC
Williams, W.M.	Pvt.	B 3rd SCVI			/ /			Con. Cem. Marietta, GA	CCM,UD2
Williams, W.W.	Pvt.	H 4th SCVC		LR	06/11/64	Trevillian Stn.	KIA		ROH,LAN

SOUTH CAROLINA DEAD IN CSA SERVICE 1861-1865

NAME	RANK	C REGIMENT	AGE	DS	DIED	WHERE	WHY	BURIED	SOURCES
Williams, W.W.	Pvt.	C 1st SCVIH		BL	05/06/64	Wilderness, VA	KIA		SA1
Williams, W.W.	Pvt.	F 1st SCVIH		GE	05/07/64	Virginia		(Dup of same in Co. C?)	SA1
Williams, W.W.	Pvt.	I 17th SCVI		LR	08/30/62	2nd Manassas, VA	DOW	(JR=DOD @ Wilmington)	JR,LAN
Williams, Wallace T.	Pvt.	H 1st SCVIG		BT	06/09/64	Ft. Delaware, DE	DOW	Finn's Pt., NJ Nat. Cem.	ROH,FPH,P5,SA1
Williams, Washington	Pvt.	A 7th SCVI		ED	12/13/62	Fredericksburg	KIA		ROH,JR,KEB
Williams, Washington A.	Cpt.	F 3rd SCVI	23	LS	09/20/63	Chickamauga, GA	KIA	(Acting Major) UD3	ROH,JR,SA2,RHL
Williams, William B.	Sgt.	A 26th SCVI	31	HY	07/30/64	Crater, Pbg., VA	KIA		ROH,BLM
Williams, William S.	Pvt.	A 1st SCVIG	19	BL	11/01/63	At home	DOD		ROH,SA1
Williams, Wilson B.	2nd Lt.	K Hol.Leg.	37	SG	09/02/62	Warrenton, VA	DOW	(Wdd @ 2nd Man.)	ROH,R48
Williamson, Bright J.	Pvt.	L 21st SCVI	25	MN	11/15/63	Pt. Lookout, MD	DIP		ROH,HMC,HAG,P1
Williamson, D.V.	Sgt.	F 4th SCVC		MN	/ /	Virginia	DOD		HMC
Williamson, David R.	Pvt.	L 21st SCVI	28	MN	01/27/65	Wilmington, NC	DOD	(PP=Goldsboro, NC)	ROH,HMC,HAG,PP
Williamson, David W.	Pvt.	F 3rd SCVIBn	50	LN	12/02/62	Richmond, VA	DOD	(PP=White Sulpher Ss)	ROH,KEB,PP
Williamson, E.	Pvt.	B 17th SCVI		FD	/ /	2nd Manassas, VA	DOW		JR
Williamson, E.J.	Sgt.	K 13th SCVI		LN	05/04/63	Guinea Stn., VA	KIA		ROH
Williamson, G.W.	Pvt.	I 26th SCVI		WG	05/20/64	Virginia	KIA		ROH
Williamson, Hiram	Pvt.	B 17th SCVI		FD	/ /	At home	DOD		JR,HFC
Williamson, J. Thomas	Pvt.	F 3rd SCVIBn	18	LN	12/11/63	Ft. Delaware, DE	DIP	Finn's Pt., NJ Nat. Cem.	ROH,FPH,P5,KEB
Williamson, James Wilds	Sgt.	B 21st SCVI		DN	03/15/65	Elmira, NY	DIP	Woodlawn N.C.#1690 Elmira	ROH,FPH,P6,HAG
Williamson, Leonard S.	4th Sgt.	L 21st SCVI		MN	07/11/63	Morris Island SC	DOW	(Wdd & POW 7/10)	ROH,HMC,HAG
Williamson, Reuben	Pvt.	B 4th SCVI		AN	09/03/61	Germantown, VA	DOD	(JR=D,P.S.S.)	JR,SA2,GMJ
Williamson, Robert L.	1st Sgt.	L 21st SCVI	27	MN	01/15/65	Ft. Fisher, NC	KIA		ROH,HMC
Williamson, S.	Pvt.	C 1st SCVA			09/21/64	Charleston, SC	DOD	Magnolia Cem. Charleston	ROH,MAG,RCD
Williamson, S.	Pvt.	I 22nd SCVI		OG	12/26/62	Richmond, VA		(Williams, S. in HC ?)	ROH
Williamson, Samuel W.	Pvt.	L 21st SCVI	24	MN	01/30/65	Pt. Lookout, MD	DOW	(Wdd Ft Fisher Dd enroute)	ROH,HMC,HAG,PP
Williamson, Solomon M.	Pvt.	L 21st SCVI	30	MN	05/09/64	Swift Creek, VA	KIA		ROH,HMC,HAG
Williamson, Thomas E.	Pvt.	A 10th SCVI		GN	12/31/62	Murfreesboro, TN	KIA	(WG ?)	ROH,JR,RAS,HOW
Williamson, W.W.	Pvt.	H 5th SC			07/04/62	Frayser's Farm	DOW		JR
Williamson, William	Cpl.	K Orr's Ri.	31	AN	06/27/62	Gaines' Mill, VA	KIA		ROH,JR,CDC
Williamson, William D.	Pvt.	A 1st SCVIG		BL	05/15/64	Wilderness, VA	DOW	(Wdd 5/5, day of dth Appx)	SA1
Williamson, William G.	Pvt.	I 26th SCVI	20	WG	/ /	Clay's Farm, VA	KIA		CTA,HOW
Williamson, William P.D.	Cpl.	K 26th SCVI	19	HY	05/20/64	Clay's Farm, VA	KIA	Blandford Church Pbg., VA	ROH,BLC,PP,CEN
Williford, W.H.	Pvt.	H 12th SCVI	39	YK	05/12/64	Spotsylvania, VA	KIA		CWC,YEB
Willingham, Edward W.	Cpl.	F 12th SCVI		FD	09/17/62	Sharpsburg, MD	KIA	(JR=DOW 10/5)	ROH,JR.HFC,CDC
Willingham, H. Warren	Pvt.	B 3rd SCVI		NY	10/23/64	Columbia, SC	DOW	Liberty Hill L.C. NY	ROH,NCC,PP,SA2
Willingham, Joseph	Pvt.	F 6th SCVC	25	FD	/ /	Fayetteville, NC	KIA		CAG
Willis, Alfred	Pvt.	G 11th SCVI		CO	04/08/64	Lake City, FL	DOD	(PP=3/8/64)	ROH,HAG,PP
Willis, Allen	Pvt.	F 21st SCVI		MO	08/01/64	Petersburg, VA	DOW	Blandford Church Pbg., VA	ROH,HOM,HAG,BL
Willis, Andrew P.	Pvt.	B 1st SCVC	23	SG	06/09/63	Brandy Stn., VA	KIA	Gordonsville, VA	ROH,HOS,GOR
Willis, C.A.	Pvt.	A 1st SCVIG		BL	05/15/64	Lynchburg, VA	DOW	(Wdd 5/5/64 @ Wilderness)	ROH,SA1,CDC
Willis, Calvin	Pvt.	I 5th SCVI		SG	/ /	Richmond, VA	KIA	(1862)	HOS
Willis, D.K.	Pvt.	I 5th SCVI		SG	/ /	Virginia			HOS
Willis, E.R.	Pvt.	A 3rd SCVI		SG	03/20/65	Bentonville, NC	KIA	PP	ROH,SA2,KEB,WA
Willis, Edward H.	Pvt.	B 13th SCVI		SG	/ /	Petersburg, VA	KIA		HOS
Willis, Francis	Pvt.	E 13th SCVI		SG	09/03/63	Ft. Delaware, DE	DIP		P40
Willis, Israel	Cpl.	E 13th SCVI		SG	/ /	Charlottesville	DOD		HOS
Willis, J.E.	Pvt.	I 15th SCVI		LN	/ /	Richmond, VA		Oakwood C.#16,Row C,Div G	ROH,OWC
Willis, James	Pvt.	I 13th SCVI	19	SG	08/06/62	Richmond, VA	DOD	Hollywood Cem.Rchmd. Q299	ROH,HC
Willis, James A.	Sgt.	C 7th SCVI	21	AE	07/01/62	Malvern Hill, VA	KIA	(JR=Savage Stn.)	ROH,JR,KEB,CDC
Willis, John C.	Pvt.	I 5th SCVI		SG	/ /		DOD	(1861)	HOS
Willis, John Q.	Sgt.	E 13th SCVI		SG	05/06/64	Wilderness, VA	KIA		ROH,HOS

SOUTH CAROLINA DEAD IN CSA SERVICE 1861-1865

NAME	RANK	C REGIMENT	AGE	DS	DIED	WHERE	WHY	BURIED	SOURCES
Willis, Joseph P.	Pvt.	C 7th SCVI	18	AE	05/06/64	Wilderness, VA	KIA		ROH,KEB
Willis, M. McK.	2nd Lt.	E 13th SCVI		SG	09/30/64	Jones' Farm, VA	KIA		ROH,BOS,HOS,R47
Willis, Milton H.	Pvt.	L 1st SCVIG		CN	09/01/63	Ft. Delaware, DE	DIP	Finn's Pt., NJ Nat. Cem.	ROH,FPH,P5,SA1
Willis, Thomas W.	Cpl.	C 7th SCVI	24	AE	07/02/63	Gettysburg, PA	KIA	(KEB=W.W.)(JR=7/3)	ROH,JR,GDR,CDC
Willis, W.		F			/ /	Griffin, GA		Griffin, Spaulding Cnty GA	UD2
Willis, W. Thomas	Pvt.	I 13th SCVI	21	SG	07/02/63	Gettysburg, PA	KIA		ROH,GDR
Willis, William	Pvt.	H P.S.S.			/ /	Frayser's Farm	DOW		JR,CDC
Willoughby, P.	Pvt.	C Ham.Leg.		CL	05/07/65	Newport News, VA		Greenlawn C. Newport News	PP
Wills, David E.	Sgt.	E P.S.S.		SR	/ /		KIA		JR
Willson, James Samuel	Pvt.	G Orr's Ri.	22	AE	05/03/63	Chancellorsville	KIA	Upper Long Cane P.C.	ROH,CAE
Willson, John H.	Pvt.	F 5th SCVI		YK	06/27/62	Gaines` Mill, VA	KIA		SA3
Wilson,	Cpt.	2nd SC			07/02/63	Gettysburg, PA	KIA	Magnolia Cem. Charleston	MAG
Wilson, A.J.	Pvt.	4th SCMil			02/08/65	Columbia, SC			PP
Wilson, Alfred	Pvt.	K 3rd SCVC	19	BL	04/02/65	At home	DOD		ROH
Wilson, Andrew	Pvt.	F 5th SCVI	23	YK	07/06/62	Gaines' Mill, VA	DOW	(On Rchmd effects list)	ROH,JR,SA3,YEB
Wilson, Andrew	Pvt.	K 12th SCVI	37	PS	05/05/64	Wilderness, VA	KIA		ROH
Wilson, B.P.	Pvt.	H 7th SCVI			/ /	Richmond, VA		Oakwood C.#89,Row B,Div B	ROH,OWC
Wilson, Benjamin	Pvt.	C 1st SCVIG		RD	02/05/64	Columbia, SC	DOD		SA1
Wilson, Brainard D.	Pvt.	F 9th SCVIB	28	SR	09/04/61	Germantown, VA	DOD		ROH,JR
Wilson, C.B.	Pvt.	A 5th SCVI		LR	06/27/62	Gaines` Mill, VA	KIA		JR,SA3,LAN
Wilson, Caleb	Pvt.	E 3rd SCVI		NY	12/25/62	Richmond, VA	DOD	(On Rchmd effects list)	ROH,JR,SA2,ANY
Wilson, Calvin	Cpl.	E 24th SCVI	37	CO	02/15/63	At home	DOD		ROH
Wilson, Charles	Pvt.	B 1st SCVA			09/03/62	Charleston, SC		Magnolia Cem. Charleston	ROH,MAG,RCD
Wilson, Charles	Pvt.	G 13th SCVI		NY	10/29/63	Ft. Delaware, DE	DIP	Finn's Pt., NJ Nat. Cem.	ROH,FPH,ANY,P5
Wilson, Charles A.	Pvt.	D 2nd SCVI		SR	08/15/61	Richmond, VA	DOD	Oakwood C.#52,Row D,Div A	ROH,SA2,OWC,KEB
Wilson, Charlton Henry	Chaplain	7th SCVC	36	DN	06/03/64	Richmond, VA	DOD	Hopewell P.C. Florence, SC	ROH,JR,TOD
Wilson, Cunningham	Pvt.	F 3rd SCVI		LS	07/01/62	Malvern Hill, VA	KIA		JR,KEB,CNM
Wilson, D.A.	2nd Lt.	A 2nd SCVIRi		AE	10/08/62		DOD		R45
Wilson, David	Pvt.	B 7th SCVIBn		FD	12/09/64	Elmira, NY	DIP	Woodlawn N.C.#1036 Elmira	FPH,P5,P65,HAG
Wilson, David	Pvt.	D 17th SCVI		CR	07/30/64	Crater, Pbg., VA	KIA	(CB=DOD)	BLM,HHC,CB
Wilson, David H.	Sgt.	F 6th SCVI	30	CR	11/15/63	Loudon, TN			ROH,HHC
Wilson, E.J.	Pvt.	Kershaw Ca			11/29/62	Richmond, VA	DOD	(On Rchmd effects list)	JR,CDC
Wilson, Edward	Pvt.	L P.S.S.			/ /		DOW		JR
Wilson, Franklin	Pvt.			NY	02/01/63	Charleston, SC		Old Tranquil M.C. Newberry	NCC,ANY
Wilson, G.	Pvt.	B 8th SCVI		CD	04/18/65	Pt. Lookout, MD	DIP	C.C. Pt. Lookout, MD	ROH,FPH,P6
Wilson, G.W.	Pvt.	A 18th SCVI		UN	07/11/62	Charleston, SC		Magnolia Cem. Charleston	ROH,MAG,RCD
Wilson, G.W.	Pvt.	I 6th SCVI		CR	06/15/62	7 Pines, VA	DOW	Oakwood C.#46,Row L,Div B	OWC,CDC,HHC
Wilson, George	Pvt.	H 24th SCVI		CR	09/20/63	Chickamauga, GA	KIA	Con. Cem. Marietta, GA	ROH,HHC,CB,CCM
Wilson, George R.	Pvt.	E 6th SCVI		DN	10/15/62	Richmond, VA	DOD	Hollywood Cem.Rchmd. F190	ROH,HC,JLC
Wilson, George W.	Pvt.	K 21st SCVI		DN	01/15/65	Ft. Fisher, NC	KIA		PP,HAG
Wilson, Gilliam	Pvt.	F 20th SCVI		NY	/ /	Charleston, SC	DOD		ANY,KEB
Wilson, Harrison	Pvt.	A 15th SCVAB			09/09/62	Charleston, SC		Magnolia Cem. Charleston	ROH,MAG,RCD
Wilson, Henry B.	Pvt.	D 16th SCVI		GE	07/22/64	Atlanta, GA	KIA	(DOW @ Forsythe per 16R)	ROH,16R
Wilson, Henry C.	Pvt.	3rd SCVABn	25	LN	11/04/63	At home	DOD		ROH
Wilson, J.	Pvt.	B 8th SCVI		CD	11/15/61	Richmond, VA	DOD	(Typhoid)(Wilkerson, J.?)	JR
Wilson, J.A.	Pvt.	D 6th SCVI		CR	/ /	Richmond, VA		Oakwood C.#32,Row 25,Div J	ROH,OWC
Wilson, J.C.	Pvt.	C 3rd SCVI		LS	07/01/62	Malvern Hill, VA	KIA	(Wilson, C. in ROH)	ROH,SA2
Wilson, J.C.	Pvt.	C 24th SCVI		CO	01/28/65	Camp Chase, OH	DIP	Con. Cem.#920 Columbus, OH	FPH,P6
Wilson, J.F.W.	Pvt.	A 20th SCVI		PS	08/01/64	Petersburg, VA	DOW	(Wdd 7/18,DofD estimated)	ROH
Wilson, J.H.	Pvt.	1st SC Res		SG	02/07/65	Columbia, SC	DOD		ROH,PP
Wilson, J.H.	Pvt.	G 14th SCVI	25	AE	03/18/65	Ft. Delaware, DE	DIP	Finn's Pt., NJ Nat. Cem.	ROH,FPH,P6,P40

SOUTH CAROLINA DEAD IN CSA SERVICE 1861-1865

NAME	RANK	C	REGIMENT	AGE	DS	DIED	WHERE	WHY	BURIED	SOURCES
Wilson, J.H.	Cpl.	D	Ham.Leg.		AN	05/31/62	7 Pines, VA	KIA		GRS
Wilson, J.L.	Pvt.	E	17th SCVI	44	YK	06/26/64	Richmond, VA	DOD		ROH
Wilson, J.N.	Pvt.	B	22nd SCVI		SG	11/11/63	Charleston, SC	DOD	Magnolia Cem. Charleston	ROH,MAG,HOS,RC
Wilson, J.N.	Pvt.		Kershaw Ca			01/18/62	Dranesville, VA	DOD	(? What unit, 6th SCVI)	JR
Wilson, J.W.	Cpl.	B	13th SCVI		SG	07/01/63	Gettysburg, PA	KIA		ROH,HOS
Wilson, Jacob Gilliam	Pvt.					10/07/64			Old Tranquil M.C. Newberry	NCC
Wilson, James	Pvt.	F	12th SCVI		FD	08/04/64	Richmond, VA	DOD		ROH,HFC
Wilson, James	Sgt.	C	24th SCVI		CO	10/14/64	Atlanta, GA	DOD	(Fairgrounds Hospital)	ROH
Wilson, James	Pvt.	C	24th SCVI		CO	09/20/63	Chickamauga, GA	KIA		EJM
Wilson, James B.	Pvt.	K	Hol.Leg.			01/23/65	Elmira, NY	DIP	Woodlawn N.C.#1609 Elmira	FPH,P6,P65,P12
Wilson, James B.	Pvt.	D	13th SCVI	18	NY	09/01/62	Ox Hill, VA	KIA		ANY
Wilson, James C.	Pvt.	C	24th SCVI		CO	01/28/65	Camp Chase, OH	DIP	Con. Cem.#920 Columbus, OH	FPH,P23
Wilson, James E.	1st Sgt.	G	Hol.Leg.	16	NY	11/05/64	Petersburg, VA	KIA		ROH,ANY
Wilson, James F.	Pvt.	D	18th SCVI		AN	05/26/64	Petersburg, VA	DOW	(Wdd 5/22, ROH=Lt.)	ROH,PP
Wilson, James M.	Pvt.		Ferguson's			/ /	Dalton, GA		(1864)	PP
Wilson, James S.	Pvt.	F	20th SCVI		NY	/ /	Strasburg, VA	KIA		ANY,KEB
Wilson, James T.	Pvt.	G	Orr's Ri.		AE	05/03/63	Chancellorsville	KIA		ROH,JR
Wilson, James William	Pvt.	E	3rd SCVI		NY	10/13/64	Strasburg, VA	KIA	Old Tranquil M.C. Newberry	NCC,SA2,ANY,KE
Wilson, Jesse	Pvt.	D	1st SCVIG		DN	/ /	Richmond, VA	DOD		ROH,SA1
Wilson, John	Pvt.	B	7th SCVIBn	27	FD	10/10/62	At home	DOD		ROH,HAG,HFC
Wilson, John	Pvt.	C	25th SCVI		WG	10/15/62	Charleston, SC	DOD	Magnolia Cem. Charleston	ROH,MAG,HAG
Wilson, John	Pvt.	G	5th SCVI		YK	01/11/63	Fredericksburg	DOD	(To hosp 12/24/62)	ROH,JR,SA3,YEB
Wilson, John	Pvt.	G	7th SCVIBn		KW	05/16/64	Drury's Bluff VA	DOW		HIC,HAG
Wilson, John	Pvt.	E	7th SCVC	28	NY	/ /	At home	DOD		ANY
Wilson, John A.	Pvt.	C	P.S.S.		AN	05/31/62	7 Pines, VA	KIA		ROH,JR,SA2,GMJ
Wilson, John Calvin	Sgt.	I	4th SCVC	40	WG	08/13/64	Richmond, VA	DOW	(Wdd @ Cold Harbor)	ROH,HOW,CTA
Wilson, John G.	1st Sgt.	A	2nd SCVIRi		AE	09/09/62		DOD		JR
Wilson, John H.	Pvt.	F	5th SCVI		YK	06/27/62	Gaines' Mill, VA	KIA		JR,SA3,CB
Wilson, John H.	Pvt.	G	2nd SCVIRi			/ /	Emory, VA		Con. Cem. Emory, VA	PP
Wilson, John H.	Pvt.				AN			DOD	(SA2=DIS,GMH=DOD '64)	SA2,GMJ
Wilson, John L.	Pvt.	C	7th SCVI	25	AE	12/13/64	Fredericksburg	KIA		ROH,JR,KEB
Wilson, John M.	Pvt.	E	20th SCVI		AN	/ /	Gordonsville, VA			ROH,KEB
Wilson, John Mc.	Pvt.	B	7th SCVIBn	40	FD	08/27/64	At home	DOD		ROH,HAG,HMC
Wilson, Joseph Edward	Pvt.	K	4th SCVI	19	RD	08/06/61	Culpepper, VA	DOW	Fairview Cem. Culpepper VA	ROH,CGH,CDC
Wilson, L.M.	Pvt.	M	P.S.S.		SG	10/20/63		DOD	(L.W.?)	ROH,JR
Wilson, Lawrence J.	Sgt. Maj.		1st SCVIH		BL	05/06/64	Wilderness, VA	KIA		ROH,SA1
Wilson, Lawson H.	Pvt.	F	5th SCVI		YK	10/07/64	Darbytown Rd. VA	KIA	(YEB notes widow's claim)	SA3,YEB,CB
Wilson, M.	Pvt.	G	1st SCVA			02/04/65	Charleston, SC		Magnolia Cem. Charleston	ROH,MAG,RCD
Wilson, M.A.W.	Pvt.	B	22nd SCVI		SG	/ /	Petersburg, VA	KIA		ROH,HOS
Wilson, McKiney	Pvt.	C	7th SCVIBn	20	RD	06/20/62	Adams Run, SC	DOD	(HAG & PP=McKenzie)	ROH,HAG,PP
Wilson, Nicholas	Pvt.	D	17th SCVI	24	CR	09/14/62	South Mtn., MD	KIA	(JR=Sharpsburg)	ROH,JR,HHC,CB
Wilson, Philip	Pvt.	F	1st SCVA			08/05/62	Charleston, SC		Magnolia Cem. Charleston	ROH,MAG,RCD
Wilson, Pinckney S.	Pvt.	F	17th SCVI	16	YK	01/16/62	At home	DOD	(CB=Virginia)	JR,YMD,YEB,CB
Wilson, R. Henry	Pvt.	G	5th SCRes	39		12/17/62	Adams Run, SC	DOD		PP
Wilson, Reuben	Pvt.	D	Ham.Leg.		AN	05/31/62	7 Pines, VA	KIA		ROH,JR,GRS,CDC
Wilson, Robert Conway	Pvt.	M	10th SCVI	28	HY	/ /	Tennessee	DOD	(See SUN NEWS 11/3/90)	RAS
Wilson, Robert J.	2nd Cpl.	F	5th SCVI	24	YK	05/06/64	Wilderness, VA	KIA		ROH,SA3,YEB,CB
Wilson, Robert McFadden	1st Sgt.	I	4th SCVC	25	WG	08/23/64	Petersburg, VA	KIA		ROH,HOW,CTA
Wilson, Samuel	Pvt.	H	19th SCVI	42	AE	11/15/64		KIA		ROH
Wilson, T.A.	Lt.	A	2nd SCVIRi		AE	08/30/62	2nd Manassas, VA	DOW		JR,CDC
Wilson, T.F.	Pvt.	D	18th SCVI		AN	05/20/64	Clay's Farm, VA	KIA		ROH

SOUTH CAROLINA DEAD IN CSA SERVICE 1861-1865

NAME	RANK	C REGIMENT	AGE	DS	DIED	WHERE	WHY	BURIED	SOURCES
Wilson, T.F. (T.J.?)	Pvt.	A		PS	07/24/64	Petersburg, VA	KIA	Blandford Church Pbg., VA	ROH,BLC
Wilson, T.J.	Pvt.	C 3rd SCVIBn		LS	02/28/65	Pt. Lookout, MD	DIP	C.C. Pt. Lookout, MD	ROH,FPH,P6,P113
Wilson, Thomas Burr	Pvt.	D 13th SCVI	24	NY	05/30/62	Richmond, VA	DOD	Hollywood Cem.Rchmd. L92	ROH,JR,HC,ANY
Wilson, Thomas L.	Pvt.	D 5th SCVI		NY	/ /	Richmond, VA	DOD	(SA3 indicates DIS in'61)	JR,ANY,SA3
Wilson, W.F.	Pvt.	H 6th SCVC			10/27/64	Burgess' Mills	KIA		CDC
Wilson, W.W.	Pvt.	H 1st SCVC		YK	03/15/62		DOD		ROH
Wilson, Wesley G.	Pvt.	I 17th SCVI	17	LR	06/11/64	Petersburg, VA	DOD		LAN,PP
Wilson, William	Pvt.	C 1st SCVIG		RD	09/20/62	Lynchburg, VA	DOD	Lynchburg CSA Cem.#4 R1	ROH,JR,SA1,CDC
Wilson, William	Pvt.	E 10th SCVI		WG	07/13/62	MS	DOD		RAS,HOW,PP
Wilson, William	Pvt.	L P.S.S.			/ /		DOW		JR
Wilson, William	Pvt.	F 5th SCVI	24	YK	11/28/63	Racoon Mtn., TN	KIA		CB,YEB
Wilson, William B.	Pvt.	D 13th SCVI	24	NY	08/19/62	Richmond, VA	DOD		ROH
Wilson, William C.	Pvt.	K 21st SCVI		DN	03/24/65	Elmira, NY	DIP	Woodlawn N.C.#2450 Elmira	FPH,P6,P65,HAG
Wilson, William E.	Pvt.	C 22nd SCVI	28	SG	05/11/65	Baltimore, MD	DIP	Loudon Pk.C. B-25 Balto MD	ROH,FPH,CV,P5,PP
Wilson, William H.	Pvt.	E 7th SCVIBn	36	SR	12/06/63	Sullivans I., SC	DOD		ROH,HAG
Wilson, William H.	Pvt.	H 24th SCVI		CR	/ /		DIP	(1864)	ROH
Wilson, William James	2nd Sgt.	G 15th SCVI	28	WG	05/08/63	Chancellorsville	KIA		ROH,JR,HOW,CTA
Wilson,Jr., William	Pvt.	K 6th SCVI		GE	09/15/61	Fairfax, VA	DOD		ROH
Wimberly, Augustus	Pvt.	C 24th SCVI	23	CO	09/12/63	Atlanta, GA	DOD	(Gate City Hospital)	EJM
Winbourne, G.W.	Pvt.	Inglis LA		DN	10/18/64	At home	DOD		ROH
Winburn, S.	Pvt.	E 8th SCVI		DN	04/27/62	Richmond, VA	DOD	(Pneumonia)	JR,KEB
Winburn, William	Pvt.	D 21st SCVI		DN	05/20/64	Drury's Bluff VA	DOW		ROH,HAG
Winchester, Isaac M.	Pvt.	A 2nd SCVI		PS	09/17/62	Sharpsburg, MD	KIA	(JR=Maryland Hts.)	ROH,JR,SA2,H2
Winchester,Sr., Willowby	Pvt.	F 22nd SCVI		PS	03/08/62	Columbia, SC	DOD		PP
Winck, P.A.	Pvt.	F 12th SCVI		FD	06/27/62	Gaines' Mill, VA	KIA	(Wilkes?)	JR
Windham, C.	Pvt.	K 10th SCVI		CN	09/20/63	Chickamauga, GA	DOW		RAS,ROH,CDC
Windham, E.	Pvt.	A 14th SCVI	20	DN	08/10/62	Richmond, VA			ROH
Windham, Edward D.	Pvt.	K 6th SCVI	25	CL	07/30/62	Richmond, VA	DOD		ROH,3RC
Windham, J.E.	Pvt.	A 14th SCVI		DN	08/03/62	Richmond, VA	DOD	(Typhoid)	JR
Windham, Moses	Pvt.	A 14th SCVI	17	DN	04/12/63	Fredericksburg	DOD		ROH,DEB
Windham, S.	Pvt.	E 8th SCVI		DN	04/27/62	Richmond, VA		Oakwood C.#173,Row J,Div A	ROH,OWC,KEB
Windham, Samuel	Pvt.	K 21st SCVI		DN	09/14/62	Georgetown, SC	DOD		PP,HAG
Windham, W.G.	Pvt.				/ /			Fredericksburg C.C. R4S13	FBG
Windhurst, L.	Pvt.	B 1st SCVA		CN	11/07/61	Port Royal, SC	KIA		ROH,JR
Windle, John H.	Color Sgt.	C Hol.Leg.	30	SG	08/23/62	Rappahanock, VA	KIA	(CDC= John W. Windall)	ROH,JR,HOS,CDC
Winfield, J.B.	Pvt.	H 6th SCVI		FD	05/31/62	7 Pines, VA	KIA		JR
Wingard, Henry	Pvt.	K 20th SCVI		LN	08/24/63		DOD	(5 Wingards in Co.K/KEB)	ROH
Wingard, James Joseph	Pvt.	K 13th SCVI		LN	09/01/62	Ox Hill, VA	KIA	(Killed by shell)	ROH,JR
Wingard, James S.	Pvt.	K 13th SCVI		LN	07/08/62	Richmond, VA	DOD		ROH,JR
Wingate, M.F.	Pvt.	23rd SCVI			12/04/61	Richmond, VA		Hollywood Cem.Rchmd. B112	HC
Wingate, Willie	QM Sgt.	C 3rd SCVABn		DN	06/15/64	Columbia, SC			ROH,PP
Wingo, George W.	Pvt.	C 13th SCVI		SG	09/02/63	Ft. Delaware, DE	DIP	Finn's Pt., NJ Nat. Cem.	ROH,FPH,P5,P115
Wingo, Ransom F.	Pvt.	C 13th SCVI		SG	05/03/65	Pts. Monroe, VA	DIP	Nat. Cem. Hampton, VA	ROH,P113,HOS,PP
Winholter, L.	Pvt.	B German A.		CN	11/07/61	Port Royal, SC	KIA		JR
Winkle, W.J.	Pvt.	E 1st SCV			04/25/62	Richmond, VA		Oakwood C.#49,Row J,Div A	ROH,OWC,CDC
Winkles, William	Pvt.	E P.S.S.		SR	/ /	Manchester, VA	DOD	(1862)	ROH
Winn, A.W.	Pvt.	G 3rd SCVI	22	LS	09/16/61	Flint Hill, VA	DOD		ROH,JR,SA2,KEB
Winn, H.	Pvt.	D 1st SCVC		CR	09/29/64	Elmira, NY	DIP	Woodlawn N.C.#424 Elmira	FPH,P5,P65,P113
Winn, James	Pvt.	E 14th SCVI		LS	08/29/62	2nd Manassas, VA	DOW	(JR=DOW @ Pt. Royal)	JR,CGS,CDC
Winn, R.	Pvt.	H 5th SCVI		UN	/ /	Frayser's Farm	DOW		JR
Winn, R.J.	Pvt.	F 5th SCVI		SG	10/12/61	Richmond, VA	DOD	Hollywood Cem.Rchmd. B237	ROH,JR,SA3,HOS

SOUTH CAROLINA DEAD IN CSA SERVICE 1861-1865

NAME	RANK	C REGIMENT	AGE	DS	DIED	WHERE	WHY	BURIED	SOURCES
Winn, Robert M.	2nd Lt.	K 24th SCVI		ED	07/20/64	Peachtree Creek	KIA		ROH,HOE,CDC,R4
Winn, W. Hill	Sgt.	B 6th SCVC		ED	02/21/65	Columbia, SC	KIA (PP=2/20/65)	UD3	ROH,HOE,BHC,PP
Winn, W.A.	Pvt.	K 24th SCVI		ED	05/11/64		DOD		HOE
Winn, William Collier	Pvt.	D 3rd SCVIBn	29	LS	05/25/64	Richmond, VA	DOW	Hollywood Cem.Rchmd. I39	ROH,LSC,KEB,HC
Winningham, Henry	Pvt.	F 3rd SCVABn	20	CN	07/03/64	King's Creek, SC	KIA		ROH
Winningham, J.	Pvt.	K 10th SCVI		CN	09/20/63	Chickamauga, GA	KIA		ROH,RAS
Winningham, Noel	Pvt.	B 11th SCVI		CO	09/11/63	Charleston, SC	DOD	Magnolia Cem. Charleston	ROH,MAG,RCD,HA
Winsen, J.A. (Winston?)	Pvt.	C 6th SCVI		KW	11/01/62			Stonewall C. Winchester VA	WIN
Winston, D.C.	Pvt.	E 15th SCVAB		FD	01/08/64	Pt. Lookout, MD	DIP		ROH,P5
Winston, J.C.	Pvt.	H 6th SCVI		FD	10/19/64	Richmond, VA			ROH
Winter, J.J.	Pvt.	A 8th SC Res		CN	02/25/65	Columbia, SC	DOD		ROH,PP
Winter, L.G.	Pvt.	F 2nd SCV		CN	/ /	Charlottesville		Univ. Cem. Charlottesville	ACH
Winting, G.A.	Pvt.	Orr's Ri.			04/23/64	Richmond, VA		Hollywood Cem.Rchmd. I97	HC
Winton, W.J.A.	Pvt.	G 22nd SCVI		AN	/ /	Petersburg, VA			ROH
Wire, W.A.					/ /			(Rchmd effects list 12/62)	CDC
Wisdom, James P.	Pvt.	A 14th SCVI		DN	04/24/62	Richmond, VA			ROH
Wise, A.J.	Pvt.	B 1st SCVIH		OG	10/01/62	Warrenton, VA	DOW (Wdd 8/30 2nd Man)		ROH,JR,SA1
Wise, A.J.	Pvt.	C Ham.Leg.		CL	07/21/61		DOD		JR
Wise, D.H.	Pvt.	D 20th SCVI		LS	10/12/64	Richmond, VA		Hollywood Cem.Rchmd. V133	ROH,HC,KEB
Wise, H.	Pvt.	B 14th SCVI		ED	10/09/64	Richmond, VA		Hollywood Cem.Rchmd. V338	HC
Wise, H.G.	Pvt.	B 1st SCVIH		OG	12/25/63	Manchester, VA	DOD		ROH,SA1
Wise, H.J.	Pvt.	E 10th SCVI			11/06/62	Knoxville, TN		Bethel C. Knoxville, TN	TOD
Wise, Henry A.	Pvt.	A 22nd SCVI		ED	09/14/62	South Mtn., MD	KIA		ROH
Wise, J.S.	Pvt.	I 23rd SCVI		CL	09/14/62	South Mtn., MD	DOW (JR=Sharpsburg)		ROH,JR,CDC,HCL
Wise, J.T.	Pvt.	I 23rd SCVI		CL	/ /	Maryland		Rose Hill C. Hagerstown MD	ROH,JR,BOD
Wise, James H.	Pvt.	G 13th SCVI		NY	09/20/61	At home	DOD		ROH,JR,ANY
Wise, John A.	Pvt.	H Hol.Leg.	34	NY	09/09/62	Culpepper, VA	DOW		ROH,JR,ANY
Wise, John C.	Pvt.	H Hol.Leg.	20	NY	11/05/64	Petersburg, VA	KIA		ROH,ANY
Wise, John G.B.	Pvt.	I 6th SCVI	35	CR	01/14/64	At home	DOD		ROH,HHC,CB
Wise, John T.	Pvt.	F 1st SCVIG		HY	11/25/62	Virginia	DOD (JR=DOD @ Sharpsburg)		JR,SA1
Wise, Lawrence W.	3rd Lt.	F 7th SCVI	28	ED	/ /	At home	MUR		HOE,KEB,R46
Wise, Lemuel E.	Pvt.	G 13th SCVI		NY	09/18/61	Camp Johnson, SC	DOD (Measles)		ROH,JR,ANY
Wise, R.	Pvt.	K 6th SCVI			08/15/64	Petersburg, VA	DOW (Wdd 7/28,DofD estimated)		ROH
Wise, T.J.	Pvt.	C Ham.Leg.		CL	07/21/61	1st Manassas, VA	KIA		JR
Wise, Theodore R.	Pvt.	E 3rd SCResB	17	CR	12/26/64	Florence, SC	DOD (Prob SC Res Bn. POW Gds.)		ROH,HHC,PP
Wise, Tyre	Pvt.	B 14th SCVI	16	ED	/ /	Petersburg, VA	DOD (1863)		HOE,UD3
Wise, V.F.	Pvt.		20	OG	/ /	Virginia	KIA (1864,Wiles, V.P. F,25th?)		ROH
Wise, W.J.	Pvt.	I 23rd SCVI		CL	09/17/62	Sharpsburg, MD	KIA		ROH,JR,HCL
Wise, William J.	Pvt.	B 14th SCVI	20	ED	/ /	Petersburg, VA	DOD (1863)		HOE,UD3
Wiseman, James M.	Pvt.	C 19th SCVI		ED	02/03/64	Rock Island, IL	DIP	C.C.#353 Rock Island, IL	FPH,P5,HOE
Wisher, John W.	Pvt.	H 24th SCVI		CR	02/24/64	Cassville, GA	DOD (John Wilburn?)		ROH
Wisher, Joseph	Pvt.	C 17th SCVI	22	YK	05/19/65	Elmira, NY	DIP	Woodlawn N.C.#2948 Elmira	FPH,P6,P65,YEB
Withers, J.D.E.	Sgt.	C 24th SCVI		CO	09/20/63	Chickamauga, GA	KIA		JR
Withers, James W.	Cpl.	G 3rd SCVIBn		FD	05/06/64	Wilderness, VA	KIA		ROH,KEB
Withers, Simpson	Pvt.	I 13th SCVI		SG	06/15/62		DOD (Typhoid)		JR
Witherspoon, J.W.	Pvt.	K 21st SCVI		DN	05/16/64	Drury's Bluff VA	KIA (HAG=Weatherspoon)		ROH,HAG,CDC
Witherspoon, James M.	Pvt.	E 2nd SCVI		KW	01/15/63	Fredericksburg	DOW		ROH,SA2,HIC,KE
Witherspoon, John A.	Cpt.	C 17th SCVI	23	YK	10/19/62	Warrenton, VA	DOW (Wdd @ Sharpsburg)		ROH,JR,YEB
Witherspoon,Jr., John K.	Pvt.	H 7th SCVC	21	KW	08/20/62	Rapidan River VA	KIA (Acting as courier)		ROH,JR,HIC,CDN
Wittemore, William	Pvt.	Ham.Leg.			/ /	Manassas, VA	DOD	Circular Ch. Charleston	MAG
Wix, Foster	Pvt.	A P.S.S.		UN	/ /		DOD		JR

SOUTH CAROLINA DEAD IN CSA SERVICE 1861-1865

NAME	RANK	C	REGIMENT	AGE	DS	DIED	WHERE	WHY	BURIED	SOURCES
Wix, Hiram	Pvt.	A	P.S.S.	23	UN	06/30/62	7 Pines, VA	KIA		ROH
Wofford, John	Pvt.	F	13th SCVI		SG	07/01/63	Gettysburg, PA	KIA		HOS
Wofford, John Henry	Pvt.	K	3rd SCVI	28	SG	05/12/64	Spotsylvania, VA	KIA		ROH,SA2
Wofford, John Young	2nd Lt.	E	13th SCVI		SG	07/02/63	Jordan's Spgs VA	DOD	(Began 1st Lt. K,3rd SCVI)	JR,HOS,R47,SA2
Wofford, Joseph W.	Pvt.	E	18th SCVI		SG	05/15/65	Pt. Lookout, MD	DIP	C.C. Pt. Lookout, MD	FPH,P6,P115
Wofford, Thomas C.	Pvt.	F	13th SCVI		SG	03/17/65	Elmira, NY	DIP	Woodlawn N.C.#1712 Elmira	FPH,P6,HOS
Wofford, William B.	4th Sgt.	K	3rd SCVI	27	SG	01/26/63	Richmond, VA	DOW	(Wdd @ Petersburg)	ROH,JR,HOS,KEB
Wofford, William Thomas	Pvt.	K	3rd SCVI	26	SG	05/12/64	Spotsylvania, VA	KIA	Spotsylvania C.H., VA	ROH,SCH,SA2,HOS
Woldrop, Thomas	Pvt.	C	18th SCVI	30	UN	07/30/64	Crater, Pbg., VA	KIA		ROH
Wolf, David	Pvt.	E	15th SCMil		FD	04/17/65	Pt. Lookout, MD	DIP	C.C. Pt. Lookout, MD	ROH,FPH,P6
Wolf, Leland	Pvt.	K	5th SCVI		SG	/ /	Chattanooga, TN	DOD	(Wolfe in SA3)	HOS,SA3
Wolf, W. Meyer	1st Lt.	G	11th SCVI	21	CO	05/09/64	Swift Creek, VA	KIA		ROH,HAG,R47
Wolf, William S.	Pvt.	B	20th SCVI	29	OG	07/15/64	Petersburg, VA	KIA	(Date appr 6/24-8/1)	ROH,KEB,CDC
Wolfe, D.W.	Pvt.	G	25th SCVI	20	OG	03/01/65	Elmira, NY	DIP	Woodlawn N.C.#2100 Elmira	ROH,FPH,P6,P65
Wolfe, J.A.	Pvt.		13th SCVI			11/03/61	Richmond, VA		Hollywood Cem.Rchmd. B128	HC
Wolfe, James D.	1st Lt.	B	Hol.Leg. C		RD	10/13/63		DOD		R48,R43
Wolfe, Milton Y.	Sgt.	D	3rd SCVIBn		LS	07/02/63	Gettysburg, PA	KIA	(JR=M.J.)	ROH,JR,GDR,KEB
Wolfe, Peter	Pvt.	G	25th SCVI		OG	01/15/65	Ft. Fisher, NC	KIA		EDR,HAG
Wolfe, Samuel H.	1st Lt.	A	18th SCVI		UN	07/30/64	Crater, Pbg., VA	KIA		ROH,BLM,R47
Wolfe, W.L.	Pvt.	I	2nd SCVA	34	OG	03/18/65		MUR	(Killed by a deserter)	ROH
Wood,	Pvt.					07/14/63	Ft. Sumter, SC	ACD	(Drowned going to Chlstn)	ROH
Wood, Allen W.	Pvt.	C	1st SCVIH		BL	05/05/64	Wilderness, VA	KIA		SA1
Wood, Benjamin	Pvt.	D	22nd SCVI		PS	07/30/64	Crater, Pbg., VA	KIA		BLM
Wood, Chesley G.	Pvt.	B	5th SCVI		YK	06/30/62	Frayser's Farm	KIA		JR,SA3,YEB
Wood, D.	Pvt.	A	1st SCSSBn			07/21/63	Georgetown, SC	DOD		PP
Wood, D.E. (D.M.?)	Pvt.	C	22nd SCVI	33	SG	05/02/65	Pt. Lookout, MD	DIP	C.C. Pt. Lookout, MD	ROH,FPH,P6,P115
Wood, E.A.	Pvt.		Ham.Leg.			/ /	Richmond, VA		Oakwood C.#156,Row N,Div A	ROH,OWC
Wood, E.H.	Sgt.	C	14th SCVI		LS	06/30/62	Frayser's Farm	KIA		ROH,JR
Wood, E.W.	Pvt.	F	22nd SCVI		PS	10/22/62			Stonewall C. Winchester VA	ROH,WIN
Wood, H.	Pvt.	G	Perenau's			12/07/61	Charleston, SC	DOD	Magnolia Cem. Charleston	ROH,MAG,RCD
Wood, J.R.	Pvt.	D	P.S.S.		SG	07/15/62	Gaines' Mill, VA	DOW	Oakwood C.#5,Row R,Div C	ROH,JR,OWC,HOS
Wood, Jacob	Pvt.	F	18th SCVI	18	LN	07/11/63	Jackson, MS	KIA	(JR=Co.A of UN District)	ROH,JR
Wood, James	Cpl.	A	17th SCVI		CR	07/30/64	Petersburg, VA	KIA		ROH,HHC
Wood, James	Pvt.	G	2nd SCVA			05/30/65	Pt. Lookout, MD	DIP	C.C. Pt. Lookout, MD	FPH,P6,P115
Wood, James	Pvt.	G	P.S.S.	22	YK	05/31/62	7 Pines, VA	KIA		JR,SA3,YEB,CB
Wood, John	Pvt.	E	7th SCVI		ED	10/28/63	Ft. Delaware, DE	DIP	Finn's Pt., NJ Nat. Cem.	ROH,FPH,P5,P40
Wood, John	Pvt.	I	22nd SCVI		OG	09/14/62	South Mtn., MD	KIA		ROH
Wood, John	Pvt.	D	25th SCVI		MN	/ /	James Island, SC	KIA		HMC,HAG
Wood, Manning A.	Pvt.	C	22nd SCVI	25	SG	12/26/64	Elmira, NY	DIP	Woodlawn N.C.#1289 Elmira	ROH,FPH,P5,P65
Wood, Oliver	Pvt.	I	13th SCVI	19	SG	06/10/65	Pt. Lookout, MD	DIP	C.C. Pt. Lookout, MD	ROH,FPH,P6,P115
Wood, R.C.	Pvt.	B	22nd SCVI		SG	07/30/64	Crater, Pbg., VA	KIA		HOS
Wood, T.J.	Sgt.	H	23rd SCVI			04/11/65	Thomasville, NC		Con. Cem. Thomasville, NC	PP
Wood, W.A.	Pvt.					/ /			Fredericksburg C.C. R8S12	FBG
Wood, W.W.	Pvt.	H	18th SCVI		YK	03/06/64	Savannah, GA		Laurel Grove C. Savannah	BGA
Wood, William J.	Pvt.	A	Hol.Leg.	30	SG	09/10/62	Warrenton, VA	DOW	(Wdd 2nd Man.)	ROH,HOS
Wood, William S.	Cpt. AQM		2nd SCVI		RD	07/30/61	Orange C.H., VA	DOD	(Typhoid)	ROH,JR,SA2,H2
Woodard, Elbert W.	Pvt.	C	3rd SCVCBn		BL	/ /		DOD	(Memorial to CNM 2/4/62)	CNM
Woodard, William	Pvt.	F	27th SCVI		CD	06/16/64	Columbia, SC	DOD		ROH,PP
Woodford, P.R.	Pvt.	A	14th SCVI		DN	08/06/62	Richmond, VA			ROH
Woodhurst, G.	Pvt.	G	3rd SCVIBn	26	AE	07/18/62	Columbia, SC	DOD		ROH
Woodhurst, George W.	Pvt.	G	1st SCVC	26	AE	07/18/62	James Island, SC	DOD	(Typhoid)	ROH,JR,PP

SOUTH CAROLINA DEAD IN CSA SERVICE 1861-1865

NAME	RANK	C REGIMENT	AGE	DS	DIED	WHERE	WHY	BURIED	SOURCES
Woodin, Charles H.A.	Cpt.	A 20th SCVI		PS	10/19/64	Cedar Creek, VA	DOW	(Head Wd. Dd in 3 hours)	ROH,KEB,R47,UD
Woodle, Hinson	Pvt.	B 24th SCVI		MO	09/20/63	Chickamauga, GA	KIA		ROH,HOM,CDC
Woodley, Alexander	Pvt.	K 8th SCVI		MO	07/12/61	Culpepper, VA	DOD	(Typhoid)	JR,HOM,KEB,CDC
Woodrow, D.M.	Pvt.	I 10th SCVI		MN	/ /	Atlanta, GA	DOD	Oakland Cem. Atlanta, GA	RAS,HMC,CVGH
Woodrow, J.	Pvt.	I 6th SCVI		CR	02/07/65	Richmond, VA		Hollywood Cem.Rchmd. W63	HC
Woodrow, John E.	1st Cpl.	I 8th SCVI		MN	/ /	Virginia	DOD		HMC,KEB
Woodruff, John	Pvt.	B 1st SCVC		SG	/ /	Upperville, VA	KIA		HOS
Woodruff, W.A.	Pvt.	K 3rd SCVI		SG	12/14/61	Centreville, VA	DOD	(Pneumonia)	JR,SA2
Woods, A.H.	1st Lt.	I 18th SCVI	28	DN	09/17/62	Sharpsburg, VA	KIA		ROH,CDC,R47
Woods, Brewer	Pvt.	Ham.Leg.	20	LS	01/11/62	Charlottesville	DOD	New Harmony P.C. LS Cty.	GEC,LSC
Woods, F.E.	Pvt.	C 7th Res Bn			02/11/65	Charleston, SC	DOD	Magnolia Cem. Charleston	ROH,MAG,RCD
Woods, J.H.	Pvt.	K 6th SCVI	23	CL	/ /		MIA		ROH
Woods, J.M.	Pvt.	I 6th SCVI		CR	/ /		KIA		CB,HHC
Woods, James N.	Pvt.	A 17th SCVI	26	CR	07/30/64	Crater, Pbg., VA	KIA	(May be John) CB	ROH,BLM,HHC,UD
Woods, Johnson M.	Cpt.	F 23rd SCVI	44	CR	07/22/64	Petersburg, VA	DOW	Family C. Broad R. Chester	ROH,R48,HHC,PP
Woods, Robert	Pvt.	L P.S.S.	40	AN	05/12/64	Liberty, GA	DOD		ROH
Woods, S.J.	Pvt.	A 8th SCVI		DN	08/02/61	Charlottesville	DOD	Univ. Cem. Charlottesville	ROH,JR,ACH,KEB
Woods, William	Pvt.	B 6th SCVI		CR	01/08/62	Charlottesville	DOD	Univ. Cem. Charlottesville	ROH,ACH,CDC,HH
Woods, William	Pvt.	B 4th SCVC		CR	/ /	Huegenot Spgs.	DOD	(1864)	CB
Woodson, J.A.	Pvt.	C 3rd SCVABn			02/03/65	Charleston, SC	DOD	Magnolia Cem. Charleston	ROH,MAG,RCD
Woodward, Furman	Pvt.	H 14th SCV		BL	/ /		DOD	(1862)	UD2
Woodward, Hansford	Pvt.	C 1st SCV		BL	12/15/62	Staunton, VA	DOD		ROH
Woodward, Lawrence B.	Pvt.	H 14th SCVI		BL	06/09/62	Crenshaw Fm., VA	DOD		JR,UD2
Woodward, Leonard	Pvt.	D 10th SCVI		MN	12/31/62	Murfreesboro, TN	KIA	(PP=DOD Meridian,MS 6/30)	RAS,HMC,PP
Woodward, T.J.	Pvt.	G 27th SCVI		SG	09/19/64	Elmira, NY	DIP	Woodlawn N.C.#501 Elmira	FPH,HOS,HAG,P5
Woodward, W.H.	Pvt.	A 1st SCVIG	21	BL	12/14/62	Fredericksburg	DOW	Beulah M.C. Georgetown SC	ROH,GNG,SA1
Woodward, W.W.	Pvt.	E 1st SCVIH		BL	11/27/64	Virginia	DOD		SA1
Woodward,Sr., J.	Pvt.	E 1st SCVA			07/03/64	Ft. Johnson, SC	KIA		ROH,CDC
Woolbright, Seaborn	Pvt.	D Hol.Leg.	23	BL	05/08/62	Adams Run, SC	DOD		PP
Wooley, Andrew	Pvt.	A 1st SCVIG		BL	07/02/63	Gettysburg, PA	DOW		SA1,GDR
Wooley, Duncan	Pvt.	I 22nd SCVI		OG	06/16/62	Secessionville	KIA		ROH,CDC,PP
Wooley, Ely	Pvt.	A 1st SCVIG		BL	07/02/63	Gettysburg, PA	KIA		ROH,JR,SA1,GDR
Wooley, George W.	Pvt.	F P.S.S.		LN	06/01/62	Fts. Monroe, VA	DOW	(Wdd @ 7 Pines)	ROH,JR,CDC,CNM
Wooley, Nathaniel	Pvt.	H 1st SCVIH		BL	10/09/61	At home	DOD		SA1
Woolford, J.J.	Lt.	F SCVI			07/02/63			Stonewall C. Winchester VA	WIN
Woolsey, James B. (D.?)	Pvt.	A 7th SCVI			12/02/62	Richmond, VA		Oakwood C.#158,Row L,Div A	ROH,OWC,KEB
Wooten, J. Litton	Pvt.	G 7th SCVI		ED	/ /	Richmond, VA	DOD	Oakwood C.#119,Row A,Div A	ROH,HOE,OWC,UD
Wooten, J.N.	Pvt.	Ferguson's			/ /	Dalton, GA		(1864)	PP
Wooten, James	Pvt.	G 1st SCVIG		ED	08/04/64		DOD		SA1,HOE
Wooten, James T.	Pvt.	F 3rd SCVC	25	BT	/ /	Columbia, SC	DOD		ROH
Wooten, M.W.	Pvt.	K 14th SCVI		ED	05/06/64	Wilderness, VA	KIA		HOE
Wooten, Samuel	Pvt.	E 8th SCVI		DN	09/13/62	Maryland Hts. MD	KIA		JR,KEB
Wooten, Shadrack	Pvt.	H 1st SCVIG	27	BT	12/15/62	At home	DOD		ROH,SA1
Wooten, W.A.	Pvt.	E 8th SCVI		DN	09/13/62	Maryland Hts. MD	KIA		JR
Wooton, James	Pvt.	E 13th SCVI		SG	11/15/62	At home	DOD		JR
Wootton, A.L.	Pvt.	B 2nd SCVIRi		PS	/ /				ROH
Wootton, W.M.	Pvt.	B 2nd SCVIRi		PS	/ /			(Dup of Warren ?)	ROH
Wootton, Warren	Pvt.	B 2nd SCVIRi		PS	/ /	Charlottesville	DOD	Univ. Cem. Charlottesville	ROH,ACH
Workman, A.H.	Pvt.	F 14th SCVI	36	LS	12/22/62	Richmond, VA	DOD	Oakwood C.#160,Row M,Div A	ROH,JR,OWC
Workman, A.T.	Pvt.	B 19th SCVI		ED	07/24/64	Richmond, VA		Hollywood Cem.Rchmd. V524	HC
Workman, Anders F.	Pvt.	B 1st SCVIG	40	NY	07/24/64	Richmond, VA	DOD		ROH,SA1,ANY

SOUTH CAROLINA DEAD IN CSA SERVICE 1861-1865

NAME	RANK	C	REGIMENT	AGE	DS	DIED	WHERE	WHY	BURIED	SOURCES
Workman, H.H.	Pvt.	D	P.S.S.		SG	/ /	Petersburg, VA	KIA		HOS
Workman, Joseph Martin	Pvt.	G	3rd SCVI	33	LS	11/06/62	Richmond, VA	DOD	Workman Fam Cem. LS	ROH,JR,SA2,RCD
Workman, Perry	Pvt.	D	P.S.S.		SG	07/15/64	Petersburg, VA	KIA		ROH,HOS
Workman, Robert	1st Cpl.	B	3rd SCVI		NY	05/06/64	Wilderness, VA	KIA		ROH,SA2,ANY,KEB
Workman, S.W.	Pvt.	F	5th SCVI		SG	08/16/61	Orange C.H., VA	DOD	(JR=D,P.S.S.)	ROH,JR,SA3
Workman, W.A.	Color Sgt.	H	12th SCVI	40	YK	05/12/64	Spotsylvania, VA	KIA	Spotsylvania C.H., VA	SCH,CWC,YEB
Worsham, J.D.	Pvt.	I	25th SCVI		CL	09/04/63	Bty. Wagner, SC	KIA	(CDC=Worsham, P.W.)	ROH,CDC
Worsham, Joseph K.	Pvt.	I	25th SCVI		CL	02/24/65	Elmira, NY	DIP	Woodlawn N.C.#2241 Elmira	FPH,P6,P65,HAG
Worth, D.M.	Pvt.	H	12th SCVI	18	YK	07/01/63	Gettysburg, PA	KIA		CWC,YEB,GDR
Worthington, William A.	Pvt.	H	1st SCVIG		LS	05/03/63	Chancellorsville	KIA		ROH,SA1
Worthy, Henry	Pvt.	D	1st SCV	21	CR	06/15/62	At home	DOD		ROH,HHC
Worthy, Thomas C.	Pvt.	B	4th SCVC		CR	05/30/63	Old Church, VA	KIA	(ROH=J.C.)	ROH,HHC
Wosen, W.	Pvt.	D	1st SC			12/06/62			Stonewall C. Winchester VA	WIN
Wray, William	Pvt.	I	5th SCVI	21	YK	/ /	Virginia	DOD		YEB
Wrede, Herman	Pvt.		Ham.Leg.		CN	08/30/62	2nd Manassas, VA	KIA		ROH
Wren, J.A.	Pvt.		19th SCVI			09/20/63	Chickamauga, GA	DOW	(10/19th Consolidated)	CDC
Wren, Thomas N.	Pvt.	A	17th SCVI	22	CR	11/18/64	Elmira, NY	DIP	Woodlawn N.C.#963 Elmira	ROH,FPH,P5,HHC
Wren, William Alexander	Pvt.	A	17th SCVI	22	CR	02/04/62	Charleston, SC	DOD		ROH,JR,HHC,CB
Wrenn, Joseph C.	Pvt.	A	6th SCVI	23	CR	07/18/61	Petersburg, VA	ACD	(Fell from RR car)	ROH,HHC,CB
Wright, Archibald Y.	1st Sgt.	G	3rd SCVI	28	LS	01/20/62	Charlottesville	DOD		ROH,JR,SA2,KEB
Wright, Bun	Pvt.	I	6th SCVI		CR	/ /		KIA		CB,HHC
Wright, Burr Harrison	Cpl.	F	23rd SCVI	24	CR	07/12/64	Petersburg, VA	DOW	Blandford Church Pbg., VA	ROH,BLC,HHC,PP
Wright, C.J.	Cpl.	E	20th SCVI		AN	07/27/64	Deep Bottom, VA	DOW		ROH,CDC,KEB
Wright, Daniel G.	Pvt.	B	24th SCVI		MO	09/15/64	Georgia	DOD		ROH,HOM
Wright, Daniel G.	Pvt.	G	8th SCVI		MO	/ /	Richmond, VA		(1863)	HOM,KEB
Wright, Daniel G.	Pvt.	G	8th SCV	25		/ /	Richmond 1863			UD2
Wright, David G.	Pvt.	K	24th SCVI		ED	/ /	(Daniel G.?)		Con. Cem. Marietta, GA	BGA,CCM,UD2
Wright, David W.	Pvt.	G	22nd SCVI	20	AN	09/08/62	Virginia	DOD		ROH
Wright, E.C.	Pvt.	H	7th SCVIBn		CR	10/29/64	Pt. Lookout, MD	DIP	C.C. Pt. Lookout, MD	FPH,P5,HHC,HAG
Wright, E.H.	Cpl.	F	23rd SCVI		CR	07/05/64	Petersburg, VA	KIA		ROH,HHC
Wright, Ephraim Fanet	Sgt.	I	6th SCVI	24	CR	06/30/62	Frayser's Farm	KIA		ROH,WDB,HHC
Wright, Farr Ellerbe	Pvt.	G	8th SCVI	24	MO	01/12/63	Lynchburg, VA	DOD	(JR=Richmond, VA)	JR,HOM,KEB,UD2
Wright, Hiram	Pvt.		Palm. LA		SR	05/25/63	Orange C.H., VA	DOD	(Convulsions)	JR,SOB
Wright, J. Wesley	Pvt.	G	7th SCVI		ED	05/06/64	Wilderness, VA	KIA		ROH,HOE,KEB,UD1
Wright, J.D.	Cpt. QM					05/05/63		DOD	(Typhoid)	JR
Wright, J.M.	Pvt.	H	18th SCVI		YK	10/20/64	Elmira, NY	DIP	Woodlawn N.C.#525 Elmira	FPH,P5,P65,P120
Wright, J.P.	Pvt.	H	22nd SCVI		GE	04/09/65	Elmira, NY	DIP	Woodlawn N.C.#2611 Elmira	FPH,P6,P65,P120
Wright, J.S.	Pvt.		2nd SC			/ /			Charlestown, VA	ROH
Wright, James	Pvt.		2nd SCVIRi			09/17/62	Sharpsburg, MD	KIA	Rose Hill C. Hagerstown MD	ROH,JR,CDC,BOD
Wright, James C.	Pvt.	K	1st SCVI		LR	02/06/64	Ft. Delaware, DE	DIP	Finn's Pt., NJ Nat. Cem.	ROH,FPH,P42,LAN
Wright, James C.	Pvt.	K	Orr's Ri.	44	AN	11/12/63		DOD	(Dup of J.C. ?)	ROH
Wright, James D.	2nd Sgt.	B	27th SCVI		CN	/ /	Fayetteville, nc			PP,HAG
Wright, John	Pvt.	B	13th SCVI		SG	07/02/63	Gettysburg, PA	KIA		ROH,HOS
Wright, John	Pvt.	H	7th SCVC		KW	/ /		KIA		HIC
Wright, John L.	Pvt.	E	Hol.Leg.	29	SG	09/14/62	South Mtn., MD	KIA		ROH,HOS
Wright, John N.	Pvt.	E	3rd SCVI		NY	09/17/62	Sharpsburg, MD	KIA	(KEB=J.M.)(JR=DOW 9/20)	ROH,JR,SA2,ANY
Wright, John W.	3rd Cpl.	I	21st SCVI		MN	05/07/64	Pt. Walthal Jctn	KIA	(HMC=Petersburg 6/24/64)	ROH,HMC,CDC,HAG
Wright, Joshua H.	Pvt.	G	7th SCVI		ED	09/17/62	Sharpsburg, MD	KIA		ROH,HOE,UD1,KEB
Wright, Lilburn H.	Pvt.	K	2nd SCVIRi	50	AN	10/28/62	Danville, VA	DOD		ROH
Wright, Obediah I. (T.?)	Pvt.	K	Orr's Ri.	18	AN	07/19/62	Richmond, VA	DOD		ROH,CDC
Wright, P.	Pvt.	A	14th SCVI	22	DN	03/25/63	Fredericksburg	DOD		ROH,DEB

SOUTH CAROLINA DEAD IN CSA SERVICE 1861-1865

NAME	RANK	C REGIMENT	AGE	DS	DIED	WHERE	WHY	BURIED	SOURCES
Wright, Richard	Pvt.	D 17th SCVI		CR	05/20/64	Clay's Farm, VA	KIA	(HHC=Howell's Farm)	ROH,HHC,CB
Wright, T.J.	Pvt.	G Ham.Leg.		SR	05/31/62	7 Pines, VA	KIA		ROH,JR,CDC
Wright, Thomas L.	Pvt.	M 8th SCVI	18	DN	07/17/62	Richmond, VA	DOD	(Measles)	ROH,JR,KEB
Wright, Thomas L.	1st Sgt.	A 5th SCVI		LR	10/01/64	Fts. Monroe, VA	DOW	(Wdd 9/30,Ft. Harrison)	SA3,LAN
Wright, W.C.	Pvt.	D 10th SCVI		MN	/ /		DOD		RAS,HMC
Wright, W.H.	Pvt.	E 2nd SCVI		KW	07/13/63	Richmond, VA	DOD	(Dysentery)	SA2,KEB,HIC,H2
Wright, W.W.	Pvt.	I 2nd SCV			/ /	Richmond, VA		Oakwood C.#10,Row 40,Div D	ROH,OWC
Wright, William	Pvt.	E 6th SC Res	42	CN	02/19/65	Charleston, SC	DOD	Magnolia Cem. Charleston	ROH,MAG,RCD
Wright, William	Pvt.	H 2nd SCVI		LR	07/02/63	Gettysburg, PA	KIA		ROH,JR,SA2,LAN
Wright, William	Sgt.	I 6th SCVI		CR	/ /	Bermuda Hundred	KIA	(Prob a later unit)	HHC
Wright, William Miles	Pvt.	K 3rd SCVI	21	SG	09/13/62	Maryland Hts. MD	KIA		ROH,JR,SA2,HOS
Wright, Wsley	Pvt.	F 18th SCVI		YK	03/25/64	Weldon, NC			PP
Wulbern, J.D.H.	Sgt.	G 3rd SCVC	27	CN	09/15/64	Hardeeville, SC	DOD	Bethany Church, Charleston	MAG,RCD
Wyatt, G.B.	Pvt.	C 5th SCV			10/11/62	Richmond, VA		Hollywood Cem.Rchmd. O260	HC
Wyatt, Henry M.	Pvt.	K P.S.S.		SG	02/03/64	Rock Island, IL	DIP	C.C.#362 Rock Island, IL	FPH,P5
Wyatt, L.J.	Pvt.	I 5th SCVI		SG	05/06/64	Wilderness, VA	KIA		HOS
Wyatt, Redmond F.	Pvt.	G 22nd SCVI	38	AN	07/30/64	Crater, Pbg., VA	KIA		ROH,BLM
Wyatt, William	Pvt.	I 6th SCVI		UN	10/10/61	Richmond, VA	DOD		ROH
Wyatt, William	Pvt.	I 5th SCVI		SG	/ /	Manchester, VA	DOD		HOS
Wylie, H. Franklin	Pvt.	E 15th SCVI	18	FD	11/07/62	Culpepper, VA	DOD	(JR=5/31/62)	ROH,JR,KEB
Wylie, Hugh	Pvt.	A 17th SCVI	20	CR	03/25/65	Ft. Steadman, VA	KIA		ROH,HHC,CB
Wylie, J. Dixon	Pvt.	G 6th SCVI	24	CR	01/25/62	Huguenont Ss. VA	DOD		ROH,HHC
Wylie, J. Ross	Pvt.	D 17th SCVI	24	CR	10/22/62	Lynchburg, VA	DOD		ROH,JR,HHC,CB
Wylie, James	Pvt.	A 12th SCVI		YK	03/15/62		DOD		CWC
Wylie, John	Pvt.	C 17th SCVI		YK	/ /	Maryland	DOW		JR,CB
Wylie, Jonathan	Pvt.	A 17th SCVI	19	CR	11/18/62	Lynchburg, VA	DOW	Lynchburg CSA Cem.#1 R2	ROH,JR,BBW,HHC
Wylie, Philip C.	Pvt.	H 24th SCVI	33	CR	08/05/64	Atlanta, GA	KIA		ROH,HHC,CB
Wylie, T. Sumter	Cpl.	D 17th SCVI		CR	11/30/64	Elmira, NY	DIP	(HHC=State Reserves)	ROH,HHC,CB
Wylie, William	2nd Sgt.	G 5th SCVI	33	YK	11/10/64	Rock Island, IL	DIP	C.C.#1607 Rock Island, IL	FPH,SA3,CDC,YE
Wylie, William T.	Pvt.	A 17th SCVI	22	CR	04/15/65	At home	DOD	(William F. in HHC?)	ROH,HHC,CB
Wyman, Hampden Hastings	Pvt.	F 11th SCVI	18	BT	05/13/64	Swift Creek, VA	DOW	Blandford Church Pbg., VA	ROH,BLC,PP
Wyndham, C.	Pvt.	K 10th SCVI		CN	09/20/63	Chickamauga, GA	KIA		ROH,RAS
Wyndham, C.R.	Pvt.	Hart's LA		CN	09/17/63	Richmond, VA			ROH
Wyrick, Frank N.	Pvt.	C 12th SCVI		FD	05/12/64	Spotsylvania, VA	KIA		HFC
Wyrick, Jesse P.	Pvt.	F 12th SCVI		FD	06/27/62	Gaines' Mill, VA	KIA		ROH,HFC,CNM
Wyrick, W.P.	Pvt.	C 12th SCVI		FD	07/25/63	David's Isl., NY	DOW	Cypress Hills N.C.#678, NY	ROH,HFC,P1,P6

SOUTH CAROLINA DEAD IN CSA SERVICE 1861-1865

NAME	RANK	C REGIMENT	AGE	DS	DIED	WHERE	WHY	BURIED	SOURCES
Yarberry, O.L.	Pvt.	K 22nd SCVI		PS	11/12/63	Camp Morton, IN	DIP	Green Lawn C. Indianapolis	FPH,P5,CV
Yarborough, Burr J.	Pvt.	D 19th SCVI	16	ED	06/17/62	Boonesville, MS	DOD		JR,UD3
Yarborough, F.L.	Pvt.	B 21st SCVI		DN	/ /			(NI HAG)	ROH
Yarborough, George H.	Pvt.	D 21st SCVI		CD	07/10/63	Morris Island SC	KIA		ROH,JR,CDC,HAG
Yarborough, J.H.	Pvt.	E 9th SCVIB		KW	09/19/61	Germantown, VA	DOD		ROH,JR,HIC
Yarborough, James M.	Pvt.	A 1st SCVIR			01/09/64	Pt. Lookout, MD	DIP	C.C. Pt. Lookout, MD	FPH,P1,P113,SA
Yarborough, John	Pvt.	I 26th SCVI	39	WG	07/15/64	Petersburg, VA	DOW	(Date approx,6/17-7/27)	ROH,HOW,CTA,CD
Yarborough, John Calvin	Pvt.	A 7th SCVIBn	23	KW	09/19/62	At home	DOD		ROH,HIC,HAG
Yarborough, John M.	Pvt.	E 7th SCVI		ED	07/09/62	Lynchburg, VA	DOD	Lynchburg CSA Cem.#4 R2	ROH,JR,UD3,BBW
Yarborough, Thomas L.	Pvt.	B 21st SCVI		CN	04/28/65	Elmira, NY	DIP	Woodlawn N.C.#2728 Elmira	FPH,P5,P65,HAG
Yarborough, William C.	Pvt.	D 21st SCVI		CD	/ /	At home	DOD	(1862)	ROH,HAG
Yarbrough, Michael	Pvt.	E 7th SCVI		ED	/ /		DOD		HOE,KEB,UD3
Yargrin, B.T.	Pvt.	F			10/23/62	Richmond, VA		(Prob Yeargin, 2nd SCVIRi)	ROH
Yates, Barney	Pvt.	G 16th SCVI		GE	11/30/64	Franklin, TN	KIA		ROH,16R,PP
Yates, John	Pvt.	E Orr's Ri.	28	PS	12/01/62	Winchester, VA	DOD		ROH,CDC
Yates, Joseph	Pvt.	A 15th SCVI		RD	10/25/62	Winchester, VA		Stonewall C. Winchester VA	ROH,JR,WIN,KEB
Yates, William	Pvt.	D 25th SCVI		MN	/ /	Charleston, SC	DOD		HMC,HAG
Yeadon, Richard W.	Pvt.	B 7th SCVC		CN	01/28/64	At home	DOD	Family Cm/Accabee Chlstn.	MAG,RCD
Yeadon,Sr., Richard	Cpl.	A Ham.Leg.		CN	05/31/62	7 Pines, VA	KIA		ROH,JR,CDC
Yeargin, E. Riley	Pvt.	B 16th SCVI		GE	07/29/62	Adams Run, SC	DOD		PP,16R
Yeargin, John B.	Pvt.	Arsenal Co			07/27/63	Columbia, SC	DOD	(PP=6/27/63)	ROH,PP
Yeargin, John H.	Pvt.	D Orr's Ri.		AN	/ /	Richmond, VA		Oakwood C.#88,Row N,Div C	ROH,OWC,CDC
Yeargin, Thomas J.	Pvt.	I 14th SCVI	22	AE	06/14/62	Coosawatchie, SC	DOD	(HOL= John A.)(Typhoid)	ROH,JR,HOL
Yeargin, William D.	2nd Lt.	F Ham. Leg.		GE	07/21/61	1st Manassas, VA	KIA		ROH,JR,CV,R48
Yeddards, David F.	Pvt.	F 2nd SCVIRi	30	AE	08/26/62	Manchester, VA	DOD		ROH
Yelldell, William Alonzo	Cpl.	I 24th SCVI	17	ED	07/27/64	Atlanta, GA	KIA		ROH
Yerger, J.C.	Pvt.	H 1st SC Res			02/15/65	Charleston, SC	DOD	Magnolia Cem. Charleston	ROH,MAG,RCD
Yon, G.A.E.	Pvt.	H 3rd SCVI		LN	09/13/62	Maryland Hts. MD	KIA	(Yonce?)	ROH,SA2,CDC
Yon, J.C.	Sgt.	I 22nd SCVI		OG	05/12/65	Newport News, VA	DIP	Newport News C. #29	P6
Yon, John E.	Pvt.	H 3rd SCVI		LN	09/17/62	Sharpsburg, MD	KIA	Rose Hill C. Hagerstown MD	JR,KEB,WAT
Yon, L.W.	Cpl.	I 22nd SCVI		OG	10/01/62		DOW	(Wdd South Mtn 9/14/62)	ROH
Yon, R.A.	Sgt.	I 27th SCVI		CN	02/12/65	Richmond, VA		Hollywood Cem.Rchmd. W278	HC
Yonce, Gabriel	Pvt.	F 24th SCVI	18	AN	10/23/63	Augusta, GA	DOW		EJM
Yonce, George	Pvt.	H 20th SCVI		LN	08/02/62		DOD	(KEB= Younce)	ROH,KEB
Yongue, J. Ross	Pvt.	G 6th SCVI	27	CR	02/26/62	Centreville, VA	DOD		ROH,HHC
Yonn, R.A.	Pvt.	H 2nd SCVA			05/25/64	Charleston, SC	DOD	(Soldiers Relief Hospital)	ROH,CDC
Yoring, Joseph	Pvt.	H 15th SCVAB			04/29/65		DIP	(POW in NC 4/15/65)	P1
Youmans, J.F.	Pvt.	F 14th SCVI		LS	08/11/62	Richmond, VA			ROH
Youmans, Oliver Johnson	Sgt.	C 2nd SCVI		RD	05/06/64	Wilderness, VA	KIA	Fredericksburg C.C. R6S13	ROH,SA2,FBG,H2
Young,	Pvt.	H Ham.Leg.	18	OG	/ /	Virginia	KIA	(1864)	ROH
Young, A.	Pvt.	1st SC			10/09/61	Richmond, VA		Hollywood Cem.Rchmd. R169	HC
Young, A. Hayne	3rd Sgt.	C 3rd SCVI		NY	05/06/64	Wilderness, VA	KIA		ROH,SA2
Young, A.M.	Pvt.	L P.S.S.			11/21/63		DOD		ROH
Young, A.M.	Pvt.	A 1st SCVA			03/02/64	Nashville, TN	DIP		P5
Young, A.P.	2nd Sgt.	G 14th SCVI	32	AE	08/29/62	2nd Manassas, VA	KIA		ROH,JR,CDC
Young, Allen	Pvt.	A 2nd SCVC		KW	03/15/65	Neuse River, NC	KIA	(UD1=Bentonville, NC)	ROH,HIC,UD1
Young, Archibald	Pvt.	D 7th SCVIBn	30	KW	05/15/62	Adams Run, SC	DOD		ROH,HIC,HAG
Young, Archibald W.	Pvt.	A Orr's Ri.		PS	03/02/64	Nashville, TN	DIP	City Cem. Nashville, TN	PCS,P2
Young, Burke	Pvt.	D Orr's Ri.		AN	06/24/62	Savage St., VA	KIA	(2nd Rpt=Gaines' Mill)	ROH,JR,CDC,CNM
Young, C.C.	Pvt.	A 18th SCVI		UN	10/01/62	Frederick, MD	DOW	Mt.Olivet C.#70 Frederick	ROH,FPH,UNC,BO
Young, Charles S.	Pvt.	K 7th SCVC		KW	08/15/64	Deep Run, VA	KIA		ROH,HIC

SOUTH CAROLINA DEAD IN CSA SERVICE 1861-1865

NAME	RANK	C REGIMENT	AGE	DS	DIED	WHERE	WHY	BURIED	SOURCES
Young, Christopher C.	Pvt.	A 18th SCVI	35	UN	02/07/65	At home	DOD	(Who buried @ Frederick?)	ROH
Young, Cyrus	Pvt.	H 4th SCVI	33	PS	08/29/61	Culpepper, VA	DOD	Fairview Cem. Culpepper VA	JR,CGH,SA2,CDC
Young, D.J.	1st Lt.	C 17th SCVI	30	YK	08/30/62	2nd Manassas, VA	KIA	Buffalo B.C. Cherokee Cty.	ROH,JR,TCC,R47
Young, F.M.	Pvt.	F 13th SCVI		SG	07/08/62	Richmond, VA		Hollywood Cem.Rchmd. L102	HC
Young, Francis M.	Pvt.	B 15th SCVI	18	UN	12/09/64	Pt. Lookout, MD	DIP	C.C. Pt. Lookout, MD	ROH,P5,P115,FPH
Young, George F.	2nd Sgt.	C 1st SCVIH		BL	08/31/62	2nd Manassas, VA	DOW		ROH,JR,SA1,JRH
Young, George W.	Pvt.	B 15th SCVI	22	KW	01/07/62	Hardeeville, SC	DOD	(1st in G, 2nd SCVI)	ROH,JR,KEB,H2
Young, Green	Pvt.	D Hol.Leg.	18	BL	03/05/62	Charleston, SC	DOD	(PP=Adams Run, SC)	ROH,PP
Young, Henry J.N.	Pvt.	H Ham.Leg.		OG	08/14/64	VA	DOW	(Globe Tavern?)	ROH,CDC
Young, J.A.	Pvt.	H 25th SCVI		CN	07/16/63	Grimball's, SC	KIA	(John's Island)	ROH,JR,CDC
Young, J.C.	Pvt.	B 7th SCVI		AE	11/06/62	Richmond, VA		Oakwood C.#150,Row L,Div B	ROH,OWC,KEB
Young, J.C.	Pvt.	L Orr's Ri.		AN	06/27/62	Gaines' Mill, VA	KIA		ROH,JR,CDC
Young, J.F.	Pvt.	B 13th SCVI		SG	07/03/62	Richmond, VA		Hollywood Cem.Rchmd. L178	HC
Young, J.H.	Pvt.	G 14th SCVI	33	AE	06/27/62	Gaines' Mill, VA	KIA		ROH,CNM
Young, J.H.	Pvt.	D SCVA		CN	03/28/62	Charleston, SC		Magnolia Cem. Charleston	JR,MAG,RCD
Young, J.M.	Pvt.	F 14th SCVI		LS	12/14/62	Fredericksburg	DOW		JR
Young, J.P.	Pvt.	K 18th SCVI	22	SG	07/30/64	Crater, Pbg., VA	KIA		ROH,BLM
Young, James	Pvt.	I Hol.Leg.		SG	/ /	Richmond, VA			ROH
Young, James A.B.	Pvt.	G Orr's Ri.		AE	08/15/64	Elmira, NY	DIP	Woodlawn N.C.#28 Elmira	ROH,FPH,P5,P65
Young, James R.	Pvt.	F 13th SCVI		SG	07/03/62	Richmond, VA		(HOS=1863)	ROH,JR,HOS
Young, Jesse F.	Pvt.	A 9th SCVIB	22	KW	08/30/61	Germantown, VA	DOD	Quaker Cem. Camden, SC	ROH,JR,LAN,PP
Young, John Brandon	Pvt.	A 18th SCVI	45	UN	10/05/62	Richmond, VA	DOD	Oakwood C. #23 Row L Div B	ROH,OWC,UNC,CDC
Young, John L.	2nd Lt.	K 18th SCVI			07/04/62				R47
Young, John M.	Pvt.	H 7th SCVIBn	20	RD	05/16/64	Drury's Bluff VA	KIA		ROH,HAG
Young, John Pigg	Pvt.	A 23rd SCVI	18	CD	08/11/64	Petersburg, VA			PP
Young, Joseph P.	Pvt.	I 5th SCVI		SG	05/31/62	7 Pines, VA	DOW	(SA3 drops on FUR home)	HOS,SA3
Young, Joseph S.	Pvt.	B 4th SCVC		CR	07/26/64	Pt. Lookout, MD	DIP	C.C. Pt. Lookout, MD CB	ROH,FPH,P6,HHC
Young, Josiah	Pvt.	E Orr's Ri.	30	PS	07/01/63	Richmond, VA	DOD	(PP=Harrisonburg 7/3/63)	ROH,CDC,PP
Young, M.J.	Cpl.	D 7th SCVIBn	25	KW	08/15/62	Adams Run, SC	DOD	(PP=J.J. 7/9/62)	ROH,HIC,HAG,PP
Young, Moses	Pvt.	K 12th SCVI	25	PS	08/15/62	Richmond, VA	DOD		ROH
Young, R.A.	Pvt.	H 2nd SCVA			/ /	Charleston, SC		Magnolia Cem. Charleston	MAG,RCD
Young, Richard	Pvt.	B 2nd SCVIRi		PS	03/29/64	Rock Island, IL	DIP	C.C.#944 Rock Island, IL	FPH,P5
Young, Robert	Pvt.	F 24th SCVI		AN	01/02/64	Kingston, GA	DOD		HOL
Young, Samuel O.	Pvt.	C 24th SCVI	35	CO	09/22/63	Rome, GA	DOD	Myrtle Hill C. Rome, GA	ROH,BGA
Young, W.D.	Pvt.	B 27th SCVI		CN	/ /	Fayetteville, NC			PP
Young, W.M.					/ /			(Rchmd effects list 12/62)	CDC
Young, William	Pvt.	I 14th SCVI	19	AE	11/13/63	Ft. Delaware, DE	DIP	Finn's Pt., NJ Nat. Cem.	ROH,FPH,P5,HOL
Young, William	Cpl.	G 24th SCVI			07/22/64	Atlanta, GA	KIA		ROH,CDC
Young, William A.	4th Cpl.	I 4th SCVI		PS	07/21/61	1st Manassas, VA	KIA	(JR=P.S.S.)	ROH,JR,SA2
Young, William H.	Cpt.	K 3rd SCVI	28	SG	07/02/63	Gettysburg, PA	KIA		ROH,JR,GDR,SA2
Young, William H.	Pvt.	F 24th SCVI	20	AN	11/19/63		DOD	Con. Cem. Marietta, GA	HOL,BGA,CCM,UD2
Young, William J.	Pvt.	G 2nd SCVI		KW	07/01/62	Malvern Hill, VA	KIA		H2,SA2,KEB
Young, William T.	Pvt.	D 17th SCVI		CR	07/30/64	Crater, Pbg., VA	KIA		ROH,HHC,CB
Youngblood, L.A.	Pvt.	D 14th SCVI	17	ED	03/08/65	Elmira, NY	DIP	Woodlawn N.C.#2368 Elmira	FPH,P5,P65,D14
Youngblood, R.C.	Pvt.	H 18th SCVI	26	YK	07/30/64	Crater, Pbg., VA	KIA	(BLM= R.G.)	ROH,BLM,YEB
Youngblood, Thomas W.	Pvt.	H 18th SCVI	23	YK	07/22/62	Charleston, SC		Magnolia Cem. Charleston	ROH,MAG,RCD,YEB
Youngblood, William H.	Pvt.	H 6th SCVI	19	YK	/ /	Germantown, VA	DOD	(1861, YEB=DOW)	ROH,YEB
Youngenser, G.	Pvt.	B 13th SCVI		SG	/ /	Richmond, VA		Oakwood C.#4, Row K,Div F	ROH,OWC
Younginger, J.	Pvt.	H 15th SCMil		UN	04/29/65	Hart's Island NY	DIP	Cypress Hills N.C.#2645 NY	FPH,P6
Zahler, J.	Pvt.			CO	04/15/65	Columbia, SC	DOD		ROH
Zahler, J.M.	Pvt.	D 4th SCVC		CN	06/04/65	Pt. Lookout, MD	DIP	C.C. Pt. Lookout, MD	FPH,P6,P115

SOUTH CAROLINA DEAD IN CSA SERVICE 1861-1865

NAME	RANK	C REGIMENT	AGE	DS	DIED	WHERE	WHY	BURIED	SOURCES
Zealy, James E.	Pvt.	I 2nd SCVI		BT	09/09/61	Falls Church, VA	DOD	Grahamville, SC Cem.	ROH,SA2,KEB,H2
Zealy, R.F.	1st Sgt.	A 15th SCVI	19	RD	06/24/64	Hanover C.H., VA	DOW	(Wdd 5/24/64)	ROH,KEB
Zedaker, John	Pvt.	A 18th SCVI		UN	07/30/64	Crater, Pbg., VA	KIA		ROH,BLM
Zehe, John H.	Pvt.	E 11th SCVI		BT	10/24/64	Elmira, NY	DIP	Woodlawn N.C.#856 Elmira	FPH,P5,P65,HAG
Zeigler, B.C.	Pvt.	B 3rd SCVC		CO	04/05/65	Thomasville, NC		Thomasville C.C., NC	CV,PP
Zeigler, D.A.	Pvt.	B 1st SCVIH		OG	08/30/62	2nd Manassas, VA	KIA	(Canister shot in chest)	ROH,JR,SA1,JRH
Zeigler, D.W.	3rd Cpl.	B 1st SCVIH		OG	03/07/63	Richmond, VA	DOD		ROH,JR,SA1,JRH
Zeigler, David F.	Pvt.	E 27th SCVI	47	OG	05/20/64	Drury's Bluff VA	DOW		ROH,HAG,CDC
Zeigler, Fred	Pvt.	F 25th SCVI	22	OG	06/03/64	Cold Harbor, VA	KIA		ROH,HAG
Zeigler, George J.J.	Sgt.	B 20th SCVI	28	OG	02/04/62	At home	DOD		ROH,CNM
Zeigler, Hayne H.	Pvt.	B 20th SCVI	21	OG	10/20/64	Cedar Creek, VA	KIA	Woodstock, VA	ROH,CV,KEB
Zeigler, J.C.T.	Pvt.	A 1st SCVIH		BL	10/12/62	Warrenton, VA	DOW	(Wdd @ 2nd Man)	ROH,SA1,CDC,UD
Zeigler, J.M.	Pvt.	H 17th SCVI		BL	07/31/64	Petersburg, VA	DOW	(Wdd 7/30)	ROH
Zeigler, Malachi C.	Pvt.	H 6th SCVI	24	OG	07/09/62	Richmond, VA	DOD	Oakwood C.#1,Row B,Div A	ROH,OWC
Zimmerman, A.O.	Pvt.	B 1st SCVIH	23	OG	04/24/64	At home	DOD		ROH,SA1
Zimmerman, D.R.	Pvt.	C 7th SCVI	30	SG	04/10/64	Rock Island, IL	DIP	C.C.#1022 Rock Island, IL	ROH,FPH,P5,KEB
Zimmerman, Dozier P.	Pvt.	B 21st SCVI	19	DN	09/02/64	At home	DOD		ROH,HAG
Zimmerman, Frank A.	Pvt.	I 13th SCVI	27	SG	08/15/62	Richmond, VA	DOD	(Typhoid)	ROH,JR,HOS
Zimmerman, G.H.	Pvt.	K 7th SCVI			10/15/62	Staunton, VA		Thornrose C. Staunton, VA	TOD
Zimmerman, Jacob N.	Cpl.	I 13th SCVI	25	SG	05/12/64	Spotsylvania, VA	KIA		ROH,HOS
Zimmerman, John M.	Pvt.	K P.S.S.	22	SG	06/30/62	Frayser's Farm	KIA	Glen Springs Cem. SG Cty.	ROH,JR,HOS,SCS
Zimmerman, Russell D.	Pvt.	F 25th SCVI		OG	05/07/64	Pt.Walthal Jctn.	KIA	(PP=5/27, Body sent home)	ROH,CV,BLC,PP
Zimmerman, Samuel E.	Pvt.	B Hol.Leg.	29	SG	07/29/63	At home	DOD		ROH,HOS
Zimmerman, W. Capers	Pvt.	F 25th SCVI		OG	/ /				ROH,HAG
Zinker, William	Pvt.	H 20th SCVI		LN	10/13/63	Strasburg, VA	KIA	(KEB=Zenkee)	ROH,CDC,KEB

SOURCE CODES AND ABBREVIATIONS

ACC- R. Wayne Bratcher, *Anderson County Cemeteries, Volume 1* (Greenville, S.C.: A Press, 1985)

- R. Wayne Bratcher, *Anderson County Cemeteries, Volume 2* (Greenville, S.C.: A Press, 1986)

- Anne Sheriff, "Anderson County Cemeteries, Volume 3." (Undated manuscript prepared by The Albemarle County Historical Society, Charlottesville, Va. Volume now in the collections of the South Carolina Historical Society.)

ACL- Mary D. Robertson, ed., *A Confederate Lady Comes of Age: The Journal of Pauline DeCaradeuc Heyward, 1863-1888* (Columbia: University of South Carolina Press, 1992)

AHB- Richard Manning Boykin, *Capt. Alexander Hamilton Boykin* (New York: Privately printed, 1942)

ALH- Louise Haskell Daly, *Alexander Cheves Haskell, Portrait of a Man* (Norwood, Mass.: Plimpton Press, 1934; repr., Wilmington, N.C.: Broadfoot Publishing Co., 1989)

ANY- John Belton O'Neall and John A. Chapman, *Annals of Newberry* (Newberry, S.C.: n.p., 1892; repr., Baltimore, Md.: Genealogical Publishing Co., 1974)

AOA- E. Prioleau Henderson, *Autobiography of Arab* (Self-published, 1901; repr., Camden, S.C.: J.J. Fox, 1991)

AR- R. A. Brock, "The Appomattox Roster," *Southern Historical Society Papers, Volume V* (1887, repr., New York: Antiquarian Press, Ltd., 1962)

- William G. Nines and Ronald G. Wilson, *The Appomattox Paroles, April 9-15, 1865* (Lynchburg, Va.: H. E. Howard, 1989)

BBC- Berry Benson, *Berry Benson's Civil War Book, Memoirs of a Confederate Scout and Sharpshooter* (Athens: University of Georgia Press, 1962; repr., Frances Benson Thompson, ed., Athens: University of Georgia Press, 1991)

BBW- Lucy Harrison Miller Baber and Evelyn Lee Moore, *Behind the Old Brick Wall* (Lynchburg, Va.: The Lynchburg Committee of The National Society of The Colonial Dames of America in the Commonwealth of Virginia, 1968)

BCI- *Berkeley County Cemetery Inscriptions* (Charleston Chapter, S.C. Genealogical Society, 1985)

BGA- James Thomas Woodward, "South Carolina Confederate Soldiers Buried in Georgia." (Undated typed manuscript in the S.C. Department of Archives and History, Columbia, S.C.)

BHC- U.R. Brooks, *Butler and His Cavalry in the War of Secession* (Columbia, S.C.: The State Co., 1909)

BIG- Mamie Yeary, *Reminiscences of the Boys In Gray* (Dallas, Tex.: Smith & Lamar, 1912)

BLC- "Known South Carolina dead buried in Blandford Church Cemetery." (A list provided by John R. Davis, Jr., chief of interpretation, Petersburg National Battlefield, National Park Service, 1990. This list is based upon City of Petersburg records of deaths in Petersburg hospitals and a record of the dead of Elliott's Brigade at the Crater. This manuscript is in the collections of the South Carolina Historical Society.)

BLM- "Blandford Church Memorial, erected by the State of South Carolina to the memory of her sons who lost their lives in the defence of their country at the Battle of the Crater, July 30, 1864, Elliott's Brigade." (Virginia Historical Inventory, Dinwiddie County, 1936-1937, by the Works Progress Administration. Copy provided by the National Park Service and now in the collections of the South Carolina Historical Society.)

BNC- "Individuals from southern states who died during the Civil War and are buried in the Beaufort National Cemetery, 1601 Boundary Street, Beaufort, South Carolina." (Typed list is in the collections of the South Carolina Historical Society.)

BOD- Steven R. Stotelmyer, *The Bivouacs of the Dead: The Story of Those Who Died at Antietam and South Mountain With Histories and Rosters of Antietam, Washington, Mt. Olivet and Elmwood Cemeteries* (Baltimore, Md.: Toomey Press, 1992)

BOS- J.F.J. Caldwell, *The History of a Brigade of South Carolinians First Known as Gregg's and Subsequently as McGowan's Brigade* (Philadelphia, Pa.: King and Baird Printers, 1866; repr., Dayton, Ohio: Morningside Press, 1992)

CAE- R. Wayne Bratcher, *Cemetery Records of Abbeville County, S.C.* (Greenville, S.C.: A Press, 1982)

CAG- Gary R. Baker, *Cadets in Gray* (Columbia, S.C.: Palmetto Bookworks, 1989)

CB- Robert J. Stevens, *Captain Bill, Book One: The Records and Writings of Captain William Henry Edwards (and others), Company A, 17th Regiment, South Carolina Volunteers, Confederate States of America* (Richburg, S.C.: Chester District Genealogical Society, 1985)

- Robert J. Stevens, *Captain Bill, Book Two: The Records and Writings of Captain William Henry Edwards (and others), Company A, 17th*

Regiment, South Carolina Volunteers, Confederate States of America (Richburg, S.C.: Chester District Genealogical Society, 1985)
- Robert J. Stevens, *Captain Bill, Book Three: A Genealogy of the Catawba River Valley of South Carolina, Chester-York-Lancaster Counties Edwards, Culp, McFadden families* (Darlington, S.C.: Self-published, 1990)

CC- William H. Krause, *The Story of Camp Chase* (Nashville, Tenn.: Publishing House of the Methodist Episcopal Church, South, 1906)

CCM- Larry O. Blair & Thomas E. Lyle, *Confederate Veterans Interred in the Confederate Cemetery, Marietta, Ga.* (Maryville, Tenn.: Printed by Byron's Graphic Arts, 1991)

CCP- Ron Chepesiuk, *Chester County, A Pictorial History* (Norfolk, Va.: The Donning Co., 1984)

CD- *Confederate Soldiers, Sailors and Civilians Who Died as Prisoners of War at Camp Douglas, Chicago, Ill., 1862-1865* (Kalamazoo, Mich.: Edgar Gray Publications, n.d.)

CDC- *Charleston Daily Courier* (Various issues 1860-1865. Microfilm in the Charleston County Library.)

CDG- *The Bulletin of the Chester District Genealogical Society, Volume XVII, No. 2* (June 1993)

CDN- Brent Holcombe, *Marriage and Death Notices From Camden, S.C. Newspapers, 1816-1865* (Easley, S.C.: Southern Historical Press, 1978)

CEN- 1860 Census schedules, M653 series Microfilm rolls, National Archives, Washington, D.C.

CGB- Richard Lewis, *Camp Life of a Confederate Boy of Bratton's Brigade, Longstreet's Corps, C.S.A.* (Charleston, S.C.: News and Courier Book Presses, 1883; repr., Gaithersburg, Md.: The Butternut Press, n.d.)

CGH- Robert A. Hodge, *A Death Roster of the Confederate General Hospital at Culpepper, Virginia* (Fredericksburg, Va.: Robert A. Hodge, 1977)

CGS- Varina D. Brown, *A Colonel at Gettysburg and Spotsylvania* (Columbia, S.C.: The State Co., 1931; repr., Baltimore, Md.: Butternut and Blue, n.d.)

CGW- R. Lockwood Tower, ed., *A Carolinian Goes to War: The Civil War Narrative of Arthur Middleton Manigault, Brigadier General, C.S.A.* (Columbia: Published for the Charleston Library Society by the University of South Carolina Press, 1983)

CIG- Larry J. Daniel, *Cannoneers in Gray: The Field Artillery of the Army of Tennessee, 1861-1865* (University: University of Alabama Press, 1984)

CKB- Charles Kelly Barrow, "Letter list of South Carolina dead buried in Forsyth, Milner, Barnesville & Thomaston, Ga." Sent to the author, 1991.

CLD- Edward L. Wells, *A Sketch of the Charleston Light Dragoons from the Earliest Formation of the Corps* (Charleston, S.C.: Lucas, Richardson & Co., 1888)

CMH5- Ellison Capers, *South Carolina*, Volume V of *Confederate Military History* (Atlanta, Ga.: Confederate Publishing Co., 1899; repr., n.p.:Blue & Grey Press, n.d.)

CML- W.J. Tancig, *Confederate Military Land Units, 1861-1865* (Cranbury, N.J.: Thomas Yoseloff, 1967)

CMO- Chester CSA Memorial Monument, erected May 7, 1938, in Richburg, S.C., by the Lafayette Strait Chapter, United Daughters of the Confederacy.

CNM- *Charleston Mercury* (Various issues, 1860-1865. Microfilm held by the Charleston County Library.)

COF- William A. Albaugh III, *Confederate Faces: A Pictorial Review of the Individuals in the Confederate Armed Forces* (Solana Beach, Cal.: Wm. A. Albaugh III and Verde Publishers; repr., Wilmington, N.C.: Broadfoot Publishing Co., 1993)

CRD- Eleanor D. McSwain, ed., *Crumbling Defences or Memoirs and Reminiscences of John Logan Black, Colonel, C.S.A.* (Macon, Ga.: The J.W. Burke Co., 1960)

CRM- "Chester Militia Roll." (A partial list of men who had gone into Confederate service from Beat No. 5, Western Battalion, 27th Regiment, South Carolina Militia, Chester District. Original document consisted of several handwritten pages from a larger ledger. The pages were purchased as memorabilia by R.W. Kirkland, transcribed, and the original document sent to a dealer for resale; it was lost in the mails. A copy of the transcription is in the collections of the South Carolina Historical Society.)

CSL- Spencer Glasgow Welch, *A Confederate Surgeon's Letters to his Wife* (New York: Neale Publishing Company, 1911; repr., Marietta, Ga.: Continental Book Co., 1954)

CSO- Joseph H. Crute, Jr., *Confederate Staff Officers, 1861-1865* (Powhatan, Va.: Derwent Books, 1982)

CTA- Danny H. Smith, *The Call to Arms* (Hemingway, S.C.: Three Rivers Historical Society, n.d.)

CUC- E.M.F. Bryan and G.H. Bryan, *Cemeteries of Upper Colleton County, S.C.* (Jacksonville, Fla.: Florentine Press, 1974)

CUS- J. Roderick Heller III & Carolynn Ayres Heller, *The Confederacy is on Her Way Up the Spout: Letters to South Carolina, 1861-1864* (Athens: University of Georgia Press, 1992)

CV- Louis H. Menarin, ed., *Cumulative Index, The*

APPENDICES

Confederate Veteran Magazine, 1893-1932 (Wilmington, N.C.: Broadfoot Publishing Co., 1990) See index for references to names of deceased soldiers, events, and places.

CVGA- Charles Kelly Barrow, "List of S.C. CSA soldiers buried in Oakland Cemetery, Atlanta & Glenwood Cemetery, Thomaston, Ga.," *Palmetto Partisan* (Winter 1992)

CWC- Douglas Summers Brown, *City Without Cobwebs (A History of Rock Hill, S.C.)* (Spartanburg, S.C.: Reprint Co., 1975)

D14- "Roll of Honor, Co. D, 14th Regiment, S.C. Volunteers" (Edgefield, S.C.: Advertiser Office, 1866)

DAR- Eliza Cowan Ervin & Horace Fraser Rudisill, *Darlingtoniana: A History of People, Places and Events in Darlington County, S.C.* (Columbia, S.C.: R.L. Bryan Co., 1964)

DEB- Bessie Mell Lane, ed., *Dear Bet, The Carter Letters, 1861-1865, The Letters of Lieutenant Sidney Carter, Company A, 14th Regiment, South Carolina Volunteers, Gregg's-McGowan's Brigade, CSA to Ellen Timmons Carter* (Clemson, S.C.: Self-published, 1978)

DEM- Robert Harley Mackintosh, Jr., ed.,*"Dear Martha..." The Confederate War Letters of a South Carolina Soldier Alexander Faulkner Fewell* (Columbia, S.C.: R.L. Bryan Co., 1976)

DOC- John Johnson, *The Defense of Charleston Harbor including Fort Sumter and the Adjacent Islands, 1861-1865* (Charleston, S.C.: Walker, Evans & Cogswell, 1890; repr., Freeport, N.Y.: Books For Libraries Press, 1970)

DRE- "Dorchester County & Township CSA Enrollment Book." (A ledger manuscript in the collections of the South Carolina Historical Society.)

EDN- Carlee J. McClendon, *Edgefield Death Notices and Cemetery Records* (Columbia, S.C.: The Hive Press, 1977)

EDR- William Valmore Izlar, *A Sketch of the War Record of the Edisto Rifles, 1861-1865* (Columbia, S.C.: The State Co., 1914; repr., Camden, S.C.: J.J. Fox, 1990)

EJM- Eugene Jones, "A History of the 24th South Carolina Volunteer Infantry Regiment." (Unpublished manuscript in possession of Mr. Jones, Goose Creek, S.C., n.d.)

ELM- C.W. Holmes, *Elmira Prison Camp* (New York: G. P. Putnam's Sons, 1912)

EMC- William A. Turner, *Even More Confederate Faces* (Orange, Va.: Moss Publications, 1983)

ETT- Eleanor Boland Owens, *Sketches of Private E.T. Tollison, C.S.A.* (Bamberg, S.C.: Kilgus Printing Co., Inc., 1992)

ETW- Walbrook Davis Swank, *Eyewitness to War, 1861-1865, Vol. 1: Memoirs of Men Who Fought in the Battle of Trevillian Station 11-12 June 1864* (Charlottesville, Va.: USAFRET Papercraft Printing & Design Co., Inc., 1990)

FBG- Robert K. Krick, *Roster of the Confederate Dead in the Fredericksburg Confederate Cemetery* (Fredericksburg, Va.: n.p., 1974)

FCP- Brent H. Holcomb & Elmer O. Parker, *Early Records of Fishing Creek Presbyterian Church, Chester County, SC 1799-1859* (Greenville, S.C.: A Press, 1980)

FLR- *For Love of a Rebel* by The Arthur Manigault Chapter of the United Daughters of the Confederacy Georgetown, S.C. (Charleston, S.C.: Walker, Evans & Cogswell, 1964; Revised ed., 1974)

FPH- Frances Ingmire and Carolyn Ericson, *Confederate P.O.W.'s Soldiers & Sailors Who Died in Federal Prisons & Military Hospitals in the North*. Compiled in the Office of the Commissioner for Marking Ground of Confederate Dead, War Department, 1912. (n.p., 1984)

FRB- John M. Carroll, *List of Field Officers, Regiments & Battalions in the Confederate States Army 1861-1865* (Mattituck, N.Y.: J.M. Carroll & Co., 1983)

GAY- D. Alexander Brown, *The Galvanized Yankees* (Urbana: University of Illinois Press, 1963)

GDR- Robert W. Krick, *Gettysburg Death Roster* (Dayton, Ohio: Press of Morningside Bookshop, 1981)

GEC- Greenville Chapter, S.C. Genealogical Society, *Greenville County Cemetery Survey, Vols. 1-5* (Greenville, S.C.: A Press, 1977-1983)

GEE- Beverly T. Whitmore, ed., *The Presence of the Past: Epitaphs of 18th and 19th Century Pioneers in Greenville County, South Carolina, and Their Descendants ...* (Baltimore, Md.: Published for the Greenville County Historical Society by Gateway Press, 1976)

GIG- Ezra J. Warner, *Generals in Gray: Lives of the Confederate Commanders* (Baton Rouge: Louisiana State University Press, 1983)

GLS- William Francis Strait III, ed., *Gilbert Matier Lafayette Strait, His Letters and His Times, 1851-1863* (Self-published, 1988)

GMJ- *General Micah Jenkins and the Palmetto Sharpshooters*. South Carolina Regimental Series. (Germantown, Tenn.: Guild Bindery Press, Inc., 1994)

GNG- *Georgetown County, S.C. Tombstone Inscriptions* (Georgetown: Georgetown County Historical Society and the Georgetown Committee of the National Society of Colonial Dames of America in the State of South Carolina, 1980)

GOR- "Gordonsville, Va. Receiving Hospital Death Roster." Manuscript held by the City of Gordonsville, copy in the collections of the

South Carolina Historical Society.)
GRG- Sol Emanuel, "An Historical Sketch of The Georgetown Rifle Guards and as Co. A of the Tenth Regiment S.C. Volunteers ..." (n.p., n.d. [1909?])
GRS- J.L. Mauldin, "Minutes of the Meeting of the Gist Rifles Survivors Association, Company D, Hampton Legion, C.S.A. at Williamston, S.C., August 15, 1883. and Company Muster Roll, From 1st Manassas to Appomattox 1861-1865." (n.p., n.d.)
GSR- "Goldsboro Surrender Paroles." National Archives Microfilm #418, held by R.W. Kirkland.
H2- Mac Wyckoff, *A History of the 2nd South Carolina Infantry, 1861-65* (Fredericksburg, Va.: Sergeant Kirkland's Museum and Historical Society, 1994)
H15- Robert B. Wilkinson, Jr., "A Brief History & Roster of the Fifteenth South Carolina Volunteer Infantry, Confederate States Army, Company C and Company I in the War Between the States, 1861-1865." (Unpublished manuscript in the Newberry/Saluda Regional Library, July 1987)
HAG- Johnson Hagood, *Memoirs of the War of Secession* (Columbia, S.C.: The State Company, 1910; repr., Camden, S.C.: J.J. Fox, 1989)
HC- Hollywood Memorial Association, *Register of Confederate Dead Interred in Hollywood Cemetery, Richmond, Va.* (Richmond, Va.: Gary, Clemmitt & Jones, 1869)
HCD- Edward McCrady, *Heroes of the Old Camden District, South Carolina, 1776-1861...* (Richmond, Va.: Wm. Ellis Jones, Printer, 1888)
HCL- Virginia K.G. Orvin, *History of Clarendon County, 1700-1961* (n.p., n.d.)
HFC- Fitz Hugh McMaster, *History of Fairfield County, South Carolina From "Before The White Man Came" to 1942* (Columbia, S.C.: The State Co., 1946)
HGC- George C. Rogers, Jr., *The History of Georgetown County, South Carolina* (Columbia: University of South Carolina Press, 1970)
HHC- Anne Pickens Collins, *Heritage History of Chester County, South Carolina* (Chester, S.C.: Self-published, 1982)
HHS- *History of the Hibernian Society in Charleston, S.C., 1799-1981* (Charleston: Self-published, 1981)
HIC- Thomas J. Kirkland and Robert M. Kennedy, *Historic Camden, Part One: Colonial and Revolutionary* (Columbia, S.C.: The State Co., 1905; repr., Camden, S.C.: Kershaw County Historical Society, 1963)
- Thomas J. Kirkland and Robert M. Kennedy, *Historic Camden, Part Two: Nineteenth Century* (Columbia, S.C.: The State Co., 1926; repr., Camden, S.C.: The Kershaw County Historical Society, 1963)
HLS- "Minutes of the Proceedings of The Reunion of the Hampton Legion Survivors Held in Columbia, S.C. on the 21st Day of July, A.D. 1875" (Charleston, S.C.: Walker, Evans & Cogswell, Printers, 1875)
HMC- W.W. Sellers, *History Of Marion County, S.C., From Its Earliest Times to the Present* (Columbia, S.C.: R.L. Bryan Co., 1902; repr., Marion, S.C.: Marion Public Library, 1956)
HOE- John A. Chapman, *History of Edgefield County From the Earliest Settlements to 1897* (Newberry, S.C.: Elbert H. Aull, 1897; repr., Easley, S.C.: Southern Historical Press, 1976)
HOF- J. W. Reid, *History of the Fourth Regiment of S.C. Volunteers From the Commencement of the War Until Lee's Surrender ...* (n.p., 1891; repr., Dayton, Ohio: Press of Morningside Bookshop, 1975)
HOL- H.A. Carlisle, *History of Lowndesville* (Danielsville, Ga.: Heritage Papers, 1987)
HOM- J.A.W. Thomas, *A History of Marlboro County, With Traditions and Sketches of Numerous Families* (Atlanta, 1897; repr., Baltimore, Md.: Regional Publishing Co., 1971)
HOS- Dr. T.B.D. Landrum, *History of Spartanburg County* (1900; repr., Spartanburg, S.C.: Reprint Co., 1960)
HOW- William Willis Bodie, *History of Williamsburg* (Columbia, S.C.: The State Co. 1923; repr., Spartanburg, S.C.: Reprint Co., 1980)
HSF- South Carolina Historical Society miscellaneous genealogical files
HSU- Anne King Gregorie, *History of Sumter County* (Sumter, S.C.: Library Board of Sumter County, 1954)
ISH- James R. Hagood, *The Immortal Six Hundred: A Story of Cruelty to Confederate Prisoners of War* (Winchester, Va.: The Eddy Press Corp., 1905; repr., Little Rock, Ark.: Eagle Press, 1986)
JES- C. Foster Smith, *Jeremiah Smith and The Confederate War* (Spartanburg, S.C.: Reprint Co., 1993)
JLC- James Lide Coker, *History of Company G, 9th S.C. Regiment, Infantry, S.C. Army and of Company E, Sixth S.C. Regiment, Infantry, S.C. Army* (Charleston, S.C.: Walker, Evans & Cogswell, 1899; repr., Greenwood, S.C.: Attic Press, Inc., 1979)
JMB- Ruth Barr McDaniel, *Confederate War Correspondence of James Michael Barr & Wife Rebecca Ann Dowling Barr* (n.p., 1963)
JR- A partial list of South Carolina Confederate dead prepared by William B. Johnston under the direction of the South Carolina legislature.

APPENDICES

This work was superseded by "The Roll of the Dead" by Professor William Rivers. The manuscript ledger is in the S.C. Department of Archives and History, Columbia.

JRH- Col. James R. Hagood, "Memoirs of the 1st SCVI in the Confederate War for Independence from April 12, 1861 to April 10, 1865." (Manuscript in the South Caroliniana Library, Columbia, S.C.)

K23- W.J. Andrews, *Sketch of Company K, 23rd South Carolina Volunteers, in the Civil War, From 1862-1865* (Richmond, Va.: Whittet & Shepperson, 1909; repr., Suffolk, Va.: Robert Hardy Publications, 1986)

KCS- Kershaw County Cemetery Survey Project, *Kershaw County, South Carolina, Cemetery Survey, 3 Volumes* (Camden, S.C.: Kershaw County Historical Society, 1991)

KEB- D. Augustus Dickert, *History of Kershaw's Brigade...* (Newberry, S.C.: Albert H. Aull Co., 1899; repr., Dayton, Ohio: The Press of Morningside Bookshop, 1976)

LAN- Frances Reeves Jeffcoat, Confederate Records, Lancaster District, S.C., gleaned from S.C. Department of Archives and History and the Lancaster *Ledger*, 1986. (Columbia, S.C.: Self-published, 1986)

LC - Robert W. Krick, ed., *Lee's Colonels: A Biographical Register of the Field Officers of the Army of Northern Virginia* (3rd ed., Dayton, Ohio: Press of Morningside House, Inc., 1991)

LCA- Arthur P. Ford and Marion Johnstone Ford, *Life in the Confederate Army and Some Experiences and Sketches of Southern Life* (New York: The Neale Publishing Co., 1905)

LED- A. Toomer Porter, *Led On! Step By Step...* (New York: G.P. Putnam's Sons, The Knickerbocker Press, 1898; repr. New York: Arno Press, 1967)

LGS- "Lexington County Genealogical Survey," in *Lexington County Genealogical Association Exchange*

LNC- Jane Anderson Seay, *Silent Cities: A Tombstone Registry of Old Lexington District, S.C.* (Self-published, 1984)

LSC- James Leland Bolt and Margaret Eltinge Bolt, *Church and Family Cemeteries, Laurens County, S.C.* (Greenville, S.C.: A Press, 1983)

LSS- W.S. Dunlop, *Lee's Sharpshooters or The Forefront of Battle...* (Little Rock, Ark., 1899; repr., Dayton, Ohio: Press of Morningside Bookshop, 1982)

MAC- *The Magazine of Albemarle County, Va. History* 22 (1963-1964, Civil War issue) (Charlottesville, Va.: The Michie Co., 1964)

MAG- *A Brief History of the Ladies Memorial Association of Charleston, S.C. ...Together With A Roster of the Confederate Dead, Interred At Magnolia and the Various City Church Yards* (Charleston, S.C.: H.P. Cooke & Co., 1880)

MCC- McCormick County Historical Society, *McCormick County Cemeteries* (McCormick County, S.C.: Dick Moon Printing, Inc., 1987)

MCF- William A. Albaugh III, *More Confederate Faces: A Pictorial Review* (Washington, D.C.: ABS Printers, Inc., 1972; repr., Wilmington, N.C.: Broadfoot Publishing Co., 1993)

MCG- Betty Couch Wiltshire, *Mississippi Confederate Graves Registration* (Bowie, Md.: Heritage Books, Inc., 1991)

MDM- Olin Fulmer Hutchinson, Jr., ed., *"My Dear Mother & Sisters," Civil War Letters of Capt. A.B. Mulligan, Co. B, 5th South Carolina Cavalry-Butler's Division-Hampton's Corps 1861-1865* (Spartanburg, S.C.: Reprint Co., 1992)

MJL- "Diary, J.L. McCrorey," 2nd Lieut., Co. B, 4th South Carolina Cavalry, 1864. Typescript in The South Caroliniana Library, Columbia, S.C.

MP- The Wade Hampton Chapter, United Daughters of the Confederacy, Columbia, S.C., *Memorial Pamphlet: Confederate Soldiers Who Died in the Service of Their Country and are Buried in Columbia, South Carolina 1861-1865* (n.p., n.d.)

MSF- Daniel E. Huger Smith, Alice R. Huger Smith, and Arney R. Childs, eds., *Mason Smith Family Letters, 1860-1868* (Columbia: University of South Carolina Press, 1950)

NCC- George Carter Abrams, ed., *Newberry County, South Carolina Cemeteries: Volumes One and Two* (Newberry, S.C.: Newberry Publishing Co. for The Newberry County Historical Society, 1982)

NHU- Alan D. Charles, *Narrative History of Union County, S.C.* (Spartanburg, S.C.: Reprint Co., 1987)

OCS- B.W. Roach and Sarah Roach, *Oconee County, South Carolina Cemetery Survey: Volumes One and Two* (Greenville, S.C.: A Press for The Pendleton Chapter of the South Carolina Genealogical Society, 1983-1984)

Px- "National Archives Selected Records of the War Department Relating to Confederate Prisoners of War, 1861-1865." (145 microfilm rolls, series M598.) In this volume the particular roll sourced is identified by "P" followed by a number identifying the specific microfilm roll of the 145 in the National Archives catalogue.

PCS- Pendleton Chapter of the South Carolina Genealogical Society, Pickens County, *South Carolina Cemetery Survey Volumes One and Two* (Greenville, S.C.: A Press, n.d.)

PDL- Joseph Woods Brunson, ed., *Pee Dee Light Artillery of Maxcy Gregg's (Later Samuel McGowan's) Brigade First South Carolina*

Volunteers (Infantry) C.S.A ... (Winston-Salem, N.C.: Stewart Printers, 1927; repr., William Stanley Hoole, ed., Dayton, Ohio: Morningside House, 1983)

PL- E. W. Beitzell, *Point Lookout Prison Camp* (n.p., n.d.)

PP- *Paths to the Past.* Confederate death and burial lists compiled in a number of bound pamphlets by the Lauderdale County (Mississippi) Department of Archives and History. These are largely based on the Watkins compilations, with added material derived from local research. Copies in the collections of the South Carolina Historical Society.

Rx- "National Archives Compiled Records Showing Service of Military Units in Confederate Organizations." 74 microfilm rolls, series M861. In this volume the particular microfilm roll sourced is identified by an "R" followed by the number of the specific roll.

RAP- Frank M. Mixson, *Reminiscences of a Private* (Columbia, S.C.: The State Co., 1910; repr., Camden, S.C.: J.J. Fox, 1990)

RAS- C. I. Walker, *Rolls and Historical Sketch of the Tenth Regiment So. Ca. ...* (Charleston, S.C.: Walker, Evans & Cogswell, 1881; repr., Alexandria, Va.: Stonewall House, 1985)

RCD- June Wells, ed., "Roster of Confederate Dead." A manuscript compiled by Agatha Aimar Simmons in 1957 with a list prepared by Yates Snowden in 1880. Includes material collected by M.C. Meigs, tombstone inscriptions by W.P.A., and private data. Copy is in the collections of the South Carolina Historical Society.

RCO- Rome *Courier* (July 17, 1866, Rome, Georgia). A list of S.C. soldiers buried in Myrtle Hill Cemetery, Rome, Georgia.

RHL- "Roll of Honor, Confederate Dead in Laurens Cemetery." A copy of a 1918 pamphlet in The South Caroliniana Library, Columbia, S.C.

RME- Richard L. Beach, ed., *Remember Me: The Civil War Letters of Lt. George Robinson and His Son Sgt. James Robinson of "The Glenn" Hamburg, South Carolina, 1861-1862* (Bowie, Md.: Heritage Books, Inc., 1991)

ROH- National Archives microfilm list of South Carolina CSA dead, 1861-1865. This microfilm made from Professor Rivers's "Roll of Honor" which had been deposited in the National Archives in 1947 after being discovered in the vaults of a bank in Charleston, S.C. The original document was returned to the S.C. Department of Archives and History in 1994.

RRT- "Rivers' Raising of Troops for Confederate Service," included in *The Report of the Historian of the Confederate Records to the General Assembly of South Carolina For the Year 1899* (Columbia, S.C.: R. L. Bryan Co., 1900)

16R- John S. Taylor, *Sixteenth South Carolina Regiment CSA From Greenville County, S.C.* (n.p., 1964)

SA1- A.S. Salley, Jr., *South Carolina Troops in Confederate Service, Volume I* (Columbia, S.C.: R.L. Bryan Co. 1913)

SA2- A.S. Salley, Jr., *South Carolina Troops in Confederate Service, Volume II* (Columbia, S.C.: The State Co., 1914)

SA3- A.S. Salley, Jr., *South Carolina Troops in Confederate Service, Volume III* (Columbia, S.C.: The State Co., 1930)

SAS- Carol Bleser, ed., *Secret and Sacred: The Diaries of James Henry Hammond, a Southern Slaveholder* (New York: Oxford University Press, 1988)

SCA- Charles Inglesby, *Historical Sketch of the 1st Regiment of South Carolina Artillery (Regulars)* (Charleston, S.C.: n.p., n.d.)

SCC- The Pinckney Chapter, South Carolina Genealogical Society, *Spartanburg County, S.C. Cemetery Survey* (n.p., n.d.)

SCH- "Register of men buried in Confederate Cemetery, Spotsylvania Court House, Va.," (repr., Confederate Cemetery Association, 1966)

SCL- Allen H. Stokes, Jr., *A Guide to the Manuscript Collection of the South Caroliniana Library* (Columbia: South Caroliniana Library, 1982)

SCS- John Amasa May and John Reynolds Faunt, *South Carolina Secedes ...* (Columbia: University of South Carolina Press, 1960)

SHS- James I. Robertson, ed., *Index-Guide to The Southern Historical Society Papers, 1876-1959* (Wilmington, N.C.: The Broadfoot Publishing Co., 1992). See index for references to specific names and battles.

SMC- Domenick A. Serrano, *Still More Confederate Faces* (Bayside, N.Y.: Metropolitan Co., 1992)

SOC- E. Milby Burton, *The Siege of Charleston, 1861-1865* (Columbia: University of South Carolina Press, 1970)

SRG- Walter Brian Cisco, *States Rights Gist: A South Carolina General of the Civil War* (Shippensburg, Penn.: White Mane Publishing Co., 1991)

SSC- Joseph R. Gainey, ed., *Some Spartanburg County Cemeteries* (Spartanburg, S.C.: Piedmont Historical Society, 1983)

SSO- Lloyd Halliburton, *Saddle Soldiers: The Civil War Correspondence of General William Stokes of the 4th South Carolina Cavalry* (Orangeburg, S.C.: Sandlapper Publishing Co., 1993)

STC- U.R. Brooks, ed., *Stories of the Confederacy* (Columbia, S.C.: The State Co., 1912)

STR- Warren Ripley, ed., *Siege Train: The Journal of a Confederate Artilleryman in the Defense of Charleston* (Columbia: Published for the Charleston Library Society by the University

APPENDICES

of South Carolina Press, 1986)

37V- J.L. Scott, *36th and 37th Battalions Virginia Cavalry* (Lynchburg, Va.: H.E. Howard, Inc., 1986)

3RC- Three Rivers Historical Society, *Survey of Cemeteries in Williamsburg, Florence and Georgetown Counties* (n.p., n.d.)

TCC- Bobby G. Moss and Dennis R. Amos, *Tombstones & Cemeteries of Cherokee County, S.C., Vols. 1-4* (Greenville, S.C.: A Press, 1984)

TOD- Manuscript research records on the CSA service of the Todd and Amick families of South Carolina plus research into the records of Companies I and C of the 15th SCVI. This collection includes a number of Confederate graveyard lists from various places in Virginia, North Carolina, Georgia, etc., and has been completed through 1994. Copy in the collections of the South Carolina Historical Society.

TRR- John K. McIver Chapter, United Daughters of the Confederacy, *Treasured Reminiscences Including accounts of the 1st, 6th, 8th, 9th, and 21st Regiments, South Carolina Volunteer Infantry, The 6th South Carolina Cavalry Regiment, and the 1st, 15th and Pee Dee Volunteer Artillery Battalions, Confederate States Army, 1861-1865* (Columbia, S.C.: The State Co., 1911)

TSC- Natalie Jenkins Bond and Osman Latrobe Coward, eds., *The South Carolinians: Colonel Asbury Coward's Memoirs* (New York: Vantage Press, 1968)

UCS- Joseph H. Croute, Jr., *Units of the Confederate States Army* (Midlothian, Va.: Derwent Books, 1987)

UD1- *Recollections and Reminiscences, 1861-1865 Through World War I, Volume One* (n.p.: The South Carolina Division of the United Daughters of the Confederacy, 1990)

UD2- *Recollections and Reminiscences, 1861-1865 Through World War I, Volume Two* (n.p.: The South Carolina Division of the United Daughters of the Confederacy, 1991)

UD3- *Recollections and Reminiscences, 1861-1865 Through World War I, Volume Three* (n.p.: The South Carolina Division of the United Daughters of the Confederacy, 1992)

UD4- *Recollections and Reminiscences 1861-1865 Through World War I, Volume Four* (n.p.: The South Carolina Division of the United Daughters of the Confederacy, 1993)

UNC- Mrs. E.D. Whaley, Sr., *Union County Cemeteries: Epitaphs of 18th and 19th Century Settlers in Union County, S.C. and Their Descendants* (Greenville, S.C.: A Press, 1976)

V4- Ron Field, *4th South Carolina Volunteers (Sloan's)* Lower Swell, Gloucestershire, U.K.: Design Folio, 1992. (A pamphlet publication in a series describing S.C. regiments and battalions.)

WAT- The Watkins S.C. Confederate Burial Papers, four folders with various unbound reports of South Carolina CSA graves around the country. Researched and reported by Mr. Raymond F. Watkins, Springfield, Va. Copies held in S.C. Department of Archives and History, Columbia.

WCT- "Williamson County Confederate Cemetery, Tennessee." (An extract list of South Carolina dead in cemetery sections 83, 84, 85, and 86. The original is lost but page 17 of a larger list survives; it probably was prepared by a Williamson County research group. Copy in the collections of the South Carolina Historical Society.

WDB- James Richmond Boulware, "The War Diary of Dr. J.R. Boulware, C. S. Army Assistant Surgeon 6th South Carolina Volunteer Infantry." (Unpublished typed manuscript in the South Caroliniana Library, Columbia, S.C.)

WIN- Lucy Fitzhugh Kurtz and Benny Ritter, *A Roster of Confederate Soldiers Buried in Stonewall Cemetery, Winchester, Virginia* (Winchester, Va.: Published through the courtesy of the Farmers & Merchants National Bank, 1962)

WLI- Washington Light Infantry Monument list of Confederate dead in Washington Park, Charleston, South Carolina.

WV- Gregory A. Coco, *Wasted Valor: The Confederate Dead at Gettysburg* (Gettysburg, Pa.: Thomas Publications, 1990)

YEB- Jo Robert Owens and Ruth Dickson Thomas, *Confederate Veterans Enrollment Book of York County, S.C.- 1902* (Glover, S.C.: Westmoreland Printers, Inc., 1983)

YMD- Brent H. Holcomb, *York, South Carolina, Newspapers Marriage and Death Notices, 1823-1865* (Spartanburg, S.C.: Reprint Co., 1981)

DISTRICTS IN 1860

AE	Abbeville	KW	Kershaw
AN	Anderson	LR	Lancaster
BL	Barnwell	LS	Laurens
BT	Beaufort	LN	Lexington
CN	Charleston	MN	Marion
CR	Chester	MO	Marlboro
CD	Chesterfield	NY	Newberry
CL	Clarendon	OG	Orangeburg
CO	Colleton	PS	Pickens
DN	Darlington	RD	Richland
ED	Edgefield	SG	Spartanburg
FD	Fairfield	SR	Sumter
GN	Georgetown	UN	Union
GE	Greenville	WG	Williamsburg
HY	Horry	YK	York

CAUSE OF DEATH

ACD	Accidental Death
DID	Died in duel
DOD	Died of disease
DOE	Died of exposure
DOW	Died of wounds
EXC	Executed following General Court Martial
KIA	Killed in action
SUI	Suicide
MUR	Murdered or killed in an argument

PLACE NAME CONVENTIONS

Appomattox, VA
Armstrong Mills, VA (12/10/64, Cavalry skirmish)
Averysboro, NC (3/16/65)
Battery Isl., SC (5/21/62, Skirmish, 24th SCVI)
Bean's Stn., TN (12/14/63)
Bentonville, NC (3/19-21/65)
Blackwater, VA
Blandford Church Pbg., VA (Burial site in Petersburg, Va.)
Boonesboro, MD (AKA South Mountain, Md., 1862 Campaign)
Brandy St., VA (8/1/63, Cavalry battle, 2nd SCVC)
Brown's Ferry, VA
Bty. Wagner, SC (8/17-26/64, 9/1-6/64)
Bull's Gap, TN (3/15/64, skirmish)
Burgess Mills, VA (10/27/64, 6th SCVC)
Burke's Stn., VA (10/28/63, 2nd SCVC)
Campbell Stn., TN (12/05/63, P.S.S.)
Centreville, VA
Chaffin's Farm, VA (9/29-10/02/64, 6th SCVC)
Chancellorsville, VA (5/5-6/63)
Charlottesville (Va.)
Chattanooga, TN
Clay's Farm, VA (5/20/64)
Cold Harbour, VA (6/1-3/64)
Crater Pbg., VA (Petersburg, Va., 7/30/64)
Culpepper Gen. Hos. (Culpepper, Va. General Hospital)
Darbytown Rd., VA (Richmond, Va. front)
Deep Bottom, VA (Richmond, Va. front, 7/27/64)
Dranesville, VA (12/20/61)
Drury's Bluff, VA (5/12/64)
Enterprise, MS
Fairfax, VA (Fairfax Court House, Va.)
Five Forks, VA (4/1/65)
Frayser's Farm (Richmond, Va. front, 6/30/62)
Fredericksburg (Fredericksburg, Va., 12/13/62)
Ft. Anderson, NC (2/19/65)
Ft. Fisher, NC (1/15/65)
Ft. Gaines, AL (Mobile Bay, Culpepper's Battery, 8/8/64)
Ft. Harrison, VA (Richmond, Va. front, 9/20-30/64)
Fts. Monroe, VA (Fortress Monroe, Va.)
Ft. Sanders, TN (11/29/63)
Ft. Stedman, VA (3/25/65 Hol. Leg.)
Fussell's Mill, VA (8/16/64)
Gaines' Mill, VA (Richmond, Va. front, 6/27/62)
Germantown, VA
Gettysburg, PA (7/1-3/63)
Globe Tavern, VA (8/21/64, Hagood's Bgd.)
Gordonsville, VA
Hatcher's Run, VA (10/27/64, 2/5-7/65)
Hawes Shop, VA (5/28/64, 4th SCVC & 5th SCVC)
Jackson, MS (5/14/63 [24th SCVI] - 7/16/63 [22nd SCVI])
James Island, SC (Various events and units)
Jarratt's Stn., VA (Jarratt's Depot or Station, 5/8/64)
Jericho Ford, VA (North Anna River, 5/23/64)
Jerusalem, VA
Kennesaw Mtn., GA (6/27-28/64)
Kinston, NC (12/14/62, Evan's Brigade, 17th SCVI, 18th SCVI, 22nd SCVI, 23rd SCVI, 26th SCVI, Hol. Leg.)
Lee's Mill, VA (6/30/64, 6th SCVC)
Lenoir's Stn., (Lenoir's Station, Tenn., 6/19/63)
Lookout Mtn., TN (11/24/63)
Lookout Valley, TN (10/28/63)
Louisa C.H., VA (Louisa Court House, Va., 5/2/64)
Lovejoy's St., GA (Lovejoy's Station, Ga., 7/29/64)
Lynchburg, VA
1st Manassas, VA (7/21/61)
2nd Manassas, VA (8/29-30/62)
Manassas Jnctn. (Mannassas Junction, Va.)
Manchester, VA (Suburb of Richmond, Va., hospital site)
N. Anna River, VA (North Anna River, Va. AKA Jericho Ford, Va., 5/23/64)
New Hope Ch., GA (New Hope Church, Ga., 5/27/64)

APPENDICES

New Kent C.H., VA (New Kent Court House, Va., 8/27/63)
New Market, VA
Noel Station, VA (5/23/64)
Orange, VA (Orange Court House, Va.)
Ox Hill, VA (AKA Chantilly, Va., 9/1/62)
Peebles Farm, VA (9/29/64)
Petersburg, VA
Pickett's Fm., VA (7/21/64, 18th SCVI)
Rappahanock Stn., (Rappahanock Station, Va.)
Ream's Stn., VA (On the Weldon Railroad, Petersburg, Va., 8/21/64 & 8/25/64, Richmond, Va.)
Sappony Ch., VA (Sappony Church, Va., 7/1/64)
Savage Stn., VA (Richmond, Va. front, 6/29/62)
Secessionville (Secessionville, James Island, S.C., 6/16/64)
Sharpsburg, MD (9/17/62)
Smith's Crnr., NC (Smith's Corner, N.C., AKA Averysboro & Smith's Ford, 3/15/65)
S. Newport, GA (South Newport, Ga. skirmish, 8/17/64)
Spotsylvania, VA (5/8-19/64)
Springplace, GA (2/27/64, 3rd SCVC)
Stony Creek, VA (4/2/64)
Sullivans I., SC (Sullivan's Island, S.C.)
Sutherland Stn., VA (4/2/65)
Swift Creek, VA (5/7/64)
Town Creek, NC (2/20/65)
Trevillian Stn. (Va., 6/11-12/64)
Walthall Jctn. (Port Walthall Junction, Va., 5/6/64)
Warrenton, VA
Wauhatchie, TN (AKA Racoon Mtn., 10/28/63)
Weldon RR, VA (8/18-22/64)
Whites Bridge, VA (11/26/63 skirmish, 2nd SCVC)
Wildcat Mtn., TN
Wills Valley, TN (8/31/63)
Winchester, VA
Wilderness, VA (5/5-6/64)
Williamsburg, VA (5/5/62)
Williamsburg Rd. (Richmond, Va. front, 10/27/64)
Wyatt's Farm, VA (9/29/64, 5th SCVC)

RANK ABBREVIATIONS

Lt. Gen. - Lieutenant General, corps commander
Maj. Gen. - Major General, division commander
Brig. Gen. - Brigadier General, brigade commander
Col. - Colonel, regimental commander or higher unit staff
Lt. Col. - Lieutenant Colonel, battalion commander or higher unit staff
Major - Regimental or higher unit staff
Surgeon - Regimental medical officer
Asst Surg. - Assistant surgeon, officer
Adj. - Adjutant, Regiment or higher unit staff
Chaplain - Regimental religious officer
Cpt. - Captain, company commander or higher unit staff
1st Lt. - First Lieutenant, company commissioned officer
2nd Lt. - Second Lieutenant, company commissioned officer
3rd Lt. - Third Lieutenant, company commissioned officer
QM. Sgt. - Quartermaster Sergeant, regimental staff
Ord. Sgt. - Ordnance Sergeant, regimental staff
1st Sgt. - First Sergeant, sometimes called Orderly Sergeant, company principal non-commissioned officer
2nd Sgt. - Second Sergeant, company non-com.
3rd Sgt. - Third Sergeant, company non-com.
4th Sgt. - Fourth Sergeant, company non-com.
5th Sgt. - Fifth Sergeant, company non-com.
1st Cpl. - First Corporal, company non-com.
2nd Cpl. - Second Corporal, company non-com.
3rd Cpl. - Third Corporal, company non-com.
4th Cpl. - Fourth Corporal, company non-com.
5th Cpl. - Fifth Corporal, company non-com.
Hosp Stwd. - Hospital Steward, surgeon's helper and nurse
Musician - Company bugler or drummer
Teamster - Wagon or ambulance driver, company or higher
Pvt. - The common soldier

UNIT ABBREVIATIONS

Ham. Leg.- Hampton Legion
Hol. Leg.- Holcombe Legion
Orr's Ri.- Orr's Rifles, AKA 1st Regiment of Rifles
P.S.S.- Palmetto Sharpshooter Regiment
1st SCVIG- First South Carolina Volunteer Infantry Regiment (Gregg's)
1st SCVIH- First South Carolina Volunteer Infantry Regiment (Hagood's)
1st SCVIR- First South Carolina Volunteer Infantry Regiment (Regulars, converted to Heavy Artillery)
2nd SCVIRi.- Second South Carolina Rifle Regiment
9th SCVIH- Ninth South Carolina Volunteer Infantry Regiment (Col. Heyward)
9th SCVIB- Ninth South Carolina Volunteer Infantry Regiment (Col. Blanding)
2nd SCVI-27th SCVI- Line infantry regiments with no identity complications
1st -3rd SCVA- Line artillery regiments. Note that the 1st SCVIR regiment served as fortification troops and is sometimes referred to as the First Atillery.
1st SCVIBn- The First South Carolina Infantry Battalion, AKA the Charleston Battalion

3rd SCVIBn- The Third South Carolina Infantry Battalion, AKA the James Battalion.

4th SCVIBn- The Forth South Carolina Infantry Battalion, AKA the Mattison Battalion.

7th SCVIBn- The Seventh South Carolina Infantry Battalion, AKA as the Enfield Rifles.

1st SCVC-7th SCVC- The seven line cavalry regiments. Note that these were formed by combining various older battalions and independant companies. The tracing of these earlier units is confusing but it should be recognized that many deaths attributed to the final regimental structure occured in one of the earlier smaller units.

SCRes- There is no established listing of the various reserve organizations called up from time to time. In some cases these are referred to as State Troops. The reserves called up late in the war seem to have been formed into battalions best known by their commander. An example is Gill's Battalion, a unit formed to guard prisoners at the Florence stockade. In this compilation an attempt has been made to assign official number identities to these units using the numbers cited in the National Archives M861 series of microfilm rolls of Confederate Units.

SCMil - South Carolina Militia organizations called up in the final days of the war to resist Federal invasion of the state. Some are identified by number such as the 14th SCMil.

SECESSION CONVENTION RESOLUTION

[On September 17, 1862,] Mr. [Jacob Pinckney] Reed offered the following resolutions, which were considered immediately, and were agreed to:

Resolved unanimously, That the thanks of this Convention are eminently due, and are hereby tendered, to the South Carolina soldiers, officers and privates, in the Confederate Army, for the patriotic gallantry with which they responded to the call of their country, and for the characteristic courage and energy with which they have borne aloft the Palmetto Banner on the bloody battle fields of Virginia, South Carolina and elsewhere, to the imperishable glory and honor of themselves and their State.

Resolved unanimously, That this Convention begs, most sincerely, to mingle its sympathies with the relatives and friends of those who have fallen in the service of their country, whether in battle, amidst the clangor of arms, from wounds received in battle, from disease, or from accident; and that the Executive authority of this State be requested to collect the names of all such, and have them transcribed into a suitable Record Book, designating the corps to which they belonged, their rank in the service, and the cause of death, to be preserved amongst the archives of the State, as a token of respect to their memories, and a legacy of inestimable value to their friends.

Resolved unanimously, That the children who have been, and may hereafter be, made orphans, by the fall of their fathers in defending their country against the invasion and devastation of a relentless and cruel enemy, are preëminently the children of the State, and it is the duty of the constituted authorities to provide, as far as practicable, for their sustenance and education, and for training them up in such a way that the State, in future years, "when asked for her jewels, may point to her sons," the offspring of fathers who fell gallantly defending the liberties of their country.

Resolved unanimously, That a copy of these resolutions be transmitted by the Clerk of the Convention to officers commanding regiments, battalions and companies of South Carolina troops, with a request that they be communicated to their respective commands.

[As reported in the *Journal of the Convention of the People of South Carolina, held in 1860, 1861, and 1862, Together with the Ordinances, Reports, Resolutions, etc.* (Columbia, S.C.: R. W. Gibbes, Printer to the Convention, 1862)]

REPORT OF WILLIAM B. JOHNSTON TO THE GENERAL ASSEMBLY

Charleston Daily Courier
December 24, 1863

SOUTH CAROLINA'S DEAD

As a matter of general interest we subjoin the report of Mr. W. B. Johnston, the agent appointed to record the names of soldiers from the State who have fallen during the present war, made to the Legislature at its recent session:

Columbia, December 1, 1863.
To the Senate and House of Representatives of the State of South Carolina:

As the agent appointed to collect and record the names of deceased soldiers from South Carolina who have fallen in battle or died during the war, I beg leave respectfully to report the progress made in the discharge of my duty.

Shortly after my appointment, I addressed a circular to the commanding officers of the regiments in service, requesting full and regular returns of the deaths in their respective commands, and have received, classified and recorded the dead of the following regiments, from the official regimental rolls.

Palmetto Sharp-shooters, Col. Joseph Walker, Commanding. Killed in battle and from wounds, 205; disease, 77; accident, 2; total, 283. [sic]

1st Regiment, Col. D.H. Hamilton, Commanding. Killed in battle and from wounds, 85; disease, 125; accident 2; total 212.

3rd Regiment, Col. J. D. Nance, Commanding. Killed in battle and from wounds, 149; disease 158; accident 2; total 309.

5th Regiment, Col. Coward, Commanding. Killed in battle and from wounds, 126; disease, 105; total, 231.

8th Regiment, Col. C.M. Weatherby, Commanding. Killed in battle and from wounds, 67; disease, 186; total, 253.

9th Regiment, Col. Blanding, Commanding. Total number of deaths, cause not given, 124.

13th Regiment, Col. Edwards, Commanding. Killed in battle and died from wounds, 153; disease, 56; total, 209.

14th Regiment, Col. McGowan, Commanding. Killed in battle and died from wounds, 88; disease, 141; total, 229.

16th Regiment, Col. W.D. DeSaussure, Commanding. Killed in battle and died from wounds, 115; disease, 167; total, 282.

17th Regiment, Col. F.W. McMaster, Commanding. Killed in battle and died from wounds, 85; disease, 122; accident, 2; total 209.

I also gave notice, in the public journals, to the families and friends of deceased soldiers to forward me the desired information. This request has been and is being generally responded to.

My report is up to the 1st of November, ult., and the record shows an aggregate loss of four thousand and eighty-nine men. Of these two thousand two hundred and thirty nine fell in battle or died from wounds, and eighteen hundred and fifty from diseases — a few from accidental causes.

The record, alphabetically arranged, as far as made, has been placed in the Library, for the inspection of the members of your honorable body. Since the report has been made up, I have received full returns from the 18th Regiment, and partial returns from other sources.

Respectfully,
W. B. Johnston,
Recording Age't

The following is the action of the Legislature on the subject:

House of Representatives, December 3, 1863:

The Committee on the Military, to whom was referred the report of W. B. Johnston, Recording Agent, report that they find the work has been faithfully executed, and that the agency should be continued. They recommend the following resolutions:

Resolved, That the agency to record the names of soldiers from this State who have died in service be continued in the same manner as was provided in the joint resolution of last session.

Resolved, That the agent do urge, by public advertisement, the families of deceased soldiers to report to him, that he may have the means of verifying and correcting regimental returns.

APPENDICES

IN THE SENATE, December 17, 1863

Resolved, That the Senate do concur in the report.

The attention of all is called to the advertisement of the agent in another column.

THE ROLL OF HONOR

TO THE FAMILIES OF DECEASED SOLDIERS

The legislature has continued the Agency to record the names of soldiers from this State who have fallen in service or died from disease in the present war. The following resolution was adopted by both branches of the General Assembly:

"*Resolved*, That the Agent do urge by public advertisement, the families of deceased soldiers to report to him, that he may have the means of verifying and correcting Regimental returns,"

In accordance with the above resolution of the General Assembly, I earnestly request the families and friends of deceased soldiers to forward to me the names of the brave men who have fallen in battle or died in service during the present war. The information required is the name, rank, number of regiment, letter of company, date of death, cause of death, in what battle, or where died.

I would also earnestly request all the commanding officers of regiments from this state to forward me official returns of the casualties in their respective commands from the beginning of the war, and to continue said returns during their term of service, so that the Roll of Honor may be as perfect and complete as possible.

Wm. B. Johnston
Recording Agent of the State

WILLIAM J. RIVERS'S ADVERTISEMENT

Charleston Daily Courier
January 25, 1865

STATE RECORD OF THE NAMES OF DECEASED SOLDIERS

South Carolina College
Columbia, January 16, 1865

UNDER APPOINTMENT BY THE LEGISLATURE to prepare this Record, I earnestly appeal to the families and friends of our deceased soldiers to send me *at once* their names, &c, while there is an opportunity to secure accurate information. Hospital registers and reports of casualties from the army are defic[i]ent in the information required; it must be obtained at home.

The record will date back to the beginning of the war, and include all who have been killed in battle or died of wounds received in battle, or from disease or accident. If you have been so fortunate as not to lose friend or relative; yet [r]emember that it is noble to rescue from oblivion the name of but one friendless youth who had gone from your neighborhood to die in our cause.

Give-1. Name in full, 2. From what District, 3. Rank, 4. Company, 5. Regiment and arm of service, 6. Died, year, month, day, 7. Cause of death and remarks (as to where he died, age, previously wounded, &c.).

Circulars and blanks to be filled will be sent to such as desire them. No fee or expense is incurred by anyone for having the record made. The State is endeavoring to fulfill a sacred obligation in securing now, and recording for posterity, the name[s] of all her sons who have fallen in this war. In 1862 the Convention unanimously resolved that this should be done, "as a token of respect to their memories, and a legacy of inestimable value to their friends," and the resolution was sent forth by their order, to be read to our regiments, battalions and companies everywhere. Many a brave soldier may have died in solitude or rushed upon the foe, with the thought in his heart that his name would be honorably preserved at home.

January 23 S.C.
Wm. J. Rivers

APPENDICES

WILLIAM J. RIVERS ON THE "ROLL OF HONOR"

The following material taken from an undated newspaper clipping (page 12, *The Sunday Ne...*) was pasted into the front of William B. Johnston's "Rolls of Honor" in the South Carolina Department of Archives and History. It includes letters written by Johnston's successor, Professor William J. Rivers, concerning his "Roll of Honor."

STATE CONFEDERATE RECORDS

LIST OF 12,000 DEAD SOLDIERS PREPARED BY PROFESSOR RIVERS

The Foundation of all the Other Work that has been Done by the State Historian Since Hampton Freed South Carolina from the Domination of Carpetbaggers and Negroes — Communication of Prof. Rivers to Col. J. P. Thomas, Confederate Historian of South Carolina.

Baltimore, Md, Nov. 15, 1897: I shall not wait for the letter you said you would write to me on your return from Charleston, for I am sure you must be much occupied, but shall send you a short account of my connection with the agency of recording names of deceased soldiers from South Carolina during the late war. The account referred to is, in part, explanatory of the "book" you inquired about in your letter.

The work to which you are appointed appears to be of higher and broader scope than that to which my effort was directed. I failed in satisfactory accomplishment, because part of the information necessary thereto was not in existence. No matter how persevering a person may be he cannot create a single part, and facts — a multiplicity of them — were what I was called upon to collect. I have a memorandum of letters I wrote to officers and others in every section of the State, and to some beyond the bounds of the State. Very many to whom I appealed for information are now dead, and the opportunities for learning what we desire to put on record are becoming, year after year, fewer and fewer. I suppose that the little I did in what I made the attempt to do is forgotten now, and perhaps it will interest you to hear from me (before I also forget) some particulars respecting my connection with the early and humbler portion of the work which (placed under your direction in broader scope) I hope you will be enabled to bring to successful completion. On page 440 of the published Journal of the Convention, September 17, 1862, is this:

"Resolved unanimously, That this Convention begs most sincerely to mingle its sympathies with relatives and friends of those who have fallen in the service of their country, whether in battle, amidst the danger of arms, from wounds received in battle, from disease, or from accident, and that the Executive authority of the State be requested to collect the names of all such and have them transcribed into a suitable record book, designating the corps to which they belonged, their rank in the service and cause of death, to be preserved among the archives of the State, as a token of respect to their memories and a legacy of inestimable value to their friends."

Under this resolution Governor Pickens appointed Mr. William B. Johnston as agent to record the names of deceased soldiers. On the 22nd of December, 1864, the committee on the military in the Legislature, to whom was referred the report of the recording agent, found "errors so flagrant" in it as to render it untrustworthy, and recommended the adoption of this resolution: "That the agency to record the names of the soldiers of this State who have been killed or died in service be continued, and that Prof. Rivers, of the South Carolina College, be appointed for that service, and that he receive the sum of twenty-five hundred dollars as compensation therefor...." I never saw compensation because with every effort on my part I could not complete the work to my satisfaction. My first determination was to visit the camps and gather information there. I applied to the Secretary of War, at Richmond, for permission to do so. He said authority and free passes would be given me provided I held the Governor's commission. Governor Magrath ordered the commission made out for me, but remarked: "You'll soon have no railroads to travel on. From private advices just received, Sherman will make only a feint on Charleston and will march on Columbia and destroy all public buildings here. Go, by my authority, to the medical bureau, who have lumber, and tell them to send you material and workmen to make boxes, and save the valuable books in the College library. Send them anywhere you think best out of Columbia." Before I could do anything more effectual than getting some boxes made, (for I had only one man to work on them,) Sherman's army was upon us. There was no opportunity for collecting the names of deceased soldiers till after the burning of the city and the State House (and most of the historic contents,) nor indeed till the war was ended. That end came in less than sixty days.

Ascertaining that no records, such as I thought, remained from the destruction of papers at Richmond, nor were among the captured Confederate papers at Washington, the task committed to me became now only possible through the help of our own people at home. Appeals were made by advertisements in newspapers, by circulars, by letters written to officers, and to every one from whom I thought information could be obtained. I said in my advertisement: "The record cannot be complete without the assistance of all who take an interest in this memorial. Especially to our returned soldiers do I now make this appeal. If it be but a single name you can furnish, send it at once."

In our destitution writing material was scarce. I was given by the Confederate medical office, (who had no further use for them) three blank books, roughly made and of coarse brown paper. In one of these I recorded the names of official or [...] sources, with a refer[...] the document [remainder unreadable].

The following was my report at the close of next year, 1866:

"To the Honorable the Senate and the House of Representatives: As soon as post offices began to be reestablished in the State the collecting of names of our deceased soldiers was resumed. Inquiries in Richmond and Washington led to the conclusion that no Government records containing lists of such names had been saved or captured, and that the only source of information left was at home. Appeals through the newspapers for the desired information have been but partly successful, and I am engaged in writing to company officers for lists of the dead. The extensive loss of papers of the army occasions delay in obtaining such lists, which, in many instances, perhaps in most, have to be made up from memory. But I look forward to large results from the interest manifested by the officers to whom appeals have been made. Lists of the dead, complete or in part, have been received from ninety-three companies. From such sources and from letters from relatives and friends, five thousand, five hundred and twenty names have been recorded. In considering the loss of papers, and lest the name of any soldier should be forgotten in the final record, I have collected in a separate volume, from published reports of adjutants and other officers at the time of the casualties, and from lists of burial places in Virginia and elsewhere, and from other sources, about three thousand, five hundred additional names. These are not entered upon the record. I have thus, in all, nine thousand names.

It is not the name only that is sought, but the district to which each soldier belonged, his rank, company, regiment and arm of service, the date of his death, the cause and place of death and his age. During the coming year, in addition to correspondence with company officers, blank forms will be furnished the tax-collectors, and it is hoped that in this way many names may be gathered that would not otherwise be sent in. Assistance is also expected from the soldiers' memorial and charitable associations forming in various parts of the State.

It is my duty to report that, of the large collection made for the State by my predecessor in this agency, amounting to more than seven thousand names, nothing has been delivered over to me.

It is impossible to avoid errors in such a work. Even parents and company officers sometimes give very different reports of the same soldier. In order to secure as great accuracy and completeness as practicable it may be necessary hereafter to verify the record by publication, so that in each district corrections may be made and omissions supplied before the final manuscript copy shall be prepared for the archives of the State. The plan of doing this, and of the arrangement of names in the record, and of the introduction and prefix of statistics that naturally belong to such a record, it is unnecessary to report upon at this time, as the collection of names cannot be finished till the close of another year, at least.

What has been done is ready for inspection, and also the account of expenditure, which, from the recent date of the appropriation for this purpose, is of small amount, and is, therefore, not embodied in this report.

Respectfully submitted,
William J. Rivers, Recording Age't

The work was continued by me the next year (1867) and then reconstruction times came upon us and all honor to dead Confederates was out of order till after years — too many years indeed for us — those times were passed. In the meanwhile the Survivors' Association was formed, with Hampton at the head, and to them I committed the result so far as I had been able to proceed in my task. In collecting the names I had put them down alphabetically, as obtained from time to time. From my manuscript record the Association caused to be made a lexicographical list (as to the first three letters in each name) so that any name could be readily referred to. An account of what the Association accomplished up to November, 1870, will be found in the Charleston Courier in a "Report of the executive board of the Survivors' Association of the State of South Carolina," signed by Edward McCrady, James Conner, James McCutchen, Ellison Capers, C. Irvine Walker,

William W. Allen. Those evil reconstruction times which crushed down all that was high and noble in the State, did not spare the South Carolina University in which I was a professor. I had to look for the support and the education of my four sons and two daughters, and there was providentially offered me a situation in Maryland, which afforded my children both a support and a good education. I was not in the State — at home — when our own people came into power again and Gen. Hampton was elected Governor.

The completion of the honor roll of deceased Confederate solders from South Carolina was again a matter of interest. The movement thereto came (I believe) from the Survivors' Association. Instead of a separate agency, the work was committed to the Adjutant General of the State. His office, as was fitting, became the permanent depository of the record and of all documents connected with it. And I think the scope of the record was enlarged so as to embrace a history of the formation of the various military organizations raised in the State for Confederate service.

I beg leave to introduce here the following letters. On my going to Maryland (1873) I left with Mr. Bryan a box of books for sale and put in the box some manuscript material relating to our history and the roll of deceased soldiers, which I thought the State, in case our people came into power again, ought to have. When studying out a subject connected, if I remember right, with the chapter on the Carolinas in the narrative of critical history of America (the Vol. V.,) I sent for the box and whatever remained in it, and so the papers came again into my keeping. This explains the introductory part of Gen. Manigault's letter.

Executive Department
Office of the Adjutant & Inspector General
Columbia, SC, July 23, 1885

Professor William J. Rivers
Chestertown, Md.

Dear Sir,
Yours of the 20th has been received, and I reply at once with many thanks for your kind offer to lend me the papers and memorandums which you are in possession of relating to the various organizations that served in the Confederate States army during the war. I will be glad for you to send them at your earliest convenience by express, as I feel sure that I will derive much aid from them. I was not aware that you had left them in Columbia or would have availed myself of them long since. After extracting what information I can the papers shall be returned.

Gen. McCrady some time since placed me in possession of one of your manuscript books and some historical manuscript of several regiments: they have been of great value to me and assisted me materially. I find great difficulty in obtaining the assistance of survivors. Out of a little more than 500 companies there are 50 or 60 rolls that the [...] have [...] enable to make any progress [rest unreadable].

    Signed by A. M. Manigault
    Office of Adjutant and Inspector General

Department for Enrollment of Troops,
furnished by S.C. for C.S.A.
    August 8, 1885

Prof. W.J. Rivers,
Chestertown Md.

Dear Sir:
I beg to acknowledge, with thanks, receipt of the package by express containing original material and general information gathered by you some years since with the view of making a correct roll of those who fell in battle or died of disease while in the Confederate States service during the late war, as well as other matter relating to the different military organizations furnished by South Carolina. Your letter of July has also been received. I have been much occupied lately with other official duties outside of the office, and have not been able to give much attention to that branch of the department relating to the rolls, but I trust that in a short time I will be able to give it almost my entire attention, and do not doubt but that I will derive much aid from the papers you so kindly sent me. I may have to keep them for a considerable period of time, but will take the best care of them and return after use.

    I am very truly yours,
    A. M. Manigault
    A. and I. General

I am glad that Gen. Manigault did not return the papers to me for I see now that their proper place of custody is where they are. You will perceive that your inquiry in your letter lately received for "A copy of a book written by" me on the history of the military commands, originated from the mention of a brief MS on the subject which the Survivors' Association received from me, and which Gen. McCrady handed over to the adjutant's office. No doubt it is there still. What I had begun was meant as part of a prefix or preface, had it been possible for me to complete satisfactorily the roll of deceased soldiers.

I was not appointed to this work till the closing months of a four-years' war. Thirty-three years (a generation) passed. Can the work be effectually done now? Can we reverse the mistake made at the beginning by not establishing then a bureau to which official reports should have been sent at or soon after the casualties, before decay and devastation began to come on the Confederacy, and on us and on the officers and their men, and on their papers and on all that belonged to them?

We have done what we could. If the record cannot be complete let blank leaves be in it for additional names; such names being added as the Legislature from time to time shall order to be enrolled with the others. It is with a sigh that I think of the Lines:

"The knights are dust,
And their good swords are rust;
Their souls are with the saints, we trust."

I wish you, again, success in bringing to completion the long-standing promise of the Convention.
    Yours truly,
    W. J. Rivers

STATISTICAL SUMMARIES

A preliminary review of the reported deaths by cause, district, and regiment produces some interesting statistics, of which the following are but a beginning.

TOTAL BY CAUSE

Died of disease	6,755
Killed in action	5,226
Died of wounds	2,647
Died in prison	1,408
Accidents	155
Murdered	28
Executed	9
Suicides	3
Died in duels	2
Died of exposure	2
Unrecorded causes	2,404

TOTAL BY REGIMENTS

1st SCVIBn	45
1st SCVIGregg's	498
1st SCVIHagood's	333
1st SCVIRegulars	187
1st SCVC	177
1st SCVA	154
2nd SCVI	490
2nd SCVIRifles	187
2nd SCVC	89
2nd SCVA	113
3rd SCVI	563
3rd SCVIBn	153
3rd SCVABn	88
3rd SCVC	59
4th SCVI	119
4th SCVIBn	20
4th SCVC	261
5th SCVI	485
5th SCVC	160
6th SCVI	583
6th SCVC	150
7th SCVI	496
7th SCVIBn	316
7th SCVC	133
8th SCVI	432
9th SCVIBlanding's	176
9th SCVIHeyward's	6
10th SCVI	519
11th SCVI	325
12th SCVI	560
13th SCVI	652
14th SCVI	624
15th SCVI	539
16th SCVI	439
17th SCVI	498
18th SCVI	506
19th SCVI	347
20th SCVI	243
21st SCVI	497
22nd SCVI	479
23rd SCVI	316
24th SCVI	479
25th SCVI	415
26th SCVI	321
27th SCVI	277
Orr's Rifles	745
Palmetto Sharp Shooters	603
Ham.Leg.	362
Hol.Leg.	371

The dead from the many independent cavalry and artillery companies have not been listed nor have those from the reserve organizations called up from time to time. They have been left off because of yet unresolved unit identification confusion. Note that there are problems in the records of the Hampton and Holcombe legions. The cavalry and artillery companies of these legions were transferred to conventional cavalry and artillery organizations and it is possible that the casualties of these cavalry and artillery companies have been credited to both the legion organization and to the cavalry and artillery organizations. The Hampton Legion records are further confused by the transfer of the surviving infantry to the Second SCVC and the renaming of the combination as the Hampton Legion Cavalry. The date of an individual's death thus must also be used to identify his unit designation at the time of his death. The figures cited here should be used with caution pending further study.

DISTRICT CASUALTY STATISTICS

DISTRICT	DEATHS	WHITE MALE POP.	DEATHS /1000
Abbeville	718	5,786	124.1
Anderson	735	7,138	103.0
Barnwell	369	6,396	57.7
Beaufort	214	3,385	63.2
Charleston	1048	14,761	71.0
Chesterfield	351	3,614	97.1
Clarendon	138	2,249	61.4
Colleton	377	4,780	78.9
Darlington	512	4,328	118.3
Edgefield	903	7,802	115.7
Fairfield	370	3,241	114.2
Georgetown	116	1,589	73.0
Greenville	666	7,280	91.5
Horry	350	2,866	122.1
Kershaw	359	2,503	143.4
Lancaster	406	3,055	132.9

Laurens	636	5,165	123.1
Lexington	560	4,630	120.9
Marion	718	5,504	130.4
Marlboro	346	2,682	129.0
Newberry	480	3,601	133.3
Orangeburg	430	4,097	104.9
Pickens	704	7,593	92.7
Richland	337	3,477	96.9
Spartanburg	1260	9,147	137.7
Sumter	242	3,429	70.6
Union	508	4,379	116.0
Williamsburg	407	2,712	150.1
York	805	4,379	183.8
(Unknown Dist.)	3483		
State	**18,666**	**146,201**	**127.5**

It is clear from these data that there are a number of missing death reports. If the low-death-rate districts were brought up to a rate near the state average, then some 3,000 more deaths have not been accounted for. This figure seems reasonable. The death figures for some units are apparently low. The Fourth SCVI, the Ninth SCVIB (Blanding), and the Fourth SCVIBn (Mattison Battalion) were disbanded because of losses, but the numbers available at this printing do not show totals that would justify such an action. These considerations suggest that there were about 21,500 deaths in state and Confederate service. It is hoped and expected that further research will permit revised editions of this register to be more complete and refined.

APPENDICES

PHOTO CREDITS

FRONT DUSTJACKET AND FIRST PAGE OF ENDPAPERS

Top row, left to right:

Col. J. R. R. Giles, 5th SCVI, killed May 31, 1862, at Seven Pines. Courtesy of the Union County Museum through the South Carolina Confederate Relic Room and Museum.

Major John S. Hard, 7th SCVI, killed September 20, 1863, at Chickamauga. Courtesy of J. S. Taylor through the South Carolina Confederate Relic Room and Museum.

Capt. Robert H. Hawthorne, Co. F, Orr's Rifles, died June 27, 1862, at Gaines' Mill, Va. Courtesy of the South Caroliniana Library through the South Carolina Confederate Relic Room and Museum.

Middle row, left to right:

Pvt. Joseph Wesley Amick, Co. I, 15th SCVI, killed September 14, 1862, at South Mountain, Md. Courtesy of Earl Eargle through the South Carolina Confederate Relic Room and Museum.

Pvt. Bartos J. P. Jeffcoat, Holcombe Legion, Co. B, 7th S.C. Cavalry. Prisoner of war, died at sea during exchange. Courtesy of W. C. Smith through the South Carolina Confederate Relic Room and Museum.

Pvt. John Fraser, Co. B, 21st SCVI, killed in action, September 16, 1864, at Petersburg, Va. Courtesy of Horace Rudisill through the South Carolina Confederate Relic Room and Museum.

Bottom row, left to right:

Pvt. Edward Henry Mellichamp, Engineer Corps, died as a prisoner of war May 25, 1865, at Pt. Lookout, Md. Courtesy of Edward H. Mellichamp IV through the South Carolina Confederate Relic Room and Museum.

Pvt. James Hunt Taylor, color bearer for 1st SCVI (Gregg's), killed June 27, 1862, at Gaines' Mill, Va. Courtesy of the South Carolina Confederate Relic Room and Museum.

Pvt. J. Robertson Davis, Co. E, 6th SCVI, died as a prisoner of war, September 16, 1864, Point Lookout, Md. Courtesy of the Darlington County Historical Society through the South Carolina Confederate Relic Room and Museum.

BACK DUSTJACKET AND SECOND PAGE OF ENDPAPERS

Top row, left to right:

Pvt. George Clark, Co. G, 7th SCVI, died of disease. Courtesy of the South Carolina Confederate Relic Room and Museum.

1st Lt. Edward B. Clinton, Co. I, 5th SCVI, died of fever at Warrenton, Va., December 24, 1861. Courtesy of Dr. Gaillard Waterfall through the South Carolina Confederate Relic Room and Museum.

Pvt. Thomas W. Fowler, Co. E, 5th SCVI, killed at 1st Manassas, July 21, 1861. Courtesy of the Union County Museum through the South Carolina Confederate Relic Room and Museum.

Middle row, left to right:

Pvt. Isaac H. Hargrove, Co. I, 1st SCVIH (Jenkins's), killed January 17, 1864, by an artillery shell at Morristown, Tenn. Courtesy of Jack Marlar through the South Carolina Confederate Relic Room and Museum.

Capt. Langdon Cheves McCord, Co. H, Hampton's Legion, died of wounds, January 23, 1863, at Richmond, Va. From the collections of the South Carolina Historical Society.

Major William C. Preston (painting from photograph as captain), CSA Artillery, killed by cannon shot at Peachtree Creek, Ga. Courtesy of the South Carolina Confederate Relic Room and Museum.

Bottom row, left to right:

1st Lt. Adj. William Mason Smith, 27th SCVI, died of wounds, August 16, 1864, at Richmond, Va. From the collections of the South Carolina Historical Society.

Corp. Thomas J. Wilson, Co. C, 3rd SCVIBn, died as a prisoner of war, February 28, 1865, at Point Lookout, Md. Courtesy of Erskine Eugene Traynham through the South Carolina Confederate Relic Room and Museum.

Pvt. Young H. E. Hitch, Co. I, 16th SCVI, killed June 19, 1864, at Kennesaw Mountain, Ga. Courtesy of Mrs. Nan Barmore through the South Carolina Confederate Relic Room and Museum.

www.ingramcontent.com/pod-product-compliance
Lightning Source LLC
Chambersburg PA
CBHW080753300426
44114CB00020B/2724